DATE DUE

DEMCO 38-296

Encyclopedia of the Second World

by George Thomas Kurian
John J. Karch
Associate Editor

Facts On File
New York • Oxford

Encyclopedia of the Second World

Facts On File, Inc.　　　　Facts On File Limited
460 Park Avenue South　　Collins Street
New York NY 10016　　　 Oxford OX4 1XJ
USA　　　　　　　　　　 United Kingdom

Library of Congress Cataloging-in-Publication Data

Kurian, George Thomas.
　　Encyclopedia of the Second World / George Kurian.
　　　　p.　　cm.
　　Includes bibliographical references and index.
　　ISBN 0-8160-1232-6
　　1. Communist countries—Dictionaries and encyclopedias.
　　I. Title.
　　D847.K82 1990　　　　　　　　　　　90-40370
　　909'.09724—dc20

A British CIP catalogue record for this book is available from the British Library.

Facts On File books are available at special discounts when purchased in bulk quantities for businesses, associations, institutions or sales promotions. Please call our Special Sales Department in New York at 212/683-2244 (dial 800/322-8755 except in NY, AK or HI) or in Oxford at 865/728399.

Composition by TSI Graphics, Inc.
Manufactured by the Maple-Vail Book Manufacturing Group
Printed in the United States of America

10 9 8 7 6 5 4 3 2 1

This book is printed on acid-free paper.

CONTENTS

INTRODUCTION

The *Encyclopedia of the Second World* is a companion volume to the *Encyclopedia of the Third World* (three volumes, Fourth Edition, 1991) and the *Encyclopedia of the First World* (two volumes, 1990). It is compiled on the same thematic arrangement and information classification schedule as the other two. Together, the three encyclopedias provide in-depth profiles of all independent nations of the world.

Taxonomy is a difficult art, particularly when applied to the classification of nations. The Second World is neither a political nor an economic term. It follows a nomenclatural scheme that came into vogue in the 1960s to describe the assorted post-World War II national groupings and alignments. First the term Third World was adopted (as a loan translation of the French *tiers monde*) to describe low-income or developing countries and, by force of logic, the First World was applied to developed countries and the Second World to socialist countries. These terms came to acquire in course of time other connotations and attributes besides the nature of the economy and the stage of economic development. An ideological component was introduced when the First World was seen as free or democratic, the Second World as unfree (being within the Pax Sovietica or Soviet sphere of influence) and the Third World as essentially nonaligned. Over the next two decades several synonyms came into popular usage, such as North and South, East and West. None of these terms was precise, but they were convenient, and for the purposes of scholarship and journalism, they imposed some kind of order on a disorderly world. In politics and economics, just as in law, terminology is often *cy pres*, or mere approximations of meaning. Although the group descriptors varied, the original concept behind them remained valid: there were three broad groups of nations in the world and their interactions followed predictable patterns.

The 11 nations of the Second World may seem, outside the context of this study, as disparate and diverse. The Second World is not a monolithic bloc and was never one except for a few years before the death of Stalin. There is very little political, economic, racial, linguistic or religious unity organically binding these countries, just as such unities do not exist in the First World or the Third World. In size these countries range from China, the most populous nation on earth, to Mongolia with only two million inhabitants, and from the Soviet Union, occupying one-sixth of the global land surface, to tiny Albania, which is only slightly larger than Maryland. Their economic status also varies widely. The Soviet Union, the second largest industrial power in the world, appears cheek by jowl with Mongolia with a GNP of only $1.7 billion. Many of these countries also are torn by historic animosities, such as between Albania and Yugoslavia, the Soviet Union and China, Germany and Poland, and Hungary and Rumania.

Yet the 11 countries were linked together until 1989 by a common adherence to Marxist ideology and a common subjection to totalitarian governments based on that ideology. With the collapse of Communism this unity has been shattered and all of them—with the exception of China and Albania—are now in the process of transition to a free-market economy and a pluralistic political system. This event ranks with the two world wars, the Bolshevik Revolution and the post-war liquidation of colonialism as one of the historic turning points of 20th century history. The nations of Eastern Europe are passing through their Thermidor—an event that seems to follow ineluctably every revolution—but it is too early to predict the extent and scope of the changes or the nature of the society that will emerge from the wreckage of Marxism. Czechoslovakia, Hungary, and Poland have proceeded more rapidly in establishing the framework of a democratic society. The Soviet Union, Rumania, Bulgaria and Yugoslavia are proceeding more slowly and have not entirely abandoned the rubrics and institutions of Communism. Mongolia, like a proper satellite, is waiting for its cues from Moscow before taking the plunge into a democracy it has never known in its history. A whole generation may pass before the forces unleashed by Gorbachev run their course and the new order is securely in place.

The changes in Eastern Europe and the Soviet Union have affected the various areas of national life covered in this encyclopedia differently. The most radical changes are taking place in nine areas:

1. In politics, the Communist parties have abandoned their monopoly of power and new nonsocialist parties have begun to appear on the political horizon. This has meant constitutional changes and the transfer of power in some cases from a moribund Communist Party apparatus to freely elected leaders. In Eastern Europe it also has meant the holding of free elections for the first time in half a century. Open dissidence is a new phenomenon in these countries where regimentation was the rule until 1989.

2. The restoration of human rights has led in almost every case to the dismantling of the security apparatus engaged in a relentless struggle against real and imagined enemies of the state as well as revisionists.

3. The repudiation of Western cultural traditions and values implicit in Marxism had created a puritanical and austere society in Eastern Europe. With the exit of official censors, Western cultural influences have free access to these societies.

4. The Communist press was a party monopoly and a propaganda weapon in the war against ideas. In almost every East European country, the press has thrown off the shackles and serves as the springboard for political and economic reforms.

5. The church has emerged as one of the strongest beneficiaries of the new order in Eastern Europe, just as it was one of the targets of a savage persecution under all Communist regimes. The "silent, suffering church" of the Communist era has become a vibrant bulwark of freedom. All East European countries now permit freedom of belief and worship and in many cases churches, seminaries and monasteries have been returned to the believers.

6. The economy has been energized by a return to the concept of private property, an anathema to orthodox Marxism. Centralized planning has been discredited as one of the principal reasons for the decline of East European economies. Subsidies for basic products are being withdrawn; party apparatchiks have lost much of their decision-making power; and prices are being set in response to the law of demand and supply in the marketplace. In some cases private banks have been permitted and foreign trade and investment regulations have been liberalized. Most East European nations have joined the IMF and World Bank and the Soviet Union is negotiating for membership in GATT.

7. In defense, the Warsaw Pact has become virtually otiose, although it continues a formal existence as a counter to NATO. Almost all East European countries have curtailed their defense spending.

8. The legal system is more difficult to change but work has begun in all East European countries to de-Socialize the system and introduce Western concepts, such as contract.

9. As Communist labor unions have lost their monopoly, free labor unions have been permitted to organize and operate without hindrance. Strikes have become legal and wage scales are being set in response to cost of living indices.

The presence of East Germany in the encyclopedia is an example of the problems I faced in compiling the work at a time of massive changes in Eastern Europe. Since the *Encylopedia of the First World* dealt only with West Germany it became necessary to include East Germany as a chapter, although the reunification of the two German states is now a reality. Yet, until the next revision of the encyclopedia, the chapter will retain a strong historical interest as a profile of the German Democratic Republic on the eve of its disappearance.

Even with its current troubles, the Second World is a formidable political entity in the political landscape of the world. It encompasses 34.8% of the global land surface, 29.4% of the global population and 21.05% of the Gross Global Product.

In terms of both population and land area, the Second World towers above the First World, but its combined GNP is only $3.895 trillion compared to $14.4 trillion for the First World.

Work on the *Encyclopedia of the Second World* started in early 1989 and the initial draft was completed in January 1990. When the work began the Second World was relatively stable (although there were a few rumblings) and there seemed no reason to doubt that it would survive in the same form not only the decade but

Country	Sq km (000)	Population (million)	GNP ($ billion)
Soviet Union	22,402	281	2,500
China	9,561	1,054	350
Albania	29	3	3
Yugoslavia	256	23.3	154
Bulgaria	111	9.0	67.6
Rumania	238	22.9	151.3
Hungary	93	10.6	26.3
Czechoslovakia	128	15.5	158.2
East Germany	108	16.6	207.2
Poland	313	37.5	276.3
Mongolia	1,565	2.0	1.7

also the approaching millennium. After all, authoritarian and closed societies are generally believed to be if not immune at least slow to change. But even as the work progressed most of the countries it describes were caught in the throes of a convulsion without parallel in modern times. Strong regimes fell like a house of cards, unbreachable walls came tumbling down, entrenched tyrants were disgraced and executed, and the bastions of power were swept away.

It is good advice never to write history when the pages of history are turning and in Eastern Europe in 1989 they were turning as in a gale. A reference book is like a still photograph. It best describes static conditions. It freezes the action. It is not like a movie which is able to portray the dynamics of movement and change. The startling events that outpaced the writing of the book posed severe burdens. Several sections had to be rewritten, then torn again and rewritten. As a result, the political sections reflect events through September 1990. Even so the book only attempts to portray Eastern Europe and China and Mongolia on the eve of the present turmoil and describe the conditions that led to these cataclysmic events. Although the book attempts to chronicle change through mid 1990, it is not a survey of the changes that still are in the offing or a profile of the Second World that will emerge from its troubles.

The fall of East European regimes has been described by some Western observers as the "end of history" in a Hegelian sense of bringing to an end the ideological conflict between Communism and capitalism and establishing the permanent triumph of the latter. Such an interpretation is typically Hesperocentric because it views all history strictly in terms of Western interests and through Western biases. It also is reminiscent of the advice given to President McKinley in 1900 by one of his officials to abolish the Patent Office because "everything that can be discovered has already been discovered." While the peripeteia in Eastern Europe does not mark the end of history, it certainly marks the end of the Cold War and of post-World War II European history. It also marks the return of these regimes to normalcy which psychologists characterize as regression to the mean after an exceptionally strenuous interlude.

These events also mark the end of prophecy because they have confounded alike prophets and pundits who have no clue to the direction in which the reborn regimes will move. The end of any dictatorship is always exhilarating as a vindication of the spirit of liberty. But in societies long subjugated to unmitigated tyranny reforms may sometimes prove more destabilizing than revolutions. The legacies of Stalinism have not been entirely obliterated and may resurface if reforms prove ineffective. The allure of a consumer society may prove equally dangerous if it means only replacing the Berlin Wall with the Wall Street.

A word of caution is necessary about the statistical component of each country profile. In Communist countries, statistics is an ideological tool; it is not necessarily user-friendly, but rather party-friendly, and as such serves a political purpose. Skepticism is necessary in interpreting data because not only are they fragmentary and incomplete (although some nations like Hungary, Poland and Rumania belong to the IMF and World Bank) but such incompleteness is officially encouraged in order to hide the regime's failures and exaggerate its successes. In many cases the data are misleading and in others their quality is unsatisfactory. Data on gross output and national income in absolute terms are not published. Official statistics on national accounts are limited to a few index series for the overall productive sector and a percentage breakdown of gross output and national income by productive sector. The arbitrary nature of the pricing system and differences in statistical methodology as compared to Western practices also preclude a direct comparison of economic growth rates with similar rates in Western countries. Data relating to money supply and foreign exchange reserves are state secrets. Defense expenditures are hidden under various rubrics and even President Gorbachev confessed that he did not know how much the Soviet Union was spending on defense. Further, because Second World countries have nonconvertible currencies with a number of exchange rates, the establishment of their dollar equivalencies is a source of unending despair for economists. Officials charged with reporting data often have vested interest in manipulating data to show that they have met production quotas set in national plans. Differences in statistical terminology pose more troublesome problems. In strict Marxian theory, the productive sector is restricted to the creation of physical goods and does not include services and public administration. National income or the Net Material Product (NMP) excludes material costs including depreciation. Additional problems arise because of prices and weights used in calculating broad economic measures. The industrial production index includes new products at substantially higher prices even when the product is unchanged from earlier models. This bias accentuates the growth rate of the industrial sector relative to other sectors. Another problem concerns investment and consumption in terms of uses of national income. Consumption is calculated at wholesale prices excluding turnover taxes. This means a consistent exaggeration of investment rates in relation to consumption.

Statistics is not the only area where data are sparse and unreliable. Information also is deficient on a number of other topics in the classification schedule. However, in these cases, the poor quality or unevenness of the data is due more to official neglect or faulty administrative mechanisms rather than willful distortions. The most common of such problem areas are:

Population: Internal and external migration
　　　　　 Population policies
　　　　　 Urbanization
Ethnic Groups and Languages: Official policy on minority groups and languages
Civil Service: Codes, size and recruitment
Local Government: Revenues and expenditures
　　　　　　　　　　 Authority of local officials
Economy: Foreign aid
Public Finance: Fiscal policy
Currency and Banking: Monetary Policy
Manufacturing: Industrial policy
Labor: Occupational distribution
　　　　 Labor legislation
　　　　 Foreign workers
　　　　 Industrial relations—Machinery and procedures
　　　　 Working conditions
　　　　 Unemployment
Transportation and Communications: Tourism
Defense: Defense production
　　　　　 Military aid
　　　　　 Deployment of armed forces
Legal System: Prisons
Law Enforcement: Incidence and types of crime
　　　　　　　　　 Secret police
Food and Nutrition: Diet

In compiling the encyclopedia I had the valuable assistance of a friend and distinguished East European specialist, John Karch. He has contributed five sections (Politics and Government, Civil Service, Foreign Policy, Parliament and Political Parties) to six chapters (Soviet Union, Poland, East Germany, Hungary, Czechoslovakia and Yugoslavia) and additional two sections (Ethnic Groups and Languages) to the Soviet Union, East Germany, Hungary and Yugoslavia.

It is always a pleasure to acknowledge the full measure of support I received in this project as well as in its predecessors from Facts On File, particularly Edward W. Knappman, whose commitment to excellence in reference books is a challenge and source of inspiration. Eleanora von Dehsen was a very supportive editor throughout and her attention to details, smooth efficiency and buoyant humor make her in many ways a model editor. My thanks also are due to William Drennan on whom fell the onerous duty of copyediting and who discharged it, as always, meticulously.

Yorktown Heights, N.Y.　　　　　George Thomas Kurian

NOTES AND INFORMATION CLASSIFICATION SYSTEM

NOTES ON TECHNICAL USAGE

The cutoff date for this work is January 1, 1990. Every effort has been made to make the statistical data in this edition current as of that date. Later information, where available, has been included where such inclusion was required for fullness of treatment. Wherever the data are older than the cutoff date it is so indicated in the text.

Throughout this work weights and measurements are shown in SI (Systeme International) units with U.S. equivalents shown in parentheses.

All years are calendar years unless noted as fiscal year, in which case a slash or virgule appears between the years, as in 78/79. Inclusive years are noted with a hyphen, as in 1978-79, signifying the full period of the calendar years noted.

INFORMATION CLASSIFICATION

Information in each country section has been arranged according to a standard, but not rigidly uniform, pattern. This classification system is central to this work and has been adhered to throughout except where the need for clarity of presentation or the nature or absence of information required modification in the scheme. The organization system has been designed not only for ease of consultation but also to provide a comparative framework essential to the study of international institutions. See note in the introduction on the quality of statistical data and certain problem areas where information is uneven. These areas have been asterisked in the classification system.

1. BASIC FACT SHEET

Official Name
Abbreviation
Capital
Head of state
Head of government
Nature of government
Population (year)
Area
Major ethnic group(s)
Language(s)
Religion(s)
Unit of currency
National flag
National emblem
National anthem
National holidays
National calendar
Physical Quality of Life Index
Date of independence
Date of constitution
Weights and measures

2. GEOGRAPHICAL FEATURES

General location
Area
Greatest distances
Borders
Coastline
Border agreements and disputes (where applicable)
Capital
Other major urban centers and population (table)
Topographical regions
Rivers and lakes

3. CLIMATE & WEATHER

Climate and seasons
Temperature ranges
Prevailing winds (where applicable)
Rainfall

4. POPULATION

Estimated population
Last official or true census
Population, year; 1990; 2000
*Immigration and emigration
Status of women
Official birth control policies (where applicable)
Birth control activities (where applicable)
Table of population growth (major countries only)
*Population dynamics (as urbanization, nuptiality, age profile, density, fertility) (major countries only)
Demographic indicators

5. ETHNIC COMPOSITION

Major ethnic groups
Ethnic aliens
Foreign communities
Table (where available)

6. LANGUAGES

Official, national or major language
Minority languages and dialects
*Language policy

7. RELIGIONS

Majority religion
Principal sects and denominations
Religious minorities
Official religious policy
Extent of religious freedom

8. HISTORICAL BACKGROUND

General history (including major wars and colonial experience) up to 1945 or date of independence

9. CONSTITUTION & GOVERNMENT

Constitutional basis of government
Basic constitutional provisions for government organization
Head of state
Executive, including head of government and cabinet
Organization of government chart
List of heads of state and government (from 1945 or date of independence)
List of cabinet members

10. FREEDOM & HUMAN RIGHTS

Constitutional basis
Basic freedoms
Discrimination
Women's rights

11. CIVIL SERVICE

*Civil service system and codes
*Structure and recruitment
*Size (where available)

12. LOCAL GOVERNMENT

Units of territorial administration
Political subdivisions and administrative centers
*Local or municipal government
Table of political subdivisions (with population and area)

13. FOREIGN POLICY

Principal determinants, goals and priorities
Evolution of foreign policy
Relations with major powers
Relations with neighbors
Formal alliances

14. PARLIAMENT

Structure and constitutional provisions
Membership, terms
Powers and relation to executive
Legistlative process
Suffrage and electoral system
Table of party composition in parliament

15. POLITICAL PARTIES

Major political parties, their ideology and party structure
Illegal political parties and extraparliamentary interest or terrorist groups (where applicable)

16. ECONOMY

Classification
Type of economy
Dominant sector
Evolution of economic sectors (major countries only)
General economic policies (major countries only)
Economic development, planning (Second and Third worlds only)
Current development plan (Second and Third worlds only)
*Foreign aid (where applicable)
Table of principal economic indicators
Table of balance of payments
Table of GDP

17. PUBLIC FINANCE

Fiscal year
*Fiscal policy
External public debt (Third World only)
National budget
National budget distribution of revenues and expenditures

18. CURRENCY & BANKING

Basic currency unit and subdivisions
Denominations
Dollar exchange rate (time series)
Monetary history
Banking system
Central bank
Commercial banking system
Table of financial indicators
*Monetary policy

19. GROWTH PROFILE

20. AGRICULTURE

Total land area
Land use
Major agricultural regions
Land tenure
Land reforms (where applicable)
Agricultural techniques (where applicable)
Mechanization
Marketing (where applicable)
Agricultural policy and programs (where applicable)
Crop production
Livestock and animal breeding
Forests
Fisheries
Table of agricultural indicators

21. MANUFACTURING

Manufacturing development
Manufacturing centers
*Industrial policy (where applicable)
Foreign investment
State manufacturing sector
Table of manufacturing indicators

22. MINING

Mineral resources
Mineral production
Foreign participation (where applicable)
State mining sector
Table of mineral production (where applicable)

23. ENERGY

Energy resources
Energy policy (where applicable)
Energy programs and projects (where applicable)
Table of energy indicators

24. LABOR

Size of labor force
Sex distribution
*Occupational distribution
*Unemployment
*Labor legislation
*Industrial relations machinery and procedures

ALBANIA

BASIC FACT SHEET

OFFICIAL NAME: Socialist People's Republic of Albania (Republika Popullore Socialiste e Shqiperise)

ABBREVIATION: AB

CAPITAL: Tirana

HEAD OF STATE: President Ramiz Alia (from 1982)

HEAD OF GOVERNMENT: Prime Minister Adil Karkani (from 1982)

NATURE OF GOVERNMENT: Communist dictatorship

POPULATION: 3,208,033 (1989)

AREA: 28,748 sq. km. (11,100 sq. mi.)

MAJOR ETHNIC GROUPS: Gegs and Tosks

LANGUAGE: Albanian

RELIGION: None; officially atheist

UNIT OF CURRENCY: Lek

NATIONAL FLAG: Red standard, at the center of which is a black double-headed eagle topped by a red gold-edged five-pointed star

NATIONAL EMBLEM: A black two-headed eagle supported on either side by golden sheaves of wheat. A red gold-edged five-pointed star appears at the top, and at the base in gold letters on a red riband is the date May 24, 1944, the date of the founding of the People's Republic of Albania.

NATIONAL ANTHEM: "Hymni i Flamurit" ("Anthem of the Flag")

NATIONAL HOLIDAYS: January 11 (Proclamation of the Republic); November 7 (Victory of the October Socialist Revolution); November 28 (Proclamation of Independence); November 29 (Liberation Day, 1944)

NATIONAL CALENDAR: Gregorian

PHYSICAL QUALITY OF LIFE INDEX: 82 (on an ascending scale with 100 as the maximum)

DATE OF INDEPENDENCE: November 28, 1912

DATE OF CONSTITUTION: December 27, 1976

WEIGHTS & MEASURES: Metric

GEOGRAPHICAL FEATURES

Albania, on the western coast of the Balkan Peninsula, is separated from the heel of the Italian boot on the southwest and the west by the Strait of Otranto and the Adriatic Sea respectively. Albania's total area is 28,748 sq. km. (11,100 sq. mi.). It shares a 1,204-km. (748-mi.) boundary with two countries: Yugoslavia (476 km.; 296 mi.) and Greece (256 km.; 159 mi.). The maximum length north to south is 340 km. (211 mi.) and the maximum width east to west is 148 km. (92 mi.). The coastline is 472 km. (293 mi.) long.

Albania's boundaries were established in 1913 and demarcated in 1923. They were drawn at first at the Conference of Ambassadors in London. The country was occupied by the warring powers during World War I, but the 1913 boundaries were confirmed at Versailles in 1921 and in the Paris Agreement of 1926. The borders were defined on the principle of nationality rather than geography. The northern and eastern borders were intended insofar as possible to separate the Albanians from the Serbians and Montenegrins, and the southeastern border to separate the Albanians from the Greeks. Allowance was made for local economic characteristics, such as markets and grazing areas attached to villages. The Macedonia lake district was divided among the three area states: Albania, Yugoslavia and Greece. The border runs generally north from the lakes following the ridges of the eastern highlands, some 16 to 32 km. (10 to 20 mi.) west of the watershed divide. The watershed divide was abandoned altogether along the northeastern boundary.

The border shared with Yugoslavia runs northward from Lake Prespa to the Adriatic Sea, connecting high points through the North Albanian Alps. There is no natural topographic dividing line from the highlands through Lake Scutari to the Adriatic, but the Buene River functions as one for part of the border. The Greek border runs from the common border near Lake Prespa southwest to the Ionian Sea.

Because the boundaries are artificial, they continue to remain disputed both by Albania and its neighbors. The Kosovo area in Yugoslavia contains a substantial Albanian population. There are Greeks and Albanians on the wrong side of the southeastern boundary.

The capital is Tirana or Tirane in the central part, about 50 km. (20 mi.) east of the Adriatic Sea. There are no other population centers with a population of over 100,000.

PRINCIPAL POPULATION CENTERS (1983)	
Tirana (Tirane, the capital)	206,100
Durres (Durazzo)	72,400
Shkoder (Scutari)	71,200
Elbasan	69,900
Vlore (Vlone or Valona)	61,100
Korçe (Koritsa)	57,100
Fier	37,000
Berat	36,600
Lushnje	24,200
Kavaje	22,500
Gjirokaster	21,400
Source: *Forty Years of Socialist Albania.*	

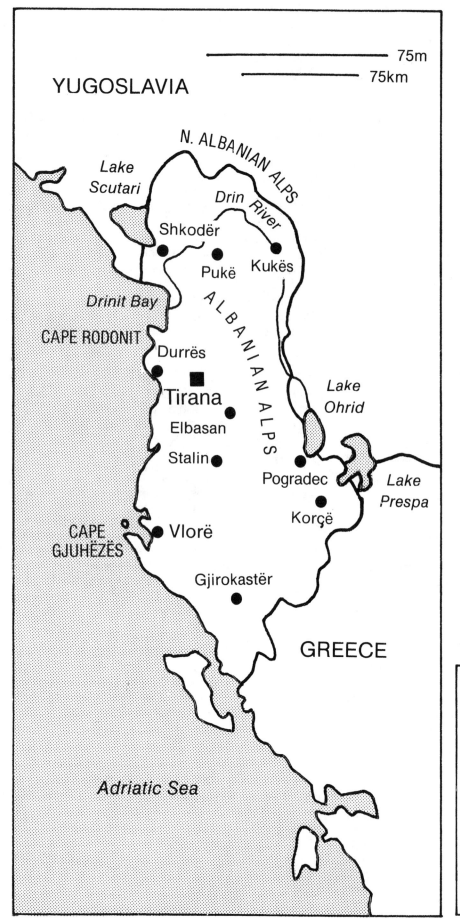

YUGOSLAVIA

75m

75km

N. ALBANIAN ALPS

Lake Scutari

Drin River

Shkodër

Pukë

Kukës

Drinit Bay

CAPE RODONIT

A L B A N I A N   A L P S

Durrës

Tirana

Elbasan

Stalin

Lake Ohrid

Pogradec

Lake Prespa

Korçë

CAPE GJUHËZËS

Vlorë

Gjirokastër

GREECE

Adriatic Sea

24 MAJ 1944

Nearly 70% of Albania is mountainous and inaccessible. The remaining alluvial plain receives only seasonal rains and is poorly drained. Much of it also is infertile. Good soil and reliable precipitation occur, however, in the river basins within the mountains in the Lake District on the eastern border and in a narrow band of slightly elevated land between the coastal plains and the mountains.

The North Albanian Alps are an extension of the Dinaric alpine chain and, specifically, the Montenegrin limestone plateau. The mountains are rugged and folded, and the rivers have deep valleys with steep sides. The southern mountains encompass the area east of Vlore and south of the Vijose River and follow the northwest to southeast trendlines characteristic of the Dinaric Alps. However, they are more gentle and accessible. The valleys are wider between the ridges, and the valley floors are arable.

A low coastal belt extends from the northern boundary southward to about Vlore, extending about 16 to 48 km. (10 to 30 mi.) deep. There are large areas of marshland and eroded badlands, but in the foothills of the central uplands the land is fertile. The lowlands are of recent geological origin, created by sediments from the many torrents that rise in the interior mountains. The sedimentation has raised the river channels above the level of the nearby terrain. Coastal hills descend abruptly to the Ionian Sea beaches along the Albanian Riviera from Vlore Bay southward to about Sarande. South of Sarande is another small area of coastal lowlands fronting on the Ionian Sea and separated from the Greek island of Corfu by a 1.6-km.-wide (1.0-mi.-wide) channel.

The central uplands region extends south from the Drin River valley to the southern mountains. In the North, from the Drin River to the vicinity of Elbasan, it is about 32 km. (20 mi.) wide. Near Elbasan it narrows to practically nothing and then broadens into a broad, triangular shape, with its base against the southern mountains. This area experiences occasionally severe earthquakes. The ridges of the uplands are extensions of the Dalmatian coastal range that enters Albania from Yugoslavia. Elevations generally are moderate, between 305 and 914 m. (1,700 and 3,000 ft.), with a few reaching about 1,524 m. (5,000 ft.)

The serpentine zone extends nearly the length of the country, from the North Albanian Alps to the Greek border south of Korce, an area 16 to 32 km. (10 to 20 mi.) wide and over 201 km. (125 mi.) in length. At Elbasan it touches the coastal plain and reaches the eastern border for nearly 80 km. (50 mi.) in and north of the lake region. The serpentine zone derives its name from its rock of dull green color and often mottled or spotted appearance.

The mountains east of the serpentine zone are the highest in the country. They occupy a narrow strip south of Lakes Ohrid and Prespa and between the White Drin River and the Yugoslav city of Debar. A peak in the Korab Range, on the border north of Debar, exceeds 2,743 m. (9,000 ft.). These ranges, generally trending north to south, are among the most rugged in the Balkan Peninsula.

The three lakes of easternmost Albania are part of the Macedonian lake district. These are Lake Ohrid, Little Lake Prespa and Lake Prespa. The lakes, at elevations of over 610 m. (2,000 ft.), are scenic and picturesque. Lake Ohrid is fed primarily from underground springs and is blue and very clear.

With the exception of one small stream, the precipitation drains through all-Albanian rivers. A considerable amount of water from Yugoslavia and Greece also drains through Albania, particularly through the Drin River. With the exception of the Drin River, which flows northward and drains nearly the entire eastern border region before it turns westward to the sea, most of the rivers in the northern and central parts of the country flow much more directly westward to the sea. They do so by cutting across ridges rather than flowing around them. Albanian rivers are typically unnavigable because of their steep gradients and irregular seasonal flow patterns. The Buene is an exception. It is dredged between Shkoder and the Adriatic and is navigable for small ships. The Drin is by far the largest and the most constant river. Fed by the melting snows from the northern and eastern mountains, its normal flow varies seasonally by only about one-third. Along its length of about 282 km. (175 mi.) it drains 5,959 sq. km. (2,300 sq. mi.) within Albania. It also collects water from the Adriatic portion of the Kosovo watershed as well as the three border lakes. The Seman and Vijose are the only other rivers over 161 km. (100 mi.) in length and with basins of over 2,591 sq. km. (1,000 sq. mi.). These rivers drain the southern regions. As is the case with the shorter streams, they are dry in the summer and virtually useless for navigation.

CLIMATE & WEATHER

For a small country, Albania has an unusually large number of climatic regions. The coastal lowlands have a typically Mediterranean climate, while the highlands have a Mediterranean continental climate. In both climatic zones, weather changes markedly from north to south and from winter to summer. The lowlands have mild winters, averaging about 45°F; summer temperatures average 75°F. Humidity is high, and therefore summers tend to be oppressive. The southern lowlands are warmer, averaging over 5°F higher than the North during summer. Inland temperatures vary more widely with differences in elevation. Cold northerly and northeasterly winds cause frigid winters. Average summer temperatures are lower than in coastal areas, but daily fluctuations are greater.

Average precipitation is high, resulting from the convergence of the prevailing airflow from the Mediterranean with the continental air mass. The central uplands receive the heaviest rainfall. Vertical currents initiated when the Mediterranean air is uplifted also result in frequent thunderstorms accompanied by torrential downpours. When the continental system is weak, Mediterranean winds drop their moisture farther inland. When there is a dominant continental air mass, it spills cold air onto the lowland areas. This occurs most frequently in the winter season. Lowland rainfall averages

1,016 to 1,524 mm. (40 to 60 in.) annually, increasing between these two extremes from south to north. Nearly 95% of the rain falls during the rainy season. Rainfall in the uplands is higher, averaging 1,778 to 2,540 mm. (70 to 100 in.). Largely because of the summer thunderstorms, the seasonal variations are not as great as in the coastal area.

POPULATION

The population of Albania in 1988 was 3,147,352, based on the last official census, in 1982, when the population was 2,766,100. Albania ranks 109th in the world in population and 126th in land size. The population is expected to reach 4,030,000 in 2000.

The most notable characteristics of Albanian demographic growth are its high birth rate fostered by the official pronatalist policy and the high ratio of males to females. In both respects it is untypical of European countries. Because of the high birth rate, the median age also is much lower than elsewhere in Eastern Europe. The higher ratio of men in the population is attributed to the high infant mortality rate among female infants, who are regarded as less desirable than male infants by their parents.

The population is highly dispersed, and the country remains one of the most rural in Europe. Immediately after World War II there was a trend toward urbanization, but in the 1960s the government initiated a number of measures to reverse this trend. Housing in the cities is greatly overcrowded and further restricts movement to the cities. Internal migration is controlled by requiring approval for persons to move from one location to another. Legal external emigration is virtually nonexistent.

POPULATION GROWTH, 1930–70 (000)

Date	Total	Males	Females
1930	1,003	—	—
1945	1,122	571	552
1950	1,219	626	593
1955	1,391	713	678
1960	1,626	835	791
1970	2,136	—	—

DEMOGRAPHIC INDICATORS, 1988

Population: 3,208,033 (1989)
Year of last census: 1982   World rank: 109
Sex ratio: Males: 51.58   Females: 48.42
Population trends (million)
  1930: 1.003   1960: 1.626   1990: 3.281
  1940: 1.088   1970: 2.136   2000: 4.030
  1950: 1.219   1980: 2.671
Population doubling time in years at current rate: 34
Hypothetical size of stationary population (million): 6
Assumed year of reaching net reproduction rate of 1: 2005
Age profile (%)
  0–15: 35.8   30–44: 17.0   60–74: 5.3
  15–29: 29.3   45–59: 11.1   Over 75: 1.5
Median age (years): 23.3
Density per sq. km. (per sq. mi.) 109.5 (283.7)

DEMOGRAPHIC INDICATORS (continued)

Annual growth rate (%)
  1950–55: 2.44   1975–80: 2.39   1995–2000: 1.75
  1960–65: 2.99   1980–85: 2.21   2000–2005: 1.59
  1965–70: 2.68   1985–90: 2.10   2010–15: 1.34
  1970–75: 2.51   1990–95: 2.08   2020–25: 1.18
Vital statistics
  Crude birth rate, 1/1,000: 26.2
  Crude death rate, 1/1,000: 5.8
  Change in birth rate: –31.6 (1965–84)
  Change in death rate: –27.1 (1965–84)
  Dependency, total: 63.6
  Infant mortality rate, 1/1,000: 48
  Child (0–4 years) mortality rate, 1/1,000: 3
  Maternal mortality rate, 1/100,000: N.A.
  Natural increase, 1/1,000: 20.4
  Total fertility rate: 3.6
  General fertility rate: 105
  Gross reproduction rate: 1.61
  Marriage rate, 1/1,000: 8.5
  Divorce rate, 1/1,000: 0.8
  Life expectancy, males (years): 67.9
  Life expectancy, females (years): 72.9
  Average household size: 5.4
  % illegitimate births: N.A.
Youth
  Youth population, 15–24 (000): 649
  Youth population in 2000 (000): 738
Women
  Of childbearing age 15–49 (000): 853
  Child-woman ratio (children per 1000 women 15–49): 501
  % women using contraceptives: N.A.
  % women married 15–49: N.A.
Urban
  Urban population (000): 1,433
  % urban, 1965: 32 1985: 34
  Annual urgan growth rate (%) 1965–80: 3.4 1980–85: 3.3
  % urban population in largest city: 25
  % urban population in cities over 500,000: 0
  Number of cities over 500,000: 0
  Annual rural growth rate: 1.1%

Settlement patterns are influenced by history and geography. Poor soil and lack of water in many areas discourage large concentrations. The rugged terrain makes land transportation difficult and reduces access. The heaviest concentration is in the district of Tirana, followed by Durres, Fier and Lushnje. The areas surrounding Korce and Shkoder also are thickly settled. Coastal cities generally have a small hinterland.

Typical mountain villages contain 70 to 100 households and are linked with the outside world only by footpaths. Houses are clustered in the South, while in the North they are dispersed. Fields and pastures are some distance from the village. During the summer, water is scarce and is limited to drinking.

ETHNIC COMPOSITION

Nearly 97% of the population is Albanian; the remaining 3% is divided among Greeks, Vlachs, Bulgars, Serbs and Gypsies.

The main cleavage in Albanian society is between two ethnic groups: Gegs and Tosks. The dividing line between the two is the Shkumbin River, but there is some spillover on both sides. Numerically, the Gegs are slightly in the majority. There are marked differences in the physical appearances of Gegs and Tosks. There also are sharp contrasts between their social systems. The Gegs, because of their greater isolation in the mountainous areas of the North, have a more closely knit tribal organization. Until the rise of the Communist state after World War II, unwritten tribal codes regulated social conduct and relations, including regulation of blood feuds. The Tosks generally were more outspoken and educated and less xenophobic than the Gegs. Ethnic distinctions began to be blurred as the Communist Party under Enver Hoxha (himself a Tosk) waged a successful struggle to extirpate vestiges of the old social order and to suppress tribal customs and rituals.

Greeks, who constitute about 2% of the population, are most numerous in the southwestern coastal area of Dhermi and Himare and in the region extending southward to the Greek border from Gjirokaster. Most of them have adopted Albanian dress and customs and speak fluent Albanian in addition to Greek. Vlachs, descendants of the Romanized Dacians or Thracians of the pre-Christian era, are most numerous in the Pindus Mountains and in the Fier, Korce and Vlore areas. Persons of Bulgar origin live mostly in the border area near Lake Prespa, and persons of Serb origin live in the Shkoder area. Gypsies are scattered all over the country.

An estimated 2 million Albanians are believed to live outside the country. Yugoslavia alone has 1 million, of whom about 70% live in the Kosovo area. Some 100,000 live in the United States, 350,000 in Greece and 250,000 in Italy. Albanians also are found in Bulgaria, Egypt, Turkey and Rumania.

LANGUAGES

Albanian, the national and official language spoken by nearly all inhabitants, is the only surviving language of the early Thraco-Illyrian group. Of the outside influences on the language, the most prominent are Latin and Italian (during the centuries of Roman domination and trade with the Venetian merchants), and Turkish and Greek (during Turkish rule). The first written documents in Albanian did not appear until the 15th century, but the repressive policies of the Ottoman rulers during the next 450 years restricted the growth of the language. The use of written Albanian was prohibited, and the language was kept alive only by émigré Albanians, particularly those in Italy after 1848. By the early 20th century more than a dozen different alphabets had developed, based on Latin, Greek, Turkish, Arabic and other scripts. A standardized orthography was adopted in 1908 using a Latin-based alphabet of 36 letters approved by a linguistic congress at Monastir. The alphabet was made official by a government directive in 1924. Despite the government's efforts to develop a uniform language, dialectal differences persist, particularly in spelling. Such differences and variants were incorporated in a dictionary of the Albanian language published by the Institute of Sciences in 1954.

The two principal dialects are Geg, spoken by about two-thirds, and Tosk, spoken by the remaining one-third. Despite considerable variations between these dialects and their subvarieties, Albanians communicate easily with each other. After the Communist takeover, the Tosk dialect, spoken by most of the party leaders, became the sole official language of the country.

RELIGIONS

Until the 1940s, Albania was the only predominantly Islamic nation in Europe, a legacy of five centuries of Ottoman rule. In 1944, the last year in which a religious count of the population was made, there were 826,000 Muslims, 212,500 Eastern Orthodox and 142,000 Catholics in a population of 1,180,500. About a quarter of the Muslims belonged to the dervish order of Bektashi, an offshoot of Shiites.

Christianity was introduced to Albania in the first century. After the division of the Roman Empire into West and East in 395, Albania became politically a part of the Eastern or Byzantine Empire but remained ecclesiastically part of Rome. However, when the final schism occurred in 1054 between the Eastern and Western churches, the Christians in the southern part of the country came under the jurisdiction of the Constantinople ecumenical patriarchate. This situation prevailed until the 14th century, when Turkish invaders introduced Islam. During the next five centuries, Islam made steady inroads, although it met with initial resistance from the Catholics. Muslim *pashas*, *beys* and *agas* were instrumental in forcibly converting whole villages in their domains. By the close of the 17th century the Catholics in the North were outnumbered by the Muslims.

At the time of independence Albania became a secular state. The Constitution declared that all religions were respected and guaranteed their freedom of exercise. The Communist Constitution of 1946 followed the same liberal tenor. It guaranteed freedom of conscience and religion to all citizens, separated church and state and even provided for subsidies to religious organizations.

However, even before the adoption of the Constitution, the first shots had been fired in the state's war against religion. The Agrarian Reform Law of 1945 confiscated the wealth and properties of all monastic orders and dioceses and seized their printing presses and libraries. In another three years, the regime enacted its first law aimed specifically at the control and regulation of all religious bodies. Known as Decree 743 on Religious Communities, it was approved by the Council of Ministers in 1949, converted into Law 773 in 1950 and amended by Decree 3660 in 1963. To organize and function, religious communities had to be recognized by the state and their statutes approved by the Council of Ministers. The heads of religious communities and sects also had to be approved by the Council of Ministers after being elected or appointed by the proper religious organs. Religious communities with headquarters outside the country were ordered to terminate their activities. Pastoral letters, messages, speeches and other religious communications were to be approved by the government. Religious institutions were forbidden to run schools, philanthropic and welfare institutions and hospitals and from owning real estate.

Although the Sunni, Bektashi, Orthodox and Catholic communities were approved as late as 1951, the regime's religious policy from the outset was aimed at their eventual destruction. To this end, religious leaders were executed as enemies of the people, assassinated, purged and terrorized. The leaders of the Bektashi clergy who were considered disloyal were killed. The primate of the Orthodox Church, Archbishop Kristofor Kisi, was deposed and jailed and replaced by a renegade priest, Pashko Vodica, who was installed as Archbishop Paisi. The Roman Catholic Church became a principal target of persecution because of its resistance to the Communization of religion. In 1945, of the 93 Catholic priests, 24 were executed, 35 imprisoned, 11 either missing or dead, 11 drafted into the army and three forced to flee. (The remaining were too elderly to be considered a threat.) The Catholic school system was completely eliminated. Both seminaries were closed, as well as 20 convents, 10 monasteries, 15 orphanages, 16 church schools and 10 charitable institutions. Catholic printing presses were confiscated, and the publication of seven religious periodicals ceased. Enver Hoxha himself spearheaded the campaign against the Catholic Church. In 1967 a total of 2,169 churches, mosques, cloisters and shrines were converted into cultural centers for young people. The government boasted that it had created the first atheist nation in the world.

The coup de grâce to organized religion was Decree 4337, which rescinded all constitutional guarantees of freedom of religion and thus in effect placed religious organizations outside the law.

Since 1967, all organized religious activity has ceased to exist in Albania. The last Catholic church, the Cathedral of Tirana, was closed in 1969. Even cemeteries were affected, and all crosses and religious inscriptions in them were removed. Younger clergymen have been forced to seek work elsewhere, and the elder clergy were ordered to return to their birthplaces, which they could not leave without permission from the authorities.

Despite these draconian measures, there is believed to be considerable religious activity underground in Albania. The Communist Party ideological organ *Bashkimi* acknowledged in 1973 that "we have by no means achieved complete emancipation from the remnants of religious influences," and the periodical *Nentori* admitted that "despite the hard blows religion had suffered through the destruction of its material institutions, religious ideology is still alive." In 1976 a new clause was inserted into the Constitution stating that Albania "recognizes no religion and supports atheist propaganda for the purpose of implanting the scientific materialist world outlook."

HISTORICAL BACKGROUND

Modern Albanians call their country Shqiperia and themselves Shqipetare. In ancient times they were known as Illyrians, and in the Middle Ages as Arberishe or Arbeneshe and their country as Arberia or Arbenia. The present names, Albania and Albanians, are derived from the names Arbanoi or Arbaniti, which appeared in the 11th century.

Until 168 B.C. Albania comprised parts of the Kingdom of Illyria, with its capital at Shkoder. Conquered by the Romans in 168–67 B.C., it remained a province of the Roman Empire until A.D. 395, when it became part of the Byzantine Empire. During the succeeding nine centuries, invasions of Huns, Bulgarians and Slavs drove the Illyrians to the mountain fastnesses on the Adriatic coast, where they are concentrated today. During the Crusades in the 12th and 13th centuries, Albania became a thoroughfare for the crusading armies, who used the port of Durres as a bridgehead. After the Fourth Crusade, in 1204, Venice received control over Albania and Epirus but yielded possession to the kings of Naples in the 13th century. In 1272 Charles I of Anjou crossed the Adriatic, occupied Durres and thus established the Kingdom of Albania, which lasted for nearly a century.

Albania's dark ages began with the defeat of the Serbs by the Ottoman Turks in 1389 in the Battle of Kosovo, after which the Turks asserted their suzerainty over the country. The native tribal chieftains were forced to submit to Turkey and convert to Islam. One of them was John Kastrioti of Kruje (a region northeast of Tirana), whose four sons were taken hostage by the sultan to be trained in the Ottoman service. The youngest of these sons, Gjergj (1403–68), soon won the sultan's favor, distinguished himself in the Turkish army, converted to Islam and was bestowed the title of Skander Bey, which in Albanian became Skanderbeg. Following the defeat of the Turks at Nish by the Hungarian king Hunyadi, Skanderbeg fled to his native land and seized from the Turks his father's fortress at Kruje. Skanderbeg's defection, reconversion to Christianity and the creation of the Albanian League of Princes in 1444, with himself as its head, enraged the Ottomans, who began a series of campaigns against him. In his wars against the Turks, Skanderbeg was aided by the kings of Naples and the popes, one of whom, Pope Nicholas V, named him Champion of Christendom.

With Skanderbeg's death, the Turks were gradually able to extend their hold over Albania, defeating both the local chieftains and the Venetians. To escape the Turks, vast numbers of Albanians fled to southern Italy and Sicily. The Turks were able to subjugate Albania politically and religiously more than any other Balkan country. Many of the Albanian *pashas* and *beys* became viziers of the empire; one, Mehmet Ali Pasha, founded an Egyptian dynasty that lasted until 1952; another, Ali Pasha Tepelena, known as the Lion of Yannina, ruled over a principality that stretched from the Gulf of Arta to Montenegro until the Ottomans defeated and decapitated him in 1822.

It was only when the Ottoman Empire broke up in 1912 that Albania became an independent nation. Virtually dismembered by the Treaty of San Stefano, Albania struggled to ward off the territorial demands of Serbia, Austria-Hungary, Italy, Russia and Montenegro. In the summer of 1912, Albanians staged a series of revolts, and a group of patriots, led by Ismail Qemal Bey, proclaimed Albania's independence at Vlore on November

28, 1912. Supported by Austria and Italy, Albania's independence was recognized by the 1912 Conference of Ambassadors at London, and its northern boundaries were demarcated by a 1913 agreement. This agreement assigned Shkoder to Albania but gave Kosovo and Metohija (Ksomet), then inhabited chiefly by Albanians, to Serbia. The southern boundaries were determined by the 1913 Protocol of Florence.

The Conference of Ambassadors drafted a constitution for the new state under the guarantees of the Great Powers; created an International Control Commission to control the country's administration and budget; and selected as its sovereign a German prince, William zu Wied. Prince William arrived on March 14, 1914, but had to flee the country within six months due to the outbreak of World War I.

At the end of World War I, Albania was occupied by the Allied armies, mostly Italian and French. Both Greece and Italy laid claims to parts of Albania, and the Tittoni-Venizelos Agreement of 1919 called for the dismemberment of the country. The Secret Treaty of London, concluded in 1915, provided for the partition of Albanian territory among Italy, Montenegro, Serbia and Greece. But President Woodrow Wilson's insistence on the restoration of an independent Albania based on the principle of self-determination saved the country from partition. In the summer of 1920 an Albanian partisan army drove the Italians from Vlore, and the Italian government recognized Albania's independence. In January 1920 a congress of representatives met in Lushnje in central Albania and created a government headed by a Council of Regency composed of representatives of the four religious denominations: The Sunnis and the Bektashis representing Muslims and the Catholics and Orthodox representing Christians. The stage was set for an internal struggle between the old, essentially Muslim, landlords, led by Ahmet Zogu and the Western-educated liberals, led by Bishop Fan S. Noli. In 1924 the liberals staged a successful coup against the conservatives, forced Zogu to flee to Yugoslavia and formed a new government under Bishop Noli. But Bishop Noli's radical policies alarmed some of his supporters and neighboring states. Meanwhile, Zogu led an army from Yugoslavia and in December 1924 entered Tirana as victor, forcing Bishop Noli to flee. Zogu ruled for the next 14 years, the longest since the time of Skanderbeg, first as President Zogu until 1928 and then as Zog I, king of the Albanians. King Zog was a moderate dictator and survived three coups against him, in 1932, 1935 and 1937. He effected far-reaching reforms both in the administration and society, particularly outlawing the traditional blood feuds and the carrying of arms. In 1926 and 1927 Zogu concluded bilateral treaties with Italy, establishing a defensive alliance between the two countries. These treaties enabled Italy to extend its sphere of influence over Albania and eventually led to the Italian invasion on April 7, 1939. King Zog fled the country, never to return. Albania was united with Italy under the crown of King Victor Emmanuel III.

In the chaotic conditions created by the Italian occupation and World War II, the Communists took the lead as the dominant resistance movement. On November 8,

1941, the Albanian Communist Party was founded under the guidance of two emissaries from the Yugoslav Communist Party, Miladin Popovic and Dushan Mugosha. Enver Hoxha, a young schoolteacher who had studied in France and Belgium, was elected as provisional and subsequently as permanent secretary general. From the outset, the strategy of the party was to conceal its Marxist character and to stress nationalism and patriotism. To this end it created the National Liberation Movement on September 16, 1942, to coordinate the activities of a number of guerrilla bands, not all of whom were Communist. In July 1943, at the Conference of Labinot, the General Staff of the Army of National Liberation of Albania was created, with Enver Hoxha as the chief commissar. Its prime objective in the 1943–44 years was to immobilize the other nationalist resistance groups, such as the Balli Kombetar (National Front) and the Legality Movement, both strongly anti-Yugoslav. Having accomplished this goal, the National Liberation Front, as the movement was by then called, sponsored the Congress of Permet to create the necessary machinery to seize power. The Congress of Berat, convened by the front in October 1944, converted the committee into a coalition provisional "democratic" government, which in the following month seized control of the whole country, and on November 28, Albania's traditional independence day, installed itself in Tirana. Yugoslavia played a major role in the Communist takeover, supplying political direction through its emissaries, although most of the war matériel was supplied by the Anglo-American command in Italy.

In August 1945 the first congress of the National Liberation Front was held, and the name of the organization was changed to the Democratic Front to make it more palatable to the public. Only Democratic Front candidates were allowed in the first postwar national elections held in the same year. The Constituent Assembly thus elected on December 2, 1945, proclaimed on January 11, 1946, the People's Republic of Albania, and on March 14 it approved the first Albanian Constitution, based largely on the Yugoslav Communist Constitution.

For events after 1945, see Chronology.

CONSTITUTION & GOVERNMENT

The Constitution of Albania was adopted on December 27, 1976. It replaced the Constitution of 1946, amended in 1948 and revised in parts since then. The Constitution of 1976 redesignated the People's Republic of Albania as the Socialist People's Republic of Albania and identified the Albanian Party of Labor (APL) as "the sole directing political power in state and society" and Marxism-Leninism as the ruling ideology. "In the construction of socialism," the Constitution declares, "Albania relies primarily on its own efforts," a reference to its hermit status in the Communist world. Private property is abolished and the "bases of religious obscurantism" and financial dealings with "capitalist or revisionist monopolies or states" are outlawed.

The supreme bodies of state power are identified as the People's Assembly and the Presidium of the Peo-

ORGANIZATION OF THE ALBANIAN GOVERNMENT

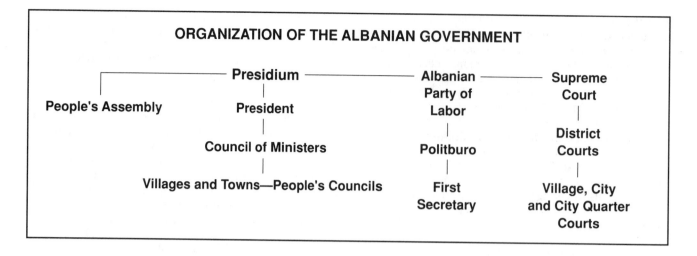

People's Assembly

Presidium — President — Council of Ministers — Villages and Towns—People's Councils

Albanian Party of Labor — Politburo — First Secretary

Supreme Court — District Courts — Village, City and City Quarter Courts

ple's Assembly. The "supreme organ of state administration" is the Council of Ministers, headed by a chairman and a vice chairman. In practice, the head of state is the president of the Presidium of the People's Assembly and the head of government or prime minister is the chairman of the Council of Ministers. In 1989 the cabinet consisted of a chairman, four deputy chairmen, 15 ministers and the chairmen of the State Planning Commission and the State Control Commission.

The interlocking of the party with the Council of Ministers is standard practice in Albania, as it was in other East European countries. Members of the Council generally are members or candidate members of the Politburo.

One atypical feature of the Albanian governmental structure is the major role assigned to the Presidium of the People's Assembly. The president of the Presidium also is the chief of state, and its members hold high party positions. Because of the infrequent and short meetings of the People's Assembly, the Presidium functions as the actual legislative branch of government. It does more than conduct the affairs of the People's Assembly between sessions; it also conducts the affairs of government. It can issue decrees and ratify international treaties, appoint diplomats, appoint the supreme commander of the armed forces, decree general mobilization and a state of war and designate ministry jurisdiction over various enterprises.

Albania is perhaps the last of the Stalinist nations in the world, with an administrative apparatus designed to perpetuate a small elitist Communist clique in office. Despite its official adherence to "scientific materialism," old ethnic and tribal loyalties and feuds still play a part in the highest levels of government. During his regime of over 40 years, Hoxha assassinated many of his lieutenants, such as Mehmet Shehu.

CABINET LIST

Chairman, Presidium, People's Assembly: Ramiz Alia
Chairman, Council of Ministers (Prime Minister): Adil Karkani
Deputy Chairman, Council of Ministers: Pali Miska
Deputy Chairman, Council of Ministers: Manush Myftiu
Deputy Chairman, Council of Ministers: Simon Stefani

CABINET LIST (continued)

Minister of Agriculture: Pali Miska
Minister of Communal Economy: Xhemal Tafaj
Minister of Construction: Ismail Ahmeti
Minister of Domestic Trade: Osman Murati
Minister of Education: Skender Gjinushi
Minister of Finance: Andrea Nako
Minister of Food Industry: Jovan Bardhi
Minister of Foreign Affairs: Reiz Malile
Minister of Foreign Trade: Shane Korbeci
Minister of Health: Ahmet Kamberi
Minister of Industry, Mines and Energy: Besnik Bekteshi
Minister of Internal Affairs: Simon Stefani
Minister of Light Industry: Vito Kapo
Minister of People's Defense: Prokop Murra
Minister of Transportation: Hajredin Celiku
Chairman, State Control Commission: Manush Myftiu
Chairman, State Planning Commission: Niko Gjyzari
Director, Albanian State Bank: Qirjako Mihali

RULERS OF ALBANIA

Heads of State (from 1914)
March–September 1914: Prince William of Wied
September 1914: Burhan Eddin
(September 1914–April 1920: Austrian, French and Italian occupations)

Regents (from 1920)
April 1920–December 1921: Aqif Pasha Elbasani/Luigj Bumci/ Mihal Turtulli/Abdi Toptani
December 1921–February 1922: Omer Vrioni/Antoine Pistulli
December 1921–January 1925: Sotir Peci/Refik Toptani
December 1922–January 1925: Xhafar Ypi/Gjon Coba

President (from 1925)
January 1925–August 1928: Ahmed Zogu

King (from 1928)
August 1928–April 1939: Zog I
(April 1939–September 1943: Italian occupation)
(September 1943–October 1944: German occupation)
(November 1944–January 1946: Provisional Government)

Presidents (from 1946)
(Chairman of the Presidium of the People's Assembly)
January 1946–July 1953: Omer Nishani
July 1953–November 1982: Haxhi Lleshi
November 1982–   : Ramiz Alia

FREEDOM & HUMAN RIGHTS

Although information on Albania is scanty, by most accounts the worst excesses of the Hoxha years are over and under President Ramiz Alia, restrictions on the average Albanian have been relaxed somewhat. Although Albanians remain isolated from foreign influences, the government tacitly allows citizens to receive foreign broadcasts. The government has liberalized issuance of visas to foreign tourists and allowed a limited number of Albanians to visit foreign countries in groups.

However, the improvement in the human rights situation is only marginal, and complaints continue to occur about violations. Although the number of political and religious prisoners has declined, physical abuse of such prisoners has not entirely ceased. Prison conditions are harsh. Long-term solitary confinement is common; cells are cramped without room to lie down, unheated, unfurnished and without sanitary facilities. The Burrel prison and the Spac and Ballsh labor camps are noted, in particular, for their harsh conditions.

The Albanian Criminal Code is explicitly ideological and is characterized officially as a weapon in the class struggle. Political crimes are loosely defined, allowing the regime to use the courts to punish any person. Of the 34 crimes listed in the Criminal Code, 12 are political crimes for which the death sentence may be imposed. The Criminal Code also provides that banishment (generally to a state farm or other state enterprise) or internment may be imposed administratively, without trial, for up to five years on persons considered to be threat to the Communist system, and on their families. Political detainees lack adequate legal safeguards during pretrial investigations. Some of these investigations drag on for years while the accused languish in prison, without access to lawyers or relatives.

The judicial system is under the total control of the Albanian Party of Labor. Courts may not render independent verdicts in conflict with the policies of the regime. Political trials are held in camera, and political prisoners are denied defense counsel. Most such trials are summary—few last more than one day—and there have been no acquittals. Estimates of the number of prisoners vary from 4,000 to 40,000, including members of the prewar elite and pro-Yugoslav, pro-Soviet and pro-Chinese sympathizers, to say nothing of alleged CIA agents.

The government uses a pervasive informer network to report on the private lives of citizens. Neither the privacy of the individual nor the sanctity of the home is respected. Contacts with the outside world are carefully monitored.

The freedoms of speech and of the press do not exist. Any citizen who publicly criticizes the government is subject to swift and severe reprisals under an article of the Constitution that forbids antistate agitation and propaganda. All news media are state-controlled and serve as mouthpieces for the regime. Even art, literature and scholarship must hew to the government line and extol the contributions of the APL to society. Information from abroad is carefully monitored, and persons having unauthorized contacts with foreigners may be jailed.

The state of religion in Albania (see Religions) reflects the thoroughness with which the regime pursues its Stalinist ideology. Describing itself as the world's first atheist state, the government has converted all the nation's buildings of worship into cultural centers, museums, sports halls and so on. A substantial number of political prisoners are priests, some of whom were arrested for conducting religious services and others for baptizing children.

The Constitution does not guarantee freedom of movement, either within the country or abroad. The Criminal Code states that flight from the country or refusal to return to the fatherland by a person sent abroad is considered treason, which may be punishable by death.

Ethnic minorities suffer a number of civil disabilities, particularly affecting their right to live in border areas. The government as well as the leadership of the APL are overwhelmingly ethnic Albanian. It is believed that the regime has advanced the rights of women in terms of their participation in the labor force.

Workers do not have the right to associate freely or

to strike. There is only one trade union federation, and that is the United Trade Unions of Albania (UTUA), an arm of the APL. It has no significant independent voice in the conduct of labor relations but plays a key role in indoctrinating workers.

CIVIL SERVICE

No information is available on the Albanian civil service.

LOCAL GOVERNMENT

For purposes of local government, Albania is divided into districts, cities, towns and villages, each administered by a people's council. As constitutional agencies, these councils wield cultural, administrative and economic powers within their jurisdictions. They are responsible for drawing up local budgets, maintaining public order and implementing laws. The Constitution also requires that councils call periodic meetings of their constituents.

Each council chooses an executive committee from among its membership. Other committees and departments may be established at the discretion of the executive committee for performance of specific tasks or for supervision of public enterprises. The councils are elected from lists of the local organizations of the Albanian Party of Labor for three-year terms.

POLITICAL SUBDIVISIONS				
		Area		Population
Provinces	Capitals	sq km.	sq mi.	(1983 est.)
Berat	Berat	1,026	396	157,300
Diber	Peshkopi	1,568	605	137,800
Durres	Durres	848	327	220,600
Elbasan	Elbasan	1,481	572	213,200
Fier	Fier	1,175	454	216,400
Gjirokaster	Gjirokaster	1,137	439	61,200
Gramsh	Gramsh	695	268	39,300
Kolonje	Erseke	805	311	22,500
Korce	Korce	2,181	842	201,300
Kruje	Kruje	607	234	94,600
Kukes	Kukes	1,331	514	88,400
Lezhe	Lezhe	479	185	54,200
Librazhd	Librazhd	1,013	391	64,100
Lushnje	Lushnje	712	275	117,800
Mat	Burrel	1,028	397	68,700
Mirdite	Rreshen	867	335	45,800
Permet	Permet	930	359	37,100
Pogradec	Pogradec	725	280	62,700
Puke	Puke	1,033	399	46,100
Sarande	Sarande	1,097	424	78,200
Shkoder	Shkoder	2,528	976	210,200
Skrapar	Corovoda	775	299	42,500
Tepelene	Tepelene	817	315	46,100
Tirana	Tirana	1,238	478	316,100
Tropoje	Bajram	1,043	403	40,900
Vlore	Vlore	1,609	621	158,200
TOTAL		28,748	11,100	2,841,300

FOREIGN POLICY

Even after independence, Albania was one of the least influential and most ignored nations in Europe. Significantly, when the fate of East European nations was decided at Yalta and Teheran after World War II, Albania was left out of the discussions. As a result, Albania's foreign relations have been characterized by disregard for the conventions of diplomatic conduct on the one hand and distrust of the motives of powerful nations on the other. Even within the Communist bloc, Albania has been an odd man out, with no permanent friendships or alliances. No nation in the postwar world has elevated isolationism as an ideology and followed it as consistently as Albania.

World War II represents a watershed in Albanian history, marking its complete break with the West. Since then Albanian foreign policy has undergone four phases. From 1945 to 1948 it was a satellite of Yugoslavia, which had helped to found the Albanian Communist Party and masterminded its rise to power. In 1948 it broke with Yugoslavia and became a full-fledged satellite of the Soviet Union, a position it retained until 1960. During this period it became a member of the Warsaw Pact and the Council for Mutual Economic Assistance. As an ardent Stalinist, Hoxha found the Cold War congenial; it gave him an opportunity to direct his blasts at the "two greatest evils in the world—revisionism and imperialism—personified by Yugoslavia and the United States, respectively."

Stalin's death in 1953 marked the beginning of the breach with Moscow, but it was not until 1960 that the Soviet phase of Albanian foreign policy ended. Hoxha was alarmed by Nikita Khrushchev's efforts to seek a rapprochement with Tito. Seeking a new ally, Albania found one in Peking. In 1960, as Khrushchev sought to line up Communist parties for a condemnation of Communist China, Albania defied the Soviet Union by declining to participate in the conference. By the end of 1961, diplomatic relations between the two countries were severed, Soviet aid ceased and Soviet technicians and advisers left Tirana, to be replaced by those of Communist China. Khrushchev became the object of violent attacks in the Albanian press, being castigated as more a revisionist than Tito. In turn, Albania became the proxy for violent propaganda blasts from Moscow obviously directed against Peking.

The Chinese phase of Albanian foreign policy was slightly different from the first two because now Albania was not a satellite but rather a client of a powerful state, which it defended in world councils. Albania was instrumental in gaining U.N. membership for the People's Republic of China. However, with the death of Mao Zedong and the post-Maoist regime's moves toward détente with the West, Albania found itself once again estranged from its patron. The estrangement culminated in China's suspension of economic and military assistance (totaling over $5 billion during a 24-year period). However, formal diplomatic relations were retained.

In the wake of the rupture with China, Albania entered the fourth phase of its foreign policy. This phase was characterized by halfhearted and sporadic moves to forge new links but faced a number of roadblocks: the Kosovo issue with Yugoslavia, the boundary and Greek ethnic minority issues with Greece, the return of Albania's prewar gold reserves held in Britain and a war-related reparations issue with West Germany. Some minor gains included establishment of a ferry service with Italy and air links with Greece and Turkey; and the establishment of diplomatic relations with a few countries, such as France, Italy, Kenya and Botswana.

When Hoxha died in 1985, no foreign delegations were permitted at the funeral, and a Soviet message of condolence was rejected. Ramiz Alia, who replaced Hoxha, has followed the independent policies of his predecessor. Albania remains hostile to the Soviet Union and has reiterated its determination not to have any relations with either the Soviet Union or the United States. However, diplomatic relations were established with Spain in 1986 and with Canada and West Germany in 1987. In 1985 several cooperation agreements were signed with Greece and the Albanian-Greek border crossing at Kakavija was reopened. In 1987 Greece formally ended the technical state of war with Albania that had existed since 1945.

PARLIAMENT

The national legislature is the 250-member People's Assembly, elected every four years from single-member districts. The Constitution refers to it as "the highest organ of state power," but since it meets only briefly twice a year, its real function is as a rubber stamp for the decrees of the Presidium and the Council of Ministers. Members of the Assembly rarely initiate legislative proposals. Bills become laws after an affirmative vote by a simple majority, but an amendment to the Constitution requires a two-thirds vote.

Suffrage is universal for all Albanians over 18 years. Candidates are selected by the Democratic Front. In 1982 a total of 1,627,959 voters voted for the party slate and only one voted against it!

There is only one political party, the Albanian Party of Labor (see Political Parties).

POLITICAL PARTIES

Since the end of World War II Albania has had only one political party, the Albanian Party of Labor (Partia e Punes e Shqiperise, APL) also known since 1948 as the Albanian Workers' Party and founded in 1941 as the Albanian Communist Party. As in other Communist parties, the real source of all power within the APL is the Politburo, composed of 13 regular members and five candidate members. The top executive branches of the Politburo are the Secretariat and the various directorates of the Central Committee. Policy guidelines adopted by the Politburo are passed on by the Secretariat to the appropriate directorate, which directs its implementation by the respective state and party organs. The

most important directorates are the Directorate of Cadres and Organizations, the Directorate of Agitation and Propaganda, the Directorate of Education and Culture, the Directorate of State Administrative Organs and the Directorate of Mass Organizations. Where important policy issues are involved, they are dealt with by special commissions created in the Central Committee. The next highest echelon in the party hierarchy is the Central Committee, composed of 61 regular and 36 candidate members. The Central Committee gives formal approval to Politburo decisions.

According to the party statutes, the highest organ is the Party Congress, convened every four years. The Congress formally reviews the party program and elects the Central Committee and the Central Control and Auditing Commission. Since the Congress meets only once in four years and the Central Committee once in four months, their impact on party activities is minimal.

This organizational setup is duplicated at the regional level. The highest regional party organ is the city and district party conference, which meets once a year. Between conferences, party affairs are managed by party committees, within which a party bureau of generally 11 members wields the real power. Party bureau members must first be approved by the party's national central committee. District or city committees not only guide the activities of all local party organizations and look after their ideological and political education but also oversee the work of local governmental bodies within their jurisdiction.

At the grass-roots level, party units known as organizations serve as the final links with the masses. Such organizations exist in factories and plants, agricultural enterprises, villages, units of the armed and security forces, state administration and schools. No official is appointed without prior approval of the appropriate party organizations.

The APL operates a number of schools and courses for its cadres as well as three research and study institutes attached to the Central Committee. The highest school is the V. I. Lenin Institute. The three party institutes are the Institute of Marxist-Leninist Studies, the Institute of Party History and the Institute for Economic Studies. The party also conducts practical courses and study groups for its activists and propagandists.

All-pervasive and all-embracing as its organization is, the APL also utilizes several mass organizations to ensure that it reaches all segments of Albanian society. The most important of these organizations are the Democratic Front, the Union of Albanian Working Youth, the Union of Albanian Women and the United Trade Unions of Albania. Hoxha once described these organizations as the "levers of the party" for mobilizing and educating the people. They also are described as "fighting reserves of the party."

PRINCIPAL ECONOMIC INDICATORS, 1988*

Gross National Product: $2.7 billion to $2.9 billion
GNP per capita: $930

*Most economic indicators for Albania have not been published.

GROSS DOMESTIC PRODUCT, 1988*

GDP average annual growth rate: 5.7% (1980–86)
Sectoral origin of GDP (%)
  Primary
    Agriculture: 34
    Mining: N.A.
  Secondary
    Manufacturing: 43
    Construction: 8
    Public utilities: N.A.
  Tertiary
    Transportation & communications:
    Trade:
    Finance:
    Public administration & defense: } 15
    Services:
    Other:

*Most data relative to Albania's Gross Domestic Product have not been published.

ECONOMY

Albania is the poorest country in Europe. Estimates of the GNP and the GNP per capita are not available, but the latter is believed to be less than $1,000. The reasons for the country's backwardness are not far to seek. It emerged from a feudal economic system only after World War I and then was beset with political and social problems, as a result of which the transition to a modern industrial economy did not take place. The Communists took over an economy in 1945 that was basically agricultural and that possessed only a rudimentary industrial sector and practically no entrepreneurial class. Ideological considerations imposed many restrictions on the pace of development; the new regime was forced to depend on its patrons—Yugoslavia, the Soviet Union and China—for priming the economy and providing the start-up capital and machinery to help Albania catch up with the rest of Europe. Because Albania switched its patrons in fairly rapid succession, the economy grew by fits and starts rather than consistently. At the same time, being a Communist nation gave the country certain advantages. Austerity and regimentation could be imposed in a way not possible in a free-market economy; draconian measures would be accepted in silence by the long-suffering populace; decisions could be made fairly quickly and enforced decisively. Opposition could be crushed and economic saboteurs dealt with summarily. It also was possible to coordinate ideology and a system of centralized planning through a series of five-year and annual plans. Albania has a state-run economy, where the dominant sector is public.

Data for Albania's balance of payments have not been published.

The first five-year plan was launched in 1951, when Albania had been three years into Soviet tutelage. It and the second five-year plan (1956–60) emphasized rapid industrial development. When the third five-year plan was launched in 1961, agriculture was suffering as a result of neglect during the previous decade, and the nation was facing a food deficit. Furthermore, Soviet aid had been suspended and China, as the new ally, was

better at agricultural than industrial aid. As a result, the third and the fourth (1960–70) five-year plans shifted the emphasis to agriculture. Both plans fell short of their targets because the peasants were not ready to relinquish the age-old farming methods and adopt modern scientific farming methods. The fifth five-year plan (1971–75) aimed at extensive capital investments and large industrial projects. During the sixth five-year plan (1976–80) the net material product (NMP) grew by 5%, industrial production by 6.8%, agricultural production by 21.4% and exports by 33%. The seventh five-year plan (1981–85) targeted an NMP growth rate of 35% to 37% but achieved a growth rate of 16%. Industrial production grew by 27%, agricultural production by 13% and exports by 29%. The eighth five-year plan (1986–90) stressed development of energy and mineral resources.

PLANNED GROWTH PERCENTAGES UNDER THE EIGHTH FIVE-YEAR PLAN (1986–90)

Global Social Product	31–33
Net Material Product	35–47
Industrial production	29–31
Agricultural production	35–37
Foreign trade	34–36
Real income	7–9
Basic investment	11–13

Albania is not involved in official development assistance programs.

After 45 years of forced economic development, the Albanian economy has been described by foreign observers as a mixture of the 14th and the 20th centuries. On the farms oxen and buffalo are found cheek by jowl with modern (but foreign-made) tractors. This dichotomy is best illustrated in the main square of the capital city, where traffic policemen stand waving their batons at a nonexistent traffic. Industry is geared not to the country's domestic needs but toward exports. The limited domestic resources are poorly developed, and the economy is heavily dependent on foreign economic assistance.

However, although austerity and regimentation still prevail, the country has achieved some measure of economic progress under the Communist regime. While Albania remains the poorest country in Europe, it clearly has outdistanced comparable countries in the Third World in creating a strong infrastructure and economic self-reliance.

PUBLIC FINANCE

Albania's public finance is shrouded in the kind of secrecy that other governments impose on military transactions. Information on budgetary practices is not available, and only such data are released annually as suits the government. Three different budgets are approved by the People's Assembly every year: a state budget, a national budget and a budget for the local government. The state budget is 7% to 8% larger than the national budget. Only about one-fourth of local budgetary revenues are derived from local taxation, and it may be surmised that the balance is paid out of the central government budget. The fiscal year is the calendar year.

Until the break with the Soviet Union in 1960, budgets usually were in surplus, a matter of great pride for the government. The amount of this surplus declined steeply thereafter but still is maintained. In 1970, annual revenues were reported as 5.21 billion leke and the expenditures as 5.11 billion leke. Annual revenues and expenditures respectively were 8.433 billion and 8.415 billion leke in 1985, 9.3 billion leke and 9.250 billion leke in 1986 and 9.350 billion leke and 9.3 billion leke in 1987. Total investment during the 1986–90 five-year plan is estimated at 24.450 billion leke, 2.8 billion leke more than under the 1981–85 five-year plan.

Revenues are listed in the budget under two headings: national economy and the nonproductive sector, and other income. In 1969 all personal income taxes were abolished. The remaining sources of income are a turnover tax on all goods, deductions from enterprise profits, and social insurance premiums. These sources yield on average three-quarters of the revenues. The balance, not shown in official statistics, consists primarily of income from agriculture in the form of compulsory deliveries and proceeds from state farm operations. By far the most important sources of revenue are the turnover tax and deductions from profits, together yielding over 70% of revenues. The turnover tax and the enterprise profits deduction fall heavily on consumers because they are reflected in the sales prices of commodities and consequently represent a hidden sales tax. It also is regressive because, unlike an income tax, it takes no account of differences in income and places a heavier burden on those least able to pay.

Budget laws specify the amount of revenue to be derived from the socialized sector, including collective farms and cooperative enterprises. This proportion has ranged between 85% and 90%. The revenue from the nonsocialized sector consists mostly of taxes imposed on the output from personal farm plots of collective and state farm workers and, to a lesser extent, of taxes on some private artisan and other activities tolerated by the government within narrowly prescribed limits.

CENTRAL GOVERNMENT EXPENDITURES, 1987

% of total expenditures
Defense: 11.3
Education: ⎫
Health: ⎬ 28.7
Housing, Social Security, Welfare: ⎭
Economic services: 54.3
Other (including administration): 1.6
Total expenditures as % of GNP: N.A.
Overall surplus or deficit as % of GNP: N.A.

CENTRAL GOVERNMENT REVENUES, 1987*

% of total current revenues
Income from state enterprises: 96.3
Other: 3.7

*Most data regarding Albanian central government revenues are not published.

EXCHANGE RATE
(National Currency per U.S. Dollar)

1979	1980	1981	1982	1983	1984	1985	1986	1987	1988
7.00	7.00	7.00	7.00	7.00	7.00	7.00	7.00	7.00	7.00

GROWTH PROFILE
(Annual Growth Rates, %)*

Population, 1985–2000: 1.8
Crude birth rate, 1985–90: 26.5
Crude death rate, 1985–90: 5.4
Urban population, 1980–85: 3.3
Labor force, 1985–2000: 2.4
GDP, 1980–85: 5.7
Energy production, 1980–86: −1.3
Energy consumption, 1980–86: 0.9

*Most data regarding annual growth rates in Albania have not been published.

Published information is also scanty on expenditures. Data are shown for some outlays, such as defense, administration, sociocultural measures and the national economy. Expenditures on these items have remained remarkably stable over the years. In 1987 defense accounted for 11.3%, the national economy 54.5%, sociocultural measures 28.8% and administration 1.5%. The largest item under the national economy is investment. The amount of investment and its sectoral distribution vary from year, depending primarily on amount of foreign assistance, sectoral performance and needs. The relative shares of sectoral investments have fluctuated widely, but generally industry receives the lion's share—up to 60%—and agriculture about 10% to 20%. Investment in housing and for social and cultural purposes has been minimal, reflecting the regime's policy of promoting rapid industrial development rather than raising the standard of living.

CURRENCY & BANKING

The national currency is the lek (plural: leke), divided into 100 quintars or quindarka. Coins are issued in denominations of 5, 10, 20 and 50 quintars and notes in denominations of 1, 3, 5, 10, 20, 50 and 100 leke.

The lek is a nonconvertible paper currency with multiple official exchange rates. There are two types of tourist or support leks applicable to nonresidents and to support and other noncommercial payments received by residents. The first applies to Western countries and the second to Communist countries. A third rate is used to balance clearing accounts under special payments and trade agreements. There also is an illegal black market rate. All currency matters are administered by the Albanian State Bank. Albania is not a member of the World Bank or the IMF, and data regarding Albania's international financial situation are not available.

The sole major banking institution is the Albanian State Bank, which functions as an arm of the Ministry of Finance. It issues currency, provides credit to all economic sectors, accepts savings deposits and serves as the country's Treasury. In addition, it helps the State Planning Commission to prepare the five-year plans and is responsible for controlling all financial activities through the use of its financial levers. The bank's annual reports disclose only some of its operations, particularly its loans to the agricultural and housing sectors. Only a fraction of these loans are granted to individual farmers.

The Directorate of Savings and Insurance accepts deposits through its 115 savings offices and 3,600 agencies.

AGRICULTURE

Albania's agricultural resources are limited. Good agricultural land amounts to only 5% of the country's total land area of 28,748 sq. km. (11,100 sq. mi.). Soils are thin or altogether lacking in the mountains of the North and East, and coarse and infertile sands and gravels are found in the intermediate mountains. The alluvial soils of the lowland plains are sterile and poorly drained. There is little land along the narrow valley floors. This leaves the inland basins and the slightly elevated land between the coastal plains and the mountains as the only regions where farming can be carried on profitably.

The government estimates that about 20% of the land is arable, but most Western sources estimate that only 11% of the land can be so categorized. Nearly half of the arable land is in vineyards and olive groves. Forests cover one-third of the land and pastures another third. About 22% of the land is unproductive, but half of the unproductive land has some potential for development.

Agriculture is organized on the Stalinist model, and farm operations are centrally planned and carried out by state and collective farms. Self-sufficiency in foods is a high priority because of the financial burden of grain imports. Special emphasis is placed on the output of bread grains, the staple of the Albanian diet, and the production of potatoes as a substitute of bread. Next to grains and potatoes, the major crops are export crops such as cotton, tobacco, sugar beets and sunflowers as well as grapes, olives and other fruits and vegetables for export.

The Albanian peasant is traditionbound and averse to changes in traditional farming techniques. In the 1950s the government socialized the land and introduced new farming methods through harsh means, although less bloody than those of Stalin. Mass mobilization of peasants did not result in better performance, and the early five-year plan targets for agriculture had to be scaled down. The major thrusts of official efforts have been to bring in additional acreage through land reclamation; mechanization and improvement of farm techniques; expansion of livestock herds and supply of fodder; and extension of the irrigation system to overcome the adverse effects of frequent droughts. The increase in the area of cultivated land since 1960 has been achieved at the expense of natural pastures and meadows. Much of the work was done manually through mobilization of large numbers of coolies, as in the Chinese system, and

with the participation of members of the armed forces. By the end of the 1980s almost all land capable of being reclaimed had been reclaimed. Expansion of the irrigation network proceeded more slowly with the use of the same manual construction methods.

AGRICULTURAL INDICATORS, 1988

Agriculture's share of GDP (%): 34
Average annual growth rate (%): N.A.
Value added in agriculture ($): N.A.
Cereal imports (000 tons): 3
Index of Agricultural Production (1979–81=100): 108 (1986)
Index of food production (1979–81=100): 108 (1986)
Index of Food Production Per Capita (1979–81=100): 97 (1984–86)
Number of tractors: 10,580
Number of harvester-threshers: 1,310
Total fertilizer consumption (tons): 9,410
Fertilizer consumption (100 g. per ha.): 1,320
Number of farms: 400
Average size of holding, ha. (ac.) 1,686 (3,491)
Tenure (%)
　State: 100
% of farms using irrigation: N.A.
Total land in farms ha. (ac.): 710,000 (1,754,410)
Farms as % of total land area: 24.7
Land use (%)
　Total cropland: 62.6
　　Permanent crops: 27.2
　　Temporary crops: ⎫
　　Fallow: ⎭ 72.8
　　Meadows & pastures: ⎫
　　Woodlands: ⎬ 37.4
　　Other: ⎭
Yields, kg./ha. (lb./ac.)
　Grains: 3,048 (2,720)
　Roots & tubers: 9,161 (8,177)
　Pulses 409 (365)
　Milk, kg. (lb.)/animal 1,410 (3,108)
　Livestock (000)
　　Cattle: 610
　　Sheep: 1,230
　　Hogs: 220
　　Horses: 42
　　Chickens: 5,000
Forestry
　Production of roundwood, 000 cu. m. (000 cu. ft.): 2,330 (82,284)
　　of which industrial roundwood (%): 31
　Value of exports ($ 000): 710
Fishing
　Total catch (000 tons): 13.7
　　of which marine (%): 73.7
　Value of exports ($ 000): N.A.

Agricultural organization consists of two types of farms: state farms under the direction of central or local governments, and collective farms. State farms, modeled on the *sovkhozes* of the Soviet Union, were established beginning in 1945 on lands confiscated from large landowners and foreign concessionaires and contain some of the most productive land in the country. Collective farms were organized through the forcible consolidation of private holdings. Begun in 1946, the collective farm program was completed only in 1968 because of strong peasant resistance. The basic features of a collective farm are: complete government control; collective use of the land and other principal means of production; obligatory common work by the members; and distribution of the net income to members on the basis of the quantity and quality of the work performed. Farm members receive as their share whatever remains after completion of compulsory deliveries to the state, provision of prescribed operating and investment funds, payment for irrigation water and machine-tractor station services, and setting aside 2% of the income for social assistance to members. The General Assembly of all the members is the highest ruling organ of a collective farm, but actual control is vested in the farm's basic party organization.

An important feature of the state and collective farms is the small private plot allotted to a member family for its own personal use. These plots vary from 0.10 to 0.15 ha. (0.25 to 0.38 ac.), depending on the location and the availability of irrigation. The collective farm statute also entitles each family to maintain a few domestic animals privately, no more than one cow or one pig and up to 10 to 20 sheep and goats.

There are 38 large centrally controlled state farms with an average of 2,915 ha. (7,200 ac.) of farmland, including about 1,943 ha. (4,800 ac.) of cultivated land. The 250 locally administered state farms have an average of less than 162 ha. (400 ac.). The average size of collective farms varies widely as new ones are created every year and existing ones are consolidated. A total of 87% of all collective farms have less than 1,000 ha. (2,470 ac.) of cultivated land each, and only 9% have more than 2,429 ha. (6,000 ac.). Highland farms are among the smallest, many being smaller than 304 ha. (750 ac.). The average size of a collective farm is about 567 ha. (1,400 ac.) of cultivated land. The 421 collective farms provide 73.6% of total agricultural production and the state sector 26.4%.

Based on available statistics, the total output of field crops rose substantially from 1960 to 1985, at the expense of livestock production. The share of field crops has risen from 44% in 1960 to over 60%, while that of livestock has declined during the same period, from 44% to less than 25%. The following table shows the changes in production of major crops from 1960 to 1985.

PRINCIPAL CROPS (000 tons)			
	1960	1970	1985
Bread grains (wheat, rye, corn)	197.1	593.0	940.0
Potatoes	23.4	475.0	136.0
Rice	4.6	24.0	13.0
Cotton	16.1	34.0	26.0
Tobacco	8.1	16.0	19.0
Sugar beets	72.7	140.0	348.0
Vegetables	71.3	224.0	186.0
Fruits	27.0	75.1	40.0
Grapes	22.3	94.4	83.0

All agricultural marketing is controlled by the state. Albania became self-sufficient in grains in 1976. By 1985 a total of 56.5% of the arable land was under irrigation. With an investment of 980 million leke, this area was to increase to 63% by the end of the 1986–90 plan period.

The Benje irrigation system, for completion in 1990, is to provide 500 cu. m. (17,657 cu. ft.) of water a year, sufficient to irrigate 100,000 ha. (247,000 ac.).

Information on livestock is more sketchy, perhaps as a result of unsatisfactory progress in this sector. One important drawback is the shortage of fodder; another is neglect by peasants of state-owned cattle.

The land officially considered as forest includes areas that contain little more than scrub. In the lower elevations forest have been ravaged by unsystematic cutting, but in the higher elevations mature trees have survived as a result of their inaccessibility. The oaks are the most important trees and make up nearly half of all the forests. They predominate between the 305-m. and 914-m. (1000-ft. and 3,000-ft.) elevations. Beech appear at all elevations between 914 m. (3,000 ft.) and the timberline. The better conifers, including several pine species in the North and fir, with lesser numbers of pine and spruce in the South, coexist with beech. True mixed woods, known as karst woods, occur at medium elevations. Usually they are almost entirely deciduous, the larger including maple, ash, beech and oak, and the intermediate varieties hawthorne, dogwood, hazel and cherry.

Fishing is an important occupation along the Adriatic. A fish cannery is in operation at Vlore.

MANUFACTURING

The manufacturing sector is almost entirely of post-1945 origin. The first manufacturing plant in the country, built in about 1949, was a textile mill, and it was followed by a number of other factories built under the five-year plans and with Soviet aid. This development was interrupted in the wake of the breach with Soviet Union in 1960 but soon resumed with Chinese aid. It is reported that the Chinese equipment was better suited to the needs of the country and of better quality than that supplied by the Soviet Union. Among the major industrial projects completed with Chinese assistance were the oil refinery at Fier, the hydroelectric power station at Vau i Dejes on the Drin River, a thermal power plant at Fier, a steel rolling mill at Elbasan, cement mills at Elbasan and Kruje, large textile combines at Tirana and Berat and a knitgoods factory at Korce. Of industrial plants in the agricultural sector, the largest were the nitrate fertilizer plant at Fier, a superphosphate plant at Lac and a plant for the manufacture of tractor spare parts at Tirana. Along with the construction of technologically up-to-date plants, others were built with outdated technology. At the same time, obsolete plants and workshops remained in use. Until recently these obsolete plants employed more than half the labor force and produced about 40% of the industrial output.

More than 16 industries are represented in the industrial sector, of which the food industry, the extractive industry and light industry account for over 70%. Capital goods predominate, in keeping with the official philosophy of deemphasizing consumer goods. Overall, the sector is poorly balanced not only technically but also because it ignores domestic needs and has no established foreign outlets. For example, the metalworking industry lags in production of spare parts for key industrial and agricultural equipment, causing frequent downtime in plants and farms. Progress toward modernization is slow because managers and workers are more comfortable with older machines and systems and also because of inadequate investment resources. The poor industrial organization and low labor productivity are reflected in the generally inferior quality of the products. At present there is no foreign investment in Albania.

Nevertheless, in terms of the number of commodities produced today in the country compared to 45 years ago, Albania has made significant industrial progress, particularly in cement, copper and, to a lesser extent, textiles.

MANUFACTURING INDICATORS, 1988*

Average annual growth rate, 1980–85: N.A.
Share of GDP: 43.1
Labor force in manufacturing: 36.2

*Most data regarding manufacturing in Albania have not been published.

MINING

Minerals generate a large share of the NMP and provide employment for a large segment of the labor force. This does not mean that the country is rich in minerals but only underscores the relative weakness of the agricultural and industrial sectors. There are considerable reserves in oil and natural gas. Chrome is the most important export commodity. Albania is the largest source of chrome in Eastern Europe. Good-quality copper ore also is available in export quantities. There are no hard coal deposits, but lignite is plentiful and accessible. Asphalt occurs in a concentrated deposit in one small area. Iron, nickel, gold and silver ores occur in less important deposits. Iron is plentiful, but the ores are of low grade. Other minor deposits include bauxite, magnesite, pyrites and gypsum. Limestone is available throughout the country and quarried in many places. The state controls all mining in the country, and there is no foreign participation in mining.

Output of chrome, the major mineral, was 250,000 tons in 1984, accounting for more than 17% of total exports. The Todo Manco mine a Bulqize in Diber District accounts for 44% of all chrome production. The major coal mine is at Memaliaj in Tepelene District. Copper smelting and processing plants are at Rubik, Kukes, Shkoder and Lac. Under the 1986–90 five-year plan, 1.1 billion leke is being invested in the chrome and copper industries. An iron and steel plant was opened at Elbasan in 1976, and a second blast furnace began production in 1981. The plant's output of steel was 14,000 tons in 1986.

ENERGY

Albania is self-sufficient in oil and natural gas. The main oil fields are at Staline (formerly Kucove), from where a pipeline transmits the oil to the port of Vlore. The crude oil, however, is high in sulfur content and is expensive to refine. Output of petroleum was 3.8 million tons in 1984.

Rapid electrification of the country is a major goal of the regime. The country's hydroelectric potential has been estimated at 3 billion kw.-hr. per year, half of which is represented by the Drin River. The first major plant on the Drin River was completed at Vau i Dejes in 1971 and a second station on that river at Fierze in 1975. Output of electric energy reached an estimated 2.850 billion kw.-hr. in 1984. The largest hydroelectric project is the Enver Hoxha station at Koman, the third on the Drin River. It was connected to the national grid in 1987. A major project of the 1986–90 five-year plan is construction of a new hydroelectric and irrigation complex on the Divoli River at Benje in Gramsh District that will generate 250 million kw.-hr. per year. The distibution system also has been rapidly extended. However, distribution of electric power is reported to be very wasteful with losses as high as 15% of total output.

ENERGY INDICATORS, 1988

Primary energy production (quadrillion BTU)
  Crude oil: 0.18
  Natural gas, liquid: 0.0
  Natural gas, dry: 0.01
  Coal: 0.03
  Hydroelectric power: 0.03
  Nuclear power: 0.0
  Total: 0.25
Average annual energy production growth rate (%): −1.3% (1980–86)
Average annual energy consumption growth rate (%): 0.9 (1980–86)
Energy consumption per capita, kg. (lb.) oil equivalent: 1,664 (3,668)
Energy imports as % of merchandise imports (%): N.A.
Public utilities' share of GDP (%): N.A.
Electricity
  Installed capacity (kw): 760,000
  Production (kw.-hr.): 3.88 billion
    % fossil fuel: 12.4
    % hydro: 87.6
    % nuclear:—
  Consumption per capita (kw.-hr.): 1,037
Natural gas, cu. m (cu. ft.)
  Proved reserves: 6 billion (212 billion)
  Production: 450 million (15.892 billion)
  Consumption: 384 million (13.561 billion)
Petroleum, bbl.
  Proved reserves: 200 million
  Years to exhaust proved reserves: 8
  Production: 26 million
  Consumption: 20 million
  Refining capacity per day: 40,000
Coal, 000 tons
  Reserves: 15,000
  Production: 2,300
  Consumption: 2.530

LABOR INDICATORS, 1988

Total economically active population: 1.5 million
As % of working-age population: 74.5
% female: 41.0
% under 20 years of age: 12.9

```
┌─────────────────────────────────────────────┐
│         LABOR INDICATORS, 1988 (continued)    │
│ % unemployed: N.A.                            │
│ Average annual growth rate, 1980–2000 (%): 2.4│
│                                               │
│ Activity rate (%)                             │
│    Total: 45.8                                │
│    Male: 53.5                                 │
│    Female: 38.1                               │
│                                               │
│ % organized labor: 40                         │
│ Hours of work in manufacturing: N.A.          │
│                                               │
│ Sectoral employment (%)                       │
│    Agriculture, forestry & fishing: 21.8      │
│    Mining:          ⎫                          │
│    Manufacturing:   ⎬ 36.2                     │
│    Construction: 11.6                          │
│    Electricity, gas & water:—                 │
│    Transportation & communication: 4.8        │
│    Trade: 7.7                                  │
│    Finance, real estate:        ⎫             │
│    Public administration & defense: ⎬ 12.5    │
│    Services:                    ⎭             │
│    Other: 5.4                                 │
└─────────────────────────────────────────────┘
```

LABOR

The labor force was estimated in 1987 at 1.5 million, compared to 932,000 in 1967. The participation rate is high, at 74.5%, and 41% of women 15 to 64 years old are employed outside the home. Despite the high participation rate, the country suffers from a labor shortage, primarily because of low productivity and a low level of mechanization. Periodically, party hierarchs complain of poor labor discipline and inefficient manpower management. An important element in the official efforts to correct this situation is political indoctrination of the workers. This task is a major function of the trade unions, which have no other significant responsibilities in the field of labor relations.

One notable feature of the Albanian labor scene is the large percentage of the labor force still in agriculture—over 60%—one of the dominant characteristics of a developing country. The industrial labor force is only one-fourth of the agricultural labor force, and the percentage in services is considerably less, at 12.5%. The core of the labor force is locked into the collective farms and, to maintain a steady growth in nonagricultural labor, workers have to be drawn away from rural areas without damaging the rural economy. One way in which this is done is to encourage young women—traditionally unpaid domestic labor—to find work outside the home and even outside their native villages.

Another major problem is the low productivity of the Albanian worker, both in agriculture and in industry. The poor level of productivity is manifested in many ways: absenteeism, loafing on the job and a general indifference toward the quality of the product. On the management side, the main shortcomings include poor organization, setting low work output norms and labor hoarding. In many enterprises the managers abuse a legal provision that allows them to employ 2% more workers than required in the enterprise plan. In some others the effective workday is only six to seven hours.

One distinctive labor practice is the mobilization of large numbers of the population for "voluntary" work on various types of construction and agricultural projects, including building railroads, housing and irrigation canals; land improvement; harvesting; and planting trees. Sometimes tens of thousands of individuals from all walks of life, including members of the armed forces, are assembled by the government to carry out specific tasks with simple tools or with their bare hands. The party uses these projects to display mass enthusiasm in the service of the nation, but observers have noted less than boundless enthusiasm among the masses for such projects.

There is only one labor federation—the Central Council of Albanian Trade Unions—founded in 1945 more as an ideological training arm of the APL than as a regular association of workers. In addition, it is charged with combating religion and promoting productivity. It has no role in safeguarding workers' interests or negotiating with management.

Organizationally the Trade Union Council is composed of three general unions representing workers in (1) industry and construction, (2) education and trade and (3) agriculture and procurement, as well as over 2,000 local unions.

```
┌───────────────────────────────────────────────┐
│         FOREIGN TRADE INDICATORS, 1988          │
│ Exports: $428 million                           │
│ Imports: $363 million                           │
│ Balance of trade: $65 million                   │
│            Direction of Trade (%)               │
│                          Imports      Exports   │
│ EEC                        28.0         22.9    │
│ U.S.A.                      4.3          1.5    │
│ East European countries    42.4         43.6    │
│ Japan                       0.1          4.8    │
│           Composition of Trade (%)              │
│                          Imports      Exports   │
│ Food & agricultural raw materials N.A.   N.A.   │
│ Ores & minerals            N.A.         26.2    │
│ Fuels                      33.3         40.3    │
│ Manufactured goods         N.A.         N.A.    │
│    of which chemicals      16.6         N.A.    │
│    of which machinery      22.2         N.A.    │
└───────────────────────────────────────────────┘
```

FOREIGN COMMERCE

Albania's foreign commerce has consistently shown a deficit. The principal exports are chromite, ferronickel ore, coal, copper wire, bitumen, tobacco and cigarettes, timber and furniture, textiles, canned foods, wine, fruits and vegetables and handicrafts. In 1988 fuels made up 40.3% of the exports and ores and minerals 26.2%. The export of electricity is increasing in volume and revenues. Albania has electricity export agreements with Austria, Bulgaria, Greece, Rumania and Yugoslavia. In the 1982–85 period electricity exports totaled 4.8 million kw.-hr.

Foreign commercial transactions are made difficult by the inflexible trade policies of the government, including a constitutional provision against acceptance of foreign credits. Albania has not yet recovered from the termination of trade agreements with China, which, until 1976, accounted for about half of foreign trade. However, a rapprochement began in 1983 when a Chinese trade delegation visited Albania, resulting in trade accords worth $5 million to $7 million. Commercial relations with both Western and Eastern European nations have improved steadily since 1980, the former accounting for 40% and the latter for 37% of total trade. Albania's main trading partners are Czechoslovakia, Yugoslavia and Italy. An exchange agreement was signed with Yugoslavia in 1985 setting the total value of their bilateral trade during 1986–90 at $680 million. Similar five-year agreements have been signed with most CMEA members (except the Soviet Union and Mongolia) and with Algeria, Argentina, Austria, China and Finland and a three-year agreement with Turkey.

TRANSPORTATION & COMMUNICATIONS

Albania has few transportation links with the outside world and, because of its mountainous terrain, internal transportation also is inadequate. This is in contrast to ancient times, when two major Roman roads crossed what is now Albania. The Via Egnatia went east from Durres (Dyrrhachium in Roman times) via the Shkumbin Valley to the lake district and thence eastward across the Balkan Peninsula to Thessaloniki and Constantinople. The Via Zenta was a north–south route built by Ragusan merchants when Ragusa (now Dubrovnik) was a Balkan mercantile power. It followed the Drin River Valley. During World War I Austrians built some 644 km. (400 mi.) of strategic roads. The Communists began the first road network in the country and by 1987 had completed 4,989 km. (3,101 mi.) of roads, which 1,287 km. (800 mi.) are paved. Although described as all-weather roads, those in the mountains generally are closed in the winter by snow.

In 1945 Albania had no railways. The first standard-gauge railroad construction began in 1947. Progress has been slow because of the terrain and lack of investment capital. By 1987 there were 500 km. (311 mi.) of railway track, with lines linking Tirana, Vlore, Sukth and Durres; Durres, Kavaje, Rrogozhine, Elbasan, Libraszd, Prenjas and Pogradec; Rroghozhine, Lushnje, Fier, Balish, Vore, Lac, Lezhe and Shkroder; and Selenice and Vlore. There is a standard-gauge line between Fier and Selenice. A new 35-km. (22-mi.) line between Fier and Vlore was opened in 1985. In 1986 work began on a railway linking Milot, Rreshen and Klos with 63 km. (39 mi.) of main line and 32 km. (20 mi.) of secondary lines.

In 1979 Albania and Yugoslavia agreed to construct a 50-km. (31-mi.) line between Shkoder and Titograd. The line was opened to international freight traffic in 1986. There are plans to link Durres with the Bulgarian Black Sea ports via the Yugoslavian cities of Skopje and Kumanovo.

The chief ports are the Enver Hoxha Port at Durres; Vlore; Sarande; and Shengjiu. Durres Harbor has been dredged to allow bigger ships. Vlore is a better natural port and the terminus of an oil pipeline. In 1980 construction began on a new port near Vlore with a cargo-

handling capacity of more than 4 million tons per year. A freight ferry service was inaugurated in 1983 between Durres and Trieste.

There is no regular internal air service and no international flag carrier. Albania has air links with Belgrade, Bucharest, Budapest, Berlin, Rome, Bari, Vienna, Istanbul and Zurich in the summer. There is a small but modern airport near Rinas, 28 km. (17 mi.) from Tirana.

Data are not available regarding tourism in Albania or travel by Albanians.

TRANSPORTATION INDICATORS, 1988

Roads, km. (mi.): 12,000 (7,456)
  % paved: 40
Motor vehicles
  Automobiles: 3,500
  Trucks 11,200
  Persons per vehicle: 146
Railroads
  Track (km./mi.) 445 (277)
  Passenger traffic (passenger-km./passenger-mi.): 291 million
    (181 million)
  Freight (freight-tonne-km./freight-ton-mi.): 127 million
    (87 million)
Merchant marine
  Vessels: 20
  Total deadweight tonnage: 79,900
Ports
  Number: 3
  Cargo loaded (tons): 1,077,000
  Cargo unloaded (tons): 626,000
Air
  Airports with scheduled flights: 1
  Airports: 11
Pipelines
  Crude (km./mi.): 145 (90)
  Refined (km./mi.) 55 (34)
  Natural gas (km./mi.): 64 (40)
Inland waterways
  Length (km./mi.): 43 (27)

COMMUNICATION INDICATORS, 1988*

Telephones
  Total (000): 4,800
  Persons per: 580
Post office
  Number of post offices: 292

*Most data concerning communication in Albania have not been published.

DEFENSE INDICATORS, 1988

Defense budget ($): 143 million
  % of central budget: 10.9
  % of GNP: 5.3
Military expenditures per capita ($): 47
Military expenditures per soldier ($): 3,404
Military expenditures per sq. km. ($): 4,974
Total strength of armed forces: 42,000
  Per 1,000: 13.3
Reserves: 155,000
Arms exports ($): 0
Arms imports ($): 0

DEFENSE INDICATORS, 1988 *(continued)*

Personnel & Equipment

Army
  Personnel: 31,500
  Organization: 1 tank brigade; 4 infantry brigades; 3 artillery regiments; 6 light coastal artillery battalions; 1 engineer regiment
  Equipment: 190 main battle tanks; 80 armored personnel carriers; 80 air defense guns; 30 reconnaissance vehicles
Navy
  Personnel: 3,300
  Equipment: 2 submarines; 32 torpedo craft; 8 patrol vessels; 2 mine warfare vessels
  Bases: Durres, Valona, Sazan Island, Pasha Liman
Air Force
  Personnel: 7,200
  Organization: 95 combat aircraft; no armored helicopters; 3 fighter ground attack squadrons; 3 fighter squadrons

---

DEFENSE

The People's Army, which encompasses the ground, naval and air arms of the regular armed forces, is under the Ministry of People's Defense. The minister of people's defense is the commander in chief. The army claims no antecedents in the forces of the pre-Communist regimes and dates itself from July 10, 1943, when a General Staff was formed within the guerrilla forces. All of the regular military forces are within the People's Army. Members of the naval and air arms are referred to as naval and air soldiers. Major subcommands, such as the army's directorates of Political Affairs and Rear Services, serve all service components.

The army has one tank brigade and four infantry brigades, all below-strength, together with six light coastal artillery battalions, three artillery regiments and one engineer regiment. The country is divided into two military districts, one in the North and the other in the South.

Conscripts make up over half of the army's total strength. Conscription is for two years in the army and three years in the navy and air force and paramilitary forces. Training is low-level because of the lack of advanced equipment. The reserve obligation is up to age 56.

Rank designations were abolished in 1966. There are no badges of rank on the uniforms.

Almost all artillery is light and small-caliber, since movement of heavy equipment is nearly impossible over much of the terrain. Additionally, heavy weapons, equipment to transport them, and their ammunition cannot be produced locally or, in the absence of permanent allies, obtained externally.

Naval units are subordinate to the Coastal Defense Command, which, although part of the People's Army, is operationally responsible directly to the Ministry of People's Defense. The senior naval officer is the commander of naval forces, who also is the commander of coastal defense and deputy minister of defense for naval affairs. Naval forces are divided into three commands: the Submarine Brigade, the Vlore Sea Defense Brigade, and the Durres Sea Defense Brigade, located at Pasha Liman, on the island of Sazan and at Durres and

Lake Scutari, respectively. Many of the ships put to sea infrequently, and many naval ensigns are part-time fishermen or farmers, many of them from the vicinities of Vlore or Durres.

The Albanian air force is the youngest of the three service branches, having been founded on April 23, 1951. The air force also is part of the People's Army and is headed by a chief of the air force who also is a deputy minister of defense. Much of the aircraft and air defense artillery and missile units were obtained first from the Soviets and later from the Chinese. Much of this equipment is obsolete. The five principal air bases are at Tirana, Shijak (about 32 km.; 20 mi. from Tirana), Vlore, Sazan Island (at the mouth of the Vlore Bay) and Stalin (about 64 km.; 40 mi. from Tirana). Helicopter bases are at Tirana, Shkoder and Vlore. Because the air force is small, with exposed bases and with equipment that is not easily resupplied, it is not expected to contribute significantly to any defense effort. More detailed information is not available.

The dual use of service personnel in peacetime is illustrated by the party slogan "the pick in one hand and the rifle in the other." They assist in construction of industrial enterprises and hydroelectric plants, land reclamation projects, crop harvests and the like.

Three military schools offer advanced officer training, of which the oldest is the Enver Hoxha United Army Officers' School. It has a university-level curriculum, and its students become commissioned officers upon graduation. The Skanderbeg Military School is a secondary or preparatory school. The third institution, a military academy, is similar to a war college in Western military establishments.

Albania receives no military aid.

EDUCATION

As the European country longest under Turkish rule, Albania was shut out of the great educational Renaissance that swept Europe in the Middle and Modern ages. As late as the 1940s over 80% of the people were illiterate. Schools in the native language were practically nonexistent until independence because the Turkish rulers prohibited use of the Albanian language. Turkish was used in the Ottoman schools for the Muslim population and Greek in the few schools maintained by the Ecumenical Patriarchate for Greek children. The first known school to use Albanian was a Franciscan seminary that opened in 1861 in Shkoder.

In 1908, after an Albanian alphabet was devised by a group of intellectuals, elementary schools teaching the alphabet were opened in various parts of the country. In 1909 a normal school was established in Elbasan to train teachers able to teach in the native tongue. Next year, in one of the cycles of repression that characterized the Ottoman regime, these schools were closed down.

The national government formed in 1920 included for the first time a Ministry of Education, and it was responsible for laying the foundations of a national educational system. The system included a number of foreign-run schools: the French Lycee and the American

Technical School (in which Enver Hoxha and Mehmet Shehu, respectively, were educated), the American Agricultural School in Kavaje and an American girls' school founded by Kristo Dako. In 1933 the Albanian Royal Constitution was amended, making education the exclusive right of the state and closing down all foreign-run schools except the American Technical School. Nationalization was followed in 1934 by a far-reaching reorganization of the entire school system, providing for compulsory education from ages four to 14; expansion of secondary, technical, vocational and commercial schools; and the strengthening of teacher education. However, compulsory education was never enforced in rural areas for the simple reason that there were no schoolhouses. There were no universities in prewar Albania. The great majority of students who sought higher education went to Rome.

Education was a high priority for the Communist regime that seized power in 1944. Its major objective was to eradicate illiteracy and to bring all children under the control of the state. The Educational Congress of Korce called for a radical reform of the educational system. The recommendations of the Korce Congress were codified in the Educational Law of August 17, 1946. The law adopted Marxist-Leninist principles in education and, further, required all illiterates between 12 and 40 to attend classes in reading and writing. It provided for seven-year obligatory schooling and a four-year secondary education. Another education law, adopted in 1948, provided for expansion of vocational and technical training. By 1950, when Albania had already passed into the Soviet orbit, secondary technical schools had been established on the Soviet model. The first steps toward higher education were the establishment of the two-year Teachers' Training College in Tirana in 1946, and the subsequent founding, in 1951, of the Higher Pedagogic Institute, the Higher Polytechnical Institute and the Higher Agricultural Institute. All these institutions, along with the Higher Institute of Medicine and the Higher Institute of Economics, were combined to form the University of Tirana in 1957. Within the next decade some 22 branches of this university had been founded.

The years 1948 to 1960 represent the Soviet phase of Albanian education. Most textbooks were Russian translations. Soviet educators were attached to the Ministry of Education. Study of the Russian language was compulsory from the seventh grade, and a number of students and teachers were sent to the Soviet Union for further training.

EDUCATION INDICATORS, 1988

Literacy
  Total (%): 71.5
  Male (%): 79.9
  Female (%): 63.1
First level
  Schools: 1,631
  Teachers: 27,387
  Students: 54,032
  Student–teacher ratio: 19.7
  Net enrollment rate (%): 98
  Females (%): 48

EDUCATION INDICATORS, 1988 (continued)

Second level
  Schools: 20
  Teachers: 1,552
  Students: 35,643
  Student–teacher ratio: 23:1
  Net enrollment rate (%): 63
  Females (%): 45
Vocational
  Schools: 313
  Teachers: 5,404
  Students: 12,379
  Student–teacher ratio: 22.9
Third level
  Institutions: 8
  Teachers: 1,502
  Students: 21,285
  Student–teacher ratio: 14:1
  Gross enrollment rate (%): 7.1
  Graduates per 100,000, age 20–24: 721
  % of population over 25 with postsecondary education: N.A.
  Females (%): 45
Foreign study
  Foreign students in national universities: N.A.
  Students abroad: 175
    of whom in Greece: 138
    Italy: 21

GRADUATES, 1984

Total: 3,248
Education: 288
Humanities & religion: 179
Fine & applied arts: 85
Law: 108
Social & behavioral sciences: 478
Natural sciences: 127
Medicine: 186
Engineering: 582
Agriculture, forestry, fisheries: 1,099
Other: 116

In 1954 the Ministry of Education was redesignated the Ministry of Education and Culture and given an expanded role in two tasks: "the Communist education of the new generation and the dissemination of culture to the masses." Regulation 55 of the Education Law of March 16, 1954, reaffirmed the exemplary character of Soviet education as a model for Albania.

The death of Stalin and the resulting break with the Soviet Union caused Albania to remap its educational directions. The Educational Reform Law of 1960 reorganized the school system on a two-tier, 8-4 basis. Another far-reaching school reform became effective on January 1, 1970, based on the recommendations of the Mehmet Shehu Committee. Its primary goal was to rid the school system of the "revisionist" Soviet influences. The preamble to the law set the ideological tone of the new system. Its aim was to create loyal Communists oriented to productive work. Its three components were listed as academic education, productivity and military education. A further reform, in 1979, was designed to improve the qualitative level of schooling and the teaching of science.

Education is free, compulsory and secular. It is compulsory for eight years, beginning at age six and ending at age 13. The medium of instruction is Albanian, but the state guarantees the right of national minorities to receive schooling in their own mother tongue. The system integrates four key elements: formal academic education, work in productive enterprises, physical education and military training. Pupils are divided into two streams: full-time and part-time. Full-timers start preschool at age three and spend a total of 15 years in school. Part-timers may complete their basic eight-year program in six years but must spend an additional preparatory year before starting third-level study. Graduates of general and vocational secondary schools must spend one full year in work enterprises before proceeding to higher education. During this probationary period they are placed under the direct supervision of workers and villagers and are subject to their approval. There are no entrance examinations for admission to the tertiary level.

The academic year runs from September through June. There are no private schools.

Preschool education begins at age three and lasts three years. Communist indoctrination starts even at this early age. There are no primary or intermediate schools, and the eight-year basic compulsory school is an integrated cycle. The graduates of the eight-year school receive a special certificate.

The four-year secondary school is divided into general secondary schools and vocational secondary schools. The structure of training is the same for both groups: six and a half months of academic study, two and a half months of productive work, one month of military training and two months of vacation. There are examinations at the end of grade 12. At the end of every year, pupils receive a certificate.

Third-level study lasts from three to five years. The University of Tirana and the higher institutes function under the control not only of the Ministry of Education and Culture but also of the Union of Albanian Working Youth. The university is headed by a rector and each of the faculties by a dean. The higher institutes are headed by directors except the Higher Institute of Agriculture, which is under a rector.

The chain of command in the educational system runs from the Party Politburo to the educational sections in the district people's councils. General guidelines are set by the Central Commission on Education. Another permanent body is the Central Committee's Directorate of Eduction and Culture which supervises the ideological content of education. At the district level, educational programs are administered by the education sections of the district people's councils through inspectors. At all levels, the branches of the Union of Albanian Working Youth have a strong influence on educational policy.

All educational expenditures are met by the state.

Albania has made dramatic progress within the past 45 years in reducing illiteracy from over 80% to 25%. All mass organizations of the APL are engaged in nonformal or continuing education.

Kindergarten and lower-eight-year schoolteachers are trained in special teacher training establishments or three-year pedagogical institutes; higher-eight-year schoolteachers and teachers for secondary schools are trained at the Pedagogical Institute.

LEGAL SYSTEM

The judicial system consists of the Supreme Court and district, village, city and city quarter courts. Until March 1966 the courts were supervised by a minister of justice. This office no longer exists, and its functions are discharged by the Supreme Court. A revised Penal Code was promulgated in 1977, followed by a Code of Criminal Procedure in 1980, a Labor Code in 1980, a Code of Civil Procedure in 1982 and a Family Code in 1982.

Court decisions are made collegially. In cases where the Supreme Court and district courts have original jurisdiction, assistant judges participate in the ruling. People's courts at the village and city levels decide cases with the participation of an assistant judge from the district court and two "social activists," who actually are local party members. If a case is before the Supreme Court by appeal, three judges make the verdict. When a case is before a district court by appeal, assistant judges participate.

The Supreme Court is elected for a four-year term by the People's Assembly. Between sessions of the People's Assembly, judges are elected by the Presidium of the People's Assembly. District court judges are elected by a secret ballot of all voting citizens. Social activists are elected for one-year terms by a people's meeting, which is similar in structure to a U.S. town meeting.

Trials normally are held in public. The accused is assured the right of defense except in political trials, and the principle of presumption of innocence is sanctioned by the Code of Penal Procedure. The judiciary, however, is not independent and must hew to the party line in all matters. A law on the reorganization of the courts passed in 1968 says clearly that "the people's courts will be guided in their activities by the policy of the party."

No information is available on prisons in Albania.

LAW ENFORCEMENT

No Communist country has as extensive a police and security organization relative to its size as Albania. All security and police forces are controlled by the Ministry of the Interior. The ministry has three police and security directorates: the People's Police, State Security and the Frontier Guards.

The People's Police has five branches: the Police for Economic Objectives, the Communications Police, the Fire Police, the Detention Police and the General Police. The Police for Economic Objectives serve as guards for state buildings. The Communications Police guard bridges, railways, power lines and so on. The Detention Police are prison and camp guards. The General Police attend to regular police functions, such as traffic, local crime and other duties. Some General Police functions overlap those of the Directorates of State Security. The General Police also watch movements of citizens, who are required to carry identification cards at all times. Local police are assisted by auxiliary policemen, who are able-bodied men required by a 1948 law to serve as police volunteers for two months.

The Directorate of State Security (Drejtorija e Sigurimit te Shtetit, commonly abbreviated as Sigurimi), modeled on Stalin's secret police, is organized into four battalions, with more plainclothes than uniformed personnel. It has seven sections: political, censorship, public records, prison camp, two sections for counterespionage, and a foreign service. The political section's primary function is to infiltrate opposition groups. The public records section is charged with the ideological supervision of public agencies.

The Frontier Guards are organized into five battalions along military lines but are more closely allied with the Directorate of State Security than with the armed forces. The stated mission of the Frontier Guards is to prevent Albanians from leaving the country and to protect the state's borders against spies and smugglers.

No information is available on incidence and types of crime in Albania.

HEALTH

One of the Communist regime's striking successes has been in the field of health—the elimination or reduction of the many diseases that had taken heavy tolls of life or debilitated large segments of the population before 1950. This success has been achieved primarily through large-scale inoculation programs and expansion of health services. Among the diseases eliminated are malaria, tuberculosis and syphilis. Progress also has been made in reducing infant mortality. The number of medical personnel has risen as a result of accelerated training programs and the establishment of the Higher Medical Institute, which later became the Faculty of Medicine of the University of Tirana. The use of mobile medical teams has played a major role in expanding and improving medical care in rural areas.

No information is available on the principal causes of mortality and health problems in Albania.

FOOD & NUTRITION

The Albanian diet reflects the harsh nature of the country. Dishes generally are high in starch content and lack variety. Most dishes are made from corn, wheat, rice or potatoes. Yogurt, cheese and prepared dry beans are among the most common food supplements. Green vegetables and fruits appear only seasonally and in limited quantities.

HEALTH INDICATORS, 1988

Health personnel
  Physicians: 3,061
    Persons per: 720
  Dentists: 900
  Nurses: 6,801
  Pharmacists: 532
  Midwives: 5,098

HEALTH INDICATORS, 1988 (continued)

Hospitals
  Number: 928
  Number of beds: 17,600
  Beds per 10,000: 62
Type of hospitals (%)
  Government: 100
Public health expenditures
  As % of national budget: N.A.
    per capita: $43.10
Vital statistics
  Crude death rate per 1,000: 5.8
  Decline in death rate: −27.1 (1965–84)
  Life expectancy at birth (years): Male 67.9; female 72.9
  Infant mortality rate per 1,000 live births: 48
  Child mortality rate (Ages 1-4 years) per 1,000: 3
  Maternal mortality rate per 100,000 live births: N.A.

FOOD & NUTRITION INDICATORS, 1988

Per capita daily food consumption of calories: 2,742.7
Per capita daily consumption of proteins, g. (oz.): 80.3 (2.8)
Calorie intake as % of FAO recommended minimum requirement: 121
% of calorie intake from vegetable products: 87
% of calorie intake from animal products: 13
Food expenditures as % of total household expenditures: N.A.
% of total calories derived from:
  Cereals: 66.4
  Potatoes: 2.6
  Meat & poultry: 5.2
  Fish: 0.1
  Fats & oils: 6.4
  Eggs & milk: 6.2
  Fruits & vegetables: 4.7
  Other: 8.4
Per capital consumption of foods kg. (lb.); l. (pt.)
  Potatoes: 47.2 (104.0)
  Rice: 5.5 (12.1)
  Fresh vegetables: 128.3 (282.9)
  Fruits (total): 42.2 (93.0)
    Citrus: 4.3 (9.4)
    Noncitrus: 37.9 (83.5)
  Milk: 114.8 (253.1)
  Butter: 1.2 (2.6)
  Cheese: 5.2 (11.4)
  Meat (total): 26.9 (59.3)
    Beef & veal: 10.3 (22.7)
    Pig meat: 3.4 (7.5)
    Poultry: 4.0 (8.8)
    Mutton, lamb & goat: 9.2 (20.2)
  Sugar: 18.6 (41.0)
  Beer, l. (pt.): 1.0 (2.1)
  Wine, l. (pt.): 2.5 (5.2)
  Alcoholic liquors, l. (pt.): 1.0 (2.1)

The vast majority of the rural inhabitants and some in the smaller cities have no access to safe water. Central sewage systems are found only in the largest towns.

MEDIA & CULTURE

The Albanian press is of postwar origin. From the beginning it functioned as an ideological tool rather than as an information medium. There are two dailies, both published in Tirana: *Zeri i Popullit* (Voice of the People), the organ of the APL, is, in the Stalinist model, the *Pravda* of the country; *Bashkimi* (Unity) is technically the mouthpiece of the Democratic Front but essentially is the voice of the government and thus the *Izvestia* of the country. The former has a circulation of 145,000 and the latter of 30,000, but circulation figures do not reflect actual readership. Many of the subscriptions are held by institutions, libraries and cultural houses rather than individuals. In some areas party agitators frequently read the newspapers aloud to groups. Thus the exposure to the print media is actually greater than indicated by circulation figures. All publications in Albania are owned by the government.

Twenty-three nondailies and 77 magazines are published under various auspices. Local party committees publish their own newspapers. Examples are *Jeta e Re* (New Life), published in Shkoder; *Prepara* (Forward), published in Korce; *Pararoja* (Vanguard), published in Gjirokaster; and *Adriatic*, published in Durres. In addition, there are wall newspapers or flash bulletins on the Chinese model, generally posted on bulletin boards in factories, farms, schools and other places.

The periodical press is more diversified than the daily press. The party, many government ministries and each of the mass organizations have their own organ. The more important journals include *Rruga e Partise* (Party Path), the theoretical journal of the party published by the Central Committee; *Ylli* (Star), a monthly illustrated review; *Nentori*, published by the Union of Writers and Artists; *Hosteni* (The Goad), published by the Union of Journalists, *Horizonti* (Horizon) and *Pionieri* (The Pioneer), published by the Union of Working Youth; *Puna* (Work), published by the Central Council of Albanian Trade Unions; and *Shqiptarja e Re* (The New Albanian Woman), published by the Women's Union of Albania.

The national news agency is the Albanian Telegraph Agency (ATA), founded in 1945. Only Xinhua news agency is represented in Tirana.

Radio was in its infancy in Albania when the Communists came to power. In 1945 there were only two transmitters in the country. Since then the electronic media have been developed under Radiotelevisioni Shqiptar. The radio services are run by Radio Tirana, which broadcasts 24 hours of programs daily from. Tirana, with regional stations at Berat, Fier, Gjirokaster, Korce, Kukes, Puke, Roghozhina, Sarande and Shkoder. All but eight of the 32 transmitters are short wave, indicative of the importance placed on external propaganda. External services are broadcast for 83 hours daily in 21 languages. In fact, Albania ranks eighth in the world among broadcasters in terms of the number of hours of external broadcasting.

Albania opened its first experimental television station in 1969 but has achieved only modest progress since then. There are television stations at Tirana, Berat, Elbasan, Gjirokaster, Kukes, Peshkopi and Pogradesc. Programs are broadcast in color in Tirana and in black and white elsewhere for five hours daily and eight hours on Sundays. Albanians can pick up Italian and Yugoslav TV channels in coastal areas.

The Albanian film industry produces an average 14 films per year, all of them on Marxist themes.

SOCIAL WELFARE

The social insurance program, introduced in 1947, is administered by the government and covers medical care, disability insurance, old-age pensions, family allowance and rest and recreation. Until 1965 much of social insurance activity was administered by the trade unions. Peasants are excluded from social insurance benefits under a law of September 13, 1966, but they receive similar benefits from their collectives. Funds for social insurance payments come from the state, and contributions are paid by state institutions and enterprises in their role as employers. Free medical care is provided for everyone, but drugs are paid by the user. Disability payments range from 85% to 100%, and party leaders receive an additional 10%. Old-age pensions are computed at the rate of 70% of the worker's average monthly wage. Special provisions cover pregnant women, sickness, children and funerals.

There is no private welfare system in Albania.

MEDIA INDICATORS, 1988

Newspapers
  Number of dailies: 2
  Circulation (000): 145
  Circulation per 1,000: 52
  Number of nondailies: 23
  Number of periodicals: 77
Book publishing
  Number of titles: 844
Radio
  Number of transmitters: 32
  Number of radio receivers (000): 210
    Persons per radio receiver: 15
  Total annual program hours: 6,600
Television
  Television transmitters: 216
  Number of television receivers (000): 52
    Persons per television receiver: 59
  Total annual program hours: 2,090
Cinema
  Number of fixed cinemas: 103
  Seating capacity: 28,000
    Seats per 1,000: 9.9
  Annual attendance (million): 4.2 (1989)
    Per capita: 1.3
Films
  Production of long films: 14
  Import of long films: 7
    28.6% from France
    14.3% from Italy
    14.3% from United Kingdom
    28.6% from Japan

CULTURAL & ENVIRONMENTAL INDICATORS, 1988

Public libraries
  Number: 45
  Volumes (000): 3,723
Museums
  Number: 2,034
Performing arts
  Facilities: 29
  Number of performances: 25,280
  Annual attendance (000): 8,654
  Attendance per 1,000: 2,884
Ecological sites: 6
Botanical gardens & zoos: 1

CHRONOLOGY (from 1946)

1946—The Constituent Assembly proclaims the People's Republic of Albania and promulgates the first Constitution.

1948—The Communist Party is renamed the Albanian Party of Labor. . . . As Yugoslavia is expelled from the Cominform, Albania breaks off relations with its former protector and sides with the Soviet Union; the powerful Koci Xoxe is dismissed and anti-Yugoslav faction leader Mehmet Shehu is rehabilitated.

1949—Albania joins the CMEA.

1953—Joseph Stalin dies, and Albania's relations with the Soviet Union begin to weaken.

1954—Enver Hoxha resigns as head of government but remains first secretary of the APL. . . . Mehmet Shehu is named prime minister. . . .

1956—The Soviet-Albanian rift widens following Soviet intervention to crush the Hungarian revolt.

1961—Albania breaks off diplomatic relations with the Soviet Union and accepts China as its new ally.

1962—Albania withdraws from the CMEA.

1967—Albania declares itself an atheist state and closes all religous establishments.

1968—Albania withdraws from the Warsaw Pact.

1972—Following reestablishment of Sino-American relations, Albania becomes disenchanted with the Tirana-Beijing axis.

1974—Gen. Beqir Balluku, the minister of defense, is executed for pro-Chinese sympathies.

1976—Albania ratifies a new Constitution.

1979—Hysni Kapo, a close associate of Hoxha, dies.

1980—Shehu is dismissed and is reported to have committed suicide; Hoxha admits to shooting Shehu in an altercation.

1982—A group of armed Albanian exiles lands on the coast but is promptly disposed of by the authorities. . . . Adil Karkani is named prime minister.

1983—China terminates diplomatic relations with Albania.

1985—Hoxha dies and is replaced as first secretary of the ALP by Ramiz Alia.

1987—Alia becomes head of state and president of the Presidium. . . . Greece ends its technical state of war with Albania following the opening of the border crossing at Kakavija. . . . Albania attends meeting of the Balkan foreign ministers in Belgrade.

1990—Thousands of Albanians take refuge in embassies in Tirana in the nation's most serious postwar crisis. . . . The regime, bowing to international pressure, allows the evacuation of the refugees to Germany, Italy, Czechoslovakia and other countries.

BIBLIOGRAPHY

BOOKS

Coon, Carleton S. *The Mountain of Giants: A Racial and Cultural Study of the North Albanian Mountain Ghegs.* Cambridge, Mass., 1950.

Griffith, William E. *Albania and the Sino-Soviet Rift.* Cambridge, Mass., 1963.

Hamm, Harry. *Albania: China's Beachhead in Europe.* New York, 1963.

Logoreci, Anton. *The Albanians: Europe's Forgotten Survivors.* London, 1977.

Marmullaku, Ramadan. *Albania and the Albanians.* Hamden, Conn., 1975.

Myrdal, Jan, and Gun Kessle. *Albania Defiant.* New York, 1976.

Pano, Nicholas C. *The People's Republic of Albania.* Boulder, Colo. 1985.

Prifti, Peter R. *Socialist Albania Since 1944.* Cambridge, Mass., 1978.

Skendi, Stavro. *The Albanian National Awakening, 1878–1912.* Princeton, N.J., 1967.

_____.*The Political Evolution of Albania, 1912–44.* New York, 1954.

OFFICIAL PUBLICATIONS

40 Years of Socialist Albania. Tirana. 1984

Portrait of Albania. Tirana. 1982

Statistical Yearbook (Annual). Tirana.

BULGARIA

BASIC FACT SHEET

OFFICIAL NAME: People's Republic of Bulgaria (Narodna Republika Bulgariya)

ABBREVIATION: BU

CAPITAL: Sofia

HEAD OF STATE: President Zhelyu Zhelev (from 1990)

HEAD OF GOVERNMENT: Chairman of the Council of Ministers Andrei Lukanov (from 1990)

NATURE OF GOVERNMENT: Socialist democracy

POPULATION: 8,972,724 (1989)

AREA: 110,911 sq. km. (42,823 sq. mi.)

MAJOR ETHNIC GROUP: Bulgars

LANGUAGE: Bulgarian

RELIGION: Bulgarian Orthodox

UNIT OF CURRENCY: Lev

NATIONAL FLAG: Tricolor of white, green and red horizontal stripes with the coat of arms of the republic in gold, green, red and white on the white stripe at the hoist

NATIONAL EMBLEM: A lion rampant is the central device on a gold-edged round blue shield. The lion appears to be turning, with its hindpaws like a treadmill in an industrial cogwheel. Golden wheat sheaves surround the shield. The national colors—white, green and red—form the upper part of a ribbon binding the sheaves. Across the base of the emblem a red ribbon carries in gold numerals two dates in Bulgarian history: 681, when Bulgars crossed the Danube to subdue the Slavs and found an empire; and 1944, when Bulgaria was liberated from Nazi control. A gold-rimmed five-pointed Communist star appears at the crest.

NATIONAL ANTHEM: "Bulgariya Mila, Zemya na Geroi" ("Dear Bulgaria, Land of Heroes")

NATIONAL HOLIDAYS: September 9–10 (National days); November 7 (Anniversary of the Bolshevik Revolution, 1917); March 3 (Liberation Day); May 24 (Education Day)

NATIONAL CALENDAR: Gregorian

PHYSICAL QUALITY OF LIFE INDEX: 93 (on an ascending scale with 100 as the maximum)

DATE OF INDEPENDENCE: October 5, 1908

DATE OF CONSTITUTION: May 18, 1971

WEIGHTS & MEASURES: Metric

GEOGRAPHICAL FEATURES

Located in the Balkan Peninsula, Bulgaria has an area of 110,911 sq. km. (42,823 sq. mi.) and extends 330 km. (205 mi.) north to south and 520 km. (323 mi.) east to west. Its total boundary length of 2,145 km. (1,332 mi.) is shared with four countries: Rumania (509 km.; 316 mi.), Turkey (259 km.; 161 mi.), Greece (493 km.; 306 mi.) and Yugoslavia (506 km.; 314 mi.). The Black Sea coastline is 378 km. (235 mi.).

As a pawn for centuries in the balance of power politics of more powerful European nations, Bulgaria's boundaries were imposed on it by others. Nevertheless, the boundaries follow logical physical divisions and do not violate natural features. None of its current borders are officially disputed. The post-World War I boundaries were established in rough detail by the Treaty of Peace signed in 1919 at Neuilly-sur-Seine, to which Bulgaria was a party. They were demarcated by international commissions between 1919 and 1922, formalized by the Treaty of Lausanne of 1923 and reconfirmed by the Treaty of Paris of 1947. As an ally of Germany in World War II, Bulgaria briefly reacquired coveted portions of Macedonia and Thrace but lost them again at the conclusion of the war.

The border with Yugoslavia follows the high ridges separating the watersheds of the Morava and Vardar River valleys in Yugoslavia from those of the Iskur and Struma River valleys in Bulgaria. The border starts in the North at the junction of the Timok River and the Danube and follows the river for about 16 km. (10 mi.). Leaving the Timok, it remains on high ground (except when crossing some river valleys) until it reaches the tripoint with Greece. The border with Greece follows higher elevations and ridges in the Rodopi. East of the Struma and Mesta River valleys, the border is at the dividing line between the Maritsa River basin and those of the streams that follow southward to the Aegean Sea. The Turkish border follows small rivers and streams for more than 40% of its length. The Rumanian border follows the Danube for about 467 km. (290 mi.), from the northwestern corner of the country to the city of Silistra, and then cuts to the east-southeast for about 137 km. (85 mi.) across the old province of Dobrudzha. The line across Dobrudzha is arbitrary and has been redrawn several times. The Danube has steep bluffs on the Bulgarian side and swamps and marshes on the Rumanian side. Most of the river islands are marshes subject to regular inundation by floodwaters and are, therefore, uninhabited.

The capital is Sofia, in a sheltered basin at the base of the Vitosha Range. It is on the direct route from Belgrade to Istanbul and also on the north–south route from the Danube to the Aegean Sea that uses the Struma and Iskut River valleys. Known as Serdica in antiquity, it was founded by the Thracians and has a history

RUMANIA

100m

100km

Vidin

Danube River

Silistra

Ruse

DOBRUDJA

Mikhaylovgrad

Iskŭr River

Razgrad

Tolbukhin

Pleven

Shumen

Vratsa

Lovech

Veliko Turnovo

Turgovishte

Varna

YUGOSLAVIA

B A L K A N   M O U N T A I N S

Gabrovo

Sliven

Sofia

Tundzha River

Pernik

Stara Zagora

Yambol

Burgas

Black Sea

Kyustendil

Pazardzhik

Plovdiv

Blagoevgrad

Maritsa River

Dimitrovgrad

Struma River

Khaskovo

R H O D O P E   M T S.

Smolyan

Kurdzhali

TURKEY

G R E E C E

of over 2,000 years. Because of its pleasant climate and strategic location, it was a contender in the selection of a capital for the Eastern Roman Empire. Destroyed by Attila the Hun in the fifth century, it was rebuilt in the sixth and seventh centuries. It declined again under the Ottomans and, in 1878, when it was liberated, had only some 15,000 to 20,000 inhabitants.

Plovdiv is the second most important city. It is older than Sofia, having been established in the fourth century B.C. by Philip of Macedon and named after him as Philippopolis. On the route from Belgrade to Istanbul, it has more rail lines radiating from it than Sofia. The old Plovdiv is typically Macedonian, and although severely damaged in a 1928 earthquake, is preserved as a national monument.

Veliko Turnovo, on the northern slopes of the central Stara Planina, was the fortress capital of the medieval Second Bulgarian Kingdom and also the site of the first Constituent Assembly, where the Turnovo Constitution for independent Bulgaria was adopted in 1879. Varna and Burgas are the chief Black Sea ports and Ruse the principal port on the Danube. Varna is a naval base, the site of a naval academy and the center of a shipbuilding industry. Burgas and Ruse also are growing rapidly. A number of new population centers have been built since World War II. They include resort cities such as Zlatni Pyassutsi, mining centers such as Madan and industrial towns such as Dimitrovgrad.

PRINCIPAL POPULATION CENTERS (est. population, 1983)			
Sofia (capital)	1,093,752	Pleven	140,440
Plovdiv	373,235	Shumen	104,089
Varna	295,218	Tolbukhin	102,292
Burgas (Bourgas)	183,477	Sliven	102,037
Ruse (Roussé)	181,185	Pernik	96,431
Stara Zagora	144,904		

Four alternating bands of high and low terrain extend generally east to west across the country. From north to south, they are the Danubian Plateau, the Stara Planina (Old Mountain) or Balkan Mountains, the Central Thracian Plain and the Rodopi (or Rhodope Mountains). The western part of the country consists almost entirely of higher land, and the eastern mountain ranges taper into hills and gentle uplands as they approach the Black Sea.

The Danubian Plateau extends from the Yugoslav border to the Black Sea and encompasses the area between the Danube, which forms most of the country's northern border, and the Stara Planina to the south. The plateau rises from cliffs along the river, typically 91 to 183 m. (300 to 600 ft.) high, and abuts the mountains at elevations of 366 to 457 m. (1,200 to 1,500 ft.). The region slopes gently but perceptibly southward to the mountains. The western portion is lower and more dissected, the eastern is more like a plateau. The southern edge of the plateau blends into the foothills of the Stara Planina, as the Bulgarian extension of the Carpathian Mountains is known. At the famous gorge of the Danube called the Iron Gate, the Carpathians sweep eastward, becoming the Stara Planina in Bulgaria.

The Stara Planina continues southeastward, becoming the northern boundary of the Sofia Basin, and then turns more directly eastward, to end at Cape Emine on the Black Sea. It is some 595 km. (370 mi) long and 19 to 48 km. (12 to 30 mi.) wide. It retains its height well into the central part, where Botev Peak, its highest point, rises to about 2,377 m. (7,800 ft.). The range still is apparent until its rocky cliffs fall into the Black Sea. Over most of its length the Stara Planina is the divide between the drainage to the Danube and to the Aegean Sea. Only small areas to the east drain directly to the Black Sea.

Separated from the main range by a long geological trench that contains the Valley of the Roses is the Sredna Gora (Middle Forest), a ridge running almost precisely east to west, about 161 km. (100 mi.) long. Because it is a narrow ridge, it appears higher than its actual average elevation of 1,524 m. (5,000 ft.).

The southern slopes of the Stara Planina and the Sredna Gora give way to the Thracian Plain. Roughly triangular in shape, the plain originates at a point east of the mountains that ring the Sofia Basin and broadens as it fans eastward to the Black Sea. It encompasses the Maritsa River Basin and the lowlands that extend from it to the Black Sea.

The Rodopi occupies the area between the Thracian Plain and the Greek border and includes the Rila mountain range south of Sofia and the Pirin range in the southwestern corner. Topographically, the Rodopi dominates not only Bulgaria but also the entire Balkan Peninsula. The Rila contains Mount Musala, whose 2,895-m. (9,500-ft.) peak is the highest in the Balkans. About a dozen other peaks in the Rila are over 2,743 m. (9,000 ft.). The Vitosha Range is an outlier of the Rila, and its 2,286-m. (7,500-ft.) peak, Mount Vitosha, is a landmark on the outskirts of Sofia. Snow covers its conical summit most of the year. The Pirin is characterized by rocky peaks and stony slopes. While the Rila is of volcanic origin, the Pirin was formed at a different time by a fracturing of the earth's crust. Therefore, some geographers refer to the western Rodopi and the Pirin as the Thracian Macedonian Massif. To the east of the Rodopi are the relatively lower Sakar and Strandzha mountains. They extend the length of the Rodopi along the Turkish border to the Black Sea but rarely exceed 457 m. (1,500 ft.) in height except in one place, where they reach 853 m. (2,800 ft.).

The greater part of the country drains to the Black Sea through the Danube, including the northern watershed of the Stara Planina, all of the Danubian Plateau and the coastal areas. Although only the Danube is navigable, there are a number of other rivers. Of the tributaries of the Danube, the most important are, from east to west, Ogosta, Iskur, Vit, Osum, Yantra and Lom. Of these, all rise in the Stara Planina but the Iskur, which rises in the Rila. The Provadiyska, Kamchiya, Fakiyska and Veleka rivers flow directly into the Black Sea. Some of these rivers are sizable streams, but the Danube gets only a little more than 4% of its total volume from its Bulgarian tributaries. As it flows along Bulgaria's northern border, the Danube averages 1.6 to 2.4 km. (1.0 to 1.5 mi.) in width. Its highest water levels usually are reached during June floods, and in normal years it is frozen for about 40 days.

The Thracian Plain and most of the higher lands in the South and Southwest drain to the Aegean Sea. The three largest rivers flowing to the Aegean Sea are the Maritsa, the Struma and the Mesta. Of these, the Maritsa, with its tributaries, is by far the largest. It drains all of the western Thracian Plain, all of the Sredna Gora, the southern slopes of the Stara Planina and the northern slopes of the eastern Rodopi. The Mesta separates the Pirin from the main Rodopi ranges. The Struma and the Mesta reach the sea through Greece.

There are no lakes of any significant size in Bulgaria.

CLIMATE & WEATHER

For a small country, Bulgaria has an unusually varied and complex climate, with six or more climatic zones. The country lies in the transition line between the East European continental and the Mediterranean climatic zones, and its mountains and valleys act as barriers and channels, respectively, to the air masses from these zones. The Black Sea affects the weather in the costal areas.

In general, the continental system prevails in the North. It is characterized by hot summers and cold winters and rainfall well distributed throughout the year, with a major portion of it concentrated in early summer thunderstorms. The Stara Planina represents the southern limits of this zone. The Rodopi marks the northern limits of the Mediterranean climate, with mild, damp winters and hot, dry, rain-free summers. The southern slope of the Rodopi has a mild climate, which was earned for it the name of Green Greece or Bulgarian California.

The area between these zones, including the Thracian Plain, is influenced by both types of climates but more of the time by the continental system. The result is a plains climate characterized by long summers and high humidity. The climate generally is more severe than that of Spain, Italy, France and Soviet Georgia, all of which are in the same latitude. Average temperatures and precipitation are erratic, varying widely from year to year.

Rainfall over the country averages about 635 mm. (25 in.) a year, with Dobrudzha, the Black Sea coastal area, parts of the Thracian Plain and the Danubian Plateau receiving less than the average. Higher elevations are the most generously watered, in places receiving 1,016 mm. (40 in.) or more. Dobrudzha and the Danubian Plateau receive most of their rainfall during the crop-growing season. However, the Thracian Plain experiences frequent and prolonged summer droughts. A few sheltered pockets in the higher mountains may remain covered with snow all year, and much of the higher land well into springtime. Lower elevations are snow-covered an average of 25 to 30 days a year. Average cloudiness is about 55%, and average relative humidity is as high as 70% to 75%.

Throughout the uplands the many valley basins frequently have temperature inversions, resulting in stagnant air. For example, Sofia occasionally is troubled by smog, although otherwise it has a pleasant climate because of its elevation. It also is sheltered from the northern European winds by the mountains that ring the basin. Its temperatures in January average −1.7°C (29°F); in August they average 21.1°C (70°F). Its rainfall is near the country average.

During winter there are many windy days and violent local storms, particularly along the Danube. The hard-blowing, hot and dry Black Wind wreaks havoc on crops. It gets its name from the quantities of dust it carries, which often darken the skies. In contrast, valleys opening to the south along the Greek and Turkish borders are as mild as the Aegean and Mediterranean coasts.

POPULATION

In 1989 the population of Bulgaria was estimated at 8,972,724, on the basis of the last census, in 1985, when the population was 8,942,976. Bulgaria ranks 68th in the world in size of population and 98th in land area. The population is expected to reach 8,998,000 in 1990 and 9,099,000 by 2000.

The first population census was held in Bulgaria in 1881, three years after it achieved partial independence from the Turks in 1878. The population in the first census was 2.008 million. It grew to 3.154 million by 1888, partly as a result of expansion of the county's borders. The 4 million mark was crossed in 1905, the 5 million mark in 1926, the 6 million mark in 1934, the 7 million mark in 1946 and the 8 million mark in 1965. Population growth has not been significantly affected by immigration or emigration, except in the case of the Turks, many of whom were periodically repatriated to Turkey during the past century. Bulgarians themselves have shown little interest in emigrating abroad. Of the approximately 1 million Bulgarians abroad, the vast majority are in Greece, Yugoslavia, Rumania and the Soviet Bessarabia. A scattering of Bulgarians are in Australia and in North and South America.

Bulgaria is one of the extremely few countries in the world where males have outnumberd females for a considerable period of modern history. Between 1887 and 1965, females have been in the majority only at two censuses: 1920 and 1947. However, the male majority began to narrow in the 1960s and by the late 1980s the ratio had been reversed. The reversal resulted from changes in life expectancy statistics.

DEMOGRAPHIC INDICATORS, 1988

Population: 8,972,724 (1989)

Year of last census: 1985	World rank: 68
Sex ratio: Males: 49.5	Females: 50.5

Population trends (million)

1930: 5.997	1960: 7.906	1990: 8.998
1940: 6.624	1970: 8.515	2000: 9.099
1950: 7.273	1980: 8.862	

Population doubling time in years at current rate: Population stable

DEMOGRAPHIC INDICATORS, 1988 (continued)

Hypothetical size of stationary population (million): 10
Assumed year of reaching net reproduction rate of 1: 2030
Age profile (%)

0–15: 20.8	30–44: 21.1	60–74: 13.7
15–29: 19.8	45–59: 20.0	Over 75: 4.5

Median age (years): 36.7
Density per sq. km. (per sq. mi.) 80.9 (209.6)
Annual growth rate

1950–55: 0.67	1975–80: 0.32	1995–2000: 0.08
1960–65: 0.83	1980–85: 0.22	2000–2005: 0.01
1965–70: 0.69	1985–90: 0.11	2010–15: −0.09
1970–75: 0.54	1990–95: 0.06	2020–25: −0.09

Vital statistics
    Crude birth rate, 1/1,000: 13.4
    Crude death rate, 1/1,000: 11.6
    Change in birth rate: −10.5 (1965–84)
    Change in death rate: 37.8 (1965–84)
    Dependency, total: 49.3
    Infant mortality rate, 1/1,000: 17.0
    Child (0–4 years) mortality rate, 1/1,000: 1.0
    Maternal mortality rate, 1/100,000: 20.1
    Natural increase, 1/1,000: 1.8
    Total fertility rate: 2.0
    General fertility rate: 63
    Gross reproduction rate: 1.07
    Marriage rate, 1/1,000: 7.3
    Divorce rate, 1/1,000: 1.1
    Life expectancy, males (years): 68.4
    Life expectancy, females (years): 73.6
    Average household size: 3.3
    % illegitimate births: 11.4
Youth
    Youth population 15–24 (000); 1,294
    Youth population in 2000 (000); 1,376
Women
    Of childbearing age 15–49 (000): 2,174
    Child–woman ratio (children per 000 women 15–49): 321
    % women using contraceptives: N.A.
    % women married 15–49: N.A.
    Abortions per 100 live births: 111
Urban
    Urban population (000): 6,786
    % urban, 1965: 46; 1985: 68
    Annual urban growth rate (%) 1965–80, 2.8; 1980–85, 1.7
    % urban population in largest city: 18
    % urban population in cities over 500,000: 18
    Number of cities over 500,000: 1
    Annual rural growth rate: (%) −2.1 (1985–90)

POPULATION GROWTH, 1881–1975

Year	Total	Males	Females
1881	2,008	1,028	980
1888	3,154	1,605	1,549
1893	3,311	1,691	1,620
1900	3,744	1,910	1,835
1905	4,036	2,057	1,978
1910	4,338	2,207	2,131
1920	4,847	2,421	2,426
1926	5,479	2,743	2,736
1934	6,078	3,054	3,024
1946	7,029	3,517	3,513
1956	7,614	3,799	3,814
1965	8,228	4,114	4,114
1975	8,728	4,358	4,370

Another unusual feature of Bulgarian demographics is the unusually large number of very old people. Over 1% of the population is over 80 years, and there are hundreds of centenarians.

More than four-fifths of the population was rural at the time of independence, and more than three-quarters still were rural in 1947. The movement to the cities was a post-World War II phenomenon, and it took place with unexpected swiftness. By 1969 urban dwellers had become a majority, and by 1987 more than two-thirds of Bulgarians were living in cities.

The national population density of 80.9 per sq. km. (209.6 per sq. mi.) compares favorably with the more densely populated Western European countries. Regions with the highest densities are the Sofia Basin and the southwestern portion of the Thracian Plain. The population is more dense than average in the western and central portion of the Danubian Plateau, in the lower eastern Rodopi and in the vicinities of Varna and Burgas and the Black Sea coast. It is least dense in the higher mountains, particularly in the western Rodopi, the Pirin, the Rila and along the narrow, high ridge of the Stara Planina.

Population growth has been comparatively steady since independence. Its rate has fluctuated, but not widely. It was high until 1910 and in the interwar period and low during the 1910–20 decade and since 1941. It entered a period of accelerated decline in 1985, and the decline is projected to continue well into the next century, reaching 0.2% by 2025.

The family is the focal unit of society, and the Bulgarian society has been characterized as familistic. The marriage rate remains high, at 7.3 per 1,000. Nearly 37.4% of the women marry under age 19 and 50% between 20 and 29. The relative percentages for men are 6.1% and 73.8%. In 1987 there were 2.627 million families, with an average of 3.3 members per family.

ETHNIC COMPOSITION

Bulgaria is characterized by a remarkable ethnic, linguistic and religious homogeneity. Approximately 85% are Bulgarian. The most significant ethnic minorities are Turks, who make up about 8.5%; Gypsies, 2.5%, and Macedonians, 2.5%. The remainder are Greeks, Rumanians, Armenians and others.

The Turks and the Pomaks (as the Islamized Bulgarians are known) are the legacies of four centuries of Turkish rule, and their numbers have been steadily reduced by emigration to Turkey. In 1950–51 alone 150,000 were expelled from Bulgaria. Many of the remaining Turks are tobacco growers or artisans living in the eastern third of the country and along the Danube. Their traditional peasant conservatism, bolstered by their Islamic faith, has made them less willing to adapt to the current social order than the rest of the population. An effort by the Zhivkov regime in the late 1980s to Bulgarianize the Turks resulted in protests by Turkey and mass emigration of Turks to Turkey. But many of the émigrés later returned to Bulgaria, as they found living conditions in Turkey more intolerable than at home. The Mladenov regime abandoned the harsher features of this policy, but historic hostilities between the Bulgarians and the Turks persist. However, the

Turks pose no serious problem to the Bulgarian government, and the Turks' cultural and other rights are guaranteed by the Constitution.

Gypsies are not considered a national minority by the government, although they consider themselves as such. As in other countries, they are strongly attached to their nomadic way of life and reluctant to settle down in a place and integrate themselves into the national society.

Macedonians are not recognized as a separate community. They are considered to be ethnic Bulgarians and their language to be a dialect of Bulgarian. They live mainly in the Pirin region in the Southwest. Rumanians fall into two groups: the Rumanian-speaking Vlachs of the Northwest, and the Greek-speaking Karakatchans, who are nomadic mountain sheperds of Rumanian origin. Another hybrid community is the Gagauzi of the Northeast who are of Turkish origin but who follow the Orthodox faith.

There are no foreign communities as such in Bulgaria.

LANGUAGE

Bulgarian, the national language, is classified as a Slavic language of the southern group, which also includes Macedonian, Serbo-Croatian and Slovenian. Old Bulgarian, also known as Old Church Slavonic, was the first Slavic language to acquire an alphabet, in the ninth century. The alphabet, created by Sts. Cyril and Methodius, two Greek missionaries, was based partly on Greek and was named Cyrillic after St. Cyril. Both the grammar and the vocabulary of modern Bulgarian show the influence of non-Slavic languages. For example, Bulgarian has no inflectional cases of nouns but expresses them by prepositions. Russian is the most popular foreign language, followed by French, German and English, in that order.

RELIGIONS

By the second century, Christianity had become established in the area that is now Bulgaria. The Bulgars, who conquered the land in about 670, were converted when Boris, their king, was baptized by the Greek clergy. The creation of the Cyrillic alphabet by the Greek missionaries Sts. Cyril and Methodius was a landmark in ecclesiastical history, enabling language, culture and religion to coalesce and intertwine. In 889 Boris abdicated to enter a monastery, while his son Simeon left a monastery to ascend the throne. Slavonic was substituted for Greek in the Bulgar liturgy. The Bulgar church was declared autocephalous, with its own patriarch. In 1018 the Bulgarian kingdom fell to Byzantine rulers, who suppressed the Bulgarian patriarchate. Bulgaria regained its independence in 1186, and the patriarchate was reestablished in 1235, following a 30-year union with Rome. In 1396 Bulgaria fell before a third wave of Muslim invaders, the Ottoman Turks.

For the next 500 years the Bulgarian land and church were under the heel of the Turkish oppressors. During this period the church was controlled by the Ecumenical Patriarchate. The church was able to reestablish itself in 1878, but a reconciliation with the Ecumenical Patriarchate was not effected until 1945.

The Bulgarian Orthodox Church has 11 dioceses, each governed by a bishop under the authority of a patriarchate in Sofia. There are three overseas dioceses, in New York; Akron, Ohio; and Detroit. The Bulgarian monastery of St. George on Mount Athos, however, is under the authority of the Ecumenical Patriarchate.

Prior to World War II and the Communist takeover, the Orthodox Church claimed a membership of 85% of the national population, but in the years since then, this percentage has dropped to below 20%. In the immediate postwar years the church lost much property, including all monasteries, but after the church leaders pledged loyalty to Communist regime in 1953, most of the property was returned to church control. Since that year the church also has received financial aid from the government. Two seminaries—Tcherepich Seminary, near Vraca, and Sofia Theological Academy—remain open. The church publishes the *Official Gazette of the Bulgarian Orthodox Church*, a monthly titled *Spiritual Culture* and a yearbook.

The Armenian Apostolic Church has 12 congregations in the country. Protestantism was introduced by American Congregationalist missionaries in 1856, American Methodists in 1857 and Russian Baptists in 1865. Pentecostalism was established in 1921 by Russian missionaries at Burgas and today is the largest Protestant denomination.

From the ninth to the 14th centuries the Roman Catholic Church made repeated efforts to bring Bulgaria into its fold, but except for a brief 30-year union, these efforts were not fruitful. The majority of Bulgarian Catholics are descendants of the Bogomils converted to Catholicism by the Franciscans in the 17th century. In 1758 the vicariate of Sofia was established, and in 1789 the diocese of Nicopoli. In 1926 an exarchate of Sofia was created for Catholics of the Byzantine rite, who number a few thousands and who are found in Sofia, Plovdiv and along the Greek border. Catholics of the Latin rite number about 50,000 and are concentrated in certain towns, such as Rokovski and Nikolaievo. Immediately following World War II the church lost all its property as it became the target of the new Communist regime's hostility. All foreign religious personnel and priests were expelled, and many were arrested, sentenced to life imprisonment or killed. However, the church survived. Unlike in Rumania, the Catholic Church has not been forcibly reunited with the Orthodox Church. Priests of both the Latin and Byzantine rites continue to function under an exarch and an apostolic vicar, respectively. There has been a thaw in relations between the state and the Catholic Church since 1975, when Todor Zhivkov, as party leader, visited Pope Paul VI in Rome.

The law regulating the juridical status and internal organization of religious communities, the Law Concerning Religious Faiths of 1949, states: "The Bulgarian Orthodox Church is the traditional faith of the Bulgarian people. It is bound up with their history and, as such, by its structure, its nature and its spirit, can be considered a church of the popular democracy." (Article 3). "All churches are free to manage their organizational structure, rites and religious buildings." (Article 5). "A Church becomes legal and receives juridical status at the time it is ratified by the Ministry of Foreign Affairs." (Article 6). "When it appears necessary, the state may subsidize the support of ecclesiastical institutions." (Article 13). "Freedom of conscience and religion are guaranteed." (Article 1). "Lay religous organizations may not carry out pastoral activity; and religious communities may not engage in the education of children or youth, nor supervise hospitals, orphanages or other similar establishments." (Articles 20 and 21).

Although the church is barely tolerated by the state, the Bulgarian Orthodox Church has been more fortunate than churches in other East European countries. It has been authorized to maintain its rural property and receives from the state an annual subsidy for construction and support of church buildings and the salaries of its clergy. Orthodox priests are paid at the same rate as teachers, and bishops at the rate of professors. However, any religious activity outside the walls of the church is liable to prosecution and punishment. All religious issues are handled by a special committee within the Ministry of Foreign Affairs known as the Committee for Questions Concerning the Bulgarian Orthodox Church and Religious Denominations.

HISTORICAL BACKGROUND

Bulgarian history begins when the Bulgars, a central Asian Turkic tribe, overran what is present-day Bulgaria in the seventh century. They mixed with the Slavs, who had settled in the region earlier, and created a common polity in which the Slavs contributed their culture and language and the Bulgars their political institutions. From this amalgam came the First Bulgarian Kingdom, with its capital at Pliska (679–1018). In the ninth century Bulgaria was powerful enough to challenge Constantinople. Twice in this period Bulgars controlled areas of Greece, Turkey, Yugoslavia, Rumania and even Russia. In 811 the Bulgars gained a stunning victory over the Byzantine emperor Nicephorus. In 924, after Serbia fell under Bulgarian rule, Simeon (893–927) claimed the title of tsar of all Bulgarians and Greeks. With territorial expansion came a resurgence of arts and letters, making Simeon's reign the Golden Age of Bulgaria. By the end of the 10th century the First Bulgarian Kingdom was in decline, a process hastened the internal struggles of the boyars against the king and the encroachments of neighbors such as the Magyars and Byzantines. After a brief revival in the late 10th century under Samuel, the First Bulgarian Kingdom vanished from history. From 1018 to 1185 all of Bulgaria was under Byzantine rule. Byzantine feudalism replaced Bulgarian feudalism, and the Byzantine Church replaced the Bulgarian Church.

The Second Bulgarian Kingdom was established in 1186 and lasted until 1396. It began when two brothers, Asan and Peter, led a revolt against Byzantium and liberated first northeastern Bulgaria and then Thrace. In 1187 Byzantine emperor Isaac Angel concluded peace, granting autonomy to Bulgaria, and followed it in 1201 with a treaty ceding all of northern Bulgaria and a large part of Macedonia to the Second Kingdom. To free the Bulgarian Church from the control of the Byzantine Church, Kaloyan, the Bulgarian ruler, brought the Bulgarian Church under the protection of Rome and had himself crowned by a papal nuncio in 1204. The alliance with Rome lasted until 1235, when the Bulgarian Patriarchate was reestablished.

In the 13th century Bulgaria became the largest state in the Balkans, extending from the Black Sea to the Adriatic Sea in the west and to the Aegean Sea in the south. Again, as in the time of Simeon, arts and culture flourished and reached a state of excellence. The first chronicle of Bulgarian history was written, and the first Bulgarian coins were minted.

By the second half of the 13th century, the Second Kingdom was in decline. Debilitated by internal unrest, it was rent apart by foreign invasions: the Byzantines from the east, and Hungarians, Tatars and Mongols from the north. At one point the Hungarian king declared himself king of Bulgaria. By this time Bulgaria was divided into three parts: one part under the Bulgarian czar, with his capital at Turnovo; the so-called Vidin Kingdom, in the far Northwest; and the principality of Dobrudzha, in the northeast.

Meanwhile, the nemeses of Christian Europe, the Turks, had crossed the Bosporus and had begun to advance on Thrace, Macedonia and parts of Bulgaria. In 1371 they captured Sofia and in 1388 beat the Serbs. By 1396 all of Bulgaria was under Turkish rule.

The 482 years of Turkish rule were the darkest in Bulgarian history, just as it was in the history of every country ruled by the Turks. Far less civilized than any of the peoples they ruled, the Turks were characterized only by an enormous capacity for brutality and sustained by a religious and political system that institutionalized such aggression. Peasants as well as nobles were forced to convert to Islam and to yield their sons and daughters to the harems and courts of the sultans, *viziers* and *beylerbeys;* all agricultural produce was subjected to requisition by Turkish soldiers; and heavy taxes and hard labor were imposed on all Christians.

It was not until the 19th century that organized resistance to Turkish oppression began to be effective. By then Ottoman power was in full retreat and large parts of Europe had already been liberated. In 1870 the Bulgarian Orthodox Church was reestablished. In 1872 the Bulgarian Revolutionary Central Committee was formed in Bucharest. As the revolutionary fervor grew, the Bulgarians turned to Russia for help.

The precursor to the liberation in 1878 was an unsuccessful rising in 1876. Thousands of Bulgarians were killed in April of that year; 15,000 were massacred in cold blood in Plovdiv alone. The savagery of these reprisals was so brutal that the Russians invaded Bulgaria soon after the Russo-Turkish War of 1877 and liquidated the Turkish army by 1877. In these battles for Bulgaria's liberation, the Russians lost over 200,000 lives.

Following the Russian intervention, Bulgaria was granted the status of an autonomous tributary of the sultan; complete independence was not established until 1908. However, the Congress of Berlin took away from Bulgaria parts of Macedonia and Thrace that the Treaty of San Stefano had granted it. This set the tone for an irredentist foreign policy that lasted well until 1945 and that led to Bulgaria's disastrous alliances with Germany in both world wars.

The government that was established after independence was based on the Turnovo Constitution of 1879—originally drafted by the Russians but rewritten by the Bulgarians—and established a democratic government and a constitutional monarchy headed by a German prince. Stefan Stambolov, prime minister from 1887 to 1894, consolidated the country's administration and economy. In 1908, when Bulgaria declared itself an independent kingdom, its king, Ferdinand, assumed the title of tsar.

Within four years Bulgaria was once again embroiled in war. It joined the anti-Turkish coalition (consisting of Greece, Montenegro and Serbia) in the First Balkan War (October 1912–May 1913), gaining its long-desired outlet to the Aegean Sea. But dispute over Macedonia pitted Bulgaria against its allies, who now joined Turkey to defeat Bulgaria in the Second Balkan War (June to July 1913). The Treaty of Bucharest (August 10, 1913) deprived Bulgaria of a large part of Macedonia.

However, Macedonia remained a sore issue for Bulgaria, which was determined to regain the land that had escaped its grasp so often. Of all the Balkan states, Bulgaria was the only one to join the Central Powers in World War I, ironically siding with its former oppressor Turkey against her friend and benefactor Russia. Although Bulgaria gained some initial victories, it emerged from the war defeated and in a worse position than before the war. Thrace and Macedonia were lost, and Bulgaria was forced to pay reparations for the Allied occupation that followed. King Ferdinand was forced to abdicate shortly before the armistice was signed. He was replaced by his son Boris III, who ruled until his death in 1943.

The interwar period was one of political unrest and Macedonian terrorism spearheaded by the Internal Macedonia Revolutionary Organization (IMRO). IMRO was responsible for the overthrow and execution of Aleksander Stamboliski, the leader of the Bulgarian Agrarian Union and prime minister from 1919 to 1923. Macedonian terrorism ended with the putsch of 1934 led by the Zveno (Link) group. As soon as it seized power, Zveno suspended the Constitution, dissolved the parliament and stripped the king of his powers. In 1935 the king, with the aid of the military, regained power and ruled the country as a royal dictator until 1943.

Bulgaria entered World War II on the Axis side and again suffered defeat. The war ended for Bulgaria when, on September 4, 1944, Soviet troops entered Sofia. The government of the Fatherland Front (Otechestven Front), a Communist organization, seized power within five days of the occupation. On October 28, 1944, an armistice was signed between Bulgaria and the Soviet Union by which the former surrendered all territories gained since 1941.

For postwar history, see Chronology.

CONSTITUTION & GOVERNMENT

The theoretical foundation of the state is the Constitution of 1971, which replaced the earlier one of 1947. The Constitution established the basic institutions of government, the National Council, the State Council and the Council of Ministers at the national level and the people's council's at the local level.

The Constitution of 1971 is a far cry from Bulgaria's first constitution—the Turnovo Constitution of 1879, which was considered by its contemporaries as one of the most liberal in the world. Whereas most European countries at that time limited suffrage in various ways, all Bulgarian citizens over age 21 enjoyed the franchise. The parliament was supreme, and the king was bound by its laws. Over the next 65 years the Turnovo Constitution was revised twice, suspended twice and violated many times. Even after the Communist takeover, the Turnovo Constitution continued to be the charter of government until the new constitution was adopted in 1947.

Known as the Dimitrov Constitution after Georgi Dimitrov, who helped to draft it, the Constitution of 1947 remained in force for 24 years. It consisted of 11 chapters and 101 articles without a preamble. It established the National Assembly as the supreme organ of state power and the Council of Ministers as the supreme executive power. However, in actual practice the Presidium of the National Assembly, which met in continuous session, was empowered with legislative, executive and judicial authority. Following the Soviet model, the first secretary of the Bulgarska Komunisticheska Partiya, BKP, (Bulgarian Communist Party) also was chairman of the Council of Ministers and, as such, the country's prime minister. The Constitution also dealt with extensively social and economic structures. It prescribed collective ownership of the means of production, empowered the government to nationalize any industry and expropriate land, and restricted ownership of private property.

The Constitution of 1971 was born at the 10th Congress of the BKP, in Sofia. It was approved by popular referendum on May 16 and proclaimed two days later by the National Assembly. The structure and functions of the organs of state power outlined in the Dimitrov Constitution remained essentially the same, except that the State Council became a more powerful body than the Presidium of the National Assembly that it replaced and overshadowed the Council of Ministers as well. One major departure was the inclusion of a preamble containing a declaration of principles. Another is a dilution of the legislative powers of the National Assembly and the expansion of the right of legislative initiative to the Supreme Court, the local people's councils and, most importantly, the State Council.

Twenty articles deal with the economic foundations of the state. The Constitution recognizes four kinds of ownership: cooperative, state, public organizations and individual. The Law on Citizens' Property abolished private ownership except of items for personal use. Basic rights and liberties of citizens get a constitutional nod, but such rights are subservient to the rights of the state.

The 1971 Constitution was a map that did not show the actual terrain of power. The locus of power lay not in the constitutional organs but in the extraconstitutional institution of the BKP, of which the actual government was only a shadow. At the highest levels there was an interlocking of offices designed to ensure party control of all important valves of power.

The State Council was the hub of the entire governmental system. It was a 24-person executive committee within the National Assembly and was elected for an indefinite term. It functioned as a collegial executive and legislative body, and its president was the head of state. It was effectively the surrogate of the legislature and the executive. Furthermore, most members of the State Council were concurrently high-ranking members of the BKP and thus wielded power at three levels.

The State Council's permanent functions included calling the National Assembly into session, drafting bills and decreeing them into law, interpreting laws and decrees, creating and eliminating administrative departments below the ministerial level, appointing and recalling diplomatic representatives, ratifying international treaties and directing the defense of the country. Acts and decrees of the State Council had the force of law and needed no confirmation by the National Assembly.

Additionally, the State Council exercised executive control over the Council of Ministers, the local people's councils and the office of the chief prosecutor and could repeal decisions of the ministries and other central departments. In the absence of the National Assembly, the State Council was empowered to sign peace treaties and amend the Constitution and to change the territorial boundaries of the country. In carrying out these functions, the Council of State was assisted by two committees.

In 1987 the National Assembly approved a number of structural reforms and personnel changes in the Council of Ministers. The number of deputy chairmen was reduced from nine to one. Other changes included abolition of four councils—Agriculture and Forestry, Economic Affairs, Social Affairs and Intellectual Development—that had been founded in 1986. Three ministries and several state committees also were abolished, including the Ministry of Trade, and four new ministries were created in their place. The National Assembly also approved extensive administrative reforms.

Following the collapse of Communism in Eastern Europe in 1989/90, Bulgaria began to dismantle the constitutional structures of the authoritarian state. The transition to a moderate socialist polity was slow but it gained momentum after the fall of Ceausescu in Rumania. First, the Communist Party was stripped of its monopoly of power, called "the dominant role" in the constitution. Zhivkov himself was arrested, and the secret police disbanded. The Communist Party lost its control over the police and the military. Constitutional amendments removed the words "Communist" and "Socialist" from the Constitution. The State Council was dissolved and an executive presidency replaced the former, largely ceremonial, office of head of state. Finally, multiple parties were permitted to stand for free national and local elections. A new constitution is being drafted by the National Assembly, and it is expected to be promulgated by 1993.

The Council of Ministers is described in the Constitution as a "supreme executive and administrative body of state power" overseeing the day-to-day functioning of the government. The Council of Ministers consists of a chairman, who also is the prime minister or head of government; one deputy chairman; 11 ministers; and several chairmen of subordinate committees. Other members of the Council of Ministers are ministers without portfolio and the deputy chairman of the State Control Committee. Within the Council of Ministers there is an inner executive committee known as the Bureau of the Council of Ministers. Its membership includes the prime minister, his deputy, the minister of finance and the chairman of the State Planning Committee. The Council of Ministers is formally elected by the National Assembly.

The functions and powers of the Council of Ministers may be grouped together as executive, legislative, economic (budget preparation), police and military. It can form committees, councils, general boards and offices and can issue orders to the people's councils. There are seven committees subordinate to the Council of Ministers and 12 supervised by it.

RULERS OF BULGARIA
Princes

July 1879–September 1886:	Aleksander
September 1886–July 1887:	Coregents: Stefan Stambolov, Petko Karavelov, Sava Mutkurov
July 1887–October 1908:	Ferdinand

Kings

October 1908–October 1918:	Ferdinand
October 1918–August 1943:	Boris III
August 1943–September 1946:	Simeon II
	Coregents: August 1943–September 1944, Prince Kyril, Nikolai Michov, Bogdan Filov; September 1944–September 1946, Venelin Ganev, Zvetko Boboshevsky, Todor Pavlov

Presidents

(Chairman of the Presidium of the National Assembly 1946–71; Chairman of the Council of State since 1971; Executive President from 1990)

September 1946–December 1947:	Vasil Kolarov
December 1947–May 1950:	Mintso Neychev
May 1950–November 1958:	Georgi Damianov
November 1958–April 1964:	Dimitar Ganev
April 1964–April 1971:	Georgi Traikov
April 1971–November 1989:	Todor Zhivkov
November 1989–July 1990:	Petar Mladenov
July 1990– :	Zhelyu Zhelev

ORGANIZATION OF THE BULGARIAN GOVERNMENT

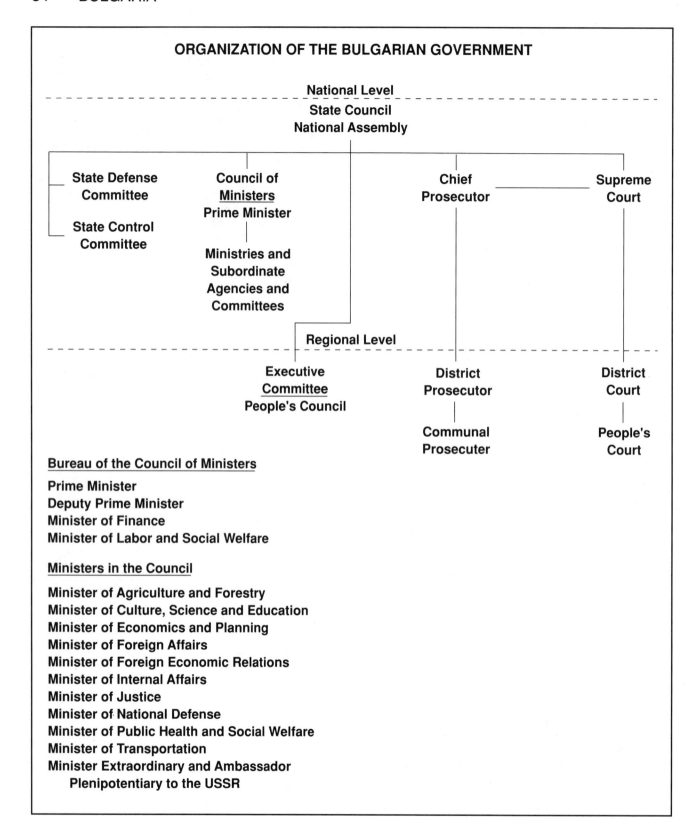

National Level

State Council
National Assembly

State Defense
Committee

State Control
Committee

Council of
Ministers
Prime Minister

Ministries and
Subordinate
Agencies and
Committees

Chief
Prosecutor

Supreme
Court

Regional Level

Executive
Committee
People's Council

District
Prosecutor

Communal
Prosecuter

District
Court

People's
Court

Bureau of the Council of Ministers

Prime Minister
Deputy Prime Minister
Minister of Finance
Minister of Labor and Social Welfare

Ministers in the Council

Minister of Agriculture and Forestry
Minister of Culture, Science and Education
Minister of Economics and Planning
Minister of Foreign Affairs
Minister of Foreign Economic Relations
Minister of Internal Affairs
Minister of Justice
Minister of National Defense
Minister of Public Health and Social Welfare
Minister of Transportation
Minister Extraordinary and Ambassador
    Plenipotentiary to the USSR

Other Members of the Council
Ministers Without Portfolio (2)
Deputy Chairman of the State Control Committee

Committees Subordinate to the Council
Administration for Microbiology and the Pharmaceutical Industry
Administration for Quality Standardization and Metrology
Commission for Economic and Scientific-Technical Cooperation
Committee for Friendship and Cultural Relations with Foreign Countries
Committee for Youth and Sports
High Certifying Commission
National Council for the Protection of Wildlife

Agencies and Committees Under the Supervision of the Council

Academy of Sciences
Bulgarian Foreign Trade Bank
Bulgarian National Bank
Bulgarian Radio and Television
Bulgarian Telegraph Agency
Central Cooperative Union

Commission on the Living Standard
Committee for Communal Services
Committee on Prices
Committee on Tourism
Coordination Council of the Central Cooperative Farm Union
Main Administration of Construction Troops

RULERS OF BULGARIA *(continued)*
Prime Ministers
(Chairman of the Council of Ministers since 1946)

July–November 1879:	Todor Burmov
November 1879–March 1880:	Archbishop Kliment
March–November 1880:	Dragan Tsankov (Liberal Party)
November 1880–April 1881:	Petko Karavelov (Liberal Party)
April 1881–July 1882:	Iohan Erenroth
July 1882–September 1883:	Leonid Sobolev
September 1883–June 1884:	Dragan Tsankov (Liberal Party)
June 1884–August 1886:	Petko Karavelov (Liberal Party)
August 1886:	Archbishop Kliment
August 1886:	Petko Karavelov (Liberal Party)
August 1886–June 1887:	Vasil Radoslavov
June–August 1887:	Constantin Stoilov
August 1887–May 1894:	Stefan Stambolov (Liberal Party)
May 1894–October 1908:	Constantin Stoilov
October 1908–March 1911:	Aleksander Malinov (Democratic Party)
March 1911–July 1913:	Ivan Gheshov (National Party)
July 1913:	Stoyan Danev
July 1913–June 1918:	Vasil Radoslavov
June—November 1918:	Aleksander Malinov (Democratic Party)
November 1918–October 1919:	Todor Todorov
October 1919–June 1923:	Aleksander Stamboliski (Agrarian Party)
June 1923–January 1926:	Aleksander Tsankov

RULERS OF BULGARIA *(continued)*

January 1926–June 1931:	Andrei Liapchev (Democratic Party)
June–October 1931:	Aleksander Malinov (Democratic Party)
October 1931–May 1934:	Nikola Mushanov (Democratic Party)
May 1934–January 1935:	Kimon Gheorghiev
January–April 1935:	Pencho Zlatev
April–November 1935:	Andrei Toshov
November 1935–February 1940:	Georgi Kiosseivanov
February 1940–August 1943:	Bogdan Filov
August 1943–May 1944:	Dobri Bozhilov
May–September 1944:	Ivan Bagrianov
September 1944:	Kosta Muraviev (Agrarian Party)
September 1944–October 1946:	Kimon Gheorghiev (Republican Party)
October 1946–July 1949:	Georgi Dimitrov (Communist Party)
July 1949–January 1950:	Vasil Kolarov
January 1950–April 1956:	Vulko Chervenkov
April 1956–November 1962:	Anton Yugov
November 1962–April 1971:	Todor Zhivkov
April 1971–June 1981:	Stanko Todorov
June 1981–April 1986:	Grisha Filipov
April 1986–February 1990:	Georgi Ivanov Atanasov
February 1990– :	Andrei Lukanov

Communist Party Leaders
General Secretary, 1946–54, and since 1981; First Secretary of the Central Committee, 1954–81

October 1946–March 1954:	Vulko Chervenkov
March 1954–November 1989:	Todor Zhivkov
November 1989–February 1990:	Petar Mladenov
February 1990– :	Alexander Lilov

CABINET LIST

President	Petur Toshev Mladenov
First Dep. President, State Council:	Angel (Angelov) Dimitrov
Chairman, Council of Ministers (Prime Minister):	Andrei Lukanov
Deputy Chairman, Council of Ministers:	Nadya Asparukhova
Deputy Chairman, Council of Ministers:	Stoyan Mirchev Mikhaylov
Deputy Chairman, Council of Ministers:	Georgi Georgiev Pirinski
Deputy Chairman, Council of Ministers:	Mincho Smilov Yovchev
Deputy Chairman, Council of Ministers:	Kiril Dimitrov Zarev
Minister of Agriculture and Forestry:	Georgi Momchev Yordanov
Minister of Construction, Architecture, and Urban Works:	Petur Marinov Petrov
Minister of Economics and Planning:	Kiril Dimitrov Zarev
Minister of Finance:	Belcho Antonov Belchev
Minister of Foreign Affairs:	Boiko Georgiev Dimitrov
Minister of Foreign Economic Relations:	Khristo Iliev Khristov
Minister of Industry and Technology:	Mincho Smilov Yovchev
Minister of Internal Affairs:	Atanas Georgiev Semerdzhiev, *Col. Gen.*
Minister of Internal Trade:	Ivan Petrov Shpatov
Minister of Justice:	Svetla Raykova Daskalova
Minister of National Defense:	Dobri Marinov Dzhurov, *Army Gen.*
Minister of National Education:	Asen Khadzhiolov
Minister of Public Health and Social Welfare:	Mincho Tsanev Peychev
Minister of Transportation:	Trifon Nenov Pashov
Minister Extraordinary and Ambassador Plenipotentiary to the USSR:	Georgi Tsankov Pankov
Chmn., State and People's Control Committee:	Georgi Dimitrov Georgiev

FREEDOM & HUMAN RIGHTS

Along with the other East European regimes, Bulgaria was one of the worst offenders against human rights from 1945 to 1989. Following the Stalinist model of repression, the Soviet-backed regime stripped Bulgarians of every basic human right guaranteed them in the Constitution. All forms of dissent were brutally suppressed in an effort to isolate the country from the West, enforce a centralized command economy, and create a Marxist society. The media, judiciary, church and educational system were all converted into agents of the state.

The Velvet Revolution that swept Eastern Europe in 1989 reached Bulgaria late. But with the fall of Zhivkov and the BKP hardliners in early 1990, Bulgaria moved decisively into the democratic camp. The words "Communist" and "Socialist" were deleted from the Constitution; the State Council was dissolved; and an executive presidency was created. BKP's monopoly of power was rescinded. The party's control over the military and police was removed, and the secret police was disbanded. Opposition groups were permitted to form and contest elections. Free and fair elections—the nation's first since 1945—were held in 1990, and the head of the main opposition group, the Union of Democratic Forces, Zhelyu Zhelev, was elected president in August 1990. The BKP itself was renamed the Bulgarian Socialist Party as a final act of renunciation of the nation's Stalinist heritage. A new constitution is being drafted by the National Assembly. It is expected to formally restore all human rights and to guarantee their exercise by all Bulgarians.

The Sofia Spring has extended to other areas as well. Torture and beatings of prisoners and politically motivated arbitrary arrests, interrogations, trials and incarcerations have been officially renounced. Human rights groups have been legitimized. Forced change of residence and internal exile have been declared illegal. Freedoms of assembly and religion have been restored. Discriminatory acts against Turks have been suspended. Regulations against foreign travel have been removed, and control over the media has been relaxed.

The Constitution declares that women and men enjoy equal rights. There is no overt discrimination against women, and statistically their role in society became more productive under the Communists. In 1988, for the first time, women were admitted to the army's Vasil Levsky Military Academy. What residual discrimination they suffer is not much more than that suffered by women in Western countries.

CIVIL SERVICE

No information is available on the Bulgarian civil service.

LOCAL GOVERNMENT

Until 1987 the country was divided into 28 *okruzi* (singular: *okrug*), translated roughly as districts containing some 200 cities and approximately 5,500 villages or hamlets. The cities and larger towns were divided into *rayoni* (singular: *rayon*), and the smaller villages were grouped together into *obshtini* (singular: *obshtina*). The *rayoni* and the *obshtini*—the urban boroughs and the village communes—were the smallest units of local government, that is, those with people's councils.

In 1987 the republic was divided into nine regions. Each region is governed by a regional people's council. The council has an elected executive committee, which is constantly in session. The executive committee is to the people's council what the State Council was to the National Assembly at the national level. The executive committee prepares regional economic plans and budgets within the framework of the state economic plan and the state budget and has general administrative oversight over the districts and municipalities within its jurisdiction.

POLITICAL SUBDIVISIONS

Provinces	Capitals	Area Sq. Km.	Area Sq. Mi.	Population (1986 est.)
Blagoevgrad	Blagoevgrad	6,490	2,506	346,266
Burgas	Burgas	7,697	2,972	449,314
Gabrovo	Gabrovo	2,035	786	175,120
Khaskovo	Khaskovo	4,007	1,547	301,249
Kurdzhali	Kurdzhali	4,036	1,558	302,578
Kyustendil	Kyustendil	3,041	1,174	190,410
Lovech	Lovech	4,136	1,597	202,708
Mikhaylovgrad	Mikhaylovgrad	3,609	1,393	223,292
Pazardzhik	Pazardzhik	4,455	1,720	326,315
Pernik	Pernik	2,391	923	174,419
Pleven	Pleven	4,332	1,673	362,130
Plovdiv	Plovdiv	5,639	2,177	754,393
Razgrad	Razgrad	2,668	1,030	198,007
Ruse	Ruse	2,570	992	304,443
Shumen	Shumen	3,390	1,309	254,789
Silistra	Silistra	2,842	1,097	174,052
Sliven	Sliven	3,614	1,395	239,479
Smolyan	Smolyan	3,523	1,360	164,223
Sofiya	Sofia (Sofiya)	7,165	2,766	305,251
Stara Zagora	Stara Zagora	5,066	1,956	411,506
Tolbukhin	Tolbukhin	4,704	1,816	257,298
Turgovishte	Turgovishte	2,732	1,055	171,167
Varna	Varna	2,825	1,477	464,701
Veliko Turnovo	Veliko Turnovo	4,680	1,807	339,120
Vidin	Vidin	3,006	1,161	166,388
Vratsa	Vratsa	3,955	1,527	287,841
Yambol	Yambol	4,110	1,587	203,754
City Commune				
Sofiya	Sofia (Sofiya)	1,194	461	1,199,405
TOTAL		110,912	42,823	8,949,618

FOREIGN POLICY

Between 1945 and 1990 Bulgaria's foreign policy was completely subordinated to that of the Soviet Union. Todor Zhivkov once acknowledged that Bulgaria was bound "to the Soviet Union in life and death." The basis of this alliance was the Treaty of Friendship, Cooperation and Mutual Aid with the Soviet Union in 1948 and renewed at periodic intervals. The bonds between the two countries are not only ideological and historical but also economic. The Soviet Union is the country's largest trading partner, and it supplies most of its needs of raw materials and technicians.

Relations with other East European states are largely governed by a series of bilateral treaties of friendship and cultural cooperation. They also are institutionalized through the Warsaw Pact and COMECON. Relations with Yugoslavia and Albania have followed Soviet initiatives. Bulgaria's irredentist claims against Greece and Yugoslavia have not been actively pressed for many decades, but combined with other ideological frictions have helped to create periodic chills in relations with these two neighbors. Another contiguous neighbor, Turkey, has been the object of Bulgaria's historic hostility, and relations between the two have verged on a state of undeclared war. Official efforts to Bulgarianize ethnic Turks living in Bulgaria have been the subject of numerous protests by Turkey. Frequent defections by Bulgarian Turks to Turkey have added to the tensions. As a strong ally of the Soviet Union, Bulgaria main-

tained its distance from Rumania's Ceausescu regime until the latter's overthrow in December 1989.

Bulgaria has maintained a low profile in international politics, and its relations with Western countries have not yet recovered from the ravages of the Cold War. Relations with Italy were strained for a number of years after Mehmet Agca, a Turkish citizen, claimed Bulgarian involvement in his assassination attempt against Pope John Paul II in 1981. Sergei Antonov, a Bulgarian airline official, was arrested in Rome in this connection but later acquitted and released for lack of evidence. The "Bulgarian Connection" was a diplomatic setback for Bulgaria.

Since the Soviet Union's detente with the West, Bulgaria has made a number of moves to improve relations with its Balkan neighbors and the West.

PARLIAMENT

The National Assembly (Narodno Sobraniye) is a 400-member unicameral legislature elected for a term of five years. The National Assembly is convened at least three times a year but its sessions are brief. The National Assembly has permanent commissions, the functions of some of which overlap those of the ministries.

The basic election law is the Law of Election for the National Assembly, adopted in 1953. It has been amended many times since then. Article 6 of the Constitution extends the right to vote to every Bulgarian citizen who has reached age 18 except those who are "under complete tutelage." Members of both national and local representative bodies are elected by direct and secret ballot on the basis of universal, equal and direct suffrage. Technically they may be recalled by the electorate.

Dates for elections to the National Assembly and the regional people's councils are scheduled generally two months after the expiration of the current term. Elections are held on weekdays and nonworking days. Elections are conducted by the Central Election Commission, comprised of representatives of various organizations such as trade unions, cooperatives, youth organizations and special-interest groups.

In 1990 Bulgaria held its first post-Communist era election to the National Assembly. The main contestants were the Bulgarian Socialist Party, successor to the BKP; the Union of Democratic Forces, an alliance of right-of-center opposition parties; the Agrarian Party, a former BKP ally; and the Movement for Rights and Freedom (MRF), representing Turkish interests. The results were as follows:

BSP	211 seats	
UDF	144 seats	
MRF	23 seats	
Agrarian Party	16 seats	
Three small parties	4 seats	
Independents	2 seats	

POLITICAL PARTIES

The ruling party in Bulgaria from 1945 to 1990 was the Bulgarian Communist Party (BKP), which enjoyed a monopoly of power under the Constitution. Following the collapse of Communism, it was renamed the Bulgarian Socialist Party (BSP). Contesting the 1990 election under that name, it gained an absolute majority of 211 seats in the 400-member National Assembly. It is thus the only Communist party to retain power in Eastern Europe after the Velvet Revolution. The party's governing statute was issued in 1962, at the Eighth Party Congress, and has been amended four times since then: at the Ninth Congress, in 1966; at the 10th Congress, in 1971; at the 12th Congress, in 1981; and at the 13th Congress, in 1986.

The party hierarchy is composed of the Politburo, the Secretariat and, to some extent, the Central Committee, the memberships of which interlock, as one person may occupy two or more positions at any time. Theoretically, the apex of the party is the five-year congress. The main functions of the party congress include amending the party statutes, electing the Central Committee and receiving reports on major government programs or reforms.

The Central Committee is elected by the congress, although in practice it merely approves the list of names provided by the party leadership. The former is a large, unwieldy body, consisting in 1988 of 188 full members and 126 candidate members. It meets only four times a year for one or two days at a time. For the performance of its duties it has 14 permanent departments and six schools and departments.

Within the Central Committee the effective loci of power are in the Politburo and the Secretariat. The Politburo generally consists of 12 members. It is a self-perpetuating body, and changes in membership are dictated by the members themselves. The Secretariat, headed by the general secretary, the most powerful man in the country, consists of eight to 10 secretaries. Some of the secretaries manage party affairs, while others direct government departments and agencies assigned to them.

The Agrarian Party, formerly the Bulgarian Agrarian Union (Bulgarski Zemedelski Suyuz, BZS), was formed in 1899 and is one of the oldest agrarian organizations in Europe. In the 1920s it became the governing party under Aleksander Stamboliski. The party split in 1931, and in 1942 the radical half of the party, known as the Pladne, joined the BKP in the Fatherland Front coalition. The BZS, which was subservient to and controlled by the BKP, had a more simplified party hierarchy than the BKP, being governed by an executive council elected by delegates of its congress, which meets every four years. The Executive Council is composed of 99 members and 47 alternate members, who elect members of a standing committee, comparable to the BKP Politburo. Other leading party organs are the Auditing Commission and the Supreme Council, consisting of members and alternates of the Executive Council, members of the various commissions and chairmen of district committees.

The Union of Democratic Forces (UDF) is a loose alliance of anti-Communist and pro-democratic right-of-center parties brought together to contest the 1990 election of the National Assembly. Although it did not win a majority of the seats in parliament, its leader, Zhelyu Zhelev, was elected president following the ouster of Petar Mladenov. Not much is known on the internal organization or ideology of the UDF. Even less is known about the Movement for Rights and Freedom, a party that represents Turkish interests.

There are no known illegal political parties or terrorist groups.

ECONOMY

Bulgaria has a centralized command economy with a massive, monopolistic public sector.

At the end of World War II Bulgaria possessed one of the least developed economies of Europe, with the lowest per capita income in Eastern Europe and with over four-fifths of its work force in agriculture. The Communist regime introduced a policy of rapid industrialization whose primary elements were concentration and centralization. In the process, huge trusts were created in industry and vast complexes in agriculture. Within a decade Bulgaria enjoyed one of the fastest rates of growth in the region. The transformation also was made possible by generous and substantial Soviet aid and credits as a quid pro quo for unwavering fidelity to the Soviet camp.

In the 1960s the government launched a program to decentralize decision-making, allowing limited market forces to operate, but political events in Czechoslovakia alarmed the leadership and prompted it to reverse the trend. A new system of central controls was reintroduced, including the organization of most firms into state enterprises. By 1971 over 60 state economic amalgamations were responsible for almost all nonagricultural production, while in the agricultural sector state collective farms had been formed as Agro-Industrial Complexes (AIC's), most encompassing 17,814 to 26,721 ha. (44,000 to 66,000 ac.).

In early 1979 the government decreed a partial return to decentralization with the adoption of the New Economic Mechanism (NEM), which called for reduced centralized planning while providing for economic accountability within state enterprises. Introduced first in agriculture with the abolition of the Ministry of Agriculture and the establishment of a National Agro-Industrial Union, the system was extended in January 1980 to other sectors of the economy.

The development of the economy faced severe limitations because of the inadequacy of domestic resources, including basic raw materials and skilled workers. It also suffered from overdependence on the Soviet Union. Efforts to overcome persistent growth-retarding difficulties led to frequent tinkering with economic mechanisms. Following the Soviet model, there also was a heavy reliance on centralized planning.

The 1975–80 five-year plan achieved an increase of 35% in industrial production and 20% in agricultural output, with three-quarters of the plan's budget spent on further modernization and reconstruction of industry. Foreign trade increased by 80%. Under the 1981–85 five-year plan the NMP rose by 20%. Its priorities were the development of heavy industry and the fusion of state and cooperative ownership. The 1986–90 five-year plan emphasizes the development of science and technology. It also provides for a restructuring of foreign trade activities, reforms in the structure and policies of domestic economic management and the establishment of over 1,500 self-governing enterprises. A major reorganization of the banking system began in 1987. Financial incentives were introduced for increased agricultural production in the private sector. By 1990 the growth rates were estimated at 30% for the NMP, 37% for foreign trade, 27% for industrial production, all above the 1985 figures. Central planning is directed by the Council of Ministers with the aid of specialized ministries and of various committees and commissions. The most important of these committees is the State Planning Committee.

PRINCIPAL ECONOMIC INDICATORS, 1988

Net Material Product: $67.6 billion
NMP per capita: $7,510
NMP average annual growth rate (%): 1.8 (1988)
NMP per capita average annual growth rate (%): N.A.
Consumer Price Index (1980=100)
  All items: 108.3 (1986)
Average annual rate of inflation: 1·8% (1987)

Data for Bulgaria balance of payments have not been published.

GROSS DOMESTIC PRODUCT, 1988

GDP nominal (national currency: 26.851 billion
GDP real (national currency): 25.923 billion
GDP by type of expenditure (%)
  Consumption
    Private: 58
    Government: 11
  Gross domestic investment: 24
  Gross domestic savings: N.A.
  Foreign trade
    Exports: } 7
    Imports: }
Sectoral origin of GDP (%)
  Primary
    Agriculture: 13
  Secondary
    Manufacturing: 60 (includes mining and public utilities)
    Construction: 10
  Tertiary
    Transportation & communications: 7
    Trade: 7
    Finance:
    Public administration and defense: } 3
    Services:

A major feature of the economy is its organization into trusts (officially known as state economic associations) that unite enterprises within branches of economic sectors along functional lines, such as metallurgy, textiles, food processing, railroads, tourism, wholesale distribution, publishing and filmmaking. In agriculture the large agro-industrial complexes unite several previously independent farms. Trusts are responsible to the economic ministries and receive instructions directly from the Council of Ministers. Each trust has several branches, as many as 106 in one instance. Formerly, trust branches had been legally and financially independent enterprises, with trusts serving as only administrative links between enterprises and ministries. However, following their reorganization in the 1970s, trusts have assumed various functions previously performed by the enterprises. Trusts now formulate economic and development policies and establish relations with suppliers, distributors and financial institutions. They also provide centralized research, operational guidance and export markets. Each branch, however, is responsible for fulfilling the quotas set by the national plan. Profits of the individual branches are pooled and redistributed by the parent organization. More productive branches have to share their profits with less productive ones.

Bulgarian economic statistics suffer from inconsistencies resulting from frequent shifts in methodologies. Because of differences in concept and coverage, national account data are not comparable with those of Western countries. The bulk of investment is channeled into the material production sector, particularly industry and state enterprises. Government policy is to shift financing progressively from the government budget to the economic trusts. However, since all investment funds remain subject to government control, the difference is only a matter of bookkeeping. Serious shortcomings are frequent in the implementation of investment programs. The main problem is the initiation of programs that exceed available capacity and resources. The situation is aggravated by poor planning, inferior design, delays in the delivery of machinery and materials, poor organization of work and slack discipline.

Bulgaria has one of the lowest debts to the West of all CMEA countries. The gross external debt rose from $4.0 billion in 1985 to $4.6 billion in 1986. In 1985 the government borrowed $470 million in three major loans from Western banks, both to help develop its electronic and high-technology industries and to offset some of the economic consequences of adverse weather conditions.

Bulgaria is not involved in official development assistance programs.

PUBLIC FINANCE

The fiscal year is the calendar year. The national budget constitutes the financial part of the annual socioeconomic plan and provides for the financial flows implicit in that plan. It is comprehensive, and its coverage extends to all economic, social and cultural activities. In line with the official policy of gradually placing economic trusts and their branches on a self-financing basis, a progressively larger share of the funds budgeted for the economy is being retained by the trusts rather than channeled to the budget. Ultimate control over the use of these funds, nevertheless, remains with the government, and their disposition is subject to the provisions of the budget.

The national budget is prepared by the Ministry of Finance and is formally approved by the National

Assembly, but as a rule only minor modifications are made during legislative review. Budgets for the local governments are included in the national budget and generally constitute about 20% of the total. The Ministry of Finance also is responsible for implementation of the budget through its corps of state and local inspectors.

CENTRAL GOVERNMENT EXPENDITURES, 1987

% of total expenditures
Defense: —
Education: ⎱ 18.8
Health: ⎰
Housing, Social Security, welfare: 18.0
Economic services: 46.4
Administration 1.6
Other: 15.2

CENTRAL GOVERNMENT REVENUES, 1987*

% of total current revenues
National economy: 92
Other: 8

*Most data regarding Bulgaria central government revenues have not been published.

Budgetary data have not been published since the 1960s. Some figures are released to the press or mentioned in speeches and articles by officials of the Ministry of Finance. The annual budgets have grown steadily larger, from 7.057 billion leva in 1973 to 20.672 billion leva in 1987. As a rule, the budgets are balanced and show a small surplus. In 1973 the expenditures were 7.035 billion leva and the surplus 22 million leva; in 1987 the relative figures were 20.662 billion leva and 10 million leva. In 1987 a total of 92% of the revenues were derived from the operations of the economy; the remainder were raised from a variety of levies. The largest single item of revenue—more than 30%—is collected from a turnover tax on sales. The second most important source consists of levies on enterprises by a profits tax, a tax on fixed capital (interest charge) and miscellaneous deductions from income. Social Security taxes based on payrolls are the third major source. About two-thirds of the revenues are derived from the industrial sector. In 1980 all income taxes for wage earners and collective farmers were abolished. Income derived from activities in the private sector remain taxable.

The largest item of expenditure is the national economy, a broad rubric whose parameters are not clearly defined. It accounted for 46.4% of the total in 1987. The next two large items are Social Security and culture (including education, science, and health and art), accounting for 18.0% and 18.8%, respectively. Administration accounts for a much smaller percentage, at 1.6%. One unusual feature of the budget is the large category of other expenditures, whose details are not disclosed. They probably include expenditures for defense, internal security and other sensitive matters. The level of expenditures reflects the government's expectations and goals about each sector of the economy.

CURRENCY & BANKING

The Bulgarian currency unit is the lev (plural: leva), divided into 100 stotinki (singular: stotinka). Coins are issued in denominations of 1 stotinka and 2, 5, 10, 20 and 50 stotinki and 1 lev and 2 and 5 leva. Notes are issued in denominations of 1 lev and 2, 5, 10 and 20 leva.

The lev is a nonconvertible currency with a variety of exchange rates usable only in domestic transactions. There are two official exchange rates and at least three clearing account rates. One official exchange rate applies to capitalist currencies and the other to ruble area currencies. The first clearing account rate applies to multilateral transactions with COMECON, the second to bilateral transactions with socialist countries and the third to bilateral transactions with Western countries.

Except for small remittances or travel allocations to other Communist countries, the lev is nontransferable for residents and foreigners who have resided in the country for more than six months. Ownership or trade in gold, foreign currencies or so-called capitalist securities is prohibited, as is the import and export of Bulgarian bank notes.

Until 1987 the Bulgarian banking system consisted of the Bulgarian National Bank and two semi-independent banks attached to it: the Bulgarian Foreign Trade Bank and the State Savings Bank. Following the reorganization of the banking sector in 1987 eight additional banks were chartered: Biokhim, Avtoteckhnika, Elektronika, Stopanskabanka, Stroitelna, Transportna and Zemedelska i Kooperativna, for special sectors such as electronics, trade, construction, transportation and agriculture. The Bank for Economic Projects or the Mineral Bank also was reorganized. Each bank is responsible for financial dealings within its sector and enjoys some independence in setting operational policies.

The banking system follows the pattern of institutional concentration in the economy. The Bulgarian National Bank is directly responsible for the financial sector, and it also oversees the financial aspects of the annual plans. In addition, it publishes the official financial statistics for the banking system. These statistics are limited to the annual data on bank credits for investment and on the volume of outstanding short- and long-term loan balances for the banking system as a whole. Debts on outstanding loans are broken down by type of borrower and, in the case of short-term loans, by purpose. With minor exceptions, no information is available on the volume of loans extended, on loan maturities, or on interest rates after 1970. The State Savings Bank publishes data on the volume of personal savings.

With the enlarged sphere of financial independence for the economic trusts since the 1970s, there has been increased lending activity. In the late 1970s there was a tightening of investment credit. Long-term loans are granted predominantly for fixed investment purposes.

Nearly 80% of the long-term loans are due from state and collective enterprises, and the balance from private individuals who had borrowed to finance home construction. Nearly 90% of the short-term loan balances are owed by state enterprises, and the balance from collective enterprises. By sector, the largest short-term borrowers are trade, industry, construction and agriculture. The State Savings Bank advances consumer loans for the purchase of durable goods. It also grants small loans to licensed private craftsmen for working capital and to workers on collective and state farms for purchase of livestock, seeds, fertilizers and small tools. The repayment record on loans by the State Savings Bank is excellent, with a delinquency rate of less than 0.01%.

Bulgaria's external foreign debt was $7.1 billion in 1989. Other data relative to Bulgaria's international financial situation are not available.

The Mineral Bank plays a major role in financing credit for large-investment projects and for foundation and expansion loans for small and medium-size enterprises. It is a joint stock company owned 50% by the Bulgarian National Bank and 50% by large economic trusts.

EXCHANGE RATE (National Currency per U.S. Dollar)									
1979	1980	1981	1982	1983	1984	1985	1986	1987	1988
—	—	—	0.850	0.980	0.980	1.00	1.230	1.310	1.310

Data regarding annual growth rates in Bulgaria have not been published.

AGRICULTURE

Natural conditions are favorable for agriculture. Fertile soils and a varied climate make possible the cultivation of a wide variety of field crops, fruits and vegetables, including warm-weather crops such as cotton, tobacco, rice, sesame and grapes. However, frequent droughts, such as the one in 1986, lead to wide fluctuations in crop yields and necessitate extensive irrigation.

The Stara Planina divides the country into several climatic and agricultural regions. The long Danubian tableland north of the Stara Planina has a continental climate, with cold, hard winters that tend to damage orchards and vineyards. The continental climate also prevails in the Sofia Basin and in the region surrounding the headwaters of the Struma River. A near-Mediterranean climate prevails in the Thracian Plain and in the valleys of the lower Struma, Mesta and Maritsa rivers, in the Arda Basin and in the southern slopes of the Rodopi. But the winters are not mild enough for the cultivation of Mediterranean crops such as olives and citrus fruits. The Black Sea coast is warmer in winter and cooler in summer, but the hot winds and frequent gale storms have an adverse influence on crops. The Plovdiv area and the coastal districts of the Dobrudzha region in the Northeast receive scant rainfall, most of it in the summer months, and the timing and amount of precipitation are unfavorable for optimum crop growth. Droughts are frequent in this region.

Good soils make up almost three-fourths of the land surface. The Danubian Plateau contains several grades of black earth, which gradually give way to gray forest soils in the foothills of the Stara Planina. Pitch soil called *smolnitsa* predominates in the Thracian Plain, the Tundzha and Burgas lowlands and the Sofia Basin. Chestnut and brown forest soils are found at higher elevations of the central region, in the Strandzha uplands, in the basins of the eastern Rodopi region and in the Struma and Maritsa valleys. Brown forest soils and mountain meadow soils occur in the Stara Planina and in the Rila, Pirin and western Rodopi. Alluvial soils are found alongside the rivers and in several basins.

Total agricultural land comprises 6,182,000 ha. (15,269,540 ac.), or 55.7% of the land area. Natural pastures constitute 20% and meadows 4.7%; field crops are 75.3%, of which 7% is devoted to vineyards, orchards and other perennial crops. Excluding pastures, the per capita acreage of farmland is among the lowest in the world. More than half the cultivated acreage is subject to erosion. Large areas degraded by erosion continue to be included in the official statistics on farmland acreage. Special laws were passed in 1967 and 1973 for the preservation of farmland, creating a special land improvement fund, and in 1970 the government established special district councils for this purpose. Under the 1973 law only land unsuitable for agricultural purposes or farmland of low productivity could be put to nonagricultural uses.

About 29% of the arable land is under irrigation, compared to 21% in 1970 and 26% in 1976. Irrigation projects have figured prominently in every five-year plan since 1960. Primitive gravity irrigation is practiced on about nine-tenths of the irrigated area. Water is distributed over the fields from unlined earthen canals by means of furrows dug with a hoe. The timing of the water application and the quantity of water used are not properly adjusted to the needs of the various crops, so that the increase in yields is only half as great as that obtained under optimum conditions and about half the water is wasted. The network of irrigation ditches also impedes mechanization. Improper irrigation and irrigation techniques have raised the groundwater level excessively in several districts, causing salinization. Modernization programs have replaced the ditches with stationary sprinkler systems in some areas, but progress has been slow in this direction.

The basic unit in agriculture is the agro-industrial complex (AIC), comprising several previously independent, contiguous collective and/or state farms having similar climatic and soil conditions. The complex also may include other units engaged in the production, processing and distribution of farm products. AIC's have carried Bulgarian agriculture to levels of concentration and size large even by Soviet standards.

Announced in 1969 as an experimental program, the AIC concept was quickly implemented nationwide. By the fall of 1972 there were 170 AIC's formed through consolidation of 845 collective farms and 170 state farms; including the private farms of collective and state farmers, they contained 92.5% of the cultivated land and accounted for 94.5% of the farm output. Only a small number of private farms in mountainous areas remained outside the system. The average AIC is composed of five or six farms having 23,887 to 27,530 ha.

(59,000 to 68,000 ac.). All farmlands are state property, and farm workers have the status of industrial workers under the Labor Code.

```
┌─────────────────────────────────────────────────────┐
│           AGRICULTURAL INDICATORS, 1988              │
│ Agriculture's share of GDP (%): 14.7                 │
│ Index of Agricultural Production (1979–81=100): 103 (1986) │
│ Index of Food Production (1979–81=100): 106 (1986)   │
│ Number of tractors: 54,180                           │
│ Number of harvester-threshers: 7,813                 │
│ Total fertilizer consumption (tons): 864,000         │
│ Number of farms: 296 agro-industrial complexes       │
│ Average size of holding, ha. (ac.): 12,431 (30,705)  │
│ Tenure (%)                                           │
│   State: 100                                         │
│ % of farms using irrigation: 29                      │
│ Total land in farms ha. (ac.): 6,182,000 (15,269,540)│
│ Farms as % of total land area: 55.7                  │
│ Land use (%)                                         │
│   Total cropland: 75.3                               │
│     Permanent crops: 7.0                             │
│     Temporary crops: ⎫                               │
│     Fallow:          ⎬ 93.0                          │
│   Meadows & pastures: 24.7                           │
│ Yields, kg./ha. (lb./ac.)                            │
│   Grains: 3,266 (2,915)                              │
│   Roots & tubers: 12,536 (11,189)                    │
│   Pulses: 980 (875)                                  │
│   Milk, kg. (lb.)/animal: 3,506 (7,729)              │
│ Livestock (000)                                      │
│   Cattle: 1,706                                      │
│   Sheep: 9,724                                       │
│   Hogs: 3,734                                        │
│   Horses: 120                                        │
│   Chickens: 38,000                                   │
│ Forestry                                             │
│   Production of roundwood, 000 cu. m. (000 cu. ft.): 4,525 │
│     (159,800)                                        │
│     of which industrial roundwood (%): 60.9          │
│   Value of exports ($ 000): 21,550                   │
│ Fishing                                              │
│   Total catch (000 tons): 109.2                      │
│     of which marine (%): 87.1                        │
│   Value of exports ($ 000): 14,250                   │
└─────────────────────────────────────────────────────┘
```

The transition of agriculture to the AIC system was completed in 1980. Initially the state farms and the collective farms maintained juridical autonomy, but eventually this was lost and they become operating sections of the AIC. Some AIC's are groupings of multiple units producing the same crop; others combine diverse crops; and still others are vertically integrated, including fertilizer production, marketing, packaging, agricultural research and sales. Originally, cooperative farms were included in the AIC network, but they were abolished in 1977. AIC's are governed by the same regulations that apply to all state economic associations or trusts.

Despite the dominance of AIC's, there is in the agricultural sector a small but vigorous sub-economy consisting of personal plots and auxiliary plots. Although Communist ideologues consider them incompatible with the socialist system, BKP leaders have time and again reaffirmed the importance of private farm plots as a reserve for the increase of farm output, particularly in livestock production. Rather than competing with the socialized agricultural sector, private farm plots supplement it. Personal farm plots are cultivated by any indi-

vidual, while auxiliary plots are market gardens run by workers in state enterprises to supply office canteens and *gastronoms*.

Leasing of small garden plots for personal use began in the 1950s as a form of compensation to farm families who had become part of collective farms. Plot size varied according to the character of use, ranging from 0.2 ha. (0.5 ac.) for intensive cultivation of fruits and vegetables to 0.5 ha. (1.2 ac.) for grain and 1 ha. (2.5 ac.) for poor-quality land. A further 0.1 ha. (0.2 ac.) is provided for each head of cattle raised. In 1974, loans were provided and income taxes remitted to encourage more people to cultivate plots, and provision of machine services, seed, fertilizer and equipment at zero or very low cost was guaranteed by the AIC. At the same time, there were strict limits on the size of the farms, the size of farm equipment used and the use of hired labor. By 1982, personal plots produced 33% of all vegetables, 51% of potatoes, 30% of milk, 40% of meat and more than half the eggs and accounted for one-quarter of agricultural output and farm family income. Much of the output is marketed through AIC channels, and such subcontracting is becoming an accepted feature of agricultural production. Total cultivated land use by individuals rose from 9.8% in 1960 to 13.8% in 1985, with most of the increase in the late 1970s. Such growth has taken place without any significant shrinkage in the size or degree of central control over the state agricultural institutions.

As in other sectors, agriculture is subject to highly centralized planning in the form of long-range (10 to 15 years), five-year and annual plans that are coordinated with national and regional plans. The plans consist of norms regarding varieties of crops and breeds of livestock, production targets and estimates of resources and labor requirements, with detailed directives for the introduction of technological improvements. The planned targets and conditions for their attainment are formulated for each individual complex by the State Planning Committee together with the Ministry of Agriculture and the regional people's councils. Seven groups of norms enter into the formulation of plan targets: the technical measures to be introduced; the physical volume of each crop and livestock product to be sold to the state; the volume of capital investment and its specific uses; consumption of materials, parts and products; allowable expenditures and labor remuneration; formation of various operating and reserve funds and for material incentives; and development of social amenities. These norms may be changed in exceptional cases only. The AIC's distribute among their constituent units these tasks handed to them from above. On the basis of the state plan, each AIC and its constituent units prepare a counterplan that sets higher goals than those officially established.

Employment in agriculture has steadily dropped from 54.7% in 1960 to 44.9% in 1965, 35.2% in 1970 and 17% in 1986. (Official figures suffer from numerous inconsistencies and serious undercounting.) The outmigration from agriculture, mostly of young people, has brought a deterioration in the age structure of the remaining farm population. There also is a corresponding decline in skilled manpower relative to the higher levels of mechanization. Farm wages are based on the overall profits of the individual farms. All farmers are entitled to a minimum wage. Work input is measured on the basis of uniform labor norms differentiated according to natural conditions. Each farm has a wage fund calculated as a percentage of its total income. The AIC work force is organized into brigades headed by first-line supervisors.

Investment in agriculture has fluctuated more sharply than in industry or other sectors. As a percentage of total investment, it rose from 12.4% in 1949 to 22.9% in 1956 and reached a peak of 29.7% in 1960. Thereafter it has steadily declined—to 19.7% in 1965, 15.8% in 1970, 14.7% in 1975, 12.4% in 1980 and 8.2% in 1985. Much of the increased investment in the 1960s was used for creation of the AIC's and construction of farm buildings, irrigation facilities and mechanization. This capital-intensive phase was completed by the 1970s, from which time the sector has received a smaller proportion of national resources.

Bulgaria has more tractor power per acre than any other East European country except Czechoslovakia. However, the level of mechanization is extremely low, except on wheat farms. Many of the tractors and combines are overage and obsolete, and there are chronic shortages of spare parts as well as of trained operators.

Marketing of farm products is geared to the five-year plan quotas for sale to the state. It is based on bilateral contracts between trusts in the food processing sector and AIC's. The price system includes bonuses for quality. These bonuses are payable only after a specified portion of the contracted quantity has been delivered and vary in relation to total delivery. The intent of the bonus is to stimulate quality without encouraging overproduction. The marketing contracts are worked out by the Ministry of Agriculture and the State Arbitration Commission. An integral part of the procurement contract is establishment of a fund by each food processing trust for improvement of farming methods and for modernization of the farm's physical facilities. Individual farmers may sell some of their produce at retail directly to consumers in cooperative markets at prices not exceeding those charged at state retail stores. These cooperative markets are subordinate to the trade organs of municipal authorities. Sale of meat, meat products and alcoholic beverages in cooperative markets is prohibited as is sale of any produce through middlemen.

The contribution of agriculture to the NMP was 14.7% in 1986 compared to 22% in 1970 and 31% in 1960. However, the annual growth rate since 1960 has exceeded 3.4%. The structural composition of farm output has changed in favor of livestock production, which has grown at a faster pace than crop production. The area under field crops also has declined since 1960. The proportion of acreage devoted to the various crops are: grains 62.5%; industrial crops 14.6%; feed crops 18.7%; and vegetables, potatoes and melons 4.2%. The acreage under bread grains has steadily declined and constitutes less than half of the total grain acreage. The area

under feed grains has remained fairly stable. Among industrial crops, the acreage under tobacco and oilseeds has expanded considerably. The area under vegetables has expanded, led by tomatoes. The potato acreage, on the other hand, has declined. The area of fodder crops has suffered a substantial decline. The acreage of apple orchards and vineyards has grown, but that under fruit trees and berries has declined. Changes in crop acreage do not always conform to government policy and indicate that market forces are operating independently of government plans.

Despite substantial increases in outputs and yields, the sector suffers from obsolete farming techniques and practices and farmers' resistance to modernization. Traditionally, a single variety of wheat has been grown in the entire country despite variations in soil and climatic conditions. Propagation of diseases such as wheat flower blight is aided by faulty cultivation practices such as excessively heavy seeding. Substantial crop losses occur through inexpert application of fertilizers and pesticides, inadequate thinning and weeding, improper crop rotation and poor harvesting methods. Climatic abnormalities also account for frequent crop failures.

Although agriculture is entirely socialized, substantial numbers of livestock are privately owned—virtually all the goats and rabbits, more than half the poultry, about two-fifths of the sheep and 20% to 30% of the hogs and cattle. Expansion of livestock herds has been hampered by inadequate feed supplies, poor herd management and substandard veterinary services. Production of meat in 1985 was 768,000 tons, of which pig meat was 340,000 tons, beef and veal 127,000 and poultry 165,000. Because of heavy exports, there are periodical shortages in domestic market supplies of livestock products.

Forests cover about 35% of Bulgaria's territory, with about 24% coniferous and 76% deciduous. The principal lumbering areas are the Rila and western Rodopi in the Southwest and the southern slopes of the Stara Planina in the center. Intensive exploitation and neglect have contributed to deterioration of the forests. Between 1960 and 1980 more than 1.4 million ha. (3.5 million ac.) were replanted as part of an afforestation program.

Fishing is a developing sector, and its operations are primarily in the Black Sea (where resources are less than abundant) and in the Atlantic Ocean. The latter accounts for two-thirds of the total catch, which grew from 5,000 tons in 1960 to 109,200 tons in 1988. Cape horse mackerel account for a little less than half the deep-sea catch. Fishing vessels are based in the ports of Varna and Burgas.

MANUFACTURING

Bulgaria faces even more severe constraints in manufacturing than it does in agriculture. The country is short of raw materials, skilled technicians and reliable export markets. To overcome these limitations, the government has adopted the same techniques it uses in agriculture: concentration and automation.

```
+-----------------------------------------------------------+
|            MANUFACTURING INDICATORS, 1988*                 |
| Share of GDP: 14.7                                        |
| Labor force in manufacturing: 20.8                        |
| *Most data regarding manufacturing in Bulgaria have not   |
|  been published.                                          |
+-----------------------------------------------------------+
```

Virtually all industry is state-owned. State enterprises account for 98.6% of industrial assets, employ 90% of industrial labor and produce 92% of industrial output. Collective enterprises account for the balance of assets, labor and output. More than half the enterprises in the state sector employ more than 500 people, and one-quarter employ more than 1,000 people. Metallurgy; glass and china; clothing; and the leather, shoe and fur industries have the largest number of workers per enterprise. Territorial distribution of industry favors the site of raw materials or major consuming centers, such as Sofia, Plovdiv, Varna, Burgas and Ruse. In 1970 the BKP laid down guidelines for a program of regional economic development. Its aim was to arrest excessive urban growth and, at the same time, to help develop backward rural areas. With these guidelines, decentralization of industry has been undertaken. Construction of new industrial plants in heavily populated areas is prohibited. Further expansion in these areas is limited to modernization of existing facilities and introduction of more advanced technology. Some industrial activity has been transferred from congested cities to rural areas.

The weakest link in the industrial chain is the supply system. The supply of raw materials and other resources to industrial producers suffers from frequent breakdowns, resulting in factory shutdowns, substitution of materials of lower quality and hoarding of scarce materials. Supply difficulties are particularly disruptive because of the stringent nature of production plans and the limited availability of resources. Although customers and suppliers enter into annual contracts, these contracts frequently are ignored by the latter.

In terms of employment shares, the largest state industry branches are machine building and metalworking, food processing, textiles, timber and woodworking, chemicals and rubber, and fuels.

The Bulgarian Industrial Association (BIA) was founded in 1982. It is actively involved in trade promotion in its role as a kind of Chamber of Commerce, but it also engages in a wide range of other activities, from management and technical consulting to creation of new enterprises. The BIA stimulates enterprise formation in areas where studies have discovered gaps in the domestic or export markets and provides venture capital to new projects. In some ways the BIA operates like a ministry, although it has no statutory standing. The BIA has strong links with the Mineral Bank, which sometimes is referred to as the "BIA Bank."

Industry's share of total investment has risen steadily since 1949, with the exception of two five-year plan periods, ending in 1960 and 1975. It started out in 1949 at 31.4%, then rose to 36.8% in 1956, dipped to 34.2% in 1960 and rose to 44.8% in 1965 and to 45.2% in 1970, fell back to 39.9% in 1975 and then rose again to 41.9% in 1980 and to 48.4% in 1985, its highest level since 1949. More than four-fifths of industrial investment is devoted to expansion of producer goods, particularly heavy industry. Beginning in 1967, substantial investment funds also have been devoted to food processing—the major export industry and earner of foreign exchange. Investment allotment to consumer goods never has exceeded 22%.

There is no foreign investment in Bulgaria.

MINING

Bulgaria contains a variety of metallic and nonmetallic minerals. A few are of good quality, but most of these occur in small quantities. The largest deposits of iron ore are in the far western Stara Planina and the Strandzha mountain range, and there are smaller deposits in the vicinity of Burgas, along the Black Sea coast and north and west of Sofia. Coal is in some 20 small deposits, of which the largest are in the Stara Planina 32 km. (20 mi.) north of Sofia and another in the extreme northwestern portion of the same range. Brown coal and lignite are more abundant. Copper, lead and zinc are mined in exportable quantities. Among East European countries, Bulgaria ranks high in the production of these three minerals. Among the other metallic ores, Bulgaria has three of the most important alloying metals—manganese, molybdenum and chromium—but the manganese is of poor quality. Uranium has been discovered in several deposits near Sofia and is extracted from one or more of them. Gold occurs in a number of places in small quantities.

Reserves of anthracite and bituminous coal are insignificant. Brown coal deposits that can be mined economically are nearly depleted. Only the lignite reserves are sizable. Lignite is mined mainly in the Maritsa Basin, near Dimitrovgrad in the Thracian Plain and in the Sofia Basin. The Maritsa Basin, particularly the area known as Maritsa-Iztok, is the richest source, contributing about 50% of the total output. Lignite output in 1984 was 32.121 million tons.

The main deposits of iron ore are at Kremitovtsi, northeast of Sofia, and at Krumovo, in the lower Tundzha Valley. The ore in the former is of low grade with a mineral content of about 33%. Reserves at Krumovo are of better grade but much smaller, and mining at the deposit was discontinued in the mid-1960s. Iron ore output in 1984 was 622,000 tons.

Copper is the major nonferrous metal, and it is mined south of Burgas, in the Sredna Gora Mountains near the town of Panagyurishte and in the western Stara Planina south of Vratsa. The ore is concentrated locally and is smelted and refined in plants in Eliseyna, Pirdop and the Medet complex. Production in 1984 was 73,000 tons.

Lead and zinc are obtained from mines near the towns of Madan and Rudozem in the eastern Rodopi and in the western part of the Stara Planina, at Eliseyna and Chiprovtsi. The Rodopi mines account for the major portion of the ore output. Production of both lead and zinc in 1984 was 160,000 tons.

Nonmetallic minerals are more abundant. Asbestos,

salt, sulfur and cement are produced in quantities large enough to allow for some exports.

All Bulgarian mining is state-owned, and there is no foreign participation in the mining sector.

ENERGY INDICATORS, 1988

Primary energy production (quadrillion BTU):
  Crude oil: 0.01
  Natural gas, liquid: 0
  Natural gas, dry: 0
  Coal: 0.50
  Hydroelectric power: 0.02
  Nuclear power: 0.14
  Total: 0.67
Electricity:
  Installed capacity (kw.): 10,243,000
  Production (kw.-hr.): 41.817 billion
    % fossil fuel: 65.6
    % hydro: 5.6
    % nuclear: 28.8
  Consumption per capita (kw.-hr.): 5,025
Natural gas, cu. m. (cu. ft.):
  Proved reserves: 5 billion (177 billion)
  Production: 150 million (5.297 billion)
  Consumption: 6.473 billion (229 billion)
Petroleum, bbl:
  Proved reserves: 13 million
  Years to exhaust proved reserves: 43
  Consumption: 94 million
  Refining capacity per day: 300,000
Coal, 000 tons:
  Reserves: 3,730,000
  Production: 35,222
  Consumption: 42,190

ENERGY

Bulgaria produces less than one-third of its energy needs. Its first nuclear power station, constructed by Soviet engineers, opened in 1974. Nuclear power, which provided 29% of electric energy in 1985, is expected to provide 40% in 1990 and 60% by 2000. Loading of the fifth reactor at the nuclear power station at Kozlodui began in 1987. When a sixth reactor is completed, this station will produce 43% of the nation's power supply. A second nuclear power station is being built at Belene on the Danube. The wind power station at the Frangen Plateau, north of Varna, is the nation's first. The major hydroelectric power stations are on the Sestrimo cascade, in the upper reaches of the Maritsa River and at the Vucha cascade southwest of Plovdiv. A thermal plant fueled by local coal is at Bobov Dol. In addition, Bulgaria imports electricity from Rumania, the Soviet Union and Yugoslavia. The electrical transmission network is connected with the power grids of Rumania, Yugoslavia and the Soviet Union.

Deposits of crude oil are at Tyulenovo in the Dobrudzha region and at Dolni Dubnik east of Pleven. Natural gas fields have been discovered near Vratsa and in the area of Lovech south of Pleven. Domestic production covers only a small fraction of national energy needs. The Soviet Union supplies over 95% of the country's crude oil requirements. Construction of a 1,635-km. (1,016-mi.) gas pipeline linking Bulgaria to the Soviet Union was completed in 1986. Soviet supply of natural gas is estimated at 5.5 million cu. m. (194.2 million cu. ft.) per year.

Crude oil is processed in two refineries, at Burgas and Pleven, whence it is transported by pipelines to the consuming centers.

LABOR INDICATORS, 1988

Total economically active population: 4.3 million
As % of working-age population: 75.3
% female: 47.6
% under 20 years of age: 4.2
Activity rate (%)
  Total: 53.7
  Male: 56.8
  Female: 50.6
Hours of work in manufacturing: 42.3/per week
Employment status (%)
  Employees: 99.2
  Other: 0.8
Sectoral employment (%)
  Agriculture, forestry & fishing: 17.0
  Mining: ⎫
  Manufacturing: ⎬ 37.0
  Construction: 7.9
  Transportation & communications: 6.8
  Trade: 8.2
  Services: 21.6
  Other: 1.5

LABOR

The Bulgarian labor force was estimated in 1988 at 4.3 million, representing a high participation rate of 75.3%. The participation rate also is high for women, at 47.6%. Four-fifths of all women working in industry are in blue-collar jobs. By far the largest proportion of women workers is in textiles, where they constitute over 75% of total employment. Women also constitute the majority in food processing.

The majority of industrial workers are paid on a piecework basis, but the prevalence of piecework has been declining and varies widely among the industrial branches. It is highest in textiles and construction and lowest in mining. Pay scales differ according to the sector; they are higher for white-collar workers, for workers in capital goods industries and for workers in state industrial units and lower for blue-collar workers, for workers in consumer goods industries and for workers in collective industrial units.

Among the reported manpower problems are maldistribution of labor, resulting in excesses in some sectors and shortages in other sectors; shortage of skilled workers, excessive turnover; high absenteeism; poor discipline; and lack of incentives. Workers have the right to quit their jobs freely but have to seek reemployment through district labor bureaus, which assign them arbitrarily.

Unemployment has never been officially admitted, but some degree of unemployment and underemployment exist in several rural areas.

The Central Council of Trade Unions, the only labor federation, was founded in 1904 and was known as the General Workers' Professional Union until 1951. Following the principle of democratic centralism, union officials are elected by the rank and file, but all candidates for union offices are screened and selected by officials at higher levels. The trade union local is the basic organizational unit at the factory or enterprise level, and above it there is an ascending hierarchical structure based on territorial divisions. There are 17 individual trade unions affiliated with the Central Council of Trade Unions, with a total membership of 4 million.

Workers are not permitted to organize outside the official union structure, nor are they allowed to strike, although disgruntled workers in Mezdra engaged in a week-long stoppage in March 1987. There is no collective bargaining. A new Labor Code, in force since January 1987, and a restructuring of unions in the spring of 1987 were touted as bringing the rank and file into the decision-making process.

The Constitution declares that every able-bodied citizen is "obliged to do socially useful work." Those who do not work may be charged with vagrancy or social parasitism. The 1987 Labor Code stipulates 16 years as the minimum age for all but certain light work. Persons between 16 and 18 years of age may not be assigned heavy or dangerous work, and their workweek may not exceed 36 hours.

In 1988 the minimum wage was $120 per month and the average wage was $210 per month. The workweek for adults is 42.5 hours (five days of 8.5 hours per day). Paid vacations range from 14 workdays annually for those who have worked less than 10 years to 18 workdays for those who have worked for over 15 years. Additional paid vacation is granted those in difficult or dangerous occupations. Participation in unpaid compulsory brigades often lengthens working hours.

Trade unions are assigned the role of promoting job safety and the general social welfare of their members. A national labor safety program exists, but standards of enforcement vary greatly. Over one-third of working women are employed in places where the hygiene is unsatisfactory, and there are few safeguards for pregnant working women.

FOREIGN COMMERCE

Foreign trade is a state monopoly. Trade policy is formulated by the Ministry of Foreign Trade, the Ministry of Finance and the Bulgarian National Bank.

There is a complex body of laws and regulations governing various aspects of foreign trade, and these are subject to frequent revisions. There are two basic types of foreign trade organizations: those attached to and serving individual economic trusts with a large export volume, and those serving several trusts with lower export volumes. These organizations retain their juridical identity and are not considered to be departments of the trusts they serve. Relations between the trusts and the foreign trade organizations are governed by contract. The latter may engage in foreign trade for the account of the trusts, on their own account or directly. Sometimes the foreign trade of a single trust may be apportioned among several foreign trade organizations.

FOREIGN TRADE INDICATORS, 1988		
Exports: $16.8 billion (1987)		
Imports: $16.9 billion (1987)		
Balance of trade: $−100 million		
Direction of Trade (%)		
	Imports	Exports
EEC	9.7	4.9
U.S.A.	0.9	0.4
East European countries	74.3	79.8
Japan	0.7	0.1
Composition of Trade (%)		
	Imports	Exports
Food & agricultural raw materials	8.5	17.1
Ores & minerals	} 43.9	} 8.0
Fuels		
Manufactured goods	47.5	74.9
of which chemicals	5.4	5.4
of which machinery	37.4	57.8

Export plans are approved by the Council of Ministers by physical and value terms, and by major trading areas graded by importance into four categories: countries in COMECON, of which Bulgaria is a member; other Communist countries, Western industrial economies and developing countries. Trusts are encouraged to adjust their output to foreign market requirements and to achieve maximum efficiency in export production. Financial incentives to surpass official foreign trade targets are provided by allocating the producers and foreign trade organizations a portion of the receipts from excess exports and a portion of the savings made on imports through import substitution. Producers are obligated both to produce the items called for by the export plan in accordance with specifications and to meet contractual delivery dates, but with few exceptions they have no direct contact with foreign buyers. It is the responsibility of the foreign trade organizations to seek out the most profitable markets and to handle the trade transactions. It is also their duty to keep producers informed about changing conditions in world markets and to make them aware of needed adjustments in production.

Standard subsidies, differing by trade area, are granted on all exports. In effect these subsidies modify the official exchange rate so that trade is actually conducted on a multiple exchange rate basis. Exports also receive subsidies from the state budget if returns from them do not cover costs.

Relations between trusts and economic organizations are determined by state regulations. Disputes between them are settled by the Ministry of Foreign Trade and the Ministry of Finance.

The great bulk of the trade is carried on with Communist countries, particularly the Soviet Union. The share of these countries has declined only slightly, from 85% in 1961 to 79.2% in 1986. The Soviet Union alone accounts for 59.5% of total trade. East Germany and Czechoslovakia are the main COMECON trading partners after the Soviet Union, but the volume of trade with these countries is much lower than that with the Soviet Union. The orientation of trade with the Soviet bloc is based primarily on political factors but also dictated by the shortage of export goods salable in Western markets and the inadequacy of foreign exchange reserves. Trade with COMECON members is conducted on the basis of bilateral clearing accounts that do not involve use of foreign exchange. In addition, the Soviet Union has supplied Bulgaria with industrial plants and equipment in exchange for the output of these plants.

Three-fourths to four-fifths of trade outside the Soviet bloc is with the EEC. Trade with developing countries and with the United States is negligible.

Over the years there has been a gradual shift from agricultural to industrial commodities and from raw materials to manufactured and semiprocessed goods in foreign trade. The share of manufactured exports rose from 25% in 1960 to 75% in 1986. Nearly half the imports also consist of industrial goods. Data on the balance of payments have never been published. It is known that Bulgaria has been the recipient of generous Soviet loans and, in turn, Bulgaria has made some loans to developing countries to help finance its exports. The trade with Western nations has been chronically in deficit and offset only partially by income from Western tourists.

The most important trade fair is the Plovdiv International Fair.

TRANSPORTATION & COMMUNICATIONS

The first railroad was built in Bulgaria in 1866 by British engineers and connected Ruse on the Danube with Varna on the Black Sea. The legendary *Orient Express* ran through Bulgaria, entering the country from Belgrade, crossing the western mountains at Dragoman Pass and continuing through Sofia and Plovdiv and down the Maritsa River valley to Edirne and Istanbul.

TRANSPORTATION INDICATORS, 1988

Roads, km. (mi.): 37,397 (23,237)
  % paved: 91
Motor vehicles
  Automobiles: 1,030,090
  Trucks: 587,400
  Persons per vehicle: 5.5
  Road freight, ton-km. (ton-mi.): 10.324 billion (7.071 billion)
Railroads
  Track, km. (mi.): 4,294 (2,668); electrified, km. (mi.): 2,342 (1,454)
  Passenger traffic, passenger-km. (passenger-mi.): 8.004 billion (4.973 billion)
  Freight, freight-tonne-km. (freight-ton-mi.): 18.327 billion (12.553 billion)
Merchant marine
  Vessels: 205
  Total deadweight tonnage: 2,302,900
  No. oil tankers: 16; GRT: 312,000
Ports
  Number: 3 sea, 3 river
  Cargo loaded (tons): 3,930,000
  Cargo unloaded (tons): 25,377,000
Air
  Km. (mi.) flown: 24.7 million (15.3 million)
  Passengers: 2 million
  Passenger traffic, passenger-km. (passenger-mi.): 2.961 billion (1.840 billion)
  Freight traffic, freight-ton-km. (freight-ton-mi.): 43.1 million (29.5 million)

TRANSPORTATION INDICATORS, 1988 *(continued)*

Mail ton-km. (mail ton-mi.): 1 million (621,000)
Airports with scheduled flights: 13
Airports: 380
Civil aircraft: 65
Pipelines
  Crude, km. (mi.): 193 (120)
  Refined, km. (mi.): 418 (259)
  Natural gas, km. (mi.): 1,400 (869)
Inland waterways
  Length, km (mi.): 471 (293)
  Cargo, tonne-km. (ton-mi.): 58.643 billion (40.167 billion)

COMMUNICATION INDICATORS, 1988

Telephones
  Total (000): 1,876
  Persons per: 4.8
Phone traffic (000 calls)
  Local: 25,800
  Long distance: 600
  International: 6,130
Post office
  Number of post offices: 2,587
  Pieces of mail handled (000): N.A.
Telegraph, total traffic (000): 7,593
Telex
  Subscriber lines: 6,030
  Traffic (000 minutes): 30,733
Telecommunications
  1 satellite ground station

TOURISM & TRAVEL INDICATORS, 1988

Total tourism receipts ($): 345 million
Expenditures by nationals abroad: ($): N.A.
Number of tourists (000): 7,295
  of whom (%) from Turkey, 36.7
               Yugoslavia, 19.7
               Czechoslovakia, 6.1
               Poland, 6.5
Average length of stay (nights): 10

The rail network, operated by the Bulgarian State Railways (BDZ), runs 4,294 km. (2,668 mi.) of track, of which 2,050 km. (1,274 mi.) are electrified. All but a few hundred miles are standard-gauge, and 823 km. (511 mi.) are double-track. Because of the terrain the system has a large number of tunnels and bridges constructed with tight curves and steep gradients. Most of the some 1,600 bridges are short, but the longest, 2.4 km. (1.5 mi.) long, crosses the Danube at Ruse. Most of the 175 tunnels also are short, the longest being 5.6 km. (3.5 mi.). In 1986 the new Sofia–Gorna–Oryakhovitsa–Varna line was opened for traffic. Construction of a 161-km. (100-mi.) Sofia subway began in 1979 and is continuing. The last steam locomotives were replaced in 1978.

Because of the terrain, roads suffer from the same problems as rail tracks in both construction and maintenance. Ice and snow close most routes at times during winter. Spring thaw and floods damage the better roads and make poorer roads impassable. About 211 km. (131 mi.) of superhighways have been constructed in recent decades.

The 471 km. (293 mi.) of the Danube is the lifeline of the country. However, the fact that the Danube leaves the country to exit into the Black Sea from Rumania limits its potential as an avenue to seagoing trade, and the fact that it flows along the northern periphery limits its usefulness to the rest of the country. Downstream from the Iron Gate, the Danube can take up to 2,500-ton vessels. It is navigable for an average of 300 days per year except for a short time in winter and early spring. Other streams are too short, too shallow or have too-steep gradients to be used as waterways. Only about 2.5% of the total ton-mileage of freight is transported using inland waterways.

The Black Sea is even more important than the Danube as a maritime outlet. Burgas and Varna are thriving ports, the latter developing rapidly and by 1970 surpassing Burgas as the major port and center of the maritime industry. The country's merchant fleet expanded five-fold in tonnage in the 1960s. There are no large passenger vessels in the fleet but several hydrofoils, having a capacity of over 100 passengers, operate between Danube River ports.

The national flag carrier is BALKAN—Bulgarian Airlines. Its planes are all of Soviet make. It conducts domestic as well external flights. The principal airport is Vrazhdebna near Sofia, and there are other international airports at Varna and Burgas.

DEFENSE

Bulgaria is militarily isolated from its Warsaw Pact neighbors because its neighbor Rumania, has prohibited movement of foreign troops across its borders. This handicap limits the usefulness of the Bulgarian People's Army (Bukgarska Norodna Armiya, BNA) to its Soviet allies. The principal orientation of the defense forces and strategy is toward its not-so-friendly neighbors to the south, west and east: Greece, Yugoslavia and Turkey, respectively.

The BNA command is organized along standard Warsaw Pact lines, with the minister of defense as the highest-ranking uniformed officer directly responsible to the head of state. Under the minister of defense are district commanders, service chiefs and a number of deputy ministers of defense, including the chief of staff and the heads of rear services, training and administration.

Military terminology distinguishes between the ground forces (called the army) and other branches, such as the air force, navy and auxiliary administrations, directorates and branches, such as rear services (logistics), training, artillery, armor, communications, engineering, chemical and political, all of which are directly responsible to the Ministry of National Defense.

The ground forces are distributed into three territorial commands having headquarters at Sofia, Plovdiv and Sliven. The basic organizational unit is the division and, as in other Warsaw Pact countries, each division has about 10,000 men. Divisions are at least of full combat strength. Each of Bulgaria's Warsaw Pact allies has a number of tank divisions, but Bulgaria has only tank

brigades. Motorized rifle divisions have one tank regiment, one artillery regiment and three motorized rifle regiments. Some units are equipped with short-range missiles and unguided rockets.

The air force is relatively modest, with some 255 combat aircraft organized in squadrons, usually with 12 airplanes each. The fighter-bomber squadrons use MiG-17's, which perform well in a ground support role. There are 40 armored helicopters. Air defense forces are positioned to protect the country's borders as well as a few cities and air installations. Early-warning radars are located mainly along southern and western borders and are linked with the Warsaw Pact air defense warning network.

Naval forces, with only 8,800 personnel, constitute less than 6% of the armed forces' personnel strength. They man a variety of vessels and include a contingent of naval infantry, or marines. Some of the smaller vessels make up the Danube River flotilla. Other than the torpedo-carrying patrol boats, the navy's offensive strength consists of Soviet-built submarines. The fleet frequently joins the Soviet fleet for maneuvers in the Mediterranean.

Conscription is mandatory, and most 19-year-old males are drafted. Occupational deferments were eliminated by law in 1970, and other deferments are granted infrequently. Those conscripted serve two- or three-year duty tours. The basic ground force tour is two years and that of special units and air and naval forces is three years. Those who have had military service and who have not reached age 50 are considered reserves. Officers remain in the reserve until 60.

The training program is patterned after that of the Red Army and is reinforced by joint Bulgarian-Soviet maneuvers that employ standard procedures and tactics. The basic program is carried on in an annual cycle and begins with individual physical training and initiation into the care and use of weapons. The recruit learns individual actions necessary in group or combat situations, ranging from personal combat techniques to exposure to gas or nuclear radiation. As the cycle progresses, the conscript becomes part of a team manning a larger weapon or a more complex piece of equipment and then proceeds to learn how to employ these weapons in coordination with other systems. The training culminates in late summer or fall in an annual maneuver in which Soviet forces may participate. Mountain and winter exercises are held to familiarize the troops with a variety of climatic and terrain conditions. Combined arms exercises are held, led by tank and motorized rifle groups engaged in mock offensive operations.

DEFENSE INDICATORS, 1988

Defense budget ($): 2.465 billion
   % of central budget: 18.5
   % of GNP: 3.6
Military expenditures per capita ($): 275
Military expenditures per soldier ($): 15,621
Military expenditures per sq. km. (per sq. mi.) ($): 22,225 (57,578)
Total strength of armed forces: 157,800

DEFENSE INDICATORS, 1988 *(continued)*

Per capita:
Reserves: 216,500
Arms exports ($): 370 million
Arms imports ($): 725 million

Personnel & Equipment

Army
 Personnel: 115,000
 Organization: 3 military districts, 1 with 2 motorized rifle divisions and 1 tank brigade; 2 with 3 motorized rifle divisions and 2 tank brigades
 Equipment: 2,550 main battle tanks; 350 reconnaissance vehicles; 60 mechanized infantry combat vehicles; 1,000 armored personnel carriers; 1,200 artillery; 450 mortars; 40 SSM launchers; 500 air defense guns; 50 SAMs
Navy
 Personnel: 8,800
 Bases: Varna (HQ); Burgas, Sozopol, Balchik; Vidin (HQ), Danube River base
 Equipment: 4 submarines; 3 frigates; 3 corvettes; 6 missile craft; 6 torpedo craft; 33 mine warfare vessels; 2 amphibious craft
 Naval aviation: 9 armored helicopters
 Coastal artillery: 2 regiments
Air Force
 Personnel: 34,000
 Organization: 2 air divisions; 7 combat regiments
 Equipment: 255 combat aircraft; 40 armored helicopters

Noncommissioned officers generally come up from the ranks, but they also may attend special schools and enter military units directly with a noncommissioned officer grade. Under any but exceptional circumstances, the graduates of these secondary schools are obligated to serve in the armed forces for at least 10 more years. Cadet programs in several university-level higher military schools provide officers for the services. Line officers for infantry or armored units and logistics officers have four-year courses. Technical special branches and candidates for air and naval careers have five-year courses.

The morale and conditions of military service are high. Service life is extolled in the media, and the vast majority of the troops enjoy a respected status and receive valuable training. Special social benefits also are available to the forces' personnel. Their dependents receive special financial aid and preference in educational and job placements. Disabled veterans get liberal pensions and free medical treatment and public transportation.

Bulgaria produces only a relatively small amount of military equipment locally. Nearly all heavier and more complex items of military hardware are obtained from the Soviet Union. Military expenditures per soldier are considerably less than those of other Warsaw Pact countries, and the amount spent on equipment and maintenance is rather austere. The armed forces are a less-than-average financial burden on the country but, because of the small population, are a greater-than-average manpower burden. The armed forces provide the youth with skills that are of value to the national economy. The disciplinary habits inculcated by the defense establishment are of positive social value, far outweighing the drain on the labor force. Military units often are called upon for field work on public projects, such as irrigation systems, and the army's heavy equipment may be put to civilian use in emergency situations, such as during droughts.

EDUCATION

Bulgaria's educational history begins with the conversion of the country to Christianity in the ninth century under King Boris I. A court school was established in the early medieval Bulgarian royal capital at Preslav. Later, St. Clement, a disciple of the missionaries Sts. Cyril and Methodius, founded a monastery school at Lake Ohrid in Macedonia that became renowned throughout the Slavic world.

The occupation of the country by the Turks from 1396 arrested the development of education, which was kept alive only in a few monastic schools. After Bulgaria's liberation in 1878, education developed fairly rapidly. Between 1878 and 1912 the first state university, an art academy, teacher training institutes, theological institutes, vocational and commercial schools, and the Academy of Sciences were established. The interwar period witnessed the founding of a new Free University; the American college, run by missionaries; and two higher schools of economics.

With the seizure of power by the Communists under Soviet aegis in 1944, the nature and structure of the system were radically altered. Private schools were abolished, and religious training was banned. Education was given a Marxist and technical bent. Article 45 of the Constitution of 1971 defined the new educational ideology:

> All citizens of the People's Republic of Bulgaria are entitled to free education in all grades and types of educational establishments, under circumstances determined by law. The educational establishments belong to the state. Education is based on the achievements of modern science and the Marxist-Leninist ideology. . . . Citizens of non-Bulgarian extraction, in addition to the compulsory study of Bulgarian, also have the right to study their own language.

The Education law of 1959 extended compulsory education to eight years and mandated "socially useful activities"—meaning technical education—for all students at all levels. Also in 1959 a law was passed decreeing expansion of nursery schools and kindergartens.

The basic or common system of education extends from grades one through 11, with education compulsory from ages seven through 16. The school year begins for elementary and secondary schools on September 15 or the next weekday. However, the length of the school year varies by grade. For grades one to three the school year ends on May 31, for grades four to 10 on June 15 and for grade 11 on June 30. The differences in length of the school year are due to the varying amounts of time allotted to field trips, "socially useful activities" and technical projects. School is held six days a week, and the school year is divided into two semesters, the first running from September 15 to January 31 and the second from February 5 to the end of the school year.

There are three vacation periods: December 31 to January 14, February 1 to February 5 and April 1 to April 10. Most crèches and nursery-kindergartens continue on a year-round basis. Higher education institutions may begin between September 1 and September 15 and continue until June 30, although if work experiences are involved, they may be open until July 20.

Pupils in grades one to three receive a written evaluation of their progress in school, rather than numerical or letter grades. No repetition of grade is permitted at this level. Instead, special tutorial sessions are provided for slow learners. Evaluation from grades four to 10 is numerical, on a six-point descending scale. To be promoted to the next grade, students must obtain at least a grade of 3 in every subject for which grades are assigned. Students receiving a grade of 2 are required to take another examination in the subject at the start of the next school year; if they fail again, they must repeat the previous grade. No pupil may repeat a particular grade more than once or repeat more than two grades during his or her school career.

The curricula for elementary and secondary schools are developed by the Ministry of National Education with the help of a committee. Highly specialized curricula for technical and vocational schools are developed by subject-matter specialists. All textbooks are published by the Ministry of Public Education and are based on the approved curricula. There is a strong emphasis on programmed learning techniques and methodologies, because they are believed to demonstrate scientific materialism in action.

Preprimary education consists of two institutions: crèches (detski jasli), administered by the Ministry of Health for children from birth to three; and kindergartens (detski gradini), for children aged three through six. Attendance is voluntary in both. The crèches serve primarily as day-care centers for infants of working parents, and fees usually are charged in them as well as in kindergartens. There are four types of kindergartens: all-day kindergartens, open from seven in the morning until five or six in the evening; half-day kindergartens, functioning either in mornings or in afternoons; seasonal kindergartens, in rural areas during periods of planting or harvesting; and boarding school kindergartens, where children remain 24 hours a day throughout the workweek.

Elementary and secondary education is provided in the general polytechnical school, a project-oriented 11-year comprehensive institution. It provides general, technical and preinduction military training and consists of three levels: the primary school (nachalno uchilishti), grades one to three; the intermediate school or progymnasium (progimnazija), grades four through eight; and the gymnasium (gimnasium), grades nine through 11. Students completing the progymnasium may either go on to the gymnasium or may enter a vocational-technical school (teknikum). Students completing this level are awarded a certificate (svidetelstvo). To enter the gymnasium they must then pass an examination in mathematics and the Bulgarian language. Students who complete the full 11-year program and have had no grade lower than 3 during their last year of school take a series of final examinations; those who are successful receive a diploma that qualifies them for admission at the university level.

Another form of the general polytechnical school is the general foreign language polytechnical school, established soon after World War II for training specialists in Russian and several major Western languages. The curriculum is similar to the regular one except for the concentration on foreign languages.

Boarding schools (internati or hostels) and extended day-care centers (poly-internati or semihostels) function as adjuncts to elementary and secondary schools for children who are unable to live at home or both of whose parents work. They are staffed by vuz-pitateli, who are both counselors and recreational leaders. A less organized and structured variant is the zanimalna, which is a study hall and extended school-care center.

Several types of institutions are responsible for vocational education. The first is the vocational technical school. Students are admitted after the completion of grade eight, and the usual curriculum lasts one to three years. General education courses are limited in these trade schools, and graduates enter the work force. The second is the secondary professional-technical school, first established in the mid-1960s. It provides a three-year or longer course of combined vocational and general education. Students are required to pass a matriculation examination (both written and oral) in Bulgarian and mathematics as well as a qualification examination in their special vocational subject that includes practical work. Successful students receive both a secondary-school diploma and a certificate of qualification (kvalifitsiran rabotnik) listing their level or grade of proficiency and entitling them to work at their particular trade or vocation. A third type of vocational school is the teknikum, where middle-level technicians are trained. The course curricula are two to four years for day students and five years for night students and those studying extramurally. One-third of the course work consists of general academic subjects. Students receive secondary-school diplomas as well as certificates of qualification as technicians after passing a state examination, both written and oral, in Bulgarian and in mathematics; completing a diploma project; and passing a practical test in his or her respective field of vocational competence. Teknikum graduates may apply to any higher-education institution. Secondary-level vocational schools also exist in music, art and ballet. The number of students enrolled in all types of vocational schools has been fairly constant during the past decade, at about 25% of total student enrollment.

Higher education is provided by two different types of institutions: the first, roughly comparable to junior colleges, give postsecondary work of one, two or three years' duration to train cadre at the semispecialist level. Examples are institutes that train librarians and teachers for primary schools. The second category also may be divided in two: universities and specialized institutes. Completion of a program of studies at either type requires four or five years. Bulgaria has three universities: Clement of Ohrid State University of Sofia, which is the largest and oldest, founded in 1888; Cyril and Methodius State University at Veliko Turnovo; and Paisii of Hilendar State University in Plovdiv. The number of specialized institutes has varied at about 25 to 30 each academic year recently as a result of expansion, reorganization and consolidation.

Admissions to institutions of higher education are highly selective and are regulated by the national economic plans, so that no more students are admitted in any one field than will meet the country's estimated manpower needs for trained personnel in that field. In addition to a secondary-school certificate *(matura)*, almost all higher schools require entrance examinations, the sole exceptions being several schools providing courses in fields having a high national priority but low student interest, such as mining. This quota system results in large numbers of applicants being denied admission—perhaps as high as 80% in any one year. By law, preference for admission to higher education is given to young people who have worked for two or more years after graduation from secondary school—50% of the available openings are allotted to them—and to youths whose parents are, according to official documents, "peasants and workers." Upon completion of their studies, most graduates are required to accept the positions assigned them by the government and to remain therein for a minimum of three years.

Although Bulgaria is officially a Communist state, the Bulgarian Orthodox Church is permitted to maintain a program of theological education for training its prospective clergy. Its theological seminary offers a six-year postprogymnasium course, which may be followed by an additional four years of work at the theological academy.

EDUCATION INDICATORS, 1988

Literacy
  Total (%):95.5
  Male (%): N.A.
  Female (%):N.A.
First & second levels
  Schools: 3,501
  Teachers: 62,188
  Students: 1,097,437
  Student–teacher ratio: 18:1
First level only
  Net enrollment rate (%): 97
  Females (%): 48
Second level only
  Net enrollment rate (%): 78
  Females (%): 49
Vocational
  Schools: 528
  Teachers: 18,692
  Students: 228,620
  Student–teacher ratio: 12:1
Third level
  Institutions: 30
  Teachers: 16,453
  Students: 109,291
  Student–teacher ratio: 7:1
  Gross enrollment rate (%): 18.4
  Graduates per 100,000 aged 20–24: 1,255
  % of population over 25 with postsecondary education: 5.2
  Females (%): 54

EDUCATION INDICATORS, 1988 *(continued)*

Foreign study
  Foreign students in national universities: 6,060
  Students abroad: 617
    of whom in
      West Germany, 105
      Hungary, 96
      Czechoslovakia, 151
      United States, 14
Public expenditures (national currency)
  Total: 1.651 billion
  % of GNP: 7.0
  % of national budget: N.A.
  % current expenditures: 89.7

GRADUATES, 1983

Total: 18,652
Education: 4,245
Humanities & religion: 1,708
Fine & applied arts: 809
Law: 265
Social & behavioral sciences: 242
Commerce & business: 2,143
Mass communication: 71
Service trades: 335
Natural sciences: 692
Mathematics & computer science: 444
Medicine: 1,904
Engineering: 4,523
Architecture: 130
Transportation & communications: 326
Agriculture, forestry, fisheries: 815

The programs of study of most higher educational institutions of full rank are four or five years in length, with six in medicine. Upon graduation, the student may continue his or her studies toward the candidate of sciences *(kandidat na naukite)* degree, which normally requires a minimum of three additional years and a thesis. The highest degree is that of doctor of sciences *(dokto na naukite)*, which requires a thesis of high originality and scholarly significance.

Each university is headed by a rector elected by the senior teaching staff for a term of usually two years. It is largely a ceremonial position. Most of the day-to-day administration is the responsibility of the chief administrative officer and the financial administrative officer, both of whom are appointed by the government. In addition, each faculty or school has a dean *(dekan)* and one or more associate deans *(prodekan)*, who are elected by members of the respective faculty or school. Most policy decisions are made by the institution's Academic Council or Faculty Council, the former presided over by the rector and the latter by the respective deans.

The most important organ in educational administration and finance is the Ministry of National Education. There is no aspect of education outside its jurisdiction and purview, other than vocational and higher education. The administration and operation of most vocational schools and some *teknicums* are the responsibility of the ministry, economic trust or other unit directly concerned with that trade or vocation. Each such unit is assisted by an interdepartmental committee at the national, regional and school levels. The Ministry of National Education, however, reviews and coordinates all vocational education programs through the Indepartmental Council for Scholastic and Vocational Guidance. The ministry also is responsible for all aspects of vocational education relating to instruction and methods, for courses for factory workers at their places of employment and for vocational schools not under the control of any other body.

Higher education is directed by the Council of Higher Education, a subunit of the National Committee for Science, Technical Progress and Higher Education.

A section of the Regional People's Council or Soviet is the regional counterpart of the Ministry of National Education. Often a special education committee of the Regional People's Council is designated to oversee this sector. It acts as a transmission belt for policies or decisions of the central ministry and also directly supervises and administers most general polytechnical schools in the region. Local bodies are charged with administering and funding kindergartens and enforcing compulsory education. The schools themselves are administered by a director, assisted by school soviet or council.

Teachers for nursery-kindergarten and primary schools obtain their training mostly in two-year teachers' institutes, which require graduation from a general polytechnical secondary school for admission. These institutes also prepare teachers for the middle grades, but a university or equivalent diploma is the preferred route to teaching positions in middle schools. Secondary-school teachers are trained in universities after enrolling in an education major.

LEGAL SYSTEM

Bulgarian law is based on Civil Law as modified by the Soviet model. The Constitution places the judiciary below the executive and legislative branches. It also lumps together the judicial bodies and prosecutors in overlapping and parallel functions. By providing for election of judges and lay assessors, the Constitution ensures political control over the judicial machinery.

The highest judicial organ is the Supreme Court, members of which are elected by the National Assembly for five-year terms. It is a court of original as well as appellate jurisdiction and is organized into civil, criminal and military divisions.

Below the Supreme Court are the regional and district (raion and okrug) courts. Judges and lay assessors in the courts are elected by their respective people's councils for five-year terms and are subject to recall by the voters. Lay assessors have equal rights with judges in deciding cases.

As in other systems following Soviet legal structure, public prosecutors play a central role in the criminal justice system. The chief prosecutor of the republic is elected by the National Assembly for a period of five years, and other prosecutors are appointed and discharged by him.

Minor special courts include the State Court of Arbi-

tration, which hears civil law disputes among state enterprises, offices and public organizations, and the Foreign Trade Court of Arbitration, which settles disputes connected with international trade.

The Criminal Code defines crimes as socially dangerous acts identified and declared by law as such. A person may be punished only when he has been found guilty of one of the listed crimes by a proper court. The age of criminal liability is 18. Courts may hand down punishments of 11 different varieties. The code sets upper and lower limits of sentences for each type of crime. The death sentence is never mandatory in peacetime but is optional for a number of crimes. The stipulated sentences for crimes against the state tend to be more severe than sentences for crimes against individuals.

The Ministry of Justice is responsible for the administration of prisons. According to regulations, the primary responsibilities of prison officials are to rehabilitate and reeducate prisoners. Reeducation involves political reorientation, general education and vocational education. The physical facilities are classified as prisons, labor-correctional institutions and correctional homes. According to the seriousness of the offense and other factors, a prisoner may be confined in light, general, strict or enforced disciplinary regimes, one of which is specified in his or her court sentence. Prisoners are separated by age, sex and disciplinary regime. Women and minors serve their sentences in separate prisons or correctional homes. Prisoners are obliged by law to work, and they receive 20% of the wages. Prisoners have legal rights, including time outdoors, exercise, visitors, correspondence, food packages, possession of personal effects and correspondence with lawyers and officials, but these rights vary according to the regimes and are subject to strict limitations. For example, correspondence and packages may be inspected, visits are monitored and personal property of prisoners may be searched. Prisoners are rewarded for good behavior and punished for bad. A number of sentences do not involve confinement, but only banishment to a certain area or prohibition from being in a certain area.

LAW ENFORCEMENT

Until the late 1950s, Bulgaria was a police state on the Stalinist model in which the security police held arbitrary powers over the lives of all Bulgarians and were an instrument of oppression and tyranny. During this period, the state security troops and the regular police forces were estimated to have a total of about 200,000 men. The most severe phase of the reign of terror lasted until 1948 and the atmosphere of repression well into the 1950s. After that time most police functions were assumed by the People's Militia, and the secret police faded into the background, greatly reduced in size but still functioning within the Ministry of Internal Affairs. The secret police was abolished in 1990.

The People's Militia is the principal law enforcement agency, operating under the Ministry of Internal Affairs with district, municipal, urban borough and village commune offices. They are charged with maintaining law and order, protecting personal and public property and regulating traffic. They monitor rules of residence, collect local taxes, rescue people, supervise observance of quarantine measures and drinking laws and combat antisocial behavior. They have unusual powers in dealing with vagabonds, beggars, prostitutes and "socially dangerous" persons whose civil rights have been curtailed. They maintain a major share of the local records dealing with vital statistics, citizenship, identification, travel visas, registration of residences, licenses, permits and employment. Laws concerning the stay of foreigners also are administered by the People's Militia.

Petty crime is widespread and rampant. Although political crimes and economic crimes have decreased since the 1950s, violent crimes have increased. Political prisoners no longer constitute the bulk of the prison population, as they did in during the early post-World War II period. The most prevalent criminal problems have their roots in alcoholism, which has resisted official countermeasures for decades. Tourism has created special problems in resort areas. It is reported to have fostered moral laxity and petit bourgeois attitudes toward moneymaking.

HEALTH INDICATORS, 1988

Health personnel
   Physicians: 26,451
      Persons per: 337
   Dentists: 5,844
   Nurses: 58,961
   Pharmacists: 4,150
   Midwives: 7,769
Hospitals
   Number: 250
   Number of beds: 87,085
   Beds per 10,000: 97
Admissions/discharges
   Per 10,000: 2,118
   Bed occupancy rate (%): 84.4
   Average length of stay (days): 16
Type of hospitals (%)
   Government: 100
Public health expenditures
   Per capita: $197.50
Vital statistics
   Crude death rate per 1,000: 11.6
   Decline in death rate: 37.8 (1965–84)
   Life expectancy at birth (years): males, 68.4; females 73.6
   Infant mortality rate per 1,000 live births: 17.0
   Child mortality rate (ages 1–4 years) per 1,000: 1.0
   Maternal mortality rate per 100,000 live births: 20.1
Causes of death per 100,000
   Infectious & parasitic diseases: 7.1
   Cancer: 163.8
   Endocrine & metabolic disorders: 17.3
   Diseases of the nervous system: 6.0
   Diseases of the circulatory system: 721.1
   Diseases of the digestive system: 36.8
   Accidents, poisoning & violence: 63.5
   Diseases of the respiratory system: 92.3

HEALTH

Public health care is provided, administered and financed by the state. Free health care is available to all citizens with the exception of medicines, the cost of which is met by the patients.

The cornerstone of the health service is the polyclinic, which provides general and specialized outpatient aid and consultation. Polyclinics may be attached to a hospital or may be independent units serving a designated geographical area. A separate network of polyclinics is attached to economic trusts and enterprises. Each polyclinic is divided into departments for the various specialties of medicine.

The major problem with health care is overcrowding. One physician sees an average of 30 patients in a four-hour period of office consultations, and another 20 in a three-hour period of house calls. The average period of consultation is only six minutes, much too short for proper diagnosis. Waiting rooms in polyclinics are jammed, and people have to wait for hours. The inefficiency of polyclinic health care has led to a flourishing private practice among doctors and specialists.

The outpatient work of the polyclinics is supplemented by a network of special dispensaries that provide long-term care for persons suffering from serious illnesses. A network of hospitals, at least one in each district, provides inpatient treatment and specialized diagnostic and clinical facilities. There are six hospitals connected with special medical research institutes and nearly 200 sanatoriums and health spas for persons suffering from chronic ailments.

Physicians and auxiliary medical personnel are civil servants but are classified as nonproductive workers and thus have lower salary scales than productive workers. This status is the cause of considerable dissatisfaction among and a serious shortage of medical personnel.

FOOD & NUTRITION

Although food expenditures account for the largest share of household expenditures in Bulgaria, the national diet is deficient in many respects. Many items, such as fruits, vegetables and dairy products are in chronic short supply. Of nine major food categories, the consumption of only vegetable oils, sugar and flour exceeds desirable levels. The consumption of the other six categories—meat, fish, milk and milk products, vegetables, fruits and eggs is less than half the desirable levels.

FOOD & NUTRITION INDICATORS, 1988

Per capita daily food consumption, calories: 3,663
Per capita daily consumption, proteins, g. (oz.): 106.7 (3.8)
Calorie intake as % of FAO recommended minimum requirement: 146
% of calorie intake from vegetable products: 76
% of calorie intake from animal products: 24
Food expenditures as % of total household expenditures: 44.3
% of total calories derived from:
   Cereals: 40.6
   Potatoes: 1.6
   Meat & poultry: 9.6
   Fish: 0.5

FOOD & NUTRITION INDICATORS, 1988 *(continued)*

Fats & oils: 14.7
Eggs & milk: 8.9
Fruits & vegetables: 5.3
Other: 18.9
Per capita consumption of foods kg. (lb.); l. (pt.)
Potatoes: 30.0 (66.1)
Wheat: 160.0 (352.8)
Rice: 4.3 (9.5)
Fresh vegetables: 37.9 (83.5)
Fruits (total): 115.0 (253.5)
    Citrus: 4.7 (10.3)
    Noncitrus: 110.3 (243.2)
Eggs: 225 (496.1)
Honey: 0.4 (0.8)
Fish: 8.2 (18.0)
Milk: 190.0 (418.9)
Butter: 2.7 (5.9)
Cheese: 11.3 (24.9)
Meat (total): 72.5 (159.8)
    Beef & veal: 11.0 (24.2)
    Pig meat: 37.1 (81.8)
    Poultry: 17.9 (39.4)
    Mutton, lamb & goat: 6.5 (14.3)
Sugar: 50.8 (112.0)
Chocolate: 2.8 (6.1)
Biscuits: 3.0 (6.6)
Beer, l. (pt.): 107.7 (227.6)
Wine, l. (pt.): 22.6 (47.7)
Alcoholic liquors, l. (pt.): 3.0 (6.3)
Soft drinks, l. (pt.): 35.0 (74.0)
Coffee: 0.1 (0.2)
Tea: 0.9 (1.9)
Cocoa: 1.0 (2.2)

MEDIA INDICATORS, 1988

Newspapers
    Number of dailies: 17
    Circulation (000): 2,834
    Circulation per 1,000: 316
    Number of nondailies: 37
    Circulation (000): 1,092
    Circulation per 1,000: 121
    Number of periodicals: 1,758
    Circulation (000): 10,211
    Newsprint consumption:
    Total (tons): 41,500
    per capita, kg. (lb.): 4.6 (10.1)
Book publishing
    Number of titles: 4,322
Radio
    Number of transmitters: 39
    Number of radio receivers (000): 1,997
        Persons per radio receiver: 4.5
    Total annual program hours: 45,332
Television
    Television transmitters: 744
    Number of television receivers (000): 1,693
        Persons per television receiver: 5.3
    Total annual program hours: 5,024
Cinema
    Number of fixed cinemas: 3,314
    Seating capacity: 717,000
        Seats per 1,000: 80
    Annual attendance (million): 96.4
        Per capita: 10.8
    Gross box office receipts (national currency): 42.7 million lev
Films
    Production of long films: 40
    Import of long films: 164
        7.9% from United States
        32.3% from USSR
        4.3% from France
        3.0% from Italy

MEDIA & CULTURE

The Bulgarian press is essentially a postwar creation, since all papers published before World War II were either suspended or nationalized after the war. Of the 17 dailies being published in the country, only three are older than the war. These are *Rabotnichesko Delo*, the BSP organ that was published as an underground paper between 1927 and 1944; *Zemedelsko Zname*, founded in 1899; and *Otechestven Front*, which predates the establishment of the people's republic by two years. Eight of the dailies are distributed nationally, including the three considered the most influential: *Rabotnichesko Delo*; *Otechestven Front*; and *Narodna Mladezh*. The five others are published in provincial centers. All except *Vecherny Novini* (*Evening News*) are publishing in the morning.

CULTURAL & ENVIRONMENTAL INDICATORS, 1988

Public libraries
    Number: 5,699
    Volumes (000): 52,100
    Registered borrowers: 2,225,000
    Loans per 1,000: 5,800
Museums
    Number: 206
    Annual attendance (000): 15,426
    Attendance per 1,000: 1,700
Performing arts
    Facilities: 65
    Number of performances: 18,469
    Annual attendance (000): 6,026
    Attendance per 1,000: 670
Ecological sites: 12
Botanical gardens & zoos: 4

PRINCIPAL DAILIES	
Daily	Circulation
Rabotnichesko Delo	850,000
Trud (Central Council of Trade Unions)	300,000
Otechestven Front	280,000
Zemedelsko Zname	165,000
Narodna Mladezh	250,000
Kooperativno Selo	193,000

Most of the provincial papers have an average circulation of less than 50,000.

Of the 37 non-dailies, 10 are weeklies and the rest appear at least twice a week. In this group are the only two non-Bulgarian publications—one in Greek and the other in Armenian. The Orthodox Church publishes one paper.

The official news agencies are Bulgarska Telegrafitscheka Agentzia (BTA) and the Sofia News Agency (Sofiapres). The former is the official voice of the government, and the latter is charged with the preparation and distribution of propaganda abroad.

Broadcasting is a state monopoly under the Committee on Art and Culture and is administered by two agencies: Bulgarian Radio and Bulgarian Television. The former operates four home service programs and a foreign broadcast service. One of the channels operates 24 hours a day. Most of the programming originates in Sofia. Experimental television broadcasts began in 1954, and a regular service was put into operation in 1959. Color was introduced in 1977. Advertising is permitted, but very little is carried. Broadcasting is supported by license fees and official subsidies. Nearly a third of television broadcasts are devoted to news and propaganda. There are few Western imports, and most of the programming comes from the Intervision network.

SOCIAL WELFARE

In addition to free medical care, all citizens are entitled to a variety of free social benefits, including sickness and disability pay, pensions, maternity benefits and family allowances. Most of these are administered by the trade unions, with the exception of pensions, which are paid by the Ministry of Finance, from the budget.

There is no waiting period for disability compensation. Payments vary, depending upon the severity of the injury and the length of service, from 30% to 100% of wages. Old-age pensions are based on length of service and the nature of the work done. The pensionable age is 55 for women and 60 for men, but early retirement is permitted for certain kinds of work. Payments range from 55% to 80% of wages, based on a scale covering the last three or five years of employment. Pregnant women receive generous maternity benefits; in addition, there is a system of monthly family allowance payments for children up to age 16.

There is no private welfare system in Bulgaria.

CHRONOLOGY

1946—The monarchy is abolished and Bulgaria is declared to be a people's republic; Georgi Dimitrov is named head of government; agriculture is collectivized.
1947—New Constitution is promulgated.
1948—Banks, industries and mines are nationalized.
1949—Dimitrov dies; Vasil Kolarov takes over as prime minister.
1950—Dimitrov's brother-in-law Vulko Chervenkov is named prime minister.
1954—Chervenkov yields post of first secretary of the BKP to Todor Zhivkov, a Khrushchev protege.
1956—Chervenkov loses post of prime minister to Anton Yugov.

1962—Yugov and Chervenkov fall from favor and Zhivkov takes over as prime minister.
1965—On Khrushchev's ouster in the Soviet Union, coup against Zhivkov is mounted by dissidents; coup is put down and is followed by a purge.
1971—Zhivkov is elevated as president and Stanko Todorov becomes prime minister. New Constitution is promulgated.
1981—Grisha Filipov replaces Todorov as prime minister.
1985—Official Bulgarianization drive is launched and is directed against ethnic Turks.
1986—Georgi Ivanov Atanasov replaces Filipov as prime minister.
1987—BKP Congress approves extensive administrative reforms, including redrawing of local government jurisdictions.
1989—Zhivkov is ousted as regime yields to Soviet and popular pressures for reform; Petar Mladenov is named president.
1990—National Assembly revokes the Communist Party's monopoly of power; the State Council is abolished; an executive presidency is created; the Secret Police is disbanded; the Bulgarian Communist Party (BKP) renames itself the Bulgarian Socialist Party; in free elections to the National Assembly the Bulgarian Socialist Party gains absolute majority by winning 211 out of 400 seats; President Mladenov steps down in the face of allegations that he ordered the shooting of protesters during anti-Communist demonstrations in 1989; Zhelyu Zhelev, leader of the opposition Union of Democratic Forces, is elected president; Andrei Lukanov replaces Atanasov as prime minister.

BIBLIOGRAPHY

BOOKS

Brown, James F. *Bulgaria Under Communist Rule.* New York, 1970.
Crampton, R. C. *Modern Bulgaria.* New York, 1987.
Gianaris, Nicholas V. *The Economies of the Balkan Countries.* New York, 1982.
McIntyre, Robert J. *Bulgaria: Politics, Economics, Society.* New York, 1988.
Osborne, R. H. *East-Central Europe: An Introductory Geography.* New York, 1967.
Starr, Richard F. *The Communist Regimes in Eastern Europe: An Introduction.* Stanford, 1967.
Welsh, William A. *Bulgaria.* Boulder, Colo., 1986.

OFFICIAL PUBLICATIONS

Prebroyavane (census of population).
Statisticheskii (statistical yearbook).

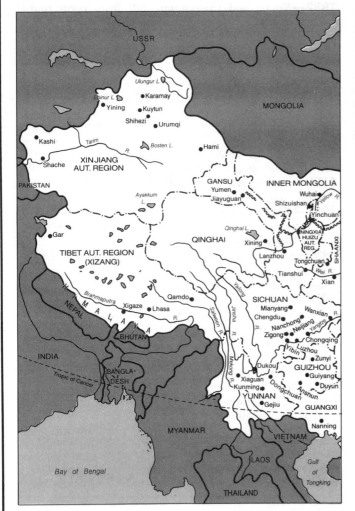

CHINA

BASIC FACT SHEET*

OFFICIAL NAME: People's Republic of China (Zhongguo Renmin Gonghehua)

ABBREVIATION: CH

CAPITAL: Beijing

HEAD OF STATE: President Yang Shangkun (from 1988)

HEAD OF GOVERNMENT: Premier of the State Council Li Peng (from 1988)

NATURE OF GOVERNMENT: Communist dictatorship

POPULATION: 1,112,298,677 (1989)

AREA: 562,904 sq. km. (3,692,244 sq. mi.)

MAJOR ETHNIC GROUPS: Han Chinese (93.3%); Zhuang, Uygur, Hui, Yi, Tibetan, Miao, Manchu, Mongol, Puyi and Korean

LANGUAGE: Putonghua (Mandarin)

RELIGIONS: Officially atheist; Confucianism, Buddhism, Taoism, Islam and Christianity

UNIT OF CURRENCY: Yuan

NATIONAL FLAG: Red flag with five yellow stars in the upper left quadrant—one large star near the hoist and four smaller ones arranged in an arc to the right.

NATIONAL EMBLEM: A large golden star partially encircled by four smaller stars, also in gold, against a circular red background, above a golden replica of Tiananmen Square. A gold decorative frame of ears of wheat and rice surrounds the emblem. At the base of the emblem is a gold cogwheel partially covered by red drapery.

NATIONAL ANTHEM: "Yi Yong Ju Jin Xing Qu" ("March of the Volunteers")

NATIONAL HOLIDAYS: National Day (October 1); May Day; Chinese New Year

NATIONAL CALENDAR: Chinese traditional and Gregorian

PHYSICAL QUALITY OF LIFE INDEX: 75 (on an ascending scale with 100 as the maximum)

DATE OF INDEPENDENCE: 1523 B.C.

DATE OF CONSTITUTION: December 4, 1982

WEIGHTS & MEASURES: Metric

*The pinyin is the preferred form of romanization. However, where a term is more commonly known by the older Wade-Giles transliteration, that system is followed; e.g., Chiang Kai-shek.

GEOGRAPHICAL FEATURES

The third-largest country in the world and the largest Asian country, China has an area of 9,562,904 sq. km. (3,692,244 sq. mi.), extending 4,845 km. (3,011 mi.) east-northeast to west-southwest and 3,350 km. (2,082 mi.) south-southeast to north-northwest. The national territory includes several islands, of which the largest is Hainan, off the southwestern coast; others are Tungsha (Pratas) and the Sisha (Paracels), Spratly, Chungsha and Nansha archipelagoes. Mainland China's 5,744-km. (3,588-mi.) coastline extends from the mouth of the Yalu River in the Northeast to the Gulf of Tonkin in the South in a sweeping arc, broken in the South by the Luichow Peninsula, projecting into the South China Sea, and in the North by the Liaotung Peninsula and the Shantung Peninsula, projecting into the Yellow Sea.

China shares its total boundary length of 28,073 km. (17,445 mi.) with 13 countries as follows:

Country	Km.	Mi.
Mongolia	4,673	2,904
Soviet Union	7,520	4,673
North Korea	1,416	880
Hong Kong	84	52

Country	Km.	Mi.
Macao	1.6	1
Vietnam	1,281	796
Laos	425	264
Myanmar	2,185	1,358
India (including Jammu and Kashmir)	1,892	1,176
Bhutan	412	256
Nepal	1,078	670
Pakistan	523	325
Afghanistan	71	44

China's borders are disputed at a number of points. That with the Soviet Union is the cause of intermittent friction. Chinese maps show substantial portions of Soviet Siberian territory as part of China. In the western sector China has claimed portions of the Pamir area where the borders of the Soviet Union, China and Afghanistan meet in Central Asia. North and east of the Pamir region, some sections of the border are undemarcated. The most serious dispute is in the Northeast, in the remote regions of Nei Monggol Autonomous Region (Inner Mongolia) and in Heilongjiang Province along segments of the Argun, Amur and Ussuri rivers. The border with India was the cause of two wars with India in which the Chinese were victorious, but major disputes remain in the Aksai Chin area of northeastern Jammu and Kashmir. Eastward from Bhutan lies another large disputed area north of the Brahmaputra River. Many islands in the South China Sea held by Vietnam, Malaysia or the Philippines are claimed by China; conversely, Vietnam claims the Chinese-held Paracel Islands. Most significantly, the PRC has been unable to assert de facto control over Taiwan, which is historically part of China.

The capital is Beijing, formerly known as Peking, Peiping or Shuntien-fu, founded by Khitan Tartars in the 10th century and the capital of China from the 15th century. There were 56 other cities with a population of 1 million or more, in the mid-1980s, of which Shanghai is the largest, with a population of over 7 million in 1990. It is by far the largest port serving the vast hinterland of the Yangtze River Valley. Tianjin is the third-largest port, on the Hai Ho at the terminus of the Grand Canal. Shenyang, formerly Mukden, is the capital of the Northeast Administrative Area and situated on a tributary of the Liao River. Shenyang was the Manchu capital

MAJOR URBAN CENTERS* (population est. in 000, 1985) (Wade-Giles or other spellings in parentheses)	
Shanghai (Shang-hai)	6,980
Beijing (Pei-ching or Peking, the capital)	5,860
Tianjin (T'ien-chin or Tientsin)	5,380
Shenyang (Shen-yang or Mukden)	4,200
Wuhan (Wu-han or Hankow)	3,400
Guangzhou (Kuang-chou or Canton)	3,290
Chongqing (Ch'ung-ch'ing or Chungking)	2,780
Harbin (Ha-erh-pin)	2,630
Chengdu (Ch'eng-tu)	2,580
Xian (Hsi-an or Sian)	2,330
Zibo (Tzu-po or Tzepo)	2,300
Nanjing (Nan-ching or Nanking)	2,250
Liupanshui	2,220
Taiyuan (T'ai-yüan)	1,880
Changchun (Ch'ang-ch'un)	1,860
Dalian (Ta-lien or Dairen)	1,630
Zaozhuang	1,590
Zhengzhou (Cheng-chou or Chengchow)	1,590
Kunming (K'un-ming)	1,490
Jinan (Chi-nan or Tsinan)	1,430
Tangshan (T'ang-shan)	1,390
Guiyang (Kuei-yang or Kweiyang)	1,380
Linyi	1,370
Lanzhou (Lan-chou or Lanchow)	1,350
Taian	1,330
Pinxiang	1,290
Suzhou (Su-chou or Soochow)	1,280
Anshan (An-shan)	1,280
Qiqihar (Chi'-ch'i-ha-erh or Tsitsihar)	1,260
Yancheng	1,250
Qingdao (Ch'ing-tao or Tsingtao)	1,250
Hangzhou (Hang-chou or Hangchow)	1,250
Fushun (F'u-shun)	1,240
Yulin	1,230
Chaozhou	1,210
Dongguan	1,210
Xiaogan	1,200
Fuzhou (Fu-chou or Foochow)	1,190
Suining	1,170
Xintai	1,160
Changsha (Chang-sha)	1,160
Shijiazhuang (Shih-chia-chuang or Shihkiachwang)	1,160

MAJOR URBAN CENTERS* (continued) (population est. in 000, 1985) (Wade-Giles or other spellings in parentheses)	
Jilin (Chi-lin or Kirin)	1,140
Nanchang (Nan-ch'ang)	1,120
Baotau (Pao-t'ou or Paotow)	1,100
Puyang	1,090
Huainan (Huai-nan or Hwainan)	1,070
Zhongshan	1,060
Luoyang (Lo-yang)	1,050
Weifang	1,040
Laiwu	1,040
Leshan	1,030
Jingmen	1,020
Ningbo	1,020
Urumqi (Urumchi)	1,000
Heze	1,000
Datong (Ta-t'ung or Tatung)	1,000

*Data refer to municipalities, which may include large rural areas as well as an urban center.

from 1625 to 1644. Wuhan is a river port in east-central China on the confluence of the Han and Yangtze rivers. Guangzhou, formerly Canton, is on the Pearl River and was one of the five treaty ports engaged in extensive trade with Western powers. Chongqing, formerly Chungking, is at the junction of the Kialing River with the Yangtze Kiang and was the capital of China during World War II. Harbin, on the southern bank of the Sungari River, was initially developed by the Russians and later by the Japanese. Chengdu, in central China, is the capital of the province of Sichuan and is on the Minkian River. Xian, formerly Sian, is the capital of Shaanxi Province and is near the Wei (Wei Ho) River. The Wei River Valley is known as the cradle of Chinese civilization.

China is geographically one of the most diverse regions of the world, including vast areas of rugged, inhospitable terrain; broad plains; deserts; lofty mountain ranges; and steppe. Geographers have identified a number of topographical regions based on terrain and relief, divided broadly into plateaus and basins, the Great Plains and the Southeast.

Western and northwestern China consist largely of great upland basins separated from each other by massive mountain systems. Of the mountain systems, the highest is the Tibetan massif, bounded on the south by the Himalayan ranges, on the west by the Hindu Kush, on the north by the Kunlun and the Astin Tagh and on the east by the mountains of Sichuan. Comprising nearly a quarter of China's territory, it contains some of the world's most spectacular terrain. The eastern rim of the plateau is crossed by several of the great rivers of Asia—the Huang, Yangtze, Salween and Mekong—flowing through gorges 4,000 m. (13,124 ft.) high in places. Southern Tibet has an average elevation of 5,000 to 7,000 m. (16,405 to 22,967 ft.). The northern highlands are only slightly lower, and here there are large basins dotted with brackish lakes. High winds sweep across the plateau almost daily, and even in midsummer sudden storms with hail and snow flurries are not uncommon.

North of the Tibetan Plateau and at a much lower general level lies the Tarim Basin. It is hemmed in by great mountain ranges: the T'ien Shan to the north, the Pamir Knot to the west and the Astin Tagh to the south. From these heights, glacier-fed streams descend, only to lose themselves in the Taklamakan Desert, which occupies the center of the basin and which is one of the most barren of the world's deserts. To the northeast of the Tarim Basin and included within the same bounds is the smaller Turian Basin.

North of the Tarim Basin is Dzungaria, yet another inland basin, descending in steplike formation to the north. It is enclosed by the T'ien Shan to the south; the Altai Mountains to the northeast, cutting it off from Outer Mongolia; and the Tarbagatai Mountains to the northwest, forming the frontier between China and the Soviet Union.

Inner Mongolia is the southern half of the Gobi, a semidesert region enclosed by the Khangai, Altai and Nan Shan to the west, the Ala Shan and In Shan to the south, the Ta Ch'ingan to the east and the Sayan and Irkutsk Mountains to the north. A number of streams, the most important of which is the Estin Gol, descend from the Nan Shan, across the panhandle of Kansu, to be lost in the heart of the desert.

The southwestern plateau comprises the whole of Yunnan and the western part of Keichow and is highly dissected.

The four great plains of China are the Hwang Ho, the Yangtze, the Si Kiang and the Northeast or Manchurian. The Hwang Ho Basin is confined between the northern axis of the In Shan and the central axis of the Tsinling. The Yangtze Basin lies between the Tsinling and the Nanling axes. After leaving the highlands, the Yangtze flows eastward through a series of lake basins: the Red Basin of Szechwan; the Central Basin of Hunan, Hubei and Jiangxi; and the delta region of Anhui and Jiangsu. These basins form the most productive and the most populated regions. The Si Kiang Basin is not as extensive a plain as the Hwang Ho or the Yangtze but is important as a subtropical area, permitting double-cropping of rice. The Northeast or Manchurian Plain is bounded on the west by the Ta Ch'ingan Mountains, on the north by the Hsiao Ch'ingan Mountains, on the east by the Eastern Manchurian Mountains and on the south by the Jehol Mountains and the sea. The plain is split into northern and southern halves by a low divide, the northern half being drained by the Sungari River and the southern half by the Liao River.

The southeastern area forms a discrete region between the lower Yangtze and the lower Si Kiang in a region of folded mountains having a northeast–southwest trend.

Mountains comprise more than two-thirds of the land area of China. They fall into three groups according to the direction in which they run: east–west; northeast–southwest; and north–south.

The east–west ranges, mainly in the western part, include the Altai, Tianshan, Kunlun, Karakorum, Gangdise, Himalayas, Qinling and Nanling. The Altai, meaning the Golden Mountains, are in the northern part of the Xinjiang Uygur Autonomous Region and have an average elevation of 3,000 m. (9,843 ft.). The Tianshan Mountains, running across the middle of Xinjiang, are 3,000 to 5,000 m. (9,843 to 16,405 ft.), with the highest peaks in the western chain rising to 7,000 m. (22,967 ft.). The massif is made up of several parallel ranges, with depressed basins between them. Aydingkol Lake, in the middle of the Turpan Depression, is 154 m. (505 ft.) below sea level and is the lowest point in China. The Kunlun Mountains extend from Pamirs in the West eastward to the Sichuan Basin. Generally the ranges are over 5,000 m. (16,405 ft.), with peaks reaching 7,000 m. (22,967 ft.). The Bayan Har Mountains, the eastern section of Kunlun, form the watershed for the Yangtze and Yellow rivers. The Qinling extends about 1,500 m. (4,922 ft.) across central China from southern Gansu in the West to the area between the lower reaches of the Huaihe River and the Yangtze River in the East. Its elevation, generally lower than those of others, is 2,000 to 3,000 m. (6,562 to 9,843 ft.). The Karakorum, meaning the "Purplish Black Kunlun" in Uigur, starts from the Xinjiang-Kashmir border in the Northwest and stretches southeastward into the northern part of Tibet. The average height is 6,000 m. (19,686 ft.), but Qogir, its main peak reaches 8,611 m. (28,253 ft.). The Nanling Range includes all the mountains between Guangxi-Guangdong and the Hunan-Jiangxi provinces. It consists of the group known as the Five Mountains: Yuecheng, Dupang, Mengzhu, Qitian and Dayu. The Gangdise, meaning "Master of All Mountains" in Tibetan, towers 6,000 m. (19,686 ft.) in southern Tibet to form the watershed between the rivers of the continental plateau drainage system and those of the Indian Ocean drainage system. Its main peak is Kangrinboque, meaning "Treasure of the Snow." The Himalayas rise above the southern rim of the Qinghai-Tibet Plateau, the main part of the range lying on the Sino-Indian and Sino-Nepali borders. The 2,500-km. (1,554-mi.) mountain chain averages 6,000 m. (19,686 ft.) above sea level, with over 40 peaks rising over 7,000 m. (22,967 ft.). The highest peak in this system is Mount Qomolangma ("Goddess Peak" in Tibetan), better known in the non-Chinese world as Mount Everest.

The northeast–southwest ranges, composed of an eastern and a western chain, are mainly in the eastern part of China. The former includes, in northeastern China, the Changbai Mountains, with an average elevation of 2,700 m. (8,859 ft.) and stretching across Liaodong and Shandong peninsulas south to Zhejiang and Fujian provinces. The western chain is composed of the Greater Hinggan Range in northeastern China, the Taihang Mountains in northern China, the heights along the Yangtze River gorges and the Xuefeng Mountains in Hunan.

The north–south ranges include the Hengduan Mountains in western Sichuan and Yunnan provinces. The former includes the Daxue, Nushan and Gaoligong mountains, averaging 4,500 to 5,000 m. (14,765 to 16,405 ft.); its highest peak, Gongga, soars 7,590 m. (24,903 ft.). This range blocks communication between eastern and western China—hence its name Hengduan, the "Barrier Mountains" in Chinese.

Since the general lie of the land is toward the east, all the great national rivers flow toward the Pacific. In the Northeast, the Amur (Hei-lung Chiang) drains a great part of the Manchurian Basin as it winds along its 4,023-km. (2,500-mi.) course. However, navigation is limited to small steamers and native craft. Other Manchurian rivers include the Liao Ho, the chief river in southern Manchuria; the Tumen; and the Yalu, the last forming the boundary between China and Korea.

The main river in northern China and the second-largest in the country is the Yellow River (Huang Ho), which acquired its name from the yellowish-muddy color of its waters—the result of its passage through the yellow loess plateau of Kansu. From Kansu it winds 4,795 km. (2,980 mi.) through the northern provinces eastward to Shantung, where it empties into the Gulf of Chihli (Ba Hai). To keep its flow channeled, the Chinese have been continually building up its embankments, with the result that its riverbed is 4.9 m. (16 ft.) or more above the general level of the surrounding plain. Along its lower course, the Yellow River floods regularly, particularly in later summer and early autumn, and there are no important towns along its banks.

Central China is drained by China's longest river, the Yangtze (Ch'ang Chiang). From its source about 80 km. (50 mi.) from that of the Yellow River, it wends 5,208 km. (3,237 mi.) to the East China Sea. From the confluence of its two headwaters in the upland of southern Tsinghai, it flows southward to southern Szechwan as the Chin-sha Chiang; beyond the great bend in northwestern Yunnan it turns sharply to the east. The Yangtze can be divided into three parts: a torrential upper course that includes many rapids and falls, a middle course where navigation is limited to junks and river steamers, and a lower course navigable by oceangoing vessels. Near Shanghai the river is divided by the Ch'ung-ming Island into two channels, of which the southern, Wu-sung, is deeper.

In central China, the Huai Ho and the Fu-ch'un Chiang are next in importance to the Yangtze. The latter is one of the main rivers along the Chekiang coast. The Huai is unique in that it is the only long river without a natural outlet and consequently floods frequently.

Important rivers that drain the southwestern coastal regions are the Min Chiang and the Chu Chiang (Pearl River). The Pearl, the fourth-largest river in China, is a general name for a network of three waterways that meet south of Guangzhou to form a big estuary consisting of many channels separated by islets. The main eastern channel, Hu Men (Boca Tigris), enters the sea near Hong Kong, while the main western channel flows close to Macao.

Farther south are two independent rivers, the Mekong (Lan-ts'ang Chiang) and the Red River (Yuan Chiang), of which only the upper courses are in China.

Pacific drainage accounts for 50% of China's total drainage area; inland drainage for 39%; and Indian Ocean and Arctic drainage the remaining 6% and 5%, respectively. The Arctic drainage is through the upper Irtysh via the Zaisan Nor. The Indian Ocean drainage is through the Salween (Nu Chiang), the Irrawaddy and the Brahmaputra (Tsangpo or Ya-lu-ts'ang-pu), but their lower reaches are in Myanmar, Bangladesh or India.

Inland drainage covers a number of upland basins in the vast dry interior of northern and northwestern Chi-na. Inland rivers generally flow into lakes or die in the desert. An example is the Tarim, the longest inland river in southern Sinkiang. However, many of them are valuable for irrigation.

China has many large canals, such as the Beijing-Hangzhou Grand Canal and the Hunan-Guangxi Canal, connecting the Yangtze River system with that of the Pearl River.

In addition to man-made lakes and reservoirs there are 380 large natural lakes, of which 130 are over 100 sq. km. (39 sq. mi.) in area. Most of the lakes are on the middle–lower Yangtze River Plain and the Yunnan-Guizhou Plateau. There also are a large number on the Qinghai-Tibet Plateau, in the Inner Mongolia-Xinjiang region and in northeastern China. If a diagonal line were drawn across China from the southern section of the Greater Hinggan Range through the Yinshan and the eastern section of the Qilian Mountain chain to the Gangdise massif, most of the salt lakes would fall northwest of this line. These lakes in the inland drainage basins have little water and no outlets, but they are rich in chemicals. Best known among them are Qinghai Lake, Nam Co and Siling Co on the Qinghai-Tibet Plateau and Lop Nur in Xinjiang. The lakes southeast of the diagonal line are freshwater ones in the exterior drainage basins with outlets through rivers. Best known among these lakes are Dongting, Honghu, Poyang, Chaohu, Taihu and Yangcheng on the middle–lower Yangtze River Plain; Baiyang, Weishan and Hongze on the Yellow–Huaihe–Haihe River Plain; and Dianchi and Erhai on the Yunnan-Guizhou Plateau. The better-known lakes in northeastern China are Jingbo and Hulun as well as Xingkai, which straddles the Sino-Soviet border.

CLIMATE & WEATHER

The diversity of China's terrain is matched only by the diversity of its climate. In a vast subcontinent such as China, with tremendous differences in latitude and longitude as well as altitude (from peaks 8 km.; 5 mi. in height to basins below sea level), there are sharp variations in climatic features. Leizhou Peninsula, Hainan Island, the South China Sea islands of Guangdong Province and the southern part of Yunnan Province have a tropical climate, where summer reigns all year long. Heilongjiang Province, in the Northeast, has a short and cool summer and a severe winter. The area around the Yangtze River and Huaihe River valleys in the east is warm and humid, with four distinct seasons. The Inner Mongolia-Xinjiang area, in the Northwest, experiences extremes of weather in a single day, giving rise to the saying "Fur coats in the morning and gossamer at noon." Some areas of the Yunnan-Guizhou Plateau, in the Southwest, have a mild winter and cool summer, as does Kunming, which is justly named "City of Spring." The Tibet Plateau has a cold, dry climate and a strong sun; in some of its areas pronounced differences in climate are found between high and low altitudes.

In spite of these differences, the one constant that characterizes Chinese climate is the monsoon rhythm arising from the continentality of the Asian landmass.

PROVINCIAL-LEVEL UNITS AND SELECTED URBAN CENTERS—PINYIN AND WADE-GILES FORMS

Pinyin	to Wade-Giles	Wade-Giles	to Pinyin
Provincial-Level Units			
Anhui	Anhwei	Anhwei	Anhui
Beijing	Pei-ching	Chekiang	Zhejiang
Fujian	Fukien	Fukien	Fujian
Gansu	Kansu	Heilungkiang	Heilongjiang
Guangdong	Kwangtung	Honan	Henan
Guangxi-Zhuang	Kuang-hsi-chuang-tsu	Ho-pei	Hebei
Guizhou	Kweichow	Hsin-chiang-wei-wu-erh	Xinjiang-Uygur
Hebie	Ho-pei	Hsi-tsang	Xizang
Heilongjiang	Heilungkiang	Hunan	Hunan
Henan	Honan	Hupeh	Hubei
Hubei	Hupeh	Kansu	Gansu
Hunan	Hunan	Kiangsi	Jiangxi
Jiangsu	Kiangsu	Kiangsu	Jiangsu
Jiangxi	Kiangsi	Kirin	Jilin
Jilin	Kirin	Kuang-hsi-chuang-tsu	Guangxi-Zhuang
Liaoning	Liaoning	Kwangtung	Guangdong
Nei Monggol	Nei-meng-ku	Kweichow	Guizhou
Ningxia-Hui	Ning-hsia-hui-tsu	Liaoning	Liaoning
Qinghai	Tsinghai	Nei-meng-ku	Nei Monggol
Shaanxi	Shensi	Ning-hsia-hui-tsu	Ningxia-Hui
Shandong	Shantung	Pei-ching	Beijing
Shanghai	Shanghai	Shanghai	Shanghai
Shanxi	Shansi	Shansi	Shanxi
Sichuan	Szechwan	Shantung	Shandong
Tianjin	Tien-chin	Shensi	Shaanxi
Xinjiang-Uygur	Hsin-chiang-wei-wu-erh	Szechwan	Sichuan
Xizang	Hsi-tsang	Tien-chin	Tianjin
Yunnan	Yünnan	Tsinghai	Qinghai
Zhejiang	Chekiang	Yünnan	Yunnan
Urban Centers			
Changchun	Ch'ang-ch'un	Ch'ang-ch'un	Changchun
Chengdu	Ch'eng-tu	Ch'eng-tu	Chengdu
Chongqing	Ch'ung-ch'ing	Ch'ung-ch'ing	Chongqing
Fushun	Fu-shun	Fu-shun	Fushun
Guangzhou	Kuang-chou	Ha-erh-pin	Harbin
Harbin	Ha-erh-pin	Hsi-an	Xi'an
Lüda	Lü-ta	Kuang-chou	Guangzhou
Nanjing	Nan-ching	Lü-ta	Lüda
Qingdao	Tsingtao	Nan-ching	Nanjing
Shenyang	Shen-yang	Shen-yang	Shenyang
Taiyuan	T'ai-yüan	T'ai-yüan	Taiyuan
Wuhan	Wu-han	Tsingtao	Qingdao
Xi'an	His-an	Wu-han	Wuhan
Yan'an	Yenan	Yenan	Yan'an

Source: Based on information from U.S. Department of Interior, Board on *Geographic Names, Gazetteer of the People's Republic of China: Pinyin to Wade-Giles, Wade-Giles to Pinyin*, Washington, D.C., July 1979.

The monsoon denotes a wind system that, in China, changes from southeast in summer to north and northeast in winter. The cold air mass established in the autumn in Siberia and Mongolia forms an anticyclone or center of high pressure and spreads southward until it meets the warm air mass of the North Pacific trades along a front to the south of the China coast known as the West Pacific Polar Front. From this great anticyclone there is an outflow of dry northerly and northeasterly winds over China, bringing prolonged and bitter winters to the northern part of the country and cold weather as far south as the central and lower Yangtze River basins. Occasionally this bitter weather is interrupted by a welcome warm spell as a few European or Atlantic storms penetrate Manchuria or North China.

But these lulls are of short duration. Frequently cyclones develop along the Yangtze River Valley, causing heavy snowfalls.

In spring the movements are reversed. The cold air mass over the heart of the continent warms up, giving place to a continental low, while a high-pressure center is established over the eastern Pacific. Northerly and northwesterly winds give way to those from the south and southeast, and a great current of warm, humid air moves in from the south. Between May and July the summer monsoon extends over the Yangtze and the North China Plain. The characteristic weather of the summer monsoon over much of China is hot, calm days of high relative humidity, which are very oppressive. Inland the winds are light, but coastal regions in the

Pinyin	to	Conventional Form of Reference		Conventional Form of Reference	to	Pinyin
Beijing		Peking		Amoy		Xiamen
Chang Jiang		Yangtze River		Amur River		Heilong Jiang
Da Hinggan Ling		Greater Khingan Range		Argun River		Ergun He
Da Yunhe		Grand Canal		Brahmaputra River		Yarlung Zangbo Jiang
Dongbei Pingyuan		Manchurian Plain		Canton		Guangzhou
Ergun He		Argun River		China, People's Republic of		Zhonghua Renmin Gongheguo
Gangdisê Shan		Kailas Range				
Guangzhou		Canton		Dzungarian Basin		Junggar Pendi
Guangzi-Zhuang Zizhiqu		Kwangsi Chuang Autonomous Region		Formosa Strait		Taiwan Haixia
				Grand Canal		Da Yunhe
Heilong Jiang		Amur River		Greater Khingan Range		Da Hinggan Ling
Huang He		Yellow River		Great Wall		Wanli Changcheng
Junggar Pendi		Dzungarian Basin		Hainan Strait		Qiongzhou Haixia
Juyong Guan		Nankow Pass		Inner Mongolia (short form); Inner Mongolian Autonomous Region		Nei Monggol Zizhiqu
Karakorum Shankou		Karakoram Pass				
Kashi		Kashgar				
Kunlun Shan		Kunlun Mountains		Kailas Range		Gangdisê Shan
Lancang Jiang		Mekong River		Karakoram Pass		Karakorum Shankou
Mu Us Shamo		Ordos Desert		Kashgar		Kashi
Nei Monggol Zizhiqu		Inner Mongolia (short form); Inner Mongolian Autonomous Region		Koko Nor		Qinghai Hu
				Kunlun Mountains		Kunlun Shan
Ningxia-Hui Zizhiqu		Ningsia-Hui Autonomous Region		Kwangsi Chuang Autonomous Region		Guangxi-Zhuang Zizhiqu
				Lesser Khingan Range		Xiao Hinggan Ling
Nu Jiang		Salween River		Manchurian Plain		Dongbei Pingyuan
Qaidam Pendi		Tsaidam Basin		Mekong River		Lancang Jiang
Qingdao		Tsingtao		Nankow Pass		Juyong Guan
Qinghai Hu		Koko Nor		Ningsia-Hui Autonomous Region		Ningxia-Hui Zizhiqu
Qing Zang Gaoyuan		Tibet, Plateau of				
Qui Ling		Tsinling Shan		Ordos Desert		Mu Us Shamo
Qiongzhou Haixia		Hainan Strait		Pearl River		Zhu Jiang
Shantou		Swatow		Peking		Beijing
Sichuan Pendi		Szechwan Basin		Red River		Yuan Jiang
Songhua Hu		Sungari Reservoir		Salween River		Nu Jiang
Songhua Jiang		Sungari River		Sinkiang Uighur Automomous Region		Xinjiang-Uygur Zizhiqu
Taiwan Haixia		Formosa Strait				
Taklimakan Shamo		Takla Makan Desert		Suchow		Xuzhou
Tarim He		Tarim River		Sungari Reservoir		Songhua Hu
Tarim Pendi		Tarim Basin		Sungari River		Songhua Jiang
Tianjin		Tientsin		Swatow		Shantou
Tian Shan		Tien Shan		Szechwan Basin		Sichuan Pendi
Tumen Jiang		Tumen River		Takla Makan Desert		Taklimakan Shamo
Turpan Pendi		Turfan Depression		Tarim Basin		Tarim Pendi
Wanli Changcheng		Great Wall		Tarim River		Tarim He
Wusuli Jiang		Ussuri River		Tibet (short form); Tibetan Autonomous Region		Xizang Zizhiqu
Xiamen		Amoy				
Xinjiang-Uygur Zizhiqu		Sinkiang Uighur Autonomous Region		Tibet, Plateau of		Qing Zang Gaoyuan
				Tien Shan		Tian Shan
Xiao Hinggan Ling		Lesser Khingan Range		Tientsin		Tianjin
Xizang Zizhiqu		Tibet (short form); Tibetan Autonomous Region		Tsaidam Basin		Qaidam Pendi
				Tsingtao		Qingdao
Xuzhou		Suchow		Tsinling Shan		Qin Ling
Yalü Jiang		Yalu River		Tumen River		Tumen Jiang
Yarlung Zangbo Jiang		Brahmaputra River		Turfan Depression		Turpan Pendi
Yuan Jiang		Red River		Ussuri River		Wusuli Jiang
Zhonghua (or Zhohgguo) Renmin Gongheguo		China, People's Republic of		Yalu River		Yalü Jiang
				Yangtze River		Chang Jiang
Zhu Jiang		Pearl River		Yellow River		Huang He

South and Southeast experience disastrous typhoons. The duration of the summer monsoon season varies between the North and the South, being shorter in the North because of the lateness of the onset.

Temperature patterns are determined by altitude, latitude and landmass. There is a difference of 9,144 m. (30,000 ft.) between Mount Everest and Turfan Basin and a difference of nearly 40° in latitude between Hainan and Moho on the Amur. In winter there is a large

and steady fall in temperature from the South to the North. Hong Kong has a January temperature of 16°C (60°F) and Harbin in Manchuria of −19°C (−2°F). The ocean has very little moderating effect on winter temperatures, since the winds outflow from the central low pressure and the cold Kamchatka Current hugs the coast in its southward flow.

There is a remarkable unity of temperature in summer, the maximum differences being only 15°F compared to 60°F in winter. Every place is hot and humid. In the desert and semidesert regions of Sinkiang, Mongolia and Dzungaria, annual temperature ranges are very great, up to 76°F, compared to 22°F in Hong Kong. The northern areas in China are much colder than comparable regions in the same latitudes in Europe, Africa and North America. For example, the January temperature in Shenyang is −13°C (8.6°F) compared to 7°C (44.6°F) in Rome, and 3.2°C (37.8°F) in Shanghai compared to 13.4°C (56.1°F) in Port Said.

Except for the small southwestern corner of Sikang, which shares the phenomenal rainfall of Assam across the border, rainfall in China shows a general decrease from southeast to northwest, ranging from 2,159 mm. (85 in.) in Hong Kong to 102 mm. (4 in.) in Kashgar. The decrease is most marked north of Tsinlang Shan, the most significant physical divide. The national average is 1,524 mm. (60 in.), with a summer maximum and a winter minimum. Even in the lower Yangtze River Valley, where rainfall is more evenly distributed throughout the year, a clear summer maximum is maintained. The seasonal variations are caused primarily by the monsoon rhythm. Yet the southeasterly monsoons do not have rain-bearing winds. The rainfall is cyclonic in origin. Cyclones act as cooling agents of condensation. Variability in the annual precipitation is another factor that increases from southeast to northwest—i.e., in inverse ratio to the amount that falls. The area with the least rainfall—the Northwest—has a variability of 30%. Even in the Yangtze River Valley, the variation is marked, ranging from 737 to 1,372 mm. (29 to 54 in.) over a 10-year period.

Climatologists have distinguished 10 climatic regions in China:

1. Hainan, South Guangxi and South Guangdong. This region has a tropical climate with long, hot and humid summers and cool, dry winters. The average January temperature is 13°C (55°F) and the annual rainfall 1,524 to 2,032 mm. (60 to 80 in.), with a marked winter maximum.

2. South China, North Guangxi, North Guangdong, Fujian and South Zhejiang. This is a subtropical region, with hot, wet summers and cooler winters. In autumn the coastal areas have a secondary maximum of rainfall caused by typhoons.

3. The Yangtze River Basin below the gorges. This region has hot summers but very cold winters. The summer heat is oppressive because of the absence of winds.

4. The Red Basin of Sichuan. For an inland region, it has an equable climate. The Red Basin is sheltered by the Tsinling and Ta Pa Shan from the bitter northern winds, and this accounts for the mild winters. The region is noted for its mists. The rainfall is gentle but ample.

5. The North China Plain, including the peninsula of Shantung. Here the temperature variation is considerable—e.g., 56°F at Beijing. Summers are very hot. Summer rains are torrential and therefore not of much value. Winters are long, cold and dry.

6. The loess region. This region has a continental climate with an annual range of temperature of up to 70°F. During the long winters, bitter northwesterly winds whip up heavy dust storms. Rainfall is sparse and variable. In years of drought, the dust storms in summer are worse than those of winter.

7. Inner Mongolia and Sinkiang. This region has a temperate desert or semidesert climate, with great contrasts in temperature between summer and winter (0°F to −20°F) and also great diurnal ranges. Rainfall is sparse, never more than 102 to 127 mm. (4 to 5 in.), and even this is uncertain. This region also is subject to heavy dust-laden winds.

8. The highland plateau of Tibet. Here the seasonal and diurnal ranges of temperature are great and rainfall is negligible, except in the southeastern corner, where Lhasa is located.

9. The Yunnan-Kweichow Plateau. This region has a delightful and almost ideal climate, with moderate summers and winters and adequate rainfall.

10. The Northeast, or Heilongjiang. This region has a continental climate, with cold winters. Rainfall also decreases to the northeast but is adequate.

POPULATION

China is the most populous country in the world and the only country with a population of over 1 billion. In 1989 the population was estimated at 1,112,298,677, based on the last official census, in 1982, when the population was 1,008,175,288. The population is expected to reach 1,253,000,000 by 2000.

The adjective most often used to describe the population of China is "teeming," but what this adjective masks is that even with its vast population, China ranks in density of population far below the United Kingdom, and the population is teeming in places only. Topography and climate limit the land on which crops can be grown so that only 11% to 12% of the land area is cultivated. As a result, some 95% of the inhabitants live on 40% of the area. The most densely populated area covers most of the Yangtze River Delta and the North China Plain. In some of the coastal areas, densities of 772 inhabitants per sq. km. (2,000 inhabitants per sq. mi.) are not uncommon, but then vast areas of China are virtually uninhabited. The four least populated provinces—Inner Mongolia, Xinjiang, Qinghai and Tibet—account for half the land area but just 4% of the population.

The uneven density has two major reasons, one geographical and the other social. Most of China is inhospitable to human habitation, being hilly and mountainous on the one hand and desert and arid on the other. These areas also have the harshest climates. The social factor involves strong attachment to family and land as well as regional dialects, which militate against migration.

Nevertheless, migration has played a significant role in the present distribution of population in those areas of high density. Sichuan represents a good example of the westward spread of the population in the modern period. Since 1650 this province has been the main beneficiary of movements of people in search of good agricultural land. The population of Sichuan increased from 8.6 million in 1787 to 44.2 million in 1850 and to 62.3 million in 1953. In some instances, populations advanced and then receded like waves in the sea, the movements being guided by the pull of economic opportunity and the push of wars, diseases, drought or political upheavals. Manchuria represents an example in which the pull of opportunity was great. Fleeing the civil wars and famines in North China, millions of Chinese fled to Manchuria beginning in 1900. During the first half of this century, as many as 30 million Chinese moved to Manchuria—one of the greatest, if little known, migrations in human history.

Since the establishment of the PRC, patterns of migration have changed. For one thing, emigration has become insignificant. Since 1949 China has had, for all practical purposes, a closed population. Illegal emigration is punishable by life imprisonment or death, and few have managed to leave the country. Exceptions are the 13,000 Tibetans who left for India in 1959 and 1960; 50,000 Kazakhs who crossed the border into the Soviet Union in 1962; and the 10,000 Chinese who flee to Hong Kong every year. Against this outflow there has been a substantial inflow of overseas Chinese immigrants, numbering in the millions, particularly from Vietnam and Indonesia. But set against China's total population, these external movements are quite insignificant. The government publishes little meaningful data regarding internal migration. There are frequent references to "large number of migrants" without actual numbers or the names of their destinations. However, three major trends may be deduced from available official documents. First, the movement was toward the northern and western provinces; much of it was officially sponsored; and their exit made no dent on the areas they left but was significant for their destinations. Official policy on internal migration had three broad purposes: to increase the cultivable land in the border provinces; to increase the industrial production capacity in the interior provinces; and to settle Han Chinese in areas populated by minorities as a means of consolidating control over them.

As with almost all statistics pertaining to the PRC, population statistics are regarded with considerable skepticism by demographers. The first true census in Chinese modern history was held in 1953, and it was marred by a number of miscalculations and improper practices. Initiated only four years after the Communists seized power and organized with Soviet help, the census proved to be a more difficult undertaking than the regime had envisioned and took over a year to complete. As the first nationwide census in Chinese history, the census was complicated by numerous problems, including the inexperience of census takers; the peculiarities of household arrangements; the ambiguities of residence; the need to convert the age of persons from the lunar calendar to the solar calendar; the impossibility of counting boat people, nomads and people in remote areas (who were eventually estimated); and the absence of proper statistical control over the huge mass of data. The result was an underenumeration or an overenumeration by several millions. The official census report showed a population on June 30, 1953, of 601,603,417, including 11,743,320 overseas Chinese and 7,591,298 Taiwanese. Also included in the report were information on the provincial distribution of population, information on urban-rural distribution and information on the distribution of national minorities. Indicative of the very tentative nature of these figures is the fact that even in 1971 the government was not sure whether the population of China was 750 million or 830 million. According to Vice Premier Li Hsien-nien, "Unfortunately, there are no accurate statistics in this connection."

The census of 1964 was a major improvement on that of 1953, but the same difficulties persisted, and the data were subject to as great a range of error. The census was not even publicized as such a major event needs to be, and it may simply have been an effort to update the neglected registers. The census of 1982, officially called the third census, followed numerous changes in the regulations regarding registration on which, in the absence of actual enumeration, the accuracy of the census depended. The 1982 figure of 1,088,175,288 has not been accepted by demographers as accurate, although it is used widely in the absence of alternative and more accurate figures. Because the Chinese make up over 20% of the world's population, inaccuracies in the Chinese data have far-reaching implications on calculations of global population.

The growth in population since 1949 has been due almost entirely to natural increase because of the negligible impacts of immigration and emigration. During the Mao years, China's annual population growth reached more than 2% because of the government's pronatalist policy as well as a rapid decline in mortality. The higher levels of mortality in the late 1950s reduced the annual growth rate, but it rose in the mid-1960s to 2.5% to 2.95%. After peaking in the 1980s, the birth rate declined once more, especially after the introduction of the one-child-per-family regulation in the 1970s. The decline has been fairly rapid in the more populous provinces, some of which have completed the transition from high-fertility to low-fertility areas within a generation. But other provinces have not reported any decline at all, and as a result it may be safely assumed that the current annual population growth is about 1.3%, as estimated by the World Bank.

The halving of the birth rate—a decline faster than that recorded in any other country in modern times—is the result of one of the most draconian birth control policies in the world. In 1956, following the 1953 census, the government announced a policy of promoting late marriage and birth limitation, but this policy was repudiated during the Great Leap Forward and was reactivated only in the 1970s. Since then China has had a highly effective fertility reduction program. Contraceptives are universally available and free, as are abortion and sterilization. The effectiveness of the policy stems from two sorts of incentives and disincentives. The first is economic: paid vacations or work points for undergoing planned birth operations; and financial allowances and priority in education, employment and housing for couples who pledge to have only one child, combined with financial penalties for those who have more than two children. The second is social pressure on couples in their reproductive years through the media and group discussions.

When the population control program began in the 1970s the government endorsed a specific set of norms with respect to childbearing, embodied in the slogan "Later, Longer, Fewer"—i.e., later marriages and childbirth, spacing of at least four years between children and a smaller total number of children per couple. Its adoption endorsed the notion that reproduction is a concern not only of the nuclear family but also of the society. The current goal of population policy is to limit the total population of China to 1.2 billion by 2000.

Administrative control of birth planning activities is under the reorganized Birth Planning Leading Group of the State Council. Planned birth offices are set up at every level down to the commune in rural areas; street committees in urban areas; and Committees on Planned Births in large enterprises and institutions. This administrative structure distinguishes China from most other developing countries, in which birth planning services are ancillary to other health services. The close ties of the top leadership also give the program an urgency that is one of the ingredients of its success. At the same time, the vertical approach is complemented by horizontal control at the local level. As a result, there is room for local initiative. However, local control also has a cost: It creates an environment in which the line between persuasion and coercion may be overstepped by local cadres.

At the local level, the actual provision of birth planning services is integrated with health care delivery services. By one estimate there is one part-time birth planning worker for every 20 to 40 households throughout rural China; most of these workers are female barefoot doctors.

The practice of contraception has become almost universal because of the availability of free contraceptives. Of the 115 million women at risk, some 75% are reported to practice contraception, compared to 68% in the United States, 23% in India, 40% in Sri Lanka and 43% in Columbia. Of the married couples using contraception, 50% use the intrauterine device (IUD), 30% sterilization (1.7% female, 12% male), 12% oral contraceptives and 7% condoms. Compared to other countries, the Chinese rely more on the IUD and much less on the Pill. Abortion was legalized in 1956. The abortion rate is about 290 per 1,000, but much higher in the cities because even rural women go to cities to have abortions performed.

The government also has mounted a major campaign to raise the urban age of marriage to 28 for males and 25 for females. In Shanghai, more than three-quarters of all husbands and wives were married above the recommended ages. In rural areas the age of marriage is 25 for men and 23 for women. The marriage age has risen more sharply in urban areas because of housing shortages, a major factor in family limitation all over the world.

Study groups at the brigade and commune levels have been set up to set up birth quotas and allocate births to couples in a particular order: first to newlywed couples who conform to the norm of late marriage and to married but childless couples, and then to couples with one child aged four or above. In addition to setting goals and monitoring progress, these study groups provide a forum for intense social pressure. The local branches of the Planned Reproduction Group are charged with maintaining for every married woman of reproductive age a Planned Reproduction Card, which shows the number of her previous births, by sex; the date of her last birth; and the type of contraception she uses. These cards form the basis for compilation by each group of the "planned birth rate."

In 1979 the government initiated a campaign for a one-child family. Its purpose is to reduce the family size in the next two decades enough to bring the birth rate down still further in view of the continuing increase in the proportion of the population entering childbearing years—a result of the baby boom years of the 1950s and 1960s.

In addition to additional vacation days for women undergoing various types of planned birth operations, there are monetary incentives as well, varying with the province. Typically these incentives consist of monthly subsidies to one-child families until the child is 14 years old, or an annual bonus of 400 work points for the same period. The child also receives priority in admission to schools and in obtaining a job, and the parents receive private plots and housing lots of a two-child standard. Disincentives apply from the birth of the third child and include deductions from wages and work points, and exclusion of that child from cooperative medical programs, which means that parents have to meet all his or her medical expenses. The incorporation into birth planning policy of such a wide array of financial and other incentives has no precedent elsewhere, and it would not have been possible for a nonauthoritarian government to impose such a policy on the people. One indicator of its success is the rapidity of the fertility decline.

While official policy has been critical in China's success in limiting its population in a dramatically short time, other factors have been at work as well. These include rising levels in education, health, personal income and urbanization, all of which universally have a negative impact on birth rates.

Growth rates are expected to fall even further in the next few decades, though at a much slower pace. According to Western projections, they will fall to 0.93% by 2000 and to 0.31% by 2030–35. The projection assumes a decline in the fertility rate to replacement level between 2000 and 2005.

There are no officially available data on age structure, but data from a large (but not nationwide) 1975 census indicates that 35% of the population was under age 15 and about 63% under age 29. Reflecting the fertility decline since the 1970s, this proportions are likely to have declined to 32% under 15, compared to 40% to 45% in high-fertility countries such as India and Mexico.

According to official data, the proportion of the urban population is relatively modest: 22% in 1985, com-

DEMOGRAPHIC INDICATORS, 1988

Population 1,112,298,677 (1989)
Year of last census: 1982   World rank: 1
Sex ratio: Males: 51.5   Females: 48.5
Population trends (000)

1930 500,000	1960 682,024	1990* 1,112.000
1940 530,000	1970 838,396	2000* 1,253.000
1950 556,613	1980 931,235	

Population doubling time in years at current rate: 50
Hypothetical size of stationary population (million): 1,681
Assumed year of reaching net reproduction rate of 1: 2000
Age profile (%)

| 0–15: 33.6 | 30–44: 17.5 | 60–74: 6.3 |
| 15–29: 29.1 | 45–59: 12.2 | Over 75: 1.3 |

Median age (years): 25.6
Density per sq. km. (per sq. mi.): 113.7 (294.4)
Annual growth rate

1950–55: 2.16	1975–80: 1.44	1995–2000: 1.17
1960–65: 1.76	1980–85: 1.17	2000–2005: 0.95
1965–70: 2.58	1985–90: 1.04	2010–15: 0.51
1970–75: 2.37	1990–95: 1.12	2020–25: 0.43

Vital statistics
Crude birth rate, 1/1,000: 21.0
Crude death rate, 1/1,000: 6.6
Change in birth rate: −51.3 (1965–84)
Change in death rate: −50.4 (1965–84)
Dependency, total: 44.4
Infant mortality rate, 1/1000: 33
Child (0–4 years) mortality rate: 1/1,000: 2
Maternal mortality rate, 1/100,000: 44
Natural increase, 1/1,000: 14.4
Total fertility rate: 2.4
General fertility rate: 63
Gross reproduction rate: 0.98
Marriage rate, 1/1,000: 8.3
Divorce rate, 1/1,000: 0.5
Life expectancy, males (years): 67.8
Life expectancy, females (years): 70.7
Average household size: 5.1 (rural); 3.8 (urban)
% illegitimate births: N.A.
Youth
Youth population 15–24 (000): 266,636
Youth population in 2000 (000): 188,928
Women
Of childbearing age 15–49 (000) 318,576
Child-woman ratio (children per 000 women 15–49): 330
% women using contraceptives: 74
Urban
Urban population (000): 249,595
% urban, 1965: 18; 1987: 38
Annual urban growth rate (%)
    1965–80: 2.3; 1980–87: 11.0
% urban population in largest city: 6
% urban population in cities over 500,000: 45
Number of cities over 500,000: 78
Annual rural growth rate: 0.7%

*estimated

pared to 13.3% in 1953. The definition of urban was officially adopted in 1955. According to it, a place is urban if it meets one of three criteria: (a) a seat of a municipal people's committee or a people's committee above the *hsien* (county) level; (b) a minimum resident population of 2,000, of which at least 50% is nonagricultural; and (c) a resident population of 1,000 to 2,000, of whom 75% are nonagricultural.

The PRC government has followed a contradictory urban policy since 1949. When it came to power, it favored rapid urbanization. According to Mao, "Tens of millions of peasants will go into the cities . . . and build a great number of large modern cities . . . a transformation in which the rural population will become the residents of cities." In addition, there were two powerful forces promoting urban growth: the pull of industrialization, and the push of enforced collectivization of the countryside. Both forces siphoned off millions of peasants from the villages, but not all of them could settle in the towns because of severe housing shortages. Many cities also enlarged their boundaries to include adjacent rural areas, thus statistically inflating their populations. As the problem became unmanageable, the government initiated a policy to "dissuade farmers from pouring into the cities." At the same time, millions of people were persuaded to "go down" to the rural areas. In 1959, the year of the Great Leap Forward, a new wave of migrants flooded the cities—among them many of the cadres and students who had been transferred to rural areas just the previous year! It is reported that the urban population of China increased by some 20 million during the Great Leap Forward, although this number is suspect. In any case, during the Cultural Revolution the tide turned again, and the new migrants were again driven back into the country. Since then, the larger cities have grown only slowly and have managed to stabilize their populations.

ETHNIC COMPOSITION

According to official data, 93.3% of the population is Han Chinese; the term Han refers to the ancient dynasty that ruled China from 206 B.C. to A.D. 220. Although there are sharp regional and cultural differences among the Han, who are a mingling of many races, they share a common language, social organization and cultural characteristics universally recognized as the core of Chinese civilization.

Han is only one of 56 nationalities that officially make up the Chinese population; the other 55 are called minority nationalities. However, even while accounting for only 6.7% of the population, these minority nationalities are distributed over 50% of the national territory, mostly along the inland borders. The distinction between Han and some of the minorities is not clear because many have been totally or partially assimilated over the centuries. Some are found only in a single region, while others are spread over many regions. In general, Xinjiang, Inner Mongolia and Tibet contain heavy concentrations of minorities, whereas minority groups in Yunnan and Guizhou provinces and the Guangxi-Zhuang Autonomous Region are more fragmented and inhabit smaller areas. By proportion of minorities, Tibet ranks first with 90%, followed by Xinjiang with 60%, Qinghai with 38%, Ningxia with 33%, Yunnan with 25% to 30%, and Inner Mongolia with 15%. There are special minority autonomous administrative regions on the Soviet model. They include five provincial-level units: Xizang, Xinjiang, Guangxi, Nei Monggol and Ningxia (named respectively for Tibetan, Uygur,

Zhuang, Mongol and Hui nationalities). In addition, there are over 29 autonomous prefectures and 73 autonomous counties.

Government policy toward minorities is premised on the somewhat contradictory goals of national unity and the protection of minority equality and identity. The Constitution prohibits discrimination against or oppression of any nationality and guarantees them equal rights and duties. The eventual goal is the assimilation of these minorities into the Han polity, but as a means toward this goal, they are allowed a modicum of self-rule and some elements of their cultural identity. Yet this policy could not work well within the framework of a strong central government. Relations with the minorities have been exacerbated by traditional Han attitudes of cultural superiority, described as Han "chauvinism." Han cadres fill all important leadership positions, and anti-Han tendencies are generally labeled as antinational or separatist. Pressures on minorities were most severe during the Cultural Revolution and the ascendancy of the Gang of Four. Although the constitutional rights of these minorities were never annulled, they were subjected to much repression during this period. After the purge of the Gang of Four in 1976, the campaign against minorities was suspended with the admission that it had caused considerable alienation. However, the emphasis on national unity and strong central control remained.

The Mongols constitute the largest ethnic group on the Mongolian steppes and are divisible into three groups: the Eastern Mongols, related to the Khalka of (Outer) Mongolia, the Western Mongols or Oirat; and the Northern Mongols or Buryat. Small numbers of Mongols also are in Manchuria, Kansu and Xinjiang. Other Mongol groups include the Daur, Orochon, Yakut, Solon and Tungusic, all of which are numerically insignificant.

The Uygurs (New Uighurs or Eastern Turks) live mainly in the southern part of Xinjiang (Sinkiang) and generally call themselves after the names of their adopted cities. The Uygurs are Muslims like many other groups in northwestern China, such as Hui, Kirghiz, Monguor, Tadjik, Tatar and Uzbek.

Depending on the geographical environment, Tibetans are grouped into nomadic and sedentary. The nomadic herders occupy the northern plateau regions, where they pasture their sheep and yaks for the greater part of the year, descending into the Brahmaputra Valley for the coldest months only. From late spring until winter the herds are moved to successively higher pastures. Winter is the time for trading, for repairing equipment, for weaving yak hair cloth and so on. The great majority of Tibetans are sedentary farmers, working mostly as tenants.

The Miao and Yao, though not closely related, are often classified together. The former are distributed widely over the mountainous areas of Kweichow and Yunnan in the West to Hunan, Kwangtung and Kwangsi in the central South. The Kwantung group, on Hainan Island, is descended from Miao soldiers brought there centuries ago by the Chinese rulers to quell the rebellious Li. The Miao are subdivided into many groups, such as Red, Black, Blue, White and Flowery Miao. The Yao inhabit the mountainous regions of Kwangtung and Kwangsi.

The Zhuang constitute the largest of the ethnic minorities. This Thai-speaking group is principally on the plains and valleys of western Kwangsi. The Yi or Lolo inhabit principally the Liang Shan on the borders of Sichuan and Yunnan. The Puyi or Chungchia inhabit the low, marshy areas around Kuei-yang and in southwestern Kweichow Province.

Many of these minority nationalities are indigenous groups that settled in their homes in ancient times, while others have moved to their present locality only in recent centuries. Although their migratory routes were different, they were generally southward.

With the exception of the Koreans, few ethnic nationalities have been able to preserve their identity in the face of the preponderance of the Han Chinese culture. Conflicts have been frequent between the majority and minority cultures, and the degree of Sinification reflects the outcome of these conflicts. The most Sinified groups are in the southeastern area and among the Tumet of former Suiyuan Province.

There are no foreign communities as such in China.

LANGUAGES

The Chinese language is spoken by more people in the world than any other language, including English. Chinese is also a much older language and one that has undergone fewer changes in the course of its history, and one of the most important changes—the introduction of *pinyin* script—is of recent date. Also, as every student of Chinese knows, it is one of the most difficult languages in the world to learn. As a result, illiteracy always has been high in the country, and literacy was among the privileges of the elite.

During the course of its evolution the spoken language has undergone more modifications than the written one, particularly in pronunciation and modes of expression. A number of dialects have developed out of these changes. The spoken language also is more receptive to foreign influences. As a result, speech communities intermingle and overlap.

Like most Sino-Tibetan languages, Chinese has a basically monosyllabic structure, which means that the basic constituents of Chinese words and phrases are single syllables. While most Chinese words consist of one syllable each, there are a number of polysyllabic words. Also like other Sino-Tibetan languages, Chinese has a system of tones, the relative pitch levels used in pronouncing the syllables. In ancient times there were four tones, which in time evolved into eight tones, not all of which are used in modern dialects. Mandarin, the standard dialect, has four tones: one upper even tone, one lower even tone, one falling tone and one rising tone. In a language that abounds in homonyms, tones are essential in distinguishing words that sound the same but have different meaning.

Of the numerous dialects, the most important in terms of the number of speakers is Mandarin, followed by Wu, Hsiang, Hui, Kan, Hakka, Min and Yueh.

LARGER MINORITY NATIONALITIES IN CHINA				
Nationalities	Distribution	Occupation	Language	Religion
Lisu	Northwestern Yunnan	Agriculture; animal husbandry and hunting	Lisu	Christianity and Polytheism
Li	Hainan Island	Agriculture	No written language	Polytheism
Thai (Paiyi)	Southwestern and southern Yunnan	Agriculture	Thai	Buddhism
Hani	Southeastern Yunnan	Agriculture	No written language	Polytheism
Kazak	Northern part of Sinkiang Uigur Autonomous Region	Animal husbandry; some agriculture	Kazak	Islam
Pai (Minchia)	Ta-li and Chien-ch'uan hsien of Yunnan	Agriculture	No written language; some Chinese	Polytheism, some Christianity
Yao	Kwangsi, Hunan, Kwangtung and Yunnan	Agriculture; some forestry	No written language	Polytheism
Tung	Area where Kweichow, Hunan and Kwangsi meet	Agriculture; some forestry	No written language	Polytheism
Korean	Yen-pien area in Kirin	Agriculture	Korean	Buddhism, some Christianity
Puyi (Chungchia)	P'an-chiang valley in southwestern Kweichow	Agriculture	No written language	Polytheism
Mongol	Inner Mongolia Autonomous Region, Kansu, Liaoning, Kirin and Heilungkiang	Agriculture; animal husbandry	Mongolian	Lamaism
Manchu	Liaoning, Kirin, Heilungkiang, Inner Mongolia and Peking	More or less similar to occupations of the Han people	Chinese (Manchu language no longer used)	Similar to religions of the Han people
Miao	Southeastern Kweichow and western Hunan	Agriculture	Miao	Polytheism
Tibetan	Tibet and western Szechwan	Agriculture; animal husbandry	Tibetan	Lamaism
Yi (Lolo)	Great and Little Liangshan areas between Szechwan and Yunnan	Agriculture	Newly created Yi language	Polytheism
Hui	Ningsia Hui Autonomous Region and numerous places throughout China	Agriculture; some small business	Chinese	Islam
Uygur	Sinkiang Uighur (Uygur) Autonomous Region	Agriculture; some handicraft and commerce	Uigur	Islam
Zhuang	Kwangsi Chuang Autonomous Region	Agriculture	No written language	Polytheism

Adapted from "Wu-kuo yu na-hsieh shao-shu min-tsu" ("What are some of the minority nationalities in our country"), *Shihshih shou-tse (Current Events Handbook)*.

Although derived from a common core language, different pronunciation and linguistic structure make most of them mutually unintelligible. Even within Mandarin, there are three groups of subdialects: Northern Mandarin, spoken in Beijing and the entire Yellow River Basin; Southwestern Mandarin, spoken in the southwestern hinterland, including the Szechwan Red Basin, the Yunnan-Kweichow Plateau and the central Yangtze River plains; and Southern Mandarin, spoken in the lower Yangtze River Valley eastward to Nanjing.

The Wu dialect had its origins in Soochow, from where it spread to the lower Yangtze and gained great importance as the dialect of Shanghai. There are six to eight tones in Wu. A group of minor dialects occur south of the Yangtze River Valley and consist of Hsiang, spoken in central Hunan; Hui, spoken in southern Anhui, and Kan, spoken in northern Jianxi. Hakka is a major dialect of the overseas Chinese, and its sphere extends on an east–west axis from Fujian to Guangxi, with offshoots in Taiwan and Hainan. Hakka and Kan are very similar, differing only in tonal systems and final consonants. The Min or Fujian dialect is divided into two groups: Northern Min and Southern Min. The former, spoken in northern Fujian, is represented by the Foochow dialect; the latter, by the Amoy dialect in southern Fujian and by the Swatow dialect in northeastern Guangdong and on Hainan Island. The Southern Min dialect also has spread to overseas Chinese communities. Yueh or Cantonese is spoken widely in Guangdong and Kwangsi and is the most popular dialect of Chinese in the United States and Southeast Asia.

The written language has changed little since the beginning of the Christian era, when the present form, known as the Regular script (*k'ai shu*), became universal. As a nonalphabetical language, Chinese has a complicated system of characters divided into six main categories: pictographs, ideographs, compound ideographs, phonetic loan characters, phonetic compounds and derivative characters. Among these, the simple pictographs and ideographs are the basic forms from which the others have derived, but the phonetic compounds constitute the largest class of Chinese words. The addition of new forms is constantly enriching vernacular (*pai-hua*) Chinese, in contradistinction to literary (*wen-yen* or *wen-li*) Chinese, based on the language of the ancient Chinese classics and preserved in scholarly writings in its pristine and inflexible style for the past 20 centuries. The literary language is characterized by a remarkable clarity, even in dealing with abstract ideas, but it differs so greatly in syntax and grammar from the vernacular as to constitute a separate language. Even more remarkable is the fact that scholars fluent in the literary mode may quite naturally turn to the dialectal vernacular for everyday speech. Pronunciation of literary Chinese depends on the dialect of the reader. Sometimes because of its terseness and because it omits particles, literary Chinese cannot be fully understood when read aloud. Certain written characters have no colloquial rendering, and certain colloquial words have no written equivalents. In the latter case, however, a character of the same meaning may be used as a substitute, or a "vulgar" character may be invented for the purpose. Despite its shortcomings, literary Chinese has exerted a tenacious influence on the Chinese mind. Modern Chinese scholars are able to read ancient Chinese texts in a way in which no modern English-speaker can read Anglo-Saxon.

The cultural bond of language has led it to become one of the rallying standards of Chinese nationalism, embodied in the cry "One State, One People, One Language." Seeking to foster unity through language, each regime since 1911 has sought to (1) adopt Mandarin as a national language, (2) popularize Chinese among the non-Han minorities, (3) simplify the written words, (4) compile a list of basic Chinese characters and words and (5) alphabetize the Chinese language. The movement was launched by Hu Shih as the Chinese Renaissance Movement in the late 1910s, seeking to establish Mandarin as the national language. It gained momentum after the Communists took over in 1949. A Committee for Chinese Language Reform was established to work toward the goal of a new written language based on the Latin alphabet. Before such a change could be introduced, uniform pronunciation had to be adopted and dialectal differences had to be minimized. In 1956 the campaign for promoting the nationwide use of Mandarin was stepped up with a draft plan for the phoneti-

cization of Chinese. At the same time, non-Han Chinese people were pressured to accept Mandarin as the "common speech" (*p'u-t'ung-hua*).

A major problem in implementing this plan was the complexity of the Chinese script. The radicals of some characters have a large number of strokes, and the compound forms are even more complicated. Several characters have as many as 20 or more strokes requiring considerable time and patience. A number of devices were adopted to simplify the script, including the use of a running hand or cursive style, adoption of simpler or variant words for complicated ones, substitution of simpler characters for complex ones having the same sound, and omission of redundant parts in a character. Using these simplified forms, which have gained wide currency, as well as newly coined forms of their own, the Committee for Chinese Language Reform has prepared several lists of simplified characters, which have been officially approved by the State Council.

Another language reform measure, which had its origin in the mass education movement of the early 1920s, is the compilation of lists of basic Chinese words, somewhat like basic English to be used in adult education.

An even more serious need was the introduction of a phonetic alphabet to replace the system of Chinese characters. In the absence of an alphabet, scholarly tools such as dictionaries, indexes, bibliographies and catalogs have traditionally been arranged on the basis of a complex system of fundamental characters (radicals) or the number of strokes in each character. Chinese characters also create special problems in other areas. Telegraphic messages have to be sent in numerical codes. Typesetting machines and typewriters are vastly more complicated than those using an alphabet.

In the 20th century, many alphabetic systems have been devised to overcome these deficiencies, ranging from romanizations to kanalike symbols used by the Japanese, shorthand systems and picture scripts. The first such alternative system was a set of 39 phonetic symbols, *chu-yin tzu-mu*, promulgated in 1918, but it proved more cumbersome than the one it was intended to replace and did not gain wide support. There also was great interest in romanization, spurred by Christian missionaries in the 19th century. From these attempts had evolved the Wade-Giles system, named for Sir Thomas Wade and Herbert A. Giles, two British Sinologists, which was the standard system of romanization until 1979, when it was supplanted by *pinyin*. Another system that attracted much scholarly attention is Gwoyeu Romatzyh (National Language Romanization) made by Chao Yuan-jen (Y. R. Chao), but it never gained popular approval. A third system was that devised by Soviet linguists and known as Latinxua (latinized script); it was propounded by two Communist scholars, Chu Ch'iu-pai and Wu Yu-chang. Interestingly, Latinxua used Latin rather than Cyrillic characters. Banned by the Nationalists, Latinxua reappeared under the Communists. A National Conference on Language Reform was held in Beijing in 1955, and in 1956 a committee of linguistic experts appointed by the Maoist regime recommended adoption of a 26-letter Latin alphabet for the Chinese written language. The new system, known as *pinyin*, was formally approved by the National People's Congress in 1958. It took another 21 years before the government decided to adopt it officially. In 1979 and following years the government issued a number of word lists and lists of places and persons with standard spellings. The switchover to *pinyin* posed problems not only for Chinese—particularly nationalists for whom language is a highly emotional issue—but also for Western readers accustomed to Wade-Giles. Because it is based on the Beijing dialect, much education had to follow its introduction in all parts of China.

As part of latinization, Chinese writing switched to left to right—i.e., horizontally—rather than in vertical lines from right to left, as in traditional Chinese. Pens and pencils also have replaced the time-honored writing brushes. Another part of the reform concerned punctuation. There were no punctuations in Chinese writing until a set of marks was introduced in the late 1910s. The new system was copied from the West, with the exception that the period is not a point but a small circle.

The introduction of a latinized script has not been an unmixed blessing. It has made classical Chinese virtually a foreign language for most Chinese and therefore constitutes a serious diminution of China's literary heritage. As it will be impossible to translate all the classic texts into the romanized form, most of them will be available only to scholars.

RELIGIONS

In China, organized religion is subordinated to a complex of folk beliefs and practices that provide the ritual setting to daily lives. They include ancestor worship; reverence for family altars and institutions; and more distinctly occult elements such as magic, sorcery and divination. Over this substratum of core beliefs and practices lies a thin veneer of ethical rules of conduct by some of the greatest of classical masters, Confucius in particular. Some elements of theology and cosmogony were added from Buddhism, which was the first of the organized religions to reach China and which ranks with Confucianism and Taoism as one of the three main indigenous religious traditions. At the fringe of this religious landscape are the two major religions of the non-Chinese world—Islam and Christianity—neither of which were grafted onto the national consciousness and thus never properly took roots in the country. To complicate the picture even further is the hovering and brooding presence of Marxism, which negates religious belief and has waged a relentless campaign to uproot all established religions.

The most pervasive and the oldest of all Chinese religious practices—the distinction between religious practice and religion is quite important in the Chinese setting—is ancestor worship. Although ancestor worship is found in a variety of other cultures, nowhere else has it been so interwoven into the social fabric as to constitute an inseparable part of daily life. The basis of ancestor worship is the assumption that the living can communicate with the dead and that the dead, although living in another realm, can influence and be influenced by events and persons in this world. Since afterlife is thus a continuum of life on earth, the Chinese shun a violent death because it will entail entering the spirit world in a mutilated form. Among the many duties of a faithful descendant, the primary duty was veneration of his or her ancestor. Most homes had a small chapel or shelf containing ancestral tablets, pieces of wood inscribed with the name, title and sometimes the birthdate and death date of an ancestor. Usually there were no idols, because gods play an insignificant role in Chinese religion. Ancestral portraits were displayed not as religious objects but as heirlooms. Ceremonies in which incense was burned and candles lighted took place before the tablets on the first and 15th days of the month in the lunar calendar. On festivals such as New Year's Day and occasions such as change of residence, promotions and the birth and death dates of ancestors of the past three generations, a complete meal consisting of rice and wine was offered, accompanied by kowtowing according to the seniority of the living family members. The home contained the main altar, but every year at the Ching-ming festival in spring, the family graveyard was cleaned and repaired and yellow paper currency was burned for the use of the departed.

The personal and familial nature of ancestor worship precluded the suprafamilial aspect of most religions from taking roots in China. Formal religions such as Christianity were rejected because it could not be reconciled with ancestor worship and because its theological aspect overshadowed its social aspect. But while strong enough to resist the inroads of other religions, it was not vigorous enough to survive the decline of the patriarchal family in 20th-century Chinese society.

Folk religious systems antedate formal religious systems and coexist with them everywhere, even in the 20th century. But in China they flourish aboveground and have fewer linkages with organized religion. The world of folk religion is a kaleidoscope of dragons, demons, ghosts, gods, animals and spirits jumbled together. The concept of the afterlife is tied in with that of two types of soul: the *p'o*, or the animating agent, and the *hun*, or the rational soul. The soul resided in the heart or the breath. A person's name was the handle to the soul, control over which was exercised through charms, curses and other devices. Shadows were believed to be real parts of the soul, and care was taken in the funeral ceremony to keep shadows out of the coffin and the grave. The belief in the spirit world was the basis for a well-developed animism. Spirits and souls might enter into or possess both animate and inanimate objects; hence the concern for *feng-shui* (literally, wind and water—i.e., occult influences). The grave was considered a fetish; so also animals such as a tiger, wolf, fox, crane, unicorn, phoenix, dragon or tortoise, and objects such as flags, books, mirrors, pictures and trees. But the most important spiritual mediums were human agents called *wu*, or shamans, essentially necromancers, geomancers, fortune-tellers and sorcerers, who enjoyed great prestige among the credulous peasants. For the peasants, constantly beset by life's mysterious and capricious forces, the shaman represented a source of knowledge and succor. Influence, bribes and placatory offerings could secure favors with the heavenly hierarchies just as they did with the imperial hierarchies. The Chinese pantheon was headed by a supreme being called Shang-ti, the Emperor Above; Tien, the Emperor of Heaven; or Yu-huang, the Jade Emperor. Under him was a host of demiurges, holding temporary office and subject to promotion or demotion, just like earthly functionaries. The titles did not vary, but the officeholders did. Some of these lesser gods were deceased men of some local importance. For their meritorious deeds they were appointed *ch'eng-huang* (the gods of walls and moats). Their temples served the same purpose in the spiritual world as the magistrate courts in this world. The rural population also worshiped *ts-ai-shen*, the god of wealth and the rain god, represented by the *lung-wang*, the dragon king and the most popular village deity. Another village deity was the *t'u-ti*, the census god.

In addition to these folk deities, every family had its own tutelary deity, the kitchen god who kept an account of the good and bad deeds of the family and reported annually to the Tien. The kitchen god's periodical ascent to heaven was made easier by the burning of incense.

Not all spirits were benevolent, and in fact evil spirits such as demons outnumbered the benign ones. The most vicious were the *kuei*, disembodied spirits of the dead. Certain animals, such as foxes and snakes, had supernatural powers. Children were particularly exposed to evil spirits and thus had to wear amulets for special protection. Days and seasons could be inauspicious, and all rituals were integrated into the almanac as to help ward off evil and invoke good. Good and pious works punctuated the life of the virtuous Chinese villager. They included copying scriptures, giving alms, freeing captive birds and fish, and repetition of the name of the Buddha.

Folk religions did not concern themselves with theology, philosophy or ethics other than in a rudimentary way. The philosophical and ethical bases were provided by Confucianism, Taoism, Buddhism and other systems, none of which was organized in terms of doctrine, clergy or believers. Although Confucianism is primarily a politico-intellectual tradition of statecraft (*ju-chia*), it was transformed by its followers into a religion with all the trappings of a cult: temples, sacrifices and priests. This religious aspect of Confucianism is known as *k'ung-chiao*. To the scholar, Confucianism established his superiority over the unlettered peasant. But its inherent religious neutrality made Confucianism too impersonal to fill the emotional needs of the common people. In the 20th century Confucianism, closely identified with the imperial power, collapsed along with the monarchy. Sacrifices in Confucian temples were discontinued in 1928. Reduced to a philosophical system, it was supplanted by Western philosophical and ethical traditions and even more so by dialectical materialism.

Taoism also is both a philosophy and a religion. Its conversion to a religion took place in the early centuries of the Christian era. Originally based on Persian Mazdaism in its early phase, it included confession of sins, healing, prayers to the spirits and an elaborate angelology. Later, as a rival to Buddhism, it adopted an order of clergy and monks. Its philosophical character was gradually diluted as it became identified with folk religion. The organization and rituals of Taoism are blatant imitations of Buddhism. By the Middle Ages Taoism had elaborate rules for monks and laity; large monasteries; and a tight parish organization with hereditary patriarchs presided over by the *t'ien-shih*, known to Western scholars as the Taoist pope. Its clergy, called *tao-shih*, were elected and ordained and were divided into two classes: monastics and nonmonastics, both committed to observing rigorous religious rules, including fasting. Unlike Buddhist monks, the *tao-shih* kept their family names as well as their hair. Strong Buddhist influences also permeated the architecture of Taoist temples, called *kuan* and *kung*, as well as liturgy and music. The Taoist pantheon was peopled by folk deities such as the Jade Emperor and lower gods and guardian spirits. The cult also embraced the rich reservoir of native superstitions such as geomancy; divination; witchcraft; astrology; communication with the dead; and, most importantly, alchemy, particularly the transmutation of base metals into gold and the manufacture of elixirs of immortality. From Indian cultures Taoism borrowed Yogic practices such as breathing controls, and special diets designed to prolong life. Taoism also quickly disintegrated in the early part of the 20th century. The official end came when the last hereditary *t'ien-shih*, presiding over Taoist headquarters in the Dragon and Tiger Mountain in Jiangxi, was expelled by the Nationalist government in 1927.

Although Buddhism originated in India and only spread into China after many centuries, it is considered a native religion for all practical purposes. Chinese Buddhism is of the Mahayana (Great Vehicle) school, which is more properly a religion than the Hinayana (Lesser Vehicle) school. In the Mahayana version, Buddha is a god whose image is worshiped and to whom sacrifices are offered. Buddhist temples and ceremonies are replicas of imperial palaces and court ceremonies. Nirvana is replaced by the Western Heaven ruled over by Amida Buddha (Amitabha). Hells and purgatories have been added as countervailing concepts. The Indian *bodhisattva* Avalokiteshvara, originally a male deity, became the goddess of mercy, Kuan-yin. The Buddhist *sanghas* or religious communities won the favor of the masses by organizing great ceremonies of penitence and sacrifices for dead ancestors.

Unlike Confucianism and Taoism, Buddhism opened up China to foreign contacts and influences. Religious ideas passed through China to Japan, Korea and other countries. The Buddhist Dhyana School, a meditative institution founded by the Indian monk Bodhidharma, grew into the Ch'an contemplative school in China and passed into Japan as Zen.

Although persecuted at times by Taoist and Confucianist emperors, Buddhism was a useful political tool for China's rulers in their efforts to control the Mongol and Tibetan peoples who adhered to Lamaism, a form of Mahayana Buddhism corrupted by native shamanism.

Suffering serious setbacks in the early part of this

century, Buddhism enjoyed a brief revival in the 1930s and 1940s through the efforts of many abbots, such as Yin-kuang and T'ai-hsu.

Islam is considered a foreign religion known as Hui Hui chiao, which means the religion of the Uygurs, the Turkic tribe of Xinjiang. About half of Chinese Muslims speak a Turkic language. Though distributed in most inland provinces, their most important traditional centers are in Yunnan, Gansu, Xinjiang, Ningxia and Inner Mongolia. The Muslim community has avoided identifying itself with Chinese culture except for the sake of political expediency. Social customs and mores also have been preserved tenaciously: Muslim graveyards are separated; Arabic and Persian phrases are preserved in polite salutations; turbans are customary; food laws are observed; and boys are circumcised at seven. Muslims generally live in secluded quarters referred to as barracks. Islam flourished under the Nationalist government when Muslims reestablished contacts with Arab countries, resulting in strong movements toward orthodoxy. The same period opened the way to political and military power for many Muslims. Even after the advent of communism, Islam has fared better than other religions. Muslims are treated as members of a nationality rather than as members of a religion and thus enjoy semiautonomy in certain areas in northwestern China. Adopting the Koranic practice of taqiyah, or dissimulation in hostile environments, the Muslims have collaborated with the Communists and have joined the army and the government in large numbers. The Chinese Islamic Association operates under government aegis and disseminates Communist propaganda in the Middle East. Muslim schools have been established as instruments of Communist indoctrination. Islam also is taught in the Central Academy of Nationalities and the Chinese Muslim College in Beijing.

There is no accepted term for Christianity in Chinese. Catholicism and Protestantism, which were introduced separately, are called respectively T'ien-chu chiao (doctrine of the Heavenly Lord) and Chi-tu chiao (doctrine of Christ). Both groups evolved in isolation and operate as two different religions.

The first Christian missionaries entered China long before they reached many of the countries in northwestern Europe. The first known missionary was the Nestorian evangelist Alopen, who arrived in Sian, the Tang capital, in 635. A Nestorian monument erected outside Sian in 781 was excavated in 1625. Known as the "Luminous Religion," Nestorianism vanished as quickly as it came, and by 845 the church had been wiped out in China.

Another eight centuries went by before the Jesuits, under Matteo Ricci, reestablished a Christian presence in Beijing and other cities in the Yangtze River Valley. They soon gained imperial favor with their mathematical and astronomical knowledge and their diligent cultivation of the Chinese language. Their success encouraged other bodies, such as the Dominicans and Franciscans, to follow them. However, the so-called Rites Controversy, and the papal decision of 1742 forbidding Chinese Christians to observe ancestor worship, meant the end of official favor and the beginning of persecution.

The third phase of Christian missionary work in China began in the 19th century when, according to the treaties China concluded with the Western nations, missionaries were granted the right to live and travel in the interior, the protection of their own governments and immunity from Chinese government interference. However, Christian success in spreading the Gospel raised considerable apprehension among the traditionbound Chinese, culminating in the Boxer Rebellion of 1900. Notwithstanding the revolt, Christianity continued to spread and take roots in the cities. Missionary efforts contributed to the ferment that gave birth to the Revolution of 1911 and the establishment of the Chinese Republic in 1911. From that time to the rise of the Communists in 1949 was a period of dramatic growth for the Chinese Christian churches. Christians were prominent in the national leadership that replaced the Confucian mandarinate. Opposition to Christianity did not disappear but found a new home among the rationalists and Communists.

In the interwar period Catholics outnumbered Protestants by three to one. There were 3 million Catholics and an almost entirely Chinese hierarchy, headed by a Chinese cardinal. Thirteen large orders representing 36 nationalities worked in mission stations throughout the country, and they also supplied half of the 5,442 priests. The Catholic Church ran 776 primary schools, 155 middle schools, three universities, 288 hospitals and 320 orphanages.

The Protestant strength was equally impressive. Over 9,000 missionaries from 170 missionary societies supplemented 2,000 Chinese ministers in maintaining 12,000 places of worship. Religious training was provided by 50 theological schools and 160 Bible schools. Protestants were mostly found in large cities and in the treaty ports along the coast, but the China Inland Mission dedicated itself exclusively to evangelism of the interior. Protestants paid great attention to education. They maintained 13 colleges and 2,301 middle schools. Medical work also was emphasized, through 216 hospitals, 23 leprosariums, 38 clinics, five medical schools and 40 nursing schools.

Almost from the time they took over the mainland in 1949, the Communists began a determined campaign against both Catholics and Protestants. Because this campaign was part of a wider campaign to eliminate all foreign influences, it became progressively severe. At the same time, it was subtle and marked by finesse and shrewdness. No Christian was openly executed. The Communists were careful not to make martyrs. They fabricated charges against Christian leaders and threw them in jail. Many simply disappeared. In the same way, they did not liquidate religious organizations but rather infiltrated them, placed pro-Communist puppets in positions of leadership and thus caused their eventual disintegration. During the land reform, all rural churches were closed as part of a general order forbidding public assemblies. After the Korean War, when the United States embargoed remittances of funds to China, all Christian schools, hospitals and other institutions were placed under direct government control. As a prelude to the creation of puppet churches, the government created the Three Autonomies in the Catholic Church, corresponding to the Three Self-Movement (self-support, self-government and self-propagation) among the Protestant churches. By 1957 the rupture between Rome and Beijing had become total, and Catholic presence after that date was limited to state-sponsored churches such as the National Patriotic Catholic Association and the Constitutional Church. During the Cultural Revolution all traces of the visible church were obliterated. By the mid-1970s the number of Catholic clergy had been reduced to about 500.

The Protestants fared equally badly. Although the government was more successful in its efforts to infiltrate Protestant denominations, they were not spared the repression. With the outbreak of the Cultural Revolution, all public Christian activities had ceased. In 1964 it became illegal to teach religion to children under 18 years of age, and Bibles were confiscated. Between 1966 and 1969 no communications were received by the outside world from Chinese Christian leaders. The church in China had finally been silenced and driven underground.

After the death of Mao there was a gradual remission in official hostility, and some signs of life appeared in the church, considered dead. A few Catholic and Protestant churches were allowed to reopen and hold public services. Reluctant to meet in their former church buildings, most Christians continued to meet in private homes as families or in small groups. Christian visitors were once again allowed into China, and their reports, although not glowing, confirmed the existence of a large body of believers in every city. A few seminaries also have opened doors and recruited students for replenishing the ranks of the clergy.

Indigenous churches—not affiliated to any foreign denomination—have flourished in China since the 19th century. The first was the quasi-Christian God Worshipers' Society (Pai Shang-ti Hui), begun in 1847 under a visionary, Huang Hsiu-sh'uan, among the impoverished peasants of Kwangsi. In 1851 Hung proclaimed a new dynasty, the Heavenly Kingdom of Great Peace (T'ai P'ing T'ien Kuo), known to the Western world as Taiping. In a short time it became syncretistic, with the addition of Confucian, Buddhist and Taoist elements. Hundreds of thousands of peasants joined the movement, which eventually became a mass revolt in which 35 million people were killed during the 17 years before it was suppressed in 1868. From 1906 further efforts to break off from foreign missions led to the founding of several churches. Their membership increased rapidly, and by 1949 there were 440,000 adherents in 30 or more denominations, including the True Jesus Church, Little Flock or Assembly Hall churches (begun by noted writer Watchman Nee) and China Jesus Independent Church. Although these churches were completely Chinese in leadership and outlook, they were among the first to be persecuted and suppressed. Watchman Nee himself was jailed for 15 years.

Russian Orthodox chaplains accompanied cossacks to Beijing in 1686, and an Orthodox mission was set up there in 1715. After the Bolshevik Revolution, many Orthodox clergy fled to China. By 1949 there were 300,000 Orthodox Christians (mostly Russian) in China and Manchuria, with five bishops; 210 parishes; 200 priests; two monasteries; and an Orthodox university, at Harbin. But with the rise of Mao to power, the Orthodox Church also went under.

HISTORICAL BACKGROUND

Although earlier civilizations, now extinct, have flourished elsewhere, China is the world's oldest nation, with a continuous history that goes back to the second millennium B.C. The Chinese therefore have a strong sense of history and have kept voluminous records since very early times. An inward-looking people, the Chinese have constructed a China-centered view of the world reflected in the Chinese name for their own country—Zhonghua, literally the Middle Kingdom or the Central Nation.

The Chinese count time not in centuries, as in the West, but in dynasties. From the very first dynasty to 1911, when the first republic was established, there were 17 dynasties, many of them with subdivisions and periods.

The origins of Chinese civilization are shrouded in the mists of time. The first prehistoric dynasty is said to be the Xia, which ruled for about 500 years (2200–1700 B.C.). The first historical dynasty about which archaeological evidence exists is the Shang (or Yin), which ruled from 1700 to 1027 B.C. Two important Shang developments were the invention of writing and the use of bronze. The last Shang ruler was overthrown by a chieftain of a frontier tribe called Zhou (Chou), settled along the banks of the Wei He Valley in modern Shanxi Province. The Zhou dynasty had its capital at Hao, near the modern city of Xian (Sian). The Zhou dynasty ruled China for a longer period than any other. However, in 771 B.C. the Zhou court was sacked and its king killed, forcing the transfer of its capital eastward to Luoyang, in the modern province of Henan. Because of this shift the Zhou period is divided into Western and Eastern eras. The latter is further subdivided into the Spring and Autumn period (722–481 B.C.) and the Warring States period (403–221 B.C.). The Eastern Zhou period was a time of the flowering of Chinese culture, represented by such philosophers as Kongfuzi (K'ung-fu-tzu) or Master Kung (551–470 B.C.), known to the West as Confucius; Mencius or Mengzi (Meng-tzu, 372–289 B.C.); Xunzi (Hsun-tzu, c. 300–237 B.C.), the legalist whose ideas were developed by Hanfeizi (Han-fei-tzu, d. 233 B.C.) and Li Si (Li Ssu, d. 208 B.C.); and Laozi (Lao-tsu or "Old Master"), the founder of Taoism, and his disciple Chuan Chu (369–286 B.C.).

The history of China as a united nation begins properly in 221 B.C. In that year the western frontier state of Qin (Ch'in, from which the name China is derived) subjugated the other warring states, and the king of Qin took on the grandiloquent title of First Emperor Qin Shi Huangdi. He set in motion a process of centralization and imperial expansion. To fend off barbarian invasions from the north, the various fortification walls built previously by the warring states were connected to make a 3,300-km. (2,051-mi.) Great Wall. The Qin dynasty did not outlast the death of its founder and lasted only 15 years—the shortest dynastic period in Chinese history.

The dynasty that replaced it was the Han—after whom the major nationality of China is named—with its capital at Chang'an, later known as Xi'an. The Han period is noted for the invention of paper and porcelain, the establishment of the Silk Route to the Roman imperial possessions in Asia Minor and the introduction of Buddhism.

The collapse of the Han dynasty was followed by nearly four centuries of rule by warlords. This period began with the Three Kingdoms (A.D. 220–80), followed by the Jin dynasty, which through its Western and Eastern branches ruled until 420. From that time until the sixth century, power was shared by four southern and five northern dynasties. This period was noted for the spread of Buddhism; the invention of gunpowder and the wheelbarrow; and numerous advances in medicine, astronomy and cartography.

China was reunified by the short-lived Sui dynasty, which ruled from 581 to 618. Their principal legacy was the Grand Canal, a monumental engineering feat. The Sui was supplanted by the Tang dynasty in 618. Most historians regard the Tang period as the high point in Chinese civilization, distinguished not only by the military exploits of its early rulers but also by the flowering of creativity in many fields. Block printing was invented, making the written word accessible to a larger audience. The Tang period also was the golden age of literature and art. The Tang rulers were the first to establish a cadre of civil servants selected through competitive examinations.

Tang power ebbed by the mideighth century, and the dynasty ended in 907. The next half century is known as the Five Dynasties and 10 Kingdoms period. This age of fragmentation gave way to a new power, the Song (Sung) (960–1279), notable for the development of cities and the mercantile class. At the same time there was a progressive revival of interest in the Confucian ideals, coinciding with the decline of Buddhism. The Confucian revival was spearheaded by Zhu Xi (Chu Hsi, 1130–1200), whose teachings became the official imperial ideology until the end of the Manchu dynasty. A rigid and unyielding creed, it stressed the one-sided obligations of obedience and compliance by subject to ruler, child to parents and wife to husband. Before or during the Song period three other dynasties held power in various other parts of China: the Liao (Kitan) dynasty (907–1125), the Western Xia (Hsia) dynasty (1032–1227) and the Jin (Nurchen) Dynasty (1032–1227).

At the beginning of the 13th century the Mongols were already ascendant in northern China. Chingiz Khan and his successors had established an empire that stretched from the Sea of Japan to the Black Sea and beyond. Kublai Khan, grandson of Chingiz Khan, began a drive against the Song, and even before the latter's extinction, established the first alien dynasty to rule all China, the Yuan (1279–1368). As in other parts of their empire, Mongol rule was brief and culturally barren. The period was notable only for the visit of the Venetian Marco Polo, whose account of his trip to Kublai Khan's court was the first Western glimpse into the fabulous land of Cathay. The Mongol rule was resented by the Han Chinese, who were discriminated against socially and politically.

Rivalry among the heirs to the Mongol khaganate, natural disasters and numerous peasant uprisings led to the collapse of the Yuan dynasty. It was supplanted in 1368 by the Ming dynasty, founded by a Han Chinese peasant and former Buddhist priest. With its capital first at Nanjing and later at Beijing, its power reached its zenith during the first quarter of the 15th century. Chinese armies reconquered Annam in Southeast Asia, and the Chinese fleet ranged the China seas and the Indian Ocean as far as the eastern coast of Africa. Many Chinese historians consider the Ming period as the most stable and prosperous of Chinese eras. However, by the first half of the 17th century Ming power had weakened enough to allow invaders from the North to grasp the throne once again. In 1644 the Manchus took Beijing and became masters of northern China, thus establishing China's second and last alien dynasty. Known as the Qing (Ch'ing), it survived until 1911.

Although non-Han, the Manchus were Sinicized to a great degree, and they adopted Chinese customs and retained most of the Ming institutions. They continued the Confucian cult rituals over which they traditionally presided. In a series of bloody and costly campaigns, the Manchus gained control over most border and other outlying areas, including Xinjiang, Yunnan, Tibet and Taiwan. A combination of military prowess and bureaucratic skills contributed to the early successes of the Manchus.

The Qing were suspicious of the Han, and Qing policy was directed toward preserving Manchu superiority. Han Chinese were prohibited from migrating to Manchuria. The Manchus were forbidden to engage in manual labor and trade, and no agriculture was permitted in northern Manchuria. Intermarriage between the two groups was forbidden. In many government positions a system of dual appointments was used, with Chinese officials being supervised by Manchus.

Even as the Manchu empire grew to include a larger area than ever before or since, it was sapped by new threats from within and without. The process of disintegration took the entire 19th century through a series of incidents that cumulatively drained its resources and eventually toppled it. Beginning in the early 19th century, localized revolts erupted in various parts of the empire. Secret societies, such as the White Lotus sect in the North and the Hung Society in the South, gained ground, combining anti-Manchu subversion with banditry. Peace and stability had caused an explosion of population, but with no industry or trade of sufficient scope to absorb the surplus, there was widespread rural discontent and urban pauperism, aided by weakening of the Manchu bureaucratic and military systems through corruption. These problems were compounded by natural calamities of unprecedented proportions, including droughts, famines and floods. These disasters were caused in part by misgovernment and neglect of public works. This was especially the case in southern

China, the last area to yield to the Qing conquerors and the first place to be exposed to Western influence. It was the site of the most famous rebellion in Chinese history—the Taiping Rebellion, led by a misguided former Protestant convert, Hong Xiuquan, who proclaimed himself the Heavenly King of the Heavenly Kingdom of Great Peace in 1851. Over 35 million people were killed before the rebellion was finally crushed in 1864.

As the empire reeled under this revolt, the Western powers trying to get a foothold grew bolder. First the Portuguese gained Macao, where they monopolized the foreign trade at Guangzhou (Canton). Soon the "Celestial Empire" was humiliated by Great Britain in the Opium War (1839–42), provoked by illegal British trade in opium, which was prohibited by imperial decree. When the Chinese government confiscated and burned 20,000 chests of opium, the British retaliated with a punitive expedition in which the imperial army was disastrously defeated. The resulting Treaty of Nanking (1842) was the first of a series of agreements with Western trading nations that the Chinese call "unequal treaties." Under its terms, the Chinese ceded Hong Kong; abolished the licensed monopoly system of trade; opened five ports to foreign trade; limited the tariff on trade to 5% ad valorem; granted British nationals extraterritoriality; and paid a large indemnity.

The treaty triggered a scramble among Western powers to carve up the vast empire. In the 1850s the Russians invaded the Amur watershed of Manchuria in violation of the Treaty of Nerchinsk (1689) and in 1860 forced the emperor to grant them all of Manchuria north of the Amur River and east of the Ussuri River. Foreign encroachments intensified after 1860 through a series of treaties imposed on China under one pretext or another. The catalog of concessions lengthened, and the foreign stranglehold on the economy deepened. The treaty ports became virtually foreign enclaves.

The official response of the tottering Manchu court to these humiliations was a series of halfhearted reforms designed to avert further decline. The first phase of the reforms was championed in the 1860s by such generals as Zeng Huofan, Zuo Zongtang and Li Hong Zhang. It attempted to reform the bureaucracy; modernize the army; expand public education; build railroads, telegraph lines and new harbors; and create an industrial base. These efforts petered out, sabotaged by the Confucian bureaucrats, who saw in them only a threat to their own entrenched powers.

As the reforms failed to take hold, the foreign powers continued to dismember the empire. France, victorious in a war with China in 1883, took Annam; the British took Burma; Russia took Turkestan; and Japan, emerging from its centuries-long seclusion, took Taiwan, Korea and the Liuqiu (Ryukyu) Islands. In 1898 the British acquired a 99-year lease over the New Territories of Kowloon.

In 1898 the second phase of the reform movement was even briefer than the first; it lasted for just 102 days, from June 11 to September 21. Like the first, it was a self-strengthening movement, aimed at sweeping social and institutional changes. Opposition to the reform was intense among the Manchu ruling elite. Supported by the ultraconservatives, Empress Dowager Cixi (Tz'u-hsi) engineered a coup forcing young, reform-minded Emperor Guangxu (Kuang-hsu) into seclusion and took over the government as regent. The reform ended with the execution of six of its principal advocates and the flight of two to Japan.

The ultraconservatives then retaliated by backing an antiforeign and anti-Christian organization known to the West as the Boxers. In 1900 this group rampaged northern China in what became known as the Boxer Rebellion. The uprising was crushed by the expeditionary forces of the foreign powers, and under the Boxer Protocol of 1901 the court was forced to pay the Western powers a large indemnity and consent to the stationing of foreign troops on Chinese soil.

The failure of the reform and the fiasco of the Boxer Rebellion set the stage for the Republican Revolution of 1911. The leader of the revolutionaries was Sun Zhongshan (Sun Yat-sen, 1866–1925), who as an exile in Japan had founded in 1905 the Tong Meng Hui (the United League or Brotherhood Society), a forerunner of the Guomindang (Kuomintang or KMT, the Nationalist Party). His followers included overseas Chinese and also military officers, among them a young cadet named Chiang Kai-shek. Sun's political philosophy centered on the Three Principles of the People: nationalism, democracy and socialism.

The Manchu dynasty fell on October 10, 1911, after having been in power for 267 years. Its anticlimactic exit was the result not of a massive popular uprising but of a minor mutiny by the imperial garrison at Wu-Ch'ang, where 3,000 soldiers rose in revolt. The city fell without resistance, and the relatively bloodless revolution spread quickly. Sun was inaugurated on January 1, 1912, in Nanjing as the provisional president of the new Chinese Republic. But power in Beijing had already passed to Yuan Shikai, the strongest warlord and commander in chief of the imperial army. To prevent possible bloodshed, Sun agreed to a united national government in Beijing under Yuan Shikai. On February 12, 1912, the last Manchu emperor, Puyi, abdicated, and on March 12 Yuan Shikai was inaugurated as provisional president of the republic.

Within two years Yuan Shikai became a virtual dictator by arranging the assassination of his political opponents and forcing Sun to flee to Japan. Yuan Shikai suspended parliament (in which the Guomindang had a majority of seats) and proceeded to establish a monarchy, and when that attempt failed, proclaimed himself president for life in 1915. He died a year later.

Yuan Shikai's death was followed by a scramble among the regional warlords for control of the Beijing government. In addition to internal chaos, the nation was threatened from without by Japan, who claimed Shandong and also sought to establish its protectorate over all of China through the so-called Twenty-one Demands. In 1917, the Beijing government conceded in a secret deal the Japanese claim to Shandong. When this sellout became public, there were massive student protest demonstrations, culminating in a national movement known as the May Fourth Movement or, in

THE CHINESE DYNASTIES

Xia (Hsia) dynasty	2200–1700 B.C.
Shang (Yin) dynasty	1700–1027 B.C.
Zhou (Chou) dynasty	c. 1066–221 B.C.
Western Zhou (Chou)	c. 1066–771 B.C.
Eastern Zhou (Chou)	c. 770–256 B.C.
Spring and Autumn period	722–481 B.C.
Warring States period	403–221 B.C.
Qin dynasty	221–206 B.C.
Han dynasty	206 B.C.–A.D. 220
Six dynasties	
Three Kingdoms period	220–316
State of Wei	220–265
State of Shu	221–263
State of Wu	222–280
Western Jin (Tsin) dynasty	265–316
Eastern Jin (Tsin) dynasty and 16 states	304–439
Eastern Jin (Tsin)	317–420
16 States	304–439
Southern and Northern dynasties	
Southern dynasties	
Song (Sung)	420–429
Qi (Ch'i)	429–502
Liang	502–557
Chen (Ch'en)	557–589
Northern dynasties	
Northern Wei	386–534
Eastern Wei	534–550
Northern Qi (Ch'i)	550–577
Western Wei	535–557
Northern Zhou (Chou)	557–581
Sui dynasty	581–618
Tang (T'ang) dynasty	618–907
Five Dynasties and 10 Kingdoms period	902–979
Later Liang	907–923
Later Tang (T'ang)	923–936
Later Jin (Tsin)	936–946
Later Han	947–950
Later Zhou (Chou)	951–960
10 kingdoms	902–979
Song (Sung) dynasty	960–1279
Liao (Kitan) dynasty	907–1125
Western Xia (Hsia) dynasty	1032–1227
Jin (Nurchen) dynasty	1115–1233
Yuan (Mongol) dynasty	1279–1368
Ming dynasty	1368–1644
Qing (Ch'ing or Manchu) dynasty	1644–1911
Republic	1912–1949
People's Republic established	1949

intellectual circles, as the New Culture Movement, which helped rekindle the fading cause of the republican revolution. In October 1919 Sun Zhongshan, who in 1917 had set up a rival government in Guangzhou in collaboration with southern warlords, reestablished the Guomindang. When his efforts to obtain aid from Western democracies failed, he turned to the new power on the international scene: the Soviet Union. In 1922 the Guomindang-warlord alliance in Guangzhou ruptured and Sun fled to Shanghai, receiving Soviet pledges of support. A new alliance was forged under Soviet auspices between the Guomindang and the Chinese Communist Party (CCP), founded in 1921. Soviet advisers helped to train political workers as well as military officers, among them Chiang Kai-shek, who received sev-

eral months' military training in Moscow. When Chiang returned in 1923 he established the Whamboa Military Academy at Guangzhou. As head of the academy, Chiang rose to prominence and became the natural successor as Guomindang leader on Sun's death in 1925. In 1926 Chiang staged a coup, ousting the left-wing CCP elements in the party, but the Soviets nevertheless continued to support him. For a time in 1927 there were three capitals in China: the warlord regime in Beijing; the CCP and leftwing Guomindang regime in Wuhan; and the Chiang Kai-shek-led right-wing Guomindang government in Nanjing, which remained the Nationalist capital for the next decade. By 1928 the Beijing regime had been eliminated and Chiang was in control of most of China, receiving prompt international recognition as head of the sole legitimate government of China. The decade of 1928 to 1937 was an era of consolidation and accomplishment by the Nationalists.

But even as the nation was beginning to experience a strong, stable central government for the first time in a century, two forces were at work that would eventually undermine Chiang's regime: the rise of the CCP and Japanese aggression.

By mid-1927 CCP fortunes were at their lowest ebb in the decade. The CCP gave up its former policy of passivity and cooperation with Chiang in favor of armed insurrection in both urban and rural areas. Attempts were made by the Communists to take cities such as Nanzhang, Changsha, Swatow and Guangzhou, and an armed rural uprising, known as the Autumn Harvest Insurrection, was staged by peasants in Hunan. It was led by a former librarian of Beijing University, Mao Zedong (Mao Tse-tung), a man of boundless energy and faith in the revolutionary potential of the peasantry. Despite the failure of the insurrection, Mao continued to work among the Hunan peasants, turning them into a powerful guerrilla force under his military commander, Zhu De. Without waiting for the sanction of the CCP Center, then in Shanghai, Mao began to establish peasant-based soviets along the border between Hunan and Jiangxi (Kiangsi) Province. By the winter of 1927–28, Mao's People's Liberation Army (PLA) had some 10,000 men. In 1931 Mao proclaimed the establishment of the Chinese Soviet Republic under his chairmanship in Ruijin (Jui-chin), Jiangxi Province. By 1932 Mao's control of the CCP was complete. Surviving a series of encirclement and extermination attacks mounted by the Guomindang forces, Mao, along with 100,000 to 190,000 supporters, began his epic retreat, celebrated in Communist legend as the Long March, for some 10,000 km. (6,215 mi.) through southwestern China to the northern province of Shanxi (Shensi), where some 20,000 survivors arrived in 1935. The Communists then set up their headquarters in Yan'an, in southern Shanxi. The Yan'an era (1936–45) was one of rapid growth for the CCP, owing to a combination of internal and external circumstances, of which World War II was the most significant.

The Japanese had initiated a policy of conquering China piecemeal as early as 1917, and had pursued that policy relentlessly since then by seizing Manchuria in 1931 and then pushing down over the Great Wall into northern China and along the coastal provinces. In the first half of the 1930s the Guomindang was more preoccupied with campaigns to exterminate the Communists than resisting the Japanese invaders. Open hostilities between the two governments began only on July 7, 1937, when a clash, carefully engineered by the Japanese, occurred between Chinese troops and the invaders at the Marco Polo Bridge near Beijing. The Guomindang and the CCP patched up their differences to face the common enemy, but the uneasy alliance crumbled after 1938. By 1940 the Japanese controlled most of coastal and northern China and the rich Yangtze River Valley. The Guomindang government moved its capital to Ch'ung-ch'ing (Chongqing). However, the Guomindang reverses greatly benefited Mao. The Communists increased their party membership from 100,000 in 1937 to 1.2 million by 1945. The PLA troops became skilled guerrilla fighters able to wear down the enemy by alternating offensive and defensive actions.

China emerged from the war greatly enfeebled, economically prostrate and politically divided. Despite massive economic aid from the United States, the economy was shattered by inflation and sabotaged by the Communists. Famines and floods left millions homeless and destitute. The civil war between the Communists and the Guomindang began in earnest within a year of the end of the war. In 1947 the U.S. mission, headed by George C. Marshall, was withdrawn from Beijing as the United States decided not to intervene militarily in the conflict. Thereafter the Guomindang collapse was swift. In 1949 the PLA entered Beijing without a fight, and within months all the major cities passed into Communist hands. In December 1949 Chiang, with a few hundred thousand of his troops, fled from the mainland to Taiwan, proclaiming T'ai-pei as the capital of his republic.

For post-1949 events see Chronology.

CONSTITUTION & GOVERNMENT

The People's Republic of China was established on October 1, 1949. For the first five years of its existence it had no constitution since, according to the regime, the revolution had not been consummated and the economy had not been completely socialized. In the place of a constitution, the state was governed by the Organic Law of the People's Republic and the Common Program of the People's Political Consultative Conference. Both documents reflected Mao's ideas on "new democracy," which was a people's democratic dictatorship, a contradiction in terms that was justified as appropriate for a transition from a semifeudal and semicolonial stage to socialism. The first Constitution was promulgated in 1954, and it was followed by three others, in 1975, 1978 and 1982, each representing a major phase of China's post-1949 political development.

The Constitution of 1954 contained a few features reminiscent of the political forms of imperial China and the structure of the Nationalist government, but it derived its concepts and wording most significantly from the Stalin Constitution of 1936 of the Soviet Union. The Constitution of 1954 is regarded favorably by China's current leadership because it is more organic than programmatic—i.e., it is less of a political manifesto than a document setting forth the norms and standards for the structure and function of government, the obligations of the citizens and the relationship between government and people. Consisting of 106 articles, the Constitution of 1954 was designed as a blueprint for an orderly transition to socialism. It defined the PRC as "a people's democratic state led by the working class and based on the alliance between workers and peasants." Article 3 stated that China is a unified multinational state but does not provide for constituent republics. It included universal articles on civil liberties and provided for a government based on elected representatives. The first function of the state in a "new democracy" was stated as the development of industry and the betterment of the economy. Another is the elimination of class antagonisms, to be achieved primarily by government regulation. Most of the general principles in the Constitution dealt mainly with the different types of ownership of the means of production. These were divided into four: state ownership, cooperative ownership, ownership by individual working people and capitalist ownership. Capitalist ownership was not eliminated, but Article 10 affirmed the state's policy of gradually restricting and eliminating it. Feudal landlords and capitalists were deprived of political rights but permitted to reform themselves through labor. The Communist Party was given no legal standing by the Constitution. Indeed, the party was mentioned only twice in the whole document, both times in the Preamble, and only with reference to its leadership of the Chinese people before 1949.

The Constitution of 1975 was a leftist document reflecting the changed political mood following the Cultural Revolution. The new version, including a fresh Preamble, was considerably shorter than the original (particularly the sections dealing with state structure), containing only 30 articles. Thus it was more programmatic than organic. China was no longer defined as a people's democratic state but rather as "a socialist state under proletarian dictatorship." It also stressed more than its predecessor party control over the state apparatus. Article 2 stated, "The Communist Party is the core of leadership of the whole Chinese people." No reference was made to the election of a people's congress. The presidency was abolished, and command of the armed forces was transferred to the chairman of the party's Central Committee. Another provision strengthening the constitutional status of the party was its right to nominate and dismiss the premier and members of the State Council. The four former categories of ownership of the means of production were reduced to two; state ownership and collective ownership, representing the Communist and socialist stages, respectively, of social evolution. Nevertheless, the peasant private plots, temporarily eliminated during the Great Leap Forward and again under attack during the Cultural Revolution, were guaranteed by Article 7. Most of the freedoms guaranteed in the Constitution of 1954 were kept intact except for the freedom to change residence. A new fundamental duty was added in Article 26, whereby all citizens were required to support party leadership.

The Constitution of 1978 represented a return to partial normalcy. By then Mao had died and the Gang of Four had been arrested. A degree of deradicalization and de-Maoization had already taken place. But the right wing under Deng Xiaoping had not yet consolidated its position. As a result, the third Constitution represented a compromise, and changes dealt more with procedures than with structural alterations. Generally it gave more power to the National People's Congress (to be elected by secret ballot) than previously but without diminishing the party's authority to control and supervise the state organs. It retained the 1975 prescription of the Chinese state as "a socialist state under proletarian dictatorship." The presidency was not revived, but the judiciary was restored. The network of the people's procuratorates was reestablished and made responsible to the people's congresses at various levels instead of being under the control of the various public security organs. The system of people's assessors also was re-created. The right of an accused to defense at his trial was restored. Of the Constitution's 60 articles, 16 dealt with the fundamental rights and duties of citizens, compared with only four in the Constitution of 1975. Freedom of residence was not restored, but a new right to strike was inserted. The right of minority peoples to preserve their own customs was returned to them, and the government organs in the national autonomous areas were required to use the language of the local minority. There was an increased emphasis on economic struggles, as contrasted to the political and class struggles prominent during the Cultural Revolution. The Preamble stressed the Four Modernizations, and to further this goal Article 10 and Article 48 sanctioned the use of material rewards. Most significantly, Mao Zedong Thought, which had guided China since 1949, was downplayed, and the people were called on only to "defend the great banner of Chairman Mao."

The Constitution of 1982, still in effect in 1990, is essentially a Deng Constitution. It often is compared rather than contrasted with the Constitution of 1954. The longest of the four constitutions, with 138 articles, it is more structural than programmatic, marking a radical departure from the heavily political preoccupations of its predecessors. The presidency was restored. China is defined as a "socialist state under people's democratic dictatorship." No reference is made to the preeminent role of the Communist Party, although it states that the state is "led by the working class." Moreover, Article 5 states, "All state organs, the armed forces, all political parties and public organizations . . . must abide by the Constitution and the law." All civil liberties were restored, with the significant exception of the right to strike. The new Constitution also reflects the post-Mao state by diminishing the political and governmental role of the people's communes by transferring their power to the townships.

The Constitution of 1982 consists of 10 sections, as follows:

Section 1: Articles 1–32, General Principles
Section 2: Articles 33–56, Fundamental Rights and Duties of Citizens
Section 3: Articles 57–78, The National People's Congress
Section 4: Articles 79–84, The President
Section 5: Articles 85–92, The State Council
Section 6: Articles 93 and 94, The Central Military Commission
Sections 7 and 8: Articles 95–122, Local Government and National Autonomous Areas
Section 9: Articles 123–35, The People's Courts and People's Procuratorates
Section 10: Articles 136–38, National Flag, National Emblem and Capital

Of the state organs specified in the Constitution, the weakest is the presidency, which is largely ceremonial. The president is the head of state. The really efficient part of national government is the State Council (Guo Wu Yuan), which, according to the Constitution, is the executive body of the National People's Congress and the "highest organ of state administration." It is chaired by the premier, nominated by the Central Committee and approved by the National People's Congress, and includes a number of vice premiers, ministers in charge of ministries and ministers heading commissions. The premier of the State Council is the head of government. The functions of the State Council are defined as exercising "unified leadership" over the entire administration, including local governments. Most if not all of the ministries, commissions, bureaus and agencies attached to the State Council are represented in some or all provincial-level administrative units and in some cases county and commune-level units.

Although the functions and powers of the State Council are exceptionally broad, policy is largely determined by the Central Committee and Political Bureau, to both of which it is closely linked by concurrent memberships. This linkage facilitates the party's control over the state but at the same time obliterates the distinction between party and government.

The membership of the State Council has varied over the years, but the general trend has been toward a high degree of compartmentalization of jurisdictions, a topheavy hierarchical structure and multiplication of units. The council is divided into ministries, commissions, bureaus, agencies and departments. With the growing number of units it has become necessary to create intermediate offices between the state council and these units. Known as staff offices, they have supervisory responsibility over a group of related units. According to a high-ranking party leader, from 1950 to 1981 the number of ministries and commissions grew from 34 to 100, the number of ministries and deputy ministries to 1,000 and departments to 5,000. Under Deng this number has been cut back but still remains unwieldy.

The State Council rarely meets as a whole. The long-standing practice is for major decisions to be made by an inner cabinet known as the Standing Conference of the State Council (Kuo-wu-yuan ch'ang-wu hui-yi), which generally consists of 15 members, including the premier and four vice premiers.

Directly attached to the State Council is the General Office, which appears to be a housekeeping organ corresponding to the Secretariat of the Central Committee. In addition, a number of specialized offices, subordinate directly to the State Council, deal with diverse matters such as science, environmental protection and family planning.

FREEDOM & HUMAN RIGHTS

The major event affecting human rights in China in 1989 was the bloodbath in Tiananmen Square in Beijing in early 1989, which set the country back some 20 years in its evolution toward a less totalitarian government. The power struggle that preceded and followed this event has witnessed a leftward and more doctrinaire shift at the very apex of the power structure. The gradual relaxation of the political atmosphere that began with the ascent of Deng in the early 1980s has consequently slowed, and some of the gains made in this period have been lost.

CABINET LIST

President: Yang Shangkun
Vice President: Wang Zhen
Premier, State Council: Li Peng
Vice Premier, State Council: Yao Yilin
Vice Premier, State Council: Tian Jiyun
Vice Premier, State Council: Wu Xueqian
State Councilor, State Council: Chen Junsheng
State Councilor, State Council: Chen Xitong
State Councilor, State Council: Li Guixian
State Councilor, State Council: Li Tieying
State Councilor, State Council: Qin Jiwei
State Councilor, State Council: Song Jian
State Councilor, State Council: Wang Bingqian
State Councilor, State Council: Wang Fang
State Councilor, State Council: Zou Jiahua
Secretary General: Luo Gan
Auditor General of Auditing Admin.: Lü Peijian
Chmn., Central Military Commission: Deng Xiaoping
Minister in Charge of National Defense Sci., Tech., and Industry Commission: Ding Henggao
Minister in Charge of State Education Commission: Li Tieying
Minister in Charge of State Family Planning Commission: Peng Peiyun
Minister in Charge of State Nationalities Affairs Commission: Ismail Amat
Minister in Charge of State Physical Culture and Sports Commission: Wu Shaozu
Minister in Charge of State Planning Commission: Yao Yilin
Minister in Charge of State Restructuring of Economic System Commission: Li Peng
Minister in Charge of State Sci. and Tech. Commission: Song Jian
Minister of Aerospace Industry: Lin Zongtang
Minister of Agriculture: He Kang
Minister of Chemical Industry: Gu Xiulian
Minister of Civil Affairs: Cui Naifu
Minister of Commerce: Hu Ping
Minister of Communications: Qian Yongchang
Minister of Construction: Lin Hanxiong

CABINET LIST (continued)

Minister of Culture: He Jingzhi
Minister of Energy Resources: Huang Yicheng
Minister of Finance: Wang Bingqian
Minister of Foreign Affairs: Qian Qichen
Minister of Foreign Economic Relations and Trade: Zheng Tuobin
Minister of Forestry: Gao Dezhan
Minister of Geology and Mineral Resources: Zhu Xun
Minister of Justice: Cai Cheng
Minister of Labor: Ruan Chongwu
Minister of Light Industry: Zeng Xianlin
Minister of Machine-Building and Electronics Industry: Zou Jiahua
Minister of Materials: Liu Suinian
Minister of Metallurgical Industry: Qi Yuanjing
Minister of National Defense: Qin Jiwei
Minister of Personnel: Zhao Dongwan
Minister of Posts and Telecommunications: Yang Taifang
Minister of Public Health: Chen Minzhang
Minister of Public Security: Wang Fang
Minister of Radio, Cinema and Television: Ai Zhisheng
Minister of Railways: Li Senmao
Minister of State Security: Jia Chunwang
Minister of Supervision: Wei Jianxing
Minister of Textile Industry: Wu Wenying
Minister of Water Resources: Yang Zhenhuai
President, People's Bank of China: Li Guixian

RULERS OF CHINA*
Emperors (Manchu dynasty)

1616–26: Ying-ming (Nurhachu)
1626–43: T'ai Tsung (Abahai)
June 1644–February 1661: Shun Chih (Fu-lin) (Regents: 1644–50 Dorgan 1650–57 Jirgalang)
1662–1722: K'ang Hsi (Hsuan-yeh) (Regency council)
1722–1736: Yung Cheng (Yin-chen)
1736–95: Ch'ien Lung (Hung-li)
1796–September 1820: Chia Ch'ing (Yung-yen)
September 1820–February 1850: Tao Kuang (Min-ping)
February 1850–August 1861: Hsien Feng (Yi-chu)
August 1861–January 1875: T'ung Chih (Tsai-ch'un) (Regent: 1861–72 Tz'u-An/Tz'u-Hsi)
January 1875–November 1908: Kuang Hsi (Tsai-t'ien) (Regents: 1875–81 Tz'u-An/Tz'u-Hsi 1881–9 Tz'u-Hsi)
November 1908–January 1912: Hsuan T'ung (P'u-yi) (later Emperor of Manchukuo) (Regent: 1908–12 Prince Chun)

Presidents

Chairman of the Republic 1949–75. From 1975 to 1983 the post of president was abolished, the ceremonial functions of head of state being conducted by the chairman of the Standing Committee of the National People's Congress.

January–February 1912: Sun Yat-sen
February 1912–June 1916: Yuan Shih-k'ai
June 1916–August 1917: Li Yuan-hung
August–September 1917: Feng Kuo-chang
September 1917–June 1922: Hsu Shih-ch'ang
June 1922–June 1923: Li Yuan-hung
October 1923–November 1924: Ts'ao K'un
November 1924–April 1926: Tuan Ch'i-jui
April 1926–June 1927: Post vacant
June 1927–June 1928: Chang Tso-lin
October 1928–December 1931: Chiang Kai-shek (Chiang Chung-cheng)
December 1931–January 1932: Ch'eng Ming Hsu
January 1932–May 1943: Lin Sen
May 1943–January 1949: Chiang Kai-shek
January–September 1949: Li Tsung-jen (acting)

RULERS OF CHINA* (continued)

October 1949–April 1959: Mao Tse-tung (Mao Zedong)
April 1959–October 1968: Liu Shao-chi
October 1968–January 1975: Tung Pi-wu (acting)
January 1975–July 1976: Chu Teh
July 1976–March 1978: Soong Ching-ling (acting)
March 1978–June 1983: Ye Jianying (Yeh Chien-ying)
June 1983–April 1988: Li Hsien-nien (Li Xiannian)
April 1988– : Yang Shangkun

Prime Ministers
Premier of the State Council since 1949

1901–3: Jung Lu
1903–October 1911: Prince Ch'ing
October 1911–January 1912: Yuan Shih-k'ai
February–June 1912: Tang Shao-yi
June–July 1912: Lu Cheng-hsiang
July 1912–March 1913: Chao Ping-chun
March 1913–14: Sun Pao-ch'i
1914–April 1916: Hsu Shih-chang
April 1916–May 1917: Tuan Ch'i-jui
July 1917: Chang Hsuin
July 1917–November 1918: Tuan Ch'i-jui
November 1918–June 1919: Ch'ien Neng-hsuin
June–September 1919: Kung Hsin-chan
September 1919–May 1920: Chin Yun-p'eng
May–August 1920: Sa Chen-ping
August 1920–December 1921: Chin Yun P'eng
December 1921–January 1922: Liang Shih-yi
January–April 1922: Yen Hui-ching (W. W. Yen)
April–June 1922: Chou Tzu-ch'i
June–August 1922: Yen Hui-ching
August–September 1922: T'ang Shao-yi
September–November 1922: Wang Ch'ung-hui
November–December 1922: Wang Ta-hsieh
December 1922–January 1923: Wang Cheng-t'ing
January–June 1923: Chang Shao-ts'eng
June 1923–January 1924: Kao Ling-wei
January–July 1924: Sun Pao-ch'i
July–September 1924: Ku Wei-chun (Wellington Koo)
September–October 1924: Yen Hui-ch'ing
November 1924–November 1925: Huang Fu
November–December 1925: Tuan Ch'i-jui
December 1925–February 1926: Hsu Shih-ying
February–April 1926: Chia Teh-yao
April–May 1926: Hu Wei-te
May–June 1926: Yen Hui-ch'ing
June–October 1926: Tu Hsi-kua
October 1926–April 1927: Ku Wei-chun
April–June 1927: Chiang Kai-shek
June 1927–October 1928: Pan Fu
October 1928–September 1930: Tan Yen-k'ai
September–November 1930: Sung Tsu-wen (T. V. Soong) (acting)
December 1930–December 1931: Chiang Kai-shek
December 1931–January 1932: Sun Fo
January 1932–December 1935: Wang Ching-wei
December 1935–December 1937: Chiang Kai-shek
December 1937–January 1938: Wang Ch'ung-hui (acting)
January 1938–November 1939: K'ung Hsiang-hsi
November 1939–December 1944: Chiang Kai-shek
December 1944–March 1947: Sung Tsu-wen
March–April 1947: Chiang Kai-shek (acting)
April 1947–May 1948: Chung Ch'un
May–November 1948: Wong Wen-hao
November 1948–March 1949: Sun Fo
March–June 1949: Ho Ying-ch'in
June–September 1949: Yen Hsi-shan

RULERS OF CHINA (continued)

October 1949–January 1976: Chou En-lai
February 1976–September 1980: Hua Kuo-feng (Hua Guofeng) (acting February–April 1976)
September 1980–November 1987: Chiao Tzu-yang (Zhao Ziyang)
November 1987– : Li Peng

Communist Party Leaders
Chairman of the Central Committee 1949–82
  General Secretary since 1982

October 1949–September 1976: Mao Tse-tung (Mao Zedong)
October 1976–June 1981: Hua Kuo-feng (Hua Guofeng)
June 1981–January 1987: Hu Yao-pang (Hu Yaobang)
January 1987–June 1989: Chiao Tzu-yang (Zhao Ziyang)
June 1989– : Chiang Tse-Min

Chairman, Military Affairs Committee (effective leader)
June 1981–December 1989: Teng Hsiao-ping (Deng Xiaoping)
December 1989– : vacant

Opposing Government 1917–27
SOUTH CHINA
Capital: Canton
Sun Yat-sen established a government in Canton that disappeared in 1927.

Presidents
August 1917–March 1925: Sun Yat-sen
March 1925–27: Hu Han-min

Secessionist State 1932–45
MANCHUKUO
Capital: Mukden
Head of State
March 1932–March 1934: P'u-Yi (*f.* Emperor of China)
Emperor
March 1934–May 1945: Kang Teh (*b.* P'u-yi)
Prime Minister
January 1932–May 1935: Chang Hsiao-hsin
May 1935–May 1945: Chang Ching-hui

Former Independent State
TIBET
Capital: Lhasa
Kings
1642–55: Gusri
1655–68: Daya Khan
1668–97: Tenzin Dalai Khan Regent: 1679–1729 Sange Gyatso
1697–1720: Lhabzang Khan
1720–28: Chinese occupation
1728–47: Phola Sonam Tobgye
1747–50: Gyurme

Rulers
(The first date is the date of birth. Enthronement dates are given in parentheses.)

1708 (1750)–1757: Kelzang Gyatso (7th Dalai Lama)
1758–1804: Jampal Gyatso (8th Dalai Lama)
1806–15: Lungtok Gyatso (9th Dalai Lama)
1816–37: Tsultrim Gyatso (10th Dalai Lama)
1838 (March 1855)–1856: Khendrup Gyaltso (11th Dalai Lama)
1856 (1873)–1875: Trinley Gyatso (12th Dalai Lama)
1876 (October 1895)–December 1933: Thubten Gyatso (13th Dalai Lama)

*Names are romanized following the Wade-Giles system.

RULERS OF CHINA *(continued)*

1935 (November 1950)–March 1959: Tenzin Gyatso (*b*. Lhamo Tontrop) (14th Dalai Lama)

March 1959–September 1965: Chokyi Gyaltsen (6th Panchen Lama)

Regents

1757–77: Demo Trulku Jampel Delek
1777–April 1791: Tsemoling Ngawang Tsultrim
1791–1810: Tenpai Gonpo Kindeling
1811–19: Demo Thubten Jigme
1819–September 1844: Jampel Tsultrim Tsemoling

Regents

1844–May 1845: Administrator: Tenpai Nyima (4th Panchen Lama)
May 1845–62: Yeshe Gyatso Rating
1864–73: Khenrab Wangchuk Dedrug
1875–86: Choskyi Gyaltsen Kundeling
1886–95: Demo Trinley Rabgyas
1895–1913: Ganden Tripa Tsemoling Rimpoche
1913–33: Rule by Dalai Lama
January 1934–February 1941: Rating Rimpoche (*b*. Jampal Yeshe)
February 1941–November 1950: Taktra Rimpoche Ngawang Sungrab

Prime Ministers

1862–September 1864: Wangchuk Gyalpo Shatra
1864–1907: Post abolished
1907–20: Changkhyim
1907–23: Paljor Dorje Shatra
1907–26: Sholkhang
1926–50: Langdun
1950–April 1952: Lozang Tashi/Lukhangwa

This setback illustrates the fundamental weakness in China's so-called political modernization program. There is an entrenched intolerance of any criticism of the CCP and its aging leadership. Change can only be initiated at the top and then trickle down to the bottom rather than vice versa. The rigidity of institutional structures is as old as Chinese society, and it has been reinforced by the harshness of Marxist dogma. The official intolerance of dissent also was underscored by the violent suppression in late 1987 and also in March 1988 and in December 1988 of demonstrations in Tibet against Han Chinese dominance. At least five people died and one Han Chinese police officer was killed during these incidents. Disappearances, common during the Cultural Revolution, have become rarer, but at least one incident was reported recently, of the disappearance of Xu Yongze, an itinerant Christian evangelist.

The Code of Criminal Procedure specifically prohibits the use of torture. In 1986 China signed the U.N. Convention Against Torture and Other Cruel, Inhuman or Degrading Treatment, and the National People's Congress ratified the Convention in 1988. But news reports of the use of torture by officials persist. However, the government continues to publicize and condemn cases of such activity and to take actions against their perpetrators. Sometimes persons convicted of serious crimes are subjected to public humiliation at "mass sentencing rallies" or by parading them through the streets. No public executions, however, have been held since 1980. Little information is available on conditions inside Chinese prisons.

The law on arrest and detention conforms to accepted norms in democratic countries. According to it, interrogation should take place within 24 hours of detention, and the detainee's family or work unit should be informed of the reasons therefor and of the place of detention. The Public Security Bureau must submit a request for formal arrest to a procuratorate within three to four days of detention, and the procuratorate must approve the application for arrest or have the detainee released within three days. Thus a detainee may be held for not more than 10 days prior to formal arrest. The period for detention during investigation after formal arrest is four months, and the time limit for trials 45 days. Since 1984, accused persons may be granted bail if they are not considered dangerous.

The law notwithstanding, persons accused of political crimes are often held for periods much longer than those sanctioned by the code. The provision requiring immediate notification of families or work units also is frequently ignored, and suspects are held incommunicado for long periods.

Under "labor education" provisions, those who commit minor theft or fraud or who have been expelled from their work units may be deprived of their civil liberties and subjected to one to four years of reform without trial. "Reform through labor" is a more severe sentence, similar to Soviet "internal exile" and imposed on those accused of more serious crimes. Offenders are often transferred to labor camps in remote areas in Xinjiang and Qinghai and are often denied permission to return to their homes even after they have completed their sentence. In addition, several forms of administrative detention were noted in Amnesty International's 1987 report titled "China: Torture and Ill-Treatment of Prisoners." Under one form, people may be detained for up to 15 days for minor public-order offenses. Under another form, known as "shelter and investigation," accused persons may be detained indefinitely for minor offenses if they have no known legal address or occupation.

There are no standing special political or security courts. The judiciary is subject to party controls enforced through political-legal committees, which may intervene in trials to secure party interests in important criminal cases. The courts function under the assumption that a person is guilty until proven innocent. Trials are essentially sentencing hearings in which the defense does not contest the charges but only pleads for mercy. Trials are preceded by extensive pretrial investigations carried out by the Public Security Bureau and the procurator. The law guarantees the right to counsel, but the defense attorney normally does not enter the case until just prior to trial. Only in less than 2% of the cases are the accused found innocent. Defendants in criminal cases have the right of appeal, but in doing so they increase their chances of a more severe sentence. According to the Criminal Procedure Code, all trials not involving state security are held in public. But such attendance requires an admission ticket, which may be withheld at official discretion.

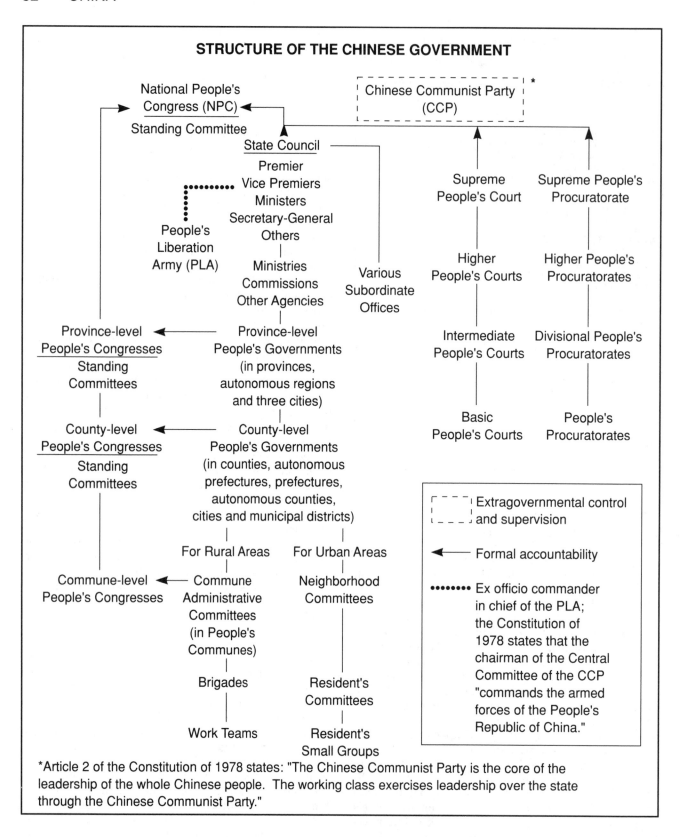

STRUCTURE OF THE CHINESE GOVERNMENT

*Article 2 of the Constitution of 1978 states: "The Chinese Communist Party is the core of the leadership of the whole Chinese people. The working class exercises leadership over the state through the Chinese Communist Party."

The regime denies that there are any political prisoners, but this is only a semantic subterfuge, since "counterrevolutionaries" are classified as common criminals. Counterrevolutionary activity is defined as "inciting the overthrow of the socialist system." The total prison population is estimated at 2 million to 5 million, and of this total 1% to 3% are political prisoners according to Western standards.

As in prerepublican China, personal and family life are extensively regulated by state and society. In urban areas, life revolves around the work unit, which not only provides employment but also often controls housing, ration coupons and permission to marry and have a child. The work unit, along with personnel in neighborhood committees, monitors a person's attitude and behavior. The unit implements party policies at the local level, but its considerable autonomy also may be used to ignore or obstruct directives from the top. Recent economic reforms, however, have weakened the unit's interference in many aspects of social life. Family planning was an area where draconian measures to limit the number of children per family to one offered much scope for arbitrary official actions. Local officials sometimes coerced women who had become pregnant without permission into having abortions. However, official policy does not permit or condone forced abortions or sterilizations.

Contacts between Chinese and foreigners had become free of official interference until the Tiananmen Square demonstrations brought a deterioration in the political climate. "English corners" where Chinese and foreigners can meet to talk in English attract large numbers of people.

The Code of Criminal Procedure allows officials wide latitude in emergency situations to enter and search living premises without warrants or notifications, use electronic eavesdropping, and to seize mail or telegrams, although these powers are used sparingly.

The gap between law and practice is nowhere wider than in relation to freedom of speech and press. Prohibition in the constitutional Preamble of criticism of the CCP or socialism takes precedence over the clause in the same Constitution providing for both freedoms. As a result of this contradiction, official policy is punctuated by periodical campaigns against so-called press excesses. In such a climate, press freedom has not been able to take roots. The bolder editors and authors who cross the bounds of officially permitted criticism are labeled as bourgeois and expelled from the party or jailed. There is a strong distrust of intellectuals among the party leadership and periods of thaw alternate with stifling constraints on intellectual freedom. Under General Secretary Zhao Ziyang of the CCP there was an attempt to remove some of the straitjackets under which Chinese culture languished, but with the rise of the hard-liners after Tiananmen, these programs have been quickly dismantled. Although more foreign books and artistic works are now available, they still are screened by authorities. More foreign films are shown on television, but most of them are politically neutral and uncontroversial. Foreign periodicals are not available in newsstands but are available to subscribers in educational institutions. Coverage of foreign news in the open media is quite extensive and professional. Chinese citizens may freely listen to foreign broadcasts, and millions do turn to the Voice of America and even Christian shortwave stations to learn or brush up on their English. Here again official policy appears erratic; foreign correspondents are invited at one time and ordered out at other times.

In violation of the constitutional provisions of freedom of assembly, municipal ordinances have been passed limiting citizens' rights to participate in marches and demonstrations by requiring application in advance and proscribing certain areas. The Tiananmen demonstration in 1989 was the acid test of the limits of government tolerance of demonstrations, and it has left a negative legacy in its wake. Similarly, the government has adopted a repressive attitude to demonstrations in Lhasa. In general, the regime feels threatened by the actual exercise of the right of freedom of assembly.

After the excesses of the Cultural Revolution, freedom of religion was one of the major freedoms to be resuscitated. Although atheism is part of the official ideology, its enforcement and propagation have met with much resistance in a culture historically permeated with religious mores. Current religious policy rests on the assumption that "it will take patient, meticulous and repeated education over a long period of time to weaken religious influence. Religion cannot be completely abolished." Such a benign attitude is more in tune with the Constitution, under whose provisions no institution or person may compel citizens to believe or disbelieve in religion or discriminate against them because of religious preference. The only major requirement is that religious bodies must not be subject to foreign domination, a proviso often used against Buddhism in Tibet and against the Catholic Church. Religious policy also forbids proselytization other than at places of worship and religious indoctrination of children by parents. However, this provision is loosely implemented, and there are no known cases of conviction under its authority.

All religious bodies are required to be affiliated with one of eight national organizations. Three of them represent the Catholic Church; two Protestant; and Buddhism, Islam and Taoism one each. The Catholic Church, however, is quite different from the universal church of that name under the authority of the Holy See. It is a Chinese national church that rejects papal infallibility and supremacy, has no ecclesastical links with Rome and supports the state policy of birth control.

Religious activities have expanded considerably in recent years, and many religious institutions closed during the Cultural Revolution have reopened. In 1988 over 30,000 churches, temples, monasteries and mosques held public worship. Officials also acknowledge the existence of a vast underground Christian church meeting in private homes. However, there is a pressing shortage of priests, ministers, monks and imams because the older generation is not being replaced by new entrants fast enough. The government also limits the number of new clergy and controls their appointments. Tibet is a special case because there are 14,000 officially approved monks and several times that number of unofficial monks, who although they live in monasteries are supported by their families. Since 1981 the authorities have permitted the establishment of seminaries to train a limited number of young people in religious orders. The Catholics run 10, Protestants nine (excluding the National Theological Institute at Nanjing), Muslims nine and Buddhists 20.

The religious associations sponsor a variety of publications for believers, including scriptures, teaching materials, theological journals and hymnbooks. Since 1980 the Protestant China Christian Council has printed and distributed over 3 million Bibles, and Xinhua, the official bookstore network, also distributes them.

Statistics present a problem in Communist China in many areas, and religion is no exception. The number of Christians is estimated from 8 million (5 million Protestants and 3 million Catholics) to 20 million, the number of Muslims at 15 million and the number of Buddhists at 10 million. The degree of error in these counts probably is very high; nevertheless, the fact that they run into millions attests to the existence of a fairly liberal religious policy, unusual for an orthodox Marxist country.

Religious freedom, however, still is not a right, but a gift of the state, and it may be withdrawn at any time. The regime does not tolerate unsanctioned religious activity, defined as "counterrevolutionary sabotage perpetrated in the name of religion." A recent example is the crackdown on Buddhist monks following political disturbances and the placing of security personnel in the major monasteries. Another target of official displeasure is the network of house churches, in which Christians outside the "patriotic church system" worship. Itinerant evangelists are harassed, and unofficial religious organizations are prohibited. In 1983 the death penalty was authorized for secret sects that spread "feudal and superstitious ideas," a broad rubric aimed at curbing any kind of religious zeal.

Although the regime continues to be concerned over divided loyalties of believers, contacts between Chinese religious leaders and their foreign coreligionists have expanded in recent years. Catholic bishops have been permitted to travel overseas and establish contacts with church officials. Billy Graham visited China in 1988 at the invitation of the official China Christian Council and spoke to Chinese congregations in Beijing and Shanghai and at a house church at Guangzhou. Muslims have been permitted to make the hajj since 1979. In addition, Chinese religious organizations are permitted to receive funds and gifts from abroad if no strings are attached to them. The government, however, remains wary of overt foreign involvement in Chinese religious affairs smacking of patronage. Missionaries are prohibited from working qua missionaries, but they may work as teachers of English and other disciplines as long as they do not engage in proselytizing. Occasionally, minor infractions of this injunction are overlooked as a gesture of goodwill. In the past, the authorities were particularly unhappy with the Vatican because of its diplomatic ties with Taiwan. Chinese priests who publicly maintain their loyalty to the pope are subject to arrest and imprisonment. Since the onset of a more liberal religious policy, many Catholic bishops imprisoned for their loyalty to the pope have been released. Chinese hostility to the Dalai Lama has not diminished with the years, particularly because he is regarded as a symbol of Tibetan nationalism.

Travel within China is restricted through various formal and informal regulations. Chinese citizens must have a written letter of introduction from their work unit to buy airplane tickets, secure hotel accommodations or acquire ration coupons for purchase of some basic foodstuffs outside their place of residence. Those who travel by train and plan to stay with relatives need not obtain such letters of introduction but still are legally required to register with the local police during their visits. In practice, however, many Chinese do not comply with these regulations. To curb such widespread noncompliance, the authorities instituted in April 1985 the first nationwide identity card system, which came into full effect in 1989. These cards must be presented whenever a citizen transacts business at a bank or post office, buys an airplane ticket or checks in at a hotel. Residents of Hainan Province and the four special economic zones are issued color-coded ID cards as a step to control unauthorized migration to those areas.

Chinese citizens may not freely change their locality of residence or workplace. They are registered as residents of a particular jurisdiction, and permission to move to another locality is granted only for a change in employment. Because of the unwillingness of work units to lose employees, such permission is rarely granted. As a result, there is virtually no labor mobility except for workers under the labor contract system, who may hire themselves out for three to five years anywhere in the country. Some steps have been taken recently to give professionals such as scientists and technicians greater mobility. Despite official restrictions, significant number of farmers are moving into small and medium-size cities as well as the larger ones. The number of unregistered residents is estimated at 1 million in Shanghai and 700,000 in Beijing.

Control on foreign travel and emigration have been relaxed since the 1970s and was further liberalized under the Citizens' Exit and Entry Control Law of 1985, which went into effect in 1986. The law authorizes exit for personal reasons but denies exit to those in criminal or civil cases or those whose exit may harm China's national security interests. Permission to travel may also be denied to the more vocal critics of the regime and to known dissidents. Restrictions on internal travel by foreigners also have been relaxed. Over 500 cities and other areas now are open to foreign visitors without special permission. Large areas in China still remain officially closed to outsiders, particularly in sensitive border regions.

According to the Constitution, the government grants asylum to political refugees. Included in this category are some 300,000 Vietnamese and Laotians of Chinese descent. Because of the current hostile relations between Vietnam and China, ethnic Vietnamese refugees have not been granted the right to resettle in China.

Although China has taken giant steps in recent years toward a more democratic polity, it still is by no means a democracy. The regime's leaders are orthodox Marxists to whom the concept of a pluralist state is anathema. Political dynamics are guided by the Leninist doctrine of "democratic centralism," which means that all decisions are made by the top leadership or major faction within that leadership and must be implicitly obeyed by the party's rank and file as well as by the population at large. The key political virtues are loyalty, unity and obedience. Policy ambiguities may be manipulated by lower-level functionaries, but by and large official pronouncements and directives are sacrosanct and immune from criticism. The major forum for debate is the National People's Congress (NPC). The NPC is a rubber stamp and rarely rejects proposed government policies or programs, although a few have been modified in deference to the expressed concerns of its delegates. The State Council and the Standing Committee of the Politburo also may join issue on the merits of some policy. Factional politics within the Communist Party provide the only source of radical breaks in policy, and, in the absence of a genuine opposition, factions function as the only alternative choices for the party faithful.

Chinese students, however, are of a different breed and have taken to the streets and squares in large numbers in the late 1980s. For 18 momentous days, from April 17 to June 5, 1989, over 1 million students poured into Tiananmen Square in Beijing in one of the most massive demonstrations in Chinese history, demanding greater democracy and the ouster of Deng and other aging party leaders. In a dramatic gesture, they erected a large statue of the Goddess of Democracy, resembling the Statue of Liberty in New York Harbor. The response of the regime, in which the hard-liners soon gained the ascendancy, was brutal and violent. Martial law was declared, detachments of the People's Liberation Army were called in and hundreds of demonstrators were killed before peace was restored. Subsequently, Zhao Ziyang, the party general secretary and leader of the moderate faction, was dismissed.

Given the government policy of repressing dissent, there are no known organizations within China monitoring human rights. Several legal journals debate questions having to do with the rights of the accused, etc., in a purely academic fashion. Generally, the Chinese government treats human rights as an internal issue and resents foreign concerns in this area. They react defensively to attempts by foreign journalists to see at firsthand conditions in places like Tibet, where human rights have suffered considerable erosion.

Although gender equality is one of the key tenets of the Communist party, women have gained few breakthroughs in the male-dominated political establishment in the past half century. In 1989 none of the 17 members of the Politburo was female, and of the 175-member Central Committee, only 10 are women. There are two women among 41 ministers and commission directors. Of the government cadres, 28.5% are women, and of the delegates to the 13th Party Congress in 1987, 14.9% were women. Of the provincial governors, only one is a woman. Not only is there an absence of equality, but also open discrimination persists in key areas of national life. Even though the share of women in the professions has increased since 1949, it is nowhere close to parity. Women are considered more expensive as employees because of maternity pay and other statutory allowances, and also less productive over the long haul. Female participation in the work force is 43.7% (compared to 7.5% in 1950), but they are concentrated in the lower-paying and less-prestigious jobs. In 1988 some 28% of university students were female. At the same time, of the 200 million illiterates, some 70% are women.

The regime has pursued an enlightened policy toward minorities. They benefit from special treatment in marriage and family planning, employment and university admission. Although only Tibet has a non-Han majority, other autonomous areas are also treated as if they had a non-Han majority. The 1984 Law on Regional Autonomy for Minorities provides that heads of government in these regions and their prefectures and counties must be members of the chief local minority. Their cultural rights are constitutionally guaranteed. Nevertheless, minority representation in the central government is far below their share of the population, and they are virtually excluded from leadership positions. The standard of living of most minorities remains substantially below that of the Han Chinese. The Tibetans have been the worst affected by the failure of the government to respect minority rights in practice. Although the Han Chinese constitute only 3% of the population in the Tibet Autonomous Region, they make up 40% of all government cadre, 40% of regional department heads, 38% of university students and 60% of factory managers.

CIVIL SERVICE

The cadre (ganbu) is the Chinese equivalent of the civil service system in other countries. The term refers to a public official holding a responsible or managerial position in various official or party institutions. He or she may or may not be a member of the party, although only party members are appointed to sensitive positions. Cadres are divided into leading and ordinary, and both these groups are divided again into technical, party and government. As a rule, all cadres are expected to be both "red" and "expert"—i.e., loyal to the party as well as skilled in the appropriate profession. Considerable criticism of the cadres appears periodically in the Chinese media, many of which are common to the bureaucracies of other countries. They refer to poor cadre performance caused by an inflexible seniority system, mistrust of new ideas, dilatoriness, arrogance, lack of discipline, sloth and favoritism. Another problem associated with the lifetime tenure of most cadres is senility, as aging bureaucrats cling to their offices until they are physically incapacitated.

No accurate counts of cadres exist. Public employees numbered 720,000 in 1949. In 1980 the number of cadres was officially placed at 18 million without further elaboration. Leading cadres were estimated at "several hundred thousand." No information is available on Civil Service codes or recruitment of lower level civil servants.

LOCAL GOVERNMENT

On the whole, the Communist regime has adopted without substantial change the previous local government divisions. Except for territorial adjustments, most of the provinces, municipalities and counties remain as they were before 1949. There are, however, two important innovations: the organization of the people's communes on or below the county level; and the establishment of minority nationality areas, consisting of autonomous regions, districts and counties.

The present system of local government is described in the Constitution of 1982 and in local government laws. Article 30 of the Constitution provides for the administrative division of the country into provinces, autonomous regions and municipalities directly under the central government; provinces and autonomous regions into prefectures, counties and cities; and counties into townships, nationality townships and towns.

With the promulgation of the Constitution of 1954, organs of administration were formally established at all subnational levels. Regional and local people's councils (*jen-min tai paio ta-hui*), directly elected on the *hsiang* (township) and *ch'u* (city district) levels, appointed the people's government council (*jen-min cheng-fu wei-yuan-hui*) of their respective units and elected delegates for the *hsien* (county) people's assembly. These in turn appointed the people's government council of the *hsien* and elected delegates to the provincial people's council.

These structures, however, broke down during the Cultural Revolution, when revolutionary committees (*ke-ming wei-yuan-hui*) replaced the people's councils at all levels. These committees were theoretically supposed to represent the revolutionary trinity: *keming san-chieh-he*, Maoist mass organizations; revolutionary cadres; and the PLA. In fact, PLA soldiers and generals dominated all revolutionary committees. By 1980 all revolutionary committees passed from the scene and were replaced by the 1954 organs. The Regional and Local Government Law of 1979 reestablished the people's councils and also renamed their heads as governors (*sheng-chang*) in the case of provinces, mayors (*shih-chang*) in the case of cities and chairmen of the people's government (*jen-min cheng-fu chu-hsi*) in the case of autonomous regions. These provisions were reconfirmed by the Constitution of 1982, which lays down terms of office for the people's councils of five years on the provincial level and three years on the *hsien* and *hsiang* levels. It also provided for direct election of the congresses to the *hsien* level by secret ballot.

The 29 administrative units on the provincial level include 21 provinces (*sheng*); the three municipalities (centrally administered cities) (*chih-hsia-shih*) of Shanghai, Beijing and Tianjin; and the five autonomous regions (*tzu-chih-ch'u*) of Xinjiang Uygur, Xizang, Ningxia Hui, Guangxi Zhuang and Nei Menggu, the home of the Uygurs, Tibetans, Hui, Zhuang and Mongols, respectively.

Between the provincial and the *hsien* levels, administrative entities without congresses have been established. There are 208 of these units: one administrative area (*hsing-cheng-ch'u*) on Hainan Island, eight leagues (*meng*) in Inner Mongolia, 29 autonomous areas (*tzu-chih-chou*) and 170 areas (*ti-ch'u*).

On the local administrative level there are 2,772 units, including three autonomous banners (*tzu-chih-ch'i*), 53 banners (*ch'i*), 71 autonomous *hsien* (*tzu-chih-hsien*), 431 city districts (*ch'u*), 214 provincially or area-administered cities (*shih*) and 2,000 regular *hsien*. On this level as well as on the *hsiang* level, the party

ADMINISTRATIVE DIVISIONS OF CHINA*			
Province	Prefectures	Counties	Cities
Hebei	10	139	9
Shanxi	7	101	7
Liaoning	3	53	11
Jilin	5	48	10
Heilongjiang	9	76	13
Shandong	9	106	9
Jiangsu	7	64	11
Zhejiang	8	65	3
Anhui	9	70	11
Jiangxi	6	82	8
Fujian	7	61	6
Henan	10	111	14
Hunan	11	90	10
Hubei	8	73	6
Guangdong	9	97	11
Shaanxi	7	92	5
Gansu	10	74	4
Qinghai	7	38	1
Sichuan	14	181	11
Guizhou	7	79	5
Yunnan	15	122	4
Autonomous Regions			
Guangxi Zhuang	8	80	6
Xinjiang Uygur	13	80	7
Nei Monggol (Inner Mongolia)	4	43	5
Xizang (Tibet)	5	71	1
Ningxia Hui	2	17	2
Municipalities			
Beijing		9	
Shanghai		10	
Tianjin		5	
TOTAL	210	2137	190

Source: Adapted from *Beijing Review*, no. 20 (1979), p. 23.

*These divisions are as of the end of 1978, and the table has not included the number of communes in each province.

wields tight control. The *hsien* magistrates, *shih* mayors, *hsiang* magistrates and village chiefs are, in almost all cases, members of their respective party committees. The exact number of *hsiang* and *chen* (country towns) is estimated as 55,000 to 60,000. The number of the lowest administrative units in the countryside—the administrative villages (*hsing-cheng-ts'un*)—probably is 700,000 to 750,000.

The structure of local government is based on that of the national government. As presently constituted, the local people's congresses suffer from the same problems as the National People's Congress. The number of deputies is too large, ranging up to 1,000, and the standing committees also are large, with an average membership of 50 to 60, most of them far advanced in age. Moreover, deputies to local people's congresses are elected in name only; most of them are coopted from other fields, such as the theater, sports, engineering or teaching. Membership on the standing committee is a reward for veteran party members. Consequently there is a high rate of absenteeism on the standing committees. Moreover, Chinese press reports reveal utter confusion in the absence of constitutional guidelines on the division of legislative authority among the various units of local government. Finally, local government organs are fifth wheels without any real power and hence burdened with a sense of superfluity. "The party has already made its decisions. Why should we go through the motions of debating them?" is a common complaint at local assemblies. Exceptions to this aura of powerlessness are the municipal people's congresses in Beijing and Shanghai, where most of China's highly skilled people are concentrated. The activities of the deputies in these two cities receive national attention. Their organization also is as extensive as that at the national level, with special sub-

committees in charge of law, finance, urban planning, etc. Since 1980, local legislation also has become increasingly comprehensive and wide-ranging.

A second noteworthy development, which took place in 1980–81, is the direct election by rural residents of deputies to county people's congresses. Before that only deputies to township (or commune) people's congresses were directly elected, and township deputies, in turn, elected deputies to county people's congresses from their own members. Although hailed as a measure to enhance democratic processes at the county level, these elections, like the others, are orchestrated by local Communist Party branches, with predictable results.

The executive arm of local government is known as the people's government. The Constitution states: "Local people's government at different levels are the exec-

POLITICAL SUBDIVISIONS

Provinces	Capitals	Area		Population (1986 est.)
		Sq. Km.	Sq. Mi.	
Anhwei (Anhui)	Ho-fei (Hefei)	139,900	54,000	51,560,000
Chekiang (Zhejiang)	Hangchow (Hangzhou)	101,800	39,300	40,300,000
Fukien (Fujian)	Foochow (Fuzhou)	123,100	47,500	27,130,000
Heilungkiang (Heilongjiang)	Harbin (Harbin)	463,600	179,000	33,110,000
Honan (Henan)	Cheng-chou (Zhengzhou)	167,000	64,500	77,130,000
Hopeh (Hebei)	Shih-chia-chuang (Shijiazhuang)	202,700	78,200	55,480,000
Hunan (Hunan)	Ch'ang-sha (Changsha)	210,500	81,300	56,220,000
Hupeh (Hubei)	Wu-han (Wuhan)	187,500	72,400	49,310,000
Kansu (Gansu)	Lan-chou (Lanzhou)	366,500	141,500	20,410,000
Kiangsi (Jiangxi)	Nan-ch'ang (Nanchang)	164,800	63,600	34,600,000
Kiangsu (Jiangsu)	Nanking (Nanjing)	102,600	39,600	62,130,000
Kirin (Jilin)	Ch'ang-ch'un (Changchun)	187,000	72,200	22,980,000
Kwangtung (Guangdong)	Canton (Guangzhou)	231,400	89,300	62,530,000
Kweichow (Guizhou)	Kuei-yang (Guiyang)	174,000	67,200	29,680,000
Liaoning (Liaoning)	Shen-yang (Shenyang)	151,000	58,300	36,860,000
Shansi (Shanxi)	T'ai-yüan (Taiyuan)	157,100	60,700	26,270,000
Shantung (Shandong)	Tsinan (Jinan)	153,300	59,200	76,950,000
Shensi (Shaanxi)	Sian (Xi'an)	195,800	75,600	30,020,000
Szechwan (Sichuan)	Ch'eng-tu (Chengdu)	569,000	219,700	101,880,000
Tsinghai (Qinghai)	Hsi-ning (Xining)	721,000	278,400	4,070,000
Yunnan (Yunnan)	K'un-ming (Kunming)	436,200	168,400	34,060,000
Autonomous Regions				
Inner Mongolia (Nei Monggol)	Hu-ho-hao-t'e (Hohhot)	1,177,500	454,600	20,070,000
Kwangsi Chuang (Guangxi Zhuang)	Nan-ning (Nanning)	220,400	85,100	38,730,000
Ningsia Hui (Ningxia Hui)	Yin-ch'uan (Yinchuan)	66,400	25,600	4,150,000
Sinkiang Uighur (Xinjiang Uygur)	Urumchi (Urumqi)	1,646,900	635,900	13,610,000
Tibet (Xizang)	Lhasa (Lhasa)	1,221,600	471,700	1,990,000
Municipalities				
Peking (Beijing)	—	16,800	6,500	9,600,000
Shanghai (Shanghai)	—	6,200	2,400	12,170,000
Tientsin (Tianjin)	—	11,300	4,400	8,080,000
TOTAL		9,572,900	3,696,100	1,045,320,000

utive bodies of local organs of state power as well as the local organs of state administration at the corresponding level." This is the "dual subordination" principle enshrined in Communist political theory. Thus in actual practice local government is dominated primarily by the party, secondarily by the central government and thirdly by the bureaucracy. Invariably a Communist Party functionary is either the top executive or his deputy; in the latter case, the deputy wields the real power.

Given the centralized administration and the economy, there is little scope for local autonomy. Because of their abject dependence on central largess and directions, there is great disparity among the provinces in the amount of development funds and manpower. The local bureaucracy also is centrally oriented, creating structures parallel to the national government, even to the point of unnecessary duplication. Much of local politics is concerned with meeting the demands of the central bureaucracy rather than representing and securing local interests.

Official efforts to improve governmental performance at the local level have included strengthening standing committees of local people's congresses at and above the county level; institution of multiple candidacies in elections to local people's congresses; and reactivation of "basic-level mass autonomous organizations" such as urban neighborhood committees, people's mediation committees and public security committees.

FOREIGN POLICY

Chinese foreign policy history exhibits a number of dichotomies and contradictions. China is a superpower without formal superpower status, it is a socialist country that does not belong to the socialist camp and it is a developing country that does not belong to the Third World proper. Reflecting the factional struggles within the party inner leadership, the policy also suffers from sudden shifts and breaks, as a result of which it lacks the consistency, coherence and predictability of the foreign policies of other major powers. Such fluctuations reflect the fact that China has no urgent goals to achieve in foreign affairs, and foreign policy is merely an extension of internal political developments. The contradictions in international relations stem from the theory of contradictions that Mao often employed to interpret society and revolution in China, and they also hark back to the *yin* and *yang* philosophy embedded in the Chinese mind, in which harmony and struggle are but different phases of the same process. Thus advance alternates with retreats, peace with violence and growth with decline. Viewed in this light, Chinese foreign policy has a coherence that often escapes the casual observer.

Since 1949 China has gone through several phases of foreign policy, each with its own salient themes. From 1949 to Stalin's death in 1953 China adopted a policy in Mao's words of "leaning to one side"—the Soviet side. In the first flush of the revolution, the new regime considered itself the harbinger and model of a series of

revolutions that would sweep the world. As the standard-bearer of the global revolution, it adopted a posture of belligerence, chauvinism and xenophobia that actually predated Marxism and harked back to the Manchu days. The United States was the object of Mao's unremitting hostility, particularly after China was drawn ineluctably into open hostilities in the Korean War and the United States brought Taiwan within its defense shield. The Korean War cost China dearly in men and equipment and also delayed its entrance into the United Nations, in which it was dubbed an aggressor in that war.

From 1953 Chinese foreign policy increasingly veered away from a dogmatic insistence on armed struggle and deemphasized hostility toward the new states in Africa and Asia that were following a "third road." The period from 1953 to 1965 was marked by a mixture of optimism, assertiveness, frustration and caution. Until 1960 China continued to act as a loyal ally of the Soviet Union and was particularly buoyed by the launching of Sputnik and the first successful testing of an intercontinental ballistic missile by the Soviet Union in 1957. Mao believed that these developments would decisively tip the balance of power in favor of the socialist camp. But by 1960 the contrasting positions of the two Communist superpowers on the issue of exporting revolution and abandoning the policy of coexistence began to loom large in acrimonious though muted exchanges. Other differences over doctrinal and policy-related issues gradually hardened into what came to be known as the Sino-Soviet dispute. The United States, which has been until then the "No. 1 enemy," was displaced by the Soviet Union, labeled a "hegemonist."

The 1953–65 phase was notable also for China's emergence as a major economic power following its successful first five-year plan, and as a major military power in Asia following its victory over India in two border wars. This period also witnessed China's increased involvement in revolutionary ferment in Third World countries and severe setbacks in its efforts to export revolution. The worst of these setbacks came in 1965, when Indonesian president Sukarno—Mao's most reliable anti-American foreign policy partner—was toppled from power shortly after Indonesian Communists failed in their bid to seize power and were brutally suppressed by the pro-American Indonesian army.

The Cultural Revolution, which started in the mid-1960s, represented an interregnum in Chinese foreign policy. During this period (1966–68) the country was isolated from the outside world, and relations with over 30 countries were disrupted. The aberration peaked in 1967, when the Red Guards sacked foreign embassies in Beijing, and lashed out at virtually every country for real or imaginary slights against the Cultural Revolution.

Isolation ended gradually after 1969 as order was restored and the machinery of government stabilized under the moderate and pragmatic influence of Premier Zhou Enlai. Mao's efforts to rekindle the revolutionary fervor under the slogans of "politics in command" had proved too chaotic for all but the most demented radicals. Moreover, the Sino-Soviet border fighting in 1969 brought home a sense of realism about the external situation.

In April 1969 the CCP Ninth National Party Congress adopted a report, delivered by the then party vice chairman and minister of defense, Lin Biao, which contained two significant foreign policy points. One expressed Chinese readiness to conduct foreign relations on the basis of peaceful coexistence. The other was a reference to the Soviet Union as a "common enemy" (along with the United States) of all peace-loving and progressive countries. With this assertion, Lin Biao initiated the strategy of "simultaneous confrontation against both superpowers," which guided Chinese policy for the next four years.

By 1971 virtually all diplomatic links broken during the Cultural Revolution had been restored, and the stage was set for the next phase of Chinese foreign policy, which matured incrementally into one espousing peaceful coexistence with all countries. The first credible clue to this new shift in policy direction came in 1970, when the Chinese resumed diplomatic relations with Yugoslavia after 12 years of hostility over ideological issues. This move also was addressed to the Third World, in which President Tito was a dominant figure.

The new approach bore fruit in October 1971, when the PRC finally was seated in the United Nations and Nationalist China was expelled from that organization. This was followed shortly thereafter in 1972 by President Nixon's historic visit to Beijing. In Nixon's words, as the U.S. president and Premier Zhou Enlai shook hands on the Beijing Airport tarmac, "one era ended and another began." In the same year China established diplomatic relations with West Germany and normalized relations with Japan.

Chinese pragmatism was not without cost, however, in its relations with Vietnam, with which it was involved in a brief, ill-conceived war. Nevertheless, particularly after the death of Mao and the rise of Deng Xiaoping, the new goals and priorities of Chinese foreign policy had become well established. After 1985, Gorbachev's *glasnost* facilitated the mending of relations with the Soviet Union after a breach that had lasted over a quarter century. The violent suppression of the prodemocracy movement in Tiananmen Square in 1989 was a major setback for Deng, but the Chinese have successfully contained any damage to their foreign relations and averted a relapse into their earlier isolation.

Chinese foreign policy thus is a product of three decades of trial and error, more failure than success perhaps, but nevertheless remarkable for snatching stability from the jaws of chaos. By 1990 Chinese foreign policy has reached a new threshold of maturity, flexibility, balance and moderation. For the first time China is able to deal on a normal basis with both superpowers and has learned the art and wisdom of isolating troublesome issues and irritations so they do not impede the major thrust of policy. Given the historical ambivalence of China about the external world, this is a major achievement.

In the evolution of foreign relations the United Na-
tions has been a positive as well as a negative influence. China had been excluded from this body for more than two decades, and its admission in 1971 rectified a major anomaly in U.N. membership. China's behavior in the United Nations has been responsible, shunning violent controversy and generally voting with the Third World on major issues.

Chinese relations with the Soviet Union have come full circle since 1950, when the two countries signed a 30-year treaty of friendship, alliance and mutual assistance. This treaty was abrogated in 1980, when relations between the two reached a nadir. In the intervening period the rift between the two Communist giants split the entire socialist camp. Even before 1956, the date usually assigned as the starting point of the rift, there were historical disagreements, particularly Stalin's support of Chiang Kai-shek after World War II, and Soviet dismantling of Manchurian industry. But the first crack in the alliance did not appear until the 20th Party Congress in Moscow, at which Khrushchev made his famous de-Stalinization speech debunking the dictator and revising Marxism-Leninism on a number of fundamental points. Since Mao considered himself the greatest Communist theorist of his time, he felt insulted, particularly because he had not been consulted beforehand. Further, the Chinese had a greater regard for the dead dictator than the Soviets did. The doctrinal revisions also offended the Chinese, especially the Khrushchevian stress on peaceful coexistence as against the Chinese road of relentless struggle against capitalism, on Mao's model. From this initial break almost every episode widened the gulf between the two countries. The most important events in the chronology of this conflict were: (1) the Sino-Indian border wars in which the Soviet Union remained neutral at first and later sided with India; (2) the Soviet Union's reneging on a promise to help build a nuclear delivery system in China; (3) withdrawal of Soviet economic assistance in 1960; (4) the Albanian issue, in which China sided with Albania; (5) the 1960 Moscow Conference of world Communist parties, in which the Soviet Union took an active role to downgrade China; (6) the partial nuclear test ban treaty between the Soviet Union and the United States; which China felt was designed to deter it from becoming a nuclear power; and (7) border disputes over 1,295,337 sq. km. (500,000 sq. mi.) taken by the Soviet Union from China through "unequal treaties."

The territorial issues were responsible for delaying a rapprochement until the mid-1980s. Dramatized by a visit by Gorbachev in 1989, the elimination of open hostility did not follow any resolution of the outstanding disputes but resulted rather from a conjunction of *glasnost* on the Soviet side and Dengian pragmatism on the other.

Significantly, relations with the superpowers has consumed much of the energies of makers of Chinese foreign policy since 1949, although their rhetoric deals more with the "nonimperialist" powers. The most troubled relations, apart from India, are with Vietnam, against which China launched a two-week "defensive" war in 1979. Hostility to Soviet-backed Vietnam was a legacy of the Sino-Soviet rift, but it was aggravated by the Vietnamese overthrow of the Chinese-backed Pol Pot regime in Cambodia and the mistreatment of ethnic Chinese in Vietnam. Relations with neither India nor Indonesia have become normal, as Beijing probably has written off both of them. China has abandoned its earlier role in Africa and Latin America as the patron saint of revolution but has been unable to assume a more positive image.

With Japan's meteoric rise to the status of an economic superpower, China has found it beneficial to establish friendly and cooperative ties, laying aside the century-old hostility. Soon after the Sino-U.S. rapprochement in 1972, Japan and China reestablished diplomatic relations. A formal peace treaty concluded between the two countries in 1978 included an antihegemony clause directed against the Soviet Union.

Following negotiations, both Portugal and Great Britain have agreed to respect the treaty clauses calling for the return of Macao and Hong Kong, respectively, to China in the later 1990s. According to the provisions of the agreement, Macao and Hong Kong will retain a special status.

PARLIAMENT

The National People's Congress (NPC) is defined in the Constitution of 1982 as "the highest organ of state power," without being identified, as in the Constitution of 1975, as "under the leadership of the Communist Party of China." Among its 15 powers enumerated in Article 62 are amending the Constitution; supervising enforcement of the Constitution and the law; deciding on the choice of premier (on the recommendation of the CCP Central Committee); electing or removing the president of the Supreme People's Court and the chief procurator of the Supreme People's Procuratorate; examining and approving the national economic plan, the state budget and the final state accounts; deciding on questions of war and peace; and approving administrative boundaries.

The NPC holds one session a year. Its deputies are elected by secret ballot for a term of five years by the people's congresses at the provincial-level administrative divisions. The provincial-level delegates themselves are indirectly elected. In 1987 the NPC had 2,978 members. Members of the National Committee of the Chinese People's Political Consultative Conference (CPPCC), a revolutionary united front organization led by the Communist Party, may be invited to attend the NPC as observers.

Because of the NPC's infrequent meetings, the Constitution provides for a Standing Committee of 133 members (in 1988) and a number of special committees appointed by the Standing Committee to carry on legislative work. The Constitution enumerates 21 powers assigned to the Standing Committee, to be exercised when the NPC is not in session. The NPC elects and has the power to recall all members of the Standing Committee: further, no member of the Standing Committee is permitted to hold any administrative or judicial post.

POLITICAL PARTIES

With a membership of 45 million—exceeding the population of all but 22 countries in the world—the Chinese Communist Party (CCP) is the largest political party in the world. It is the pivot of the Chinese political system, eclipsing even the government, and despite the debacle of the Cultural Revolution appears to be more firmly entrenched than at any time since 1949.

Despite apparent structural similarities with Communist parties in other countries, the CCP is unique in several respects. First, the distinction between party and state is considerably blurred to the point where the two systems are identical. The post-Mao leadership has attempted with some success to re-create the distinction between party and state, but so pervasive is the party's power that the latter appears only as a shadow of the former. Another important distinction is the role of the military in the political system, a role that has been reduced in the Soviet Union to a purely professional one. At the top in China, many leaders hold concurrent civilian and military posts; the military also plays a large part in CCP activities at all subnational levels.

The CCP is built on orthodox Leninist principles of organization. These principles are enshrined in the party Constitution, the most recent of which was adopted at the 11th Party Congress, in 1977, and supplemented by the Guiding Principles for Inner Party Political Life, adopted in 1980. According to the Constitution the highest organ of the party is national party Congress. The number of delegates to the Congress is not fixed by the Constitution but, together with procedures governing their election and replacement, is left to the Central Committee to determine.

Thirteen party congresses have been held since the party was founded in 1921.

NATIONAL PARTY CONGRESSES AND PARTY GROWTH				
Congress	Venue	Year	Delegates	Party Strength
First	Shanghai	1921	12	57
Second	Shanghai	1922	12	123
Third	Canton	1923	27	342
Fourth	Shanghai	1925	20	950
Fifth	Hankow	1927	80	57,900
Sixth	Moscow	1928	118	40,000
Seventh	Yenan	1945	752	1,210,000
Eighth	Beijing	1956	1,021	1,734,000
Ninth	Beijing	1969	1,512	20,000,000
10th	Beijing	1973	1,249	28,000,000
11th	Beijing	1977	1,510	35,000,000
12th	Beijing	1982		N.A.
13th	Beijing	1987		45,000,000

The party Congress is elected for a term of five years, but this term may be extended or reduced by the Central Committee. Although the party Constitution of 1956 called for annual sessions of the Congress, subsequent constitutions contemplate only one session per Congress. Thirteen years elapsed between the initial meeting of the Eighth (which actually met in two sessions) and the convening of the Ninth, but only four years elapsed between the Ninth and 10th and between the 10th and 11th, and five years between the 11th and 12th and between the 12th and 13th.

The 11th Congress was the last public Congress attended by foreign observers and media representatives. Subsequent congresses have been convened in secrecy, and no foreign observers have been invited to attend. No publicity materials were released until each Congress had adjourned.

Although described as "the highest leading body," the Congress is in fact an otiose institution. The party Constitution of 1956 assigns to the Congress four tasks: (1) to hear and examine the reports of the Central Committee and other central organs, (2) to determine the party's line and policy, (3) to revise the party Constitution and (4) to elect the Central Committee. The present Constitution contains no article dealing with the powers and functions of the Congress but refers to the subject obliquely by stating that the Central Committee is elected by the Congress. The Congress's main and perhaps only useful function is to give regional functionaries and activists an opportunity to meet and hear the party leadership in person.

The Central Committee is composed of two categories of personnel: full members with voting rights and alternate members with no voting rights. In 1989 it consisted of 175 full members and 110 alternate members for a total of 285 members, a reduction from a peak of 342 members for the 11th Central Committee. Prior to the Cultural Revolution, ranking alternates were elevated to full membership when vacancies occurred. This is no longer the practice. The growing tendency is to reserve full membership for the leading functionaries at all levels and to elect as alternates rising figures whose work merits recognition.

Rank within the party is critical. Formerly rank was determined by the number of votes received in the election of the Central Committee; now it is decided by the Political Bureau. Party rank is indicated by a carefully devised pecking order relative to the location of the chairman on public occasions or in official listing of leaders on certain occasions. In the latter case, rank may be hidden by listing the names according to the number of strokes in Chinese characters (the Chinese equivalent of alphabetization).

The chairman of the Central Committee is the de facto chairman of the party and the commander in chief of the PLA, in contrast to other Communist countries in which the general secretary is the most powerful figure, a tradition set by Stalin in 1922. The post of chairman was created at the party's Seventh Congress, in the first major effort to create a cult around Mao.

The Central Committee does not sit in continuous session, nor is it required to convene with any regularity. The Constitution states simply that it will meet when convened by the Political Bureau. The number of plenums has varied from three for the Ninth and 10th to 12 for the Eighth. These figures are somewhat misleading as indicators because meetings called "working conferences" are not included in the numbered plenum series. Some sessions are known as "enlarged sessions," when they include specialists who contribute to the primary topics under discussion.

The Central Committee is only slightly less unwieldy as a legislative or policy-making forum. Most of its members reside outside Beijing and have other responsibilities, making it difficult to hold frequent or extended meetings. Therefore it elects the Political Bureau (Politburo) from among its own members. The Politburo consists of 17 full members, all of whom reside in Beijing, and is the heart of the political system. Meetings of the Politburo are not ordinarily reported in the media, although its decisions are noted with all solemnity. Until about 1960 the Politburo functioned as a harmonious body in which members spoke freely and debated issues, but practicing the principle of democratic centralism, presented a united front once decisions were reached. This cohesiveness was later destroyed during Mao's Cultural Revolution and subsequent purges and has never been resorted to quite the same degree. To avert a relapse into intraparty struggles, the party Constitution has a provision that the Politburo must operate on the principle of collective leadership.

Decisions of the Politburo are issued in its name or in that of the Central Committee and are in the form of resolutions, directives and circulars, commonly referred to as Politburo decisions or Central Committee documents. Those relating to party matters are sent to the party committees at the provincial level, those relating to state matters to the State Council and those relating to military matters to the Military Commission of the Central Committee.

Because even the 17 members of the Politburo constitute an unwieldy number for collegial decisions, there is an inner or kitchen cabinet within the Politburo known as the Standing Committee. In 1989 it consisted of five members including the premier and the party general secretary.

The party Constitution authorizes the Central Committee to establish "necessary organs that are compact and efficient" to attend to the day-to-day work of the party and the PLA. These organs are directed and supervised by the Politburo. Eleven of these are currently active:

- Central Committee for Discipline Inspection
- Secretariat
- Central Advisory Committee
- Central Military Commission
- General Office
- International Liaison Department
- Organization Department
- Propaganda Department
- United Front Work Department
- Work Committee for Government Organs
- Work Committee for Party Organs

Prior to the Cultural Revolution the most important of these organs was the Secretariat, which was the housekeeping organ operating under a chief of staff.

The main source of its power was its ability to influence personnel appointments. The Secretariat disintegrated when its general secretary, Deng Xiaoping, fell into disgrace, and even after it was revived when he returned to power, some of its functions were taken over by the General Office.

The Propaganda Department also was a casualty of the Cultural Revolution, and was revived in 1976. It is in charge of all media activities, particularly publication of *Renmin Ribao* (People's Daily) and *Hongqi* (Red Flag).

The Central Military Commission, headed by Deng until late 1989, is the directive organ for the PLA. As chairman of this commission, Deng was addressed as *chu-hsi* (chairman), the only such office in the PRC.

The Third Plenum of the 11th Central Committee set up the Central Commission for Inspecting Discipline. In name and form the commission resembled the discipline inspection committees that existed between 1949 and 1955 and that were attacked and abolished during the Cultural Revolution. The importance attached to the new body, set up in 1978, is evident from the list of its 69 members. Its area of concern is more far-reaching than the term "discipline" would suggest. The commission has played an important role in restoring normalcy to the party and correcting the aberrations of the Cultural Revolution. For example, it was responsible for the posthumous rehabilitation of Liu Shaoqi. Together with the Organization Department it supervises the discipline inspection organizations at the subnational levels. The commission also was responsible for drafting the Guiding Principles of Inner Party Political Life, which was aimed at curbing the personality cult.

Relations with other Communist parties in good standing with the CPC are conducted through the International Relations Department. The mission of the United Front Work Department is to promote national policies by securing the support and involvement of the masses in party projects. It deals with the various mass organizations and the democratic parties active within the Chinese People's Political Consultative Conference (CPPCC).

Since there are no retirement provisions in the CCP, the Central Advisory Committee was added as a halfway house for aging leaders (who have been CCP members for at least 40 years). In 1989 it had 200 members.

The organizational structure of the CCP below the national level has the form of a pyramid, at the base of which are the party branches *(tang-te chich-pu)* or, in the case of a larger membership in the membership units, general branches *(tsung-chi-pu)* and basic organizations *(chi-ts'eng tsu-chih)*. The basic organizations hold annual members' congresses and are led by a committee and a secretary. In the cities, the basic organizations usually are established according to the functional principle—i.e., in factories, schools, shops, offices and PLA companies. Other organizations are established on the territorial principle—i.e. streets, wards, etc. In the countryside both principles are combined, with basic organizations in people's communes cooperatives, state farms and villages. The number of these branches rose from 1 million in 1959 (with an average membership of 13) to 1.46 million in 1982 (with an average membership of 27). At the higher levels the party macine is organized strictly according to the territorial principle. All levels have their party congress, elected by the party congresses of the respective lower level, which, in turn, elect party committees. The committees then appoint a secretariat under the leadership of a first secretary *(ti-i shu-chi);* a Disciplinary Investigation Commission; and—on the provincial level only—an Advisory Commission. Party congresses on the county level are held every three years and on the provincial level every five years.

The next level consists of party organizations in the townships, counties, autonomous counties, banners and municipalities, which are in turn directed by organizations in the 208 autonomous areas, leagues and an administrative area. Immediately above them are the party organizations in the 21 provinces, five autonomous regions and three directly administered cities.

The provincial secretaries wield enormous influence and may exert pressure when the center is paralyzed by interfactional squabbles. Generally they are full members of the Central Committee.

There is one exception to the principle of territorial rather than functional organization at the higher levels. The PLA has its own pyramid of party organizations, rising from the "base" in the companies through battalions, regiments, divisions and corps up to the 11 military regions. It is only on the central level that the civilian and military party machines combine.

In its efforts to enlist broad popular support, the CCP relies as much on mass organizations and "democratic parties" as on its own mechanisms. These are the transmission belts to the 96% of the Chinese population who are not Communists. The activities of the mass organizations are technically represented by CPPCC but actually are directed by the United Front Work Department of the Central Committee. The CPPCC addresses its efforts particularly to intellectuals without party affiliation and to overseas Chinese. The eight constituent "democratic" parties are: the Revolutionary Committee of the Guomindang, the China Democratic League, the China Democratic National Construction Association, the China Association for Promoting Democracy, the Chinese Peasants' and Workers' Democratic Party, the China Zhi Gong Dang, the Ji San Society and the Taiwan Democratic Self-Government League.

Among the better-known mass organizations included in the CPPCC are the All-China Federation of Trade Unions, the Communist Youth League, the All-China Women's Federation, the All-China Federation of Literacy and Arts Circles, the All-China Federation of Youth, the All-China Students' Federation, the All-China Federation of Industry and Commerce and the Chinese People's Association for Friendship with Foreign Countries.

ECONOMY

China has a centrally planned economy in which the dominant sector is public: China is one of the 42 low-income countries of the world, ranking slightly lower than India in per capita income and above it in aggregate GDP. China also has an economy characterized by great diversity and complexity. Because of the great variety of geographic zones and the broad spectrum of technologies in use, there are wide differences among areas in economic activities, organizational forms and prosperity. Even within a given city, enterprises range from tiny, collectively owned handicraft units, earning marginal incomes for their members, to high-technology facilities. Similarly, the agricultural sector is diverse and ranges from prosperous suburban communes to fishing collectives on the seacoast, herding collectives in Inner Mongolia and struggling grain-producing brigades in the arid mountains of Shaanxi. Because technological development has been haphazard, a wide range of technological levels is in use simultaneously; state-of-the art plants exist cheek by jowl with machinery 30 years behind the times. The economy is further characterized by limited interregional economic integration. Consequently, although the central administration coordinates the entire economy and redistributes resources among regions when necessary, in practice most economic activity is decentralized, and there is relatively little flow of goods and services among areas.

The CCP came to power in 1949 with the fundamental long-range goal of transforming China into a modern, powerful socialist nation. In economic terms this goal meant industrialization, improvement of living standards, narrowing of income differences and production of modern equipment. As years passed, this goal still held, but the economic strategies necessary to achieve them were dramatically altered a number of times in response to internal as well as external pressures. The major conflict) was between those leaders who felt that the economic goal should receive priority and others (including Mao) who held that politics should be in command. Nearly two decades of economic development were sacrificed in this struggle before the pragmatist faction finally gained control and initiated a program of economic modernization in the 1980s.

An important characteristic in the development of economic policies and the underlying economic model was that each new policy period, while differing significantly from that which preceded it, nonetheless retained most of the existing economic organization. Thus the economic model at any given point in post-1949 history reflected both the economic philosophy of the ruling faction as well as the structural foundation built up during the preceding period.

At least nine phases can be distinguished in China's economic history under the Communists. The first was the recovery from World War II and the Civil War that followed it (1949–52). At the time of the establishment of the People's Republic, China was virtually destitute. Mines, transportation systems, factories, power systems and communications had been totally or partially destroyed, and about half of the machinery in the major industrial area of the Northeast had been dismantled and shipped to the Soviet Union. Food production was some 30% below prewar levels. Finally, the nation was reeling under the worst inflation in its history. Within three years the new regime restored the economy to normal working order; established price stability; and restored commerce, industry and agriculture to their prewar levels. The banking system was nationalized and centralized under the People's Bank of China, and inflation was brought under control by 1951. The monetary system was unified, credit was tightened, government budgets were trimmed and the value of the currency was guaranteed by the government. Commercial activity was revived by establishing state trading companies, which competed with private traders. The transformation of ownership in industry proceeded more slowly. About a third of the industrial enterprises had been state-owned under the Nationalists, and they became the nucleus of the state sector. Another 50% was brought under state control by 1952. Agriculture was changed more rapidly. Under a nationwide land reform program, titles to about 45% of the arable land were redistributed to the 60% to 70% of peasant families who previously owned little or no land. Once the land reform was completed, peasants were encouraged to cooperate in some phases of production through formation of small mutual aid teams of six or seven households each.

The second phase was the first five-year plan (1953–57). Having restored a viable economic base, the regime embarked on an intensive program of industrial growth and socialization. For this purpose it borrowed the Stalinist economic model, with its three principal thrusts: state ownership in the modern sector, large collective units in the agricultural sector and centralized economic planning. In the first five-year plan the primary emphasis was on development of heavy industry and capital-intensive technology at the expense of agriculture. Not only was the plan formulated with the help of Soviet planners but also Soviet engineers helped to install the industrial plants and equipment. By 1956 private ownership of industry ceased to exist. Of all modern industrial enterprises, two-thirds were state-owned and one-third were under joint public-private ownership. During the same period handicraft industries were organized into cooperatives.

Agriculture also underwent extensive organizational changes. To facilitate the mobilization of agricultural resources, improve the efficiency of farming and increase state access to farm products, peasants were organized into large socialized collective units. From the loosely structured small mutual aid teams, villagers were encouraged to join lower-stage agricultural prducer cooperatives in which they received some income on the basis of the amount of land they contributed and eventually to advanced cooperatives, or collectives, in which they received only wages. Each family, however, was allowed to retain a small private plot for its own use. By 1957 a total of 93.5% of all peasant households belonged to the advanced cooperatives.

The first five-year plan was one of the most successful of all economic plans, laying a solid foundation for heavy industry and building over 156 major facilities. Industrial production increased at an average annual rate of 16% and GNP at a rate of 7%.

The third phase was the Great Leap Forward (1958–60). Before the end of the first five-year plan the growing imbalance between growth in industry and agriculture and dissatisfaction with inefficiency and lack of flexibility in the decision-making process convinced Chinese leaders—particularly Mao—that the Soviet model was not appropriate for China. In 1957 the government adopted measures to decentralize a great deal of the authority for economic decision-making to the provincial, county and local administrations. In 1958 the government abandoned the second five-year plan in favor of an approach that relied on spontaneous heroic efforts to produce an explosive "Great Leap" in production for all sectors of the economy at once. Further reorganization of agriculture was regarded as the key to greater productivity. In the absence of adequate investment funds for both industry and agriculture, it was decided to utilize the one resource that China had in abundance: surplus rural labor. They were to be employed building huge irrigation and water control works on the one hand and on the other setting up thousands of small-scale, low-technology backyard industrial projects in farm units. Such a mobilization was achieved by a sudden leap to the final stage of agricultural collectivization: the formation of people's communes. Communes were created by combining some 20 or 30 advanced producer cooperatives with an average of 20,000 to 30,000 members, although the actual numbers varied from 6,000 to 40,000. Communes comprised three organizational levels: the central commune administration; the production brigade, the equivalent of a village; and the production team, of some 30 to 40 families. Ideally commune members lived in dormitories and ate in communal mess halls. By 1960 the commune administration was found to be too unwieldy, but the brigades and teams survived.

In the industrial sector, enterprises were politicized and factories were placed under the command of party branches. Central planning was deemphasized in favor of spontaneous, politically inspired production decisions from individual units.

The result of the Great Leap Forward was disaster on all fronts. By 1962 China was on the brink of famine, and starvation was averted only by using the country's foreign exchange reserves to import grain. The withdrawal of Soviet aid in 1960 following the Sino-Soviet rupture caused industrial growth to plummet to a level just 5% above the 1957 level.

The fourth phase was the Agriculture First experiment (1961–65). In 1961 the government abandoned the Great Leap Forward in favor of a new strategy to restore agricultural output. Planning and economic coordination were revived—although in a less centralized form—to bring order and efficient allocation of resources back to the economy. The rate of investment was reduced and investment priorities reversed—agriculture first, light industry second and heavy industry third. Organizational changes in agriculture involved mainly placing greater responsibility on production teams and restoring private plots to peasant families. The sector received considerable state support in the form of reduced taxes, higher prices and increases in inputs such as fertilizers and machinery. Control over industry remained for the most part in the hands of provincial and local-level governments. Planning rather than politics once again guided production decisions, and material rewards rather than revolutionary enthusiasm became the leading incentives for efficient production. Imports of foreign technology and machinery, which had come to a halt with the withdrawal of Soviet aid in 1960, were initiated with Japan and West European countries.

By 1965 the economy had recovered, and production in both agriculture and industry surpassed the 1960 levels. Between 1961 and 1965 agricultural output grew at an average annual rate of 6.6% and industrial output by an average of 17.3% annually. Contributing to this growth were a host of small-scale rural industries, particularly fertilizer plants and hydroelectric plants.

The fifth phase was the Cultural Revolution (1966–68). Although primarily a political upheaval, the Cultural Revolution virtually suspended all industrial growth for three years. Fortunately, the turmoil did not spread to rural areas and agriculture was not directly affected. The modern sector was paralyzed in several ways, most directly through the political activity involving students and workers. Transportation was disrupted as trains and trucks were requisitioned to carry the Red Guards. Output at many factories suffered from shortages of raw materials and other supplies. Production declined when factories were placed in the hands of revolutionary committees. In addition, many engineers, managers, scientists, technicians and other white-collar personnel were "criticized," "demoted," "sent down" to the countryside to do manual work or even jailed. Imports of foreign equipment were curtailed by violent antiforeign outbreaks. Probably the most serious and long-lasting effect on the economy came from the closure of universities, thus drying up the flow of skilled personnel for many years.

The sixth phase was the return to normalcy (1970–74) under the direction of Premier Zhou Enlai, the main proponent of the "Four Modernizations" (of industry, agriculture, defense, and science and technology). The revolutionary committees were dispossessed of their power, universities were reopened, skilled personnel were restored to their jobs and foreign contacts were resumed. There was a significant increase in investment during this period, including the signing of many contracts with foreign firms, particularly one for 13 of the world's largest chemical fertilizer plants.

The seventh phase was the Gang of Four period (1974–76). The ascendancy of the Gang of Four—Jiang Qinq (Mao's wife), Zhang Chunquio, Yao Wenyuan and Wang Hongwen, all of them Mao's proteges—had a paralyzing effect on the economy, since they opposed the Four Modernizations in favor of a more primitive Communist society. The instability was exacerbated by the death of Zhou Enlai and Mao in 1976, and the subsequent second purge of Deng. The period came to an end with the arrest and disgrace of the Gang of Four.

The eighth phase was the revival of the Four Modernizations (1976–78) under the leadership of the rehabilitated Deng. A battery of new policies was adopted for this purpose. The authority of the managers and professionals was stengthened at all levels at the expense of that of party officials. Expertise was emphasized over ideology. Material rewards such as bonuses and wage increases were given a central role in the incentive system. Production of consumer goods was expanded in an effort to achieve a better quality of life. Research and education became prominent once again, and the victims of the Cultural Revolution were rehabilitated. Interaction with foreign countries played a major part in the modernization drive. Foreign equipment, plants and designs were imported in large numbers, along with foreign technicians. Chinese students were permitted to go abroad for higher study, and foreign experts were hired to teach in China. Coastal areas were given the right to establish commercial contacts with foreign countries. A draft 10-year plan (1976–85) was adopted at the Fifth National People's Congress, in 1978.

The ninth phase was the Period of Readjustment (1979–present). At the third plenum of the party's Central Committee in 1978, a shift in economic policy was announced. The 1976–85 plan was abandoned—although many of its elements were retained—and the 1979–81 period was designated as one of readjustment, during which crucial imbalances in the economy would be corrected and the foundation laid for a modernization program. In addition, several important new policies were initiated. Investment in construction was reduced. Light industry was expanded because it created consumer goods and required less investment than heavy industry and because new facilities could go into production much more quickly. Foreign trade procedures were greatly eased, allowing individual corporations and enterprises to engage in negotiations with foreign firms and even to set up joint ventures. To increase agricultural output, procurement prices for agricultural goods were raised and farm units were guaranteed autonomy in decision-making. Farmers were permitted to lease land from the state, and free peasant markets were established not only in the countryside but also in urban areas. Enterprises were allowed to retain a portion of their profits for reinvestment and distribution to workers as bonuses. This set of new policies was described in four words: adjustment, reform, consolidation and improvement.

The seventh five-year plan (1986–90) continued the modernization of the economy, giving priority to the expansion of the "open door" policy. Target growth rates were lower than during the previous plan. The GNP was planned to increase by an average of 7.5% annually and agricultural and industrial output by 6.7% annually. In the first year of the plan, the reforms produced excessive growth in some areas, requiring a series of measures to slow the growth rate. Since the Tiananmen Square suppression of the prodemocracy movement and the subsequent imposition of martial law (lifted in 1990), the economy has experienced severe problems as a result of lower foreign investment and balance-of-payments deficits.

China's economic management system is, by international standards, extraordinarily centralized and char-acterized by strict vertical control, with relatively few horizontal linkages. Commands flow constantly downward and information upward. The response of the units at the bottom to changes in policy at the top is remarkably quick and uniform. In accordance with the Constitution, a major portion of the governmental apparatus is devoted to managing the economy; all but nine of the 39 ministries and eight commissions are concerned with economic matters.

Perhaps the most outstanding feature of the Chinese economic system is its ability to mobilize resources, both physical and human, for achieving a clearly defined goal. Through central control of resources the system can generate very high rates of savings and regulate the growth of consumption but at the same time provide a reasonably secure basic level of consumption for all inhabitants.

Another distinguishing feature of the system is its well-organized multi-level structure, which is closely integrated with the political structure of the country. This facilitates the effective and quick transmission of directives from above during periods of strong central government and is remarkable for its ability to deliver basic social services effectively and efficiently to the vast majority of the population. At the same time, the system apparently can continue functioning on a decentralized basis when the central government becomes weak. For example, the food grain distribution system, although provincially organized, is able to move supplies to other regions quickly in response to need. Another feature of the economy is the successful use of mass campaigns using moral incentives to achieve economic goals, although some of these campaigns have been carried to excess with unintended consequences.

The numerous economic failures in the past five decades illustrate the sheer difficulty of monitoring and regulating all economic activity by a central authority, given the insufficiently developed communications system. The Chinese themselves have been the first to admit these deficiencies and call for reform. The pressure for reform recognizes the fact that future development must be based on increasing efficiency of resources rather than on mere mobilization of resources, as in the past. Maintaining growth and modernization in isolation from international technological development has become increasingly difficult for China. The similarities between debates on system reform in China and Eastern Europe are striking but hardly surprising because both share the five key features of all command economies: (1) virtually exclusive public ownership of the means of production, (2) centralization of economic decisions, (3) strictly hierarchical planning, (4) the passive role of money and prices in resource allocation and (5) state monopoly of foreign trade, and insulation of the domestic price structure from the world market price structure.

A highly centralized command economy can succeed only with taut management—something beyond the capability of the Chinese. Consequently the planners have found it difficult to match production with demand. Bottlenecks and supply shortages are frequent.

Large inventories are accumulated of goods in excess supply (or of such poor quality as to be useless), but they continue to be produced. For example, steel has to be imported, while 20 million tons of it are stockpiled. The Chinese system of material balances used to balance supply and demand has apparently not worked well because of its crude application in plan preparation. Preparation of the annual plan usually begins with a target for output for a key commodity, usually an intermediate good such as steel, from which the output targets for the other major commodities are derived. From these targets total industrial production follows, and then total income, investment and finally consumption, derived as a residual. In these calculations, the previous year's rates of use are used, with minor adjustments. Delays in preparing the plan result frequently in material allocations being made before the plan is finalized and approved. The system also suffers from underallocation of materials and nondelivery of allocated materials. Thus most enterprises attempt to stockpile materials, and there is a significant exchange of materials among enterprises outside the official allocation process. Bureaucratic behavior aggravates these problems, since it is generally preoccupied with the size of the output rather than its quality and the needs and satisfactions of consumers. It also discourages product innovation and cost reduction because they might disrupt the primary objective of meeting quantitative targets.

In principle China's annual plan, especially its annual investment plan, forms part of a detailed five-year plan and a broader 10- or 20-year plan. In practice, however, there is little effective medium- or long-term planning. Even within specific sectors there is no objective method for evaluating the benefits and costs of investment proposals. Investment decisions on even large national projects have been made without any economic or technical analysis.

Each plan consists of several interlocking plans within it, including a production plan, a material allocation plan, a wage and labor plan, etc. At the center the preparation of the plan is the responsibility of the State Planning Commission, and its implementation is supervised by the State Capital Construction Commission for large capital construction projects, the State Economic Commission for industry and transportation, and the State Agricultural Commission. The planning bureau in each province and county prepares a similar local plan. County plans are guided and integrated by the provincial planners, and provincial plans by the State Planning Commission. The provincial plans include targets for goods not included in the national plan but important for the provincial economy. Many goods not treated at the provincial level are similarly added to the county and city plans.

Beneath the general planning umbrella, responsibility for commodity flows is divided among several agencies, chiefly according to the nature of the goods concerned. Industrial producer goods come under the jurisdiction of the State Material Supply Bureau or, for more specialized items, the relevant industrial ministries; food and edible oil under the Food Ministry; and nonstaple

food, other consumer goods and services and a few producer goods under the Commerce Ministry. The supply and marketing cooperatives handle nonfood agricultural output, producer goods for agriculture and sales of consumer goods in rural areas. Each of these agencies has subordinate or counterpart units at the provincial and county levels whose duty is to disaggregate the allotments among the units beneath them. The process is reversed for requisitions. For example, the communes, county-controlled enterprises, construction units and departments initiate the process by individually submitting requisitions for the coming year to their next immediately higher agency, which aggregates them for review by the next level.

The channels through which goods are actually distributed, once the allocation has been determined, vary somewhat. Large allocations (more than one railroad car in volume) and specialized equipment are handled by direct bilateral transfer between producer and user. Smaller allocations of more standardized items flow through a network of wholesale and retail organizations.

The rural economy, comprising some 53,000 communes, is the largest sector in China. Each commune consists of four units: the family, a production team of some 30 to 40 families, a production brigade of some seven to eight teams and a people's commune of some 15,000 people or 12 to 13 brigades. The economic activities of the family include work on the private plot (currently about 8% of total cultivated land); husbandry of small animals, especially pigs; collection of animal manure, the main source of fertilizer; and a wide range of sideline activities. The importance of these family activities is greater than the estimated 30% of total agricultural income they represent, since they provide most families with the bulk of their cash income and most of the vegetables and meat.

The team is the basic production unit. Above it comes the brigade, which is responsible for large-scale and more technical operations and also the delivery of social services to the rural population. The commune is responsible for organizing large construction projects and capital-intensive industrial enterprises, and it also oversees civil administration as the lowest level of the state apparatus. It collects taxes and farm products for the state, delivers public services and passes down planning and political guidelines.

The commune economy is remarkably isolated from the rest of the economy, most directly by restricting migration from the commune. Thus, in principle, a person born in a commune dies in that commune. The state's control over the sector is mainly through the supply and marketing system. First, a large proportion of the above-subsistence output is procured by the state according to fixed quotas and prices, the proportion varying with the product. For example, some 50 million tons of grain, accounting for 15% to 20% of the output, are procured in three forms: (a) agricultural tax paid in kind, (b) quota procured at an officially set price and (c) an above-quota procurement at a negotiated price above the official price. The total grain thus procured accounts for 90% of the total marketed output. Second, the commune receives virtually all its farm and nonfarm inputs—including consumer goods and fertilizers—through the plan material allocation system. Credit is provided by the Agricultural Bank. With such a broad array of controls, the state is able to assign detailed acreage targets to the production units while at the same time allowing them considerable discretion in determining the means to achieve these targets.

The modern secondary sector is entirely state-owned with the exception of a few private businesses and collectives. The activities of each economic organization revolve around its annual plan, sometimes subdivided into periods as short as 10 days. This plan usually is summarized in a set of physical and financial targets. Because the plan does not fulfill itself, the issue of managerial motivation is important. Unlike the Soviet Union, China offers few financial incentives to its managers to achieve or surpass plan targets. Greater reli-

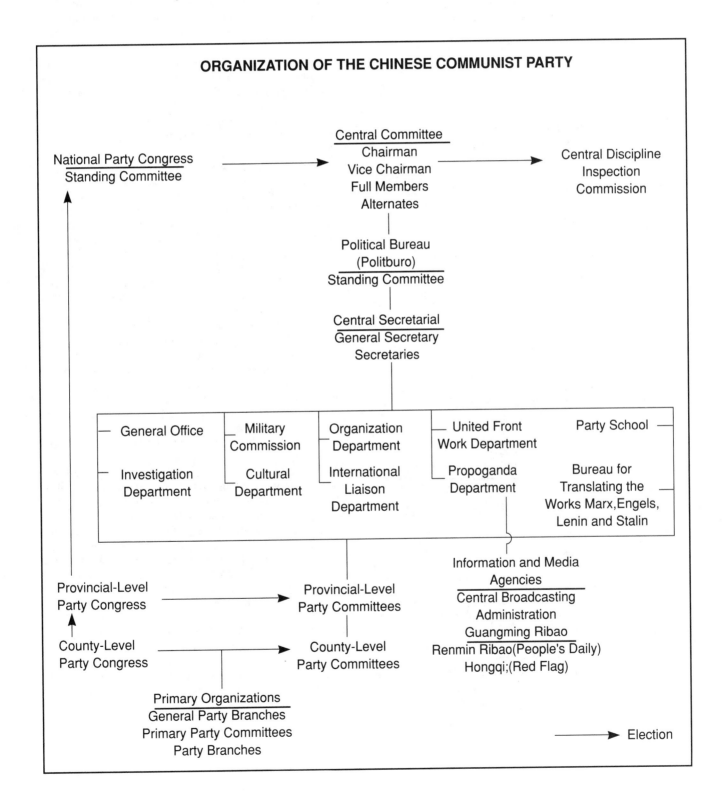

ORGANIZATION OF THE CHINESE COMMUNIST PARTY

ance is placed on nonmaterial rewards (such as praise and promotion) and to a lesser extent on penalties (criticism and demotion).

Over the past three decades the structure of China's economy has altered substantially. At current prices the share of agriculture in NMP has dropped by 21% while that of industry has risen by 26%. As a result, the share of agriculture is significantly smaller in China than in other low-income developing countries, though it is more than double that in middle-income countries. The share of industry, however, is much greater—nearly twice the share of other low-income countries and about 25% higher than in middle-income countries. The share of services is small—more than half that in other low-income countries and less than half that in middle-income countries.

INTERNATIONAL COMPARISON OF PRODUCTION STRUCTURE (%)					
Sector	China	India	Indonesia	Low-Income Countries	Middle-Income Countries
Agriculture	31	38	30	38	15
Industry	47	27	33	24	38
Services	22	35	38	38	48

Economic growth since 1949 has varied from 17% during 1949–52 to −3.7% during the Great Leap Forward. But even during the period of turmoil from 1957 to 1979, the average annual rate of growth was 3.5%, higher than the average for other low-income countries and not far below the average of 3.7% for middle-income and industrialized countries.

INTERNATIONAL COMPARISON OF NATIONAL INCOME		
Countries	Average Annual Growth 1965–87 (%)	Level, 1987 ($)
China	5.2	290
India	1.8	300
Indonesia	4.5	450
Sri Lanka	3.0	400
Low-income countries	3.1	290
Middle-income countries	2.5	1,810
Industrialized countries	2.3	14,430

Although China's per capita GNP appears lower than that of India, in terms of real per capita income China ranks much higher than India, although lower than the Philippines or Malaysia.

China has a high rate of savings and investment, estimated at about 34% of the GNP, a rate surpassed by only a few other countries. However, owing to the low level of GNP, even this high rate of investment secures only a small amount of resources relative to the population. China's actual savings rate is considerably higher than the figures suggest. Whereas in other low-income developing countries more than a quarter of the investment

has been financed by inflows of external funds, China has not received any foreign capital since 1960 and, in fact, has maintained a substantial foreign aid program. (Data for this program are not published.) Official data on sectoral allocation of fixed investment are incomplete in important respects. But unofficial estimates suggest that about 20% went into agriculture, 55% into industry (about four-fifths of this into heavy industry) and the remainder into transportation, commerce, housing or social services. The proportion of total investment accounted for by inventories and works in progress is inordinately high, at 30%, due to mismatches between demand and supply and lack of incentives to economize on working capital.

Material consumption per capita is estimated to have grown in real terms at an annual rate of 4.7% from 1952 to 1957 and 1.9% from 1957 to 1979. Total consumption (including nonmaterial services) is estimated to have grown at an average annual rate of 1.9% during 1957–79.

There are marked interprovincial disparities in real income and output. Since 1952, interprovincial differences in per capita industrial output have narrowed in proportional terms, mainly because growth has deliberately been kept below the national average in the old industrial centers and above the national average in the interior and border provinces and in Beijing. Interprovincial inequalities of per capita industrial output are clearly much greater than those of agricultural output but have much less effect on inequalities of personal consumption and income. One reason for this is that real wages in state industry are in principle uniform throughout China. Another is the centralized budgetary system, as a result of which industrialized provinces do not receive commensurately higher levels of expenditures. On the other hand, interprovincial differences in agricultural output per capita are of major distributional significance. Most agriculture is in the hands of communes; commune industry revenues accrue directly or indirectly to commune members and are taxed lightly.

Thus while urban incomes are relatively uniform, rural incomes vary widely and are lowest in agriculturally poor provinces, such as Gansu. Nationwide urban per capita income is about 2.2 times the rural income. In money terms, the urban-rural income ratio is the same in 1980 as it was in 1957. In real terms, however, since the cost of living has risen faster in rural than in urban areas, the gap appears to have widened considerably. Urban per capita incomes are estimated to have increased between 1957 and 1979 at an annual average rate of 2.9%, as against 1.6% in rural areas. This has occurred despite official efforts to reduce the gap by holding down urban wage rates—the average real wage in state organizations in 1979 was slightly lower than in 1957—and by raising agricultural procurement prices. But physical productivity per worker in agriculture has risen very little, and the participation rate in urban areas has increased faster than in rural areas. Available statistics confirm a substantial gap between rural and urban living standards. The one possible exception is housing, of which there is an acute shortage in cities.

Families frequently have to share accommodations, and the average floor space per person is only 3.6 sq. m. (39 sq. ft.)—not much larger than a double bed. In rural areas there apparently is less crowding, and the average peasant household is reported to have 3.8 rooms. But urban rents are very low, and urban areas have better sanitation and water.

One of the major achievements—and one of its earliest—of the Communist regime was the reduction of income inequalities in Chinese society. In urban areas in 1980 the poorest 40% of the urban population received about 30% of the total income, the richest 20% about 28% and the richest 10% about 16%. By international standards, China has become one of the most egalitarian societies in the world. The share of the poorest 40% is roughly double the average for other developing countries, and the share of the richest 10% roughly half. There are many reasons for this state of affairs. First, there is no private property income (rents, dividends, etc.), which tends to be distributed highly unequally in other countries. Second, there is almost no income from self-employment, which also causes a high degree of inequality in other countries. Third, the distribution of wages and salaries is comparatively equal because managerial and professional employees are less well paid than in other countries. Last, the rationing system and the low prices of basic necessities relative to luxuries also have a leveling effect. What inequality persists among households is caused primarily by variations in participation rates.

Income inequalities are slightly higher in rural areas because although land is owned in common, there is wide variation in the quality of the land in each commune, and the richer production teams earn and save more. Further, China has eliminated an important equalizing force present in most other developing countries: migration. Restrictive migration has closed the door for poorer peasants seeking to improve their lot in different pastures. National data for 1981–83 on differences in annual income among teams showed that 16% of teams had an income of Y40 or less while 25% had an income in excess of Y100. This implies that the poorest 40% received 20% of total rural income, the richest 20% received 39% and the richest 10% received 23%. Although rual income distribution is more unequal than urban income distribution, there is much less rural inequality in China than in any other comparable developing country.

Overall, the poorest 40% of the people receive 18% of personal income, the richest 20% receive 39% and the richest 10% receive 23%. Significantly, the data confirm the large gap between average urban and average rural incomes. Although urban people are only about 15% of the total population, they constitute about half of the richest 20%. Likewise, the poorer half of the population is virtually 100% rural.

As in other Marxist economic systems the price system is extremely rigid, and prices have been ignored as a tool of economic management. Not only has the general level of prices remained remarkably stable but also few adjustments have been made to the relative prices of different goods and services. Prices are determined by a variety of methods and administrative levels, which generally are correlated with the planning system. Prices of most goods controlled in detail by the central economic plan are set at the national level. These include rationed consumer staples and centrally controlled industrial products, and their prices change infrequently. Prices of goods allocated by plans drawn up at lower administrative levels usually are set by planning and commercial agencies at those levels. Such prices are more flexible and change more often. Goods that are covered by plans only in a general way are exchanged between units at prices that are mutually agreed on, within limits established by commercial departments. All prices in rural and urban free peasant markets are determined by supply and demand, as are prices for goods and services supplied by individual laborers.

Prices of individual products go through several stages. Producing units are paid a price by commercial departments that are intended to cover all current producing costs, depreciation, taxes and a small profit. To minimize the need for subsidies, these prices usually are set high enough so that profits would accrue even to inefficient producers. Commercial departments then sell the goods to retail outlets or other producers at a wholesale price that includes cost, freight and a margin of profit. The prices are marked up again by the retailer. Rationed commodities, including grain and edible oils, are purchased and retailed at prices fixed by the central government. In some cases purchase prices are raised to encourage production, but retail prices are held constant through subsidies.

PRINCIPAL ECONOMIC INDICATORS, 1988

Gross National Product: $356.49 billion
GNP per capita: $330
GNP average annual growth rate (%): 10.5 (1980–88)
GNP per capita average annual growth rate (%): 9.2 (1980–88)
Consumer Price Index (1980=100)
  All items: 139.0 (1987)
Wholesale Price Index: N.A.
Average annual growth rate (%) (1980–87)
  Public consumption: 4.9
  Private consumption: 6.1
  Gross domestic investment: 19.0
Income distribution: N.A.
Average annual rate of inflation (1980–87): 4.2

BALANCE OF PAYMENTS ($ million), 1987

Current account balance: 300
Merchandise exports: 34,734
Merchandise imports: −36,395
Trade balance: −1,661
Other goods, services & income: 5,413
Other goods, services & income: −3,676
Private unrequited transfers: 249
Official unrequited transfers: −25
Direct investment: 1,669
Portfolio investment: 1,191
Other long-term capital: 3,032
Other short-term capital: 212
Net errors & omissions: −1,481
Counterpart items: −154
Total change in reserves: −4,768

GROSS DOMESTIC PRODUCT, 1988

GDP nominal (national currency): 779 billion
GDP per capita ($): 274
GDP average annual growth rate: 9.8% (1980–86)
GDP by type of expenditure (%)
  Consumption
    Private: 49
    Government: 13
  Gross domestic investment: 38
  Gross domestic saving: 38
  Foreign trade
    Exports: } 6
    Imports: }
Sectoral origin of GDP (%)
  Primary
    Agriculture: 41
  Secondary
    Manufacturing: 41 (includes mining & public utilities)
    Construction: 6
  Tertiary
    Transportation & communications: 3
    Trade: 8
Average annual sectoral growth rates (%)
  Agriculture: 7.4
  Industry: 13.2
    Manufacturing: 12.6
  Services: 7.6

Prices have little or no effect on the production and distribution of goods. Enterprises are allocated fixed quantities of goods, whatever the cost. The price of such a good does not affect the amount used by an enterprise. However, in the case of unallocated goods treated only in general terms by the plan, prices have an influence on purchasing decisions because enterprises purchase these goods themselves out of capital funds or via short-term loans. Prices also have an influence on nonrationed goods whose retail prices are adjusted periodically to balance supply and demand. Prices of luxury items are set much higher than their costs to discourage excess consumption.

The price mechanism works imperfectly in the agricultural sector. In the first place, farm prices are much lower than prices for industrial goods, thus depressing farm incomes. Second, the cost of increasing agricultural output has been rising steadily, reflecting the cost of higher inputs, such as for pesticides and fertilizers. Finally, price incentives are the basic means of expanding agricultural production. For all these reasons the government has raised procurement prices for agricultural goods and instituted subsidies to maintain retail prices at the same level. In the 1980s food prices were allowed to rise as the subsidies were curtailed. The price of many other primary products has not been raised in the past two decades, even though they are in short supply. By contrast, the prices of industrial consumer goods have not been lowered despite significant declines in production costs, so the consumer goods industries now enjoy huge profit margins. Profits as a percentage of fixed capital are over 61% for watches, 45% for rubber goods, 40% for bicycles, 38% for dye and petroleum products, 33% for pharmaceuticals and 32% for textiles but only 5% for chemicals, iron ore, coal, shipbuilding, agricultural tools and cement. A major

thrust of the post-1980 reforms was to revise prices on the basis of real costs.

For the first 30 years of its existence, the PRC had a remarkable track record in holding down inflation to less than 1% annually. However, as the economy developed, inflationary pressures became evident as pent-up demand fueled by large holdings of personal savings caused a steep jump in prices of consumer goods. Budget deficits in the mid-1980s and excessive money and credit growth also contributed to galloping inflation. From a rate of 5% in the second quarter of 1986, the Market Price Index rose steadily until at the end of 1987 it was rising at an annual rate of 19.6%. Prices for food items, which account for 50% of the average urban household budget, rose even more rapidly. In 1988 food and vegetable prices in large and medium-size cities were up 24.2% and 48.7%, respectively, over the same period in 1987. The benchmark National Retail Price Index rose by 11% in the first quarter of 1988. According to the State Statistical Bureau, about 21% of the urban households experienced a decline in their real income.

PUBLIC FINANCE

The fiscal year is the calendar year. The state budget is the principal instrument of financial control over the economy and accounts for about 30% of the GDP. Provincial and county governments, with their own budgets, collect more than 80% of all revenues and carry out 50% of all expenditures. In form, however, the state budget is consolidated, with county budgets incorporated into the provincial budgets and they, in turn, incorporated into the state budget. In substance there has likewise been strong central control not only over tax rates and policies but also over the level and composition of local expenditures.

The precise degree of state control over provincial budgets has varied almost annually since the 1950s in an attempt to find the right balance between two sets of conflicting requirements. On the one hand, the central government wishes to maintain substantial control, especially over investment, and to avoid large disparities in expenditure levels among provinces. On the other hand, incentives are needed for provincial governments to mobilize revenues, economize on expenditures and adapt their expenditure pattern to local needs.

During the periods of decentralization (starting in 1958, 1970 and 1980) the basic principle has been to allow each province to retain a predetermined portion of its revenues and to give the provincial government substantial freedom in deciding the composition of its expenditures. At other times the central government has maintained control over both the total and the composition of provincial revenues and expenditures, and there has been little connection between revenues and expenditures (except that in many years the provinces have been permitted to retain a proportion of their above-plan revenues or expenditure savings as discretionary funds). Even during periods of decentralization, moreover, the extent of local discretion has remained circumscribed, especially over investment, as the central government has continued to set tax rates and to issue guidelines on the composition of expenditures.

An important and consistent feature of the budget is the transfer of resources from the more prosperous to the poorer regions. Some provincial budgets show surpluses, and some deficits and funds are transferred from the former to the latter. As a result, the highly industrialized regions pay a much higher rate of net taxation than others, and the least-developed regions are heavily subsidized. Shanghai, Liaoning and Jiangsu pay 90%, 82% and 70% of their taxes, respectively, to the central government, while the autonomous regions of Xizang (Tibet) and Ningxia Hui pay no net taxes to the center but receive over half of the funds required for budgetary expenses from the center. The Xinjiang Uygur Autonomous Region is subsidized for about a third of its expenditures and Yunnan Province for about 15%.

Among the post-1980 reforms was one to improve the flexibility of the planning system by allowing province-level and local administrations greater control over their budgetary expenditures. Resembling a revenue-sharing system, its details vary somewhat among provinces, but the basic principle is to allow each province to retain a fixed proportion of the revenues it collects and within that amount to give them more freedom than hitherto in choosing the composition of its expenditures. The reform is designed to stimulate provincial revenue-gathering efforts. For this reason most provinces are permitted to retain in addition to a specified fraction of industrial and commercial tax revenues, all the profits of the provincially and subprovincially controlled enterprises. To stimulate enterprise efficiency, tax collection and the elimination of waste further, each

---

CENTRAL GOVERNMENT EXPENDITURES, 1987

% of total expenditures
Defense: 8.3
Education: ⎱15.8
Health: ⎰
Housing, Social Security, welfare: ⎱26.7
Economic services: ⎰
Other: 49.2

CENTRAL GOVERNMENT REVENUES

% of total current revenues
Taxes: 92.2
Special funds: 7.4
Government consumption as % of GNP: 13
Annual growth rate of government consumption: 4.9%

EXTERNAL PUBLIC DEBT, 1988

Total: $23.659 billion
  of which public (%): 40.5
  of which private (%): 59.5
Debt service total: $2.381 billion
  of which repayment of principal (%): 57.4
  interest (%): 42.6
Debt service rate: 7.9%
External public debt as % of GNP: 8.1
Ratio of external public debt to international reserves: 1:4

EXTERNAL PUBLIC DEBT, 1988 (continued)

Debt service as % of GNP: 1
Debt service as % of exports: 7.1
Terms of public borrowing
  Commitments: $9.210 billion
  Average interest rate: 6.6%
  Average maturity: 15 years

---

province is encouraged to extend revenue-sharing principles down to the county level.

The largest single source of revenue comes from enterprise profits partly because they are high and are remitted virtually in full to the state. The second-highest source of revenue is the industrial and commercial tax, which accounts for three-quarters of all tax receipts. Industry and commerce are the main catchment areas of taxes. The only agricultural tax—a combination of production and land tax—now accounts for less than 3% of total revenues. There is no personal income tax.

Taxes on goods discriminate between those needed by consumers and luxuries. Basic necessities such as grain are not taxed at all and are, indeed, subsidized. Producer goods such as coal and fertilizer, are taxed at low levels. Nonessential consumer goods such as radios are taxed heavily, and items such as liquor and tobacco are taxed punitively. The central government collects additional revenues directly, from customs duties, railways, the merchant marine and so on.

On the expenditures side, the distinctive feature is the large amount of investment. Over the past two decades, grants for fixed and working capital formation have accounted for half of total budgetary expenditures. Control of investment is shared between the Ministry of Finance and the State Planning Commission. The plans generally envisage more investment than can actually be financed. In most years, therefore, the budget cuts the total amount of investment. Among other items of expenditure, defense and cultural items stand out. The pattern of expenditure varies according to the level of government. Defense does not figure in the provincial budgets; on the other hand, social expenditures (health, education and culture) and administrative costs account for a third and a quarter, respectively, of provincial expenditures, compared to 6% and 2%, respectively, in the central budget.

Well into the 1980s Chinese budgets were balanced but, deficit rose to Y17.1 billion or 1.6% of the GNP in 1987. The deficit is financed by net foreign borrowing, domestic bonds and overdrafts from the People's Bank of China. Banking data indicate that net lending by the central bank to government financial departments rose by Y15 billion in 1987, placing the net budgetary deficit at 2.2% of the GNP. In 1983 official figures for China's foreign debt were published for the first time. They

---

EXCHANGE RATE
(National Currency per U.S. Dollar)

1979	1980	1981	1982	1983	1984	1985	1986	1987	1988
1.496	1.530	1.745	1.923	1.981	2.796	3.201	3.722	3.722	3.722

FINANCIAL INDICATORS, 1988

International reserves minus gold: $18.541 billion
  SDR's: 586
  Reserve position in IMF: 407
  Foreign exchange: $17.548 billion
Gold (million fine troy oz.): 12.7
Central Bank:
  Assets (%)
    Claims on government: 11.3
    Claims on private sector: 0.9
    Claims on banks: 82.2
    Claims on foreign assets: 5.5
  *Liabilities (%)
    Reserve money: 84.0
    Government deposits: 9.6
    Foreign liabilities: 1.2
    Capital accounts: 6.3
Money supply
  Stock in billion national currency: 421.5
  M^1 per capita: 400
Private banks
  Assets
    Loans to government: 80.9 ⎤
    Loans to private sector: ⎦
    Reserves: 16.0
    Foreign assets: 3.1
  Liabilities (%)
    Deposits (billion national currency): 1,005
      of which
      Demand deposits: 26.6
      Savings deposits: 24.4
      Foreign liabilities: 3.1

*Total over 100% reflects excess liability

GROWTH PROFILE (Annual Growth Rates, %)

Population, 1985–2000: 1.3
Crude birth rate, 1985–90: 17.1
Crude death rate, 1985–90: 6.8
Urban population, 1980–87: 11.0
Labor force, 1985–2000: 1.4
GNP, 1975–88: 10.5
GNP per capita, 1965–88: 9.2
GDP, 1980–86: 9.8
Inflation, 1980–87: 4.2
Agriculture, 1980–87: 7.4
Industry, 1980–87: 13.2
Manufacturing, 1980–87: 12.6
Services, 1980–87: 7.6
Money holdings, 1980–87; 25.9
Manufacturing earnings per employee, 1980–85: N.A.
Energy production, 1980–87: 5.5
Energy consumption, 1980–87: 4.4
Exports, 1980–87: 11.7
Imports, 1980–87: 14.2
General government consumption, 1980–87: 4.9
Private consumption, 1980–87: 6.1
Gross domestic investment, 1980–87: 19.0

showed a debt of $3 billion, mainly to the IMF, the World Bank and Japan. By 1988 net foreign debt had risen to $23.659 billion.

CURRENCY & BANKING

The national monetary unit is the yuan (Y), officially called renminbiao (People's Bank dollar) or jiao (chiao) and divided into 100 fen or cents. Coins are issued in denominations of 1, 2, and 5 fen and notes in denominations of 10, 20 and 50 fen and 1, 2, 5 and 10 yuan.

The core of the banking system is the People's Bank of China (PBC), which was created in 1949 in the wake of the socialization of the banking sector. Since then, although the banking sector itself, like the economy, has gone through various and conflicting phases, the PBC has not lost its preeminence. It serves as the government Treasury, the main source of credit for enterprises, the clearing center for financial transactions, the holder of enterprise deposits, the national savings bank, the financial underwriter of economic plans, the controller of the money supply and the issuer of currency. One of its principal functions is the supply of short-term and medium-term credit to industrial and commercial enterprises, and credit of all durations to agricultural units. Personal loans also are granted on one-year maturity. All monetary transactions in the state sector are made through the bank. This practice effectively minimizes the need for currency, which is used only for wage payments and retail sales.

With one of the highest savings rates in the world, China uses its bank network to soak up urban and rural savings. Branch offices of the PBC handle urban savings. In the countryside, savings are deposited with the rural credit cooperatives, which exist in most communes and brigades.

Of the 14 other domestic banks, only six were founded before 1980. These are the Bank of China, the Agricultural Bank of China, the Bank of Communications (the oldest of the current banks, founded in 1908), the China and South Sea Bank, the China International Trust and Investment Corporation and the People's Construction Bank. The restructuring of the banking sector that began in 1980 has led to the founding of eight banks: the China State Bank, the China Investment Bank, the Guangdong Provincial Bank, the Industrial and Commercial Bank of China, the Kimcheng Banking Corporation, the National Commercial Bank, the Sin Hua Trust Savings and Commercial Bank and the Yien Yieh Commercial Bank. There are 23 foreign banks and branches.

AGRICULTURE

Agriculture is the lifeblood of China. There are fields in the Chang Tiang Valley that have been cultivated for over 3,000 years. Chinese society also has evolved around the farm as its core, and farm cycles govern the life cycles of not only the peasant but also every Chinese.

Although China sometimes is visualized as a vast paddy field, only about 15% of the land area is cultivable; the total land area in farms is 143,600,000 ha. (354,835,600 ac.). Even within this relatively small area, the weather is a source of uncertainties and constant hazards, and can be as erratic and capricious as any

Ming emperor. Despite these limitations, the Chinese agricultural economy is by some measurements the largest in the world. Accounting for less than 8% of the arable land, it provides enough food for 22% of the world's population. Even more dramatically, with only one-third of the arable land in the United States, it feeds five times the U.S. population. With 75% of its labor force in agriculture, China accounts for 30% of the world's farming population, larger than India, Indonesia and Brazil combined. Historically a leader in agricultural technology, it is renowned for its intensive use of arable land, based on extremely high man/land ratios.

Evidence from eastern China indicates the existence of an agricultural economy based on cereals from at least 7000 B.C. and one based on sustained field cropping from 1000–700 B.C. The first recorded land tax dates from 594 B.C., and by 400 B.C. substantial works for irrigation, drainage and flood control had already been constructed. There was further rapid development of agricultural technology between A.D. 800 and 1200, particularly in southern and eastern China. These included sophisticated land preparation and transplanting techniques, improved seeds, mechanical methods of lifting water, and gravity-flow irrigation and flood-control systems. Thereafter there were few technological improvements; rather there was a progressive expansion of the arable area coupled with some intensification through double-cropping and irrigation. This pattern persisted until 1949, although Western influences and commerce brought about some changes, such as maize and peanut cultivation in northern China, improved strains of cotton and tobacco, and market gardening. China also contributed to the rest of the world new crops such as tea and soybeans and new technology such as sericulture.

By about 1750 the social structure of agriculture had evolved toward landlord-tenant systems and small-scale owner-cultivators. Within the limits of available technology, the extraordinary skills of the farmer and the high standards of crop husbandry sustained a remarkably high level of land productivity. From as early as the 17th century, rice yields exceeded 2 tons per hectare (0.8 ton per acre), which has yet to be reached in many other developing countries. But even minor aberrations of the weather upset the food balance, at a cost of millions of lives. Internal upheavals and wars also took their toll. The landless peasantry remained a sectoral as well as a political problem until the rise of the Communists.

In large parts of China agriculture is severely limited by terrain and rainfall. Much of the country is too mountainous or too dry or too remote from the main population centers and markets. If the country is roughly divided along long. 103° E, over 90% of the population and about the same proportion of agricultural output are in the eastern half.

Climate and topography together define a variety of agricultural regions, the major factors being soils, rainfall and the length of the growing season. Seven regions have been distinguished (nine by the Ministry of Agriculture), but given the size and diversity of China, several dozen separate zones are needed to map accurately

areas with similar production sytems. Significant differences in farming systems occur moving from north to south and from east to west. The intensity of cultivation increases in four distinct stages from north to south: (1) single-crop, spring-sown temperate cereals in the Northeast; (2) a winter wheat/summer crop cycle (three crops in two years) on the North China Plain; (3) double-cropping with a summer rice crop in the Chang Jiang Basin of central China; and (4) double-cropping (and occasional triple-cropping) in the tropical southern coastal areas. Intensive farming systems are practiced on the North China Plain, the Chang Jiang Basin, the upland basin of Sichuan and the southern coastal areas. Close to half the arable area is irrigated (49 million ha.; 121 million ac., or nearly triple the area in 1949). Moving southward, grain yields increase sharply, with double-cropped or triple-cropped land producing four to five times as much as areas in the colder, drier Northeast and Northwest. China's range livestock (sheep, goats, cattle, camels) are found largely on 200 million ha. (494 million ac.) of grassland in the northern and western border regions. However, most animal production is accounted for by pigs and poultry, which are reared on private plots and integrated with crop production.

Agricultural incomes and living standards tend to vary according to productivity and market proximity. Probably the most disadvantaged areas are the northern uplands (Gansu, Ningxia, Shaanxi, Shanxi and Henan) and southern and western upland areas. Low-income areas are also found in some of the lowlands, e.g., the saline areas of the North China Plain and flood-prone areas of Anhui. The most favored areas incude northeastern, central and eastern China, where agricultural incomes are two to three times higher than in the poorer areas.

The northeastern region comprises the provinces of Heilongjiang, Jilin and Liaoning, accounting for 10% of the gross agricultural output and 7% of the rural population. About 12% of the area is irrigated. Agricultural output is 30% above the national average. Spring wheat is the dominant crop in the northern and western portions of this region, and corn is important in one-third of the region. Millet is a transition crop between corn and wheat areas, and soybeans are concentrated along the Songhua and Liao rivers. The region is China's major sugar beet area. Some sorghum (gaoliang) is produced, and rice cultivation has been pushing northward with the advent of high-yielding, short-season varieties. Single-cropping predominates over most of the region. Grain production has grown rapidly because of the good soils. The cultivated areas are mainly in the rolling plains and valleys, where extensive swamp drainage has taken place.

The border provinces region comprises Nei Monggol, Ningxia, Gansu, Xinjiang, Xizang (Tibet) and Qinghai. With 50% of the land area, the region accounts for only 6% of the farm population and 5% of the gross agricultural output. Grain production is only 80% of the national average. Agriculture is dominated by seminomadic herding of sheep, goats and horses on the extensive rangelands. The region sustains some 95 million sheep and goats (52% of the national herd). Farming is limited to summer cropping of irrigated land along the upper reaches of the Huang He and its tributaries, and of oasis-type irrigated areas in Xinjiang and sheltered valleys in Xizang and Qinghai. Rain-fed cropping is largely limited to the southern part of Gansu. Northeastern Nei Monggol is an important forest area.

North China is the most important agricultural region. It includes five provinces (Shandong, Shanxi, Shaanxi, Hebei and Henan) and two municipalities (Beijing and Tianjin) with 27% of the rural population and accounting for a similar percentage of production. The major problems in this region are the easy erodibility of the loess soils in Shaanxi and Shanxi and the poor drainage along the coast of northern Shandong and in the Huang He Delta. Winter wheat is the dominant crop and is grown in about 30% of the arable area, in rotation with summer crops—grain, sorghum or millet in the Northwest and millet, sorghum, corn, soybeans, cotton, rice and sweet potatoes on the plains. Peanut is a major crop in Shandong, which is the most important center for this crop in China. Much of the growth of grain production north of the Huang He is associated with improved varieties of winter wheat. About half of the arable area is irrigated.

The East China region comprises the provinces of Anhui, Jiangsu and Zhejiang and the municipality of Shanghai. Accounting for 20% of total agricultural production, this region is second only to the Northeast as the breadbasket of China. The Chang Jiang crosses the central part of the region and provides much of the irrigation that permits intensive land use. The region is divided into three broad plains: the Jianghua Plain to the north, the Jiangnan Plain to the south and the Chang Jiang Delta. With an annual growing season of 230 to 250 days and with well-distributed rainfall throughout the year, Zhejiang has the highest cropping intensity in China. Rice is the dominant crop, but cotton, wheat, corn, sorghum and vegetables also are important. Most of the area is double-cropped (wheat/rice), and in some locations a three-crops-in-two-years system is used. The lower Chang Jiang Plain is one of China's most important cotton-producing areas. Some 69% of the area is irrigated, again the highest percentage in China.

The south-central region comprises the provinces of Hubei, Hunan and Jiangxi, in the middle reaches of the Chang Jiang Basin. It accounts for 16% of the rural population and 15% of the gross agricultural output. The annual growing season ranges from 240 to 320 days. With favorable alluvial soils and moisture conditions, the land is intensively cultivated, and its cropping index of 225% is the highest regional average in China. Rice is the most important crop, generally double-cropped with wheat. Cotton is grown in the drier parts, and tea is an important upland crop in the southern areas. Intensive aquaculture is practiced in the lakes. The region offers good prospects for further diversified growth.

South China comprises the provinces of Guangdong and Fujian and the autonomous region of Guangxi Zhuang, lying mainly in the humid subtropics. It accounts for 12% of the rural population and 10.6% of the gross agricultural output. Agriculture is concentrated in the numerous river valleys and small floodplains, of which the largest is formed by the Zhu Jiang Delta. The growing season lasts nearly year-round, with over 350 frost-free days per annum. Rice is the dominant crop, occupying 60% to 65% of the cultivated area, but other important crops include sweet potatoes and corn. Most of the rice is double-cropped with sweet potatoes, rapeseed or wheat grown during the dry season. The region also is a center for tropical crops such as pineapples, sugarcane, rubber and cocoa.

The southeastern region comprises the provinces of Sichuan, Yunnan and Guizhou, mostly mountainous uplands with the exception of the upper inland basin of Chang Jiang, the so-called Red Basin of Sichuan. The region accounts for 17% of the rural population but only 12.6% of the gross agricultural output. The region has the lowest sown area per capita and the lowest rural income; in fact, Guizhou is the poorest province in China. The yearly growing season lasts 260 to 340 days in the Red Basin, where many crops are grown—wheat, rapeseed and barley in winter and rice, corn, cotton and sweet potatoes in summer. Outside of the Red Basin, output and productivity are low. Grain production per capita is significantly below the national average, and growth is limited by a reduction in cultivated acreage in the Red Basin.

China's important contributions to the world agricultural economy are evidenced by its large share in the production of several major commodities. It produces more than 10% of the world's annual output of rice, wheat, corn, sorghum, soybean, cotton, peanuts, rapeseed and tea and accounts for more than 25% of the world's tuber crops. With some 17% of the world's grain production in recent years, China's annual grain output is only fractionally below that of the United States. China ranks first in the world in rice production by a considerable margin. In livestock, China has the world's largest goat population, largest pig population and second-largest (after Australia) sheep population. Crop yields are typically 30% to 70% above average world levels, although 30% to 50% below the levels found in developed countries. In cereals, only France and the United States exceed China in yields per acre.

A major difference between the experience of China and that of many other developing countries relates to the availability of new arable land. Since 1965 the reported cropped acreage has been roughly constant, with new land available through irrigation or land development in the border areas being offset by losses to residential or industrial uses in other regions. Scarcity of land has forced China to concentrate on rice, wheat and corn, which together have accounted for 90% of total cereal production in recent years. For other cereals, such as millet and sorghum, and for other competing field crops, such as soybean, the cropped acreage has declined considerably. For the same reason China has performed poorly in certain other field crops, such as cotton and peanuts. On the other hand, crops that do not compete with food grains for land use, such as tea, mulberry and tuberous root crops, have done well.

Intense and increasing pressure on a narrow arable

land base has been a major element in China's agricultural experience since 1949. China has the highest person/arable land ratio in the world—about 10 persons per ha. (4 persons per ac.), which is 300 times that of the United States and double that of India. Of necessity, therefore, China's arable land is intensively farmed. About 45% of the arable land is irrigated, more than double the proportion in other developing countries and roughly a quarter of the world's total irrigated land. Application of chemical fertilizers exceeds 125 kg. per ha. (112 lb. per ac.), more than three times the average for other developing countries.

As a result of these developments, not only have food supplies been generally adequate, but also food security is enforced through nationwide food procurement and rationing in urban areas. Food imports have been negligible—except during the disastrous Great Leap Forward—and rarely have exceeded 5% of domestic production.

The social revolution that accompanied the establishment of the people's republic in 1949 was the first real transformation in Chinese agriculture in its entire history. It overthrew the ownership class that had prevailed for centuries and created a new class of peasant leaders. Agrarian reform was the most successful program initiated by the Communists, and it proceeded in several phases. In general, the Communists adopted a practical attitude, working out different timetables to fit different areas and classes. The Agrarian Reform Law of 1950 preserved the institution of private ownership of land while confiscating the holdings of the landlords only. Land thus confiscated—some 45 million ha. (110 million ac.), or roughly 45% of the total land area under cultivation at that time—was redistributed to over 300 million peasants—or 60% to 70% of the rural population. Each peasant received 0.06 to 0.2 ha. (0.15 to 0.45 ac.).

The land reform was not an end in itself but only the first step to the eventual collectivization and nationalization of agriculture. This was accomplished in three more stages: mutual aid teams organized under a 1951 law; the transformation of these teams into agricultural producer cooperatives; and collective farms, the highest form of socialized farming. Within a single decade, in the 1950s, the historic fabric of Chinese agriculture had been completely replaced by a new system. The remarkable change had been achieved with less disruption and brutality than in the Soviet Union, and, moreover, did not affect the growth of output. Traditional agricultural techniques were not abandoned but rather were intensified and rationalized. It was only when the leadership embarked on the Great Leap Forward and organized the communes that the sector ran into difficulties. The peasants became exhausted from the unremitting pressure to produce. Adverse weather during 1959–61 combined with political excesses caused a severe agricultural crisis, forcing China to import grain. During the "Agriculture First" period in the early 1960s, agriculture recovered quickly from the disastrous Great Leap Forward. Along with greater decentralization and restoration of private plots, the regime promoted modernization through massive inputs of chemical fertiliz-

ers, high-yielding seed varieties and farm equipment. These improvements were focused on the more productive areas, designated as "high and stable yield areas," covering one-third of the country, much of it in the lower Yangtze River Valley. At the same time, the government urged poorer areas to rely mainly on their own efforts. This was symbolized by a campaign called "Learn from Dazhai." Dazhai was a village in the Northwest that had overcome poverty to become relatively wealthy by Chinese standards through self-reliance. The set of policies based on the Dazhai model formed the framework for agricultural development from the early 1960s until the post-Mao era. Relatively isolated from the Cultural Revolution, agriculture emerged intact from this destructive era and became one of the cornerstones of the "Four Modernizations."

Under Deng, agricultural policy has been reoriented toward a greater role for private initiative. The role of free farm markets has been expanded, and the prices of many commodities have been allowed to rise in response to market conditions. High prices combined with tax and procurement adjustments have brought greater farm revenues. The responsibilities of production teams in decision-making have been increased, and the link between effort and reward has been strengthened. In many areas small work groups were established and given the use of team land and other resources under a contract that scaled remuneration to output. Individual and household production through private plot and sideline activities was encouraged. To maximize efficiency in production and marketing of some important food crops and livestock, specialized production bases were established. Twelve of the largest specialized in grain, and smaller ones on other food crops and livestock. This was a major departure from the former policy of local self-sufficiency. On some state farms, vertical integration was introduced, combining production, processing and marketing.

The core of the current agricultural system is the commune, governed by the Work Regulations for Rural People's Communes of 1962. At the lowest level in the commune structure is the production team, generally made up of 20 to 50 families (the national average is 34) from one neighborhood or locality and often with strong family ties among its members. There are over 5 million production teams comprising some 175 million peasant families, or 807 million people. Collective activities include farming the commune holding (an average of 15 to 20 ha.; 37 to 49 ac.); sidelines such as piggeries, orchards, herb gardens and apiaries; and other forms of employment. The team usually owns small tools and equipment such as pedestrian tractors, threshers and irrigation pumps, and obtains larger machinery from the production brigade on a service-fee basis. These activities are managed by an elected team leader and other officials, including accountants and storekeepers. Farm surpluses (after various deductions) accrue to the team and are distributed annually. Of the total gross output, costs of purchased inputs average 32%; of the balance, some 50% is distributed as collective income to team members. The remainder, about 18% represents collective withholdings, taxes, reserves and a welfare fund. Reserves, used for both investment and emergency relief, are quite limited among the poorer teams. Decisions on allocations are subject to official guidelines.

Distributed collective income (cash and grain) is allocated to individual household heads within the team according to their accumulated work points and through the use of a basic per capita grain allocation. The latter helps to maintain all commune members above dire need and, in the case of the poorest teams, absorbs virtually all team income. Work points are based on official guidelines but allow some latitude for team decisions. Most combine time and rate assessments tempered by skill and other quality differentials, but a few are based solely on piecework. These assessments may be revised periodically, as when a new crop is introduced into the farm plan or when a new team-operated sideline enterprise is established.

Recent reforms have introduced contractural arrangements into this system. Most commonly, these contracts involve a small group of workers within a team undertaking a task with a specified output target, work points and material output allocation. Work points also may be accumulated through participation in activities at the production, brigade or commune level (or sometimes in state or urban employment), where the benefits do not accrue directly to the worker's team. In some areas the tendency is now to pay cash wages to workers, with some supplementary payments being made to the workers' teams from enterprise profits. Households with few working members or many ill or elderly members receive grants from team welfare funds. Where crop failure reduces the available food supply below acceptable levels, relief grain is provided (usually on a loan basis) under the food security system managed by the Ministry of Food.

About 30% of total agricultural income is generated by private plots and sideline activities. They provide the main source of cash income in the peasant economy. The range of household sideline activities, mostly undertaken by female members of the household, is large. The main restriction is that no extra household employment or hiring of labor is permitted. The output of private plots and sidelines is sold through local markets and state agencies. The limit is 15% of the output for private plots. Some provinces also have allowed households increased access to collective land, roadsides or uncultivated land on a temporary basis.

The middle tier of the commune structure is the production brigade, which encompasses either one large village or several smaller ones. There are over 700,000 production brigades, with seven to eight teams per brigade on average, with some as large as 12 and others as few as three. Basically, the brigade is a coordinating mechanism for activities requiring several teams to act together. The brigade may organize specialized teams—e.g., in construction. The brigade is the locus for basic social services and also is the lowest level at which the party is organized. Brigade enterprises have multiplied in recent years in the more populated areas. Nationally there are two enterprises per brigade.

At the apex of the peasant economy are the com-munes. Currently there are 53,000 communes, roughly 25 per county, each serving an average of 12 to 13 production brigades. Thus the average population of a commune is 15,000 people, with arable land resources averaging 1,800 ha. (4,446 ac.). Many commune managers receive salaries from the provincial governments, and the commune center—generally a rural township—offers a variety of higher-level services, such as secondary schools and hospitals. Working in tandem with party functionaries, the commune staff provides leadership and direction to commune activities as a whole, and disseminates and monitors policy and program directives from higher authorities. General administrative duties include collecting taxes, maintaining public security, collecting data, writing official reports, registering births and deaths and performing marriage ceremonies. Local services controlled at the commune level include education, communications, marketing, procurement, health and agricultural extension. The communes manage numerous enterprises, such as tractor service pools, chemical and cement plants, machine shops, canneries and small-scale hydroelectric plants. Each commune manages an average of six such enterprises, whose employees are paid monthly wages.

The state sector is much smaller in agriculture than in industry. The first state farms were established in the 1950s, mostly as pioneer settlements in border areas, with ex-army personnel making up most of the labor force. State farms continue to be concentrated in border areas and in reclamation and development work. Currently state farmlands comprise some 30 million ha. (74 million ac.), of which some 4.5 million ha. (11 million ac.) are arable lands under cultivation—equivalent to 4.5% of the nation's total cultivated area. With 2,047 farms in operation, the average cultivated area is some 2,700 ha. (6,669 ac.), rather more than the area in an average commune, where the average population is three times as large. Over half of the cultivated area, some 2.4 million ha. (5.9 million ac.), is in the Northeast, mainly in Heilongjiang, where the average size of a state farm exceeds 20,000 ha. (49,400 ac.). Xinjiang, in the extreme Northwest, and coastal lands of Jiangsu and Hebei in northern China also have large state farms. Almost all of China's natural rubber production comes from state farms in the South. State farms have many characteristics that set them apart from communes: a higher contribution to state procurement of grains (45%); larger farm industrial enterprises; per capita income three times the nationwide average for communes; and a high rate of mechanization, with 85% of the cultivated area machine-plowed, 50% machine-harvested and 76% machine-plowed.

Marketing of agricultural products was socialized in the 1950s. By the mid-1950s, when private marketing was progressively restricted, three types of supply and marketing channels were developed. For major crops—Category I, consisting of grains, oilseeds, cotton and sugar—purchase and distribution were limited to state-managed procurement agencies at centrally determined prices. These agencies also were charged with collecting the agricultural tax, which was (and is) paid in kind, mainly as grain. Category II crops, including livestock products, were sold to marketing cooperatives under a quota system, and the surplus was sold in free markets. Prices for most of these crops also were set nationally, with some provincial variations. Minor crops such as vegetables were sold through rural markets at regulated prices. This system has remained in force for the past three decades, although since the 1980s the free markets have gained in importance and scope. The two most prominent marketing agencies are the Ministry of Food, which procures and distributes grain and oilseed crops; and the All-China Federation of Supply and Marketing Cooperatives (S&M Federation), which markets cash crops and distributes some agricultural inputs and tools. Some products, including sugar, pigs and rubber, are handled by the Ministry of Commerce.

The Ministry of Food procures about 50 million tons of grain annually, or 18% to 20% of total food grain output. Since the 1950s procurement has been based on quotas, which account for 45% to 55% of total grain procurement. The balance comes from tax grain (20%) and above-quota purchases, the latter negotiated with the production teams on an annual basis and for which there is a 50% price premium. Quota and tax grain assessments were made in the 1950s and have not been revised upward, so their burden is much lower today.

The major emphasis in food grain policy has been to assure adequate supplies throughout the country at stable and uniform prices. In the urban areas grain and edible oils are rationed. Grain rations vary with the locality—being higher in the North than in the South—and also with age and type of activity. In the rural areas, supplies are much more variable, although the authorities maintain a floor consumption level. Restrictions on the sale of surplus grain in free markets at negotiated prices were lifted in 1978. It is estimated that some 5 million tons of grain now enter these markets, often grain of superior quality or of specialized types.

The S&M Federation is essentially a state trading corporation with some 3.6 million workers and 600,000 licensed agents who buy and sell on a commission basis. In the countryside, 36,000 separately organized marketing cooperatives form a nationwide network. The S&M Federation also purchases most of the industrial crops, including cotton, wool and jute, processed vegetables and medicinal herbs, spices and honey. Like the Ministry of Food, the S&M Federation operates within state-determined prices and purchase quotas for some of the leading crops. Where the prices do not cover costs, the agency receives special subsidies.

Credit for agricultural development is largely the responsibility of the Agricultural Bank of China, but some funds for rural development also are provided by the People's Bank of China and the People's Construction Bank. The work of these banks is complemented by some 59,000 local credit cooperatives, organized at the commune and brigade levels.

The structure and functional responsibilities in the agricultural sector are broadly similar in various levels of government. In both the center and in the provinces

THE AGRICULTURAL REGIONS OF CHINA						
Name	Provinces	Rainfall, mm. (in.)	Growing season, months	Percent of land cultivated	Crops	Comments
Spring wheat region	N. Hebei, Shaanxi, Shanxi, Gansu, S. Liaoning, Ningxia, Inner Mongolia	350 (13.8) variable	6.5	18	Main crop, wheat; also millet, potatoes, kaoliang, barley, peas	Sparsely populated
Winter wheat-millet region	Shanxi, Shaanxi, Gansu	430 (17.0)	7–7.5	22	Wheat, millet, cotton, kaoliang	Loess country; most fertile areas are the valleys of the rivers Fen and Wei
Winter wheat, rice, kaoliang region	Henan, Hebei	600 (23.6)	8	68	Wheat, kaoliang, cotton, millet, corn, soya beans	The North China Plain; considerable rice now grown, especially in Honan, and some double-cropping
Yangtze rice-wheat region	Hubei, Anhui, Jiangsu	1,000 (39.4)	10	35	Rice, wheat, cotton, mulberry trees for silk farms	Very rich, with many important nonfood crops; increasing multiple-cropping
Rice-tea region	Hunan, Jiangxi, Zhejiang, Fujian	1,500 (59.0)	10–11	18+	Rice, tea, rapeseed, mulberry trees	Rich; hilly terrain keeps cultivated area low
Szechuan rice region	Sichuan	1,000 (39.4)	11–12	33.3	Rice, wheat, corn, rapeseed, sugarcane	Traditionally a big exporter of grain to other regions
Double-cropping rice region	Guangdong, Guangxi, Fujian, Jiangxi	1,750 (68.9)	12	13	Rice, sweet potatoes, sugarcane, fruits	Cultivated land, very productive, but many hills and intense population pressure
Southwest rice region	Yunnan, Guizhou	1,150 (45.3)	12	7	Rice, corn, peas, beans, rapeseed	One of the fastest-growing regions for grain production since 1949
Soya bean-kaoliang region	Heilongjiang, Jilin, Liaoning	500–800 (20.0–31.5)	5	c. 16	Wheat, kaoliang, soya beans	An area where new land has been brought into cultivation and rice is now grown

are agricultural ministries whose work is coordinated by agricultural commissions. At the center are five agricultural ministries, dealing with agriculture (including animal husbandry); water conservancy; forestry, agricultural machinery state farms and land reclamation; aquatic products; and meteorology. These ministries supervise a network of research institutions and stations.

A central feature of the agricultural system is the comprehensive planning at all levels of government. The broad array of planning instruments includes marketing and supplies, prices, allocation of resources and capital construction. Indicative or indirect planning leans heavily on material incentives and pricing adjustments and accords considerable discretion to lower units, while physical planning or planning by directives assigns physical outputs and hectarage targets and allocates resources. The current emphasis is on the former type of planning.

The apex organization for agricultural research is the Chinese Academy of Agricultural Sciences (CAAS), which operates a network of national research institutes. Currently there are 31 national research institutes—13 in Beijing and 18 in the provinces. Some are organized by discipline (such as the Plant Protection Institute) and some by commodity (such as the Tea Institute and the Cotton Institute). Each province is served by a local research network, with a provincial academy of agriculture as the lead institution. At the provincial level these networks are substantial and complex. Below the provincial level are some 20 prefectural-level institutes and over 170 county-level establishments. Nationwide there are some 1,300 large research institutes and facilities above the prefectural level that are concerned with agriculture in some way. Research work is closely coordinated with extension activities. This linkage was reinforced after the Cultural Revolution on the basis of a "seven-level" scientific network. The three higher levels—national, provincial and prefectural—are concerned with research, and the four lower levels—county, commune, brigade and team—are concerned with extension activities. Under the Agricultural Education Department are seven national agricultural colleges; a further 38 institutions are supervised at the provincial level. Secondary-level technical education for agriculture is provided through a system of senior secondary schools in which, in principle, entrants are graduates of lower secondary schools.

Although agricultural investment has lagged behind that of industry since the 1950s, the sheer size of total public investment outlays has ensured a substantial flow of funds into agriculture after the 1960s. In addition, substantial funds were mobilized from the moderate incomes of the peasantry as well as large contributions in labor. Despite such inflow, investment priorities were not always well selected. Faulty decisions affected the quality of fertilizers and agricultural machinery. Because of poor farm management, much land fell into disuse for arable purposes.

Extensive efforts to improve the land base; extend irrigation, drainage and flood prevention systems; and develop new lands have been the main foci of rural investment. Since 1949 some 86,000 reservoirs have been constructed, with a storage capacity estimated at 400 billion cu.m. (14.126 trillion cu. ft.), close to 15% of the total water runoff. Total irrigation development is estimated at 45 million ha. (111 million ac.), up from 16 million ha, (40 million ac.) in 1949. With major investments in water conservancy, grain production has become progressively less subject to year-by-year fluctuations due to weather. Except for large dams, almost all water conservancy is done by hand, using wheelbarrows, small carts, shoulder poles and baskets. Projects with tens of thousands of workers are common.

Major problems in land development are erosion, siltation and salinity. Some 15% of the total irrigated area is affected by salinity. Massive silting is an age-old problem of the Huang He, and continuous silting on the North China Plain has required dike structures to be raised progressively. Erosion control is made difficult by the removal of vegetative cover for fuel.

AGRICULTURAL INDICATORS, 1988

Agriculture's share of GDP (%): 31
Average annual growth rate (%): 7.4 (1980–87)
Value added in agriculture ($): 90.102 billion
Cereal imports (000 tons): 15,897
Index of Agricultural Production (1979–81 = 100): 134 (1986)
Index of Food Production (1979–81 = 100): 134 (1986)
Index of Food Production Per Capita (1979–81 = 100): 124 (1985–87)
Number of tractors: 866,463
Number of harvester-threshers: 30,945
Total fertilizer consumption (tons): 16,851,600
Fertilizer consumption (100 g. per ha.): 1,740
Number of farms: 1,650,000
Average size of commune holding (ha/ac): 15–20 ha; 37–49 ac.
Tenure (%)
   State: 10
   Cooperative: 90
% of farms using irrigation: 44
Total land in farms, ha.(ac.): 143,600,000 (354,835,600)
Farms as % of total land area: 15
Land use (%)
   Total cropland: 100
      Permanent crops: 2.6
      Temporary crops: $\left.\right\}$ 97.4
      Fallow:
Yields, kg./ha. (lb./ac.)
   Grains: 3,977 (3,550)
   Roots & tubers: 16,091 (14,362)
   Pulses: 1,322 (1,180)
   Milk, kg.(lb.)/animal: 1,774 (3,911)
Livestock (000)
   Cattle: 66,925
   Sheep: 94,210
   Hogs: 338,074
   Horses: 11,000
   Chickens: 1,796,000
Forestry
   Production of roundwood, 000 cu. m. (000 cu. ft.): 268,385 (9,478,008)
   of which industrial roundwood (%): 35.1
   Value of exports ($000):525,879
Fishing
   Total catch (000 tons): 8000.1
   of which marine (%): 58
   Value of exports ($000): 645,813

Because of China's large manpower, mechanization has not been a major priority. It is important in those areas of northern and northwestern China that have short and viable growing seasons and thus need rapid land preparation and harvesting, and in areas of double-cropping and triple-cropping. Elsewhere tractors are used essentially for transportation.

Research development has focused mainly on rice and wheat. China was the first nation to develop and popularize a rice hybrid. The rice varietal improvement program has stressed yield and early maturation as the main breeding objectives, but many of the popular varieties also are resistant to diseases. Research has contributed to significant advances in wheat and corn production as well. To widen the genetic resources, spring wheat cultivars were introduced from abroad, particularly Mexico. Apart from crop-specific research, China has done much pioneering work in other areas, such as the use of azolla and green manures, the development of biogas and the use of forages and agricultural residues in livestock-fattening systems.

China's animal husbandry sector is not well developed, and the livestock population is small in relation to the size of the pastureland, occupying 34% of the total land area. Most communes raise pigs and some poultry. Meat consumption is relatively low, and the main source of meat is pork. Some dairy cows are kept, but the level of consumption of dairy products also is low. Sheep and goats are found mostly in the large herding regions, such as Nei Monggol and Xinjiang, outside the main agricultural areas. Sheep are raised both for meat and as a source of wool. Large animals, mostly water buffalo but also oxen, cattle, horses, mules and donkeys, provide draft power for cultivation and transportation.

Fishing makes up less than 2% of the gross value of agricultural output. However, China has excellent coastal fisheries in addition to 260,000 sq. km. (100,360 sq. mi.) of inland lakes and ponds. The principal fisheries are on the coasts of southern and southeastern China.

Forests cover some 13% of the total land area, mostly in the remote inland regions, where lack of transportation makes exploitation difficult. Coniferous stands are mainly in Manchuria and Nei Monggol and deciduous stands in Sichuan and Yunnan. The government has an extensive afforestation program. Reported failure rates in afforestation are high because young trees need watering for several years before they are well established. Trees have been successfully established in only 20% of the replanted areas.

MANUFACTURING

In contrast to the agricultural economy, in which China has a history of thousands of years, the industrial economy is less than half a century old. Within this short span of time it has made enormous strides and achieved impressive gains, almost all of which were made under the Communist regime.

Statistics for manufacturing are not separated in China from those of a wider group of activities subsumed under the heading "industry" and covering manufacturing, electric power, mining and mineral extraction, logging and transportation of timber, and services provided to workers and staff within industrial enterprises. Chinese data for industry cover all state enterprises and, in addition, urban collective and commune-owned enterprises that meet three tests: they have at least 10 workers, have buildings and equipment and operate at least three months in a year. Output from rural industrial enterprises owned by production brigades or production teams and from commune enterprises too small or seasonal to meet these tests, is counted in agricultural output, while manufacturing on a very small scale within such units as households generally goes unrecorded.

According to official estimates, gross industrial output has increased in real terms more than 40-fold since 1949, implying an average growth of over 13% per annum. If the 1949–52 recovery period is omitted, the rate for 1952–79 is 11.1% per annum. Especially rapid growth was achieved in two periods: 35% per annum between 1949 and 1952 and 18% per annum between 1952 and 1957. Between 1952 and 1979, despite political turmoil, gross output continued to grow at nearly 10% per annum. Net output in current prices has grown more slowly than gross output in constant prices, at rates averaging 8.6% in 1957–79 and a little less since 1970. But in real terms this growth may have paralleled that of gross output, since there has been a slow downward drift of industrial prices since 1957.

The broad picture of remarkable growth suggested by these figures is confirmed by available evidence. However, there may be mild upward biases in the growth rates given in the official series, since Chinese prices and accounting conventions give greater weight to fast-growing sectors. Prices of industrial products are higher on average, by international comparative standards, for the newer products, whose output has grown faster than for old ones, whose output has grown more slowly. There also are problems in creating links in the series where products change. Computation of gross output is biased toward more modern sectors such as iron and steel, machine-building and chemicals. In contrast to the practice in many other countries, gross output does not include the value of raw materials used in such activities as grain milling, slaughtering and cotton ginning, except in the largest urban enterprises.

A further problem is that over time, and as a result of changing priorities and technologies, the output mix has shifted, as has the relationship between final output and intermediate inputs such as steel, coal or electricity. In some years more than others, a significant share of output has remained unused, stockpiled or wasted. Thus trends in useful final output may have varied from those in measured output. Moreover, since gross output is the leading target at all levels, many reporting units probably have tended to make choices that have raised their measured gross output performance.

Net output, too, suffers from distortions. About a fourth consists of labor costs, which were held down from 1957 to 1977 by granting almost no wage increases. Since, with minor exceptions, there is no charge for the use of capital, over two-thirds of the net output consists of indirect taxes and planned profits, based on prices that do not reflect demand and supply but make profits seem higher in some industries than in others. Compared to market economies, these price markups and indirect taxes at successive stages of manufacturing are relatively high, while price markups and indirect taxes in commerce are generally small, with the effect that much of the national income shows up as net output in industry rather than services. Low prices of foodstuffs and most services add to the relatively heavy weight of industry. Indeed, Western concepts used in national accounting and in aggregating output were never designed for such a price and tax system, so inferences based on these concepts may be misleading.

The neglect of consumer goods industries over long periods also is not revealed in the official figures. The per capita production of most consumer goods remains very low, and even where considerable gains have been made in numbers, the quality of these goods remains below average.

By force of circumstances, China has had to rely on itself to attain a fair degree of industrial self-sufficiency. In practically every significant industry, major plants have been created in several parts of the country. An extensive machine-building capability has been achieved by encouraging enterprises to build their own machinery. Special efforts have been made to spread manufacturing into backward regions and rural areas, where no industry existed prior to 1949. As a result, there is a foundation of engineering experience and a breadth of technical expertise, unusual in a developing country. The Chinese also have used ingenuity in the absence of foreign capital or know-how. Small plants using outdated methods were built as a means of acquiring basic skills and obviating problems in building larger plants.

The Chinese classification of branches of industry is based on the Soviet approach of the 1950s. Industries are arranged approximately according to the international classification system, with some minor exceptions.

Of the gross industrial output, about 89% in 1985 came from manufacturing. The share of gross manufacturing is significantly lower in net output because a very large share of the gross output in manufacturing represents the cost of purchased current inputs—such as energy, materials and components—rather than value added (such as wages and profits) in the industry itself. As a result, manufacturing share of net output probably is about 80% to 83%.

To translate Chinese data in GDP terms, it is necessary to add depreciation, switch net output in brigade industries from agriculture to industry and reassign wages of people engaged in services or other nonindustrial activities within industrial enterprises. The net effect of these adjustments would raise the industrial share of the GDP to 43.6% and the manufacturing share of the GDP to 35% at Chinese prices.

China is one of the few countries in the world that has sustained industrial growth rates as high as 10% per annum for more than 20 years. (Japan, Korea, Thailand and Nigeria are among the others.) As a result, the industrial sector is unusually large relative to the rest of the economy. However, if international prices were used and indirect taxes were excluded, as they are in other countries, the industrial sector's share in China probably would be roughly comparable to those in middle-income countries. By international standards the industrial output per capita is small, about 25% of the average for middle-income countries and 4% of the average for industrialized market economies. But it is three times higher than the average in low-income countries.

In terms of total output China ranks among the world's major industrial countries. The net value of manufacturing production (at Chinese prices and official exchange rates) is about a seventh that of the United States. Quantitatively China leads the world in output of cotton yarn and fabric. It ranks third in output of cement, coal and sulfuric acid, fifth in steel and seventh in electric power. Its output of radios is second only to that of Hong Kong. Comparisons based on physical output of basic intermediate goods are biased in China's favor, however, since Chinese manufacturing tends to be wasteful of energy and materials. For example, the conversion efficiency of primary energy in China is 28%, compared to 51% in the United States and 57% in Japan. In China final products probably involve less fabrication and have a lower average value relative to the materials used than goods manufactured in advanced countries. In some branches of output, moreover, China still is only a small producer by world standards. For example, its output of motor vehicles is only 0.4% of the world total.

China's industrial labor is estimated at 53.4 million (63 million counting brigade industrial labor), surpassing in numbers that of the EC and North America combined. However, as a percentage of the population, the share of industrial labor in China is 6%, compared to 10% to 11% in the industrial market economies; 13% to 14% in the industrialized, centrally planned economies; and 1% to 2% (or less) in the least-developed countries. In net output per workers, China trails most countries except the poorest. Excluding automobiles, not a significant factor in Chinese industry, manufacturing derives a higher share of its output from heavy industry than most developing countries. In many respects China has an industrial structure similar to that of Brazil and India but has a higher share of textiles, machinery and metal products than both but a lower share in food, beverages and tobacco. The latter anomaly is caused by the exclusion of brigade and very-small-scale enterprises from the Chinese statistics.

The basic organizational unit in the industrial sector is the enterprise. This usually is a single plant, often a small one, but large manufacturing enterprises are not uncommon. A basic distinction among enterprises is their legal ownership. The more important ones are owned by the state ("the whole people"). The rest, collectively owned, are either collective enterprises or commune enterprises. There are no private industrial enterprises.

At the core of the industrial sector are about 60,000 independent accounting units belonging to the state, with an average of well over Y5 million worth of gross fixed assets and 371 workers each. The much smaller collective enterprises average Y210,000 worth of gross fixed assets and 133 workers each, and the still smaller commune enterprises average Y75,000 of gross fixed assets and 50 workers each. State enterprises, although less than 25% of the total in numbers, produce nearly 82% of the total output, compared to 11.7% coming from urban collective enterprises and 6.3% from commune enterprises. Information on the value of assets, profits and taxes is available for independent accounting units only, primarily in industry. In the units covered, which produced 96% of the net total output in 1985, the state sector accounted for 91.1% of gross fixed assets, 83.1% of working capital or circulating funds, 88% of net fixed assets and 87% of profits and taxes. Conversely, the collective enterprises weigh more heavily in employment, with 42% of total industrial employment. Capital per worker or staff member in 1985 averaged Y11,217 in state enterprises but only Y2,416 in urban collective enterprises and about Y1,730 in rural commune enterprises.

Production brigades are excluded from industrial statistics. According to the Ministry of Agriculture, there are about 580,000 industrial enterprises in production brigades, with a total of 9.73 million workers and staff, or about 17 workers each. Gross output per worker was Y12,000 in state enterprises, Y4,800 in urban collective enterprises, Y2,600 in rural commune enterprises and Y1,680 in production brigade enterprises. However, many of the workers in production brigades work only part time in industry. If brigade enterprises are counted, China has over 935,000 industrial enterprises.

The basic structural division in industry is between light and heavy industry. Light industry includes all consumer goods, food products, processed agricultural products and textiles plus many producer goods—e.g., paper and pulp, synthetic fibers and simpler types of farm equipment. Heavy industry includes steel, cement, machine building, electric power, timber extraction and all mining other than salt mining. Heavy industry, using nearly 83% of net fixed assets, produces nearly 62% of net output. Its share of industrial employment is slightly over 58%. Heavy industry also generates 60% of the profits and taxes from industry. For each Y100 of capital invested, light industry yields Y47.7 in profits and taxes compared to Y19.1 from heavy industry. However, the net output per person employed is about 15% higher in heavy industry, which also produces slightly more profits per worker. Despite the sizable overall profits in industry, about 23% of all state industrial enterprises operate at a loss.

In light industry, enterprises in the state sector produce 76% of the gross output, with 55,000 units, 8.46 million workers and Y51.6 billion in fixed assets. Similarly, the 30,000 state enterprises in heavy industry generate 85% of the gross output and employ 85% of the gross fixed assets in the state sector and 72.2% of the state sector's average employment. With nearly twice as much fixed capital per worker as light industry, heavy industry produces only about half as much gross output per worker.

Over half of the work force in state industrial enterprises is employed in machine building. Over 60% of the collective enterprises' work force is in light industry. Production brigades also are oriented to light industry.

The major state institutions overseeing the industrial sector are the State Economic Commission (SEC) and the State Planning Commission (SPC), both in the same building. The SEC has the prime responsibility for executing the annual plans, setting up priorities, controlling quality and maintaining standards. The SPC draws up annual and longer-term plans and approves major investment projects, which then are carried out under the State Capital Construction Commission. Other commissions involved in this sector are the Energy Commission, the Machine-Building Industry Commission and the Import-Export Control Commission. Below these supraministerial bodies, 14 central government ministries are primarily engaged in manufacturing. These include eight ministries of machine building and six others, dealing with agricultural machinery, the building materials industry, the chemicals industry, the metallurgical industry, the textiles industry and light industry.

In addition, industrial enterprises are found under practically every other ministry. There is a widespread pattern of vertical integration and self-reliance within these units. The Building Materials, Chemicals and Metallurgical Industry ministries have their own mining operations; the Ministry of the Textiles Industry has its own petrochemical complexes to produce synthetic fibers; the Ministry of Coal Mining makes coal mining machinery; the Ministry of Railways makes railway equipment; the Ministry of Geology makes geological instruments; the Ministry of Posts and Telecommunications makes telephone equipment; the Ministry of Communications builds ships; and so on. Practically all ministries have machine-building enterprises. The Ministry of Agriculture exercises indirect supervision over brigade and commune industries, while the Ministry of State Farms oversees 6,100 industrial enterprises on state farms. Many Ministry of Defense factories produce civilian consumer goods such as clothing, footwear, radios and sunglasses.

One of the most important ministries is the Ministry of Light Industry, which contains 18 industrial departments and supervises 10,600 state enterprises and 55,600 urban collective enterprises. In heavy industry the sphere of each ministry is narrower, but supervision is more direct. For example, the First Ministry of Machine Building has six general bureaus, and supervises 4,240 state enterprises and 2,200 urban collective enterprises producing 20,000 kinds of products.

This central organization is mirrored, on a smaller scale, in each province and independent municipality. Each has industrial bureaus (Shanghai and Liaoning have 11 each). Each enterprise has a dual responsibility to the central ministry and its corresponding local or regional organ, although in some cases there is a single chain of supervision. The unit of government that has supervisory power over an enterprise often acquires a sense of proprietorship. However, enterprises sometimes change hands, being shifted from central to regional control or vice versa. Enterprises also sometimes pass from one ownership category to another, as, e.g., from collective into state enterprises. As a result of the interaction of several levels of authority on each enterprise, decision-making processes tend to become complex and often extend beyond the primary channel of supervision. Enterprise managers must constantly interact with various state authorities and be guided by national policies and standards. Some degree of entrepreneurship is exercised by central bureaus for particular industries that have substantial influence in shaping economic policies. This degree of administrative centralization is higher for heavy and defense industries—e.g., out of the 17,000 state-owned independent accounting units in machine building, 12,000 are directly under central ministries, in most cases jointly with provincial authorities. Conversely, light industry is almost entirely under the direct control of regional or local authorities. The level of governmental supervision also depends on the level of technical competence and industrial experience of the local authorities.

Differences appear between state and collective enterprises mainly in the wage levels and the way in which profits are divided. Wages in the latter are lower than those in comparable jobs in state enterprises, and there are substantial regional variations. In state enterprises all profits belong, in principle, to the state. By comparison, collective enterprises pay a graduated income tax, which in the larger enterprises amounts to 55% of the profits after indirect taxes. The remainder is divided according to a formula that varies among localities. The norm in Beijing was 40% to the municipal bureau, 30% to the parent corporation and 20% to 30% (i.e., 9% to 13.5% of total profits) to the enterprise itself. The collective enterprise's share of its profits after taxes was raised to 50% to 70% in 1981. Half of the enterprise profits are plowed back into investments, and the other half are used for welfare services and bonuses.

Each enterprise prepares an annual plan whose broad outlines are passed down from above but fleshed out from below. Each plan specifies a target along with detailed instructions and constraints on resources, workers, labor, etc. In addition to the physical quantity of output, the targets also include quality, profits, fulfillment of contracts and labor productivity, but these are secondary to the output. Additional targets may be decreed by the latest policies and campaigns, such as saving energy and reducing consumption of raw materials.

The plan gives the enterprise little scope for varying its technology or substituting one input for another. Raw materials, the sources and channels through which they are to be delivered and the recipients of the output are all specified. However, when an enterprise does not receive its planned allocations on schedule, it must cultivate alternative supply channels to provide for such contingencies. The authorities informally permit various types of barter deals among enterprises to cope with these difficulties. Also, plans often are changed

and reallocations and reductions made to reflect revised priorities. Fixed capital in production is inflexible, but additional funds may be borrowed for working capital. A principal 1981 reform was to allow enterprises greater latitude in securing capital funds.

Nonmonetary rewards and peer pressure are used more often to motivate workers and managers. Bonuses have been reintroduced, but they are small and tend to be shared equally, with managers getting no more than the average. A worker's pay is practically never reduced, and no one is discharged. Pay differentials are generally narrow within age and skill groups. Chinese managers generally earn only a little more than ordinary workers—e.g., about Y100 a month compared to about Y65.

China is noted for the important role played by rural small-scale units in the industrial economy and also for the coexistence of enterprises of different sizes, exemplifying the principle of "walking on two legs." While this approach has allowed China to achieve a high degree of self-sufficiency, it has at the same time reduced per capita productivity and lowered per-unit efficiency. The definitions of "large," "medium" and "small" vary with the industry, and the total number of large and medium-size enterprises also varies with the definition used. Prima facie, the importance of small industrial enterprises is not large or uncommon by international standards. However, they are unusual in that many of them, dispersed throughout the country, are characterized by large economies of scale. As a result, China has quite an unusual structure of production within particular industries. Cement is an example, where about two-thirds of the national output comes from small enterprises using vertical kilns in which cement is cooked in batches. This technique became obsolete many decades ago in the West because it presents difficulties in controlling quality, but it is particularly adapted to China because of low investment costs, simplicity of process and savings in transportation costs. China now has over 3,400 of such plants, their output varying from 80,000 tons per annum to 2,000 tons per annum. However, these vertical kilns have a serious disadvantage in that they use double the energy per ton as in developed countries. In the nitrogenous fertilizer industry also about two-thirds of the output comes from small plants, using technology based on partial oxidation using coal, another technique long abandoned in the West. Typically, these plants have an ammonia production capacity of 3,000 to 5,000 tons, about 1/100th of large plants, and their energy consumption per ton is about 2.4 times that of large plants. Because ammonia bicarbonate is unstable, and decomposes when exposed to moisture or temperatures above 20°C (68°F), there are serious difficulties in storing, transporting or applying it. Energy consumption and quality differences also are substantial between large and small plants in the iron and steel industry. Small plants are found in a wide range of other industries as well, such as paper, ball and roller bearings and automobile parts.

When the people's republic was established, China's industries were heavily concentrated in the coastal provinces. Industry still is disproportionately concentrated in the older industrial centers, but many industries have been built in the intervening period throughout the country, and especially in the interior. The leading industrial region is East China, particularly Shanghai, Jiangsu and Zhejiang, which together produce roughly a quarter of the national industrial output. Shanghai leads in both heavy and light industries. A second leading industrial region is the Northeast, which still is the strongest base for heavy industry, with a share of industrial capacity considerably larger than indicated by its one-sixth share of total output. A third major industrial region is North China, particularly Beijing, Trianjin and adjacent Hebei Province. In some ways, nearby Shandong and Hunan provinces are part of this zone. This third zone links the other two so that one could almost say that there is an industrial corridor, roughly from Harbin down to a little south of Shanghai, containing about 60% of China's industries. Other concentrations of industry are in central China, particularly Hubei and Hunan; in the Southwest; and in Guangdong, on the southeastern coast.

Since 1949 each of the 29 principal geographical divisions appears to have increased its gross industrial output, with the exception of five regional units: Shanghai, Tianjin and the three provinces of the Northeast. A long contiguous belt on the eastern coast from Guangdong in the South through Fujian, Jianxi, Zhejiang, Anhui, Jiangsu, Shandong and Hebei roughly maintained its shares; Moving west toward the interior, the area from Guangxi in the South through Hunan, Hubei and Shanxi north to Nei Monggol and westward to Shaanxi, Gansu, Ningxia and Qinghai increased its share; the capital district of Beijing more than doubled its share of industrial output. Counting also the modest increases achieved in Sichuan and Guizhou, a very slight increase in Xinjiang and the beginnings of industry in Xizang (Tibet), all of interior and western China expanded its industrial output faster than the national average of 400%.

Industry is the second of the Four Modernizations launched in the 1980s, and the shift in policy it represents has already affected the sector profoundly. Previously, light industry was badly neglected, along with agriculture and nonproductive investments. Between 1966 and 1978, of the total amount of investment in capital construction, heavy industry took up more than 55%, agriculture about 10% and light industry about 5%. Production remained divorced from customers' needs, and shortages were endemic. Industrialization programs placed a premium on immediate gains in output at the expense of quality and efficient use of resources.

The new policy framework first announced in 1979 is designed to counteract these problems. It had a number of primary thrusts: (1) to slow the rate of growth in heavy industry; (2) to increase the supply of consumer goods; (3) to promote the efficient use of resources; (4) to adjust output to consumer needs; (5) to give enterprises somewhat greater autonomy; (6) to create a wider division of labor, including networks of parts suppliers; and (7) to foster competition among enterprises serving the same markets. The authorities also reasserted central control over investments at lower levels in an effort to curb uncoordinated investments in light industry in poor and backward areas. These industries had been established wherever local resources and prerogatives permitted using local raw materials formerly shipped to distant industrial centers. While such investments were enormously attractive in improving local incomes, living standards and supplies of goods, they made no sense from a national point of view when they added to an already redundant capacity.

The new reforms are aimed to strengthen the enterprises' sense of "operation, market, competition and service." Within industries, reorganization is based on principles of rationalization, efficiency, cooperation and specialization. An enormous effort is devoted to technological transformation, mastering new products and raising the technical level of industry. Energy conservation, lower costs of production and quality are central themes. Energy-inefficient products are being phased out. Much emphasis is placed on improving testing equipment, design, quality control and technical and scientific research work as well as information on markets. Another change being pursued is toward economies of scale by producing in larger quantities and achieving specialization in production.

The difficulties in implementing these reforms has exposed the many problems and weaknesses as well as the strengths of the industrial sector. Like other sectors in China, industry abounds in contradictions and paradoxes. Some of the weaknesses and inefficiencies in the system relate to the country's level of development; others relate to the socialist economic system. Most of the light industries are described as backward by international standards, with low capacity; obsolete equipment; small plants, many causing serious pollution; low technical and managerial competence levels; and uninspiring product designs. Most equipment tends to be 20 or 30 years out of date, and energy-inefficient. Only a small fraction of the machine tools are special-purpose or high-precision types. This problem is aggravated by low levels of technical know-how in moving from new product designs to series or mass production. This reflects both inexperience in designing assembly lines and difficulties in designing and building the specialized components and machinery required. Even though China tries to make most of its own equipment, many sophisticated items have to be imported from hard-currency areas. Wasteful errors have been made in the planning and design of even the largest industrial plants, as a result of which expensive plants in industries, such as steel, chemical fertilizers and petrochemicals have had to idle for lack of raw materials, energy or other basic requirements. Pipelines have been built for natural gas that could not, in fact, be produced.

While machinery is abundant in most plants, a high proportion stands idle most of the time or is used only occasionally in a backup capacity. Factory buildings are nearly always poorly maintained and ill designed for efficient performance. Another problem is that factories are in the middle of workers' housing, or in residential areas, aggravating environmental pollution. Many factories are converted buildings originally de-

MANUFACTURING INDICATORS, 1988

Average annual growth rate, 1980–87: 12.6
Share of GDP: 34%
Labor force in manufacturing: 17.7%
Value added in manufacturing: $91.463 billion
  Food & agriculture: 13%
  Textiles: 13%
  Machinery: 26%
  Chemicals: 10%
Index of Manufacturing Production (1980=100): 158.6 (1988)

signed and built for other purposes. Because no worker may be laid off, worker utilization is low, and a large part of the work is done by a small proportion of the employed work force, while others stand partly idle. Because of compartmentalization, technological and management improvements do not spread among industries and organizations. Thus while cotton spinning and weaving plants are highly efficient, garment factories are backward and have low rates of machine utilization. While the machine tool industry is strong, the automobile industry has only rudimentary facilities. There is a wide range in the quality of machinery in various industries. Laboratory equipment and general-purpose machine tools are more competitive in design than textile machinery and paper machinery. Despite significant advances in manufacturing technology, the Chinese have difficulties in producing large, complex systems and in introducing numerical controls. China is particularly backward in two areas: computers and telecommunications—areas that constitute the leading edge of technology in advanced countries. Only small numbers of computers are being produced, and they are not standardized, which hampers software development. Industry also is hampered by the lag in high-quality professional and technical manpower, caused by the hiatus in higher education from 1966 to 1976. Faced with a shortage of technical specialists, many plants retrain workers with mixed success.

Chinese industry has severe pollution problems, which now are being taken seriously after being ignored in the past. Probably the heaviest polluters are the large integrated steelworks. In the larger cities pollution control programs have been developed, and some relocation of plants is planned.

While industrial managers are generally dedicated and energetic, they are relatively passive in making major decisions regarding investment and allocation of resources. They also are hampered by lack of economy-wide information necessary to make analytical choices.

A further source of inefficiency at all levels is the system of prices, taxes and charges, which distorts the relationship between capital and labor. Prices do not reflect true scarcity values. Enterprises make expensive items for themselves to keep their costs down and produce more of the products in excess supply while trying to use those in scarce supply.

New measures have been introduced since 1978 to attract foreign capital to assist in China's industrial development. Several new types of arrangements have been introduced, including processing of foreign-supplied materials or assembly of foreign-supplied components; compensation trade in which foreigners supply equipment and assistance in exchange for part of the output; joint ventures; and cooperative production in Chinese facilities. Special export processing zones have been set up on the southeastern coast, near Hong Kong. Thus far these new arrangements account for only a small fraction of manufactured exports.

MINING

Coal is China's most abundant mineral resource, with proven resources of over 600 billion tons, of which 90% is bituminous and 35% is coking coal. Coal supplies are considered adequate for many decades of economic growth. There are, however, problems of quality and location. The quality is variable, requiring coal treatment plants to produce coal useful for the metallurgical industry. The location problem is reflected in the distribution of both production and reserves. About 65% of known reserves are concentrated in Shanxi Province and Nei Monggol, but they account for only 10% of the current output. Even within eastern China, reserves and output are concentrated in the Northeast, so that supplying coal to the industrial cities of southern and central China requires long haulage. As a result, coal accounts for 40% of all rail freight.

Coal mining was one of the few economic activities that had been substantially developed in pre-Communist China. Before 1949 the highest level of output was 66 million metric tons, in 1942. Thereafter output fell and did not recover until 1952. Expansion of coal mining was a major goal of the first five-year plan. The state invested heavily in modern mining equipment and in the development of large, mechanized mines. A special technique known as long-wall mining was widely adopted. By 1957 output had reached 130 million tons. Much of the growth in output during this period came from increased production by small, local mines. A temporary but serious setback followed the Tangshan earthquake, which severely damaged China's most important coal center, the Kailuan mines. Currently the coal mining industry consists of 30 large mines, each producing over 300,000 tons a year; a large number of medium-size mines; and over 20,000 small mines. Some one-third of the coal output is accounted for by small mines operated by local units at county or lower levels. Although there are a few open-pit mines, such as the Old Fushun West mine in Liaoning Province, the majority of the mines are underground shafts. Most of the coal is mined by conventional blasting and hauling techniques, and only a small percentage of the mines are mechanized.

A program to expand and modernize coal mining in the 1980s has led to the construction of eight major coal bases, at Huolinhe in Nei Monggol, Datong in Shaanxi Province, Huainan-Huaibei in Anhui, Yanzhou in Shandong, Xuzhou in Jiangsu, Liupanshui in Guizhou, Pingdingshan in Henan and Kailuan in Hebei.

Iron ore is the other major mineral resource, with known reserves of 44 billion tons. Large deposits are widely distributed in 18 provinces and autonomous regions. Most of the important mining areas are north of the Chang Jiang. There is relatively little exploitation of the deposits in Gansu, Guizhou, southern Sichuan and Guangdong provinces. Most of the ore mined has an iron content of only about 30% and requires substantial refining or beneficiation before smelting. Few mines have plants for converting low-grade iron ore into highly concentrated pellets.

CHINA'S RESOURCES OF MINERALS, METALS AND FUELS				
Commodity	Deposits/Reserves Size	Quality	Adequacy of Current Output*	Comments
METALS				
Aluminum	Considerable; huge	Poor	—	Substantial importer from France, Canada, Japan and elsewhere
Antimony	Largest in the world	Excellent	+	Can easily satisfy own demand and export
Bismuth	Huge	Good	B	Small exporter
Chromite	Small	Unknown	—	Seriously deficient, has to import
Copper	Modest	Poor	—	Produces only 30% to 50% of requirements; accounts for three-fifths of nonferrous metal imports
Gold	Modest	Variable	B	At present a very-small-scale producer by world standards
Iron ore	Huge	Poor	—	Importer
Pig iron Steel scrap Finished steel			—	Importer
Lead	Modest	Unknown	—	Net importer
Manganese	Huge	Good	B	Small exporter, mainly to Japan
Mercury	Huge	Excellent	B	Small exporter
Molybdenum	Huge	Excellent	+	Exporter, mainly to Eastern Europe
Nickel	Small	Unknown	—	Heavily dependent on imports, which account for one-fifth of all nonferrous metal imports
Tin	Large	Fair	+	Important exporter, particularly to the United States
Tungsten	Largest in the world	Good	+	Important exporter
Zinc	Modest	Unknown	—	Net importer
NONMETALIC MINERALS				
Asbestos	Large	Fair	B	Minor exporter
Barite	Huge	Good	+	Exporter
Fluorspar	Huge	Good	+	World's largest producer; two-thirds of output exported
Graphite	Large	Poor	B	Very small amount available for export
Magnosite	Huge	Good	B	Small exporter
Phosphates	Medium	Unknown	B	Small importer
Pyrite	Modest	Unknown	B	Self-sufficient
Salt	Huge	Good	+	World's second-largest producer; 10% exported
Sulphur	Large	Fair	—	Net importer
Talc	Huge	Good	+	Half of output exported, mainly to Japan
MINERAL FUELS				
Coal	Huge	Variable	B	Small exporter, but overall situation very tight, especially coking coals
Petroleum (crude)	Huge	Poor	+	Marginal exporter at present
Natural gas	Small	Unknown	B	
Hydroelectricity	Huge		B	

Sources: This table is based mainly on material in K. P. Wang and John Ashton, *JEC* (1967), pp. 167–95, 297–315; CIA, *China's Minerals and Metals Positions in the World Markets* (Washington, D.C., 1976); and Peter D. Weintraub, "China's minerals and metals," *U.S.-China Business Review* (Nov.-Dec. 1974), pp. 38–53.

*+ = current production surplus to domestic requirements.
 − = imports necessary.
 B = approximate *balance* between domestic supply and requirements.

MINING IN CHINA				
(Unofficial estimates unless otherwise indicated)				
Substance	Quantity Unit	1982	1983	1984
Hard coal*	000 metric tons	641,360	687,630	759,120
Brown coal (incl. lignite)*	000 metric tons	24,970	26,900	30,110
Crude petroleum*	000 metric tons	102,123	106,068	114,613
Iron ore*†	000 metric tons	53,660	56,695	63,350
Bauxite	000 metric tons	1,600	1,600	1,600
Copper ore†	000 metric tons	175	175	180
Lead ore†	000 metric tons	160	160	160
Magnesite	000 metric tons	2,000	2,000	2,000
Manganese ore†	000 metric tons	479	479	479
Zinc ore†	000 metric tons	160	160	160
Salt (unrefined)*	000 metric tons	16,384	16,127	16,419
Phosphate rock	000 metric tons	11,720	12,500	11,800
Potash‡	000 metric tons	26	29	40
Sulphur (native)	000 metric tons	200	200	200
Iron pyrites (unroasted)	000 metric tons	4,100	5,200	4,700
Natural graphite	000 metric tons	185	185	185
Antimony ore†	metric tons	12,000	15,000	15,000
Mercury	metric tons	700	700	700
Molybdenum ore†	metric tons	2,000	2,000	2,000
Silver†	metric tons	78	78	78
Tin concentrates†	metric tons	16,000	17,000	17,500
Tungsten concentrates†	metric tons	12,530	12,530	13,500
Gold†	kg.	55,986	57,541	59,097
Natural gas*	billion cu. m. (billion cu. ft.)	11.933 (421.414)	12.212 (431.266)	12.425 (438.789)

Sources for unofficial estimates: For tin, Metallgesellschaft Aktiengesellschaft (Frankfurt am Main, Federal Republic of Germany); for all other minerals, U.S. Bureau of Mines.
Official estimates (000 metric tons): coal (incl. brown coal), 872,284 in 1985, 870,000 in 1986; crude petroleum, 124,895 in 1985, 131,000 in 1986; salt, 14,789 in 1985; natural gas, 12.927 billion cu. m. (465.517 billion cu. ft.) in 1985.
*Official estimates.
†Figures refer to the metal content of ores and concentrates.
‡Potassium oxide (K_2O) content of potash salts mined.

The program for expansion and modernization of iron ore mining includes mines at Shuicheng and Shijiaying, north of Tangshan, both in eastern Hebei Province; the Jidashan, Dong Anshan, Xi Anshan and Dagushan mines near the Anshan Iron and Steel Company; the Nanfen mine near the Benxi steelworks; the Paiyuan mine near the Baotou steel mill; the Egou mine near the Taiyuan steelworks; the Daye mine at the Wuhan steel mill; and the Jiangshan and Yanbei mines in Shanxi Province.

Considerable geological exploration since 1949 has led to the discovery of over 132 useful minerals. China is among the world leaders in proven deposits of tin, tungsten, molybdenum, antimony, mercury, zinc and lead. Among the rare earth metals and ferroalloys, beryllium, tungsten, molybdenum, barium, manganese, mercury, niobium, zirconium and titanium are present in large quantities. China is seriously deficient in chrome and nickel.

There is no foreign participation in mining in China.

ENERGY

China is the world's third-largest consumer of commercial energy (behind the United States and Soviet Union) and, at least at present, produces more than it consumes. Industry is the dominant energy consumer, accounting for 72% of the total, followed by households and commercial users with 14%, agriculture with 6% and transportation with 5%. Coal is the main source, accounting for 70%, oil the second-largest, with 24%; natural gas third, with 3%; and hydroelectricity last, with 3%. Noncommercial energy sources—mainly rice straw, firewood and animal wastes—supply over 250 million tons of coal equivalent (Mtce). China is a net exporter of energy, virtually all of it oil.

Among the three principal subsectors—oil, coal and hydroelectric power—the respective roles of the central ministries vis-à-vis provincial and local authorities vary. Petroleum is the most centralized, under the Ministry of Petroleum Industry. In contrast, roughly 40% of the coal is produced by small mines controlled at or below the provincial level. For electric power five regional grids come under the central Ministry of Electric Power, but other grids are controlled jointly by the center and the provinces. Other ministries also are involved with energy. The Ministry of Railways handles about two-thirds of the coal production and most of the refined petroleum production. The Ministry of the Chemicals Industry operates a number of refineries. The Ministry of Geology is active in exploration of energy resources.

The prices of several forms of energy are at the official exchange rate, still well below international prices. They include fuel oil, coal, crude oil and industrial electricity. The exceptions are gasoline, kerosene and electricity for household lighting, which are above international prices. Energy pricing appears to be used primarily to generate and distribute revenues rather than to influence supply and demand.

The extent to which these prices affect the level or composition of energy supply and demand is not clear, as fuels and electricity are distributed through administrative allocations. The per capita consumption of commercial energy is about 3.5 times the average of other low-income developing countries, one-third short of the middle-income average. This level of consumption of commercial energy is very high in relation to economic activity—about 2.5 times as much per unit of GNP as the average for other developing countries and about 1.5 times the average for other centrally planned economies. China shares a high reliance on coal with the Soviet Union and East European economies. China's per capita consumption of motor fuels and electricity combined is almost double that of Indonesia or India, so that the high share of coal does not reflect a shortage of other premium forms of energy. Although industry is generally more energy-intensive than other sectors, the share of industry in the Chinese GDP is close to the average for middle-income countries and thus does not entirely account for the high energy consumption. The real reason appears to be that China uses energy a good deal less efficiently than other developing countries. China has had only limited access to fuel-saving techniques over the past three or four decades. Further, incentives to economize energy have been lacking.

Based on available information, China may be a net importer of oil by the 1990s, and the energy trade balance may deteriorate as a result of declining oil production and continued growth in consumption. Unfortunately, oil data are among the weakest of all Chinese industrial data. Only fragmentary data are available, pieced together from statements by officials and press reports, often noting only percentage increases. Thus output figures, estimates and future projections are subject to considerable error.

Until 1949 China consumed little oil and produced only 10% of what it consumed. Production was only 70,000 tons per annum plus 50,000 tons yearly of shale oil. The major turning point was the discovery in 1959 of the Daqing field, one of the world's major oil fields, in the Songhua Jiang-Liao He Basin. Since then Daqing has led the industry in China. Further important discoveries, including the major fields of Shengli, Dagang, Huabei, Nanyang and Renqiu, have enabled China not only to meet domestic needs and eliminate imports but also to export oil to earn hard currency. Exports peaked at 13.5 million tons in 1978. From 1957 to 1975 oil production grew at an average rate of 24.7% but declined to 8.3% between 1975 and 1979.

Oil reserves are very large and widely dispersed. In general, development is concentrated on deposits close to major industrial centers. Deposits in remote areas such as the Tarim, Dzungarian and Tsaidam basins have remained largely unexplored. The quality of oil from major deposits varies considerably. A few deposits, such as the Shengli field, produce generally low-quality oil suitable mainly for burning as fuel. Most of the oil produced from the big fields in the North and Northeast

is low in sulfur and high in paraffin content, making it difficult and expensive to refine. In the 1980s light oil was produced at the Dongpu field, along the border between Shandong and Henan provinces. Newer deposits have been found of high-quality, light oil in some of the less accessible oil basins, including the Zhu Jiang estuary of the South China Sea and Tsaidam Basin in Qinghai Province.

Oil experts believe that offshore deposits are extensive and eventually could equal onshore reserves. Offshore drilling began in the 1970s, mainly using foreign technology, but by the 1980s China was producing some of its own rigs. Exploration contracts for areas in the South China Sea and the Gulf of Tonkin were signed were various Western oil companies, and in the shallow waters of the Bo Hai with the Japanese National Oil Company. Of these, drilling in the Bo Hai has been the most promising. The continental shelf between Taiwan and Japan is considered by some experts as one of the most prolific oil reservoirs in the world. Major offshore oil production is unlikely before the 1990s.

Exploration is done by about 300 seismic crews and 500 drilling rigs, which annually drill about 2,000 to 3,000 wells. The last major discovery was in the Renqiu area, in 1975. Onshore only about 13% of the potential oil-bearing wells have been fully explored, and 60% have hardly been explored at all.

A total of 80% of the crude oil production is moved by pipeline and the remainder by rail, which also carries most of the refined products. The first oil pipeline was laid from Daqing to the port of Qinhuangdao. It was 1,152 km. (716 mi.) long and went into operation in 1974. The following year it was extended to Beijing; a second line connected Daqing to the port of Luda and branched off to North Korea. A pipeline from Linyi in Shandong Province to Nanjing was completed in 1978, linking the oil fields of Shengli and Huabei to ports and refineries of the lower Chang Jiang region. The total 6,800-km. (4,226-mi.) network of oil pipelines is not extensive in relation to China's size and the distribution of production and markets. The high pour point of most of the crude oil, fuel oil and the heaviest grades of diesel fuel complicates their transportation, and all pipelines, railroad tank wagons and oil tankers need heating equipment.

A rudimentary petroleum refining industry was established with Soviet aid in the 1950s, and modernized and expanded thereafter with Japanese and European equipment. Refinery capacity is about 93 million tons, with a throughput of some 73 million tons. There are 46 refineries, most of them small by international standards. Only 31 have capacities of 500,000 tons per annum or more, and even the largest—at Daqing, Fushun, Shanghai and Yanshan—have a capacity of about 1 million tons only.

Natural gas still is a relatively minor source of energy, and its production is declining. There is only one large producing basin, in Sichuan Pendi. Production is almost equally divided between nonassociated gas and associated gas dissolved in the oil and produced with it.

Reserves of oil shale are reported unofficially to be about 400 billion tons and may be much larger, since

ENERGY INDICATORS, 1988

Primary energy production (quadrillion BTU):
    Crude oil: 5.61
    Natural gas, liquid: 0
    Natural gas, dry: 0.65
Coal: 17.74
Hydroelectric power: 0.96
Nuclear power: 0
Total: 24.96
Average annual energy production growth rate (%): 5.5
    (1980–87)
Average annual energy consumption growth rate (%): 4.4
    (1980–87)
Energy imports as % of merchandise imports: 2
Electricity
    Installed capacity (kw.): 87,000,000
    Production (kw.-hr.): 444.13 billion
        % fossil fuel: 77.5
        % hydro: 22.5
    Consumption per capita (kw.-hr.): 423
NAtural gas, cu. m. (cu. ft.)
    Proved reserves: 856 billion (30.23 trillion)
    Production: 20.499 billion (723.922 billion)
    Consumption: 14.023 billion (495.222 billion)
Petroleum, bbl.
    Proved reserves: 22.3 billion
    Years to exhaust proved reserves: 23
    Production: 978 million
    Consumption: 761 million
    Refining capacity per day: 2.2 million
Coal (000 tons)
    Reserves: 737,100,000
    Production: 880,000
    Consumption: 873,920

the geological environment is favorable for their formation in many of the sedimentary basins. Deposits of 100 million tons or more, containing 5 billion to 10 billion tons of oil, are reported in Heilongjiang and Hebei. The grade of most oil shales is fairly low (less than 10%), but a few deposits have 10% to 20% of oil by weight. Before 1958, shale oil accounted for almost half of oil production, but the proportion has declined rapidly as normal crude oil production has increased.

One of Communist China's most impressive achievements is the development of electric power. From 1,964 mw. of generating capacity in 1952, the country had developed a 110,000-mw. capacity by 1988, an average growth of 13.7% per annum, compared to 10% in all developing countries. All the more impressive is the fact that China manufactures all equipment needed for power generation, transmission and distribution. Electrification has reached nearly 90% of the communes and 63% of the brigades. Figures for electrification at the household level are not available. Industry consumes 79.0% of electricity; agriculture, 15.8%; residential, commercial and municipal users, 4.8%; and transportation, 0.6%. Despite rapid growth, the system cannot meet the demands of the economy, and power shortages are common, causing much disruption to industrial plants.

The power-generating facilities consist of nearly 90,000 plants. About 88,000 are small hydroelectric plants, which together supply only about 10% of the total kilowatt-hours. At the other end of the scale 61 of the larger power stations have capacity exceeding 250 mw. Thermal generation is used by about 75% of the larger plants, with coal as the predominant fuel. Most of the coal-fired plants are near the big coalfields in the northern, northeastern and central parts of the country. Hydropower is dominant in the mountainous regions of the South, Southwest and Northwest and accounts for about 30% of the total generating capacity.

Transmission grids are small by Western standards, but three-fourths of generation is concentrated in 12 large grids, of which the five largest account for 47% of the total capacity. Transmission voltages are of three kinds: 110 kv. (62,000 km.; 38,533 mi. of lines); 220 kv. (26,000 km.; 16,159 mi.); and 330 kv (801 km.; 498 mi.). Because transmission voltage is relatively low, lines often are overloaded.

China's most important potential source of power growth is hydroelectricity. Its hydropotential is estimated at some 571,000 mw. of generating capacity, of which only 3% is being used. Fuller exploitation of this potential, however, is hampered by the fact that hydroelectric projects require seven to 14 years for completion, as against 18 months for thermal stations.

Geothermal resources are widely distributed, since China has a relatively high geothermal gradient. Most occurrences seem to be relatively low-temperature groundwater suitable for space heating. High-temperature manifestations suitable for power generation are more frequent in the mountainous western parts of the country, such as Yunnan and Xizang (Tibet). Geothermal energy has not yet been developed to a significant extent. Its role is likely to be limited to some urban heating systems in the colder parts of the country, such as Beijing, and to power generation in regions such as Xizang that lack other energy sources. Of noncommercial fuels, rice straw is the most important, as firewood is scarce.

LABOR

Manpower is China's largest resource. Its labor force, estimated at 513 million in 1988 is larger than the population of any country in the world except India. The occupational structure of the labor force is determined partly by historical legacies and partly by the imperatives of socialist planning. At the same time, the Chinese labor force shares may of the dominant characteristics of its counterparts in developing countries, particularly the relatively high share of workers in agriculture—75%—and the low share in services. Females constituted 43.7% of the work force in 1988.

Employees of state organizations—who, together with members of urban collectives, are referred to as "workers and staff"—are paid according to centrally prescribed wage scales. These scales, which have remained virtually unchanged since 1956, vary from place to place, among industries and occupations in the same place and within industries, according to the size of the enterprise and the level of government that controls it. The wages of industrial workers have eight grades, with a wage range (from the highest to the lowest grade) of about three to one. There is a 16-grade scale for technicians and engineers, a 26-grade scale for government administrators and so on, with the widest wage range of the order of 15 to one. Young people joining the labor force are paid below the standard scale for the first two or three years, but once on the scale are usually promoted to the second grade within a year or so. In urban collectives the applicable scales are not centrally prescribed but must be approved by local labor bureaus.

Both in state organizations and in urban collectives, wages are supplemented by bonuses, usually 10% to 12% of wages, distributed in a variety of ways but not always according to work performance. In contrast to the Soviet Union, piecework payment systems are rare. The worker's welfare fund, another 11% of the wage bill, finances pensions, sickness and disability benefits, etc. There are no paid vacations, apart from seven public holidays per year.

Most labor is allocated by central and local labor bureaus. An annual labor plan, subject to approval by the planning agencies at each level, specifies the disposition of new entrants to the labor force among different organizations and enterprises. It also specifies the permitted amount of migration, if any, from communes to urban areas. Managerial appointments are handled by a separate hierarchy of personnel bureaus.

Each enterprise and organization is obliged to employ the number of people specified in the plan. Employers have little choice about whom to hire and are obliged to hire anyone sent by the labor bureau. Once on the payroll, it is virtually impossible to discharge a worker, no matter how unsatisfactory his or her conduct. By the same token, employees are expected to spend their entire career in the agency or organization that hired them initially. Technical and professional staff sometimes may be transferred in the service of the same organization, but interorganizational transfers are extremely rare.

In general there is no labor market because both labor allocations and wage levels are determined by the administrative process. But the process is not as arbitrary as it appears. People have some choice in choosing the skills they want to acquire in school and, occasionally, labor bureau allocations may be refused. As a result, despite an overall surplus of labor, shortages are experienced in unattractive jobs.

Trade union activity is organized under the aegis of the Communist Party. The All-China Federation of Trade Unions, with 89 million members, is organized on an industrial basis, with 15 affiliated national industrial unions and 29 affiliated local trade union councils. In the mid-1980s it drafted a new trade union law permitting the rank and file greater voice in union affairs. Trade union membership is not compulsory, although it brings many benefits with it. The union's primary function is to promote labor discipline, enhance labor productivity, hold periodical campaigns and conduct political indoctrination. Unions also perform, as in the Soviet Union and East European countries, a variety of welfare functions, such as handling pensions and disability benefits, operating schools and sanatoriums, and running clubs and eating facilities.

Strikes are illegal, except as a response to intolerable working conditions. During the first half of 1988 there were 49 officially reported strikes. In addition, informal work stoppages and slowdowns are not uncommon and apparently are tolerated for brief periods as long as vital services and national security industries are not affected. It also appears that authorities are more tolerant of strikes in the special economic zones.

LABOR INDICATORS, 1988

Total economically active population: 513 million
As % of working-age population: 83.7
% female: 43.7
% under 20 years of age: 9
Average annual growth rate, 1985–2000 (%): 1.4
Activity rate (%)
  Total: 52.3
  Male: 57.3
  Female: 47.0
% organized labor: 65% of urban work force
Sectoral employment (%)
  Agriculture, forestry & fishing: 60.1
  Mining: 0.2
  Manufacturing: 17.7
  Construction: 6.6
  Electricity, gas & water: 1.0
  Transportation & communication: 2.6
  Trade: 5.0
  Finance & real estate: 0.3
  Public administration & defense: 1.8
  Services: 3.8
  Other: 2.8

Under the labor contract system, which was instituted in 1986, and now covers over 7 million workers, individual workers are permitted to negotiate with management over some contract terms. In practice, however, only university graduates have the privilege of doing so.

Collective bargaining is not permitted. Most large and medium-size enterprises have workers' councils with some advisory functions. However, they convene only once or twice a year, and most of their work is related to welfare rather than production. A law passed in April 1988 enlarged their powers in state enterprises.

China has not yet ratified ILO Convention 105 on forced labor. Child labor is a serious problem in both rural and urban areas and has eluded government efforts to curb it.

The normal and maximum workweek is 48 hours. Some work time may be spent in political study.

In the workplace occupational safety and health are constant themes of posters and campaigns, but progress in this area has depended on construction of modern facilities to replace the older noisy and dirty ones built with Soviet assistance in the 1950s. Every production unit of any size has a health and safety officer, who receives training under ILO auspices. Nevertheless, every year state procurators deal with thousands of negligence and accident cases involving civil or criminal liability.

FOREIGN COMMERCE

Historically the Chinese have disliked foreign trade, and they have managed well for thousands of years without it. This does not mean, however, that trading activities did not exist. As early as the Western Han dynasty (206 B.C.–A.D. 24), Chinese envoys pioneered the "Silk Route" through central Asia. During later dynasties Chinese ships traded throughout Asia and as far as Africa. But under the Qing dynasty (1644–1911), foreign trade was officially discouraged. According to Qing emperors, China "possessed all things in abundance" and did not need anything from abroad.

The commercial doors of China were forced open by Western traders in the 19th century. But foreign trade continued to remain small in relation to the whole economy. Revolutions, civil wars and World War II hampered the expansion of external trade in the first half of the 20th century, and the embargo by Western countries after the start of the Korean War, the embargo by the socialist bloc after the breakup with the Soviet Union and its allies after 1960, the Cultural Revolution and other events had the same effect in the third quarter of the 20th century. The net result was that China entered the international trade scene in the 1980s virtually as a newcomer. Further, the domestic market had been so thoroughly insulated against world market influences that its products were not adapted to or compatible with international standards. As a corollary to self-sufficiency, the regime viewed trade deficits with horror and made every effort to maintain imports and exports in balance.

Since the late 1970s the former trade policies have been gradually relaxed and trade has been recognized as among the critical avenues of modernization. Exports have been accorded high priority, and foreign investment has been welcomed rather than shunned, as formerly. Even with these changes, China's foreign trade in 1987 accounted for only 13.7% of the GDP, considerably lower than those of comparable large countries.

China's trade accounts for less than 1% of world trade. Except in the trade of some nonferrous metals, such as tungsten, antimony and tin, and medicinal herbs (of which China is an important supplier in the world market), China's influence on the world market is small.

There are neither quantum indexes nor appropriate deflators to determine the trends in China's imports and exports in real terms, but an indication may be gained by using the rates of change in the International Price Index. Using 1953 as the base year, China's exports increased from 1953 to 1980 from $1 billion to $18 billion, or at an annual growth rate of about 5.3%, and imports at 4.5% in real terms. Much of this growth took place after 1970, when the value of both exports and imports in current dollars increased at slightly 23% a year on average, or at 9% in real terms.

China's trade history has by no means been smooth and reflects the interruptions and breaks in its political development. The main phases coincide with the nine phases of its economic evolution (see Economy).

Among the many changes that took place in the 1970s were not only the volte-face in official policy but also the emergence of petroleum as a major export revenue earner; the receipt of favorable credit terms from Japan, the United States and Western Europe; and the resumption of trade, albeit on a modest scale, with socialist countries. With the rise of Deng to power, trade has been accepted as an "engine of progress." Many of his reforms have related specifically to trade, particularly the creation of special economic zones, promotion of foreign investment and decentralization of foreign trade management. The increase in the total value of exports since 1980 has been spread fairly evenly among all commodity groups. Most impressive has been the growth of manufactured exports, in which China traditionally was weak. During this period imports have accelerated faster than exports, turning former trade surpluses into deficits.

Changes in commodity structure of trade reflect to a large degree the transformation of the economy and the scope of the development strategy. Under central planning, trade has only a balancing role; imports make up domestic production shortfalls, and exports are viewed mainly as means to pay for imports. It is only recently that trade has been viewed as a developmental process.

Changes in the structure of imports reflect China's industrial strategies since the Revolution. Between 1949 and 1960 imports of producer and capital goods accounted for over 90% of imports, and consumer goods (including food items) the remainder. In the 1960s, following the disastrous Great Leap Forward, an acute agricultural crisis forced China to import several million tons of food grains, mainly wheat, and also more fertilizers to step up agricultural production. With the rapid buildup of industrial capacity in the 1950s and 1960s, imports of machinery and equipment declined, but those of intermediate goods, such as iron and steel and raw materials, rose. In the 1970s Chinese planners pursued import-substitution still further, this time focusing on intermediate goods, especially steel, chemical fertilizers and synthetic fibers. In the case of manmade fibers and petrochemicals, imported equipment virtually created new industries, but import substitution was less successful in steel. Contracts for whole plants and technology imports surged again under Deng, but a number of these contracts were canceled or postponed in the early 1980s. Another important change in the 1970s was the change from being a petroleum importer to a petroleum exporter. Cereals constitute the second-largest item in imports and cotton the third-largest.

Changes in the export structure also reflect shifts in economic policy and strategies. In 1953 about 82% of total exports were agricultural or processed agricultural products. With rapid industrial development and growing domestic consumption, this share has fallen to 16%. On the other hand, exports of light manufactured goods, particularly textiles, have sustained a steady long-term increase, reaching 66% in 1987.

The great swing in the direction of trade was away from centrally planned economies and toward market economies. In 1953, when the delivery of Soviet aid equipment was well under way, 70% of China's trade was with centrally planned economies. By 1966, with the final repayment of Soviet aid, the share of centrally planned economies fell to 22%, and trade with the Soviet Union virtually ceased. As China increasingly turned to the market economies for both imports and exports, the share of the centrally planned economies declined still further, to 12%.

Since then there has been little change in the direction of trade, except for a rise in Japan's share. Hong Kong is the largest single export market, accounting for about a quarter of all exports. An unknown but substantial proportion of Chinese exports to Hong Kong is reexported. Japan is the second-largest export market, with a share of 20%. Other industrialized countries, led by the United States, take 20%, and a further 20% goes to developing countries. About one-fourth of the total imports come from Japan and another 20% from the United States.

In general, China has a small trade surplus with the centrally planned economies; a large trade surplus with developing countries (excluding Latin America); and a huge deficit with market economies, particularly Japan, West Germany and the United States.

A full-fledged state trading system was established only in 1956, seven years after the establishment of the republic. There were no further organizational changes until 1978, when the organizational framework was made less rigid and slightly decentralized.

At the apex of the foreign trade system is the Ministry of Foreign Trade (MOFT), which controls 16 Foreign Trade Corporations (FTC's), each of which has a monopoly over the export and import of a specific group of commodities. Other agencies under the MOFT include the China Council for the Promotion of International Trade. Each province, autonomous region and centrally administered municipality has a Foreign Trade Bureau (FTB).

This system worked well in prereform China, where foreign trade was not a major economic desideratum, but it was too cumbrous and inefficient in a reform setting. It became necessary to decentralize foreign trade management in two directions: laterally to other ministries, and vertically or geographically to local government levels. Additionally, new agencies had to be established to fill in gaps in responsibility. At the supraministerial level, two new commissions were added: the Foreign Investment Control Commission (FICC) and the Import-Export Commission (IEC). The role of the FICC is clear from its title; the IEC is concerned primarily with foreign trade policy guidelines, treaties and laws, foreign trade agreements, large foreign trade ventures and special trade practices. Another new agency is the China International Trust and Investment Corporation (CITIC), which negotiates foreign ventures and coordinates introduction of foreign technology.

At the ministerial level several new import and export corporations have been established to conduct foreign trade directly. The authority to conduct foreign trade directly also has been granted to several provincial- and municipal-level governments, such as Beijing, Tianjin and Shanghai; the coastal provinces of Guangdong, Liaoning, Fujian and Hebei; and Guangxi Zhuang Autonomous Region. In addition, several local trust and investment corporations have been set up to interest foreigners or overseas Chinese in investing in local enterprises. Special economic zones have been established in the two coastal provinces of Guangdong and Fujian. The zones are designed to attract foreign investment in light manufacturing industries catering to export markets and receive preferential tax treatment. They are administered directly by the provincial authorities, with a simplified bureaucracy and broad investment guidelines. Nevertheless, the bulk of China's foreign trade still is carried out by the FTC's.

Four measures for promoting foreign trade and investment deserve special mention. The first is export processing, under which arrangement foreign firms supply raw materials, semifinished goods, packaging materials and/or components, while the Chinese enterprises process or assemble products according to foreign contractors' designs, specifications and quality requirements. The Chinese enterprises receive only a processing fee, from which the cost of specific equipment and machinery supplied by the contractors is deducted. Imported materials and components are exempt from duties and taxes.

The second measure is compensation trade, under which mode China provides factory building and labor while foreign firms supply capital, equipment, technology, training, designs and possibly supervisory personnel. Foreign firms are paid directly by the goods produced or indirectly by other products mutually agreed on.

The third measure is cooperative production, which arrangement is halfway between compensation trade and joint ventures. It is a form of technology transfer whereby a foreign firm helps a Chinese enterprise to set up a factory and produce an item under license by giving extensive technical assistance in stages. No equity investment by the foreign partner is involved, as the facilities are entirely Chinese-owned. In its early stages such ventures involve only assembly of imported parts and components, but gradually the Chinese enterprise manufactures the product entirely or mostly from its own materials and components. Payment is often made by supplying over an extended period a share of the output generated by the facilities.

The fourth measure is joint venture under the Joint Ventures Law of 1979. In general the share of foreign investment should not be less than 25%, with no maximum. In practice, the Chinese share is invariably 50% or more. After-tax profits are shared by the Chinese unit and the foreign firm according to their respective capital shares. The profits may be remitted outside China. The chairman of the board of a joint venture must be Chinese, but the position of general manager is rotated between foreign and Chinese nominees. The law provides a 33% corporate income tax and an additional 10% tax on profits remitted outside China. Favorable tax treatment is extended for reinvestment of profits in China; for joint ventures scheduled to operate for more than 10 years; and for joint ventures engaged in farming or forestry or located in remote, underdeveloped areas. Priority is given to joint ventures that (a) modernize or restructure existing industries using a relatively small amount of capital but achieving high yields quickly as well as generating additional foreign exchange, (b) develop energy resources or install energy-saving devices, (c) construct critical infrastructure facilities or (d) develop remote backward areas. The priority sectors are defined as agriculture, energy, transportation, urban development, textiles and light industries, machinery and electronics industries, building materials and the tourist industry.

Despite these efforts, progress has been slow, and most investment is by overseas Chinese from Hong Kong in medium-size or small enterprises, without much significant transfer of modern technology. For larger multinationals, investment in China appears to be like charting an unfamiliar sea. Another problem is the Chinese insistence on foreign exchange earnings rather than sales in the domestic market.

The planning of foreign trade is an essential part of central economic planning, whose framework has remained virtually unchanged since the 1950s. The current practice is first to promote exports, then to determine the level of imports based on expected foreign exchange earnings, thereby maintaining the current account in balance. The foreign trade plan is in turn incorporated into the foreign exchange plan, which is reviewed quarterly. Since 1979 some flexibility in foreign exchange planning has been allowed by the introduction of a foreign exchange retention system that encourages local authorities and trade corporations not under the MOFT to earn more foreign exchange by retaining a proportion of the foreign exchange earned in their jurisdictions, varying from 15% to 40%.

The State Price Bureau under the State Council fixes prices for both domestic and foreign goods in accordance with a set of uniform criteria. The basic principle is that domestic prices are isolated from world market prices for the dual purpose of maintaining domestic price stability and of protecting domestic industries. The domestic prices of imported goods are made consistent with prices of similar domestically produced goods but may be revised upward or downward to reflect differentials in quality.

Since 1978 import duties and profits on foreign trade have been separated. Import duties under the general tariff fall into 25 categories, ranging from 5% to 200%. In general the tariff rates are relatively low on imports of the means of production (raw materials and capital goods) but high on consumer goods. The tariff rates for most consumer goods range from 15% to 80% ad valorem. Import duties affect resale prices for the 20% of imports for which similar domestically produced goods do not exist; for the remaining imports, the duty affects MOFT's profits only.

Imports are purchased at world market prices and sold at the prevailing domestic price, while exports are purchased at the domestic prices and sold at world market prices. Since domestic prices on the average exceed both import prices and export prices, most imports make an accounting profit while most exports make an accounting loss. These differences are evened out within the whole state trading system.

In 1980 a new foreign exchange trading system was introduced for selected enterprises. Unlike the official rate, which is pegged to the value of a basket of currencies, the new rate is pegged to the dollar and applies only to foreign trade and trade-related invisible transactions. Since 1980 enterprises earning foreign exchange in a few areas have been permitted to sell foreign exchange through the People's Bank of China.

In recent years China has shifted from a policy of "no debt" to a policy of accepting foreign borrowing to foster modernization. Foreign loans must be approved by the SPC (State Planning Commission), which reviews them in cooperation with the Import-Export Commission and the Foreign Investment Control Commission.

FOREIGN TRADE INDICATORS, 1988

Exports: $57.1 billion
Imports: $52.0 billion
Balance of trade: $5.1 billion
Annual growth rate (%), exports: 11.7 (1980–87)
Annual growth rate (%), imports: 14.2 (1980–87)
Ratio of international reserves to imports (in months): 6.7
Value of manufactured exports ($): 19.997 billion
Terms of trade (1980 = 100): 87
Exports of goods as % of GDP: 19.0
Imports of goods as % of GDP: 17.7

Direction of Trade (%)

	Imports	Exports
EEC	16.8	9.8
U.S.A.	11.1	7.7
East European countries	7.1	7.2
Japan	23.4	16.2

Composition of Trade (%)

	Imports	Exports
Food & agricultural raw materials	13.4	20.4
Ores & minerals	1.3	1.6
Fuels	1.2	11.5
Manufactured goods	84.0	66.5
of which chemicals	11.6	5.7
of which machinery	33.9	4.4

Different foreign trade data are provided by the People's Bank of China and the MOFT. Both sets of figures exclude certain types of data outside their jurisdictions. However, both data indicate that merchandise trade has shifted from a surplus into deficit since 1980. China has consistently had a surplus on its service account because of the large receipts from shipping and tourism. During the past several years the Chinese merchant fleet has grown faster than that of any other country, and the share of China's trade handled by its own fleet is reportedly 70%, the highest percentage in the world. Receipts from transportation and insurance have grown at an average annual rate of 43%. Tourist receipts and interest receipts also have increased rapidly in recent years. A traditional major factor in China's balance of payments has been remittances from overseas Chinese, estimated at about $680 million in 1980. Surpluses in invisibles have helped China to offset its trade deficits in the 1980s. Foreign aid and loans to Third World countries, which dominated the capital account from the mid-1960s until recently, have shrunk to about $253 million and no longer are important in the balance of payments.

In a broader perspective, Chinese trade remains quite small in relation to total world trade and, in fact, has declined in the past 50 years. In the early 1920s China accounted for 2% of world trade; in the later 1950s this share had fallen to 1.5% and by the 1980s to less than 1%. This decline reflects China's lack of trade growth during the troubled 1960s, a period in which world trade was expanding rapidly. By comparative standards, too, China's trade is small. In 1988 its exports, at $57.1 billion, were almost $2 billion less than that of Taiwan.

For many years the Canton Fair has played an important role in China's foreign trade. The fair is held twice a year and attracts over 30,000 visitors a year, of whom about a quarter are traders and the rest are Chinese visitors.

China is not a member of any trade blocs or customs unions.

TRANSPORTATION & COMMUNICATIONS

Technologically, China has a dual transportation system. Traditional means such as pack animals, human porters, animal- or coolie-drawn or pushed carts, rickshas and wind-powered sampans coexist with a relatively modern transportation system. These traditional forms remain important, especially in the densely populated parts and provide an alternative to the more expensive modern means. Another major characteristic of Chinese transportation is the dominance of the rail system to a degree not found elsewhere in the world—surprising in a country where the first rail line, laid in 1876 between Shanghai and Woosung, had to be removed because of local opposition and taken to Taiwan. A third characteristic is the virtual absence of private automobiles and the absence of heavy motor traffic and standardized modern highways. Utilization of the transportation system is relatively high. This is particularly true of the rail system, which is generally regarded as among the most efficient in the world.

For a large country, China has a remarkably immobile population—about 200 passenger-km. (124 passenger-mi.) per capita per year by modern transportation, compared with 710 (441) in India and 993 (617) in the Soviet Union. The low mobility in China results in part from the low density of the transportation network and its limited capacity. There is only one railway passenger car for 65,000 people and one passenger bus for 30,000 people. One benefit from such a low transportation density is that the sector consumes only 5% of national energy—the lowest percentage in the world. In other low-income countries, the transportation sector accounts for 10% to 20% of national energy. Gasoline consumption is largely limited to trucks and buses in road transportation.

The railway system is the major carrier in the modern sector and has more than doubled its size over the past 30 years, from some 22,000 route-km. (13,673 route-mi.) to 52,500 route-km. (32,629 route-mi.). Other than for a small length of meter-gauge line near the Vietnam border and narrow-gauge lines elsewhere, the system is uniform and technically integrated. On the standard-gauge lines, 9,400 km. (5,842 mi.) are double-track and 4,400 km. (2,735 mi.) are electrified. While the rail freight is now the third-largest in the world (after the Soviet Union and the United States) and the rail network the fifth-longest in the world, they still are modest in relation to the territorial area and population. For example, the rail system is about 20% the size of that in the United States, a country of similar geographical size and with a highly developed nonrail sector; about 35% of that in the Soviet Union; and 20% smaller than that in India, a country about one-third the geographical size of China.

About 60% of the total 22,000 route-km. of rail lines in 1949 were concentrated in the northeastern and central coastal regions and were made up of different gauges and types. The pattern of rail construction under the Communists reflected economic, national integration and strategic considerations. Rail penetration of Xinjiang, for example, was influenced by the search for petroleum. One of the most impressive achievements is the line linking Chengdu and the Sichuan Basin with Paochi on the Wei River and so with the east–west Lunghai Railway. It follows almost exactly the ancient courier "trestleroad" of the later Han dynasty. It attracted much attention because of the engineering feats involved in surmounting the formidable slopes of the Tsinling and Ta Pa Shan.

In the first decades of the PRC the railways absorbed well over 50% of all new investments in the transportation sector, and most of it was for new line construction. Although the rail system was important before 1949, the "railway age" in China matured only after then—ironically at a time when the importance of railways was declining in almost all other countries. One consequence of China's late railway development is that the system has avoided uneconomic branch lines that in other countries were built before road transportation was a competing alternative.

China's railways are exceptional among the world's major railways in that 78% of the locomotive fleet consists of steam locomotives, with 20% being diesel and 2% electric. Steam locomotives add to the low fuel efficiency of the system. Passenger accommodations range from inexpensive hard seats to luxurious soft sleepers used by a fraction of the passengers, including most foreigners.

Financially, Chinese railways are reported to be very profitable. Tariffs are said to be high in relation to costs except for short-distance trips. Tariffs are uniform throughout the country and thus result in substantial interprovincial and commodity cross-subsidization. Passenger trains are classified as super express, express and ordinary. There is little specialized suburban equipment and stations. A 24-km. (15-mi.) subway serves Beijing, and a new one was opened in Tianjin in 1984. On-time performance is high, reportedly 95% for passenger trains and 90% for freight trains.

The network of motorable roads increased 10-fold, from 80,000 km. (49,720 mi.) in 1949 to over 980,000 km. (609,074 mi.) in 1988 and was maintained mainly by provincial, county and commune governments. Design standards for all roads are low, and main roads do not permit fast traffic. There are less than 200 km. (124 mi.) of four-lane intercity highways.

TRANSPORTATION INDICATORS, 1988

Roads, km. (mi.): 980,000 (609,074)
    % paved: 20
Motor vehicles
    Automobiles: 794,452
    Trucks: 2,231,981
    Persons per vehicle: 341
    Road freight, tonne-km. (ton-mi.): 35.5 billion (24.315 billion)
Railroads
    Track, km. (mi.): 56,600 (35,200); electrified, km. (mi.): 4,400 (2,735)
    Passenger traffic, passenger-km (passenger-mi.): 284.3 billion (176.7 billion)
    Freight, freight tonne-km. (freight ton mi.): 947.1 billion (648.7 billion)
Merchant marine
    Vessels: 1,773
    Total dead weight tonnage: 18,484,200
    No. oil tankers: 179; GRT: 1,476,000
Ports
    Number: 8 major
    Cargo loaded (tons): 59,580,000
    Cargo unloaded (tons): 70,680,000
Air
    Km. (mi.) flown: 101.2 million (62.8 million)
    Passengers: 7.3 million
    Passenger traffic, passenger-km. (passenger-mi.): 18.6 billion (11.6 billion)
    Freight traffic, freight tonne-km. (freight ton-mi.): 660 million (450 million)
    Airports with scheduled flights: 80
    Airports: 330
Pipelines
    Crude, km. (mi.): 6,500 (4,036)
    Refined, km. (mi.): 1,100 (683)
    Natural gas, km. (mi.): 4,200 (2,608)
Inland waterways
    Length, km. (mi.): 109,500 (68,055)
    Cargo, tonne-km. (ton-mi.): 757.2 billion (518.639 billion)

COMMUNICATIONS INDICATORS, 1988

Telephones
    Total (000): 7,059
    Persons per: 149
Phone traffic (000 calls)
    Local:
    Long distance: } 903,200
    International: 17,660
Post office
    Number of post offices: 50,969
    Pieces of mail handled (000): 4,959,433
    Telegraph, total traffic (000): 198,595
    Telex
        Subscriber lines: 5,391
        Traffic (000 minutes): 12,360 (international)
Telecommunications
    3 domestic satellites; 1 Indian Ocean INTELSAT; 1 Pacific Ocean INTELSAT

TOURISM & TRAVEL INDICATORS, 1988

Total tourism receipts ($): 1.530 billion
Expenditures by nationals abroad ($): 314 million
Number of tourists (000): 12,852
    of whom from
        United States, 239,600
        Japan, 470,500
        United Kingdom, 71,400
        Australia, 78,100

There are no private automobiles. Chinese trucks do not use diesel, and they have low fuel efficiency, with fuel consumption 15% higher than for similar vehicles in other countries. The main product of the domestic truck manufacturing industry is a four-ton truck. China is the 10th-largest commercial-vehicle producer in the world. About 30 motor vehicle plants are reported to be in operation, but only four have any significant production capacity. About 38 different models are locally manufactured, and many other models are imported. However, trucks neither larger than eight-ton nor smaller than two-ton are readily available. Buses provide public transportation in towns and cities and in many rural areas. Cars and jeeps are used mostly as taxis. Three-wheeled motorcarts and bicycle carts are common means of lightweight transportation in urban areas. The ubiquitous bicycle may be considered China's national vehicle; there are over 100 million of them, almost as many as there are cars in the United States. Animal-drawn carts are the most common vehicles in rural areas, and whether two-wheeled or four-wheeled, they are drawn by a variety of animals—horses, mules, donkeys, cows, oxen and camels. Carts pulled by human beings have not entirely vanished.

The road network is characterized by the limited extent of paving, due in part to a shortage of good materials such as asphaltic binders, and in some areas because of the absence of natural gravel or rock. Chinese crude petroleum has a high paraffin content and does not yield true asphalts but rather a type of oiled gravel. They are reasonably satisfactory for low pavement loadings but have limited strength and cannot normally be used for highways with heavy traffic. Portland cement pavements are used in some cases, but the costs are prohibitive. Mudbound macadam also is used extensively as a final surface but is much rougher than gravel surfaces. Severe congestion is apparent on many roads, particularly in cities and larger villages, despite the relative low volume of motor vehicles. This is due to the slow nature of the traffic flow. Slow-moving vehicles consume from five to 10 times as much road capacity as fast-moving vehicles because of their own slow speed and their hindrance to faster vehicles.

Water transportation is historically the oldest means of transportation in China. About 109,500 km. (68,055 mi.) of waterways are navigable, of which 57,000 km. (35,426 mi.) have a usual water depth of 1 m. (3.3 ft.) or more and 2,700 km. (1,678 mi) are navigable in vessels of 1,000 tons or more. The greater part of the system is in the southern half, where the Chang Jiang and the Zhu Jiang and their tributaries account for two-thirds of the country's total. The Chang Jiang is the longest and the most important. Together with its major tributaries, the Jialing Jiang, Chuan Jiang, Wu Jiang and Han Jiang, it has 80,000 km. (49,720 mi.) of navigable length and is the main transportation artery connecting southwestern and central China to eastern China. Among the many ports and industrial cities it serves are Chongqing, Wuhan, Wuhu, Ma'anshan, Nanjing and Shanghai. The Zhu Jiang system has 12,000 km. (7,458 mi.) open to navigation, mostly on the Xi Jiang, which runs west through Guangxi. Other rivers with navigable stretches include the Huang He, Huai He, Hai He and Min Jiang. The Heilong Jiang and the Songhua Jiang provide access to Heilongjiang but are closed by ice in the winter. The ancient Grand Canal, originally constructed to carry tribute grain from Hangzhou in the Chang Jiang Valley to the imperial court in northern China, is usable for 1,100 km. (684 mi.) of its total length of 1,800 km. (1,119 mi.). Barges and tugs up to 600 tons may be used on parts of the Grand Canal. Ships as large as 10,000 tons could ascend the lower Chang Jiang to Wuhan in the high-water season. Smaller modern vessels ply the shallower stretches of the rivers, particularly junks and sampans, the traditional Chinese craft, many of them motorized.

Along the 18,000 km. (11,187 mi.) of coastline are 15 ports engaged in foreign commerce, of which the most important are Luda, locally known as Dalian, at the southern tip of the Liaotung Peninsula; Quinhuangdao, in eastern Hebei Province; Tianjin, on the Hai He; Qingdao, in Shandong; Lianyungang, a coal port on the eastern terminus of the Longhai Railway; Huangpu, the harbor of Guangzhou; and Shanghai, the largest port in China and one of the world's major ports.

China's merchant fleet is the ninth-largest in the world. It is managed by the China Ocean Shipping Corporation.

The major international airports are at Beijing and Xiamen. The airports at Shanghai and Chengdu have been expanded in the 1980s.

China's aviation is underdeveloped. For example, it has only 40,000 domestic flights, compared with 85,000 in India. Operated by the General Administration for Civil Aviation (CAAC), it operates over 160 domestic and 11 international routes. The CAAC is being restructured and its operations divided among six new airlines (Air China, China Eastern Airways, China Southern Airways, China Southwestern Airways, China United Airlines and China Capital Helicopter Service). In air transportation as in other areas, China suffers from limited access to modern technology. For example, airplanes do not operate in bad weather because of the lack of proper navigational aids and landing systems.

DEFENSE

The Chinese Communist Party came to power not through an election or revolution but through the successful military mission of the People's Liberation Army (PLA). The PLA is the world's largest standing army and has the world's third-largest air and naval forces. It provides China with a credible conventional defense-in-depth on land, at sea and in the air but lacks offensive capability more than a short distance beyond its borders and is vulnerable to nuclear, biological and chemical attack, particularly from its superior neighbor the Soviet Union. The small but effective nuclear deterrent is based on the policy of "no first use."

Deterrence is enhanced by a huge and well-organized population that can be mobilized at short notice. Coastal defense consists of successive rings of submarines, missile destroyers and frigates supported by smaller missiles and torpedo boats. There are no military bases

in foreign countries. The air force is strong in numbers but weak in equipment.

The PLA underwent its own version of the Cultural Revolution with Mao's insistence of a "people's war" in contrast to modernization. With the death of Mao, the scales have tipped in favor of modernization, and a fragile consensus has been restored in both the military and the political leadership.

The PLA is organized as the armed forces of the party and remains under CCP control. The Common Program, the prescursor of the Constitution, placed control of the armed forces in the hands of the 22-member People's Revolutionary Military Council. Later constitutions confirmed this precedent, and the State Constitution of 1978 designated the party chairman as commander in chief of the armed forces. Until his resignation in 1989 Deng, although the virtual leader of the party, had no other official position than as chairman of the Military Affairs Committee. The chairmanship is currently vacant.

The PLA traces its history to the Nanchang Uprising of August 1, 1927, led by Zhou Enlai, Zhu De, Peng Dehuai and Lin Biao, and the equally ill-fated Autumn Harvest Insurrection, led by Mao Zedong. The survivors of these and other incidents came together in the spring of 1928 to form the First Workers' and Peasants' Army, a ragged collection of dedicated Communists, bandits and deserters from Chiang's army that was the real beginning of the PLA. When the PLA became a national army in 1949, it was a swollen, unwieldy mass of over 5 million men. In 1950 a massive demobilization of ill-trained or politically unreliable troops reduced this number to about 3 million, with another 60,000 and 10,000 in the fledgling navy and air force, respectively. After an unsuccessful attempt in 1949 to take the island of Quemoy from the Nationalists, the PLA engaged in a year-long conquest of Tibet, which was completed only in 1951. The Korean War (1950–53) was a watershed in the evolution of the PLA and its first confrontation with an external enemy under modern battlefield conditions. Although it fought the mighty United States and its allies to a standoff, its deficiencies were demonstrated all too painfully. The lightly equipped Chinese troops were slaughtered in human wave attacks against the United Nations' modern firepower, and their "people's war" tactics could not be utilized on the narrow Korean peninsula. Troops often were short of food, medical supplies and ammunition. The obvious need for heavier weapons, air power and a more efficient logistical system provided the impetus to modernize the PLA with Soviet advice and weapons. A 30-year-treaty of friendship, alliance and mutual assistance signed with the Soviet Union in 1950 made possible the transformation of the PLA from a guerrilla army to China's national armed forces. The National Defense Council and the Ministry of National Defense were established in 1954, and military ranks and titles along the Soviet model were introduced in the next year. By 1956 China was producing small arms and artillery, and its air force had MiG-15 and MiG-17 fighters and IL-28 light jet bombers.

The momentum of modernization was lost in the

"wasted years" of the Great Leap Forward and the Cultural Revolution and was not regained until the 1980s. The PLA's disastrous preformance during its invasion of Vietnam illustrated its relative inferiority and lack of offensive capability.

Mao's doctrine of "people's war"—borrowed from fourth-century B.C. Chinese strategist Sun Tzu, Lenin and others—was a formula for protracted psychological and economic struggle. It emphasized the military advantages of manpower rather than firepower. It called for infiltration and stealth as basic tactics and favored an active defense in depth with incessant counterattacks—"luring the enemy in deep" to extend and disperse his forces in order to annihilate them piecemeal. It was a strategy that in the West is known as Fabianism, after Fabius the Cunctator, a Roman general. The doctrine prescribed three phases of protracted warfare—strategic defensive, stalemate and offensive—and mobilization of the entire population. Mao organized his forces into "main" and "regional" forces, the former available for operations in any region whenever necessary and the latter concentrating on defending its own localities and attacking the enemy there in cooperation with the local militia and self-defense corps. Tactics emphasized deception, surprise, psychological warfare, close combat and night fighting to negate the enemy's advantage in weapons. The troops remained dispersed except before an attack.

In the early 1950s Mao's doctrine was modified to accommodate the shift from revolution to national defense and changed again in the 1960s to reflect global advances in technology, requiring defense against nuclear as well as conventional attacks. The new doctrine, "people's war under modern conditions," was a marriage of old and new, mixing grand strategy and small-unit tactics and retaining the enduring factors of force size, structure, composition and mission. Nuclear deterrence was premised on two factors: a guarantee that China will not use nuclear weapons first; and China's relative ability to survive a nuclear attack, given the vast territory and the dispersal of its industrial and military bases. China's missiles are liquid-fueled and require lengthy preparations before launch. But they are deployed secretly and may be moved from their garrisons during crises. Because they are relatively inaccurate, they could be used only against cities and other large-area targets. China has been dispersing, hardening and camouflaging military installations since at least 1961. However, the basic principles of Mao's doctrine still guide China's military theorists because of China's nuclear inferiority. The exported version of Mao's doctrine forms the theoretical basis of guerrilla operations in many African and Latin American countries.

Since the Korean War, the PLA has engaged in only two external wars: the Sino-Indian War of 1962 and the Vietnam War of 1979. Described as "counterattacks" (even though there were no initial attacks from the enemy), they were shallow, ground-forces incursions lasting three or four weeks. Thus, since 1949 the doctrine of "people's war" has not been tested in the crucible of battle.

At the apex of the military organization is the Military Commission of the CCP Central Committee. The chairman and 10 members of the commission are all members of the Politburo. Responsible to the commission are the General Staff Department (GSD—operations); the General Political Department (GPD—indoctrination) and the General Logistics Department (GLD—logistics). Below the department level run parallel chains of command for operational, political and logistical matters, each with its separate communications facilities. The Ministry of National Defense provides administrative support. It has no policy-making or implementation responsibilities but is concerned only with planning, manpower, budget, foreign liaison and training.

Military policies and decisions originating in the Military Commission flow through the GSD to the Military Regions (MR) and thence to the main force units. Orders to regional forces also pass through the military district level. Headed by a chief of staff, the GSD contains directorates for eight service arms: the air force, navy, and II Artillery Corps (the strategic missile force), Armored Corps, Artillery Corps, Engineer Corps, Capital Construction Engineer Corps and Railway Engineer Corps. The GSD also is functionally organized for operations, training, intelligence, mobilization, unit organization, surveying, communications and military schools. The GSD itself serves as headquarters for the army. The directorate for the navy controls the North, East and South Sea fleets, while the other directorates generally exercise control through the commanders of the 11 military regions.

The GPD is headed by the PLA's top commissar and is responsible for loyalty, political indoctrination and the administration of military justice. These responsibilities are carried out through a formal chain of commissars, equal in authority to the commanders at each echelon. Virtually anyone in a position of authority in the PLA is a party member. There is a party or Communist Youth League member in every unit down to the smallest maneuver element. Party committees exist at all organizations of battalion level or higher, while companies have a party branch in each.

The GLD is charged with logistical functions, including production, supply, transportation, housing, pay and medical support. Logistics is the weakest sector in military capability.

Each of the 11 MR's contain one to four military districts, which are geographically identical to the provinces. Nuclear forces are directly subordinate to Beijing. Conventional, main, regional and militia units are controlled administratively by MR commanders, but the GSD at Beijing could contact directly and command any main-force unit at will. The PLA organization and echelons are: squad, platoon, company, battalion, regiment, division and army, organized triangularly. The largest tactical formation in peacetime is the army—roughly equivalent to a corps in the U.S. Army.

Over 80% of the PLA is made up of the ground forces. Main forces include about 40 armies, including one airborne army. Independent divisions number 11 armored, about 40 artillery and antiaircraft artillery and 15 or more engineer, plus 150 independent regiments of

Military Regions	Military Districts
Lanchow	Gansu, Ningxia-Hui, Shanxi, Qinghai
Xinjiang	Xinjiang
Chengdu	Sichuan, Xizang
Kunming	Guizhou, Yunnan
Wuhan	Henan, Hubei
Foochow	Fujian, Jiangxi
Nanjing	Anhui, Zhejiang, Jiangsu
Guangzhou	Hunan, Guangdong, Guangxi
Shenyang	Heilongjiang, Jilin, Liaoning
Beijing	Hubei, Nei Monggol, Shanxi
Tsinan	Shandong

mostly support troops. Regional forces include about 85 divisions of border defense, garrison and internal security troops, plus 130 independent regiments. Each main-force army includes 43,000 troops in three partially motorized infantry divisions and two regiments of artillery and antiaircraft. Each division has over 12,000 personnel in three infantry regiments, a regiment each of artillery and armor, and one antiaircraft battalion. Organization is flexible, and higher echelons are free to tailor forces for combat around any number of infantry divisions. Each division has its own armor and artillery, which may be apportioned as needed among its units. The one airborne army is technically part of the air force and consists of three lightly equipped divisions of about 9,000 men each. Once delivered to a battle area, it becomes an infantry force with mortars and recoilless guns. The 11 armored divisions each have up to 300 medium tanks. Armored personnel carriers are few, and self-propelled guns are virtually nonexistent. Artillery forces emphasize towed guns and howitzers as well as truck-mounted multiple-rocket launchers.

Regional forces are full-time troops organized as independent divisions for border defense, garrison and internal security missions. Border defense units are reconnaissance forces deployed along China's long land borders, while garrison divisions perform the same role along coastlines exposed to attack. The ground forces are deficient in tactical nuclear weapons, antitank guided missiles and tactical surface-to-air missiles.

The part-time militia is trained and led by the PLA and organized in three categories: The best-trained is the armed militia; the next is the "basic" or "backbone" militia, and the least-trained is the "ordinary" militia. Organization is nominal at the national and regional levels. Real control rests with the provincial party committees and military district headquarters, under which there are divisions at the county level, regiments at commune levels, battalions at production brigade levels and companies at production team levels. Urban militia units are organized at plants, schools, etc. In general the militia does not function as units of larger than company or battalion size. Armed militia units have a full range of infantry weapons, light antiaircraft guns and antitank artillery. Armed militia units near the borders and coastline perform patrols and guard duty, while urban militia units have internal security responsibilities.

The air force has five branches: air defense, ground attack, bombing, reconnaissance and airborne troops. In peacetime it is controlled by the GSD via the army headquarters located with or in communication with each of the 11 MR headquarters. In wartime the control probably would revert to the regional commanders. The primary mission of the air force is defense; it has only limited interdiction, airlift and reconnaissance capabilities. Each fighter-bomber and bomber division has three regiments, a typical air defense regiment consisting of three squadrons of about 12 aircraft each. The air force also controls SAM sites, antiaircraft guns and air base radars. Most aircraft have unsophisticated avionics, as a result of which most navigation is visual. Chinese pilots rarely fly at night or in bad weather.

Although the navy comprises less than 10% of the PLA's strength, it is the third-largest navy in the world. Like the ground forces, it is organized into main forces (three fleets), regional forces (patrol gunboats) and militia (armed fishing trawlers). It also includes the naval air forces. The main elements of naval defense are submarines, destroyers and frigates with antiship missiles, missile and torpedo patrol boats and naval shore batteries. China's only amphibious operation of any distance has been its occupation of the Paracel Islands in 1974. The navy's lack of shipborne SAM's and effective antisubmarine warfare (ASW) sensors and weapons has delayed its development into an open-ocean force. It has to operate within range of shore-based aircraft or stay in the shallow waters of the continental shelf to reduce threat from submarines.

China possesses a small but credible nuclear deterrent force. Although it claims it never will use nuclear missiles first, it has consistently expanded its capabilities and now has operational ICBM's, first tested in 1980. The missiles are operated by the II Artillery Corps and are under the direct command of the highest levels of the Military Commission. China detonated its first atomic device in 1964 and since then has conducted a number of nuclear tests.

Because living standards and career opportunities are generally better in military than in civilian life, the PLA has an abundance of willing recruits. By law, conscription is in effect. The Constitution states, "It is the lofty duty of every citizen to defend the motherland and resist aggression. It is the honorable obligation of citizens to perform military service according to law." The Chinese appear to take this obligation seriously and even use illegal means to get accepted into the PLA. Each year after the autumn harvest conscription quotas are set for the individual provinces and military subdistricts. Only about 10% of those reaching the conscription age of 18 annually are actually drafted. The initial obligations are three years for nonspecialists in the ground forces; four years in the air force, land-based naval units and technical units in the ground forces; and five years for those serving aboard ship. Upon completing military service, most conscripts return to their homes and civilian employment, and all are assigned to the militia. Service with the PLA is a ladder to success and promotion in the party and government. As there are no ranks in the PLA, promotion consists of transfer to a more responsible position, generally up a unit's chain of command. Selection takes place two echelons above the vacancy to be filled and is based on party recommendations. Often a member of a selection committee will sponsor a particular candidate, a practice that greatly contributes to cliques within the PLA.

Uniforms are notable for their distinctive Maoist cut and lack of insignia. The only service not wearing Maoist-style uniforms is the navy, which returned to traditional dress in 1974. Naval duty dress is dungarees and a striped T-shirt. The ground forces wear olive drab trousers and a jacket buttoned to the neck. Navy personnel wear blue, and air force personnel wear an olive drab tunic with blue trousers. Rank insignia was abolished in 1965, but subtle distinctions provide a clue to the ranks of officers, such as red collar tabs, the number of ball point pens displayed in the pockets and the number of jacket pockets (four for officers and two for enlisted personnel).

After the aberrations of the Maoist period, military training has returned to its normal professional standards. The PLA's first military academy, called the Anti-Japanese Military and Political College, was formed in 1936 in Yan'an. By 1949 the PLA ran at least three military academies, all of which were closed in the mid-1960s and were not reopened until 1978. Currently there are three levels of military education. The top-level academies are controlled by the Ministry of National Defense. At the intermediate level are the service colleges, such as Beijing Air War College and Luda Naval Academy. At the tertiary level are technical schools. The top institutions in professional military training are the PLA Military Academy, the Academy of Military Science and the Beijing Institute for International Strategic Studies.

The average PLA soldier is technically less proficient than his Western counterpart. Offsetting this disadvantage is his toughness and readiness to fight long and hard with a minimum of supplies or amenities. He is highly disciplined, superbly motivated and well led, but also poorly equipped, inadequately serviced and insufficiently trained. All PLA soldiers, from private to noncommissioned officer, are called "fighters." The code of conduct and discipline has not changed since the 1920s. The soldier must obey his superior but at the same time may criticize any regardless of rank during political discussions. He is included in small-unit planning and may offer advice on the execution of unit plans. Morale is traditionally high. There have been fewer than a handful of deserters during the many military conflicts since 1949. Only three or four Communist pilots have flown to Taiwan, despite large sums of money reportedly being offered as inducements.

The PLA has a peculiar hierarchy, and its lexicon of titles is one of the most unusual among modern armies. A commander is any officer who commands at least a company; officers below that level are called leaders. A political commander or leader is called a commissar. The commissar system was introduced by the Soviets at Whamboa Military Academy in the 1920s. The relative statuses of the commander and the commissar indicate the extent of CCP control over the military apparatus.

In the heyday of the Cultural Revolution, with "politics in command," the commissars wielded more power than the commanders. Since then the pendulum has swung back. Despite such swings, the supremacy of the party over the PLA never has been in doubt, and commanders have been required to abide by the "mass line." Nevertheless, regional commanders have great influence in party councils, and their signals are closely watched before critical decisions are taken.

DEFENSE INDICATORS, 1988

Defense budget ($): 16 billion
% of central budget: 33.6
% of GNP: 6.7
Military expenditures per capita ($): 23
Military expenditures per soldier ($): 5,000
Military expenditures per sq. km. (sq. mi.) ($): 1,667 (4,319)
Total strength of armed forces: 3.2 million
   Per 1,000: 2.9
Reserves: 1.2 million
Arms exports ($): 1.1 billion
Arms imports ($): 140 million

Personnel & Equipment

Army
  Personnel: 2.3 million (1,075,000 conscripts)
  Organization: 11 military regions; 26 military districts (provincial regions); 1 independent military district; 3 garrison commands; 22 integrated group armies comprising 80 infantry divisions; 11 armored divisions; 5–6 field and antiaircraft artillery divisions; 50 independent engineer regiments
  Equipment: 9,000 main battle tanks; 1,200 light tanks; 2,800 armored personnel carriers; 14,500 towed artillery; 1,250 multiple-rocket launchers; 15,000 air defense guns; also mortars, SSM launchers, antitank guided weapons, SAM's.

Navy
  Personnel: 300,000
  Organization:
    North Sea Fleet; 9 coastal defense districts
    Bases: Qingdao (hq.), Dalian (Luda), Huludao, Weihai, Chengshan
    East Sea Fleet; 7 coastal defense districts
    Bases: Shanghai (hq.), Wusong, Dinghai, Hangshou
    South Sea Fleet; 9 coastal defense districts
    Bases: Zhanjiang (hq.), Shantou, Guangzhou, Haikou, Yulin, Beihai, Huangpu, outposts on Paracel and Spratley islands
  Equipment: 115 submarines, including 1 SSBN; 19 destroyers; 34 frigates; 850 patrol and coastal combatants, including 10 corvettes, 235 missile craft, 185 torpedo craft, 420 patrol craft (91 coastal, 380 inshore, 50 riverine), 128 mine warfare vessels, 76 amphibious vessels, 104 support and miscellaneous vessels
Coastal regional defense forces: 38,000
Marines: 4,500
Naval air force: 30,000; 900 shore-based combat aircraft; 12 armored helicopters

Air force
  Personnel: 470,000; 3 airborne army divisions: 27,000
  Equipment: 6,000 combat aircraft, 120 medium bombers (some nuclear-capable), 500 fighter ground attack craft, 4,000 fighters, 130 reconnaissance aircraft, 420 transport aircraft, 400 helicopters
  Organization: 7 military air regions
    Antiaircraft artillery: 16 divisions, 28 independent air defense regiments, 16,000 AA guns
  Strategic forces
    Offensive: 90,000 strategic rocket units, 6 ICBM, 60 IRBM, 50 MRBM
    Defensive: Tracking stations: Xinjiang and Shanxi; phased-array radar complex; ballistic missile early-warning system

Under Mao there was a symbiotic relationship between the PLA and the people. Although this relationship was strained during the excesses of the Cultural Revolution, the PLA always considered itself the protector and friend of the masses. Although it has a reputation as a productive force in civilian public works, its actual contribution to the civil economy has been minimal. Except in the Xizang and Xinjiang military districts, it has not been engaged in public works projects since 1954. Its most public-spirited programs have been the provision of free medical and veterinary services and local disaster relief. Instead of directly supporting the civil economy, the PLA has tried to be as self-sufficient as possible by running its own farms and small factories. It supplies much of the food and equipment it needs. On a per capita basis the PLA is the least expensive standing army in the world. The civil population, however, benefits from the military modernization drive in an unexpected way. Defense industries are encouraged to turn to civil production to sop up excess plant capacity, employ more workers and generate profits to buy modern equipment.

China produces a vast range of military armaments and equipment, including tanks, artillery, armored personnel carriers, nuclear missiles and aircraft.

EDUCATION

Traditional education has a 2,500-year history in China, but modern education dates only from the Revolution of 1911. The May 4 Movement of 1919, led by students, signaled the shift from the former Japanese-model education system to a Western one stressing cultural modernization and educational reform. Hu Shih, an American-trained Chinese educator, was the important spokesman of this movement. Before much progress could be made, civil wars and World War II intervened, and the educational system was in considerable disarray when the Communists took over in 1949.

Even after the establishment of the people's republic, the course of education was marked by twists and turns as the regime sought to tailor education to suit ideology. The years of the Cultural Revolution (1965–76) were a hiatus in Chinese educational history, when the regime closed schools and colleges and students roamed the country as Red Guards, creating havoc and reciting verses from Chairman Mao. This phase came to an end with the death of Mao and the rise of the pragmatists, but the educational system still bears the scars of the decade of anarchy.

Three articles in the Constitution of 1982 relate to education. Article 19 places on the state the responsibility of "developing socialist educational undertakings in order to raise the scientific cultural level of the whole nation." Article 46 states that citizens "have the duty as well as the right to receive education." Article 4 makes Putonghua (known as Mandarin in the West) the national language but guarantees minorities the right to employ their own language under certain conditions.

Compulsory education covers in principle all of primary school, but in rural areas the goal of universal primary education has yet to be attained. Each academic year is divided into two parts: spring and fall semesters. Classes are held six days a week, with half a day on Saturday, nine months per year. Each semester there are two examinations at every grade level—midterm and final examinations—and assessment of student performance is based on the outcome of these examinations. The grading system is from 0 to 100, with 60 as the passing grade. In some schools a nonnumerical grade is used, with *you* (excellent); *liang* (good); *zhong* (fair) and *cha* (poor) used to represent grades.

Since the end of the Cultural Revolution, private schools have reappeared, but they still maintain a low profile. Most of them teach foreign languages, but a few prepare students for examinations at various levels. They are funded mostly by private individuals, particularly overseas Chinese.

Kindergartens are available for children aged three to six. They function under the auspices of government authorities, army units, factories or agricultural production units, neighborhood communities, communes or production brigades. Kindergartens are available from four to eight or 10 hours a day. Some provide boarding facilities, while others are temporary, being set up, for instance, during the harvest. Fees are charged to meet the cost of meals and medical care. Kindergarten activities are largely determined by the wealth of the community and the teachers' qualifications.

Primary education expanded rapidly after 1949. The net enrollment rate of 118% is close to those of advanced countries and 30% above the average rate for the rest of the developing world. A considerable proportion of students in primary schools are over- or underage. The proportion of overage students in primary schools, estimated at 33%, is higher than that in other comparable countries, where it is 13% to 21%. Some overage students are repeaters, but most are late school entrants. Girls comprise 44% of the students in primary schools, implying that most of the appropriate age group not in school are girls. Grade promotion in primary schools is not automatic. No official information is available on repetition rates, but data from selected schools show an average repetition rate of 5%. Generally, primary schools are easily accessible, even in rural areas. The average commune has 15 primary schools, usually within walking distance. Access is difficult only in the remote areas of the North and West, partially inhabited by nomads.

About 64% of the students who begin their education complete primary schooling. This completion rate is about 20% higher than in the rest of the developing world. There is an urban-rural and sex disparity in retention rates. Rural girls are most often taken out of school prematurely for economic rather than academic reasons. Chinese educators believe that five years of schooling are needed to achieve reasonable literacy in the Chinese language, defined as the ability to recognize and write some 3,000 characters. This implies that 36% of primary-school children who drop out of school are illiterate or semiliterate. About 83% of the urban and 79% of the rural primary-school graduates proceed to junior secondary education. These are high percentages by international standards, approach those of advanced countries and are 13% above the median for the LDC's.

A common primary-school curriculum has been developed but local authorities may adjust the basic curriculum somewhat to meet their specific needs. Chinese and mathematics account for as much as two-thirds of the scheduled hours. The curriculum is weak in the natural and social sciences, which together occupy 8% of the school time, with the remaining hours devoted to physical education, music and art. Foreign languages may be offered in grades four and five, but the shortage of teachers is a constraining factor, except in urban areas. The scheduled class week of six workdays comprises 24 to 27 periods, lasting 45 minutes each for each grade. This is above the average in many advanced countries, where often the schedule is light in the early school years. There are, in addition, seven to eight hours per week in each grade of extracurricular activities, including productive labor, private study, Young Pioneer activities and outdoor sports. Productive labor, which has been de-emphasized since the Cultural Revolution, still is a compulsory school activity and involves students in maintaining school facilities, working in nearby factories or cultivating school gardens.

Students are expected to meet a portion of the costs for their schooling. Tuition fees are modest, but supplementary fees for books, transportation, food and heating are collected. Fees have no readily apparent deterrent effect. In fact, it is suggested that modest fees encourage parents to treat schooling seriously and to be certain that their children attend.

Community-run or *minban* schools combining part work and part study date back to the party's guerrilla warfare days in Yan'an. They are operated by a village, brigade, factory or neighborhood committee and funded by student tuition and funds generated by student labor. Even though they are self-supporting, *minban* schools are subject to the administrative control of the education authorities, and the qualifications of their teachers are certified by the country-level education bureau. *Minban* schools are run for widely different purposes, such as reducing the enrollment load of regular schools, absorbing children with behavior problems and graduates of the regular school system who are not admitted to the next level, and developing local initiative in rural areas.

Chinese educators feel that the school week is too long and that primary children are overburdened. The general trend is toward reduced homework. First-grade children are not given any homework; homework for the second and third grades does not exceed 30 minutes per day, and for fourth and fifth graders one hour per day. A certain amount of homework is assigned during vacations.

Some 36% of primary school teachers are civil servants, and 64% are *minban* teachers. Only 47% of the primary-level teaching staff are qualified. The primary-level student–teacher ratio of 27:1 is closer to that of advanced countries and is better than the average ratio in other LDC's of 38:1 to 34:1. This ratio is caused by the

staff's low teaching load. The average of 19 to 20 scheduled class contact periods per week is five to 10 periods a week less than in many other countries. The average size class of 27 students is bigger than the classes in advanced countries but is not particularly large compared to classes in other LDC's. China uses the subject–teacher method of instruction in primary schools, in contrast to the norm of one teacher handling all subjects in primary classes. The government justifies this method by citing the high number of unqualified teachers, for whom it is easier to master one or two subjects rather than the eight in the curriculum. Chinese teachers also appear to specialize by grade and teach in only one or two of the five primary grades. The subject–teacher method also increases the demand for teachers and the minimum size at which a school can operate economically.

Most primary schools, even those in Beijing and Shanghai, have poor facilities. Lighting and heating are insufficient, and rural schools often lack windowpanes because glass is in short supply. In some remote regions, schools are housed in caves dug out of the hills and mountains, and are potentially dangerous because of the risk of sudden collapse. Some 35% of the primary schools in some prefectures lack furniture. Benches and desks are made of dry clay in areas where wood is scarce. Teaching equipment is sparse, except for a few posters, one or two wall maps and a chalkboard. The supply of textbooks, however, is ample, even though the students have to pay for them. The textbooks are of poor quality, printed on rough paper with few illustrations.

Learning the Chinese script, which occupies 40% of the scheduled primary week, requires an unusual amount of rote learning. In the traditional style, students recite in unison the Chinese symbols on the chalkboard. But the teachers are eager to teach and the students are eager to learn, and disciplinary problems are almost nonexistent. Chinese students probably are farther advanced in mathematics than school children of their age in many other countries.

Secondary education has developed even more rapidly than primary education. The secondary enrollment rate has risen from 2% in 1949 to 37%. The rate compares favorably with the 26% enrollment ratio for 92 other developing countries but is lower than the 60% in China's East Asian neighbors or the 80% in OECD countries. Secondary education is biased toward general training. Less than 5% of the schools are vocational or technical, and they enroll 12% of the secondary-school population. Thus secondary schools prepare students for higher academic education rather than for the labor market, even though only 37% of junior secondary graduates (from grade eight) proceed to senior secondary schools and a maximum of 10% of senior secondary school graduates (from grade 10) proceed to postsecondary institutions. The neglect of technical and vocational education is a fallout of the Cultural Revolution, during which 62,000 vocational and technical schools were dismantled. As a result, China trails not only Europe and the Soviet Union (where the percentage of technical/vocational students is 27.1% and 42.1%, respectively) but also LDC's, where the relative percentage is 10.9%.

The academic secondary school system suffers from serious teacher shortages. In junior secondary school only 11% of the teachers have a college degree, and in general senior secondary schools only 51%. The situation is better in technical/vocational and normal schools, where 90% and 75%, respectively, of the teachers are qualified. Utilization of teachers also is low in secondary schools. In the academic schools, the student–teacher ratio is a low 18:1 and in technical/vocational schools 11:1. The major reason for the low ratios is low teaching loads rather than small classes. In many schools only 12 to 13 class periods are scheduled per week for each teacher, as against a norm of 20 to 25 in other countries. Also at the secondary level, each teacher teaches only one subject. As a result, not only are teachers underemployed, but also the necessary coordination between related subjects, such as mathematics and physics, becomes more difficult.

Junior secondary education (grades six through eight) is extensive with a gross enrollment of rate of 75% and a female enrollment rate of 41%. Of the 144,000 general secondary schools, 104,000 offer junior secondary education only, while most of the others are vertically integrated. Ethnic minorities are less well represented at this level than at the primary level. The enrollment of Han Chinese is almost 40% higher, measured as a percentage of the total population or even higher measured as a percentage of the relevant age groups.

The internal efficiency—the retention rate—of junior secondary schools is even higher than that of primary schools. Enrollment statistics indicate a 5% to 6% dropout between grades and an 85% graduation rate. Repetition rates also appear to be low, at 0% to 10%. In contrast, wastage rates in secondary education amount to 28% to 46% in other LDC's at the same income level.

The curriculum in junior secondary schools is common throughout China. Chinese and mathematics account for 38%, foreign languages (usually English) 16% and nine other subjects 46%. In addition to the 30 to 31 scheduled class periods per week, students are required to spend time on private study, productive labor, sports and other extracurricular activities. The social sciences and the experimental aspects of the natural sciences occupy a weak position in the junior secondary curriculum. Further, science teaching is made difficult because of a general shortage of laboratories and equipment. Students can conduct experiments in only 10% of the junior secondary schools, and teacher demonstrations are possible in only 25%. Because of the shortage of buildings, many schools use a double shift system. The quality of the buildings and furniture is higher than in primary schools, but equipment is substandard and lighting is poor.

General senior secondary education covers grades nine through 11. It enrolls 29% of the 15 to 16 age group, with girls making up 39%. The 40,000 secondary schools with senior grades are in towns. The general senior secondary school curriculum offers essentially one study option. The program is strong in the natural sciences and mathematics, which occupy about half of the scheduled time with 30% devoted to Chinese and a foreign language and the remaining 18% shared among three other subjects. Senior secondary school students appear well advanced in mathematics and sciences and in grade 10 deal with mathematical problems that in many other countries are taught in higher grades or are studied by gifted students only. However, parts of the syllabi are outdated, and many modern concepts are missing.

Since the 1970s, tests have again become an important part of school life, and much of the teaching is geared toward tests and university examinations. Students are given midterm as well as final examinations each semester, and report cards are issued regularly. Nonscheduled activities continue to include productive labor, which at this level comprises four weeks per year in industry and agriculture. It often provides the school with an income.

The formal technical and vocational senior secondary and postsecondary system consists of 2,000 schools administered by the various ministries and 3,000 administered by enterprises. Enrollment in technical and vocational schools is low in all areas but particularly so in agriculture, although agriculture occupies 75% of the labor force. Agronomy is one of the lowest choices of secondary school graduates. Few students from rural backgrounds have a desire to become farmers, a problem common to most LDC's. The output from trade and industrial schools also falls far short of the country's needs. Enterprises therefore run their own vocational schools to meet some of their urgent manpower needs. However, the limited intake to the universities of senior secondary school graduates has forced an increasing percentage of these graduates to apply to technical/vocational schools. Thus many technical/vocational schools have courses following senior secondary education.

China has 633 universities and other institutions of higher learning; the Ministry of Education directly manages 35, municipalities and provinces run 392 and 12 ministries run 206. Responsibility for research is shared between the Ministry of Education and the Chinese Academy of Sciences. Only 24% of college enrollees are women, a lower proportion than in the rest of the developing world (33%). In technical fields, the more prestigious institutions play a critical role. They enroll 45% and 60% of students in science and engineering, respectively, and graduate 56% and 70%, respectively, of all scientists and engineers.

Graduate education began only in the 1950s and was one of the casualties of the Cultural Revolution. Graduate institutions reopened in 1978, but the curriculum pattern was not fully defined for many years. Enrollment in graduate courses is low not only in agriculture but also in finance, law, business, trade, economics and administration. Overall enrollment in higher education is very low by international standards. For formal university institutions, the enrollment rate is 1.2%, rising to 1.7% if nonformal and other postsecondary institutions are included, compared to 4.4% in the rest of the developing world and 23% in advanced countries. China has only 10.5 university students per 10,000 population, while the United States has 500; other developed countries have 200; and India, another developing country, has 60. There is a striking contrast between China's quantitative performance in primary and secondary education and its performance in higher education.

The key universities recruit their students nationwide. Many other universities also recruit from outside their province. Until recently universities provided boarding for all their students. Some day students have been accepted in the past decade, but the percentage is low and restricted by lack of transportation in many university towns.

After 1976 a number of steps were initiated to improve the quality of higher education. First, order and stability were reestablished by ending political struggle on university campuses. Second, 88 institutions were selected as "key" universities and provided with special funding, top students and faculty members. Third, entrance examinations were reinstituted to recruit the most academically qualified students. Of these, the last was the most controversial, as a throwback to one of China's oldest cultural legacies—the civil service examinations for the imperial mandarinate. The entrance examinations are rigorous and result in the acceptance of only 5% of the candidates. A preselection examination is given to reduce the number of national-examination-takers to three to five times the places allotted. Each province is assigned a quota of students who would be admitted to the key universities, a second quota who would attend normal universities within the province and a third quota of students from other provinces who would be admitted to provincially run universities. There are separate quotas for minority students. The schools have the option of making the selection among the applicants who make the minimum test score. In addition to the written examination, applicants have to pass a physical examination and a political screening, but only a small number are excluded for either reason. Normally students with a peasant background are favored and in fact constitute 53% of higher education enrollment.

The length of postsecondary courses, which was shortened to three years in the early 1970s, was restored to four years in the 1980s and further increased to five or six years for some programs. The emphasis is again on basic and theoretical subjects, and these make up two-thirds of university curricula. Many subjects abolished during the Cultural Revolution have now been restored. Although manual labor is no longer part of the curriculum, college students are advised to spend four weeks a year in productive work related to their studies. Bachelor's, master's and doctoral degrees also were restored in 1981. Undergraduate curricula remain relatively inflexible, with few elective subjects.

All sectors of research and teaching are hampered by outmoded equipment and facilities. The absence of the latest technology is evident in most laboratories. In engineering and science the applied-method approach is favored over fundamental research. Certain subjects are neglected, such as immunology and genetics in the life sciences. There is a heavy concentration on physi-

cal chemistry at the expense of organic and inorganic chemistry. The universities also are deficient in computers and software.

The student–teacher ratio in higher education is low, at 5:1, compared to 10:1 in many other countries. In the key institutions, which employ 50% of all staff, overemployment is even more serious, with a student–teacher ratio of 3:1. The number of full professors is, nevertheless, low and accounts for only 5% of total staff, as against 62% lecturers and 33% assistants. Assistants primarily grade papers and tutor undergraduate students; lecturers primarily teach; associate professors do research; and full professors are not always active in either teaching or research, doing mostly administrative work. The teaching load generally is low. The percentage of staff with postgraduate-level research is low, and the percentage of staff who have not completed undergraduate studies is high. About two-thirds of the staff are over 40 years of age. There is no compulsory retirement age for university professors, which accounts for the high percentage of older teachers. Another characteristic is low staff mobility. Most university teachers spend their entire academic life in the same institution, and few have traveled outside China on exchange programs.

The absence of campus master planning, a heavy compartmentalization, and inappropriate scheduling prevent full use of laboratories, classrooms, libraries and other facilities. There is little provision for interlibrary loans, and libraries lack an adequate supply of postgraduate literature.

In a country of China's size, the management of education is a formidable task, even more so because of the constant shifts in educational objectives and financing methods. Most of China's over 90 ministries and commissions at the cabinet level are involved in education activities. Preeminent among them is the Ministry of Education, which is responsible for primary and general secondary schools and primary teacher training institutions as well as many technical schools and universities, and for overall education policy. The Ministry of Education comprises two offices; nine major departments; eight separate bureaus; and units dealing with the TV university, publishing and research. Several departments and bureaus cut across levels of education. The ministry appears, however, not to be overstaffed and employs only some 500 professional staff.

Provincial and local educational administration also is quite complex. Each province, autonomous region and directly administered municipality has a bureau of education, with offices for primary, secondary and higher education, adult education, planning and finance, personnel, productive labor, audiovisual media and student affairs. Each prefecture within a province has an office of education, with units for education, planning and finance, and personnel. Since prefectures have no income of their own, their funds come from the provincial bureaus. Each county has a county education office, with responsibilities for primary schools, junior secondary schools and spare-time institutions. The counties have some income from local taxes, a minor part of which is allocated to education. The communes no longer have any responsibility for education but provide some office staff. The same is true of the brigades, although they pay *minban* teachers in kind.

Educational planning, by means of long-term and annual plans, is directed by the Ministry of Education but involves all levels of educational authorities. The plans set detailed quotas for enrollment, construction of new facilities, personnel, etc. The procedure differs much from what prevails in other planned economies. It is highly participatory and comprehensive but also cumbersome, time-consuming and expensive.

Financial responsibility for education is divided among the central ministries, provinces, municipalities, counties, communes, brigades, enterprises, parents and adult students. Unusual for a socialist society is the burden borne by parents and adult children, estimated at 8% of all educational expenditures. Considerable income also is produced by student productive labor activities. Under self-help programs, brigades contribute voluntary labor in building school facilities. Brigades and enterprises contribute to recurrent costs by paying the wages of *minban* teachers and vocational school instructors. The central government share of recurrent costs is paid on a per capita basis to each school. The trend is toward greater financial responsibilities for localities.

The unit cost of education is low at the primary and secondary levels but high at the tertiary level. The last is caused by a generous boarding policy and very low student–teacher ratio. Total public expenditure on education as a percentage of the GNP is estimated at 2.9, which is less than the median percentage of 3.9% for 82 selected developing countries and the median percentage of 5.7% for developed countries. Government expenditure on education as a percentage of total expenditures also is low, at 8.1% compared with 15.1% in other developing countries and 15.6% in developed countries. Public expenditure on education per student in LDC's and advanced countries is 143% and 389%, respectively, of the Chinese figure. Low teacher salaries, charges paid by parents as fees and for books, and local contributions explain the low level of public spending on education.

Because of the considerable economies in conducting nonformal education, this sector is considerably developed, almost on a level with advanced countries. Nonformal education at the primary, secondary and tertiary levels adds 15%, 8% and 59%, respectively, to the educational enrollments.

EDUCATION INDICATORS, 1988

Literacy
  Total (%): 72.6
  Male (%): 83.5
  Female (%): 61.2
First level
  Schools: 820,846
  Teachers: 5,414,000
  Students: 131,825,000
  Student–teacher ratio: 24:1
  Net enrollment rate (%): 118
  Females (%): 44

EDUCATION INDICATORS, 1988 (continued)

Second level
  Schools: 92,967
  Teachers: 2,758,000
  Students: 48,899,000
  Student–teacher ratio: 18:1
  Net enrollment rate (%): 37
  Females (%): 40
Vocational
  Schools: 17,751
  Teachers: 550,000
  Students: 6,074,000
  Student–teacher ratio: 11:1
Third level
  Institutions: 1,054
  Teachers: 372,000
  Students: 1,880,000
  Student–teacher ratio: 5:1
  Gross enrollment rate (%): 1.7
  Graduates per 100,000 age 20–24: 168
  % of population over 25 with postsecondary education: 1.0
  Females (%): 28
Foreign study
  Foreign students in national universities: 2,593
  Students abroad: 16,985
    of whom in
      United States, 8,637
      West Germany, 723
      Japan, 5,185
      Canada, 654
Public expenditures (national currency)
  Total: 15.192 billion (1983)
  % of GNP: 2.9
  % of national budget: 8.1
  % current expenditures: 84.2

GRADUATES, 1984

Total: 289,241
Education: 84,842
Humanities & religion: 14,596
Fine & applied arts: 1,343
Law: 3,163
Commerce & business: 15,036
Natural sciences: 16,433
Mathematics & computer science: 5,178
Medicine: 32,257
Engineering: 90,917
Architecture: 855
Transportation & communications: 3,631
Agriculture, forestry, fisheries: 18,569
Other: 2,421

At the primary level, adult education's targeted groups are dropouts and illiterates. Secondary education is mostly technical or vocational, offered by enterprises and spare-time schools. The most impressive growth of nonformal education has been at the tertiary level. Because the output from traditional universities and colleges is limited, TV universities, correspondence universities, night schools and enterprises have taken up the slack. Virtually every large enterprise runs workers' colleges or TV colleges with full-time instructors. The TV universities deserve special mention. They are joint creations of the Ministry of Education and the central broadcasting authorities. Each province and autonomous region except Xizang has its own television university, but the Central Broadcasting and TV University in Beijing plays the leading role. The local organizer of the class usually is an enterprise, and it pays all associated charges, including the salaries of local tutors and instructors. The program offers the equivalent of a two-year degree course. The curriculum is highly technical, but the most popular course is English, which has a wide unenrolled audience as well, estimated in the millions. Students may enroll for full-time or part-time study. Students in the former are released from their job for three years to complete the program; students in the latter study for a few hours each day. Students enter a TV university by passing one of two examinations. Nonformal education outside a TV university is the responsibility of the National Bureau of Worker-Peasant Education.

Teachers are trained in 186 normal universities and teachers colleges. Preservice primary-level teacher training is conducted in three-year courses at the senior secondary level and in two-year courses at the postsecondary level in 1,053 normal schools. In-service training and upgrading of primary-level teachers, whether formally qualified or not, take place at 2,000 training institutions, which are separate from the normal schools. The in-service teacher training system is well developed by international standards.

LEGAL SYSTEM

The State Constitution of 1982 and the Organic Law of the People's Courts provide for a four-tier court system. At the apex is the Supreme People's Court, which is not only the highest appellate forum of the land but also the supervisor of the administration of justice by subordinate courts. Local people's courts—the courts of first instance—handle civil and criminal cases. They consist of (1) higher people's courts at the level of provinces, autonomous regions, and municipalities directly under the central government; (2) intermediate people's courts at the level of prefectures; autonomous prefectures; and municipalities under the central government, provinces or autonomous regions; and (3) basic people's courts at the level of autonomous counties, towns and municipal districts. Special courts adjudicate military, railway transportation, water transportation, forest and economic cases. The president and judges of the Supreme People's Court are elected by the National People's Congress and serve no more than two consecutive five-year terms. Local people's courts are similarly elected by the local state organs at their level.

China is perhaps the only major society without a written criminal or civil code. Although there are selected statutes, there is no comprehensive code. Law plays the dual role of resolving disputes between people and suppressing "enemies of the people." The definition of "enemies" varies with the times but has always included rightists, counterrevolutionaries, "bad elements" and revisionists. Although the Constitution guarantees the independence of the judiciary, such independence is only a political fiction, and interference by party organs in judicial organs is common. The conception of equality before the law is seen as violating the Marxist theory of class struggle.

The court system is complemented by a structure of people's procuratorates, from the Supreme People's Procuratorate at the top to lower procuratorates established at the corresponding levels of the courts. The procuratorates represent the state in criminal proceedings and ensure that the judicial process of the courts and the execution of judgments and orders in criminal matters conform to the law.

Prisons were separated from the Ministry of Public Security and placed under the Ministry of Justice in 1983. The majority of the prisoners are sentenced to hard labor, of which there are two kinds: criminal and administrative. The former is for a fixed number of years, while the latter is for an indeterminate period, but usually three or four years. Both categories may be found at state farms, mines and factory prisons. Prisoners are required to work eight hours a day, six days a week. They are forbidden to read anything not provided by the prison; to speak dialects not understood by the guards; or to keep cash, gold or jewelry. Mail is censored, and generally only one visitor is allowed per month. Sentences may be reduced for up to half the original sentence, but at least 10 years of a life sentence have to be served. Both probation and parole are granted when certain conditions are met.

No detailed information is available on the criminal justice system.

LAW ENFORCEMENT

The Ministry of Public Security within the State Council is the central police authority. The ministry consists of an administrative office and functionally separate departments for political security, economic security, communications security, intelligence and police operations. Subordinate to the ministry are public security departments at the provincial level (including the three special municipalities); public security bureaus in the prefectures and large cities; public security subbureaus in counties and municipal districts; and stations at the commune, village or town level. The police appear to wield progressively greater influence at each lower level of government. Each office has sections for population control, pretrial investigations, welfare, fire fighting and traffic control; a detention center; and sections for other activities. Some sections, such as those for fire fighters, are all but technically independent. The public security station—the police element in closest contact with the people—is supervised by the public safety subbureau as well as by the local people's government and the procuratorate. The procuratorate supervises investigations conducted by the public security station and may assume direct responsibility if it so chooses.

A public security station generally is smaller than a police station in the West but has considerably broader responsibilities. In rural areas it has a chief, a deputy chief, a small administrative staff and a small police force. In urban areas it has more administrative personnel and seven to 18 patrolmen. Criminal law activities include investigation, apprehension, interrogation and temporary detention. The station's household section maintains a registry of all persons living in the area. Births, deaths, marriages and divorces are recorded and confirmed through random checks. The station regulates all hotels and registers all hotel guests who stay beyond a certain number of days. It also controls theaters, cinemas, radios and printing presses; regulates explosives, guns, ammunition and poisons; directs traffic and fire fighting; monitors public health and sanitation; and protects important public offices and installations. Controlling changes of residence is another important police function.

Public security officials can impose administrative sanctions. They can apprehend vagabonds and people who repeatedly breach public order and sentence them to "reeducation through labor" for a maximum of two years. They may apply admonitions; fines; and detention for up to 15 days. Offenders also may be coerced into "volunteering" for extra work, and illegal goods in their possession may be confiscated.

Supplementing the work of the police are a variety of neighborhood and workplace committees. They were first established in the 1950s and retained in the post-Mao period. Most relevant to law enforcement are the security defense committees, composed of three to 11 members and subject to the direction of the local police.

Each policeman is responsible for approximately 600 residences in his area. The relationship between the patrolman on his beat and the people is close. He lives in the neighborhood and is expected to know everyone who lives there. The census police, particularly, are rarely transferred and spend most of their career in one neighborhood. His task is not only to prevent and punish crime but also to promote desirable social behavior. The positive side of his duties is a year-round responsibility and is enhanced annually by a "cherish the people" month. He may mediate in minor disputes, supervise individuals recently released from prison and intervene in the careers of potential deviants. Regular police wear a khaki-green uniform with red piping (supplemented by fur-collared greatcoats in winter) and usually work six days a week, their eight-hour shifts interrupted by a two-hour lunch break. The traffic police work night shifts as well as day shifts and are assigned to police booths at intersections or on main roads. These booths are connected by telephone to district or neighborhood stations. Citizens, few of whom have private telephones, report incidents to the police from one of these booths. Members of the public security police do not carry weapons on a regular basis.

Police patrol activities take place almost entirely on foot or bicycles. Traffic police are making increased use of sidecar motorcycles. Jeeps are used for transportation and crowd control, while trucks are employed to move large numbers of personnel.

In the absence of a modern communications system, police command and control are not highly developed. Most patrolmen frequently work on their own and must make decisions independently without the help of a two-way radio or a telephone. However, this does not appear to present a major problem in apprehending fugitives, since the lack of mobility within the country, combined with the system of resident registration, make it difficult for a criminal to go far from the scene of his crime.

The Armed People's Police is a specialized branch of the public security forces, and its personnel are armed with heavier weapons. Trained by the PLA, they protect public buildings, including foreign embassies. Secret police operations employ agents, informers and "roving spies." Agents in plain clothes are posted at bus and railway stations and other public places. Police informers denounce "bad elements" and assist in surveilling suspected political dissidents. A "roving spy," ever watchful for sabotage, is a special category of informant in factories and workplaces. The Ministry of State Security, established in 1983, is in charge of intelligence and counterespionage. It has vastly greater powers than the police to investigate, detain and arrest potential enemies of the socialist system.

Criminal identification facilities and laboratories are limited and ill-equipped. Fingerprinting is not used extensively, and computers are being introduced only slowly. It is not clear whether there is any central criminal record facility, although the police are helped tremendously by the detailed records maintained by the census police.

Personnel for the police are drawn from every segment of the population, and there is no apparent dearth of recruits. The pride of the police training system is Public Security University in Beijing. Each of the 29 provinces and the three major municipalities also has a police college.

Crime statistics are not very reliable and vary from source to source. Post-1984 estimates range from four to five crimes per 10,000. The major problem crimes are drug trafficking, gambling, prostitution and economic crimes.

HEALTH

The Chinese health-care policy has three distinctive features. One is a strong emphasis on preventive measures and on improving the environment through vaccination and infectious disease vector control and by strict enforcement of the elementary aspects of private and public sanitation. An important aspect of the preventive emphasis has been a strong vertical organization, with central authorities responsible for campaigns against specific diseases, combined with effective use of clinical services in support of prevention measures. A second feature is the wide diffusion of basic curative care, most notably by the "barefoot doctors" at the team and brigade level backed up by referral of difficult cases to better-equipped and better-trained personnel at commune health centers and county hospitals. A third feature is the continued reliance on traditional Chinese medicine.

The ratio of population to medical personnel is more satisfactory in China than in other LDC's or middle-income countries: 724 per qualified doctor and 365 per other qualified personnel, in contrast to 9,900 and 8,790, respectively, in low-income countries and 4,310 and 1,860, respectively, in middle-income countries. In part because the pay of medical personnel is very low by international standards, the total annual medical expenditure per capita is only $4.30 (of which $4 is public expenditure), of which almost two-thirds are for drugs. Thus China has been able to achieve virtually universal health coverage at a fraction of the cost in developed countries.

The main contributors to China's superior performance in the health field are fourfold. First, the food rationing system has almost eliminated acute malnutrition, which contributes to one-third to two-thirds of all child deaths in other developing countries. Second, near-universal basic curative and preventive health care has greatly reduced the incidence and fatality rates of common respiratory and diarrheal diseases. Third, widespread primary education, primarily of women, has contributed to improved nutrition and health practices in childrearing. Finally, lower fertility rates have created conditions conducive to the health of mothers and children. China's population policy has thus had important health benefits.

Life expectancy is perhaps the best indicator of a country's health status, and the dramatic declines in the death rate since 1949 have pushed China's life expectancy to a level that would be expected of a country with several times its per capita income. China's life expectancy of 69 years far exceeds the average of both low-income countries and middle-income countries. However, there is substantial variation across provinces—from 59 years in Guizhou to 72 years in Shanghai.

The patterns of mortality indicate that China is well on its way through what is called the "epidemiological transition," in which mortality from infectious and parasitic diseases is much reduced and the incidences of cancer and circulatory diseases are much increased. On this transition scale, China is midway between low-income and high-income countries.

Although little detailed information is available on morbidity, great progress has been achieved in controlling diseases that were rampant in pre-1949 China, such as cholera, plague and venereal diseases. Tuberculosis and schistosomiasis remain major problems. The apparent prevalence of roundworm infection, although not a major concern in itself, suggests that much progress remains to be made in hygiene in rural areas.

Compared to virtually all other countries, China has strongly emphasized public preventive over curative health services. Major campaigns were mounted shortly after 1949 to improve environmental sanitation; to eliminate the then "four pests"—rats, flies, mosquitoes and bedbugs; to vaccinate against infectious diseases; and to control the vectors of major endemic disorders such as malaria and schistosomiasis. With the success of these campaigns, some emphasis has been shifted to the provision of minimal curative care. As a corollary, China has emphasized lower-level professional care rather than highly skilled care. Preventive measures and low-level professional personnel also place greater

responsibility on local communities. As the basics of community involvement in preventive health have become more established, it has become necessary to upgrade the skills of health professional to deal with more complicated medical problems.

The primary health-care system today in rural China is a three-tiered system, relying on three levels of the health-care establishment: the brigade's cooperative medical center, the commune health center and the county general hopsital. The system rests on the idea that it is impossible for a country with a vast and low-income population to have a fully qualified medical doctor in each town or village, but that it is possible to have one or more paramedical workers in each community, providing walking-distance service to all its members. China has made major gains toward this goal by avoiding creation of a separate bureaucracy for the health-care system and imposing the health-care system on the existing politico-administrative structure. Thus the divisions of county, commune, brigade and production team have become the focal points for the operations of the various levels of the health-care program.

At the commune and county levels, and to some

HEALTH INDICATORS, 1988

Health personnel
  Physicians: 1,482,000
    Persons per: 724
  Nurses: 718,000
  Pharmacists: 33,800
  Midwives: 76,000
Hospitals
  Number: 60,429
  Number of beds: 2,685,000
  Beds per 10,000: 22
Admissions/discharges
  per 10,000: 182
  Bed occupancy rate (%): 82.7
  Average length of stay (days): 16
Type of hospitals (%)
  Government: 100
Public health expenditures
  As % of national budget: 2.%
  Per capita: $4.30
Vital statistics
  Crude death rate per 1,000: 6.6
  Decline in death rate: −50.4 (1965–84)
  Life expectancy at birth (years): male, 67.8; female, 70.7
  Infant mortality rate per 1,000 live births: 33
  Child mortality rate (ages 1–4 years) per 1,000: 2
  Maternal mortality rate per 100,000 live births: 44
Causes of death per 100,000
  Infectious & parasitic diseases: 23.7
  Cancer: 113.0
  Endocrine and metabolic disorders: 6.3
  Diseases of the nervous system: 9.4
  Diseases of the circulatory system: 251.1
  Diseases of the digestive system: 25.9
  Accidents, poisoning & violence: 31.3
  Diseases of the respiratory system: 43.0
% population with access to safe water: 50

extent at the brigade level, the patient may choose between Western-oriented medical care and traditional Chinese care. Both are available, and both are components of the government's health-care system. Despite the apparently easy coexistence of both systems, there appears to be relatively little attempt to integrate them. Perhaps the best-known exception is the use of acupuncture in Western surgery, but even this is less common than it used to be, except when other anesthetics are contraindicated.

The medical station at the brigade level is financed cooperatively, through payment of premiums by members of the production brigade. It also receives contributions from the welfare funds of the brigade; receipts from the sale of medicinal herbs; fees from the users of this service; and various subsidies from the commune, county, province and state. Government subsidies for the brigade's cooperative medical service are limited and take the following forms: (1) the price of Western drugs is set artificially low, (2) vaccines and contraceptives are provided free and (3) the cost of training barefoot doctors is subsidized.

The commune health center, which typically is a small hospital, is financed in the same way but generally receives more subsidies from the state. Administratively it comes under the leadership of the local commune management committee and party committee, but its medical services are supervised by the three county-level health-care units: the general and maternity and children's hospitals and the antiepidemic station.

At the county level there are three health-care units—the county general hospital, the county antiepidemic station and the county MCH station, under the overall administrative leadership of the county health bureau. Staffed by a college-trained physician, the county hospital serves as the general referral hospital for the entire county, treating cases referred to it by the commune health centers. In addition, it conducts training courses to upgrade the quality of the commune physicians. The county antiepidemic station is responsible for disease control and preventive health. All three county units are fully funded from the state's regular budget.

Although this system maximizes local resources in health care, it has led to marked disparities in the quality of health personnel and access to health care. There is a 3–1 ratio between the best- and worst-off provinces in terms of population per barefoot doctor.

China has paid relatively less attention to provision of dental care than of other medical services, although there exists a curative program paralleling the three-tiered health-care system and making heavy use of paraprofessional staff. However, little emphasis is placed on prevention, particularly oral hygiene and fluoridation of water.

In urban areas, places of employment provide a range of clinical services that, depending on the size of the employer, can include general hospital services. In addition, "street" and "lane" health stations staffed by carefully supervised paramedics provide preventive and simple curative services. Referrals from these sta-

tions go to county-level hospitals or specialized hospitals.

Actual expenditures on health care as a percentage of total government expenditures have changed little from the early 1950s, when they were 2%. The costs estimated are for direct health-care services; water supply and sanitation measures and the costs of free contributions of labor are excluded. Two-thirds of all costs are for drugs. Although the level of public expenditures is relatively high for a developing country, so is the availability of resources.

FOOD & NUTRITION

Average food consumption in China compares well with that in other developing countries—higher than that of India and other low income countries and not far below the average for middle-income countries. Evidence suggests, however, that the Chinese diet contains an unusually low proportion of meat and fats. Nevertheless, in terms of the relative consumption levels of low-income groups, China is way ahead of both low-income and middle-income countries. In urban areas staple foods are rationed, with monthly entitlements that vary with age, sex and occupation but that provide for an adequate (although spartan) level of consumption. Food prices are so low that almost all families can afford their full allotment. In rural areas the allotments are more generous and invariably are supplemented by food grown in private plots. Rural meat rations, however, are only a quarter to half of those in urban areas.

FOOD & NUTRITION INDICATORS, 1988

Per capita daily food consumption, calories: 2,602
Per capita daily consumption, proteins, g. (oz.): 61.3 (2.2)
Calorie intake as % of FAO recommended minimum requirement: 133
% of calorie intake from vegetable products: 91
% of calorie intake from animal products: 9
Food expenditures as % of total household expenditures: 56.3
% of total calories derived from
  Cereals: 71.3
  Potatoes: 0.9
  Meat & poultry: 6.5
  Fish: 0.4
  Fats & oils: 4.6
  Eggs & milk: 1.1
  Fruits & vegetables: 2.3
  Other: 12.9
Per capita consumption of foods, kg. (lb.), l. (pt.)
  Potatoes: 52.3 (115.3)
  Wheat: 55.6 (122.6)
  Rice: 147.5 (325.0)
  Eggs 3.7 (8.1)
  Honey: 0.1 (0.2)
  Milk: 12.1 (26.6)
  Butter: 0.1 (0.2)
  Cheese: 0.1 (0.2)
  Meat
    Beef & veal: 0.3 (0.6)
    Pig meat: 16.2 (31.3)
    Poultry: 1.7 (3.7)
  Sugar: 5.4 (11.9)
  Beer, l. (pt.): 1.3 (2.7)
  Wine, l. (pt.): 0.1 (0.2)

Acute malnutrition has been virtually eliminated, although in some rural areas children suffer from growth retardation as a result of poor diet.

MEDIA & CULTURE

The Chinese press consists of 2,191 newspapers, including 222 dailies, with an estimated circulation of about 150 million. The flagship of the press is *Renmin Ribao* (People's Daily), the Communist Party organ whose editorials reflect official thinking on the issues of the day. Each province and municipality has its own daily as also each economic sector. The other principal dailies include *Jiefangjun Bao* (Liberation Army Daily), organ of the PLA; and *Guangming Ribao*, a small-circulation newspaper devoted mainly to science, culture and education. None of the other newspapers approaches these three in prestige and authoritativeness. *Hongqi* (Red Flag), the theoretical organ of the CCP Central Committee, is the ideological weather vane of the party. Another important organ of information is *Can Kao Xiao Xi* (Reference News), which carries foreign news in Chinese translations.

Mass publications are propaganda media and tools "to serve the interest of proletarian politics, the party's class struggle and mass line." Characteristically, openness is discouraged in communications because "we cannot expose our weakness to our enemies." Thus what constitutes information in China is often an interpretation of events designed to promote governmental programs and policies. Timeliness is far less important than correctness from the party's point of view.

Private ownership of the press is illegal. All dailies are owned either by the Central Committee of the Communist Party or by the corresponding provincial committees. When there is more than one daily in a city, one, usually the evening paper, is owned by the municipal party committee. Nondailies are owned either by district party committees or county party committees. The more populous or prosperous administrative units between the provincial and county levels also may have their own dailies. The numerous departments and committees of the State Council may publish their own nondailies, weeklies or periodicals. All dailies or nondailies identified with the title Ching Nian (Youth) belong to the Chinese Youth League. Periodicals may be published by academic institutions and government agencies with the approval of the party committee of the district.

Distribution of all print media is handled by the post office; distribution of books, by the New China Book Store. Mail service generally is tardy, with the result that dailies reach readers many days after publication. Advertisements in print and electronic media reappeared in 1979 after a break of several years and now have become regular features. Official advertising bureaus provide full services to their clients.

Unlike the Soviet Union, China has no official censorship but rather employs party ownership of the media to achieve the same effect. The official in charge of propaganda in each party committee controls the press in

PRINCIPAL DAILIES	
National	Circulation (approx.)
Renmin Ribao (People's Daily), Beijing	5,000,000
Jiefangjun Bao (Liberation Army Daily), Beijing	100,000,000
Nongmin Ribao (Peasants' Daily), Beijing	1,000,000
Can Kao Xiao Xi (Reference News), Beijing	3,600,000
Gongren Ribao (Workers' Daily), Beijing	1,800,000
Jiefang Ribao (Liberation Daily), Shanghai	1,000,000
Zhongguo Qingnian Bao (China Youth News), Beijing	3,000,000
English-Language	
China Daily, Beijing	120,000
World Economic Herald, Shanghai	300,000
Provincial Dailies	
Beijing Ribao, Beijing	1,000,000
Dazhong Ribao, Shandong	600,000
Guangzhou Ribao, Guangzhou	N.A.
Guizhou Ribao, Guizhou	N.A.
Hebei Ribao, Hebei	N.A.
Hubei Ribao, Hubei	N.A.
Jiangxi Ribao, Jianxi	N.A.
Jiefang Ribao, Shanghai	N.A.
Qingdao Ribao, Shandong	N.A.
Shanxi Ribao, Shanxi	N.A.
Sichuan Ribao, Sichuan	N.A.
Tianjin Ribao, Tianjin	N.A.
Xin Hua Ribao, Nanjing	N.A.
Yangcheng Wanbao, Guangdong	N.A.

his jurisdiction. Further, all journalists are recruited by the party, and while they need not be party members, they are required to be "loyalists." Although routine material does not require "clarification" (meaning approval) from party authorities, important editorials and news stories require prior endorsement by the party committees. For example, all editorials appearing in *Renmin Ribao*, *Hongqi* and *Jiefangjun Bao* are vetted by the top leaders of the Politburo and the Central Committee. However, factional infighting at the leadership levels may—and often does—subject the editors to conflicting orders, and some of them may lose their jobs—or their heads—in the process.

There are two news agencies: Xinhua (New China News Agency), founded in 1931; and Zhongguo Xinwen She (China News Service), founded in 1952. Xinhua is an active arm of the Communist Party; its personnel are on the party payroll, and its director is an official of the Propaganda Department of the Central Committee. It is the sole foreign news distributor in China and joins with Zhongguo Xinwen She in reporting domestic news to the outside world. But Zhongguo Xinwen She does not serve any client inside China. The principal foreign news agencies in Beijing are AFP, ANSA, AP, dpa, Jiji, Reuters, TASS and UPI.

The organizational structure of the electronic media is three-tiered: central, provincial and local. In 1949 the Central People's Broadcasting Station came into being as a network of four stations, all in Beijing. Stations I and II broadcast in Mandarin; Station III aims its programs at Taiwan; and Station IV broadcasts in minority languages. Also under the supervision of the Central Broadcasting Administration is Radio Beijing, one of the five largest international radio stations in the world. There is at least one radio station in each provincial capital, and in larger cities, such as Shanghai. The local broadcasting system is a wired operation of radio receiving networks. The system uses a central receiver, with an amplifier and a switchboard housed in the studio. The broadcasts are picked up by the receiver; amplified; and sent through the switchboard to loudspeakers in village squares, school playgrounds, marketplaces, rice paddies, factories, mines, communal mess halls, dormitories and even on treetops and telephone poles.

MEDIA INDICATORS, 1988

Newspapers
  Number of dailies: 222
  Number of nondailies: 224
  Circulation (000): 46,089
  Circulation per 1,000: 45
  Number of periodicals: 3,100
  Circulation (000): 138,852
  Newsprint consumption
    Total (tons)1,315,100
    Per capita, kg (oz.): 1.2 (2.6)
Book publishing
  Number of titles: 52,000
Radio
  Number of transmitters: 571
  Number of radio receivers (000): 253,900
    Persons per radio receiver: 4.2
Television
  Television transmitters: c. 5,400
  Number of television receivers (000): 92,140
    Persons per television receiver: 12
Cinema
  Number of fixed cinemas: 143,650
  Annual attendance (million): 18,250
    Per capita: 18.1
Films
  Production of long films: 130

CULTURAL & ENVIRONMENTAL INDICATORS, 1988

Public libraries
  Number: 2,406
  Volumes (000): 261,000
  Registered borrowers: 117 million
  Loans per 1,000: 154
Museums
  Number: 900
Performing arts
  Facilities: 1,756
  Number of performances: 743,891
  Annual attendance (000): 723,222
  Attendance per 1,000: 690
Ecological sites: 62
Botanical gardens & zoos: 47

Television was introduced in 1958. Today 47 stations serve every province and autonomous region except Xizang. Two channels are in operation in Beijing. Channel 2 televises its news programs through a microwave network of 169 relay stations. Channel 8 is directed to Beijing residents. Both Channel 8 on Mondays, Wednesdays and Fridays and Channel 2 on weekday mornings telecast educational programs that constitute the curriculum of the TV universities.

SOCIAL WELFARE

Social welfare is administered primarily at the commune level out of welfare funds set apart for this purpose. There is no unemployment insurance or a program of family allowances. Old-age benefits, invalidity and death benefits, sickness benefits and maternity benefits are administered by the Ministry of Labor and Personnel and are extended to all employed persons in state-run enterprises (optional for state farm workers). For old-age pensions, and invalidity and death benefits there is a 3% payroll deduction; for the other benefits the state meets the entire cost. The age of pension is 60 for men and 55 for employed women. The old-age pension is 60% to 90% of the last month's earnings. In 1985 the invalidity pension was 40% of earnings and the sickness benefit 60% to 100% of earnings.

There is no private welfare system in China.

CHRONOLOGY

1945—Japan surrenders, bringing World War II to a close.

1946—CCP-KMT representatives meet with Marshall mission; CCP-KMT civil war resumes.

1947—Marshall mission ends.

1948—CCP forces defeat KMT is many areas.

1949—CCP forces seize most major cities; People's Republic of China is established in Beijing; Chiang Kai-shek flees to Taiwan along with remaining KMT forces and sets up Republic of China, with seat at Taipei.

1950—North Korea invades South Korea; Chinese "people's volunteers" enter the fighting and push U.N. troops back into South Korea. . . . China invades Xizang (Tibet).

1951—China announces completion of the occupation of Xizang.

1952—Land reforms conclude. . . . The Three Anti and the Five Anti campaigns begin.

1953—Korean armistice is signed.

1954—Soviet-style collective farms are established.

1957—The Hundred Flowers campaign is launched.

1958—Mao launches Great Leap Forward campaign. . . . Communes are established. PRC forces shell Quemoy and Matsu. . . . Tibetan revolt against PRC rule is crushed, and Dalai Lama flees to India.

1960—PRC breaks with the Soviet Union; Soviet and Chinese troops clash on the Xinjiang border.

1962—Sino-Indian War erupts over Chinese occupation of areas in northern Kashmir.

1964—China conducts its first atomic test.

1965—Cultural Revolution begins; Many Chinese leaders, including Liu Shaoqi, Zhu De and Deng Xiaoping, are disgraced.

1967—China explodes its first hydrogen bomb.

1969—Chinese and Soviet troops clash on the Wusuli Jiang border.

1971—PRC is seated in the Chinese seat at the United Nations, and the Republic of China is expelled. . . . Vice Chairman Lin Biao dies under mysterious circumstances in a plane crash, following an abortive coup attempt.

1972—President Richard Nixon visits Beijing.

1975—Chiang Kai-shek dies.

1976—Zhou-Enlai dies; Mao Zedong dies. . . . The Gang of Four is arrested. . . . Tangshan is devastated by an earthquake. . . . Hua Guofeng is sworn in as premier.

1978—China ends aid to Vietnam.

1979—United States recognizes PRC and breaks relations with Republic of China (Taiwan); China invades Vietnam in a brief war.

1981—The Gang of Four is convicted.

1982—Deng Xiaoping emerges as paramount ruler.

1983—China adopts new economic policy and strengthens relations with the West.

1984—U.S. president Reagan visits China. . . . Sino-British agreement is signed on reversion of Hong Kong to China in 1997.

1986—China launches "anticorruption" campaign.

1987—Hu Yaobang resigns as CCP general secretary and is replaced by Zhao Ziyang. . . . At the 13th National Congress, reformists led by Zhao gain the upper hand as only 90 of the 209 members of the outgoing Central Committee are reelected; Deng retires from the Central Committee but retains influential post of chairman of the Military Affairs Committee; Li Peng is named acting premier in place of Zhao Ziyang.

1988—Violent anti-Chinese demonstrations in Xizang are suppressed by force.

1989—Soviet president Gorbachev visits Beijing. . . . Prodemocracy demonstrators, numbering several thousands, gather in Tiananmen Square in Beijing and press for reforms; after initial vacillation, regime sends in the army and crushes the protest; China faces mounting international criticism for using force to quell the prodemocracy movement; antireform faction within the Politburo and the Central Committee gains strength; Zhao Ziyang is ousted and replaced by Jiang Zemin as party general secretary. . . . Deng resigns as chairman of the Military Affairs Committee.

1990—Martial law is lifted. . . . Dissident scientist Fang Lizhui is allowed to go into exile in the United Kingdom.

BIBLIOGRAPHY

BOOKS

Andors, Stephen. *China's Industrial Revolution.* New York, 1977.

Arendrup, B. *China in the 1980s and Beyond.* London, 1986.

Barnett, A. Doak. *Cadres, Bureaucracy and Political Power in Communist China.* New York, 1967.

———. *China's Economy in Global Perspective.* Washington D.C., 1981.

———. *Chinese Communist Politics in Action.* Seattle, 1969.

———. *The Making of Foreign Policy in China: Structure and Process.* Boulder, Colo., 1985.

———. *Uncertain Passage: China's Transition to Post-Mao Era.* Washington, D.C., 1974.

Baum, Richard. *China's Four Modernizations: The New Technological Revolution.* Boulder, Colo., 1980.

Bernstein, Richard. *From the Center of the Earth: The Search for the Truth About China.* Boston, 1982.

Blecher, Marc. *China: Politics, Economics and Society.* Boulder, Colo., 1986.

Bonavia, David. *China the Unknown.* New York, 1985.

———. *The Chinese.* New York, 1980.

Brugger, Bill. *China Since the Gang of Four.* New York, 1980.

Bullard, Monte. *China's Political-Military Evolution: The Party and the Military in the PRC, 1960–84.* Boulder, Colo., 1985.

Bush, Richard C. *Religion in Communist China.* Nashville, Tenn., 1970.

Butterfield, Fox. *China: Alive in the Bitter Sea.* New York, 1982.

Camilleri, Joseph. *Chinese Foreign Policy: The Maoist Era and Its Aftermath.* Seattle, 1980.

Chang, Luke T. *China: Boundary Treaties and Frontier Disputes.* Dobbs Ferry, N.Y., 1982.

Chen, Jerome. *Mao and the Chinese Revolution.* New York, 1965.

Chen, King C. *China and the Three Worlds: A Foreign Policy Reader.* Armonk, N.Y., 1979.

Chen, Nai-Ruenn, and Walter Galenson. *The Chinese Economy Under Communism.* Chicago, 1969.

Cheng, Chu-Yuan. *China's Economic Development: Growth and Structural Change.* Boulder, Colo., 1981.

Cheng, J. Chester. *The Politics of the Red Chinese Army.* Stanford, Calif., 1966.

Chow, Gregory. *The Chinese Economy.* New York, 1984.

Chu-yuan, Cheng. *China's Economic Development: Growth and Structural Change.* Boulder, Colo., 1980.

Chubb, O. Edmund. *Twentieth-Century China.* New York, 1972.

Cooper, John F. *China's Global Role.* Stanford, Calif., 1980.

Coye, Molly Joel, and Jon Livingston. *China: Yesterday and Today.* New York, 1979.

Croll, Elisabeth. *The Family Rice Bowl: Food and Domestic Economy in China.* London, 1983.

Dixon, John. *The Chinese Welfare System, 1949–79.* New York, 1981.

Domes, Jurgen. *China After the Cultural Revolution.* Berkeley, Calif., 1977.

_____. *The Government and Polity of People's Republic of China*. Boulder, Colo., 1985.

Donnithorne, Audrey. *China's Economic System*. New York, 1967.

Eberhard, Wolfram. *A History of China*. Berkeley, Calif., 1977.

Eckstein, Alexander. *China's Economic Revolution*. New York, 1977.

Farrish, Raymond O., and James C. Hsiao. *China's Modern Economy*. New York, 1986.

Feuchtwanger, Stephen. *The Chinese Economic Reforms*. New York, 1983.

Garside, Roger. *Coming Alive: China After Mao*. New York, 1981.

George, Alexander L. *The Chinese Communist Army in Action: The Korean War and Its Aftermath*. New York, 1967.

Ginsburg, Norton, and Bernard Lalor. *China: The Eighties Era*. Boulder, Colo., 1984.

Gittings, John. *The Role of the Chinese Army*. New York, 1967.

Godwin, Paul S. *Armed Forces of the People's Republic of China*. Boulder, Colo., 1989.

Goldstein, Steven. *China Briefing*. Boulder, Colo., 1985.

Goodman, David S. *Groups and Politics in the People's Republic of China*. Armonk, N.Y., 1984.

GPO. *China Under the Four Modernizations: Selected Papers*. Washington, D.C., 1982.

Griffith, William E. *The Sino-Soviet Rift*. Cambridge, Mass., 1964.

Gungwu, Wang. *China and the World Since 1949*. New York, 1977.

Harding, Harry. *Chinese Foreign Relations in the 1980s*. New Haven, Conn., 1986.

Harris, Louise C. *China's Foreign Policy Toward the Third World*. New York, 1985.

Harris, Peter. *Political China Observed*. New York, 1980.

Hinton, Harold C. *The PRC: A Handbook*. Boulder, Colo., 1979.

Ho, Ping-ti, and Tang Tsou. *China's Heritage and the Chinese Political System*. Chicago, 1968.

Hook, Brian, ed. *Cambridge Encyclopedia of China*. New York, 1982.

Howe, Christopher. *China's Economy: A Basic Guide*. New York, 1978.

Hsiao, Katherine. *Money and Monetary Policy in Communist China*. New York, 1971.

Hsiung, James C. *China's Independent Foreign Policy*. New York, 1985.

Hsu, Immanuel L. Y. *The Rise of Modern China*. New York, 1975.

Hsueh, Chun-tu. *China's Foreign Relations: New Perspectives*. New York, 1982.

Hu, Chang-tu. *China: Its People, Its Society, Its Culture*. New Haven, Conn., 1960.

Information China. Elmsford, N.Y. 1989.

Jian, Song. *Population Control in China: Theory and Application*. New York, 1985.

Kaplan, Frederic M., and Julian M. Sabin. *Encyclopedia of China Today*. New York, 1981.

Karnow, Stanley. *Mao and China: From Revolution to Revolution*, New York, 1972.

Kirby, Edward Stuart. *Contemporary China*. Hong Kong, 1956.

Kraus, W. *Economic Development and Social Change in PRC*. New York, 1982.

Leeming, Frank. *Rural China Today*. Armonk, N.Y., 1984.

Leung, C. K., and Norton Ginsburg. *China: Urbanization and National Development*. Chicago, 1980.

Lewis, John Wilson. *Party Leadership and Revolutionary Power in China*. London, 1970.

Li, Dun J. *The Ageless China: A History*. New York, 1971.

Lippitt, Victor P. *The Economic Development of China*. Armonk, N.Y., 1987.

Liu, Sheng, and Song Jian. *China's Population: Problems and Prospects*. Beijing, 1981.

Lui, Alan P. *How China Is Ruled*. Englewood Cliffs, N.J., 1986.

MacInnes, Donald E. *Religious Policy and Practice in Communist China*. New York, 1972.

Maxwell, Neville. *China's Road to Development*. Elmsford, N.Y., 1979.

Meisner, Maurice. *Mao's China: A History of the People's Republic*. New York, 1977.

_____. *Mao's China and After*. New York, 1986.

Moody, Peter R. *China's Politics After Mao: Development and Liberalization, 1976–83*. New York, 1983.

_____. *Opposition and Dissent in Contemporary China*. Stanford, Calif., 1977.

Mosher, Steven W. *Broken Earth. The Rural Chinese*. New York, 1984.

Muller, David G. *The Chinese Military System: An Organizational Study of the Chinese People's Liberation Army*. Boulder, Colo., 1977.

Myers, Ramon H. *The Chinese Economy: Past and Present*. Belmont, Calif., 1980.

Nathan, Andrew. *Chinese Democracy*. Berkeley, Calif., 1986.

Nee, Victor, and David Mozingo. *State and Society in Contemporary China*. Ithaca, N.Y., 1983.

Nelsen, Harvey. *The Chinese Military System*. London, 1977.

O'Leary, Greg. *The Shaping of Chinese Foreign Policy*. New York, 1980.

Orleans, Leo. *Every Fifth Child: The Population of China*. Stanford, Calif., 1972.

Perkins, Dwight H. *China's Modern Economy in Historical Perspective*. Stanford, Calif., 1975.

Price, R. F. *Education in Communist China*. New York, 1970.

Prybyla, Jan S. *The Chinese Economy: Problems and Policies*. Columbia, S.C., 1981.

Pye, Lucian W., *China: An Introduction*. Boston, 1972.

_____. *The Dynamics of Chinese Politics*. Boston, 1978.

Qi, Wen. *China: A General Survey*. Beijing, 1984.

Richman, Barry M. *Industrial Society in Communist China*. New York, 1969.

Saich, Anthony. *China: Politics and Government.* New York, 1981.

Scalapino, Robert A. *Elites in the People's Republic of China.* Seattle, 1972.

Segal, Gerald. *The China Factor: Peking and the Superpowers.* New York, 1981.

Spence, Jonathan D. *The Gate of Heavenly Peace: The Chinese and Their Revolution, 1895–1980.* New York, 1981.

Stavis, Benedict. *Making Green Revolution: The Politics of Agricultural Revolution in China.* Ithaca, N.Y., 1974.

Sutter, Robert. *Chinese Foreign Policy Development After Mao.* New York, 1985.

Teiwes, Frederick C. *Politics and Purges in China.* Armonk, N.Y., 1979.

Terrill, Ross. *The China Difference.* New York, 1979.

———. *Eight Hundred Million: The Real China.* Boston, 1972.

———. *Flowers on an Iron Tree: Five Cities of China.* Boston, 1975.

Thornton, Richard C. *China: A Political History.* Boulder, Colo., 1981.

Townsend, James R., and Briantley Womade. *Politics in China.* Boston, 1986.

Treager, T. R. *Economic Geography of China.* New York, 1970.

———. *Geography of China.* Boston, 1963.

U.S. Defense Intelligence Agency. *Handbook of the Chinese Armed Forces.* Washington, D.C., 1976.

Wagel, Srinivas. *Finance in China.* New York, 1980.

Waller, Derek. *Government and Politics of the People's Republic of China.* New York, 1982.

Wang, James C. *Contemporary Chinese Politics.* Englewood Cliffs, N.J., 1985.

Whyte, Martin K. *Small Groups and Political Ritual in China.* Berkeley, Calif., 1983.

——— and William L. Parish. *Urban Life in Contemporary China.* Chicago, 1984.

World Bank. *China: Socialist Economic Development* (3 vols.). Washington, D.C., 1983.

Wu, Yuan L. *China: A Handbook.* New York, 1977.

———. *The Economy of Communist China.* New York, 1965.

Yang, Ch'ing-k'uan. *Religion in Chinese Society.* Berkeley, Calif., 1961.

Youdes, Pamela. *China.* New York, 1982.

Young, Graham. *China: Dilemma of Modernization.* Wolfeboro, N.H., 1985.

Yu-ming, Shaw. *Mainland China: Politics, Economics and Reform.* Boulder, Colo., 1985.

———. *Power and Policy in the People's Republic of China.* Boulder, Colo., 1985.

OFFICIAL PUBLICATIONS

China: A Statistical Survey (annual).
People's Republic of China Yearbook (annual).
Statistical Yearbook of China (annual).

CZECHOSLOVAKIA

BASIC FACT SHEET

OFFICIAL NAME: Czech and Slovak Federative Republic (Ceska a Slovenska Federativni Republika)

ABBREVIATION: CZ

CAPITAL: Prague

HEAD OF STATE: President Vaclav Havel (from 1989)

HEAD OF GOVERNMENT: Prime Minister Marian Calfa (from 1989)

NATURE OF GOVERNMENT: Socialist democracy

POPULATION: 15,658,079 (1989)

AREA: 127,877 sq. km. (49,373 sq. mi.)

MAJOR ETHNIC GROUPS: Czechs and Slovaks

LANGUAGES: Czech and Slovak

RELIGIONS: Roman Catholic, Protestant, Orthodox

UNIT OF CURRENCY: Koruna

NATIONAL FLAG: A white stripe over a red stripe with a blue triangle extending from hoist to midpoint

NATIONAL EMBLEM: The ornate white lion of the royal house of Bohemia. On the lion's shoulder is displayed a small red and blue shield featuring a flaming grenade against a stylized outline of Mount Krivak. The large red shield is of unusual heraldic shape—square at the bottom and triangular at the top.

NATIONAL ANTHEM: Two anthems: a Czech section called "Kde Domov Muj?" ("Where Is My Native Land?") followed by a Slovak section called "Nad Tatrou sa Blyska" ("It Storms over the Tatra")

NATIONAL HOLIDAYS: May 9 (Anniversary of the Liberation); October 28 (Nationalization Day); December 26 (St. Stephen's Day); Labor Day; New Year's Day; Christmas; Easter Monday

NATIONAL CALENDAR: Gregorian

PHYSICAL QUALITY OF LIFE INDEX: 94 (on an ascending scale with 100 as the maximum)

DATE OF INDEPENDENCE: October 28, 1918

DATE OF CONSTITUTION: July 11, 1960

WEIGHTS & MEASURES: Metric

GEOGRAPHICAL FEATURES

A landlocked country in east-central Europe, Czechoslovakia consists of the Czech lands (Bohemia and Moravia), with an area of 78,863 sq. km. (30,449 sq. mi.), and Slovakia (49,014 sq. km.; 18,924 sq. mi.). Extending 767 km. (477 mi.) east to west and 468 km (291 mi.) north to South, Czechoslovakia has a total land area of 127,877 sq. km. (49,373 sq. mi.). It shares its total boundary length of 3,472 km. (2,157 mi.) with six countries: Poland, 1,310 km. (814 mi.); Soviet Union, 98 km. (61 mi.); Hungary, 679 km. (422 mi.); Austria, 570 km. (354 mi.); and Germany, 815 km (507 mi).

Czechoslovakia's boundaries are mostly mountainous. The border with the Soviet Union runs along the Carpathian ranges, the Polish border along the Carpathians and the Sudetes, the border with Germany along the Krusne Hory, the Cesky Les and the Sumava, and the Austrian border along the Sumava Mountains. The Danube and its tributary the Ipel comprise part of the Hungarian border. There are no current border disputes.

The capital is Prague, situated on both sides of the Vltava (Moldau) River, near the center of Bohemia. Although one of the newest national capitals of Europe, it is one of the Continent's oldest and most picturesque cities, founded, according to legend, by Libusa, ancestress of the House of Premysl.

MAJOR URBAN CENTERS (est. population, 1986)	
Prague (Praha, the capital)	1,193,513
Bratislava	417,103
Brno	385,684
Ostrava	327,791
Kosice	222,175
Plzen (Pilsen)	175,244
Olomouc	106,086
Liberec	100,917
Hradec Kralove	99,571
Pardubice	94,451
Ceske Budejovice	94,206
Havirov	91,873
Usti nad Labem	91,703
Zilina	91,444
Gottwaldov (Zlin)	86,210
Nitra	85,276

Czechoslovakia divides historically as well as topographically into three major areas: Bohemia, Moravia, and Slovakia. Bohemia consists of the five western political divisions (known as regions or *krajs*), with names ending in *cesky*; Moravia of the two central political divisions, with names ending in *moravsky*; and Slo-

EAST GERMANY

Elbe River

KRUŠNÉ HORY

Usti Nad Labem

Liberec

C Z E C H

SUDETEN MOUNTAINS

POLAND

SEVEROČESKÝ

Mladá Boleslav

Karlovy Vary

Kladno

Labe River

Hradec Králové

80 m

80 km

Prague

PRAHA

ZÁPADOČESKÝ

STŘEDOČESKÝ

VÝCHODOČESKÝ

Pardubice

S O C I A L I S T

BOHEMIAN FOREST

Příbram

Plzeň

Opava

Ostrava

Olomouc

SEVEROMORAVSKÝ

Frýdek Mistek

BESKIDS

HIGH TATRA

WEST GERMANY

JIHOČESKÝ

Jihlava

BOHEMIAN-MORAVIAN HEIGHTS

JIHOMORAVSKÝ

Vltava River

Brno

Gottwaldov

Žilina

Váh River

CARPATHIAN MTS.

VÝCHODOSLOVENSKÝ

Hornád River

Prešov

České Budějovice

WHITE CARPATHIANS

R E P U B L I C

Znojmo

STŘEDOSLOVENSKÝ

Trenčín

Banská Bystrica

Košice

U.S.S.R.

Danube River

S L O V A K   S O C I A L I S T   R E P U B L I C

ZÁPADOSLOVENSKÝ

Zvolen

Banská Štiavnica

Hron River

Trnava

Nitra

BRATISLAVA

Bratislava

AUSTRIA

Komárno

Nové Zámky

Tisza River

RUMANIA

H U N G A R Y

vaki of the three eastern political divisions, with names ending in *slovensky.*

The two main physical features of the country are the Bohemian Massif and the Carpathians, representing the Hercynian and Alpine elements. The two zones are separated by a zone of subsidence occupied by the upper Oder and the Morava rivers. The Bohemian Massif is the most stable and compact core of the Hercynian system in central Europe and consists of three main components: the Sudetes; the Krusny Hory or the Ore Mountains; and the Sumava Mountains.

The Sudetes occupy the northeastern part of the Bohemian Massif and form six main ranges: Jesenik, Orlicke, Bystricke, Jilove, Krkonose and Jizerske, all running parallel to each other. The ranges, partly narrow ridges and partly domes, reach their highest elevation in the North in Snezaka (1,603 m.; 5,258 ft.) and Sisak (1,506 m.; 4,940 ft.). The Krusne Hory rise steeply above the central depression and are gently tilted in the Northwest. Their outer ridge is known as the Cisarsky Les Mountains. Between the inner and outer ridges is the Ohre River, a tributary of the Elbe. The highest elevation of the Krusne Hory is the 1,244-m. (4,080-ft.) Mount Klinovec. The foothills of the Krusne Hory are noted for many thermal springs.

The southwestern part is known as the Sumava Mountains. Its hilly ranges, known as the Cesky Les, join the Krusne Hory. This part of the Bohemian Massif is not very impressive, but the mountains in the Southeast attain an elevation of 1,457 m. (4,780 ft.) at Mount Javor. The rim of the massif is less pronounced in the southeastern part, where the Moravian Heights reach 835 m. (2,739 ft.) at Mount Javorice. The area is crossed by several passes.

The central part of the Bohemian Massif is the Plain of Polabi. The southern part consists of the upland basins of Trebon, drained by the Luznice River, and Ceske Budejovice, drained by the upper Vltava. The basins of the northern part of the plateau include the Kladno, Labe and Plzen (Pilsen). The convergence of rivers, fertile soils and coal deposits account for the economic importance of the region.

The Moravian region, enclosed between the Moravian Heights and the western Carpathians, is a topographic borderland between Bohemia and Slovakia and a corridor between Hungary and Silesia. The Moravian Heights are easily accessible through lower areas stretching athwart the plateau, such as the Gate of Trebova. The easternmost part of the Moravian Heights, north of Brno, has a distinct topography developed during the Paleozoic era, including the gorge at Macocha, the Katerinske Caves and the Masaryk Dome. The Moravian Gate, in the northern part of the depression, is one of the most important gateways of central Europe, constituting a frontier between the Hercynian and Alpine mountain systems. In the East, Moravia is limited by the Carpathian ranges of Bile Carpaty (White Carpathians) and the Javorniky Mountains. To the east of the Morava River the land is called Carpathian Moravia.

The Carpathians extend into northern Slovakia, starting near the Danube as the Little Carpathian Range. It joins with the White Carpathians, the Javorniky Moun-

tains and the Bezkydy Mountains to form the first Carpathian bow. Their mildly elevated ranges are dissected by numerous river valleys and passes. The Orava and Vah valleys separate the outer Carpathians from the inner crystalline zone. Several intermontane basins— the Liptov, the Turiec, the Poprad and the Hornad— separate the Carpathians into fragments. The High and the Low Tatra mountains have an atypical Alpine landscape. They extend in a narrow ridge along the Polish border and are a popular summer resort. The highest peak in the country—Gerlochovka, also known as Stalinov Stit (2,655 m.; 8,711 ft.)—is in this ridge. The tree line is at about 1,500 m. (4,922 ft.). An icecap extended into this area during glacial times, leaving pockets that became mountain lakes. The southern part of the Carpathian bow is defined by fractures marked by the volcanic hills of the Slovenske Krusnohorie (Slovak Ore Mountains), characterized by steep slopes. Finally, a typical region is formed by the Slovak lowlands on the northern fringes of the Danube Basin, known as the Little Alfoeld, or parts of the Big Alfoeld to the east, where the Ipel and Kosice basins are much smaller.

Czechoslovakia's location across the main European divide explains the pattern of its drainage. The Elbe and the Oder drain toward the north and together with the basin of the Vistula cover an area of some 50,000 sq. km. (19,300 sq. mi.). The rest of the country belongs to the Danubian drainage system. Bohemia constitutes one hydrographic unit around the Vltava-Elbe. Similarly, Moravia forms a distinct hydrographic unit with an axis along the Morava River. The Danube system does not represent a single unit, as its many tributaries tend to flow parallel in their upper courses.

The Elbe extends 364 km. (226 mi.) in Czechoslovakia and originates in the Krkonose Mountains. The Elbe's average flow is three times greater in the spring than in the fall. Both the Elbe and its tributary the Vltava are navigable in their lower reaches but freeze up to 60 days a year.

The Czechoslovak sector of the Danube is 172 km. (107 mi.) long. Although the river is fed by Alpine glaciers, there is considerable difference between high and low water levels. Averaging about 3m. (10 ft.) in depth, the Danube presents several navigation problems requiring constant dredging. In winter the river freezes and small river barges are threatened by floating ice. The main tributaries of the Danube are the Morava; the Vah; the Nitrah; the Hron; the Ipel; and the tributaries of the Tisza, of which the Hornad is the most important. As it leaves Bratislava, the Danube divides into two channels, the main channel being the Danube proper, and the northern channel the Little Danube (Maly Dunaj). The Little Danube flows eastward to join the Vah River just north of Komarno, where the Vah joins with the main Danube. The land between the Little Danube and the main Danube is known as Great Rye Island (Velky Zitny Ostrov).

A complex of lakes is found in central Bohemia in the Trebon and Budejovice basins. A number of small lakes of glacial origin are in the mountains, including Certovo and Cerne Jezero in the Sumava Mountains and Strbske and Popradske Pleso in the Carpathians.

CLIMATE & WEATHER

Continental weather systems prevail throughout the country, but western regions are more often under the influence of the maritime weather of Western Europe, with Slovakia under the influence of the continental system predominant in Eastern Europe. When the systems to the north are weak, Mediterranean weather may occasionally brush southern parts of the country.

Winters are fairly cold, cloudy and humid. High humidity and cloud cover tend to be more prevalent in the valleys and lower areas. Light rain or snow is frequent. The mountains are snow-covered from early November through April, with deep accumulations in some places. Lower elevations rarely have more than 150 mm. (6 in.) of snow cover at a time. Summers are generally pleasant. December, January and February are the coldest months and June, July and August the warmest. Spring starts late, and fall may come abruptly in September. At lower elevations, even in Slovakia, frosts are rare between the beginning of April and the end of October.

About 60% of the winds are westerly. Generally, wind velocities are low, and in intermontane basins air movements tend to stagnate. The most important local wind is the foehn, which occurs in northeastern Bohemia and in the piedmont areas of the Carpathians. It raises temperatures and causes winter thaws.

The mean annual temperature nationwide ranges from 6°C to 10°C (43°F to 50°F). It is lower in the isolated mountain areas, especially in the Tatras and the Sudetes. The warmest parts of the country are the basins and lowlands, such as the Polabi in Bohemia, the Moravian Plains, and the lowlands along the Danube and the Tisza. The Polabi Basin is warmer than the southern Bohemia, and the lowlands of Slovakia are warmer than the western parts of the country. Due to fragmentation of relief, cold and hot pockets are found. In the mountains the northern slopes, which are exposed to the westerly and northwesterly winds, are warmer than the southern slopes. Spring is generally cooler than the fall. In the more continental eastern parts temperature variants are greater in the spring than in the fall.

Rainfall is influenced by elevation, the direction of exposure, shelter from the winds and situation on the windward or leeward side. Generally, rainfall increases toward the east. In the lowlands maximum precipitation occurs in the summer, but with increasing altitudes it tends to be better distributed throughout the year. The lowlands exposed to the south, particularly the Moravian and Danubian plains, have a second maximum in October as a result of Mediterranean influences.

Generally, elevations of up to 250 m. (820 ft.) have the least precipitation and the leeward locations even less. Although the western parts have less rainfall, aridity is more common in the eastern Danubian lowland because of the seasonal distribution of rainfall.

The more elevated hilly regions and piedmont areas receive up to 1,372 mm. (54 in.) of rainfall a year and the mountains up to 1,397 mm. (55 in.) annually. The lower but westwardly situated Sumava Mountains receive as much precipitation as the higher Tatra Mountains, chiefly due to Atlantic influences.

The annual average number of days with snowfall is 45 in the West and 27 to 30 in the East. Winter temperatures are more uniform in Slovakia than in Bohemia.

POPULATION

The population of Czechoslovakia in 1989 was 15,658,079, based on the last official census, in 1980, when it was 15,283,095. Czechoslovakia ranks 50th in the world in size of population and 69th in land area. The population is expected to reach 15,664,000 in 1990 and 16,086,000 in 2000.

The Czech region comprises 62% of the area and 72% of the population and the Slovak region 38% of the area and 28% of the population. Historically, the population density always has been higher in the Czech region than in the Slovak region. Within the Czech region, Moravia-Silesia is more densely settled than Bohemia, and within the Slovak region Bratislava is the most densely settled. The lowest density in the country is in the Presov region of Slovakia.

The population of Czechoslovakia in 1947 was approximately equal to the number of inhabitants of the same territory in 1900.

POPULATION GROWTH, 1900–47	
Year	Population (000)
1900	12,159
1910	13,000
1921	13,003
1930	13,998
1939	14,612
1947	12,165

There was almost no increase from 1900 to 1921—a period that included World War I and the influenza epidemic of 1918–19. Between 1939 and 1947 there was a loss of 2.45 million as a result of war losses—estimated at 250,000—and the expulsion of the great majority of the German ethnics under the terms of the Potsdam agreement. The decline was heaviest in the Czech regions, where it amounted to 18%, compared to a 2.4% rise in the Slovak regions. The most affected were the three southwestern regions of Karlovy Vary, Usti nad Labem and Liberec, where the decline ranged up to 52%. The expulsion of the Germans led to a substantial internal migration of Czechs to the lands vacated by them. In addition to the Germans, 800,000 Ruthenians resided on land ceded to the Soviet Union, 92,000 Magyars were expelled to Hungary; and all but 16,000 of the 55,000 Jews who survived the war had emigrated, mostly to the United States. Since 1947 the principal migratory event was the exodus following the Soviet invasion in 1968. There is no significant immigration to Czechoslovakia.

Outside Czechoslovakia, the principal concentration of Czechs and Slovaks is in the United States, where their present population is estimated at 500,000.

DEMOGRAPHIC INDICATORS, 1989

Population: 15,658,079 (1989)
Year of last census: 1980   World rank: 50
Sex ratio: males, 48.71;   females, 51.29
Population trends (million)

1930: 13.998	1960: 13.654	1990: 15.664
1940: 14.713	1970: 14.334	2000: 16.086
1950: 12.389	1980: 15.265	

Population doubling time in years at current rate: Over 100 years
Hypothetical size of stationary population (million): 5
Assumed year of reaching net reproduction rate of 1: 2030
Age profile (%)

0–15: 24.2	30–44: 22.6	60–74: 11.7
15–29: 21.0	45–59: 15.7	Over 75: 4.8

Median age (years): 33.6
Density per sq. km. (per sq. mi.) 122 (316)
Annual growth rate

1950–55: 1.10	1975–80: 0.68	1995–2000: 0.56
1960–65: 0.73	1980–85: 0.43	2000–2005: 0.53
1965–70: 0.29	1985–90: 0.40	2010–15: 0.44
1970–75: 0.60	1990–95: 0.44	2020–25: 0.37

Vital statistics
Crude birth rate, 1/1,000: 14.2
Crude death rate, 1/1,000: 11.9
Change in birth rate: −10.4 (1965–84)
Change in death rate: 18.0 (1965–84)
Dependency, total: 54.1
Infant mortality rate, 1/1,000: 14
Child (0–4 years) mortality rate, 1/1,000: Insignificant
Maternal mortality rate, 1/100,000: 8
Natural increase, 1/1,000: 2.2
Total fertility rate: 2.0
General fertility rate: 62
Gross reproduction rate: 1.06
Marriage rate, 1/1,000: 7.7
Divorce rate, 1/1,000: 2.4
Life expectancy, males (years): 67.3
Life expectancy, females (years): 74.7
Average household size: 2.9
% illegitimate births: 7.0
Youth
Youth population 15–24 (000): 2,343
Youth population in 2000 (000): 2,542
Women
Of childbearing age 15–49 (000): 3,946
Child–woman ratio (children per 000 women 15–49): 329
% women using contraceptives: 66
% women married 15–49: N.A.
Abortions per 100 live births: 56.5
Urban
Urban population (000): 11,079
% urban, 1965: 51; 1985: 66
Annual urban growth rate (%) 1965–80: 1.9; 1980–85: 1.4
% urban population in largest city: 12
% urban population in cities over 500,000: 12
Number of cities over 500,000: 1
Annual rural growth rate: −1.5%

The Czech urban tradition dates from approximately the ninth century and was led by Prague, then both a bishopric and a princely seat, and the site of the famed Hradcany Castle. Prague and a host of secondary towns flourished until the defeat of the Bohemian nobles in the Battle of the White Mountain in 1620. Thereafter until the 19th century the cities languished. Slovakia, under Hungarian rule, fared worse. The 19th century saw a surge in both nationwide and urban population. Between 1800 and 1910 the population doubled, but emigration absorbed much of this natural increase. In 1910 a total of 8% of all Czechs lived in Vienna and 5% of all Slovaks lived in Budapest. The population in towns of more than 2,000 inhabitants grew from 18% to 45% between 1843 and 1910. Prague's population grew sevenfold, Plzen's 13-fold and Ostrava's 167-fold. The process continued, although at a slower rate, through the First Republic. The Communist government that seized power after World War II has tried, with some success, to reverse this trend. In fact, Prague's rate of growth during the 1970s was the lowest of all six major cities and only one-tenth that of Bratislava. A redefinition of the criteria by which settlements are classified as urban also helped to reduce the magnitude of urbanization. Prague and the six largest cities account for half of the urban population. Beyond this, however, there is little concentration. About 60% of all Czechs and Slovaks live in population centers of 10,000 or less.

The demographic and social characteristics of the population have not changed significantly since 1947, based on vital statistics data. Children under 14 constitute 24% today as against 24.2% in 1947, but the proportion of persons over 60, which is 16.5% today, is about one-third higher than in 1947. The high disparity in the sex ratio has been reduced from 94.4 males per 100 females to a more equitable 48.7 males per 51.3 females. The Czech and Slovak regions have a marked difference in their sex ratios stemming principally in the large migration of Slovak men to the Czech regions.

There are 5.288 million households, and the average household, with 2.9 members, is much larger than its counterpart in Western European countries. Women marry much younger: A total of 27.3% marry under 19, compared to only 6.7% of men under 19. On the other hand, 73.1% of men marry between 20 and 29, compared to 57.4% of women in that age range.

No detailed information is available on population policies and programs.

ETHNIC COMPOSITION

Since 1918 Czechoslovakia has been a multinational state. The ethnic composition changed dramatically after World War II. The population structure over 70 years is reflected in the accompanying table.

ETHNIC COMPOSITION, 1921–87

	1921	1937	1948	1987
Total population (million)	13.4	14.4	12.3	15.6
Nationality percent of total				
Czech	52.6	52.8	68.1	63.0
Slovak	15.2	16.9	25.7	31.6
Hungarian	5.0	4.4	3.2	3.8
Polish	0.8	0.7	0.6	0.5
German	24.6	23.2	1.5	0.4
Ruthenian	0.8	0.9	0.5	0.4
Others	1.0	1.1	0.4	0.3

Of the nation's population in 1987, a total of 10.36 million lived in the Czech lands and 5.2 million in Slovakia. The Czechoslovakia that emerged after

World War I included only a bare majority of Czechs, and unrealized expectations of other nationalities and great power politics resulted in the country's dismemberment.

In 1945 Czechoslovakia was restored to its prewar borders. During 1946 some 2.5 million Germans were expelled. Ruthenia was annexed by the USSR in June 1945, and there was a partial population exchange between Slovakia and Hungary. By 1948 Czechoslovakia was essentially a state of two nations: the Czechs and the Slovaks.

In late 1960s the Communist Party of Czechoslavakia claimed to have solved the nationality problem, with Czech-Slovak relations "truly equal." However, this continues to be the major problem. The Constitution itself contradicts this claim. Czechoslovakia is a unitary state with a centralized structure controlled by the Czechs. Under the federal system Slovakia has not realized self-determination, and many Slovaks, including Communist leaders, have fallen victim to charges of "bourgeois nationalism" for promoting Slovak rights.

The Constitutional Act of 1968 provided "effective guarantees" to citizens of Hungarian, German, Polish and Ruthenian origin. The act specified representation to elected bodies, education and media in their languages, the right to have cultural and social organizations, and freedom from discrimination. The largest of the ethnic groups is the Hungarian, with about 600,000 people living along Slovakia's southern boundary. Slovak-Magyar relations always have been troublesome, given the history of Hungarian domination over the Slovaks, but the large majority of Hungarians prefer to remain in their present homes.

Following the deportation and emigration of the Germans, only about 63,000 are left, compared to 3.3 million in 1938, who had lived in areas Germans had inhabited for centuries. The Germans resented Prague's treatment and agitated for political reform, but a substantial number were for secession, which Hitler exploited. Those remaining after the war regained their citizenship in 1953. Poles, numbering 78,000, live in the Tesin area. Only a small number of Ruthenians remained in the country following the USSR's annexation of Carpatho-Ukraine. Today about 62,000 Ruthenians live in eastern Slovakia. The ethnic groups are requesting greater resources for education, media and cultural development. They especially feel discrimination in the political sphere.

The Constitution does not recognize the Jews and the Gypsies as ethnic groups, and both have experienced discrimination and injustices. Of the 300,000 Jews in Czechoslovakia before World War II, only about 40,000 remained at its end. With emigration there are only 5,000 to 6,000 today. The Gypsies had been considered as a "nationality" during the First Republic, but the Communist regime rejected that status. Numbering about 275,000 (estimates range up to 400,000), most live in Slovakia. Gypsy leaders campaign for legal status and object to denigration and to policies such as "dispersion." Czechoslovakia has about 70,000 foreign workers and specialists from numerous countries, including Vietnam (about 18,000), Yugoslavia, Cuba, Poland, Mongolia and Hungary. There are, in addition, a substantial number of foreign students, many from Africa. Reports indicate problems, including racism, involving certain foreigners, especially the Vietnamese.

LANGUAGES

The Czech, Slovak and all other ethnic groups use their own languages. There is no "Czechoslovak" language. According to the Constitution, the Czech and Slovak languages "should be used equally in the promulgation of laws and other generally legal regulations," and both are equal in all state organs and proceedings and in contacts with citizens.

Czech and Slovak are separate western Slavic languages. They are related and contain dissimilarities as well as similarities. Basically, each is understood by the other. Czech is the language of people in Bohemia and Moravia, and Slovak of people in the Slovak Socialist Republic. Both use the Roman alphabet, although there are differences. The two languages developed separately under different cultures and histories. In past centuries German was used in the Czech lands and Magyar in Slovakia. Both flowered during the 19th-century "national awakening," the Slovaks surviving the intensely imposed policy of "Magyarization," which included education in the Magyar language only.

There are marked differences in Czech throughout Bohemia but especially in Moravia; Slovakia has its western, central and eastern versions. Local dialects still are widely spoken, especially in rural areas, but increasingly the grammatical, literary languages are employed. In recent years both Czech and Slovak have been infused with foreign words, especially Russian and English, to the dismay of literary purists. Many Czechs speak German; many Slovaks, Magyar. Russian is taught in school, but English has become the most desired foreign language in the universities.

The Constitution recognizes the right of the Hungarian, German, Polish and Ukranian (Ruthenian) ethnic groups to education in their own language, the right to use their language in official communication in areas inhabited by the respective ethnic groups, and the right to their own press and to information in their own language. Each ethnic group thus should have in its territory the means and facilities for development of its educational, cultural and social affairs. There is dissatisfaction by all the ethnic groups of the regime not living up to the Constitution in providing adequate resources to maintain and develop their ethnic identity. The Jews, who speak the language of the area for general communication, use Yiddish in their own community. The Jews particularly have been deprived of access to their own media. The Gypsies speak their own language as well as the language of the area.

RELIGIONS

Christianity was first propagated by German Catholic missionaries, and later by Orthodox Slav missionaries in the South. Moravia was Christianized in the ninth and 10th centuries by Cyril and Methodius. The Kingdom of

Bohemia became Catholic under King Wenceslas. The Catholic Church met one of the earliest pre-Reformation challenges in Bohemian Protestant martyr John Huss, who combined nationalism with a call to purity of faith and practice. A second Protestant movement developed when a number of Christians left Prague in 1457 to establish a Christian community known as Unitas Fratrum (Unity of Brethren), later the Moravian Brethren. In 1573 these two movements joined with Lutheranism to form a united confession. From 1621, when the Catholic Habsburgs took control of Bohemia and Moravia, to the Edict of Toleration of 1781, Protestantism was suppressed. It was only in 1848 that Protestants were granted equal rights with Catholics.

Roman Catholicism is the majority religion, although a deeply persecuted one from 1947 to 1990. Of all the East European Soviet satellites, Czechoslovakia was the most implacable foe of the Catholic Church. Until 1990 many of the Catholic archdioceses have had no residential bishops because the papal nominees were prevented from exercising their office. In their stead, the regime appointed its own nominees, chosen from a Communist front organization called the *Pacem in Terris* Association, successor to the Priests for Peace Movement. Religious orders and congregations were dissolved in 1950. They were reinstated briefly in 1968, but after the fall of Dubcek their activities were closely watched. In Slovakia, the activities of religious personnel were limited to pastoral work by brothers and to social welfare by sisters. Only two seminaries or faculties of theology were tolerated, and their staffs were appointed and controlled by the government. The Czech seminary is the Faculty of Sts. Cyril and Methodius at Litomerics; that for the Slovak region is the Faculty of Sts. Cyril and Methodius at Bratislava. A numerus clausus was imposed on the number of candidates to be admitted each year to these seminaries, this provision being particularly aimed against the entry of more brilliant or technically competent students. As a result of persecution, the proportion of younger clergy has diminished. Further, numerous priests were prevented from exercising their office, and many parishes were vacant. The principal instrument of government interference in church activities was the *Pacem in Terris* Association, founded in 1971 by renegade priests. The association was engaged in limited charitable work and even more limited publishing, but its membership was heavily infiltrated by Communist spies.

The Greek Catholic Church of the Byzantine Rite suffered a worse fate and now is limited to the diocese of Presov. In 1950 the government engineered a merger of the Uniate and the Orthodox churches, although only 46 out of 246 congregations and 28 out of the 311 Greek Catholic priests accepted such a merger. From 1968 the Greek Catholic Church was the target of a concerted attack by party and government functionaries.

Lutheranism is the dominant Protestant tradition. It consists of two bodies: The Slovak Evangelical Church of the Augsburg Confession, established in 1530; and the Silesian Evangelical Church, also of the Augsburg Confession; this church is a Polish-speaking denomination found in Tesin, Karvina and Ostrava border areas.

The Evangelical Church of Czech Brethren is the result of the union in 1918 of the former Lutheran and Czech Reformed churches. The Reformed Christian Church also dates from 1918, when Slovakia was severed from Hungary.

The second-largest denomination after the Roman Catholic Church is the Czechoslovak Hussite Church, which broke off from the Catholic Church after World War I over certain issues, such as the use of vernacular and the relaxation of priestly celibacy. While adopting a Hussite emphasis, it has retained many Catholic features, such as apostolic succession, and it considers itself a Reformed Catholic rather than a Protestant Church.

The first Orthodox communities were established in Prague in 1863. Until it was declared autocephalous in 1951, the church functioned under the jurisdictions of the patriarchs of Serbia, Constantinople and Moscow. In the conflict between the state and the Greek Catholic Church, the Orthodox Church received support from the former, although for less than spiritual reasons.

Church-state relations were governed by the Constitution of 1960, Article 32, which restates the article of the same number in the Constitution of 1948. The wording is very general: "Freedom of religion is guaranteed. One may profess any religion or no religion. Religious practices may be observed insofar as they do not transgress the law. . . . Religious faith or convictions cannot be used as a pretext for refusing to carry out individual civil responsibilities fixed by law."

All religious issues are handled by the Federal Office of State for Ecclesiastical Affairs within the Ministry of Culture. Created in 1949, it is given the task of "watching over ecclesiastical and religious life to see that it develops in harmony with the Constitution and the principles of the popular democratic regime." All religious communities require official recognition from the Federal Office. After 1968 the Federal Office was divided into Czech and Slovak sections, and these were further divided into districts.

State-church relations have undergone four distinct phases since the 1948 coup that brought the Communists to power. The first 20 years were characterized by bitter persecutions, directed mostly against the predominant Catholic Church. In the first year the religious press was totally suppressed; the landed properties of the church were confiscated; all church schools and hospitals were nationalized; all Catholic organizations, including Catholic Action, were disbanded; the leading clergyman were arrested; and diplomatic relations with the Holy See were severed. Church-state relations were regulated by several decrees. Decree 118/49 stated: "Activities of a sacred character proper to churches and to religious societies can only be exercised by those who have received permission from the state." Decree 219/49 stated: "Priests must be persons loyal to the demands of the state, not laying themselves open to criticism and responding to the general conditions required for entering into the service of the state." In the absence of state permission, ecclesiastical posts are considered vacant. At the same time, the state pays a salary to recognized priests who fulfill official conditions. With the suppression of religious orders and congregations, the religious were forced to enter secular life as workers. Decree 112/50 suppressed Catholic theological seminaries and faculties and replaced them with two state seminary faculties, and a numerus clausus was imposed, restricting the number of seminarians. From 1950 to 1960 church leadership was decimated by deportations, house arrests and refusals to permit episcopal vacancies to be filled. All priests, pastors and bishops had to swear allegiance to the state and in addition were forced to serve only in designated parishes or in a specified job of a nonparochial nature. Religious instruction was permitted in state primary schools for one hour a week after school hours and only by authorized priests or pastors and only on the written request of parents. Because of the insufficient number of priests, this apparent concession was a dead letter.

The "Prague Spring" of 1968 brought a respite to the suffering church. Church affairs were returned to church control, the rights of the church were recognized and condemned churchmen and laymen were rehabilitated. The numerus clausus was lifted from church seminaries, a free religious press was resurrected and religious education was tolerated.

With the Soviet invasion and the replacement of Dubcek by Gustav Husak as Communist Party leader, the campaign against the church resumed in earnest. There was a concerted effort to eradicate religion, and the heavy hand of the state fell not only on the Catholic Church but also on smaller groups, such as the Evangelical Church of Czech Brethren. Government appointees, who were mostly hardened Marxists and noted anticlericalists, were placed in positions of authority within the church. Children receiving religious education declined from 62% of the student population in 1968 to 48% in Slovakia and 22% in Bohemia and Moravia in the 1980s. Religious meetings, retreats and religious youth camps, which had blossomed in 1968–69, were all prohibited.

A year after the Soviet invasion, the Ministry of Culture prepared a document entitled, "A Plan for Limiting the Activity of the Churches," ostensibly limited to Slovakia but intended for the whole country. It called for a strict application of the antireligious laws of 1948–50. It recommended that six of the seven Catholic episcopal seats be left vacant. It created a new pro-Communist group of mercenary clergymen known as the *Pacem in Terris* Association, whose function was specified as paralyzing "the irritating influence of the Vatican." Religious press, admission to seminaries and religious instruction in schools were to be curtailed as before. The Orthodox, Lutheran and smaller Protestant churches also were placed under surveillance. Finally, ecumenical activities and foreign influences were to be severely controlled. In 1973 the Vatican reached a partial and still uneasy settlement with the regime regarding filling episcopal sees with *Pacem in Terris* Association members. In 1978 Frantisek Cardinal Tomasek was named archbishop of Prague; the position had been vacant for 30 years. A new Catholic province of Slovakia also was set up.

The fourth phase of church-state relations began with the collapse of Communism and the restoration of democracy in Czechoslovakia in 1989. Cardinal Tomasek played a leading role in the events that led to the final overthrow of the Communist regime. Relations between church and state have been normalized; the regulations against religious activities have been rescinded; and freedom of worship has been restored. The church appears to have risen from the rubble stronger than ever.

The traditional pilgrimages to Levoca and to Nitra were attended in 1989 by 20,000 and 50,000 pilgrims respectively. The most important religious event in 1989 was the canonization of Blessed Agnes of Bohemia in Rome in November. This ceremony was carried live by Czechoslovak Television, the first time in 45 years that official media had publicized such an event. When the first non-Communist majority government was formed under Marian Calfa, one minister was Richard Sacher, representing the Stream of Rebirth, a Catholic-inspired revival group in the Czechoslovak People's Party.

In 1990 Pope John Paul II visited Prague, and diplomatic ties between the Vatican and Czechoslovakia were restored.

There are no reliable figures on religious affiliation. Estimates based on limited surveys indicate that Roman Catholics continue to predominate, accounting for roughly half of the population. Not surprisingly, the number of those without religious profession has increased dramatically in the socialist era. A sociological survey in 1980 in Moravia, which is traditionally less devout than Slovakia, showed 30% as Catholic, 30% as atheist and 40% as undecided. The most provocative information was that after several decades of persecution, scientific atheism had not caught on as much as the regime had hoped. In Slovakia 71% identified themselves as believers. Atheism was highest among the 25- to 39-year-olds, but only 14% of the 14- to 24-year-olds were atheists. Religious sentiments were influenced by social background. Nine-tenths of all farmers were believers, as were three-fourths of all workers and slightly more than half of all employees. Perhaps most disconcerting for the Communist Party was the realization that after decades of denunciation of clerical meddling in politics, 28% of those surveyed thought that clergy should have a public and political role.

HISTORICAL BACKGROUND

The earliest inhabitants of the present-day Czech and Slovak lands were Celtic tribes such as the Boii, who settled in Bohemia as early as 500 B.C., and the Cotini, who settled farther east in Moravia and parts of Slovakia. The Celts were displaced in time by seminomadic German tribes, such as the Marcomans in Bohemia and the Quadi in Moravia and Slovakia. In the fourth century the Germans began to move westward, and by the fifth century the region became a Slavic domain. The sixth century witnessed the onslaught of the Avars, a pastoral people speaking a Ural-Altaic language. They were repelled by Samo, who unified the Slavic tribes and established in 625 the Samo Empire, which lasted until 658 as the first Czech polity. Early in the ninth century a Moravian polity developed under Mojmir, chief of the Holasovici, who founded the Moravian Empire. During his reign German Catholic missionaries were dispatched to spread Christianity among the Slavs, and Mojmir and his fellow chieftains were baptized at Regensburg, Germany. Rotislav (850–70), Mojmir's successor, fearing German influences as a threat to his rule, turned to Emperor Michael of Byzantium, who dispatched the Orthodox missionaries Cyril and Methodius, who devised the Cyrillic script and who inculcated the Eastern rites and liturgy in the Slavic language. But beginning with the reign of Svatopluk (871–94), Rotislav's successor who chose to ally with the Germans, the Moravian Empire was permanently drawn to the German sphere of influence.

The Moravian Empire disintegrated with the Magyar invasions. The Czech tribes broke away and swore allegiance to the Frankish king Arnulf, while the Slovaks remained for many centuries under Magyar rule. Magyar authority over Slovakia was greatly augmented as a result of the influx of Magyar refugees following the defeat of the Hungarian armies by Ottomans at Mohacs in 1526.

The political center of gravity shifted as a result of the breakup of the Moravian Empire to Bohemia, where a new kingdom was formed under the Premyslid Dynasty. In the 10th century the Premyslid chiefs—members of tribe called Cechove, from which Czech is derived—unified neighboring tribes under their authority. The third ruler of this dynasty was Saint Wenceslas (d. 929), the national saint and hero whose statue dominates Prague Square. The Bohemian kingdom existed in the shadow of the Holy Roman Empire and in 950 became a fief of Holy Roman Emperor Otto I and its king became one of the seven secular electors of the emperor. In 973 the bishopric of Prague was founded subordinated to the archbishopric of Mainz. In the 13th century, as the authority of the Holy Roman Emperor began to wane and the Magyars and Poles were absorbed in warding off Mongol invasions, the Premysl rulers became more assertive. In 1212 King Otakar I (1198–1230) extracted a golden bull from the emperor confirming the royal title on himself and his descendants in perpetuity and acknowledging his authority over Bohemia. Otakar II (1253–78) married a German princess, Margaret of Babenberg, and thereby became duke of Austria and master of upper and lower Austria and Styria. He conquered the rest of Styria and parts of Carinthia and Carniola. All of Otakar's German possessions were lost in 1276 in a struggle with Emperor Rudolf. Wenceslas II (1276–1305) acquired the Polish territories of Teslin and Cracow in 1290 and 1291 respectively and in 1300 became king of Poland. His son Wenceslas III was elected king of Hungary in 1301 but was murdered in 1306, and with his death the Premysl line came to an end. After a four-year civil war John of Luxemburg, son of Emperor Heinrich, married Premyslid Princess Elizabeth and claimed the throne of Bohemia. During his weak rule the nobles won a charter of privilege known as Domazlice Agreement.

The reign of the second Luxemburg king, Charles IV (1342–78), is known as the Golden Age of Czech history. During his rule Prague was made into an archbishopric independent of Mainz and its archbishop was given the right to crown Bohemian kings. A supreme court was created in Prague. Brandenburg, Lusatia and Silesia were made into fiefs of the Czech crown, while Bohemia itself ceased to be a fief of the emperor. In 1347 Charles was elected Holy Roman Emperor. Prague became an imperial city, and extensive building projects were undertaken, including the founding of New Town; the rebuilding of Hradcany Castle, the royal palace; the Charles Bridge across the Elbe; and the University of Prague in 1348.

When Charles died in 1378, his kingdom was divided among his three sons, with Wenceslas IV inheriting Bohemia, Silesia and part of Lusatia. During his reign the Hussite Movement was spawned, and it dominated Czech history for the next 100 years. In 1403 John Huss (Jan Hus) became rector of the University of Prague. A reformist preacher, described as a "pale, thin man in mean attire," Huss espoused the antipapal teachings of John Wycliffe, rejecting the corruption, wealth and hierarchical tendencies of the Roman Catholic Church of that day. Hussitism advocated purity and poverty for the clergy and insisted on communion under both kinds, bread and wine, for the laity. Hussites were divided into two camps: the moderates, or Utraquists; and the radical Taborites, who rejected much of the church doctrine and upheld the Bible as their sole authority. The Hussite controversy began at the university but soon involved the court and the people. In 1414 Huss was summoned to the Council of Constance to defend his views. The council condemned him as a heretic and burned him at the stake in 1415. His death sparked generations of religious warfare, pitting Catholics against reformers and Germans against Czechs. At first the Taborites, led by John Zizka, imposed a reign of terror, massacring many Catholics, storming monasteries and churches, expelling the Catholic clergy and expropriating ecclesistical lands. Dynastic squabbles added to the general chaos. Attempts at compromise, particularly the Basle Compact, were rejected by the pope. From 1471 to 1526 Bohemia was governed by the Polish Jagellon kings, who governed as absentee monarchs. In 1526 King Louis died at the Battle of Mohacs aginst the Ottomans, and the Diet elected Archduke Ferdinand, younger brother of Emperor Charles V, to succeed him, thus uniting the crowns of St. Stephen and St. Wenceslas under the Austrian scepter. Austrian rule lasted for 392 years, until 1918.

The reign of the early Hapsburgs—Ferdinand, Maximilian II (1564–76), Rudolf II (1576–1612), Matthias (1612–17) and Ferdinand of Styria—were marked by intensification of the nationalist struggle between the Czechs and the Germans and the religious struggle between the Catholics and the Protestants. Armed conflict broke out between the Czech estates and Ferdinand in 1547 in which victory went to the latter. In the reprisals that followed, the Hussites were bitterly persecuted. After Ferdinand became the Holy Roman Emperor in 1556, he founded the Jesuit Academy in Prague and attempted to expand the influence of Catholicism. In 1618, with Ferdinand of Styria on the throne, Czech rebel forces once again confronted the monarch. On November 8, 1620, the Czechs were decisively defeated at the Battle of the White Mountain. From then on, Hapsburg rule was secure.

For the Czechs, the defeat was disastrous. Many Czech nobles were executed; more than five-sixths of them went into exile, and their properties were confiscated. In 1622 the University of Prague was merged with the Jesuit Academy, and the entire educational system was placed under Jesuit control. In 1624 all non-Catholic priests were expelled by royal decree. Hapsburg rule was buttressed by large-scale immigration of Catholic Germans, who received most of the confiscated lands and who came to constitute the new nobility. They took over commerce and industry as well. The Czech peasantry was enserfed by royal patent.

The Czech provinces suffered greatly in the Thirty Years' War (1618–48) during which foreign armies laid waste villages and towns. The Treaty of Westphalia, which ended this war, incorporated the Bohemian Kingdom into the Hapsburg imperial system. During the reign of Maria Theresa (1740–80) and her son Joseph II (1780–90), Austrian hegemony was strengthened further through a policy of centralization and bureaucratization. The Czech and Austrian provinces were welded together; their separate chancelleries were abolished and replaced by a joint Austro-Bohemian chancellery. The Czech diets were stripped of the last vestiges of autonomy. German became the official language.

In other respects the rule of Maria Theresa and of Joseph II proved enlightened. The power of the Catholic Church, particularly in education, was curtailed, and feudal social structures were dismantled. Joseph II abolished serfdom altogether, and in 1781 his Edict of Toleration extended freedom of worship to Lutherans and Calvinists. Industry was encouraged, and new urban settlements were formed. The population of Bohemia and Moravia quadrupled during this period.

During the reign of Leopold II (1790–92) and Francis II (1792–1835) a reactionary movement caused many of these gains to be reversed. But the ferment caused by the Napoleonic wars had a profound impact on the empire. The Holy Roman Empire was dissolved and replaced by the Austrian Empire, which from 1815 was dominated by the reactionary policies of Prince Metternich.

The first half of the 19th century witnessed a reawakening of Czech national consciousness. The earliest phase of this national movement was philological and led to the rebirth of the Czech language as a literary medium. The Czech revival acquired an institutional foundation with the establishment of the Museum of the Bohemian Kingdom in 1818 as a center for Czech scholarship. A major figure in this movement was Frantisek Palacky, whose monumental five-volume *History of the Czech People* became the inspiration for several generations of nationalists. The Slovaks experienced an analogous national revival. A Slovak literary language was developed by a Jesuit priest, Anton Bernolak.

Meanwhile, the Protestant Slovaks adopted a different literary language developed by Jan Kollar and Pavel Safarik, which combined Czech grammar with elements of the central Slovak dialect. One of their students, L'udovit Stur, refined their work and developed the *sturovcina*, which was purely Slovak in character.

The major political event in the 19th century was the Revolution of 1848, which was crushed by the imperial forces. Absolutism was restored under Hapsburg emperor Francis Joseph (1848–1916).

The expulsion of Austria from the German Confederation and the establishment of the Dual Monarchy did not bring any concessions to the Czech or Slovak nationalists. The Germans on the one hand and the Hungarians on the other thwarted all attempts by the Czechs to gain autonomy. In 1905 Professor Tomas Masaryk founded the Czech Progressive Party, calling for an independent united Czech and Slovak nation.

In July 1914, when Austria went to war on the side of Germany, the Czechs intensified their efforts to break away from the empire. Czech and Slovak leaders joined to create the Czech National Council in Paris and set up centers of resistance in Vienna, Prague, Budapest and Bratislava. In the fall of 1918 the Allies granted formal recognition to the Czech National Council as the government of an independent republic. The Paris Peace Conference, convened in January 1919, was attended by Karel Kramar and Edvard Benes, respectively prime minister and foreign minister of the provisional Czechoslovak government. The conference approved the establishment of the Czechoslovak Republic, including the historic Bohemian kingdom (Bohemia, Moravia and Silesia), Slovakia and Ruthenia. The predominantly Polish Tesin was divided between Czechoslovakia and Poland. Only the Czech claim to Lusatia was rejected by the conference.

Czechoslovakia was established on October 28, 1918, with Masaryk as presidnt. In the next month a provisional constitution was drafted and a provisional National Assembly was inaugurated. The new nation had a population of 13 million. It received 70% to 80% of all industry of the former empire, including the Skoda Works of Plzen [Pilsen], producing heavy armaments, locomotives, automobiles and machinery and the chemical industry of northern Bohemia. A total of 7% of all Hungarian industry also fell to the new republic. Czech and Slovak were recognized as co-official languages, but national minorities were assured special protection under the aegis of the League of Nations. In an effort to defuse potential separatist movements, the government was highly centralized and provincial assemblies had only nominal powers.

Between 1918 and 1938 Czechoslovakia had relatively stable governments. Excluding the period from March 1926 to November 1929, a coalition of five Czech parties, known as the Petka, constituted the backbone of the government. These were the Agrarians, the Social Democrats, the Socialists, the Populists and the National Democrats.

The new government soon was locked into a struggle with the Sudeten Germans. Its early policies, intended to correct social injustice and effect a moderate redistribution of wealth, fell more heavily on the Germans. Although German minority rights were carefully protected, local hostilities were engendered by efforts to restore Czech cultural presence in areas dominated by Germans. Sudeten nationalist feelings ran high in the early years of the republic, and the Constitution of 1920 was drafted without Sudeten participation. From 1926 to the rise of Hitler, a policy of rapprochement brought the Sudetens into a working alliance with the Czechs. Only the Sudeten Nazi Party—highly popular among German youth in Czechoslovakia—remained in opposition. By 1935, encouraged by Berlin, the Nazis, led by Konrad Heinlein, formed a new party, the Sudeten German Party (Sudetentdeutsche Partei, SdP), which soon became the fulcrum of German nationalism. The SdP endorsed the fuehrer, mimicked Nazi banners and slogans and uniformed troops, and co-opted the German youth in the Kameradschaftsbund. By 1937 SdP leaders openly supported Hitler's pan-Germanism.

In 1935 Benes succeeded Masaryk as president. On March 13, 1938, Austria was annexed by the Third Reich, a union known as the Anschluss. Almost immediately thereafter, Czechoslovakia became Hitler's next target in his pursuit of *Lebensraum*. His strategy was to use Sudetenland as a bridgehead into Eastern Europe. Neither Britain nor France desired war or were capable of fighting Germany at this time and at Berchtesgaden and later at Munich capitulated to Nazi demands for a swift return of Sudetenland to the Germans. The Munich agreement stripped Czechoslovakia of 38% of Bohemia and Moravia. It also yielded 11,882 sq. km. (4,586 sq. mi.) to Hungary and southern Tesin to Poland. Meanwhile, encouraged by Hitler, both Slovakia and Ruthenia asserted their autonomy. In November 1938 Emil Hacha succeeded Benes as president of the new Second Republic, consisting of three autonomous units: Bohemia-Moravia; Slovakia; and Carpatho-Ukraine, as Subcarpathian Ruthenia was renamed. Still unsatisfied, Hitler planned to eliminate Czechoslovakia first before embarking on war with Poland. On March 15, 1938, Hitler persuaded Hacha to capitulate. On March 16, Hitler, ensconced in Prague's Hradcany Palace, proclaimed Bohemia and Moravia German protectorates.

The protectorate, legally subordinate to the Third Reich, was placed under protector: first Baron Konstantin von Neurath; later the notorious Reinhard Heydrich; and then Col. Gen. Kurt Daluege. German rule was moderate at first but after the student demonstrations of November 15, 1939, became brutal. Meanwhile, Benes organized a government-in-exile in London, and Czech and Slovak resistance was active throughout the war.

The postwar settlement resulted in numerous boundary and population changes. Ruthenia was ceded to the Soviet Union. All Sudeten Germans were expelled. Individual acts of retaliation against Germans and precipitous expulsions under harsh conditions characterized the immediate aftermath of the occupation. The Potsdam agreement provided for the resettlement of Sudeten Germans in Germany under the supervision of the Allied Control Council. Territory ceded to Poland was

returned to Czechoslovakia. The Magyar minority was resettled on the basis of an exchange-of-population agreement with Hungary.

For postwar history, see Chronology.

CONSTITUTION & GOVERNMENT

Czechoslovakia was an artificial creation following World War I. The new state was populated by Czechs, Slovaks, Ruthenians, Germans, Hungarians, Poles, Jews and Gypsies. The Czechs and Slovaks had separate histories following the collapse, in the 10th century, of the Great Moravian Empire. The Slovaks fell to the invading Hungarians (Magyars) and existed under oppressive Magyar rule for 1,000 years. The Kingdom of Bohemia came under Hapsburg rule beginning in 1526, but its absolutism allowed political reforms for the Czechs.

The "national awakening" of the 19th century permeated the Czech and Slovak nations, but the demand upon Hungary by the "Slovak nation" for self-government was rejected, as was a Czech proposal to Vienna. However, following external setbacks, Emperor Francis Joseph accepted changes affecting the Czechs. The February Constitution of 1861 provided for a Czech Diet and a measure of self-government. Hungary refused this right to Slovakia.

World War I afforded opportunities to promote independence. Separate councils were formed, including the National Council in Paris, headed by Tomas Masaryk, Edvard Benes and the Slovak Milan R. Stefanik. Among understandings reached by Czech and Slovak leaders, the Pittsburgh agreement of June 30, 1918, signed by future president Masaryk, provided for a state of the Czech lands and Slovakia, but "Slovakia shall have her own administrative system, her own Diet and her own courts." Independence was proclaimed October 28, 1918, by the Czechoslovak National Council in Prague, and two days later the Slovak National Council, meeting in Turciansky Svaty Martin, agreed to participate in a "Czecho-Slovakia" with a "right of national self-determination." The Ruthenians, on condition of self-government, agreed to be included in the new Republic on May 8, 1919. With the help of President Woodrow Wilson's Fourteen Points, Czechoslovakia was recognized as an independent state by the Treaty of Versailles on June 28, 1919. A tragic airplane crash on May 4, 1919, killed General Stefanik, a war hero and minister of war, robbing the nation of an outstanding champion for Slovak rights.

The Constitution of 1920 provided for a president, a government, and a bicameral National Assembly. Although considered by the outside world as a representative democracy in a sea of dictatorships, Czechoslovakia was plagued by serious disputes revolving around the non-Czech nationalities. Slovakia and Ruthenia did not achieve self-determination, and Sudeten German discontent was fanned by Nazi Germany. In this multinational state, the government system was centralized and the Czechs, led after the 1937 death of Masaryk by President Benes, maneuvered political alignments for effective control. After the 1938 Munich Conference ceded Sudetenland to Germany, the Second Republic, of "Czecho-Slovakia," granted autonomy to Slovakia and Ruthenia (Podkarpatska Rus). In March 1939 Hitler invaded Bohemia and Moravia, establishing them as protectorates. Slovakia declared its independence, as did Ruthenia, but the latter was incorporated into Hungary, which also seized southern areas of Slovakia. The Slovak Republic was led by Monsignor Jozef Tiso until the war's end.

The political structure for the post-World War II Czechoslovakia was prepared abroad. After resigning as president on October 5, 1938, Benes fled the country and organized a government-in-exile in London. Benes was especially influenced by the Soviet position regarding Munich and Moscow's rapid recognition of his government. In 1943 he concluded a treaty with the Soviet Union and in 1945 returned to his country by way of Moscow, where he made significant concessions to Czech Communists for the postwar government, which was organized in April 1945 at Kosice in eastern Slovakia.

The Communist Party of Czechoslovakia (Komunisticka Strana Ceskoslovenska, KSC) obtained key ministerial positions, and Soviet-controlled "national committees" were established in liberated communities for administrative purposes. In the 1946 national elections the Communists received 38% of the votes, a plurality resulting in KSC leader Klement Gottwald becoming prime minister. However, in Slovakia the Slovak Democratic Party received 62% of the votes and the Slovak Communist Party 30%. Gottwald had declared at Kosice that "the Slovaks should be masters in their Slovak country," but the authority of the Slovak National Council was severely limited, an arrangement to which the non-Communists and Benes agreed. Through a variety of repressive measures, especially by the Ministry of the Interior, the KSC precipitated a government crisis, resulting in the February 28, 1948, coup d'etat, made easier by the resignation of non-Communist ministers and Benes's misdirected behavior. Foreign Minister Jan Masaryk, son of the country's first president, was found dead on March 10, 1948.

The National Assembly adopted a constitution on May 9, 1949, known as the Ninth of May Constitution, which declared Czechoslovakia a "people's democracy," with the KSC accorded the leading role. Benes resigned and Gottwald became president. Czechoslovakia was a unitary state, relegating Slovakia to an inferior position. The supreme organ of state power was the unicameral National Assembly, elected for six years, which elected the president, the head of the republic, for the traditional seven years. He in turn appointed the prime minister, who headed the Council of Ministers, the executive organ of power responsible to the National Assembly. The Czechs and Slovaks were assigned separate governmental structures. In Slovakia legislative power lay in the Slovak National Council, elected for a six-year term, and executive authority in the Board of Commissioners, appointed by the central government and responsible to the Slovak National Council and to Prague. This formal framework concealed the extent of central control over Slovakia.

Due to "major revolutionary changes" in "socialist construction," the National Assembly adopted a new constitution on June 11, 1960, which proclaimed Czechoslovakia a "socialist republic" (Ceskoslovenska Socialisticka Republika, CSSR), the first Soviet bloc country to elevate itself to a "higher" ideological stage. This constitution also assigned a leadership role in society to the KSC. There was no discernible change in the structure of government. Between sessions of the National Assembly, party policies were given formal legislative stamp by the 24-member Presidium, created in 1953 and incorporated into this constitution. The concept of the unitary state continued, and Slovakia suffered a setback as the Slovak National Council became both the legislative and the administrative organ, with limited responsibilities. Also, the national committees were under the control of the central government rather than under the Slovak National Council.

Following Communist seizure of power, the regime was one of the most subservient to Moscow. Nationalization and collectivization of agriculture were pursued forcefully, and election returns became the familiar 99% variety. Fear prevailed throughout the country. Dissatisfaction was not assuaged by the Constitution of 1960, and in many cases, including Slovaks and minorities, even increased. Discontent mounted, reaching crisis proportions after the mid-1960s. Stalinist first secretary Antonin Novotny was replaced as Communist Party leader by Alexander Dubcek, a Slovak party veteran, on January 5, 1968. In March retired general Ludvik Svoboda succeeded Novotny as president.

Dubcek's leadership undertook necessary reform measures, adopting in April an "action program" intended to achieve socialist-humanitarian democracy. This involved meaningful reforms and real human rights. The dynamic movement became known as the "Prague Spring," receiving worldwide attention but not Soviet acceptance. The world was shocked when during the night of August 20–21, 1968, the Soviet-led Warsaw Pact invasion of Czechoslovakia crushed Dubcek's "socialism with a human face." The country was forced to return to prereform Stalinist-type policies. On April 17, 1969, Dubcek was ousted as Communist Party leader and replaced by Gustav Husak, a Slovak with a nationalistic past that included incarceration but now selected by Moscow to purge both party and society in reestablishing orthodoxy.

One pressing problem was self-determination for Slovakia. The KSC accused the interwar "Czech bourgeoisie" of applying the theory of a "Czechoslovak nation." The party now claimed a solution to the nationality question. Thus, with an October 27, 1968, amendment to the Constitution, effective January 1, 1969, Czech-Slovak relations became "truly equal." Czech-controlled power was to be diminished. A summary of the Constitution of 1960, the Constitutional Act of 1968 regarding the Czechoslovak federation, and subsequent amendments follow.

The Constitutional Act of 1968 declared Czechoslovakia to be a "federal state of two equal fraternal nations, the Czechs and the Slovaks." The federal republic consisted of the Czech Socialist Republic (Ceska Socialisticka Republika, CSR) and the Slovak Socialist Republic (Slovenska Socialisticka Republika, SSR), both having "equal positions and mutually respecting each other's sovereignty." All three republics the—CSSR, the CSR and the SSR—were based on the principle of "democratic centralism." State power was exercised through the Federal Assembly, the Czech National Council, the Slovak National Council and national committees. CSSR organs exercised jurisdiction in statewide matters, while the Czech and Slovak republics maintained control over their own national activities. Citizenship was of the unitary Czechoslovakia, and Czech and Slovak languages were officially equal.

The central government had jurisdiction over foreign policy, defense, currency, federal stockpiles, federal legislation and administration, and protection of federal constitutional rule. The legislative, executive/administrative and judicial organs of state power had jurisdiction in these areas. The CSSR and the two national republics had joint jurisdiction over planning; finance; banking; price control; foreign economic relations; industry; agriculture and food; transportation; mail and telecommunications; development of science and technology; labor, wages and social policy; socioeconomic information; regulations governing socialist enterprises; internal order and state security; the media; and control. The areas of control by central organs were specified either in the Constitution or by acts of the Federal Assembly.

The CSSR maintained the traditional executive structure, with the president and the government (Council of Ministers) sharing responsibilities. The head of the republic was the president, chosen by the KSC and elected for a five-year term by the Federal Assembly. The president was the head of state, commander in chief of the armed forces and represented the country in foreign relations. He received and accredited diplomats; convened the Federal Assembly, which he might dissolve; signed laws; and reported to the Federal Assembly on the state of the republic and on political questions. He appointed and recalled the prime minister, individual ministers, high officials, generals, and professors and rectors, the latter recommended by the Czech and Slovak national councils. The president might attend and chair meetings of the Council of Ministers and request reports from it as well as from individual ministers. Finally, the president made awards, grants amnesties and pardons and proclaimed a state of war. The Constitution did not provide for a vice president. In the event of a vacancy, the prime minister assumed the responsibilities of the presidency until a new president was elected by the Federal Assembly. Party leader Husak became president in 1975. Despite losing his KSC leadership in March 1987, Husak remained president until December 10, 1989, when, under intense popular pressure, he was forced to resign. On December 22 an agreement was reached between the Communist Party and the opposition Czech Civic Forum movement; its Slovak counterpart, the Public Against Violence; and other political groups on playwright Vaclav Havel as the next president of the Federal Republic. Also, the accord provided for "Prague Spring"

hero Dubcek to be chairman of the Federal Assembly. On December 28 Dubcek was elected unanimously by the Federal Assembly as chairman, saying, "this is a continuation of Prague Spring" and that the Federal Assembly "will become a place where people's wishes will come true and their rights will be respected." The next day Havel was elected president of the country, the first non-Communist president since 1948.

The supreme organ of state power is the government, consisting of the prime minister as head of government, and other ministers. The government is appointed by the president and is responsible to the Federal Assembly. Following its appointment, the government presents to the Federal Assembly a policy statement and requests a vote of confidence. It may submit its resignation to the president, who would recall the government in the event of a no-confidence vote by a chamber of the Federal Assembly. Ministerial resignations are submitted to the president. The government carries out laws and decrees, implements domestic and foreign policy, prepares economic plans and the federal budget, appoints government officials specified by law and implements any other measures pursuant to legislation. The government establishes a Presidium to assist in decision-making. The Constitution directs the government to cooperate with the Czech and Slovak governments when negotiations of international treaties and activities of international organizations affect the jurisdiction of the republics. The government issues decrees, and its ministers regulations, in conformity with legislation. The ministries conduct activities in exclusively federal and joint jurisdictional spheres. State organs of the republics implement Federal Assembly legislation in their territories unless assigned to federal organs, and the central government may suspend republic measures it deems contradictory to federal measures.

Ministries and other central organs are established by the Federal Assembly. The Constitutional Act of December 20, 1970, confirmed the following federal ministries: Foreign Affairs, National Defense, Interior, Finance, Foreign Trade, and Labor and Social Affairs. The act established ministries of Technological and Investment Development, Fuels and Energy, Agriculture and Food, Transportation and Communications. The act also established the State Planning Commission; the Committee of Public Control to conduct inspections; and the Price Bureau.

The governments of the Czech and Slovak republics make decisions on bills, their own decrees, implementation of their policies, approval of applicable international treaties, individual republic economic plans and budgets, individual republic economic policy measures, and appointments of officials provided by law.

The government of each republic may establish a Presidium. The government issues decrees and regulations to implement the National Council's legislative acts and, if authorized, acts of the Federal Assembly. The government of each republic is the supreme executive organ, with a prime minister, deputy prime ministers and ministers. The principle of no confidence applies to the government and its members. In his oath every member swore loyalty to the CSSR and to "socialism."

Up to December 1989 the federal prime minister was Ladislav Adamec, promoted in October 1988 from his position as the Czech Republic Premier. A veteran KSC and government functionary, Adamec was considered a moderate conservative. There were two first deputy prime ministers, five deputy premiers, ten ministries, a minister without portfolio and two chairmen of ministerial rank.

The Dubcek reforms were retracted in 1968 and reformists replaced by pro-Soviet conformists. Centralization reduced Slovak constitutional gains. However, dissidents, led by intellectuals, resumed and increased their activities, demanding the regime implement provisions for human rights specified in the Constitution and in international documents. The reaction of KSC and the government—essentially the same leadership—was increased repression. The deteriorating economy through the 1970s and especially into the latter 1980s was in more urgent need of reform than it was 20 years earlier. Generally there was widespread dissatisfaction and mounting agitation for real political, economic and other reforms.

Despite the conservative makeup of the country's leadership and the combination of domestic pressures and Gorbachev's urging, there was in 1989 hope for real changes in Czechoslovakia, which would be reflected in a new constitution. In October 1988 the KSC Central Committee established the Commission for the Preparation of the New Constitution, headed by General Secretary Jakes. A draft was to be completed for the 18th Party Congress, in May 1990. The new constitution was considered essential for restructuring and for incorporating the various amendments into one document. Although greater democratization was anticipated, the primacy of the KSC was likely to continue. One indication of possible political reforms occurred in April 1989, when the KSC-controlled National Front submitted multiple candidates—rather than one—in by-elections for nine seats in the Federal Assembly. The experiment was considered by reformers as a prelude to a new electoral law permitting multiple candidacies. Non-Communist activists and Slovaks indicated skepticism about any dramatic improvement.

In line with an agreement between the Communist Party and the opposition groups Czech Civic Forum, Public Against Violence and others, the Federal Assembly on November 29 deleted from the Constitution the article recognizing the primacy of the Communist Party in the society. The drafting of a new constitution was undertaken by the Civic Forum, which presented a first draft to the Federal Assembly during the first week of December 1989. The draft then was made public for nationwide discussion. Its principles proposed "a democratic, socially just state governed by law. . . ."

The demands by reformers escalated as the year progressed, the relatively small groups joined by the masses, including students, with demonstrations throughout the country involving hundreds of thousands. Events moved rapidly. On November 12 party leader Jakes told a Communist youth conference that the party would not tolerate protests or relax its control. November 17 witnessed the most massive demonstration in Prague since 1968. That evening a peaceful protest by several thousand students calling for free elections and access to Prague's Wenceslas Square was suppressed brutally by police. This provoked great emotion throughout the country, resulting in heightened demands for reform.

Politically, the various opposition groups, with reform-minded Communists among them, organized into the Civic Forum on November 19, with branches in other parts of the Czech lands. In Slovakia, Public Against Violence was formed, headed by Jan Carnogursky, a human rights activist who had been jailed for his activities. The Civic Forum leadership included Vaclav Havel, the playwright and human rights activist who was a leader of Charter 77 and jailed several times for voicing violations and calling for reforms.

The Civic Forum immediately demanded the resignation of the Communist leaders responsible for the 1968 Warsaw Pact invasion of Czechoslovakia and for "the 20 years of subsequent decline." Dubcek returned to the capital and addressed a huge number of demonstrators in Wenceslas Square on November 24. Radio and television began live coverage of developments. On November 25 Havel spoke on television, outlining Civic Forum's goals contained in its program issued the following day, calling for:

- a democratic constitution
- democratic institutions
- equality for all political parties
- free elections
- an end to the Communist Party's power monopoly
- equality for all nationalities
- integration of Czechoslovakia into the "common European home"
- economic competition and equality for different types of ownership
- social justice
- emancipation of the churches
- protection of the environment
- freeing of culture, the sciences and education from ideology and state control

The demands issued on November 26 by the Slovak Public Against Violence were similar. The success of the November 27 general strike indicated that both the Civic Forum and Public Against Violence were powerful political entities with nationwide support. On November 28 discussions between the Civic Forum and Public Against Violence on the one hand and the regime on the other resulted in an agreement for a new government, to be completed December 3, to consist largely of experts and professionals. Also, the regime initiated limited changes. On December 3 the regime's new government, which consisted of 16 Communists and five non-Communists, was rejected by the opposition. Prime Minister Adamec resigned on December 7 and was succeeded by First Deputy Prime Minister Marian Calfa, a 43-year-old Slovak. Three days later the Council of Ministers was assembled, with the Communist Party in the minority for the first time since its seizure of power in 1948. The new federal government was sworn in by President Husak, who then resigned. Its composition was as follows:

Prime Minister Calfa had been a member of the Communist Party since age 18, holding high-level positions under Husak and Jakes leadership, but on January 18 he resigned from the party but continued as head of the government. Other party members resigned during this period, including deputy premiers Vladimir Dlouhy and Valtr Komarek. Calfa and Dlouhy joined the Public Against Violence and the Civic Forum respectively.

Calfa's resignation left the Communists with only seven ministerial positions. The party's number was reduced to six with the resignation of Czech Republic premier Frantisek Pitra, who was simultaneously deputy prime minister of the federal government.

The government's main responsibility was to prepare for free and democratic elections, which were held June 8–9, 1990. The Civic Forum and the Public Against Violence won 47% of the votes and a parliamentary majority. After intensive negotiations following the elections for the Federal Assembly, a new coalition federal government was formed, as were governments for the Czech Republic and Slovak Republic. On June 12 Havel requested Prime Minister Calfa to form a new government, which was sworn in on June 29 by the president. Calfa was a strong supporter of economic reform and had impressed Havel with his leadership of the government of "national understanding" during the transition period.

The new federal cabinet, characterized by Havel as a "government of sacrifice," had 16 members compared to the earlier 23. A 17th minister, representing the Christian Democratic Movement (CDM), was to be named subsequently but was still unannounced at the end of August 1990. Also in the cabinet were deputy premiers, including prime ministers of the two republics who were automatically federal deputies. Nine of the ministers held portfolios in the previous government. The Communist Party received no positions. The government, reflecting objectives of the Civic Forum and the Public Against Violence, was designed to hasten economic reform and administrative reorganization. The federal cabinet, with incumbents' nationalities and political affiliations, follows.

The makeup of the government reflected Havel's emphasis on "experts" and "professionals." Consisting of ten Czechs and six Slovaks, the new government also reflected the country's population ratio. In his June 29 address to the Federal Assembly, Havel characterized seven members—Calfa, Dienstbier, Vales, Miklosko, Rychetsky, Vacek and Langos—as the "backbone" of the government who would be the "focal point of executive power." Jan Carnogursky, Havel's counterpart in the Slovak Public Against Violence movement, declined to continue in the federal government. He had been first deputy prime minister in the transition cabinet. Now, as leader of the CDM, Carnogursky became deputy premier in the Slovak Republic government.

The new Czech government was also sworn in on June 29, while the Slovak government was installed two days earlier. The Czech cabinet consists of 21 members: the prime minister, Petr Pithart; three deputy premiers; and 17 ministers. Fourteen Czech ministers are new.

FEDERAL GOVERNMENT June 29, 1990			
Position	Name	Nationality	Political Affiliation*
Prime Minister	Marian Calfa	Slovak	PAV
Deputy Prime Ministers:			
Economic reform	Vaclav Vales	Czech	I
Legislation	Pavel Rychetsky	Czech	CF
Human rights, religion, culture	Jozef Miklosko	Slovak	CDM
Foreign affairs	Jiri Dienstbier	Czech	CF
Ministers:			
Defense	Miroslav Vacek	Czech	I
Internal affairs	Jan Langos	Slovak	PAV
Finance	Vaclav Klaus	Czech	CF
Foreign trade	Slavomir Stracar	Slovak	PAV
Labor and social affairs	Petri Miller	Czech	CF
Transporation	Jiri Nezval	Czech	I
Telecommunications	Theodor Petrik	Slovak	CDM
Economy	Vladimir Dlouhy	Czech	CF
Strategic planning	Pavel Hoffmann	Slovak	I
Environment	Josef Vavrousek	Czech	I
Control	Kvetoslava Korinkova	Czech	I

*CF—Civic Forum (Czech); CDM—Christian Democratic Movement (Slovak); PAV—Public Against Violence (Slovak); I—Independent.

Eleven represent the Civic Forum, including the prime minister; two are from the People's Party; and one is from the Movement for Self-Administrative Democracy-Society for Moravia and Silesia. Seven are independents.

The Slovak government consists of 23 members: the prime minister, Vladimir Meciar; one first deputy premier, Jan Carnogursky; three deputy premiers; and 18 ministers. Thirteen Ministers belong to the Public Against Violence, seven to the CDM, and three to the Slovak Democratic Party. Both the Czech and Slovak governments include one minister whose sole responsibility is to ensure republic-federal cooperation.

The new political leadership addressed the historically unsettled and fundamental question of Czech-Slovak relations. With freedom and democracy came Slovak demands for meaningful political realignment of the two nations. The Federal Assembly and the Czech and Slovak Councils face the urgent tasks of drafting the

FEDERAL CABINET LIST

Prime minister:	Marian Calfa
First deputy prime minister:	Valtr Komarek
First deputy prime minister:	Jan Cernogursky
Deputy prime minister:	Frantisek Pitra

FEDERAL CABINET LIST (continued)

Deputy prime minister & chairman of the State Commission for Scientific, Technical and Investment Development:	Frantisek Reichel
Deputy prime minister & chairman of the State Planning Commission:	Vladimir Dlouhy
Deputy prime minister:	Josef Hromadka
Deputy prime minister & minister of agriculture & food:	Oldrich Bursky
Minister of foreign affairs:	Jiri Dienstbier
Minister of national defense:	Miroslav Vacek
Minister of finance:	Vaclav Klaus
Minister of labor & social affairs:	Petr Miller
Minister of foreign trade:	Andrej Barcak
Minister of transportation & communications:	Frantisek Podlena
Minister without portfolio:	Robert Martinko
Minister without portfolio:	Richard Sacher
Minister of metallurgy, machine building & electrical engineering:	Ladislav Vodrazka
Minister of fuel & power:	Frantisek Pinc
Minister-chairman of the Committee of People's Control:	Kvetoslava Korinova
Minister in charge of the Federal Price Office:	Landislav Dvorak

three constitutions. The major issue is self-determination for Slovakia. The responsibility for drafting the federal constitution lies with deputy prime minister for legislation, Pavel Rychetsky.

After heated debates the Federal Assembly on April 20, 1990 changed the country's offical name from the Czechoslovak Socialist Republic to the "Czech and Slovak Federative Republic" (CSFR). This structure has detractors among a significant segment of the Slovak population. Proposals on the future of Slovakia range from the current federal system (supported by the Public Against Violence), through a Czech-Slovak confederation with Slovakia participating in European affairs as a "sovereign equal entity" (favored by the Christian Democratic Movement), to a "sovereign, autonomous, and independent" Slovakia (advocated by the Slovak National Party and the Movement for Independent Slovakia). However, the federal leadership faces discontent among the Czechs as well. The Czech government program promotes "new Czech statehood" while a movement in Moravia-Silesia is campaigning for its own government within a federal state. Moreover, polemical arguments exacerbate the already serious tensions. Clearly the drafters of the constitution face a monumental task. Although the federal, Czech, and Slovak governments agreed in August that by January 1, 1991 federal power will be reduced and that of the Czech and Slovak republics strengthened, a substantial segment of the Slovak people and political leadership are not expected to be mollified. The constitution must receive three-fifths approval in both chambers.

RULERS OF CZECHOSLOVAKIA
Presidents (from 1918)

October 1918–December 1935: Tomas Masaryk
December 1935–October 1938: Edvard Benes
October–November 1938: Jan Syrovy (acting)

RULERS OF CZECHOSLOVAKIA (continued)
Presidents (from 1918)

November 1938–March 1939: Emil Hacha
March 1939–March/May 1945: German occupation
March 1945–June 1948: Edvard Benes (in Kosice March–May 1945)
June 1948–March 1953: Klement Gottwald
March 1953–November 1957: Antonin Zapotocky
November 1957–March 1968: Antonin Novotny
March 1968–May 1975: Ludvik Svoboda
May 1975–December 1989: Gustav Husak
December 1989– : Vaclav Havel

Prime Ministers (from 1918)

October 1918–July 1919: Karel Kramar
July 1919–September 1920: Vlastimil Tusar (Social Democratic Party)
September 1920–September 1921: Jan Cerny
September 1921–October 1922: Edvard Benes (National Socialist Party)
October 1922–March 1926: Antonin Svehla (Czech Agrarian Party)
March–October 1926: Jan Cerny
October 1926–February 1929: Antonin Svehla (Czech Agrarian Party)
February 1929–October 1932: Frantisek Udrzal (Czech Agrarian Party)
October 1932–November 1935: Jan Malypetr (Czech Popular Party)
November 1935–September 1938: Milan Hodza (Slovakian Agrarian Party)
September–December 1938: Jan Syrovy
December 1938–March 1939: Rudolf Beran (Agrarian Party)
March 1939–March/May 1945: German occupation
March–April 1945: Jan Sramek (in Kosice)
April 1945–June 1946: Zdenek Fierlinger (Socialist Party) (in Kolsice April–May 1945)
July 1946–1948: Klement Gottwald (Communist Party)
June 1948–March 1953: Antonin Zapotocky (Communist Party)
March 1953–September 1963: Vilem Siroky
September 1963–April 1968: Jozef Lenart
April 1968–January 1970: Oldrich Cernik
January 1970–October 1988: Lubomir Strougal
October 1988–December 1989: Ladislav Adamec
December 1989– : Marian Calfa

Communist Party Leaders (from 1948) (First Secretary, 1948–71; General Secretary, 1971–89; Chairman since December 1989)

February 1948–March 1953: Klement Gottwald
March 1953–January 1968: Antonin Novotny
January 1968–April 1969: Alexander Dubcek
April 1969–March 1987: Gustav Husak
March 1987–November 1989: Milos Jakes
November 1988–December 1989: Karel Llrbanek
December 1989– : Ladislav Adamec

FREEDOM & HUMAN RIGHTS

Until December 1989 Czechoslovakia was ruled by a totalitarian Commmunist regime that was considered one of the harshest in Eastern Europe. With the collapse of the Communist regime in that month, the human rights situation has become normal. The election of human rights activist, Vaclav Havel, as president and the appointment of Jan Carnogursky, a former dissident, as deputy prime minister, signaled the dismantling of the security apparatus that had been primarily responsible for the numerous human rights violations since 1949. All primary freedoms, including those of religion, association, free speech and assembly have been fully restored. Arbitrary detention and interference with privacy, family, home and correspondence have ceased. Czechs and Slovaks have now the freedom to travel within the country, and also to travel abroad and to emigrate without harassment. With the holding of the first free elections in the country since World War II, these freedoms have become broadly comparable to those prevailing in Western Europe.

Since the beginning of March 1990 the Czechoslovak Federal Assembly has approved a number of laws that guarantee certain human rights, such as freedom of association, freedom of assembly, the right to petition, and freedom of the press. Parliament has also adopted amendments to the penal code that eliminate references to political "crimes" and abolish the death penalty in Czechoslovakia. More new laws are being discussed, most notably a law on freedom of travel. Under the outsted Communist regime, only state-approved organizations were considered legal. A new law on freedom of association that was approved by the Federal Assembly on March 27 and took effect on May 1 gives all Czechoslovak citizens the right to belong to any interest group they choose or to set up their own groups. Newly formed organizations are required only to register with the authorities. The same stipulation applies to political parties and organizations, whose legal status is regulated by a separate law passed in January 1990.

The authorities will no longer scrutinize organizations as closely as they did in the past. The principle of "duplication of interests," for example, which the Communists adopted to ensure that only one state-controlled organization pursued a specific issue or brought together people sharing a particular interest, has been eliminated. In fact, the authorities' only task now will be to determine whether or not organizations have met all the administrative requirements for registration. One such requirement is that at least three people, one of them over the age of eighteen, sign the organization's application for registration. It will be up to the new groups themselves to make sure that their activities do not violate the law.

On March 22 the Czechoslovak government recommended two changes in the penal code. First, it advocated abolishing the death penalty in Czechoslovakia. Second, it urged that a number of activities, such as "subversion" and "damaging the interests of the republic abroad," cease to be classified as political crimes. The death penalty was replaced by life imprisonment for the severest crimes and by imprisonment for between 15 and 25 years for other crimes that previously could have been punished by the death penalty. Prisoners serving life sentences could be paroled after 20 years for good behavior. Government officials said that 53 death sentences had been passed since 1968 and 46 executions carried out. Parliament also approved the possibility of releasing defendants on bail during pretrial hearings. The amount of bail would vary, depending on the nature of the charge, from 10,000 to 1,000,000 koruny (the average monthly income in Czechoslovakia is about 3,000 koruna). Such a step marks the introduction of yet another legal instrument extending the civil rights of Czechoslovak citizens.

In the past five months the post-Communist authorities have observed all basic human and civil rights, ignoring those parts of the existing law (such as some provisions of the Penal Code) that violate international norms and international agreements to which Czechoslovakia is a signatory. Most of the new laws therefore only reflect the *de facto* situation. During the assembly's discussions of these new laws, some deputies criticized the legislation for not going far enough, fearing that it could be abused by an undemocratic regime should such a government be reinstated in Czechoslovakia.

On April 23 the Federal Assembly approved a separate law regulating the activities of Czechoslovak trade unions. The law frees trade unions from the control of both the state and employers and permits more than one union to organize in a work place. Trade unions now have the right to be consulted by the government on some important new laws, in particular those affecting workers. Furthermore, the new law states that trade unionists' rights, as stipulated by the International Agreement on Trade Union Freedoms and approved by the International Organization of Labor, may not be superseded by any Czechoslovak law.

On March 27 a new law governing freedom of assembly was passed. According to the law, Czchoslovak citizens have the right to gather at public places, organize rallies and demonstrate, without being required to obtain the authorities' permission. In the future, organizers are only required to inform their local authorities at least five days in advance of the time and place of public rallies and demonstrations. The new law acknowledges that these public gatherings are an important means of making constitutional rights—in particular freedom of speech—a reality. One slight alteration was made to the original draft of the law: the version passed by the Federal Assembly stipulates that no public rallies and demonstrations may be held within 100 meters of courts and buildings used by legislative bodies.

Also on March 27, the assembly passed a new law on petitioning that gives all Czechoslovak citizens the right to gather signatures and submit petitions to state authorities. The law stipulates that citizens submitting a petition cannot be prosecuted either for their actions or for the petition's contents.

On March 27 an amendment to the existing press law was also approved. The amendment, which abolishes censorship, allows private citizens and foreigners to publish periodicals in Czechoslovakia. Czechoslovak citizens and corporations will not require state approval to publish periodicals and need only register with the authorities. Foreigners, on the other hand, are required both to obtain the state's approval and to register. An application for registration can be submitted only by people over 18 and must detail the contents of the planned periodical, its price, the number of copies that will be printed and the publication's address. The state authorities must respond to the application for registration "within a reasonable period of time." Despite these changes, the assembly left intact the constitutional provision making radio, television and the film industry state property. According to the Czechoslovak media, the amendment eliminated "only the most urgent deformations of the past," and a new press law is being prepared.

Now that censorship has been eliminated and there are no restrictions governing what periodicals can and cannot contain, questionable or false information may occasionally be published. The law therefore stipulates that if citizens feel they have been wronged by information published in a periodical, they may ask that the periodical publish a correction within two months. If the periodical does not comply with this request, a libel suit may be filed, but complainants are not required to request that the misinformation be corrected before filing a suit. To make libel suits effective, the assembly approved an amendment to the Civil Code making it possible to claim damages in such cases.

The new law on freedom of travel takes the liberalization process begun by the previous regime one step further. According to the new law, Czechoslovak citizens have the right to leave Czechoslovakia freely, remaining abroad as long as they wish and returning to Czechoslovakia at any time. The law stipulates that every Czechoslovak citizen must be issued a passport on request and greatly simplifies the administrative procedure necessary to obtain one. The law names only three groups of people that may be denied passports: those seeking to avoid paying child support; those against whom criminal proceedings have been initiated; and, during a military alert or a period of increased military tension, draftees.

At the beginning of 1990, the government decided that once a year every Czechoslovak citizen may buy hard currency to the value of 2,000 koruny (about $50) from the Czechoslovak State Bank for travel abroad. People who want to travel to the West more than once a year will have to rely on their own hard-currency resources, but having hard currency is not a prerequisite for travel to the West.

On March 27 the Federal Assembly passed an important law on citizenship that affects Czechoslovak exiles in the West and people who decide to live abroad permanently in the future. According to the law, Czechoslovak citizens may now be deprived of their citizenship only at their own request; they may not be deprived of it by the state for any other reason. Thousands of people who under the previous regime lost their citizenship for political reasons or after "illegally" leaving Czechoslovakia and settling in the West can now regain their citizenship. They must apply for it by the end of 1993.

CIVIL SERVICE

As the "guiding force" in the state, the KSC exercised executive power at the federal, republic and lower levels. In the highly structured system, the federal, Czech and Slovak governments appointed higher-ranking officials selected by the party. The KSC had its own bureaucracy, operating in Slovakia through the KSS. As elsewhere in the Soviet bloc, the government had no comparable Office of Personnel Management, as in the United States. On the federal and republic levels, min-

istries and other organs have a personnel office (previously *kadrovy* and now *personalni odbor* odbor) that handles personnel matters.

The KSC was deeply involved in appointments to government positions at all levels, with the Central Committee Secretariat "approving"—in effect, selecting—the personnel under the *nomenklatura* system. In Slovakia the KSS Central Committee "proposed" for KSC approval regional public officials. The regional and district party organizations controlled and placed through the commissions staffers in the administrative structure of the national committees. With the organization of the new government in December 1989 the KSC's powers in personnel matters were reduced drastically.

The deterioration of political power, especially following the June 1989 elections, sharply curtailed Communist influence in the state administration and the economic sector. Exclusion from the cabinet robbed the KSC of appointments to higher-level positions. However the KSC's entrenched position throughout the federal bureaucratic structure and at the lower levels poses a serious problem for Havel's leadership. Some in the Civic Forum, the Public Against Violence, and other groups, want to oust Communists from managerial and other positions, including the media. Others favor an evolutionary process. The controversy continues with Communist members clinging to their positions and networking.

Czech Prime Minister Pithart warned against "collective guilt," saying that "decent experts" should be retained. President Havel, acknowledging their decades-long entrenchment, noted that many Communists supported the Civic Forum and the government's programs. He suggested that a "second revolution" was requuired to quickly implement economic reforms. The president preferred this method, rather than radical purges, to progressively erode Communist power. Critics of Havel's approach, including members of his Civic Forum, are concerned with Communist organizational skills and obstructionist tactics.

Unlike domestic ministries, the foreign ministry under Dienstbier has witnessed remarkable changes, especially among its diplomatic personnel. Within six months a substantial number of ambassadors and other diplomats were replaced, the intelligence function of its embassies was curtailed, and its diplomats became more responsive to legitimate requests from the media. The new diplomatic attitude is contributing to the government's positive image abroad.

Czechoslovakia has no training institution to prepare students specifically for public service. The natural sources are the university-level institutions, technical institutes and secondary schools. The ministries maintain close contact with educational institutions for more effective transition to employment. Charles (in Prague), Brno, Olomouc, Komensky (Comenius) in Bratislava and Kosice universities are the more prominent. Recently Charles University created a Faculty of International Affairs and Languages, intended, at least partly, to prepare students for careers in foreign-service–oriented organizations. An Institute for Government

Management, under the federal government, conducts training programs for government officials.

LOCAL GOVERNMENT

Czechoslovakia consists of two republics: the Czech Socialist Republic and the Slovak Socialist Republic. Each has a unicameral legislative body known as the National Council, an executive branch known as the government, and a judiciary consisting of the Supreme Court and a prosecutor. The seat of the Czech Socialist Republic is in Prague, and the seat of the Slovak Socialist Republic is in Bratislava. The two national governments are clearly subordinate to the federal government. The federal government may invalidate national government initiatives. There also is an interlocking of offices within the two levels: for example, the two republic premiers are deputy premiers in the federal government, and the chairman of each national council is a member of the Presidium of the Federal Assembly. The Czech National Council has 200 delegates and its Slovak counterpart 150. Deputies are elected to five-year terms of office, and each national council holds two sessions annually. In the Czech Socialist Republic the Presidium of the National Council consists of 25 members, and in the Slovak Socialist Republic 21—including, in both cases, a premier, three deputy premiers and the chairmen of the Planning Commission and the People's Control Commission.

Each republic is divided into 10 regions, 114 districts and several thousand municipal and other local units. The principal organ of government at these levels is known as the national committee, with membership ranging from 15 to 25 at the lowest level, 60 to 120 at the district level and 80 to 150 at the regional level. These members are popularly elected to five-year terms of office. Each national committee elects a council from among its membership as the coordinating and controlling body. The council also may establish other commissions and subcommittees.

The national committees are assigned particular areas of jurisdiction, including protection of socialist ownership and implementation of economic and planning directives.

FOREIGN POLICY

Czechoslovakia's foreign policy had revolved around the Soviet Union since the Munich agreement, when Moscow's verbal support made an indelible impression on President Benes and other leaders, and the Kremlin's early recognition of Benes's government-in-exile solidified pro-Soviet feelings. On December 12, 1943, Benes concluded in Moscow a Treaty of Friendship, Mutual Assistance and Postwar Cooperation with Stalin. In January 1945 Benes recognized the Soviet-sponsored Lublin Committee, prompting the Polish government-in-exile to break relations with Czechoslovakia. Benes returned to Czechoslovakia by way of Moscow, where he held discussions with Soviet officials and KSC leaders as the Red Army was proceeding with liberating

POLITICAL SUBDIVISIONS				
Republics and Regions	Capitals	Area Sq. Km.	Sq. Mi.	Population (est. 1986)
Czech Socialist Republic	Prague			
Jihocesky	Ceske Budejovice	11,345	4,380	695,066
Jihomoravsky	Brno	15,028	5,802	2,058,020
Severocesky	Usti nad Labem	7,819	3,019	1,183,145
Severomoravsky	Ostrava	11,067	4,273	1,958,877
Stredocesky	Prague	10,994	4,245	1,137,086
Vychodocesky	Hradec Kralove	11,240	4,340	1,244,452
Zapadocesky	Pizen	10,875	4,199	873,239
Slovak Socialist Republic	Bratislava			
Stredoslovensky	Banska Bystrica	17,986	6,944	1,581,144
Vychodoslovensky	Kosice	16,196	6,253	1,463,333
Zapadoslovensky	Bratislava	14,492	5,595	1,715,861
Capital Cities				
Prague	—	496	192	1,193,513
Bratislava	—	367	142	417,103
TOTAL		127,905	49,384	15,520,839

Czechoslovakia. The Kosice Program confirmed that the alliance with the Soviet Union was the cornerstone of Prague's foreign policy. Thus the security of Czechoslovakia was "guaranteed" by the Soviet Union. In June 1945 the government ceded Ruthenia to the USSR. After first accepting unanimously participation in the Marshall Plan (July 1947), the still non-Communist government reversed its decision when Stalin declared opposition to it.

Soviet pressure over Ruthenia, overruling Prague on the vitally needed Marshall Plan aid, and giving assistance to the KSC to seize power, all demonstrated Moscow's unchallenged position. The Communist Party became a member of the Communist Information Bureau (Cominform) in October 1947, and in January 1949 the government was a founding member of the Council for Mutual Economic Assistance (CMEA), through which Moscow coordinates the economies of its members. Soviet control of the country's defense was illustrated in May 1950 during the purge of Czechoslovakia's armed forces. On May 14, 1955, Prague became one of the seven signatories to the Treaty of Friendship, Cooperation and Mutual Assistance; the Warsaw Treaty Organization (WTO), or the Warsaw Pact, as it is commonly known, was established for 20 years, extended in 1975 for 10 years and in 1985 renewed for another 20 years. The WTO consists of the Political Consultative Committee, Foreign Ministers Committee, Defense Ministers Committee and joint armed forces, with a Soviet marshal serving as commander in chief. Czechoslovakia participates in WTO military maneuvers, some of which are held annually on its territory. As a result of CSCE's Stockholm accord January 1, 1987, foreign, including U.S., inspectors have observed exercises in Czechoslovakia.

Czechoslovakia continued to be a loyal ally of the Soviet Union. With a comparatively developed industry, Czechoslovakia has been an important supplier of military weapons to its WTO partners and other countries in support of Soviet objectives.

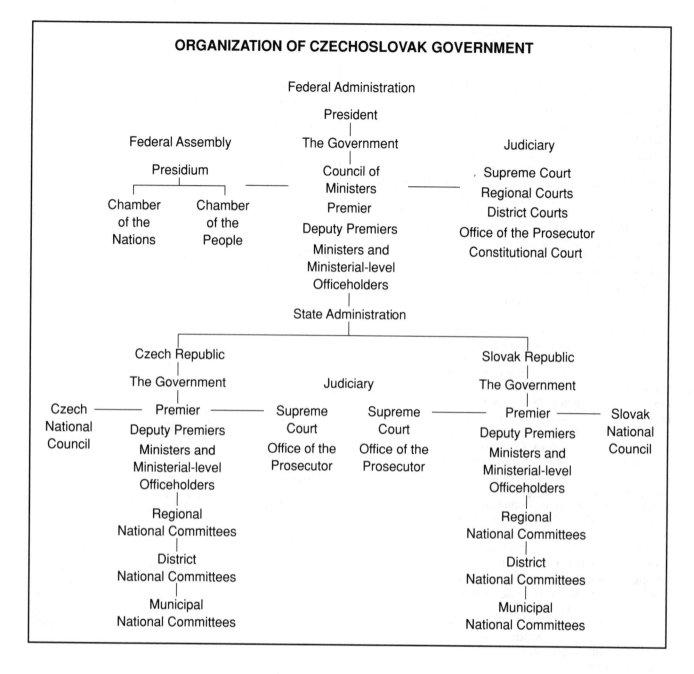

ORGANIZATION OF CZECHOSLOVAK GOVERNMENT

Federal Administration

President

Federal Assembly   The Government   Judiciary

Presidium   Council of Ministers   Supreme Court
    Premier   Regional Courts
Chamber   Chamber   Deputy Premiers   District Courts
of the   of the   Ministers and   Office of the Prosecutor
Nations   People   Ministerial-level   Constitutional Court
    Officeholders

State Administration

Czech Republic   Slovak Republic

The Government   Judiciary   The Government

Czech   Premier   Supreme   Supreme   Premier   Slovak
National   Court   Court   National
Council   Deputy Premiers   Office of the   Office of the   Deputy Premiers   Council
    Ministers and   Prosecutor   Prosecutor   Ministers and
    Ministerial-level   Ministerial-level
    Officeholders   Officeholders

Regional   Regional
National Committees   National Committees

District   District
National Committees   National Committees

Municipal   Municipal
National Committees   National Committees

The slow pace of economic and political improvement coupled with intraparty struggle resulted in Alexander Dubcek's replacement of Stalinist KSC leader Antonin Novotny in January 1968. However, Dubcek's "Prague Spring" program was criticized by the Soviet-controlled Warsaw Pact, with only Rumania supporting the CSSR leader, who proceeded with his wide-ranging reforms. During the night of August 20–21 the world was shocked to learn of the Soviet-led Warsaw Pact invasion and rapid troop deployment throughout the country. Czechoslovakia offered no military resistance to the forces from the USSR, East Germany, Poland, Hungary and Bulgaria. The public's response was overwhelmingly anti-Soviet, and demonstrations continued for some time. Rumania opposed this military action, sharply criticizing the invasion, as did Yugoslavia, Albania (which withdrew from the WTO as a result) and

China, as well as other governments around the world. The new regime, led by Gustav Husak as Communist Party leader, justified the invasion as "rendering international assistance" against "counterrevolutionary forces." The Husak leadership began a process of "normalization." In October 1968 Prague signed a status-of-forces treaty with Moscow providing for stationing of Soviet military forces in Czechoslovakia. Prague already had or would conclude treaties of friendship, cooperation and mutual assistance with all other WTO members: Poland (March 1967), East Germany (March 1967), Bulgaria (April 1968), Hungary (June 1968), Soviet Union (May 1970) and Rumania (August 1970). A web of such accords was created by all members with each other. Soviet military presence on the territory of Czechoslovakia was further enshrined by the Treaty of Friendship, Cooperation and Mutual Assistance of May

26, 1970, cited above. Moreover, Soviet military advisers were attached to Czechoslovakia's higher commands.

The non-Soviet troops departed but Soviet military forces remained, and Moscow soon indicated to all WTO allies strict limits on an independent course. In November 1968 Soviet general secretary Leonid Brezhnev declared in Warsaw the right to intervene in "friendly socialist countries" by WTO military forces if a regime is determined to be in danger; while the "Brezhnev Doctrine" of limited sovereignty had not been renounced officially by Gorbachev, there was no evidence of Soviet intention to intervene militarily in Czechoslovakia during the revolutionary changes taking place in that country in November–December 1989. At a meeting of the heads of state of the Warsaw Pact on December 4 in Moscow, its members acknowledged that the 1968 invasion was interference in the internal affairs of Czechoslovakia and thus "illegal." They pledged not to interfere again in each other's affairs.

Following the U.S.-USSR Intermediate-Range Nuclear Forces (INF) Treaty of December 1987, Moscow withdrew its SS-12 nuclear weapons from Czechoslovakia. In early 1989 Soviet forces in Czechoslovakia totaled 80,000, part of the Central Group of Forces. In his December 7, 1988, address before the United Nations, Gorbachev announced Soviet troop reductions within two years, including 5,000 tanks in six divisions, 50,000 troops, artillery and aircraft from East Germany, Hungary and Czechoslovakia. After 20 years of "temporary" presence in the country, Soviet officials indicated that by the end of 1990 they planned to withdraw 5,300 troops, 700 tanks, one tank division and 20 aircraft from Czechoslovakia. The general population had long hoped for a complete end to what they consider Soviet occupation.

The foreign minister of the new government of Czechoslovakia, Jiri Dienstbier, declared on December 14, 1989, that the status-of-forces agreement with the Soviet Union, providing for the stationing of Soviet military forces in Czechoslovakia, is illegal because it was concluded by compulsion. As a result of negotiations, Moscow agreed to withdraw "a substantial part" of the 70,000 to 75,000 troops stationed in Czechoslovakia by the end of May, before Federal Assembly elections set for early June 1990.

In his 1990 New Year's address President Havel declared that the country should "never again be an appendage or a poor relative of anyone else." CSSR-Soviet negotiators agreed on February 22 in Prague for total Soviet troop withdrawal from Czechoslovakia, and four days later in Moscow Havel and Gorbachev agreed on a three-stage pullout of the 73,500 Soviet troops to be completed by July 1, 1991. At a news conference Havel said that CSSR-Soviet relations assumed a "new character," with Moscow officials being "very critical" of the 1968 invasion.

Prague continues to be a friendly member of WTO, favoring its continuation but proposing changes freely. For example, in April Foreign Minister Dienstbier suggested a three-stage conversion to an all-European system. The character—perhaps the foundation—of the pact is changing from confrontational to "constructive cooperation" with NATO and other European countries. According to the June 7 declaration of the Political Consultative Committee meeting in Moscow, the pact favors "the formation of a new, all-European security system and the creation of a single Europe of peace and cooperation." Recognizing the new situation in Europe, the participants "find it necessary to reconsider the character and functions of the Warsaw Treaty." They renounced the pact's "ideological enemy image" of NATO and decided "to review the character, functions, and activities of the Warsaw Treaty." The members then pledged to begin the "transformation" of WTO into a "treaty of sovereign states with equal rights, formed on a democratic basis." The members created a provisional commission to prepare "concrete proposals" for the transformation for the Political Consultative Committee before the end of October. Prague favored these unfolding alliance policies. Clearly the pact's direction was European, through the Helsinki process, a step considered beneficial to its members. Havel called the conference "historic."

At the June 14–15 Berlin meeting, the pact's defense ministers discussed the implementation of the "transformation" of WTO into a greater political alliance, expressing desire for closer cooperation with NATO. However, the Soviet defense minister charged NATO's strategy to be "aggressive" and its military power threatening, and he called on his partners "not to slacken our allied ties." Subsequently the temporary commission convened in Prague to prepare proposals for WTO transformation.

In addition to the close political and military alignment with the Soviet Union, Czechoslovakia's trade shifted from Western to Eastern orientation with the establishment of the CMEA in 1949. The preponderance of Prague's trade had been with CMEA countries, about half with Moscow, on whom it relied for critical energy supplies and raw materials; in return, Czechoslovakia exported machinery, equipment and manufactured consumer products. Moscow's increase of oil prices impacted strongly on Czechoslovakia, causing a search for other markets, including Iran and Libya. In the latter half of the 1980s Prague was developing a stronger trade relationship with Western countries and reducing its high intra-CMEA trade, but it also cooperated for greater CMEA integration.

Czechoslovakia has extensive bilateral and multilateral relations with Eastern bloc countries, including exchanges, in all sectors. Ideologically, Husak's regime had been most closely identified with Erick Honecker's East Germany, which was severely critical of Dubcek's policies. With the rise of Solidarity in Poland, Czechoslovakia's relations with this northern neighbor had deteriorated, partly out of Prague's fear of democratic "infection." In 1981 Husak approved imposition of martial law in Poland, and in 1989 the Milos Jakes leadership perceived the Warsaw developments as a duplication of Dubcek's "Prague Spring." Both Husak and Jakes were outspoken critics of Solidarity. In a similar fashion, Czechoslovakia's southern neighbor Hungary was criticized on ideological grounds for its economic and especially political developments toward democratic pluralism. This had been viewed as a threat to KSC monopoly rule, as was the public airing of interviews with Dubcek on Hungarian TV in April 1989 discussing the "Prague Spring" and its similarity to Gorbachev's reforms; the interviews drew an official protest from the Jakes regime. In addition, Budapest's decision in May 1989 to suspend, at least temporarily, construction of the Gabcikovo-Nagymaros Danube Dam exacerbated the already poor relations between Czechoslovakia and Hungary.

The post-Communist leadership of President Havel has sought to improve relations with Germany. Havel's first visit abroad as president was in January 1990 to East Germany and the Federal Republic of Germany (FRG). He approved of German unification providing the new country was a "peaceful and democratic state."

Havel then visited Poland on January 25, 1990, and Hungary the following day. In Warsaw he proposed that Czechoslovakia, Poland and Hungary hold discussions in Bratislava on closer political and economic ties. As a group the three countries would approach Western Europe "offering spiritual values and brave peace proposals." In a program address to the Federal Assembly, Prime Minister Calfa said that the CSFR was planning talks with the GDR and Poland on a joint initiative regarding the institutionalization of the Helsinki process. Calfa considered indispensable the "guarantee of the inviolability of the western Oder-Neise Polish state frontier." With less dependence on the Soviet Union for their security the CSFR and Poland are strengthening their bilateral military cooperation.

The Hungarian minority in Slovakia and Slovaks in Hungary have always been a source of tension between the two countries. Arpad Goncz, president of Hungary, paid an informal visit to Prague and Bratislava July 12, 1990. The two presidents discussed joining efforts toward the European Community and, in their communique, they agreed that both sides appoint their national sections in the CSFR-Hungarian intergovernmental mixed commission for nationalities. The commission's principal task is to monitor the development of minority nationalities in their countries and propose legal and institutional conditions for their rights. Also, they agreed on the construction of a new Hungarian cultural center in Bratislava. In the Slovak capital, Goncz and Slovak premier Meciar exchanged views on minorities, the completion of the Danube water project, and Hungarian relations with the CSFR and the Slovak Republic.

Since Rumanian criticism of the WTO's 1968 invasion Czechoslovak-Rumanian relations had been on a formal basis only, but improved after the Communist downfall in both countries. Yugoslavia, not a member of the WTO, also opposed the invasion, but its economic and other relations with Czechoslovakia remained basically unchanged. Prague's contacts with China mirrored Sino-Soviet relations, except for Beijing's condemnation of the 1968 invasion. In the 1980s, relations improved in economic, political and other fields. Prague viewed the "restoration" of relations with China as mutually beneficial and "strengthening socialism"

and portrayed the June 1989 Beijing massacre as a justifiable necessity to suppress a "counterrevolution." Czechoslovakia had developed favorable relations with Vietnam, Laos and Cambodia, helping the regimes ruling those countries to "liquidate remnants of colonialism." Prague assisted North Korea materially during the 1950–53 war and they continue to have cordial relations. Cuba, too, had received assistance from Czechoslovakia.

Over the decades one of Prague's major policies had been support of "national liberation movements" in Africa, Asia and Latin America by supplying "effective aid." Many revolutionaries had been trained in Czechoslovakia, which extended military, economic and other assistance, including thousands of specialists. Prague also had supported Moscow's policies toward South Africa and the Arab states for the PLO and against Israel.

Iraq's invasion of Kuwait had an impact on the CSFR's economy. Prague criticized Iraq's aggression, continued to recognize the legitimate Kuwaiti government, adhered to UN's embargo, and halted arms shipments to Iraq, which, in 1990, owed the CSFR about $300 million. Prague's relations with Cuba were exacerbated in July 1990 over Cuban refugees in the CSFR Embassy in Havana. The previous month President Havel called on Fidel Castro to release all political prisoners in Cuba, a suggestion Castro labeled as "interference in Cuban affairs." About 30 CSFR women and children of diplomats left Cuba, and the refugees surrendered to Castro's authorities.

Albania was critical of the "velvet revolution" but relations remained correct. Five days before the Havana incident 51 Albanian refugees at the CSFR Embassy in Tirana were flown to Prague, where they were given political asylum. One reason for this response was Tirana's volume of trade with CSFR. The two governments signed a comprehensive economic agreement in May 1989 and raised their diplomatic representation to ambassadorial level the following September.

President Havel's official visit to Israel April 25–27 inaugurated a new phase of relations with the resumption of diplomatic relations that were broken in 1967. Earlier (April 12–13) PLO president Yasir Arafat visited Prague, where Havel assured him of "humanitarian assistance to the Palestinian people" in the form of scholarships and medical treatment.

Czechoslovakia considers the United Nations as an important forum for strengthening peace and international security and has been an active member in international organizations. Prague maintains diplomatic relations with about 130 countries and has membership in over 60 governmental and 1,250 nongovernmental organizations. It is a charter member of the United Nations and is a member of many of its specialized agencies, including IAEA, UNIDO, WHO, ILO and FAO. Prague also is a member of the General Agreement on Tariff and Trade (GATT) and of UNCTAD and has applied to join the International Monetary Fund (IMF), the World Bank, and the Council of Europe. Prague is planning to sign a trade and cooperation agreement with the European Community. There is a UNESCO Cooperation

Commission and a U.N. Association in Prague. Czechoslovakia was a member of the U.N. Security Council in 1964 and during 1978–79. It has signed the U.N. Convention on the Law of the Sea and is a member of the U.N. Commission for Disarmament and its Committee for Peaceful Exploitation of Space, among other bodies. During Communist rule the United Nations also has served as a forum for Czechoslovakia's support of Moscow's propaganda themes.

Prague had been a favored locale for Communist front organizations such as the Soviet-controlled *World Marxist Review*, the theoretical monthly journal of international communism; the Christian Peace Conference (CPC); the International Organization of Journalists (IOJ); the International Radio and Television Organization (OIRT); the International Union of Students (IUS); and the World Federation of Trade Unions (WFTU). The World Peace Council, with headquarters in Helsinki, has an active office in Prague.

In line with its multilateralism, Czechoslovakia was an active participant in the 1975 Helsinki conference on Security and Cooperation in Europe (CSCE) and in its follow-up conferences, in the NATO-WTO Mutual and Balanced Force Reduction (MBFR) negotiations in Vienna (1973–89), and it continues to participate in the Conventional Armed Forces in Europe (CFE) talks, also in Vienna. Its relations with non-Eastern bloc countries increased in the 1970s and expanded in the 1980s in pursuit of Brezhnev's and Gorbachev's policy of detente, and Czechoslovakia has promoted closer CMEA relations with the European Community (EC), resulting in formal relations in June 1988; Prague signed an individual agreement in December 1988. This association was motivated by Czechoslovakia's need for convertible currency for modernization of its industry.

Unlike the interwar period, relations between Czechoslovakia and the United States since the 1948 Communist coup have been troublesome. President Woodrow Wilson's Fourteen Points and support for Czech and Slovak independence, as for other nations, was imbedded in the new country's memory. Its Constitution was modeled on the American, and the United States was a land of opportunity for Slovaks and Czechs. Of the millions of American citizens who trace their roots to the Czech lands and Slovakia, the majority are Slovak. The United States extended recognition to Benes's government-in-exile, contributed to the country's liberation and in 1947 invited Prague to participate in the Marshall Plan.

Following the Communist coup in 1948 the U.S. consulate was closed in Bratislava, the Slovak capital, and relations were strained. After the Warsaw Pact invasion in 1968 the United States raised the question before the U.N. Security Council that it was a violation of the U.N. Charter and an infringement of Czechoslovakia's sovereignty. Poor relations worsened, but after several years bilateral negotiations were conducted on several issues, including consular convention, trade, financial settlement, exchanges and consulates. Serious questions remained unsolved, and the negotiations failed. However, in 1982 Washington and Prague concluded an agreement on compensation of U.S. citizens for property nationalized after the war, and on the return to Czechoslovakia of gold recovered from Germany after the war and held in custody by a U.S.-U.K.-French commission. In 1986 the governments signed an agreement for exchanges in culture, education, science and technology. Over the years Prague had resented denial of most-favored-nation tariff treatment by the United States, which bases its decision on qualification. By early 1990 prospects for improved relations appeared promising, with Washington welcoming developments in that country in late 1989.

During his visit to the USSR and Eastern Europe, Secretary of State James Baker presented to Havel an assistance program that included a pledge to eliminate U.S. trade barriers, make Prague eligible for U.S. trade credits, and to increase bilateral cultural, educational and diplomatic contacts. In a speech at Prague's Charles University Baker proposed a four-point program of U.S. support for Eastern Europe: help for the free elections; economic aid to rebuild economies; political and economic cooperation; and a redefinition of military policies.

President Havel visited Canada and the United States. He held talks with President George Bush and made an impressive address before the joint session of Congress on February 21. President Bush confirmed the U.S.'s desire to assist the country's "democratic rebirth," revealing that he had signed a waiver to the Jackson-Vanik amendment clearing the way for Czechoslovakia to receive most-favored-nation treatment in trade. Bush promised to support Prague to obtain aid from international financial institutions. However, he disagreed with Havel's proposal to abolish both NATO and the Warsaw Pact, saying that NATO has a "vital role in assuring stability and security in Europe." Before Congress, Havel said he looked to a future when Europe would be responsible for its own security, undivided by ideology, restated his idea for an international peace conference and suggested that U.S. support for Soviet liberalization would "help us most of all."

On April 12 the two countries signed the U.S.-Czechoslovak Trade Agreement, extending most-favored-nation status to that country. The accord lowers tariffs, encourages economic ties and increases tourism.

In the spirit of Gorbachev's policy of coexistence and "common European home," Czechoslavakia's conservative leadership, its reluctance tempered by economic necessity, normalized its relations with a number of West European countries. Prague ceased jamming Radio Free Europe broadcasts in December 1988. Despite the tragedy of World War II, Czechoslovakia's continual charges of "revanchism" and East German considerations, West Germany became its most important trading partner. The outstanding issue had been the Munich agreement. Following nearly three years of negotiations, Prague and Bonn signed an accord in December 1973, ratified in June 1974, which proclaimed Munich null and void, recognized the inviolability of the existing borders, established diplomatic relations, and laid the ground for expansion of exchanges and development in various fields. In 1975 and 1979 the countries concluded agreements for economic and cultural cooperation. Trade increased more rapidly than activities in other areas, largely because of East-West relations over such issues as the Soviet invasion of Afghanistan, deployment of nuclear weapons and human rights. For example, the imprisonment of playwright Vaclav Havel (then a Charter 77 activist) in February 1989 prompted West Germany's Bundestag to pass a resolution charging Prague with violating the Helsinki provisions. The Jakes regime considered this action interference in Czechoslovakia's internal affairs.

With Austria numerous problems required solution. In December 1975 the governments settled the long-delayed financial and property question, established a bilateral commission to develop relations and raised diplomatic missions to embassies. This resulted in an Austrian presidential visit to Prague in 1979, but improvement of relations was hampered by several issues, including civil rights in Czechoslovakia, espionage, divided families and border incidents. However, 1985–86 meetings of foreign ministers and presidents presaged positive developments, especially official contacts, exchanges and trade; Austria is Czechoslovakia's second-largest non-CMEA trading partner.

Austria applauded Czechoslovakia's transition to democracy, but Havel's visit to Austria in July 1990 created controversy, despite its "unofficial" nature. Havel met with Austrian president Kurt Waldheim at Salzburg's 70th annual music festival, which Havel opened. He criticized the rewriting of history but questioned the West's isolation of Waldheim. Havel also met with Chancellor Franz Vranitzky, with whom he discussed a nuclear power plant under construction near the Austrian border that is criticized by Austrian environmentalists.

Roman Catholicism is the predominant religious affiliation in Czechoslovakia, the proportion higher in Slovakia than in the Czech lands. Consequently, relations with the Vatican were necessarily of some importance for the atheistic regime as well as for the believers. The organized Roman Catholic Church became an object of Communist persecution, which gave rise to an underground church. In 1950 the Uniate Church (Catholics of the Eastern Rite), mostly in eastern Slovakia, was forcibly incorporated into the small Orthodox Church, thus severing the former's ties with the Vatican. Under Dubcek religious freedom flourished and gave the Uniates hope for reinstatement. But the "Prague Spring" was short-lived, and persecution was reinstated instead.

Among other problems, many bishoprics became vacant. The infrequent contacts with the Vatican showed little improvement. However, the regime's failure to create an atheistic society, the determined resistance of believers and resurgence of religious fervor among young people coupled with international condemnation of antireligious policies (for example, violation of the CSCE agreement) and Gorbachev's *glasnost* forced the regime to rethink its repressive policy. Finally, in April 1989 a Vatican delegation reached a provisional agreement with Prague on 10 of the 13 vacant bishoprics in the country and provided for further official discussions on outstanding issues. The accord came two months before the 90th birthday of Frantisek Cardinal Tomasek, the archbishop of Prague who for decades struggled for religious and other freedoms. As a result, Pope John Paul II named bishops to several sees, but by mid-1989 six remained vacant. However, the Vatican appeared optimistic that the remaining vacancies probably would be filled by 1990. With the establishment of the non-Communist government in December 1989, additional appointments were made and the new government decided to restore diplomatic relations with the Vatican.

After 40 years, full diplomatic relations with the Vatican were reestablished in April 1990. During April 21–22 Pope John Paul II visited the CSFR, his first to an East European country outside of Poland. Despite a rainstorm, some 300,000 attended the pope's mass outside Prague, and on April 22 about 1 million people attended an outdoor mass in a muddy field outside Bratislava. Pope John Paul announced plans to hold a synod of bishops from east and west Europe. Saying "the night is over, day has dawned anew," the pope visualized "a common European home from the Atlantic to the Urals."

PARLIAMENT

In Czechoslovakia the bicameral Federal Assembly (Federalni Shromazdeni) is the supreme organ of state power, consisting of the Chamber of the People and the Chamber of the Nations, both equal. Concurrent decisions normally are required for passage of laws. The Chamber of the People (Snemovna Lidu) has 200 deputies elected by countrywide vote. The 150-member Chamber of the Nations (Snemovna Narodu) represents each republic equally: 75 members from the Czech Socialist Republic and 75 from the Slovak Socialist Republic. ("Socialist" was deleted following the fall of the Communist regime.) The Constitutional Act of 1968 specified four-year terms of office for deputies to the Federal Assembly. The term was changed to five years by the Electoral Law of 1971 to coincide with that of the KSC Congress. The KSC-controlled National Front presented a single list of candidates. Despite reports of substantial rejections by voters, the official results continued to be in the 99% range. All citizens 18 years of age or over have a legal right to vote. Deputies to the Federal Assembly are elected by universal, equal, direct and secret vote. The last elections under Communist control were held in May 1986.

The Federal Assembly is convened by the CSFR president at least twice yearly, in spring and fall, and prorogued by him. A joint session is required for the election of the CSFR president, the chairman and deputy chairmen of the Federal Assembly and to consider policy statements. Generally the sessions are to be public.

The Federal Assembly enacts the Constitution and legislation; discusses domestic and foreign policies; approves economic plans and the federal budget; elects the president and considers his reports; discusses policy and activities of and confidence in the government;

elects and recalls members of the Constitutional Court; establishes by constitutional act federal ministries and by act other federal organs; declares war; and ratifies treaties. Both chambers elect from their membership a 40-member Presidium, 20 from each Chamber, with those in the Chamber of the Nations comprising 10 each from the CR and the SR. The Presidium exercises the functions of the Federal Assembly between sessions. Each chamber has its own Presidium of three to six members, elects its own chairmen and establishes its own committees and control organs. The Federal Assembly elects a chairman, first deputy chairman and deputy chairmen from among its Presidium members. KSC members predominated during Communist rule. Finally, the Presidium decides on elections to the Federal Assembly.

Chapter Seven of the Constitution is devoted to state organs of the Czech Republic and the Slovak Republic. The Czech National Council (Ceska Narodni Rada) and the Slovak National Council (Slovenska Narodna Rada) represent the "national sovereignty and independence" of each nation and are the supreme organs of state power—legislative and administrative—in the republics. The Czech National Council has 200 deputies and the Slovak National Council 150 deputies, also elected for five-year terms. As with the Federal Assembly, the councils also meet at least twice yearly, in fall and spring. Under the Communist regime it was for very short sessions, essentially to bestow legality to party programs. The national councils adopt constitutional and other acts for their republics, approve applicable international treaties, discuss domestic policy questions, approve and oversee economic plans and budgets, discuss their government's policies, establish ministries and other organs of state administration and elect and recall members of their constitutional courts. Laws are adopted by majority vote and constitutional acts by three-fifths vote.

Each National Council elects from its members a Presidium consisting of a chairman, deputy chairmen and members; it exercises the National Council's responsibilities between its sessions. The Presidium appoints and recalls the premier and other members of the republic government. The chairman of the National Council represents that body, signs its acts and those of the Presidium, and convenes and presides over the National Council's meetings. Committees such as Agriculture and Food, Culture and Education, and Health and Social Affairs are established by each National Council.

During the revolutionary changes in November–December 1989 the new government established the probable date for new national elections and filled vacancies in the Federal Assembly. In December 22 talks between the Civic Forum and Public Against Violence as well as other groups and the Communist Party, agreement was reached on filling 23 seats in the Federal Assembly left vacant by resignations and expulsions from the Communist Party. Sixteen delegates were to represent the Civic Forum, five the Slovak Public Against Violence and two the Communist Party.

On March 6, 1990 parliament formally scheduled free multiparty national elections in June. The election laws passed earlier included proportional representation in the 12 regions and two-year terms for deputies. Over 3,500 candidates competed for the 300-seat Federal Assembly's two chambers: House of the People (101 from the Czech Republic and 49 from Slovakia) and the House of the Nations (75 from each republic). About 1,700 candidates ran for the 200-seat Czech National Council, and some 1,100 for the 150-member Slovak National Council. Altogether 22 parties participated, some only in the Czech lands (4) and some only in Slovakia (6). Each voter cast three ballots—one for each of the federal chambers and one for a national council. Votes were cast only for party lists. A 5% vote was required for a party, movement or coalition to be represented in parliament.

The results were generally surprising. Although the Civic Forum-Public Against Violence won a plurality (46.3%), the expectation had been for a larger majority, while the Communist Party, although a distant second, received a higher vote (13.6%) than predicted. Also, the conservative Christian Democratic Union—a coalition of the People's Party, Czech Christian Democratic Party and the Slovak Democratic Party—had hoped for much higher support than its third-place showing. The smaller parties received less than 10% of the total vote. The Civic Forum won a majority in the Czech National Council, while the Public Against Violence obtained a plurality in the Slovak National Council.

On June 27 the Federal Assembly elected Dubcek as chairman and on July 5 Havel as president for a two-year term by a vote of 234 to 50. The Federal Assembly's mandate is to adopt a new constitution by 1992. The Czech and Slovak republics are also drafting new constitutions.

POLITICAL PARTIES

As in other Soviet bloc countries, the KSC was both a political party and a constitutionally recognized organization assigned the leadership role in society. In fact, it was the source of all power in the state—legislative, executive and judicial—controlling all levels of power and nearly all organizations.

Formally, Czechoslovakia has had a multiparty system since the April 1945 Kosice Program. An agreement between Benes's government-in-exile and the Communist leaders in Moscow resulted in the Czechoslovak National Front, a coalition of four Czech and two Slovak political parties friendly to the Soviet Union. Two were the KSC and the Slovak Communist Party (KSS), and the others were soon to be purged of all real or potential adversaries. In mid-1989 six political parties were functioning: KSC, KSS, Czechoslovak Socialist, Czechoslovak People's, Slovak Freedom and Slovak Revival Party. With reform taking place in the USSR, Poland and Hungary, increasing demands were made for "real" political parties.

The Czechs and Slovaks began to organize political parties in the late 19th century. These, and others that followed (altogether about 20, including the KSC), developed and functioned during the First Republic. The multiparty system distinguished interwar Czechoslovakia from other East European countries. However, a coalition of five parties—the Petka, as it was known—held the reins of government in a disciplined arrangement that excluded all others. The Petka consisted of the Czechoslovak Agrarian, Social Democratic, National Socialist (Benes's), People's and National Democratic parties. The Slovak People's Party was formed in 1918 and led by a Catholic, Father Andrej Hlinka, who campaigned for Slovak autonomy at Versailles, then demanded it from Prague, as he strongly opposed centralization. The most popular of the pre-World War II political parties—the Czechoslovak Agrarian and, in Slovakia, the People's Party—were abolished, as were all others, by the 1945 Kosice Program. In the May 1946 elections the KSC received a plurality of 38%, while in Slovakia the KSS managed only 30% compared to the Slovak Democratic Party's 62%.

Following the Communist coup in 1948, the non-Communist political parties were purged and virtually destroyed in the KSC's drive for monopoly of power. Only remnants of the parties remained, if at all. The National Socialist became the Czech Socialist, the Slovak Democratic the Slovak Revival, and the Social Democratic merged with the KSC in June 1948. Over the next 40 years, in addition to the KSC and the KSS, the Czechoslovak Socialist, the Czechoslovak People's, the Slovak Revival and the Slovak Freedom parties participated in the Communist-controlled National Front. As such they had been of no consequence.

Following its abortive "revolution of the proletariat" in December 1920, the left wing of the Social Democratic Party, with other radicals, created the KSC in May 1921, announcing its membership in the Communist International (Comintern). The KSC participated in the free elections, receiving about 10% of the popular vote. There was an earlier, short-lived group of Czechs in Moscow—former prisoners of war—who in May 1918 declared themselves a Communist Party and proclaimed a socialist republic. In the 1925, 1929 and 1935 elections the KSC sent respectively 41, 30 and 30 deputies to the 300-member National Assembly. The party's clear objective was a pithy threat made in 1929 by the newly elected general secretary, Klement Gottwald: "We go to Moscow to learn from the Russian Bolsheviks how to wring your necks." During the interwar period, KSC survived intraparty ideological and leadership differences, and criticism by Moscow. The KSC was banned by the new government following the Munich Conference, and most of its members fled the country. The future leadership of the KSC spent the war years in Moscow, but some (for example, the Slovak Vladimir Clementis) were in London, and others in the underground. Those in the West were considered unreliable by Moscow and were ultimately purged. Clementis, who followed Jan Masaryk as foreign minister, was executed in 1952.

As with other Societ bloc Communist parties, the KSC's guiding principle for the organizational structure and the activity of the party was "democratic centralism," which also applied to the government framework. Party statutes were considered by members in reverent terms. Basic KSC statutes were approved by the 12th Party Congress, in 1962, and amended by subsequent congresses, including the 17th, held March 24-28, 1986. The statutes made clear that democratic centralism required all organizations and members to implement party policy and decisions of the leading party organs. Under democratic centralism all leading party organs were elected from the bottom to the top. The organs were accountable to the higher and lower party organizations, and decisions made by the superior organs were unconditionally binding for all lower organs. In reality, the KSC Presidium was the determining authority in Czechoslovakia.

According to the statutes, the supreme organ of the KSC was the Party Congress, convened by the party's Central Committee every five years, but an extraordinary Congress could be assembled. The Central Committee announced the date of the meeting and the agenda eight weeks in advance, allowing time for discussion of issues. Deliberations were held by party organs in sessions at the republic, regional and lower levels. The Central Committee decided on the rules for representation and the manner of electing delegates. For the 17th Party Congress, 1,545 delegates were elected, but four less attended, compared to 1,421 at the 16th Congress. The Congress heard a favorable presentation by its general secretary and other positive reports, then adopted a resolution endorsing the reports. The 17th Congress declared General Secretary Gustav Husak's to be the "mandatory policy line," and it approved the Central Committee's written report on the fulfillment of the previous Congress's decisions. The resolution instructed the Central Committee to implement the decisions and all party organs and members to follow the policy line. The 18th Party Congress was planned for May 1990, but the dynamic events of the "Velvet Revolution" forced an emergency Congress December 20–21.

The Congress elected the Central Committee and the Central Control and Auditing Commission. The 17th Congress elected 135 full and 62 candidate members, an increase of 12 and seven, respectively, over the 16th Congress. The Central Committee met at least three times annually. Representing the Congress between sessions, the Central Committee developed and implemented policies adopted at the Congress at the federal, republic and lower levels; the government; the National Front; and other organizations. The Central Committee also maintained contact with other parties.

The statutes provided for the election by the Central Committee of the Presidium, the Secretariat, the general secretary and the secretaries. In reality the Presidium established the KSC's, and thus the country's, policies. The 17th Congress announced Gustav Husak as general secretary and 10 others as full and six as candidate members of the Presidium; 13 secretaries, headed by the general secretary; and the chairman of the Central Control and Auditing Commission. In mid-1989 the top KSC organizational structure was as follows: the Central Committee (as above); the Presidium of 13 full and three candidate members; the 11-member Secretariat, consisting of the general secretary (Milos Jakes), four secretaries, and six members; and the chairman of the

Central Control and Auditing Commission. The Central Committee departments were: Agitation and Propaganda; Agriculture, Food, Forestry and Water Resources; Culture; Economic Administration; Economics; Education and Science; Industry, Transportation and Construction; International Politics; Mass Media; Party Work in Industry, Transportation, Construction and Trade; Political Organization; Social Organizations and National Committees; and State Administration. Moreover, there were a chairman and two secretaries on the Committee for Party Work in the Czech Socialist Republic.

According to party statutes, the territorial organization of the KSC in Slovakia was the Communist Party of Slovakia (KSS), consisting of regional organizations. The KSS was directed "to follow in its activity the decisions of the Congress and of the Central Committee of the KSC." The KSS's structure paralleled that of its Czech counterpart. At the pinnacle was the Congress, meeting every five years with the "consent" of the KSC prior to the KSC Congress. The election of delegates at regional conferences was by KSS rules. The Congress considered and approved reports of its Central Committee, the Central Control and Auditing Commission and others; considered the tasks of the KSS; elected its Central Committee, which met at least three times yearly, and the Central Control and Auditing Commission. The KSC statutes instructed the KSS Central Committee to implement the decisions of the KSC Central Committee in Slovakia; assign personnel to supervise regional organizations, promote societal harmony and submit regular reports to the KSC; propose to the KSC Central Committee Slovak employees for higher positions; and implement its own budget.

The KSC statutes assigned to the KSS Central Committee the role of guiding and controlling the Slovak National Council, the government and social organizations. The Central Committee met at least three times yearly. It elected from among its members a Presidium to direct political, organizational and educational work between sessions of the Central Committee; a Secretariat to direct the organization, implement decisions and select personnel; and the first secretary. In mid-1989 the KSS's Presidium had nine members, and the Secretariat, with Ignac Janak as first secretary, three secretaries and two members. The Slovak inferior position in the KSC was also reflected in their having only 30% of the high-echelon KSC positions.

In the Czech and Slovak republics there are 12 regions (kraj), including Prague and Bratislava, which have regional status. Seven are in Bohemia-Moravia and three in Slovakia. Each region convoked a conference every two to three years, electing a committee that in turn elected from its members a Presidium and a Secretariat with a leading secretary, other secretaries and a Central Control and Auditing Commission. Each region was divided into districts (okres). The district conferences, also meeting every two to three years, elected a Presidium, a committee and the Central Control and Auditing Commission. The next lower level consisted of municipal and enterprise committees, where several primary organizations functioned. Committees were el-

ected for two to three years at conferences or plenary party meetings. Each committee elected a chairman and a Central Control and Auditing Commission. At the lowest rung were primary organizations—the "foundations" of the party, as the statutes characterized them—formed at all basic levels of activity. It was here that the party had direct, live contact with people. The directing organ was the party meeting, held monthly. An annual plenary session elected a committee for two to three years; this committee elected its chairman.

All party organizations, functioning on the principle of democratic centralism, were guided by KSC statutes and the resolutions of its Congress and the Central Committee in implementing policies and regulations. District party committees then directed primary organizations and municipal enterprises in implementation of the political, ideological and economic requirements of the party. The major duties of the regional and district organizations were to implement the economic plan; direct ideological indoctrination; "guide and control" the work of the national committees, trade unions and other social organizations; and select, assign and train personnel for supervisory positions in industry, agriculture and the national committees. The lower organs continued the implementation of party programs in their jurisdictions.

Membership in the Communist Party of Czechoslovakia had been one of the highest in the world on a per capita basis. During the interwar period the KSC was legal and began with an impressive 350,000 membership at its founding in 1921, increasing to over 400,000 shortly thereafter. However, a major purge, the first of many during the next 50 years, reduced membership to below 100,000 by 1925. At issue were doctrinal questions of self-determination and nationalism debated in Moscow. Attrition through purges, resignations and disinterest reduced membership to approximately 50,000 in 1938. It was less than 30,000 at war's end, but with the Red Army's liberation of most of Czechoslovakia and the establishment of national committees throughout the country, KSC membership became an attraction for many. Party rolls jumped dramatically to 1,160,000 before the May 1946 elections, in which the KSC gained a parliamentary victory. The number was 1,355,000 in February 1948, but following the coup d'état and merger with the Social Democratic Party on June 27, 1948 full membership reached 1,788,400. With more than 500,000 additional members the total was 2,311,000 in May 1949, the highest it was to reach.

Purges and resignations involving hundreds of thousands of members were conducted periodically, usually following a crisis. For example, 300,000 members were purged and 200,000 resigned during late 1968 and early 1971. Thus party members and candidates numbered 1.6 million in 1960, then increased, but reached a new low of 1.1 million, or 7.4% of the population, in early 1975. At the 16th Party Congress, in April 1981, General Secretary Husak reported a membership of 1,538,179 as of January 1. The 17th Party Congress, in March 1986, cited membership of 1,674,918, or one out of seven citizens over 18 years of age. According to the report of the KSC, active and retired workers accounted for

44.6% and cooperative farmers for 6% of the membership. Women's percentage rose to 28.9, a third of all members were under age 35 and over half joined the party since 1970. In mid-1989 KSC membership was slightly over 1.7 million. Civic Forum leader Vaclav Havel cited a figure of 1.7 million on December 6. At the Extraordinary Party Congress on December 20 General Secretary Urbanek reported that since November 17 some 66,000 members had left the party and 3,300 party organizations had been dissolved. The Group for Independent Social Analysis in Prague estimated that 600,000 to 800,000 members had abandoned the party by mid-January 1990. The Slovak Communist Party had reported 451,445 members and candidate members as of October 1 and that by mid-December 5,796 had returned their membership cards.

The composition of all organs at the 17th Party Congress assured continuing conservative policies, and officially there was no indication of problems either in the society or the party. In the ensuing period the regime's ambivalent position on Gorbachev's policies of *glasnost* and *perestroika* became obvious. At the Central Committee session in December 1987 Husak was replaced by Milos Jakes, a veteran Czech KSC functionary who was not a reformist but a conservative or, at best, a centrist. There were other personnel changes during 1988–89, as well as rhetorical references to *glasnost* and *perestroika*, but no real policy changes despite admissions of stagnation. In May 1988 the KSC published measures to improve information within the party, but the KSC's primacy was continually emphasized. Dubcek, in foreign media, called reform a necessity, but the regime rejected his proposals.

At the October 1988 Central Committee plenum Prime Minister Lubomir Strougal and Deputy Prime Minister Peter Colotka resigned from the Presidium. Five new members were announced, increasing its membership to 15, and changes also were made in the Secretariat. However, these developments were within the conservative sphere. The June 1989 Central Committee session confirmed this.

The momentous events during November and December 1989 led to the resignation on November 24 of party leader Jakes, who was replaced by Karel Urbanek. An Extraordinary Congress was held on December 20 with 1,524 delegates, including only 18 members of the Central Committee. The delegates voted to abolish the post of general secretary of the Communist Party and to establish the position of chairman of the party. The Congress also provided for a first secretary of the Central Committee, electing Vasil Mohorita to this post.

The transition of KSC's predominant position in the country to a party of opposition began in December 1989. The Extraordinary Congress (December 20–21), attended by 1,500 delegates, apologized "to all citizens who suffered from repression and those who were ousted from the party in 1968." The post of general secretary was abolished and Ladislav Adamec, considered a realist, became KSC's chairman, a title discarded decades earlier. Even the election process took on a new look. Instead of automatic approval of preselected leader, six candidates competed, with Adamec winning

about 60 percent of the votes in secret balloting. The Congress established another new position, that of first secretary, and elected ideologist Vasil Mohorita, a young reformist who had been chairman of the Socialist Youth Association. The first secretary is to administer the party's internal affairs while the chairman is responsible for contact with other political parties and organizations.

The Congress adopted a program to review the 1968 "Prague Spring," accept political pluralism and pursue democratization of the party. The Workers' Militia, a paramilitary organization that served the party, was abolished. The Secretariat was reduced from nine to four secretaries, but more dramatic changes were made at the January 6, 1990 plenum. The KSC's powerful Presidium was replaced by a Political Executive Committee, consisting of 24 members, and chaired by Jan Siroky. It is made up of the KSC chairman, the four secretaries, and nineteen members elected by the CC. The CC itself had been reduced from nearly 200 before the December Congress to 140 members. At the August 1990 CC plenum Adamec resigned as chairman of KSC and was replaced by Mahorita as interim chairman.

The KSS's Extraordinary Congress, held December 8, 1989, replaced its Presidium with an Executive Committee, consisting of a chairman and three secretaries. Jan Siroky was elected chairman but on January 20, 1990 was replaced by Peter Weiss, formerly a KSS secretary.

Despite the repressive political environment in Czechoslovakia, far removed from Hungary and Poland and lagging behind the Soviet Union, an increasing number of groups and associations became organizationally active, especially during 1988–89. The organizations were spawned in the main by intellectuals, youths and specialists generally promoting reforms, especially human rights, or special sectors, including workers. The oldest, best known and most influential is Charter 77 (Charta 77), in existence since 1977, which demands that the regime observe domestic and international laws. Several of the other groups are: Christian Union for Human Rights; Obroda: Club for Socialist Restructuring; Peace on Earth: Association of Believing Catholic Laymen; Polish-Czechoslovak Solidarity (since 1978); Open Dialogue; Association of Friends of the U.S.A.; Brno Initiative; and Group for Labor Union Solidarity. No formal announcement of an independent political party was observed in mid-1989 but the announced objective of some groups included political reform—for example, Movement for Civil Liberties, and Democratic Initiative.

There was one flicker of public discontent, not in evidence since Dubcek, by an existing party leader. In May 1989 the leading secretary of the Czechoslovak Socialist Party, Jan Skoda, expressed in a carefully phrased statement a desire for greater democratization. Other groups emerged in subsequent months. Events were moving so rapidly that parties and associations appeared to lag behind the public masses rather than lead them. Neither the National Front political parties nor any one of the associations or groups was capable by itself of acquiring sufficient political power to challenge the Communist Party. However, progressive developments in Eastern Europe, without Soviet military intervention, created an environment that resulted in mass demonstrations for reform, including political pluralism, which the Communist regime was unable to contain.

In this milieu the Civic Forum, an umbrella organization of Charter 77 and other associations, was formed in Prague for the Czech lands on November 19. The following day its Slovak counterpart, Public Against Violence, was established in Bratislava, capital of Slovakia. These two organizations maintained close contact and were the leading actors that negotiated historic agreements with the Communist regime. The Civic Forum and Public Against Violence represented the masses, leading them in thunderous demonstrations and a countrywide general strike on November 27.

In the formation of the new government on December 10, leaders from the Civic Forum and Public Against Violence identified themselves as "without political affiliation." The most notable leader of the Civic Forum, Vaclav Havel, was elected president of the republic, and the leader of Public Against Violence, Jan Carnogursky, was appointed first deputy prime minister. The prime minister was a member of the Communist Party, as were some ministers. Others awarded ministerial portfolios were from the Czechoslovak People's and the Czechoslovak Socialist parties.

Some leading party members (e.g. premier Calfa) have resigned while others have been purged. The December Congress suspended membership of 22 former officials and expelled former Presidium hardliner Vasil Bilak. At the February 17 plenum the CC expelled the 22, including former general secretary and the country's President Husak. The CC denounced them for "grave political mistakes" and "abuse of power."

In early January 1990 the KSC claimed membership to be 1,658,000. However, at the party plenum on February 17 chairman Adamec announced that 20 to 30% of the members left the party after November 17, 1989. In March KSC cited a figure of 1,099,000, reduced still more in succeeding months with estimates of 760,000 and lower in mid-1990.

Regional KSC committees were abolished. Among the CP's changes, the basic organizations (e.g. at an enterprise became publicly inactive. The CC abolished all party units throughout the government structure, including the military. However, the extent of these changes remained unclear since some units continued to function and others transformed themselves into other categories, such as clubs.

In November–December that flicker became a flame as Groups and movements became dynamic political forces. Two major groups emerged in November—the Civic Forum (CF) and the Public Against Violence (PAV). The CF, organized on November 19, 1989, by several hundred activists, functioned in the Czech lands while PAV, established November 20 by cultural figures and leaders in the professions, operated in Slovakia. They organized mass demonstrations and strikes that brought about the fall of the Communist dictatorship.

The CF, comprising a broad political spectrum, was clearly the strongest in Bohemia-Moravia, while the PAV early enjoyed the same in Slovakia.

Following the political transition to a multi-party system, numerous parties, movements, and coalitions emerged in vying for seats to the Federal Assembly and to the Czech and Slovak National Councils.

The Czechoslovak Socialist Party, Czechoslovak People's Party, Slovak Freedom Party, and the Slovak Revival Party had functioned under Communist control and were of no political consequence. The once powerful Czechoslovak Social Democratic Party was reestablished in November and held its constituent congress in March. In December a Slovak Social Democratic Party was established, but in March the two parties decided on a joint coordinating committee. In April the two agreed to participate in the elections as one party. The new election law placed a minimum of 10,000 members in a party to be eligible to submit candidates. The Christian Democratic Party (CDP) in the Czech Republic decided in March to choose an independent course from the Civic Forum.

Of the numerous parties representing the agricultural sector four formed a coalition, including the Czechoslovak Agrarian Party, and two ran candidates under the CF umbrella, and one joined with the People's Party, itself in coalition with the Christian Democrats. The Czechoslovak Socialist Party, having been under Communist control, tried to benefit from its past when as the National Socialist Party it was identified with Masaryk and Benes. At its March congress the Green Party showed a quick rise in membership but did not join any coalition.

The KSC—and the KSS in Slovakia—continued to have relatively large memberships and country-wide organizations, particularly meaningful factors at local levels. The Slovak Renewal Party reverted to the Slovak Democratic Party, a major party in Slovakia during 1945–48. There were still other parties.

For elections each party was allowed up to 20 candidates on its ticket for the Federal Assembly's House of People and 15 candidates for the Czech chamber for the House of Nations, and 30 for the Slovak chamber of the Nations. The following 23 parties submitted candidates:

*Parties, Movements and Coalitions
in the 1990 Elections*

1. Both Republics:
—Communist Party
—Socialist Party
—Social Democratic Party
—Green Party
—Free Bloc
—Coalition of All-People Democratic Party and Association for the Republic
—Alliance of Farmers and the Countryside
—Coexistence
—Czechoslovak Understanding Movement
—Czechoslovak Democratic Forum
—Coalition of Special-Interest Unions
—Civic Freedom Movement

2. Czech Republic
   —Civic Forum
   —Chrisitan and Democratic Union
   —Movement for Autonomous Democracy in Moravia
     and Silesia
   —Friends of Beer Party
   —Organizaton of Independent Rumanians
3. Slovak Republic
   —Public Against Violence
   —Christian Democratic Movement
   —Freedom Party
   —Democratic Party
   —Slovak Nationalist Party
   —Party of Gypsies (Romanies)

The majority of these parties did not receive the necessary five percent for seats in the federal parliament and some that qualified were disappointed. Only seven won seats in the federal parliament, the same number in the Slovak National Council, and five in the Czech National Council. The victorious Civic Forum and the Public Against Violence are both undergoing philosophical and structural changes. The KSC is revising its statutes and discussing further structural revisions, aimed to project a united party with a favorable image. Of the three Christian partners, who had expected a much higher percentage of votes, the CDM and the People's Party declined to be included in the federal government. The Slovak CDM participates in Slovakia and the People's Party is included in the Czech Republic's government.

The nine political parties that failed to win the required five percent minimum of votes in the June elections on July 30 established an "extraparliamentary assembly." This body, representing 17 percent of the electorate, will enable parties to voice their views and comment on the performance of the Federal Assembly as well as the Czech and Slovak National Councils.

PRINCIPAL ECONOMIC INDICATORS

Gross National Product: $142.55 billion (1986)
GNP per capita: $9,180 (1986)
GNP average annual growth rate: (%) 1.4 (1988)
Consumer Price Index (1980 = 100)
    All items: 111.1 (1988)
    Food: 114.5 (1988)
Average annual rate of inflation: 0.9% (1987)

GROSS DOMESTIC PRODUCT, 1986

GDP nominal (national currency): 562.2 billion
GDP real (national currency): 580.7 billion
GDP average annual growth rate: 3.1% (1980–86)
GDP by type of expenditure (%)
    Consumption
        Private: 68
        Government: 8
    Gross domestic investment: 19
    Foreign trade
        Exports: } 5
        Imports: }

GROSS DOMESTIC PRODUCT, 1986 (continued)

Sectoral origin of GDP (%)
    Primary
        Agriculture: 8
    Secondary
        Manufacturing: 60
        Construction: 11
    Tertiary
        Transportation & communications: 5
        Trade: 16
        Finance: }
        Public administration & defense: } 1
        Services: }

ECONOMY

Czechoslovakia is among the largest industrialized countries in Eastern Europe. However, the economy suffers from the constraints imposed upon it by the former Communist regime, including apathetic labor, frequent shifts and turns in economic policy, relative neglect of agriculture and infrastructure in favor of heavy industry, and mismanagement of foreign trade.

The Czechoslovak economy emerged from World War II relatively unscathed. Industry was the largest sector, and the quality of Czech products was comparable to those of the West. Unlike Bulgaria or Rumania, Czechoslovakia was not an underdeveloped country that needed Communist bootstraps to raise its standard of living. It was already well developed, and the transformation of the economy from 1948 was more political than economic.

Planning started in 1949 on the eve of the Korean War, in which Czechoslovakia was a major supplier of heavy armaments to the Communist forces. Foreign trade with non-Communist countries dropped sharply after the 1950s, and the share of Communist countries in total trade rose to over 80% by 1970. Distortion in the economy surfaced in the 1950s as real wages increased and the efficiency of capital dropped. The unrealistic goals of the first five-year plan were not met. The second five-year plan attempted to deal with the failures of the first plan. The third five-year plan (1961–65) was ambitious but equally unrealistic and was abandoned after two years. By this time Czechoslovakia was in the midst of a full-blown recession, caused partly by internal disequilibrium and partly by external factors, such as the cancellation of Chinese orders as a fallout from the Sino-Soviet dispute.

The Soviet development model as used in Czechoslovakia in the early decades of the Communist era suffered from two principal deficiencies. One was its total insulation from market forces and the other the flaws in its statistical system. Production goals were calculated in physical units known as material balances, with no regard to quality or salability. The system stifled innovation and did not provide a basis for evaluating alternatives or increasing productivity. Development was conceived in terms of more factories and production units rather than in terms of their efficiency. The pressure for greater investment and defense production depressed private consumption, which grew more slowly than the GNP, resulting in chronic shortages and long lines in the stores. Plants and construction firms held large inventories of materials to compensate for irregular deliveries from suppliers, and completion of most investment projects required an inordinate amount of time. As the efficiency of capital declined, more investments had to be pumped in to produce the same amount of GNP. Agriculture was the Cinderella sector in that it was neglected. Prices were set by planners arbitrarily and reflected neither scarcity nor cost and bore little rational relationship to each other in the domestic market or to world prices. The Soviet model worked well for the Soviet Union in its early years because it was the only Communist nation and it had immense resources, which could be squandered without reference to the laws of supply and demand. But after World War II the system was faced with the dilemma of over 10 Communist economies, among which no meaningful exchange rates could exist, and no foreign trade could flourish on the basis of arbitrary prices that had no relevance outside national borders. The Soviet model treats foreign trade as a residual in planning. Imports are what is needed to meet the material balances for the economy, while exports consist of products that are useless for the economy. Cost is no real consideration because there is no economic basis for estimating costs. Such inefficiencies do not materially affect the Soviet Union because of its size, but this was not so in Czechoslovakia, where foreign trade played a greater role and affects both growth rates and wages.

The second deep-rooted problem with the Stalinist model is its use of statistical idiosyncrasies to cover up shortfalls in performance and production. The broadest measure of the economy is the social product, which aggregates immediate and final gross production in the "productive" sectors—that is, excluding such services as public administration and professional activities that do not contribute directly to material production. Social product includes double-counting inputs, turnover taxes and replacement of depreciated fixed capital. National income or the net material product excludes material costs, including depreciation. It comes closest to the value-added concept of non-Communist economists, although it is restricted to physical goods and material services. Generally, national income would be expected to increase more rapidly than the GNP because national income does not include some of the slower-growing service sectors.

Additional problems arose because of prices and weights used in calculating broad economic measures. For example, estimates of the Czechoslovak Academy of Sciences sometimes were double and sometimes were half those of official data. The Industrial Production Index included new products at substantially higher prices, although the product itself was unchanged from the earlier model. This kind of bias accentuated the growth rate of industrial sectors relative to others that produced only standard products. Another problem concerned investment and consumption in terms of uses of national income. Consumption was calculated at retail prices and investment at wholesale prices excluding turnover taxes. This meant a consistent exaggeration of investment rates in relation to consumption.

With the death of Stalin in 1953 the trend toward economic reform became strong in all Communist countries, and Czechoslovakia was no exception. However, most of these changes were administrative or technical and posed no threat to party control over the economy. One purpose of the reform was to close the widening technological gap between the West (including Japan) and the Eastern bloc countries. After 1968 the reform movement gained strength under the leadership of Ota Sik. His remedy was to combine the strengths of planning and market forces. The latter would provide immediate signals of imbalances and inefficiencies, while the former would provide broad guidelines of development.

The reform program consisted of several elements. Economic controls were decentralized by expanding the authority and responsibility of enterprises. The central planning authority concerned itself only with long-term overall targets and general guidance for achieving them. Enterprises themselves determined short-term production goals. Enterprises were required to become financially viable and to realize a profit from their sales after covering all costs and various state levies. State subsidies were gradually eliminated, and loss-making firms were shut down. The economic performance of enterprises was judged by realized profits rather than the fulfillment of planned output targets. The change made the enterprises more competitive and more responsive to the needs of consumers. At the same time, the producers were progressively exposed to foreign competition, thus forcing them to increase productivity and lower prices. A realistic system of prices was introduced based on actual costs and reflecting supply-demand conditions and world prices. The system included three categories of prices: fixed, flexible and free. Fixed prices applied to important raw materials and basic consumer goods. Flexible prices were set by producers at a level calculated to maximize their profits but within the limits prescribed by authorities. Free prices, primarily on luxury items and goods in ample supply, were subject to the laws of the marketplace.

The free grant of investment funds out of the state budget was discontinued. Enterprises were required to finance their own investments either from their own resources or through bank loans. Enterprises also were subjected to a capital tax—that is, an interest charge on their total capital investment. All investment projects had to be justified fully with regard to need, effectiveness and cost. Investment by the state was limited to key development projects. The wage and salary system was revised to make it less egalitarian. Under the revised system, wages and salaries consisted of a fixed element determined by an officially set schedule and a flexible increment based on the employee's performance and the level of profits attained by the enterprise. A greater spread was permitted between the remuneration of managerial and technical personnel and the wages of blue-collar workers.

As a means of earning hard currencies, exports to Western countries were stimulated through incentives, including the right of an enterprise to retain a portion of the foreign currency profit. To facilitate the adaptation of domestic producers to world market requirements, enterprises were allowed under certain conditions direct access to foreign markets rather than through foreign trade organizations.

To promote greater specialization and concentration of industrial production, enterprises were organized into branch associations resembling trusts or cartels and under the supervision of branch directorates. The directorates served as links between the enterprises and ministries and were responsible for the performance of the enterprises under their jurisdiction and the provision of such services to them as research, testing, design and marketing.

The reform program had been only partially implemented when the "Prague Spring" was cut short by the Soviet invasion. By the early 1970s all traces of the reforms had vanished and the economy was back on its original track.

In the decade following the Soviet invasion the economy experienced a high growth rate, partly as a result of the earlier stimulation provided by the reforms and partly as a result of a high rate of investment, which reached 33% during the sixth five-year plan (1976–80). Most plants had accumulated stock to draw on, thus eliminating the shortage of consumer goods by the early 1970s. By the late 1970s the situation had deteriorated again. Long lines appeared again, corruption became rampant and black markets flourished. The slowing of the growth rate also was explained by the declining supply of new workers. Whereas 400,000 workers were added during the fifth five-year plan, the labor force increased by only 250,000 during the sixth five-year plan. By 1976 there were 200,000 vacancies in the older industrial establishments.

During the fifth five-year plan (1971–75) the NMP rose by 31.1% and industrial production by 37.5%. Both growth rates declined, the former to 11.3% and the latter to 14.8%, during the seventh five-year plan (1981–85). The eighth five-year plan (1986–90) envisages a growth rate in NMP of 19% and in industrial growth rate of 15.8%, but both are projected to fall far short of the targets. In 1987 Mikhail Gorbachev visited Prague in an apparent effort to persuade the Czech hard-liners to adopt some of the new Soviet-type reforms but without much success.

In 1990 Czechoslovak State Bank president Jan Mitro announced that several large industrial corporations were insolvent and that 38 of them would have to be restructured. The total insolvency was estimated at $1.5 billion. This pessimistic conclusion was confirmed by the secretary of the Committee for Planned Management, Jaromir Matejka, according to whom 30% of Czechoslovak industry was "hopelessly uneconomic and fit only for closure or complete overhaul." A report of the Forecasting Institute of the Academy of Sciences, "Detailed Forecasts about the Czechoslovak Socialist Republic until 2010," predicted that unless market forces were reintroduced, Czechoslovakia would sink to the level of the Third World. An analysis by the distinguished economist Milos Zeman showed that during the 40 years of Communist rule, Czechoslovakia had dropped from the 10th to 40th place among the industrial powers; in the development of professional skills it had dropped to the 50th place, behind Nepal, and 30% of its environment was devasted by pollution.

CENTRAL GOVERNMENT EXPENDITURES, 1986
% of total expenditures

Defense: 7.7
Housing, Social Security, welfare: 26.9
Economic services: 24.2
Other: 41.2

CENTRAL GOVERNMENT REVENUES, 1986
% of total current revenues

Taxes: 9.2
Receipts from enterprises: 72.1
Other: 18.7

PUBLIC FINANCE

Very little information is available on the national budget. The fiscal year is the calendar year. Small surpluses are believed to be more common than deficits. The budget for 1988 was balanced at 394 billion koruny, 3.3% more than in 1987. The major revenue item is the category "From Socialist Economy," which apparently refers to income derived from state economic organizations and the turnover tax. Taxes provide only 20% of the revenues. On the expenditures side, the major categories are National Economy, Culture and Social Welfare, Science and Technology, Defense, and Technical Services, accounting for 38.6%, 41.1%, 3.9%, 11.7% and 2.7%, respectively. The budgets of local administrative organs are included in the central budget. State enterprises are theoretically autonomous, but the government absorbs almost all the surplus funds of the more profitable ones and subsidizes the less profitable or money-losing ones.

The turnover tax originally was employed in the Soviet Union, and it is a uniquely Communist mechanism for influencing consumption patterns and raising revenues at the same time. Applied to goods intended for retail sale, the tax is the difference between producers' costs plus profits and the selling price. The tax is set arbitrarily, with nominal or no taxes on essential products and penal taxes on items such as sugar, tobacco and alcoholic beverages.

CURRENCY & BANKING

The national monetary unit is the koruna (plural: koruny), divided into 100 haleru (singular: haler or heller). Coins are issued in denominations of 5, 10, 20 and 50 haleru and 1, 2 and 5 koruny and notes in denominations of 10, 20, 50, 100, 500 and 1,000 koruny.

The koruna is a nonconvertible currency used only for domestic transactions. It is legally defined in terms of 123 mg. (.004 oz.) of gold. There are two exchange rates: one the official or commercial rate, and the other the noncommercial or tourist rate.

Currency in fact plays only a small role in the economy. Financial transactions are quick and simple, aided by the fact that the state owns everything and there is little risk involved. The process is assisted by the fact that there is only one bank effectively in operation. The State Bank, Statni Banka Ceskoslovenska, is a central bank, commercial bank, investment bank and clearing agent, all combined. It supervises the other banks in the system, although they are in theory and practice subsidiaries of the state bank. The Commercial Bank is primarily the bank for foreign currency transactions. In addition, there are two savings banks, one for each republic, and a smaller bank, Zivnostenska Banka, for small business. Insurance similarly is handled by two companies, one for each republic. Individuals have only savings accounts and no checking accounts. In the absence of checks, collection notices are sent to the payee's bank. There is virtually no consumer credit, and money or capital markets do not exist.

The principal function of this rudimentary system is only as a bookkeeper, because the government controls all investments and the national plan regulates productive facilites. The State Bank does extend credits to enterprises but only to meet targets specified in the plans. If a request for a loan fits into a plan, credit is automatic, giving the State Bank little initiative. Interest rates are employed primarily as a charge to cover bank costs and reflect neither the cost of capital nor the priorities of investment.

The five-year plans have financial counterparts known as financial plans, which express in money terms what the plans do in terms of goals and targets. These financial plans regulate all banking activity. They include allocations to consumption and investment, foreign and domestic financing, and wage and price changes.

Czechoslovakia's external public debt was $8.5 billion in 1990.

EXCHANGE RATE
(National Currency per U.S. Dollar)

1979	1980	1981	1982	1983	1984	1985	1986	1987	1988
10.44	10.94	11.94	12.44	12.84	12.11	11.32	9.71	9.40	8.96

GROWTH PROFILE (Annual Growth Rates, %)

Population, 1985–2000: 0.3
Crude birth rate, 1985–90: 15.2
Crude death rate, 1985–90: 11.2
Urban population, 1980–85: 1.4
Labor force, 1985–2000: 0.7
GNP, 1988: 1.4
GDP, 1980–86: 3.9
Inflation, 1987: 0.9
Energy production, 1980–86: 0.9
Energy consumption, 1980–86: 0.8

AGRICULTURE

Of the total land area of 12.8 million ha. (31.6 million ac.), 6.924 million ha. (17.102 million ac.) are considered agricultural land. Agricultural activity is spread throughout the country. Nearly 70% of the agricultural land is classified as cropland; the remainder consists of fields for hops, vineyards, meadows and pastures.

The major agricultural regions are the western grainlands in the Vltava basin north of Prague, the flatlands in southern Slovakia, the Great Rye Island between the Danube and the Little Danube, and the central and southern Moravian lowlands.

Agriculture depends primarily on rainfall, which is generally adequate, although variations in amount and timing adversely affect cropping. Irrigation facilities cover roughly 4% of the farms, much of them developed after 1975. In addition, 630,000 ha. (1,556,100 ac.) of waterlogged land require drainage before they can be cropped.

Before World War II agricultural land was almost entirely in private hands. From 1919 to 1938 a moderate redistribution of land took place without altering the basic structure of ownership. According to the 1930 census agricultural holding under 50 ha. (123.5 ac.) comprised 80.4% of all agricultural land, and these holdings accounted for 87.4% of the total grain output, 67.6% of the sugar beet production and 69% of the potato crop.

The agricultural sector suffered less during the war than its counterparts in neighboring countries. However, in the aftermath of the war profound changes took place. The first was the loss of Ruthenia to the Soviet Union which led to the loss of 7% of the agricultural land. The second was the decline in agricultural population as a result of the deportation of the Sudeten Germans. The per capita agricultural land increased, but there were fewer people to till this land.

Immediately after the war the government launched a series of land reforms. These reforms may be classified into three phases: the Land Transfer of 1945; the Communist land reforms of 1947; and the New Land Reform Act (also Communist) of 1949.

The Land Transfer of 1945 was a consequence of the expulsion of the Germans and the confiscation of their property. Confiscated farms were redistributed among Czechs and Slovaks, with a ceiling of 13 ha. (32.1 ac.) per farmer. None of the confiscated land was retained by the state. Recipients of the new farms did not receive title deeds immediately but were expected to pay the state the value in one to 15 years.

The first land reform still was under way when the Communists demanded a more radical land reform. The demand was designed to break the power of the politically influential large landowners. The new law provided for the expropriation of all farmland exceeding 50 ha (123.5 ac.). Land obtained through this law was redistributed among small peasants and Communist sympathizers. The reform bill was passed in 1947 despite strong resistance from non-Communist parties.

After the Communist seizure of power in 1948, an early piece of legislation was the New Land Reform Act of 1949, which confirmed the 1947 revision. The 1949 act mandated that no person could own a farm unless he tilled it himself. It also launched an extensive program of collectivization, which was completed by 1950. Both political and economic objectives were involved in the collectivization of agriculture. The main economic motives were the rationalization of agriculture through introduction of large-scale farming and improved state-controlled marketing. Labor shortages in agriculture were to be overcome by mechanization. The government also justified its move by basing it on the cooperative tradition, which was strong in Czechoslovakia even before 1948. Indeed, the official name for collectives is "unified agricultural cooperatives," thus representing collectives as an advanced evolutionary stage of the older cooperative movement rather than as a radical departure from it.

Four types of collectives exist, each representing a different degree of integration of work and property. Types I and II are described as the lower types and types III and IV as the higher types. Although a uniform charter was issued in 1953, distinctions among these types persist.

AGRICULTURAL INDICATORS, 1987

Agriculture's share of GDP (%): 8
Cereal imports (000 tons): 428
Index of Agricultural Production (1979–81 = 100): 119 (1986)
Index of Food Production (1979–81 = 100): 119 (1986)
Index of Food Production Per Capita (1979–81 = 100): 118 (1984–86)
Number of tractors: 138,731
Number of harvester-threshers: 20,606
Total fertilizer consumption (tons): 1,734,000
Fertilizer consumption (100 g. per ha.): 3,365
Number of farms: 1,391,000
Average size of holding, ha. (ac.): 8.1 (20.0)
Size/class
    Below 1 ha. (2.47 ac.): 89.9
    1–5 ha. (2.47–12.35 ac.):
    5–10 ha. (12.35–24.7 ac.):
    10–20 ha. (24.7–49.4 ac.):   } 9.9
    20–50 ha. (49.4–123.5 ac.):
    50–200 ha. (123.5–494 ac.): 0.0
    Over 200 ha. (over 494 ac.): 0.2
Tenure (%)
    Owner-operated: 6.0
    State: 30.8
    Collective: 63.2
Activity (%)
    Mainly crops: 34.3
    Mainly livestock: 24.4
    Mixed: 41.3
% of farms using irrigation: 4
Total land in farms, ha. (ac.): 6,924,000 (17,102,280)
Farms as % of total land area: 54.1
Land use (%)
    Total cropland: 75.3
        Permanent crops: 2.6
        Temporary crops: }
        Fallow: } 97.4
    Meadows & pastures: 24.7
Yields, kg./ha. (lb./ac.)
    Grains: 4,699 (4,194)
    Roots & tubers: 17,187 (15,340)
    Pulses: 2,066 (1,844)
    Milk, kg. (lb.)/animal: 3,857 (8,503)
Livestock (000)
    Cattle: 5,073
    Sheep: 1,104
    Hogs: 6,833
    Horses: 46
    Chickens: 47,000

AGRICULTURAL INDICATORS, 1987 (continued)

Forestry
    Production of roundwood, 000 cu. m. (000 cu. ft.): 18,959 (669,537)
        of which industrial roundwood (%): 92.7
    Value of exports ($000): 401,666
Fishing
    Total catch (000 tons): 20.7
        of which marine (%): 0.0
    Value of exports ($000): 2,879

In Type I, neither land nor livestock is pooled, and machines are the only means of production that may become common property. For agricultural operations collectively performed income is distributed according to the work and services contributed by each member.

In Type II, land may be pooled. However, even if private property in land is maintained, sowing, plowing and harvesting are performed in common, and all field operations are carried out as if the farms formed a single enterprise. The boundaries of individual fields are abolished, but livestock is not collectivized.

In Type III, all land is pooled except for small private plots, which may never exceed 1 ha. (2.5 ac.). All implements and farm buildings are pooled except for small tools, private residences, and stables for livestock. Livestock is pooled, but each member may retain one cow, three goats, two pigs, five sheep and an unlimited number of poultry and rabbits. No compensation is paid for the land, but 80% of the value of livestock, implements and buildings is repaid, according to the ability of the collective. A member is free to withdraw, in which case he may receive land equal in size to that with which he joined, in the same or a different location. The business of the collective is conducted by a general assembly through an elected board of managers. The work performed by members is measured in working units or "workdays." Up to 15% of the collective's net cash proceeds may be paid in form of rent based on the acreage contributed by the members.

Type IV is similar to Type III except that no rent is paid. Type IV is the most unpopular category because it abolishes all private property.

Some state farms had existed in Czechoslovakia even before World War II, but between 1936 and 1976 their size grew from 38,000 ha. (93,860 ac.) to 2.1 million ha. (5.2 million ac.). Under the socialist regime they became models of large-scale production. State farms are engaged in mixed farming, raising both crops and livestock. They also specialize in production of certified seeds and plants, and they possess breeding and experimental stations for livestock. There are two groups of state farms: the first includes large units of confiscated lands; the second, amalgamations of small farms. State farms enjoy priority in the allocation of machinery and fertilizers. They employ hired labor who are rewarded on the basis of achievement.

The Law on Mechanization of 1949 created state tractor stations (STS) with a monopoly in the ownership of agricultural machinery. STS's work closely with collectives, providing them with the services of tractors, combines, threshers and other heavy machinery as well as participating in planning their work. They also assist private farmers. State farms have their own machinery and therefore do not normally avail themselves of STS services.

Government policy encourages cooperation and specialization among agricultural units. In the 1970s joint agricultural enterprises (JAE's) were created, each specializing in a particular activity, such as fattening hogs or cattle, egg production or production of feed mixtures. Some offer agrochemical, construction, land improvement and marketing services. Others are organized geographically, engaging in multiple activities within a single district. These enterprises are particularly important in the production of pork, poultry and eggs.

Management of most large farms is organized hierarchically on three levels. A board of managers consisting of a director and a team of specialists is responsible for the operation of large state farms. In large cooperative farms, management is theoretically vested in a general assembly of members, but its authority has declined over the years and responsibility has become concentrated in boards of economic management consisting of a chairman and a staff of experts. A second echelon of management has responsibility for smaller operations in either a geographical area or in a particular area of production; the latter basically include subfarms in which a degree of specialization occurs in crop production. The third level organizes the labor force, such as the field brigades. In actual practice, the second and third tiers merely carry out the directives of the first. Thus the quality of management is critical, especially on large farms.

The size and complexity of the large farms hamper the flexibility of farm managers. Availability of machinery, fertilizers and livestock feed are beyond the control of management. In addition, the state plan and its targets impose a relatively rigid production schedule. Since the first five-year plan, agricultural planning has involved central direction of production. This was comparatively easy with regard to state farms and collectives, but in the private sector special methods had to be devised to make individual farms conform to central planning. An elaborate production plan devised for the entire country is broken down into regional and local plans, and these, in turn, into farm plans. Each plan contains exact targets, stating the proportion of farm lands sown to individual crops, the yields to be attained and the quantity of fertilizers to be applied as well as the number of livestock and their quantity, weight and milk yields. The plans also provide for compulsory delivery quotas. At the farm level, the plan is enforced in the form of a contract between the producer and the state.

A well-organized system of agricultural statistics was one of the early by-products of agricultural planning. However, resistance by the peasants to exaggerated demands led to great distortion in reporting and gravely disrupted agricultural statistics in general. Thus Czechoslovak agricultural statistics are deficient on even important types of information, such as land under crops.

The government sets prices for nearly all inputs and production in the agricultural sector. Despite periodic price increases, the state subsidizes various inputs and at least some retail food prices. Many state farms require budget subsidies to operate because of low productivity. Farm product prices remain politically sensitive, forcing the regime to agonize over every decision to hike the prices of essential foodstuffs such as milk and beef.

Crop cultivation has become less important than livestock breeding; in 1960 both branches were equal in value of output, but since then the former has lost some 10 percentage points while the latter has gained correspondingly. More than half the cropped area is sown with grains, both coarse grains and bread grains. Although there has been only a small increase in the grain acreage since 1960, there has been a pronounced shift in the grains cultivated, with wheat and barley expanding at the expense of rye. The remaining acreage is devoted to a variety of crops, of which clover, alfalfa and other fodder are the most important. Land planted with hops, fruits and vegetables has increased, while acreage under potato and sugar beet has declined. The reduction in agricultural land and the steady decline in the agricultural labor force have been only partially made up by increases in productivity. Severe periodic droughts also depress agricultural output. As a result, Czechoslovakia has to import between 1 million and 2 million tons of grains annually, most of it for livestock feed.

Cattle and sheep make up most of the livestock herd. Sheep are largely confined to hilly areas with poor pastures and are raised by private farmers. Although some sheep are slaughtered for meat, wool is the primary product. After the collectivization of agriculture, raising livestock has become an increasingly large-scale operation. The major constraint in this sector is the shortage of fodder and feed mixtures, requiring imports from non-Communist countries. Unfavorable weather also has a direct and pronounced effect on livestock conditions, especially on the weight of animals for slaughter. Czechoslovakia's meat consumption, one of the highest in Europe, has been outpacing production for a number of years. Hogs constitute the main source of meat, accounting for half of all meat consumption.

Forests cover about 25% of the land area of Czechoslovakia (38% in Slovakia), thus making it one of the most forested countries in Europe. Conifers make up about 85% of the total forested area in Bohemia, 62% in Moravia and 31% in Slovakia. The forests suffered during World War II from destructive exploitation. Moreover, the loss of Ruthenia, which accounted for 14% of the prewar forest area, deprived the country of some of its richest forestland. In 1950 almost all forestland was nationalized and placed under the Administration of State Forests. Cutting and processing of timber are performed by state enterprises.

As a landlocked country, Czechoslovakia has a negligible fishing sector. Production is derived mostly from pond cultivation and, to a lesser extent, from rivers, mostly the mountain rivers in Slovakia and Bohemia. Carp, tench, pike, eel and trout are among the most common species of fish caught. Domestic needs are supplied mostly by imports.

MANUFACTURING INDICATORS, 1986

Average annual growth rate, 1.2% (1987)
Share of GDP: 16%
Labor force in manufacturing: 37.3%
Value added in manufacturing (million 1980 $): N.A.
    Food & agriculture: 9%
    Textiles: 11%
    Machinery: 38%
    Chemicals: 8%
Index of Manufacturing Production (1980=100): 128 (1988)

MANUFACTURING

Czechoslovakia inherited the bulk of the industrial assets of the Austro-Hungarian Empire after World War I. Industrialization continued in the interwar years, and the country became noted for its armament and heavy industries. The industrial sector came through World War II relatively intact, and on the eve of the Communist takeover Czechoslovakia was one of the most industrialized countries in central Europe.

Following orthodox Communist strategy, the new rulers assigned the lion's share of investment funds to this sector, which became the leading edge of the economy. The share of light industry declined to 14% for food and tobacco goods and to 9% for textiles, leather and clothing but rose to 30% for engineering and metalworking, 11% for metallurgy and 11% for energy. The industrialization of Slovakia has been a feature of postwar programs. The East Slovak Iron Works near Kosice is the largest integrated steel mill in the country.

Although the official Indexes of Industrial Production record substantial annual increases since 1960, independent studies show a steady decline during each of the five-year plans after 1961–65. Deficiencies in the industrial sector include the country's low natural resource base, lack of specialization in production lines, the low level of technological innovation and failure to retire obsolete equipment. Machinery is the main export, but Czechoslovakia is committed by specialization and joint investment agreements with other Comecon members to specific long-term obligations in particular production branches. In the 1970s the government introduced several measures to stimulate the industrial sector. Enterprises were granted limited autonomy in areas other than investments, and enterprises in the same or closely related branches were merged in the form of cartels or trusts. Changes also were introduced in the wage and price system. The net effect of these measures, however, was modest.

A fresh effort was made in the early 1980s to revive the industrial sector. Industrial policy was formulated in a series of directives targeting certain sectors for priority development. This program of "most important structural changes" (MISC) originally covered some 60 sectors and subsectors that were accorded priority access to capital and labor. The most attractive and largest of these subsectors was the nuclear energy industry. Among the major participants in this program were Vitkovice Iron Works in Ostrava, Sigma of Olomouc and Skoda of Plzen. Other large MISC's were automobiles and trucks, computers, semiconductors and integrated circuits. Presumably due to the difficulties of allocating resources to the priority sectors, the number of MISC's was reduced to 31 for the 1981–85 five-year plan. Enterprises were prohibited from undertaking investment projects not included in the plan, and central authorization was required for all industrial construction projects.

MINING

Czechoslovakia's mineral supplies are relatively poor. It has adequate supplies of coal, antimony, magnesite, mercury, uranium, graphite, kaolin and other clays, glass, sands, limestone and common building materials. The outputs of iron ore and other ferrous ores cover only a small part of the domestic requirements. Deposits of nonferrous metals are limited or nonexistent. As a result, the expanding metallurgical industry has to obtain all its supplies from foreign sources.

The mining industry also has been affected by a perennial shortage of skilled labor in the face of a brawn drain from the mining industry into more attractive branches. The high labor turnover is responsible for the high percentage of unskilled workers in mining, estimated at one-third to one-half. To compensate for the labor shortage, the government uses a variety of emergency measures, such as lengthening the workweek, the use of temporary work brigades, shock workers and obligatory overtime.

Four types of coal are mined in the country: anthracite, bituminous brown coal and lignite. Anthracite is mined in southern Bohemia; bituminous coal west and northwest of Prague in an arc extending from Plzen to Kralupy on the Vltava, in northeastern Bohemia and in southwestern and northeastern Moravia; brown coal in western and northwestern Bohemia, in three separate basins extending along the Ore Mountains to the right bank of the Elbe and in Slovakia in the neighborhood of Handlova; and lignite in western Bohemia and the Handlova region in Slovakia. The bulk of the bituminous coal output comes from the Ostrava-Karvina Basin and the brown coal output from the North Bohemian Basin. Nearly all the mines now in operation were opened prior to World War I. All of the bituminous coal output comes from underground mines, and nearly all the brown coal and lignite from strip mines. Until 1948 Czechoslovakia was an exporter of coal, but since then reduced output has forced it to import coal, particularly from the Soviet Union.

Iron ore deposits occur principally in the Nucice-Zdice deposits in the Silurian Basin of Bohemia and the Slovak Ore Mountains west of Kosice. Slovakia produces more than 80% of the total production of iron ore. Most of the output comes from underground mines.

This fact combined with the low average quality of the ore, inadequate mechanization and shortage of skilled workers contribute to high operating costs. As in other minerals, Czechoslovakia is not self-sufficient in iron ore.

Of the minor ferrous metals, the most important is manganese, found in eastern Bohemia, in the Iron Ore Mountains in the Ostrava region and in the vicinity of Kysovce in Slovakia.

Among the nonferrous minerals only antimony, mercury and uranium deposits are large enough for commercial exploitation. The deposits of copper, tin, lead and zinc that had been mined for centuries are largely depleted. Antimony is the most abundant nonferrous metal. Czechoslovakia is the largest antimony producer is Eastern Europe. Major deposits are in the Slovak Ore Mountains. Data on uranium production are classified as secret information.

There is no foreign participation in Czechoslovak mining operations.

ENERGY

Czechoslovakia's energy resources are meager. The principal domestic energy resource is coal. Numerous small oil and gas fields have been dug throughout the country, but production is insignificant and supplies less than 1% of consumption. The expanding needs for energy are met primarily through oil imported from the Soviet Union through pipelines. Although Soviet oil prices are revised annually to reflect world prices, they are substantially below world market prices—according to some sources, less than one-fourth of world oil prices. The Soviet Union also extends credit to Comecon countries to buy its oil.

Prior to World War II, 90% of electric power production came from thermal plants. Because of the postwar coal shortage increasing emphasis was placed on hydroelectric power. Between 1949 and 1960 a total of 23 hydroelectric plants were built. The largest thermoelectric plant is at Ervenice. The power transmission network is based on a 220,000-volt main transmission line extending from Ervenice in northern Bohemia to Nove Mesto and Vahom in western Slovakia. Like much of Eastern Europe, Czechoslovakia lacks sufficient reserve power capacity for peak demand, often requiring curtailment of supply to industrial and commercial customers. The nation's first nuclear power plant (of Soviet design) began operation at Jaslovske Bohunice in 1980. In 1986 two new power units were built at the nuclear station at Dukovany, and in 1987 a fourth reactor was put into operation. Construction of a new unit at Mochovce was completed in 1989, and a unit at Temelin is due for completion in 1992. The proportion of nuclear power in the total power output is expected to reach 50% by 2000. The first hydroelectric generator of the Gabcikovo Nagymaros Danube barrage program, a joint project with Hungary, began operation in 1990.

LABOR

The labor force in 1988 was estimated at 8.2 million, up from 7.29 million in 1979. Czechoslovakia has one of the tightest labor markets in the world, with shortages in virtually every sector. Various official measures to counter the steady decline in the number of workers have had only limited success. Since women already make up 48% of the labor force, further supplies from this source are unlikely. Further, new workers gravitate toward the service sectors rather than the productive sectors. Most large enterprises are able to fill only half of their newly created jobs. Officials also complain of growing absenteeism as well as alcoholism and poor discipline.

The national labor federation is the Revolutionary Trade Union Movement (Revolucni Odborove Hnuti, ROH) whose governing body is the Central Council of Trade Unions. Membership in a ROH-affiliated union is obligatory for all workers. An attempt to establish an independent trade union movement was suppressed in the early 1980s.

Although there is no forced labor (as there was in the early days of the Communist regime), politically suspect persons are forced to do menial work under a constitutional clause that affirms work as a duty. The average workweek is 42.5 hours. Beyond 45 hours workers are paid overtime, and there are some additional bonuses for shift and overtime work. The retirement age is 57 for women and 60 for men. The average pension is 55% of the average wage. A welfare system exists to supplement the pension if need can be demonstrated.

Working conditions are generally acceptable. There is no statewide legally mandated minimum wage. Individual ministries set wage scales in the enterprises under their control.

Amendments enacted in 1988 to the Labor Code generally strengthened the powers of management, which now may terminate a worker's employment within two (instead of six) months, giving no reasons; terminate a worker's employment for any serious infringement of work discipline (rather than for repeated serious infringements, as formerly); search the work force coming to and leaving work; check for alcohol intoxication and drug use; reduce workers' wages for producing substandard products; and extend a worker's probationary period from one to three months.

FOREIGN COMMERCE

An important characteristic of the Czech economy and one it shared with other Soviet bloc countries was the isolation of the economy from the rest of the world. This was partly accomplished by severely restricting foreign currency transactions and confining them to official channels at fixed and favorable exchange rates. Further isolation was achieved by creating state-owned foreign trade companies to serve as buffers between foreign companies and domestic exporters and importers. Gains and losses between foreign and domestic prices were channeled through the government budget. The net effect was to create an autarkic bias in foreign trade that was largely restricted to Comecon countries. Within a decade of the Communist era, the negative effects of such a policy began to be felt, particularly in

MINERAL PRODUCTION, 1983–85

Mineral	1983	1984	1985
Hard coal (000 metric tons)	26,915	26,421	26,223
Brown coal (000 metric tons)	98,878	101,084	98,633
Lignite (000 metric tons)	3,538	3,659	3,682
Kaolin (000 metric tons)	662	668	675
Iron ore			
Gross weight (000 metric tons)	1,903	1,869	1,824
Metal content (000 metric tons)	507	494	N.A.
Crude petroleum (000 metric tons)	93	91	123
Salt (refined) (000 metric tons)	241	243	243
Magnesite (000 metric tons)	662	660	654
Antimony ore (metric tons)*	753	763	N.A.
Copper concentrates (metric tons)*	28,382	29,608	29,296
Lead concentrates (metric tons)*	5,270	5,129	5,244
Mercury (metric tons)	144	152	158
Tin concentrates (metric tons)*	307	425	507
Zinc concentrates (metric tons)*	14,199	14,370	14,441

*Figures refer to the metal content of ores and concentrates.

ENERGY INDICATORS, 1987

Primary energy production (quadrillion BTU)
Natural gas, dry: 0.03
Coal: 1.89
Hydroelectric power: 0.05
Nuclear power: 0.14
Total: 2.11
Average annual energy production growth rate (%): 0.9 (1980–86)
Average annual energy consumption growth rate (%): 0.8 (1980–86)
Energy consumption per capita, kg. (lb.) oil equivalent: 4,845 (10,681)
Electricity
Installed capacity (kw.): 20,371,000
Production (kw.-hr.): 84.775 billion
% fossil fuel: 74.2
% hydro: 4.7
% nuclear: 21.1
Consumption per capita (kw.-hr.): 5,518
Natural gas, cu. m. (cu. ft.)
Proved reserves: 9 billion (318 billion)
Production: 744 million (26 billion)
Consumption: 11.404 billion (403 billion)
Petroleum, bbl.
Proved reserves: 18 million
Years to exhaust proved reserves: 18
Production: 1 million
Consumption: 116 million
Refining capacity per day: 455,000
Coal, 000 tons
Reserves: 5,560,000
Production: 126,429
Consumption: 126,870

LABOR INDICATORS, 1988

Total economically active population: 8.2 million
As % of working-age population: 78.9
% female: 46
% under 20 years of age: 4.1
% unemployed: N.A.
Average annual growth rate, 1980–2000 (%): 0.7
Activity rate (%)
Total: 49.8
Male: 55.2
Female: 44.7
% organized labor: 97

LABOR INDICATORS, 1988 (continued)

Hours of work in manufacturing: 43.2 per week
Employment status (%)
Employers & self-employed: 0.1
Employees: 91.2
Unpaid family workers: 8.5
Other: 0.2
Sectoral employment (%)
Agriculture, forestry & fishing: 12.8
Mining: ⎱ 39.1
Manufacturing: ⎰
Construction: 10.1
Transportation & communication: 6.7
Trade: 11.2
Public administration & defense: 2.2
Services: 18.0

FOREIGN TRADE INDICATORS, 1987

Exports: $23.5 billion
Imports: $23.9 billion
Balance of trade: −$400 million

Direction of Trade (%)

	Imports	Exports
EEC	9.8	9.8
U.S.A.	0.2	0.4
East European countries	74.5	72.0
Japan	0.4	0.2

Composition of Trade (%)

	Imports	Exports
Food & agricultural raw materials	10.6	5.5
Ores & minerals	3.7	0.4
Fuels	30.4	3.5
Manufactured goods	55.4	90.5
of which chemicals	6.7	6.0
of which machinery	32.2	54.2

the slowing of the introduction of new technologies and a serious lag in the competitive design and packaging of industrial products.

In the mid-1970s the economy's structural deficiencies were compounded by rapidly deteriorating terms of trade. Adjustments in the price basis for valuation of imports and exports raised the price of fuels and raw materials (the primary imports) relative to that of manufactured goods (the primary exports). As the terms of trade worsened, more and more exports were required to purchase the same volume of imports. The structure of imports and exports reflects these imbalances. Of the total imports, fuels and raw materials account for over half, machinery and equipment for 36% and agricultural products and manufactured consumer goods for the balance. The single most important import is fuel, and as its major fuel supplier, the Soviet Union dominates imports. Of the exports, machinery and equipment account for a little over half, fuels and materials for over one-fourth and manufactured consumer goods and agricultural products for the balance. Historically the country has been an exporter of armaments and military equipment, but these transactions are not included in trade statistics.

Czechoslovakia does not publish balance-of-trade statistics, but trade with both East and West has long been in deficit. Income from tourism, transit traffic and other services and remittances from Czechoslovaks abroad are not substantial enough to offset these trade losses. Czechoslovakia has received credit from West European sources to finance trade deficits. Although information on these credits is not published, Czechoslovakia's indebtedness is considerably less than that of neighboring countries such as Poland and Hungary, and Czechoslovakia's international credit standing has not suffered. In the 1980s the regime also introduce modest reforms permitting direct transactions between domestic producers and foreign non-Communist markets. The pricing mechanism also was streamlined to facilitate cost-effective development of export products.

Since the collapse of Communism the government has encouraged changes in CMEA's mechanism, and President Havel proposed a regional organization in east-central Europe between Germany and the Soviet Union with ties to Western Europe. In 1990 Prague's trade with the Soviet Union was still over 40% of total, including 37% of its energy supplies. In late July Moscow refused to disclose the quantity of future oil exports to Eastern Europe, but about a one-third reduction was expected during the remainder of the year. In early August, in contravention of their 1989 trade agreement, Moscow indicated a reduction of its exports of raw materials to the CSFR.

The major factor in the reduction of trade with CMEA countries was the currency reform in 1989, devaluing koruny for both tourists and commercially. Hard currency from tourism, which rose 85% between 1989 and 1990, has become a growing source of income. On January 4, 1990, the commercial rate was devalued further, intended to increase exports. Prague's objective is to make the koruna a convertible currency on January 1, 1991. During 1989 exports to non-CMEA countries increased markedly, especially to developing countries, prompted by higher retention of hard currency by producers. Foreign trade monopolies have been abolished.

The principle trade fair is held at Brno.

TRANSPORTATION & COMMUNICATIONS

Czechoslovakia's railroad history began with the building of the first track for steam-powered trains in Moravia between 1839 and 1848. It ran from Breclav along the Morava River through the Moravian Gate and along the Oder River to Ostrava-Bohumin. Called Ferdinand's Nordbahn, it was part of a trunk line connecting Vienna with Cracow. Almost simultaneously with the main line, several branch lines were built, extending from Breclav to Brno, from Prerov to Olomouc and from Ostrava to Opava. In 1845 the Olomouc line was extended westward through Ceska Trebova to Prague and in 1849 to Brno, the capital of Moravia. Prague was connected in 1851 with Dresden, giving the Bohemian capital access to Hamburg, and in 1861 with Nuremberg by a line running through Plzen.

Between 1855 and 1880 private entrepreneurs took over railroad construction. The rail network of the major coal basins and Sudetenland dates from this period. In 1880 the Austrian government resumed its interest in railroads and built a number of secondary lines in the rural regions. Slovakia's railroad system centered on two main lines—Kosice to Bohumin and Bratislava to Zilina, the latter line built by the Hungarian government. In the interwar period, rail links between the Czech lands and Slovakia were strengthened by two new lines running across the Carpathians—one running from Horni Lidec to Puchov and the other from Veseli nad Moravou to Nove Mesto and Vahom. In Slovakia four new lines were added, providing access to the mining and timber regions. Of the total length of trackage, 71% was in Czech lands, which had double the average density of the rail network in Slovakia. Overall, the average rail density was fourth in Europe, preceded only by Belgium, Great Britain and Germany.

At the close of World War II all railroads passed into state ownership and were placed from 1952 to 1954 under the Ministry of Railways and since 1954 under the Ministry of Transportation. With the change of the main flow of trade from the West to the East, freight had to be hauled over longer distances; also, the rapid industrial expansion under the five-year plans placed additional burdens, requiring construction of several new lines. The most important of these new lines were from Brno to Havlickuv Brod, from Vizovice to Horni Lidec in eastern Moravia and from Roznava to Turna nad Bodvou in eastern Slovakia. To meet the transportation needs stemming from increased freight traffic with the Soviet Union, the Kosice to Bohumin railroad was double-tracked, and new transloading facilities and installations for switching of railroad car axles from standard European to Soviet wide gauge were built at the frontier station of Cerna nad Tisou. A program of electrification was begun, which by 1988 had electrified 3,530 km. (2,192 mi.) of track. The length of double tracks has risen to 2,868 km. (1,782 mi.). The railroads suffer from a variety of operational problems, some of which can be traced to the inferior construction of the secondary lines in the 19th century. Others are due to inadequate additions of new equipment, poor maintenance, lack of spare parts and shortage of skilled workers. Maintenance generally is postponed until a breakdown forces repair.

Since its founding Prague has been a focal point in central European communications, and transcontinental trade routes crossed present-day Czechoslovakia's territory since the early Middle Ages, running generally in a north-to-south direction. Among these the Amber Road, the route through the Moravian Gate, provided the passageway between the plains of northern Europe and the Danubian valley. Postal roads and military roads were added from the 17th to the 19th centuries. However, until 1918 the roads were unsuitable for motor traffic. It was only in the interwar period that serious road-building was undertaken. A number of main and secondary roads were broadened and paved with stone, concrete or asphalt; bridges were rebuilt or reinforced; and numerous connections between Moravia and Slovakia were built. After the Communist takeover the major effort has been the building of a 317-km. (197-mi.) superhighway linking Prague, Brno and Bratislava. The government claims that 98% of all villages and towns are within 2 km. (1.2 mi.) of a railroad or bus station. However, the road system, outside of the super-highway, is in a state of disrepair as a result of poor maintenance. Public transportation is operated by the Czechoslovak State Road Transport with 11 regional head offices.

TRANSPORTATION INDICATORS, 1988

Roads, km. (mi.): 73,316 (45,556)
  % paved: 100
Motor vehicles
  Automobiles: 2,694,994
  Trucks: 425,174
  Persons per vehicle: 5.0
  Road freight, ton-km. (ton-mi.): 12.201 billion (8.357 billion)
Railroads
  Track, km. (mi.): 13,116 (8,150); electrified, km. (mi.): 3,530 (2,192)
  Passenger traffic, passenger-km. (passenger-mi.): 19.935 billion (12.387 billion)
  Freight, freight tonne-km. (freight ton-mi.): 69.401 billion (47.536 billion)
Merchant marine
  Vessels: 18
  Total deadweight tonnage: 220,400
Air
  Km. (mi.) flown: 23.4 million (14.5 million)
  Passengers: 980,000
  Passenger traffic, passenger-km. (passenger-mi.): 2.203 billion (1.369 billion)
  Freight traffic, freight tonne-km. (freight ton-mi.): 58.3 million (39.9 million)
  Airports with scheduled flights: 14
  Airports: 130
  Civil aircraft: 40
Pipelines
  Crude, km. (mi.): 1,448 (900)
  Refined, km. (mi.): 1,500 (931)
  Natural gas, km. (mi.): 8,000 (4,968)
Inland waterways
  Length, km. (mi.): 475 (295)
  Cargo, tonne-km. (ton-mi.): 4.825 million (1.438 million)

COMMUNICATIONS INDICATORS, 1988

Telephones
  Total (000): 3,707
  Persons per: 4.2
Phone traffic (000 calls)
  Local: 5,651,000
  Long distance: 415,000
  International: 7,770
Post office
  Number of post offices: 6,634
  Pieces of mail handled (000): 77,288
Telegraph: Total traffic (000) 9,366
Telex: Subscriber lines: 11,119
  Traffic (000 minutes): 77,286
Telecommunications
  1 satellite ground station

TOURISM & TRAVEL INDICATORS, 1988

Total tourism receipts ($): 307 million
Expenditures by nationals abroad ($): 229 million

COMMUNICATIONS INDICATORS, 1988 (continued)

Number of tourists 16,605,700
  of whom (%) from
  East Germany, 47.8
  Hungary, 19.5
  Poland, 17.6
  Soviet Union, 2.3
Average length of stay (nights): 2.9

Inland waterways play a relatively minor role in domestic traffic but figure prominently in foreign trade. Czechoslovakia controls the upper reaches of some major European waterways: the Vltava (Moldau), which runs its full course within the national boundaries; the Elbe (Labe), connecting the country with the North Sea; and the Danube, connecting the country with the Black Sea. The Oder, which has its source in Northern Moravia, can accommodate only small vessels. The major waterways are not connected. The construction of a canal linking the Danube, Oder and Elbe has been planned for close to a century.

Prior to World War II the Elbe-to-Vltava waterway accounted for the bulk of Czechoslovak riverborne freight. Both rivers are fully navigable for 220 to 260 days a year, but traffic comes to a virtual halt in the winter, when the rivers freeze and again in the summer, when the water level drops. From Devin to Szob, a distance of over 161 km. (100 mi.), the Danube forms the southern boundary between Czechoslovakia and Hungary. Bratislava and Komarno, the two Danube ports on the Czechoslovak side, have been trading centers since Roman times. The importance of the Danube has increased since the postwar shift in trade from West to East.

The first regular international air service was established in 1920 by a Franco-Rumanian corporation. It was followed in 1923 by the first regular domestic air service from Prague to Bratislava by the state-owned Czechoslovak State Airlines (Ceskoslovenske Statni Aerolinie, CSA). In 1924 the flight was extended to serve Kosice and in 1926 Brno. In the 1930s there were three airlines: CSA, with 18 aircraft, Czechoslovak Air Transport Company, with 14; and Zlin Air Transport Company (owned by the shoe manufacturer Bata), with six to eight. In 1946 CSA was reestablished as a state monopoly. After 1948, flights to countries outside the Soviet orbit were curtailed. Domestic services also were sharply reduced. Since the 1950s all CSA aircraft have been Soviet-built Ilyushins Tupolevs or Yaks. Of the 130 airports, the largest is Ruzvne, seven miles outside Prague.

DEFENSE

The Constitution of 1960 specifies the "defense of the country and its socialist order" as "the supreme duty and a matter of honor for every citizen." Service in the armed forces is a civic responsibility, and the law mandates a system of universal conscription.

The president is the titular head of the armed forces by virtue of his constitutional designation as commander in chief. Defense policy is formulated by the Council of Defense, established in 1969. Although this council is a governmental body, the interlocking nature of state and party organs ensures that it is amenable to party directions. Its membership is never revealed, but it is believed to include the president, the minister and deputy minister of defense and selected members of the Presidium. In peacetime the council has the responsibility of evaluating threats to national security and determining responses to such threats as well as drawing up the annual defense budget. In wartime the council would oversee national mobilization plans, the direction of the armed forces and civilian resistance. Defense councils also are established at both republic levels. Their purpose and composition are not clear.

The Ministry of National Defense, which operates at a lower level and is subject to both the Council of Defense and the Council of Ministers, is responsible for organization, equipment, training, planning and the allocation of funds designated for defense in the national budget. The minister of national defense customarily is a serving officer, the only four-star general on active duty.

When the military was restructured on the Soviet model in the 1940s, a parallel political network was superimposed on the military organization. Political officers subordinate to the armed forces' Main Political Directorate were assigned to all units, down to and including battalions. The chief of the directorate was one of the four general officers serving concurrently on the Central Committee. However, political officers were subject to normal command of their military commanders. Political indoctrination courses were part of the curricula at military schools and academies and figured prominently in training programs. Common propaganda themes were the leading role of the party and the armed forces in the building of socialism and the contribution of the Soviet Union to the liberation of the country from the Nazis.

Until 1968 and to a lesser extent after that year, the armed forces were strongly influenced by the Soviet Union. The Czechs and the Slovaks are among the few peoples of Eastern Europe who did not harbor ill will against the Russians, and Russophilism was reinforced by the abandonment of Czechoslovakia by the Western powers at Munich in 1938. The armed forces did not resist the Communist coup of 1948, and most troops voted Communist in the first postwar elections in 1946. Under Gen. Ludvik Svoboda, the armed forces were restructured on the Soviet model, with Soviet-made weapons and training programs. By the time the Warsaw Pact was formed in 1955, the Czechoslovak defense forces had gained a reputation of being one of the most efficient and loyal units of the pact forces.

The 1968 Soviet invasion was a tragic interregnum for the armed forces, although they were not called upon to fight the invaders. In the initial period Czechoslovak troops were confined to their barracks but not disarmed. Even after the non-Soviet units in the Warsaw Pact forces were withdrawn, there was a pervasive sense among the professional soldiers of having been stabbed in the back. Some 60% of the officers under age 30 left the service of their own volition. About 11,000 officers and NCO's were expelled from the party and from the service, half of them for having supported Dubcek. In the post-Dubcek era the armed forces suffered from the apathy of the populace. Many observers even questioned whether in a general East-West conflict the Czechoslovak armed forces would remain loyal to the Warsaw Pact.

National defense legislation enacted in 1949 provided for universal male conscription. Most personnel enter the service through conscription—a little more than 70% of the ground troops and 33% of the air force personnel. Since 1968 half of the annual class of draftees has been called up in the spring and half in the fall. The basic term of service is two years in the ground forces and three years in the air force, but those who go into technical training opt for longer terms. The law makes no provision for conscientious objection. The penalty for evasion of military service is a prison sentence of up to five years in peacetime and up to 15 years in a state of emergency. Women also are enrolled in the armed forces but are not subject to conscription.

Reserve obligations for conscripts who have completed their active duty generally last until age 50. Upon discharge the conscript is enrolled in the so-called First Reserve, where he remains until reaching age 40. For the next 10 years he is carried on the rolls of the Second Reserve, who are liable for call-up only in times of absolute emergency. Like other Warsaw Pact nations, Czechoslovakia holds periodic mobilization exercises at the local rather than the national level.

About 72% of armed forces personnel serve in the ground forces (commonly referred to as the army). The army is divided into three categories: arms (*zbrane*), auxiliary arms (*pomocne*) and services (*sluzby*). The first include infantry, armor, artillery and engineers; the second chemical, signal and transportation branches; and the third medical, verterinarian, ordnance, quartermaster, administration, justice and topographic. Tactical organization follows the Soviet pattern, with some minor variations and modification for differences in equipment of local manufacture. There are two military districts: the Western Military District at Tabor and the Eastern Military District at Trencin. The headquarters of the First Army is at Pribram. The five tank divisions are based at Slany, Brod, Tabor, Topolcany and Presov. Additional units are the five motorized rifle divisions, one airborne regiment, two antitank regiments, two conventional artillery brigades, three surface-to-surface missile brigades and two antiaircraft artillery brigades. Three of the tank divisions and three of the motorized rifle divisions as well as the brigades and regiments are considered combat-ready—that is, manned at 75% strength. The remaining units are manned at 50% or lower strength.

The Czechoslovak air force is tactical in nature. About one-third of the air force personnel are conscripts. Many of the combat aircraft are equipped with air-to-air missiles. The air force is rated third among those of Warsaw pact nations in combat-readiness and competence.

DEFENSE INDICATORS, 1988

Defense budget ($): 5.36 billion
% of central budget: 23.9
% of GNP: 3.38
Military expenditures per capita ($): 342
Military expenditures per soldier ($): 2,721
Military expenditures per sq. km. (per sq. mi.) ($): 4,191 (10,858)
Total strength of armed forces: 197,000
  Per capita: 12.6 per 1,000
Reserves: 280,000
Arms exports ($): 1.1 billion
Arms imports ($): 460 million

PERSONNEL & EQUIPMENT

Army
  Personnel: 145,0000
  Organization: Two military districts, 1 with 2 army headquarters; 1 with 3 motor rifle divisions and 1 tank division; 1 with 2 motor rifle divisions and 1 tank division; 1 with 2 tank divisions
  Equipment: 3,400 main battle tanks; 1,250 reconnaissance vehicles; 1,150 mechanized infantry combat vehicles; 2,500 armored personnel carriers; 1,000 towed artillery; 975 self-propelled artillery; 400 multiple-rocket launchers; 36 surface-to-surface missile launchers; 575 air defense guns; 175 SAM's
Air force
  Personnel: 52,000
  Organization: 2 air armies; 4 air divisions; 12 combat regiments
  Equipment: 450 combat aircraft; 45 armored helicopters

Military officers undergo a training course that begins upon graduation from military secondary schools or graduation from regular secondary schools after taking basic premilitary subjects. Also part of the requirement for candidates is a five-month tour of duty. There are several schools and academies within the armed forces. The most important are the Klement Gottwald Military Political Academy at Bratislava, which awards Doctor of Social Political Science degrees, and the Jan Evangelista Purkyne Military Medical Research and Advanced Studies Institute at Hradec Kralove, which awards doctorates in pharmacy and medicine. Five other higher military schools award the title of engineer to their graduates. These are the Antonin Zapotocky Military Academy at Brno, the Ludvik Svoboda Higher Military School of the Ground Forces at Vyoska Morava, the Higher Military Aeronautical School of the Slovak National Uprising at Kosice, the Higher Military Technical School of the Czechoslovak-Soviet Friendship at Liptovske Mikulas and the military faculty of the Higher School of Transportation and Communications at Zilin. Only the first offers postgraduate instruction in all subjects. The Jan Sverma Higher Military School of Rear Services and Technical Support at Zilin offers subjects with an economic rather than a technical orientation.

Following the Soviet model, the program of training is rigorous from the start. The training year is divided into four phases. The first is devoted to individual physical training and live firing practice of weapons. The second phase emphasizes platoon and company training and handling of crew-served weapons. The third phase stresses battalion-level exercises. The culmination of the training year is the large unit—division or higher—exercise, where combined arms operations are conducted under conditions as near to actual combat as possible. There are few frills for the trainees: Free time, furloughs and recreational programs are minimal or nonexistent.

The acme of the training cycle is reached during the increasingly frequent Warsaw Pact exercises of all pact member countries or of the northern tier countries (Poland, Czechoslovakia and the Soviet Union).

From 1968 to 1990 five divisions of the Soviet Central Group were stationed in Czechoslovakia. Although Soviet troops maintained a low profile, their presence was much resented by the local populace. In 1990, agreement was reached with the Soviet Union on the complete withdrawal of Soviet forces from Czechoslovak territory.

Czechoslovakia has a thriving arms industry, producing a wide range of military equipment, making it the most important Warsaw Pact arms producer outside the Soviet Union. The Skoda factory at Plzen is one of Europe's oldest quality arms producer, and its gun named Brno became the model of what is known in the English-speaking world as the Bren gun. Although most of the equipment is of Soviet design, many, like the BM-21, are substantial improvements, and some, like the Tatra and Praga vehicles, are of original Czechoslovak design. Czechoslovakia exports over $1 billion worth of military arms and equipment annually, particularly the famed T-55 tanks.

EDUCATION

Czechoslovakia occupies a special place in the educational history of Europe. The first university in central Europe was established at Prague in 1348, and the famous religious reformer John Hus was one of its early chancellors. His tradition of liberal inquiry was carried on by Jan Amos Komensky (Comenius), who laid the systematic foundation of modern education in his didactic works and who also was an active teacher and organizer of schools in several countries. However, in the Catholic-Protestant conflict in the 17th century, the reformers lost, and education was taken over by Catholic religious orders, notably the Jesuits. In the following century the central state proclaimed the principle of general compulsory schooling—in German in Bohemia and in Hungarian in Slovakia. In addition to general and humanistic studies, the Hapsburgs promoted secondary and tertiary technical learning. The first higher school for engineering in central Europe was established in 1707. After World War I the new Czechoslovak republic took over the existing school system without any radical change in structure. During this time secondary enrollment was less than 8% and tertiary enrollment considerably less. Compared to the Czech lands, schooling in Slovakia was underdeveloped. There were only 276 Slovak-language schools with 390 teachers for a population of 2 million. During the First Republic (1918–39) the school system became centralized under the federal government. The Language Law of 1920 permitted national minorities to educate children in their own language.

With the 1948 Communist coup, the structure of education underwent its first radical change in modern times. All schools were nationalized and reorganized on Marxist principles and on the Soviet model. The new system stressed political indoctrination and "socially useful learning" and established a close relationship between education and work. The legal foundations of the system are laid down in the Constitution of 1960, which granted all citizens the right to a free education. Two other constitutional clauses had an important bearing on education. The first granted Hungarian, German, Polish and Ukrainian minorities the right to an education in their own language. The second established separate educational jurisdictions in the Czech Socialist Republic and the Slovak Socialist Republic, each with its own ministry of education.

Since 1948 six school laws have been passed. The first, ratified in 1948 soon after the Communist coup, nationalized the school system, extended compulsory education to nine years, elevated Marxism-Leninism as the ruling education philosophy and provided universal access through a single-track system. The second, dated May 24, 1953, reduced the duration of compulsory education to bring it into line with the Soviet model. The law of December 15, 1960, stressed the technical character of general education. An additional law, in 1968, extended the general upper secondary school, the *gymnasium*, from three to five years, bringing the duration of preuniversity schooling to 13 years. Higher education is governed by Law 39 of April 10, 1980. The present system is based on the sixth school law, of March 22, 1984, which shortened elementary schooling from five to four years but extended compulsory education from nine to 10 years.

Compulsory education starts with the school year following the sixth birthday of the pupil. However, on application of the parents, exceptions may be made and schooling may be advanced or delayed by one year. The school year starts on September 1 and ends on June 30. The school week is five days, Monday through Friday. In higher education institutions the academic year is divided into two semesters, the first starting the first week in October and ending the second week in January, and the second starting the first week in February and ending in early June. In commemoration of Comenius, March 28 is celebrated as Teachers' Day.

Compulsory education is completed after 10 years of school, usually after the first two years in any of the three main types of secondary school. There are exceptions for children who did not pass elementary school; gifted children who complete elementary school in less than eight years; and handicapped children, who receive a 11-year education.

The expansion of education is reflected not only in enrollment figures but also in changes in the content of the curricula. In 1948 apprentice training was integrated into the educational system by law, and most of the secondary vocational schools were upgraded to become full upper secondary schools, leading to a combined general/professional maturity certificate. In practice, however, the integration took time. Similarly, the secondary vocational schools only gradually came to provide a complete secondary education.

Enrollment figures for women show their growing participation in formal education. Generally, girls prefer secondary grammar and boys secondary vocational schools. This development has given rise to the phenomenon known as "feminization of the *gymnasium.*" As a result, girls receive a proportionately longer and higher formal secondary education than do boys.

The language of instruction is Czech in Czech lands and Slovak in Slovakia. There is no separate provision for Czechs living in Slovakia and for Slovaks living in Bohemia and Moravia. Among minorities, only the Hungarians are numerous enough to use the constitutional right to separate-language schools. As in other areas, the Gypsy-Roms, officially not considered a minority, suffer from discrimination as well as neglect.

There are no private schools of any kind. Even the theological faculties—two for Catholics, two for Protestants, one for the Hussites and one for the Orthodox—are run by the state.

The grading system consists of the following terms and numbers: 1, *vyborny* (excellent); 2, *chvalitebny* (very good); 3, *dobry* (good); 4, *dostatecny* (satisfactory); and 5, *nedostatecny* (unsatisfactory). All children in the first grade are promoted automatically. From grades two through seven pupils are not promoted if they fail in two successive school terms and/or fail to receive acceptable marks in the language of instruction and mathematics.

Preschool institutions include crèches or day nurseries for children up to age three and nursery schools for children between three and six. Crèches are organized by factories and farms under the supervision of the Ministry of Health. They are open primarily to children of employed mothers. Nursery schools are designed to provide pre-elementary education, and their curricula stress acquisition of basic skills suitable for a head start in the primary school.

Primary education is provided in the elementary school *(zakladnil skola),* divided into two levels of four years each. In the first level children are taught by subjects by a single teacher; in the second level they are taught by a team of teachers, each handling a different subject. The curriculum is preparatory and strongly linked with that of secondary schools. Although the curriculum is uniform, instruction in certain subjects can be extended using optional classes and interest circles. Children with learning problems receive intensive care. After-class activities and problem-solving in groups also are used as means of collective, ideological and moral education.

Secondary education is divided into three main streams: Predominantly general education is given in the secondary grammar schools or *gymnasia,* mixed general and vocational education is provided in the secondary vocational schools and predominantly professional education is given in secondary vocational training centers. The ideal integration of general and vocational education, long extolled by educational thoreticians, has not yet taken place. Access to secondary education is in principle guaranteed to all students, but the choice of the school and the study course are limited by the number of available schools. Whereas secondary grammar schools attract fewer applicants than there are seats, some professional courses are extremely crowded, and entry is governed by entrance examinations.

Secondary grammar schools prepare students for higher studies, and approximately 60% to 70% of their graduates apply to higher educational or professional institutions. However, few of them are technically competent in any field and thus are excluded from a variety of jobs. The average enrollment in a secondary grammar school is 200, although there are schools with enrollments of up to 700. Most schools are in the larger cities, but no village is more than 20 km. (12.4 mi.) from one.

Secondary vocational schools offer about 100 technical specializations in addition to general education. Approximately 25% of those receiving the maturity certificate move on to higher education. Secondary vocational schools have a much larger average enrollment of 460, and many of them have hostels.

Secondary vocational training centers, which offer apprenticeship training on the basis of schooling and training contracts between pupils and companies, are equipped with facilities in three areas of education: general, specialized theoretical and practical. About 23% of the courses offered are for two years, 62% are three-year courses and 15% are four-year courses. For companies faced with a shortage of skilled workers, these centers provide a useful catchment area of recruitment.

Higher education is provided in five types of higher schools (*vysoke skoly*): 13 universities, including pedagogical faculties; 10 higher technical schools; two schools of economics; five agricultural schools; and six art schools. Pedagogical faculties are either parts of universities or independent in regions without a university. In addition, universities may have single faculties as branches in other cities.

EDUCATION INDICATORS

Literacy
    Total (%): 100
    Male (%): 100
    Female (%): 100
First level
    Schools: 6,274
    Teachers: 97,385
    Students: 2,088,750
    Student–teacher ratio: 21:1
    Net enrollment rate (%): 87
    Females (%): 49
Second level
    Schools: 343
    Teachers: 9,723
    Students: 134,103
    Student-teacher ratio: 14:1
    Net enrollment rate (%): 42
    Females (%): 63
Vocational
    Schools: 561
    Teachers: 174,044
    Students: 257,968
    Student–teacher ratio: 15:1

EDUCATION INDICATORS (continued)

Third level
    Institutions: 36
    Teachers: 19,459
    Students: 169,011
    Student-teacher-ratio: 9:1
    Gross enrollment rate (%): 15.5
    Graduates per 100,000 aged 20–24: 1,087
    % of population over 25 with postsecondary education: 6.0
    Females (%): 43
Foreign study
    Foreign students in national universities: 4,007
    Students abroad: 1,212
        of whom in
        USA, 59
        West Germany, 586
        Switzerland, 168
        Hungary, 169
Public expenditures (national currency)
    Total: 27.131 billion
    % of GNP: 5.1
    % current expenditures: 95.1

GRADUATES, 1983

Total: 35,241
Education: 5,821
Humanities & religion: 422
Fine & applied arts: 605
Law: 1,345
Social & behavioral sciences: 658
Commerce & business: 4,766
Mass communication: 279
Natural sciences: 542
Mathematics & computer science: 465
Medicine: 2,293
Engineering: 12,800
Architecture: 221
Transportation & communications: 1,069
Agriculture, forestry, fisheries: 3,817
Other: 138

The universities are headed by rectors appointed by the president of the republic on the advice of the respective national government. The deans and heads of faculties are nominated by the rector and appointed by the minister of education.

Admission to higher education is regulated by special provisions. In principle, applicants have to take entrance examinations, but these may be omitted at the dean's discretion, especially where there are fewer applicants than seats. In certain fields, admissions are restricted by quotas. Each year students have to take a maximum of five examinations. In the case of failure, single examinations, or the whole year, may have to be repeated, the latter only twice during a whole course of study. Studies are completed with a final examination in which the defense of a thesis plays a central part. Upon successful completion of a course, titles as well as professional qualifications are awarded. For schools of technology, economics and agriculture, the title is engineer; for art schools, painter or sculptor; and so on. The higher schools are bound to help their graduates find jobs in their corresponding professions—a privilege guaranteed by a common law for the graduates of all professional schools.

Commissions for school education and culture exist at the highest level in each of the federal and republic parliaments. The ministries of education have only the higher schools under their direct administration. The secondary schools are run by 12 national committees; the elementary schools, by their local administration units at the district level.

Nonformal education is conducted in a variety of ways and through various organizations, such as the mass media, cultural agencies, companies and factories, and educational institutions. Secondary and tertiary schools conduct broad programs in adult, continuing and recurrent education. All schools accept pupils from the workplace.

Kindergarten teachers are trained in four-year secondary pedagogical schools. Primary-level teachers (grades one to four of the elementary school) and teachers of nonvocational subjects in secondary schools are trained in universities and independent pedagogical faculties. The former study for four years and the latter for five years. Teachers of vocational subjects are trained in five-year courses in specialized schools. The unified training program for all secondary teachers has given the individual teacher greater mobility.

LEGAL SYSTEM

Constitutionally, the judiciary is an independent branch of government. Judges of the Supreme Court are elected by the Federal Assembly to serve 10-year terms of office. The Federal Assembly also elects a chairman and a vice chairman of the Supreme Court. By law one of these offices must be held by a Czech and the other by a Slovak, and the judges themselves must be drawn equally from the two republics. The Supreme Court has three councils, one each for civil, penal and military cases. The chairman of each council is designated concurrently as a deputy chairman of the Supreme Court. The decisions of the court emanate from "benches," which consist of the chairman and four justices in some instances and the chairman and two justices in other instances.

In each republic there is a Supreme Court with the same structure as the federal Supreme Court. Their judges are elected by their respective national councils for 10-year terms of office. They decide appeals against first-instance decisions from the regional courts.

Regional civil courts sit in the capitals of each of the 10 regions and in Prague. The lowest courts are called district courts and are located in each district. They consist of one professional judge and two assessors or "people's judges." Regional and district professional judges are chosen by the Czech and Slovak national councils; lay assessors are chosen by the district national committees.

Another arm of the judiciary is the Office of the Prosecutor. The federal prosecutor is called the general prosecutor and is appointed and removed by the president. Each republic has its own prosecutor, but they are subordinate to the general prosecutor.

For the first 32 years of its existence—except under the Nazi interregnum—Czechoslovakia operated under two different penal codes. One, used in Bohemia and Moravia, was the Austrian Penal Code; the other, used in Slovakia, was the Hungarian Penal Code. After the 1949 coup the Communists hastily improvised a uniform code, which was in true Stalinist fashion harsh and repressive. Amendments in the 1950s eliminated some of its worst aspects, and a revision in 1961 even guaranteed civil rights—but only on paper. During the "Prague Spring" of 1968 Dubcek published a new Penal Code that effectively safeguarded basic rights, but with his downfall, it was replaced by one even more repressive than the original Code of 1950. A 1973 amendment was more draconian. Subversive activity, sedition, criticism of the Soviet Union and similar offenses could result in prison sentences of up to 12 years. The Penal Code reflected the regime's paranoia about further democratization attempts similar to that of 1968. For example, imprisonment could be invoked against anyone who "publicly defames the republic, the Federal Assembly, the Czech or Slovak National Council or their presidiums or governments, the president or another leading representative of the republic, or a state belonging to the world socialist system or its leading representative." The Penal Code was used effectively by the regime to crush the Charter 77 Movement. Even worse than harassment and imprisonment was denial of means of livelihood. More than 500,000 Dubcek supporters were dismissed from the party and denied employment or the right to practice any profession. Not only were these apostates denied employment, but also the discrimination was carried a stage farther and their children were denied entry into schools and universities. Amendments to the Penal Code in 1973 raised the maximum allowable prison sentence from 15 to 25 years for anti-socialist crimes. Penalties were increased for fleeing the country, and the death penalty was extended to cover many more crimes.

No information is available on prisons or the administration of criminal justice.

LAW ENFORCEMENT

In Czechoslovakia the term "security" is used in preference to "police," and thus the main police agency is the National Security Corps (Sbor Nardodni Bezpecnosti, SNB), which comprises two branches: Public Security (Verejna Bezpecnost, VB) and State Security (Statni Bezpecnost, StB). The VB is a uniformed force that performs routine police duties, while the StB, the former Secret Police, is a nationwide plainclothes force that is at once an investigative agency, an intelligence agency and a counterintelligence agency. The SNB is an armed force subject to military discipline and under the jurisdiction of the military courts. Ranks in the SNB correspond to those in the military. It is a volunteer service, although conscription was used in the immediate post-Dubcek period to rebuild it. The SNB operates its own training institute: the Advanced School, which occupies a large complex in Prague.

VB personnel are the most visible at all levels from federal to local, although it is reported to be a relatively small force. They wear olive drab uniforms identical to the military uniforms, but red shoulder boards and red trimming on hats distinguish them from the military. Public security vehicles are yellow and white, with the initials VB. Both the VB and the StB are deployed throughout the country, with units at the regional and district levels.

No information is available on crime.

HEALTH INDICATORS, 1988

Health personnel
  Physicians: 48,414
    Persons per: 321
  Dentists: 8,307
  Nurses: 146,952
  Pharmacists: 7,375
  Midwives: 6,792
Hospitals
  Number: 377
  Number of beds: 122,842
  Beds per 10,000: 99
Admissions/discharges
  Per 10,000: 1,809
  Bed occupancy rate (%): 81.3
  Average length of stay (days): 13
Type of hospitals (%)
  Government: 100
Public health expenditures
  Per capita: $329.30
Vital statistics
  Crude death rate per 1,000: 11.9
  Decline in death rate: 18.0 (1965–84)
  Life expectancy at birth (years): male, 67.3; female, 74.7
  Infant mortality rate per 1,000 live births: 13.9
  Child mortality rate (ages 1–4 years) per 1,000: 16
  Maternal mortality rate per 100,000 live births: 10.2
Causes of death per 100,000
  Cancer: 238.8
  Diseases of the nervous system: 8.8
  Diseases of the circulatory system: 651.4
  Diseases of the digestive system: 47.0
  Accidents, poisoning & violence: 78.0
  Diseases of the respiratory system: 86.7

FOOD & NUTRITION INDICATORS 1988

Per capita daily food consumption, calories: 3,473
Per capita daily consumption, protein, g. (oz.): 100 (3.5)
Calorie intake as % of FAO recommended minimum requirement: 140
% of calorie intake from vegetable products: 66
% of calorie intake from animal products: 34
Food expenditures as % of total household expenditures: 26.4
% of total calories derived from
  cereals: 30.2
  potatoes: 4.2
  meat & poultry: 13.7
  fish: 0.4
  fats & oils: 17.0
  eggs & milk: 9.8
  fruits & vegetables: 4.0
  Other: 20.7
Per capita consumption of foods, kg. (lb.), l. (pt.)
  Potatoes: 79 (174)
  Wheat: 155 (342)
  Rice: 3.8 (8.3)
  Fresh vegetables: 62.4 (137.5)

FOOD & NUTRITION INDICATORS 1988 (continued)

Fruits (total): 65.8 (145)
  Citrus: 9.0 (19.8)
  Noncitrus: 56.8 (125.2)
Eggs: 32.8 (72.3)
Honey: 0.8 (1.7)
Fish: 5.0 (11.0)
Milk: 9.4 (20.7)
Butter: 8.9 (19.6)
Cheese: 12.3 (27.1)
Meat (total): 88.9 (196)
  Beef & veal: 24.3 (53.5)
  Pig meat: 53.4 (117.7)
  Poultry: 10.5 (23.1)
  Mutton, lamb and goat: 0.7 (1.5)
Sugar: 51.6 (113.7)
Chocolate: 3.0 (6.6)
Margarine: 5.5 (12.1)
Biscuits: 4.6 (10.1)
Beer 1 l. (pt.): 260.1 (549.8)
Wine, l. (pt.) 13.5 (28.5)
Alcoholic liquors, l. (pt.) 3.4 (7.1)
Soft drinks, l. (pt.) 22 (46.5)
Mineral waters, l. (pt.) 15.0 (31.7)
Coffee: 0.2 (0.4)
Tea: 1.9 (4.1)
Cocoa: 1.0 (2.2)

HEALTH

The health service covers virtually 100% of the population. Foreigners also have free health coverage under certain bilateral reciprocal agreements. Although there is a federal Ministry of Health, there is no health budget at the federal level. All health institutions are established and run by local authorities—that is, regional and district committees. A few facilities are operated by the republics' ministries of health. Some federal ministries run their own hospitals out of their budget; others have peripheral interests, such as the Ministry of Agriculture in nutrition policy, the Ministry of Finance in subsidies to the pharmaceutical industry and the Ministry of Labor in sickness and maternity benefits. Specific intervention by federal authorities is reserved to the People's Control Board.

The local health authorities are the Krajski Narodny Vybor (KNV), the regional committee; the Okresni Narodni Vybor (ONV), the district committee; the Krajsky Ustav Narodnlho Zdravi (KUNZ), the regional institute of health; and the Okresni Ustav Narodnlho Zdravi (OUNZ), the district institute of health. Each district is divided into health communities served by the community physician and his staff. The pharmaceutical industry operates as a service under the district and regional institutes of health. There are three levels of hospitals: the teaching hospitals, of which there is at least one or two in each region; super district hospitals, each serving a group of three or four districts; and county hospitals, serving each district.

FOOD & NUTRITION

The average Czechoslovakian consumes 3,473 calories and 100 g. (3.5 oz.) of protein per day. Of the caloric intake, vegetables provide 66% and animal products

34%. Expenditures on food account for 26.4% of total household expenditures. Of the total caloric intake, 30.2% is derived from cereals, 4.2% from potatoes, 13.7% from meat and poultry, 0.4% from fish, 9.8% from eggs and milk, 4.0% from fruits and vegetables, 17.0% from fats and 20.7% from other foods.

MEDIA & CULTURE

The publication of the first journal in Czech coincided with the national revival in the 18th century. Although newspapers were published in German in the territory that is now Czechoslovakia long before then, *Prazske Noviny*, which appeared in 1817, was the first to be printed in Czech. The first Slovak paper, *Prespurske Noviny*, appeared in 1783 in Bratislava, which was then known by its German name of Presspurske or Pressburg.

When Emperor Joseph II lifted the censorship briefly in the 18th century, a spate of new journals and magazines was spawned in response. The most important among them were *Svetozor* (*World Outlook*), edited by Pavel Safarik; *Casopis Cheoeho Museum*, edited by Frantisek Palacky; and *Slovenskyi Narodne Noviny*, edited by L'udovit Stur. Meanwhile, in Prague, the old *Prazske Noviny* had acquired a new editor in 1846— Karol Havlicek, who was to become known as the father of Czech journalism. Havlicek founded the first Czech-language daily, *Narodni Noviny* (*National News*), which soon became the spokesman of the middle-class liberals. The principal voice of the opposition Radical Democrats was *Prazski Vezerni List* (*Prague Evening Page*), which became the most widely circulated paper of the day, with a press run of 5,000. By the end of 1848 a total of 66 newspapers and periodicals were being published in Prague alone.

The next year, the liberal interlude ended with the reimposition of censorship. Most of the papers were suspended, and Havlicek himself was hounded out of town, arrested, convicted of treason and exiled. By 1852 only two Czech-language papers were being published in Prague and one in Moravia. By 1860 the number had dwindled to one, *Prazske Noviny*, with a circulation of 2,000.

In 1860 the authorities relented enough to grant permission to two new journals: the first was *Cas* (*Time*), published by Alois Krasa; the second was *Narodni Listy* (*National Pages*), published by Julius Gregr. *Cas* was the voice of the conservative upper classes; and *Narodni Listy* was the voice of the patriots grouped around Palacky. An ally appeared in 1862 when a group of writers started *Hlas* (*The Voice*), which merged with *Narodni Listy* in 1865.

Despite official harassment, the last quarter of the 19th century witnessed a rapid growth in the number and quality of newspapers. Two of the best-known dailies in the national press were founded during this period: *Pravo Lidu* (*People's Right*), the official voice of the Social Democrats; and *Lidovi Noviny* (*People's News*). By 1900 the number of dailies in Bohemia and Moravia reached 37. In addition, 329 other publications, classified as political periodicals, were published. On the eve of World War I the relative figures rose to 59 and 702.

When the First Republic was established in 1918, its president, Thomas Masaryk, praised the press as one of the forces responsible for its creation. Accordingly, the

---

MEDIA INDICATORS, 1988

Newspapers
Number of dailies: 30
Circulation (000): 4,372
Circulation per 1,000: 280
Number of nondailies: 118
Circulation (000): 1,239
Circulation per 1,000: 80
Number of periodicals: c. 1,500
Circulation (000): 22,123
Newsprint consumption:
Total (tons): 68,200
Per capita, kg. (lb.): 4.4 (9.7)
Book publishing
Number of titles: 8,718
Radio
Number of transmitters: 126
Number of radio receivers (000): 4,209
Persons per radio receiver: 3.7
Total annual program hours: 42,975
Television
Television transmitters: 81
Number of television receivers (000): 4,368
Persons per television receiver: 3.5
Total annual program hours: 9,650
Cinema
Number of fixed cinemas: 2,787
Seating capacity: 861,000
Seats per 1,000: 56.2
Annual attendance (million): 76.6
Per capita: 4.9
Gross box office receipts (national currency): 415.9 million koruny
Films
Production of long films: 63
Import of long films: 177
10.2% from U.S.A.
9.0% from France
22% from Soviet Union
3.4% from West Germany

CULTURAL & ENVIRONMENTAL INDICATORS, 1988

Public libraries
Number: 9,453
Volumes (000): 56,577
Registered borrowers: 2,908,000
Loans per 1,000: 6,447
Museums
Number: 314
Annual attendance: (000): 21,335
Attendance per 1,000: 1,400
Performing arts
Facilities: 81
Number of performances: 21,361
Annual attendance (000): 8,549
Attendance per 1,000: 550
Ecological sites: 28
Botanical gardens & zoos: 42

Constitution of the new state guaranteed press freedom. But as the state began to be assailed by threats from within, particularly from Slovak secessionists and German Sudeten irredentists, freedom of the press was curtailed and prior censorship was imposed. Meanwhile, all the major political parties founded their own dailies: *Cheske Slovo* (*Czech World*) of the National Socialists, *Venkov* (*Countryside*) of the Agrarian Party, *Lidove Listy* (*People's Pages*) of the Catholic Populist Party and *Rude Pravo* of the Communist Party. Not all the papers were political. *Lidovi Noviny* had emerged as one of Europe's best dailies, with a circulation of over 100,000. Another politically unattached daily was *Narodni Politika* (*National Politics*). By 1930 the Czechoslovak press included 115 dailies, 88 papers published every other day and 423 weeklies. This was the high watermark of a free press in Czechoslovakia.

Throttled by the Nazis, the press emerged from World War II much debilitated. One of the first acts of the postwar government, which included Communists, was to ban private ownership of newspapers and to give the Ministry of Information (controlled by the Communists) control over licensing and other press affairs. Through this ministry the Communists controlled the national news agency, Ceteka, the broadcasting agency and the Bureau of Publications. Thus the press was seized by the Communists long before they actually seized political power through the 1948 coup. A new law was passed making membership in the Communist-controlled Czech or Slovak journalists' unions a condition for employment in the media. All opposition papers were suppressed. Of the 44 papers published before the coup, only half survived, and they were reorganized on the Soviet model, with *Rude Pravo* as the flagship.

With the exception of the brief interlude during the 1968 "Prague Spring," the Czechoslovak press remained until 1990 one of the most regimented in Eastern Europe. Press history during the Communist era was one of constant purges of journalists who refused to do the party's bidding or who offered even the slightest criticism of official policies.

There are 30 dailies (although official circulation statistics list only 28), including nine in Prague and nine in Bratislava. The parallel breaks down when it comes to the smaller provincial papers, of which the Czechs have about 60%. Overall, 11 dailies are printed in Slovak, one in Hungarian and the rest in Czech. All are full size, and there are no tabloids. *Rude Pravo* and other major newspapers usually run eight pages an issue, while the smaller provincials average four. About 500 other periodicals and magazines appear weekly and another 1,000 at less frequent intervals. Most of the dailies are published in the morning; Prague and Bratislava have evening papers; the others appear about noon. Most newspapers appear every day of the week, although some skip Mondays. There are no special Sunday editions and no magazine sections. The press is so structured that no paper strictly competes against another. Except for *Uj Szo* (*New World*) (the Hungarian-language daily in Bratislava) and *Prager Volkszeitung* (a German-language weekly in Prague), all major publications are in either Czech or Slovak.

By far the largest in circulation and most influential paper is *Rude Pravo*, the party organ in Prague, followed by *Pravda*, the party organ in Bratislava. The leading dailies are as follows:

Daily	City of Publication	Circulation
Rude Pravo (Red Right)	Prague	950,000
Zemedelske Noviny (Farmer's News)	Prague	342,000
Pravda (Truth)	Bratislava	330,000
Mlada Fronta (Youth Front)	Prague	325,000
Prace (Labor)	Prague	317,000
Praca (Labor)	Bratislava	230,000
Svobodne Slovo (Free World)	Prague	228,000
Lidova Democracie	Prague	217,000
Ceskoslovensky Sport	Prague	185,000
Smena (Shift)	Bratislava	129,000

The post-Communist media in Czechoslovakia are run with a kind of revolutionary fervor, unusual in the West. *Lidovi Noviny* (*People's News*), the organ of the Civic Forum, the new government party, is the most important publication to emerge from the Velvet Revolution. Named after the paper closed down by the Communists in 1952, it was the monthly of the underground Charter 77 Group, and its board of governors included Vaclav Havel and Foreign Minister Jiri Dienstbier. It is published biweekly with a press run of 380,000 copies. Another opposition paper that has emerged aboveground is *Servis/Sport*, the sport in the title being that of baiting the authorities. The paper's 50,000 copies are distributed by students, and there are just three paid staffers, plus 15 to 20 volunteers. Another fledgling newspaper is *Svobodny Zitrek* (*Free Tomorrow*), edited by a well-known journalist, Irena Gerova. There are counterparts of *Lidovi Noviny* in the capitals of the two other federal states: *Verejnost* in Bratislava and *Moravske Noviny* in Brno. The newly created Syndicate of Journalists has sponsored the reappearance of the monthly *Reporter*, a title identified with the 1968 Prague Spring.

The biggest of the provincials is *Nova Svoboda* published in the coal and steel center of Ostrava and with a circulation of 198,000.

As a command media, the Czechoslovak press was insulated from the economic pressures of the marketplace. There is more advertising than is common in the East European press. Most of the ads are placed by state enterprises. The Czech and Slovak journalists' unions have a combined membership of about 5,000. Most journalists are underpaid and therefore have to free-lance to make a decent income.

The national news agency is CTK (Ceskoslovenska Tiskova Kancelar), better known as Ceteka. It was founded in 1918 as a government agency and has remained so ever since. A much smaller and specialized agency, Orbis, supplies information on Czechoslovakia to the foreign media on a commercial basis.

Broadcasting is a state monopoly; radio is operated by Czechoslovak Radio and television by Czechoslovak Television, both under the control of the Press and Information Office. Domestic radio is divided into five networks: Radio Prague, Radio Bratislava, Radio Hvezda, Radio Vltava and Radio Devin. The first two are heavy on information; Radio Hvezda features light entertainment; and the last two feature high-quality programming on the order of BBC's "Third Programme." Originally radio and television were administered jointly, but they were split in 1964. The first television service started in 1954 and the second—in color—in 1970. Except on special occasions, the second channel operates only in the evenings. On weekdays the regular programming begins in midafternoon and continues until 11:00 P.M. or midnight. On weekends it runs from 9:00 A.M. to midnight, with a break in the early afternoon. The principal television programming centers are at Prague, Brno, Ostrava, Bratislava and Kosice. About a third of television programs are devoted to news and information. Both services are supported by license fees and by state subsidies and some advertising. Czech television is linked to the Soviet bloc's Intervision network and also imports television features from Western Europe (though Eurovision) and from the United States. Television programming was dull and full of the banalities of Communist propaganda in the early days; however, spurred by complaints and the challenge of better programming from nearby nonsocialist countries, the dosage of unmitigated ideology has been reduced to allow room for more genuine entertainment.

No information is available on film production.

SOCIAL WELFARE

Czechoslovakia has a comprehensive and universal system of Social Security. Everyone is entitled to free medical care and medicine. Nearly one-quarter of the population receives some kind of pension—the elderly, widows, orphans and the disabled. Because of the shortage of labor, a substantial minority of the elderly are employed.

Women workers enjoy the full complement of maternity and child-care benefits: maternity leave at 90% of pay for 26 weeks with an additional nine weeks in the case of multiple births or single mothers; two years of unpaid leave for child-rearing; and three days of annual leave in case of children's illnesses. There are substantial family allowances in addition to direct grants to families headed by single parents or with handicapped children. Unmarried mothers, widows and divorced mothers cannot be fired if they have a child under three years of age or children between three and 15. After a minimum of 25 years of employment men are pensionable at 60 and women at 53 to 57, according to the number of children reared. Maximum retirement pensions are calculated at 50% to 60% of the average earnings during the preceding five or 10 years. In addition, there are disability pensions, widows' pensions and orphans' pensions. Pensions of private farmers are based on their contributions. There are family allowances for each child.

There is no private welfare system in Czechoslovakia.

CHRONOLOGY (FROM 1945)

1945—President Benes arrives in Moscow and establishes the framework of a provisional postwar government. . . . Soviet tanks enter Prague, and the provisional government begins formal administration. . . . Government decree expropriates all land held by Germans, Hungarians and Czech collaborators. . . . Czechoslovakia cedes Ruthenia to the Soviet Union. . . . All trading companies, industries, mines, banks and insurance companies are nationalized. . . . United States and Soviet Union complete withdrawal from Czechoslovak territory.

1946—Czechoslovak-Hungarian population exchange agreement signed in Budapest. . . . Communists poll 38% in general elections. . . . President Benes is reelected for the third time. . . . Klement Gottwald forms Communist-led coalition government. . . . United States suspends aid to Czechoslovakia. . . . Paris Peace Conference approves Czechoslovak request for a Danubian bridgehead opposite Bratislava.

1947—People's War Crimes courts are dissolved.

1948—Charging non-Communist parties in the National Front, particularly the Social Democrats, with subversion, the Communists stage a coup, seizing government offices, factories, schools and newspapers. . . . All-Communist cabinet is sworn in by Benes; Foreign Minister Jan Masaryk commits suicide. . . . People's courts are reactivated. . . . All non-Communists, estimated at 4,800, are purged from the government. . . . New electoral law is approved, limiting voter choice to a single list. . . . All enterprises employing over 50 persons are nationalized along with the building industry, apartment houses and broadcasting. . . . National Assembly adopts new Constitution. . . . Benes resigns the presidency and is replaced by Klement Gottwald. . . . Benes dies. . . . Antonin Zapotocky is named prime minister. . . . Slovak and Czech Communist parties are merged. . . . Government decree abolishes the provinces of Bohemia, Moravia and Slovakia, replacing them with 19 administrative regions *(kraje)*. The first five-year plan is promulgated.

1949—Council for Mutual Economic Aid (CMEA) is set up. Government issues new Church Law, taking over church property and requiring government sanction of all church appointees. State Office for Church Affairs is established by law. . . . Over 10,000 are arrested in anti-Titoist purges.

1950—Government bans all books published in Czechoslovakia before May 5, 1948. . . . Most monastic houses are confiscated. . . . Government dismisses Gustav Husak, chairman of the Slovak Board of Commissioners. . . . Ministry of State Security is created. . . . New Criminal Code is passed.

1951—In mass purges, members of the Central Committee, including Rudolf Slansky are arrested, tried and executed.

1953—Stalin dies. . . . Gottwald dies within days of returning from Stalin's funeral. Antonin Zapotocky is named president and Vilem Siroky is named prime minister.

1954—Husak is sentenced to life imprisonment.

1955—State of war with Germany is ended.

1957—Zopotocky dies and is succeeded in office by Antonin Novotny.

1960—New Constitution is promulgated. . . . The official name of the state is changed to Czechoslovak Socialist Republic.

1963—Jozef Lenart succeeds Siroky as prime minister.

1968—As proreform Communists gain strength in the Central Committee, Alexander Dubcek is named first secretary, Oldrich Cernik prime minister and Ludvik Svoboda president. . . . The "Prague Spring" is heralded by a number of reforms doing away with the harsher aspects of the Communist regime. . . . An alarmed Soviet Union and its Warsaw Pact allies invade Czechoslovakia and occupy the country. . . . In "normalization" programs, thousands are dismissed, exiled, arrested or executed. Dubcek is replaced as Communist Party leader by Gustav Husak.

1969—Czechoslavkia is declared to be a federal republic consisting of two units.

1975—Husak is elected president in addition to being leader of the party.

1977—Charter 77 is issued by dissidents and restive intellectuals.

1985—Czechoslovakia celebrates the 11th centenary of St. Methodius's bringing the Gospel to the country.

1987—Husak resigns as Communist Party leader and is replaced by Milos Jakes, an economist.

1989—Following the debacle of hard-line communism in Eastern Europe, the Czechoslovak Communist Party gives up its monopoly of power; Husak resigns as president and is replaced by human rights activist and playwright Vaclav Havel; a new cabinet is sworn in under Marian Calfa; non-Communists hold the majority of portfolios in the cabinet.

1990—In national elections, Civic Forum and its Slovak sister party, Public Against Violence, captures 46.3% of the national vote and an overall 170 seats in the 300-seat National Assembly; the Communist Party wins 13.6% of the vote and 47 seats; and the conservative Christian Democratic Union wins 11.6% of the vote and 40 seats. . . . Calfa is renamed premier. . . . Czechoslovakia adopts new official name, Czech and Slovak Federative Republic. . . . Pope John Paul II visits Prague in his first official visit to a Warsaw Pact country outside Poland. . . . Diplomatic ties with the Vatican are restored. . . . Havel hosts meeting of Adriatic-Danube group of nations, consisting of Poland, Hungary, Italy, Austria, Yugoslavia and Czechoslovakia. . . . Havel is reelected president and Alexander Dubcek is elected chairman of the National Assembly.

BIBLIOGRAPHY
BOOKS

Bradley, J. F. *Politics in Czechoslovakia, 1945–71.* Lanham, Md., 1981.

Burke, John Frederick. *Czechoslovakia.* London, 1976.

Busek, Vratislav, and Nicolas Spulber. *Czechoslovakia.* New York, 1957.

Glaser, David. *Czechoslovakia: A Critical History.* Caldwell, Idaho, 1961.

Golan, Galia. *The Czechoslovak Reform Movement: Communism in Crisis, 1962–68.* London, 1971.

Jancar, Barbara Wolfe. *Czechoslovakia and the Absolute Monopoly of Power: A Study of Political Power in a Communist System.* New York, 1971.

Kaplan, Karel. *The Communist Party in Power: A Profile of Party Politics in Czechoslovakia.* Boulder, Colo., 1985.

Korbel, Josef. *Twentieth-Century Czechoslovakia: The Meanings of Its History.* New York, 1971.

Kusin, Vladimir V. *From Dubcek to Charter 77: A Study of Normalization in Czechoslovakia, 1968–78.* New York, 1978.

Mamatey, Victor S., and Radomia Luza. *A History of the Czechoslovak Republic, 1914–48.* Princeton, N.J., 1973.

Marek, Miroslav. *Cultural Policy in Czechoslovakia.* Paris, 1970.

Oddo, Gilbert L. *Slovakia and Its People.* New York, 1960.

Paul, David W. *Czechoslovakia: Profile of a Binational Socialist Country.* Boulder, Colo., 1981.

Pelikan, Jeri. *Socialist Opposition in Eastern Europe: The Czechoslovak Example.* New York, 1976.

Sik, Ota. *Czechoslovakia: The Bureaucratic Economy.* White Plains, N.Y., 1972.

Skilling, H. Gordon. *Czechoslovakia's Interrupted Revolution.* Princeton, N.J., 1976.

Suda, Zdenek. *The Czechoslovak Socialist Republic.* Baltimore, Md., 1969.

———.*Zealots and Rebels: A History of the Communist Party of Czechoslovakia.* Standford, Calif., 1980.

Szulc, Tad. *Czechoslovakia Since World War II.* New York, 1971.

Taborsky, Edward. *Communism in Czechoslovakia, 1948–60.* Princeton, N.J., 1961.

Ulc, Otto. *Politics in Czechoslovakia.* New York, 1974.

Wallace, William V. *Czechoslovakia.* Boulder, Colo. 1976.

Wanklyn, Harriet. *Czechoslovakia.* New York, 1954.

Wheeler, George S. *The Human Face of Socialism: The Political Economy of Change in Czechoslovakia.* New York, 1973.

Windsor, Philip, and Adam Roberts. *Czechoslovakia 1968: Reform, Resistance and Repression.* New York, 1969.

EAST GERMANY

BASIC FACT SHEET

OFFICIAL NAME: German Democratic Republic (Deutsche Demokratische Republik)

ABBREVIATION: GDR

CAPITAL: Berlin (East)

HEAD OF STATE: Chairman of the Council of State Sabine Bergmann-Pohl (from 1990)

HEAD OF GOVERNMENT: Chairman of the Council of Ministers Lothar de Maiziere (from 1990)

NATURE OF GOVERNMENT: Parliamentary democracy

POPULATION: 16,586,490 (1989)

AREA: 108,179 sq. km. (41,768 sq. mi.)

MAJOR ETHNIC GROUP: German

LANGUAGE: German

RELIGIONS: Evangelical Lutheranism and Roman Catholicism

UNIT OF CURRENCY: DDR Mark

NATIONAL FLAG: Tricolor of black, red and gold horizontal stripes with the coat of arms superimposed on the middle red stripe

NATIONAL EMBLEM: A circular red shield surrounded by a garland of yellow wheat sheaves tied at the bottom by a ribbon in the national colors, displaying as its central device a stylized gold hammer and a pair of compasses or dividers

NATIONAL ANTHEM: "Auferstanden aus Ruinen" ("From the Ruins Newly Arisen")

NATIONAL HOLIDAYS: National Day (October 7); New Year's Day; Labor Day; Christmas (December 25 and 26); Good Friday; Easter Monday; Pentecost Monday

NATIONAL CALENDAR: Gregorian

PHYSICAL QUALITY OF LIFE INDEX: 95 (on an ascending scale with 100 as the maximum)

DATE OF INDEPENDENCE: October 7, 1949

DATE OF CONSTITUTION: April 9, 1968

WEIGHTS & MEASURES: Metric

Note: On October 3, 1990 the German Democratic Republic officially ceased to exist when it merged with the Federal Republic of Germany (FRG). The following chapter, written in part before the collapse of the Communist regime in GDR in December 1989, is a profile of the country on the eve of this historic event. It is retained without change for its historical interest.

GEOGRAPHICAL FEATURES

East Germany, or the German Democratic Republic (GDR), is in north-central Europe and has an area of 108,179 sq. km. (41,768 sq. mi.), including East Berlin with 404 sq. km. (156 sq. mi.). The GDR extends 533 km. (331 mi.) north-northeast to south-southwest and 324 km. (201 mi.) east-southeast to west-northwest. It has a total boundary length of 2,607 km. (1,619 mi.) shared with three countries: West Germany (1,381 km.; 858 mi.), Poland (456 km.; 283 mi.) and Czechoslovakia (430 km.; 267 mi.). The Baltic coastline is 340 km. (211 mi.) long.

The GDR was carved from the remnants of the Third Reich and represents the Soviet occupation zone among the four Allied occupation zones. The border with Czechoslovakia is the only one that conforms to the pre-1937 borders. The border with West Germany was delimited by the Potsdam Agreement, which also established the Oder-Neisse river line as the boundary with Poland. The Oder-Neisse line is not officially disputed but neither is it irrevocably guaranteed by the GDR or FRG. The border with West Germany extends from Lubeck Bay on the Baltic Sea southward following prewar state boundaries, tracing the course of the Elbe River for a short distance before traversing southward through the Harz Mountains and then twisting eastward through the Thuringer Wald. In 1972 a Boundary Commission was set up to settle boundary questions between the two states. A bilateral frontier agreement was reached in 1973 to care for frontier waterways and handle environmental problems.

The capital is East Berlin, constituting the former Soviet sector of occupied Berlin. There are no other cities with a population of over 1 million, but the GDR includes three of most noted cities of prewar Germany: Leipzig, Dresden and Chemnitz (now Karl-Marx-Stadt).

MAJOR URBAN CENTERS (population est. 1985)	
East Berlin (capital)	1,215,600
Leipzig	553,700
Dresden	519,800
Karl-Marx-Stadt (Chemnitz)	315,500
Magdeburg	285,000
Rostock	244,400
Halle an der Saale	235,200
Erfurt	216,000
Potsdam	135,500
Gera	131,800
Schwerin	127,500
Cottbus	124,800
Zwickau	120,200
Jena	107,400
Dessau	103,600

East Germany lies in the heart of the northern European plain. The terrain is gentle, and the landscape is marked by few sharp contrasts. There are no significant natural boundaries, and landforms merge into one another. However, the country may be broadly divided into two geographic regions. The northern plain covers most of the country and contains the coastal areas of the far North and lowlands of the center. The uplands consist of mountains and the rolling hills that cover the southern section.

The district of Rostock stretches along the entire length of the Baltic coast. The coastline is uneven but generally flat and sandy. The continuous action of wind and waves has created sand dunes and ridges along the coast, and sandbars have formed, connecting the mainland with some of the offshore islands. The northern sections of Schwerin and Neubrandenburg districts, which also are characterized as coastal, are dotted with marshes and numerous lakes. Although its soils are poor, the coastal regions contain some of the most intensively cultivated agricultural land.

Much of the country consists of the central lowlands, including the districts of Frankfurt, Potsdam and Cottbus as well as portions of Schwerin, Neubrandenburg, Magdeburg, Halle, Leipzig and Dresden. Formed by glacial action during the Quaternary period, the lowlands are dominated by rolling hills and low ridges that rarely reach elevations over 91 m. (299 ft.) above sea level. Numerous lakes cover the landscape, particularly in western Neubrandenburg and around Berlin. Broad valleys, carved as glaciers receded, crosscut the plains, providing natural transportation routes.

The Börderland, a fertile belt of rolling countryside, forms a transition zone from the central lowlands to the uplands in the South. Extending in an arc from Magdeburg and Halle southeast through parts of Leipzig and Dresden, its broadest sections lie along the Elbe and Saale rivers.

The uplands cover about 20% of the southern section, including portions of the districts of Magdeburg, Halle, Leipzig and Dresden as well as Erfurt, Suhl, Gera and Karl-Marx-Stadt. The Harz forms the northwestern section of the uplands, with its highest peak at Brocken (1,141 m.; 3,744 ft.). In the Southwest, extending some 104 km. (65 mi.), is the Thuringer Wald, a narrow ridge of thick woodland. To the southeast, forming the border with Czechoslovakia, is the Erzgebirge, with elevations to 1,213 m. (3,980 ft.).

CLIMATE & WEATHER

The GDR has a temperate climate. The Northwest, open to the maritime westerly winds, experiences little variation, but the Southeast, exposed to the continental influences, has warm summers and cold winters. Daily temperature variations are slight. Mean temperatures in Berlin are 1°C (34°F) in January and 18°C (64°F) in July. Dresden, in the South, averages 0°C (32°F) in January and 19°C (66°F) in July, with an average annual temperature of 9°C (48°F). The average annual precipitation is 610 to 640 mm. (24 to 25 in.), mostly in the summer. The major departure from the average is in the Harz Mountains, where the annual precipitation is as high as 1,470 mm. (58 in.).

POPULATION

The population of the GDR in 1989 was 16,586,490, based on the last official census, in 1981, when the population was 119,145 higher, at 16,705,635. The GDR ranks 101st in the world in land area and 47th in population. The population is expected to decline even further, to 16,552,000 by 1990 and to 16,371,000 by 2000.

Population decline is a phenomenon that began in the aftermath of World War II and has steadily reduced the number of East Germans from a peak of 19.1 million in 1948. The country has experienced a negative growth rate ever since (with the exception of a small increase in the 1960s in the wake of the building of the Berlin Wall). By 2030 the GDR population is expected to stabilize at about 15 million.

The structure and dynamics of the population concern the social planners even as much as the absolute decline in numbers. These problems include a sex ratio highly skewed in favor of females, rapid aging of the people, a shrinking family and a declining share of the under-15-year-olds in the total population. Some of these problems are common to all European countries, but they are much more accentuated in GDR.

The population pyramids of both the GDR and the FRG (West Germany) still reflect—and will continue to reflect well into the next century—the casualties suffered in the two world wars. The lower birth rates began to distort the pyramids even during the interwar years. The GDR has felt these negative effects more severely than the FRG because of the additional losses suffered through emigration to the latter. The number of German civilian and military deaths resulting from World War II is estimated at 3.5 million to 4.5 million, most of them males in the 20-to-44 age group. As a result, the ratio of women to men was already 5:4 in 1950. The surplus of women was especially marked in the 21-to-35 age group, where women outnumbered men by more than 2:1.

Compounding the problem was the expulsion of over 11.7 million ethnic Germans from Eastern Europe. Of these, only 2.2 million finally settled in the GDR. There was a parallel emigration from the GDR to the FRG, consisting primarily of young people of working age. Between 1950 and 1961 a total of 2.7 million to 3.9 million East Germans left for FRG, and the flow was not stanched until the Berlin Wall was built in the latter year.

To these historical and political factors were added natural demographic processes the GDR shares with its neighbors, such as declining fertility, late marriages, increasing popularity of single lifestyles, smaller families, more widespread availability of contraceptives and abortions. Official policy turned pronatalist to counter these alarming trends, and material incentives are offered for larger families. Women receive a one-year paid leave after the birth of a second child. The peak marriage rate of 11.7 per 1,000 was reached in 1970. Even though there was a growing tendency from the 1970s for women to marry young, this gain was offset by one of the highest divorce rates in the world. The GDR also has a high death rate, resulting primarily from an unfavorable age structure. The age structure is lopsided, with over one-fifth of the population over pensionable age in 1986 compared to 14% in 1950.

It is estimated that the GDR will achieve a normal population pyramid by the first decade of the 21st century. The proportion of the elderly is expected to decrease to 15% in the 1990s, while the proportion of those under 15 is expected to decrease initially and then begin an upward trend, thus reducing the dependency ratio. The sex ratio also is expected to improve, and men are expected to outnumber women in the working-age population before 2000.

Like most European countries, the GDR has a high population density. In the North, where few towns of historical significance are found, the density generally is less than in the South. The southern industrial districts have the heaviest concentration of population in the country. The only exceptions to this pattern are the newly developed ports of Rostock, Stralsund and Wismar.

In the central third of the country, East Berlin overshadows all other cities in size and importance. Its population, however, is relatively older than that of the other major centers. In the central region, the other major urban centers are Magdeburg, one of Germany's oldest cities; Potsdam; Brandenburg; and Frankfurt. Potsdam and Brandenburg are geographically close to East Berlin, but Frankfurt lies near the Polish-German border.

Some of the largest urban concentrations are in the southern third of the country; the historic cities of Leipzig and Dresden are there, in addition to eight other cities with a population of over 100,000: Cottbus, Dessau, Halle an der Saale, Karl-Marx-Stadt, Zwickau, Erfurt, Jena and Gera.

Although 80% of all East Germans live in urban areas, only one-quarter live in cities of over 100,000. Historically, Germany has been a country of small and medium-size towns, and the devastation of World War II dampened the trend toward megalopolises experienced in Italy, France, the United Kingdom and other countries. In the immediate postwar period there also was some internal migration from towns along border areas. In keeping with the socialist pattern of urban planning, government efforts are directed toward developing urban centers throughout the country through dispersion of industry. In practice, however, planners have not been successful in reducing rural-urban disparities or in achieving balanced growth among districts. There are no official restrictions on internal movement. However, a shortage of housing and the difficulty of switching jobs have prevented large-scale internal migration. Most migration takes place from small rural areas or small urban centers to medium-size or large municipalities within the same district.

ETHNIC COMPOSITION

The population of the GDR is virtually homogeneous. Germans make up over 99 percent of the population,

---

DEMOGRAPHIC INDICATORS, 1988

Population: 16,586,490 (1989)
Year of last census: 1981   World rank: 47
Sex ratio: males: 47.5;   females: 52.5
Population trends (million)

1930: 15.4	1960: 17.24	1990: 16.552
1940: 16.8	1970: 17.058	2000: 16.371
1950: 18.387	1980: 16.737	

Population doubling time in years at current rate: Population is declining
Hypothetical size of stationary population (million): 15
Assumed year of reaching net reproduction rate of 1: 2030
Age profile (%)

0–15: 19.2	30–44: 19.6	60–74: 11.0
15–29: 22.0	45–59: 19.9	Over 75: 8.3

Median age (years): 36.2
Density per sq. km. (per sq. mi.): 153.1 (396.6)
Annual growth rate

1950–55: −0.49	1975–80: −0.13	1995–2000: −0.01
1960–65: −0.26	1980–85: −0.11	2000–2005: −0.03
1965–70: −0.06	1985–90: −0.07	2010–15: −0.09
1970–75: −0.26	1990–95: −0.05	2020–25: −0.17

Vital statistics
  Crude birth rate, 1/1,000: 13.4
  Crude death rate, 1/1,000: 13.4
  Change in birth rate: −17.0 (1965–84)
  Change in death rate: −1.5 (1965–84)
  Dependency, total: 47.6
  Infant mortality rate, 1/1,000: 11.0
  Child (0–4 years) mortality rate, 1/1,000: Insignificant
  Maternal mortality rate, 1/100,000: 15.6
  Natural increase, 1/1,000: 0
  Total fertility rate: 1.6
  General fertility rate: 50
  Gross reproduction rate: 0.80
  Marriage rate, 1/1,000: 8.3
  Divorce rate, 1/1,000: 3.2
  Life expectancy, males (years): 69.5
  Life expectancy, females (years): 75.4
  Average household size: 3.5
  % illegitimate births: 33.8
Youth
  Youth population 15–24 (000): 2,187
  Youth population in 2000 (000): 2,089
Women
  Of childbearing age 15–49 (000): 4,026
  Child-woman ratio (children per 000 women 15–49): 246
  % women using contraceptives: N.A.
  Abortion ratio per 100 live births: 35.0
Urban
  Urban population (000): 13,231
  % urban 1965: 73; 1985: 76
  Annual urban growth rate (%) 1965–80: 0.1; 1980–85: 0.6
  % urban population in largest city: 9
  % urban population in cities over 500,000: 17
  Number of cities over 500,000: 3
  Annual rural growth rate: −1.5%

---

with the Sorbs officially the "only" minority. According to government statistics the Sorbs number about 100,000 people. Other minorities living in this territory before World War II became victims of Nazi atrocities. There are approximately 400 Jews, most living in East Berlin. They are organized in the Union of Jewish Communities in the GDR, which has struggled to combat anti-Semitism.

The Sorbs (also known as Wends and Lusatians) are descendants of Slavic people who trace their heritage to the seventh century. They live in the southeastern

GDR, near the Czech and Polish borders, in some 160 cities and villages in and around Cottbus, Bautzen and Hoyerswerda. The Sorbs have managed to preserve their national identity, culture and language, although they appear to be integrated into East German society. According to Article 40 of the Constitution "the Sorbs have the right to cultivate their mother tongue and culture," and the government's Office of Sorbian Culture provides information about these interesting people. In Sorb schools German is the secondary language, but the Sorbs speak German fluently. Teachers study at the Sorbian Teacher Training College and at the Institute for Sorb Language and Culture at Karl Marx University.

In mid-1989 GDR had about 170,000 foreigners from many countries. The majority are guest workers (*Gastarbeiter*) from communist-ruled countries, especially Vietnam, Mozambique, Cuba, Angola and China. About 10% of the total are students or trainees. Some 6,500 Poles are day workers. With increased emigration of Germans, the GDR requires even greater numbers of foreign workers. The life of the *Gastarbeiters* in GDR has been unhappy. They experience loneliness, segregation, hostility, neofascism and racism—officially nonexistent phenomena. Only recently, with *glasnost*, has attention been focused on this German behavior in the media and, reluctantly, in the regime. In March 1989 the Volkskammer passed a law giving foreign residents over 18 years of age the right to vote, claimed to be evidence of official opposition to hatred, racism and prejudice; but in the months since then there has been no evidence of changed behavior.

LANGUAGES

German is the official language of the GDR, spoken not only in East and West Germany, but also widely throughout Western and Eastern Europe. It also is the official language of Austria and an official language of Switzerland and Luxembourg. German belongs to the Indo-European family of languages and is one of the most influential in the world, particularly in science, literature and philosophy. Specialists generally consider two major divisions of the German language: High German (Hochdeutsch), spoken in the higher regions of central and southern Germany; and Low German (Plattdeutsch), of the northern flatlands. The differences lie in the pronunciation of consonants, spelling and idioms.

While regional variations—e.g., Bavarian or Bayerische—and local dialects are numerous, High German is spoken by the intelligentsia, taught in schools and employed in literature and by the media. As in other cultures, purists have been concerned with the infusion of foreign words and idiomatic expressions into German usage.

The Sorbian minority speaks a Slavic language. Article 40 of the GDR Constitution extends to the Sorbs the right to their mother tongue and cultural development.

RELIGIONS

The region of the former united Germany that now constitutes the GDR is precisely the region that was historically most Protestant since the Reformation. Thus, although there are no official statistics on religious affiliations—it being awkward for a professedly Marxist regime even to acknowledge the existence of religious affiliations—it may be safely said that most East Germans are Protestant. That proportion, however, has been steadily declining for many reasons and now is estimated at about 50%. Another 8% is Roman Catholic. The proportion of non-Christian religions is quite insignificant. Like Poland and unlike some other East European regimes, GDR rulers have not been militantly antichurch, and both Protestants and Catholics enjoy considerable and real freedom.

Most Protestants are affiliated with one of eight territorial Lutheran churches that are members of the Federation of Evangelical Churches in the GDR (Bund der Evangelischen Kirchen in der Deutschen Demokratischen Republik, BEK, formerly the Union of Protestant Churches). Four are United Lutheran-Reformed churches (Berlin-Brandenburg, Greifswald, Gorlitz and Saxony); three are Lutheran (Saxony, Thuringia and Mecklenburg); and the eighth is the Evangelical Church of the Union, which serves Anhalt and also is Lutheran-Reformed in tradition. Prior to 1968 all these churches were members of the All-German Evangelical Church of Germany. In 1968, under pressure from the government, the East German churches withdrew from the all-German organization. A major organization that supported the break was the Association of Protestant Clergy in the GDR, established in 1958 with state support.

The formation of the federation has not led to any doctrinal or organizational unity. On the other hand, the churches suffer more from internal decline than from official pressures. Traditionally the Lutheran churches have retained a great deal of autonomy and administrative independence from one another, and differences in theology and structure have been preserved as the means of maintaining such autonomy. Each of the territorial churches elects its own bishop and has its own synod. Elections and administrative matters are wholly independent of state control.

Another dilemma facing the churches is that of declining membership, compounded by a shortage of pastors and decreasing numbers of divinity students. Almost half the churches in many regions are without a regular pastor or pastoral visitation—a situation that contributes to a general decline in religious practice and lay participation. As the pressures of secularization take their toll, baptisms and church weddings have been reduced to one-fourth and one-fifth, respectively, of their number in the 1940s. Only one in 10 attends church regularly and less than 1% is actively involved in church affairs. The disaffection is particularly strong among the young—an ominous sign of the times, portending a greater decline in the future. The creation of the BEK has enabled the churches to present a common front to the regime, but as yet the churches do not speak with a common voice and lack the moral authority to retrieve leadership in society.

Besides the BEK churches, there are smaller groups of Protestants, the largest of which are the Baptists and the Methodists.

The Roman Catholic Church did not normalize its status until the signing of the 1970 treaty between West Germany and Poland and until the 1973 basic treaty between the two Germanys removed all barriers to a reorganization of the dioceses. The ancient archepiscopal office of Gorlitz, attached until then to the Polish archdiocese of Wroclaw (Breslau), was made independent, and the diocese of Berlin, also a suffragan to Wroclaw, was made directly dependent on the Holy See. Three new apostolic administrators were appointed for the territories of Erfurt-Meiningen, Magdeburg and Schwerin. The Catholic Church has shared in the general decline of the faith in GDR, but the absence of statistics makes it difficult to assess the pastoral situation. Because of the advanced age of most priests, lay deacons have been ordained in many areas as auxiliaries to take over pastoral duties.

The Protestant churches are financed through offerings and a voluntary income tax on members. The churches also own about 202,429 ha. (500,000 ac.) of land that the government has not expropriated, and they operate 50 agricultural enterprises. A substantial portion of church financing is contributed by churches in West Germany and is used primarily for renovation of old buildings and construction of new churches. The government offers support for charitable institutions, such as hospitals, homes for the aged and day-care centers. The Catholic Church operates 40 hospitals and 167 special homes and centers.

The Constitution of 1968 as amended in 1974 has three provisions regulating church-state relations:

Article 39, paragraph 1 states: "Every citizen of the GDR has the right to freedom of conscience and to the free practice of the religion of his choice." Paragraph 2 states, "The churches and other religious communities regulate their affairs and exercise their activities within the structure of the constitutional and legal regulations of the GDR. The regulations in detail may be defined in special conventions." Article 20, paragraph 1 also grants "freedom of conscience and religious opinion." Article 6, paragraph 5 prohibits "manifestations of hate against creeds, races and peoples." However, unlike the Constitution of 1949, the Constitution of 1968 did not acknowledge the juridical personality of the churches. All religious matters come under the State Secretariat for Religious Questions.

Although the churches have experienced great difficulties since the assumption of power by the Communists, they have not been the object of brutal repression in the same manner as in Czechoslovakia. Church leaders had fought the Nazis during the war, and many had been imprisoned along with Communists. No top church leaders have been jailed in the GDR. In fact, the church has experienced less persecution under the Communists than during the *Kulturkampf* in the 19th century. The churches were exempted from the agrarian reforms and they did not lose their charitable and

educational institutions. All churches receive regular state subsidies for their charitable institutions. The state also provides materials for the reconstruction of old churches destroyed during the war, and more rarely for the construction of new ones. Protestant and Catholic seminarians are exempt from military service, and the universities of Berlin, Leipzig, Halle, Jena, Rostock and Greifswald each retain a faculty of Protestant theology. Moreover, the Christian Democratic Union (CDU) is one of the legal political parties in the GDR.

This is not to say that state-church relations were entirely smooth and that the church did not suffer from real discrimination. In practice, the regime discouraged participation in religious practices by an approach that was more carrot than stick. The best jobs and educational opportunities were open only to card-carrying party members and were denied to professing Christians. All religious activities organized outside religious buildings required official permission. The principal religious ceremonies (baptism, confirmation, marriage) were rivaled by parallel rites with socialist ceremonies. The most significant of the socialist rituals was the *Jugendweihe* (youth dedication), which took place on the 14th birthday and thus corresponded to the confirmation or the bar mitzvah. The child received ideological initiation instruction before his or her formal initiation, which included a vow of loyalty to the state.

Once the critical issue of the disaffiliation of GDR churches from their West German counterparts was solved, the state was prepared to grant more concessions to the churches. President Walter Ulbricht did so in the 1960s, and his successor Erich Honecker did so in 1978. Among the major concessions were:

• grant of weekly radio and television time to both Catholic and Protestant churches
• ending of discrimination against children of believers in education and public service
• access to prisons for part-time chaplains
• eligibility of clergy and church workers for state pensions
• support for church-run kindergartens
• payment of rent to the church for the use of some 40,486 ha. (100,000 ac.) of its agricultural land by the state
• support for church cemeteries
• permission for the clergy to visit old people's homes outside visiting hours
• support for construction of new churches
• permission to import some church literature from the West

HISTORICAL BACKGROUND

Germanic tribes first appeared in European history in the first century B.C., when the Cimbri and Teutons clashed with Roman legions in Gaul and on the Alps. Later, as the Roman Empire began to disintegrate, the Alemanni, Burgundians, Franks, Lombards, Ostrogoths and Visigoths settled in the region between the Rhine and the Elbe. However, it was not until Charlemagne (768–814) that the Germans acquired a political unity. After Charlemagne's death, his empire soon fell apart. In the course of various inheritance divisions, a western and an eastern realm developed, with the eastern realm being called Deutschland, or the land of Deutsch-speakers. Germany's western frontier was fixed relatively early and has remained fairly stable. But the eastern frontier was pushed eastward for hundreds of years until it contracted in the 20th century.

The transition from East Franconian to German Reich usually is dated from 911, when Conrad I was elected the first German king. The official title was Frankish king; later Roman king while the name of his realm was first Roman Empire, and later Holy Roman Empire, to which the words "of the German Nation" were added. It was an electoral monarchy that later became dynastic. Otto I, the greatest of his dynasty, unified Germany and Italy and was crowned first holy Roman emperor in 962. His successors were engaged in constant struggles within Germany as well as with the papacy, and it was not until the new Salian dynasty that a new upswing occurred. Under Henry III (1039–56), German power reached its zenith, only to decline once again. In 1138 a century of rule by the Staufer or Hohenstaufen dynasty began. Its most brilliant ruler was Frederick I "Barbarossa" (1115–90), who led the empire into a new golden age. Under his successors, the empire broke up. With the end of Hohenstaufen rule in 1268, the temporal princes became sovereign land dukes. Germany did not again become a true nation-state until the 19th century.

The Hapsburgs took power in the 13th century under Rudolf I (1273–91). The Golden Bull or the imperial Constitution issued by Charles IV in 1356 regulated the election of the German king by seven electors privileged with special rights. These sovereign electors and their towns gradually gained in power and influence. The towns linked into leagues, the most important of which, the Hanseatic League, became the leading Baltic power in the 14th century. The power of the emperors was curtailed and increasingly eroded by capitulations, which they negotiated at their elections with the various princes. The empire was further weakened in the 16th century by the Reformation, which led to the division of Germany into two camps. In 1522–23 the Reich knights rose in revolt and in 1525 the Peasants' Revolt broke out, the first revolutionary movement in German history. The dukes profited most from the Reformation when they were given the right to dictate the religion of their subjects by the Treaty of Augsburg of 1555. The Treaty of Augsburg did not end the conflict between the faiths, although four-fifths of the country had become Protestant. In the following decades the Catholic Church was able to recapture many areas. A local conflict in Bohemia triggered off the Thirty Years' War (1618–48), which widened into Europe's worst and perhaps last major religious conflict. Not only did the war devastate and depopulate much of Germany, but also the 1648 Treaty of Westphalia ceded territories to France and Sweden and confirmed the withdrawal of Switzerland and the Netherlands from the Reich.

In the 18th century, Prussia rose to become the premier German state, especially though the military brilliance of Frederick II (The Great), its ruler from 1840 to 1876. During the French Revolution and the Napoleonic wars German nationalism resurfaced and triumphed briefly in the Frankfurt Parliament of 1848. The next few decades witnessed the rise of Prussia under its autocratic prime minister, Otto von Bismarck. After a series of successful wars (1864–71) with Denmark, Austria and France, Bismarck brought about the union of German states (excluding Austria) into the Second Reich in 1871. In 1871 Wilhelm I was proclaimed the German emperor in the Versailles Hall of Mirrors, signaling the fall of France and the rise of Germany as a European superpower. Bismarck avoided further wars but instead created an elaborate system of alliances. With the advent of Wilhelm II as German emperor and the dismissal of Bismarck, the delicate international equilibrium was disturbed after 1890. Under Wilhelm II Germany undertook a collision course with the other major imperial powers, leading to World War I, in which it suffered an ignominious defeat. Both the military and the monarchy collapsed, and Wilhelm II abdicated and fled the country. Germany became a republic in 1918.

The new state, known as the Weimar Republic, was more anarchy than republic. The Social Democratic Party, which as the majority party was charged with the transition to the new political order, left the political structure of the Second Reich untouched. The armed forces still were under the command of the imperial officer corps, while the reactionary bureaucracy entrenched themselves in the administration. In 1925 Field Marschal Paul von Hindenburg was elected president. Bedeviled by inflation, the Ruhr occupation by France, and Communist and Nazi coups, the Weimar Republic's final death blow came with the world economic crisis of 1929.

Not only did the Weimar Republic die unmourned, but it also begat a monster in Adolf Hitler, whose star was in the ascendant. On January 30, 1933, Hitler became Reich chancellor. The 12 years that followed were among the blackest in German history. It witnessed one of the most brutal dictatorships, the virtual annihilation of the Jews in Germany and the bloodiest war in military annals. The Third Reich was consumed in ashes in a vast *Götterdämmerung* in comparison with which all other historical disasters paled into insignificance. Most of Germany lay in ruins and under the heels of its conquerors. It appeared to have no future.

For postwar history, see Chronology.

CONSTITUTION & GOVERNMENT

The German people have a long and rich history, but the history of the German Democratic Republic (GDR; Deutsche Demokratische Republik, DDR) dates only from its establishment in October 1949. The GDR's 41-year history was one of dual control, German and Soviet, the former by the Socialist Unity Party (Sozialistische Einheitspartei Deutschland, SED). At the Yalta and Potsdam conferences (1945) the victorious Allies agreed to a protocol dividing Germany and Berlin into zones of occupation. German institutions would be reconstructed on democratic principles, but the Soviet practice of democracy proved totally different from that of the Western Allies. As a result of Soviet policy of exercising totalitarian control over Eastern Europe, including the Soviet Zone of Germany, the U.S., U.K. and French zones were united in September 1949 into the Federal Republic of Germany (FRG), and on October 11 the Soviet Zone was proclaimed as the German Democratic Republic. The GDR was immediately recognized by the Soviet Union and its Communist allies. In the multiparty governmental structure the SED held undisputed control, supported by the Soviet Union and its powerful military forces on GDR territory.

The GDR had two constitutions—1949 and 1968—and extensive constitutional amendments, adopted in 1974. Its first Constitution, drafted by the SED in 1946 and redrafted on May 30, 1949, was adopted on October 7 of that year. It established an "antifascist" parliamentary form of government with a multiparty system. Although the Constitution was democratic in form, resembling the Basic Law of the FRG and even the Weimar Constitution of 1949, the SED was the ultimate authority. The Constitution provided for two houses—the State Chamber (Länderkammer), or upper house; and the 400-member People's Chamber (Volkskammer), or lower house. The *Länder* were the traditional units of German government, with varying degrees of autonomy. A single largely ceremonial president was elected by the strongest group in the Volkskammer and recalled by a two-thirds vote of both houses. Four days later, the two chambers in a joint session elected Wilhelm Pieck as president. Thus administration of East Germany was formally transferred from the Soviet military to the GDR. The State Chamber proposed laws, but the Volkskammer possessed formal legislative authority. The latter elected the government (Regierung), with the largest party proposing the prime minister. The SED was assured of controlling the government, but any party or mass organization with at least 40 delegates was given constitutional assurance of representation.

The legislature was of no real significance in the GDR. Elections were held every four years, the single list of approved candidates assuring the SED of unanimity in their short sessions, devoted to speeches and formal approval of laws. In July 1952 the SED announced an ideological event: the building of socialism. Without a referendum or constitutional amendement the Länder were replaced by 14 administrative districts (*Bezirke*) with East Berlin the 15th. Without the Länder the State Chamber was itself abolished in 1958, contributing to the centralization of the SED's power. In the 1950s constitutional amendments affected the government as well. With the death of President Pieck in 1960 the SED undertook major political changes designed to strengthen the role of its leadership, particularly that of Walter Ulbricht, its first secretary. The Volkskammer replaced the office of the president with the Council of State (Staatsrat), a collective presidency with enhanced powers, especially accruing to its chairman, Ulbricht. The Council of State discharged the responsibilities of the Volkskammer between its sessions, directed its committees, issued orders, interpreted laws and supervised the Council of Ministers. Moreover, the Volkskammer created the National Defense Council with Ulbricht as chairman, responsible to the Council of State. The Staatsrat appointed at least twelve other members of the Defense Council, approved its decisions and was empowered to mobilize in the event of a national emergency.

The Seventh Congress of the SED (1967), at Ulbricht's request, called for a new Constitution to reflect societal developments. Accordingly, a commission of the Volkskammer was established in December of that year to produce a draft. After the formality of a public debate and a referendum, the new Constitution was promulgated on April 9, 1968. Having incorporated previous amendments, the basic law contained no dramatic changes: The GDR was declared a "socialist state of the German nation," ideologically at the same level as the Soviet Union and some other East European allies; the SED was accorded the leading role in the state; the economy was based on "socialist ownership of the means of production"; and inheritance was restricted to "personal property." The National Defense Council became responsible to the Volkskammer as well as to the Council of State.

The Constitution of 1968 repeated most of the provisions pertaining to human rights, extending some but constricting others. For example, the former right of emigration was withdrawn, residence was restricted to the GDR, strikes were abolished and organizing other trade unions was forbidden. The other rights were conditioned on their exercise with "the principles of the Constitution."

Within several years, however, substantial changes were made in the Constitution, stemming from adoption of new policies and SED leadership disputes. First Secretary Ulbricht became an obstacle to improved Soviet-FRG and GDR-FRG relations. Moscow engineered his removal as party leader and chairman of the National Defense Council in 1971. He was succeeded in both posts by Erich Honecker. The Council of Ministers reduced Ulbricht's powers as chairman of the Council of State—the head of state—in 1972. After Ulbricht's death in 1973, Willi Stoph became head of state. This and other significant changes were incorporated into the amended Constitution of October 7, 1974, adopted without a referendum, as required by the Constitution. The reference to a "German nation" in the Constitution of 1968 was deleted in 1974. Article 1 pronounced the GDR as a "socialist state," to be "led by the working people and its Marxist-Leninist party"—i.e., the SED. According to Article 47, the state's structure was implemented on the basis of "democratic centralism," the same operational principle in the party statutes.

The responsibility of the Council of State, elected for five years, of acting for the Volkskammer between sessions was withdrawn, as were the Council of State's powers to issue decrees, interpret laws, determine constitutionality of laws, direct the Volkskammer's committees and propose the prime minister. The remaining powers approximated those of the president under the

Constitution of 1949 but became the province of the Staatsrat, not its chairman. The Council of State's authority regarding the National Defense Council, the Supreme Court and the procurator-general remained essentially unchanged.

The executive branch of the government consisted primarily of the Council of Ministers (Ministerrat) or the government. Not only terminology but also authority changed over the years, with the powers of the Council of Ministers increasing while those of the Council of State decreased. SED leader Honecker, its general secretary, became chairman of the Staatsrat in 1976 following changes in leadership, and Politburo member Willi Stoph became prime minister; the latter had been prime minister earlier, from 1964 to 1973. While other parties had formal representation in both bodies, the preponderance of power was firmly in the hands of the SED, with Honecker heading the party, state and National Defense Council, as had Ulbricht.

Under the Constitution of 1949 the government was elected by the Volkskammer, with the prime minister proposed by the largest group. In 1950 the government came to be called the Council of Ministers, similar to the situation in the Soviet Union and other East European countries. A 1954 law provided for a Presidium of the Council of Ministers, also in the pattern of the Eastern bloc countries, and consisting of fewer members meeting more frequently between the full Council sessions. The Presidium acquired substantial executive authority. The decrees of the Council of Ministers and of individual ministers had the force of law. In 1972 the Council of Ministers became the highest organ of executive and administrative power.

Chapter 3 of the amended Constitution of 1974 was devoted to the Council of Ministers. As the government, the Council of Ministers directed the execution of the state's policy pertaining to the political, economic, cultural, social and defense sectors. The Council ensured the development and administration of the national economic plan. In supervising the execution of foreign policy, the government expanded universal cooperation with the USSR and the other socialist states and guaranteed the GDR's "active contribution to the strengthening of the community of socialist states." The Council concluded and denounced treaties; defined domestic and foreign policies; submitted bills and drafted regulations to the Volkskammer; directed, coordinated and supervised the activities of the ministries, other state organs and district councils; and issued decrees having the effect of law.

The Council of Ministers was composed of the chairman or prime minister, the head of government; deputy prime ministers; and ministers. The prime minister was nominated by the largest group in the Volkskammer; he then organized the Council of Ministers, all of whom were formally confirmed by and responsible to the Volkskammer for a five-year term. The Council of Ministers selected from among its members a Presidium, which guided the day-to-day activities of the Council. The prime minister directed the activities of the Presidium as well as of the whole Council.

Thirty-eight political parties and groups registered to participate in the first free and democratic elections in East German history on March 18, 1990. A three-party coalition Alliance for Germany, supported by FRG's Christian Democratic Union (CDU), registered a 48% vote, a resounding popular voice for unity, economic reform, political pluralism and democracy. Despite its former alliance with the SED, the East German CDU received 41% of the total vote. The German Social Union (DSU), allied with the Bavarian Christian Social Union, obtained 6%, and the Democratic Awakening (DA) less than 1%. The Social Democratic Party (SPD), which had high expectations, and the previously Communist but reformed Party of Democratic Socialism (PDS), received 22% and 16% respectively. The latter two parties had substantial support in East Berlin.

A coalition was required to form a government. Following lengthy negotiations, complicated by charges of collaboration by candidates with secret police, a grand coalition materialized. On April 9, the conservative alliance, led by CDU, which won a plurality in the March 18 elections, and the Social Democrats decided to form a government that was approved by the Volkskammer four days later. CDU leader Lothar de Maiziere (50) became prime minister. The coalition included the following parties and their share of the 24 ministerial posts: CDU (11), SPD (7), Liberals (3), DSU (2), and DA (1). Among the ministers were Protestant clergy (leaders of the SPD, DSU, and Democratic Awakening).

The new government was approved by a vote of 247 to 109, with 23 abstentions. The premier received a higher margin (265-108-9 respectively). The coalition government agreed on a one-for-one (Bonn proposed two-for-one) DDR mark conversion for DM when unity was achieved, to obtain five of 18 voting seats of the FRG's central bank, and to support membership in NATO only if that pact revoked its forward defense and flexible response policies. Also, the government agreed to military reductions of both East and West German armies and recognized the border with Poland. The Party of Democratic Socialism (PDS), which succeeded the former Communist Party and received 66 of the 400 parlimentary seats, was excluded from the government.

A political compromise was reached with the parliament approving August 22–23 the date of October 3 on which to hold unification elections. Also, the Volkskammer ratified the treaty for all-German elections scheduled for December 2. On August 30 the FRG government and the opposition parties settled the last obstacle for the Bundestag's ratification of the unification treaty—the abortion issue. East Germany was able to preserve its permissive law—allowing abortion on demand—through 1992. After arduous negotiations the treaty was signed by East and West German governments on August 31.

SPD's concurrence was required for ratification of the comprehensive document—some 1,000 pages—by two-thirds in the legislatures. The two Germanys agreed on Berlin as the capital with the proviso that the all-German parliament would decide the locale for the government and the parliament. All East German laws outside FRG's Basic Law, the European Community or the treaty, are to be compatible with West German laws within five years. Bonn's Basic Law was amended to recognize the achievement of unity. This internal unification treaty paved the way for formal unity on October 3. On September 12 the foreign ministers of the four World War II Allies and the two Germanys—the "Two-plus-Four"—signed a treaty ending the Four Power rights in Germany, "suspending" them as of October 1. The agreement became formally effective when all governments ratified it. On September 20 both German parliaments ratified the accord, the FRG's Bundestag by 442 to 47 and the GDR's Volkskammer by 299 to 80, with one abstention. The latter met for the last time on October 2—to lower the East German flag.

Until November 1989 non-SED parties were represented in the government in a subservient role, with each of the four parties allotted one ministerial-level position. Obviously, these parties were in a minority position and operated within SED policies. The SED held the preponderance of the posts, including the significant ones for control. Mounting public pressure for economic reform, political pluralism, travel and human rights intensified by mass demonstrations and flight during the fall of 1989 resulted in a leadership crisis. The unprecedented pressure forced the resignation of the GDR's government on November 7 and a major shakeup of the SED's Politburo. The surprising and dramatic resignation of the entire 44-member Council of Ministers, including Prime Minister Stoph, followed rejection by the Volkskammer's Constitution and Legal Committee of the government's draft law on travel, which provided for 30 days abroad annually. As tens of thousands of East Germans streamed across Hungary and Czechoslovakia, the committee declared for visa-free, unrestricted travel.

The following day, November 8, Hans Modrow, a new Politburo member but a reformer and himself a demonstrator in Dresden, was proposed by new General Secretary Egon Krenz as the new prime minister. Modrow, who headed the SED's Dresden branch since 1973, opposed Honecker's resistance to change. Before a mass demonstration on October 26 in Dresden, Modrow declared prophetically, "The pace of change that has started will cause a revolutionary transformation." The next day, November 9, the GDR ended its travel and emigration restrictions to the West. By November 16 Modrow had organized a coalition government that was reduced from 44 to 28 members, with the four non-Communist parties increasing from four to an unprecedented 11 positions. However, no new group was included. On November 18 the Volkskammer confirmed the government, with five deputies voting against confirmation and six abstaining. The composition of the Council of Ministers by parties was as follows: SED, 17 positions; Liberal Democrats, four, including one of three deputy prime ministers; Christian Democrats, three; National Democrats, two; and Farmers' Party, two. Clearly, the preponderance of power continued to be in the hands of the SED, whose leadership, however, undertook constitutional and legislative changes toward liberalization. These included joint ventures in the economy, foreign investment, a more meaningful separation of powers, downgrading of state security, a greater role for women, reorganization of the GDR's administrative districts and a new election law. However, the Politburo members also indicated a determination to maintain a power position in the GDR.

RULERS OF EAST GERMANY
President
Chairman of the Council of State since 1960
October 1949–September 1960: Wilhelm Pieck
September 1960–August 1973: Walter Ulbricht
August–October 1973: Post vacant
October 1973–October 1976: Willi Stoph
October 1976–October 1989: Erich Honecker
October–December 1989: Egon Krenz
December 1989–March 1990: Manfred Gerlach
March–December 1990: Sabine Bergmann-Pohl
Prime Ministers
October 1949–September 1964: Otto Grotewohl
September 1964–October 1973: Willi Stoph
October 1973–October 1976: Horst Sindermann
October 1976–November 1989: Willi Stoph
November 1989–April 1990: Hans Modrow
April–December 1990– : Lothar de Maiziere
Communist Party (Socialist Unity Party) Leaders
Secretary-General, 1950–53
First Secretary, 1953–76
General Secretary since 1976
July 1950–May 1971: Walter Ulbricht
May 1971–November 1989: Erich Honecker
November 1989–January 1990: Egon Krenz
January 1990– : Gregor Gysi

CABINET LIST, JULY 1990

Position	Incumbent	Affiliation
Prime Minister	Lothar de Maiziere	CDU
Deputy Premier and Minister for Internal Affairs	Peter-Michael Diestel	CDU
Ministers:		
Argiculture, Forestry, and the Food Industry	Peter Pollack	SPD
Construction, Housing, and Urban Development	Axel Viehweger	BFD
Culture	Herbert Schirmer	CDU
Disarmament and Defense	Rainer Eppelmann	DA
Economic Affairs	Gerhard Pohl	CDU
Economic Cooperation	Hans-Wilhelm Ebeling	DSU
Education and Sciences	Hans-Joachim Meyer	I
Environment, Energy, and Reactor Safety	Karl-Hermann Steinberg	CDU
Family and Women	Christa Schmidt	CDU
Finance	Walter Romberg	SPD
Foreign Affairs	Markus Meckel	SPD
Health and Social Services	Juergen Kleiditzsch	CDU
Justice	Kurt Wuensche	BFD
Labor and Social Affairs	Regine Hildebrandt	SPD
Media Policy	Gottfried Mueller	CDU

CABINET LIST, JULY 1990 (*continued*)		
Position	Incumbent	Affiliation
Post and Telecommunications	Emil Schnell	SPD
Regional and Local Affairs	Manfried Preiss	BFD
Research and Technology	Frank Terper	SPD
Trade (Domestic) and Tourism	Sybille Reider	SPD
Transportation	Horst Gibtner	CDU
Youth and Sports	Cordula Schubert	CDU
Chairman, Prime Minister's Office	Klaus Reichenbach	CDU

BFD: Union of Free Democrats—The Liberals
CDU: Christian Democratic Union
DA: Democratic Awakening
DSU: German Social Union
I: Independent
SPD: Social Democratic Party

FREEDOM & HUMAN RIGHTS

The GDR is geographically on the westernmost edge of the Soviet zone of influence in Europe. This position has determined its human rights policies.

In 1987 the GDR ratified the U. N. Convention Against Torture. Specific laws are on the statute books against abuse of prisoners. A new law made it a crime with penalty of up to 10 years' imprisonment for a state official to mishandle a person, either physically or psychologically. However, Amnesty International in its 1988 report cited reports from former prisoners who claimed that they had been beaten, chained, and held for prolonged periods in solitary confinement. The same charges were made by the Council of Europe in its 1986 report.

Security agencies had blanket authority to detain and interrogate citizens on suspicion alone. Politically active opposition group members were sometimes harassed through recurrent police interrogations and arrested with or without warrant. Although the Criminal Procedure Code set a limit of three months on investigatory proceedings, prosecuting authorities had no difficulty extending this period. The right of an accused to a defense attorney from the beginning of an investigative proceeding and to notification of all interested family members in the case of an arrest existed on paper but was commonly overlooked by the officials. Recent legal developments in these areas have worked in favor of the accused.

Because the Penal Code was deliberately vague defining political crimes, the defense always was at a disadvantage in proving the innocence of the accused. For example, "antistate agitation" and "asocial behavior" were broad catchphrases that could be applied in a variety of situations in which no crimes were committed.

Generally, the public was excluded from trials involving security and political issues. Although the accused could select their own attorneys, such attorneys were hard to find in a system where lawyers were themselves at the mercy of the government. However, official attitudes regarding the rights of the accused are changing; excessive pretrial detention is falling into disfavor, and the rights of defense attorneys to obtain copies of investigative documents and to discuss with their clients are being strengthened.

The government never admitted to holding any political prisoners, nor did it publish criminal statistics under this category. However, the FRG Ministry for Inner-German Relations announced that it bought freedom for 1,500 political prisoners in the GDR in 1986, for 1,247 in 1987 and for 506 by October 1988. The Salzgitter Center, an FRG government office that monitors GDR human rights abuses, registered some 25,000 prosecutions for political offenses in the GDR over the past 25 years, over half of them for attempts to emigrate illegally. The sentences for such offenses ran from 18 to 24 months. Under a general amnesty in 1987 a total of 24,621 persons were released, including all prisoners except those convicted of murder, espionage or war or Nazi crimes. The number of political prisoners was esti-

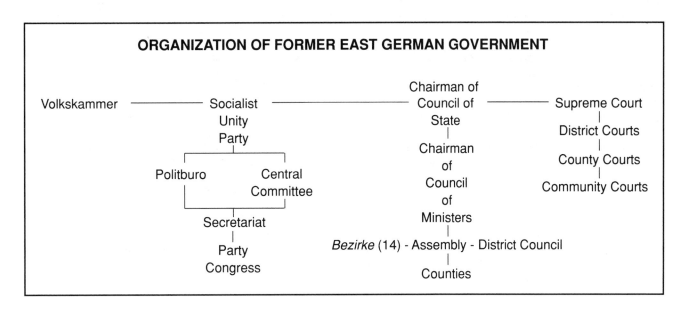

ORGANIZATION OF FORMER EAST GERMAN GOVERNMENT

mated in 1988 at over 1,000 by official West German sources; at 6,000 to 7,000 by the International Society for Human Rights; and at 7,000 to 10,000 by Helsinki Watch.

Assisted by informers, the Secret Police could open mail; install listening devices; and place people under surveillance, subject them to interrogation and intimidation and arrest them without due process. Evidence obtained through phone tapping and interception of mail was admissible in court. Police could enter and search a house without a prior warrant and obtain court approval retroactively. Young people were not forced to join the official Free German Youth but were pressured in other ways to do so. GDR citizens had to obtain government approval to marry foreigners. Persons holding professional positions were not permitted Western contacts or to travel abroad. Beginning in 1989, East Germans had the right to challenge in local county courts administrative acts affecting their civil rights, such as travel, emigration, property rights, compensation for damages and applications to obtain a building permit or to open a private shop or business.

Freedom of speech remained severely circumscribed. Public dissent could lead to prison sentences. However, in keeping with government efforts to cultivate a less repressive image, the authorities were increasingly reluctant to punish publicly dissenting speech. In most cases those engaging in free speech were merely picked up, detained for a while and then released without charges being filed. In a similar vein, periodicals were becoming bolder in their treatment of subjects formerly taboo. From time to time samizdats appeared on the scene, but generally they had a short life before they were uncovered and muzzled. The circulation or importation of most printed materials required an official import. More recently these controls have been relaxed for most publications other than those patently anti-GDR. Ironically, the restriction against foreign publications had been used since 1987 against Soviet magazines, such as *Sputnik*, for "distorting" certain events in Soviet-German relations in the Stalin era. Travelers were interrogated or arrested simply for possessing unlicensed printed material. Western newspapers and magazines were generally unavailable at public newsstands. Western journalists could not travel without prior permission or contact potential sources directly. For the average East German, contact with Western journalists was technically illegal. Western reporters covering politically sensitive events or even rock concerts were roughed up and their cameras were smashed by the security police.

West German television was viewed by 80% of the East German population, and West German radio was heard throughout the country. The government did not attempt to jam or otherwise interfere with these broadcasts.

Book publishing houses practiced self-censorship and promoted only works with a positive socialist content. All works had to receive official clearance before publication, performance or exhibition. Some works were banned completely, while others were published only outside the country under contracts negotiated by state-run agencies; still others were permitted to be published, performed or exhibited only in mutilated form.

However, beginning the late 1980s there was a limited relaxation of official controls and more openness toward new cultural expression. At the quadrennial Writers' Conference in 1987, authors were more outspoken than they had been for years. Similarly, the Filmmakers' Congress called for more innovative themes. Some previously banned books began to appear in East German editions, and some controversial plays were performed without official interference.

Academic freedom was severely limited by law. All areas of academic inquiry were strictly controlled. Teachers who allowed open classroom discussion of unapproved themes or topics or who deviated from the party line were disciplined. Many prohibited books were kept under lock and key in university libraries and loaned only to carefully screened and authorized personnel.

The constitutional freedoms of assembly and association extended only to party-affiliated organizations. The only exceptions were the church assemblies that were permitted to hold periodic congresses. All professional associations were headed by loyal party members in good standing, and dissidents and critics were summarily expelled.

Religion was the one area where human rights survived relatively unscathed. Despite the official commitment to atheism and numerous bureaucratic restrictions, the churches maintained their position as the only non-Communist voices in the GDR. The evangelical churches also were the only institutions bold enough to plead on behalf of those persecuted or discriminated against by the government. Relations with religious minorities improved during the late 1980s. The state took an unprecedented and active role in the 50th-anniversary commemorations of *Kristallnacht*, the Nazi pogrom against the Jews, and supported restoration of Berlin's largest synagogue and the establishment of a Jewish museum and cultural center. A new Mormon temple was dedicated in Berlin in 1988 with official participation, and Mormons as well as Christian Scientists experienced no interference. Western clergy were permitted to attend Evangelical Lutheran Church synods and lay conventions, and some GDR religious leaders were permitted to attend similar meetings in the West.

Restrictions on religious activities were relatively minor. All church-sponsored events and publications were monitored closely, and the government conveyed its displeasure with some of their tenor. After the Evangelical Lutheran and Catholic churches held their first ever ecumenical conference in 1988, during which some of the participants expressed sharp criticism of official policies, the state attempted to pressure church newspapers into printing only highly expurgated accounts. This censorship and the Evangelical Lutheran Church's efforts on behalf of would-be emigrants strained church-state relations briefly.

Most citizens were free to travel anywhere within the country, except within special border zones or near military installations. Technically they were not free to change their place of residence without government approval, but normally this required only registration with the police.

Women were underrepresented at both the lower and upper levels of the ruling Socialist Unity Party and the government. Of the 26 members and candidate members in the Politburo, two were female; in the 161-member Central Committee, 16 were female; in the 30-member Council of State, six were female; and there was one woman in the Council of Ministers.

CIVIL SERVICE

Possessing the leading role in the GDR, the SED exercised executive-administrative power at the national, district, county and lower levels. In the tightly structured system, upper-level appointments and assignments in the government reflected the SED's direct involvement. As in other Communist countries, the SED had its own vast bureaucracy, operating at all levels of government administration. Also, as elsewhere in Communist countries, there was no comparable Office of Personnel Management, as in the United States. At the national level, ministries and other organs had a personnel office *(Personalbüro)*, which had responsibility for personnel matters.

The SED's involvement in government personnel was through its Central Committee Secretariat's Cadre Department, to ensure loyal and disciplined public servants. The Politburo and the Secretariat determined the election or appointments of officials at the highest echelons. The Secretariat's Cadre Department communicated horizontally and vertically through the hierarchical party apparatus.

The GDR had no particular educational institution to prepare candidates for civil service specifically. As in other Communist countries, the primary sources were the universities (Berlin, Leipzig, Halle, Jena, Rostock, Greifswald and Dresden), the numerous colleges and technical institutes, and the secondary schools. The Academy for State and Law, in Potsdam, prepared students for the Foreign Affairs Ministry. In November 1989 several ministries and offices were combined into the Ministry of Education and Youth. Various ministries maintained close contact with educational institutions, and at the universities the SED and Free German Youth (Frei Deutsche Jugend, FDJ) representatives were members of councils functioning at all sections (formerly faculties). All of these links participated in varying degrees in identifying potential prospects for public service.

LOCAL GOVERNMENT

For purposes of local government the GDR was divided into 14 districts *(Bezirke)*, each of which was named for its principal city. East Berlin, claimed as the capital, also was a district, although its incorporation into East Germany was not officially recognized by Britain, France and the United States, three of the four powers that technically continued to control the entire city.

The mayor of the city was a member of the Council of Ministers.

Each district had an elected district assembly, which elected a district council as its executive. The district assembly had as many as 200 deputies, depending on the population. The council usually had 18 to 20 members, of whom the Socialist Unity Party members were the majority. To a large extent, the district councils functioned more as organs of the central government than as popular representative institutions.

Districts were subdivided into counties *(Kreise)*, of which there were more than 200, including the East Berlin counties. Each county had a county assembly and an elected executive organ, the county council. Counties were classified as urban *(Stadtkreise)* or rural *(Landkreise)*. The smallest unit of local government having a representative body and a council was the community *(Gemeinde)*, of which there were more than 9,000.

POLITICAL SUBDIVISIONS				
		Area		Population
Districts	Capitals	Sq. Km.	Sq. Mi.	(1986 est.)
Berlin, capital city	—	403	156	1,215,586
Cottbus	Cottbus	8,262	3,190	883,308
Dresden	Dresden	6,738	2,602	1,775,574
Erfurt	Erfurt	7,349	2,837	1,235,546
Frankfurt	Frankfurt	7,186	2,774	707,100
Gera	Gera	4,004	1,546	741,320
Halle	Halle	8,771	3,386	1,790,835
Karl-Marx-Stadt	Karl-Marx-Stadt	6,009	2,320	1,875,918
Leipzig	Leipzig	4,966	1,917	1,378,456
Magdeburg	Magdeburg	11,526	4,450	1,252,143
Neubrandenburg	Neubrandenburg	10,948	4,227	619,623
Potsdam	Potsdam	12,568	4,853	1,121,099
Rostock	Rostock	7,075	2,732	901,722
Schwerin	Schwerin	8,672	3,348	592,231
Suhl	Suhl	3,856	1,489	549,598
TOTAL		108,333	41,827	16,640,059

FOREIGN POLICY

The foreign policy of the former German Democratic Republic was cast in its Constitution. According to Article 6, the GDR "pursues a foreign policy serving socialism and peace, international friendship and security. The GDR is forever and irrevocably allied with the USSR." Also, "The GDR is an inseparable part of the community of socialist states," it is "faithful to the principles of socialist internationalism," it supports "peaceful coexistence" and it "works for security and cooperation in Europe." Article 7 provided for the GDR's National People's Army "close comradeship-in-arms with the armies of the Soviet Union and other socialist states." The GDR had a special relationship with the Soviet Union since World War II, and unique contacts with the Federal Republic of Germany (FRG). Mikhail Gorbachev's policies of glasnost and perestroika, permitting increased flexibility in expanding relations with Western countries, were implemented more forcefully in the GDR by the momentous political changes in the fall of 1989. The new leadership began to depart from the hard-line policy of Erich Honecker.

The GDR's alliance with the Soviet Union and the East European Communist countries had been the bedrock of its foreign policy. Following the war, the Soviet Union, in accordance with international agreements, occupied and its military administration governed the eastern zone of Germany. Nothing of importance was undertaken without Soviet authority. The 1946 forced merger of the Social Democratic Party with the Communist Party into the Socialist Unity Party (SED), the establishment of the *Länder* governments in the same year and the organization of an economic commission in 1947 were early Soviet-sponsored developments. The Constitution of 1949 establishing the GDR was created under Soviet tutelage, as was the development of the SED-controlled government, which was immediately recognized by Moscow and its East European allies. The USSR granted full sovereignty to the GDR in 1954.

During the early postwar period the Soviet Union levied economic reparations upon its zone, which included factories, industrial goods, rolling stock, livestock and timber totaling as high as $20 billion, or about half of its prewar industrial capital. The Soviet Union then extracted reparations from production for about 10 years. Consequently, the East German economy was not only depleted but also increasingly removed from its natural marketplace—West Germany—and became closely linked to the Soviet bloc. The GDR became a member of the Council for Mutual Economic Assistance (CMEA) in 1950, a year after its establishment. The CMEA undertook economic integration of its members in 1954.

As a response to the FRG's membership in NATO and the signing of the Austrian State Treaty, the Soviet Union created the Treaty of Friendship, Cooperation and Mutual Assistance on May 14, 1955. Also known as the Warsaw Treaty Organization (WTO) and the Warsaw Pact, the treaty contributed to Moscow's control of the members' military forces as well as furnishing legal authority to continue the stationing of its military forces in the GDR, Poland, Hungary and Rumania. The WTO was established for 20 years, extended in 1975 for 10 years and in 1985 renewed for another 20 years. The GDR was a founding member of the WTO, which consists of a Political Consultative Committee, Foreign Ministers' Committee, Defense Ministers' Committee and joint armed forces, with a Soviet marshal as commander in chief. The strategically important GDR participated in WTO military maneuvers, some of which were held annually on its territory. As a result of Helsinki Conference on Security and Cooperation in Europe (CSCE) accords, foreign, including U.S., inspectors have observed exercises in the GDR in recent years.

Subsequent to the Hungarian uprising in October 1956, the Soviet Union concluded status-of-forces treaties with its WTO allies. The GDR-USSR treaty was signed in March 1957 and included a provision not contained in others: In the event of a "threat to the security of the Soviet forces" on GDR territory, the Soviet High Command in East Germany "may apply measures for the elimination of such a threat." The two countries concluded a Treaty of Friendship, Cooperation and Mutual Assistance in 1964 and again in 1975, and similar agreements were signed with the WTO allies: Czechoslovakia (March 1967), Poland (March 1967), Hungary (May 1967), Bulgaria (September 1967) and Rumania (October 1970). Such a system of accords was concluded by all Soviet bloc members with each other.

Despite the treaty with Czechoslovakia, the GDR opposed the reform movement of Alexander Dubcek and participated in the Soviet-led Warsaw Pact invasion of Czechoslovakia during the night of August 20–21, 1968; the other "allies" in the invasion were Poland, Hungary and Bulgaria. Rumania opposed this military action, sharply criticizing the invasion, as did Yugoslavia, Albania (which withdrew from the WTO as a result), China and most West European Communist parties, as well as governments around the world. The GDR leadership, along with WTO members, justified the invasion as furnishing assistance against "counter revolutionary forces." All non-Soviet troops departed soon after crushing Dubcek's "Prague Spring," except Moscow's military forces, which remain in Czechoslovakia to this day. In November 1968 General Secretary Brezhnev declared in Warsaw the right to intervene in "friendly socialist countries" by WTO military forces if a regime is determined to be in danger.

The Soviet Union has maintained massive military might in East Germany since World War II. As of mid-1989 the forces numbered 380,000 in the Western Group of Forces (WGF), previously known as Group of Soviet Forces in Germany (GSFG). Their numbers, types and capabilities were far beyond Soviet defense needs. Following the U.S.-USSR Intermediate-Range Nuclear Forces (INF) Treaty of December 8, 1987, Moscow withdrew its mandatory nuclear weapons from the GDR and Czechoslovakia in the first half of 1988, but the WGF in 1989 had a full complement of SS-21 short-range nuclear missiles not covered by the INF Treaty.

In his December 7, 1988, address before the United Nations, Gorbachev announced Soviet troop reductions within two years, including 50,000 troops, 5,300 tanks in six divisions, artillery and aircraft from East Germany, Czechoslovakia and Hungary. In January 1989 Honecker revealed the envisaged schedule of Soviet withdrawals from the GDR. Before the end of 1989 they were to be two tank divisions, two independent tank training regiments and eight independent battalions. The following were earmarked for 1990: two tank divisions; an air assult brigade; three training regiments, including one for tank troops; and three independent battalions. The motorized infantry and tank divisions remaining in the GDR were to be reorganized for defensive operations. According to Moscow, by June 1, 1989, nearly 9,000 troops, 2,100 tanks and 300 artillery pieces had been withdrawn from the GDR, Poland and Hungary, but apparently not full divisions. The net result in mid-1989 was the reality that the Soviet armed forces in the GDR, totaling 380,000, continued to be substantial and modernized with enormous firepower, including five brigades of the modern SS-21 short-range nuclear systems, which are noted for their accuracy, reliability and range.

In addition to the close political and military alignment with the Soviet Union, the GDR's trade, following reparations and the dislocation of its forced shift toward the East, grew impressively, as did its economy, following construction of the Berlin Wall in 1961, halting emigration. Ultimately the country became the most industrialized and with the highest standard of living in the Soviet bloc. As noted, the GDR joined CMEA in 1950; the GDR's planned economy was dictated by the SED, which was subservient to Moscow's economic policies. From the 1950s up to unification the GDR's major trading partners were the Soviet Union (about 40%) and the East European countries (about 25%), principally Czechoslovakia, Poland and Hungary. Basically, the GDR exported manufactured goods and imported raw materials. The GDR, as other East European countries, was dependent on the Soviet Union for imports of fuel; in 1975 Soviet oil prices, following the 1973 oil crisis, were increased markedly, posing a problem for the GDR as well as for the other Eastern bloc countries. In 1982 Moscow reduced oil deliveries to East Germany, which was forced to increase its imports from other countries. In 1985 the GDR signed an agreement with the Soviet Union to increase the trade turnover by 28% during the 1986-90 five-year plan.

Of the East European countries, relations with Poland were the most sensitive, largely because of the former German territories east of the Oder-Neisse line awarded to Poland by the Allies at Potsdam following World War II; Poland also received the port of Stettin (Szczecin) and the Swine Channel plus a small additional area. The GDR recognized the inviolability of the Oder-Neisse in 1950, but the FRG delayed until 1970. Despite the GDR's rapid recognition of the Oder-Neisse line and bilateral and mutilateral treaties, its relations with Poland had not been particularly harmonious. In 1967 Ulbricht pressured Poland, Czechoslovakia, Hungary and Bulgaria into bilateral mutual assistance treaties with the GDR, and the Ulbricht Doctrine obliged these governments not to improve relations with the FRG unless Bonn extended official recognition to the GDR. However, the 1970 Soviet-FRG Nonaggression Treaty confirmed the Oder-Neisse line, permitting improved relations between the FRG and East European countries, which Ulbricht resisted. He was removed as the SED's first secretary the following year. Relations under Ulbricht's successor, Erich Honecker, were not without concern. For example, it took three years to reach agreement, signed May 22, 1989, on a border dispute over Pomeranian Bay, and decades for the GDR to acknowledge the secret protocol of the 1939 Nazi-Soviet Pact. The long-delayed admission, coming after Moscow's, appeared in the daily *Junge Welt* on August 23, 1989. In an interview an historian from the Marxism-Leninism Institute acknowledged the secret provision but defended the Nonaggression Pact as essential for the Soviet Union to gain territory and time. As under Ulbricht in 1968 regarding Czechoslovakia, the GDR during 1980–81 under Honecker voiced strong opposition to Poland's Solidarity and the party's reform policies, favoring Soviet intervention. Until he was deposed, Honecker continued opposition to reform in Hungary and in Poland in 1989 on ideological and political grounds; both Ulbricht and Honecker perceived the trends as undermining communism and threatening stability as well as their dominance.

Each bilateral Treaty of Friendship, Cooperation and Mutual Assistance with its WTO allies contained a provision regarding the inviolability of frontiers as determined after World War II, including the GDR-FRG boundary, and that West Berlin was not a constituent part of the FRG. The latter complicated relations with West Germany, which was of importance to the GDR as a trade partner. The GDR's reflection of pro-Soviet orientation was well illustrated in relations with Yugoslavia. With the creation of the GDR in 1949, Yugoslavia, expelled from the Communist Information Bureau (Cominform) the previous year and under virulent attack by the Soviet bloc, including the GDR, established diplomatic relations with the FRG. As relations between Moscow and Marshal Tito improved, Belgrade extended diplomatic recognition to the GDR in 1958, thereby raising the ire of the FRG, which promptly severed diplomatic relations with Yugoslavia. The GDR developed friendly relations with Belgrade, seemingly to lure Tito back into the Soviet bloc. Marshal Tito visited East Berlin in 1974, and Honecker reciprocated in 1977. In December 1988 Honecker signed a long-term Agreement for Economic and Scientific-Technological Cooperation with the visiting chairman of the Presidium of Yugoslavia.

The GDR appeared to be preparing the groundwork for a possible rapproachement with Albania, which severed diplomatic relations with the USSR in 1961 over ideology and which left the WTO following the invasion of Czechoslovakia. The foreign minister of East Germany, Oskar Fischer, made an official visit to Tirana in June 1989; he was the highest East European official to do so since 1961. On this occasion the countries signed two agreements—one on economic, industrial and scientific-technological cooperation, and the other on health services and medical sciences. The Albanian first secretary characterized Fischer's visit as of "great significance." Both sides expressed a desire to expand cooperation in all areas, including political.

As in the case of Yugoslavia, the SED served as Moscow's trusted emissary for establishing a rapproachement with China. Honecker officially visited Beijing in October 1986 to usher improved Soviet bloc relations with China. The Chinese responded with Prime Minister Zhao Ziyang's five-state visit in June 1987, beginning in East Germany. SED officials supported the Chinese regime over the June 1989 massacre on Tiananmen Square, characterizing the "recent events" as an internal affair: "There were plans to use the peaceful rallies of students in Beijing for a counterrevolutionary overthrow of the people's government."

After becoming a full member of the United Nations in 1973, the GDR established diplomatic relations with over 131 countries. It participated actively but selectively at the United Nations and with other international organizations in support of Soviet foreign policies and proposals. In addition to the WTO, the CMEA and other Eastern bloc groups, East Germany was a member of IAEA, ICES, ILO, IMO, IPU, ITU, UNESCO, UNICEF, UPU, WHO, WIPO and WMO. The GDR had not gained membership in certain multilateral organizations such as IMF and GATT, and by choice FAO and other U.N. specialized agencies. In line with Soviet policies, East Germany's support of the United Nations' programs and activities had been spotty. It had not supported the peacekeeping force in Lebanon nor the Palestinian refugees, and its donations to the U.N. Development Program and to UNICEF had been parsimonious, substantially lower than contributions from smaller, poorer states. In 1979 the GDR was elected to a two-year term as a nonpermanent member of the Security Council, where it also supported the Soviet position—e.g., vetoing a resolution for the withdrawal of foreign military forces from Afghanistan.

The GDR was a major actor in Soviet bloc propaganda activities. For example, in 1976 it organized the Conference of Communist and Workers' Parties of Europe, exhibiting its successes with great fanfare. During June 20–22, 1988, an International Meeting for Nuclear-Weapon-Free Zones was held in East Berlin with claimed 1,034 participants from 113 countries; this allegedly was the biggest such meeting ever held. East Berlin was the headquarters for the Women's International Democratic Federation. This Soviet-supported Communist front organization claims 142 affiliates in 124 countries and a membership of 200 million. Also in East Berlin was the World Federation of Teacher's Unions.

According to the Constitution, the GDR "works for security and cooperation in Europe." Thus it was an active participant in the 1975 Helsinki CSCE and in its follow-up conferences. Helsinki was of particular significance because of recognition by signatories of the inviolability of boundaries. The GDR assigned a competent delegation to the NATO-WTO Mutual and Balanced Force Reduction (MBFR) negotiations in Vienna (1973–89) and continued its active participation in the Conventional Armed Forces in Europe (CFE) talks, also in Vienna. East Germany continued to propagate Soviet policies under Gorbachev, promoting closer relations with the European Economic Community (EEC) and the general secretary's "common European home." Likewise, the GDR had been a leading voice for Soviet disarmament policies, itself initiating such proposals as the 1987 nuclear-weapons-free corridor in Central Europe.

Strategically and economically, East Germany was the most important East European country for the Soviet Union. The GDR was a creation of the Soviet Union, administered through the SED. While Moscow's allies dutifully extended official recognition to the GDR, the regime was generally politically isolated for the next two decades from Western Europe and much of the rest of the world, including the established Afro-Asian states. West Germany's "Halstein Doctrine," adopted in 1955, brought severance of diplomatic relations with any country that recognized the GDR, which was considered an artificial entity. The exception was Moscow,

which recognized the FRG without obtaining reciprocity for the GDR. In 1957 Bonn broke off diplomatic relations with Yugoslavia and in 1963 with Cuba when they recognized the GDR. As a result of the changing international situation and the FRG's policy of *Ostpolitik* (active relations with the East), the GDR's diplomatic isolation came to an end. In August 1970 with the Soviet Union, and in December of the same year with Poland, the FRG concluded treaties under which, among other provisions, Bonn accepted the postwar boundaries. A series of official meetings between East and West German leaders was initiated.

Earlier, in March 1970, the United States, the United Kingdom, France and the USSR discussed the status of Berlin, resulting in the September 1971 Quadripartite Agreement, which continued the special status of Berlin and paved the way for recognition of the GDR. The following year, on November 9, 1972, the four powers declared their agreement for membership of both the FRG and the GDR for U.N. membership, reserving their previous "rights and responsibilities." With the March 19, 1970, meeting of the two German prime ministers, a long process of negotiations resulted in the December 21, 1972, "treaty on the basis of relations between the FRG and the GDR." The event was a milestone in the GDR's struggling political history and in its bilateral relations. In the "Basic Treaty" (Grundvertrag) the signatories essentially recognized the inviolability of existing boundaries and the sovereignty of each state, as well as providing for the development of their relations. The FRG agreed to cease its policy of representing both German states. Although Bonn demurred on de jure recognition, it did agree to a "special relationship" with the GDR. On March 19, 1974, the two Germanys established permanent deplomatic missions, short of embassies. These bilateral steps, together with the GDR's admission to the United Nations, caused a proliferation of diplomatic activity, resulting in the GDR establishing diplomatic relations with 124 countries, including the FRG, by July 1978.

The FRG was the GDR's most important trading Western partner, and overall second only to the USSR. Inter-German trade amounted to up to 60% of the GDR's total trade with Western countries. The two countries had a special trade arrangement that included provisions for free duty, accounting units, rebate of the value-added tax and interest-free "swing credit" provided by Bonn for purchase of FRG goods.

The East German leadership was reminded of limits of its foreign policy in the mid-1980s as Honecker's desire to visit West Germany was frustrated by the Kremlin. With Gorbachev's policy of permitting East European officials a greater role in foreign relations, the SED leader finally made an unprecedented official visit to the FRG during September 7–11, 1987. The visit spurred not only lagging economic relations but also agreements in other sectors—science and technology; culture; environment; nuclear safety; and various projects, including an electric power grid linking the GDR and West Berlin with the FRG's grid. To those East Germans fleeing to West Germany or, after November 9, 1989, allowed to travel freely, the FRG government's policy was to grant 100 marks in "welcome money." While millions enjoyed their newfound freedom to travel, most of them intended to return to their homes.

The economic benefits that the GDR gained from its special relationship with West Germany were not sufficient to solve the GDR's economic problems. The centrally planned economy, linked as it was to the CMEA, was faced with unwelcome problems from the European Community as 1992 neared. Required was a restructuring (Gorbachev's *perestroika*) of the GDR's economy, long resisted by Honecker. In late 1989 the new SED leadership appeared more realistic, admitting to previously repressed inflation and consumer goods problems. However, the GDR's infrastructrue, relations with the FRG and potential for quality production, if unleashed by reform toward a market economy with joint ventures, was given a chance of greatly expanding its trade with Western markets.

During the momentous events of 1989 the question of reunification was discussed broadly, and addressed by the leadership of both FRG and the GDR. The "German question" was complicated. Reunification was not simply a resolution of two parties, the FRG and GDR, but also of Eastern and Western alliances; of the United States and the Soviet Union; and of individual countries concerned with postwar boundaries, especially Poland. In the fall of 1989, as the East German masses streamed across borders, FRG chancellor Helmut Kohl said, "We have less reason than ever to be resigned to the long-term division of Germany into two states." Kohl repeated his promise of substantial aid to the GDR if the latter undertook real reforms. However, the new SED leadership, headed by Egon Krenz, maintained the traditional GDR position of a separate, sovereign East Germany. Citing Modrow, FRG chancellor Kohl presented to the Bundestag on November 27, 1989, a 10-point proposal for a German confederation leading to a federation and unification of the two Germanys. The prerequisite was a "legitimate democratic government in East Germany" resulting from free elections. Common institutions would be established for various sectors, then a confederative structure leading to a federation and a united Germany. Kohl emphasized fitting such a structure into the "architecture of Europe." The chancellor declared that the FRG would approve immediately the conclusion of a trade and cooperation agreement with the GDR that would expand and guarantee East German access to the Common Market even beyond 1992, when the European Community comes into existence.

Reaction from the GDR was mixed and cautious. SED leader Krenz said a federation was possible only of "two sovereign states," adding that "unity is not on the agenda." Moscow characterized Kohl's proposal as a "clear attempt to push the recently started process of renewal in East Germany in a nationalist direction." Also, a Soviet spokesman opined, "There is not one country in Europe today that would thirst for German reunification because of the questions it raises for stability. It is not on the agenda." On November 17, prior to Kohl's proposal, Gorbachev rejected German unification until "historical conditions" in Europe change. The U.S. Department of State said Kohl's proposal was "not a blueprint for German reunification, but rather a coherent approach to a rapidly changing situation in the GDR and its relations with the Federal Republic. . . . It should be no cause for concern that the chancellor has laid out his vision for the future of Germany."

Beginning in the 1970s, establishment of diplomatic relations with Western countries was followed by expansion of economic cooperation exchanges in various fields. For example, in 1984 the GDR concluded a cultural agreement with France and Great Britain, a trade accord with Austria in the same year and economic and cultural agreements with Italy in 1985. Honecker also met with Pope John Paul II in 1985 and concluded a trade arrangement with Sweden in 1986. In building the "common European home," the GDR considered highest-level meetings with West European officials of major importance.

The GDR established diplomatic relations with the United States on September 4, 1974. A consular convention was signed in 1979, and the two countries concluded fisheries, parcel post and cultural agreements. Their bilateral relations had been formal and not particularly warm. However, the last several years have witnessed an improvement. Trade with the United States increased rapidly following 1974, with U.S. exports reaching $558 million in 1980, but the bulk ($534 million) was in agricultural products. With GDR's sharp reduction of grain imports (down to $32 million in 1987), trade decreased. However, exports of both countries have increased in the past two years, resulting in two-way trade in 1988 of over $200 million. In 1989 U.S. exports to East Germany amounted to $94 million, and imports $139 million. The U.S. Department of Commerce estimated that American sales through European subsidiaries may be several times larger than these reported figures. Up to the fall of 1990 the GDR failed to obtain most-favored-nation treatment from the United States because of unsettled claims and human rights violations.

During Communist rule the GDR had been a significant contributor to Marxist-Leninist movements and to others throughout the Third World. According to the Constitution, the GDR, "faithful to socialist internationalism," pledged support to peoples "fighting against imperialism and its colonial regime." In other words, it pledged support for "wars of national liberation." Pursuing this objective, East Germany over the years had established a substantial record of active relations with governmental and nongovernmental organizations such as the Palestine Liberation Organization (PLO), the African National Congress and the Union of Arab Maghrab. The GDR had supported the Arabs over Israel, characterizing the latter as an aggressor. The PLO established an office in East Germany as early as 1973. The GDR and Israel had no official relations. In addition to diplomatic aid, East Berlin provided development assistance, civilian specialists, military advisers, propaganda materials, training, troops and arms. East Berlin extended what it called "active solidarity," especially to trouble spots in Africa and the Middle East, but also to Latin America.

In 1989 GDR advisers operated in Algeria, Angola,

Ethiopia, Guinea, Iraq, Libya, Mozambique, South Yemen, Syria and Zambia. An indication of the diversity of its involvement may be gleaned from the following. In June 1977 the GDR signed an agreement with Ethiopia to supervise internal security of the Communist regime. An "important milestone" for East Germany was reached in 1989 with the visit of Mengistu Haile Mariam, general secretary of the Workers' Party of Ethiopia, who expressed gratitude to Honecker for the GDR's assistance. Mozambique was another country with a comprehensive economic, scientific, technological and cultural cooperation agreement with the GDR. During his May 1989 visit to East Berlin, Mozambique president Joacquim Alberto Chissano thanked Honecker for GDR specialists and for the training of personnel from Mozambique.

Soviet bloc support of guerrilla movements in Central America was through Cuba. In June 1980 the GDR concluded a friendship and cooperation treaty with Cuba, providing for economic asssistance as well as civilian and military advisers to Havana. Moreover, East Germany promised to support those elements throughout Latin America fighting to overthrow existing governments. It established diplomatic relations with the Sandinistas immediately following the overthrow of Somoza in 1979. In early 1989 Honecker complimented Cuba on its "steadfast and principled attitude under the complicated conditions of international class struggle."

With victory in the March 18, 1990 elections, the Christian Democratic coalition proceeded rapidly, in concert with Chancellor Kohl's government, toward unification. The previous month, foreign ministers of the four World War II Allies (U.S., U.K., France and the USSR), together with those of the two Germanys, meeting in Ottawa, Canada, agreed "to discuss external aspects of the establishment of German unity, including the issues of security of the neighboring states."

At its first session following the first post-Communist free elections, the Volkskammer passed a unanimous resolution acknowledging German responsibility for Nazi atrocities, an act refused by the previous Communist regime. The parliament admitted guilt for the genocide of Jews, Poles, Soviet people, the Sinti and Roma. It asked forgiveness from Jews, pledging compensation, and from Israel for "the hypocricy and hostility" of past GDR policy. The "terrible suffering" inflicted by Germans upon the Soviet people has not been forgotten, the parliament said, pledging a process of reconciliation and German integration into a European security system. It expressed gratitude to the Soviet Union for making transformation in Germany possible. The Volkskammer apologized for the GDR's unlawful participation in the 1968 Warsaw Pact invasion of Czechoslovakia, and reaffirmed the "inviolability of the Oder-Neisse borders" with Poland as the basis for the "peaceful coexistence of our people in a common European home."

The two Germanys agreed to a treaty establishing a monetary, economic and social union effective July 1, and on August 31 a comprehensive treaty covering all aspects of unification. The latter marked the GDR's

accession into the Federal Republic according to Article 23 of the Basic Law, amended with completion of unity. This included recognition of the inviolability of borders, especially meaningful to Poland. The two parliaments ratified the treaty on September 20. They agreed to October 3 for formal unification and December 2 for all-German elections.

At a meeting September 12 in Moscow, the foreign ministers of the four World War II Powers and of the two Germanys—the "Two-plus-Four"—signed a treaty ending the Four Power rights in Germany. This granted full sovereignty to the unified Germany. The GDR's Volkskammer and the FRG's Bundestag ratified the treaty on September 20 by large margins. On October 3 the East German states of Mecklenburg-Vorpommerania, Brandenburg, Saxony-Anhalt, Saxony and Thuringia became part of the Federal Republic, with Berlin as its capital, pending a parliamentary decision following the December 2 elections.

The "Two-plus-Four" treaty—formally the Treaty on the Final Provisions Regarding Germany—contained 10 articles on the external questions of German unification. Its features are:

- Grant of full sovereignty to unified Germany, consisting of the FRG, GDR, & Berlin;
- Rejection of biological, chemical and nuclear weapons;
- Limiting of German defense forces to 370,000;
- Withdrawal of Soviet troops from the present GDR by the end of 1994;
- Foreign troops and nuclear weapons are not to be stationed and deployed in that part of Germany;
- U.S., U.K. and French troops are to remain in West Berlin until complete Soviet withdrawal; and
- Germany is to choose the military alliance it prefers.

With the Soviet president present at the signing ceremony, East German prime minister and acting foreign minister de Maiziere characterized the treaty as the cornerstone of an age of peace, freedom and cooperation, and complimented "the courageous policies of Mikhail Gorbachev" regarding Eastern Europe.

German sovereignty was not to be achieved without internal and external costs. On September 13 the FRG and Soviet foreign ministers initialed a comprehensive treaty—Treaty of Good Neighborliness, Partnership and Cooperation—covering economic cooperation, financial transition and the withdrawal of Soviet troops. The two countries reaffirmed the inviolability of all borders in Eastern Europe, pledging they will "never and under no circumstances be the first to use military force against each other or against third states." The FRG obliged itself to pay 13 billion DM (about $10 billion) to the Soviet Union by the end of 1994 to finance the 380,000 Soviet troops and their 220,000 dependents on the GDR territory until 1994, and for building 36,000 apartments to accommodate returning Soviet personnel.

Following unification East Germany ceased being a member of international organizations and its foreign policy and relations became those of unified Germany. The effect on the Warsaw Pact and CMEA is potentially disastrous—the erosion of the first and possibly disintegration of the second. In mid-September 1990, as the transformation to a political WTO continued, the East Germans departed from its headquarters in Moscow, and did not attend a CMEA meeting in Bucharest called to discuss reforms. President Gorbachev accepted the FRG's continued membership in NATO and, as of October 3, the approximate 90,000 troops of GDR's Nationale Volksarmee (NVA) were integrated into FRG's Bundeswehr but the majority of them were to be retired, partly to maintain the mandatory limit of 370,000 troops in the treaty for unified Germany.

In economic relations the former GDR, as part of Germany, became integrated into the European Community automatically but existing agreements with CMEA and East European countries are being honored until the end of 1990. With regard to trade with the United States, East German goods continue, temporarily, to be subject to tariffs. The U.S. country of origin (goods "Made in East Germany") and tariff regulations continue to apply, and the former GDR still does not qualify for MFN tariff treatment although it is a part of the FRG.

PARLIAMENT

Theoretically the highest organ of state power in the GDR was the People's Chamber (Volkskammer), a unicameral legislative body. In 1958 the upper house—the State Chamber (Länderkammer)—was abolished, giving greater prominence to the People's Chamber, as did the weakening of the Council of State (Staatsrat) under the 1974 constitutional amendments. In reality, supreme authority continued to reside in the SED. The 500-member People's Chamber was elected every five years (four years under the previous constitutions) by universal, direct, free and secret vote of citizens age 18 or over, on election day; the same age qualified one to be a member of the SED. The National Front of political parties and mass organizations organized and conducted the election process, including a single list of candidates, with predictable results: a 99.94% voter turnout in the June 8, 1986, elections. The group (*Fraktion*) composition of the Volkskammer was as follows:

Group (before March 1990)	Seats
Socialist Unity Party	127
Christian Democratic Union	52
Democratic Farmers' Party	52
Liberal Democratic Party	52
National Democratic Party	52
Free German Trade Union Confederation	61
Free German Youth	37
Women's Democratic League	32
Cultural League	21
Mutual Farmers' Aid Association	14

Elections, March 1990	Seats
Christian Democratic Union/Democratic Awakening	167
Social Democratic Party	88
Party of Democratic Socialism	66
German Social Union	25
Association of Free Democrats—The Liberals	23
Alliance 90/The Greens	20
Democratic Farmers' Party/Women's Democratic League	10
United Left	1

Sixty-six representatives were from East Berlin. According to the Constitution the next national elections were to be held in 1991.

However impressive the multiparty organizations' representation may appear, the political reality has been the SED's monopolistic control, a situation similar to that in other East European Communist multiparty systems. The People's Chamber met at least twice annually for short periods of time—one or two days each session in recent years—mainly to hear speeches and officially to ratify legislative measures by (except on rare occasions) unanimous vote. Decisions were by majority vote, and constitutional amendments required a two-thirds vote of the deputies. After 1974 its formal powers had been substantial.

According to the Constitution the People's Chamber was the sole constituent and legislative organ. It was to determine and implement state policy executed through the Council of State, the Council of Ministers, the chairman of the National Defense Council, the Supreme Court and the procurator-general, all elected by and responsible to the People's Chamber. The Volkskammer enacted laws presented by its deputies, its committees, the Council of State, the Council of Ministers and the Free German Trade Union Confederation. The committees considered the bills before submitting them to the plenary session of the People's Chamber. Before passage the drafts of Basic Laws were to be submitted to the people for discussion; the 1974 constitutional amendments were not. Also, the People's Chamber determined the state plans for social development, approved treaties, decided on the state of defense and decided on holding plebiscites.

Article 55 of the Constitution provided for a Presidium, elected by the Volkskammer for the duration of the legislative term—five years. The Presidium was composed of the president of the People's Chamber, a deputy president, and other members: three SED, two LDPD, one each from the other parties, and two each from the mass organizations. The Presidium conducted activities of the Volkskammer between its sessions and convened the Volkskammer into sessions. Formally, the Volkskammer's committees were to "cooperate closely" with the voters to discuss draft laws, and to monitor the enforcement of laws, but in practice their authority was minimal. The same could be said for individual members, whose constitutional responsibilities to citizens generally had not been carried out.

As directed by the 1974 constitutional amendments, the People's Chamber elected from among its members the Council of State (Staatsrat). With the death of Wilhelm Pieck in 1960, the office of president, which he had occupied since October 1949, was replaced by this collective presidency. The People's Chamber amended the Constitution to create the 26-member Council of State, which was empowered to convene the Volkskammer, appoint the National Defense Council and organize the country's defense, represent the GDR in external affairs, appoint and receive diplomats and declare amnesties and pardons. Party leader Walter Ulbricht became chairman and, as the occasion warranted, acted on behalf of the Staatsrat. The 1974 constitutional amendments diminished the chairman's power by eliminating the following provisions of the Staatsrat: to act for the People's Chamber between sessions, issue decrees, direct the Volkskammer's committees, determine constitutionality of laws, interpret laws and propose the prime minister. The result was essentially a return to the previous range of authority of the single presidency.

Articles 66–75 were devoted to the Council of State, which was an organ of the People's Chamber, with functions assigned by the Constitution or laws and decisions of the People's Chamber, to which it was accountable. The Staatsrat was composed of the chairman, deputy chairmen, members and the secretary, all elected for five years by the People's Chamber at its first session. The largest group (SED) in the People's Chamber proposed the chairman, who directed the work of the Staatsrat. The Council of State represented the GDR, ratified and denounced treaties, oversaw lower governmental organs, called for elections, decided on the country's defense and appointed the members of the National Defense Council, exercised control over the constitutionality and legality of the activities of the Supreme Court and the procurator-general, and declared amnesties as well as pardons. The chairman directed the work of the Staatsrat and appointed and received diplomats. As noted earlier, the chairman's powers were severely reduced by the Council of Ministers in 1972 and by the 1974 amended Constitution, which specified his role to direct the work of the Council of State and to appoint and receive diplomats.

In the fall of 1989 the Council of State consisted of the chairman, eight deputy chairmen, 17 members, a secretary and the head of the chairman's Chancery. Although other parties were represented, the SED's leadership, including the prime minister, were assured of domination. Erich Honecker, chairman of the Council of State since 1976, was replaced by Egon Krenz as chairman as well as SED general secretary in November 1989; Krenz, in turn, was displaced as SED general secretary in December 1989 by Gregor Gysi.

When the non-Communist opposition became a majority government in January 1990, national elections were scheduled for March 18, the first free, democratic elections since the establishment of the GDR in 1949 and, indeed, since 1933. The parliament passed a new electoral law on February 20, providing for a 400-member Volkskammer elected to a four-year term, for pro-portional representation, and for a no minimum vote requirement. Voters would cast ballots for candidates submitted by parties and groups. Within a week 38 organizations filed lists for registration, which required certification by the electoral commission.

Outside of the extreme right, excluded by laws on parties, organizations representing the political spectrum sought participation. In addition to the traditional political parties—led in East Germany as well as in the West by the Christian Democrats and Social Democrats—groups represented trade unions, youth, women and others. West German parties not only identified with their counterparts in the East but assisted them during the campaign, the FRG promising shortly before elections to exchange East marks for DMs on a 1:1 basis, heretofore opposed by Bonn's central bank, which proposed a 1:2 exchange. The objective of the Christian Democratic Union, led by Lothar de Maiziere, was rapid unification under Article 23 of the FRG's Basic Law, or its constitution—i.e., transfer the FRG system to the GDR.

The East German voters responded with a dramatic turnout in favor of conservative candidates, German unity and a market economy. Chancellor Kohl characterized the elections as a "historic event." The conservative Alliance for Germany, composed of Christian Democrats, German Social Union and Democratic Awakening, received 48.2% of the total votes and 193 seats in the 400-member parliament. The former SED, renamed Party of Democratic Socialism (PDS), gained 16.3% and 65 seats, having received strong support in East Berlin.

Parliamentary groups were formed with at least 10 members in the Volkskammer. In addition to CDU/DA other groupings were: The Liberals, composed of the Association of Free Democrats, the Free Democratic Party and the German Forum; Alliance 90/The Greens, consisting of the New Forum, Initiative for Peace and Human Rights, Democracy Now and the Green Party; and Democratic Farmers' and Women's Democratic League. On April 5 Dr. Sabine Bergmann-Pohl (CDU) was elected president of the Volkskammer and, simultaneously, acting head of state. The Presidium of the Volkskammer consisted of the president, six deputies and 13 other parliamentary members representing the various coalitions and parties. On April 9 the parliament established 26 committees to conduct the day-to-day activities of the legislature concerned with various branches of society.

As previously noted the parliament approved Lothar de Maiziere's coalition government on April 12. On April 30 the first joint meeting of presidiums of the Volkskammer and FRG's Bundestag—headed by Dr. Bergmann-Pohl and Prof. Rita Suessmuth respectively—took place in both East and West Berlin. They established a joint parliamentary committee on German unity. The committee's primary task was to contribute to the negotiations of the unification treaty, especially involving the constitution and citizens. The meeting of the presidiums in West Berlin took place in the symbolic Reichstag building. On September 20 the Volkskammer ratified the unification treaty, signed by the "Two-plus-Four" September 12, by a vote of 299 to 80, with one abstention. The opposition consisted of Party for Democratic Socialism, Alliance 90 and the Greens.

At a special session August 22–23 the parliament approved (294 to 62, with 7 abstentions) October 3, a compromise date, for unification, and ratified the treaty for the December 2 all-German elections. Also, the legislature accepted (by a vote of 295 to 74) Bonn's election rule requiring a political party to receive a minimum of 5% of total votes to be eligible for parliamentary representation. According to the unification treaty the Volkskammer would be represented by 144 members in the Bundestag until the election of an all-German parliament. The 5% requirement was a blow to small parties and splinter groups but a provision for "joint ticket" gave them hope, especially to New Forum and Alliance 90, which spearheaded the popular demonstrations in 1989. Prospects for the reconstituted Communist party, the Party of Democratic Socialism, appeared slim.

POLITICAL PARTIES

East Germany had been ruled by the Soviet Union through the Socialist Unity Party of Germany (Sozialistische Einheitspartei Deutschland, SED) since 1946. Since the creation of the GDR in 1949, other political parties had functioned, but their existence had been a formality and up to the fall of 1989 they had been of no political consequence. As in other Soviet bloc countries, the Communist Party was enshrined—again, until the fall of 1989—in the Constitution as the leading force in the society and in the construction of advanced socialism. Within Soviet domination, the SED had been the source of all power in the state—legislative, executive and judicial—possessing all levers of control. Its aim was the creation of a Communist society. The SED's obeisance to the Soviet Communist Party and fidelity to Marxism-Leninism—explicitly documented in the Constitution—was never in doubt.

The founding of the Communist Party of Germany (Kommunistische Partei Deutschland, KPD) dates back to 1918. As with other Communist parties outside Russia and the Soviet Union during these early years, the KPD was under the control of Moscow's leadership, promoting Soviet policies. Under Hitler the KPD was driven underground and its leadership fled to foreign countries, especially the Soviet Union. Walter Ulbricht, who became the dominant SED figure in East Germany after World War II, operated out of France (1933–38), then went to the Soviet Union (1938–45). Some members became victims of Stalin's purges, but many survived to prepare with Soviet officials for a Communist takeover in Germany. For example, in 1943 Ulbricht was a cofounder of the National Committee of Free Germany (NKFD), becoming head of the "Ulbricht Group" of Communists who returned to Germany in April 1945 to assist the Soviet Military Administration in Germany to organize the administrative structure. Also organized—more accurately, reorganized—in the Soviet Zone was the KPD and, with Soviet concurrence, three other parties: the Social Democratic Party of Germany (Sozialistische Partei Deutschland, SPD), the Christian Democratic Union (Christich-Demokratische Union Deutschland, CDU) and the Liberal Democratic Party of Germany (Liberal-Demokratische Partei Deutschland, LDPD).

The SED was established at the Unification Congress in April 1946 in the Soviet Zone of Germany with the forced merger of the SPD and the KPD. The SPD was led by Otto Grotewohl and the KPD by Wilhelm Pieck. Pieck and Grotewohl became cochairmen of the SED. The unification was a major factor in developing one-party rule in East Germany, reflected in local elections held in September 1946 with the SED obtaining 57.1% of the vote, the LDPD 21.1%, the Christian Democratic Union(CDU) 18% and mass organizations the remaining 3%. In the five Länder elections the following month, the SED polled 47.5% and an SED-controlled farmers' group 3.5%. However, the other parties were victimized by various repressive measures, including arrests, in the election process.

Following the creation of the GDR in 1949 the typical Communist front was established in January 1950, composed of permitted political parties and SED-led mass organizations. Thereafter elections were to be prepared and conducted by the National Front with a single list of candidates. Through the fall of 1989 election results were barely short of unanimity for the SED-led list of candidates. Leading the GDR were Pieck as president (until 1960) and Grotewohl as prime minister; Walter Ulbricht, deputy chairman of the SED since 1946, became its Secretary-general in July 1950. Sovietization of East Germany was proceeding rapidly during these postwar years.

Nationalization, central planning and collectivization resulted not in the orientation of the society's construction of socialism but in low production, reduced productivity and food shortages, all leading to strikes and demonstrations, which in June 1953 were brutally suppressed by the East German police and the Soviet military. In 1960 the regime proceeded with further nationalization of agriculture prompting another serious reaction, this time in flight to West Germany. To halt the "brain drain" as well as the exit of factory and farm workers, the SED on August 13, 1961, began construction of its "wall of shame" in Berlin, stopping the mass flow. However, economic development came at a heavy price: the universal revulsion of the society in denial of human rights. In addition, the SED experienced serious intraparty controversies.

Walter Ulbricht, a veteran Communist who spent the war years in the Soviet Union, was the embodiment of the "cult of personality," not unlike his mentor, Stalin. In addition to heading the SED as secretary-general—renamed first secretary July 1953—Ulbricht became chairman of the Council of State (the president) following Pieck's death in 1960, as well as chairman of the National Defense Council, also in 1960. The internal party and societal problems subsided in the early 1960s, assisted in no small measure by policies adopted by the Soviet 22nd Communist Party Congress. The SED's Sixth Party Congress, in 1963, embarked on the "comprehensive building of socialism," adopting the New

Economic System. The result was a noticeable improvement in the East German economy, and West Berliners were allowed to visit relatives in the GDR. The new Constitution of 1968 assigned to the SED a leading role in society, which was declared to have developed economically from a "democratic republic" in 1949 to a higher level ideological stage: "socialism."

Ulbricht, considering Dubcek's "Prague Spring" a threat to the SED and to himself, encouraged the Warsaw Pact invasion to crush Dubcek's popular reform program. The international situation was changing. Under Chancellor Willy Brandt's *Ostpolitik*—opening to Eastern Europe—and improved Soviet relations with the FRG, Ulbricht faced challenges, especially Moscow's displeasure, which he was unable to overcome. Officially Ulbricht resigned, but in reality he was deposed as SED first secretary in May 1971 and as chairman of the National Defense Council, to be replaced by Erich Honecker. Ulbricht was accorded the title of chairman of the SED and continued as chairman of the Council of State, albeit with decreased responsibilities, and as chairman of the National Defense Council. He died in August 1973 at 80.

The stern Honecker was born in the Saar region, and joined the Communists as a youth and the KPD in 1929. He visited Moscow with an SED youth group in 1931. Arrested by the Nazis in Berlin in 1935 and sentenced to 10 years in jail, he was freed by the Red Army. During 1946–55 Honecker was chairman of the Free German Youth (Frei Deutsche Jugend, FDJ). With the party's Central Committee (CC) since 1946, he became a candidate member of the Politburo in 1950 and a full member eight years later. Honecker was in the Soviet Union during 1956–57 for political training and, upon his return, was placed in charge of Central Committee Secretariat's important national security and defense section. His title of first secretary was changed to general secretary at the Ninth Party Congess, in 1976. He was an associate and friend of Ulbricht's, supporting his mentor in the intraparty struggles, with the Berlin Wall and concerning the Warsaw Pact invasion of Czechoslovakia. As Ulbricht, Honecker was scornful of *Ostpolitik* and opposed movements such as Poland's Solidarity. Unlike Ulbricht, he was sufficiently flexible in gauging correctly Moscow's intention to improve relations with the FRG. Honecker and the SED were loyal supporters of the Soviet Union in policy and interpretation of Marxism-Leninism, both cast in the East German Constitution.

The Honecker era began on a high note. The Eighth Party Congress, in 1971, announced the SED's policy of dialogue with the FRG, increased the power of the Council of Ministers and approved a modicum of liberalism in art and literature. The Allied agreement on Berlin, the signing of the GDR-FRG "Basic Treaty" and membership in the United Nations, followed by a flood of diplomatic recognitions and the Helsinki accords, all contributed to the GDR's long-sought legitimacy and to Honecker's stature. At the Ninth Party Congress, in 1976, Honecker indicated even a greater role for the SED in building what he had termed "real existing socialism," with concentration on "increased efficien-

cy, scientific-technical progress and higher labor productivity." In October of that year Honecker became chairman of the Council of State, replacing Willi Stoph, who became prime minister once again. However, euphoria was mixed with concern over problems such as the GDR's relations with the FRG and the stationing of U.S. intermediate-range nuclear forces in Western Europe as a response to Soviet nuclear deployments.

The 10th Party Congress, in April 1981, witnessed continuity in leadership and internal and external policies, with Honecker stressing that the "SED is linked forever with the party of Lenin"—i.e., the Soviet Communist Party. On the GDR's path toward communism, Honecker emphasized even greater productivity, rewarding exemplary workers. The SED congratulated itself on its efficiency, comparing its preformance with that of the Polish Communist Party's handling of Solidarity. Honecker pledged to the Polish party and "Polish patriots" the SED's support as he denounced reforms advocated by Solidarity.

At the 11th Party Congress, in 1986, the SED considered the GDR to be a "politically stable and economically efficient socialist state." Honeker was praised by the Congress in the presence of the Soviet general secretary, whose attendance was construed as approval for the party and its leader. Gorbachev pointed to the GDR as an example of a successful centrally planned economy. The Soviet leader was especially critical of West German participation in the U.S. Strategic Defense Initiative and of Bonn's "revanchism," a recurring theme.

The economic progress that was officially applauded materialized at a steep price: discontent within East German society. Externally, in the latter 1980's, the SED and Honecker departed from their formally unequivocal policy alignment with the Soviet Union. They were unwilling to apply Gorbachev's policies of *glasnost* and *perestroika* and the "new thinking" to the GDR. While they supported reforms within the Soviet Union, the SED and Honecker demurred from implementing reconstruction within the GDR, explaining its own "independent policy." The mounting pressures for economic reform, human rights and political pluralism ultimately toppled not only the SED-led government but the SED leadership as well.

As a Marxist-Leninist party the SED is the "organized vanguard" in the GDR, with the Soviet Communist Party organization as its model. The guiding principle of the organizational structure and activity of the party was "democratic centralism," which also applies to the government. The SED was a highly structured monolith guided by its party statutes. Democratic centralism required that all organizations and members implement party policy and decisions of leading party organs. Party organs were elected from the bottom to the top, and decisions of the superior organs were binding unconditionally on all lower entities. In reality, the SED Politburo had been the determining authority in East Germany.

According to the SED statutes, adopted in 1976 and amended, the supreme organ of the SED was the Party Congress (Parteitag), convened by the CC after 1971 every five years; but an extraordinary congress was able to be held. The last Congress before the 1989 revolution was the 11th, held in 1986. The next was to be scheduled five years hence, in 1991. The CC determined the rules for the election of delegates, who numbered well over 2,000, many elected for the first time. Past Congresses had been unexciting and predictable. The general secretary made a detailed, highly favorable presentation. Others also were laudatory, and foreign delegations brought fraternal greetings. The Congress approved the CC report and adopted a program that comprehensively covered domestic and foreign issues and called for implementation of the party's policies.

The Party Congress elected the CC, the Secretariat and the Central Auditing Commission. The 11th Party Congress elected 165 full and 57 candidate members for the CC, an increase of nine, and 27 were new. The CC wielded considerable power. It could call a Party Conference between Congresses if serious events warranted a rare occurrence in the past. Meeting at least once every six months, the CC acted on behalf of the Congress between sessions. The Central Committee was the highest executive body of the SED, implementing policies and decisions of the Congress and of the Politburo. The CC functioned with various commissions, and in its sessions considered Politburo and Secretariat reports. In reality the Politburo was the ultimate authority. The CC represented the SED in contacts with other parties and organizations, approved candidates for the People's Chamber, referred members to state and economic bodies, monitored the performance of state and social organs through their party organization, appointed the editors of central party organs, decided on appointments to the Control Commission and elected the Politburo.

Although formally elected by the Central Committee, the Politburo was unquestionably the most powerful body in the SED, setting policy and making decisions affecting not only the party but also the government and the entire society. The Politburo normally met weekly. At the 1986 Congress the CC elected 22 full members and five candidate members, a large number that was reduced drastically in the fall of 1989. Up to this critical year the Politburo was a rather self-perpetuating body. In 1989 the most senior members were Willi Stoph, a member from 1954, and Honecker, a full member from 1958 but a candidate since 1950. Both were deposed in 1989. As with Ulbricht and Honecker and certain other first or general secretaries, the party leader had been an authoritarian or dictatorial ruler.

The Politburo's policies were implemented by the Secretariat, which was elected by the Central Committee. At the last Party Congress the CC elected 11 members to the Secretariat, which was chaired by the general secretary and met weekly. The secretaries had broad responsibility: international relations; party organs; agriculture; culture and science; agitation and propaganda; church affairs; trade and supply; security affairs; youth; sports; women's affairs; the economy; and East Berlin. They had a vast bureaucracy, with over 1,000 staffers, under their jurisdiction.

Below the national level, the SED was organized parallel to the government structure. Each *Bezirk* (district) had an organization similar to the state, with a conference electing a committee, which in turn elected a secretariat headed by a first secretary. Below the *Bezirk* the SED had organizations at the *Kreis* (county) level, where the structure was similar to that of the *Bezirk*, and in smaller towns and villages that lacked secretariats. On the lowest level of party organization were the approximately 80,000 primary organizations existing at enterprises, farms, institutes, higher educational institutions, residences, government offices, the military, diplomatic missions, and anywhere else having three party members. The basic units had a secretary and were responsible to the *Kreis* organization.

Despite energetic recruiting after World War II and applications from opportunists who visualized an East Germany dominated by the Soviet Union and the Communist Party in its zone, the KPD still was not the largest party, with 620,000 members compared to the SPD's 680,000. The ranks swelled with the 1946 merger of the two parties into the SED, which then conducted a recruiting drive over the next two years, reaching 1.8 million membership by the Second Party Congress, in 1947, to reflect a popularly supported political party. The number changed slightly—to 1.75 million—in 1950. With numerous socialists and other questionable members, the SED conducted a purge, a recurring phenomenon in Communist histories. The Fourth Party Congress, in 1954, reported a membership of 1.4 million. While membership still was high, the SED became a more selective, disciplined and elitist party rather than a mass organization, with concentration on attracting youth. In 1963 less than 10% of party members were under 25, a lower figure than in 1948.

At the Sixth Party Congress, in 1963, First Secretary Ulbricht unfolded a new admissions policy to promote younger, better-educated, managerial and technical members into higher echelons, including the Central Committee in the "comprehensive building of socialism." Membership totaled about 1.8 million in 1967, approximately 1.9 million in 1971 (during the Eighth Party Congress) and slightly over 2 million in 1986 (during the 11th Party Congress), full and candidate members. On January 11, 1989, the SED announced a membership of 2,324,995. The 11th Party Congress reported that 63,000 members had been expelled since the previous Congress.

SED membership included about a fifth of the labor force in the country. The party's determined effort to increase the percentage of workers in its ranks materialized. However, the figures were unrealistic in at least one aspect. The category "industrial workers" included many officials, administrators and supervisors. Although women made up nearly half of the working force in the state, their membership in the SED was only slightly over one-third.

Decades-long discontent in Eastern Europe erupted during 1989 into enormous demonstrations for reform. Seizing on Gorbachev's policies of *glasnost* and *perestroika*, the masses overwhelmed even the power structure of the hard-line SED. Hundreds of thousands, including Communists, poured into the streets and squares demanding basic human rights, political pluralism and economic reform. They shouted for democracy and change in the Communist leadership. The SED was incapable of denying the public.

On October 18, 1989, at a special session of the 163-member Central Committee, Honecker, with only his abstention, was removed as general secretary of the SED. He was replaced by Egon Krenz, frequently mentioned as Honecker's successor, who was not previously considered as a reformer but rather as a hard-liner. A member of the Politburo and the Secretariat in charge of security affairs, youth and sports, Krenz acknowledged certain shortcomings by the SED. He pledged to "regain the political and ideological offensive." On October 24 the Volkskammer confirmed Krenz as chairman of the Council of State, but there were 52 abstentions. A week later, he visited Moscow. After conferring with Gorbachev, Krenz announced his support for *perestroika* for East Germany. Meanwhile, mass demonstrations and emigration continued. On November 3, five of the 18 Politburo members were purged, while 500,000 people demonstrated in East Berlin demanding, among other changes, freedom to travel, free elections and Krenz's resignation. In response Krenz resigned in December 1989 and Gregor Gysi was elected as general Secretary in his stead.

Three days after the Liberal Democratic Party called for its resignation, the government resigned on November 7. The next day the Politburo surprisingly followed suit. Politburo member Hans Modrow, a Dresden reformist, was proposed as prime minister, and Krenz was reelected as general secretary of the SED. The new, smaller Politburo consisted of seven previous members and four new ones. On November 9 the regime opened the Berlin Wall and border areas to free travel. During the next several days an estimated 2 million East Germans took advantage of this new opportunity. Prime Minister Modrow organized his Council of Ministers, reducing the number from 44 to 28 and including 11 non-SED ministers, a higher number than previously. He pledged radical changes, and the SED leadership proposed discussions with opposition groups. The party began to take stern measures against certain party leaders, on November 23 expelling Günter Mittag, former economic head in the SED Secretariat, for mismanagement. Also, an investigation of former general secretary Honecker was undertaken.

Removing the constitutional provision of the SED's leading role in the society was a popular objective. On December 1 the Volkskammer amended the Constitution to this effect. The SED called an emergency session and apologized to Prague for participating in the 1968 Warsaw Pact invasion of Czechoslovakia. In December a Politburo candidate member resigned, explaining that he could not function credibly. At a Central Committee emergency session an unprecedented event occurred: General Secretary Krenz, the Politburo and the Central Committee all resigned, in preparation for an extraordinary Party Congress scheduled for December 15–17. Before resigning, the CC expelled Honecker from the SED.

In January 1990 SED was renamed the Socialist Unity Party—Party of Democratic Socialism (SED—PDS) as a prelude to the March 1990 elections.

ECONOMY

The GDR has a socialist economy where no significant economic activity is privately owned. Western economists label it a centrally planned economy (CPE) in which all economic decisions are centrally determined. Production targets, allocation of resources and prices are established administratively, and the means of production are almost entirely socialized. In the case of the GDR, about 97% of all net national income is earned by state-owned enterprises or collectives.

According to its advocates, this basic organizational form has its advantages. First, the economy can be harnessed to serve the political and economic objectives of the governing elite. Consumer demand can be restrained in favor of greater investment in basic industry or channeled into public sectors such as buses rather than private automobiles. Second, CPE's can maximize the continuous utilization of all available resources. Neither unemployment nor idle plants should exist beyond minimal levels, and stable development of the economy, unimpeded by inflation or recession, should be achievable. Third, social values and goals direct the economy rather than vice versa, and wealth serves social rather than private purposes.

According to its critics, CPE's have characteristic problems that make their performance inferior to free-market ones. The first stems from the very complexity of the planning process, for not every detail in a modern society is reducible to a figure in a draft plan, nor can all eventualities be covered in advance. Second, CPE's have built-in obstacles to innovation and efficiency in production. Managers with limited discretionary authority follow the line of least resistance and prefer the safety of fulfilling the plan targets—even regardless of cost—to the risks involved in developing or implementing new techniques or diversifying their product lines. Third, the system of allocating goods and services in CPE's is inefficient. The total mix of products is distributed according to the plan's System of Material Balances and is not related to actual market needs. The result is that some goods are overproduced and others are in short supply. Managers tend to hoard whatever they have and then to make informal trades when they are in need. Finally, no satisfactory means exist in CPE's to determine how to maximize economic utility with a given mix of available resources. In market economies, prices are fixed on cost, and utility considerations permit such a determination, albeit imperfectly. In CPE's, prices are set administratively on the basis of criteria unrelated to cost. Once they are set, they tend to persist. Thus prices vary significantly from the actual social or economic value of the products, and there is no valid basis for comparing the relative value of two or more products to society.

Like other socialist states of Eastern Europe, the GDR is tied through its membership in COMECON to a larger Soviet-dominated trade and production system.

The implications of COMECON membership extend to all facets of the GDR economy. Each member of COMECON is assigned certain productive specializations and is bound to deliver certain quotas of these outputs to the others. The priority areas assigned to the GDR are chemicals, industrial machinery and sophisticated electronic and optical equipment.

The GDR is relatively resource-poor. Aside from low-grade coal and potash, most of its raw materials must be imported. According to West German calculations, the GDR has to import about 80% of its high-grade coal; 96% of its crude oil; 97% of its iron ore; and all of its bauxite, chromium, manganese and phosphate. It also must import large quantities of chemicals, cotton, lumber and grain. Even its water supply is barely sufficient for its needs. Some 25% to 30% of the country's GDP is exported to pay for these basic products. Lack of natural resources is compounded by the country's small population and lack of adequate manpower. As a result, it has had to specialize in some products at the expense of others to take advantage of the efficiencies of mass production. Not only is the labor force relatively small, but also it is disproportionately aged and female. Over 20% of the population is past retirement age, and they are being replaced only slowly because of the low birth rate. Given this limitation, the regime has mobilized its entire labor force, first by bringing all available women into the productive sector and second through reducing the agricultural labor force. As a result, the GDR has a very high participation rate. Only 21.3% of its population of working age is not employed, compared to 31% in West Germany.

Despite the many constraints, the GDR's economy has developed impressively since 1949, and by any standard it stands at the top of the socialist world in performance and growth. Among all Communist countries, it has the highest per capita income, the most autos and hospital beds per capita, the highest labor productivity, the highest yield per worker in agriculture, the highest per capita electricity consumption and the most television sets and radios per capita.

The state of the economy is all the more remarkable considering the circumstances under which it was achieved. Although the term "economic miracle" has been primarily applied to West Germany, the term describes the GDR economy also, although in a more limited sense. The country was virtually devastated during World War II and suffered from the harsh Soviet occupation more than West Germany did under the more humane Allies. The country's political ostracization by the West militated against a rapid recovery, and its population loss before the construction of the Berlin Wall was an important drain on much-needed labor resources. The country's economic history since 1945 may be divided into four distinct periods:

- the period of reparations payments, 1945–53
- the period of population decline until 1961
- the period of reforms in the 1960s
- the period of increasing external economic difficulties until the early 1980s

During the first period, the GDR had a productive capacity of only 50% of the prewar level of the area that is now East Germany. Nearly 26% of the plants and machinery were dismantled by the Soviets, compared to 12% by the Allies in West Germany. During the first four years deliveries to the Soviet Union absorbed as much as 15% of the GDR's real national income, which was more than the share of gross investment. Further, the division of Germany had left the GDR with few basic industries, forcing it to build them rather than concentrating on traditional domestic lines of production. The aim of the first medium-term economic plan, the two-year plan of 1949–51, was not only to get industrial production back on its feet but also to fulfill reparation deliveries to the Soviet Union. The first five-year plan, of 1951–55, was designed to produce extensive structural changes in the industrial sector; they have persisted to this day.

The end of the reparations period in 1953 allowed the economy to catch up for lost time. However, by this time the political and economic gap between West Germany and the GDR had become so large that a mass exodus had begun to the former. In response, the second five-year plan, of 1956–60 (which did not come into operation until 1957 and which later was superseded by the seven-year plan of 1959–65) was planned to bring the standard of living in the GDR on a par with West Germany and halt the loss of skilled manpower. The ambitious plan could not be realized. During the late 1950s real per capita income in the GDR was some 30% below that of West Germany. Economic growth rates in fact declined in the GDR, and there were widespread shortages. This crisis prompted the regime to build the Berlin Wall.

The failure of the 1959–65 plan (which was abandoned in 1962) demonstrated the need for radical economic reforms. For the 1964–70 seven-year plan (Perspektivplan), the State Planning Commission abandoned the unrealistic goals of the earlier plans in favor of lower but more attainable goals that allowed greater scope for individual and collective initiative. To remove the growing distortions in output and prices, the government introduced the New Economic System (NES) in January 1963. It combined long-term central planning with indirect control of enterprises through economic levers, largely in the form of monetary instruments. Within certain limits, decision-making authority was delegated from the central economic agencies to the newly established combines of nationalized industrial concerns. For the first time in the economic history of the GDR, managers of state factories were encouraged to maximize profits and the power to use these profits partly within the enterprise itself to achieve further expansion. The state factories were made economically accountable, their fixed assets were revalued and depreciation levels were set at more realistic levels. In the monetary sector the rate of interest began to play a more decisive role.

The NES encompassed two economic plans, covering 1964–70 and 1966–70. However, after a promising initial success, new problems emerged. Productivity rises were unequally distributed over the industrial sector, and the economy began to suffer from serious dislocations. Toward the end of the 1960s the NES was suspended, and a period of consolidation followed. The 1970s encompassed two plans, 1971–75 and 1976–80, and at the end of the latter period balance-of-payments deficits reached unprecedented levels. As a result, the supply of consumer goods had to be cut back, and the standard of living declined.

The 1976–80 plan achieved an increase of 25.4% in the NMP, and industrial production rose by 32% and foreign trade by 61%. During the 1981–85 plan the country's NMP at 1980 prices for the five-year period totaled DDR-M 1.087 trillion. Labor productivity rose by 38%, crop production by 11% and foreign trade by 50%. The 1986–90 plan set further ambitious goals, including a 24% to 26% increase in the NMP, a 46% to 51% increase in industrial production and a 10% increase in livestock production. Investment during the five-year period was DDR-M 346 billion.

The GDR economy falls under the direction of the State Plan Commission (SPK), a very large national agency with branches in the counties and districts. The SPK continually charts the desired evolution of the economy. The SPK's directives are expressed in the medium-range (five-year) plans and in short-term (annual) plans. For each economic sector, tentative plan targets are annually separated from the national plan and transmitted to the central economic ministries. From here the targets are further divided and sent to the subordinate bodies.

Directly below the ministries are the centrally directed trusts, or *Kombinate*, and a few remaining Associations of Publicly Owned Enterprises. The latter are being phased out and absorbed into the former, which were introduced in 1978–80. The 130 *Kombinate* have become the predominant form in the industrial sector. The general idea behind their establishment was that greater efficiency and more rational management could be achieved by concentrating authority in the hands of middle-level leadership. Their responsibilities are essentially administrative, and they serve as links in the chain of operational command. The trend toward amalgamation is strong even at the level of the producing units, whose number has been reduced by over one-third since 1960.

A supplementary hierarchy of organs reach down from the SPK to territorial rather than functional subunits. Regional and local planning commissions and economic councils operate at the local level, where they concern themselves with environmental protection, housing, location of industry and other matters. The agricultural sector is integrated into the economy a little differently. Collective farms are formally self-governing but nevertheless subordinated to the Ministry of Agriculture. At the local level, party organs mobilize support for the plan targets and promote mass participation by workers and farmers.

In addition to the annual and medium-range plans there are other mechanisms that control supplies and establish accountability. One of these implements the System of Material Balances, which is an allocation of materials, equipment and consumer goods. As such it

acts as a rationing system that assures each element of the economy access to the basic goods it needs to fulfill its obligations. The guidance provided by the monetary devices is based on the practice of assigning prices to all goods and services, which are then used to calculate expenses as well as receipts. These prices guide decision-making because they determine profits and bonuses.

The private sector of the economy is small although not entirely insignificant. In terms of primary employment, only about 2% of the labor force is outside the socialized sector—mostly artisans, farmers and storeowners. Their contributions to the economy are acknowledged by the regime. But more important than the open private sector are two unofficial private sectors. The first consists of moonlighters, such as collective farmers who cultivate private plots, and professionals such as artists and doctors who work in their spare time. The second group is much larger and consists of people engaged in the underground "second economy." Another common practice is that of giving underhand compensation to suppliers of goods in short supply or special favors. This problem is compounded by the fact that the West German deutschemark is a much-sought-after currency and fuels a flourishing black market.

PRINCIPAL ECONOMIC INDICATORS, 1988

Gross National Product: $207.2 billion
GNP per capita: $12,500
GNP average annual growth rate: (%) 1.8 (1988)
Consumer Price Index (1980 = 100)
  All items: 100.3 (1986)

No data are published regarding balance of payments in East Germany.

GROSS DOMESTIC PRODUCT, 1988

GDP nominal (national currency): 252.2 billion
GDP by type of expenditure (%)
  Consumption
    Private: 57
    Government: 11
  Gross domestic investment: 18
  Foreign trade
    Exports: ⎱ 13
    Imports: ⎰
Cost components of GDP (%)
  Net indirect taxes: 10
  Consumption of fixed capital: 9
  Compensation of employees: 40
  Net operating surplus: 41
Sectoral origin of GDP (%)
  Primary
    Agriculture: 8
  Secondary
    Manufacturing: 70 (includes mining & public utilities)
    Construction: 6
  Tertiary
    Transportation and communications: 4
    Trade: 9
    Finance: ⎱ 3
    Public administration & defense: ⎰

As in other Marxist states, the economy is the all-pervasive preoccupation of GDR politics. Vast resources are devoted to economic education, and economic questions dominate every political speech and party congress. Under Erich Honecker the nation made a transition from the Ulbricht era of planning and reform to one of management and innovation. Since the mid-1970s the economy has enjoyed relative organizational stability. Central planning has become more cautious and more realistic. Economic success is the paramount element in the GDR's quest for legitimacy, and party leaders continually emphasize the nation's role as the showcase of socialism and its place among the 10 most industrialized nations of the world.

CENTRAL GOVERNMENT EXPENDITURES, 1988

% of total expenditures
Defense: 5.4
Education: 3.6
Health & social welfare: 18.2
Housing: 5.6
Economic services: 33.8
Subsidies & price supports: 17.0
Other: 16.4

CENTRAL GOVERNMENT REVENUES, 1988

% of total current revenues
Revenues from state-owned enterprises: 69.0
Taxes & dues: 7.1
Social insurance contributions: 6.4
Health care contributions: 3.2
Other: 14.3

EXCHANGE RATE
(National Currency per U.S. Dollar)

1982	1983	1984	1985	1986	1987	1988
2.5	2.7	3.05	2.6	2.0	1.65	1.67

GROWTH PROFILE (Annual Growth Rates, %)

Population, 1985–2000: 0
Crude birth rate, 1985–90: 12.3
Crude death rate, 1985–90: 12.9
Urban population, 1985–90: 0.3
Labor force, 1985–2000: 0.2
Energy production, 1980–85: 3.2
Energy consumption, 1980–85: 1.5

PUBLIC FINANCE

The fiscal year is the calendar year.

GDR budgets are generally balanced or in surplus. The national budget was slightly in surplus in both 1987 and 1988, with revenues of DDR-M276.779 billion and expenditures of DDR-M276.614 billion in the former year and revenues of DDR-M291.180 billion and expenditures of DDR-M291.005 billion in the latter. Of the revenues, a broad item called state economy provides 70%, taxes and dues 7% and social insurance 6.5%. Of the expenditures, state economy again is the largest item, with 27.7%, followed by price support, 16.5%; social

insurance, 12.64%; housing construction, 5.7%; defense, 5.4%; health care, 5.3%; and public education, 3.3%. The share of these categories has not changed materially in recent years.

CURRENCY & BANKING

The national unit of currency is the DDR-Mark (Mark der Deutschen Demokratischen Republik), divided into 100 Pfennige. Coins are issued in denominations of 1, 5, 10, 20 and 50 Pfennige and 1, 2, 5, 10, and 20 DDR-Marks, and notes in denominations of 5, 10, 20, 50, and 100 DDR-Marks.

As in other Communist nations, banking plays a low-key role in the economy. The central bank is the State Bank of the GDR. There are only three other banks, all state-owned; one handles agricultural credit and the other two export-import trade.

East Germany's external public debt was $20.4 billion in 1988.

AGRICULTURE

Like Soviet agriculture, GDR agriculture is organized into collective farms and subject to central planning but, unlike its Soviet counterpart, GDR agriculture is an efficient economic sector and is able to feed the population at adequate levels.

The total land area is 108,179 sq. km. (41,768 sq. mi.). Agriculture is carried out in most areas, although the land available for farming is steadily decreasing. More and more small or marginal parcels of land are being incorporated into existing farms. Because almost all available land is being intensely cultivated, great importance is placed on soil conservation. Water, in critically short supply, also is being conserved by the Water Use Law of 1981, under which user fees are levied.

Before 1945 the territories forming the GDR were noted for large landholdings. Private landholdings over 100 ha. (247 ac.) accounted for almost a third of the agricultural area in 1945. These lands, comprising 3.25 million ha. (8 million ac.), were expropriated without compensation and redistributed to landless rural farmers, farmers with nonviable holdings and refugees. Once the land redistribution was accomplished by 1952, collectivization was initiated with three types of agricultural production cooperatives, with Type III being the least collectivized and Type I the most. Each member family also received a 0.5-ha. (1.2-ac.) private plot. Collectivization covered 80% of the total land area by 1960. However, collectivization was not the final organization of the system. In the 1970s an industrialized agricultural system (*Industriemassiges*) was introduced to improve productivity through specialization and economies of scale. Collectives were divided into crop collectives and livestock collectives. Both types were further divided by specialization. For example, crop collectives include horticultural collectives and livestock collectives include fattening stations. In certain rural districts there also are agrochemical centers, construction units, irrigation and land improvement units and drainage units. These enterprises perform their specialized functions for all the collectives in a district. To avoid overspecialization, the government encourages the formation of cooperative councils. In some regions, to counter the increasing size of the units, each village is being set up as a territorial unit. These cooperation councils appear destined to become the main administrative units in agriculture.

State farms occupy 9.7% of the farm area and occupy a much less important position in the economy.

In Type I collective farms only the plowland is collectively used; all other land and productive resources are private. On Type II collective farms all farmland is cooperatively used (except for small private plots), and members surrender all machinery and equipment to the farm management. Type III farms are completely collectivized (except for the small private plots and a few head of cattle). To become a member of a Type III collective a farmer must contribute real property of a specified value or discharge this obligation by contributing a portion of his earned income over a period of time. Farmers retain legal ownership of the property they contribute. The distribution of income is based on the acreage surrendered by each member and the amount of work performed for the collective. Each collective farmer is obligated to perform a minimum annual amount of work, nonperformance of which entails penalties in the form of deductions. These work norms are designed to assure that members devote their time primarily to the collective sector rather than to their own private plots.

Most of the cultivated land is devoted to food or feed grains. The principal traditional crops are grains (especially rye), potatoes and sugar beets. Since 1945 they have been supplemented by barley and wheat as well as industrial and feed crops. Productivity has risen significantly, thus offsetting the loss of farm labor to other sectors. Grain yields per hectare have more than doubled under the Communist regime. The 1986 harvest of grain (cereals and pulses) reached a record 11.7 million tons, and the 1987 harvest was 11.5 million tons. In tonnage, the largest harvests in 1985 were 11.5 million tons of potatoes, 6.7 million tons of sugar beets, 4.4 million tons of barley, 3.8 million tons of wheat and 2.5 million tons of rye.

Traditionally, the livestock sector has accounted for two-thirds of the gross value of output in the agricultural sector. The livestock herd was drastically reduced during the war and the early years of collectivization but has since surpassed prewar levels. Pork, veal and beef dominate the meat output, and some meat and dairy products are exported. Livestock production is extensively mechanized and concentrated in large-scale organizations.

Forests account for 28% of the total land area. Pine is the most important variety, followed by spruce, oak and beech. Forests suffered from excessive exploitation during the war and compulsory deliveries of forest products to the Soviet Union during the reparations period. Afforested and reforested areas have declined since 1952 as a result of pressures on land for other purposes.

The chief commercial species of fish harvested from the Baltic are herring and sprat, codfish, coalfish, sea carp, red perch, salmon and haddock. There are over 700 fishing collectives in all coastal and river areas. The GDR is not self-sufficient in fish catch, and fishing generally is a neglected sector.

AGRICULTURAL INDICATORS, 1988

Agriculture's share of GDP (%): 11.3
Cereal imports (000 tons): 2,776
Index of Agricultural Production (1979–81 = 100): 110 (1986)
Index of Food Production (1979–81 = 100): 109 (1986)
Index of Food Production per capita: (1979–81 = 100): 110 (1984–86)
Number of tractors: 161,515
Number of harvester-threshers: 17,461
Total fertilizer consumption (tons): 1,638,900
Fertilizer consumption (100 g. per ha.): 3,296
Number of farms: 4,800
Tenure (%)
  State: 9.7
  Collective: 90.3
Activity (%)
  Mainly crops: 30.0
  Mainly livestock: 68.5
  Mixed: 1.5
% of farms using irrigation: 3
Total land in farms, ha. (ac.): 6,208,000 (15,339,968)
Farms as % of total land area: 57.3
Land use (%)
  Total cropland: 75.9
  Meadows & pastures: 20.1
  Other: 4.0
Yields, kg./ha. (lb./ac.)
  Grains: 4,531 (4,044)
  Roots and tubers: 24,565 (21,925)
  Pulses: 1,857 (1,657)
  Milk kg. (lb.)/animal: 4,600 (10,141)
Livestock (000)
  Cattle: 5,827
  Sheep: 2,857
  Hogs: 12,946
  Horses: 105
  Chickens: 50,000
Forestry
  Production of roundwood, 000 cu. m. (000 cu. ft.): 10,868 (383,803)
    of which industrial roundwood (%): 94.8
  Value of exports ($ 000): 108,100
Fishing
  Total catch (000 tons): 208.9
    of which marine (%): 90.6

MANUFACTURING

The GDR is one of the world's largest industrial powers and ranks second in COMECON (after the Soviet Union) in aggregate output. Before World War II, the area that later became East Germany was less industrially advanced than the western parts of Germany. Compounding the problem was the lack of industrial raw materials, the massive destruction of industrial plants during the war and the Soviet dismantling and removal of the few factories that survived the war. The building of an industrial base began after the end of the reparations deliveries in the early 1950s and was intensified after the halting of the tide of emigration in 1961.

The GDR's principal industrial products and product areas are chemicals and petrochemicals, including plastics, synthetic fibers, potash fertilizers, phosphates, ferrous and nonferrous metallurgy, heavy machinery (especially machine tools and processing machinery), automotive equipment, shipbuilding, electrical engineering and electronics (including computers, microelectronics and robotics, television sets and stereo equipment), precision and scientific instruments, equipment ranging from miniature lathes to industrial photogrammetry, and textile and printing machinery. The largest industrial sector covers mechanical engineering and vehicle-building, which includes foundries and shipbuilding.

MANUFACTURING INDICATORS, 1988

Share of GDP: 63.9%
Labor force in manufacturing: 40.6%
Value added in manufacturing
  Food & agriculture: 13.5%

  Textiles:
  Machinery } 86.5%
  Chemicals

The GDR traditionally spends about half of its investment funds on machinery and equipment. The high-priority investment sectors are, first, R&D in energy, chemicals and metallurgy; second, processes and machinery that will help to conserve energy and raw materials; and third, production of high-quality exportable goods.

Over 90% of industrial production is accounted for by 126 centrally managed *Kombinate* (combines). There also are some 66 district-managed *Kombinate*. Both types are organizations of enterprises or factories that produce similar products, use similar technologies or carry out sequential production stages for a given product. They report directly to the appropriate industrial ministry. Although *Kombinate* were a feature of the industrial scene for years, they were established as the dominant industrial organization only in the 1980s. They may be horizontal, vertical or mixed in structure, depending on the needs of the industry. In the food processing, consumer goods and construction industries, *Kombinate* usually are horizontal, while those in the heavy industries generally are vertical. The shipbuilding and ship repair industry, represented by VEB Schiffbaukombinat, is an example of a mixed type.

The purpose of the *Kombinat* is to provide a streamlined chain of command in the decision-making processes. They enjoy a great deal of autonomy in all day-to-day operations, including costs, relations with suppliers, labor, raw materials and spare parts. They supervise enterprise-level economic planning and coordinate it with national plans. Economic planning at the *Kombinat* level is quite detailed and involves at least 100 technical and economic indicators. Some 70% of total scientific research for specific or commercial purposes is carried out by *Kombinat* research laboratories and design institutes. Most innovations are incorporated rapidly into the production lines; others are offered by the Central License Office to foreign firms for hard currency. Much of this research also is coordinated with university and academic research institutes on the one hand and with similar entities in CMEA countries on the other. The *Kombinate* have direct interest in foreign trade. As a result, they are more responsive to world market considerations than was the case before the 1980s.

MINING

The GDR is poor in minerals except for an abundance of brown coal or lignite, of which it is the world's largest producer, and potash. Reserves of brown coal are estimated at 24 billion tons, of which 92% is suitable for open-pit mining. The major portion of the workable reserves are in the upper and lower Lausitz areas in the Cottbus and Dresden districts adjoining the Polish border. Other important deposits are in the Halle and Leipzig districts. Production was 296 million tons in 1984. The GDR is a world leader in coal gasification and the development of coal carbide. Lignite is used, in addition, for thermal electric power stations. The state controls all mineral production.

Iron ore deposits are widely scattered in areas unfavorable to mining. Ore seams are thin and have an iron content of only 20% to 35%. Nonferrous metals, including copper, lead, zinc and tin, are mined in small quantities. Virtually all other minerals are imported.

ENERGY

Apart from coal and much smaller outputs of petroleum and natural gas (42,000 tons and 8 billion cu. m.; 283

ENERGY INDICATORS, 1988

Primary energy production (quadrillion BTU)
  Crude oil: 0
  Natural gas, liquid: 0
  Natural gas, dry: 0.18
  Coal: 2.62
  Hydroelectric power: 0.02
  Nuclear power: 0.14
  Total: 2.96
Average annual energy production growth rate (%): 3.2 (1980–85)
Average annual energy consumption growth rate (%): 1.5 (1980–85)
Energy consumption per capita, kg. (lb.) oil equivalent: 5,915 (13,040)
Electricity
  Installed capacity (kw.): 22,059,000
  Production (kw.-hr.): 115.291 billion
    % fossil fuel: 89.0
    % hydro: 1.5
    % nuclear: 9.5
  Consumption per capita (kw.-hr.): 6,928
Natural gas, cu. m. (cu. ft.)
  Proved reserves: 187 billion (6.604 trillion)
  Production: 13 billion (459 billion)
  Consumption: 8.329 billion (294 billion)
Petroleum, bbl.
  Proved reserves: 4 million
  Years to exhaust proved reserves: 20
  Production: 200,000
  Consumption: 164 million
  Refining capacity per day: 470,000
Coal, 000 tons
  Reserves: 21,000,000
  Production: 311,260
  Consumption: 317,955

billion cu. ft., respectively), the GDR has no energy sources and therefore imports the bulk of its needs. Much of the uranium output is exported to the Soviet Union.

About 80% of the electric power is produced thermally from lignite, and 9.5% is generated by the two nuclear plants at Rheinsberg and Greifswald (Rostock).

LABOR

The GDR labor force in 1988 was 8.96 million, compared to 6 million in 1952. The most striking characteristics of the labor force are the shortage of labor in most productive branches; the high proportion of women, only slightly less than at parity with men; and the continued distinction in official statistics between those working in the material branches of production and those working in the "unproductive" branches. Productivity is the highest among all Communist countries. Another characteristic of the labor force is its small size relative to the manpower needs of the economy. As a result, the entire force is mobilized, and the participation rate is one of the highest in Europe. Unemployment is marginal and exists in small pockets only. The participation rate of women, at 49.1%, also is one of the highest in Europe.

Workers do not have the right to establish or join unions of their choice. The Free German Trade Union Confederation (FDGB), an appendage of the Socialist Unity Party, consists of 16 unions representing 87.7% of the work force. Its role is to enforce and promote official party policies rather than to promote the interests of its members. Workers do not have the constitutional right to strike. This right, granted in the Constitution of 1949, was deleted from the Constitution of 1968 and was not restored in the 1974 constitutional amendments. There is no legal provision for collective bargaining. Worker representatives sit on the boards of enterprises and collectives, but their presence is merely cosmetic.

East Germany has a foreign work force estimated at 170,000. The vast majority of them are from other countries in the Communist bloc, such as Cuba, Angola, China, Vietnam and Mozambique. There is also a small group of Poles who are mostly day workers. Foreign workers face harsh working and social conditions. They were given the right to vote only in 1989.

Forced labor is illegal. However, there is a requirement that teenagers must work at least one summer for the state, for which they receive a small compensation. Children from age 14 may work part time during vacations and full time with parental permission. Youths under age 18 may not be employed on night shifts.

Under the law, a full-time worker is entitled to a minimum wage of approximately $216 per month. The maximum workweek is 43¾ hours, one of the highest in Europe. All GDR citizens have constitutional guarantee of a job. Except under extraordinary circumstances, overtime is limited to 120 hours a year. A two-day weekend is common.

Levels of training of the labor force have steadily risen since the end of World War II. Nearly two-thirds of the economically active population has some vocational training. The proportion is even higher for the younger group, in which the share of graduates of technical colleges exceeds 50%.

FOREIGN COMMERCE

The GDR's foreign trade presents some unusual features. Official statistical publications give only figures for the turnover of foreign trade and not for imports and exports separately. Neither does the GDR publish a balance of payments. Thus its trade performance can be gauged only from statistics of its main trading partners.

Official turnover figures reveal that nearly two-thirds of the foreign trade is conducted with centrally planned economies, with the Soviet Union alone accounting for two-fifths. The share of trade with developed-market economies (basically OECD countries) is just under 30%. Developing-market economies account for a mere 8%.

After 1973 the GDR was badly hit by the worldwide rises in prices for raw materials and energy. The much more modest rise in the GDR's export prices resulted in a disquieting fall in the terms of trade, leading to serious balance-of-payments deficits. From 1971 to 1981 the shortfall in the balance of payments was estimated at $11.4 billion. Because of the chronic shortage of convertible currencies (common to all East European regimes), these deficits could be settled only by borrowing in Western financial markets. By 1981 the GDR had the second-highest external debt, after Poland, among all East European countries. Rising interest rates on this debt absorbed almost one-quarter of the GDR's total exports to OECD countries. Trade with the Soviet Union also showed substantial deficits beginning with the first oil shock in 1973, although these could be financed through more favorable credits.

In an effort to reduce the debt burden, the 1981–85 five-year plan emphasized the need to reduce overall consumption levels, particularly in the consumption of energy, and rapidly to increase exports to convertible-currency countries. Although the export growth rate fell short of planned targets, the GDR was successful in markedly reducing the trade deficits and realizing sizable surpluses from 1981, even at the cost of a downturn in the standard of living.

Of particular significance in GDR trade is its trade relations with West Germany, begun with the Berlin Agreement of 1951. This agreement was not so much between the two countries as between the two currency areas—the D-Mark and the DDM-Mark. Despite the political ill will between the two countries, the agreement has survived intact for sound economic reasons. In essence, the agreement provided the GDR with trade concessions applicable only to EEC members. Trade between the two German states is not subject to trade barriers. Even more important for the GDR is the fact that trade deficits with West Germany do not have to be settled in convertible currencies. To retain these advantages the GDR has made some important political concessions in its treatment of dissidents. The basic agreement is a safety valve for the GDR in case of a Western embargo or bottlenecks in industrial supplies from its

COMECON partners. Although the actual level of inter-German trade has not exceeded 10% of total GDR trade in recent years, it is strategic because of these considerations. The GDR generally runs deficits in this trade. These deficits extend to the invisible trade or services account, which includes shipping, and the use of West German ports.

Inter German trade is conducted under special rules: Exports to West Germany bear no duty; trade is conducted on the basis of accounting units (*Verrechnungseinheiten*); the value-added tax is rebated; and trade is financed through the use of an interest-free "swing credit." The GDR exports mainly oil products, chemicals, textiles, clothing, steel and nonferrous metals to West Germany, and imports from it machinery, mining equipment, high-technology products, steel and chemicals. The GDR is the largest importer of Western goods among CMEA countries outside the Soviet Union, buying $10.8 billion worth in 1987–88, of which almost half came from West Germany.

The Soviet Union still is the GDR's largest trading partner, accounting in 1988 for 39% of total trade. The trade, valued at 15 million transferable rubles, consists of GDR imports of Soviet oil, coal, steel and cotton, and exports of machine tools, ships, computers and railroad cars.

GDR foreign trade is a state monopoly coordinated by the Ministry of Foreign Trade. The state determines the volume of trade, the composition of exports and the geographical distribution of trade. Actual buying and selling usually are conducted by about 51 specialized Foreign Trade Enterprises (FTE's). The major decision-making bodies above the Ministry of Foreign Trade are the Council of Ministers and the State Planning Commission, both of which are actively involved in this sector.

With certain specific exceptions, only FTE's are authorized to negotiate and sign contracts with foreign firms. They enjoy the rights of juridical persons and as such are legally independent economic organizations. They operate within the framework of the overall foreign trade plan and negotiate contracts according to the instructions and guidelines of the responsible ministries and other end users, such as the *Kombinate*. Although mainly intermediaries, they have some decision-making power, particularly in evaluation of proposals. A Western firm has little choice of the FTE with which it does business. Normally FTE's invite from foreign firms at least three bids, which are then assessed on the basis of commercial criteria such as price, delivery dates, payment terms and quality. Political considerations also may play a part in the final decisions. About half of the FTE's are organizationally part of a special *Kombinat*, and its director-general would concurrently be a deputy director of the *Kombinat*. A second type of FTE coordinates the product lines of several *Kombinate* and reports directly to a given industrial ministry as well as to the Ministry of Foreign Trade. A third type of FTE handles several different kinds of product lines, cutting across industrial sectors. All three types are subordinate to one of the 11 industrial ministries as well as to the Ministry of Foreign Trade, whose permission they must obtain before signing any contract with suppliers or buyers. Any losses sustained by FTE's in the fulfillment of contracts approved by the Ministry of Foreign Trade will be made up from the public Treasury.

In addition to the FTE's there are a number of special foreign trade service enterprises. These include the Chamber of Foreign Trade; the national Chamber of Commerce, responsible for international economic relations and trade promotion; and the International Trade Center, Berlin, which offers a full range of advice, facilities and services.

The semi-annual Leipzig Trade Fair is the most important trade promotion event in the GDR. It is one of the oldest in Europe, dating back about 800 years, and also the largest in CMEA countries and among the three largest horizontal fairs in the world. The spring fair takes place about the second week of March and the autumn fair about the first or second week of September. The former, which is the larger of the two, is focused on heavy industry (metallurgy, heavy machinery and machine tools), materials handling equipment, electronics, telecommunications, data processing equipment, agricultural machinery, precision instruments and laboratory equipment, and air-conditioning equipment. The autumn fair concentrates on chemicals, chemical plants, plastics, textile production equipment, printing equipment, automotive products, medical and surgical equipment and light industry.

The GDR does not levy customs duties or other taxes on commercial imports. Duties are applied only to noncommercial goods or to certain goods imported or exported by tourists. The GDR is not a party to the GATT. All foreign exchange transactions are handled by the Foreign Trade Bank or the Trade Bank.

The Law on International Commercial Agreements (GIW), and a second law affecting international commercial agreements in areas where the GIW is silent, superseded the old Commercial Code and related laws, some of whose terms went back to 19th-century imperial Germany.

FOREIGN TRADE INDICATORS, 1988

Exports: $30.8 billion
Imports: $31.0 billion
Balance of trade: $200 million

Direction of Trade (%)*

	Imports	Exports
EEC	13.0	N.A.
U.S.A.	0.4	N.A.
East European countries	63.3	N.A.
Japan	0.7	N.A.

*Figures are for total trade. Separate export figures are not published.

Composition of Trade (%)

	Imports	Exports
Food & agricultural raw materials		
Ores & minerals	55.4	23.7
Fuels		
Manufactured goods	44.6	76.3
of which chemicals	8.6	13.2
of which machinery	29.5	46.7

TRANSPORTATION & COMMUNICATIONS

The GDR inherited a transportation system from the Third Reich that included a good railway network, although damaged by the war. The prewar network included 18,500 km. (11,498 mi.), but it was reduced to 14,300 km. (8,888 mi.) at the end of the war. Its density of 13.2 km. per 100 sq. km. (8.2 mi. per 38.6 sq. mi.) does not differ materially from the relative figure for West Germany, but the quality is hardly comparable. In West Germany double tracks make up two fifths of the total, compared to one-fifth in the GDR. The transition to diesel and electrical traction was completed in the 1980s, and the last steam trains were withdrawn from service in that decade. Nearly one-tenth of the entire line is electrified, compared to one-third in West Germany. In the 1980s the Dresden–Schona, Muldenstein–Berlin and Dresden–Berlin lines were electrified. The difference in quality between the two German rail systems is crucial in the context of the dominant role that railways play in the GDR's transportation economy.

Hitler's major transportation legacy were the *Autobahnen*, which were built in the 1930s primarily for military use. They remained important for private and commercial users after the war. The road density of 112 km. per 100 sq. km. (70 mi. per 38.6 sq. mi.) is comparable to that of West Germany, but the quality is far less comparable. Major postwar additions to the *Autobahn* system are the 74-km. (46-mi.) Dresden–Leipzig and 270-km. (168-mi.) Berlin–Rostock sections.

Urban transportation has undergone structural change since the 1960s. Tramways dominated the city transportation systems, but they have been converted in many places into high-speed systems. In Berlin, there are *S-Bahns* and *U-Bahns* (elevated and underground electric trains, respectively).

The inland waterways were well developed even before World War II. The Elbe River, which is navigable from Hamburg to Prague, provides the north–south axis of the system, and a series of canals from the Polish border near Eisenhuttenstadt to the inter-German border and beyond provides the east–west axis. Magdeburg, where the two axes meet, is the hub of the system.

The Baltic seaports of Rostock, Wismar and Stralsund were largely destroyed during the war but were reconstructed and considerably enlarged. Rostock now ranks fourth among Baltic seaports. Its position has been consolidated with the completion of the Berlin–Rostock *Autobahn*. The other seaport is at Stassnitz. The GDR merchant marine now ranks third among CMEA countries.

The national aviation flag carrier is Interflug. The country's principal international airport is Berlin-Schonefeld; international air traffic also is handled by Dresden, Leipzig and Erfurt airports.

The Oder River port of Schwedt is the GDR terminus of the Friendship Pipeline, which carries crude oil from the Soviet Union. Domestic pipelines carry the crude oil to the port of Rostock and to the refinery city of Leuna, west of Leipzig.

While the volume of private transportation has risen, it still is only 38% that of West Germany. Motorcycles and mopeds make up about two-thirds of the entire stock of motor vehicles. The price of gasoline is much higher than in Western countries. The most popular automobiles are the Trabant and the Wartburg. Waiting times for delivery of new cars are long, and as a result the autos are kept on the road much longer than in the West, and the need for repairs and spares is correspondingly greater. Spare parts account for more than a quarter of new production in automobile plants, but even so there is an acute shortage of spare parts. There is no system of regular official vehicle tests. The absence of tests contributes to the rising number of road accidents. The slow growth of private motor transportation and the relative strength of public transportation systems have inhibited the kind of traffic density and congestion that is a major feature of West German traffic. The ratio of private to public transportation is 1:4. Most public transportation is heavily subsidized, and their fares cover less than half of the operating costs.

LABOR INDICATORS, 1988

Total economically active population: 8.96 million
As % of working-age population: 67.0
% female: 49.1
% under 20 years of age: 8.6
Average annual growth rate, 1985–2000 (%): 0.2
Activity rate (%)
    Total: 51.4
    Male: 55.0
    Female: 48.1
% organized labor: 87.7
Sectoral employment (%)
    Agriculture, forestry & fishing: 10.8
    Manufacturing: 40.6
    Construction: 6.7
    Transportation & communication: 7.3
    Trade: 10.3
    Finance, real estate: ⎫
    Public administration & defense: ⎬ 24.2
    Services: ⎭

TRANSPORTATION INDICATORS, 1988

Roads, km. (mi.) 124,615 (77,434)
Motor vehicles
    Persons per vehicle: 4.3
    Automobiles: 3,462,184
    Trucks: 425,049
    Road freight, tonne-km. (ton-mi.): 7.559 billion (5.177 billion)
Railroads
    Track, km. (mi.): 14,005 (8,702); electrified, km. (mi.): 2,754 (1,710)
    Passenger traffic, passenger-km. (passenger-mi.): 22.402 billion (13.920 billion)
    Freight, freight tonne-km. (freight ton-mi.): 58.881 billion (40.328 billion)
Merchant marine
    Vessels: 377
    Total deadweight tonnage: 1,880,000
    No. oil tankers: 5; GRT: 36,000
Ports
    Number: 4 sea, 4 river
    Cargo loaded (tons): 11,982,000
    Cargo unloaded (tons): 13,141,000
Air
    Km. (mi.) flown: 34.2 million (21.2 million)
    Passengers: 1,446,000
    Passenger traffic, passenger-km. (passenger-mi.): 2.649 billion (1.646 billion)

TRANSPORTATION INDICATORS, 1988 (continued)

Freight traffic, freight ton-km. (freight ton-mi.): 70.7 million (48.4 million)
Mail tonne-km. (mail ton-mi.): 71.6 million (44.4 million)
Airports with scheduled flights: 4
Airports: 160
Civil aircraft: 45
Pipelines
  Crude, km. (mi.): 1,301 (808)
  Refined, km. (mi.): 500 (310)
  Natural gas, km. (mi.): 2,150 (1,335)
Inland waterways
  Length, km. (mi.): 2,319 (1,441)
  Cargo, tonne-km. (ton-mi.): 2.437 billion (1.669 billion)

COMMUNICATIONS INDICATORS, 1988

Telephones
  Total (000): 3,755
  Persons per: 4.4
Phone traffic (000 calls)
  Local: 1,351,300
  Long distance: 776,779
  International: 13,321
Post office
  Number of post offices: 11,972
  Pieces of mail handled (000): 1,453,628
Telegraph, total traffic (000): 13,333
Telex
  Subscriber lines: 16,724
  Traffic (000 minutes): 9,353 (international only)
Telecommunications
  1 satellite ground station

TOURISM & TRAVEL INDICATORS, 1988

Number of tourists (000): 1,500 (1984)
  of whom (%) from
  Czechoslovakia, 36.6
  Soviet Union, 18.9
  Poland, 7.6
  Hungary, 2.3
Average length of stay (nights): 3

DEFENSE

The National People's Army (Nationale Volksarmee, NVA) was founded in 1956 with the passage by the People's Chamber of the Act on the Foundation of the National People's Army and the Ministry of National Defense. The NVA incorporated the Garrisoned Police, the Naval Police and the Air Police into a single armed force having three branches: ground, naval and air. Ironically, the new armed forces follow more the traditional German military heritage than the Soviet model. The officers and men wear Wehrmacht-style uniforms and practice the Prussian-style drill and goose step march. NVA was fully integrated with the Warsaw Pact forces from the inception of the pact in 1955. The close association of the NVA with the Red Army and the defense forces of other East European Communist countries is reflected in the NVA's military oath: "I swear to be always ready, side by side with the Soviet Army and the armies of our socialist allies, to protect socialism against all enemies and to risk my life for the achieve-

ment of victory." The Constitution, too, is equally emphatic about the GDR-Soviet military ties, and Article 7 refers to the "close comradeship-in-arms" between the NVA and the Red Army. The NVA is perhaps the only army in the world so constitutionally bound to the armed forces of another state. As a consequence, the NVA is trained to fight only as part of a Soviet or Warsaw Pact army group. Similarly, the NVA's navy operates in close coordination the Soviet Baltic Fleet in peacetime and would be absorbed by it during wartime. The NVA's air force is completely integrated into the Soviet air defense system.

The NVA is administered through the Ministry of National Defense, headed by the minister of national defense, with headquarters at Strausberg. He is assisted by a collegium of eight deputy ministers, who are each assigned a separate division, as follows: Frontier Troops; People's Navy; Technology and Weaponry; Rear Services; Main Political Directorate; Air Force/Air Defense; Ground Forces; and Main Staff. Some Soviet officers also are assigned to the ministry.

Ground forces make up nearly two-thirds of the NVA. They are deployed in three military districts: Military District I, headquartered at Strausberg, which being only 35 km. (22 mi.) west of Berlin is essentially the capital district; Military District III, embracing the southern half of the country and headquartered at Leipzig; and Military District V, headquartered at Neubrandenburg and embracing the northern half of the country. Military District I includes the Ground Forces Command. The organization of tactical troops is patterned on the Soviet model. All divisions are maintained at full strength.

The key agency of the NVA appears to be not so much the Ministry of National Defense but the Commission on National Security, which is linked to the Security Department of the SED's Central Committee. Party control over the NVA is more thorough than in other Warsaw Pact countries, including the Soviet Union. The Main Political Administration, headed by one of the eight deputy ministers, has a unique dual status as a division of both the Ministry of National Defense and a department of the SED's Central Committee. Reportedly all officers and about 80% of the troops are party members. The State Security Service, responsible to the Ministry of the Interior, acts as a check on the political administration, with a network of agents and informers throughout the NVA. Political education is compulsory and lasts four hours weekly for soldiers and eight hours monthly for officers.

The formal staff structure of the NVA is unlike that of a Western army. Because the Nuremburg Tribunal declared the German General Staff a criminal organization, the NVA has no general staff in the proper sense. The field force is commanded directly by the minister of national defense. The Main Staff approaches most nearly the status of a general staff, but it has no preeminence over the other subdivisions of the ministry of national defense. This arrangement also enables the Soviets to wield close operational control of the NVA. In the event of an actual war Military District V would be absorbed by the Soviet Group Forces (GSFG), headquartered at the old German Army headquarters at

Wunsdorf-Zossen; and Military District III would come under the Soviet Northern Group, headquartered at Legnica in Poland. The NVA is subordinate to the Soviet command even in peacetime—the only Warsaw Pact defense force to be so. Soviet forces have unlimited freedom of movement within the GDR—a right they do not have in any other Eastern bloc country—and their supreme commander can unilaterally declare a state of emergency with the nominal requirement to inform the GDR government. Soviet army officers are within the functional chain of command in the GDR Ministry of National Defense and participate in high-level planning discussions. Within the Warsaw Pact the NVA is the force most completely integrated with the alliance's group of forces—the price of being in the front line, according to GDR strategists. Since 1965 the NVA has belonged to the 1st Strategic Echelon, earmarked for immediate operations against NATO in the event of an actual conflict. Its field force is sufficient to form two Soviet-style armies operating at the level of three full-size divisions.

As a postwar creation, the NVA has arms of service organized in a simple manner uncomplicated by historical traditions. The main branches are infantry, armor, artillery and rocket troops, engineers and technical troops, and signals. These are known as the operational troops. The rear services are procurement, supply and transportation. Medical, administrative and political services are separate.

The tactical unit organization is almost entirely of Soviet origin. The frontier regiments consist of four company battalions, the alert units of battalions with five companies each and the combat groups of general or heavy battalions, each organized into three platoons of three sections each.

The navy consists of four flotillas and several supporting units, all stationed within Military District V. The navy functions under the command of the Soviet Baltic Fleet. Subsidiary organizations within the navy include the Naval Aviation Branch; the Coastal Border Brigade; and an amphibious unit, the Ernst Moritz Motorized Rifle Regiment.

The air force is fully integrated with the Soviet and Warsaw Pact air defense system and has little independent capability.

To counterbalance the NVA, a number of paramilitary organizations function as checks on its power. These include

• The Border Troops, with their own chain of command within the Ministry of National Defense.

• The Frontier Command, a separate organization with headquarters at Plauen, near Karl-Marx-Stadt. They are under the regional commands of the People's Police. Frontier Command North patrols the east–west border from Lubeck Bay to Nordhausen. Frontier Command South guards the border from Nordhausen to the Czechoslovak border. The seacoast is patrolled by the Coastal Border Brigade. The Polish and Czechoslovak borders are patrolled by an independent border regiment. The northern and southern commands are identical except that the former is reinforced by the Domitz

Boat Section along the Elbe River and the Water Police. The Frontier Command Center operates in and around Berlin and includes the Frontier Crossing Regiment, controlling access points to West Berlin.

• The Hundreds and Battalions of the paramilitary Combat Groups of the Working Class, organized in all urban centers.

Until 1962 service in the NVA was voluntary. Today about 40% to 50% of its military personnel are volunteers; the remainder were drafted under a 1962 conscription law. The term of service is 18 months, and would-be regulars enlist either for the short three-year period or for full-career (12-year) service. Although conscription is technically universal, the full contingent is not recruited each year. The GDR is the only East European country that recognizes conscientious objection, and those who refuse to bear arms for religious or other reasons are conscripted into construction units. Officers are recruited from secondary schools (in which case they are exempt from basic service) or are chosen from suitable conscripts or volunteers. Officers serve for 10 years, the age limits varying from 35 for captain to 65 for major general. The NVA takes pride in the fact that its officer corps is largely proletarian in origin.

Conscripts are called up (and released) twice a year, at the beginning of December and June. Their first four weeks are spent in a recruit unit; at the end of this period they are received into their operational units in a ceremonial oath-taking parade. They then receive their personal weapon from a member of the local combat group, a symbolic act representing their full integration into the NVA. Conscripts then proceed to half-year periods of individual, section, unit and formation training. Conscripts spend much of their time outdoors and are expected to attain very high standards of physical fitness. About a quarter of all training is devoted to political indoctrination.

NCO's selected during their first half-year training period are sent either to the NCO training regiment of their military district or to the NCO training company of their unit. The emphasis of NCO training is on the technical side. Since 1963 officers are trained at the Ernst Thalmann Officer School at Lobau, near Dresden. The course lasts four years and is run on Soviet lines. Final examinations are equivalent to those in the highest civilian schools and qualify graduates for careers in civil administration should they leave the army. More advanced training is provided in the Soviet Union, which receives more officers from the GDR than from any other East European country. Higher military training of officers of colonel and superior ranks is at the Friedrich Engels Military Academy in Dresden (formerly in Berlin). The course, which lasts two years, is modeled on that of the Frunze Academy in Moscow.

The military obligation under the conscription law extends from the ages 18 to 50 for soldiers and to 60 for officers. The reserve is divided into two groups, the first of men up to age 35. Reservists are liable for military training of 21 months spread over several years. Those men who are not conscripted at 18 because numbers exceeded requirements also are liable for training as reservists on the same terms as ex-conscripts. Party functionaries, skilled workers and students, who are largely exempted from conscription, are particularly required to perform reserve training. Party functionaries who complete this training are granted military rank commensurate with their political status.

The GDR has no arms industry of any significance—a result of deliberate Soviet policy. Some small arms are produced locally, but otherwise all equipment and weapons are imported from the Soviet Union or other Warsaw Pact nations.

Proportionate to the population, the NVA remains the smallest of the Warsaw Pact armies. It also is one that has been completely indoctrinated and one more motivated by ideological than nationalist traditions. Because virtually all East German males pass through military or paramilitary training, it also provides the regime with an opportunity to inculcate the populace in socialist virtues. The morale of both enlisted personnel and officers does not appear to be strained. As a whole the army suffers from excessive political supervision, and the senior ranks are filled with men whose commitment to the party exceeds their military talent. It is not basically apathetic to the Soviet Union, as the armed forces of most other non-Soviet Warsaw Pact nations are.

DEFENSE INDICATORS, 1988

Defense budget ($): 12.753 billion
% of central budget: 10.7
% of GNP: 6.4
Military expenditures per capita ($): 657
Military expenditures per soldier ($): 74,145
Military expenditures per sq. km. (per sq. mi.) ($): 117,723 (304,982)
Total strength of armed forces: 172,000
  Per 1,000: 10.4
Reserves: 390,000
Arms exports ($): 220 million
Arms imports ($): 525 million

Personnel & Equipment

Army
  Personnel: 120,000
  Organization: 2 military districts; 1 army headquarters; 2 motor rifle divisions; 1 tank division
  Equipment: 2,850 main battle tanks; 1,000 reconnaissance vehicles; 950 mechanized infantry combat vehicles; 3,750 armored personnel carriers; 870 towed artillery; 230 self-propelled artillery; 207 multiple rocket launchers; 71 SSM launchers; 250 mortars; 270 SAM's
Navy
  Personnel: 15,000
  Bases: Peenemünde; Warnemünde; Dranske-Bug; Sassnitz; Wolgatz
  Vessels: 19 frigates; 37 patrol and coastal combatants; 24 mine warfare vessels
  Naval aviation: 1,000 personnel; 25 combat aircraft; 13 armored helicopters
Air force
  Personnel: 37,000
  Organization: 2 air divisions; 2 ground attack fighter regiments; 1 reconnaissance squadron; 1 transportation regiment; 3 helicopter regiments; 6 fighter regiments; 7 SAM regiments; 2 radar regiments
  Equipment: 330 combat aircraft; 100 armored helicopters

EDUCATION

When the schools reopened in the Soviet Zone of Germany in 1945, nearly three-fourths of the teachers in the schools were removed from their jobs for their associations with the Nazi Party. In an effort to achieve a classless school system, the former three-school system was abolished in favor of a single school *(Einheitsschule)*. The equal right of all citizens to education was guaranteed in the Constitution of 1949. It was reiterated as a basic right in Article 25 of the Constitution of 1968. The first law restructuring the educational system was the Law on the Democratization of the Education System of 1946, setting up the *Einheitsschulen*, which all children attended for the first eight years before proceeding to the *Oberschule*, which replaced the former *Gymnasium*. Two other changes completed the radical break with the past: All private schools were abolished; and religious instruction, traditionally a required subject in the curriculum, was first relegated to a voluntary one and then done away with altogether. A more socialist direction was given to education in the early 1950s, when a new 10-year school was introduced alongside the eight-year *Einheitsschule* and the *Oberschule*. Polytechnical education began in the late 1950s to complement factory-based vocational training. From these polytechnics developed the general polytechnical high school, begun in 1964. A 1959 law created a second way of obtaining the *Abitur* (diploma), which hitherto could be obtained only at the *Oberschule*. Pupils finishing the 10th grade could enter vocational training programs with a university-preparatory component and thus simultaneously learn a trade and obtain the *Abitur*. In keeping with the general cultural policy of the time (the so-called Bitterfeld Way, a two-pronged effort to integrate the proletariat and the intelligentsia), graduates from the *Oberschule* (now renamed the *Erweiterte Oberschule*, EOS) were required to undertake a one-year apprenticeship in a trade.

The last modifications of the school system, giving it its present form, were made in 1965 with a law introducing "the uniform socialist system of education" *(das einheitliche sozialistische Bildungssystem)*, which covered the entire system of education and which is the most comprehensive education law enacted in the GDR. It increased compulsory education to 10 years, created the 10-year common school as the core of the system, reduced the EOS to a two-year program and made vocational training part of compulsory education. The law introduced the idea of differentiation *(Differenzierung)*, allowing the creation of special classes and schools for gifted children.

GDR educational philosophy is based on the Marxist-Leninist theory of personality, which holds that the goal of education is to develop a socialist society. For this purpose, classroom instruction is integrated with practical and productive work. This principle pervades the curriculum and all school activities. Schools are closely connected with the social and economic forces of the community, and industrial and agricultural enterprises have a role in education not found outside the Communist world.

A second basic principle is equality of educational opportunity for all citizens, particularly between urban and rural children and between the sexes. By the 1960s the traditional one-room rural schools were abolished. Today there are neither structural nor curricular differences between urban and rural schools. Similarly, there is no distinction between the sexes in regard to the curriculum or educational opportunities. Boys and girls take exactly the same courses in regular schools and polytechnical programs. Girls are eligible for all apprenticeships and other vocational training programs. A third basic principle of GDR education is lifelong education. Both workers and professionals are urged (in some cases obligated) to refresh their skills and master new developments in their field.

Compulsory education begins at age six and ordinarily extends through grade 10 and two- to three-year vocational training or three-year training in a technical college (Fachschule) or a two-year EOS, for a total of 12 or 13 years. The obligation to learn a vocation is binding on all young people except the handicapped.

The only exception to the state ownership of educational facilities is church-related education, consisting primarily of seminaries and also a scattering of kindergartens and training programs for teachers, nurses and others employed in church institutions.

The academic year runs from September through June, with 35 weeks of instruction, six days a week. Vacations are spread over the year: one week in the fall; 10 days at Christmas (which is called "vacation at the changing of the years"); three weeks later in the winter; a week or 10 days in the spring; and two months in the summer, for a total of some 96 days.

German is the universal medium of instruction except for the Sorbs, a Slavic minority living in Upper and Lower Lusatia. There are two schools, one in Cottbus and the other in Bautzen, in which Sorbian is the language of instruction.

The grading system uses numbers rather than letters. The highest grade is 1 and the lowest is 5. All examinations are state-administered and lead to the appropriate diploma or certificate: the Abschluss at the end of the 10th grade; the Abitur on completion of the EOS or a vocational training program with a university preparatory component; the Facharbeiterbrief at the end of a course for skilled workers; and the Fachschulabschluss on completion of courses at a technical college.

All educational materials are prepared by the Ministry of Public Education. Textbooks are not free, but their prices are heavily subsidized by the state.

In contrast to the traditional German education system in which the sole function of the school was to teach, the present system places considerable value on socialization. Such socialization takes place not merely on an informal basis but also through state youth organizations such as Pioneers (Pioniere) and Free German Youth (Frei Deutsche Jugend). The Youth Initiation (Jugendweihe) is a formal ceremony designed to supplant religious confirmation and at which 14-year-olds swear an oath of allegiance to socialism and the state.

Although compulsory education does not begin until age six, there is an extensive network of preschool

---

EDUCATION INDICATORS, 1988

Literacy
    Total (%): 100
    Male (%): 100
    Female (%): 100
First level
    Schools: 5,649
    Teachers: 58,406
    Students: 859,830
    Student–teacher ratio: 15:1
    Net enrollment rate (%): 98
    Females (%): 49
Second level
    Schools: 5,711
    Teachers: 112,076
    Students: 1,140,391
    Student–teacher ratio: 10:1
    Net enrollment rate (%): 87
    Females (%): 53
Vocational
    Schools: 4,500
    Teachers: 55,234
    Students: 378,761
    Student–teacher ratio: 7:1
Third level
    Institutions: 293
    Teachers: 42,336
    Students: 432,672
    Student–teacher ratio: 10:1
    Gross enrollment rate (%): 30.5
    Graduates per 100,000 age 20–24: 2,581
    % of population over 25 with postsecondary education: 17.3
    Females (%): 55
Foreign study
    Foreign students in national universities: 91
    Students abroad: 741
        of whom in
            United States, 31
            Italy, 49
            Hungary, 186
            Czechoslovakia, 375
Public expenditure
    % of GNP: 5.4

GRADUATES, 1983

Total: 129,760
Education: 15,133
Humanities & religion: 2,508
Fine & applied arts: 1,038
Law: 1,128
Social and behavioral sciences: 4,955
Commerce & business: 9,879
Mass communication: 668
Service trades: 736
Natural sciences: 1,870
Mathematics & computer science: 914
Medicine: 18,896
Engineering: 19,366
Architecture: 298
Industrial programs: 15,981
Transportation & communications: 1,298
Agriculture, forestry, fisheries: 6,622
Other: 28,470

---

facilities run by communities, factories, collectives and churches. Kindergarten is a three-year program, with children divided into three different classes according to age. The entire program is paid for by the state except for a small charge for the meals. For the benefit of working parents, kindergartens are all-day facilities, and some are open into the early evening. Kindergartens have a medical function as well because children undergo regular medical checkups; receive adequate physical exercise; and are screened for possible maladies and incipient health problems.

At age six, children enter—after being certified by a doctor that they are mentally and physically fit to do so—the first grade of the general polytechnical high school (Allgemeinbildende Polytechnische Oberschule), with its emphasis on both "general" and "technical." The 10-year course of study is divided into three levels: grades one to three (lower); grades four to six (middle); and grades seven to 10 (upper). The lower level concentrates on German and mathematics. The fourth grade serves as a transition year during which pupils are introduced to specialized instruction. In the fifth and sixth grades instruction is begun in a foreign language, usually Russian, as well as natural science and social studies. Chemistry and civics are added in the seventh grade, by which time the curriculum is fully developed. In 1978 a controversial program of military instruction (Wehrunterricht) was added to the curriculum of the ninth and 10th grades and consisting of four double hours of instruction throughout the year. In addition, there is a 14-day course in military training for boys and civil defense for girls at the end of the ninth grade, and a three-day practical program for all pupils during the 10th grade.

An important aspect of the curriculum is its polytechnical component, which is introduced in the first grade and which becomes increasingly intensive until the end of school. In the upper level polytechnical education assumes a vocational orientation and is associated with productive industries. Almost all collective farms and industrial enterprises are involved in this phase of education. In grades seven and eight, instruction includes the courses "Introduction to Socialist Production," "Technical Drawing" and "Productive Work." In the ninth and 10th grades, instruction is differentiated into 10 categories (corresponding to major industrial sectors, such as chemicals and engineering), and the scope of instruction is determined by the available facilities. Besides teaching respect for work and the working class, polytechnic education is designed for a number of other purposes as well: to reduce the schism between the intelligentsia and the working prople; to integrate theory and practice; to intensify the teaching of science and technology; and to help young people make realistic career choices.

Although elementary education is uniform, differentiation in curriculum begins as early as the seventh grade, when pupils may opt for a second foreign language or join study groups doing special projects. Pupils selected to attend the EOS are placed in separate classes starting in the ninth grade, and especially gifted pupils may be enrolled in special classes or in special schools. Fewer than 10% of those completing the eighth grade drop out of school. At the end of the 10th grade there is a battery of examinations, upon passing which the high-

school diploma (Abschluss) is awarded. The examination consists of a written test, an oral test and a physical education test.

Secondary schooling is offered in one of three programs: A small number go on to the EOS; a larger group enrolls in specialized colleges (Fachschulen) for professional training; and the majority begin apprenticeship training leading to qualification as a skilled worker, some programs of which also grant the Abitur.

The EOS is a two-year program for which only the best and most competent pupils are selected. Preference is given to children from the working class, and care is taken to balance the numbers of boys and girls. The initial selection is made in the eighth grade, and those selected receive special training in the last two years of the Oberschule. Pupils who take required additional course work may be selected during a second round in the 10th grade. The number of pupils admitted to the EOS is centrally determined, in keeping with projected needs for university-trained personnel. Approximately 10% of the pupils in a given 10th-grade class may go on to the EOS. The EOS curriculum is an extension of the Oberschule, and the emphasis on practical polytechnic training is continued. At the end of the two-year program there are final examinations with written, oral and physical education components.

All graduates of the Oberschule who do not go on to the EOS or the Fachschulen are expected to enter a vocational training program, which takes the form of two-year apprenticeships in some cases and three-year university preparatory study leading to the Abitur in others. Training is offered in some 300 professions with some 600 areas of specialization. Women are excluded from 30 of these programs because of a perceived health risk to them. If interest in a given program is greater than the number of places allotted, a selection is made. All school-leavers, however, are guaranteed a place in some program and also a job on completing their training.

Each vocational training program contains a theoretical and a practical component, and all apprentices participate in paramilitary training for about 17 days. The proportion of theoretical and practical instruction varies with the vocation being learned, but the theoretical component in all programs has been increased in recent years and now averages about a third of the curriculum. Vocational training is carried out in plants (which frequently have their own schools) and in vocational training centers. Training is free, and apprentices also receive a monthly wage paid by the plant, 24 days of vacation and free medical care. At the end of the program apprentices are examined in basic education subjects and in vocation-related subjects. They also must write and defend a paper on a topic dealing with their profession. Individual grades are recorded on the diploma, Facharbeiterbrief. The curricula and examinations are drawn up by vocational commissions and are supervised by the State Secretariat for Vocational Training.

Higher education consists of two levels: technical or specialized colleges (Fachschulen), and universities and specialized institutions of higher learning (Hochschulen).

There are 240 *Fachschulen* teaching a total of 254 professions. Engineering and technical schools are the most numerous (95), followed by colleges of medical technology (65) and teachers' colleges (52). *Fachschulen* can be divided into two basic groups according to their requirements for admission. The first group requires completion of the *Oberschule* plus qualification as a skilled worker *(Facharbeiter);* the second requires only completion of the *Oberschule.* The course of study for each type ranges from three to four years, with two 18-week semesters per year. The degree granted, *Fachschulabschluss,* is a professional degree qualifying recipients for university study. The technical colleges are under the central direction of the Ministry of Higher and Technical Education or, more precisely, of the Institute for Technical College Education within this ministry. The program goals, curricula and degrees are drawn up by central commissions and are uniform for all colleges of a given type. The specialized colleges provide a high level of professional training while at the same time building on the general education received in the *Oberschule.* Considerable emphasis is placed on practical work experience in addition to on-the-job training. Internship is required in all fields, and students write a final thesis based on their internship experience. The technical colleges are the most widely attended form of higher education.

Universities and specialized institutions that emphasize scholarship, research and teaching represent the more prestigious of the the two levels of higher education. There are 53 *Hochschulen,* only 13 of which predate the founding of the state: the University of Berlin (Humboldt Universitat), The University of Leipzig (Karl-Marx-Universitat), the University of Halle/Wittenberg (Martin Luther Universitat), the University of Rostock (Wilhem Pieck Universitat), the University of Greifswald (Ernst-Moritz-Arndt-Universitat), the University of Jena (Friedrick Schiller Universitat), the Bergakademia in Freiberg, the Technical University in Dresden and five fine arts academies. The 40 *Hochschulen* established since 1949 comprise 16 technical universities and schools of engineering, three medical academies, two schools of agriculture and foresty, nine pedagogical universities, six fine arts academies, three schools of economics and law, and one school of physical education.

The *Abitur* or its equivalent is the basic prerequisite for admission to university-level institutions. Additional criteria for admission include work experience and practical knowledge or a completed program of vocational training, a one-year internship for applicants without vocational training, active participation in the shaping of socialist society and a willingness to defend the achievements of the state. The number of positions allotted in the various fields of study is determined by the central government in keeping with future projections. The state also endeavors to maintain a male-female parity and to provide adequate participation to students from working-class families.

University courses leading to the *Diplom,* the first-level professional degree, are four to five years in duration, depending on the field. The curriculum is divided into three parts: general education (including Marxism-Leninism and dialectical and historical materialism), specialized general education and area of specialization. In addition, students are expected to participate in summer work programs *(Studentensommer)* in industry and agriculture organized by the Free German Youth. At the end of their course of studies students take a comprehensive examination *(Hauptptrufung)* in the major and related subjects and in Marxism-Leninism and also write and defend a research thesis.

Postgraduate study leads to two levels of doctorate degrees: Doctorate A *(Promotion A),* the doctoral degree in a specific subject; and Doctorate B *(Promotion B),* or Doctor of Sciences *(Doktor der Wissenschaften). Promotion A* can be pursued as an assistant with teaching and research duties in a university department *(Sektion);* as a research student *(Forschungsstudent);* or as a returning student with some years of professional experience *(Aspirant).* Generally, work for the degree is completed in three to four years. In addition to course work, candidates must complete a program in foreign languages and in Marxism-Leninism and write and defend a scholarly dissertation. *Promotion B* is the highest academic degree and is a prerequisite for top-level teaching positions, with the rank of full professor, at the university level. It is awarded to persons with *Promotion A* on completion of a second dissertation of high academic quality.

Each university or *Hochschule* is headed by a rector, a full professor elected for a three-year renewable term by the Academic Council (Wissenschaftlicher Rat) and confirmed by the minister of higher and technical education. He is assisted by two councils: the Academic Council representing the faculty, assistants, students, the Socialist Unity Party, trade unions and the Free German Youth; and the Societal Council (Gesellschaftlicher Rat), which includes representatives from external organizations with ties to universities. The parliament of a university, the *Konzil,* is made up of representatives from all branches of the university and meets once a year. The organizational unit is the academic section *(Sektion),* which contains several related areas of study and is headed by a director.

Tuition is free for all students, and all regular students receive a stipend from the state. They receive free medical insurance, subsidized housing and low-cost meals in student cafeterias.

The educational system is centrally directed and centrally funded. Two ministries in the national government are concerned with education: the Ministry of Public Education and the Ministry of Higher and Technical Education. Other central organs in the sector include the State Secretariat for Vocational Education, an agency of the Council of Ministers that deals with the training of skilled workers and vocational guidance; the Ministry of Health, which supervises the crèche system of prekindergarten child care; the industrial ministries, which oversee polytechnical instruction and the vocational and technical training of factory workers; the Ministry of National Defense, which directs the program of military instruction in schools and the civil defense and paramilitary summer camps; the Ministry of Culture; and the State Secretariat for Physical Culture and Sports.

The Ministry of Public Education is ultimately responsible for primary and secondary education in consultation with the Academy of Pedagogical Studies, the central agency for educational research. The Ministry of Higher and Technical Education oversees the universities, technical schools and most other institutions of higher learning.

The GDR has a broad network of continuing education facilities that provides both general education courses and vocational and technical training. More than 1.5 million adults participate in these programs annually. The most important of these programs are the *Betriebsakademien*, the *Volkshochschulen* and distance and evening education programs.

Betriebsakademien exist in 1,500 factories and other enterprises and are concerned mainly with vocational training, the training of unskilled workers and the continued training of skilled workers for promotion to the rank of master craftsmen, and master craftsmen to supervisory or management positions. There are 200 *Volkshochschulen* spread throughout the country and responsible for providing general education leading to the *Abitur* or completion of the *Oberschule*. Distance education, evening education and refresher courses are offered by engineering and technical colleges as well as universities to persons unable to participate in the regular programs of postsecondary study. All fields of study can be pursued; the degree expectations are the same as for the regular courses and can be completed in four to five years without interruption of employment. Distance and evening students are often sent by their companies, and all receive release time from their jobs with pay. Enrollment is much higher at technical colleges than at universities. Distance education also takes the form of a directed self-study program supplemented by consultations in seminar groups that meet every two weeks for an all-day session. In addition, Urania (the Society for the Dissemination of Scientific Knowledge) and Kammer der Technik, an organization of scientists, technicians and economists, hold regular seminars, lectures and colloquiums for their members.

The training of teachers is divided into two levels: (1) training programs for kindergarten teachers, teachers of grades one to four and teachers of practical vocational subjects, and available at 24 teachers' colleges; and (2) training programs for teachers in grades five to 12, *Volkshochschule* teachers, teachers in vocational training programs granting the *Abitur* degree, teachers of theoretical vocational training subjects, and administrators and other school personnel, and offered at the nine pedagogical universities and in educational programs at the six regular universities—the Universities of Berlin, Leipzig, Halle/Wittenberg, Rostock, Greifswald and Jena. All graduates are guaranteed a teaching position.

The program of study includes four years of study at the first level and five years at the second level, practical teaching experience and internship. In the first years of teaching, all teachers are advised by mentors, or older in-service teachers. The number of teaching hours per week varies slightly with the teaching level, from 25 for teachers in grades one through 8, 24 for teachers in grades nine through 12 and vocational teachers and 23 for *Volkshochschule* teachers. Virtually all teachers are members of the national teachers' union, Gerwerkschaft Unterricht und Urziehung (Union for Instruction and Education). June 12, the anniversary of the 1946 school reform, is celebrated annually as Teachers' Day. On this occasion all teachers receive a bonus and some receive special awards and state titles.

LEGAL SYSTEM

Under the Constitution, legal jurisdiction is exercised by three levels of courts: the Supreme Court, district courts and county courts. Outside the regular court system are the military tribunals and an extensive system of community courts, also known as arbitration commissions in local neighborhoods and on collective farms and as conflict commissions in factories.

The Supreme Court, as the highest organ of legal competence, directs the jurisdiction of all lower courts. As the highest appellate court it may issue general legal directives. The internal organization of the Supreme Court consists of the Assembly, the Supreme Court Presidium, and three functional administrative divisions, known as collegiums, for civil, family and labor law; criminal justice; and military justice. The Assembly consists of the 15 directors of the district courts, the chairmen of the higher military courts and all professional judges. The Assembly is directed in its plenary session by the Supreme Court Presidium.

Each district court is presided over by a professional judge and two lay jurors in cases of original jurisdiction and by three professional judges in cases of appellate jurisdiction. The district courts have appellate jurisdiction in civil cases and original jurisdiction in criminal cases.

The lowest court in the regular court system is at the county level; at least one of these courts exists in each of the more than 200 counties. Each county court is presided over by a professional judge and two lay assessors. The great majority of all civil and criminal cases are tried at this level.

Community courts were created to relieve the regular courts of minor civil and criminal cases and to deal with problems of deviation from prescribed socialist conduct. Each of these social tribunals is composed of lay jurors, who are elected by their particular constituencies. Party interference is most acute at this level.

Although the Constitution asserts the independence of the courts, it also subordinates the judiciary to the political authorities. Judgeship is restricted to SED loyalists. Law and justice are tools in the building of socialism, and legal and judicial organs are agencies for the promotion of party goals. Thus the party is not merely an extralegal institution above the law but also shapes the law to serve its own ends.

As in most of continental Europe, the legal system is based on the Napoleonic Code, which differs in two ways from Anglo-Saxon law: the Napoleonic Code does not subscribe to the adversary system, and it does not recognize common law or precedent. As an example of the former, the prosecutor *(Procurator)* is responsible for presenting all the evidence, both for and against the defendant, and judgment is based solely on his presentation. The defense attorney is subordinate to the prosecutor; the defense attorney's only function is to ensure balance in the presentation. As an example of the latter, the judge is bound only by written or statutory law, which he may interpret as he sees fit.

The current Penal Code was promulgated in 1968 replacing the German Code of 1871. The 1968 code has been amended many times, notably in 1974 and 1977. The code is divided into nine sections: crimes against the sovereignty of the regime and against peace, humanity and human rights; crimes against the regime; offenses against the individual; offenses against youth and the family; offenses against socialist property; offenses against personal and private property; offenses against general security; offenses against the regime and public order; and military offenses. Of these nine sections, it is significant that five deal primarily with offenses against the regime and the social system.

The Ministry of the Interior is responsible for prisons and jails and for death sentences (by shooting). Prison sentences are administered by the Department for the Execution of Sentences. All adult prisoners are expected to work and are paid 18% of normal wages, from which they have to pay for their food and board. Parole may be granted by an order of the court on the basis of an assessment by the prison authorities. The Law on Reintegration of 1977 provides guidelines for the restoration of prisoners to useful social work.

LAW ENFORCEMENT

The GDR police predate the NVA. As early as December 1945, in violation of the Potsdam and Yalta agreements, local and state police forces were placed under the central control of the Administration of the Interior. In January 1946 the term *Volkspolizei* (People's Police) was applied to the new police force. Included in the structure of the People's Police was a special group called the Barracked People's Police, consisting mostly of former officers of the Wehrmacht who had undergone conversion to communism while prisoners in the Soviet Union.

The Volkspolizei is a centrally administered force headed by the deputy minister of the interior. The principal branches of the force include: Criminal Police, Traffic Police, Water Police, Transport Police, Factory Guards, Fire Department, Railway Police and Customs Police. The larger municipalities are covered by the City Police forces and rural areas by the special police. In East Berlin there is a separate Police Presidium, with inspectorates in each of the city's eight administrative sectors. The police uniform is gray-green for the general police, dark blue for the Transport Police and firemen, and white for the Traffic Police.

Intelligence and counterintelligence work is undertaken by the State Security Service (Staatssicherheitsdienst, SSD) and espionage work by the Chief Administration for Reconnaissance (Hauptverwaltung fur

Aufklarung, HVA). The Ministry of State Security has a dedicated riot control regiment named after Felix Dzerzynski, the founder of the Soviet Cheka.

HEALTH

The GDR is the only East European country to maintain an insurance basis for the bulk of the health-care finance. All citizens are insured—a tradition that dates back to Bismarck's compulsory health insurance of 1883. Health facilities provide services for the insured under general contract with the insurance fund and are subsidized in the case of state and municipal institutions. The existence of this system explains the availability of private physician practice.

Each district has at least one health center and a number of outpatient clinics and nursing posts. A family doctor system was developed in the late 1960s and now is quite extensive. There are 161 district hospitals providing primary inpatient care; 29 county hospitals providing both primary and specialized care; and teaching and research hospitals attached to universities such as Berlin, Leipzig, Jena, Halle/Wittenberg and Greifswald. Under the Protection of Mother and Child and Rights of Women acts, there are 858 antenatal clinics, where all expectant mothers are registered and examined, and 9,858 postnatal clinics, where mothers and their children receive medical attention for up to three years after delivery. There are 164 sanatoriums and convalescent homes for adults and children.

HEALTH INDICATORS, 1988

Health personnel
  Physicians: 39,157
    Persons per: 424
  Dentists: 12,185
  Pharmacists: 3,871
Hospitals
  Number: 542
  Number of beds: 169,179
  Beds per 10,000: 102
Admissions/discharges
  Per 10,000: 1,383
  Bed occupancy rate (%): 74
  Average length of stay (days): 21
Type of hospitals (%)
  Government: 85.2
  Private nonprofit: ⎫
  Private profit: ⎭ 14.8
Public health expenditures
  Per capita: $234.50
Vital statistics
  Crude death rate per 1,000: 13.4
  Decline in death rate: −1.5% (1965–84)
  Life expectancy at birth (years): male, 69.5; female, 75.4
  Infant mortality rate per 1,000 live births: 9.2
  Child mortality rate (ages 1–4 years) per 1,000: Insignificant
  Maternal mortality rate per 100,000 live births: 15.6
Causes of death per 100,000
  Infectious and parasitic diseases: 4.9
  Cancer: 211.6
  Endocrine & metabolic disorders: 38.1
  Diseases of the nervous system: 9.8
  Diseases of the circulatory system: 797.2
  Diseases of the digestive system: 31.1
  Accidents, poisoning & violence: 37.9
  Diseases of the respiratory system: 84.3

FOOD & NUTRITION

The average East German is better fed than his West German counterpart, consuming 3,709.7 calories (3.2 g.) and 106.3 g. (3.7 oz.) of protein per day, as against 3,430.7 calories and 91.3 g. (3.2 oz.) of protein per day for the average West German. Of the per capita caloric intake—which represents 142% of the FAO's recommended minimum requirement—36% is derived from animal products and 64% from vegetable products. Expenditures on food account for 41.4% of total household consumption expenditures. Of the total caloric intake, 25.1% is derived from cereals, 7.1% from potatoes, 14.6% from meat, 0.9% from fish, 9.2% from eggs and milk, 4.2% from fruits and vegetables, 18.3% from fats and oils and 20.6% from other sources.

FOOD & NUTRITION INDICATORS, 1988

Per capita daily food consumption, calories: 3,709.7
Per capita daily consumption, proteins, g. (oz.): 106.3 (3.7)
Calorie intake as % of FAO recommended minimum requirement: 142
% of calorie intake from vegetable products: 64
% of calorie intake from animal products: 36
Food expenditures as % of total household expenditures: 41.1
% of total calories derived from:
  Cereals: 25.1
  Potatoes: 7.1
  Meat & poultry: 14.6
  Fish: 0.9
  Fats & oils: 18.3
  Eggs & milk: 9.2
  Fruits & vegetables: 4.2
  Other: 20.6
Per capita consumption of foods, kg., l. (lb., pt.)
  Potatoes: 144.0 (317.5)
  Wheat: 97.5 (214.9)
  Fresh vegetables: 92.3 (203.5)
  Fruits (total): 55.6 (122.6)
    Citrus: 8.4 (18.5)
    Noncitrus: 47.2 (104.0)
  Eggs: 301 (663.7)
  Honey: 0.4 (0.9)
  Fish: 5.7 (12.5)
  Milk: 100.9 (222.4)
  Butter: 16.5 (36.4)
  Cheese: 7.9 (17.6)
  Meat (total): 110.0 (242.5)
    Beef & veal: 25.0 (55.1)
    Pig meat: 74.0 (163.1)
    Poultry: 9.6 (21.1)
    Mutton, lamb & goat: 1.4 (3.0)
  Sugar: 45.5 (100.3)
  Chocolate: 3.7 (8.1)
  Margarine: 7.7 (16.9)
  Biscuits: 5.0 (11.0)
  Beer l. (pt.): 141.6 (299.3)
  Wine, l. (pt.): 10.3 (21.7)
  Alcoholic liquors, l. (pt.): 10.3 (21.7)
  Soft drinks, l. (pt.):
  Mineral waters, l. (pt.): } 89.3 (188.7)
  Fruit juices, l. (pt.):
  Coffee: 0.1 (0.2)
  Tea: 3.5 (7.7)
  Cocoa: 4.2 (9.2)

MEDIA & CULTURE

Medieval Germany was the birthplace of the printing press as well as of newspapers. The first newspaper in the part of Germany that is the GDR appeared in Leipzig in 1650. The GDR's press traditions particularly go back to *Rheinische Zeitung für Politik, Handel und Gewerbe*, Germany's first socialist newspaper, edited by Karl Marx himself and that lasted for from 1848 to 1849. After a period of eclipse, the socialist press revived in the 1860s and 1870s. By 1878, when they were banned again, there were 43 social democratic papers; after the ban was lifted, in 1890, the number jumped to more than 60 (including 19 dailies) and to 90 by 1914.

The German press was virtually destroyed under the Nazis, and only a few publications survived the war. After the division of Germany into zones of occupation, the press revived more quickly in the Western zones. The first newspaper in the Soviet occupation zone was *Tagliche Rundschau*, printed on the presses of the former *Volkischer Beobachter* and that remained the voice of the Soviet Union in the GDR until 1955. Shortly afterward the Soviets started *Berliner Zeitung*, which they subsequently turned over to the Berlin municipal government. Meanwhile, the Communist *Deutscher Volkszeitung* merged with the Social Democratic *Das Volk* to become *Neues Deutschland*, which is now the country's most influential daily. Four other political dailies were sanctioned: *Neue Zeit* of the Christian Democrats; *Der Morgen*, voice of the Liberal Democrats; *National Zeitung* of the National Democrats; and *Bauern Echo* of the Farmer's Party. With the establishment of regional papers and the addition of two more national dailies—*Tribune*, official organ of the trade unions, and *Junge Welt*, voice of the Free German Youth—the GDR press took on the basic form it has today. Perhaps the most significant change was the closing down of the last of the independent papers, *Nacht-Express*, and its replacement by *Berliner Zeitung (BZ) am Abend*.

The only significant developments since the 1950s have been the cycles of repression and thaw that have characterized the press in the GDR in the same manner as in the rest of Eastern Europe. The principal periods of thaw have been from 1953 to 1956, 1961 to 1966, 1971 to 1976 and since 1985.

Most GDR dailies are morning papers, although *BZ am Abend* and several of the regionals are afternooners. Many publish several editions. Together the 39 dailies print nearly 300 separate editions, most of them by the SED papers, which enjoy a favored position in regard to allocation of newsprint. There are no Sunday editions and no magazine sections. Most dailies are full size and present a Spartan appearance. Two of the Berlin dailies, *Berliner Zeitung* and *BZ am Abend*, popularize their makeup a bit by using two-color headlines on page one, a variety of photos and varied typographical gimmicks. The major dailies follow an almost standard pattern of news presentation. Discussion of ideological problems and reports and analyses of international economic and political trends dominate their pages. A good deal of space is devoted to party affairs. Letters to the editor, even critical ones, are encouraged. But criticism must deal only with the operation of the system, not with the system itself. Regional papers are less serious and carry much more advertising.

Each of the major dailies is addressed to a specific audience: *Bauern-Echo* to farmers, *National Zeitung* to professional sodiers and veterans, *Der Morgen* and *Neue Zeit* to the middle classes and intelligentsia, *Junge Welt* to young people and *Deutsche Sport-Echo* to sports fans. (The first three of these dailies have relatively low circulations and thus are not listed in the accompanying table.) In addition to Berlin, seven GDR cities have more than one daily: Dresden, Halle, Karl-Marx-Stadt, Leipzig, Potsdam, Rostock and Schwerin. However, because they are all owned by the state or its organs, they do not compete with one another in an economic sense.

The *Pravda* of the GDR is *Neues Deutschland*, which is reported to have a circulation of 1,093,234. As the official voice of the SED, it is the country's most influential daily, although in circulation it is second behind *Junge Welt*, which sells 1,325,122. Many regional papers outsell the Berlin dailies outside of *Junge Welt* and *Neues Deutschland*. Despite the absence of multimillion-copy sales, total circulation of GDR dailies is impressive and yields a per capita circulation of close to 500 per 1,000, one of the highest in Europe.

Most of the nondailies are published by factories or other enterprises. The periodicals press is 500 titles strong, with a total circulation exceeding 16 million.

The economic framework of the press is comparable to those of other East European countries, except that, as in other sectors, it is more pragmatic and less doctrinaire. Although the ideological imperatives are inflexible, their practice is moderated by realism and redeemed by characteristically German efficiency and thoroughness. In theory opinion is more important than news, and the role of the media is "to stir people to activity" and "promote socialist consciousness." Although nothing in the Constitution prohibits private ownership of publications, various laws and regulations make it virtually impossible. By the same token, the media are exempt from the normal laws of the marketplace and of competition that prevail in the West. There is no popular or sensationalist press as such, although *Berliner Zeitung* and *BZ am Abend* have a light, popular gloss. Production also is highly centralized. The SED enterprise Zentrag is responsible for the production of all major publications and controls about 94% of the daily press circulation. In addition, it owns two of the largest paper mills, controls the import and export of all books and holds a monopoly of all advertising and publicity. Deutsche Post handles the distribution of papers by mail and also the street sales through the newsstands it operates throughout the country. Newsprint is not available on the open market. Supplies are allocated to the various publishing enterprises by the Press Office of the president of the Council of Ministers—the all-powerful government bureau that supervises all media activities. Advertising exists in both print and electronic media but is an influential factor only in the regionals and the two Berlin dailies *Berliner Zeitung* and *BZ am*

Abend, which devote significant space to ads. All journalists are members of the GDR Union of Journalists, and the party must approve all applications for membership in that organization. In addition, editors of SED papers must be approved by the Agitation and Propaganda Section of the Central Committee, and editors of non-SED papers by the Press Office.

The constitutional guarantees of freedom of speech and press are in effect nullified by the socialist ownership of the print media and the responsibility of the media to serve the state and promote socialism. Although the state virtually owns both print and electronic media and the sole national news agency, press laws govern all aspects of the media. First, all publications need a license to operate; for national publications, the license is issued by the Press Office and for regional publications by the chairman of the provincial councils. Second, controls over what is presented and how are very thorough. The main lines of publication policy—including detailed specifications of the format and the kind of news on every page—are drawn up by the Agitation and Propaganda Section. Broad outlines cover a five-year period, and these are supplemented by annual plans. On the basis of these plans, the editors draw up quarterly plans, which must be approved by the Agitation and Propaganda Section for SED papers and the Press Bureau for non-SED papers. The same process is repeated for monthly plans. The editors are free to set up only weekly and daily plans. The first two pages, including space devoted to local news, are exempt from supervised planning, but even here the papers are not free to do what they please. All papers receive daily directives from the party or Press Office regarding what news to print and what comments to make. In addition, the press closely watches the themes emphasized in *Neues Deutschland* for clues on official thinking on any subject. The extent of state control is reinforced by the right of the government to dismiss an erring journalist from membership in the GDR Union of Journalists.

There is no precensorship in the ordinary sense of the word, but in the context of the press structure, it is not necessary. Most of what appears in print or in the electronic media are dictated by the party. For news not specifically covered by party directives there are general guidelines, compliance with which is mandatory. Postpublication analyses and critiques are conducted by the same control bodies, and woe betide any editor whose work deviates from the directives or guidelines. Bad news is anything that detracts from socialist achievements; good news is anything that extols them. A journalist who does not know the difference between the two would soon be an outcast. Criticism does appear in the media, but these are "constructive" criticisms—i.e., limited to the minor inconveniences of life in a socialist society.

The official national news agency is the state-owned Allgemeine Deutsche Nachrichtendienst (ADN), originally set up by the Soviet Military Administration in 1946 and turned over to GDR control in 1953. It operates under the Press Office. Among the major foreign news bureaux represented in Berlin are AFP, ANSA, CTK, dpa, Tanjug, Prensa Latina, Reuters, TASS, and Xinhua.

MAJOR GDR DAILIES BY CIRCULATION

Daily	City	Circulation
Junge Welt	Berlin	1,325,122
Neues Deutschland	Berlin	1,093,234
Freie Presse	Karl-Marx-Stadt	652,278
Freiheit	Halle	580,400
Sachsische Zeitung	Dresden	560,800
Leipziger Volkszeitung	Leipzig	479,350
Volksstimme	Magdeburg	446,482
Tribune	Berlin	410,964
Das Volk	Erfurt	396,600
Berliner Zeitung	Berlin	393,000
Markische Volksstimme	Potsdam	340,942
Ostsee-Zeitung	Rostock	288,880
Lausitzer Rundschau	Cottbus	287,254
Volkswacht	Gera	235,200
Neuer Tag	Frankfurt a.d. Oder	206,500
Schweriner Volkszeitung	Schwerin	199,000
Berliner Zeitung (BZ) am Abend	Berlin	198,961
Freie Erde	Neubrandenburg	198.797
Deutsches Sport-Echo	Berlin	181,916
Freies Wort	Suhl	175,401
Neue Zeit	Berlin	103,876

MEDIA INDICATORS, 1988

Newspapers
  Number of dailies: 39
  Circulation (000): 9,300
  Circulation per 1,000: 559
  Number of nondailies: 30
  Circulation (000): 9,302
  Circulation per 1,000: 556
  Number of periodicals: 541
  Circulation (000): 21,410
  Newsprint consumption
    Total (tons): 139,000
    Per capita, kg. (lb.): 8.3 (18.3)
Book publishing
  Number of titles: 5,655
Radio
  Number of transmitters: 130
  Number of radio receivers (000): 6,699
    Persons per radio receiver: 2.5
  Total annual program hours: 49,257
Television
  Number of transmitters: 576
  Number of television receivers (000): 6,182
    Persons per television receiver: 2.7
  Total annual program hours: 7,962
Cinema
  Number of fixed cinemas: 2,163
  Seating capacity: 346,000
    Seats per 1,000: 20
  Annual attendance (million): 70.8
    Per capita: 4.2
Films
  Production of long films: 16
  Import of long films: 118
    5.9% from United States
    30.5% from Soviet Union
    6.8% from West Germany
    5.1% from France

CULTURAL & ENVIRONMENTAL INDICATORS, 1988

Public libraries
  Number: 6,912
  Volumes (000): 46,631
  Registered borrowers: 3,964,000
  Loans per 1,000: 5,470
Museums
  Number: 714
  Annual attendance (000): 34,322
  Attendance per 1,000: 2,070
Performing arts
  Facilities: 84
  Number of performances: 84,693
  Annual attendance (000): 29,155
  Attendance per 1,000: 582
Ecological sites: 13
Botanical gardens & zoos: 119

Radio and television are state agencies administered by Staatliches Komitee für Rundfunk beim Ministerrat der DDR and Staatliches Komitee für Fernsehen, respectively. Radio domestic services are Radio DDR I and Radio DDR II, Berliner Rundfunk and Stimme (Voice) der DDR. External services consist of Radio Berlin International and Radio Volga, the latter operated by the Soviet Military Command in the GDR. Berliner Rundfunk is directed mainly at East Berlin. Radio DDR I and Radio DDR II are the principal national services, and they are linked with provincial transmitters, eight of which also provide regional programming during certain hours of the day. One provides special services for the Sorb minority. Stimme der DDR is a 24-hour information and entertainment service.

Fernsehen der DDR transmits on two regular television broadcasting channels and has an educational service. It is a highly sophisticated operation, the best in the Soviet bloc and on a par with any of the Western European systems. There are 13 transmitters, which broadcast 96 hours a week on Program I and 61 hours a week on Program II. News is broadcast at least three times daily. About 80% of East Germans can receive programs from West Germany, and it is estimated that 80% of that percentage watch West German newscasts.

SOCIAL WELFARE

A unified social insurance system has been in operation since 1951 under the aegis of the Free German Trade Union Confederation and covers all workers except collective farmers, private craftsmen, private entrepreneurs and certain other groups insured under the German Insurance Institution. Social insurance is supervised by the Central Social Insurance Board and administered locally by enterprises. Workers make a compulsory contribution equivalent to 10% of their gross earnings, with a monthly ceiling; employers contribute 12.5% except for mining enterprises, which contribute 22.5% of gross earnings; and the state contributes the balance. University and trade school students, workers in cooperatives and family labor contribute according to special rates. Pensioners are insured without contributions.

Health services are available free to all insured and their dependents and include hospitalization, medical and dental treatment, prosthesis and spa therapy. There are no prescription charges. A recent expansion of health services has strengthened the role of industrial and enterprise clinics and of rural outpatient dispensaries. The maternity benefit for a working woman is 100% of earnings payable for six weeks before and for 20 weeks after confinement. Sick workers receive payments equal to 90% of their net earnings. The disability pension for occupational injuries is 100% of net earnings.

The age of pension is 65 for men and 60 for women, but those continuing in employment receive both pension and pay. Because of the low birth rate, a graduate allowance for every child consists of a basic grant, with a monthly allowance of up to DDR-M70 for the fifth child.

There is no private welfare system in the GDR.

CHRONOLOGY

1945—The Wehrmacht surrenders at Rheims and Berlin Karslhorst.... Allied Control Commission is set up in Berlin, and the four victorious powers—the United States, the Soviet Union, the United Kingdom and France—divide Germany into occupation zones.... The Social Democratic Party and the Communist Party are restructured. Berlin is divided into four sectors under the Interallied Military Kommandatura. The Anti-Fascist bloc is set up by the five parties allowed by the Soviet Military Administration.... Potsdam Conference draws up plans for postwar Europe.... The Soviet Military Administration establishes 11 central administrations in the Soviet Zone; Erich Honecker is elected chairman of the Central Youth Committee.... Land reforms permit large-scale confiscation of land and industrial enterprises.

1946—The Free German Trade Union Confederation is founded.... The Socialist Unity Party (SED) founded through the merger of the Communist Party and the Social Democratic Party.... *Neues Deutschland* appears.... *Land* and provincial governments are formed in the Soviet Zone, and local elections are held.

1947—Prussia ceases to exist, and the provinces of Saxony-Anhalt and Neubrandenburg are each made a *Land*.... The SED rejects the Marshall Plan.... The Society for German-Soviet Friendship is founded.

1948—The three Western zones are fused into one zone preparatory to a possible German reunification. ... The German Economic Commission takes over management of the economy of the Soviet Zone.... The Allied Control Commission disbands itself as East-West differences escalate and the Soviet Union walks out of the Berlin Kommandatura. ... West Germany initiates currency reforms marking the beginning of its economic miracle.... Soviet troops block access routes to Berlin; Berlin airlift begins; East Germany initiates currency reforms.... East

Berlin establishes its own separate city government, headed by Friedrich Ebert.

1949—COMECON is founded in Warsaw.... Berlin blockade and the Berlin airlift end. ... NATO is founded.... West German Basic Law (Constitution) takes effect.... Bundestag and Bundesrat meet in Bonn and elect Theodore Heuss federal president and Konrad Adenauer federal chancellor.... GDR is founded; provisional Volkskammer declares independent state with own constitution.... West Germany and GDR sign agreement on inter-German trade.... Soviet Military Administration is dissolved.... Wilhelm Pieck is elected president and Otto Grotewohl prime minister.... GDR enters into diplomatic relations with the Soviet Union and eight other Communist states.

1950—The German Academy of the Arts and the German Writers' Union founded.... Agreement on the Oder-Neisse line signed by the GDR and Poland. The voting age is reduced from 21 to 18.... The GDR becomes a member of COMECON. Walter Ulbricht is elected secretary-general of the SED.

1951—Volkskammer passes the GDR's first five-year plan, 1951–55.... The GDR rejects plan for United Nations-supervised all-German elections.

1952—German Treaty is signed by West Germany and the three Western occupation powers.... The GDR is divided into 14 *Bezirks;* the five *Länder* remain but lose much of their authority.... People's Police are formally commissioned.

1953—Chemnitz is renamed Karl-Marx-Stadt.... Soviet Control Commission is disbanded. ... Politburo announces introduction of new course, raising work norms and strengthening state powers.... Rationing of textiles, shoes and food is ended. ... Strike by building workers culminates in a bloody uprising, which is brutally suppressed with Soviet help. ... State of emergency is declared.... Reparations to the Soviet Union end. ... Diplomatic missions to and from the GDR are renamed embassies instead of high commissions.

1954—Soviet Union recognizes GDR sovereignty.... First German Workers' Conference is held in Leipzig. ... The National Front receives 99% of the popular vote in elections to the Volkskammer and the Bezirkstage.

1955—State of war between the GDR and the Soviet Union is ended.... Warsaw Pact is formed.... Model statutes on collective farms are passed. ... Soviet Union and West Germany establish diplomatic relations.... Constitution is amended to make creation of armed forces constitutional.

1956—The National People's Army (NVA) is created. ... West Germany bans the Communist Party.

1957—The GDR and the Soviet Union conclude agreements on trade and the stationing of Soviet troops in the GDR. ... Volkskammer imposes controls on inter-German travel.... First atomic reactor, at Rossendorf, goes on stream.

1958—The Soviet Union forgoes support costs of Soviet troops in the GDR. ... New government is formed, with Otto Grotewohl as chairman and Walter Ulbricht as deputy chairman of the Council of Ministers.

1959—Friedrich Engels Military Academy opens in Berlin. . . . Comprehensive educational law is passed by Volkskammer, establishing the 10-class general polytechnical high school as the basic school.

1960—National Defense Council is formed. . . . On the death of President Wilhelm Pieck new Council of State is formed to provide collective leadership, with Walter Ulbricht as chairman.

1961—Berlin Wall is erected. . . . Travel between West Germany and the GRD is closed to GDR citizens. . . . Stalin's name is expunged from GDR place names.

1963—Friendship Pipeline from the Soviet Union to Schwedt on the Oder River is placed in operation.

1964—Treaty of Friendship, Mutual Aid and Cooperation is signed between the GDR and the Soviet Union. . . . Volkskammer confirms Willi Stoph as chairman of the Council of Ministers following the death of Otto Grotewohl.

1965—The International Olympic Committee decides to admit the two Germanys as separate nations. . . . Volkskammer passes Family Law.

1967—Volkskammer passes law on GDR citizenship.

1968—New Criminal Code is passed by the Volkskammer. . . . Volkskammer presents new Constitution, which is approved in referendum and becomes effective. . . . GDR joins Warsaw Pact nations in invading Czechoslovakia.

1969—Eight *Länd* churches unite; the first synod of the Union of Protestant Churches is held in Potsdam.

1970—West German chancellor Willy Brandt and GDR chairman of the Council of Ministers Willi Stoph meet in Kassel.

1971—The three Western powers and the Soviet Union sign agreement on Berlin. . . . Radio station Voice of the DDR begins broadcasting.

1972—Basic Treaty is signed by West Germany and the GDR. . . . The GDR and West Germany are admitted to the United Nations.

1973—Walter Ulbricht dies; Volkskammer elects Willi Stoph as chairman of the Council of State and Horst Sindermann as chairman of the Council of Ministers.

1974—Volkskammer passes new amendments to the Constitution removing the term "German nation." . . . The name of the national currency is changed to Mark der DDR from Mark der Deutschen Notenbank.

1975—The GDR signs the Helsinki Act.

1976—Honecker, SED general secretary, is elected chairman of the Council of State in place of Willi Stoph, who is designated chairman of the Council of Ministers. . . . Sindermann is demoted to be president of the Volkskammer.

1979—The GDR and the United States sign a consular agreement.

1987—Honecker visits Bonn and holds talks with Chancellor Kohl.

1989—Mass exodus of East Germans into West Germany through Hungary triggers political crisis; protests in Leipzig and other cities are crushed under Honecker's orders; Honecker is ousted along with other hard-liners, including economic chief Guenter Mittag; Egon Krenz is named leader of the SED. Regime announces new reforms, including free elections with multiple political parties and free trade unions. . . . Berlin Wall is torn down and free travel between East and West Germany is restored. . . . Krenz is dismissed as SED leader and the entire party Central Committee resigns. . . . Gregor Gysi is named party leader, Manfred Gerlach head of state and Hans Modrow prime minister; SED relinquishes monopoly of power. . . . As exodus into West Germany continues, West Germany and East Germany begin talks on reunification.

1990—GDR holds its first free national elections. . . . The alliance of pro-reunification parties, led by the Christian Democratic Union, gains absolute majority in the Volkskammer with 303 out of 400 seats. . . . Lothar de Maiziere, the leader of the Christian Democratic Union, is elected premier and pledges early reunification. . . . Sabine Bergmann-Pohl is elected president of the Volkskammer and the nation's acting president. . . . D-Mark and DDR-Mark are united as the former is introduced as the national currency of GDR. . . . The city of Karl-Marx-Stadt readopts its previous name, Chemnitz. . . . West German chancellor Helmut Kohl reaches accord with Gorbachev on German reunification. . . . The Federal Republic of Germany and the German Democratic Republic are united and the GDR disappears from the annals of history.

BIBLIOGRAPHY
BOOKS

Childs, David. *East Germany.* New York, 1969.
———. *Honecker's Germany* (London, 1985).
Cornelson, Doris. *Handbook of the Economy of the German Democratic Republic.* Westmead, Eng., 1979.
Dickinson, Robert Eric. *Germany: A General and Regional Geography.* New York, 1953.
Hanhardt, Arthur M., Jr. *German Democratic Republic.* Baltimore, 1968.
Kirsch, Henry. *German Democratic Republic: A Profile.* Boulder, Colo., 1985.
Letgers, Lyman. *The German Democratic Republic: A Developed Socialist Society.* Boulder, Colo., 1978.
McCardle, Arthur W. *East Germany: A New German Nation Under Socialism.* Lanham, Md., 1984.
McCauley, Martin. *East Germany: The Dilemmas of Division.* London, 1980.
———. *German Democratic Republic Since 1945.* New York, 1983.
Moreton, N. Edwina. *East Germany and the Warsaw Alliance: The Politics of Détente.* Boulder, Colo., 1970.

———. *Marxism-Leninism in the German Democratic Republic: The Socialist Unity Party.* New York, 1979.

Sanford, Gregory W. *From Hitler to Ulbricht: The Communist Reconstruction of East Germany.* Princeton, N.J., 1982.

Scarf, C. Bradley. *Politics and Social Change in East Germany: An Evaluation of Socialist Democracy.* Boulder, Colo., 1984.

Schneider, Eberhard. *The GDR: History, Politics, Economy and Society of East Germany.* New York, 1978.

Schulz, Eberhard. *GDR Foreign Policy.* White Plains, N.Y., 1982.

Sonthermer, Kurt, and Wilhelm Bleek. *The Government and Politics of East Germany.* New York, 1977.

Starrels, John M., and Anita M. Mallinckrodt. *Politics in the German Democratic Republic.* New York, 1975.

Steele, Jonathan. *Inside East Germany: The State That Came in from the Cold.* New York, 1977.

Stolper, Wolfgang Frederick. *The Structure of the East German Economy.* Cambridge, Mass., 1960.

Viney, Deryck. *The East German Army.* London, 1981.

Von Beyme, Klaus. *Policy Making in the German Democratic Republic.* New York, 1982.

Wilkens, Herbert. *The Two German Economies.* London, 1981.

Woods, Roger. *Opposition in GDR Under Honecker.* New York, 1986.

OFFICIAL PUBLICATION

Statistisches Jahrbuch (Statistical Yearbook), annual.

HUNGARY

BASIC FACT SHEET

OFFICIAL NAME: Republic of Hungary (Magyar Koztarsasag)

ABBREVIATION: HU

CAPITAL: Budapest

HEAD OF STATE: President Arpad Goncz (from 1990)

HEAD OF GOVERNMENT: Prime Minister Jozsef Antall (from 1990)

NATURE OF GOVERNMENT: Socialist democracy

POPULATION: 10,566,944 (1989)

AREA: 93,032 sq. km. (35,920 sq. mi.)

MAJOR ETHNIC GROUP: Magyar

LANGUAGE: Hungarian

RELIGIONS: Roman Catholic, Calvinist, Lutheran

UNIT OF CURRENCY: Forint

NATIONAL FLAG: Tricolor of red, white and green horizontal stripes

NATIONAL EMBLEM: A shield displaying the national colors—red, white and green—on a round light-blue background illuminated by gold rays emanating from a capping gold-edged red star. The design is wreathed in green and gold wheat ears tied at the base with a ribbon in the national colors.

NATIONAL ANTHEM: "Isten aldd meg a magyart" ("God Bless the Hungarians")

NATIONAL HOLIDAYS: Anniversary of the 1848 Revolution (March 15); Liberation Day (April 4); Labor Day (May 1); Constitution Day (August 20); October 23 (the first day of the 1956 Revolution); Christmas (December 25 and 26); Easter; New Year's Day

NATIONAL CALENDAR: Gregorian

PHYSICAL QUALITY OF LIFE INDEX: 93 (on an ascending scale with 100 as the maximum)

DATE OF INDEPENDENCE: November 16, 1918

DATE OF CONSTITUTION: August 20, 1949

WEIGHTS & MEASURES: Metric

GEOGRAPHICAL FEATURES

Hungary, a landlocked country in the Carpathian Basin of central Europe, has a total area of 93,032 sq. km. (35,920 sq. mi.), extending 268 km. (167 mi.) north to south and 528 km. (328 mi.) east to west. Its total boundary length of 2,242 km. (1,393 mi.) is shared with five countries: Czechoslovakia (608 km.; 378 mi.), Soviet Union (215 km.; 134 mi.), Rumania (432 km.; 268 mi.), Yugoslavia (631 km.; 392 mi.) and Austria (356 km.; 221 mi.). The Danube and Ipoly rivers mark the western portion of the northern border and the Drava and Mura rivers a considerable portion of the southwestern border. Some 16 km. (10 mi.) of the northern boundary cross Lake Ferto. Elsewhere the borders do not follow natural terrain features. Most of the boundaries were established in 1920 by the Treaty of Trianon after the country's defeat in World War I. The treaty stripped Hungary of over 70% of its prewar territory, including Transylvania, with a large Hungarian population. Although the borders are not officially disputed, there is strong irredentism calling for the return of the lost territories.

The capital is Budapest, on both banks of the Danube and consisting of two cities, Buda on the west bank and Pest on the east bank, united as a city in 1873. There are no other cities approaching it in population.

The country is generally divided into four topographic regions: the Great Hungarian Plain (Nagy Magyar Alfold), more commonly called the Great Plain; Dunar

MAJOR URBAN CENTERS (1987)

Budapest (capital)	2,093,487
Debrecen	214,836
Miskolc	211,156
Szeged	185,559
Pecs	179,051
Gyor	130,194
Nyiregyhaza	118,179
Szekesfehervar	112,703
Kecskemet	103,944
Szombathely	86,682
Szolnok	80,921
Tatabanya	76,463

Tul, the Hungarian name for Transdanubia; the Little Plain; and the Northern Mountains. The Great Plain accounts for about half of the total land area and comprises the lowlands east of the Danube. It has a mean elevation of little more than 91 m. (300 ft.), with the largest deviation from the average elevation on the plateau between the Danube and the Tisza rivers and in an area in the Northeast along the Rumanian border. The plateau is about 30 to 46 m. (100 to 150 ft.) higher than the floodplains of the rivers, and the northeastern hills reach approximately 183 m. (600 ft.).

Transdanubia consists of rolling country, with uplands to the west, at the foothills of the Alps. Lake Balaton, the last remnant of the ancient Pannonian Sea, is roughly in the center of this region. To its east and extending to the Danube is the lowland known as the

CZECHOSLOVAKIA

SOVIET UNION

Fertő Tó

Sopron

AUSTRIA

GYÖR-SOPRON

Györ

Esztergom

KOMÁROM

BORZSONY

Vác

Salgótarján

NÓGRÁD

MÁTRA

BORSOD-ABAÚJ-ZEMPLÉN

Miskolc

SZABOLCS-SZATMÁR

Nyíregyháza

Eger

HEVES

Tisza River

Debrecen

HAJDÚ-BIHAR

Budapest

PEST

SZOLNOK

Szombathely

Pápa

Székesfehérvar

VESZPRÉM

VAS

Veszprém

FEJÉR

BAKONY

Dunaújváros

Cegléd

Szolnok

Kecskemét

GREAT HUNGARIAN PLAIN

Békéscsaba

BÉKÉS

ZALA

Lake Balaton

Nagykanizsa

SOMOGY

TOLNA

Danube River

BÁCS-KISKUN

CSONGRÁD

Kaposvár

Szekszárd

Szeged

MECSEK HILLS

Pécs

Baja

BARANYA

80 m

80 km

YUGOSLAVIA

RUMANIA

Mezofold. To the south are the Somogy or the Transdanubian Hills and the Mecsek and Villany mountains. On the Austrian border the alpine foothills rise to over 914 m. (3,000 ft.). The Transdanubian Central Mountains extend along the northern side of Lake Balaton. The chain consists of several minor ranges ranging from 213 to 762 m. (700 to 2,500 ft.).

The Little Plain, bordering Czechoslovakia and Austria, is mostly agricultural land. The Northern Mountains are the lower volcanic fringe of the Carpathian Mountains and extend northeastward from the gorge of the Danube near Esztergom for about 225 km. (140 mi.). Their highest point, Mount Kekes in the Matra Range, is about 1,006 m. (3,300 ft.).

The entire country is in the middle Danube Basin. Local rivers in northern Transdanubia and the Little Plain flow into the Danube within Hungary, but others drain into its tributaries the Drava and the Tisza, and join the Danube in Yugoslavia. The length of the Danube within Hungary is 386 km. (240 mi.). As it flows through Hungary, the Danube falls very little: It is about 134 m. (440 ft.) above sea level as it enters Hungary and drops 34 m. (110 ft.) between the Czech border and Budapest and another 15 m. (50 ft.) between Budapest and the Yugoslav border. The slight fall and the irregular water flow cause periodic devastation upon the river cities and the adjacent plains. Floods occur regularly twice each year. The first, known as the white flood, occurs in April or May, when snow melts at the lower elevations up the river and its ice breaks up. Ice plugs develop, and the backed-up water and ice often prove destructive, as, for example, during the white flood of 1838. The second, or green, flood usually occurs in June, when the river tributaries are swollen with the heavy rains during late spring and much of the melting snow from the higher elevations. At Budapest the river may rise 8 m. (25 ft.) or more above its normal level.

The Tisza is the Danube's second-largest tributary, and it meanders across the Great Plain. In contrast to the Danube, its streambed is flat, and it has virtually no valleys. Its flow is highly irregular, and during early and late spring floods it may carry 50 times as much water as it does during summer. During the green flood the Tisza's waters, combined with those of the Danube, may back up for the Tisza's entire length and cause severe damage.

The Drava, smaller than the Tisza by only a slight margin, accumulates most of its volume in Austria, flows across the northern tip of Yugoslavia, forms part of the Hungarian-Yugoslav border for about 129 km. (80 mi.) and turns back into Yugoslavia again for about 64 km. (40 mi.) before joining the Danube. It may have four annual floods, but the higher terrain on its northern shore prevents much damage.

There are three large and well-known lakes in the country. Lake Balaton, about 72 km. (45 mi.) long and 13 km. (8 mi.) wide, is the largest. It averages little more than 3 m. (10 ft.) in depth and has a maximum depth of 11 m. (35 ft.). It slopes toward the north, with the result that there are sand beaches in the South for 0.8 km. (0.5 mi.) or more from the shore.

Lake Ferto (Neusiedler See in German), on the northwestern border, is shared with Austria. The lake has an average depth of only 0.9 m. (3 ft.) and freezes entirely in winter. Lake Velence is filled artificially to maintain proper depths for fishing and bathing.

CLIMATE & WEATHER

Hungary experiences three weather systems: continental air polar air masses dominate the weather about 65% of the time in winter and 20% of the time in summer; maritime or Atlantic weather prevails about 30% of the time in winter and 65% of the time in summer; and subtropical Mediterranean weather prevails for the remainder—about 5% in winter and 15% in summer.

Geography and topographic relief account for the lesser influences from the maritime and Mediterranean systems. The country is more than 1,126 km. (700 mi.) from the Atlantic Ocean, from which it is separated by the Alps. It is nearer the Mediterranean, but also separated from it by high terrain. On the other hand, clear, dry air from the high-pressure polar and continental air masses circulating clockwise enter the country from the southern quadrants. The low hills of the eastern Carpathians provide little resistance to its entry into the Danube Basin but once there it tends to be trapped and is difficult to dislodge. Nevertheless, the weather that reaches Hungary from the Atlantic and the Mediterranean is moderating and brings in a great portion of the country's precipitation.

Rainfall averages 711 mm. (28 in.) per year in the western part of the country and 559 mm. (22 in.) in the eastern part. Even the most arid portions of the Great Plain receive about 508 mm. (20 in.). However, the seasonal distribution of rain differs widely and may be higher or lower.

The mean average temperature for the country as a whole is about 10°C (50°F). Budapest and the extreme southeastern regions are warmer and higher elevations

POPULATION GROWTH (000), 1850–1970			
Hungary: Transleithania			
Date	Total	Male	Female
1850	13,192	6,520	6,672
1857	14,349	7,379	6,970
1869	15,512	7,848	7,764
1880	15,739	7,800	7,939
1890	17,578	8,783	8,796
1900	19,255	9,582	9,672
1910	20,886	10,345	10,541
Hungary: Trianon Territory			
Date	Total	Male	Female
1910	7,615	3,794	3,821
1920	7,990	3,876	4,114
1930	8,688	4,250	4,438
1941	9,317	4,561	4,756
1949	9,205	4,423	4,781
1960	9,961	4,804	5,157
1970	10,322	5,004	5,318

cooler than average. July is the hottest month with an average of 21°C (70°F), and January the coldest, with an average of −2°C (29°F). Winters are warmer and summers are cooler in Transdanubia than in the Great Plain. The highest temperature recorded in the country over a 175-year period was 41°C (106°F) in Pecs in southern Transdanubia in 1950; the lowest, −34°C (−29°F) in Debrecen in 1942. Typical annual extremes are about 35°C (95°F) and −26°C (−15°F).

The surrounding mountains isolate Hungary from strong winds. Over the greater part of the country winds are most frequently from the north and northwest. East of Tisza and in the eastern portion of the Northern Mountains they are most often from the northeast.

The annual average of sunshine is about 5.5 hours per day, or 2,000 hours per year. The range varies from an hour and 15 minutes per day in December to nine hours and 40 minutes per day in August. In general, western regions are slightly less sunny than those in the East, and the plateau between the Danube and the Tisza experiences the most sunshine.

POPULATION

The population of Hungary in 1989 was 10,566,944, based on the last official census, in 1980, when the population was 10,709,463. The population is expected to decline to 10,554,000 by 1990 and to 10,370,000 by 2000. Hungary ranks 61st in the world in population and 105th in land area.

The size of the Hungarian population has varied considerably during its long history, as a result of wars, epidemics and migrations. Large losses seem to have occurred during the Turkish wars. After the Turks were finally expelled at the beginning of the 18th century, much of the Great Plain was relatively unpopulated. Within the next 70 years the vacant lands were filled by large numbers of Germans, Serbians and other foreign ethnic groups. As a result, the population more than doubled during this period, reaching 8 million at the time of the census of 1785–87. Subsequent censuses, such as those of 1850 and 1857, were too unreliable to measure the fluctuations in population growth. The first accurate count of the population was the census of 1870. A census has been taken each decade since then.

In the century between the censuses of 1787 and 1881, the average annual growth rate was 0.6%. Then a period of moderate growth followed. Between 1881 and 1911 the population grew at a rate of 0.9%, primarily as a result of a steep decline in the death rate. This period also witnessed a heavy stream of overseas emigration. Between 1902 and 1913 Hungary lost 808,000 citizens to emigration. The period of growth ended abruptly with World War I, the annual growth rate dropping to 0.5% between 1911 and 1949. Hungary suffered heavy casualties in both world wars, although there was no fighting on Hungarian soil. More important than the rise in mortality was the decline in births. The deficit was so great that births were more than offset by deaths during World War I. The war also altered the size of the population by the population transfers it caused. Losses during World War II were of a different nature than losses in its predecessor. There was almost no deficit of births. Military losses were less, but civilian losses were much heavier. Further losses were caused by transfers of population and territory at the end of the war.

A rise in the birth rate since the end of World War II not only reversed the wartime decline but also brought it up to the level of the early years of the Depression. There was no birth boom immediately after the war, as in other European countries, but the sharp increase began in 1952, with the birth rate going above 23 per 1,000. This proved to be a temporary phenomenon, and by the 1960s the birth rate had resumed its downward course.

The end of World War II had been followed by a mass exodus of refugees, principally Jews. A second exodus followed in 1956 upon the Soviet invasion that quelled the Hungarian Revolution. The number of refugees who fled Hungary at this time is estimated at 200,000.

The rules for legal emigration have been substantially relaxed. A Hungarian may claim a right to emigrate for family reunification under certain conditions. The law provides for exceptions to all restrictions in individual cases on humanitarian grounds. Those who are refused permission may appeal and reapply. Those who do not receive permission to emigrate normally suffer no official sanctions, such as loss of employment or housing. Persons who have emigrated legally from Hungary may apply for resettlement, but the right to return is not guaranteed.

Since 1987 Hungary has offered refuge to over 20,000 persons from Rumania, most of them ethnic Hungarians who cite bleak economic conditions in that country, declining opportunities for Hungarian-language education and cultural expression, an ultranationalistic and repressive political climate and job- and housing-related discrimination. About 10% of these refugees are Rumanians or Gypsies, and many of them have been forcibly repatriated to Rumania to face beatings, jail sentences, work without pay and forfeiture of property. Such repatriations have come under criticism from human rights advocates.

The principal feature of population distribution is the preeminence of Budapest, which accounts for 37% of the national population, although its share has declined since 1960, when it was 45%. Excluding Budapest, the population is distributed fairly evenly throughout the country. Distribution of the rural population is even more uniform. This uniformity reflects the largely rural character of the population. It was only in the 1970s that the urban population crossed the 50% mark, but even so, Hungary ranks well below most Western European countries in urbanization. Many places defined as urban contain sizable rural or agricultural populations. The Hungarian commune bears a greater resemblance to a New England town than to a commune elsewhere in Europe, in that the population does not reside wholly in the central settlement but spreads out from it into the open countryside. Thus a typical commune is extensive in area, with one-fifth of its inhabitants scattered to the periphery.

Hungary's urban population thus tends to be overstated except that the error is offset by the omission of certain places from the urban category. Only places having the status of a city or town (varos) are officially defined as urban. The distinction between cities and towns on the one hand and villages on the other is often based on historical accident and not the size of population. While all large settlements are classified as cities, some communes with populations of over 10,000 are classified as rural and some settlements with less than 10,000 inhabitants are classified as urban.

Below Budapest, none of the middle-sized cities approaches even one-fifth of the capital's population. Of these, 17 are in Transdanubia, eight in the North and 28 in the Great Plain. The cities are rather evenly distributed throughout the country. Cities in the North and in Transdanubia are compact and typically Western in character, while those of the Great Plain, by contrast, are sprawling agricultural communities.

All communes are called villages (kozseg) and are treated as rural areas. Since 1937 they have been classified as "citylike" (varosias jellegu kozsegek) or as "other." The former are expanding village settlements in which less than half the workers are farmers. Villages attain this status by government decree. The number of "other" communes has tended to decline steadily through the incorporation of suburbs into towns, the consolidation of smaller communes and the separation of isolated outlying portions of existing communes to form new communes.

Each commune includes, in addition to the central built-up area, tracts of adjacent agricultural land. In censuses, the central area is distinguished as belterulet and the outlying territory as kulterulet. The latter includes all settlements (tanya) within 0.5 km. (0.3 mi.) of the central settlement. The Communist regime tried to draw the population of the scattered settlements into villages. A Council of Outlying Settlements was established in 1949 to create larger communes and secondary settlements as nuclei for growth.

Of the secondary cities, the largest are Debrecen, Miskolc, Szeged and Pecs. The fastest-growing city since 1945 has been Miskolc, the iron and steel metropolis of the North. Pecs, Debrecen and Szeged are the regional capitals of southern Transdanubia and the northern and southern portions of the Great Plain, respectively. The only other major city is Gyor, in northern Transdanubia.

Some modest changes have taken place in the regional distribution of the population in the past half century. Only Budapest has consistently gained through internal migration. This has helped the capital to regain much of the population loss it suffered during World War II. Subsequent political changes and industrialization have caused important shifts in the distribution of population by county. The urban population outside Budapest grew four times as rapidly as in prewar years. A considerable part of this urban expansion was the result of migration from rural areas; the rate of growth in rural areas has barely maintained the replacement level. Migration from the villages helped to offset the low crude birth rates in the cities, particularly Budapest. In general, the rate of natural increase tends to be high in the rural areas in the Northeast and Northwest, low in the Southeast and Southwest and intermediate in the central and north-central counties.

The considerable population movement during the late 1940s had only a marginal effect on the geographic distribution of population. In 1951 and 1952 large numbers of people were moved by force from one part of the country to another. These included Slavic minorities and others considered politically unreliable. The flight of refugees to the West after the October 1956

DEMOGRAPHIC INDICATORS, 1988

Population: 10,588,271

Year of last census: 1980	World rank: 61
Sex ratio: males: 48.4	Females: 51.6

Population trends (million)

1930: 8.649	1960: 9.984	1990: 10.554
1940: 9.280	1970: 10.353	2000: 10.370
1950: 9.338	1980: 10.709	

Population doubling time in years at current rate: Population is declining

Hypothetical size of stationary population (million): 10

Assumed year of reaching net reproduction rate of 1: 2030

Age profile (%)

0–15: 21.1	30–44: 29.1	60–74: ⎫
15–29: 19.5	45–59: 11.8	Over 75: ⎬ 18.5 ⎭

Median age (years): 36.4

Density per sq. km. (per sq. mi.): 113.8 (294.8)

Annual growth rate

1950–55: 1.02	1975–80: 0.32	1995–2000: 0.14
1960–65: 0.33	1980–85: 0.16	2000–2005: 0.10
1965–70: 0.40	1985–90: 0.04	2010–15: 0.0
1970–75: 0.36	1990–95: 0.03	2020–25: −0.05

Vital statistics
 Crude birth rate, 1/1,000: 11.8
 Crude death rate, 1/1,000: 13.4
 Change in birth rate: −10.7 (1965–84)
 Change in death rate: 29.2 (1965–84)
 Dependency, total: 51.8
 Infant mortality rate, 1/1,000: 17.4
 Child (0–4 years) mortality rate, 1/1,000: Insignificant
 Maternal mortality rate, 1/100,000: 19.2
 Natural increase, 1/1,000: −1.6
 Total fertility rate: 1.7
 General fertility rate: 54.0
 Gross reproduction rate: 0.95
 Marriage rate, 1/1,000: 6.2
 Divorce rate, 1/1,000: 2.9
 Life expectancy, males (years): 65.3
 Life expectancy, females (years): 73.2
 Average household size: 2.9
 % illegitimate births: 9.2

Youth
 Youth population 15–24 (000); 1,485
 Youth population in 2000 (000); 1,569

Women
 Of childbearing age 15–49 (000): 2,599
 Child–woman ratio (children per 000 women 15–49): 298
 % women using contraceptives: 73
 % women married 15–49: N.A.
 Abortions rate per 100 live births: 67.0

Urban
 Urban population (000): 6,528
 % urban, 1965: 43; 1987: 59
 Annual urban growth rate (%) 1965–80, 2.0; 1980–87, 1.4
 % urban population in largest city: 37
 % urban population in cities over 500,000: 37
 Number of cities over 500,000: 1
 Annual rural growth rate: −1.6 (1985–90)

Revolution was selective by way of origin. The city of Budapest and Gyor-Sopron County lost nearly 5% of their population, and four other counties lost 1% to 2.5%. Five-sixths of the refugees were registered as residents of Budapest or Transdanubia.

A major feature of Hungarian demography is the numerical edge of females in the population, which has persisted for decades. The last time the sexes were balanced was in 1911. Migration was the most important factor tending to depress the sex ratio before World War I. Military losses in both world wars also levied a heavier toll on the males than on the females. The sex ratio does not vary smoothly with age but exhibits several eccentricities. The male deficit begins by about age 15 and persists for the remaining age cohorts. The deficit is higher in urban areas because of the heavier migration of females to the cities.

The current age structure is both a consequence of past rates of population growth and a determinant of future rates. As in many Western nations, the Hungarian population exhibits signs of rapid aging, reflecting the long-term decline in fertility and increase in longevity. Thus the age structure no longer resembles a pyramid, as in developing societies, but a rectangle. The female population is a little older than the male population both according to the median age and to the percentage distribution by age. The rural population is younger than the urban population, reflecting the higher fertility in rural areas. While the burden of dependency of children on the adult population of working age has shown a generally downward trend, that of older people has shown a consistent increase.

The institution of marriage remains strong. Nearly 97% of the males and 95% of the females are married by age 65. Women tend to marry at an earlier age than men. Nearly 30% of the women marry before 19, compared to 6.4% of the men. However, the marriage rate has steadily dropped, from a peak of 11.7 per 1,000 in 1949 and 10 per 1,000 in 1957 to 6.2 per 1,000 in 1986. The Communist regime has followed a pronatalist policy for many years, outlawing abortion and providing subsidies for families.

ETHNIC COMPOSITION

About 96% of the population is Magyar, the proper term for Hungarian. This category includes both true Magyars and those who have assimilated Magyar culture. The principal national minorities, who constitute about 4%, include Germans, Slovaks, Serbs, Croats, Rumanians and Ruthenians. Over two-thirds of each of these minority groups are peasants living in villages dispersed across the country, where rural life offers them a better climate for preserving their individuality. There is little evidence of interethnic friction, although constitutional provisions for bilingual education for minorities are not entirely enforced.

There are a few thousand Gypsies in Hungary, who are not considered an ethnic minority by the state. Prejudice against Gypsies is long-established and strong.

LANGUAGES

Hungarian or Magyar is the national language. Written in Latin characters, Magyar belongs to the Finno-Ugric family, a branch of the Ural-Altaic language group. Magyar has a heavy admixture of Turkish, Slavic, German, Latin and French words. Since World War II many Hungarians have learned to speak one or more second languages, such as Russian, German or English.

RELIGIONS

Christianity in Hungary traces its history to the third century, when the Pannonian and Dacian provinces of the Roman Empire were Romanized. Arian, Roman and Orthodox missionaries were active in this region. Catholics who worked in Moravia introduced the Greek rite and translated the liturgy and Bible into Slavic languages. Moravian converts were later dispersed, spreading the Byzantine rite throughout Bulgaria and Russia and the Roman rite throughout Hungary. Roman Catholicism became the official religion of the land in 1001 under Stephen, who was given the title of apostolic king by the pope. Both Stephen and his son were canonized. The dark ages of Hungary's history began with the Mongol invasion of the 13th century followed by the Turkish invasion of the 16th century and the Turkish occupation of the country until the late 1600s. During the Reformation period Hungary was divided into three regions: the West under the control of the Austrian Hapsburgs, the Great Plain under the Turks and Transylvania under independent princes.

The Lutheran Reformation made rapid headway under the influence of reformers such as Wittenberg. Beginning in 1545, the Hungarian church adopted first the Augsburg Confession, the Lutheran Catechism (1550), the Second Helvetic Confession (1567) and the Heidelberg Catechism. By the close of the 16th century the majority of Hungarians had become Protestants. By the end of the 17th century the Hapsburgs had driven out the Turks and united the country under their crown. At the same time, the Hapsburgs launched a Counter-Reformation, which was invigorated by two events: the failure of the War of Liberation of Ferenc Rakooczi II (1703–11) and the arrival of Catholic settlers in regions vacated by the Turks. By the close of the 18th century the Lutheran population had been reduced to one-third of the population. However, the Edict of Toleration of Joseph II and the royal decree of 1780 granted Protestants a degree of religious freedom they had not experienced hitherto, and further steps toward religious equality were taken progressively in the 19th century. Following World War I, in which Hungary gained its independence but lost much of its territory, the Lutheran Church lost more than half its membership. World War II, the rise of communism and industrialization further reduced its influence.

Catholics are mostly in Transdanubia, in the area between the Danube and the Tisza rivers and in the mountains of the North. They form the majority in 70% of the towns and are particularly strong among minorities such as Croats, Germans and Slovaks. The church survived the bitter persecutions of the early postwar years under Matyas Rakosi and remains active and influential both in the rural areas and among intellectuals. Masses are well attended, and pilgrimages are frequent. External piety is no longer concealed or engaged in merely as a form of political protest. Folk religion has had a revival since the 1950s. However, the number of clergy has declined sharply, and their median age has risen to over 60.

Discrimination against Protestant churches officially ended with the Communist takeover. The new government made individual agreements with each body and subsidized the reconstruction of churches extensively damaged during the war. Religious education is subsidized by the state. The Reformed Church of Hungary, with about 19% of the population, has 2,000 autonomous parishes in four districts or dioceses; two theological seminaries; several institutions of higher learning; and 20 charitable organizations. The Evangelical Lutheran Church, with about 4% of the population, is divided into two districts with 500 parishes forming 16 seniorates; one theological academy; and 18 social service institutions. The largest of the smaller denominations is the Baptist Church, which was established in Hungary in 1846. It has 500 congregations, one theological seminary and three social service institutions. Methodists entered Hungary in 1900 and now have 55 congregations and one charitable institution.

The Orthodox Church has 10 parishes, serving mostly Serbian and Rumanian minorities in Szentendre and Budapest. Hungarian Orthodoxy is under the Moscow Patriarchate.

Church-state relations are governed by the 1972 revision to the Constitution of 1949 and by a series of laws regulating religious practice. The Constitution guarantees freedom of conscience and freedom of worship. The most significant laws relating to religion are:

1. Decree 600 of 1945, nationalizing ecclesiastical estates, half of which became state lands; the other half was distributed among peasants.

2. Law 33 of 1948, nationalizing all church-run schools. Eight Catholic schools and two Protestant schools were returned to their respective churches in 1950.

3. Law 34 of 1950, ordering the dissolution of religious orders and congregations, with the exception of Benedictines, Franciscans, Piarists and congregations of sisters engaged in public teaching, who still are authorized to operate Catholic schools and to recruit two novices each year.

4. Decree 170 of 1951, creating a fund for churches of $4 million, to be distributed to the churches according to their numbers.

5. Agreements between the state and the Lutheran and Reformed churches in 1948 and the Catholic Church in 1950, providing for the involvement of the churches in economic affairs.

6. Agreements with the Holy See in 1964, 1969 and 1972. That of 1964, the first of its kind concluded between the Holy See and a Communist state, recognized the right of the former to nominate bishops approved by the government and modified the oath of loyalty taken by bishops to the people's republic. It also permitted the reopening of the Hungarian Institute in Rome.

The churches may collect voluntary contributions from their members, amounting in the case of the Catholic Church to 1% of the income of each head of family. Church property is exempt from taxes. All clergy must take an oath of loyalty to the state to the effect that they regard the regime as lawful. Except for the free churches, the salaries of Protestant and Catholic clergy are partially subsidized by the state. In the case of the former, the state contribution amounts to about 25% of their total stipend. Religious instruction may be offered in state primary schools in the form of optional courses outside regular school hours for pupils up to 14 years of age. About 60% of schools offer such courses and about 23% of Hungarian youth participate in them. Priests and laypersons teaching such programs draw a salary from the state. There is no teaching of religion in state secondary schools, although religious training for older youth prior to confirmation is common, consisting in the case of Catholics of a six-week accelerated course and in the case of the Reformed Church of a 10- to 12-week course over a two-year period. Religious courses are compulsory in church schools. Teachers in confessional schools receive their salary from the state, but other school expenses are met by contributions from parents.

The State Office for Ecclesiastical Affairs was created in May 1951, and except for 1957 and 1959, when it was temporarily suspended, continued to function until 1990. Headed by a minister, the office exercised strict control over all activities of the churches and the religious press, suggested or opposed appointments, supervised admission to seminaries and provided subsidies to church schools and the expenses of religious education in state schools. Its delegates were present at festivals and religious ceremonies and participated in synods.

The Protestant churches, which are termed national ecclesiastical communities, have succeeded better than the Catholic Church in accommodating to the Communist regime. The latter was bound historically to the old regime politically as the official church and also economically, as exemplified in its feudal character. The struggle of the Catholic Church against the new regime began in 1945 and was conducted personally under the direction of Cardinal Mindszenty, who was finally arrested on December 25, 1948, and sentenced the following February to life imprisonment. Between 1950 and 1956 the church was engaged in passive resistance, but a more liberal course began to manifest itself, involving elements of collaboration with the regime by groups such as the Movement of Priests for Peace. A definite thaw in state-church relations began in 1960, with the government granting priests and bishops the right to travel outside the country and the religious media to publish books. This trend has become even more marked since 1971, when the Hungarian Catholic

Church celebrated its millennium, with the government permitting the organization of local pilgrimages, authorizing for the first time the publication of a children's catechism and relaxing its control over the appointment of lower clergy. Priests accused of collaborating with the regime were no longer subject to excommunication, and the number of imprisoned priests began to diminish. An important factor in the détente was the growing role of Opus Pacis, the general secretary of which was at one time a member of the Supreme Presidium. Of equal importance has been the new policy of reconciliation toward Eastern European regimes began under Pope John XXIII and continued under his successors. In 1990 diplomatic relations with the Vatican were finally reestablished.

At its session on January 24, the National Assembly enacted a new Law on the Freedom of Conscience, Religion, and the Churches. The law went into effect on February 12, and shortly thereafter the agreements of 1948 and 1950 that had given the state full control over Hungary's Churches were revoked. In its preamble, the law states that "freedom of conscience and religion is a basic human right" as well as a "prerequisite for renewing a political system . . . that reflects the pluralism of ideas in society." It goes on to describe Hungary's church organizations as "outstanding members of society," which, in addition to fulfilling their spiritual mission, have also played an important role in promoting charitable and cultural activities. The law guarantees Hungarians the freedom to choose their "world view," as well as parents' right to decide whether they want their children to be educated in state or religious schools. The law also guarantees the right of both elementary and high school students to receive religious instruction at their parents' request. It prohibits discrimination against individuals for their religious convictions and affirms the separation of church and state, specifically forbidding the state to interfere in the churches' activities in any way.

The new law also recognizes churches as legal entities, establishes the equality of all Hungarian churches in the eyes of the law, and guarantees freedom of association for their members. These provisions allow the churches to set up lay organizations, social charities and cultural institutions, as well as to revive religious orders. Moreover, the new law requires the state to provide religious schools and institutions with the same financial support it gives state schools and institutions. The law guarantees members of the clergy fulfilling pastoral duties free access to hospitals, prisons, reformatories and military institutions. Military personnel are allowed to worship freely under the new law, individually on military premises and collectively beyond those premises. The law also states that a minimum of 100 people is required in order to found a new denomination; the only requirement for state recognition is that the new organization observe the Constitution. The courts will register all new churches and the churches themselves will be free to choose their own leaders (previously the state had approved all clerical appointments).

In May the outgoing government, led by the Hungar-ian Socialist Party, annulled both the life sentence pronounced on Jozsef Cardinal Mindszenty in 1949 and the 15-year sentence given to Hungary's second-highest Catholic prelate, Archbishop Jozsef Groesz, in 1951. Admitting that the charges had been fabricated, the HSP declared the two men's sentences null and void. Mindszenty and Groesz had been symbols not only of the persecution Hungarian churches suffered under Communism but of resistance to that persecution.

Both the outgoing and the new coalition government subsequently rehabilitated other Catholic and Protestant clergymen convicted on fabricated charges that the Communist authorities had brought against them. Other clergymen were rehabilitated by means of official apologies.

Between 1945 and 1952, the Communist state divested Hungary's churches of their assets, which it then nationalized. Farmland, real estate, buildings used to house charitable institutions and cultural establishments, and almost all church schools were seized. The churches are currently seeking to have all their assets returned, with the exception of former land holdings. They hope to reclaim many of the buildings that housed schools, hospitals and religious orders.

The churches reportedly want to reclaim 4,500 to 5,000 of their former buildings. Prime Minister Jozsef Antall's government is currently negotiating an agreement with church representatives to return church assets in two phases. During the first phase, to be completed by the end of 1991, some 800 buildings that the churches consider vital to performing basic functions would be returned. In the second stage, which, according to the government, might take as long as 20 years, the churches would become the registered owners of the remaining buildings but could not repossess them until the current occupants had been rehoused. Draft legislation that would govern this process is also being discussed with leaders of the various denominations.

On July 13 the Ministry of Culture and Education reached an agreement with delegates from all recognized churches in Hungary to reinstate religion as an optional subject in state schools, beginning this fall. Under the agreement, religious education classes will be scheduled on an extracurricular basis; they will not conflict with mandatory instruction. The schools will provide classrooms and other necessary facilities, while the churches will approve the textbooks and both clerical and lay teachers. These teachers will not be considered regular members of staff but "teaching partners," who will be consulted only on issues pertaining to religious instruction. The state rather than the schools themselves will pay their salaries.

Hungary's major churches (Catholic, Reformed and Lutheran) are also experiencing a crisis of confidence. Many leaders had discredited themselves in the eyes of religious believers by their subservience to the former Communist state. Consequently, grassroots movements within the Reformed and Lutheran churches are demanding that compromised church leaders be replaced by new leaders democratically elected by the congregations. Spokesmen for these movements are rallying support under the motto "Democracy for Our Church."

Catholics are also beginning to call for the resignation of compromised Church leaders.

HISTORICAL BACKGROUND

The Magyars arrived in the Carpathian Basin at the end of the ninth century, and this event generally marks the beginning of the Hungarian nation. The early Magyars were a seminomadic, pastoral people who lived in the Khazar state north of the Black Sea, to which they had migrated probably from the region between the great bend of the Volga River and the Ural Mountains. The Magyars were one of many warlike, nomadic hordes who swept into Europe from the East, bent on conquest and plunder. They consisted of seven tribes led by a chieftain known as Arpad, and they easily defeated the Slavs and other peoples living in the Carpathian Basin. The successors of Arpad later became kings of Hungary, and the Arpad dynasty lasted until the male line died out at the beginning of the 14th century. In the course of time the Magyars ceased their depradations and became sedentary; in turn, their land was subject to invasions by other marauding armies. Finally, the Magyars were decisively defeated by a coalition of forces of the Holy Roman Empire at Augsburg.

In 972 Prince Geza, great-grandson of Arpad, became the leader of the entire Hungarian confederation. To solidify the Western orientation of the country, he caused his son Istvan (Stephen) to be baptized a Roman Catholic. Stephen succeeded to the throne, and through his efforts Hungarians were converted to Roman Catholicism. As a reward Stephen received a crown from the pope (a story doubted by some modern historians but indelibly inscribed in Hungarian legend). Later he was canonized, and as St. Stephen and the first king of Hungary, he is revered as the father of the Hungarian nation, and his crown is considered the symbol of its sovereignty.

During Stephen's reign Transylvania was brought under Hungarian hegemony and the Latin script was adopted by the Magyar language. Stephen built forts in uninhabited territories between existing settlements, and in time towns grew up around them.

Although Stephen established a unitary state in which the royal authority was supreme and crown lands extensive, the power of his successors was challenged in 1222, when the small landholders compelled the king to sign the Golden Bull, which has been compared to the Magna Carta. The Golden Bull set limits on the king but did nothing to alleviate the condition of the landless peasants.

The 13th century was one of troubles for the nation. In 1241 the Mongols invaded Hungary, devastating and depopulating the countryside. The death of Endre III, the last Arpad in the direct male line in 1301, intensified the troubles of the realm. During the next two centuries until the Turkish invasion, Hungary was ruled by various European royal houses. A Bohemian king gave way to a Bavarian, and he, in turn, to Charles Robert of Anjou. Charles's son Louis the Great enjoyed a successful reign and is remembered for his many financial, administrative, military and commercial reforms. The

next to wear the crown of St. Stephen was Sigismund of Luxembourg, but because he was also the Holy Roman emperor, his interests were diffused relative to those of Hungary. At the same time, the Ottoman Turks were becoming more menacing around the fringes of the Hungarian domains. They were turned back at Belgrade in 1456 by Matyas Hunyadi, one of Hungary's great heroes. After Hunyadi's death, his son Matyas was elected king. Known to historians as Corvinus Matthias, he gave Hungary a period of prosperity, peace and national glory from 1458 until 1490. He established a mercenary standing army, restored public finances and reduced the power of masters over serfs. While keeping the Turks in check, he extended the kingdom over Bohemia, Silesia, Moravia, Lower Austria and other principalities.

After the death of Matyas, the inevitable power struggle culminated in the election of a weak king. Many of the foreign territories broke away, and the nobles became restive once more. In 1514 a serious serf uprising was suppressed with great loss of life. Under these conditions, in 1526 the Turkish and Hungarian armies met once again, in the Battle of Mohacs, in which the latter was disastrously defeated. It signaled the beginning of 150 years of Turkish rule. Hungary was partitioned, with the western and northern sections under Austrian rule, the central area under direct Turkish rule and Transylvania governed by Hungarian princes under Turkish suzerainty.

When the Turks were finally forced to withdraw from Hungary, the three-way partition was replaced by Hapsburg dominion rather than independence. The economy was in a shambles as a result of Turkish extortionate taxation. The population was sharply reduced, and most of the people who survived were in a condition of servitude. Only Transylvania, ruled by a series of able Hungarian princes, was able to maintain the national culture. The principality also enjoyed a measure of religious tolerance unique in Europe at that time.

Although conditions were desperate, the national will to independence survived. Toward the end of the 18th century a national renaissance began to enhance Hungarian pride in native culture and language. In about 1830 a great reform movement began, led by Count Istvan Szechenyi, a moderate, on the one hand and Lajos Kossuth, a landless noble and revolutionary, on the other. These two leaders became the opposite poles of the Hungarian response to the revolutionary ferment of the 19th century. Szechenyi wanted to educate the masses and reform the system, but Kossuth wanted to unleash the masses and topple the system. Szechenyi was led by critical realism and Kossuth by nationalistic idealism.

When repression followed the demand for moderate reforms, Kossuth gained ascendancy. Influenced by the news of revolution in Paris, Kossuth in 1848 demanded the abolition of serfdom, popular representation and the replacement of control from Vienna by a Budapest-based government. These demands were placed before King Ferdinand, who responded favorably by appointing Count Lajos Batthyany as president of a Hungarian council. The Diet was established as a bicameral legislature to be elected for three years, but suffrage was limited to Hungarian-speakers with certain property and educational qualifications. The king was bound to act as a constitutional monarch through responsible ministers.

The success was short-lived. Austrian reactionaries and Hungarian counterrevolutionaries set national minorities against the Hungarians, and there were violent conflicts between Hungarians on the one hand and Croats, Serbs, Rumanians and Slovaks on the other. King Ferdinand was forced to abdicate, and his successor, Francis Joseph, stated that he was not bound by the concessions of his predecessor. On April 14, 1849, Kossuth declared Hungary's independence and set up a national government. The Austrians backed by the Russians then moved with direct military force and crushed the revolt. Kossuth was exiled. Hungary was incorporated into the empire as a province, but some of its historic lands, such as Transylvania and Croatia, were separated from it to destroy its unity and strength. The next 16 years were characterized by an absolute regime by imperial decree. The period of reaction was dominated by Alexander von Bach, minister of internal affairs and a revolutionary agitator turned tool of absolutism. Repression and persecution fostered development of an intense national patriotism accompanied by a hatred of everything Austrian. The nationalist groups were united in their opposition to Vienna but divided in the methods they espoused. Both the old conservatives and the moderates, the latter led by Ferenc Deak, wanted a return to the constitutional arrangements of 1847–48, while the radicals and emigres, led by Kossuth, wanted nothing less than the expulsion of Austrians. Meanwhile, Austria's defeat in the wars against Italy, France and Prussia and its growing isolation, especially from Russia, led it to moderate its own stand and adopt the Compromise of 1867. In effect it established a dual monarchy with a common king but two governments. Parliamentary bodies functioned in both states, and ministers involved with matters of common concern—finance, defense and foreign affairs—were responsible to equal delegations from the two parliaments sitting alternately in the two capitals. Agreements concerning commerce and customs were made subject to periodic revisions every 10 years.

Although the emperor remained loyal to the compromise until his death in 1916, the Austrian officialdom was adamantly obstructive and caused problems to the Hungarian government. Moreover, the problem of minorities remained a thorn on the side of Hungary. That involving the Croats was the most critical. The onset of World War I, the subsequent defeat of Austria, and the death of Francis Joseph in 1916 sounded the death knell of the compromise.

In 1918 Count Mihaly Karolyi, a leader of the left wing of the Party of Independence, was appointed prime minister and formed a cabinet consisting of Social Democrats, radicals and members of his own party. He declared Hungary a republic. However, the Allies accepted Italian, South Slav, Rumanian and Czech territorial demands against Hungary and ordered the country's dismemberment. Gradually the Karolyi government was infiltrated at all levels by Communists, who

had in many instances returned from Russian prisoner-of-war camps, where they were influenced by Leninists. In 1919 Karolyi was forced to step down in favor of Bela Kun, a Communist, who unleashed a reign of terror that lasted for five months until he was ousted by a reactionary regime led by Admiral Miklos Horthy de Nagybanya, who was declared regent. In 1920 Hungary was forced to accept a dictated war settlement embodied in the Treaty of Trianon. By this treaty, which most Hungarians considered savage and unjust, Hungary lost 72% of its territory and 64% of its population to the so-called successor states to the dual monarchy.

The interwar years were characterized by reaction and reconstruction. The Depression and the influence of the rise of national socialism in Germany were keenly felt in the evolution of political and social institutions. The prime ministers during this period were Count Istvan Bethlen of the Party of Unity, who held office until 1931; Gyula Karoli, from 1931 to 1932; General Gyula Gombos, who held power until 1936; Kalman Daranyi, 1936–38; Bela Imredy, 1938–39; and Count Pal Teleki, 1939–41. Although Teleki was determinedly anti-German, Hungary received from Germany through the first and second Vienna awards 11,917 sq. km. (4,600 sq. mi.) of territory from Czechoslovakia and 41,451 sq. km. (16,000 sq mi.) and 2.5 million people of northern Transylvania.

During the war Hungary became a virtual German satellite. Teleki was driven to suicide, and the next prime minister, Laszlo Bardossy, collaborated with the Nazis in promoting Hungarian participation in the war. Horthy dismissed Bardossy for declaring war against the United States without his consent and appointed Miklos Kallai as prime minister. When Kallai began negotiating with the Allies, Hitler occupied Hungary. In 1944 Horthy arranged an armistice and broke off his alliance with the Nazis, for which he was arrested. By Christmas 1944 Soviet troops had occupied Budapest and the nation's second Communist government in modern history was set up.

For postwar history, see Chronology.

CONSTITUTION & GOVERNMENT

During its history of over 1,000 years, Hungary has experienced governing other nations and being itself subject to foreign rule. Hungary was a great empire but suffered repeated defeats. It has been an absolute monarchy, a constitutional monarchy, feudal, fascist and Communist. The Magyars sought freedom but denied it to others. The people have savored but brief periods of democracy and closed the 1980s clamoring for political reform.

As the Soviet armed forces marched into Hungary, a Committee of National Liberation was established and in January 1945 the provisional government, consisting of several parties of the Hungarian Independent Front, signed an armistice in Moscow that provided for an Allied Control Commission whose chairman was to be a Soviet marshal, Kliment E. Voroshilov. Within three years the Communist Party, with Soviet intervention, succeeded in achieving complete control of the Hungarian government. The provisional government decreed a massive land reform, supervised by the Communist minister of agriculture, Imre Nagy. Nevertheless, in elections of November 1945, considered the freest in Hungary's history, the Communist Party (CP) received only 17% of the popular vote. The Smallholders' Party, with a majority of 57%, normally would have organized the government, but by a prior agreement engineered by Voroshilov, all Front parties participated in the new government. The prime minister was from the Smallholders, but the CP was given the Ministry of the Interior, headed by Imre Nagy. In February 1946 the National Assembly established Hungary as a republic. The leader of the Smallholders' Party, Zoltan Tildy, became president, and Ferenc Nagy succeeded him as prime minister. The obstacle to total CP control was clearly the Smallholders' Party, which became the object of CP and Soviet propaganda, repression and terrorism. In June 1948 the CP and the Social Democratic Party merged, forming the Hungarian Workers' Party. In August of that year Tildy was replaced as president by a pro-Communist and the government was completely controlled by the CP, which, in February 1949, organized the Hungarian Independent People's Front, consisting of pro-Communist political parties and mass organizations similar to other East European fronts. In the ensuing elections in May 1949, the typical single slate received 96.5% of the vote. The National Assembly adopted a Soviet-type Constitution.

The Constitution of 1949 "laid down the foundation for socialism," and the 1972 amendment declared Hungary to be a "socialist" state. Gratitude was expressed to the Soviet Union for its "liberation" of Hungary and for "opening the road to democratic development for the Hungarian people." Hungary became a "people's republic" in which "all power belongs to the working people," but Article 3 stipulates that "The Marxist-Leninist party of the working class is the leading force of society." Ideologically, the Constitution places the working class in the leading role, but it is to cooperate with the peasantry, the professionals and other working strata. Article 6 permits the "liquidation of the exploiting classes" and places "social ownership of the means of production" as the base of the economic order. Nationalization of property was instituted and the state established agricultural collectives, but the state also permitted establishment of "small-commodity producers" as "useful economic activities."

The Constitution provides for a unicameral system, with the National Assembly as the highest organ of state power. According to Article 19, the National Assembly "exercises all rights deriving from the sovereignty of the people; guarantees the constitutional order of society; and determines the organization, direction and conditions of government." It enacts the Constitution and laws; draws up the economic plan; prepares the state budget; approves the government's program; ratifies treaties; declares a state of war and concludes peace; elects the Presidential Council; elects the Council of Ministers; creates ministries; elects the president of the Supreme Court and the chief prosecutor; and supervises observance of the Constitution.

In the June 1985 elections to the National Assembly the 387 members consisted of 352 members from multicandidate constituencies and 35 from the national list. About 70% were HSWP members, while only 77 were workers and four were peasants. A new electoral law provided for open nomination and a minimum of two candidates for each seat to the National Assembly and to the councils, and for a national list of 35 unopposed candidates selected by the People's Patriotic Front (PPF). The latter sparked protests against irregularities, hostility toward "spontaneous" nominations and resulted in widespread apathy among youth in the nominating process. The National Assembly elects from its members a president, a speaker, deputy presidents and secretaries; from its members it forms standing committees, such as Agriculture, Foreign Affairs, National Defense and Culture. The National Assembly is obliged to convene at least twice annually; before 1989 the deputies generally met for one or two days to approve CP decisions. Resolutions are passed by a majority vote, but a two-thirds vote is required to amend the Constitution.

The members of the National Assembly are elected by universal, equal and direct suffrage, and by secret ballot for five-year terms. In like manner citizens elect members of communal, town and Budapest district councils, while the members of the Budapest council are elected by the Budapest district councils, and members of the county councils by the town and communal councils. Constituents are given the right of recall.

The composition of the National Assembly, elected in 1985, was of the prereform era, with many deputies representing the HSWP conservative wing. By the late 1980s the National Assembly registered poorly in public esteem, and pressure for change, including new elections, mounted. At the March 8–10, 1989, session the president, a deputy president and four other deputies were pressured into resignation. The new president, Matyas Szuros, although a veteran Communist functionary, was identified with the reformist wing of the HSWP.

The Constitution provides for fundamental rights and duties. The guarantees include the right to work; rest; old age support; education; the freedom of scientific and artistic creative activity; freedom of conscience and worship; freedom of speech, press and assembly; the right of association; and personal freedom and inviolability of citizens. As elsewhere in the Soviet bloc countries, the duties outweigh the rights. The Constitution demands that "civic rights must be exercised in harmony with the interests of the socialist society; the exercise of rights is inseparable from the performance of civic duties." For example, freedom of speech, press and assembly must conform "to the interests of socialism." Mass organizations and movements exist only for the "protection of the order and achievements of socialism."

According to the Constitution, the National Assembly, at its first session, elects from among its members a Presidential Council (Elnoki Tanacs), consisting of a president, two vice presidents, a secretary and seventeen members. The prime minister and others of the

Council of Ministers are forbidden to hold positions in this body. The Presidential Council establishes the date for National Assembly elections and convenes its sessions; initiates legislation; may decree a plebiscite; concludes and ratifies treaties; accredits and receives ambassadors and other diplomats; elects professional judges; appoints high-ranking state officials and military officers; and grants pardons. It supervises the enforcement of the Constitution and discharges the duties of the National Assembly between sessions, except for amending the Constitution. The Presidential Council also has constitutional supervision over the councils at various levels, setting dates for elections and dissolving the councils when their activities are deemed unconstitutional or when they imperil the interests of the people. In case of war or extreme danger, the Presidential Council may establish a Council of National Defense vested with extraordinary powers and also proclaim a state of emergency. Despite these seemingly impressive powers and the potential of policy-making, the Presidential Council has essentially only perfunctory capabilities, with its president acting as head of state.

As Hungary entered the 1980s the leadership admitted that its Constitution was basically a reflection of the 1936 "Stalinist" Soviet Constitution and decided that in the light of the country's political transformation a new, "European type" Constitution must be enacted. Constitutional experts began its preparation in 1982 by studying modern foreign constitutions, including the U.S. document. The first draft, made public on November 30, 1988, reflected a continuation of the one-party (HSWP) system and provoked widespread criticism by the reformists—the alternative organizations and associations—who demanded deletion of references to "socialist society" and the leading role of the HWSP.

The second draft, published on January 30, 1989, provided for a parliamentary democracy based on a multiparty system. The following month the HSWP's Central Committee agreed to the exclusion of its mention in the Constitution. The Central Committee favored the state system to be characterized as "free, democratic and socialist Hungary," the country to continue to be a "people's republic" and its flag to reflect national traditions. At its March 8–10, 1989, session, the National Assembly endorsed the further codification of the second draft, and in 1990 it will consider the final draft, after public discussion, for adoption by referendum.

On September 19, 1989, the government and opposition parties agreed on a multiparty system in 1990. No one party can hold a monopoly of power; the only condition levied on parties is that their goals and activities must accord with the Constitution. There should be a division of power—that is, power should be shared by the president, the National Assembly, the Council of Ministers responsible to the National Assembly, local governments, independent courts and a Constitutional Court.

However, positive developments toward democratic principles continued to be initiated in preparation for the Constitution's formal adoption in 1990. The National Assembly passed a law on economic associations, including those with foreign businesses, to attract foreign capital, and a law extending rights to non-Hungarian investors. Of particular significance was legislation for multiparty democracy and for freedom of association and assembly, permitting the formation of associations by as few as 10 people for any purpose within constitutional limits. Demonstrators were to give notice but required no authorization. Other laws included the right to strike, motion of no confidence and plebiscite were enacted, all leading to a more democratic Constitution.

The highest organ of state administration is the Council of Ministers (Miniszter Tanacs), which is elected by and is responsible to the National Assembly. According to the Constitution, the Council of Ministers (or government) consists of the prime minister, the head of government; deputies; ministers of state; ministers; and the chairman of the National Planning Office.

Article 35 of the Constitution enumerates the Council of Ministers' responsibilities and authority: It safeguards and guarantees the political and social order of the state and the rights of the citizens; enforces the laws and decrees; directs and coordinates the work of the ministries and other organs; directs and supervises the councils at lower levels; arranges for and implements the economic plans; sets policy and provisions for scientific and cultural development; establishes and ensures the functioning of social and health services; concludes and approves international agreements; and performs other functions assigned by law. The Council of Ministers is empowered to organize government committees and to establish special organs to administer any sector of activity. The Council of Ministers or individual ministers may issue decrees in the performance of their duties. The Council of Ministers functions by issuing decrees and passing resolutions. It has authority to annul or amend measures enacted by subordinate organs deemed an infringement on laws or a violation of public interest, and ministers direct the subordinate organs to conform to rules of law and resolutions of the Council of Ministers.

On October 1989 the National Assembly adopted an amendment to the Constitution in the form of a basic law. The new Constitution:

• renamed the country as the Republic of Hungary
• declared the republic a parliamentary democracy with a multiparty system and a socially sensitive market economy
• permits the free formation of political parties
• recognizes the inviolability and inalienability of basic human rights
• provides for plebiscite and popular initiative
• permits Western-type parliamentary vote of no-confidence in the Council of Ministers or individual ministers
• abolished the State Office for Church Affairs.

Two new institutions have been established by the Constitution. They are the Constitutionality Court and the office of the ombudsman. The Constitutionality Court oversees the constitutionality of legislation, or a decree or statute. Its 15 members are elected by the National Assembly but may not belong to any political party. The ombudsman is an officer of the National Assembly, elected by it on the recommendation of the president of the republic.

RULERS OF HUNGARY
Kings/Queens (from 1000)

December 1000–August 1038: Istvan I (St. Stephen)
August 1038–41: Peter
1041–44: Samuel
1044–46: Peter
1046–47: Interregnum
1047–60: Andras I
1060–63: Bela I
1063–74: Salamon
1074–77: Geza I
1077–June 1095: Laszlo I
June 1095–February 1116: Kalman
February 1116–31: Istvan II
1131–41: Bela II
1141–61: Geza II
1161–62: Istvan III
1162–63: Laszlo II
1163: Istvan III
1163–65: Istvan IV
1165–73: Istvan III
1173–96: Bela III
1196–1204: Imre
1204–5: Laszlo III
1205–35: Andras II
1235–54: Bela IV
1254–May 1270: Bela IV/Istvan V
May 1270–72: Istvan V
1272–July 1290: Laszlo IV
July 1290–1301: Andras III
1301–8: Interregnum—claims by Laszlo and Otto not recognized
1308–July 1342: Karolyi I
July 1342–September 1382: Lajos I
September 1382–85: Maria
1385–February 1386: Karolyi II
February 1386–95: Maria
1395–1437: Sigismund
January 1438–October 1439: Albrecht I
October 1439–November 1444: Ulaszlo I
November 1444–November 1457: Laszlo V
January 1458–May 1490: Matyas I
May 1490–June 1508: Ulaszlo II
June 1508–March 1516: Ulaszlo II/Lajos II
March 1516–August 1526: Lajos II
1526–1848: Austrian rule

Regent (1849)
April–August 1849: Lajos Kossuth
Kings (from 1867)
February 1867–October 1918: Emperors of Austria
Presidents (1919)
January–March 1919: Mihaly Karolyi
March–July 1919: Sandor Garbai
Regents (from 1919)
July–August 1919: Archduke Joseph
August 1919–May 1920: Post vacant
May 1920–October 1944: Miklos Horthy de Nagybanya
October 1944–April 1945: Ferenc Szalasi (acting; styled leader)
November 1945–February 1946: Bela Zsedenyi (acting)

RULERS OF HUNGARY (continued)
Presidents (from 1946)
(Chairman of the Presidential Council since 1949)

February 1946–July 1948: Zoltan Tildy
August 1948–April 1950: Arpad Szakasits
April 1950–August 1952: Sandor Ronai
August 1952–April 1967: Istvan Dobi
April 1967–June 1987: Pal Losonczi
June 1987–September 1988: Karoly Nemeth
September 1988–October 1989: Bruno F. Straub
October 1989–May 1990: Matyas Szueros
May 1990–   : Arpad Goncz

Prime Ministers (from 1848)
March–September 1848: Lajos Batthyany
September 1848–April 1849: Lajos Kossuth
April–August 1849: Bertalan Szermere
August 1849–February 1867: Post abolished
February 1867–November 1871: Gyula Andrassy
November 1871–December 1872: Menyhert Longay
December 1872–March 1874: Jozsef Szlavy
March 1874–February 1875: Istvan Bitto
March–October 1875: Bela Wenckheim
October 1875–March 1890: Kalman Tisza
March 1890–November 1892: Gyula Szarpary
November 1892–January 1895: Sandor Wekerle
January 1895–February 1899: Deszo Banffy
February 1899–June 1903: Kalman Szell
June–November 1903: Karolyi Khuen-Hedervary
November 1903–June 1905: Istvan Tisza
June 1905–April 1906: Geza Fejervary
April 1906–January 1910: Sandor Wekerle
January 1910–April 1912: Karoly Khuen-Hedervary
April 1912–June 1913: Laszlo Lukacs
June 1913–June 1917: Istvan Tisza
June–August 1917: Moric Esterhazy
August 1917–October 1918: Sandor Wekerle
October 1918: Janos Hadik
October 1918–January 1919: Mihaly Karolyi
January–March 1919: Denes Berinkey
March–June 1919: Sandor Garbai
June–August 1919: Antal Dovcsak
August 1919: Gyula Peidl
August–November 1919: Istvan Friedrich
November 1919–March 1920: Karolyi Huszar
March–July 1920: Sandor Simonyi-Semadam
July 1920–April 1921: Pal Teleki
April 1921–August 1931: Istvan Bethlen
August 1931–September 1932: Gyula Karolyi
September 1932–October 1936: Gyula Gombos
October 1936–May 1938: Kalman Daranyi
May 1938–February 1939: Bela Imredy
February 1939–April 1941: Pal Teleki
April 1941–March 1942: Laszlo Bardossy
March 1942–March 1944: Miklos Kailai
March–August 1944: Dome Szotjay
August–October 1944: Geza Lakatos
October 1944–April 1945: Ferenc Szalasi
April–November 1945: Bela Dalnoki-Miklos
November 1945–February 1946: Zoltan Tildy
February 1946–May 1947: Ferenc Nagy
May 1947–December 1948: Lajos Dinnyes
December 1948–August 1952: Istvan Dobi
August 1952–July 1953: Matyas Rakosi
July 1953–April 1955: Imre Nagy
April 1955–October 1956: Andras Hegedus
October–November 1956: Imre Nagy
November 1956–January 1958: Janos Kadar
January 1958–September 1961: Ferenc Munnich
September 1961–June 1965: Janos Kadar
June 1965–April 1967: Gyula Kallai
April 1967–May 1975: Jeno Fock
May 1975–June 1987: Gyorgy Lazar
June 1987–November 1988: Karoly Grosz

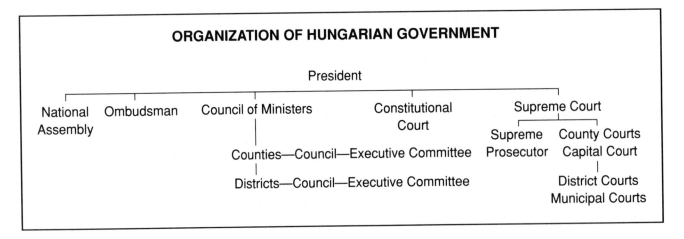

ORGANIZATION OF HUNGARIAN GOVERNMENT

President

National Assembly — Ombudsman — Council of Ministers — Constitutional Court — Supreme Court

Council of Ministers:
Counties—Council—Executive Committee
Districts—Council—Executive Committee

Supreme Court:
Supreme Prosecutor — County Courts — Capital Court — District Courts — Municipal Courts

---

RULERS OF HUNGARY (continued)
Prime Ministers (from 1848)
November 1988–May 1990: Miklos Nemeth
May 1990–   : Jozsef Antall
Communist Party Leaders (from 1949)
(Secretary General, 1949–53;
First Secretary, 1953–85;
General Secretary since 1985)
August 1949–July 1953: Matyas Rakosi
July–November 1953: Triumvirate: Matyas Rakosi/Lajos
  Acz/Bela Veg
November 1953–July 1956: Matyas Rakosi
July–October 1956: Erno Gero
October 1956–May 1988: Janos Kadar
May 1988–   : Karoly Grosz

CABINET LIST

President: Arpad Goncz
Premier, Council of Ministers: Jozsef Antall
Minister of Agriculture & Food: Jozsef Ferenc Nagy
Minister of Culture & Education: Bertalan Andrasfalvy
Minister of Defense: Lajos Fur
Minister of Environmental Protection and Water Management:
  Sandor K. Keresztes
Minister of Finance: Ferenc Rabar
Minister of Foreign Affairs: Geza Jeszenskzky
Minister of Industry and Trade: Peter Akos Bod
Minister of Interior: Balazs Horvath
Minister of Justice: Istvan Balsai
Minister of Transportation and Communications: Csaba Siklos
Minister of International Economic Relations: Bela Kadar
Minister of Labor: Sandor Gyorivanyi
Minister of Public Welfare: Laszlo Surjan

FREEDOM & HUMAN RIGHTS

Hungary is one of the Communist states that has evolved measurably from the Stalinist model to an open society. There has been significant progress in Hungary's human rights record. In 1988 unofficial groups organized the largest peaceful demonstration in recent years to commemorate the 1958 hanging of former prime minister Imre Nagy. An independent scientific and technical workers' union, an independent youth organization and several new opposition groups were founded. A new passport law made it possible for 2.5 million Hungarians to obtain new passports valid for worldwide travel as of September 30, 1988.

In recent years there have been no reported instances of political killings, disappearances or torture. In principle, citizens may bring complaints against the police. There are three levels of punitive incarceration: the "workhouse," which allows some privileges, such as visiting, outside work and leave; jail; and prison or penitentiary. Although there does not appear to be systematic mistreatment of prisoners, there are reports of isolated instances when prisoners were beaten.

Citizens are not generally subject to arbitrary arrest. A detainee must be informed in writing of the offense he or she is charged with and may be held at the police station for no longer than 72 hours before charges are filed. There is no provision for bail or provisional pretrial liberty. The Hungarian Penal Code contains a law on incitement that permits officials to prosecute for a wide range of utterances or statements. There are few closed trials, and the Constitution stipulates that all court proceedings must be open except in cases involving national security, which term is not defined. In general, judicial procedures are investigatory rather than adversarial in nature. There is no trial by jury. In mid-1988 the Ministry of Justice was assigned to draft a new Constitution allowing the judiciary a greater degree of independence.

The Constitution provides for personal freedom as well as inviolability of the home, personal correspondence and privacy. House searches may be conducted only under court orders and with proper warrants and in the presence of at least two witnesses. A written inventory of items removed from the premises must be prepared. Since the 1960s the authorities have become more tolerant of private activities.

Hungarians may subscribe to Western publications freely. Parents who provide religious instruction to their children at home are not harassed.

The Constitution guarantees free speech and a free press. On the 140th anniversary of the Hungarian Revolution of March 15, 1848, the government media for the first time gave attention to opposition events. The 1956 Revolution was the subject of three feature films and a documentary at the Budapest Film Festival in 1988. The documentary *Duanal* contained an unvarnished portrayal of the event, and it was shown on prime-time Hungarian television in December 1988. The 1958 hanging of Imre Nagy was commemorated by a massive public demonstration. The authorities sanctioned a ceremony at Nagy's unmarked gravesite and a church service. In 1989 Nagy's body was exhumed and reburied in a marked grave in a ceremony unprecedented for its crowds in modern Hungarian history. Nagy's rehabilitation was accompanied by exposure of the machinations of his enemies, particularly Andras Hegedus, who had preceded Nagy as prime minister and had "requested" Soviet intervention.

In 1988 the regime changed its policy of suppressing samizdat journals. In late 1988, along with a proliferation of clubs and protoparties, a number of independent or quasi-independent publications, such as *Reform*, *Kapu* (Gate) and *Hitel* (Credit), were allowed to appear.

The Hungarian media, although mostly state-owned and-monitored, have expanded their coverage to such controversial subjects as the meetings of the Democratic Forum, popular demonstrations protesting discrimination against Rumania's Hungarian minority, opposition to the Bos-Nagymaros Dam on the Danube and the trial of Gyula Kristaly for distributing leaflets critical of the government. Leading political figures hold televised press conferences. In September 1988 the first edition of *Reform* carried a detailed account of the Conrad spy case, involving Hungarian spies living in Sweden. The press also reports the views of groups such as the Independent Union of Scientific and Technical Workers and the independent youth organization FIDESZ. Films enjoy the greatest degree of freedom from political control.

The Constitution guarantees freedom of assembly and the right to form associations. These freedoms, however, were long suppressed until a new draft law was published in 1988. The new law prohibits assemblies and associations "that may violate the security of the state, public order, public morals, or may result in danger to public health or the rights and freedom of others." The security of the state is defined as including "the independence, territory and alliance system of the Hungarian People's Republic." The law requires three days' advance notice for all public gatherings, which the police may then ban if they so choose.

Freedom of conscience and of religious practice are affirmed in the Constitution. Virtually all major religious denominations—the Mormon Church most recently—are now officially recognized. The government has generally maintained good relations with the hierarchies of major denominations, many of which have representatives in the National Assembly.

Religious denominations have unrestricted access to religious materials, including Bibles and prayer books, which in many cases they print. They also publish newspapers and periodicals. In the summer of 1988 an International Bible Society Conference was held in Hungary.

Churches do not serve as nuclei for dissent, and no clergy are in prison. Growing numbers of young believers have formed loosely affiliated grass-roots organizations called "basic communities," which function outside official church structures. Officially some 159 young people are serving prison terms of up to three years each for refusing obligatory military service for religious reasons. The right of conscientious objection is broadly recognized for only two denominations—the Nazarenes and the Seventh-Day Adventists—because it is one of their basic precepts.

Hungary maintains and fosters active contacts with foreign religious communities. In 1989 Billy Graham held another crusade in Budapest. Pope John Paul II was invited to visit Hungary, and Hungarian Catholics were permitted to travel to Austria to participate in the pope's 1988 visit to the village of Darazsfalva. Also in 1988 the Emanuel Foundation dedicated a Holocaust memorial in Budapest's main synagogue.

With the new passport law, Hungary became the first Communist country to make available on demand for its citizens passports for worldwide travel. In 1988 Hungarians made 7,677,328 trips abroad. The government has announced proposals to eliminate passport disability for 1956 offenders.

The role of women in political life is limited. However, women's share in the professions has been substantially increasing, although they are less prominent in the top echelons of management.

Both in theory and in practice Hungary is sensitive and responsive to the cultural aspirations and rights of its recognized ethnic minorities. Schools providing instruction in their mother tongue and varieties of cultural expressions are encouraged. A major reason for this policy is the hope that its "demonstration effect" will indirectly benefit the millions of Hungarians living as minorities in the neighboring countries. Although Gypsies are not recognized as an official minority, the government is engaged in many programs to improve their living standards and educational attainments. Some popular but not official prejudice against them still exists.

CIVIL SERVICE

Hungary has no comparable Office of Personnel Management, as in the United States. Ministries and councils have a staff office *(szemelyzeti)*, which is responsible for personnel matters. Hungary has a three-year College for State Administration in Budapest, but the majority of civil servants originate from universities, colleges, technical schools and secondary schools. Law faculties have been especially favored sources. Civil service has not been particularly attractive in Hungary.

In the early years of party rule, the bureaucracy was characterized by centralization, overemployment, unqualified staffers and arrogance. Periodic attempts to curb shortcomings have succeeded only partly. The civil service rose from 20,000 in 1938 to 86,000 in 1953 but was reduced to 55,000 in 1957. The decrease at the lower levels was only half that in the ministries. In 1976 the number nationwide was 58,000, of whom 41,000 worked in the councils.

Qualifications of civil servants have been upgraded in recent years, but the professional and educational levels still are lower than desired. A total of 32% have completed university/college-level education, 52% secondary school and 8% have only elementary education. A total of 10% of the professional employees have a law degree, 6% have an economics degree and 6% have a teaching degree. The proportion of those with higher education is substantially higher in the ministries than at lower levels, but the unqualified still are too numerous.

Turnover is too high, especially among the better educated and at higher echelons. This is due to difficulty of the positions, especially for new employees; boredom; unsatisfactory working conditions; and few promotion opportunities. Those holding higher positions of responsibility cite, in addition to promotion, poor organization and an uneven work load. Lower-level staffers especially find it impossible to cope with the volume of decrees. Very few vacancies in the higher ranks are publicized, and half of them are filled by transfers, resulting in the main from personal contacts. While those of working-class or peasant origin are claimed to hold about half of the supervisory positions, the trend favors the intellectuals. In the lower councils, where shortages are higher, those of working-class or peasant origin are approximately 70%.

LOCAL GOVERNMENT

Hungary is administratively organized into counties (*megye*, formerly *varmegye*); the counties, in turn, are divided into districts (*jaras*) and communes (*kozseg*). Typically, the commune is a rural unit, in contrast to the cities which are under municipal governments. In all there are 19 counties; 128 districts; and 3,259 places, comprised of five autonomous cities (including Budapest), 57 autonomous towns and 3,197 communes (of which 2,842 are large communes and 355 are small communes). For statistical purposes, the area of each place is divided into the central settlement (*belterulet*) and the outlying territory (*kulterulet*).

In each of these levels the unit of government is the council, functioning both as an arm of the central government and as a popular local body. According to the Electoral Law of 1970, council members on the district and village levels are popularly elected, while county-level councils are elected by the district councils. The term of office for all council members is four years. Each council elects from its own ranks a president and an executive committee, who must be approved by the council on the next higher level. In addition to the executive committees, councils at the county and district levels have a secretariat with specialized departments, such as for agriculture, industry, retail trade, housing, public utilities, education, health, and child and youth welfare and sports. The councils also have some responsibilities in financial administration, economic planning and labor management.

POLITICAL SUBDIVISIONS				
		Area		Population
Counties	Capitals	Sq. Km.	Sq Mi.	(1986 est.)
Baranya	Pecs	4,487	1,732	432,000
Bacs-Kiskun	Kecskemet	8,362	3,229	558,000
Bekes	Bekescsaba	5,632	2,175	422,000
Borsod-Abauj-Zemplen	Miskolc	7,248	2,798	791,000
Csongrad	Szeged	4,263	1,646	457,000
Fejer	Szekesfehervar	4,374	1,689	426,000
Gyor-Sopron	Gyor	4,012	1,549	428,000
Hajdu-Bihar	Debrecen	6,212	2,398	551,000
Heves	Eger	3,637	1,404	342,000
Komarom	Tatabanya	2,250	869	321,000
Nograd	Salgotarjan	2,544	982	233,000
Pest	Budapest	6,394	2,469	985,000
Somogy	Kaposvar	6,036	2,331	353,000
Szabolcs-Szatmar	Nyiregyhaza	5,938	2,293	578,000
Szolnok	Szolnok	5,608	2,165	436,000
Tolna	Szekszard	3,704	1,430	266,000
Vas	Szombathely	3,337	1,288	280,000
Veszprem	Veszprem	4,689	1,810	388,000
Zala	Zalaegerszeg	3,784	1,461	313,000
Capital City				
Budapest		525	203	2,080,000
TOTAL		93,036	35,921	10,640,000

FOREIGN POLICY

Hungary has followed a pro-Soviet foreign policy since the end of World War II, the lone exception being the 1956 uprising, which was suppressed by Soviet military forces. Soviet troops have been on Hungarian territory since 1944, but plans for limited withdrawal in 1989–90 are anticipated as a result of Mikhail Gorbachev's policy of troop withdrawal from East Germany, Czechoslovakia, Hungary and Poland. Moreover, Moscow's allies have been given greater latitude during Gorbachev's policies of *glasnost* and *perestroika* in establishing and expanding closer contacts with Western and other countries.

Following the war, Communist-led Hungary, along with the other East European countries, became a satellite of the Soviet Union. The peace treaty with Hungary was signed on February 10, 1947. Budapest became a member of the Communist Information Bureau (Cominform) in October 1947, and during 1948–49 Hungary concluded 20-year treaties of friendship, cooperation and mutual assistance with the Soviet Union (February 18, 1948), Bulgaria, Czechoslovakia, Poland and Rumania.

Hungary was one of the six original members of the Soviet-sponsored Council for Mutual Economic Assistance (CMEA) in 1949. As Moscow's answer to the Marshall Plan, CMEA subsequently became a Soviet-controlled mechanism for coordinating the economies of its members. A treaty of friendship followed with East Germany in 1950. On May 14, 1955, Hungary was one of seven signatories to the formation of the Warsaw Treaty Organization (WTO). The Warsaw Pact, as it is popularly known, was established for 20 years, extended in

1975 for 10 years and renewed in 1985 for another 20 years. The WTO gave legal justification for the continuation of Soviet troops in Hungary and Czechoslovakia, which, with the conclusion of the state treaty with Austria on May 15, 1955, would have been withdrawn. The pact provides for a Political Consultative Committee; Foreign Ministers Committee; Defense Ministers Committee; and for joint armed forces, with a Soviet marshal serving as commander in chief.

Encouraged by Nikita Khrushchev's denunciation of Stalin and in sympathy with events taking place in Poland, Hungarian demonstrations for de-Stalinization in their country developed in October 1956 into a popular uprising that returned Imre Nagy as prime minister. When Nagy declared Hungary's neutrality and his government's intention to withdraw from the Warsaw Pact and to hold free, multiparty elections, the Soviet Union, which was negotiating the withdrawal of its troops, instead crushed the revolutionaries in early November. Nagy was arrested as a "counterrevolutionary" and subsequently tried secretly and hanged (along with others). Within months Moscow concluded status-of-forces treaties with six East European countries—Hungary in May 1957—providing for the stationing of Soviet troops on their territories. Hungary participated in the 1968 Soviet-directed invasion of Czechoslovakia that crushed Alexander Dubcek's "Prague Spring." In mid-1989 Soviet forces in Hungary numbered about 62,000.

In his December 7, 1988, address before the U.N. General Assembly, Gorbachev, announcing Soviet troop reductions within two years, said that 5,000 tanks in six divisions, 50,000 troops, artillery and aircraft would be withdrawn from East Germany, Czechoslovakia and Hungary. In early 1989 the Hungarian defense minister said that a Soviet air regiment would be withdrawn by the end of 1989, and Soviet officials indicated that by the end of 1990 Moscow intended to pull out 10,000 troops, 450 tanks and perhaps 40 aircraft from Hungary. Hungarian reformers were not impressed with these numbers, voicing instead a demand for complete withdrawal of Soviet forces from their country.

Recent years have witnessed new directions in Hungarian foreign policy, especially prompted by the forces of reform, although the changes have been made with Soviet concurrence. Budapest has been a member of the United Nations since December 1955 and served on its Security Council during 1968–69. Recently Budapest has emphasized multilateralism, has participated in the 1975 Helsinki Conference on Security and Cooperation in Europe (CSCE) and hosted the CSCE's Cultural Forum in 1985. The United States considers Budapest's record on reunification of divided families among the best in Eastern Europe. Hungary initiated and supports greater contacts and cooperation between East and West and was an active participant in the NATO-WTO Mutual and Balanced Forces Reduction (MBFR) negotiations in Vienna (1973–89), as it is in the Conventional Armed Forces in Europe (CFE) talks. It is establishing more active relationships with the Western economies, including the European Economic Community (EEC), with which Hungary concluded a major agreement on

November 23, 1988, to assist with Hungary's long-term development as well as current economic recovery. This was the first agreement between the EEC and a CMEA member. Such approaches to the West were born of financial necessity, including need of foreign capital. In 1989 Hungary's foreign debt was $17 billion, the highest per capita debt in Eastern Europe, and Budapest was negotiating not only with Western but other countries as well, such as Taiwan and South Korea.

Hungarian economic performance deteriorated to such a degree that on May 15, 1989, the International Monetary Fund told Budapest it would receive the last $65 million of a $350 million loan only if agreed-on economic targets were achieved. The July 15, 1989, communiqué concluding the seven-nation economic summit in Paris, focused on Eastern Europe: "We recognize that the political changes taking place in these countries will be difficult to sustain without economic progress." Accordingly, the Western leaders promised assistance in support of political and economic reforms, in Hungary and Poland, with the EEC as coordinator.

Hungary's bilateral relations improved with the West, including the United States, and were extended to other areas, reaching an understanding in the fall of 1988 to establish diplomatic relations with Israel and South Korea, the latter causing a strained relationship with North Korea. In view of the Hungarian regime's persecution of the Roman Catholic Church following the Communist seizure of power, Budapest's relations with the Vatican since the mid-1960s have been more impressive. On September 15, 1964, Hungary became the first Communist country to conclude an agreement with the Vatican, providing for appointment of bishops, oaths of allegiance to the state by the clergy and the operation of a state-supported Hungarian theological college in Rome. Twelve years later appointments to vacancies included Lazlo Cardinal Lekai as Archbishop of Esztergom, the see of the primate of Hungary made famous by Joszef Cardinal Mindszenty, whose arrest and trial (1948–49), life imprisonment (1949–56), freedom (during the 1956 uprising), refuge at the American legation/embassy (1956–71) and exile to the Vatican (1971) all received worldwide attention. While pardoned by the government, Cardinal Mindszenty was not permitted to return to Hungary; he relinquished his primacy in 1974 and died in Vienna the following year. Cardinal Lekai was credited with improving church-state relations and the establishment of diplomatic relations between Hungary and the Vatican in 1977; he died in 1986. On June 28, 1988, Laszlo Cardinal Paskai was appointed primate of Hungary.

Since World War II Hungarian relations with the United States have progressed from strained to favorable. Diplomatic relations were established on October 23, 1945, and representation on the legation level on January 26, 1946. Relations worsened during and after the 1956 uprising and improved only slowly. In November 1966 the bilateral missions were raised to embassies; a consular convention was signed in 1972; Hungary agreed to U.S. nationalization claims the following year and paid its debt to Washington in 1976; and the two countries concluded an agreement on exchanges and cooperation in culture, education, science and technology. This was followed, in January 1978, by the return to Hungary of the nationally symbolic crown of St. Stephen, held by Washington since World War II. A trade agreement extended to Hungary most-favored-nation status in July of that year. Cultural exchanges have been especially active, and visits by ranking U.S. officials were crowned by President George Bush's visit on July 11–12, 1989; he was the first U.S. president to visit Hungary. The president pledged modest economic assistance in recognition of Hungary's political and economic reforms, saying, "For the first time, the Iron Curtain has begun to part, and Hungary . . . is leading the way." The president also proposed an increase in U.S.-Hungarian trade; cultural and scientific exchanges; and promised to send Peace Corps personnel to Hungary, the first European country in which the volunteers would be assigned—to teach English.

Hungarian policy toward China has paralleled Moscow's, becoming closer in recent years and resulting in 1987 in the first visit to Hungary by a Chinese party leader, Zhao Ziyang, and First Secretary Janos Kadar's visit to Beijing later that year. The party leaders expressed their mutual agreement on their foreign policies and on internal economic reform. However, during the 1989 Chinese demonstrations, Hungary criticized Beijing's use of armed forces and other repressive measures. China, in turn, ignored the June 16, 1989, reburial in Budapest of former prime minister Imre Nagy.

Hungarian relations with its Communist neighbors have been less than satisfactory. Not surprisingly, the most tension-filled have been with Rumania, principally over the Hungarian minority, numbering about 2 million, living primarily in Transylvania, a historically disputed territory. Hungary accuses Rumania of "systematization"—that is, the forced relocation of rural inhabitants and the elimination of thousands of villages (see the chapter on Rumania). Budapest considers this a "brutal policy" intended to liquidate ethnic Hungarians and other minorities in Rumania. Official Hungarian accusations of discrimination have been made not only bilaterally but before international bodies as well. Relations have deteriorated to such an extent that Hungary has charged Rumania with "crimes against humanity." Rumania, on the other hand, continually recalls Hungarian oppression of Rumanians before 1918 and during 1940–44. Thousands of refugees, including some Rumanians, stream into Hungary, adding to Budapest's internal problems. Diplomatic expulsions followed the June 1988 anti-Rumanian demonstrations by some 50,000 people in front of the Rumanian embassy in Budapest, and Bucharest closed the Hungarian consulate in Cluj. A summit meeting in August 1988 in the Rumanian town of Arad between Rumanian president Nicolae Ceausescu and Hungarian prime minister Karoly Grosz failed to resolve their dispute. In 1989 Budapest tore down the wire barrier on the Austrian border and, declaring Rumania an "enemy," transferred troops to the Rumanian border area.

The Antall government's foreign policy is to restore the country's links with the West without alienating the Soviet Union. An agreement has been reached with Moscow on the complete withdrawal of Soviet troops in Hungary by June 30, 1991. At a meeting of the Warsaw Pact's Consultative Committee Antall announced Hungary's decision to leave the Warsaw Pact in accordance with Imre Nagy's 1956 declaration and also the recent resolution approved by the National Assembly.

PARLIAMENT

The National Assembly (Orszaggyules) is a unicameral body consisting of 386 members elected by direct universal suffrage. It is the supreme organ of state power and popular representation in the Republic of Hungary. It exercises all the rights deriving from the sovereignty of the people, guarantees the constitutional order of society and determines the organization, the course and the conditions of government. It enacts laws and decides on the economic plan and social policy of the nation. It draws up the balance sheet for public finances, and approves the state budget and its implementation. It decides about the government program and concludes international treaties of prime importance. It decides on matters of war and the conclusion of peace, and in certain cases it declares a state of emergency and sets up a National Defense Council. The National Assembly decides about the deployment of the armed forces, elects the president of the republic, the Council of Ministers, the Constitutionality Court and the holders of other important offices. It can initiate national plebiscites.

The National Assembly is elected for a term of four years. MPs enjoy parliamentary immunity. According to the amended Constitution, the National Assembly meets for at least two legislative sessions a year: from February 1 to mid-June, and then from September 1 to mid-December every year. The first session of the National Assembly is convened by the president of the republic within one month after the elections, and the convening of the subsequent sessions is within the competence of the president of the National Assembly. The president of the republic is empowered to adjourn the meeting of the National Assembly only once during the same session and for a period of not more than 30 days. Upon the written request of one-fifth of the representatives, Parliament must be convoked for an extraordinary session. In the National Assembly, half of the members constitute a quorum. Decisions are generally made by a simple majority, though in certain cases a majority of two-thirds is required. The rules governing the work of the National Assembly are laid down in detail in the standing orders.

The president of the republic, the Council of Ministers, the parliamentary committees and MPs themselves have the authority to initiate legislation. Once passed by the National Assembly, laws are promulgated by the president of the republic within 15 days. The president has the power to return a law once to the National Assembly, which is then obliged to give it a second reading. If this second reading of the bill is adopted by the National Assembly, the president is bound to promulgate it. When sent a law, the president may decide to refer it to the Constitutionality Court for expert opinion. If this court finds it unconstitutional, the president returns the law to the National Assembly.

Simultaneously with the calling of general elections, the president of the republic is empowered to dissolve the National Assembly if the legislators have withdrawn their confidence from the Council of Ministers or did not vote the new Council of Ministers confidence at least four times within a period of 12 months during its term. The president of the republic can exercise this right only two times while he is in office. The National Assembly may dissolve itself. However, it cannot dissolve itself or be dissolved if there is a state of emergency. Whatever has led to the dissolution of the National Assembly, elections must be held within three months afterwards.

On April 8, 1990, the Hungarian Democratic Forum won the second round of Hungary's first free elections in more than 40 years by a surprisingly large margin. Whereas in the first round it had polled only 25% of the vote, in the second and final round it received almost half of the votes cast. Voters elected representatives to the National Assembly from three different lists: individual, regional and national. In addition to six parties represented in the National Assembly, six independent candidates and four others jointly endorsed by parties also gained seats. A further eight deputies representing ethnic minorites were coopted.

Name of Party (Alliance)	Number of Seats
Hungarian Democratic Forum	164
League of Free Democrats	92
Independent Smallholders' Party	44
Hungarian Socialists' Party (ex-Communist)	33
League of Young Democrats	21
Christian Democratic People's Party	21
Agrarian Alliance	1
Independents	6
Single candidates representing two parties	4
TOTAL	386

The 1990 National Assembly has 10 standing and four special committees as follows:

- Constitutional, Legislative and Judicial Affairs
- Self-administration, Public Administration, Internal Security and Police
- Foreign Affairs
- Defense
- Budgetary, Tax and Financial Affairs
- Economics
- Social Welfare, Family and Health Affairs
- Environmental Protection
- Culture, Education, Science, Sport, Television and the Press
- Human Rights, Minorities and Religious Affairs

The four special committees are:

- Steering
- Electoral and Mandates
- Immunity and Incompatibility
- National Security

The standing committees have from 23 to 26 members each and the special committees from 12 to 14 members each.

On October 20, 1989, the Hungarian National Assembly passed a new electoral law that provides guidelines for the nation's first multiparty elections in over four decades. The first section of the law provides for secret ballots and universal suffrage, although voting has not been made compulsory. The voting age is 18, but not everyone age 18 and over is eligible to vote. People who have no registered abode are not allowed to cast ballots. This regulation bars the rather large number of homeless from voting, although a party has recently been formed to represent the interests of this group. There is no absentee voting. The many Hungarians who have left the country over the years are entitled to vote if they have retained a registered abode in Hungary, but not if they have asked the Presidential Council to terminate their citizenship. People serving prison terms are also not allowed to vote.

The electoral system, which is somewhat similar to the West German system, can perhaps be best described as "personalized" proportional representation. Of the 386 seats, 176—almost half—will be filled by deputies chosen by voting districts. These deputies can either be nominated by parties or run as independent candidates. The winning candidate must gain the majority (50% plus 1) of the votes, as in France, rather than a plurality, as in Germany. This requirement may cause problems. For example, since some 10 parties are contesting seats in each voting district in Budapest, it is unlikely that any party will gain a majority in these districts in the first round of voting.

Some 152 seats will be filled by deputies running on party lists in the counties, although this number could change slightly in the course of the elections. These seats will be divided proportionally, according to the number of votes the individual parties receive. The calculation of these proportions will be complicated. In order for a part to set up a regional list, it must run candidates in at least a quarter of the individual districts in that region or county. For example, Budapest, a city with county status, has 32 districts. If a party wants to start a regional list, it must run candidates in eight of these districts. Nograd County has four districts, but candidates must be run in two districts, since two is the minimum number required. If not enough candidates are elected on the county level to fill each of the 152 seats, the seats left open will be automatically transferred to the national list, thereby increasing the number of candidates on that list. Those parties that do not win at least 4% of the votes cast for the regional lists will not be able to secure a position for their parties on the national list. This regulation, which will affect the small parties in particular, was introduced to reduce the number of parties in parliament.

The national or country list was allegedly introduced to prevent votes from being lost. Before a party can appear on the national list, it must start at least seven regional lists. Some 58 parliamentary seats will be allocated to candidates appearing on this national list and will be distributed proportionally after the leftover votes, that is, those votes received by individual parties that were not counted toward winning a seat, have been added up. A party can acquire leftover votes in two ways. First, when it receives more than the number of votes necessary to win a seat, the extra votes will be added to the national list. Second, a party may receive fewer votes than necessary to win even one seat on the regional level. However, the votes that the party has received will not be lost but transferred to the national list. After the 58 seats have been apportioned among those parties that have the right to appear on the national list, the parties will select candidates who will automatically become members of parliament. This process resembles one aspect of Hungary's former electoral system, which utilized a country list to get certain candidates into parliament unopposed.

The previous electoral system called for meetings at which candidates were chosen. Each district held three such meetings, allowing candidates to introduce themselves and answer questions. Local citizens attending the meetings voted for candidates at the end of each meeting, and those candidates who received the required number of votes were allowed to run. Although this system proved effective in the multiparty by-elections held last year, it was changed by the new law.

Under the present system, each voter receives a nomination card, on which he can endorse the candidates of his choice. Each candidate running on an individual list in a voting district has to be endorsed by at least 750 voters from that district. The candidate, or a representative of his party, visits the voter to request endorsement. If the voter agrees, the candidate's name and party (or independent status) are noted on the card, along with the voter's name, address and identification number. Many people are opposed to this sytem, fearing that in the event of a radical turnaround in the present democratization process, they might be persecuted for having endorsed an anti-Communist party, even though the authorities have said they intend to destroy the cards 90 days after the elections. The new law stipulates that voters not be harassed and that cards not be collected at workplaces, in hospitals, on the public transport system, or in army units. Some parties have included addresses on their campaign leaflets to which voters can mail their cards. The disadvantage of this system of mailing cards is that the voter has no opportunity to meet or put questions to candidates.

POLITICAL PARTIES

The Hungarian Socialist Workers' Party (HSWP)—Magyar Szocialista Munkaspart—had its beginning as the Hungarian section of the Russian Communist (Bolshevik) Party in March 1918. The Party of Hungarian Communists was formed in November of that year. Led by Bela Kun (1886–1939), a former prisoner of war in Russia, the Communists in March 1919 proclaimed the Hungarian Soviet Republic. Although the Communists possessed no power base, they were strengthened by some Social Democrats, also former prisoners of war, and by the resignation of Count Mihaly Karolyi as the head of government after Hungary was proclaimed a republic in November 1918.

Kun instituted a policy of nationalization but, inexplicably, not of land reform. Unable to cope with overwhelming internal problems and allied military problems, especially Rumanian, Kun's repressive dictatorship collapsed in August 1919. The new government outlawed the CP, and Kun with others fled the country. Most settled in the Soviet Union, but some remained in the underground. Among the latter were Janos Kadar (1912–89) and Laszlo Rajk, who were to play important roles after World War II. During the interwar period several political parties existed, but the regime of Regent Admiral Miklos Horthy de Nagybanya exercised authoritative power. Horthy's driving objective was the repeal of the Trianon Treaty and the recovery of prewar territories. Thus Hungary was drawn into the Axis orbit.

Although small in number, the Hungarian Communists, supported by Moscow, gained immense power as the "Moscovites" marched with the Red Army in 1944 to "liberate" Hungary. The postwar CP leadership emerged from the Soviet faction, led by Matyas Rakosi (1891–1971). The party was assisted directly by the chairman of the Allied Control Commission, Kliment Voroshilov, a Soviet marshal. Communist-controlled Committees of National Liberation were established in liberated cities and towns. A Communist-socialist agreement placed the trade unions under Communist control, and in November 1944, a provisional government was formed consisting of Moscow-approved political parties in the Independent Front, composed of the CP, the Social Democratic Party and the Smallholders' Party. The National Peasant Party also participated. This provisional government concluded an armistice with Moscow. Real power was exercised by the Soviet occupation army.

Despite a massive land reform administered by the CP, the Smallholders' Party received a majority vote of 57% in the November 1945 free elections, a stunning victory in a multiparty system and an occupation environment. Prior to the general election, Marshal Voroshilov offered to the Smallholders 47.5% of a single ballot. The offer was refused, but the parties agreed that whatever the outcome, all would participate in the government. The CP received the portfolios of the Ministry of Defense and of the Interior when Voroshilov overruled the coalition's decision to award the important Interior position, controlling the police, to the Smallholders' Party. Laszlo Rajk became the minister of the interior and Rakosi a deputy prime minister. Nevertheless, the Smallholders' Party possessed impressive strength—the president of the National Assembly, the prime minister and eight ministerial posts. With the establishment of Hungary as a republic in February 1946, the secretary general of the Smallholders' Party became president.

Numerically, the Communists were in an inferior position, but the combination of Soviet occupation, Marshal Voroshilov, control of the police and the national committees throughout the country gave the CP control of the government and the country. These forces employed various tactics—propaganda; terrorism; blackmail; intimidation; and uncovering "spies," "traitors" and "conspirators"—directed especially against the Smallholders. During this period Kadar was first chief of Budapest's police, then in 1948 minister of the interior in charge of the national police network.

The fiction of political parties continued. For the 1947 general elections the Allied Control Commission approved six opposition parties. Terrorism increased against real or potential adversaries of the CP, but the CP managed only 22% of the votes in the fraudulent voting. The 49 Independent Party deputies were branded as "fascists" and denied their seats in the National Assembly. The Democratic People's Party, a Catholic organization, lasted a year. The leadership of the Smallholders deteriorated, and the Social Democratic Party merged with the CP in June 1948 to form the Hungarian Workers' Party. The multiparty facade remained, but the only real authority was the CP. This reality was reflected in the May 1949 elections, wherein the People's Front, controlled by the CP, reportedly obtained 95.6% of the total vote. Hungary was ruled by one of the most repressive, Stalinist-type regimes, led by Rakosi. Among his victims were, by imprisonment, the primate of Hungary, Jozsef Cardinal Mindszenty and, by execution, Rajk, branded a "Titoist," in 1949. Rajk's execution order was cosigned by Kadar, a friend from the underground. In 1951 Kadar himself was jailed by Rakosi but proved to be a survivor.

Prompted by the "New Course" policy in the Soviet Union following Stalin's death, Hungary's de-Stalinization and collective leadership was led by Imre Nagy (1896–1958) during 1953–55. This led to a popular outpouring of discontent, sparked by intellectuals and students, which culminated in the thunderous October 1956 uprising. Rakosi had been ousted as CP first secretary in July 1956, but the leadership passed to another Stalinist, Erno Gero. Nagy was recalled to head a coalition government, while the CP, led by Kadar beginning on October 25, ceased effective functioning. On October 23, 1956, thousands demonstrated, displaying sympathy for Polish events and making demands on the regime for reforms and for Soviet withdrawal. When Nagy declared neutrality and intention to withdraw from the Warsaw Pact, Kadar shifted toward Moscow, and the Soviet Union crushed the popular uprising in early November. Nagy, with others, was arrested in 1956 and executed in 1958. Kadar was installed by Moscow as first secretary of the renamed Hungarian Socialist Workers' Party (HSWP) on November 1, 1956. A period of repression followed. Many considered Kadar a traitor, but some as a pragmatist. The CP was purged, non-Communist parties were suppressed, many were imprisoned and some were executed. For 30 years the HSWP was essentially intact and in absolute control of a one-party regime, but under Kadar's leadership, Hungary recovered and the first secretary gained a modi-

cum of respect within the party, the general population and abroad, steering the country toward limited economic reform. In the 1960s Kadar pursued modernization, which included involvement of nonparty talent to build a socialist society. In 1962 he conducted another purge, and the Eighth Party Congress adopted his appealing slogan "He who is not against us is with us," and party statutes were amended to permit criticism within the party. In 1968 the HSWP embarked on the imaginative New Economic Mechanism (NEM), which sought to decentralize economic responsibility, and Hungary prospered. However, this policy antagonized many hard-liners within the party, and the 11th Party Congress, in 1975, decided against party dissent. The following year the party leadership conducted a card exchange, which reduced the opposition. Limited tolerance and reforms, including some private enterprise, continued into the 1980s but the economy stagnated, then deteriorated into a crisis requiring drastic measures. Spurred by Gorbachev's policies of *glasnost* and *perestroika*, demands in the late 1980s focused on economic reform and multiparty constitutionalism. The conservative wing of the HSWP resisted the dramatic changes this foreshadowed, initially, in May 1988, agreeing to political pluralism only within a one-party structure. However, the combination of HSWP reformers, resurgent political parties, independent associations and the public pressured the HSWP to accede to their demands. Accordingly, the National Assembly, in its January 1989 session, passed a law on freedom of association, and the party Central Committee (CC) in February 1989 adopted a resolution on the multiparty system.

The 32-year Kadar era essentially ended on May 22, 1988, when a special HSWP conference replaced the aging (76) and ill Kadar as general secretary with a younger (58) and seemingly more realistic Karoly Grosz, whom Kadar had promoted to prime minister in June 1987. Kadar was appointed to a new, honorary position: party president. The conference appointed to the Politburo two others who were to play major roles in the unfolding political history: Rezso Nyers (65), a respected economics reformer; and Imre Pozsgay (54), the forward-looking chief of the Patriotic People's Front (PPF). Kadar's stature plummeted when he was retired as president and removed from the CC, a victim of failing political, physical and mental health. He died on July 6, 1989, and on July 14 was given a state funeral at which he was eulogized by Grosz. In an irony of history, Kadar collapsed three days following the public reburial of Imre Nagy and four of his associates, the culmination of domestic and foreign pressure. In early 1989 the HSWP organized a committee to reexamine the past 40 years of Hungary's history, an unprecedented step.

An agreement to hold negotiations on significant subjects requiring urgent solutions was reached in June 1989 by the HSWP, the Opposition Round Table (ORT) and the Third Side. The ORT, which agitated for such negotiations, represented nine opposition organizations. The Third Side represented largely Communist-controlled mass organizations, although several (for example, youth, trade unions and the PPF) were undergoing reforms of their own. Discussions were held continually, and the first plenary session, carried live by TV and observed by many domestic and foreign media representatives, was conducted on June 13. The conservative-minded Grosz led the HSWP delegation, and little was accomplished. The second plenary negotiations were conducted on June 21, with reformist Pozsgay heading the HSWP's representatives. Important agreements were concluded: Economic as well as political questions were to be discussed, and new laws, especially those affecting the proposed Constitution, would be passed only with prior ORT approval.

As in other Soviet bloc countries, the HSWP's organizational setup and policies are contained in the party statutes, and the party functions on the principle of "democratic centralism"—that is, the organizational units at lower levels are subordinate to the next higher echelons, and decisions made at the higher levels are binding on the lower units. Although discussion of issues is formally permitted, once a decision is made at the top it becomes completely binding on all members and subordinate organs.

The highest level in the structure is the Party Congress, convening every five years, where major policy statements are made and a Central Committee is elected. Before 1989 the CC, in turn, elected the Politburo and the Secretariat. The CC, which normally meets three or four times annually, carries out the policies decided at the Congress; oversees the party's activities; and decides on appointments within the party and, until April 1989, the government. In reality, the Politburo, which decided the country's policies, was the most powerful body, and the Congress approved rather than elected the CC.

The HSWP had serious political, economic and ideological difficulties within its own ranks, especially over the issue of a multiparty system. At the May 1988 CC session the 108-member CC, with 38 new incumbents, changed the composition of the Politburo, as it replaced seven other members, in addition to Kadar, with six new members, for a total of 11. In February 1989 the CC accepted the concept of pluralism, a real multiparty system. At its closed session on April 12, 1989, the CC made more dramatic changes. After the Politburo resigned, General Secretary Grosz was reappointed but four were not, including the party's ideologist, Janos Berecz. The makeup of the new Politburo, reduced to nine members, and the appointment of 10 new members to the CC—now at 114—reflected the nationwide pressures for political reforms.

The HSWP reformers accomplished further structural changes at another closed CC session, held June 23–24, 1989. The CC created a four-member Presidium consisting of Rezso Nyers, president; Karoly Grosz, general secretary; Imre Pozsgay, minister of state; and Miklos Nemeth, prime minister. All were members of the Politburo, which was replaced by an expanded (21-member) CC Political Executive Committee. Grosz was considered a conservative and the three others reformers. No one emerged as the leader publicly but, calling the Presidium a "collective leadership," Nyers said that as

president he was "first among equals." His responsibilities include chairing the sessions of the major party organs, control of foreign relations and supervision of HSWP relations with other political forces. The Presidium appeared to be the policy-making body, with the general secretary administering party affairs.

Thus in mid-1989 the HSWP organization was as follows: a 114-member CC; a four-member Presidium; a six-member Secretariat; a 21-member Political Executive Committee, which includes all Presidium and Secretariat members; and the Central Control Committee. In addition, the CC had five standing committees—International, Legal and State Management Policy; Working Groups; Economic Strategy; Party Policy; and Social Policy—in addition to an advisory body to the CC. The working groups consisted of Cooperative Policy; Educational and Cultural Policy; Party-Building; and Science Policy. The CC contained the following departments: Agitation and Propaganda; Economic Policy; International Party Relations; Party Policy; Party Management and Administration; Public and General Administration; and CC Party History Institute. Below the national level, CP organizations in the 19 counties, including Budapest, all have committees which are elected by the district conferences. The lowest rung consists of the primary party organizations.

Party membership in 1919 was only about 10,000. The number of the "Muscovite" Communists also was small, and membership in early 1945 was about 30,000. Although membership increased sharply, the CP suffered a stunning defeat in the 1945 elections. Membership rose markedly after the CP achieved complete power—to nearly 900,000 in 1948—and to over 1.5 million following the merger with the Social Democratic Party that year. After a widespread purge the total dropped to approximately 850,000, the number before the 1956 uprising when the CP seemed to disintegrate, falling below 100,000. Following the uprising, thousands of Communists of the Rakosi stripe were expelled and a new core was established. In the early 1960s the membership climbed to about 500,000; then to over 750,000 in 1975; and the 13th Party Congress, in 1985, reported 870,992. Periodically the HSWP leaders have alternated purges and recruitment. At the end of 1988, membership was 817,000, of whom 40.2% were industrial workers, 7.2% collective farmers, 44.7% intellectuals and white-collar workers and 7.9% others. Women comprised 30.5% of the total. With trends toward a multiparty system, HSWP ranks were diminishing, the membership falling below 800,000 by mid-1989.

Hungary's Law on Political Parties came into effect on October 31, 1989. Only political parties that recognize and observe the constitutional order of the Republic of Hungary can operate in the country. The licensing of a political party depends on the fulfillment of four requirements: it must have a distinct program, a membership of at least 10 people, an official leader and a bank account.

The Law on Political Parties says that parties can be registered with legal continuity only within three months following the promulgation of the law. Out of the 53 parties that have appeared on the Hungarian political scene so far, 43 were registered by the designated deadline.

In Hungary the establishment of a multiparty system started only recently, and the immature political structure that has evolved is marked by two striking features. One of them is that the parties already formed, instead of having been called to life by some social layer or group for the expression of its political interests, are seeking for members to represent. (Exceptions are the Entrepreneurs' Party organized to mediate the interests of people engaging in private ventures [largely merchants and tradesmen] and the Party of the Generations as a body supporting old-age pensioners.) Actually there is but little distinction among the parties in their political practice and in regard to the social groups and ideologies they wish to represent. This has led to the strange situation that some groups of several different parties have more in common ideologically with each other than with the other wing of their own party.

The reason lies in the fact that in 1988–89, the reform wing within the Hungarian Socialist Workers' Party, the single ruling party, gained ground very fast and the opposition forces of society mustered strength simultaneously. In this way the change in the political system was legally instituted in less than 18 months.

The other wing of the state party, which adheres to traditional Marxism, has reorganized its own Hungarian Socialist Workers' Party. The wing that follows a modern socialist-social democratic line has formed the Hungarian Socailist Party (MSZP, after the Hungarian initials).

The emergence of political parties within the opposition took place in a much more complicated manner. On the other hand, the so-called historical parties that wish to revive and continue the kind of parliamentary democracy that existed in Hungary during the 100 years from 1848 to 1949, are distinctly different from those that grew on the political soil of the 1970s and 1980s. On the other hand, these two types of the Hungarian opposition parties are linked by three important ideological goals: all champion a Hungarian-centered popular-national scale of values, Christian ideals and radical liberalism.

It adds to the complications that the newcomers include the Green movement, which had no counterpart among the ranks of the historical parties. At the same time, some historical parties (e. g., the Hungarian Legitimist Party) and party unions (e. g., the Christian National Union–Anti-Marxist National Coalition) cherish conservative traditionalist endeavors that find no response among the newly formed opposition parties.

HUNGARIAN SOCIALIST WORKERS' PARTY (MSZMP)

Formation: According to its own assessment, the party is a continuer of the Hungarian Socialist Workers' Party reorganized after November 4, 1956.
Membership: 120,000
Program: the MSZMP defines itself as an up-to-date Marxist party, the leading force of a strong left to be organized, a party which is striving for popular cohesion against the restoration of

---

HUNGARIAN SOCIALIST WORKERS' PARTY (MSZMP)
(continued)

capitalism and the dictatorship of the petty bourgeoisie. In these goals it is ready to cooperate with the MSZP, which was the reform wing of the earlier MSZMP.

The party represents the interests of those who live on their wages and salaries and above all the interests of industrial workers. It accepts an economy of mixed ownership with the dominance of social property. It opposes an economic policy that impoverishes the working people, and is against unemployment. It demands security of living. It links the fostering of the national values with the strengthening of friendship among the peoples.

HUNGARIAN SOCIALIST PARTY (MSZP)

Formation: October 7, 1989
The special congress of the Hungarian Socialist Workers' Party met from October 6 to 9, 1989, and this was also the first congress of the newly founded Hungarian Socialist Party (MSZP). MSZP is, according to its own views, the legal successor to the Hungarian Socialist Workers' Party founded on October 30, 1956.
President: Rezso Nyers (b. 1929), economist and ex-minister of state.
Membership: 60,000
Program: MSZP defines itself as a political organization that accepts the values of democaratic socialism and stands for a socialist future, accepting the foremost Communist, socialist and social democratic traditions of the working-class movement, but repudiating the dictatorship of the proletariat, both the Stalinist and Leninist versions of state socialism.

As a party of socialist and social democratic orientation it is no longer a class party but a people's party, the party of the little people. It accepts—and in fact initiated the return to—a constitutional democratic state, political pluralism and a market economy based on mixed ownership. It strives to build a socialist state according to the Scandinavian pattern, and in this framework it promises a secure livelihood for the worker, success for the entrepreneur, an up-to-date school system, professional administration, respect for knowledge and talent, the purity of public affairs, and protection and equality for every minority.

PATRIOTIC ELECTION COALITION

Formation: December 12, 1989
This is a party alliance for the elections whose formation was initiated by the Patriotic People's Front (formed in 1950). It rallies the Central Council of Trade Unions and an additional 15 social organizations and associations.
Membership: figure unknown
President: Istvan Asztalos
Program: This coalition wishes to rely chiefly on the strata consisting of socially active non-party people in the period of the party state, largely on people living outside of Budapest. It professes leftist ideals but is engaged in practical action. In this spirit it wishes above all to enliven the Hungarian economy. It places considerable emphasis on the development of the infrastructure and agrarian economy. It is an adherent of strongly protective social welfare provisions. It holds that the development of local self-governments is of determinative importance. The Patriotic Election Coalition's pragmatic leftism is close to the views of the Hungarian Socialist Party, the Hungarian Agrarian Union, and of the Independent Social Democratic Party.

SOCIAL DEMOCRATIC PARTY OF HUNGARY (MSZDP)

Formation: January 9, 1989
The party's 36th—refounding—congress was held from November 3 to 5, 1989. It declared the party decision of 1948, which permitted unification with the Communist Party of Hungary on a Communist platform, null and void. Consequently, the MSZDP of today is not only a legal sucessor to, but also a direct continuer of, the pre-war Hungarian Social Democratic Party founded in 1890.
Membership: 16,000-17,000
President: Anna Petrasovits, economist
Program: The party defines itself as the party of social democracy which represents little people—chiefly the working middle strata. It believes in a welfare state achieved through a socially sensitive market economy, according to the pattern of European social democracy. Motto: Market economy and social solidarity. It professes: centralized manpower and welfare policy covered from a differentiated tax system. It sees trade-union action and the participation of industrial workers and employees in public affairs as the combined means by which the anomalies of the market principle it professes will be eliminated. The party as a people's party of the center left—this its own definition—regards the League of Free Democrats, the League of Young Democrats, and the trade union and the workers' autonomies as long-term partners.

LEAGUE OF FREE DEMOCRATS (SZDSZ)

Formation: November 13, 1988
SZDSZ started its development with the appearance on the scene of the civil-democratic, radical and social democratic opposition and of the civil rights movement after 1977. Its markedly liberal program was adopted by the first assembly of delegates on April 19, 1989.
Membership: 8,500
President: none
The League is led by a board of 12 members.
Program: The League defines itself as a social liberal organization. It takes a more definite stand than many other parties adhering to the general civil-democratic ideology, for the political and social rights of individuals. It rejects every version of the "third road" that combines capitalism and state socialism. It sees the future of the country best assured through the building of a market economy combined with an advanced social welfare system, through the dominance within a mixed-ownership economy of private ownership, through as close an adherence to the European Community as possible, and through the neutrality of the country.

LEAGUE OF YOUNG DEMOCRATS (FIDESZ)

Formation: March 20, 1988
The establishment of an independent organization for radical university students, secondary school students and of young intellectuals was first raised at a students' camp in Szarvas, central Hungary. The younger generation of the democratic opposition adopted its platform on November 20, 1988.
Membership: 3,500–4,000
President: There is no president. A board of 13 members directs the organization.
Program: The platform, which accepts the challenge of liberal and European values and within it the protection of the rights of the individual, is closely associated with the SZDS program. It would complement a market economy with extensive social welfare provisions. It is a distinctive feature of FIDESZ that it stands for a policy that champions the interests of young people. It believes in nonviolence, but, in accordance with its support of a policy of action, it does not reject peaceful forms of civil disobedience.

INDEPENDENT SMALLHOLDERS' PARTY (FKgP)

Formation: February 18, 1988. The political organization founded in 1930 and operating as a majority party from 1945 to 1947; it was politically reactivated on this day.
Membership: between 40,000 and 50,000
President: Vince Voros
Program: The party defines itself as a national democratic center party, the party of provincial and rural Hungary, which interprets its representation of the interests of "smallholders" broadly. In its view, a smallholder is not only someone living out of the land but any independent self-employed person: merchant, tradesman and small-scale entrepreneur. It accepts all the general features of the Europeanization and democratic transformation of the country—constitutionality, pluralistic popular representation and independent media. Its program is distinguished by the economic demands it sets. The party believes in the expansion of private property and an economic policy that increases domestic demand. It has worked out a new development program for infrastructure and links settlement development with the freedom of small properties and local autonomies based on cooperative ownership. Through price and tax reforms it wishes to ensure the equality of the agrarian and industrial sectors.

NATIONAL SMALLHOLDERS' PARTY (NKgP)

Formation: December 29, 1989
The radical wing of the Smallholders' Party (FKgP), whose adherents live chiefly in the Great Plains, held its constituent meeting in Szeged.
Membership: number unknown
President: none. The organization, which has its headquarters in Szeged, is directed by a board of 15 members.
Program: Although it relies on common traditions with the Independent Smallholders, NKgP puts more stress on Christian, national and civil values. The National Smallholders intend to restore the landed property according to ownership in 1947. Apart from the new distribution of land, it urges the full reprivatization of services.

HUNGARIAN DEMOCRATIC FORUM (MDF)

Formation: September 3, 1987.
The intellectuals who initiated the formation of the party represented chiefly provincial and rural Hungary but not only those living out of the land. Between October 20 and 22, 1989, the second national meeting approved the program and elected a new president.
Membership: 22,000 (based on an authentic survey taken in December 1989)
President: Jozsef Antall, prime minister
Program: The party has defined itself as a national and European center party, which, relying on the moral, intellectual and political traditions of the Hungarian people and of Europe, is striving for creating a civil democratic society. In the field of the economy it wishes to see a radical though gradual reform of ownership relations: its aim is an economy based on mixed ownership, the equality of opportunities for the various ownership forms, the freedom of enterprise and an up-to-date socially minded market economy. The program professes the need for the democratic self-administration of the country regulated by the Constitution, and takes a stand for the equality of minorities both at home and abroad.

HUNGARIAN PEOPLE'S PARTY

Formation: June 14, 1989
The revived organization is legal successor to the National Peasant Party created in 1939 and of the Petofi Party, which had a brief renaissance in 1956. Its program was approved by the party's national board on November 18, 1989.

HUNGARIAN PEOPLE'S PARTY (*continued*)

Membership: 10,000
President: Gyula Fekete, writer
Program: It defines the position of the party as a representative of the low-paid brackets, the backward regions of Hungary, and of the Hungarian minorities abroad. As an organization of the center-left, it has set three strategic principles for itself: through working out a specifically Hungarian course it wants to protect national interests; it wishes to ensure the observance of civil rights and liberties, and expects to work for a welfare society built on a market economy of mixed ownership. Its economic policy stresses the need for the upswing of agriculture. It holds that each settlement should decide for itself how it wants to transform the ownership of land. As it believes that local self-administration will trim off the undesirable effects of market economy, the party supports the transformation of ownership.

CHRISTIAN DEMOCRATIC PEOPLE'S PARTY

Formation: September 30, 1989
With the reorganization of the party, a political grouping formed in autumn 1944 by Istvan Barankovics and dissolved in 1948 to be briefly revived again in 1956, it is continuing its work.
Membership: 2,000
President: Sandor Keresztes, lawyer
Program: The Christian state ideal, which rests on the principle of *bonum commune*. It recognizes the rights of the personality, the principles of solidarity and mutual support, of participation and of freedom. Its practical demands place the party as a moderate center party that wishes to gain the support of the religious middle strata. To this end, it emphasizes the need for a market economy combined with social welfare policy and mixed ownership forms as determined by the local self-governments. On the basis of Christian moral principles, family protection is an important part of the program.

INDEPENDENT HUNGARIAN DEMOCRATIC PARTY

Formation: June 8, 1989
The party was originally formed by Pater Istvan Balogh, Ph. D. in 1947. The organization, which suspensed its activities in 1951, resumed work in 1989.
Membership: 5,000
President: there is no president, the leadership consists of a board of five.
Program: "God, family and fatherland" is the motto of the party. Thus, it wishes to see to the representation of the religious middle strata of Hungary, largely outside of Budapest. Similarly to other national Christian parties, it wishes to realize market economy in combination with a strong social welfare policy, family protection and local self-governments.
 The party is a founding member of the National Union of Center Parties and is its most populous member party. Four smaller political organizations also belong to the party union.

THE GREEN PARTY OF HUNGARY

Formation: February 18-19, 1989
Membership: 200-300
No president. The organization is directed by a board of eight members.
Program: Active nature protection. The organization, similarly to the more extensive and influential Green social movement in Hungary, professes to be part of the international movement of the Greens. In accordance with the conditions that exist in Hungary, it opposes the industrial lobby and the agricultural oligarchies, seeking support from the local autonomous communities. It pursues a policy of action, the peaceful forms of civil disobedience included.

ECONOMY

The Hungarian economic system differs substantially from those of other members of the CMEA. Although a socialist country, it is significantly decentralized and allows many important economic decisions to be shaped by market forces rather than by quantitative planning. The change from centralized planning began after the 1956 Revolution, when some decision-making was moved from the ministerial level down to the enterprise level and somewhat more emphasis was given to foreign trade and consumer goods at the expense of self-sufficiency and industry, the former emphases. The economy remained unresponsive, and a major overhaul of the economy was undertaken in the mid-1960s based on an elaborately designed market system operating within a framework of socialist ownership. At the same time centralized control was retained over international economic relations, distribution of income and certain other areas. The reforms, known collectively as the New Economic Mechanism (NEM), were put into effect on January 1, 1968.

The principal features of the NEM were as follows:

• The central administrative specifications of enterprise production and sales programs were abandoned, and each enterprise was permitted to determine its production pattern on the basis of contacts with customers.

• Central administrative allocation of material inputs also was ended, with a few minor exceptions.

• One-year operational plans were discontinued, and five-year plans became the chief steering mechanisms for the economy.

The practice of fixing wage scales was ended, but average wage levels of enterprises were severely restrained by a new tax on wage increases.

• The predominantly central allocation of resources for investment was changed to a system in which self-financing from profit complemented central investment activity.

• The chief objective of enterprise activity was to be the pursuit of profit, and incentives for managers and workers were linked to profit. The two main enterprise funds were the sharing fund (to finance wage increase and bonus payments) and the development fund (to finance enterprise investment).

• Separate foreign-trade multipliers for CMEA and Western market trading areas were introduced to link domestic production and overseas markets. However, the traditional system of taxes and subsidies on exports and imports, involving price equalization funds, was retained.

• A comprehensive price reform adjusted relative producer prices and introduced greater flexibility into price determination.

The basic aspect of the NEM was the decentralization of economic management while retaining planning and direction as functions of the central government. The traditional system of assigning a mass of detailed targets for each enterprise was replaced by an interrelated system of mostly indirect economic regulators. These regulators were divided into six groups.

The first group reflects the official price policy. It calls for a high degree of stability in the majority of retail prices but seeks to develop competitive conditions in which producer prices for goods other than most essential raw materials can be set through freely negotiated contracts between buyers and sellers. The policy also aims to achieve a closer relation between prices and costs and between domestic and world market prices.

The second group of regulators supports official policy regarding the growth of personal incomes. Through budgetary controls and rules concerning the use of enterprise incomes, the state regulates aggregate incomes, although the enterprises themselves retain some measure of freedom in determining wages and salaries. National economic plans include projections about long-term growth rates of personal incomes.

The third group of regulators is designed to help implement the government's investment policy. Under this policy a substantial part of total investment is undertaken on the initiative of individual enterprises. The state's influence in this area is exercised through investment credits and also through budgetary allocation of investment funds.

The remaining three sets of economic regulators establish the framework for credit operations, foreign trade, and fiscal and budgetary management.

An elaborate system of income and wage regulations complements these regulators. Enterprise profits are separated into three distinct funds: the development fund, the profit-sharing fund and a reserve fund. A complex system of taxation diverts a large portion of the profits to the state budget.

Even by the first decade of Communist rule, ownership of the means of production was almost entirely socialized. Nevertheless, a certain amount of private property is allowed. With about 5% of the economically active population, the private sector accounts for less than 2% of national income. The socialized sector is divided into three subsectors: the state sector, accounting for over 70% of national income; the cooperative sector (23%); and "the other socialist sector," comprising cooperatives of small-scale individual producers (5%).

Individual enterprises constitute the basic units of the economic management pyramid. They are grouped into economic and industrial branches, and they are subject to the supervision of ministries and agencies. Although enterprise managers have considerable autonomy under the NEM and are authorized to make major internal decisions, workers' self-management through workers' councils does not exist. Agency or ministry control consists in ensuring enterprises' adherence to applicable regulations and targets and through the power to appoint, dismiss or reward managers. The extent of ministerial involvement varies among branches of the economy. The 40 or 50 largest enterprises that account for a considerable portion of the industrial output receive greater scrutiny.

Economic management is the subject of considerable criticism in the Hungarian press. The shortcomings most often cited include overcentralization, excessively long chains of command and a poor level of middle-level management.

Various measures to encourage the further development of private enterprise have been implemented since 1982. In 1983 new measures permitted the establishment of customs-free zones for joint ventures between Hungarian enterprises and foreign companies. In 1986 taxes on the profits of such joint ventures were reduced and the licensing system was simplified. By early 1988 more than 100 joint ventures had been entered into with Western countries, particularly Austria and West Germany.

In 1985 further radical reforms were introduced in the system of management. In about 80% of the companies, managers are to be elected. In large and medium-size companies election will be by newly formed enterprise councils, and in small companies directly by employees. New regulations allow successful enterprises to pay higher wages and to streamline the labor force if necessary, while loss-making companies face the possibility of liquidation. A new bankruptcy law, applicable to both companies and cooperatives, took effect in 1986. State aid, which amounted to 80 billion forints between 1980 and 1985, will be phased out gradually.

Planning is the basic mechanism for directing the economy. There are three levels of national plans: the long-term 10- to 20-year plans, the five-year plans and the annual plans. After the 1968 reforms, the economic plans are no longer compulsory in the sense that individual plan targets are not set in concrete. They prescribe only the general direction, and a great deal of flexibility is permitted within limits. The national plan is formulated by the National Planning Office and the planning units of ministries, local governments and enterprises. Based on the national plans, each enterprise draws up its own annual and five-year plans, usually more than one variation or model. It also makes all decisions concerning development, except in the capital goods sector, where the government makes between 35% and 40% of all development decisions.

Hungarian planning has been beset with the same kind of problems that most command economies face. The government has been unable to develop a system of accounting and statistical reporting necessary to provide planners with reliable data. Enterprises are severely handicapped in formulating realistic plans by frequent changes in the regulators, particularly those governing prices and supply of raw materials. Another difficulty is that of anticipating market trends. Most enterprises emphasize higher output at the expense of greater efficiency, improved use of resources or better marketing. Most enterprises lack the managerial expertise for long-term planning.

The price system established under the NEM was intended to promote the rational use of resources, adaptation of production to effective demand, product innovation, equilibrium between demand and supply, and price stability. The prices were raised with the intention of eliminating production subsidies and enabling enterprises to create investment funds out of profits. Retail prices, however, were left virtually unchanged because the regime attached great importance to the maintenance of a retail price level in order to ward off public protests. The spread between producers' prices and retail prices was absorbed by the budget through price subsidies. The prices are of four different types: fixed; maximum; variable between fixed limits; and free. The more basic or scarce the product, the more rigid the price. All except free prices are set by the government through the National Material and Price Control Office. Effective supervision of prices by the authorities is hampered by the complexity of the price regulations and the lack of legal penalties except admonitions for violations. Illicit price increases are common, especially by enterprises with a monopoly position. However, retail prices are generally lower than producer prices for consumer goods because of state subsidies. Thus the price structure displays a dichotomy between the prices of consumer goods and the prices of capital goods on the one hand and the prices of agricultural goods and the prices of industrial goods on the other.

The regulation of wages has proved to be one of the most intractable and controversial problems in economic management. The wage system introduced in 1968 was intended primarily to contain the total rise in purchasing power within planned limits. It linked profits and wages and set a limit on the average annual wage bill of an enterprise. Wages and salaries consist of a fixed base pay supplemented by a share in enterprise profits. The wage schedule is based on seven levels of skills and four categories of working conditions. The profit-sharing fund is subject to a progressive tax system that imposes limits on the total amount of profits that may be distributed to each personnel category. Although managers fare better than workers under this system, workers' incomes are better protected than incomes of other personnel in loss-making enterprises.

The wage system has had many unintended consequences. The wide disparity in profit levels has brought about an inequality in workers' and managers' earnings. The linkage of wages and profits penalizes not only inefficient enterprises but also efficient ones operating under conditions of fixed or maximum prices. Many of these enterprises are in essential industries. The disparity in workers' earnings, coupled with the tight labor market, encourages excessive labor turnover.

The development of an effective wage system has eluded the government, as evidenced by the periodic shifts in policy, reforms and innovations, and retreats and advances, all hampered by contradictory policy aims and the egalitarian imperatives of a socialist society. Dissatisfaction with the wage structure is particularly strong among the better qualified because their superior skills are not adequately recognized or compensated. There also is a lack of a generally accepted concept and measure of labor productivity.

The failure of the NEM to redress economic imbalances is reflected in the flourishing "second economy" (the private economy), in which, according to unofficial sources, two of three workers are engaged. Much of this activity is tolerated by the government, as it contributes to the maintenance of a higher standard of living than would be possible otherwise. At the same time, the second economy is cited as one of the main reasons for the low productivity of Hungarian workers.

Significant reforms occurred in 1988, including a new Law on Corporate Association, which by permitting joint-stock and limited liability companies, set up new operating rules for both foreign and domestic firms, and a Foreign Investment Act that allowed 100% foreign ownership of Hungarian businesses, simplified registration procedures, and conversion of soft currency profits into foreign exchange for repatriation. The former regime also established the first personal and value-added tax systems in Eastern Europe and took steps towards a reform of the wage and price systems. The CMEA's only operating stock and bond markets are in Budapest. Also in 1989, the government reduced import regulations, continued the development of a modern banking sector and announced cuts in some government consumer and production subsidies.

Hungary also hopes the ongoing trade negotiations stemming from its 1988 agreement with the European Community will result in improved market access. With an eye toward promoting trade and investment, Hungary has also expanded its political ties with Israel and South Korea.

Despite the former regime's reform efforts, economic results in Hungary in 1988 and 1989, like those of the previous two years, remained disappointing. GDP—63% of which still passes through the central budget—stagnated in 1988 and fell slightly in 1989, while government deficits continued to exceed government projections. Inflation, officially 17% in 1989 and running above 20% so far in 1990 (but considered by many to be higher), and the reduction of consumer subsidies with resulting price hikes continue to be serious political issues. In 1988, real wages dropped by 8%, and consumption by 3%. Although wages in 1989 on average grew slightly in real terms, a further erosion in living standards for some segments of the population is expected as obsolete industries shut down; a full fifth of the population lives below the official poverty line. Concern also is growing that the government's restructuring program may push unemployment above 100,000 by the end of 1990.

Moreover, profitability of state firms remains a particularly elusive goal. Some estimates put the number of state and cooperative enterprises operating in the red as high as 500 and loss-making cooperative farms at over 100, yet only a small percentage of these (and mostly smaller units) have been forced into bankruptcy. Subsidies to others, in spite of some cuts, remain stubbornly high. Debts between companies are estimated to total nearly $1.2 billion. In addition, Hungary's $21.7 billion gross hard currency debt is a constraint that will grow as medium- and long-term debt matures.

In sum, all the reform and austerity-oriented activities undertaken by the previous regime have not added up to dramatic results. Moreover, the new government, while committed to the objective of a free-market economy, may have to move slowly in the face of popular resistance to the pain that needed reforms will bring.

PRINCIPAL ECONOMIC INDICATORS, 1988

Gross National Product: $2.603 billion
GNP per capita: $2,460
GNP average annual growth rate: (%) 1.6 (1980–88)
GNP per capita average annual growth rate: (%) 1.8 (1980–88)
Consumer Price Index (1980 = 100)
   All items: 165.5 (1988)
   Food: 157.5 (1988)
Average annual rate of inflation: 5.7% (1980–87)
Average annual growth rate (%) (1980–87)
   Public consumption: 0.9
   Private consumption: 1.7
   Gross domestic investment: −1.8
Income distribution: Highest 20% 35.8%; Lowest 20% 6.9%.

Throughout 1989, the volume of Hungary's industrial production fell slightly compared to projected stagnation. This decline was most severe in the state sector, which predominates with nearly two-thirds of all production, but was also characteristic of cooperative enterprises. The mining and light industry sectors, both subject to cutbacks in government subsidies, were the hardest hit, while metallurgy, thanks to a 10% increase in aluminum production due to high world prices, registered the highest growth, 4%. Government planners were most concerned with stagnation in the chemical and machinery/engineering sectors, which are expected to form the foundation of a restructured Hungarian economy but which do not yet show signs of change.

Recognizing that production from Hungary's small private sector remained the most dynamic, Hungary's former government took steps throughout 1989 to allow for an economy based on mixed ownership. To encourage existing firms to take advantage of the new forms of ownership opportunities allowed in the 1988 Law on Corporate Association, the National Assembly passed the Law on Economic Transformation in May 1989, which set up the conditions under which a state-owned or cooperative firm may convert to other forms of ownership, including limited liability or joint stock. In a formula based on the type of state company involved, part of the revenues from the sale of the state assets would be returned to the firm as an incentive to convert ownership structure, with the rest going into a State Fund for Privatization. By loaning investment capital from this fund, the government hoped to find buyers for additional state assets.

Creatively using the new opportunities, a handful of former state companies have successfully denationalized. In one well-publicized case, the employees of a Budapest retail chain took equity in the company, while other enterprise councils voted to sell their firms to foreign investors to get needed capital and know-how. For the most part, Hungary's commercial banks and other financial institutions rather than private citizens or foreign firms remain the major investors in local companies. In spite of the new possibilities, many state firms have been reluctant to denationalize—managers and employees often see only the risks of lost jobs and influence rather than the opportunity. The pace of denationalization may accelerate in the near future as foreign investors and the Hungarians themselves become

more used to the process. However, many Hungarians resist rapid privatization out of fear that many state enterprises will be sold to foreigners at undervalued prices.

Largely through increased convertible currency exports, Hungary reduced its convertible currency current account deficit from $1.41 billion in 1986 to $847 million in 1987 and $810 million in 1988. After this two-year improvement, however, the deficit ballooned back up to $1.4 billion in 1989, mainly as a result of increased travel of Hungarians to the West. The tourist surplus, traditionally a significant source of hard currency earnings, dipped to a mere $3 million in 1988. Throughout 1989, government officials worked with customs regulations and domestic supplies to reduce Hungarian "shopping tourism" in Austria and Western Europe, without restricting popular travel opportunities available to the population with the adoption of liberal passport laws in 1988.

The trade balance remained a star performer during this period, somewhat counterbalancing the tourist outflows. With over 50% of GDP tied to trade, export success remains key in efforts to balance accounts while simultaneously encouraging industrial restructuring. In both 1988 and 1989, convertible currency export volumes increased by 9%. The 1989 trade surplus was $540 million, up from $490 million in 1988, thanks to a 17% rise in export values. Convertible currency imports rose 18% last year, however, probably as a result of the liberalization of import licensing requirements. Many government officials worry that Hungary's recent trade performance stems more from luck—higher world prices for traditional Hungarian exports—than from any successful economic restructuring.

BALANCE OF PAYMENTS ($ million), 1988

Current account balance: −580
Merchandise exports: 9,826
Merchandise imports: −9,659
Trade balance: 166
Other goods, services & income: 2,246
Other goods, services & income: −3,098
Private unrequited transfers: 106
Other long-term capital: 852
Other short-term capital: −1,087
Net errors & omissions: −75
Total change in reserves: 890

Hungary's trade is now divided almost evenly between convertible currency and CMEA markets, with the Soviet Union, West Germany and Austria ranking as the country's top three trading partners. Hungary buys 80% of its energy and raw material imports from the Soviet Union. In a move to reduce Hungary's growing ruble surplus in its CMEA trade in order to free up more resources for Western export, Hungary revalued the forint-ruble exchange rate in September 1989. Hungary and the Soviet Union have agreed to base bilateral trade on a convertible currency basis by 1991, and the CMEA as a whole has similar plans.

Although Hungary's convertible currency debt of $21.7 billion is the highest per capita in Eastern Europe,

Hungary has been able to maintain a high level of international lender confidence through a strong commitment to its debt obligations. Central bankers have worked consistently to trade short-term debt for loans with longer maturity and to diversify the sources of currency fluctuations. U.S. holding of Hungarian loans and bonds is minimal, while Japan, with nearly half of the total debt, is Hungary's largest creditor. Hungary's debt-service obligations are expected to rise substantially, beginning in 1991 and 1992, to an estimated $3 billion. Hungarian officials hope that by then the effects of restructuring efforts will show through substantially increased hard currency exports, although not everyone anticipates this result.

In March 1990 Hungary concluded a standby agreement with the International Monetary Fund (IMF). Continued international lender confidence in Hungary will be strongly influenced by the government's ability to abide by the principal terms of this agreement, which are to shrink the current account deficit and reduce the government's large budget deficit. Moody's investor service has rated Hungary Aa2, identical to that of Spain.

GROSS DOMESTIC PRODUCT, 1988

GDP nominal (national currency): 1.088 trillion
GDP real (national currency): 798.9 billion
GDP per capita ($): 1,933
GDP average annual growth rate: 1.7% (1980–87)
GDP by type of expenditure (%)
  Consumption
    Private: 63
    Government: 10
  Gross domestic investment: 27
  Gross domestic saving: 26
  Foreign trade:
    Exports: 42
    Imports: −40
Sectoral origin of GDP (%)
  Primary
    Agriculture: 12
  Secondary
    Manufacturing: 39
    Construction: 10
    Public utilities: 1
  Tertiary
    Transportation & communications: 7
    Trade: 12
    Finance
    Public administration & defense: } 19
    Services:
Average annual sectoral growth rates (%), 1980–87
  Agriculture: 2.5
  Industry: 1.3
  Services: 1.8

Although Hungary remains closely tied politically to the Soviet Union, the relative popularity of the post-Kadar regime has permitted it not only to experiment broadly with market incentives but also to develop commercial and financial relations with the West. For example, the National Bank of Hungary joined a consortium of six foreign banks—from Austria, West Germany, Japan, France and Italy—to form an East-West trade bank, the Central European International Bank, in which Hungary has a 34% interest; headquar-

---

FINANCIAL INDICATORS, 1988

International reserves minus gold: $1.867 billion
  Foreign exchange: $1.867 billion
Gold (million fine troy oz.): 1.593
Central bank
  Assets (%)
    Claims on government: 17.9
    Claims on banks: 61.5
    Claims on foreign assets: 20.6
  Liabilities (%)
    Reserve money: 38.3
    Government deposits: 3.6
    Foreign liabilities: 88.8
    Capital accounts: 2.3
Money supply
  Stock in billion national currency: 306.1
  M^1 per capita: 28,900
Private banks
  Assets (%)
    Loans to government: 46.5
    Loans to private sector: 32.9
    Reserves: 17.2
    Foreign assets: 3.4
  Liabilities (%)
    of which
      Deposits (billion national currency): 863.4
      Demand deposits: 16.8
      Savings deposits: 32.9
      Foreign liabilities: 9.4
      Other: 40.9

EXCHANGE RATE
(National Currency per U.S. Dollar)

1979	1980	1981	1982	1983	1984	1985	1986	1987	1988
35.578	32.213	34.430	39.610	45.545	51.199	47.347	45.927	47.454	50.413

---

ters are in Budapest. Unlike Poland, where price increases for consumer goods have met with popular opposition, Hungary also has been able to raise prices substantially on basic food items as well as gasoline, tobacco, beer and newspapers to reduce subsidies and allow market forces to reflect real price increases.

During the fourth five-year plan (1971–75), Hungary's NMP rose by 35% over the previous plan period, industrial production rose by 38% and agricultural output rose by 18%. During the fifth five-year plan (1976–80) the NMP rose by 20%, industrial production by 18% and agricultural production by 13%. During the sixth five-year plan (1981–85) the NMP grew by 7% and industrial production and agricultural production by 12% each. Per capita income rose by 7% to 8%, slightly more than planned. Exports and imports rose by 27% and 6%, respectively. The seventh five-year plan (1985-90) has had only modest success because of the political and economic turmoil of the late 1980s.

PUBLIC FINANCE

The fiscal year is the calendar year. Official information is not available on the country's public finance. Only fragmentary data may be gleaned from press reports, the annual budget presentation to the National Assembly, and reports on the fulfillment of the budget as published in the *Official Gazette.*

Hungarian budgets are chronically in deficit. After 1968 the imbalances were caused primarily by excessive investment and an upsurge in consumption at state-subsidized prices. The elimination of budgetary deficits is not considered politically desirable because it would slow down the economy and unfavorably affect the standard of living.

In 1986 a total of 64% of the revenues were derived from state and collective enterprises and 15% from the turnover tax. Levies on enterprises include a tax on profits; a 5% charge on the use of capital; and taxes on wages, salaries and Social Security contributions amounting to an average of 25% of the total wage bill. Turnover taxes, levied mainly on consumer goods at the wholesale or manufacturing stage, are declining in importance. Other levies on enterprises include a production tax that is akin to a rental charge; withholding of 40% of depreciation allowances; and customs charges. A substantial portion of revenue derived from enterprises is absorbed by subsidy payments. About 20% of the revenues are collected from other sources, including direct taxes. The proportion of direct taxes has steadily risen from about 5% in 1970. Direct taxes are levied mainly on private artisans, retail merchants and intellectuals. They also are directed at stopping real-estate speculation.

Information on the distribution of budgetary expenditures is more scarce than data on receipts. The major items of expenditure in 1986 were: investment (87.5 billion forints or 12%); industrial enterprises and agricultural cooperatives (141.7 billion forints or 19.4%); Social Security (142.1 billion forints or 19.5%); consumer price subsidies (59.8 billion forints or 8.2%); defense (40.9 billion forints or 5.6%); health and social welfare (38.3 billion forints or 5.2%); culture (66.8 billion forints or 9.1%); and economic activities (53.0 billion forints or 7.2%). Between 1983 and 1986, while investment expenditures have remained relatively stable, the largest increases were reported for industrial enterprises and agricultural enterprises (106.4 billion forints to 141.7 billion forints) and Social Security (120.0 billion forints to 142.0 billion forints). Other items have grown only slightly.

CURRENCY & BANKING

The Hungarian monetary unit is the forint, divided into 100 fillers. Coins are issued in denominations of 10, 20 and 50 fillers and 1, 2, 5, 10 and 20 forints, and notes in denominations of 10, 20, 50, 100, 500 and 1,000 forints.

The forint is not convertible and is usable only in domestic transactions. There are several rates of exchange, each applying to a different set of financial transactions. In foreign trade so-called price multipliers used for accounting purposes were introduced in 1968. They serve to determine the amount of state subsidies or other financial adjustments provided by the governments for exports and imports. Bilateral ruble clearing accounts are used in trade with CMEA partners. Trade with less-developed countries also is based on bilateral clearing accounts.

Strict government controls are in effect over all foreign exchange transactions. Trading in gold is illegal, and the export or import of diamonds or jewelry is prohibited.

CENTRAL GOVERNMENT EXPENDITURES, 1987
% of total expenditures

Defense: 4.0
Education: 2.3
Health: 3.6
Housing, Social Security, welfare: 26.2
Economic services: 37.7
Other: 26.1
Total expenditures as % of GNP: 59.6
Overall surplus or deficit as % of GNP: −3.6

CENTRAL GOVERNMENT REVENUES, 1987
% of total current revenues

Taxes on income, profit & capital gain: 18.0
Social Security contributions: 24.2
Domestic taxes on goods & services: 31.5
Taxes on international trade & transactions: 6.5
Other taxes: 11.1
Current nontax revenue: 8.8
Total current revenue as % of GNP: 55.3
Government consumption as % of GNP: 10.0
Annual growth rate of government consumption: 0.9 (1980–87)

EXTERNAL PUBLIC DEBT, 1986

Total: $13.567 billion
  of which public (%): 10.6
  of which private (%): 89.4
Debt service total: $3.943 billion
  of which
    repayment of principal (%): 71.8
    interest (%): 28.2
Debt service ratio: 35.9
External public debt as % of GNP: 63.5
Ratio of external public debt to international reserves: 4.3
Debt service as % of GNP: 12.9
Debt service as % of exports: 26.7
Terms of public borrowing:
  Commitments: $2.744 billion
  Average interest rate: 7.2%
  Average maturity: 9 years

The Hungarian financial system was restructured in the late 1980s. In January 1985 the functions of issue and credit at the National Bank were separated. Under reforms implemented in January 1987 the central banking and commercial banking functions were separated and the banking system reorganized on three levels. The Bank of Hungary, as the bank of issue, continues to participate in the formulation of economic policy, and its foreign exchange authority and total assets remain unchanged. At the second tier are the commercial banks, with nationwide and general financial authority. They establish their own policies and terms within the limits of the central banking regulations and also may engage in investment. The commercial banks are: General Banking and Trust Company, Hungarian Credit Bank, Budapest Bank, Hungarian Foreign Trade Bank and Commercial and Creditbank. At the third tier are the so-called specialized financial institutions, which may undertake all banking services but may not keep the accounts of their clients. The principal institutions in this sector are: Agricultural Innovation Bank, General Bank for Venture Financing, Innovation Bank for Construction Industry, General Financial Institution for Innovation, Development Credit Corporation for the Development of Foreign Trade, Bank for Technical Development, Development Bank of Industrial Cooperatives, Bank for Small Ventures and Hungarian Industrial Bank Corporation.

The National Savings Bank and the savings cooperatives function as public banks, the latter at the local level. Since 1985 the cooperatives have maintained accounts for small enterprises and private entrepreneurs and have provided mortgage facilities to individuals. Minimum registered capital is 2 million forints at each cooperative. In 1987 there were 260 cooperatives represented in the National Council of Consumer Cooperatives.

In addition to the Central European International Bank, established in 1979 as the first Hungarian coventure with Western banking consortia, a joint Hungarian-U.S. bank, Citibank, was founded in 1986 as a collaborative effort of Citibank of New York and Central Exchange and Credit Bank of Budapest. The U.S. share in this venture is 45%. In 1987 a third joint venture, Unicbank, commenced operations with 45% foreign capital, from Western Europe.

The issue of bonds to finance construction is becoming increasingly common. Offering a higher rate of interest than the National Savings Bank, bonds were first issued on a large scale in 1983 and available initially to enterprises and later to individuals. In 1984 the State Development Bank (now the State Development Institution) began repurchasing and reselling bonds, thus giving rise to a domestic bond market. By 1986 local councils and enterprises had issued 130 bonds for a total value of 8 billion forints; about 70% of the bonds were purchased by private citizens. The bond market expanded rapidly in 1987, and 200 bonds worth 24.320 billion forints were in circulation. In January 1988 the state guarantee for bonds was terminated, thus making the issue of bonds difficult for small organizations. The state also began to issue Treasury bills to finance budget deficits.

On June 21, 1990, the Hungarian Stock Exchange resumed full-time operations as the first regular securities market in Eastern Europe since World War II. The stock exchange, which had been established in 1864, was closed in 1948. It had been partially reopened in 1983, but was hamstrung by state regulations. On January 25, 1990, Parliament passed the Stock Exchange and Stock Law, which also provided guarantees for investors and brokers and recommended the setting up of the State Stock Agency as a regulatory organ. Most importantly, the new law requires that issuing firms disclose extensive details about their finances before listing and trading. From 1993 banks will not be permitted to act as brokers or deal in shares. In order to encourage the participation of private domestic capital, the new law exempts one-third of personal income from

tax if invested in stocks. Three foreign-owned and 14 jointly owned brokerage firms are members of the exchange.

```
GROWTH PROFILE (Annual Growth Rate, %)

Population, 1985–2000: 0.2
Crude birth rate, 1985–90: 12.8
Crude death rate, 1985–90: 12.4
Urban population, 1980–87: 1.4
Labor force, 1985–2000: 0.3
GNP, 1980–85: 1.6
GNP per capita, 1980–88: 1.8
GDP, 1980–87: 1.7
Inflation, 1980–87: 5.7
Agriculture, 1980–87: 2.5
Industry, 1980–87: 1.3
Services, 1980–87: 1.8
Money holdings, 1980–87: 7.5
Manufacturing earnings per employee, 1980–86: 1.5
Energy production, 1980–87: 1.8
Energy consumption, 1980–87: 1.1
Exports, 1980–87: 3.9
Imports, 1980–87: 1.5
General government consumption, 1980–87: 0.9
Private consumption, 1980–87: 1.7
Gross domestic investment, 1980–87: −1.8
```

AGRICULTURE

The agricultural sector comprises state, collective and private farms. Since 1968 farm enterprises have had the freedom to plan production and investment—but not marketing—within a framework of government incentives and regulations. However, even with these incentives, sectoral growth has been unsatisfactory because of the primacy of industry in planning targets and generally low prices and profitability. The farm output covers almost all domestic food consumption and about one-fourth of the country's exports. Agricultural imports to the extent of about half the volume of exports are necessary to make up deficiencies in livestock feed and chemicals.

Natural conditions are generally favorable to agriculture. The country is well endowed with fertile soils, and the climate is warm enough for the cultivation of such crops as wheat, rice and grapes. However, significant variations in the volume of annual output are caused by periodic droughts and floods as well as by changes in the seasonal pattern and rainfall. The principal soils are the black earth (chernozem) in the Great Plain east of the Tisza River and in the eastern portion of Transdanubia; the alluvial meadow soils along the rivers; and the brown forest soils of most of Transdanubia and the Northern Mountains. Fruits and vegetables are grown in light, sandy soils between the Danube and Tisza rivers.

In 1988 agricultural land comprised 7,413,000 ha. (18,317,523 ac.), or 79.7% of the country's total land area. About 71.7% of the agricultural land is arable; 17.3% is comprised of meadows and pastures and 11.0% of other surfaces. The proportion of arable land to total land area is one of the highest in Europe. Agricultural land is being continually lost to industrial and urban uses, but the loss is made up by the reclamation of sandy soils. Grains occupy about 64% of the sown area, including 25% under corn. Official policy favors the expansion of the acreage under corn by reducing the acreage under wheat.

Collective farms constitute the dominant form of agricultural organization. They account for 74.5% of the agricultural land and 80% of the arable acreage. State farms and farms under the jurisdiction of the local governments contain 13.8% of the farmland and 14% of the arable area. The remaining acreage consists of unfavorably located tiny private farms.

State farms enjoying strong government support and considered as showcases of socialized agriculture number about 180, each with an average of 4,858 ha. (12,000 ac.), three-fourths of which are arable. In size they range from 2,024 ha. (5,000 ac.) to over 10,121 ha. (25,000 ac.). They have at their disposal a disproportionate share of farm buildings and machinery. Under the NEM state farm managers have considerable discretion to determine the structure of production and investments. The state, however, may intervene to direct the farms to expand production of items in short supply. State farms also have high vertical integration combining production, processing and marketing.

Collective or cooperative farms exist in several forms. By far the most important are the so-called agricultural producer cooperatives, which are large-scale farms engaged in mixed farming. The other types are mostly specialized agricultural cooperatives concentrating on one product; for example, grapes. Numbering about 2,500, collective farms cover 5.1 million ha. (12.5 million ac.) of agricultural land (76% of which is arable). About 13% of the acreage consists of small plots allotted to farm members. The 500 smallest farms have less than 1,012 ha. (2,500 ac.), while the largest 37 average 5,061 ha. (12,500 ac.).

Collective farms own all their productive resources, but barely one-third of the land they cultivate is held in common. More than half is owned by individuals, including collective farm members, and 13.5% is owned by the state. Private land is transferred to collective ownership at the time of a member's death. The legal status, organizational form, operating methods and income distribution of collective farms are governed by the Farmers' Cooperative Law of 1967, the Standard Cooperative Law of 1971 and other decrees. The laws grant collective farms equality with state enterprises and protection against interference by state administrative organs. Under the NEM collective farms have freedom of decision within the framework of the national economic plans in such matters as production and ancillary activities. In practice, however, the government intervenes in farm affairs quite frequently.

Each collective farm is governed by a general assembly of all its members. The assembly elects a management body including a president and several specialized committees, three of which are mandatory under law: the control or supervisory committee, the arbitration committee and the women's committee. The financial operation of the farm is audited by an outside accountant. Collective farms are organized into regional associations, which in turn are federated in the National Council of Producers' Cooperatives, which is represented in the National Cooperative Council.

Farmers are remunerated in three ways: a rental payment for the land they contributed to the collective; a share in the distribution of the farm's net income after taxes based on the actual number of days worked; and income derived from crops and livestock raised on personal plots.

Most collective farms operate at a loss, particularly in years of poor harvests, droughts and floods. These are dependent on state aid for their continued survival. As a result some 35% of collective farm workers receive an annual income about half of that of their counterparts in state farms.

Personal plots make a substantial contribution to the national food supply as well as to the income of farmers. Although they constitute only 13% of the collective farm acreage, they account for over one-third of the output of collective farms and about one-fourth of the national food supply. These family plots are encouraged by the collective farm management by providing them with tools, technical assistance and low rates of interest.

Collective farms engage in a wide range of ancillary activities, particularly food processing and marketing, as well as industrial, transportation and service undertakings unrelated to agricultural production. These activities permit many collectives to provide full, year-round employment to their members. A 1971 law allows the government to forbid or restrict some of the activities.

On collective farms the labor situation has been deteriorating steadily since the 1960s, and the pace of mechanization has not kept pace with the loss of able-bodied workers. More than half the collective farmers are over 60 and about 40% are over 65. The main reason for the exodus from farms is the disinclination of the young to join the farm work force, where working conditions are harsher, social benefits fewer and working hours longer. On state farms the labor situation is more stable.

Collective farms absorb about 75% of agricultural investment and state farms 25%. On the basis of acreage, investment in state farms is about 75% higher than in collective farms. Investment funds are provided from three sources: the budget, farm income and bank credits. It is difficult to disaggregate these sources because in official statistics investments on farms are lumped together with those on water management and forests. Investment and production credits are made available to farms through the Agricultural Innovation Bank. The cost of credit places a heavy burden on agriculture, which, unlike industry, cannot pass on the cost to consumers because the prices for most agricultural products are fixed by the government. Credits to agriculture have a maximum maturity of 15 years and carry an interest charge that varies with the purpose. Credits for investment in cattle- and hog-raising, truck farming and irrigation are subject to matching funds from the recipients' own resources. State farms were financed entirely through the state budget until 1967; since then they have been on a self-financing basis and have been eligible for bank loans.

AGRICULTURAL INDICATORS, 1988

Agriculture's share of GDP (%): 15
Average annual growth rate (%): 2.5 (1980–87)
Value added in agriculture ($): 4.022 billion
Cereal imports (000 tons): 660
Index of Agricultural Production (1979–81 = 100): 109 (1986)
Index of Food Production (1979–81 = 100): 109 (1986)
Index of Food Production Per Capita (1979–81 = 100): 110 (1985–87)
Number of tractors: 53,947
Number of harvester-threshers: 11,475
Total fertilizer consumption (tons): 1,338,000
Fertilizer consumption (100 g. per ha.): 26
Number of farms: 798,000
Average size of holding, ha. (ac.): 8.3 (20.5)
Tenure (%)
   Owner-operated: 6.8
   State: 13.8
   Cooperative: 74.5
% of farms using irrigation: 4
Total land in farms, ha.(ac.): 7,413,000 (18,317,523)
Farms as % of total land area: 79.7
Land use (%)
   Total cropland: 71.7
      Permanent crops: 11.8
      Temporary crops: 86.1
      Fallow: 2.1
   Meadows & pastures: 17.3
   Other: 11.0
Yields, kg./ha. (lb./ac.)
   Grains: 4,964 (4,431)
   Roots & tubers: 15,927 (14,216)
   Pulses: 1,996 (1,782)
   Milk, kg. (lb.)/animal: 4,819 (10,624)
Livestock (000)
   Cattle: 1,766
   Sheep: 2,465
   Hogs: 8,280
   Horses: 98
   Chickens: 63,000
Forestry
   Production of roundwood, 000 cu. m. (000 cu. ft.): 6,229 (219,977)
      of which industrial roundwood (%): 55.9
   Value of exports ($000): 110,380
Fishing
   Total catch (000 tons): 36.1
      of which marine (%): 0
   Value of exports ($000): 9,095

Since farm income is too low to provide adequate funds for modernization and expansion, a system of state subsidies has been devised to bridge the gap. Subsidies for approved projects are disbursed before the start of construction. The amount of the subsidy is based on a percentage of the estimated cost and is differentiated according to the project's priority rating.

Mechanization has been slow because about 80% of the tractors must be imported. Machinery inventory is complicated by the lack of spare parts and their rising prices. Even with state subsidies, many collective farms cannot afford tractors or harvester-threshers. Consequently, they continue to run obsolete machinery, even though the parts for these machines are expensive and there are no subsidies for their purchase. Domestic production also is unable to meet the need for fertilizers, and about one-third of the required tonnage has to be imported.

State farms deliver their products to state procurement agencies. Collective farms and private producers sign delivery contracts with state purchasing and food-processing industries, sell directly to retail stores or restaurants or bring their produce to the free markets for direct sale. The predominance of state trade and the absence of local farm markets result in excessive cross-hauling of produce, with resultant loss of quality. Products often move from villages to state purchasing centers and back again to the points of origin for sale through state retail outlets. With few exceptions the prices of farm products are regulated by the government. There are three price categories: fixed, variable and free. The government's policy of maintaining stable prices notwithstanding, numerous price adjustments are made periodically, generally upward.

Crop production between 1984 and 1986 showed an increase in the output of corn (from 6.686 million tons to 7.261 million tons) but a decline in virtually every other major crop, particularly wheat (from 7.392 million tons to 5.793 million tons), sugar beets (from 4.360 million tons to 3.760 million tons), barley (from 1.220 million tons to 857,000 tons) and potatoes (from 1.551 million tons to 1.264 million tons). Production of vegetables has steadily declined, requiring substantial imports from the Soviet Union.

The expansion of livestock is an important facet of agricultural policy, not only to meet domestic requirements but also to secure hard-currency export earnings. Over the years livestock production has faced major obstacles, such as shortage of feed and fodder; obsolete physical facilities, including slaughterhouses; and low selling prices. A total of 90% of the cattle consists of the native piebald breed, which produces only half the average quantity of milk produced by cows in Western countries. There is an extensive program for livestock breeders, including subsidies for every calf and every quart of milk sold, and for the construction and modernization of barns, silos, granaries and feed-processing installations. Cattle-raising on private farm plots also benefits from these subsidies.

As a landlocked country, Hungary never has had a developed fishing sector. The main areas of inland fishing are the Danube and Tisza rivers and Lake Balaton.

State forests account for 16.5% of the total land area. Oak, ask and beech are the most important varieties. Due to the small forest area and the high rate of exploitation, timber is imported.

MANUFACTURING

Virtually all manufacturing is state-owned. State enterprises account for 99% of industrial assets and produce 93% of the output. Collective industrial enterprises account for 6% of the output, and independent private artisans contribute the balance.

In 1984 there were 1,264 industrial enterprises employing 1.261 million workers and generating 1.029 trillion forints in gross output. One-third of the enterprises were very large in size, generally employing 1,000 to 5,000 workers, while a few employed over 10,000 work

```
┌─────────────────────────────────────────────────┐
│         MANUFACTURING INDICATIORS, 1988           │
│ Average annual growth rate, 1980–87: 1.3%        │
│ Share of GDP: 47.2%                               │
│ Labor force in manufacturing: 31.4%              │
│ Value added in manufacturing                      │
│    Food & agriculture: 6%                         │
│    Textiles: 11%                                  │
│    Machinery: 37%                                 │
│    Chemical: 11%                                  │
│ Earnings per employee in manufacturing: 1.5% (1980–86) │
│    Growth Rate Index (1980 = 100): 111 (1986)    │
│ Total earnings as % of value added: 35           │
│ Gross output per employee (1980 = 100): 111 (1986) │
│ Index of Manufacturing Production: (1985 = 100): 105.2 (1988) │
└─────────────────────────────────────────────────┘
```

ers. By contrast, only about 10% employed less than 100 and 20% between 100 and 300 workers. Food processing plants employed the fewest workers. The large size of many enterprises places them in a monopoly position.

In 1989 Hungary became the second nation in Eastern Europe (after Poland) to open its doors to foreign investors. Citicorp of New York financed the first known management buyout in the country when it purchased one-third ownership of Apisz, a state-owned retail paper supplier, for $12 million. Italian financier Carlo De Benedetti established a holding company in Hungary to buy shares in Hungarian firms. Bear, Stearns & Co., a New York-based security house, and International Finance Corporation, a World Bank affiliate, established an equity investment fund in Hungary known as the First Hungary Fund, the first of its kind in Eastern Europe. In 1990 General Motors Corporation of the United States formed a joint venture with Raba, a Hungarian state-owned manufacturer of trucks and engines, to build cars and engines in Szentgotthard. It is difficult to estimate the amount of convertible currency currently being directly invested in Hungary. What is known is that an array of multinationals—including General Motors, Suzuki, General Electric, Digital Equipment Corporation, Allianz AG and the Tengelmann Group—have concluded or are very close to concluding major business contracts. Besides the large corporations, several smaller companies have also established joint ventures.

In 1989 close to 1,000 joint ventures were organized, mostly by Austrian and West German firms, to take advantage of the Foreign Investment Act, which allowed profit repatriation in convertible currency for the first time. Ironically, these liberalized joint-venture regulations were a major factor behind Hungary's record outflow of convertible currency in 1989, which caused a $1.5 billion balance-of-payments deficit. According to an article in the business daily *Vilaggazdasag*, profit repatriation reached close to $500,000,000 in 1989. Examples of other direct capital investment include the recent purchase of 50% of the Hungarian state recording enterprise Hungaroton by the British firm Thorn EMI for $15,000,000 and the formation of a joint venture by the Italian AGIP firm and the state gasoline distribution enterprise AFOR to build new gasoline stations. Both examples have raised concerns inside and outside Hungary. Hungarian critics assert that the "national

wealth" is being sold off below its real value, while some Western observers have written about carpetbaggers—speculators interested in a quick profit rather than serious long-term investment—descending on Hungary.

Manufacturing is highly concentrated in Budapest and its environs within a radius of 32 km. (20 mi.). Roughly half the industrial workers are employed in this area. Two other areas—one with its center at Gyor and the other centered on Miskolc—employ a further 30%. The least-developed industrial areas are Szeged and Debrecen. In the 1960s the government embarked on a program to encourage geographic dispersion of new manufacturing investments through selective use of credits, building permits and incentives.

The relative importance of the various industrial groups has remained stable since the 1960s. In terms of employment, the proportions of the industrial branches are: heavy industry, 58.3%; light industry, 27.1%; food industry, 10.5%; and others, 4.1%. In the heavy industry group, the share of metallurgy, building materials and vehicle production has declined slightly, while that of machine building and chemicals has increased correspondingly. A very small decline also has occurred in the relative share of textiles.

Under the NEM state ownership of manufacturing has been coupled with a significant measure of autonomy for the enterprises and trusts. Nevertheless, the state retains the right to create new enterprises and liquidate obsolete and inefficient ones. Frequently the government orders internal reorganizations and mergers and changes the affiliations of enterprises with ministries. Authority to engage in foreign trade transactions requires government permission. Of the ministries responsible for manufacturing, four are preeminent: the Ministry of Heavy Industry, the Ministry of Metallurgy and Machinery Industry, the Ministry of Construction and Urban Development and the Ministry of Light Industry.

The distribution of industrial investment among industry branches initially followed the typical Stalinist emphasis on heavy industry at the expense of consumer industries. This emphasis has been moderated in recent years to achieve a better balance, to improve the supply of consumer goods and to increase the potential for food exports. Enterprise investment policy favors new building construction and expansion of capacity at the expense of modernizing production technology. One of the consequences of this policy is the coexistence in many industrial plants of modern machines imported from the West with obsolete older equipment.

One important aspect of Hungarian manufacturing is that although Hungary ranks well above Poland and East Germany among Soviet bloc countries and almost all Western countries in the share of plants employing over 1,000 workers in total industrial employment, the largest Hungarian enterprise does not even appear in the top 500 industrial companies of Europe. A second feature concerns the horizontal and vertical diversity of production and the tendency toward proliferation of parts and intermediate goods. As a result, even large enterprises do not enjoy economies of scale. Large plants, in fact, are only conglomerations of small plants, and they prefer to make parts and subassemblies themselves rather than buy them. This tendency originates in a long-standing fear of dependence on outside suppliers. The net result is the slow growth of background industries and the lack of product integration among enterprises.

Hungarian enterprises conduct only a minimum amount of basic research. Most contract out their basic research to external institutions. The R & D network is organized along sectoral and functional lines, with each ministry having its own research institute. The State Committee for Technical Development wields overall responsibility in this field.

MINING

Hungary's mineral resources include significant quantities of bauxite and smaller quantities of coal, uranium, iron, copper, maganese and lead. Some gold appears in the local copper ores along with small deposits of silver. Of the nonmetallic ores, sulfur and arsenic are the most important.

The bauxite reserves exceed those of the Soviet Union and are second in Europe only to those of France. Deposits are located along the northwestern edge of the Bakony and Vertes hills. Two-thirds of these deposits are contained within a triangle formed by the towns of Kislod, Sumeg and Tapolca at the southwestern tip of the Bakony hills. The ore occurs in thick beds close enough to the surface to allow open-pit mining. Major production centers are in the Gant field in the Vertes hills and at Iszkaszentgyorgy, Halimba and Nyirad in the Bakony hills.

The only source of domestic iron ore is a deposit in the vicinity of Rudabanya in the northern mountains. The ore seam is thin and the quality of the ore is low— less than 25% pure. Hungary imports 90% of its ore needs, principally from the Soviet Union and India.

Uranium is found in two areas of the Mecsek Mountains in southern Transdanubia. The deposits are expected to be exhausted by 1990. Black anthracite coal is mined in small quantities in the Mecsek Mountains. Lignites and brown coal are much more plentiful, the former in the southern part of the Northern Mountains and the latter in the Transdanubian Central Mountains.

ENERGY

Hungary's oil and natural gas resources are insignificant. The major oil fields are in the alpine foothills in the western county of Zala and some minor ones on the Great Plain. Natural gas is more widely distributed. The most important deposits are in Hajdszoboszlo southwest of Debrecen and in the area of Szeged. Total output in 1987 was 7.020 billion cu. m. (247.911 billion cu. ft.). Imports in the same year from the Soviet Union totaled 4.900 billion cu. m. (173.043 million cu. ft.).

Hungary is deficient in electric power. The efficiency of the power plants is low and the cost of electricity is above the average for European countries. The Paks nuclear power station, built with Soviet assistance and inaugurated in 1983, produces almost half of the country's electricity output. Hungary's domestic uranium is sufficient to supply the Paks station until 2020. In 1985 Hungary decided to proceed with the Gabcikovo (Boes)-Nagymaros Danube barrage project, a joint undertaking with Czechoslovakia. Austria decided to participate in the project in 1986. It is scheduled for completion in 1993. The project's two hydroelectric power stations are expected to supply a total of 3.6 billion kw.-hr. per year. The total cost of the project is estimated at 70 billion forints.

ENERGY INDICATORS, 1988

Primary energy production (quadrillion BTU)
  Crude oil: 0.08
  Natural gas, liquid: 0.04
  Natural gas, dry: 0.29
  Coal: 0.29
  Nuclear power: 0.08
  Total: 0.78
Average annual energy production growth rate (%): 1.8 (1980–87)
Average annual energy consumption growth rate (%): 1.1 (1980–87)
Energy consumption per capita, kg. (lb.) oil equivalent: 3,062 (6,750)
Energy imports as % of merchandise imports (%): 18
Public utilities' share of GDP (%): 0.6
Electricity
  Installed capacity (kw.): 6,242,000
  Production (kw.-hr.): 28.063 billion
    % fossil fuel: 72.8
    % hydro: 0.5
    % nuclear: 26.5
  Consumption per capita (kw.-hr.): 3,610
Natural gas, cu. m. (cu. ft.)
  Proved reserves: 125 billion (4.414 trillion)
  Production: 7.116 billion (251 billion)
  Consumption: 10.808 billion (382 billion)
Petroleum, bbl.
  Proved reserves: 290 million
  Years to exhaust proved reserves: 21
  Production: 14 million
  Consumption: 58 million
  Refining capacity per day: 220,000
Coal, 000 tons
  Reserves: 4,661,000
  Production: 23,129
  Consumption: 25,348

LABOR

In 1988 the labor force was estimated at 4.75 million, of whom 20.2% were engaged in agriculture, forestry and fishing; 33.0% in mining and manufacturing; 7.1% in construction; 8.2% in transportation and communication; 10.4% in trade; 4.7% in public administration and defense; 15.5% in services; and 1.0% in other activities. The distribution of labor is typical of other East European countries. The female participation rate is 46%, but females are better represented in the collective and private sectors than in the state sector. The labor force growth rates are different for the three main sectors and even within sectors among the branches. Thus almost two-thirds of employment in the socialized sector is in heavy industry and more than half in the machine building branch.

Industrial labor supply has a paradoxical aspect: the coexistence of a labor shortage along with underemployment. Wage regulations introduced by the NEM have led many enterprises to hoard excessive numbers of low-paid unskilled workers to whom the regulations do not apply. The resulting labor shortage varies from 5.7% to 7.8% of total work force, while the percentage of surplus workers in certain sectors is estimated at 12%. Mechanization could free a large number of workers now engaged in handling, warehousing, etc. The labor shortage has stimulated an excessive turnover, estimated at a third of the work force.

Both the absolute level and the rate of growth of productivity are low in comparison with West European countries as well as with other East European countries. Many industrial plants are technologically obsolete and available machinery is only partially utilized. More than half the industrial workers use no power-driven machinery or equipment whatever on the job but use only their bare hands for most physical labor. Productivity also has suffered from low worker morale, lack of work discipline and poor personnel management. Dismissal of workers is shunned because of the government's full employment policy.

LABOR INDICATORS, 1988

Total economically active population: 4.75 million
As % of working-age population: 72.5
% female: 46.0
% under 20 years of age: 5.4
Average annual growth rate, 1985–2000 (%): 0.3
Activity rate (%)
   Total: 46.0
   Male: 51.4
   Female: 40.9
% organized labor: 76
Hours of work in manufacturing: 33.9 per week
Employment status (%)
   Employers & self-employed: 3.4
   Employees: 80.5
   Unpaid family workers: 2.4
   Other: 13.6
Sectoral employment (%)
   Agriculture, forestry & fishing: 20.2
   Mining:
   Manufacturing: } 33.0
   Construction: 7.1
   Transportation & communication: 8.2
   Trade: 10.4
   Public administration & defense: 4.7
   Services: 15.5
   Other: 1.0

Another important feature of the labor market is the extensive size of the "second economy," in which over 2 million persons, including pensioners, are engaged, working their private farm plots, producing small goods and working on weekends and holidays and even while on "sick leave." Some even become temporarily unemployed to work in the second economy. The second economy thus affects the first economy by creating shortages of labor and trends toward higher wages. As a

result, the Hungarian labor market operates essentially in a market manner, with freedom to choose and change jobs.

In theory the sole representative of Hungarian workers is the National Council of Trade Unions (Szakszervezetek Orszagos Tanacsa, SZOT), representing some 3.6 million workers. SZOT is governed by a National Congress, which convenes every four years and consists of delegates chosen by member unions. Between Congresses the federation is directed by a 35-member Presidium headed by a president and three vice presidents and assisted by a secretary general as the chief executive.

The new labor code adopted to coincide with the introduction of the NEM in 1968 revised the function of the SZOT, which formerly was limited to mobilizing the workers to rally behind the party. Since then unions have enjoyed veto powers over enterprise managers in some cases. Collective agreements are now negotiated between the union and the individual enterprise management within specified guidelines. Significantly, the Labor Code describes the union as an organ for representing and protecting the interests of workers rather than as a party organ working to increase production. However, since SZOT leaders are also leading party members, there has been little change in the general party-trade union relationship. The SZOT has continued to reflect the party's ideological and political direction and to emphasize national economic development over worker interests.

In 1988 workers were given the option of declining automatic deduction of union dues from their pay, and since then SZOT membership has declined by 10%. The decline has affected all of the SZOT's 19 affiliated unions.

Hungary's first independent union, a grouping of scientific and technical workers (TDDSZ), was launched in the spring of 1988, and it has been followed by two more independent white-collar unions (teachers and motion-picture employees), with prospective groupings of lawyers and journalists in the offing. Despite apparent tolerance of these unions, there is considerable official uneasiness over the directions these unions would follow.

In 1988, the SZOT appeared to be endorsing selective strikes and work stoppages designed to let off steam and secure concessions. In August about 1,500 Pecs coal miners participated in Hungary's first officially acknowledged strike in 43 years. The strike was officially endorsed by the miners' union.

Wages are centrally mandated and are not subject to collective bargaining. Managers have some flexibility in job categorization and in payment of allowances. The Criminal Code provides that persons having no visible means of support and those who are convicted for the second time within two years for refusing to work may be sentenced to imprisonment, reformatory work, fine or internal exile. Annually, some 2,000 persons are convicted under this provision.

The minimum age for employment is 15 years. All workplaces are required by law to provide workers with safe working conditions; a hot meal at heavily subsidized prices; and pay-related benefits, such as overtime. Workers have the right to 15 days of paid vacation every year and one additional day for each year of service. The minimum wage is equal to $57 per month at the official exchange rate. All workers receive free health care and pensions. The average workweek is 45 hours.

Institutionalized unemployment has occurred as a result of efforts to restructure inefficient industries and rationalize labor resources. Workers who lose their jobs as a result of restructuring receive 100% of their pay for six months, 75% for the next three months and 60% for a further six months.

FOREIGN COMMERCE

A dearth of natural resources makes Hungary heavily dependent on foreign trade, which contributes 20% to 25% of national income. One of the main problems of expanding foreign trade, in which Hungary generally runs a deficit, is the poor quality of Hungarian goods competing in world markets. Most industries prefer to produce for the domestic market, where the risks are lower and the earnings higher. Foreign trade also suffers from a lack of flexibility because over half of it by volume is with COMECON countries and determined by long-term bilateral trade agreements, in effect constituting barter trade. This limitation on the freedom of trade serves to perpetuate the existing structure of industry.

Under the NEM, foreign trade was reformed to bring the pressure of foreign competition to bear on the domestic economy, with a view to stimulating greater efficiency through cost reduction and via improvements in the structure and quality of output. However, liberalization has been a slow process because of the potential for price instability and increased balance-of-payments deficits.

State monopoly of foreign trade is maintained through a system of economic regulators intended to guide foreign trade activities. However, innumerable exceptions to the general provisions have been made for individual enterprises for diverse reasons. These regulators consist of what are known as foreign exchange multipliers (in effect, foreign exchange rates used for domestic accounting purposes) and various financial "bridges" that help span the gap between domestic and foreign prices. These bridges include state subsidies, import and export taxes, government rebates and tax remissions, price fluctuation reserve funds, and a customs tariff applicable to Communist countries. Administrative controls include export and import quotas, foreign trade licensing and discretionary credit administration. Different exchange multipliers and financial bridges are applied to the ruble and dollar trading areas because trade with the former is conducted on the basis of bilateral clearing accounts for predetermined lists of commodities at specified prices. Because of the conceptual imperfections and faulty administration of the financial bridges, they have not been as effective as planned. Fluctuations in world market prices have led to wide-ranging changes in profitability. In the years immediately following the NEM, growth in trade reached 40% for exports and 66% for imports, but since then growth rates have been considerably lower and more erratic.

Virtually all trade with Communist states is with COMECON members. The Soviet Union is by far the most important trading partner, accounting for 32.7% of the exports and 28.5% of the imports in 1987. In trade with the West, West Germany, Italy, Austria, the United Kingdom and France account for over 22% of total foreign trade. Foreign trade with the Third World is insignificant because of foreign exchange difficulties. In 1980 Hungary achieved its first balance-of-payments surplus since 1973, but a trade deficit of more than $400 million was recorded in 1986 and a deficit of $361 million in 1987. The current account deficit in convertible currency fell from $1.420 billion in 1986 to $900 million in 1987. The deficit on trade with COMECON countries was eliminated in 1985 and a surplus of 280 million transferable rubles was recorded in 1987.

In 1990 Hungary announced the suspension of all export licenses based on the Soviet ruble. This step was taken to reduce Hungary's trade surplus with the CMEA countries. By March 1990 the Hungary's trade surplus with the Soviet Union approached 1 billion rubles. Contributing to this phenomenon was the decline in the value of Soviet energy deliveries caused by the sag in the world oil prices.

Hungary's trade surpluses with the Soviet Union have caused problems in recent years. One problem stems from the fact that Hungarian exports for the Soviet Union have been produced using imported materials for which Hungary has to pay in hard currency. Another is that these exports contribute to higher inflation since the government subsidizes enterprises producing for the CMEA markets. Large firms dominate these ex-

---

FOREIGN TRADE INDICATORS, 1988

Exports: $9.9 billion (1989)
Imports: $9.5 billion (1989)
Balance of trade: $400 million
Annual growth rate (%), exports: 3.9 (1980–87)
Annual growth rate (%), imports: 1.5 (1980–87)
Ratio of international reserves to imports (in months): 2.9
Value of manufactured exports ($): 6.45 billion
Terms of trade: (1980 = 100): 89
Export Price Index (1985 = 100): 132.3
Import Price Index (1985 = 100): 144.4
Exports of goods as % of GDP: 36.7 (1987)
Imports of goods as % of GDP: 37.8 (1987)

Direction of Trade (%)

	Imports	Exports
EEC	22.8	17.5
U.S.A.	2.0	2.3
East European countries	50.9	54.1
Japan	1.5	0.5

Composition of Trade (%)

	Imports	Exports
Food & agricultural raw materials	12.4	22.5
Ores & minerals	1.6	0.9
Fuels	20.4	4.0
Manufactured goods	65.6	72.6
of which chemicals	13.7	10.9
of which machinery	28.3	35.1

ports, and they are also the most inefficient because quality controls are not strict.

The Soviet-Hungarian memorandum of agreement of 1990 provided for the continued supplies of Soviet energy to Hungary (6.47 million tons in 1990). Starting in 1991 Hungary's ruble surpluses will be converted into dollar reserves and Soviet-Hungarian trade will be accounted for in dollars.

Significant shifts have taken place since 1971 in the composition of imports, from industrial and agricultural raw materials, semifinished products and foods to finished capital goods and manufactured consumer goods. Most of the increase in machinery imports occurred in 1971 after the removal of a high protective tariff against their import from the West. The composition of exports has remained somewhat more stable. Manufactured capital and consumer goods account for almost half the exports, agricultural and food products one-fourth and raw materials and semifinished products another one-fourth.

The commodity pattern of exports reflects the state of Hungary's industrial development. A high proportion of manufactures, machinery, transportation equipment and other capital goods goes to Communist countries, while a larger proportion of agricultural and industrial raw materials and foods go to the West.

Budapest is the site of two major trade fairs: the International Consumer Goods Fair and the International Technical Fair.

TRANSPORTATION & COMMUNICATIONS

Budapest, the hub of the transportation system, is a primary point on the major pipelines and is by far the busiest of the river ports. The highway network brings every town within a half-day's driving distance of the capital, and all major air traffic touches on it. The Danube determined the original location of the city, and that river is part of the city's history and legends.

The rail system is operated by Hungarian State Railways except for the Railway of Gyor–Sopron–Ebenfurt, which is jointly owned and run by Austria and Hungary. Of the total trackage, 7,513 km. (4,669 mi.) are standard gauge, 221 km. (137 mi.) are narrow-gauge and 35 km. (22 mi.) are broad-gauge, connecting with the Soviet lines in the Northeast; 1,128 km. (701 mi.) are double-track; and 1,918 km. (1,192 mi.) are electrified. There is a subway with a network of 28 km. (17 mi.) in Budapest.

The road network consists of 141,163 km. (87,733 mi.), of which 29,796 km. (18,518 mi.) are concrete, asphalt or stone block. Of the country's roads, 66% are unpaved. Superhighways are 297 km. (185 mi.) long and other main or national roads 6,371 km. (3,960 mi.) long. Construction of the Budapest ring superhighway was begun in 1987 and is to be completed in 1990. Intercity bus routes carry nearly half the long-distance passenger traffic. Budapest is one of the few cities in Europe with streetcars, and its per capita streetcar traffic is among the highest in the world. The number of private cars grew from 200,000 in 1970 to 1,660,300 in 1988.

About 1,287 km. (800 mi.) of rivers and canals are

TRANSPORTATION INDICATORS, 1988

Roads, km. (mi.): 141,163 (87,733)
  % paved: 98
Motor vehicles
  Automobiles: 1,660,300
  Trucks 201,890
  Persons per vehicle: 5.7
  Road freight, tonne-km. (ton-mi.): 9.716 billion (6.655 billion)
Railroads
  Track, km. (mi.): 13,133 (8,160); electrified, km. (mi.): 1,918 (1,192)
  Passenger traffic, passenger-km. (passenger-mi.): 11.224 billion (6.974 billion)
  Freight, freight tonne-km. (freight ton-mi.): 22.092 billion (15.131 billion)
Merchant marine
  Vessels: 16
  Total deadweight tonnage: 109,400
Ports
  Number: 2
Air
  Km. (mi.) flown: 18.5 million (11.5 million)
  Passengers: 1,116,000
  Passenger traffic, passenger-km.(passenger-mi.): 1.286 billion (799 million)
  Freight traffic, freight tonne-km. (freight ton-mi.): 15.9 million (10.9 million)
  Airports with scheduled flights: 4
  Airports: 80
  Civil aircraft: 22
Pipelines
  Crude, km. (mi.): 1,204 (748)
  Refined, km. (mi.): 600 (373)
  Natural gas, km. (mi.): 3,800 (2,360)
Inland waterways
  Length, km. (mi.): 1,770 (1,100)
  Cargo, tonne-km. (ton-mi.): 1.914 billion (1.311 billion)

COMMUNICATIONS INDICATORS, 1988

Telephones
  Total (000): 1,609
  Persons per: 6.6
Post office
  Number of post offices: 3,218
  Pieces of mail handled (000): 1,821,847
Telegraph, total traffic (000): 12,371
Telex
  Subscriber lines: 11,345
  Traffic (000 minutes): 172,017
Telecommunications
  1 satellite ground station

TOURISM & TRAVEL INDICATORS, 1988

Total tourism receipts ($): 611 million
Expenditures by nationals abroad ($): 241 million
Number of tourists (000): 9,724
  of whom (%) from
    Czechosovakia, 36.6
    Poland, 14.1
    East Germany, 11.2
    West Germany, 8.0
Average length of stay (nights): 4.6

---

considered permanently navigable, and an additional 322 to 483 km. (200 to 300 mi.) are navigable for limited use at certain times of the year. Even the Danube is frozen over for a month or so during severe winter seasons. Seasonal water flow variations are large. There is no interconnection between the major rivers, and cargo destined for Budapest from points on either the Tisza or the Darava must take long detours into Yugoslavia before reaching the Danube. Within Hungary the Danube is 418 km. (260 mi.) long and the Tisza 442 km. (275 mi.) long. Alternate channels of the Danube provide another 105 km. (65 mi.). The remaining waterways are made up of the Koros, a tributary of the Tisza; the Sio Canal; and the Sarvis, the latter two connecting Lake Balaton with the Danube. The Danube can take large river ships between its middle and lower courses, and small seagoing vessels can navigate a canal that bypasses the Iron Gate cataracts. Shipping on the Danube is fairly dependable, as the channels are deep enough, although ice and floods halt traffic at times in winter. The Tisza is less dependable, as it freezes for longer periods, its channels are shallower and the variations of water flow are greater. However, river controls undertaken since mid-19th century have eliminated over 100 curves and shortened its length by about 467 km. (290 mi.). Most craft on the Danube are barges.

The earliest pipelines were laid just before World War II. A section of the COMECON Friendship Pipeline branches off from its east–west line in Czechoslovakia and brings crude oil from the Soviet Union to Szazha- lombatta, southwest of Budapest. A second international pipeline brings natural gas from Rumania.

The national airline is MALEV (Magyar Legikozleked- esi Vallalat), founded in 1946. Its external traffic covers both Eastern and Western Europe. The main international airport of entry is Ferihegy Airport, on the southeastern outskirts of Budapest. There are no domestic flights.

DEFENSE

The Hungarian People's Army was formed soon after the Communist takeover in 1948. It was thoroughly reorganized in 1956 because some of the army units supported the revolution led by Imre Nagy.

The defense establishment is presided over by the minister of defense, who is the highest-ranking officer in the armed services. Under him the line of command runs through the chiefs of army and air and air defense and a chief of general staff (who also is a deputy minister of defense) to a number of inspectorates and directorates, all headed by deputy ministers of defense. Hungary is the only Warsaw Pact nation not to follow the Soviet pattern of forming military districts.

Military manpower is a major drain on the labor force in a country that faces a serious shortage of workers. On the other hand, the several military training schools help to introduce new skills to the conscripts and help to upgrade their skills by the time they return to civilian life.

About 78% of defense personnel are in the ground forces. Ground force combat units consist of six divisions (the largest basic units in the services) and a few special-purpose units. The major units are not maintained at full strength. Divisions are patterned after the Red Army and have the same regimental structure. Four

motorized-rifle divisions each have one tank regiment, one artillery regiment and three motorized rifle regiments. Two tank divisions each have one artillery regiment, one motorized rifle regiment and three tank regiments.

Deployment is as follows:

5th Army headquarters: Szekesfehervar
III Corps headquarters: Cegled
5th Tank Division: Tata
17th Motorized Rifle Division: Zalaegerszig
9th Motorized Rifle Division: Kaposvar
27th Motorized Rifle Division: Kiskunfelegyhaza
12th Motorized Rifle Division: Gyongyos
8th Motorized Rifle Division: Nyiregyhaza
SCUD Missile Brigade: Tapoica

The air force is relatively small, and its air defense mission is shared with the ground forces. Although a landlocked country, Hungary has a long-established navy (its Nazi leader during World War II was Admiral Horthy de Nagybanya). The naval fleet consists primarily of patrol boats, gunboats, minelayers and minesweepers patrolling the Danube.

About 60% of servicemen are two-year conscripts; the remainder are extended-service and regular NCO's and regular officers. Preconscription military training is compulsory.

DEFENSE INDICATORS, 1988

Defense budget ($): 2.67 billion
% of central budget: 8.1
% of GNP: 4.4
Military expenditures per capita ($): 322
Military expenditures per soldier ($): 26,969
Military expenditures per sq. km. (per sq. m.) ($): 27,725 (71,826)
Total strength of armed forces: 99,000
   Per 1,000: 9.4
Reserves: 127,000
Arms exports ($): 200 million
Arms imports ($): 100 million

Personnel & Equipment

Army
   Personnel: 77,000
   Organization:
   1 army; 3 corps headquarters; 5 tank brigades; 10 motor rifle brigades
   Equipment: 1,300 main battle tanks; 100 light tanks; 700 reconnaissance vehicles; 350 mechanized infantry combat vehicles; 375 towed artillery; 110 self-propelled artillery; 50 multiple-rocket launchers; 24 SSM launchers; 100 mortars; 200 antitank guided weapons; 125 recoilless launchers; 150 antitank guns; 130 air defense guns; 490 SAM's
Navy: (Danube River flotilla)
   10 patrol boats, gunboats, minelayers and minesweepers.
Air force
   Personnel: 22,000
   Organization: 1 air division
   Equipment: 135 combat aircraft; 40 armored helicopters

Hungary is a member of the Warsaw Pact, and the alliance requires the standardization of training programs, weapons and tactical doctrines. The annual training cycle culminates when the troops are ready to participate in the large-scale summer or autumn maneuvers. Most noncommissioned officers receive their training in special technical schools. The main base for general administrative noncommissioned officer training is the Central Noncommissioned Officer School. Military academies training officers have the standing of universities. The highest of these academies is Miklos Zrinyi Military Academy, which is a command and general staff college. A second trains air force officers and a third both regular armed forces personnel and police and border force personnel.

Enlisted men remain in the reserves until 50 and officers until 60. The Hungarian National Defense Association directs a large portion of defense reserve activities outside regular military units. A five-year national military educational program was introduced into primary and secondary schools beginning in 1968–69.

EDUCATION

The modern history of Hungarian education goes back to Empress Maria Theresa's *Ratio Educationis*, a codex that created the first unified state school system, comprising a three- or four-year primary school, a three-year middle school and a two-year secondary school. Following the Compromise of 1867 some minor changes were introduced into the system and the duration of schooling was increased to 15 and later reduced to 13 years. A three-year teachers' training college was established, and in 1883 a new type of science-oriented secondary school, the *real iskola*, was authorized. The next radical renewal in the system took place after World War II. The School Act of 1948 laid the foundations of the educational system of Hungary as it exists today.

The constitutional foundations of Hungarian education are found in several documents. The Constitution of 1949 declares the right to education as a fundamental right of all Hungarian citizens. Law 3 of 1961 modernized the curriculum and introduced a new type of school, the technical secondary school (*szakkozepiskola*). Act 13 of 1963 fixed the compulsory 10-year school attendance, starting from September following the child's sixth birthday. Act 6 of 1966 created a new type of technical secondary school (*szamunkakepzo iskola*). Act 24 of 1973 linked higher academic studies and productive work.

Schooling is compulsory for 10 years, from ages six to 16. The school year runs from the beginning of September to the end of June. Higher education is similarly organized, with the curricula divided into annual units, with periods set apart for "production work."

There are no private schools as such. However the churches are permitted to maintain general secondary schools. There are 10 such Catholic, Calvinist or Jewish schools. Although enjoying a certain amount of curricular autonomy, they are fully incorporated into the public school system with regard to admissions and certification procedures as well as the financing and appointment of teachers.

The medium of instruction is Hungarian, but there are separate schools for Germans, Slovaks, Yugoslavs and Rumanians living in Hungary. There are 20 schools where the teaching is entirely in the native language of the students and 267 schools where non-Hungarian languages are used as the medium for certain subjects. A special problem is posed by the Gypsies, who are not considered as a minority nor as a distinct ethnic group.

Kindergartens (*ovodak szama*) enroll preschool children aged three to six. The enrollment rate is as high as 90% in certain urban areas, and many classrooms are overcrowded. Kindergartens also are maintained by factories, companies and institutions.

Primary education is eight years long, divided into a four-year lower and a four-year upper division. The lower division classes are taught by a single teacher; in the upper division each subject is taught by a different teacher, generally a specialist. Those who repeat grades have to remain in elementary school until they reach 16. In 1978 a new law made every other Saturday free for students. Owing to the 11-day teaching cycle, lesson schedules are not broken down by weeks. Gifted students are placed in intensive courses, where the number of class hours per week is higher. Singing and music begin from the first grade, Russian from the fourth grade and other foreign languages and mathematics from the upper grades. Promotion is automatic if the student attends school regularly.

Secondary education is organized in a series of middle schools, with the general secondary school making up the academic sector and the technical secondary schools and the trade schools comprising the vocational sector. The general secondary school or the *gimnazium* is the most traditional type of school in Hungary. It includes training schools and experimental schools that enjoy great prestige. Some secondary schools have divisions for pupils with aptitudes in special learning areas. More than half of all secondary students work in study groups, and each year national competitions are held for competitors from these groups in subject areas such as history or geography. At the end of four years *gimnazium* students take maturity examinations.

Technical secondary schools are divided into four-year schools and three-year schools. Workshop practice may take place either at school or in participating factories. The four-year school offers a diploma, which allows students to pursue postsecondary studies. The three-year school trains skilled workers but does not provide full secondary education. Training is provided in 126 trades.

Disabled children are not integrated into regular classrooms but are taught in special institutions. Hungarian special education, extending back 150 years, has achieved international reputation in several areas. Another educational sector in which Hungary has excelled is music, where Zoltan Kodaly has become one of the most influential names. His method of music education—relative solmization—has been adopted around the world and particularly in two schools that bear his name: one in Budapest and the other at Kecskemet, the composer's birthplace.

Higher education is run by the state and is not a quasi-independent sector, as in many Western countries. Col-

```
EDUCATION INDICATORS, 1988

Literacy
    Total (%): 98.9
    Male (%): 99.2
    Female (%): 98.6
First level
    Schools: 3,540
    Teachers: 90,925
    Students: 1,277,300
    Student–teacher ratio: 14:1
    Net enrollment rate (%): 97.1
    Females (%): 49
Second level
    Schools: 186
    Teachers: 8,368
    Students: 125,811
    Student–teacher ratio: 15:1
    Net enrollment rate (%): 69
    Females (%): 48
Vocational
    Schools: 758
    Teachers: 22,467
    Students: 373,187
    Student–teacher ratio: 17:1
Third level
    Institutions: 54
    Teachers: 15,302
    Students: 99,025
    Student–teacher ratio: 7:1
    Gross enrollment rate (%): 15.4
    Graduates per 100,000 age 20–24: 929
    % of population over 25 with post secondary education: 7.0
    Females (%): 53
Foreign study
    Foreign students in national universities: 2,520
    Students abroad: 844
        of whom in
            United States, 96
            West Germany, 333
            Austria, 80
            Switzerland, 83
Public expenditures (national currency)
    Total: 51,361,490,000 forints
    % of GNP: 5.4
    % of national budget: 6.4
    % current expenditures: 89
```

```
GRADUATES, 1984

Total: 25,089
Education: 9,705
Humanities & religion: 679
Fine & applied arts: 235
Law: 1,387
Social & behavioral sciences: 508
Commerce & business: 1,863
Service trades: 218
Natural sciences: 308
Mathematics & computer science: 289
Medicine: 2,496
Engineering: 2,276
Architecture: 980
Industrial programs: 2,219
Transportation & communications: 361
Agriculture, forestry, fisheries: 1,421
Other: 144
```

lege admissions are based on the results of a college entrance examination. The administration of universities is vested in the rectors and deans, who share their powers with university councils and faculty councils. Universities and colleges represent the two stages of a continuum. The former trains students for research with greater theoretical inputs, while the latter trains specialists for practical purposes. Female participation in higher education is much higher than that of males because males tend to follow technical opportunities during collegegoing years. Enrollment is limited not only by the capacity of the institutions but also by forecasts of labor demand by economists. There are too many candidates in the case of certain institutions and faculties. While school education is free, students pay a fee for higher education, but 90% of students receive some kind of grant support. In addition to traditional study scholarships, social scholarships are granted to students who contract to work in rural areas for five years.

The central body controlling national education is the Ministry of Education. Its principal advisory organ is the National Education Council. Elementary schools are maintained by local councils and secondary schools by county councils. Counties exert partial influence on the content of schooling and have some role in the distribution of funds within the framework of the annual national budget. While limited decentralization of educational administration has strengthened initiative and innovation at the local level, it has been criticized for widening inequalities between rich and poor districts.

Adult education is conducted primarily through evening and correspondence courses. On a more informal level, many cultural institutions are actively involved in promoting lifelong learning, through study circles, exhibitions, lectures, literacy theaters, and symposia.

Secondary teachers have been trained in universities since 1959. Teachers of grades five to eight study in four-year teacher training colleges; teachers of the first four grades of the elementary school study in a three-year teacher training institute, and kindergarten teachers are trained in a two-year teacher training institute. Teachers are organized in the Teachers' Union, which is primarily concerned with working conditions. The Hungarian Pedagogic Society functions as a kind of in-service training agency.

LEGAL SYSTEM

The Hungarian legal system has both civil law and common law elements. The civil law system derives from the Civil Code of 1960. The Supreme Court has the power to declare legislative acts unconstitutional.

The judicial system functions under a law promulgated in 1973 that substantially reformed a law of June 1952. The system comprises local courts, labor courts, county courts, the Capital (Metropolitan) Court and the Supreme Court. Among the changes introduced under the 1973 law was an expansion of the jurisdiction of the courts to deal with two categories of essentially economic disputes: those involving individual workers and employers and those between state enterprises. Until 1973 labor disputes had been handled almost exclusively by enterprise arbitration committees in the first instance and by regional committees on appeal, and disputes between enterprises by economic arbitration committees. The 1973 law also permits citizens to appeal to the courts the decisions of the state administrative organs, and the courts to review decisions of these organs on the basis of legality.

At the base of the court hierarchy are the local courts (district courts in Budapest and municipal courts in other cities). The county courts and the Capital Court in Budapest hear appeals from the decisions of these courts. The county courts act as courts of first instance in certain serious criminal cases as well as for civil suits of a certain magnitude.

The Supreme Court is primarily a court of appeal, but it also may function as a court of first instance in important cases. Its decisions may be appealed to a council of the Supreme Court. When the Supreme Court acts as a court of appeals it is divided into councils, such as civil, criminal, economic, labor or military. Appeals from these councils on points of law may be heard by the Presidential Council.

Courts are manned by two kinds of officers: professional judges and lay assessors, except when appeals or certain kinds of civil cases are heard, when only professional judges sit on the bench. According to law, lay assessors have the same rights and obligations as professional judges. Appeals are heard by three professional judges. The president of the Supreme Court is elected by the National Assembly for a term of five years. Judges are elected by the Presidential Council for an indefinite period. Lay assessors are elected by local municipal councils.

The 1973 law as modified in 1979 gives the plenum of the Supreme Court the power to issue "guiding principles or decisions in principle" when such guidance is necessary "in the interests of guaranteeing uniformity of judicial practice or on questions of legal interpretation." Three officials—the president of the Supreme Court, the minister of justice and the supreme prosecutor—may propose that the Supreme Court consider specific matters for the purpose of issuing such decisions. The minister of justice and the supreme prosecutor may attend the plenum of the Supreme Court with advisory powers. The minister of labor and the secretary general of the National Council of Trade Unions attend when labor matters are being considered. The guiding principle and the decisions in principle are binding on the lower courts. By contrast, the decisions of the Supreme Court acting as an appeals court in specific cases are not binding as legal precedent, although they may in practice influence the decisions of the lower courts.

In matters that do not require issuance of a guiding principle but may require a statement of position by the Supreme Court, one of the councils or collegia of the Supreme Court may state such a position on issues within its field of competence. Such statements of position are not binding on lower courts.

The general operation of the court system is supervised by the minister of justice. In the case of labor affairs, his authority is exercised in consultation with the minister of labor and the secretary general of the National Council of Trade Unions. The law explicitly states that the minister of justice must not violate the principle of the independece of judges in the course of carrying out his responsibilities nor directly or indirectly influence decisions in cases under consideration by the courts. The most important task of the minister of justice is to "evaluate the social effect of the judgment activity of the courts, analyze the social causes of the violation of law and take or initiate measures to end them."

Supervision over observance of the law is vested in the supreme prosecutor, who heads a hierarchy of public prosecution offices organized on the national, county and district levels. Among his chief responsibilities are criminal investigation and prosecution and supervision of the legality of the actions of state, social and cooperative organs. The three highest organs of state—the National Assembly, the Presidential Council and the Council of Ministers—are excluded from his jurisdiction. Theoretically, the prosecutor's office is not subject to control by any other state organ. He is elected by the National Assembly to a four-year term and is constitutionally accountable to it for his performance. The deputies of the supreme prosecutor are appointed by the Presidential Council. The chief military prosecutor functions as one of his deputies. The supreme prosecutor is authorized to attend in an advisory capacity sessions of the National Assembly, the Presidential Council, the Council of Ministers, the Central People's Control Committee and plenary sessions of the Supreme Court. He can initiate actions to suspend the immunity of National Assembly deputies and to institute criminal proceedings against a professional judge.

The Penal Code was amended in 1989 to conform with the democratic nature of the new Constitution. No one may be executed for crimes against the state. Amendments to the law on criminal procedure enhance the rights of the suspect and extend the scope of the defense counsel. They also abolished prolonged prison terms for certain recidivists.

There are four classes of prison regimes: three classes of penitentiaries, and local jails. The same prison complex may include more than one class of prisons, either in separate buildings or in different sections of the same building. Rehabilitation programs vary widely, depending on the facilities available. However, all inmates are required to work. Labor camps, a familiar phenomenon in the early decades of the Communist regime, no longer exist. The prison population has declined sharply, since many antistate activities have been decriminalized. There are few inmates serving time for political or economic crimes.

In 1990 the National Assembly passed a law amnestying thousands of prisoners in Hungarian jails. All prisoners serving first sentences of less than one year were released. Prison terms of between one and three years were reduced by one-third and those of over three years by one-quarter. All pregnant women, women with small children artd the terminally ill serving any sentence also were released. Those sentenced for serious offenses, such as rape, murder or terrorism, did not benefit from the amnesty.

LAW ENFORCEMENT

Hungary's transformation from one of the most repressive Stalinist states in Eastern Europe to one of its most liberal is nowhere more clearly reflected than in its law enforcement apparatus. The hated Security Police, the first target of the 1956 Revolution, was abolished in the same year. Although rebuilt after 1957, it was gradually shorn of its powers, and the civil police asserted itself in all areas of law enforcement activity.

The Civil Police or the People's Police (Rendorseg) function in local jurisdictions but are centrally organized under the Ministry of the Interior. Various types of special units exist within the force, such as the Air Police and the Water Police. The People's Police also issue identification cards and maintain records on all nationals and aliens. Operationally, the force is divided into towns, districts, boroughs and stations. Training is provided at the Police Officers' Academy, established in 1971.

The People's Police are assisted by a number of para-police organizations. The first is the Workers' Militia or Workers' Guard (Munkas Orseg), formed in 1957 to suppress the 1956 revolutionaries. Organized along the lines of a national guard, the militia was drawn from workers with party credentials. Unit commanders are trained at the militia's central school in Budapest.

Internal security troops (belso karhatalom) have existed since the earliest days of the Communist regime. Its personnel are most frequently referred to as interior troops and occasionally as the constabulary. They are lightly armed but have considerable mobile equipment, as they must be able to respond to calls from any part of the country. Career men may serve on a voluntary basis, but recruits are acquired from the annual draft of 18-year-olds. The conscripted youth serve from two to three years. Interior troops are a uniformed force and operate in typically military units. Uniforms are the same as those worn by army personnel but are distinguished by blue backgrounds on rank shoulder boards and collar insignia.

The Industrial Guard and the Government Guard Command also are elements formed after the 1956 Revolution. Industrial Guard units are charged with preventing sabotage rampant during the postrevolution period in 1956 and also with containing pilferage. Now the men serve as full-time guards on a regular, salaried basis. The Government Guard Command (Kormanyarseg Parancsnoksag), formed in 1972 under the Ministry of the Interior, serve in the capital as an elite unit on ceremonial occasions.

Although the Security Police is officially known under the initials BKH, people still refer to it by its old hated initials, AVH. Its fangs drawn, it generally conducts its operations unobtrusively.

The Frontier Guard is similar to the Security Police in personnel strength, organization, training and equipment. They also wear army uniforms. The force is deployed on the land boundaries with Yugoslavia, Rumania and Austria.

The State Security Service, the primary agency responsible for the police, began to disintegrate in late 1989 following the breakup of the monolithic Communist regime. Most of the 30,000 policemen had belonged to the HSWP. Some 30 to 40 policemen left the party and the service every day during late 1989 and early 1990. Older policemen in senior positions retired early making it necessary to appoint new chiefs of police in 17 out of 19 county police headquarters. After a wiretapping scandal involving the State Security Service, policemen started leaving en masse. Further, 120 top policemen were dismissed for their role in various anti-human-rights activities. The difficulty in finding replacements for policemen who are leaving the service has made it necessary for the Antall government to employ former agents of the State Security Service.

The insecurity within the police service has contributed to a rapid increase in the crime rate, which in 1989 rose by more 21%. Some 230,000 crimes were committed during the year, most of them robberies and theft. Only about 40% of the cases were solved.

Although crimes against private and socialist property have decreased since the 1950s, violent crimes have increased sufficiently to cause official concern. Alcohol is a factor in about a fourth of all crimes and in about a half or more of attempted murders, crimes against juveniles and crimes against public order. Hungary's suicide rate is the highest in the world, and at least half of all suicides are committed during or after heavy drinking. On-the-job drinking has become such a problem that plant managers are required to use breath analyzers on workers before each work session.

HEALTH

Standards of health and longevity have risen remarkably since the end of World War II. Before the war Hungary had the highest mortality rate in Europe from tuberculosis. After the war high priority was given to fighting this disease, and by the late 1980s its incidence had been controlled, along with that of other dreaded diseases, such as syphilis, typhoid and malaria. Suicide still ranks high, as the fifth most important cause of death, and it is the single most important cause of death among youths between ages 15 and 20.

The state has the constitutional responsibility to provide free health care for all its citizens. Under that provision, the national health service is administered and financed by the central government. The service is free for all state workers, but cooperative workers have to pay a small monthly fee and self-employed persons must pay the full costs.

The cornerstone of the health service is the district physician, who acts as the family physician for all inhabitants in his area. At the next level is the polyclinic, which provides outpatient services in specialized fields. Polyclinics exist in most districts. The services of the district physician and the polyclinic are supplemented by factory health services in larger economic enterprises. A hospital network rounds out the health service by providing inpatient facilities. The hospital network is hierarchically organized, with the district or municipal hospitals at the base, county hospitals above them and specialized national institutes at the top. The general hospital network is supplemented by extended care facilities for patients suffering from serious or chronic diseases, as well as by maternity homes.

One peculiar feature of the health care system is the traditionally important role of medical baths. The chemical composition of the Hungarian spas is reputed to be particularly effective for rheumatism, arthritis and other ailments, and the spas attract visitors from all over Europe.

Considerable emphasis is placed on health education and regular checkups of special groups, such as schoolchildren and factory workers. Specialized mobile units periodically screen the rural population for early detection of any health problem.

Physicians and auxiliary medical personnel are state employees. Physicians are allowed to see private patients in their free time, and many physicians have lucrative private practices. Persons in higher income groups prefer to use the services of a physician of their own choosing rather than one assigned to them by the health service.

HEALTH INDICATORS, 1988

Health personnel
  Physicians: 30,924
    Persons per: 343
  Dentists: 4,499
  Nurses: 43,579
  Pharmacists: 4,506
  Midwives: 2,605
Hospitals
  Number: N.A.
  Number of beds: 104,824
  Beds per 10,000: 99
Admissions/discharges
  Per 10,000: 2,091
  Bed occupancy rate (%): 76.7
  Average length of stay (days): 13
Public health expenditures
  As % of national budget: 3.6
  Per capita: $36.70
Vital statistics
  Crude death rate per 1,000: 13.4
  Decline in death rate: 29.2 (1965–84)
  Life expectancy at birth (years): males, 65.3; females, 73.2
  Infant mortality rate per 1,000 live births: 17.4
  Child mortality rate (ages 1–4 years) per 1,000: Insignificant
  Maternal mortality rate per 100,000 live births: 19.2
Cause of death per 100,000
  Infectious & parasitic diseases: 9.8
  Cancer: 277.2
  Endocrine & metabolic disorders: 21.2
  Diseases of the nervous system: 11.2
  Diseases of the circulatory system: 739.3
  Diseases of the digestive system: 75.7
  Accidents, poisoning & violence: 122.2
  Diseases of the respiratory system: 72.4

FOOD & NUTRITION

Food and nutrition standards, although lower than those in Western Europe, compare favorably with those

---

FOOD & NUTRITION INDICATORS, 1988

Per capita daily food consumption, calories: 3,536
Per capita daily consumption, protein, g. (oz): 95.3 (3.4)
Calorie intake as % of FAO recommended minimum requirement: 132
% of calorie intake from vegetable products: 64
% of calorie intake from animal products: 36
Food expenditures as % of total household expenditures: 39.5
% of total calories derived from:
  cereals: 30.2
  potatoes: 2.6
  meat & poultry: 13.7
  fish: 0.3
  fats & oils: 19.1
  eggs & milk: 8.2
  fruits & vegetables: 4.3
  Other: 21.7
Per capita consumption of foods, kg. (lb.); l. (pt.)
  Potatoes: 58 (127.9)
  Wheat: 112.0 (247.0)
  Rice: 3.7 (8.1)
  Fresh vegetables: }
  Fruits (total):   } 155.0 (341.7)
    Citrus: 6.3 (13.9)
  Eggs: 320 (705.6)
  Honey: 0.1 (0.2)
  Fish: 2.5 (5.5)
  Milk: 179.9 (396.7)
  Butter: 2.8 (6.1)
  Cheese: 4.3 (9.5)
  Meat (total): 76.5 (168.6)
    Beef & veal: 6.9 (15.2)
    Pig meat: 42.8 (94.4)
    Poultry: 50.1 (110.5)
    Mutton, lamb & goat: 0.4 (0.9)
  Sugar: 49.5 (109.1)
  Chocolate: 3.2 (7.0)
  Margarine: 8.0 (17.6)
  Beer, l. (pt.): 92.0 (194.5)
  Wine, l. (pt.): 25.0 (52.8)
  Alcoholic liquors, l. (pt.): 5.4 (11.6)
  Soft drinks, l. (pt.): 11.0 (23.2)
  Mineral waters, l. (pt.): 17.0 (35.9)
  Coffee: 0.2 (0.4)
  Tea: 3.0 (6.6)
  Cocoa: 0.9 (2.0)

---

in Eastern Europe. The staple food in most diets is bread, which is consumed in large quantities. Bread is generally made from wheat flour blended with rye, corn or potato flour. The other major dietary item is soup in myriad forms. The most popular is goulash (gyulas), which is a heavy soup rather than a stew. The supply of meat is limited, and meat consumption is low. Pork is the most widely consumed meat, followed by poultry and beef. Consumption of fish and milk also is low. Fresh milk is seldom consumed, even by children, but is used in considerable quantities with coffee. The consumption of eggs is more satisfactory and accounts for much of the protein intake. Fruits and vegetables are primary export items, and in times of short supply their prices are beyond the reach of large segments of the population. A high percentage of fruits and vegetables is grown by peasants in their private plots and, because demand usually is high, they tend to sell their production rather than consume it themselves.

Wine and beer are the most popular beverages. Because of the incidence of alcoholism, alcoholic beverages are taxed highly in an effort to discourage their consumption.

MEDIA & CULTURE

Hungarian press historians consider a publication called *Mercurius Hungaricus*, printed in Latin between 1705 and 1710, as the nation's first newspaper, but others reserve this title for a weekly called *Nova Poseoniensis*, also in Latin, which first appeared in 1721. Although the first newspaper in Hungarian, *Magyar Hirmondo*, did not appear until 1780, a number of Hungarian-language periodicals appeared in the mid-18th century, mostly published in Vienna or Pozsony (Bratislava, then the capital of Hungary). The reform era of the 19th century was a prosperous period for Hungarian journalism. There was a great demand for political newspapers beginning in the early 1800s. The ferment preceding the Revolution of 1848 saw the birth of a number of short-lived but significant publications, including two published by Lajos Kossuth, the leader of the 1848 uprising: *Orsaggyulesi Tudositasok (Parliamentary Information)* and *Pesti Hirlap (News of Pest)*. The failure of the uprising, however, marked a setback for the press. The laws of March 1848 pertaining to freedom of the press and abolition of censorship were rescinded, and many newspapers were suppressed. But after the Compromise of 1867, conditions improved again. The labor movement launched some major newspapers, the most notable of which was *Nepszava* in 1877. It still is being published by the National Council of Trade Unions.

In the early 20th century the typical daily emerged. By 1906 a total of 1,787 publications were being published in the country, compared to 109 in 1867. In Budapest the reader had a choice of 39 dailies—30 in Hungarian and nine in German. The largest in terms of circulation was *Az Ujsag*. This growth was remarkable if only for the fact that a large part of the population was illiterate.

Between the two world wars the press suffered, first at the hands of Bela Kun's Communist regime and then at the hands of the fascist regime of Admiral Miklos Horthy de Nagybanya. The latter reimposed prior censorship and drove Communist papers underground. Newspapers were forced to seek permits for publication. Newsprint supply was controlled, and subsidies from the Press Fund were used to keep newspapers from straying from the government line. During the late 1930s Horthy de Nagybanya became more and more openly dictatorial and carried out a series of "purifications" of publications and journalists. Most of the older papers were weeded out one by one. Only two of the independent newspapers survived the last of these "purifications" by the time of the Nazi occupation in 1944. Despite all these restrictions, the Hungarian press probably was the most diverse and most interesting in southeastern Europe before World War II.

With the Communist takeover in 1948, the Hungarian press again lost its freedom. Whereas there had been 101 dailies, the press was reduced to four dailies, all run by the Hungarian Workers' Party or its mass organiza-

---

MEDIA INDICATORS, 1988

Newspapers (1990)
  Number of dailies: 29
  Circulation (000): 3,045
  Circulation per 1,000: 288
  Number of nondailies: 94
  Circulation (000): 6,007
  Circulation per 1,000: 562
  Number of periodicals: 1,678
  Circulation (000): 13,278
  Newsprint consumption
    Total (tons): 66,200
    Per capita, kg. (lb.): 6.2 (13.7)
Book publishing
  Number of titles: 8,206
Broadcasting
  Annual expenditures (national currency): 3.1 billion
  Number of employees: 5,307
Radio
  Number of transmitters: 51
  Number of radio receivers (000): 5,500
    Persons per radio receiver: 1.9
  Total annual program hours: 23,603
Television
  Television transmitters: 109
  Number of television receivers (000): 2,958
    Persons per television receiver: 3.6
  Total annual program hours: 4,472
Cinema
  Number of fixed cinemas: 3,600
  Seating capacity: 558,000
    Seats per 1,000: 51.2
  Annual attendance (million): 68
    Per capita: 6.4
  Gross box office receipts (national currency): 606.8 million
Films
  Production of long films: 23
  Import of long films: 198
    20.2% from United States
    9.6% from France
    19.2% from USSR
    6.6% from Italy

CULTURAL & ENVIRONMENTAL INDICATORS, 1988

Public libraries
  Number: 9,647
  Volumes (000): 49,405
  Registered borrowers: 2,261,000
  Loans per 1,000: 5,370
Museums
  Number: 661
  Annual attendance (000): 19,572
  Attendance per 1,000: 1,840
Performing arts
  Facilities: 41
  Number of performances: 12,960
  Annual attendance (000): 5,957
  Attendance per 1,000: 560
Ecological sites: 36
Botanical gardens & zoos: 14

---

tions. Ownership of all printing plants was transferred to the people, a common euphemism for the Communist Party. By 1953 the now totally muzzled press had been enlarged to 22 dailies and 88 weeklies. Most important of these was *Szabad Nep (Free People)*, which was modeled closely on *Pravda*. All newspapers were operated under the tight control of the Information

Bureau and under the supervision of the Agitation and Propaganda Section of the party's Central Committee.

A dissident press soon appeared, led by *Irodalmi Ujsag (Literary Gazette)*, the organ of the Hungarian Writers' Association. It received a great deal of the blame for the 1956 Revolution and also paid dearly through mass trials, arrests and deportations of journalists. After the uprising, the regime clamped down even more severely than before, and it was not until the late 1960s that the controls were relaxed, and even then very cautiously.

The Hungarian press in 1990 consists of 29 dailies, six of which are published in Budapest and the others in the provincial capitals or other major cities. Most of the Budapest papers circulate nationally. All major dailies are printed in Hungarian, although the small-circulation Budapest daily *Daily News/Neuste Nachrichten* appears in both English and German. Each of the national minority groups—German, Slovak, Yugoslav and Rumanian—has a publication in its own language; all of these publications are weeklies, except that in Rumanian, which appears every two weeks. Unlike in other Communist countries, the religious press is active, with 16 publications.

Of the total circulation of 3,045,198, provincial dailies account for 1,328,000.

```
┌─────────────────────────────────────────────────┐
│               PRINCIPAL DAILIES                 │
│ Daily                             Circulation   │
│ Daily News                             15,000   │
│ Esti Hirlap (Evening Journal)         200,000   │
│ Magyar Hirlap (Hungarian Journal)      55,000   │
│ Magyar Nemzet (Hungarian Nation)      105,000   │
│ Nepsport (People's Sport)             275,000   │
│ Nepszabadsag (People's Freedom)       705,000   │
│ Nepszava (Voice of the People)        295,000   │
└─────────────────────────────────────────────────┘
```

Napszabadsag is the principal daily as the central organ of the Hungarian Socialist Workers' Party. The paper most respected for the quality of its news coverage is *Magyar Nemzet*. Some 80% of the dailies are sold by subscription. The circulation of the papers enables them to maintain high standards of production. Further, the state gives the press—even the religious press—direct subsidies. There is no private ownership of publications, but in the 1980s many independent publishing organizations began to receive licenses. Most dailies run six to 12 pages, usually broadsheet size, although some are tabloids. Only one, *Esti Hirlap*, is an evening paper. Most publish six days a week, printing on Sundays but skipping Mondays. The Sunday editions are large and well produced, with numerous sections and supplements.

Weekly papers enjoy considerable popularity and large circulation. The largest-selling are *Radio es Televizioujsag (Radio and Television News)*, 1,350,000; *Nok Lapja (Women's Journal)*, 975,000; *Szabad Fold (Free Soil)*, 600,000; *Kepes Ujsag (Illustrated News)*, 400,000; *Ludas Matyi*, 352,000; *Vasarnapi Hirek (Sunday News)*, 320,000; and *Orszag-Vilag (Land and World)*, 208,000.

Specialized publications include 42 cultural publica-

tions, 35 medical journals, 108 scientific journals, 24 agricultural papers and 16 religious publications.

The NEM has had little impact on the economic framework of the media other than to enhance the role of advertising. In comparison with other Eastern bloc capitals, Budapest is awash with neon signs and poster ads. Newspapers carry whole pages of ads, mainly of the small classified type. Advertising also exists on radio and television, although to a much smaller extent. The state-run Hungarian advertising agency, known as Mahir, handles about a third of all advertising in the country.

Hungary has a vigorous samizdat publishing sector. Official moves against it appeared to grow fewer in 1988. A number of independent or quasi-independent publications were allowed to appear in 1988, including *Kapu (Gate)*, *Hitel (Credit)* and *Reform*.

In 1990 the Hungarian press underwent a major transformation. Foreign investors now own major shares in three of the country's four major dailies and a number of provincial newspapers. These investors include Rupert Murdoch, Robert Maxwell, and the Springer chain and the Bertelsmann group of Germany. The most independent major publication is *Datum*, founded in April 1989. Other independent papers include such general-interest publications as the weeklies *Vilag (Words)* and *Beszelo (Speaker)* as well as the satirical biweekly *Magyar Narancs (Hungarian Orange)* of the Free Democratic Union. The big success story of the press is the lively color tabloid *Reform*, in which Rupert Murdoch holds a 50% interest. At 400,000 copies weekly, it has become one of Hungary's most important publications.

The official status of the press is in a state of transition and therefore subject to some ambiguity. There is no specific censorship office and no mandatory censorship. This does not mean the absence of controls. Even so, published criticisms are as trenchant as those published in the Western press. Kadar himself was satirized on national TV and made the butt of cartoons until his exit. Comments that would be taboo in neighboring Communist countries are published as a matter of course without fear of reprisal. Hungarian journalism also is free of the kind of cant and shibboleth that is a hallmark of the Communist press elsewhere. This does not mean the absence of propaganda, but it has to compete with free opinion. The latitude in terms of government control is greater in media perceived to have less direct political impact—book publishers, libraries and films—and more stringent on mass media such as press, television and radio.

Unlike the Constitution of 1949, which declared all media to be the property of the state, the 1972 revision puts only radio and television in that category. Freedom of speech and press are "guaranteed" in accordance with the interests of socialism. Under the Penal Code, incitement, warmongering, dissemination of rumors, and libel against living or dead persons constitute offenses. Correction of false or misleading statements is required under law. Another government decree requires government offices to answer written requests from the media for information.

The media are under the direct control of the Information Bureau (IB), which has overall responsibility for all state information activities, its head is the principal spokesperson for the government.

Foreign publications are readily available in the country. There is no jamming of foreign broadcasting. Newspapers in western Hungary actually carry regularly the schedules of Austrian TV programs for the benefit of their readers. A foreign correspondent faces few official hurdles in obtaining special visas or accreditation necessary to work in Hungary. He may file whatever he pleases, although consistently unfavorable reporting may result in a rejection of a subsequent visa request.

The national news agency is Magyar Tavirati Iroda (MTI), an arm of the Information Bureau. MTI is composed of four major departments: cultural and internal policy, economics, agriculture and sports. It also publishes the Budapest daily *Daily News/Neuste Nachrichten* and a number of special bulletins. HTI receives the regular services of some 20 foreign agencies but relies heavily on Tass.

Standard radio broadcasting started in Hungary on December 1, 1925. The Hungarian Broadcasting Company, which operated the system, was virtually destroyed in World War II, and its Budapest antenna tower, one of the tallest in Europe, was demolished. Radio Budapest was on the air again in 1945.

The radio network, Magyar Radio, is part of Magyar Radio es Televiz (MRT). Its two principal radio stations are both in Budapest; Radio Kossuth, which transmits Program I, is broadcast on medium wave 24 hours a day. Radio Petofi transmits Program II broadcasts on medium wave during the morning hours and on ultra short wave in the evening. In addition, Radio Bartok, a very-high-frequency transmitter, broadcasts musical and literary programs. There are daily broadcasts in English, German and five other foreign languages and separate programs for Hungarians living abroad. Radio licenses were abolished in 1980.

Television was introduced in 1957. Magyar Televizio has two channels: The first broadcasts about 66 hours a week; the second about 20 hours a week, mostly in color. There are over 100 relay stations.

Book publishing has a long history in Hungary. By the 14th century some Hungarian libraries had as many as 200 to 300 manuscript volumes. The first Hungarian printing press was established in Buda in 1472 by Andras Hess. The first book printed in Hungary, *Chronica Hungarorum* (History of Hungary), appeared in 1473 in Latin. By the time of the Revolution of 1848 the largest publishing houses were owned by the Roman Catholic Church in Budapest and the Calvinist Church in Debrecen. The book publishing sector was reorganized in 1948. All large publishing companies were nationalized, and the National Book Office was founded. In 1949 book publishing was separated from printing and bookselling and placed under the Ministry of Culture. In 1959 the Publishing House of the Hungarian Academy of Sciences was reorganized. Smaller publishing houses were placed under specialized ministries under the broad direction of the Committee of Ministerial Publishers. The Publishers' Council was founded in 1953 and the Publishers' Board in 1954. Import and export of books are handled by Kultura.

The earliest known library was the Bibliotheca Corvina, established by King Matyas I, who reigned from 1458 to 1490. This library is believed to have had 7,000 volumes. The 18th and 19th centuries witnessed rapid growth of libraries as new universities were established. Ferenc Szechenyi founded the National Library in 1802 with his donation of 25,000 books and 2,000 manuscripts. Josef Teleki founded the Library of the Hungarian Academy of Sciences with a donation of 30,000 books. By 1885 there were 2,270 libraries with a total stock of 7.3 million works. Within the next century the number of libraries grew fourfold. They included nine major national libraries, public education libraries (owned by trade unions and local councils), university libraries, technical libraries and so on. Both the Roman Catholic Church and the Reformed Church have ancient libraries with valuable collections. Particularly, the Central Main Library of the Benedictine Order of Pannonhalma and the Chief Catholic Library in Esztergom have priceless codices and manuscripts.

The first original Hungarian film, *A Dance*, was made in 1901. In the interwar years avant-garde films began to be produced. The Horthy de Nagybanya regime subsidized film production and eventually founded the Hunnia Film Studio Company. As American and British films were banned during the war, domestic film production flourished. In 1948 the film industry was nationalized. Since the 1960s the film industry has enjoyed more freedom of expression than any other medium in Hungary. There is virtually no censorship, and Western films may be imported freely. Some films deal with politically controversial subjects, such as the 1956 Revolution and Stalin's excesses.

SOCIAL WELFARE

In addition to receiving complete or partial free medical care, 98% of the population is covered by social insurance, which includes sickness and disability benefits, pensions, maternity benefits and family allowances. Only self-employed persons are excluded from this coverage.

Men are pensionable at 60 and women at 55. The number of pensioners has been growing since the end of World War II as a result of longer life expectancy and thus has put a heavy burden on the government, which is the main source of pension funds. Even so, the vast majority of pensioners do not receive a subsistence income.

In an effort to stanch the decline in population growth, women receive generous maternity allowances and child payments. Another inducement for larger families is the system of family allowances. The payment scale favors three or more children, and a supplement is paid to handicapped children. Social insurance is administered by the trade unions through their local branches. It is financed by the central government and by contributions from employers. The pension fund receives contributions from the insured.

The social insurance programs, which are national in scope, are supplemented by a variety of social aid programs undertaken by local governments. Most of these involve short-term emergency assistance and aid to indigents.

The Ministry of Health and Social Welfare was set up in 1988. In the same year the National Assembly passed a law establishing the Social Security Fund. One of the first acts of the fund was to protect the real value of pensions for Hungary's 2.450 million pensioners. Parliament also extended family allowances to non-employed parents.

CHRONOLOGY

1946—Hungary promulgates a republican Constitution.

1947—Hungary signs a peace treaty with the Allied powers giving up all territories acquired after 1937.

1948—The Hungarian Workers' Party seizes power under Matyas Rakosi.

1949—The Constitution of 1946 is replaced by a new Constitution, under Communist aegis.

1953—Rakosi yields the prime ministership to Imre Nagy, who initiates liberal reforms.

1956—Hungary throws off the Soviet yoke in a revolution; Soviet troops invade Hungary and crush the uprising; Nagy is deposed and later executed; Janos Kadar is named to head a Soviet puppet regime; the Hungarian Workers' Party is renamed the Hungarian Socialist Workers' Party (HSWP).

1958—Kadar yields the prime ministership to Ferenc Munnich.

1961—Kadar begins his second term as prime minister.

1965—Kadar resigns as prime minister in favor of Gyula Kallai but remains first secretary of the HSWP.

1967—Jeno Fock replaces Kallai as prime minister.

1968—The regime initiates a series of reforms known as New Economic Mechanism (NEM), decentralizing authority.

1972—The Constitution of 1949 is revised and a new Constitution is promulgated.

1975—Gyorgy Lazar takes over as prime minister.

1985—The 13th Party Congress reelects Kadar as leader, with the new title of general secretary.

1987—Karoly Grosz is named prime minister in place of Lazar, who becomes deputy general secretary of the Central Committee.

1989—Imre Nagy's body is exhumed and reburied in a massive public ceremony attended by over 250,000 Hungarians, including members of the government. . . . President George Bush visits Budapest and announces a program of U.S. economic assistance. . . . Hungarian Communist Party is renamed Hungarian Socialist Party.

1990—Hungary signs pact with the Soviet Union on pullout of Soviet troops. . . . Vatican ties are restored. . . . In first free elections since World War II, the center-right Democratic Forum together with its allies, the Independent Smallholders' Party and the Christian Democratic People's Party, gain nearly 60% of seats in Parliament. . . . Jozsef Antall, the leader of the Democratic Forum, heads new cabinet as premier. . . . Soviet military forces begin complete withdrawal from Hungary.

BIBLIOGRAPHY

BOOKS

Berend, Ivan R. *Hungarian Economy in the 20th Century.* New York, 1983.

Boldiszar, Ivan. *Hungary.* Budapest, 1969.

Erdey, Ferenc. *Information Hungary.* Elmsford, N.Y., 1968.

Halasz, Zoltan. *Hungary.* Budapest, 1963.

Hare, P. G. *Hungary: A Decade of Economic Reform.* London, 1981.

Helmreich, Ernest. *Hungary.* New York, 1957.

Ignotus, Paul. *Hungary.* New York, 1972.

IMF. *Hungary: An Economic Survey.* Washington, D.C., 1982.

Kovrig, Bennett. *The Hungarian People's Republic.* Baltimore, 1970.

Macartney, C. A. *Hungary: A Short History.* Edinburgh, 1962.

Pesci, Martin, and Bela Sarfalvi. *The Geography of Hungary.* Budapest, 1964.

Siegel, Jacob S. *The Population of Hungary.* Washington, D.C., 1958.

Volgyes, Ivan. *Hungary: A Nation of Contradictions.* Boulder, Colo., 1982.

OFFICIAL PUBLICATIONS

Evi Nepszamlalas (Census of Population).
Statisztikai Evkoryu (Statistical Yearbook).

MONGOLIA

BASIC FACT SHEET

OFFICIAL NAME: Mongolian People's Republic (Bügd Nayramdakh Mongol Ard Uls)

ABBREVIATION: MO

CAPITAL: Ulan Bator (Ulaanbaatar)

HEAD OF STATE: Chairman of the Presidium of the Great People's Khural Punsalmaagiyn Ochirbat (from 1990)

HEAD OF GOVERNMENT: Chairman of the Council of Ministers Sharavyn Gunjaadorj (from 1990)

NATURE OF GOVERNMENT: Socialist democracy

POPULATION: 2,125,463 (1989)

AREA: 1,565,000 sq. km. (604,248 sq. mi.)

MAJOR ETHNIC GROUP: Mongol

LANGUAGE: Mongolian

RELIGION: None (formerly shamanism and Buddhism)

UNIT OF CURRENCY: Togrog or Tughrik

NATIONAL FLAG: A light blue vertical stripe between two red stripes; in gold, on the red stripe nearest the hoist, is a five-pointed star surmounting the soyonbo, the national coat of arms.

NATIONAL EMBLEM: An *arat* or steppes rider, dressed in white, riding a white horse and holding a *wrager* (a lasso with a wooden handle), rides toward the east and a rising sun against a blue sky illuminated by the rays of the sun, with forested hills and snowcapped mountains. Modern Mongolia is represented by a silver cogwheel at the base of a round shield and ears of wheat. A gold-rimmed red star joins the ears of wheat at the top. Within the red star is the national symbol, *soyonbo*, an ideogram of geometric figures representing fire, earth, water and air. Together these ideograms represent the ritual dagger of Buddhist lamaism used in exorcising evil spirits. Bands of gold, red and blue, the national colors, tie the emblem together at the base and carry the Cyrillic initials of the nation's name.

NATIONAL ANTHEM: "Bugd Nayramdakh Mongol Ard Ulsyn, Ulsyn Suld Duulal" ("Anthem of Our Country, or Our Free Revolutionary Land")

NATIONAL HOLIDAYS: Mongol Revolution Day (July 11); Constitution Day (June 30); Naadam (three days in summer); Bolshevik Revolution Day (November 7); May Day (May 1); New Year's Day; Mongol New Year's Day

NATIONAL CALENDAR: Gregorian

PHYSICAL QUALITY OF LIFE INDEX: 77 (on an ascending scale with 100 as the maximum)

DATE OF INDEPENDENCE: March 13, 1921

DATE OF CONSTITUTION: July 6, 1960

WEIGHTS & MEASURES: Metric

GEOGRAPHICAL FEATURES

Located in east-central Asia, Mongolia has an area of 1,565,000 sq. km. (604,248 sq. mi.), extending 2,368 km. (1,471 mi.) east to west and 1,260 km. (783 mi.) north to south. A landlocked country, it shares its total boundary length of 7,678 km. (4,771 mi.) with two neighbors: the Soviet Union (3,005 km.; 1,867 mi.) and China (4,673 km.; 2,904 mi.). The border with the Soviet Union remains essentially as it was agreed in the Treaty of Kyakhta of 1727, with the exception of the Soviet absorption of Tannu Tuva in 1924. The boundary with China was demarcated by the Sino-Mongolian Treaty of 1962. There are no current boundary disputes.

The capital is Ulan Bator (Ulaanbaatar) (known as Urga until 1924), on the historic route between Russia and China on the right bank of the Tula. Ulan Bator also is the chief industrial center because of its proximity to the Nalaikha mines. In 1987 Ulan Bator had a population of 515,000. There are no other population centers with over 100,000 inhabitants. The only one designated a city other than the capital and the *aimak* (province) centers is Darkhan. Called the smithy of New Mongolia,

Darkhan was founded in 1961 and grew rapidly to 74,000 in the next 25 years. Tsetserleg (Ara Khangai) and Choibalsan are traditional monastic centers, while Sukhe Bator, Sain Shanda, Dzun Bayan, Undur Khan, Ulan Gom and Somon are new towns that grew in importance after the people's republic was founded. Erdenet, the third most populous city, had a population of 45,400 in 1986.

Most of the northern, western, southwestern and central Mongolia consists of mountains, plateaus and depressions. Mongolians divide their country into a Khangai zone and a Gobi zone, but Russians enumerate five natural regions: the mountainous Altai; the Great Lakes Depression; the mountainous Khangai-Khentej; the uplifted eastern plains; and the nearly treeless Gobi. Nowhere lower than 457 m. (1,500 ft.) above sea level, Mongolia has an average elevation of 914 to 1,524 m. (3,000 to 5,000 ft.). In the extreme West, in the Altai Range, Tabun Bogdo peak soars to 4,358 m. (14,298 ft.). There is some glaciation. Elevations decline from the Northwest to the Southeast, from alpine snow peaks to low hills and flat plains. One-third of the country consists of the Gobi, a desert stretching southeast into Chi-

287

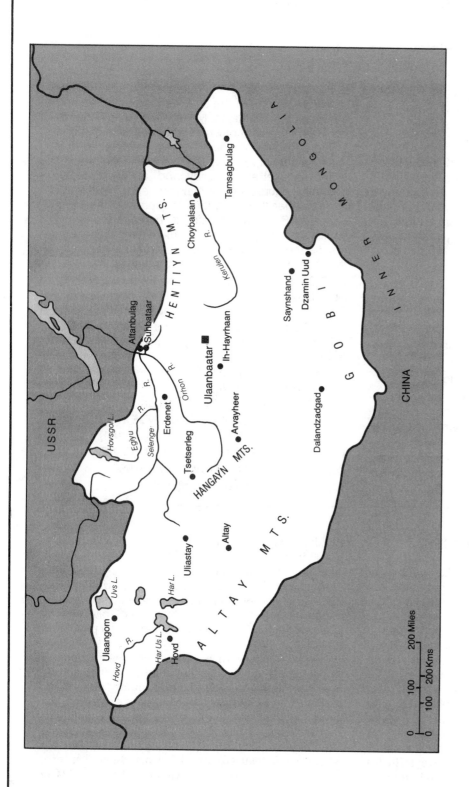

nese Turkestan. Particularly in the East it is a rocky desert of claylike soil blanketed thinly by shifting sand.

In the North, in the Arctic Basin, a considerable river system exists. The Selenga rises in the Khangai uplands and flows into Baikal; about 595 km. (370 mi.) of the river lie within Mongolia. Among its numerous tributaries are the Orkhon (1,126 km.; 700 mi.) and the Tula (703 km.; 437 mi.). Also originating in this region is the Yenisei and a minor affluent of the Irtysh. In the East, the area of Pacific drainage, the longest river is the Kerulen. In the Great Lakes Depression and in the Central Asian Basin flow the Dzabkhan (805 km.; 500 mi.), the Tes (563 km.; 350 mi.) and the Khobdo (499 km.; 310 mi.). Rivers in the Gobi region vanish in the salt lakes. Only two sizable rivers are of foreign origin: the Khalkhyn, in the extreme East, and the Khobdo, in the extreme West. With the exception of the Selenga, most waterways are not suitable for navigation and are used mainly for floating timber, for watering cattle and for irrigation.

Mongolia has hundreds of lakes, and those with outlets have fresh water. Most of the biggest lakes are in the Northwest. Fed by 200 rivers and rivulets, the bitter Ubs Nur (3,368 sq. km.; 1,300 sq. mi.) is the largest saline lake without an outlet. Forty-six rivers empty into the alpine Lake Khubsugul (2,591 sq. km.; 1,000 sq. mi.), the deepest (maximum depth, 518 m.; 1,700 ft.) and the largest freshwater lake, sometimes called the Mongol Sea. There are over 300 lakes in the Great Lakes Depression. In the East, the largest lake is Buir Nor. There also are over 200 natural mineral-water springs, hot and cold.

CLIMATE & WEATHER

Mongolia has a typically severe midlatitude continental climate characterized by very low rainfall and by wide and constantly variable diurnal, seasonal and yearly extremes in temperature. In the winter the area is encompassed by great masses of cold air forming huge high-pressure zones. In the short and relatively warm summer the remnants of the southwestern monsoon combine with low-pressure systems to produce modest precipitation, often in the form of brief and localized cloudbursts. January temperatures range from −15°C to −30°C (5°F to −22°F), with the extreme below −46°C (−50°F), and July temperatures from 10°C to 27°C (50°F to 80°F), with extremes over 38°C (100°F). The average annual temperature in Ulan Bator is a little below freezing. The total annual precipitation (some 70% to 80% occurring in July and August) varies from 254 to 381 mm. (10 to 15 in.) in the mountainous northern regions (where Khubsugul receives the most snowfall) to less than 127 mm. (5 in.) in the Gobi. The mean annual rainfall in Ulan Bator is 208 mm. (8.2 in.). The sun shines for 250 days a year, making Mongolia "the land of the Everlasting Blue Sky." Annual average relative humidity is benign, varying from 45% to 75% year-'round. Except for sudden blizzards, the winter winds are weak and local, mainly from the north. In the summer and autumn moister winds emanate from the southwest.

POPULATION

The population of Mongolia in 1989 was 2,125,463, based on the last official census, in 1979, when the population was 1,594,800. Mongolia ranks 18th in the world in land area and 121st in population. The population is expected to reach 2,150,000 by 1990 and 2,778,000 by 2000.

Decimated by wars and adverse natural conditions, the Mongols were near extinction for many centuries, and it was not until the 20th century that this decline was arrested. In recent decades the population growth rate has averaged 2.6% to 3.0%, which is relatively high even by Asian standards. Almost all the factors that formerly contributed to low growth—disease, poor sanitation, high mortality rates, low fecundity and a high proportion of celibate monks—have been reversed. A high birth rate is actively encouraged by the government, which awards gold medals to mothers with numerous offspring.

The most significant demographic characteristic is the thin and uneven distribution of the population. The national density is 1.3 per sq. km. (3.4 per sq. mi.); excluding the Ulan Bator agglomeration, the density is only half that figure. The highest concentration is in the Ulan Bator region and the lowest in the Gobi region, with the Southwest and the Northeast also poorly settled.

Traditionally the Mongols have been nomads, and even today nomadic herders live in households (khadons) comprising three or four gers (felt tents). In the Gobi region the nomadic circuit might involve 40 to 50 moves a year, except in the winter, with the herders immobilized. Despite the rapid modernization of the country, vestiges of this lifestyle persist, and a substantial portion of the rural population still lives in tents.

ETHNIC COMPOSITION

Although tribal divisions have weakened in the 20th century, they survive. About 76% of the population are Khalkha Mongols who live in the vast heartland from the east to the Altai and the valleys of the Great Lakes. West Mongols (also known as Oirat, Durbet, Olot and Torgut) account for about 5%. The largest minority, the pastoral nomad Kazakhs (a Muslim people of Turkish origin), number another 5% and are located in the far West, in their own national aimak of Bayan Uluguei. Lesser minorities, none of whom comprises more than 3%, include Buryats, Tuvinians and Darigangas, generally found in pockets to the West, Northwest and East, respectively. Nonnatives such as Russians and Chinese, each comprising about 2%, live mainly in urban areas. The Chinese are mostly the Mongolized descendants of the ruling Chinese group of pre-independence days.

There is virtually no national minority problem. However, some 4 million Mongols live outside Mongolia, mostly in Inner Mongolia, China, as well as in the Soviet Union. Pan-Mongol sentiments were strong in the early years of autonomy (1911–21) but since then have disappeared among the younger generation.

Ethnolinguistic differences are relatively unimportant, primarily because the national minorities are small and because of the great similarity in traditional social and economic organizations among all groups. Virtually all are nomadic herdsmen in social background. Further, the government has promoted the erosion of distinctive cultural traits. In the early days of the republic there was some opposition to the Khalkha dominance, particularly among the western or Oirat peoples. As a concession to the non-Khalkhas, a Nationalities Commission was established. These nationalities are defined almost wholly in terms of their language affiliations rather than their ethnic differences.

DEMOGRAPHIC INDICATORS, 1988

Population: 2,125,463 (1989)
Year of last census: 1979   World rank: 121
Sex ratio: males, 50.1;   females, 49.9
Population trends (million)

1930: 0.725	1960: 0.931	1990: 2.150
1940: 0.750	1970: 1.248	2000: 2.778
1950: 0.747	1980: 1.663	

Population doubling time in years at current rate: 26
Hypothetical size of stationary population (million): 6
Assumed year of reaching net reproduction rate of 1: 2020
Age profile (%)

0–15: 42.7	30–44: 16.1	60–74: 4.4
15–29: 26.2	45–49: 9.7	Over 75: 0.9

Median age (years): 19.9
Density per sq. km. (per sq. mi.): 1.3 (3.4)
Annual growth rate

1950–55: 1.94	1975–80: 2.82	1995–2000: 2.00
1960–65: 2.68	1980–85: 2.66	2000–2005: 1.85
1965–70: 3.08	1985–90: 2.55	2010–15: 1.52
1970–75: 2.93	1990–95: 2.28	2020–25: 1.13

Vital statistics
  Crude birth rate, 1/1,000: 36
  Crude death rate, 1/1,000: 9.2
  Change in birth rate: −15.5 (1965–84)
  Change in death rate: −35.0 (1965–84)
  Dependency, total: 75.2
  Infant mortality rate, /1,000: 47.0
  Child (0–4 years) mortality rate: 1/1,000: 43
  Maternal mortality rate, 1/100,000: 140
  Natural increase 1/1,000: 26.8
  Total fertility rate: 5.0
  General fertility rate: 132
  Gross reproduction rate: 2.14
  Marriage rate, 1/1,000: 6.3
  Divorce rate, 1/1,000: 0.3
  Life expectancy, males (years): 61.4
  Life expectancy, females (years): 65.5
Youth
  Youth population 15–24 (000): 143
  Youth population in 2000 (000): 171
Women
  Of childbearing age 15–49 (000): 528
  Child–woman ratio: 626
Urban
  Urban population (000): 1,281
  % urban, 1965: 42; 1985: 55
  Annual urban growth rate (%):
    1965–80 4.5; 1980–85: 3.3
  % urban population in largest city: 52
  % urban population in cities over 500,000: 52
  Number of cities over 500,000: 1
  Annual rural growth rate: 0.9

LANGUAGES

The standard Mongolian language is that spoken by the Khalkha, the dominant social group. Some 14% of the population speak Mongol languages differing only slightly from Khalkha, such as the Oirat, Buryat, Dariganga and Darkhat. The remaining speak non-Mongolian languages belonging to the same Altaic branch of the Ural-Altaic language family. Of these the most important are the Turkic and Tungus-Manchu languages. Turkic-speakers include numerous linguistically distinctive groups, mainly in the Khobdo region. They are the Tuvanian-speakers of Uriankhai and Kazakh (also called Kazakh-Kirghiz), Khotons, Uzbeks and Uigurs. Culturally there is little difference between Mongol- and Turkic-speakers with the striking exception of the Khotons, a Muslim group of sedentary agriculturists in Ubsa Aimak. The Tungus-Manchu languages are represented by the Tungus, specifically the Khamnegans, related to the Manchus, the former overlords of Mongolia. The Khamnegans have been completely Mongolized for centuries.

Mongolian is technically divided into four groups: Eastern Mongolian; Buryat or Northern Mongolian; Khalkha and Barga; and Western Mongolian or Oirat, which is spoken mainly outside Mongolia. Khalkha, the dominant form, has a number of dialects, the most different being Khotogoitu, spoken in the *aimak* of Khubsugul. Oirat is distinctive and so are its speakers, being physically smaller than the Khalkha, more voluble and friendlier. The differences between the Khalkha and the Oirat were encouraged by the Manchus, who ruled both separately. Oirat is spoken by seven groups in the Khobdo *aimak:* Durbets, Torguts, Baits, Uriankhas, Dzakachins, Mingats and Dambi-Ulets.

Minor Mongolian languages include Darkhat, spoken in the Darkhat region around Lake Khubsugul; Dariganga, spoken in the Southeast; and Buryat, spoken by Soviet Mongols.

The old written language used by all literate Mongols until 1931 was written in a vertical script, influenced by Chinese and adapted from the horizontal Turkic Uigur in the 13th century. The letters of the script reflected a way of pronunciation that was several centuries out of date; and as a result, writing was extremely difficult to learn. Phonetic scripts, some in Roman and some in Cyrillic, were introduced in 1931. By 1941 the Cyrillic form was recognized officially, with added symbols to indicate the two front vowel sounds found in spoken Mongolian but not in Russian. After the war the script was officially enforced in publications. The adoption of the new script strengthened Khalkha versus the other language forms, particularly in education, media and public transactions. The new script also had the additional advantage of making the acquisition of Russian easier, and it made communications with China, whose Mongols still used the old script, that much harder. At the same time, Mongolian, being a herdsman's language, is not particularly suited for complex scientific or political terminology, which must still be expressed in borrowed words. Russian is a strong second language for most Mongols and is a major qualification for officials who have to deal often with their Soviet counterparts. English is not entirely excluded, as evidenced by the number of translations from Standard English-language authors such as Shakespeare and Poe.

RELIGIONS

The difference between old Mongolia and the new Mongolia is nowhere more complete and dramatic than in religion. Until 1911 Mongolia was a theocratic state where the local religion was a mixture of Shamanism and Buddhism. By the late 19th century more than a quarter of the inhabitants were monks, theoretically celibate and thus contributing to the decline of the population.

The Buddhist establishment was in effect a state within a state, and monks constituted the most influential special-interest group. The Buddhist dignitaries, known as the "yellow" lords (from the color of their headgear), occupied a position of importance equal to that of the "black" or secular lords. Some monasteries were autonomous territories not under civil authority. These had not only temples, assembly halls and quarters for monks but also colleges of theology and folk medicine. Monks were recruited in two ways: They might join voluntarily as adults, or they might be presented by pious parents as children. A novice assigned to a master might eventually attain full status and might even become wealthy. Greater opportunities for upward mobility existed within the church than in the outside secular society. However, most monks spent their entire lives in lowly positions within the monastery and were actually no more than servants. Nevertheless, the monks enjoyed two distinct advantages: exemption from military service and access to learning and wealth.

Parallel with this system there existed vestiges of older shamanism, which was the original religion of the Mongols. By heredity, training, spontaneous vocation or election by supernatural beings, the shaman was a combined medicine man, wizard and priest with special magical powers, such as the ability to leave his body at will and to communicate with the supernatural world. The shaman's most important function was healing. He also functioned as guardian of tribal lore and as oral historian. All natural phenomena were sacred and inhabited by minor spirits, who needed to be placated constantly. Shamans performed this function, offering the idols food and drink; Shamans also prophesied the future; foretold eclipses; repelled evil spirits; and fixed auspicious days for marriages, military operations and business. Buddhism incorporated many elements of shamanism when it became the national religion, particularly the pharaphernalia of superstitions and the phalanx of demons. Shamanism, with its appeal to ignorance and mystery, has proved extremely difficult to eradicate even in the 20th century.

Buddhism was introduced into Mongolia in the eighth, ninth and 15th centuries. In Buddhism's heyday in Mongolia the country was covered with a network of monasteries presided by living saints, called *khubilgan* or, if especially distinguished, *khutukhtu*, who presided over establishments with thousands of monks (called lamas by some English writers, although the term is properly applied only to one kind of monk). In 1924 there were 14 *khutukhtus*, of whom the chief was the head of the monastery at Urga (later Ulan Bator), the Jebtsun Damba Khutukhtu, the Living Buddha. At the same time, there were 747 monasteries and 1,818 temples with 180,000 monks and 90,000 lay servants, contributing some 20% of the national livestock and a third of the national wealth. Since the monks had a monopoly of both medicine and learning, they had a vested interest in restricting the spread of both. Many of the high abbots lived in luxury, and monastic life was corrupted by concubinage, homosexuality and venereal diseases. The ruling Manchus exploited this state of affairs, since it helped to keep the Mongols weak and divided and subject to a web of demoralizing superstitions. In an effort to reduce the influence of the tribal khans, the Manchus recognized the Jebtsun Damba Khutukhtu as the temporal as well as the religious leader.

Thus when the Communists seized power with Soviet help in the early 1920s the Buddhist Church was one of the earliest targets. By the outbreak of World War II Buddhism was all but liquidated. The monks were divided into two classes: The ruling hierarchy were jailed and often shot; the middle-level monks and the simple monks were assimilated into the economy. At first there was no direct attack on Buddhism. Instead, in 1926 the government launched a campaign around the slogan "For a Purer Buddhism," aiming to reduce the monkish influence by a return to the original teachings of the Buddha, who did not recognize monasteries, property or ceremonies. Little by little the government deprived the monks of their political rights, denied them the right to travel and the right to vote, taxed them and eliminated monastery schools. In 1930 the state condemned the monks as a parasitic class of feudal society. Thereafter antireligious propaganda became strident and destructive. Special agents were assigned to individual monasteries to control and supervise enforcement of official regulations. Construction of new monasteries was prohibited. Religious titles were abolished. Existing monasteries were transformed into museums—a program copied from the Soviet Union.

The worst excesses against religion took place under Kharlogiyn Choibalsan, but the destruction of Buddhism continued under his successors. By the 1980s there were only three or four monasteries in the whole country, maintained more for their historical or propaganda value. Many of the older monasteries are in ruins, but some of them have been restored as historical monuments by the state.

The war against religion was more successful in Mongolia than in the Soviet Union and its other former satellites. Despite the extensive religious structures, Buddhism had shallow roots in the country, and even without the ruthless and harsh methods employed by the party, religious traditions and practices had become moribund. The government has boasted that Mongolia is today one of the world's most atheistic nations and that most cities are free of religious superstitions and piety. Few younger Mongolians feel any attachment to religious customs and values and tend to regard Buddhism as absurd and even embarrassing. Practicing Buddhists still exist, limited to the older generation in the rural areas, where Buddhist statues and pictures still hang on the walls of the *gers*. Once this generation passes away, Buddhism would have been completely eliminated as an influential force in national life.

HISTORICAL BACKGROUND

The Mongols are believed to be descended from the nomadic tribes of central Asia in the pre-Christian era. The most warlike of these nomadic groups was the Hsiung Nu, against whom the Chinese emperor Shih Huang Ti built the Great Wall in the third century B.C. In the second century B.C. the Hsiung Nu found that the wall was not a serious obstacle and overran northern and western China north of the Yangtze until they were driven back once again by Chinese Emperor Wu Ti, known as the martial emperor. During the following century there was incessant warfare between the Chinese and the Hsiung Nu, who forced their way back to Kansu and the northern part of modern Sinkiang. During the last three decades of the first century A.D. the Chinese general Pan Ch'ao pushed them back into Mongolia and established Chinese sovereignty in central Asia as far as the Aral Sea and possibly to the Caspian Sea. The Hsiung Nu never again seriously threatened China, but their place was taken within 10 years by another Mongoloid or Turkic tribe, the Hsien Pi. As the Han empire declined in the following century, all of China north of the Yangtze was overrun by barbarians: Hsien Pi from the north, remnants of the Hsiung Nu from the northwest and the Ch'iang from Kansu and Tibet. By the end of the fourth century the region between the Yangtze and the Gobi was dominated by the To Pa tribe of the Hsien Pi under the Northern Wei dynasty. But by the beginning of the sixth century they were overthrown by a new nomadic group of marauders known as the Gougen, who had established a powerful empire under their leader, Toulun. In turn, the Gougen were overthrown by the Turks, a subject people in the Altai region. The Turkish empire soon was split into a number of warring principalities, such as the western Turks, the eastern Turks and the Uighur Turks. It was not long before the western Turks and the eastern Turks followed the trail of the Hsiung Nu, the Hsien Pi, the To Pa and the Gougen into China, but they were repulsed by the T'ang emperors, who formed an alliance with the Uighurs to reestablish Chinese sovereignty over Sinkiang. As Chinese allies and vassals, the Ulighurs conquered much of western and northern Mongolia until, by the middle of the eighth century, their empire extended from Lake Balkash to Lake Baikal. At about this time the rising tide of Islam reached central Asia. Although the Chinese were ejected by Muslims from the Oxus Valley, the Chinese repulsed Muslim efforts to penetrate into Sinkiang. Thereafter the power of the Uighurs waned as the Kirghiz and the Karluk Turks drove them north to the Tarim Basin.

The decline of the Uighurs coincided with the ascendancy of a new Mongol tribe, the Khitans of northern Manchuria. By 925 the Khitans ruled eastern Mongolia, most of Manchuria, and much of China north of the Yellow River. Soon they established themselves of emperors of North China and were known as the Liao Dynasty.

As the stage was being set in the 11th and 12th centuries for the most momentous era in the history of the Mongols, the Mongols and the Tartars held sway over the northern and eastern areas; the Turks over western Asia and southeastern Europe; and the Tanguts, who were partly related to the Tibetans, in eastern Sinkiang, Kansu and western Inner Mongolia. Both the Tanguts (who were also known as Hsi-Hsia, or western Hsia) and the Uighur Turks were allied with the Chinese or nominally under Chinese rule.

Early in the 12th century a new Tungisic people, the Juchen, moved southeastward from central Mongolia and destroyed the Khitan empire in a violent seven-year war (1115–22) and then turned on their former allies the Sung Chinese. The Juchen leader proclaimed himself the leader of a new imperial dynasty, the Chin. Meanwhile, the defeated Khitan leader fled with a small remnant of his army to the Tarim Basin, where he allied himself with the Uighurs and established the kingdom of the Kara Khitai or western Liao, which soon controlled both sides of the Pamirs.

In central Mongolia, following the migration of the Juchen, the Borjigin Mongols emerged as the leading clan of a loose federation of Mongols. Its leader was Kabul Khan, to whom was born in 1162 a grandson known as Temuchin. When Temuchin was only 12, his father was treacherously killed by the Tartars, and he was left to die in a semidesert mountainous region. However, he survived, and by age 20 became the leader of the Kiut subclan and by 1190 the undisputed leader of the Borjigin Mongols. Allying himself with the Keraits, he first subdued the region north of the Gobi. Later he broke with the Keraits and in a series of campaigns defeated all of the Mongol and Tartar tribes in the region from the Altai to Manchuria. His principal opponents in the struggle had been the Maiman Mongols, and he selected their capital, Karakorum, as the seat of his new empire. In 1206 Temuchin was formally acknowledged as the leader of all Mongols by the *khuraltai* (council) of Mongol chieftains with the title of *khagan* (great khan). They also gave him the honorific title of Chingis (or Genghis), the name by which he is known to history.

Chingis Khan was perhaps one of the greatest military leaders in history. He developed an extraordinary military system and one of the most formidable armies that the world has ever seen. Building on a permanent base of 30,000 warriors under arms at all times, Chingis could, by levies on the Mongol tribes, raise armies of more than 300,000 men on short notice.

Chingis Khan's campaigns spanned a period of over 25 years, beginning in 1205 with the defeat of the Tangut forces in Kansu and Ninghsia; followed by the defeat of the Chin forces, the occupation of North China and the siege, capture and sack of Beijing (then known as Yenching or Chungtu) in 1213; the defeat of the Naiman Mongol leader Kushluk, who had seized the throne of Kara Khitai; the conquest of Khwarezm after defeating its Turkish rulers, Alaud-Din Mohammed and Jellaluddin, and sacking and razing to the ground Samarkand, Otrart and Kohojend; smashing the Cumans, capturing Astrakhan and annihilating a combined Russian-Cuman army on the banks of the Kalka River; and finally, the defeat of the combined Chin-Tangut armies in 1226 in a great battle on the banks of the frozen Yellow River. After accepting the surrender of the Tangut emperor, Chingis started back to Karakorum but died en route.

In accordance with the will of the dead emperor, the *khuraltai* chose his son Ogatai as *khagan*. The new ruler completed the conquest of the outlying territories of the western Hsia and the Chin Empire, and in 1231 he sent an expedition to conquer Korea. Under Ogatai the Mongol empire stretched from the Sea of Japan to Russia in the west and Syria in the south, although the Mongols themselves probably numbered less than 1 million. One of the most incredible empires in history, it was at this point the largest imperial power in the world. The sheer audacity with which the Mongols embarked on these wars—considering the paucity of their natural resources—was almost as remarkable as the success that invariably attended their operations. The empire was divided among the four descendants of Chingis under the overall authority of Khagan Ogatai: Batu, son of Juji, was the ruler of the region to the north and west of Lake Balkash; Chagatai, the region comprising modern Afghanistan, Turkestan and central Siberia; Ogatai, China and East Asia; and Tuli, the youngest, central Mongolia, the homeland, in accordance with Mongol custom.

In 1235 or 1236 Ogatai authorized two more expeditions: one against Tibet led by his son Godan, which was completed in 1239, and the second against Europe, which was led by Batu and Subotai, one of the most brilliant of Chingis's generals. The expedition started in 1237 with an army of 150,000 crossing the frozen Volga. For the next two years the Mongols spread death and destruction through Russia. In 1240 Subotai crossed the Dnieper and stormed and conquered Kiev. The Mongols then continued westward, advancing on a typically broad front in three major columns. To the north, the horde (a force roughly equivalent to a modern army corps and consisting of several *tumens* or divisions) of Prince Kaidu went through Lithuania and Poland; after destroying Boleslaw V of Poland at Cracow, Kaidu crushed at Leignitz a combined army of Germans, Poles and Teutonic Knights led by Prince Henry of Silesia. The southern horde, led by Prince Kadan, went through Transylvania into the Danube Valley and thence into Hungary. Meanwhile, Subotai and Batu, leading the central horde across the Carpathians, destroyed the army of King Bela IV of Hungary at the Sajo River. The Mongols then seized Pest. In 1241 the Mongols crossed the Danube, and their scouting parties reached Venice and Vienna. But swiftly the advance halted. The word had come, by way of the incredibly swift Mongol messenger service, that Ogatai had died. The princes, required by the law of Chingis Khan to return to Karakorum to take part in the election of a new *khagan*, led their armies back, never to return.

In 1246 the *khuraltai* selected Kuyuk, a son of Ogatai, as the *khagan*. However, within two years Kuyuk died. His successor was Mangu, eldest son of Tuli. Mangu resumed Chingis's plans for world conquest. Mangu himself, together with his brother Kublai, took the field against China. Another brother, Hulagu, was sent to Persia, where he became the first of the Ilkhans. He encouraged his cousin Batu to renew Mongol raids into central Europe. Mangu and Kublai—the later appointed viceroy of China—swept through China as far as Hanoi, which fell in 1257. When Mangu died in 1259 Kublai was elected *khagan*. After a two-year war against his brother Arik-Buka, who had opposed his election, Kublai turned his attention to the completion of the conquest of China. Assisted by Bayan, grandson of Subotai, he captured Hangchow in 1256, and in another three years all the outlying provinces were subdued. The last action in the war took place in 1279: a naval battle in the Bay of Canton in which all the Sung ships were sunk by the Mongol fleet.

Meanwhile, to the west, the first signs of decline appeared in the vast imperial domains. In the absence of Hulagu Khan, who had returned to Karakorum on the death of Mangu, his deputy was defeated and killed at the Battle of Ain Jalut by a larger Mameluke force. This was the first significant Mongol defeat in 70 years. This defeat went unavenged as both Hulagu and Kublai devoted their attention to rounding off their conquests elsewhere and suppressing dissidence. There were two abortive invasion attempts against Japan (1274 and 1281) and a brief invasion effort on Java (1292–93). Kublai had moved his capital from Karakorum to Beijing in 1263 and, after the Sung dynasty was destroyed in 1279, he established himself as the emperor of a united China, the first ruler of the Yuan dynasty. When he died in 1294, he was mourned by both the Mongols and the Chinese. The golden age of the Mongols was over.

The Yuan dynasty lasted in China until overthrown by a leader of a robber band, Chu Yuen-chang, who proclaimed himself Emperor Hung-wu, the founder of the Ming dynasty. With an army of 250,000 men he pursued the defeated Yuan armies into Mongolia and won a decisive victory at the Battle of Puir Nor in 1388. Karakorum was destroyed, and 70,000 Mongols were made prisoner.

Meanwhile, Bereke, brother of Batu, the leader of the Golden Horde, had been converted to Islam, and he allied himself with the Mamelukes against Hulagu. This chain of events marked the end of Mongol expansion in southwestern Asia. The successors of Hulagu gradually yielded their powers to the Turkish viceroys, and the Ilkhan empire fell apart before the end of the 13th century.

The Golden Horde, the khanate of the Kipchak, had a longer life than the others. Under Bereke, the court at Sarai on the Volga became a prosperous center of commerce. The Mongols mixed with the Turks of the steppes to become the Tartars of Russia. But the power of the khans declined after the princes of Moscow, former vassals and tributaries of the Mongols, asserted their independence under Ivan III in 1480. One cause of the decline was the rise of Tamerlane, or Timur the Lame, during the latter part of the 14th century. This Turkish conqueror claimed to be a descendant of Chingis Khan through the family of Chagatai, and he reunited Turkestan and the khanate of the Ilkhans under his rule. In 1391 he invaded Russia and defeated the Golden Horde and again ravaged the Caucasus and southern Russia in 1395. The khanate thereupon split into three separate kingdoms: Astrakhan, Kazan and the Crimea. That of Astrakhan, the main Golden Horde, was destroyed in 1502 by the combined armies of the Crimean Mongols and the Muscovites. The last reigning descendant of Chingis, Shanin Girai, khan of the Crimea, was deposed by the Russians in 1783.

By the middle of the 15th century the Mongol empire had shrunk to a number of independent warring tribes, particularly the Khalkhas and the Oirats. The latter gained ascendancy under Essen Tayi Khan, who defeated the Ming forces in 1449, and Dayan Khan, leader of a confederation covering north-central Asia between the Ural Mountains and Lake Baikal. Early in the 16th century the three independent sultanates of Khwarezm (Khiva), Ferghana and Yarkand were overwhelmed by the Uzbek Turks. Despite the internal bickering among the Mongol tribes, they continued their hostilities with the Ming. The leaders in the struggle were the Chahar Mongols, among whom the line of the *khagans* had continued, although the title itself had by now become meaningless. In the middle of the 16th century, Altan Khan, leader of the Tumed clan of the Khalkhas, reunited most of Mongolia. Tiring of the war with China, he concluded peace with the Ming emperor, thus ending a struggle that had lasted for three centuries, perhaps the longest war in history. During an invasion of Tibet, Altan was converted to Buddhism, and in 1577 he proclaimed Buddhism as the state religion of Mongolia.

From the 17th century Mongolia was hemmed in by the westward expansion of the Manchus and the eastward expansion of the Russians. The evolution of the art of war involving the use of muskets and cannon also had reduced the Mongols' military capabilities. Nevertheless, Mongolia produced several leaders who tried both to unite their people and to repel the incursions of the Russians and the Manchus. Among them were Ligdan Khan of the Chahar Mongols; Tsogto Taji, the national hero of this era; and Galdan Khan or Bushtu Khan of the Dzungar tribe. Because of the high quality of their leadership at this time the Dzungars dominated the history of Mongolia for much of the 17th century. After conquering most of Kashgar, Yarkand and Khotan from the Kirghiz, Galdan turned eastward in about 1682, intending to conquer the Khalkhas. In 1688 the hardpressed khalkhas appealed to the Manchus for aid. The Manchus were more than pleased to respond, and a Chinese army was sent to Mongolia. This led to the calling of a khuraltai in 1689 at Dolonor, where most of the Mongol tribe accepted Manchu sovereignty against the Dzungars, thus marking the end of independent Mongolia for over 200 years.

In 1696 the Chinese host crushed the Dzungar forces of Galdan near Chao-Modo (Urga, now Ulan Bator). This ended Dzungar influence in Mongolia, although they retained control of the western regions and parts of Sinkiang and Tibet. The Dzungars continued to trouble the Manchus for another 20 years. In 1720 they were driven out of Tibet and defeated again in 1732.

Meanwhile, the Chinese and Russian empires continued their expansions into central Asia. They found it expedient to delimit their respective areas of influence through the Treaty of Nerchinsk in 1689 and the Treaty of Kyakhta (1727), which regulated Russian-Chinese boundaries for another 175 years. During the 18th and 19th centuries the Chinese generally neglected most of Mongolia. The southern provinces, Suiyuan, Chahar and Jehl, known as Inner Mongolia, were in time absorbed into China.

The greatest single influence on Mongol life and culture during this period was Buddhism. In 1635 the khan of the Tushetu tribe proclaimed that his son was the reincarnation of the Buddha, and thus was born the tradition of the Living Buddha, or Jebtsun Damba Khutukhtu. Until the office was abolished in the 1920s, all reincarnations of the Living Buddha were from this tribe. To reduce the power of the tribal khans, the Manchus treated the Living Buddha as both the temporal and spiritual spokesman of the Mongols. Contributing to the increasingly theocratic nature of the society was the fact that over one-quarter of the male inhabitants were monks.

The train of events that led to the birth of the modern Mongolian People's Republic began with the overthrow of the Ch'ing dynasty by the Republicans on October 10, 1911. In the wake of the Manchu collapse, on November 18, 1911, Mongolia proclaimed its independence on the basis that its allegiance had been to the Ch'ing dynasty and not to China. The new government in Peking refused to recognize Mongolian independence but was too busy with internal discord to do anything about enforcing its sovereignty. The Jebtsun Damba Khutukhtu was named Bogdo Khan, or ruler. Russia moved rapidly to take advantage of the situation by signing the Russo-Mongolian Treaty in 1912, creating in effect a Russian protectorate over Outer Mongolia. Additional treaties were signed in 1913 and 1915, but Russian involvement in World War I gave an opportunity to the Chinese to reassert their sovereignty. In 1919 the Chinese reoccupied Urga and disbanded the new Mongol army. Meanwhile, the tides of the Russian Civil War spilled over into Mongolia from the North as the White Russians under Baron Roman von Ungern-Sternberg moved into Mongolia from Siberia and drove the Chinese from Urga. Opposition to the "Mad Baron" led Mongolian national leaders Sukhe Bator, Danzan Khorlo and Khorlogiyn Choibalsan, with the blessing of the Living Buddha, to appeal to Moscow for assistance. In response, the Revolutionary Provisional Government of Mongolia was established at Kyakhta, just inside Siberia from Mongolia, on March 13, 1921. This government's military force, comprising mostly of Red troops, defeated the Mad Baron at the border town of Altan Bulak and then marched on Urga and occupied the capital. The Communist victors established a new national government at Urga with the Living Buddha as the nominal head of state and a government headed by a monk named Dogsomyn Bodo and controlled by the three national leaders. On November 5, 1921, a new Mongolian-Soviet treaty of friendship was signed, which recognized the People's Government of Mongolia as the only legal government and ceded the northwestern portion of Outer Mongolia in the Altai Mountains to the Soviet Union. Dogsomyn Bodo, who opposed the extension of Soviet influence, was executed in 1922, and the next year Sukhe Bator died under mysterious circumstances, followed by the death of the Living Buddha in 1924. The People's Government forbade the selection of a successor to the Living Buddha. In the same year Danzan Khorlo, the last remaining anti-Soviet nationalist leader, was shot. With the elimination of all opposition, the stage was set for the formal withdrawal of the Soviet forces and the establishment of a puppet state. On November 26, 1924, the Mongolian People's Republic was proclaimed with a new constitution on the Soviet model. At the same time Urga was renamed Ulan Bator, or Red Hero.

From 1924 to 1928 the leftists consolidated their power without any frontal assault on the two rival national institutions: the abbots and the nobles. A new currency and a new national bank were set up, a standardized tax system was instituted and a Soviet-equipped and Soviet-trained Mongol army was created. A decisive clash between the nationalists or rightists and the Soviet-leaning leftists came in 1928 at the Seventh Party Congress of the Mongolian People's Revolutionary Party. All rightists were expelled, and the leftists seized control of the party and the government. They rushed headlong into a series of radical reforms, including confiscation of all feudal estates and a relentless war against the Buddhist clergy. Forcible collectivization followed on Stalin's model. These brutal measures caused bloody uprisings. The government responded with still harsher measures and new party purges. The government banned all private enterprise, forced craft workers to join cooperatives and nationalized all foreign and domestic trade and transportation. Extremism produced a near disaster as the nation came to the verge of a civil war. The angry and frightened nomads slaughtered their animals rather than hand them over to the state. There was widespread famine as the food supplies failed. Finally the government was persuaded by the Soviets to retreat and end its extremism. The party rejected its own earlier "left-wing deviation" and expelled several top leaders as "left-wing adventurers." The collective farm experiment was dropped, the worker cooperatives were abandoned, the cattle tax was reduced and the herdsmen and peasants were again allowed to hold private property.

The new policy of gradualism continued through World War II until late 1947. This period witnessed the successful elimination of Buddhism as a national institution. Choibalsan consolidated his power through purges in which scores of top administrators and party and army officials were imprisoned or executed. The threat of Japanese invasion led to increasing concentration on building up the defense forces. Over 10% of the national population had been conscripted by the time Mongolia joined the Soviet Union in declaring war on Japan on August 8, 1945.

For events after 1945, see Chronology.

CONSTITUTION & GOVERNMENT

The first Constitution of the Mongolian People's Republic (MPR) was adopted by the Great People's Khural on November 26, 1924, the same day on which the MPR was established. The Constitution was modeled on that of the Russian Soviet Federated Socialist Republic and represented the triumph of the pro-Russian leftists over the nationalists in the party.

The Preamble cites the death of the Living Buddha who was the chief of state from 1921 to 1924, and the overthrow of his despotism. Chapter One is devoted to the Declaration of the Rights of the Mongolian People. Chapter Two enumerates the organs of government: the Great People's Khural, the Small Khural, the Presidium, the Council of Ministers. Chapter Three's four articles deal with local self-government by *khurals* at the province, city and lower levels. Chapter Four deals with voting rights, which are denied to monks, nobles and money lenders. The Constitution also laid down certain fundamental principles, such as "proletarian internationalism," which meant, in fact, loyalty to the Soviet Union; cancellation of debts owed to and agreements with non-Communist governments; state control of the economy; separation of church and state; and the introduction of free education as a means of indoctrinating the young.

The next 16 years witnessed the transition of Mongolia from a feudal society to one of the most radical Communist states in the world. From 1924 to 1940 the so-called Choibalsan years were a mirror image of the Stalinist reign of terror in the Soviet Union. The changes that had been effected in Mongolian society as a result of these unprecedented events necessitated a new Constitution. The revised Constitution of 1940 was ratified by the Eighth Great People's Khural and, like the one that preceded it, it was modeled on the Soviet Constitution, particularly the Stalin Constitution of 1936. The new Constitution included some additional provisions. The right of citizens to private ownership of cattle and other goods and the right of inheritance were guaranteed. The authority of the Council of Ministers was enlarged, and the number of ministries was expanded. Another new section related to the courts. Chapter Nine, devoted to the electoral system, retained many of the former restrictions against "undesirable" persons. The Fundamental Rights and Duties of Citizens enumerated in Chapter 10 were considerably expanded to reflect developments since 1924. Article 80 guaranteed equal rights to women "in all spheres of life."

Between 1940 and 1960 the Constitution was amended five times: in 1944, 1949, 1951, 1957 and 1959. The 1944 amendment restored voting rights to those to whom the Constitution had denied them; the 1949 amendment altered the electoral system to include general instead of multistage elections and secret instead of open balloting; the 1951 amendment abolished the Small Khural. The remaining two amendments reorganized the local governmental system by abolishing the *bag*, the former unit of local administration, and replacing it with the *somon* (district).

The present Constitution, which replaced that of 1940, was approved by the Great People's Khural on July 6, 1960. Unlike the 1940 document, the Constitution of 1960 assigns a dominant role to the party as "the guiding and directing force of society." Like other Communist constitutions, it is rife with contradictions. Chapters Seven and Eight deal with fundamental rights and duties and guarantees all citizens equal rights irrespective of nationality, religion, etc., but the same articles forbid the advocacy of nationalism. In practice only the Khalkha occupy key positions in the party and in the administration, and Buddhists are excluded from all walks of life. Article 87 guarantees the freedoms of press, speech and assembly, but only "in conformity with the interests of the working people, in order to strengthen the socialist state system of the MPR." Further, these freedoms may be enjoyed only after the government grants "the material requisites for their realization." Similarly, the Supreme Court of the Republic has the obligation to guarantee the fulfillment of the Constitution but has no right of judicial review. The Constitution is a flexible document because only a two-thirds majority decision in the Great People's Khural is needed to amend it. The most novel feature of the Con-

stitution, not duplicated in any other Communist constitution, is contained in Chapter 10. It calls for the eventual abolition of the Constitution when the state itself is no longer necessary for the building of communism and is replaced by a Communist association of working people.

The head of state is the chairman of the Presidium of the Great People's Khural. The Presidium combines extraordinary legislative, executive and military powers. The highest executive and administrative body is the Council of Ministers, headed by a chairman, who

---

CABINET LIST

Chairman, Presidium, Great People's Khural: Jambyn Batmonh
Chairman, Council of Ministers: Dumaagiyn Sodnom
Deputy Chairman, Council of Ministers: Bat-Ochiriyn Altangarel
Deputy Chairman, Council of Ministers: Sharabyn Gungaadorj
Deputy Chairman, Council of Ministers: Puntsagiyn Jasray
Deputy Chairman, Council of Ministers: Myatabyn Peljee
Deputy Chairman, Council of Ministers: Choynoryn Suren
Minister of Agriculture and Food: Sharabyn Gungaadorj
Minister of Communications: Irbudziyn Norobjab
Minister of Culture: Budyn Sumyaa
Minister of Defense: Luvsangombyn Molomjamts
Minister of Finance: Demchigjabyn Molomjamts
Minister of Foreign Affairs: Tserenpilyn Gombosuren
Minister of Foreign Economic Relations and Supply: Punsalmaagiyn Ochirbat
Minister of Health: Choyjiljabyn Tserennadmid
Minister of Justice: Origiyn Jambaldorj
Minister of Light Industry: Nyam-Osoryn Dagbadorj
Minister of Nature and Environmental Protection: Uthany Mablet
Minister of Power, Mining Industry and Geology: Sodobyn Bathuyag
Minister of Public Security: Agbaanjantsangiyn Jamsranjab
Minister of Social Economy and Services: Tumengiyn Demchigdorj
Minister of Trade and Procurement: Badrachiyn Sharabsambuu
Minister of Transportation: Dogoogiin Yondonsuren
President, Academy of Sciences: Namsrain Sodnom
Chairman, People's Control Committee: Chubaandorjiyn Molom
Chairman, State Bank Board of Directors: Gochoogiyn Huderchuluun
Chairman, State Building Commission: Luvsanbaldangiyn Nyamsambuu
Chairman, State Commission for Information, Radio and Television: Lhagbajabyn Dzantab
Chairman, State Commission for Physical Culture and Sports: Dabaagiyn Dashdobdon
Chairman, State Commission for Planning and Economy: Puntsagiyn Jasray
Chairman, State Commission for Science, Technology and Higher Education: Mangaljabyn Dash
Chairman, State Commission for Standards: Osoryn Sampil

RULERS OF MONGOLIA
Head of State (from 1911)

December 1911–November 1919: Jebstun Damba Khutukhtu (Bogdo Gegen Khan)
November 1919–February 1921: Chinese occupation
July 1921–May 1924: Jebstun Damba Khutukhtu (Bogdo Gegen Khan)

Presidents (from 1924)
(Chairman of the Presidium of the People's Khural)
November 1924–July 1932: M. Gendun
July 1932–March 1936: Amor
1936–1939: Damsranbelegiyn Doksom
1939–July 1940: Post vacant
July 1940–September 1953: Gonchigiyn Bumatsende
September 1953–July 1954: Post vacant
July 1954–May 1972: Jamsarangiyn Sambu
May 1972–June 1974: Sonomyn Luvsan (acting)
June 1974–August 1984: Yumjagiyn Tsedenbal
August–December 1984: Nyamyn Jagvaral (acting)
December 1984–April 1990: Jambyn Batmonh
April 1990–   : Punsalmaagiyn Ochirbat

Prime Ministers (from 1912)
(Chairman of the Council of Ministers since 1924)
1912: Tserenchimit
November 1912–April 1919: Sain Noyan Khan
November 1919–February 1921: Chinese occupation
February–July 1921: Dambinbadzar (Jalhansa Khutukhtu)
July 1921–January 1922: Dogsomyn Bodo
August 1922–July 1923: Dambinbadzar (Jalhansa Khutukhtu)
1923–February 1928: Balingiyn Tserendorji
1928–July 1932: Amor
July 1932–March 1936: M. Gendun
March 1936–1938: Amor
1939–January 1952: Kharlogiyn Choibalsan
January 1952–June 1974: Yumjagiyn Tsedenbal (acting January–May 1952)
June 1974–December 1984: Jambyn Batmonh
December 1984–April 1990: Dumaagiyn Sodnom
April 1990–   : Sharavyn Gunjaadorj

Communist Party Leaders (from 1921)
(Chairman of the Central Committee 1921–40, General Secretary 1940–58, First Secretary since 1958)
March 1921–August 1924: Danzan
August 1924–October 1928: Tserenvacharyn Dambadorji
October 1928–1939: Darzavyn Losol
April 1940–April 1954: Yumjagiyn Tsedenbal
April 1954–November 1958: Dashiyn Damba
November 1958–August 1984: Yumjagiyn Tsedenbal
August 1984–April 1990: Jambyn Batmonh
April 1990–   : Gombojavyn Ochirbat

OPPOSING GOVERNMENT
(*Headquarters:* Kyakhta, Russia)
Prime Ministers (1921)

March 1921: Chakdorjab
March–July 1921: Dogsomyn Bodo

performs the role of prime minister, the head of government. The Council of Ministers is subordinate to both the Great People's Khural and its Presidium, to which it is formally accountable.

The work of the government ministries and departments is based on the principle of personal ministerial responsibility. Most members of the cabinet are either members or candidate members of the party's Central Committee.

Mongolia faithfully hewed to the official Soviet line during the Stalin era, and so it has during the Gorbachev era. In 1988 the Mongolian party began an unprecedented attack on both Stalin and former Mongolian leaders, particularly Kharlogiyn Choibalsan and Yum-

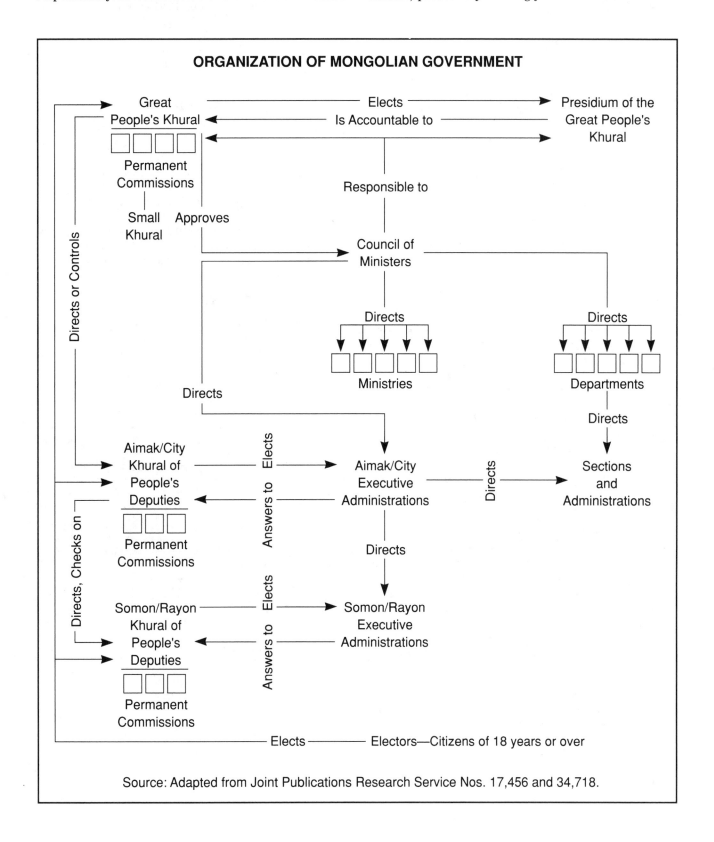

ORGANIZATION OF MONGOLIAN GOVERNMENT

Source: Adapted from Joint Publications Research Service Nos. 17,456 and 34,718.

jagiyn Tsedenbal. Choibalsan was implicated in the mysterious deaths of his rivals in the 1920s and the purge and death of thousands of other party and army officials in the 1930s. Under Jambyn Batmonh both *glasnost* and *perestroika* became the watchwords of the Mongolian administration.

A series of dramatic pro-democracy protests and the beginnings of unprecedented opposition political activity led the Mongolian Communist Party to relinquish its constitutionally guaranteed monopoly of power on April 15, 1990. The decision paved the way for a transformation of Mongolia from a one-party system into a multiparty state. Thus Mongolia became the first Asian Communist country to adopt the type of political reforms that had swept Eastern Europe in the preceding six months. Batmonh stepped down from his dual positions as head of state and general secretary of the party and was replaced by Gombojavyn Ochirbat as general secretary and by Punsalmaagiyn Ochirbat as president. Premier Dumaagiyn Sodnom also was ousted, and Sharavyn Gunjaadorj appointed in his stead.

FREEDOM & HUMAN RIGHTS

Under both Kharlogiyn Choibalsan and Yumjagiyn Tsedenbal the party was so successful in wiping out human liberties and suppressing all opposition that there are few manifestations of either. Political and social life is controlled and monitored by various government organizations, particularly the Ministry of Public Security. Although fundamental criticism is barred, criticism is permitted in certain areas and on certain topics, although this often is ritualistic. Letters published in the official press are a form of managed criticism serving to create an illusion of popular participation. Mongolians have little access to Western media.

The only sign of organized religion is the showcase Gandan monastery, maintained to prove the official contention that there is freedom of religion. The monastery has some 200 monks in addition to another 100 itinerant monks attached to it. Two or three novices are permitted to enroll annually.

Freedom of travel is tightly controlled. The major destination of travelers on official business or students on educational exchange programs is the Soviet Union. As many as 40,000 Mongolian youths are trained in the Soviet Union every year. All Mongolians over 16 must have internal passports issued by the Ministry of Public Security to travel within the country. Changes in places of residence or employment must be approved by the Ministry of Public Security and must accord with central planning goals.

In 1983 some 2,000 to 3,000 Chinese were expelled from Ulan Bator and its environs for various trumped-up reasons. With the improvement in Sino-Mongolian relations in recent years, such expulsions have ceased. Despite Batmonh's endorsement of *perestroika*, political rights still are virtually nonexistent. Women, however, have fared well within the limited political context. They constitute 48.5% of the labor force, 30.0% of the party membership, 49.8% of the trade union member-

ship, 33.9% of the membership of the local *khurals* and 25.0% of the membership of the Great People's Khural.

With the abandonment of Communist monopoly of power in 1990, some measure of political freedom has begun to flourish. Opposition parties are permitted to function; demonstrations and assemblies are tolerated; and free elections have been held at both the national and local levels. The new MPR general secretary, Gombojavyn Ochirbat, has stated that in the new Mongolia "democracy should develop, all human rights should be ensured, and social justice must prevail."

CIVIL SERVICE

There is no formally constituted permanent civil service. Since the government is the only employer in the country, all secondary-school and postsecondary graduates eventually become civil servants. Almost all those in higher or management positions are party members who are chosen for their loyalty rather than their skills.

Civil servants have a general reputation for efficiency and discipline, but, according to press reports, suffer from excessive arrogance and bureaucratic elitism.

LOCAL GOVERNMENT

Mongolia is divided into *aimaks* (provinces), *somons* (districts) and cities for purposes of local government. There are 18 *aimaks* and over 300 *somons*. The latter, which correspond to districts in the Western sense, are

POLITICAL SUBDIVISIONS				
		Area		Population
Provinces	Capitals	Sq. mi.	Sq. km.	(1984 est.)
Arhangay	Tsetserieg	55,000	21,000	83,800
Bayanhongor	Bayanhongor	116,000	45,000	69,500
Bayan-Olgiy	Olgiy	46,000	18,000	84,000
Bulgan	Bulgan	49,000	19,000	46,000
Dornod	Choibalsan	122,000	47,000	67,800
Dornogovi	Saynshand	111,000	43,000	47,400
Dundgovi	Mandalgov	78,000	30,000	44,100
Dzavhan	Uliastay	82,000	32,000	88,100
Govi-Altay	Altay	142,000	55,000	62,500
Hentiy	Ondorhaan	82,000	32,000	60,500
Hovd	Hovd	76,000	29,000	71,600
Hovsgol	Moron	101,000	39,000	96,600
Omnogovi	Dalandzadgad	165,000	64,000	35,500
Ovorhangay	Arvayheer	63,000	24,000	93,200
Selenge	Suhbaatar	42,000	16,000	76,400
Suhbaatar	Baruun-urt	82,000	32,000	47,200
Tov	Dzuunmod	81,000	31,000	90,200
Uvs	Ulav Gom	69,000	27,000	81,400
Autonomous Municipalities				
Darhan	—	200	100	63,600
Erdenet	—	800	300	40,500
Ulan Bator	—	2,000	800	470,500
TOTAL		1,565,000	604,000	1,820,400

the basic units and are coextensive with the agricultural collectives. At each level there are legislative councils called *khurals*, deputies to which are elected by their populations for two-year terms. Regular sessions of *aimak* and city *khurals* are convened at least twice a year and those for *somons* at least three times a year.

The principal tasks of the local bodies are to guide the economic, political and cultural development of their respective territorial divisions and to ensure strict implementation of the decisions transmitted from Ulan Bator. Higher *khurals* may amend or annul decisions of lower ones.

FOREIGN POLICY

As the oldest satellite of the Soviet Union, Mongolia never has had an independent foreign policy. Fear of the Chinese had driven the Mongols into the Soviet embrace in the 1920s, and that fear has been strong enough to keep them in the Soviet camp ever since. The Soviet Union, for its part, has long treated the MPR as a protectorate and a convenient buffer against China. Until after World War II the republic had no formal diplomatic relations with any nation except the Soviet Union. As Eastern Europe came into the Soviet orbit after World War II, Mongolia entered into diplomatic exchange with them, as it did with other Communist nations in Asia. Recognition of the first non-Communist state was that of India in 1955. Admission to the United Nations in 1961 was a landmark in the history of the republic's foreign relations. In 1962 Mongolia joined COMECON. Another landmark was the initiation of diplomatic relations with the United States in 1987 and the establishment of the U.S. embassy in Ulan Bator in 1988. President Batmonh sent a congratulatory message to President Bush on his election as U.S. president, and the official youth newspaper carried a favorable article about him.

The thaw in Sino-Soviet relations has favorably affected Mongolia's relations with China. A consular treaty was negotiated in 1987, followed by a trade agreement, a new border treaty and a joint railway agreement. The warming relationship is reflected in the change in tone in the Mongolian press in its treatment of Chinese news. Nevertheless, Mongolia has remained at odds with China over some minor issues, particularly Cambodia. Mongolia has given full support to Gorbachev's initiatives both at home and abroad.

PARLIAMENT

The national legislature is a bicameral body consisting of the Great People's Khural, of 430 members elected directly for five-year terms, and the Small Khural of 53 members. The right of nominating deputies is reserved for social organizations, trade unions, party organizations, youth organizations, nomads' unions, cultural societies and other working-class bodies.

Although Article 19 of the Constitution assigns the Great People's Khural plenary legislative power, legislation may be initiated by its standing commissions, its Presidium, the Council of Ministers or the Supreme Court. The formal legislative procedures of the Great People's Khural are purely academic because it is in effect a rubber stamp. Its powerlessness is attested to by the fact that it meets only once a year, for a week or less. The real function of the deputies, besides approving all bills submitted by the Presidium, is to propagandize the new laws in their constituencies. Theoretically the powers of the Great People's Khural are vast and include election of the Presidium, amendment of the Constitution, formation of the Council of Ministers, scrutiny and approval of economic plans and state budgets, and confirmation of decrees passed by the Presidium in its absence.

While the Great Khural meets only about once a year, much of the legislative work is done by the Small Khural. Seats in the Small Khural are distributed proportionately based on a nationwide party preference vote.

In contrast to the Great People's Khural as a body, its Presidium wields substantial powers. Its chairman is invariably the chief of state; in addition to him, there are six members. Most of its powers relate to foreign affairs and local government.

Mongolia held its first free elections in modern history in August 1990. The ruling MPR retained control of both houses of parliament. In the 430-seat People's Great Khural the Communists won 343 seats, the main opposition parties 34 seats and independents 25 seats. Twenty-eight seats remained unfilled because no candidate won a majority. In many constituencies there was no contest because opposition parties could not field any candidates. Communists were allotted 60% of the seats in the 53-seat Small Khural. Turnout was estimated at 92% of the 1 million eligible voters.

A carnival atmosphere surrounds elections, and the masses are mobilized by party cadres, with redoubled propaganda barrages. Technically, balloting is universal, direct and secret. Voters have the right to cross out the only names that appear on the ballot. The Central Election Commission tabulates and announces the results with much solemnity.

POLITICAL PARTIES

Since 1921 Mongolia has been ruled by one party—the Mongolian People's Revolutionary Party (MPRP). From 1924 until 1952 the party was dominated by Mongolia's Stalin, Marshal Kharlogiyn Choibalsan. His death was followed by a period of de-Choibalsanization, although the Mongols permitted their dead dictator to remain in his mausoleum. Yumjagiyn Tsedenbal, who succeeded him, was less of a dictator, although he, too, engrossed power in his own hands. Tsedenbal's successor, Jambyn Batmonh, also belongs to the same mold as his predecessors, although more of a pragmatist. Thus the MPRP has evolved under the prod of three hard-line Marxists and has come to be one of the least developed and least progressive Communist parties in the world. Another equally significant influence on the party has been the unrelenting influence of the Soviet Communist party, which determines policies, chooses leaders, decides on who should be expelled or executed and sets economic and political priorities. Since 1921 the MPRP's leaders have been willing tools of Moscow—a fact, however, that influenced Moscow in its decision to establish a satellite government in Ulan Bator rather than to annex the country. Another characteristic of the MPRP is the small number of elite leaders at the top—not only because of the nature of the Communist state, but also because of the small size of the literate population. Economists generally predominate, and Russophilism is an essential quality. The number also is kept small through frequent purges, which since the days of Choibalsan have become part of the reality of Mongolian politics. However, purges since 1952 have not led to executions. Although opposition is not allowed, rivalries exist within the party and erupt periodically. There is a fairly sizable changing of the guard at a level just below the top echelon. The extent of centralization of power at the top also is indicated by the fact that only a handful of *aimak* party or government officials are on the Central Committee.

The principal institutions of the MPRP are the Politburo of seven members and two candidate members; the Central Committee of 85 members and 65 candidate members; and the Party Congress, which may include over 700 delegates. The Politburo is the most powerful party organ, and its first secretary is generally also the head of state.

Two satellite party organizations are the association of labor unions and the youth organization Revsomols. The latter once was a major independent force within the party, and it was the springboard that launched Choibalsan into power. With an agreement reached for the withdrawal of 50,000 Soviet troops, Mongolia is slowly emerging from its satellite status. Although the Mongolian People's Revolutionary Party remains entrenched in power, it has followed the Soviet Communist Party in giving up its monopoly on power. A fledgling pro-democracy movement has gained strength through a series of protest rallies attended by thousands in the capital. The movement, named the Mongolian Democratic Union, is led by a 27-year old Moscow-trained professor, Sanjassuran Zorig, who poses the first serious challenge to the government since the Communist seized power in the 1920s. Zorig has called for a multiparty system, free enterprise, and an end to Soviet hegemony.

Another important body is the party's Control Commission, which is charged with implementation of party directives. This commission also ferrets out dissenters within the party's ranks and subjects them to appropriate punishment. Party control mechanisms have increased in sophistication over the years, with the result that there are virtually no indigenous reform movements of this kind found in Gorbachev's Soviet Union.

ECONOMY

Few nations in modern history have started from scratch as Mongolia did. In 1921 its total industrial pro-

duction was zero; in about 70 years it has reached the respectable stature of a semi-industrial state with a GNP of $2 billion, of which industry contributes over one-third. However, industry is heavily biased toward the production of livestock and animal products, the historic strengths of the economy. Almost all durable consumer goods are imported from the Soviet Union and other fellow CMEA members. Mongolia has a centrally planned economy in which the dominant sector is public.

Although Mongolia's modern economic history began in the 1920s, it was only in the 1950s that it embarked, with Soviet aid, on serious industrialization programs. It took almost 30 years for an industrial proletariat to emerge and the *arats* (herders) to change their lifestyles and attitudes. The discipline of the industrial life could be inculcated only slowly to some of the world's most untamed nomads who constituted the bulk of the population. From the 1950s Mongolia also started to receive generous aid from the Soviet Union and China, making Mongolia in per capita terms the most intensely aided country in the world. Aid from the Soviet Union took many forms. It included whole factories; machinery; trucks; tractors; free provisions of technicians, planners, engineers, geologists and others; military aid, particularly military hardware, training and advisers; and extensive training programs for Mongolian youth in the Soviet Union and other East European countries, with most of the expenses being assumed by the host country. Trade with the Soviet Union also is of paramount importance, since Mongolia has no production capacity for major machinery as well as machine tools, motors, rolling stock, mining equipment and most consumer durables. From 1921 until 1952 the Soviet Union was the sole trading partner; since then trade has diversified to include other Communist nations.

In its internal industrial development, Mongolia has placed major emphasis on the creation of infrastructure—roads, communications, power generation, mining and education. Because of the concentration on infrastructure as well as animal processing, production of consumer goods has been relatively neglected.

Livestock remains the major national resource, as it has for centuries. In 1921 almost the entire productive labor force was engaged in livestock raising; there was a nonproductive and nonworking group of some 105,000 to 120,000 monks, of whom some 40,000 lived in monasteries, and in addition there were some 90,000 laymen who were servants or serfs of the monks. More than a quarter of the national herd belonged to or were pledged to the monasteries as security for loans and thus never entered the economy, to which the monks contributed nothing. Indeed, some of the larger monasteries received substantial tax support. Livestock represented both capital and income as well as a measure of wealth; a medium of exchange; and almost the only source of food, clothing and shelter. However, in the winter, hundreds of thousands of livestock froze, starved or were killed by wolves. Thus the productive capital of the country was severely depleted every few years.

On seizing power, the Communists were faced with a

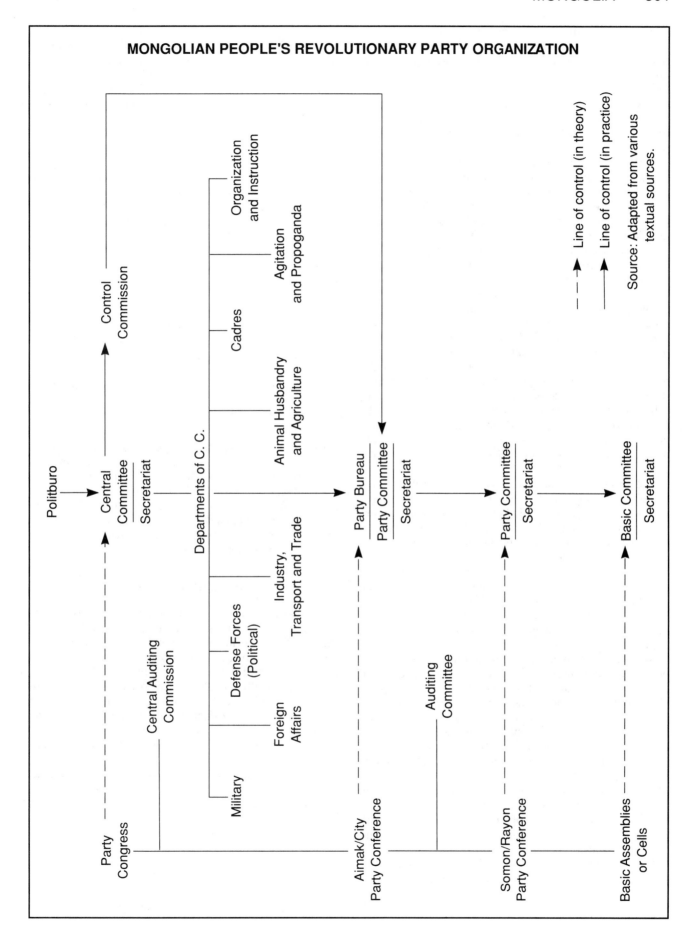

MONGOLIAN PEOPLE'S REVOLUTIONARY PARTY ORGANIZATION

Politburo

Central Committee / Secretariat

Control Commission

Departments of C. C.

Organization and Instruction

Agitation and Propoganda

Cadres

Animal Husbandry and Agriculture

Industry, Transport and Trade

Defense Forces (Political)

Foreign Affairs

Military

Central Auditing Commission

Party Congress

Party Bureau / Party Committee / Secretariat

Party Committee / Secretariat

Basic Committee / Secretariat

Auditing Committee

Aimak/City Party Conference

Somon/Rayon Party Conference

Basic Assemblies or Cells

Line of control (in theory)

Line of control (in practice)

Source: Adapted from various textual sources.

dilemma. According to classic Marxist theory, a Communist state was ushered in after the armed proletariat overthrew the capitalist exploiters and grasped the means of production. But in Mongolia there was no industry, no capitalist class and no proletariat. Lenin therefore advised the Mongolian revolutionaries that their country should bypass capitalism and proceed to the Communist stage. This is the program that Mongolia has followed since.

Initially Mongolia had no planning cadres and the party leaders had no previous planning experience or knowledge of basic economics. Thus the country's early plans were misguided, botched and ill suited to the peculiar economic conditions prevalent outside the cities. To achieve the rash targets they had set for themselves, the leaders resorted to force, expropriation and punitive taxation. Widespread uprisings forced the government to cancel its plans in 1932 and to permit the nomads to resume their ancient ways.

The next attempt at comprehensive economic planning did not take place until 1947, when the first five-year plan was unveiled. This time the government abandoned forcible collectivization in favor of voluntary cooperation. However, since stock raising, the main economic activity, was outside the socialized sector, the government could not gain control of the economy. When the taxes became too heavy the nomads simply consumed their livestock and thus reduced the national herd. The government was unable to resolve this dilemma, and thus the first plan failed to achieve any of its goals.

The second five-year plan was more realistic, increasing efforts at collectivization on the one hand and using taxation powers more equitably. Nevertheless, the plan fell behind targets in all sectors. But the marked expansion of Soviet and Chinese economic aid beginning in 1955 enabled Mongolia to fulfill most of its goals by the plan's end in 1957. Whole factories were sent from the Soviet Union, which also lowered the prices of its exports to Mongolia and raised the prices of imports from it. At the same time, China furnished funds to build roads and bridges as well as factories making paper, glass, textiles and plywood.

At the insistence of the Soviet Union the government put off the commencement of its third five-year plan until 1961 and adopted an interim three-year plan (1958–60). The purpose was to synchronize the Mongolian plans with the Soviet ones. By this time the Soviets had taken over management of the Mongolian economy and the planning process. The Soviets imposed their own aims on the economy, including the total collectivization of the nomads and the greater integration of Mongolia with other COMECON economies. In regard to the former, success was virtually complete. In the sphere of industrial development the results were impressive, but the success reflected not so much the vigor of the domestic economy as much as the magnitude of Soviet and Chinese aid. Beginning with the third five-year plan (1961–65), planning became purely an exercise in aid, consisting of entire industrial plants, public health facilities, electric power line grids, agricultural machinery, building materials, trucks, combine harvesters and purebred livestock. In addition, the Soviet Union maintained at its expense a horde of technicians, planners, agricultural experts and industrial managers; granted Mongolia a loan of 645 million rubles; and postponed repayment of a previous loan of 245 million rubles. As a result, Mongolia made considerable progress during this period. Compared with 1960, industrial production rose by 60%, electric power generation by 100%, coal production by 70%, light industry by 33%, heavy industry by 11.4%, wool products by 100%, footwear by 50%, nonferrous metals by 400%, grain production by 50% and land under cultivation by 100%. Average national income rose by 50% and workers' incomes by 25% in this period.

Succeeding five-year plans have maintained this momentum. The seventh five-year plan (1981–85) and the eighth five-year plan (1986–90) led to the following increases:

	Seventh (%)	Eighth (%)
NMP	37	26–29
Gross industrial production	56	30–34
Gross agricultural production	18	18–20
Foreign trade	100	20–25

Despite this progress, Mongolia has not become a full-fledged industrial country, and its economy remains tied to the livestock sector. With a livestock-to-human ratio of 9:1, the highest in the world, the sector has obviously reached its production limits. The economy's greatest strength lies in the generosity of the Soviet Union in underwriting the lion's share of the country's investment needs.

PUBLIC FINANCE

The fiscal year is the calendar year. The constitutional provisions relating to public finance are very detailed. It requires the government to exercise strict control over the economy through state economic plans having the force of law and through annual budgets drawn up in accordance with the plans. It also calls for establishment of a social fund that has first claim on national expenditures. The Council of Ministers is authorized as the chief architect of the national plans and budgets, with plenary powers over money, banking and credit.

PRINCIPAL ECONOMIC INDICATORS*

Gross National Product: $1.7 billion (1985)
GNP per capita: $880 (1985)
GNP average annual growth rate (%): 3.6 (1976–85)

*Additional data for Mongolia's principal economic indicators are not available.

Data regarding Mongolia's balance of payments have not been published.

GROSS DOMESTIC PRODUCT, 1988*

Sectoral origin of GDP (%)
Primary
    Agriculture: 16
Secondary
    Manufacturing: 32.4 (includes mining)
    Construction: ⎫
    Public utilities: ⎭ 5
Tertiary
    Transportation & communications: 11
    Trade: 33
    Finance: ⎫
    Public administration & defense: ⎬ 2
    Services: ⎭

*Additional data regarding Mongolia's Gross Domestic Product are not available.

Mongolia does not provide official development assistance to other countries.

CENTRAL GOVERNMENT EXPENDITURES, 1986
% of total expenditures

Defense: 13.5
Education: ⎫
Health: ⎬ 38.7
Housing, Social Security, welfare: ⎭
Economic services: 42.6
Other, including administration: 5.2

CENTRAL GOVERNMENT REVENUES, 1986
% of total current revenues

Taxes on income, profit & capital gain: 0.7
Social Security contributions: 3.5
Domestic taxes on goods & services: 62.7
Deductions from profits: 29.9
Other: 3.2

Both the central budget and the local budgets are prepared under the direction of the Ministry of Finance. The unified budget is a composite of the central government budget, the *aimak* and municipal budgets and the social insurance budget. However, statistical information is available only for the central and the unified budgets. The central budget finances national activities, such as defense; the local budgets finance education, housing, health and local services; and the social insurance budget finances pensions, social welfare and disability. Revenue sources also are divided into central and local. The former include turnover, profits and income taxes, bond sales and income from the socialized sector. Local sources include sales taxes, property taxes and licenses. And the social insurance sector receives payroll deductions from all enterprises.

According to a 1960 decree the Ministry of Finance has four main tasks: to expand budgetary capital and revenue reserves; to enlarge socialist property; to improve the country's economic potential; and to provide for the people's welfare. Specifically, it drafts and implements the state budget; estimates revenues; sets domestic prices; prepares financial plans for all state enterprises and determines their revenue contributions; assesses and collects taxes; inspects the expenditures and efficiency of state enterprises; administers curren-

cy reserves and currency rates; keeps track of foreign loans and payments; supervises the accounting and statistical work of all sectors; pays salaries; mints coins and prints currency; and reports to the Council of Ministers on the general economic health of the nation. Within the Ministry of Finance are a number of advisory bodies and statutory agencies; including the State Accounting and Statistical Inspection Administration and the Auditing Administration.

The first central budget dates from 1921, when the expenditures were reported as 1.7 million tugriks. But it was not until 1934 that the first true budget appeared, particularly following a change in recording taxes and expenditures in kind to monetary taxes and expenditures. In the 1930s defense expenditures accounted for the bulk of budget expenditures. After the war, as defense expenditures declined, development expenditures rose. A turning point in this direction came after 1954, when the Soviet aid program was stepped up. Expenditures on the national economy rose from 21.9% in 1940 to 42.6% in 1986 and sociocultural expenditures from 19.7% to 38.7% during the same period. Administrative expenditures remained relatively low (6.3% in 1940 and 4.1% in 1986), but defense expenditures rose from 6.4% in 1960 to 13.5% in 1986. Budgetary expenditures remain fairly stable except for an occasional hike in wages, pensions and relief payments, and the prices of agricultural and consumer products.

Taxation was used in the early budgets primarily as a punitive measure and as a means of confiscation of wealth hoarded by monks and nobles. Widespread disaffection forced the government to reverse its taxation policies. The government then tried to meet its deficits by overissuing paper money, and when this also failed, resorted to a number of new and innovative taxes: income tax, housing tax, profits taxes on state enterprises, lotteries, sale of bonds and sales taxes. Many were taxes in kind, payable in sheep, cattle, wool and grains. After the war the turnover or sales tax became the most important revenue provider, reflecting the growing productivity of the national economy. Meanwhile, almost all investment funds were provided by the Soviet Union and other COMECON nations. As both foreign aid and sales taxes increased their share of total revenues, income tax rates have been slashed to about 5%. Information is lacking on the relative shares of industry, agriculture and services within the socialized sector.

CURRENCY & BANKING

The national monetary unit is the togrog (formerly tughrik), divided into 100 mongo. Coins are issued in 1, 2, 5, 10, 15, 20 and 50 mongos and 1 togrog and notes in denominations of 1, 3, 5, 10, 25, 50 and 100 togrogs.

Before the establishment of the first Mongolian bank in 1924, all economic transactions were carried on through barter. In place of a monetary unit, bricks of tea, sheep, hides, goats and salt were used as mediums. In all commercial transactions, a variety of foreign currencies was used, such as U.S. dollars, English pounds, Russian rubles and Chinese yanchans. There were no national banks, and currency transactions were handled by foreign banks, such as the Ta Ching Bank, the Russo-Asiatic Bank and the Chun-kuo Yin-han. The monks were the main sources of credit, and usurious rates of 60% were common. In 1919 the Chinese currency became the national monetary medium and remained so until the Communist regime introduced the tughrik in 1925. The new government added to the chaotic conditions by canceling all debts, personal and national.

The absence of a cash economy did not bother the *arats* too much because all their daily needs were met by their livestock or themselves. There were no taxes or other monetary obligations. The few consumer goods that the *arats* needed, such as tea, sugar or salt, could be obtained through barter. Wealth was measured in the number of livestock. In such a society money was irrelevant.

The transformation of Mongolia from a cashless society to one with a modern banking and monetary system occurred in three stages: the establishment in June 1924 of the Mongolian National Bank (commonly called the MongolBank); the inauguration of the national currency called the tughrik, announced on February 22, 1925; and the gradual introduction of the tughrik into circulation from 1925 to 1928. From 1928 the tughrik became the sole currency, and other foreign currencies were not legal tender. In 1929 private lending was made illegal. Further bank reforms took place between 1933 and 1934, making the MongolBank the sole banker for all state and cooperative enterprises and eliminating cash transactions outside the household level.

Initially public finance was rigidly separated in theory from the MongolBank. The government was permitted to borrow from the MongolBank only by depositing previous metals and foreign exchange as collateral for 50% and short-term Treasury bills for the remaining 50%. An absolute limit on the total allowable government drawing from the bank was set at 25% of the total note issue outstanding. The rules were more often observed in their breach. Deficit financing became common through bookkeeping credits and currency issues. By 1933, with the advent of the ruble as the dominant currency, the entire money and credit system was centralized in government hands and the MongolBank ceased to have independent powers.

The MongolBank grants short-term credits to cooperative and state enterprises and also extends long-term credits to capital investments in the industrial sector. However, the amount of loans granted to any borrower is within the parameters of the five-year plan.

The MongolBank has 65 branches throughout the country in every *aimak* and major town. The MongolBank is governed by a central board.

Mongolia's external public debt in 1988 was $4.396 billion. Other data regarding Mongolia's financial indicators are not available.

AGRICULTURE

By tradition, Mongols are livestock herders, not farmers. The harsh climate, low precipitation and poor soil

EXCHANGE RATE (National Currency per U.S. Dollar)									
1979	1980	1981	1982	1983	1984	1985	1986	1987	1988
—	—	—	—	—	—	3.6	3.6	2.83	—

GROWTH PROFILE (Annual Growth Rates, %)*

Population, 1985–2000: 2.3
Crude birth rate, 1985–90: 31.9
Crude death rate, 1985–90: 6.5
Urban population, 1980–85: 3.3
Labor force, 1985–2000: 2.8
GNP, 1975–85: 3.6
Energy production, 1980–86: 6.7
Energy consumption, 1980–86: 3.9

*Other data regarding annual growth rates in Mongolia are not available.

discourage farming. The Communist regime therefore has devoted its efforts under the five-year plans to developing a farming sector and to making Mongolia self-sufficient in grains. This goal had been achieved by the 1980s.

In the first decade of the MPR over 90% of the population was engaged in animal husbandry and almost the entire export trade consisted of unprocessed livestock products. This proportion has changed only slightly since then. The principal livestock products include butter; sheep wool; goat down; horse, goat and yak hair; sheep, goat, lamb, kid, calf, foal and antelope skins; cattle, horse and camel hides; and tails. The breakdown of the livestock population by number is cattle 13.6%, sheep 75.0%, horses 11.0% and hogs the remainder. However, the expansion of livestock can be sustained only through large-scale agriculture and the production of fodder. A major objective is to ensure livestock feed supplies in winter. This has required the abandonment of nomadism and its replacement by a settled way of life characteristic of farming.

Livestock raising is favored by the fact that about 84% of the country is suitable for pasturage and about 25% contains pastures of high-yield grass. The best pastures are in the eastern and central *aimaks*, in Arhangay and in northern Bayanhongor. The western lake region contains pastures of average quality, and the Gobi region has low-quality pastures.

Sheep raising is undertaken in all parts of the country and accounts for 40% to 50% of livestock production by value. Where the fodder resources are inferior, such as in mountainous areas and semidesert regions, the tough goat takes over. Over half the cattle are raised in the Khangai wood steppe. Small horned cattle are raised in the Southwest. Particularly in the high mountainous regions and in the West, the yak and the *khainag* (a superior hybrid of bull yak and cow) are raised for milk, butter, meat and for pack and riding purposes.

Although horses are distributed rather evenly, most are in the steppes of the South and Southeast. The swift riding horse was the favorite animal of Chingis Khan and his successors. The two-humped Bactrian camels are in the desert and semidesert areas of the South and Southeast. Camels are raised for wool, milk and meat, but their use in overland pack and riding has been diminishing. Minor herds of deer and reindeer are raised in the Northwest, especially in the forests of Khubsugul. Mongols also are turning to poultry, bees, hogs, rabbits and sables.

Most of the arable land suitable for plowing is in the river basins of the Orkhon and Selenga in the northern and north-central districts. At the time that Nikita Khrushchev launched his ill-fated "virgin lands" scheme in the Soviet Union, Mongolia followed suit with a similar program in the Bulagan, Selenga and Tub *aimaks* and has since claimed much success. In the West, South and East only irrigation agriculture is possible.

Apart from food and fodder crops, vegetables are grown in single lots, mainly in riverine or inundated districts, such as in the Onon River Valley or in the outskirts of Ulan Bator. Horticulture is encouraged in the northern *aimaks*.

After some initial setbacks in its efforts at collectivization of agriculture, the government managed to eliminate the private sector completely except for small permissible herds belonging to individual members of the cooperatives. Formal state ownership is restricted to state farms (which account for 70% of crop acreage and over 80% of the crop yield) as well as the mechanized livestock stations that serve about half of the agricultural cooperatives. After 1959, when the collectivization program was completed, the main thrust of official policy has been toward consolidation. All farm workers are required to carry a labor record book, a lifetime record of wages, hours, punishments, charges, bonuses, approval of good work, etc. The state sets procurement prices; issues agricultural machinery, including tractors; extends loans on easy terms; and facilitates artificial insemination of livestock. Through the Ministry of Water Conservancy the government provides watering and irrigation facilities in pasturelands.

Instead of the quantitative increases in livestock population planned by the Mongolian government, the number of reported livestock declined from some 23 million in the early 1960s to 22.6 million in 1986. Some of the decline may be due to undercounting or underreporting by the *arats*, but a major reason is the high rate of exports of livestock on the hoof to the Soviet Union. Droughts, poor water and fodder reserves, floods, storms and diseases have historically limited livestock growth. The government has devoted much of its attention to introducing new water supplies, improving veterinary services, constructing new cattle pens and improving selection and breeding.

Farming, the "new branch of the economy," has enlarged its share of the gross value of agricultural output as a result of the opening of virgin lands and the expansion of water resources. Large-scale mechanization also has played an important part.

The four principal crops are wheat, barley and oats, for which the 1986 production figures were 664,000 tons, 146,000 tons and 49,300 tons, respectively. The wheat harvest reached a record 890,000 tons in 1985, enabling Mongolia to meet its own internal demand and to export excess wheat to Siberia. In 1987 production of potatoes was 137,900 tons, that of vegetables 45,600 tons and that of fodder 291,000 tons. In the same year

there were 225 collectives, 52 state farms and 17 fodder farms.

Forests account for 9.6% of the total land area of 1,565,000 sq. km. (604,248 sq. mi.). About four-fifths of the forests are concentrated in the North. Khubsugul and Khentai possess vast forest potential. Birch, cedar, larch and fir trees predominate. Sawn-wood production increased from 10,800 cu. m. (381,402 cu. ft.) in 1952 to 470,000 cu. m. (16,598,035 cu. ft.) in 1985. Since 1960 a number of new mills have started producing plywood, matches, newsprint, furniture, etc. Exploitation of the immense timber resources possesses an impressive potential.

Fishing is limited to the Buir Nur, Khubsugul and other rivers, from which the most important fish catch consists of sturgeon, salmon, trout and grayling.

AGRICULTURAL INDICATORS, 1988

Agriculture's share of GDP (%): 16
Cereal imports (000 tons): 55
Index of Agricultural Production (1979–81 = 100): 110 (1986)
Index of Food Production (1979–81 = 100): 113 (1986)
Index of Food Production Per Capita (1979–81 = 100): 97 (1984–86)
Number of tractors: 11,100
Number of harvester-threshers: 2,800
Total fertilizer consumption (tons): 16,100
Fertilizer consumption (100 g. per ha.): 137
Number of farms: 300
Average size of holding, ha. (ac.): 385,000 (950,950)
Tenure (%)
  State: 16.0
  Collective: 84.0
% of farms using irrigation: 3
Total land in farms, ha. (ac.): 124,587,000 (307,729,690)
Farms as % of total land area: 79.6
Land use (%)
  Total cropland: 0.9
    Temporary crops: 66.8
    Fallow: 33.2
  Meadows & pastures: 99.1
Yields, kg./ha. (lb./ac.)
  Grains: 1,422 (1,269)
  Roots & tubers: 11,333 (10,115)
  Pulses: 1,050 (937)
  Milk, kg. (lb.)/animal: 421 (928)
Livestock (000)
  Cattle: 2,408
  Sheep: 13,249
  Hogs: 56
  Horses: 1,971
Forestry
  Production of roundwood, 000 cu. m. (000 cu. ft.): 2,390 (84,403)
    of which industrial roundwood (%): 43.5
  Value of exports ($ 000): 70
Fishing
  Total catch (000 tons): 0.4
    of which marine (%): 0

MANUFACTURING

Food processing accounts for approximately half the total value of industrial output and three-fourths of the export trade, excluding minerals. The other two categories of manufacturing are light industries and handicrafts, and consumer goods. There has been no attempt to build a heavy industry sector.

MANUFACTURING INDICATORS, 1988

Share of GDP: 32.4% (includes mining)
Labor force in manufacturing: 10.2%
Value added in manufacturing:
  Food & agriculture: 26.8%
  Textiles: 43.2%
  Machinery: 6.6%
  Chemicals: 23.4%

The major segments of the food processing industry are milk products and meat processing. Milk products include butter, cottage cheese and pasteurized milk as well as the fermented *airag*, the national drink. The meat combine at Ulan Bator is one of the largest mechanized food processing enterprises built with Soviet aid. There is another meat processing combine, built with the help of East Germans. Among newer food industries are bakeries, flour mills, confectioneries, breweries and distilleries. Dairy products, meat and meat products, and fish are exported.

Light industries include textiles and woolen fabrics (both knit and felt) and leather goods. The largest of such enterprises is the Choibalsan industrial combine at Ulan Bator. Begun in 1934 and rebuilt in 1958, the combine includes tanneries, shoe and boot factories, wool washing and felt manufacture. Other industries are numerous but generally small, and produce matches, industrial alcohol, porcelain and carpets. Poland has helped build a factory for timber processing, and Hungary a large veterinary pharmaceutical works.

Consumer and household goods are produced by artels from waste and by-products, substandard raw materials and various locally available resources. Initially these artels employed ex-monks who had been forced out of the monasteries. Consolidation of the smaller artels and the introduction of mechanization has helped to expand the output of these cooperatives. Among the large variety of consumer goods produced by them are clothing leather, china, enamelware, plywood, salt, screws, glue and *ger* (the Mongolian felt tent). Artels also have expanded into repair services, dry cleaning, construction and transportation. Some artels composed of artisans skilled in carving, engraving and embroidery are producing traditional folk art and jewelry.

Manufacturing is organized generally along Soviet lines, with government ministries and commissions responsible for administering and running industrial enterprises. Legislation on the workweek, compensation, hours, etc., also is modeled on that in the Soviet Union. There are party cells in each plant, and managers are subject to detailed supervision by both party officials and the appropriate ministry officials. In the 290 industrial plants built by the USSR, Soviet advisers and technicians play a major role in the operation and have a large degree of autonomy.

Until the early 1960s industrial production was concentrated in Ulan Bator, which still accounts for 50% of the industrial production. Ulan Bator includes many of the nation's older industries. Among the newer industrial centers are Darkhan, Choibalsan and Erdenet.

Darkhan, close to the Soviet border and formerly a pastureland, has been under development since 1961 and now includes a city that has in addition to a large grain elevator, factories producing asphalt, wood products, bricks, cement, concrete and meat products. The nearby coal mines at Sharyn Gol have permitted creation of the most powerful thermoelectric power complex in the country. Another growing industrial city is Choibalsan, capital of Dornod Province. Choibalsan is a large, coal-centered complex specializing in wool and meat products. The fastest-growing industrial area is Erdenet, the third most populous city, where a combined copper-molybdenum works reached full production in 1983. Its 20-million-ton output accounts for 40% of Mongolia's total exports.

MINING

Although Mongolia has rich mineral deposits, mining is limited because the country has yet to be intensively prospected. Besides coal, which is the principal mineral, gold, tungsten, fluorite, wolfram, lead, zinc, copper and uranium deposits also are reported, and some of them are being mined.

Before the revolution, coal mining at the Nalaikha mines near the capital was the largest industry, employing 40 predominantly Chinese workers. The coal reserves cover over 78 sq. km. (30 sq. mi.), connected with Ulan Bator via a broad-gauge railroad. In 1964 or early 1965 the Sharyn Gol open pit mine near Darkhan commenced operations and together with Nalaikha now supplies 80% of the total coal output. The remaining coal comes from Choibalsan, which has a potential of several billion tons. There are other sizable deposits scattered throughout the country, particularly in the *aimaks* of Sukhe Bator, Central Gobi, Ubsa and Bayan Ulugei. Total coal and lignite production in 1986 was 6,964,000 tons.

Fluorite is mined principally at Borondor and exported to the Soviet Union. Large-scale copper mining and concentrating began at Erdenet in 1978, and the copper-molybdenum plant came on stream in 1983. Its production is likely to dwarf that of all other mineral resources.

ENERGY

Mongolia's energy resources are scanty. Oil was discovered in the Gobi in the early 1940s, and in 1948 an agreement was signed with the Soviet Union providing for geological prospecting. Oil wells have been operating in Sain Shanda since the early 1950s. In 1957 the Soviets turned over the joint petroleum company Mongolneft to national hands. There is a small refinery at Dzun Bayan. Currently there is no oil production. Oil imports from the Soviet Union constitute a heavy drain on the economy.

The first power plant was opened in Ulan Bator in 1924 with an output of 60 kw. The output grew to 110 kw. in 1928, 500 kw. in 1934, 5,500 kw. in 1939 and 24,000 kw. in 1960. A 350-km. (218-mi.) high-voltage power line was completed in 1967 linking Ulan Bator, Darkhan and Sukhe Bator in a single grid. Mongolia's fourth power station went into operation in Ulan Bator in 1985. Its capacity of 380 mw. doubled the country's generating capacity. The station is fueled by coal from Baga Nur.

ENERGY INDICATORS, 1988

Average annual energy production growth rate (%): 6.7 (1980–86)
Average annual energy consumption growth rate (%): 3.9 (1980–86)
Energy consumption per capita (kg. oil equivalent): 1,195
Electricity
    Installed capacity (kw.): 760,000
    Production (kw.-hr.): 2.8 billion
        % fossil fuel: 100
    Consumption per capita (kw.-hr.): 1,530
Coal, 000 tons
    Reserves: 24,000,000
    Production: 6,000
    Consumption: 5,750

LABOR

There was no labor force as such in Mongolia until the establishment of the republic in the 1920s. The semi-independent nomads led an unregulated working life, with each family comprising a self-contained unit. The skills necessary to function in a modern economy were irrelevant, and the discipline and work regimen of industrial life were totally alien. The creation of a modern labor force in such a context remains a singular achievement of the Communist regime. The distinction between "workers" in the official sense and *arats* (the traditional herdsmen or craftsmen) still is maintained. Whereas in 1924 the percentage of the latter was 100%, it is now in the single digits.

The creation of a modern labor force faced other constraints as well. The first was the small size of the national population, less than 1 million in the 1920s. The second was the even smaller size of the urban population, who form the core of any industrial labor. The third was the high rate of illiteracy and the typical nomad's disdain of formal learning. As a result, growth was slow in the early decades. In 1932 there were only 2,335 workers; by 1939 the number had risen to 31,098, by 1948 to 55,500 and by 1964 to 167,700. In 1988 the labor force was estimated at 894,000, of whom 60.8% were in agriculture, one of the highest percentages in the world. About half of the industrial work force is employed in enterprises with less than 200 workers. One significant feature is the high rate of female participation—48.5%—which reflects the historic role of women in economic activities. As the postwar generation of workers has come of age, there are fewer problems of adjustment to the industrial work ethic.

Most workers in the state industries are drawn from two sources: from state and collective farms where many of them gain their first mechanical experience; and from among conscripts who have finished their tour of compulsory duty in the army. Large numbers of industrial personnel are sent to the USSR for training.

Hundreds of Soviet technicians remain in the country, although they keep a low profile for political reasons. Technicians and engineers turned out in domestic schools are reportedly quite competent.

The Mongolian Labor Code is modeled on that of the Soviet Union. The differences between the two reflect the peculiar circumstances of Mongolia as a developing country. Because of the negative attitude of Mongolian workers to work regulations, a scale of harsh penalties is prescribed for those flouting plant regulations, such as leaving work without authorization, idleness, tardiness, leaving early or performing low-grade work. These penalties are matched by a corresponding system of incentives and benefits, such as bonuses for honest and conscientious work and the designation of "shock worker" for those who make strenuous efforts to exceed an established work norm or production goal. They also receive generous benefits from the social insurance fund.

LABOR INDICATORS, 1988

Total economically active population: 894,000
As % of working-age population: 82.2
% female: 48.5
Average annual growth rate, 1985–2000 (%): 2.8
Activity rate (%)
    Total: 46.9
    Male: 50.9
    Female: 42.8
% organized labor: 47.5
Sectoral employment (%)
    Agriculture, forestry & fishing: 60.8
    Mining: 1.9
    Manufacturing: 10.2
    Construction: 3.3
    Transportation & communication: 4.1
    Trade: 4.7
    Services: 11.8
    Other: 3.2

Wages usually are calculated on a piece-rate basis, with some quality controls in addition. The quotas are sufficiently low that the ordinary worker can meet them without undue effort. The system is so constructed that the norm rises as the output increases. There are Soviet-style "socialist competitions" in which badges, premiums and other awards are made. Salaries usually are increased automatically after a specified period on a particular job, called "prolonged meritorious service." The worker has few opportunities for moonlighting or other means of increasing earnings outside of regular work. Nor is there much need to do so, since the state takes care of his medical, educational and other extraordinary needs.

As in other Communist countries, the political leadership always is complaining of the poor productivity of the worker and the low quality of the goods. One problem is that the workers are able to handle complex machinery as long as it runs well. Once it breaks down, they are unable to fix it, resulting in long and costly delays.

Although agricultural workers are theoretically "members" of cooperatives, they are in fact employees who are paid according to the number of labordays as recorded in their labor books—a system borrowed from the Soviet Union.

The first trade union congress was held in August 1927, with a membership of 4,056. As there was no industrial tradition in Mongolia when the Communists seized power, so there was no trade union tradition. Thus, trade unions are creations of the state, not its adversaries or equals. They are organized not for collective bargaining or to influence general political and economic policies. As in the Soviet Union, the principal trade union activity is the administration of social insurance. Women constitute 49.8% of the trade union membership.

The principal labor federation is the Central Council of Mongolian Trade Unions (CCMTU), which is an arm of the MPRP. There is no specific provision for collective bargaining. Local worker committees and people's courts are empowered by law to form "commissions for labor disputes" to settle labor grievances.

The legally prescribed workday is eight hours for adults, seven hours for those between 16 and 18 and six hours for those aged 15. Those under 18 are forbidden to do arduous work, and those aged 15 may work only with permission of the local trade union committee.

FOREIGN COMMERCE

From 1921 to 1952 the Soviet Union was Mongolia's sole trading partner. During the next decade China was first added and then discarded as a trading partner, but more durable trade relations were established with other COMECON members and non-COMECON Communist nations. Trade with non-Communist nations is insignificant. However, the total extent and direction of trade can be gleaned from scattered data only. Mongolia does not publish a balance-of-payments statement or other comprehensive data on foreign trade. Neither do its principal trade partners reveal much about their export and import dealings with Mongolia.

Although the Soviet Union's share of total trade has declined since 1952, there is no doubt that Soviet trade is the economic lifeline for the country. From the standpoint of the Soviets, there is little distinction between trade and aid. Its trade terms are very liberal, and sizable trade deficits on the Mongolian side are allowed to accumulate until Mongolia is able to settle them. The USSR virtually underwrites Mongolian trade needs, almost as if Mongolia were one of its constituent republics. The composition of trade is governed by the periodical trade pacts as well as by the synchronized five-year plans of the two countries. Mongolia's exports are heavily in primary products—42.6% from the mineral sector and 39.9% from the livestock sector in 1988. Imports cover a wide spectrum of goods not produced in Mongolia, including heavy capital goods, durable comsumer goods, advanced technological products and pharmaceuticals. The pattern had been stable since the 1950s, changing only after exports of copper-molybdenum became a major revenue earner in the 1980s.

FOREIGN TRADE INDICATORS, 1988		
Exports: $388 million		
Imports: $1 billion		
Balance of trade: −$612 million		
Direction of Trade (%)		
	Imports	Exports
EEC	—	—
U.S.	—	0.7
East European countries	96.8	90.7
Japan	0.1	1.3
Composition of Trade (%)		
	Imports	Exports
Food & agricultural raw materials	10.4	39.9
Ores & minerals		
Fuels	28.7	42.6
Manufactured goods	59.5	17.5
of which chemicals	6.0	—
of which machinery	36.2	0.1

TRANSPORTATION & COMMUNICATIONS

Before 1924 only a primitive communications and transportation system existed. Most princes maintained horse relay stations in their domains. There were few roads, nor, in view of the flatness and hardness of the steppe, was there any real need for them. The great caravan routes crossed Mongolia at several points, providing the principal outlets to the rest of Asia.

Although a public transportation agency was established after 1929, horse relay stations continued to be the main modes of transport well after World War II. It was only in 1950 that the state began to take its duty to provide a national transportation system seriously. Under the five-year plans, quotas for road-building were funded. As of 1988 47,600 km. (29,584 mi.) of roads had been laid, of which only 900 km. (559 mi.) have hard surfaces. Both the Soviets and the Chinese were active in road-building as part of their aid packages.

The first railroad was built in 1939 by the Soviets as a spur of the Trans-Siberian Railroad to Choibalsan. In 1949 a railroad was built from the Russian border to Ulan Bator; the railroad was extended in 1957 to China, thus becoming the Trans-Mongolian Railroad. A 100-km. (62-mi.) spur from the Trans-Mongolian Railroad at Darkhan to the coal mines at Sharyn Gol was opened in 1963, followed by similar spurs to Erdenet, Baga Nur and Borondor.

There is a small amount of lighter and barge traffic on the Selenga, the country's only navigable river, and somewhat more on Lake Khubsugul.

Internal air transportation is provided by the Mongolian Civil Air Transport. The major airport is Buyant-Uhaa, at Ulan Bator.

DEFENSE

The Mongols are proud inheritors of one of the grandest martial traditions in history, and their horse-mobile, nomadic forefathers ruled over an empire that stretched from the Danube to the Yellow Sea. Their military culture declined after the discovery of firearms in the 14th century, but the prime event that signaled the enfeeblement of this martial race was its conversion to Buddhism in the late 17th century. Eventually a third to a half of the male population escaped military service by joining monasteries. Nevertheless, the Mongols could be fierce, well-disciplined fighters when called on by the Manchus to participate in counterinsurgency and in actions against foreign invaders in the 19th century.

The modern Mongolian People's Army (MPA) traces its descent not from the hordes of Chingis Khan but from the Mongolian People's Revolutionary Army (MPRA), founded by Sukhe Bator and Kharlogiyn Choibalsan in 1921, thus predating the founding of the MPR. The MPRA was transformed into the MPA on the founding of the republic but was built up in the face of widespread reluctance to enlist. Most recruits were illiterate; were afflicted with various diseases such as venereal disease, trachoma and tuberculosis; and further, were indoctrinated against military service by the monks, who themselves were exempt from it. Restive by nature, most recruits deserted, and they were impossible to apprehend in the vastness of the steppe. It was not until the new Military Council put teeth into the military service enforcement provisions of the Legal Code, abolished all but a few monasteries, returned monks to civilian life and prohibited young men from becoming monks that the foundations of an effective army were laid in the 1930s. The MPA performed well against the Japanese in the conflicts before and during World War II but since then has seen no military action.

As in the Soviet Union, the army and the party are closely interwoven, with parallel command structures in the government and the party, the latter clearly being dominant. Because the army is trained and directed under Soviet aegis, it tends to be more pro-Soviet than other sectors. Thus the MPA is both an instrument of the party and an agency to keep the party entirely amenable to Soviet direction.

Although the minister of defense is the technical head of the armed forces, a little-known body known as the Military Council plays a central role in control of the MPA. The Military Council was one of the first agencies set up by the Soviets under the Mongolian-Soviet Defense Accord of 1921. The council, which includes the minister of defense and the chief political commissar of the army, works in close conjunction with the Special Military Department of the party's Central Committee. Because all members of the council also are key party members, its directives carry the weight of party decisions. Party control is reinforced by the fact that 90% of the officers and 30% or more of the soldiers are members of the party or of its youth group, the Revsomol. Although there have been a number of purges in top army personnel since 1924, there have been no reported attempts at revolt or coup against the regime.

The army's role in developing the economy is fourfold: inculcation of a political consciousness and discipline among a people historically alien to concepts of organization; literacy; teaching of transferable technical skills; and the use of army units as a disciplined labor force for construction projects in a labor-short country.

Because of the small population, even the present reported level of 24,500 men under arms is a burden on the economy.

The MPA is a true satellite army in the sense that it is totally dependent on the Soviet Union for equipment and training. The mutual relations between the Red Army and MPA are governed by defense protocols, the first of which was signed in 1936; and defense pacts, the first of which was signed in 1946. The Soviet umbrella has been beneficial to Mongolia, enabling it to maintain a lower defense posture than otherwise. There are no foreign military bases as such in Mongolia.

Little is known of the command structure of the MPA. The minister of defense, who generally holds the rank of a colonel general, is the commander in chief. Assisting him is the chief of general staff. The staff formation consists of directorates and inspectorates on the Soviet model. The directorates are broken down into administrative and technical divisions. There is a provincial military office, which is responsible for conscription, mobilization and reserves. Of the military districts the most important is that of Ulan Bator, which includes a garrison under a general. The Military Construction Administration and the air force also are under MPA command.

Under the conscription laws, some 5,000 to 10,000 men are called up every year, and this call-up provides the basic source of manpower. It is not known how the cadre is obtained nor the source of officers.

Training is provided in a number of military academies, of which the most notable is the Sukhe Bator Military Academy. All academies and other military schools are run under the aegis of a school command, the Military Institute. The training is by Soviet army standards and is supervised by Soviet instructors and advisers or by MPA instructors who have been thoroughly trained in Soviet army standards.

EDUCATION

There was no organized education in Mongolia before 1924. The first secular school was established in Urga (now Ulan Bator) by Jamtsarano, a Russian Buryat, during the first period of Russian hegemony from 1912 to 1917. The monks and the nobles objected to the school and its successors as sacrilegious and subversive, and they were forced to close. Buddhist influences continued even after the establishment of the MPR, but clearly secular education was on the ascendant. The People's University was set up in 1924 with 70 students. Also in 1924, the Central Party School was established; it provided free education to 100 students from poor families. The 1940s and 1950s were landmark decades in the history of education in Mongolia. In 1955 attendance at the four-year elementary school became compulsory. Even while employing harsh methods, the new regime achieved its goal of creating a literate Mongolia. In the process it also created a new generation of workers skilled in the basics of industry and technology. Today there are no private schools in Mongolia.

TRANSPORTATION INDICATORS, 1988

Roads, km. (mi.): 47,600 (29,584)
  % paved: 2
Motor vehicles N.A.
  Road freight, ton-km. (ton-mi.): 2.046 billion (1.401 billion)
Railroads
  Track, km. (mi.): 1,748 (1,086)
  Passenger traffic, passenger-km. (passenger-mi.): 467 million (290 million)
  Freight, freight tonne-km. (freight ton-mi.): 6.333 million (4.338 million)
Air
  Passenger traffic, passenger-km. (passenger-mi.): 322 million (200 million)
  Freight traffic, freight tonne-km. (freight ton-mi.): 7.1 million (4.9 million)
  Airports with scheduled flights: 1
  Airports: 80
  Civil aircraft: 22
Inland waterways
  Length, km. (mi.): 397 (247)
  Cargo, tonne-km. (ton-mi.): 4.3 million (2.9 million)

COMMUNICATIONS INDICATORS, 1988

Telephones
  Total (000): 49
  Persons per: 38
Post office
  Number of post offices: 382
Telecommunications
  1 satellite ground station

No data are available regarding tourism to or travel from Mongolia.

DEFENSE INDICATORS, 1988

Defense budget ($): 249.44 million
  % of central budget: 13.5
  % of GNP: 14.6
Military expenditures per capita ($): 117
Military expenditures per soldier ($): 10,181
Military expenditures per sq. km. (per sq. mi.) ($): 159 (412)
Total strength of armed forces: 24,500
  Per 1,000: 12
Reserves: 200,000
Arms exports ($): 0
Arms imports ($): 10 million
Personnel & Equipment
Army
  Personnel: 21,000
  Equipment: 650 main battle tanks; 135 reconnaissance vehicles; 420 motorized infantry combat vehicles; 450 armored personnel carriers; 650 towed artillery; 100 air defense guns; 300 SAM's
Air force
  Personnel: 3,500
  Equipment: 30 combat aircraft

The rights of all Mongolian citizens to an education is spelled out in Article 80 of the Constitution of 1960. Free tuition is guaranteed, and discrimination against women was removed.

As in other areas, the Soviet imprint is strong in education. In the early days, most teachers were Soviet, and textbooks are translated verbatim from Russian. Russian is compulsory as a second language, and study abroad is almost entirely in the USSR. In 1941, on Stalin's orders, Cyrillic was adopted as the script for Mongolian.

The educational ladder begins with nursery schools and kindergartens, followed by an eight-year middle school or general polytechnic, divided into a four-year primary and junior cycle leading to a two-year special school or senior school or a four-year technical and vocational school. The special-school and the senior-school tracks culminate in a university or in technical or professional institutes.

Schooling is compulsory for eight years. Schooling in the sparsely populated rural areas is a major problem. In many such areas only partial schools are available. The percentage of dropouts is high, and almost one-quarter of the children fail to complete the fourth year. Only one in five general-school dropouts continue their education at the university level.

The school year runs from September through June. Instruction time varies from 24 hours a week in the first three grades to 34 hours a week in the final four. The curriculum has two major emphases: technical subjects and dialectical materialism.

Higher education is provided primarily by the Mongolian State University at Ulan Bator, the country's only university. There are 12 higher institutes: Higher Agricultural School, Higher Fine Arts School, Higher Medical School, Higher Polytechnic Institute, Higher Russian-Language School, Higher Russian-Language Teachers' School, Higher School of Troops of the Ministry of Public Security, Higher Teachers' School, Higher Theological School, State Higher Teachers' School, Sukhe Bator Combined Arms Higher School and Sukhe Bator Higher Party School.

Students in higher-education institutions follow a five-year course. The academic year officially opens on September 1, but first- and second-year students are required to work on state farms during September, and for them classes begin on October 1. Students are graded on a five-point scale.

The education system at all levels is controlled and financed by the state. At the national level, the control is exercised by the minister of education who is formally under a deputy prime minister who heads the Commission on Special, Middle and Higher Education. At the aimak level, there are local education authorities who prepare budgets for schools under their jurisdiction. Some special schools are administered by ministries other than the Ministry of Education.

Adult education is provided by number of institutions, such as trade unions, the Revsomol and other groups. Evening classes also are included.

Teachers are trained in two pedagogical schools. Outstanding teachers are rewarded with the title "propagator of culture" and receive cash prizes.

LEGAL SYSTEM

As in other Communist states, law serves the purpose of building up socialism and is embedded in Marxist-Leninist ideology. As a result, certain institutions that

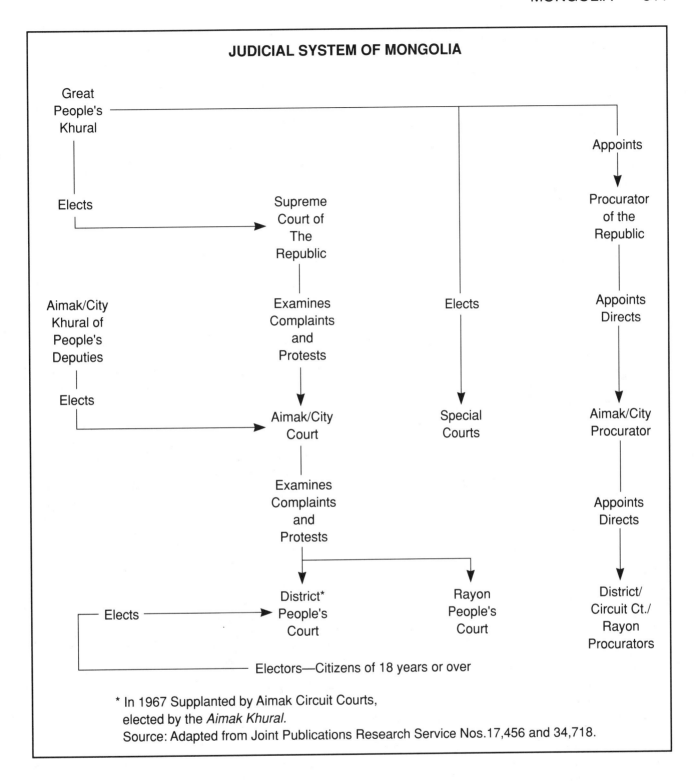

JUDICIAL SYSTEM OF MONGOLIA

Great People's Khural

Elects → Supreme Court of The Republic

Appoints → Procurator of the Republic

Aimak/City Khural of People's Deputies

Elects → Aimak/City Court

Supreme Court of The Republic — Examines Complaints and Protests → Aimak/City Court

Elects → Special Courts

Appoints Directs → Aimak/City Procurator

Aimak/City Court — Examines Complaints and Protests → District* People's Court / Rayon People's Court

Appoints Directs → District/ Circuit Ct./ Rayon Procurators

Elects → District* People's Court

Rayon People's Court

Electors—Citizens of 18 years or over

* In 1967 Supplanted by Aimak Circuit Courts, elected by the *Aimak Khural.*

Source: Adapted from Joint Publications Research Service Nos.17,456 and 34,718.

are legal in non-Communist nations, such as churches and private property, have no legal standing. Also, the emphasis is on the social rather than the private aspects of law, and penalties accordingly are more severe in the former than in the latter.

The Ministry of Justice was abolished in 1959. Present control of the judicial system is vested in the Supreme Court of the Republic and in the procurator's offices.

The courts have a dual function of enforcing laws and of educating the public in Communist morality and legality. The independence of the courts is more fiction than fact. The Constitution states that the courts are subordinate only to the laws, but since the party makes the laws, the courts become instruments of the party, not impartial agents. Law is thus the enforcer of socialist discipline and the protector of socialist property, both of which take precedence over individual rights.

EDUCATION INDICATORS, 1988

Literacy
    Total (%): 89.5
    Male (%): 93.4
    Female (%): 85.5
First level
    Net enrollment rate (%): 99
    Females (%): 49
Second level (includes first level)
    Schools: 678
    Teachers: 17,000
    Students: 428,000
    Student–teacher ratio: 25:1
    Net enrollment rate (%): 84
    Females (%): 51
Vocational
    Schools: 40
    Teachers: 1,200
    Students: 27,700
    Student–teacher ratio: 23:1
Third level
    Institutions: 8
    Teachers: 1,500
    Students: 24,500
    Student–teacher ratio: 16:1
    Gross enrollment rate (%): 25.5
    Graduates per 100,000 age 20–24: 2,297
    Females (%): 63
Foreign study
    Students aboard: 296
      of whom in
        West Germany, 10
        Czechoslovakia, 199

GRADUATES, 1981

Total: 8,000
Education: 800
Humanities & religion: 400
Fine & applied arts: 200
Law: 200
Social & behavioral sciences: 300
Commerce & business: 1,300
Service trades: 100
Natural sciences: 300
Mathematics & computer science: 100
Medicine: 1,300
Engineering: 600
Architecture: 600
Transportation & communications: 600
Agriculture, forestry, fisheries: 1,200

The judicial hierarchy consists, from top to bottom, of the Supreme Court of the Republic, *aimak* courts, city courts, district or circuit courts and special courts. All cases are tried by permanent judges sitting with people's assessors or representatives who sit on the bench with judges. They may question the witnesses and the accused and participate in findings and sentences. When a question of law or its interpretation arises, however, the judges' opinions rule. Thus their functions are different from those of jurors in Anglo-Saxon countries.

The Supreme Court of the Republic is defined in the Constitution as "the highest judicial body charged with the guidance of all other judicial bodies" (Article 65). It is elected by the Great People's Khural for three-year terms. As head of the judicial sector, the Supreme Court formulates national legal policies. The court must hold a general session at least once a month, attended by the procurator or his deputy. Such sessions may review or reverse previous decisions.

The Supreme Court may sit either as a plenary body consisting of the chairman, deputy chairman and members, or as one of three judicial chambers, the first dealing with criminal cases, the second with civil cases and the last overseeing the work of all judicial organs.

Aimak circuit courts have supplanted the district courts. There are 100 *aimak* courts, five to seven in each *aimak*, serving the *somons* and the *khorons* (subdivisions of towns). They have summary jurisdiction over both civil and criminal cases. The judges and the jurors are elected for two years; the judges by the *aimak khural* and the jurors by direct election. The *aimak* and city courts are similar to the circuit courts. Special courts include railroad and military courts.

The Constitution establishes the office of the procurator and vests him with supreme supervisory power over strict observance of the laws. The procurator is appointed by the Great People's Khural for a three-year term; he in turn appoints the *aimak*, city and district procurators for three-year terms. The procuratorial system parallels that of the courts. The procurator is authorized to review the activities of the Ministry of Public Security and its field organs, all military agencies and all judicial agencies. He reviews all cases and sentences and assesses prison conditions. He supports the public prosecution work in each locality, issues arrest warrants, confirms indictments and ensures that all laws and regulations are constitutional and legal. He is assisted by the deputy procurator and the assistant procurator, who are appointed by the procurator subject to the confirmation of the Great People'e Khural.

The legal basis for the criminal justice system is the Criminal Code of 1961. The maximum prison sentence is 15 years, but sentences generally range from six months to 10 years. The death penalty is imposed for serious crimes, such as espionage, murder and armed banditry. Probation may be granted.

Mongolia maintains both prison camps and correctional or educational colonies. The latter are designed to rehabilitate prisoners through socially useful labor. Since alcoholism is the most widely prevalent crime, there are local jails into which intoxicated persons are thrown.

LAW ENFORCEMENT

The Mongolian police force is the Militia, an arm of the Ministry of Public Security. The Militia is responsible for a broad range of law enforcement functions, including issuance of passports for internal travel. A militia department in each *aimak* and district conducts criminal investigations under the supervision of the *aimak* or district procurator. Frontier guards and security police also come under the Ministry of Public Security.

In a number of towns, police brigades exist as auxiliaries to help the militia in crime detection and prevention. The most important of these bodies are the Crime Prevention and Crime Fighting Councils.

Data are not available on incidence and types of crime in Mongolia.

HEALTH

At the turn of the century, the Mongolians were believed to be a dying people—partly as a result of the frequent famines caused by the periodical destruction of the herds, and partly as a result of high infant mortality, which claimed almost half of all Mongolian babies before they were three. The average Mongolian family in the early 1920s had only 1.8 children, which was very low for the time, especially considering that Mongolians practiced no form of birth control. The low birth rate also was due to the widespread prevalence of venereal diseases.

Today's average Mongolian is much healthier than his ancestors. Epidemic diseases, syphilis, rheumatism and trachoma have been wiped out, primarily as a result of better sanitation; better nutrition; better medical facilities; and better ventilation, heating and lighting of the felt-made dwellings known as gers. Sanitation problems were particularly severe in former times. In the remoter areas people never took a bath in the winter, and some never took a bath in their whole lives because of the scarcity of water. Where water was available, it was contaminated by both people and animals and was used for both drinking and washing without purification. Dysentery was widespread. Persons stricken with contagious diseases were not quarantined. There has been a great improvement in these conditions in the past generation. Bathrooms have been built in most new apartments and houses, and larger towns have modern sewage facilities.

There was not a single trained doctor in the country at the time of the revolution. Monks were the closest things to doctors in historic Mongolia, and their practices and healing arts combined occult sorcery and folk medicine, doing more harm than good. By the 1930s the process of supplanting folk medicine with modern medicine was well under way. In the next half century hundreds of hospitals, polyclinics and medical stations were built, at least one in every aimak, industrial facility and state farm. In doctors per capita, Mongolia now lags behind only Japan in Asia. Most doctors are nationals, trained in the Mongolian State University's Higher Medical School.

FOOD & NUTRITION

The average Mongol eats almost entirely animal products. He rarely eats fruits, cereals or most vegetables and is prejudiced against fish and eggs. Sheep, cattle, yaks, horses, camels and goats are the sources, one way or another, of all he eats. Milk—yak and fermented mare's milk—is consumed by almost everyone, along with butter, cheese and yogurt. Mutton is the most popular meat; horsemeat is popular with the Kazaks, and yakmeat and beef are eaten more selectively. Onions and potatoes are the only vegetables consumed in any quantity.

The average Mongolian consumes 2,966.3 calories and 76 g. (2.7 oz.) of protein per day. This intake represents 113% of the FAO's suggested minimum. By food categories, 56.6% of total calories is derived from cereals, 2.7% from potatoes, 21.9% from meat and poultry, 0.1% from fish, 3.3% from eggs and milk, 0.6% from fruits and vegetables, 5.8% from fats and oils, and 9.1% from other sources.

The national drink is airag, called kumiss in Russian and Tartar. It is effervescent and slightly intoxicating and tastes something like champagne and buttermilk. Another favorite drink is tea, bolstered by milk, butter and salt, in the summer. In the capital vodka is becoming a customary drink among the elite.

The most typical Mongolian dish is boz, a national dish that combines chopped mutton dumplings and cucumbers. The blood and intestines of sheep are the chief ingredients of a popular sausagelike meat. Fat from sheeps' tails has historically been considered a great delicacy.

Given the distances separating the various regions, it is surprising that there are few differences in the Mongolian diet. Such differences as do exist reflect buying power and social and physical divisions. Goats are the least valued of all animals because Mongolians like fat (goatmeat has much less fat than sheepmeat). In arid regions, however, goats, being hardier, are more numerous. In the mountains the yak is the most important animal. When animals are slaughtered, their meat usually is dried. On balance, the Mongolian diet is extremely healthy (barring the deficiencies in vegetables and fruits) and high in protein. Mongolians eat better than the neighboring Chinese.

HEALTH INDICATORS, 1988

Health personnel
  Physicians: 4,400
    Persons per: 356
  Dentists: 200
  Nurses: 7,932
  Pharmacists: 300
  Midwives: 963
Hospitals
  Number: 1,659
  Number of beds: 21,200
  Beds per 10,000: 112
Admissions/discharges
  Per 10,000: 2,508
  Bed occupancy rate (%): 89.1
  Average length of stay (days): 14
Type of hospitals (%)
  Government: 100
Public health expenditures
  Per capita: $14.7
Vital statistics
  Crude death rate per 1,000: 9.2
  Decline in death rate: −35.0% (1965−84)
  Life expectancy at birth (years): Males, 61.4; females, 65.5
  Infant mortality rate per 1,000 live births: 47.0
  Child mortality rate (ages 1−4 years) per 1,000: 4.3
  Maternal mortality rate per 100,000 live births: 140
Causes of death per 100,000: N.A.
  Although statistical data are not available, the major diseases include brucellosis, helminthiasis, bacillary dysentery, amoebiasis, enteritis, cerebrospinal meningitis, trachoma, and tuberculosis.

MEDIA & CULTURE

The Mongolian press is a 20th-century phenomenon. The first metal-type press was imported from Russia in 1912, and a small publishing house called the Mongolian Publications Committee was set up in Urga. In 1921, on the eve of the Communist revolution, it employed seven workers and had three machines. After the revolution these facilities were expanded to fulfill the party's propaganda needs. From this time date most major newspapers published today: *Unen*, the official party paper founded in 1920; *Dzaluuchuudyn Unen*, the Revsomol paper founded in 1924; *Hodolmor*, the trade union journal founded in 1928; and *Ulaan Od*, founded in 1930 as the organ of the Ministry of Defense. Interestingly, the titles of all these papers are literal translations of the Soviet counterparts. *Unen* is *Truth*, *Dzaluuchuudyn Unen* is *Youth Truth*, *Hodolmor* is *Labor* and *Ulaan Od* is *Red Star*. There are 31 other newspapers, most of them small *aimak* newspapers or specialized newspapers such as *Nayramdlyn Dzam*, published by the railroad; *Pionyeriyn Unen*, published by the Young Pioneers; *Shine Hodoo*, published by the Ministry of Agriculture; *Sportyn Medee*, published by the State Committee of Physical Culture and Sports; and *Utga Dzohiol Urlag*, published by the Writers' Union. Although described as dailies, most of these papers are published typically 12 times a month or 144 times a year. *Ulaanbaataryn Medee (Ulan Bator News)* is published 208 times a year. Because of the confusion regarding periodicity, some of the papers are described as periodicals and some of the periodicals are described as newspapers.

While all papers are owned and controlled by the party, specific control is exercised by the State Committee for Information, Radio and Television. This committee is responsible for editorial direction, finances, distribution and allocation of newsprint.

The national news agency is Montsame (Mongol Tsahilgaan Medeeniy Agentlag, Mongolian Telegraph Agency), founded in 1957.

Radio broadcasting began in 1934 and television broadcasting in 1967. The former is conducted by Ulan Bator Radio and the latter by Mongoltelevidz. Transmissions include local programs as well as relays of Soviet programs received via the Ekran satellite or the Molniya satellite.

SOCIAL WELFARE

Social welfare programs are administered by the Ministry of Health. There appears to be no central agency for the administration of welfare benefits not associated with health.

Mongolia has one of the broadest programs of social insurance, rivaling those in advanced countries. It includes a full range of medical benefits, disability payments, disability and old-age pensions, unemployment insurance, aid to expectant mothers, burial costs, access to health resorts, and relief payments for persons prevented from working because of illness or injury suffered by other members of the family. All these benefits are constitutionally guaranteed. As a pronatalist nation, aid to mothers, both during and after pregnancy, is paid on a scale rising with the number of children up to eight or more.

```
MEDIA INDICATORS, 1988
Newspapers
   Number of dailies: 2
   Circulation (000): 96
   Circulation per 1,000: 85
   Number of nondailies: 35
   Circulation (000): 718
   Circulation per 1,000: 387
   Number of periodicals: 38
   Circulation (000): 663
   Newsprint consumption
      Total (tons): 3,800
      Per capita, kg. (lb.): 2.1 (4.6)
Book publishing
   Number of titles: 861
Radio
   Number of transmitters: 22
   Number of radio receivers (000): 194
      Persons per radio receiver: 9.7
Television
   Television transmitters: 20
   Number of television receivers (000): 88
      Persons per television receiver: 21
Cinema
   Number of fixed cinemas: 59
   Annual attendance (million): 17.7
      Per capita: 9.4
Films
   Production of long films: 6
```

```
CULTURAL & ENVIRONMENTAL INDICATORS, 1988
Public libraries
   Number: 397
   Volumes (000): 8,700
Museums
   Number: 4
   Annual attendance (000): 7,400
   Attendance per 1,000: 4,400
Performing arts
   Facilities: 21
   Annual attendance (000): 3,600
   Attendance per 1,000: 1,700
Ecological sites: 4
```

CHRONOLOGY (From 1945)

1945—Mongolia declares war on Japan. . . . In national plebiscite, 100% vote for independence from China; vote is recognized by China.

1946—Treaty of friendship and mutual assistance is concluded with the Soviet Union.

1949—Railroad from the Soviet Union to Ulan Bator is completed.

1952—Marshal Kharlogiyn Choibalsan dies in Moscow; Yumjagiyn Tsedenbal is elected chairman of the Council of Ministers. . . . Mongolia signs 10-year economic and cultural agreement with China.

1957—Railway line from Ulan Bator to Peking is opened. . . . Soviet Union hands over joint Soviet-Mongolian enterprises to Mongolia.

1960—New Constitution is promulgated.

1961—Mongolia is admitted to the United Nations.

1962—Mongolia joins COMECON. . . . Frontier agreement is concluded between Mongolia and China.

1972—Jamsarangiyn Sambu, president since 1954, dies; Tsedenbal assumes the position of president and yields the chairmanship of the Council of Ministers to Jambyn Batmonh.

1984—Tsedenbal is removed from all party and state posts; Batmonh replaces Tsedenbal as president and party first secretary; Dumaagiyn Sodnom is named chairman of the Council of Ministers.

1987—Mongolia and the United States establish diplomatic relations.

1988—Before the fifth plenum of the 19th Central Committee of the Communist Party, Batmonh attacks Choibalsan and Tsedenbal for their personality cults and violation of socialist democracy.

1990—Yielding to reformist pressures within the MPR, Batmonh steps down as general secretary of the party and head of state and is replaced by Punsalmaagiyn Ochirbat as head of state and Gombojavyn Ochirbat as general secretary. . . . Sharavyn Gunjaadorj is appointed chairman of the Council of Ministers in place of Sodnom. . . . In the first free national elections in the country's history, MPR retains control of government with an absolute majority in the Great People's Khural. . . . Opposition parties are permitted to form and contest elections, marking the beginning of a new era in Mongolian politics.

BIBLIOGRAPHY

BOOKS

Ballis, William. *The Mongolian People's Republic.* New Haven, Conn., 1956.

Heaton, William. *Mongolia.* Boulder, Colo., 1989.

Lattomore, Owen. *Nomads and Commissars: Mongolia Revisited.* New York, 1962.

_____. *Nationalism and Revolution in Mongolia.* New York, 1955.

Masslennikov, Vasili A. *Contemporary Mongolia.* Bloomington, Ind., 1964.

Montague, Ivor G. S. *Land of Blue Sky: A Portrait of Modern Mongolia.* London, 1967.

Murphy, George G. S. *Soviet Mongolia.* Berkeley, Calif., 1966.

Petrov, Victor P. *Mongolia: A Profile.* New York, 1970.

Rupen, Robert R. *How Mongolia Is Really Ruled: A Political History of the Mongolian People's Republic, 1900–1978.* Stanford, Calif., 1971.

_____. *Mongols of the Twentieth Century.* Bloomington, Ind., 1964.

Sanders, Alan J. K. *People's Republic of Mongolia: A General Reference Guide.* New York, 1968.

_____. *Mongolia.* New York, 1987.

Shirendev, B., and B. Sanjdorj. *The History of the Mongolian People's Republic.* Cambridge, Mass., 1957.

OFFICIAL PUBLICATION

National Economy of the MPR.

Baltic Sea

Pomeranian Bay

SOVIET UNION

Gulf of Gdańsk

SŁUPSK

Gdynia

Gdansk

GDAŃSK

Elbląg

OLSZTYN

SUWAŁKI

Koszalin

POMERANIA

KOSZALIN

Szczecinek

Vistula River

ELBLĄG

Olsztyn

BYDGOSZCZ

Grudziądz

SZCZECIN

Szczecin

Oder River

PIŁA

Bydgoszcz

Toruń

TORUŃ

CIECHANÓW

ŁOMZA

Białystok

BIAŁYSTOK

GORZÓW

WŁOCŁAWEK

Płock

OSTROŁĘKA

Gniezno

PŁOCK

SIEDLCE

EAST GERMANY

Poznań

Zielona
Góra

POZNAŃ

KONIN

SKIERNIEWICE

Warsaw

WARSAW

BIAŁA
PODLASKA

ZIELONA GÓRA

LESZNO

Kalisz

ŁÓDŹ

Łódź

RADOM

Bug River

LEGNICA

KALISZ

SIERADZ

PIOTRKÓW

Radom

LUBLIN

Lublin

CHEŁM

Legnica

WROCŁAW

Wrocław

SILESIA

Kielce

Chełm

JELENIA GÓRA

CZĘSTOCHOWA

Częstochowa

KIELCE

TARNOBRZEG

ZAMOŚĆ

Wałbrzych

Opole

Gliwice

Bytom

WAŁBRZYCH

OPOLE

Sosnowiec

RZESZÓW

PRZEMYŚL

Zabrze

Katowice

CRACOW

TARNÓW

Rzeszów

Przemyśl

80 m

80 km

KATOWICE

Cracow

BIELSKO

NOWY SĄCZ

KROSNO

GALICIA

CZECHOSLOVAKIA

BESKIDS

HIGH
TATRA

Poland

BASIC FACT SHEET

OFFICIAL NAME: Republic of Poland (Polska Rzeczpospolita)

ABBREVIATION: PO

CAPITAL: Warsaw

HEAD OF STATE: President Wojciech Jaruzelski (from 1985)

HEAD OF GOVERNMENT: Chairman of the Council of Ministers Tadeusz Mazowiecki (from 1989)

NATURE OF GOVERNMENT: Socialist democracy

POPULATION: 38,169,841 (1989)

AREA: 312,677 sq. km. (120,725 sq. mi.)

MAJOR ETHNIC GROUP: Poles

LANGUAGE: Polish

RELIGION: Roman Catholicism

UNIT OF CURRENCY: Zloty

NATIONAL FLAG: Two horizontal stripes, the upper white and the lower red

NATIONAL EMBLEM: Silver eagle on a red shield

NATIONAL ANTHEM: "Jeszcze Polska nie Zginela" ("Poland Is Not Yet Lost")

NATIONAL HOLIDAYS: National Holiday (July 22); Labor Day; All Saints' Day; Christmas (December 25 and 26); Easter Monday; Corpus Christi; New Year's Day

NATIONAL CALENDAR: Gregorian

PHYSICAL QUALITY OF LIFE INDEX: 94 (on an ascending scale with 100 as the maximum)

DATE OF INDEPENDENCE: November 11, 1918

DATE OF CONSTITUTION: July 22, 1952

WEIGHTS & MEASURES: Metric

GEOGRAPHICAL FEATURES

Poland, in eastern Europe, is bounded on the north by the Baltic Sea and the Soviet Union, on the east by the Soviet Union, on the west by Germany and on the south by Czechoslovakia and the Soviet Union. Poland has a total area of 312,677 sq. km. (120,725 sq. mi.), extending 689 km. (428 mi.) east to west and 649 km. (403 mi.) north to south, making it almost a perfect square. It shares its total boundary length of 3,708 km. (2,304 mi.) with the Soviet Union (1,244 km.; 773 mi.), Czechoslovakia (1,310 km; 814 mi.) and Germany (460 km.; 286 mi.). Poland's Baltic coastline is 694 km. (431 mi.) long.

The capital is Warsaw (Warszawa), on both banks of the Vistula River south of the influx of the Narew River. Warsaw had an estimated population of 1,664,700 in 1986. There are no other cities of over 1 million in population, but there are 39 cities of between 100,000 and 1 million inhabitants.

On relief maps, Poland appears as an unbroken plain from the Baltic in the North to the Carpathians in the South. However, the land shows great complexity and variety, especially in east-to-west bands, accounting for wide variations in land utilization and population density. The southern foothills and mountains contain most of the country's mineral wealth and much of the fertile soils and thus have the greatest population density. The fertility of the soils and the density of population proportionately decline toward the north.

Most of Poland lies in the northern European plain that extends from the North Sea coast of the Netherlands to the Ural Mountains, dividing Europe from Asia.

MAJOR URBAN CENTERS (est. population, 1986)			
Warsaw		Tychy	185,900
(Warszawa)	1,664,700	Bielsko-Biala	176,900
Lodz	847,400	Ruda Slaska	167,200
Crakow (Kracow)	744,000	Olsztyn	152,200
Wroclaw	640,000	Rzeszow	144,900
Poznan	578,100	Chorzow	140,500
Gdansk	468,400	Walbrzych	140,400
Szczecin	395,000	Rybnik	139,200
Bydgoszcz	369,500	Dabrowa Gornicza	138,900
Katowice	367,300	Opole	127,500
Lublin	329,700	Elblag	119,600
Sosnowiec	258,100	Wloclawek	117,800
Bialystok	255,700	Gorzow	
Czestochowa	250,700	Wielkopolski	117,600
Gdynia	248,200	Tarnow	117,100
Bytom	239,500	Plock	116,300
Radom	219,100	Zielona Gora	112,200
Gliwice	211,200	Wodzislaw Slaski	110,500
Kielce	205,900	Kalisz	105,000
Zabrze	198,900	Koszalin	103,300
Torun	194,600	Jastrzebie Zdroj	101,400

The only highlands are in the far South and Southwest, where Poland shares the Carpathian and Sudeten mountains with Czechoslovakia. The average elevation is 173 m. (568 ft.). More than 90% of the national territory lies below 300 m. (948 ft.), and only 3%, chiefly in the South, rises about 500 m. (1,641 ft.). Rysy, the highest peak at 2,499 m. (8,199 ft.), is on the Czechoslovak border in the Tatry Range of the Carpathians. Six other peaks on the Polish side of the Tatry Mountains rise above 1,900 m. (6,234 ft.). The Sudeten Mountains are lower, with only one peak exceeding 1,600 m. (5,250 ft.).

The lowest land in the country is just south of the Gulf of Danzig, where some 60 sq. km. (23 sq. mi.) lie below sea level.

Geographers usually divide the country into five topographic zones, each extending east to west. The largest, accounting for three-fourths of the national territory, is the great central lowlands area. It is narrow in the west but expands to both the north and the south as it extends eastward. At the eastern border it stretches from the northeastern tip to about 200 km. (124 mi.) of the southeastern border.

To the south of the central lowlands, extending across the country, parallel to the southern border in a belt roughly 90 to 120 km. (56 to 75 mi.), is an area of mountain foothills, blending into the mountains in the extreme South and in the southwestern corner. The mountains constituting the third zone are not very rugged except in the Tatry Mountains. North of the central lowlands is the fourth zone, the Lake District, created by the recession of the most recent glacier millennia ago. This district extends for 200 km. (124 mi.) or more inland from the Baltic Sea in the western part and for a much shorter distance in the eastern section. Glacial action has led to the formation of many lakes and low hills, and much of the area is forested. The fifth zone is the narrow band of coastline in the far North where the soils generally are less fertile.

By far the greatest part of the country drains northwestward to the Baltic Sea by way of the Vistula (Wisla) and Oder (Odra) rivers. Most of the rivers join the Vistula and the Oder systems, but a few in the Northeast reach the sea through Soviet territory.

The Vistula and its tributaries drain a basin almost double the size of the Polish sector of the Oder basin and include practically all of the southeastern and east-central regions and much of the northeastern region. The Vistula rises in the Tatry Range of the Carpathians and flows into the Gulf of Danzig. Most of the Vistula's tributaries flow into it from the east, rising in the Soviet Union, and one of them, the Bug, forms about 280 km. (174 mi.) of the Polish-Soviet border.

The Oder, which with the Neisse (Nysa) forms most of the border between Poland and Germany, is fed by several other streams and rivers, including the Warta, which drains a large section of western and central Poland. The Oder reaches the Baltic through the bays north of Szczecin.

Much of the inland area is poorly drained, and its swamplands are difficult to reclaim. Most of the lakes in the Lake District are small and shallow, the largest two being no larger than 100 sq. km. (39 sq. mi.).

CLIMATE & WEATHER

For much of the year the climate is continental, dominated by high-pressure polar air masses, but the moderating influence of Western Europe's maritime weather helps to offset some of the harsher features of the continental system. Maritime influences are stronger in the winter than in the summer, and there are long, overcast periods of fog, frequent precipitation and high humidity. It is less humid when the polar high-pressure systems are dominant, but it can be extremely cold at such times. Nighttime temperatures fall occasionally into the low −4°C (25°F) range. In mountainous regions during periods of nearly calm winds cold air sinks to the valley floors, making them oppressively cold.

The summer, from June through August, has frequent showers and thunderstorms. Humidity generally is lower than in winter. When winds are from the south and southeast, it is warm and dry. Weather varies widely during both spring and autumn. Winter cold may linger until early April. Early autumn usually is bright, clear and crisp, but by November the weather may turn unpleasant, rainy and cold.

With few exceptions, mean temperatures range between 19°C and 8°C (67°F and 46°F), with marked seasonal variations among regions. The Baltic coastal areas, particularly in the West, have warmer winters and cooler summers than interior regions. The greatest differences between average winter and average summer temperatures occur in the Southeast, near the Soviet border. Although winter temperatures here average about 4.5°C (40°F) colder than in the western part, the annual mean is about the same because of higher summer temperatures. The growing season is approximately 40 days longer in the Southwest (where spring arrives early and autumn is late) than in the Northeast (where spring arrives late and autumn arrives early).

Precipitation averages 500 to 650 mm. (20 to 26 in.) annually over most of the plains, a little higher in the southern uplands and up to 1,300 mm. (51 in.) at isolated places in the mountains. Only small areas receive less than the national average, the largest of these being the city of Szczecin, the Ukrainian border and a corridor along the Vistula from Warsaw to the sea. Throughout the country, summer precipitation is double that of winter.

POPULATION

The population of Poland in 1989 was 38,169,841, based on the last census, in 1978, when the population was 35,061,450. Poland ranks 64th in the world in land area and 26th in population. The population is expected to reach 38,257,000 in 1990 and 39,866,000 in 2000.

World War II demographically affected Poland more than any other European country with the exception of Germany. Population losses during the war and in its immediate aftermath totaled roughly 6 million of a population of some 34 million. A substantial number of Jews perished in concentration camps, and a great many Poles died in combat or through Nazi reprisals against Polish uprising. As a consequence of the Yalta and Potsdam conferences, Poland lost more territory to the Soviet Union than it gained from Germany. The territorial changes led to a massive exodus of non-Poles who had lived in prewar Poland, compensated only partially by the movement of Poles from the areas ceded to the Soviet Union. The net results of these transfers of population were, first, that the 1945 population of Poland was considerably less than the 1939 figure, and second, that the central region of Poland, historically overpopulated, became more crowded as refugees from the East pushed west.

DEMOGRAPHIC INDICATORS, 1988

Population: 38,169,841 (1989)
Year of last census: 1978   World rank: 26
Sex ratio: males, 48.7;   females, 51.3
Population trends (million)
    1930: 29.5   1960: 29.561   1990: 38.257
    1940: 31.5   1970: 32.657   2000: 39.866
    1950: 24.824   1980: 35.578
Population doubling time in years at current rate: Over 100 years
Hypothetical size of stationary population (million): 49
Assumed year of reaching net reproduction rate of 1: 2020
Age Profile (%)
    0–15: 25.7   30–44: 22.0   60–74: 10.1
    15–29: 22.1   45–59: 16.1   Over 75: 4.0
Median age (years): 32.6
Density per sq. km. (per sq. mi.): 121.1 (313.6)
Annual growth rate
    1950–55: 1.89   1975–80: 1.03   1995–2000: 0.58
    1960–65: 1.27   1980–85: 0.95   2000–2005: 0.53
    1965–70: 0.72   1985–90: 0.76   2010–15: 0.40
    1970–75: 0.82   1990–95: 0.61   2020–25: 0.30
Vital statistics
    Crude birth rate, 1/1,000: 17.0
    Crude death rate, 1/1,000: 10.1
    Change in birth rate: 9.2% (1965–84)
    Change in death rate: 29.7% (1965–84)
    Dependency: total, 53.6
    Infant mortality rate, 1/1,000: 18
    Child (0–4 years) mortality rate, 1/1,000: Insignificant
    Maternal mortality rate, 1/100,000: 14.2
    Natural increase, 1/1,000: 6.9
    Total fertility rate: 2.3
    General fertility rate: 67
    Gross reproduction rate: 1.07
    Marriage rate, 1/1,000: 6.9
    Divorce rate, 1/1,000: 1.4
    Life expectancy, males (years): 66.8
    Life expectancy, females (years): 75.1
    Average household size: 3.6
    % illegitimate births: 5.0
Youth
    Youth population 15–24 (000): 5,363
    Youth population in 2000 (000): 6,523
Women
    Of childbearing age 15–49 (000): 9,596
    Child-woman ratio (children per 000 women 15–49): 358
    % women using contraceptives: 75
    Ratio of abortions per 100 live births: 20
Urban
    Urban population (000): 24,179
    % urban, 1965, 50; 1987, 61
    Annual urban growth rate (%): 1965–80, 1.9; 1980–87, 1.5
    % urban population in largest city: 15
    % urban population in cities over 500,000: 47
    Number of cities over 500,000: 8
    Annual rural growth rate (%): −0.6 (1985–90)

The first postwar census enumerated less than 24 million within the country's new boundaries. It was the 1950s before the population crossed the 25 million mark and the 1960s before it surpassed the 1939 population. The early postwar years were marked by a spurt in the annual rate of growth, which reached a peak of 1.95% in 1953 before dropping to 1.7% from 1955 to 1960, to 1.1% from 1960 to 1965 and to 0.8% to 0.9% after

1965 (although it rose briefly, to 1.0%, in the early 1980s). These rates were higher than comparable rates for all European countries except Albania, Ireland and Iceland. The early surge in the growth rate was principally due to a rise in the birth rate, but later, as the birth rate fell, the decline in the death rate helped to maintain the growth rate. After the 1960s the birth rate began to decline more steeply than the death rate. The only exception to this pattern is caused by the pass-along effects of the baby boom of the late 1940s and early 1950s, which appear as a slight bulge in the population pyramid at a 20- to 25-year interval.

Next to the events that led to postwar Poland becoming ethnically homogeneous, the most important demographic trend was the urbanization of the population. The last prewar census showed 72.6% of the population as rural and that 59.6% depended on agriculture for a livelihood. In 1950 about 63.4% still were rural, and 47.1% depended on agriculture as their chief source of income. By the 1980s the ratio had been reversed, with 40% rural and 20% dependent on agriculture. The rapid pace of urbanization is surprising because in general cities had suffered greater population losses in World War II than rural areas. The cities, especially those in the center of the country, were the scenes of the heaviest fighting as well as centers for the German policy of systematic extermination. The greatest population loss was suffered by the *voivodship* (province) of Warsaw. The southern cities showed a relatively smaller population loss. In the former German territories the German population was expelled, and since they tended to concentrate in urban areas, both Wroclaw and Szczecin sustained heavy population losses. All cities had surpassed their prewar population by the 1980s.

Despite these population shifts, the patterns of population density have remained fairly constant. The area of greatest concentration lies along the southern borders, especially along the industrial belt from Wroclaw through Cracow, with Katowice as the hub. There are three other regions of heavy density: Lublin in the southern uplands; the major cities of the central plain, Warsaw and Lodz, along with a number of smaller cities, such as Poznan; and the ports of Gdansk and Gdynia along the Baltic Coast.

Poland had been a major exporter of population to France, Germany and the United States from around the turn of the century (when population counts began to be maintained) until World War II. Migration seems to have a direct correlation to domestic birth and fertility rates. Between 1895 and 1939 Poland had the highest birth rates in its history since censuses began. In the first decade of the 20th century it reached 1.8% per year. Some 22 million Poles are reported to have left their country between 1871 and 1915, making them one of the largest emigrant groups in the world at that time. About half of the emigrants went to the United States. The emigrants consisted predominantly of young adult males, thus causing great loss to the manpower economy. World War I brought emigration to a dead halt, and it was not resumed until about 1923, at a much diminished rate. France replaced the United States as the principal destination. The Polish peasant, chronically underemployed because of shortage of land, was a reservoir of labor for neighboring countries. At the end of the great wave of free emigration, there were reported to be 3 million persons born in Poland who were living abroad, excluding Poles domiciled in Russia, Germany or Austria. However, the Great Depression halted this second wave of emigration. The number of Poles returning actually exceed the number of emigrants during the first two years of the Depression. Nevertheless, Jews continued to emigrate because of a rising tide of anti-Semitism.

After the war, with the Polish population reduced by nearly a third, the Polish government waged a vigorous campaign to induce Poles abroad to return to their homeland. This campaign met with only limited success and was more than offset by numbers fleeing the Communist regime.

ETHNIC COMPOSITION

Poland emerged from World War II as an ethnically homogeneous nation, with Poles constituting over 98% of the population. Between the two world wars, ethnic minorities had made up 30% of the population, or about 10 million people. They included Germans, Jews, Ukrainians, Belorussians, Lithuanians and others, few of whom shared the national faith of Roman Catholicism or spoke the Polish language as a mother tongue. For many Poles, this development is one of the few good things that came out of the otherwise ruinous World War II. Even so, the historic animosities against non-Poles have not entirely died out.

Poles are descended from various Slavic tribes who settled in and around the area of present-day Poland well before the eighth century. Regional distinctions among Polish peasants in dialect, dress, manners and customs follow very roughly the old tribal traditions. Many of the old tribal names persist in modified form. The Polanie (plainsmen) who lived in the neighborhood of modern Poznan gave their name to the whole nation; the Mazowszanie were presumably the ancestors of the Mazurs, who live in the area around Warsaw and northward through Olsztyn to the Soviet border. In the region between these two are the Kujawanie in the area now known as Kujawy around Wloclawek and Inowroclaw. To the north, along the Baltic shore, the area called Pomorze (seaboard) and known in English as Pomerania was inhabited both by the Pomorzanie and by a closely related tribe, the Kaszubie (Kashubs). The Slazanie, in the hilly southwestern part of the country, gave their name to Slask, now Katowice in Silesia. Under German rule some of the Kashubs and Mazurians were converted to Protestantism, and the Germans tried to identify them as non-Polish.

For 1,000 years Germans have been living in Poland, and between the two world wars their number was estimated at 741,000 (according to the Poles) to 1.7 million (according to the Germans). Before the rise of Prussia in the 17th and 18th centuries, Poles had little ill feeling toward the Germans, whom they looked on as stolid and unimaginative and lacking in social graces, but nevertheless able and industrious and highly successful as farmers, artisans and administrators. Under Prussia the Germans seized much of Poland and tried to Germanize the Poles under their rule. But the Poles perceived the Germans as more enlightened than the Russians, and anti-German feeling was not strong among the peasantry. Until World War I intermarriage between Germans and Poles was fairly common, with the German partner generally adopting the faith and language of the Polish spouse rather than vice versa. Such families called themselves Polish or German according to convenience. Those Germans who did not leave German areas ceded to Poland after World War II have been objects of discrimination, and memories of German brutality still linger as a barrier between the two peoples.

After the eastern provinces were ceded to the Soviet Union in 1945, some 300,000 Belorussians still lived in Poland. Never as nationalistic as the Ukrainians, they show little dissatisfaction with their minority status.

The largest minority group in interwar Poland, the Ukrainians were found chiefly in the southeastern provinces, where they constituted a majority in the rural areas although major cities such as Lwow (now Lvov) were predominantly Polish. With the cession of the eastern provinces, the number of Ukrainians was reduced to a little over 100,000. Because the Ukrainians were highly restive, with a history full of uprisings, and frequent pacifications by Polish troops, the cession of the territory relieved Poland of a major minority problem.

Before World War II there were 3.5 million Jews in Poland, over 10% of the national population. Today there are less than 50,000. Jews have been an important social element in Poland since medieval times. For centuries they found the country a refuge from the persecutions inflicted on them in Western Europe. Under the Polish kings they received the right to semi-autonomy in their own communities and with the rise of commerce and cities, they began to flourish as traders and shopkeepers, despised occupations for the majority of Christians. However, the Jews remained outsiders, generating considerable hostility because of their different appearance, language, customs and religion. In the 19th century their predominance in commerce came under attack through semi-official discriminatory legislation. Although anti-Semitism was widespread, persecution was not systematic or universal, and the worst pogroms were limited to the eastern provinces. Jews in Warsaw, Cracow and elsewhere were partially assimilated and spoke Polish rather than Yiddish. The liberation of Poland in 1918 raised new problems for the Jews. Included in the new republic were large numbers of Russian Jews, concentrated in such cities as Grodno, Baranowicz, and Pinsk. They were unassimilated to either Russian or Polish culture, and further, were suspected of being generally leftists. Thus the Jews were considered to be a politically dangerous minority as well. However, the Minorities Treaty of 1919 and a statute in 1927 gave them considerable autonomy. Despite these laws, anti-Semitism flourished in Poland throughout the interwar period. Mobs attacked Jews in various towns in 1919. Institutions of higher learning introduced quotas restricting enrollment of Jewish students. Jews were barred from certain trades and from government service. Pogroms took place in 1937 under Nazi inspiration. The entire community was wiped out under the Nazi occupation with the exception of a few scattered survivors.

The prominence of Jews in the immediate postwar Communist governments only served to intensify the hatred toward the survivors. Since the time of Wladyslaw Gomulka, few Jews have been active in public life. Incidents of anti-Semitism continue to be reported in the Polish press and radio. At the same time, Jewish culture has managed to survive; there are Jewish cultural associations; books, newspapers and radio broadcasts in Yiddish; and a state Jewish theater.

The Karaites, or Karaim, is a separate Jewish sect considered as a separate nationality by the government. More assimilated than other Jews, they are regarded as Gentiles by other Jews and as outsiders by ethnic Poles.

The Polish radio reports that there are about 30,000 Gypsies in Poland, but population counts of Gypsies are notoriously inaccurate. The wandering Gypsy is a familiar figure in the countryside, and Gypsy tinkers and horse traders appear at local fairs. In general Gypsies have acquired a rather disreputable but romantic aura throughout history.

Other small minorities include scatterings of Lithuanians; Russians; Czechs; Slovaks; and Muslims of Turkish or Tatar origin.

LANGUAGE

The Polish language belongs to the western branch of the Slavic language group, in which it is the third most widely spoken after Russian and Ukrainian.

Although related to all Slavic languages, Polish cannot be understood by other Slavic peoples, even by the Czechs and Slovaks who also speak West Slavic. Polish is the only major Slavic language that preserves the old Slavic nasal vowels. It also is characterized by two sets of shushing sounds by a modification of the common Slavic hard *l* into a sound similar to the English *w*.

Like many other western Slavs, Poles use the Latin rather than the Cyrillic alphabet—a result of their conversion to Roman Catholicism. To provide for Polish sounds not found in Latin, accents and other diacritical marks have been added, and special values have been given to certain consonant combinations, most of which involve the letter *z*. The result is a written language that looks like a riot of *z*'s and *c*'s. Even words borrowed from Latin and other Western languages are spelled according to the Polish orthography.

Standard literary Polish had its origins in the speech of the Polish upper classes of about the 16th century. Until that time Polish had virtually no literature, and most official and literary documents were written in Latin. From the time of the Reformation there was a flowering of literary and secular language. The 16th-century poet J. Kochanowski is regarded as the midwife of the language, and since he was a citizen of Cracow, the language he used was the Cracow dialect. In the next three centuries Polish borrowed heavily, first from Latin, then from German and Italian, and later from French, until educated Poles spoke a macaronic language interlarded with foreign words and phrases. A movement for cleansing the language of foreignisms began in the late 19th century, inspired by the poet Adam Mickiewicz. Like Roman Catholicism, Polish has become one of the hallmarks of Polish national identity.

Polish has several dialects. The most divergent from the standard is Kashubian, which is considered by some as a separate West Slavic language. Kashubian has a separate orthography and literature. The remaining five dialects are: Great Polish, spoken near Poznan; Kuyavian, spoken near Inowroclaw and Wloclawek; Little Polish, spoken around Cracow; Silesian, spoken around Katowice and Wroclaw; and Mozovian, spoken around Warsaw and extending north and east. Within these major divisions various subdivisions also are found. There is no standard dialect for the whole country, but the Cracow variety is regarded as the best and that of Warsaw the least desirable. Middle-class Warsaw speech reflects many localisms and is reputed to have a Jewish flavor. Some dialects, such as Mazovian, are the butts of jokes among the educated classes.

Minority languages are rarely employed in public.

There is no language policy as such today.

RELIGION

In terms of its influence on national life, Poland is perhaps the most Catholic country in the world, surpassing in this respect even Ireland, Italy and Spain, in all of which the church has suffered severe erosion of authority in recent years. With a Polish pope in the Vatican, Polish Catholicism is flowering at a time when the church apparently is in retreat in the rest of the world.

Poles have been predominantly Roman Catholic since the 10th century, and since that time the church has been guardian of the national flame—of its customs and morals as well as its political and intellectual integrity. For the majority of the people, Catholic faith and ritual are not merely theological traditions but also part of the national heritage. The Poles have also clung to Catholicism as a symbol of their resistance to the assimilationist pressures from Orthodox Russia and Protestant Germany. Throughout history the ecclesiastical hierarchy has served as an element of unity in times of national stress and division.

Poland's history as a Christian nation began in 966, when the duke of Mieszka was converted to Christianity by his wife; in 968 the first bishopric was established, in Poznan. Under Mieszka's son Boleslaw Chobry, the church grew rapidly with the help of German missionaries. In 1000 Gniezno was made an independent archbishopric, with three suffragan bishops. After Boleslaw's death a reaction set in against the church, and it was not until the 14th century that it became ascendant once again, under the Jagiello dynasty. The founding of the University of Cracow in 1364 and the work of German missionaries also contributed to this revival. The

15th century came to be known as the century of saints in Poland.

Lutheranism spread to Poland in 1518 with Poznan as its center, and Calvinists followed in 1848. Within the next century there arose over 900 Protestant centers, and Catholic influence in government was accordingly diminished. In 1587, shortly after the overthrow of the Jagiello regime and the establishment of the Sejm, Roman Catholicism was declared to be the official church. Catholic-Protestant conflicts among the nobility led to the country being overrun by Russia, Austria and Prussia. In the Russian sector Catholics were severely persecuted, and many bishops and priests were deported to Siberia. The church became a symbol of resistance to the Russians and the Germans, and nationalism and Catholicism fueled one another. In 1656 the Polish-Lithuanian Commonwealth was dedicated to the Black Madonna of Czestochowa. The Madonna was crowned queen of Poland, and since then Poles have annually renewed their vows to her. The Madonna and St. Stanislaw, the nation's patron saint, have become the foci of national unity and hope.

When Poland regained its independence after World War I, the church regained its place of honor in the political system as well. Supporting the government, it, in turn, received considerable official privileges. Its "leading position" was acknowledged by the Constitution of 1921. Religious instruction was made compulsory in all elementary and secondary schools. The Catholic University of Lublin, founded in 1918, exercised a strong influence on the nation's academic life. The church operated 80 seminaries, innumerable monastic institutions and welfare agencies. It also published over 200 periodicals. Poland received special attention at the Vatican after Achille Ratti, the papal nuncio in Warsaw, was elected Pople Pius XI in 1922.

After World War II, the new Communist leaders initially pursued a moderate and conciliatory policy. Cardinal Hlond, interned by the Germans during the last phase of the war, returned to head the ecclesiastical administration. Catholic educational institutions, publications and charitable establishments were quickly reestablished. Numerous churches were rebuilt with state assistance. Religion was included in the curriculum of primary and secondary schools much as before the war. Church estates were exempted from the agricultural reform of 1945. Government dignitaries attended religious functions. When Boleslaw Bierut was elected president, he took a religious oath, and many Communist leaders continued to give their children religious education. All this was accompanied by a revival of religious practice; the shrine at Czestochowa was attended by 2 million pilgrims in 1945.

For its part, the church did not explicitly repudiate the Communist regime, and it eschewed an open confrontation with the atheistic leaders. The first break in the facade of cooperation and goodwill came with the death of Cardinal Hlond in 1948 and the elevation of Cardinal Stefan Wyszynski as primate of Poland. The regime fired the first shots by attacking the Holy See for its confirmation of German clergy as administrators of dioceses in Polish territories seized by the Nazis. In 1949 the regime began to sponsor various groups of so-called patriotic or progressive priests who sided with the government against the Vatican and a lay group of Social Catholics who sought to reconcile Marxism with Catholicism. These groups operated a government-controlled publishing house known as PAX.

From 1949 to 1956 church and government were engaged not in skirmishes but in open war. In 1949 the Vatican issued a decree barring from the sacraments all Catholics who either belonged to the Communist Party or were its willing adherents, and excommunicating Communist activists. The government retaliated by passing a law providing prison sentences for up to five years for any clergyman refusing sacraments to citizens because of their political beliefs or activities. Religious associations and orders were required to register with the government, and possession of religious property was made dependent on government sanction. The pressure on the church was intensified in 1949 through a series of Communist-inspired strikes among workers on church estates. In 1950 Caritas, the church's largest welfare organization, was nationalized. Simultaneously, about 500 priests, nuns and monks were arrested and charged with graft, embezzlement, espionage and sabotage. The Sejm passed a bill calling for the seizure of all church estates over 101 ha. (250 ac.).

In April 1950 church and state reached an agreement. In return for the Vatican's recognition of the Oder-Neisse line as Poland's permanent western boundary and the Polish hierarchy's submission to state laws, the government agreed to refrain from interference with public worship, Catholic associations and publications, and other spiritual activities. The truce lasted for three years before the government renewed its campaign. Fresh arrests of bishops and clergymen followed. Religious instruction was removed from the schools and confined to churches. A 1953 decree drastically limited the authority of the pope in matters of church jurisdiction and gave the government control of all ecclesiastical appointments. A large number of Catholic publications were suspended, some of which later reappeared under new proregime editorial boards. When Cardinal Wyszynski and the Polish episcopate protested against the continuing violation of the 1950 agreement, the government responded with even harsher measures. Wyszynski was suspended from his functions, and two of his auxiliaries, nine bishops and several hundred priests were arrested. The majority of the seminaries were closed, and Catholic universities were placed under state supervision.

The church once again became a rallying point for the nation. The Poles filled their churches for political as well as religious reasons. Attendance at Mass became an act of protest against the regime. Thus when Wladyslaw Gomulka returned to power in 1956, he was faced with a divided nation. To heal the division, Gomulka released Cardinal Wyszynski, reined in PAX activities and gave in on several issues that the government had previously fought most bitterly. Religious instruction was reintroduced; suspended Catholic newspapers were permitted to resume publication; and state veto over church appointments was relinquished except in the most serious cases. The church, for its part, did its best to unite the people behind the new government.

Despite occasional friction, this "October Agreement" formed the basis of church-state relations for over two decades. Then as the 1980s dawned, two events transformed the position of the church. One was the election of the archbishop of Cracow, Karol Wojtyla, as Pope John Paul II; the second was the rise of the Solidarity movement, many of whose leaders, including Lech Walesa, were devout Catholics. These two events have enhanced the role of the church in Poland to that of a national arbiter and the unofficial conscience of the nation. As the Communist hold has weakened, so correspondingly the magisterium of the church has become secure and unassailable.

The proportion of practicing Catholics in the population is greater in Poland than in any other European country. The lowest estimate is about 80%, but the figure commonly accepted is closer to 90%. There are over 20,000 priests, 4,500 members of religious orders and 80 bishops serving over 30 million Catholics. The 46 seminaries enroll about 4,600 students. The episcopate consists of 80 bishops in 27 dioceses. Its president, called the primate of Poland, is named by the pope as archbishop of Poland's oldest see at Gniezno, and since 1945 the office has been held by men of great national stature: Hlond, Wyszynski and Josef Glemp. Each of the 4,700 parishes serves, on average, 4,000 parishioners. There are over 15,000 church buildings today, compared with 7,257 in 1937. Part of this increase was due to the acquisition of 3,297 churches in the former German territories ceded to Poland. Although the state supports and often funds the building of churches, most churches are built by parishioners. An example is the church at Nowa Huta, Poland's largest steel city, built according to Soviet specifications as a Communist stronghold. When originally planned, the city was not to have a church, but the government was forced by public pressure to permit the building of one. A new church at Lodz is almost as big as St. Peter's Basilica and holds 5,000 people.

In the words of one analyst, Jan Nowak, "Catholicism in Poland exudes a greater dynamism than in any other Catholic country in the world." Polish Catholicism has been described as emotional, traditional and unintellectual, but by any standard the Poles are the most devout of all Europeans. In Poland the pressures of secularization, urbanization and the spread of secular education have been offset by attachment to the church as the embodiment of the nation and as a bulwark against all kinds of repression. Patterns of religious commitment and participation are only marginally less for the better educated, the young and the politically active. About 75% of the skilled workers, generally the most unchurched group in other countries, are believers. A survey of workers in four new industrial centers—Pulawy, Kazimierz, Plock and Nowa Huta—shows a high percentage of believers, ranging from 82.4% in Nova Huta to 93.7% in Kazimierz. The cumulative frustrations of life in Poland under the Communist regime obviously

have had the unintended consequence of reinforcing adherence to the church. The Solidarity movement often has used Christian symbols in its public meetings, which invariably open with prayer. One of its principal demands was the broadcast of Sunday Mass over the radio.

Catholicism is less rooted among the intelligentsia and the white-collar professionals, among whom the proportion of believers is estimated at 60%. Roughly the same proportion obtains among university students. Catholic intelligentsia do not feel themselves bound to the doctrines and practices of the church to the same extent as peasants and workers do and generally are lax about religious obligations such as attendance at Mass. However, while they may question the authority of the church in some area or interpret some doctrines differently from the clergy, they do not exhibit any degree of anticlericalism because of a common bond of embattlement.

Polish Catholicism has historically tended to be more mystical then intellectual. It is noteworthy that the Polish church has produced few theologians or philosophers. According to Cardinal Wyszynski, the chief feature of Polish Catholicism is the cult of Mary, whose shrine at the Czestochowa monastery of Jasna Gora is the spiritual center of Poland. It reflects the simple, direct and uncomplicated faith of the people.

The Polish church also is one least affected by the changes introduced by Vatican II. The only major change appears to be the use of Polish in the liturgy. This may be due to the precarious status of the church in a Communist country and the desire not to stress internal disputes in the face of a hostile state. The tension between younger lay Catholics and traditional laity, older clergy and the hierarchy exists but in a muted form.

Church-state relations are regulated by the Bureau of Religious Affairs under the president of the Council of Ministers, with branches in each province. The church receives no subsidy from the government. The church and its institutions are not recognized as public bodies and thus are taxed similar to private enterprises, but with the abolition of compulsory annual listing, these taxes have been reduced somewhat. The church continues to operate a few secondary schools as well as the Catholic University of Lublin. Poland is the only Communist country that permits military chaplains in the armed forces, the chief chaplain having the grade of colonel.

Despite protests from Poland's tiny Protestant minority, public schools began voluntary classes in religious education in 1990. In the 45 years of Communist rule, religious education was permitted in the schools in the years immediately after World War II and again in the late 1950s. But since then, classes in religion were limited to after-school sessions in local churches. About 80% of elementary school students attended, but there was a sharp dropoff among high school and vocational school students. Under the new agreement reached between the church and the Solidarity government, parents will decide whether elementary school children join the twice-weekly, one-hour classes. Students in the upper grades will attend only if both the parents and the children agree.

The autocephalous Orthodox Church of Poland traces its origin to the 10th century. From 1772 to 1948 it was part of the Russian Orthodox Church. With the cession of the eastern provinces to the Soviet Union, the church was reduced to 10% of its former size.

Of the various Protestant denominations, only about one-third are recognized by the state as churches. The rest are listed as "religious organizations," which have no right to build places of worship in Poland. Upper Silesia is the most Protestant part of the country. The largest Protestant body is the Lutheran Church, followed by the Reformed Church and the United Evangelical Church.

There are several non-Roman Catholic churches, the products of several schisms. The largest is the Old Catholic Mariavite Church, founded in 1906. The most important non-Christian religion is Judaism.

HISTORICAL BACKGROUND

The ancestors of modern Poles were West Slavs who lived in the Oder and Vistula valleys. In the seventh century these tribes coalesced—under pressure from the Avars and later the Germans—under the leadership of the Polanie, a tribe occupying the valley of the Upper Varta River, and led by Duke Mieszko; this event marked the formation of the Polish nation. Duke Mieszko (962–92) traced his descent from Piast, and hence the line he established is known by that name. Responding to the challenge from the numerically superior Germans, Mieszko sealed an alliance with neighboring Bohemia by marrying a Czech Catholic princess, whose religion he adopted. Latin missionaries soon arrived to undertake the task of evangelizing the Poles. This event linked the destiny of Poland with that of Western Europe rather than with that of Orthodox Kiev or Constantinople. Mieszko's policies were carried forward by his son and successor, Boleslaw I the Brave (992–1025), who in 1000 concluded an agreement with Holy Roman Emperor Otto III, organizing Polish dioceses under the jurisdiction of an archepiscopal see at Gniezno, thus removing Poland from the German orbit. Boleslaw, who in 1025 took the title of king, deeded his country to the pope, to be held by the Piasts as a fief of the papacy. Thereafter assimilation of Latin cultural traditions was rapid, and Poland emerged as a bulwark of Western Christian civilization.

Although the strong clan system worked against the development of feudal structures, political and social classes began to take shape at this time. The chieftains of the more powerful clans formed the nucleus of Poland's knightly estate, which gradually emerged as noble class, the *szlachta*. Among the *szlachta*, the wealthier families qualified as magnates *(mozni)*. Because the rule of primogeniture never took root in Poland, all children of nobles inherited the rank, and consequently the nobility grew in numbers, composing, by the end of the 15th century, 10% of the population. The nobles constituted "the nation," and only they enjoyed political rights.

The descendants of King Boleslaw III (1102–38) were locked in a fratricidal struggle that enabled German emperors to seize Polish lands with impunity and the pagan Prussians to threaten Mazovia. In 1226 Mazovia's Duke Konrad called for aid from the Teutonic Knights, who thereupon established an autonomous state that eventually comprised the entire region between the mouths of the Vistula and the Nieman rivers. Meanwhile, the Tatars, swarming across Russia and Kiev, menaced Poland but were stopped in 1241 at the Battle of Legnica, in which Henry the Pious of Silesia and a large segment of the Polish nobility perished. The devastation resulting from the Tatar raids opened up the depopulated countryside to mass colonization by German settlers.

This chapter of troubles ended with the unification of Poland under Kasimierz (Casimir) III the Great (1333–70). A brilliant administrator, he fostered trade, reformed the currency, protected the Jews, codified the law and founded the University of Crakow. Kasimierz, who had no male heirs, designated as his successor his nephew King Louis I of Hungary (1370–82), under whom Poland and Hungary were united. After his death the nobles chose his 10-year-old daughter Jadwiga (1384–99) as "king."

In its struggle against the Teutonic Knights, who controlled most of the southeastern shores of the Baltic Sea, Poland found an ally in Lithuania. To cement this alliance, "King" Jadwiga was married to Grand Duke Jagiello of Lithuania, and the latter was baptized taking the Christian name of Wladyslaw II (1389–1434). The union of Poland and Lithuania—referred to as the Commonwealth—bore fruit when their combined armies defeated the Teutonic Knights at the Battle of Grunwald. Wladyslaw II was succeeded by his son Wladyslaw III (1434–44), who in 1440 was chosen as king of Hungary. He led a crusade against the Turks and died in the Battle of Varna in 1444.

Meanwhile, the oppressive rule of the Teutonic Knights had precipitated a revolt in Prussia against the order, and in 1454 Poland-Lithuania intervened on Prussia's side and inflicted a second defeat on the knights. The Treaty of Torun of 1466 divided the territory of the knights between royal Prussia (which was directly incorporated into Poland) and the eastern territories (later called ducal Prussia), which were ruled by a reorganized order as a fief of the Polish crown. The port of Gdansk was granted the status of a free city under Polish suzerainty.

The Polish monarchy emerged from the war against the Teutonic Knights much debilitated. To secure the military aid of the nobles, King Kasimierz IV (1447–92) was obliged to agree to the Statutes of Nieszawa (1454), regarded as Poland's Magna Carta, in which he pledged to make no laws or binding decisions without their consent.

The late 15th and 16th centuries have been called Poland's golden age, associated with some of the country's greatest sons: Nicolaus Copernicus (Mikolaj Kopernik), astronomer; Andrzej Frycz Modrzewski, political and eductional thinker; and Jan Kochanowski, poet. The first Sejm or diet was convened in 1493 and was composed of deputations from the regional nobility. According to the Constitution adopted by the Sejm in 1505, all legislation thereafter required parliamentary assent. Members of the noble class enjoyed an impressive list of rights and privileges confirmed by the Sejm, including freedom of expression and immunity from arbitrary arrest. Before the end of the 16th century each nobleman was enfranchised to cast a vote in the election of his king. With the nobility comprising about 10% of the population, Poland had one of the most representative governments in Europe at that time. Political freedom was paralleled by religious tolerance, also unequalled in Europe. While fierce persecutions and religious wars waged elsewhere, Poland was "a state without stakes" and a recognized "haven for heretics."

Protestantism made little headway until 1540, when it gained converts among the upper nobility, including some of the wealthiest and most powerful families, who cast covetous eyes on church lands. The high tide of the Polish Reformation came in the late 1550s, when Protestants gained control of the Sejm, enacting legislation favorable to the new religious dispensation and penalizing the Catholic hierarchy. However, the disunity of the Protestant sects helped the Catholics to regain their ascendancy, and in 1564 the Sejm reenforced the decisions of the Council of Trent and reestablished Roman Catholicism. At the same time, the Sejm recognized the principle that no one could be prosecuted, much less persecuted, for their religious beliefs, and religious toleration was made a cardinal legal precept in 1573. The last Jagiellonian king, Zygmunt II (1548–72), refused to curb religious dissent, saying, "I am not the king of souls." Protestantism was an aristocratic and urban phenomenon in Poland and never touched the life of the masses. By the middle of the 17th century the nobility with very few exceptions had returned to Roman Catholicism, and the Counter-Reformation was completely successful.

Religious toleration was extended to the Jews as well. The great influx of Jews had begun in the 14th century, when persecution drove thousands from Germany to seek refuge in Poland. Kasimierz III granted them special privileges as "servants of the Treasury" and gave them charters of self-government in their own communities under the protection of the crown. Their numbers grew from 50,000 in 1500 to about 1.5 million in 1650.

The growing threat posed to the Baltic states and to Ruthenia by Muscovy and the Tatars persuaded a majority of the Lithuanian boyars to seek closer ties with Poland. Through such union, the Lithuanian nobles sought their own emancipation from the power of the grand duke, whose legal authority in Lithuania was much greater than that which he exercised in Poland as king. The Polish nobles, for their part, saw in the merger an opportunity to acquire rich estates in Ruthenia. The Protocol of Lublin in 1569 established the formal union of Poland and Lithuania under the Polish crown. The union had a common diet and a common foreign policy but separate civil and military administrations. As part of the agreement the Lithuanians ceded the largest portion of their Ruthenian provinces to Poland. The union

guaranteed the equality of the Greek Orthodox hierarchy with its Roman Catholic counterpart, but the Catholic monarch Zygmunt III promoted a union with Rome that was acknowledged by a majority of the Orthodox bishops in a synod at Brest in 1596. Gradually the church in Ruthenia became Greek Catholic while retaining its separate Byzantine liturgy and ecclesiastical jurisdiction.

The failure of Poland's political institutions in the 17th and 18th centuries can be traced to the deterioration of socioeconomic conditions in the late 15th and 16th centuries, during which the privileged nobility grew wealthy and powerful and the peasantry was enserfed and their lands expropriated. The closing of the eastern Mediterranean to European commerce after the fall of Constantinople and the opening of the Vistula for exports through Gdansk to northern Germany, the Netherlands and England introduced new opportunities for the Polish landowners. The profitable grain trade was reserved by the Sejm as a monopoly for the nobility. Since serfs were required to buy all their needs from factories on the manorial estates, cities were deprived of much of their trade. The nobles dominated the Sejm and the local diets, and their only goal was to enhance their own "golden freedoms," as the body of aristocratic privileges was known, and to hobble the authority of the monarch, whom they relegated to the role of a "crowned president of a royal republic." Averse to fighting and corrupted by luxury, the nobles had no interest in defending Poland from its increasing number of enemies.

The immediate successors of Zygmunt II were all nonnative: Henryk (Henry III of France) (1573–74); Stefan I Batory (1575–86), prince of Transylvania; and Zygmunt III Vasa (1587–1632), heir to the Swedish throne whose mother was a Jagiellonian princess and who later was disposed as king of Sweden in 1598 when he tried to overthrow Protestantism and reimpose Catholicism in that country. Vasa moved the capital of Poland from Crakow northeastward to Warsaw, an important grain market linked to Gdansk by the Vistula, to improve his line of communications with Lithuania and Sweden. His continuous efforts to recover the Swedish crown drew Poland into a disastrous conflict with the rising power of Sweden.

For three centuries, from the fall of Novgorod in 1476, the Commonwealth and Muscovy were in direct conflict. The goal of Muscovy was to recover the western lands of the old Kievan state destroyed by the Tatars. Beset by a Swedish invasion of Poland in 1655, the Commonwealth struck a compromise with Muscovy. The Truce of Andrusovo (1667) partitioned the Ukraine between Poland and Muscovy along the Dneiper River.

In 1665 Poland was invaded by Sweden, and Swedish forces soon occupied about half of the country, including Warsaw and Crakow. Deserted by the nobility, King Jan II Kasimierz sought temporary refuge in Hapsburg Silesia, where he surrendered sovereignty over ducal Prussia to the elector of Brandenburg, head of the Hohenzollern line. Poland also lost territory in Livonia. In addition to the loss of prestige and territory, Poland was left prostrate by the wars, with its best farmland devastated and its grain trade ruined. The election of Jan III Sobieski (1674–96) seemed to augur a revival in Poland's fortunes, but only briefly. The power of the nobles rendered the "royal republic" weak relative to the rise of the highly autocratic kingdoms of Russia, Germany and Austria. The weakness of political system made Poland vulnerable to foreign intervention. Bribery and corruption were rampant, and the country as a whole was without fiscal management.

Jan III Sobieski's successor was a protege of Peter the Great: August II (1697–1733), a German prince and elector of Saxony. He promptly committed Poland to an alliance with Russia, Saxony and Denmark against Sweden. But Sweden's young soldier-king Charles XII quickly took the offensive in what came to be known as the Great Northern War (1700–21), again invading Polish territory and installing the Swedish nominee, Stanislaw Leszczynski, on the throne briefly (1704–9) as Stanislaw I. Poland became a cockpit, its territory pillaged by both sides. However, after the Russian victory over the Swedes at Poltava in 1709, Swedish fortunes began to ebb, and by the Treaty of Nystad of 1721, Russia was awarded Sweden's holdings in the Baltic provinces, including the former Polish territory of Livonia.

After the death of August II, a convention of 12,000 nobles rejected the Saxon connection and reelected Stanislaw I Leszczynski, father-in-law of Louis XV of France. Russia and France then intervened in favor of the late king's heir August III (1733–63), who was named king by a rival Lithuanian-led convention. The Russian invasion of Poland, forcibly ejecting Leszczynski, touched off a general European conflict, the War of the Polish Succession (1733–35). The peace that ended this war left August III on the throne but otherwise was advantageous to the Bourbons.

During the reign of the inept, pleasure-loving Saxon kings there was virtually no central government, and the magnates abetted by the foreign powers ruled their small fiefdoms much as they willed. Shifting political alliances were managed by powerful families of magnates—known as the Familia—headed by the Czartoryskis, the Potockis and the Radziwills.

By the time of the death of Peter the Great in 1762, Poland was virtually a Russian satellite state. As a successor to August III, Catherine II of Russia and Frederick II of Prussia agreed on the election of one of the Familia, Stanislaw Poniatowski, as Stanislaw II (1764–95). Before his installation, the leader of the Familia, Michal Fryderyk Czartoryski, attempted to force through reforms that would have limited the liberum veto and introduced a ministerial government appointed by the crown. The opposition nobles, fearing a strong central government, formed the Confederation of Radom and appealed for Russian intervention to protect their liberties. Russia was only happy to do so and used the occasion to arrest Catholic leaders and impose harsh conditions on the Catholic majority. With French support, the patriotic nobles joined together in the Confederation of Bar to mount armed resistance to Russian occupation. One of the leaders of the confederation was Kazimierz Pulaski, who later made his way to the American Colonies, where he organized the Continental Army's cavalry early in the Revolutionary War before dying in Savannah in 1779. The rising finally was put down after four years when Frederick II proposed a partition of Poland among the neighboring powers Austria, Prussia and Russia in order to put an end to Poland's anarchy. For the first partition in 1772 Poland was compelled to give up nearly one-third of its territory and one-half of its resources and population. Prussia obtained most of Polish Pomerania, except Gdansk and Torun; Russia all of Livonia, and Byelorussia east of the Dvina River and the valley of the Upper Dnieper; and Austria most of southern Poland, excluding Crakow. The partitioning powers also imposed on Poland a new Constitution, which vested executive authority in a council of the Sejm elected by the delegates and thus introduced an element of stability that had been lacking throughout Polish history. All actions of the Polish government became subject to review by the three occupying powers.

The shock of the first partition galvanized the Poles into a series of reforms embodied in the Constitution of May 1791 by the so-called Four-Year Sejm. It converted Poland into a hereditary monarchy with a cabinet of ministers responsible to the Sejm, nullified the anarchic liberum veto and introduced the principle of majority rule. Serfdom was limited as the first step toward its abolition. Cities once again became self-governing, and townsmen were enfranchised. State finances were reorganized, and the royal army was modernized. A modern secular school system was introduced, and the commercial vitality of the cities was restored.

The possibility of a resurgent Poland threatened Catherine II, and she found an opportunity to strike at Poland again when a group of reactionary magnates opposed to the progressive reforms formed the Confederation of Targowica and petitioned Catherine for Russian aid in restoring the old Constitution. With this semblance of legality, Catherine ordered 100,000 of her troops under her most seasoned general, Alexander Suvorov, to march into Poland in May 1792. Prussia, bound by treaty to come to Poland's aid, deserted it and joined Russia. The Poles, outnumbered on both east and west, sued for peace. Poland was partitioned a second time, in 1793. Russia appropriated most of the Belorussian and Ukrainian territory west of the Dnieper, while Prussia seized the long-coveted cities of Gdansk and Torun and the western province of Posnania. Poland as a state was mutilated and crippled. A popular uprising led by Tadeusz Kosciuszko was crushed by the combined armies of Prussia and Russia. The failure of the insurrection was followed by the abdication of Stanislaw II and a third partition, which erased Poland from the map of Europe. Austria took the ancient city of Crakow and the region around Lublin and Sandomierz. Prussia obtained central Poland, including Warsaw. Russia appropriated Courland and the remainder of Lithuania and the Ukraine. The once-proud Commonwealth ceased to exist.

At the time when Poland disappeared from the map, the star of Napoleon was rising in France, and among his staunchest friends were Polish exiles. The Polish

Legion, formed in Italy, followed Napoleon in his campaigns in Italy, Spain, Egypt and Haiti—and finally when his army entered Poland in 1806. After the defeat of the Russian-Prussian coalition in 1807, the French and Russian emperors agreed as part of the Treaty of Tilsit to the creation of an independent Polish state, designated the duchy of Warsaw, to which Galicia was added after the defeat of Austria in 1809. The title of duke of Warsaw was bestowed on Napoleon's loyal ally Frederick August I, king of Saxony. However, the real ruler was the French resident minister in Warsaw, whose main task was to requisition men and matériel for the war effort. He fielded an army of 100,000 Poles for the ill-fated Russian campaign, of whom three-fourths perished.

After Napoleon's defeat at Waterloo, the Grand Duchy was swept away at the Congress of Vienna, which confirmed the partition of Poland. Out of the remnants of the duchy, Czar Alexander I created a small Kingdom of Poland—generally known as the Congress Kingdom—and the Congress made the city of Crakow and its environs a free republic. It was annexed by Austria in 1846.

At the Congress of Vienna the partitioning powers had agreed to respect the rights of their Polish subjects. But Prussia and Austria embarked almost immediately on a policy of repression. Initially Alexander I played the role of a benign monarch. The czar was represented by a governor, who exercised executive authority through an appointed Polish Council of State. The Constitution provided for a bicameral diet with a directly elected lower chamber summoned at the discretion of the czar. The Polish army served under the Polish flag, and the Roman Catholic Church was accorded official status. A Polish judicial system administered a Polish legal code that guaranteed Poles liberties not enjoyed elsewhere in the Russian empire.

The Polish nationalists were not appeased by such token acts of benevolence and wanted nothing short of the expulsion of the Russians. In November 1830 a military insurrection led by junior officers broke out in Warsaw and quickly spread to garrisons throughout the kingdom. It ended a year later in utter defeat. The uprising was followed by ruthless Russification. The Congress kingdom was made an integral part of the Russian empire and ruled directly by a government department in St. Petersburg. Martial law was imposed; the use of Polish in schools was prohibited; the Polish universities were closed; civil rights were curtailed; Polish units were integrated into the Russian army; and the Catholic Church was singled out for particularly harsh treatment. Defeat and oppression combined to set off the so-called Great Emigration in which over 10,000 Poles, the flower of the country's intelligentsia, left the country, including Fryderyk Chopin and the poet Adam Mickiewicz. Official Russian policy softened after the accession of Alexander II in 1855, but the proposed conscription of Poles into the Russian army set off a new insurrection, in 1863. Lacking the army that had defied the Russians in 1830, the insurrection consisted of a series of uncoordinated small-scale guerrilla activities that were doomed from the start. Nevertheless, it took

two years for the Russians to suppress it completely. It was the last Polish attempt at armed opposition until 1914.

For the next half century the national mood was one of silent resignation to and acceptance of the Russian yoke. Many sought an outlet for their creative energies in "organic labor"—support of internal economic and social reconstruction. Poles cooperated in administrative reforms and development of municipal and civic institutions. The change in the moral and intellectual climate was promoted by the rapid industrial development of Russian Poland. When in 1851 Poland was included in the Russian tariff system, its industry gained favored access to a huge market. Poland became the most important industrial region in the Russian empire. Industrialization stimulated the growth of cities and the emergence of a prosperous bourgeoisie. Poles began to occupy a number of important positions in the Russian economy.

Austrian Poland, or Galicia, was economically the most backward of all Polish lands. Much of its soil was poor, and many areas suffered from overpopulation. However, despite limited economic progress, the Austrian Poles won important political privileges. After a defeat by Prussia in 1866, the Austrian government needed to secure greater political support from its Slavic subjects. Serfdom was abolished in 1848. Poles were introduced into the provincial administration, and a provision was made for seating local assemblies after establishment of the Dual Monarchy in 1867. From this date Galicia was fully integrated into the political life of the Hapsburg monarchy. Galicians served as governors and cabinet ministers and rose to high positions in the army, the diplomatic corps and the bureaucracy. Polish delegates exercised a key role in the Vienna parliament, where no party had an absolute majority. In the course of time Galicia became an important artistic and cultural region centered in Crakow and Lwow.

Prussian Poland experienced the most oppressive rule of all. Eastern Pomerania was incorporated directly into the Kingdom of Prussia in 1815 as the province of West Prussia, but Posnania was recognized as a semi-autonomous grand duchy under Prussian sovereignty, with the Prussian ruler Frederick William III as the grand duke of Poznan. This limited autonomy was curtailed after 1827, and in 1848 the grand duchy was abolished and Posnania became a Prussian province. A Germanization campaign was launched as part of Bismarck's campaign to rid Germany of all un-German elements, particularly Slavic and ultramontane elements—a program known as *Kulturkampf*. Courts and schools were conducted exclusively in German. Catholic schools were closed, and restrictions were placed on the activities of the church and its hierarchy. Poles were subjected to legal discrimination and economic pressures. Polish Catholics responded by redoubling their religious and national zeal. Turning their energies to the economy, they achieved commanding positions in the industrial and agricultural sectors. They organized a number of self-help institutions, including a farmers' bank; an industrial bank; and the Union of Cooperative Banks, founded in 1886 through a merger of cooperative societies. The Poznan area became the richest and economically the most highly developed of all Polish lands. German efforts to colonize their Polish dominions failed because of Polish resistance.

At the outbreak of Word War I, Polish sympathies were split into two camps: one Pro-Russian and the other pro-Austrian. Russia was supported by Roman Dmowski's National Democracy (ND) Party. In Galicia there was considerable pro-German sentiment, since Austria was recognized as the most benevolent of the occupying powers. The Poles in Galicia set up the Supreme National Committee (Naczelny Komitet Narodowy, NKN) to fight for Austria. It was headed by Wladyslaw Sikorski, and one of its three brigades was commanded by Jozef Pilsudski. Poland was one of the war's major battlegrounds. Warsaw was under German occupation between 1914 and 1915. Both Austrian and Russian armies carried out scorched-earth strategies during their withdrawals. By 1916 a total of 2 million Poles were fighting on either side, and Polish war casualties exceeded 450,000. After Russia signed the Treaty of Brest-Litovsk with Germany in 1918, ending Russian participation in the war, Poles turned to the Allies for support. In 1917 Polish exile leaders formed a National Committee in Paris. In 1918 President Wilson, prompted by his friend pianist Ignacy Jan Paderewski, proclaimed his Fourteen Points, the 13th of which said,

> An independent Polish state should be erected which should include the territories inhabited by indisputably Polish populations, which should be assured a free and secure access to the sea and whose political and economic independence and territorial integrity should be guaranteed by international covenant.

Inside Poland an anti-Russian independence movement took shape under Pilsudski, which, with the collapse of the Central Powers, quickly organized a Polish government in Moscow. It came into conflict with the representatives of the Polish National Committee, which was strongly pro-Russian and conservative. The breach between the two groups was healed by the arrival in Poland of Paderewski, who was nonparty and was backed by the United States. He became prime minister and foreign minister in Poland's first independent government in over a century.

The first order of the day was the settlement of the boundaries. By the 1919 Versailles Treaty Poland recovered the main part of the lands formerly under Polish rule, but access to the Baltic Sea was limited to a narrow strip of land that terminated at the almost wholly German city of Danzig, (now Gdansk), which was made a free city under the protection of the League of Nations. East Prussia remained a German enclave separated from the rest of Germany by the Polish Corridor, which Germans had to cross in sealed trains. By plebiscite Silesia was partitioned between Germany and Poland, the latter receiving the most important industrial regions. The Cieszyn (Teschen) region in the southern fringes of Silesia was an ethnically mixed area with a Polish majority and a Czech minority. It was parti-

tioned, with Czechoslovakia obtaining the larger and richer area south of the Olza River. The city and region of Vilna, to which both Poles and Lithuanians had laid claim, became part of Lithuania in 1920, but was occupied by Poland in 1922 over the protests of Britain and France.

The settlement of Poland's eastern frontier with the new Soviet Union was more difficult. The Poles insisted on the historic frontier of 1772 rather than the eastern frontier of the Congress kingdom known as the Curzon Line. An offensive to liberate the Ukraine from the Soviets was undertaken by Pilsudski in alliance with Simon Petlyura, the Ukrainian military leader in 1920. Polish forces captured Kiev but soon were compelled to retreat in the face of a Soviet counteroffensive. The Red Army counterattacked, soon reaching the gates of Warsaw, but a counteroffensive by Pilsudski and Sikorski turned them back. The 1921 Riga Peace Treaty divided the disputed territory in Belorussia and the western Ukraine between Poland and the Soviet Union, and the Soviets also agreed to pay compensation to Poland.

Poland adopted a democratic constitution in March 1921. Based on the French model, it installed a parliamentary system in which executive authority was vested in a government responsible to a bicameral legislature comprising the Sejm and the Senate. The presidency was weak and mainly ceremonial, in an apparent move to curb Pilsudski's power. The parliamentary electoral system encouraged a multiplicity of parties. About 30 parties contested elections in 1920, and about 15 won parliamentary seats regularly. Inasmuch as no party or bloc received a parliamentary majority, changes of government were frequent. Pilsudski, the first president of the republic, had no political party backing but owed his position to his great personal popularity. His power base consisted of socialists, the military, left-wing peasants and ethnic minorities. His main opposition was ND, the largest party on the right, which wanted a strong, all-Polish central government that excluded national minorities, particularly Ukrainians, Germans and Jews. In the center was the Piast Party, formally the Polish Peasant Party, which had its stronghold in rural Galicia. The Polish Communist Party, founded in 1918, was never politically significant in the interwar years.

Following Paderewski's resignation after less than a year in office, there were 13 short-lived cabinets until 1926. Three of these were led by Wincenty Witos of the Piast Party and two by Wladyslaw Grabski. From 1921 to 1926 the country was plagued by economic problems, including massive unemployment, inflation of food items approaching 1,200% and plummeting value of the Polish mark. Efforts to foster a recovery were dealt a death blow by the tariff war with Germany that erupted in 1925, affecting one-quarter of all Polish trade. A financial panic ensued.

The apparent breakdown of the economy and the parliamentary process prompted Pilsudski to leave the sidelines and mount a coup d'etat in 1926. With the units sympathetic to him, he seized control of the country after several days of street fighting and forced the resignation of both the prime minister and the president. Pilsudski refused the presidency but nonetheless established himself as the virtual dictator. His authoritarian government operated under the facade of a democratic government, and he retained the post of minister of war in successive cabinets headed by his loyal lieutenants and served as prime minister from October 1926 to June 1928. Pilsudski refused to consider one-party rule and relied for organizational support in the legislation on a political alliance called the Nonparty Bloc for Cooperation with the Government (Bezpartyjny Blok dla Wspolpracy z Rzadem, BBWR), which offered slates of progovernment candidates at election times. His regime was supported by the army, the political left and trade unions. However, he offered no political program beyond cleansing *(sanacja)*, a term that became the regime's label, and the introduction of better public administration. With the help of a large group of technocrats, the Pilsudski regime carried through a modest economic recovery. The government took an active role in stimulating economic growth through public investment, central planning and state participation in vital industries and services. The port of Gdynia on the Baltic was developed as an alternative to Danzig.

The impact on Poland of the Great Depression beginning in 1929 was immediate and severe. In the four years from 1928 to 1932 industrial output dropped by nearly one-half, and unemployment rose to 20% by 1932. Labor unrest and terrorism by Ukrainian nationalists added to the government's problems. Parliamentary opposition to the regime also was mounting, and it culminated in a walkout of non-BBWR members in 1934. BBWR members then introduced legislation that led to the promulgation of a new Constitution in 1935. The main feature of the Constitution of 1935 was the shift of executive authority from the legislature to the presidency, which was responsible "only to God and to history." The army came directly under the command of the president, and it was independent of civilian control. The office was designed with Pilsudski in mind, but he died in 1935, and there was no potential successor of equal stature to replace him. The Constitution of 1935 had reduced the size of the legislature and had restricted suffrage. The legislative elections held later in the year were boycotted by more than half the voters.

The BBWR was dissolved after the 1935 elections and replaced by a new progovernment party, the Camp of National Unification, with a more right-wing and anti-Semitic cast. The army itself was divided into two camps, the regime's opponents rallying around Sikorski and Josef Haller.

Poland had followed a conciliatory policy toward Germany during the early 1930s. As the threat of German expansion increased, it shifted to an independent policy, trying to maintain a balance between its two historic enemies, the Soviet Union and Germany. In 1938 Poland gave up its seat on the Council of the League of Nations. The German absorption of Czech lands foreshadowed Poland's destruction. In 1939 Poland accepted a British guarantee of its independence and concluded a military alliance that obligated the United Kingdom to come to the aid of Poland in case of external aggression. Hitler believed that this pact was a bluff and countered it with a secret pact with Stalin calling for the dismemberment of Poland.

On the morning of September 1, 1939, Germany attacked Poland. Britain and France lived up to their treaties and declared war against Germany on September 2. Soviet forces invading Poland on September 17 met hardly more than token resistance. Germany and the Soviet Union partitioned Poland along a line that roughly corresponded to the Curzon Line.

The period from 1939 to 1945 was the most tragic in the history of Poland. In those years more than 6 million Poles died, or about 15% of the prewar population. Of the 6 million, about 700,000 died in war-related actions and reprisals, and tens of thousands perished from starvation or other hardships. From the start the German pursued a ruthless policy of genocide. Hans Frank, the German governor of Poland, said, "From now on, the Polish nation is ended and the very concept of Polak will be erased. . . . Poles will become slaves of the German empire." For Hitler, Poland was a reservation, a vast labor camp. About 1 million Poles were deported and another 2.5 million sent to labor camps in Germany. The Russians were equally brutal. They deported some 1.5 million Poles to labor camps in Siberia, and about 100,000 Polish soldiers and officers were executed and buried in a mass grave in the Katyn Forest near Smolensk.

A Polish government-in-exile was set up in 1939 with General Sikorski as prime minister and commander of a Polish division of 100,000 men. After the fall of France, he regrouped 20,000 men in Britain. Polish ground units fought under the British command in the Middle East and Italy. In May 1944 the Poles captured the fiercely contested German stronghold at Monte Cassino, over which they hoisted the Polish flag. By 1945 the Poles constituted the fourth-largest Allied contingent in Europe. Polish cryptanalysts were responsible for breaking the German Code "Enigma," thus enabling the Allies to read the orders Hitler sent to his field commanders. On the Eastern Front, the Kremlin had formed a front group, the Union of Polish Patriots, which grew by 1944 to field army strength under the command of Gen. Zygmunt Berling. In Poland two underground armies, the Home Army (Armia Krajowa, AK) and the People's Army (Armia Ludowa, AL) constantly harassed the Germans and on the eve of the liberation of Warsaw led the ill-fated Warsaw Uprising.

Following the liberation of Poland by the Red Army, the Communist-backed Polish Committee of National Liberation (Polski Komitet Wyzwolenia Narodowego, PKWN) proclaimed itself as the sole legal authority in liberated areas. It was led by two longtime Communists, Wladyslaw Gomulka and Boleslaw Bierut.

The Poland that emerged from the war was a different country physically as well as politically. According to the decisions made by the Allies at Yalta and Potsdam, Poland's new western frontier lay along the Oder and Neisse rivers, adding over 100,000 sq. km. (38,600 sq. mi.) of German territory including Silesia and Pomerania and the southern portion of East Prussia, which contained Masuria. At the same time, Poland was forced to cede to the Soviet Union 180,000 sq. km.

(69,480 sq. mi.), including Vilna and Lwow, and to Czechoslovakia the part of Cieszyn Silesia seized by Poland in 1938. As a result of these territorial adjustments Poland's physical center moved westward, accompanied by a large-scale transfer of population. The Polish population fell from 35 million in 1939 to 25 million in 1950.

For events after 1945, see Chronology.

CONSTITUTION & GOVERNMENT

Poland has a proud history of parliamentary government. The Poles cite 1493 as the beginning of the Sejm (parliament or diet), consisting of a Chamber of Deputies and a Senate. The Kingdom of Poland joined with Lithuania in 1386 to create the Jagiellonian dynasty (1386–1572). In 1503 the Sejm adopted the *nihil novi* (nothing new) constitution, a significant development requiring the king to obtain permission, at least in principle, from the senators and the gentry *(szlachta)* deputies to change a law. The Sejm grew in importance as power was being centralized. In 1569 the Union Act established the "Republic of Two Nations" and unified the Sejm.

However, the monarchy was never to reach the golden age of the Jagiellonian dynasty, falling victim to outside pressures from Prussia, Sweden, Austria and Russia. Internally, the gentry impeded the development of a strong monarchy, most notably by adopting the liberum veto whereby unanimity was required for the Sejm's passage of legislation. The combination of external forces and internal weaknesses, particularly the liberum veto, inexorably led Poland into disintegration.

Efforts were made in the 18th century, under a Polish king, to reform and strengthen the political system. In 1776 the Sejm created the Permanent Council of 30 members to function between its sessions, and in 1791 it passed the Government Act, known as the May 3 Constitution, which sought to reform the political system in Poland. This document is held in high esteem to this day. Among its other provisions, the Constitution "abolished forever" the debilitating liberum veto provision. However, these attempts became academic as Poland was partitioned by Russia, Prussia and Austria in 1772, 1793 and 1795, the latter wiping Poland off the map of Europe.

During the early 19th century the Sejm functioned albeit in severely limited capacity and temporarily: In 1807 Napoleon permitted the Sejm in the Duchy of Warsaw; following the Congress of Vienna (1815); and during the uprising against Russia (1830–31). Also, Austria allowed a partially autonomous Sejm to exist in Lwow.

During World War I President Woodrow Wilson highlighted independence for Poland, which was regained on November 11, 1918. An Electoral Law for elections to the Sejm—the most democratic in its history—was announced on November 26, 1918, by Marshal Jozef Pilsudski the provisional president and chief of state. Elections were held in January 1919. In another democratic development the constitution adopted March 17, 1921, provided for a bilateral 444-member Sejm. The presi-

dent appointed the government, which was responsible to the Sejm. However, the period of parliamentary democracy was brief as political controversies led to an early departure of Prime Minister Ignacy Jan Paderewski, an eminent pianist, and the retirement of Pilsudski.

With the country in serious political and economic difficulties that 14 governments since independence had been unable to solve, Marshal Pilsudski engineered a successful coup d'état and established authoritarian rule, which lasted until 1939. Pilsudski, who died in 1935, was succeeded by what was characterized as "the colonels." The legislature functioned, but it was ineffectual, particularly under the Constitution of 1935. In addition, the country was beset by ethnic dissatisfaction, exploited by Germany and the Soviet Union. The government was ill prepared to defend against foreign military powers. Following the Nazi-Soviet Pact of August 23, 1939, which contained a secret provision for the partition of Poland, Germany launched a massive invasion of the country, followed by the Red Army's occupation on September 17.

The government went into exile, joined later by military contingents that fought with distinction on the side of the Allies. Using the Katyn massacre as a pretext, Moscow severed diplomatic relations with the Polish government-in-exile in London in April 1943, and began the political preparation of installing Communist control in Poland. In December 1943 it established the Home National Council, controlled by the Polish Workers' Party (PPR), organized by the Communists the previous year. The Soviet Union then formed the Polish Committee of National Liberation (PKWN) on July 22, 1944, in effect the provisional "government," at Lublin. It was recognized officially by Moscow in January 1945.

The Yalta Conference of February 1945 provided for the Provisional Government of National Unity, essentially the PKWN, with participation of the government-in-exile. An element of the London government, headed by Stanislaw Mikolajczyk, leader of the Peasant Party, participated. He became a deputy premier. This "coalition" was formed June 28, 1945, and the United States and the United Kingdom extended recognition to it the following month, withdrawing their recognition from the London government. The Mikolajczyk group was entirely too small and too weak to compete against Communist domination at the national and lower levels. Yalta's provision for "free and unfettered elections" as soon as possible was outrageously violated. The Communist Party delayed parliamentary elections until January 19, 1947, preparing for victory by a variety of tactics, including control of local government and mass organizations, propaganda, infiltration, intimidation and arrests.

In the provisional government the PKWN controlled 16 of the 20 ministerial positions, including police and defense. In this controlled election the single list of proregime candidates, not surprisingly, was declared the winner by the substantial margin of 80 percent, with 417 of 444 delegates. Moscow-trained party veteran Boleslaw Bierut, at this time also president of the PKWN, became president of the republic, and Jozef

Cyrankiewicz, leader of the pro-Communist wing of the Polish Socialist Party (PPS), the prime minister. All high-level positions were occupied by either Communists or their collaborators. Mikolajczyk was forced into exile. A Provisional Constitution was enacted in 1947, essentially continuing the governmental structure. The Communist Party forced a merger with the PPS in December 1948, the new organization becoming the Polish United Workers' Party (Polska Zjednoczona Partia Robotnicza, PZPR).

As in other Soviet bloc countries, the new Constitution, adopted on July 22, 1952, was patterned after the Soviet Constitution of 1936, with a collective presidency. Bierut became the prime minister of the Polish People's Republic. The Sejm passed a number of amendments in subsequent years. The PZPR initiated a major draft revision of the Constitution in 1976 affecting the Sejm, the government, civil rights, the judiciary and other areas.

For many years (1947–52, 1954–70) the government was headed by Prime Minister Jozef Cyrankiewicz, the leader of the Polish Socialist Party until the 1948 merger with the Polish Workers' Party. During 1952–54 he was deputy premier while Bierut was prime minister. The discontent throughout the country betrayed this seeming continuity. Cyrankiewicz was succeeded as prime minister by Piotr Jaroszewicz, who was followed by Edward Babiuch (1980) and Jozef Pinkowski (1980–81). To combat the potential power of Solidarity, the government was taken over on December 13, 1981, by the Military Council for National Salvation, which became the country's supreme authority. The Military Council was headed by Gen. Wojciech Jaruzelski, who interned former prime minister Jaroszewicz in 1981. Jaruzelski also held the positions of prime minister (since February 1981), defense minister and first secretary of the PZPR. The Military Council, composed of 21 high-ranking military officers, was abolished in July 1983. Jaruzelski relinquished the prime ministership in November 1985 to Zbigniew Messner, an economist who failed to improve the economic and political situation. He was replaced in August 1988 by Mieczyslaw F. Rakowski, whose performance was widely criticized as well.

As of September 1989 the Constitution of the Polish People's Republic was a consolidated document comprising the Constitution of 1952 with amendments adopted in 1976, 1980, 1982, 1983 and 1987. Since 1976, and in Chapter 1 of the Constitution, the Polish People's Republic has been officially designated a "socialist state." State authority is vested in the Sejm and the People's Council. Also in 1976, following heated controversy, the PZPR was enshrined in the Constitution as "the guiding political force of society in building socialism." Similarly controversial was the reference to the Soviet Union. Both references to PZPR and the USSR were included only after scaling down the language. The basic law declares that the foreign policy of Poland is to "consolidate friendship and cooperation with the USSR and other socialist countries" and that Poland's relations with other countries are based on the principle of "peaceful coexistence and cooperation."

Chapter 2 details the social and economic system of Poland. The socialist economic system is based on socialized means of production. Foreign trade is the monopoly of the state, which develops the economic and cultural life of the country by a national socioeconomic plan. Property is nationalized, but small-scale private property, including agricultural, exists with provisions for inheritance. Work is a duty as well as a right of every citizen. Chapter 4 covers the Constitutional Tribunal, the Tribunal of State and the Supreme Chamber of Control. Next are the main organs of state administration and the local organs of state power and administration. The court system and Prokuratura are in Chapter 7, the fundamental rights and duties of citizens are covered in detail in Chapter 8 and the principles of electoral law are in Chapter 9. Chapter 11 specifies that the Constitution can be amended by the Sejm by two-thirds of the votes, with at least half the members present.

The Sejm appoints and recalls the Council of Ministers (cabinet) and individual members. Between the Sejm's sessions that authority is vested in the Council of State, which acts on the recommendation of the prime minister, who is the head of government. Formal approval is given by the Sejm at its next session. The Council of Ministers is the highest executive and administrative organ of state power. It is responsible to the Sejm or the Council of State. Until 1989, at least, practical policy control resided with the PZPR's Politburo. The government is composed of the prime minister, deputy prime ministers, ministers, and chairmen of commission and committees established by law. The prime minister and deputy prime ministers constitute the government's Presidium, but additional members can be appointed by the Council of Ministers. The prime minister is chairman of both the Council of Ministers and the Presidium. He issues orders and regulations.

The responsibilities of the Council of Ministers are:

• coordinate the activities of ministers and other organs
• adopt the annual budget estimates and the draft of a multiyear socioeconomic plan, submitting both to the Sejm
• adopt the annual national socioeconomic plan
• supervise execution of the budget and the plan
• ensure the protection of public order, of state interests and of the rights of citizens
• give general guidance on foreign relations
• give general guidance on the country's defense and on the organization of the armed forces, and specify the annual conscription
• supervise the work of organs of administration

Ministries are established by law to direct branches of state administration. In carrying out the laws, ministers issue orders and regulations, which can be abrogated by the Council of Ministers.

The dynamic changes in Poland during 1989, sparked by a resurgent Solidarity, led to an unprecedented leadership change in the government. After furious negotiations the Sejm approved, by a vote of 237 to 173,

Minister of the Interior Gen. Czeslaw Kiszczak, on the recommendation of Gen. Jaruzelski, Chairman of the Council of State, to be prime minister. Kiszczak's efforts to form a "grand coalition" government, to include Solidarity representatives, failed as Solidarity refused to participate. Solidarity feared a nominal role in the government and opposed Kiszczak because of his repressive measures against the union during martial law. After decades of subservience the United Peasant Party (UPP) and the Democratic Party (DP) also refused to support the Communist nominee, for the first time.

Following extensive negotiations and compromise, including the involvement of Soviet General Secretary Mikhail Gorbachev, Jaruzelski nominated Tadeusz Mazowiecki as prime minister to form a new government. The Soviet leader faced a dilemma: approve a non-Communist or invoke the "Brezhnev Doctrine" of military intervention. Gorbachev gave his assent and, after intense negotiations, the PZPR's demands for particular ministries were satisfied. On September 12, 1989, the Sejm voted 402 to 0, with 13 absentions, in favor of the new government. This was an historic development, unprecedented in the Soviet bloc since Communist seizure of power in the 1940s in Eastern Europe—the first majority non-Communist government. Mazowiecki is a Catholic writer and high official in Solidarity. He had served in the Sejm (1960–72), representing a small Catholic opposition group, and was an outspoken critic of the regime. He was imprisoned for one year during martial law. In recent years he has been a close adviser

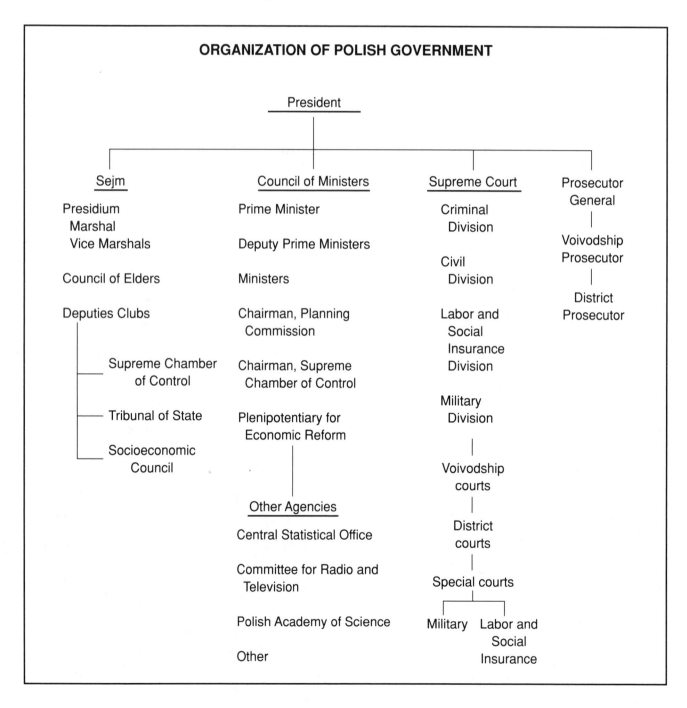

ORGANIZATION OF POLISH GOVERNMENT

President

Sejm	Council of Ministers	Supreme Court	Prosecutor General
Presidium Marshal Vice Marshals	Prime Minister	Criminal Division	Voivodship Prosecutor
Council of Elders	Deputy Prime Ministers	Civil Division	District Prosecutor
Deputies Clubs	Ministers	Labor and Social Insurance Division	
Supreme Chamber of Control	Chairman, Planning Commission	Military Division	
Tribunal of State	Chairman, Supreme Chamber of Control	Voivodship courts	
Socioeconomic Council	Plenipotentiary for Economic Reform	District courts	
		Special courts	
	Other Agencies	Military Labor and Social Insurance	
	Central Statistical Office		
	Committee for Radio and Television		
	Polish Academy of Science		
	Other		

to Solidarity leader Lech Walesa and editor of the union's quarterly journal *Tygodnik Solidarnosc* (Solidarity Weekly).

Four parties participated in the formation of Mazowiecki's government: Solidarity, the UPP, the DP and the PZPR. Each of them was awarded the post of deputy prime minister, reflecting formal equality, with each deputy prime minister also in charge of a ministry. In addition to its leadership role, Solidarity possessed a ministerial superiority in the 25-member Council of Ministers. The distribution of ministerial-level positions was as follows:

```
Prime Minister

Minister of Administration, Local
Economy and Environmental Protection
                |
        Voivodships (49)
                |
    Voivods and City Presidents
         |                    |
    Departments         People's Council

Agriculture and        Chairman
  Forestry             Vice Chairmen (2)
Education              Presidium
Finance               Committees
Labor and Social
  Welfare
Local Economy
Planning
Public Transportation
Religious Affairs
Trade and Services
Other
        └──────────┐
          Communes (over 1,500)
          Urban Districts (21)
            Towns (about 800)

        Chiefs and Town Chiefs
         |                    |
    Secretariat          People's Council

General                Chairman
Administrative         Vice Chairmen
  Affairs              Councillors
Agriculture Service
Local Schools
```

Solidarity
  Prime minister
  Deputy prime minister
  Ministries
   • National Education
   • Culture and the Arts
   • Finance
   • Industry
   • Country Planning and Building (Housing)
   • Labor and Social Policy
  Head, Office of the Council of Ministers
  Chairman, Government Economic Committee
  Chairman, Central Planning Office
  Chairman, Territorial Management
  Chairman, Contact with Political Parties (outside the Sejm)
United Peasant Party
  Deputy prime minister
  Ministries
   • Agriculture, Forestry and Food Industry
   • Justice
   • Health and Social Welfare
   • Administration, Local Economy and Environmental
     Protection
Democratic Party
  Deputy prime minister
  Ministries
   • Home Market (Domestic Trade)
   • Comminications (to be organized)
  Office for Scientific-Technological Progress and Application
Polish United Workers' Party
  Deputy prime minister
  Ministries
   • National Defense
   • Internal Affairs
   • Transportation, Shipping and Communications
   • Foreign Economic Relations
Independent
  Ministry
   • Ministry of Foreign Affairs

During the formation of the government it was unclear whether the traditional Presidium of the Council of Ministers, consisting of the prime minister and deputy prime ministers, would continue. Surprisingly, the Ministry of Foreign Affairs, a highly desired post, was given to an independent, Krzysztof Skubiszewski, a specialist on international law and Polish-German relations who was a member of the Consultative Council. Solidarity also headed the Committee for Radio and Television, a nonministerial but an important position in society.

All cabinet members were new except the PZPR's ministers of National defense and internal affairs, Gen. Florian Siwicki and Gen. Kiszczak. Unquestionably, these—in charge of armed forces and the police, respectively—are considered the two most important ministerial positions. Most of the new ministers were from the professions and all, or nearly all, of the non-PZPR members were former Communists who had been dismissed for their outspoken criticism and radical reforms, especially in the economic sector. All political leaders agreed that the composition of the government was the beginning of an era but that it would be Solidarity's performance on which judgement would be made.

RULERS OF POLAND
Kings/Queen (from 966)

(some referred to as dukes before the 14th century)

966–92: Mieczyslaw I
992–June 1025: Boleslaw I
1025–34: Mieczyslaw II
1034–November 1058: Kasimierz I
November 1058–1079: Boleslaw II
1079–1102: Wladyslaw I Herman
1102–October 1138: Bolesaw III
October 1138–1146: Wladyslaw II
1146–73: Boleslaw IV
1173–77: Mieczyslaw III
1177–94: Kasimierz II
1194–98: Leszek I
1198–1202: Mieczyslaw III
1202–27: Leszek I
1227–79: Boleslaw V
1279–89: Leszek II
1289–90: Wladyslaw I
1290–96: Przemysl
1296–1305: Waclaw I (Vaclav II of Bohemia)
1305–6: Waclaw II (Vaclav III of Bohemia)
1306–33: Wladyslaw I
1333–November 1370: Kasimierz III
November 1370–September 1382: Lajos I (also King of Hungary)
September 1382–1384: Interregnum
1384–86: Jadwiga (daughter of Lajos I)
1386–89: Jadwiga/Wladyslaw II Jaglello
1389–June 1434: Wladyslaw II Jagiello
June 1434–November 1444: Wladyslaw III (also Ulaszlo I of Hungary)
November 1444–1447: Interregnum
1447–June 1492: Kasimierz IV
June 1492–June 1501: Jan I Olbracht
June 1501–1506: Aleksander
1506–30: Zygmunt I
1530–April 1548: Zygmunt I/Zygmunt II August
April 1548–July 1572: Zygmunt II August
July 1572–May 1573: Interregnum
May 1573–May 1574: Henryk (Henri III of France)
May 1574–1576: Interregnum
1576–86: Stefan I
1586–August 1587: Interregnum
August 1587–April 1632: Zygmunt III (Sigismund of Sweden)
May 1632–May 1648: Wladyslaw IV
May 1648–August 1668: Jan II Kasimierz
August 1668–1669: Interregnum
1669–1673: Mikola
1673–May 1674: Interregnum
May 1674–June 1696: Jan III
June 1696–September 1697: Interregnum
September 1697–1704: August II (Elector Friedrich August I of Saxony)
1704: Stanislaw I
1709–February 1733: August II
February–October 1733: Stanislaw I
October 1733–October 1763: August III (Elector Friedrich August II of Saxony)
October 1763–September 1764: Interregnum
September 1764–November 1795: Stanislaw II August
1795–1918: Poland partitioned among Austria, Prussia, and Russia

---

Presidents (from 1918)
(Chairman of the Council of State since 1952)

November 1918–December 1922: Jozef Pilsudski
December 1922: Gabriel Narutowicz
December 1922–May 1926: Stanislaw Wojciechowski
May–June 1926: Maciej Rataj (acting)
June 1926–September 1939: Ignacy Moscicki
September 1939–January 1945: German occupation
January 1945–November 1951: Boleslaw Bierut
November 1951–August 1964: Aleksander Zawadski
August 1964–April 1968: Edward Ochab
April 1968–December 1970: Marian Spychalski
December 1970–May 1972: Josef Cyrankiewicz
May 1972–November 1985: Henryk Jablonski
November 1985–   : Wojciech Jaruzelski

Prime Ministers (from 1917)
(Chairman of the Council of Ministers since 1952)

November 1917–February 1918: Jan Kucharzewski
February–August 1918: Antoni Ponikowski
August–September 1918: Jan Steczkowski
September–October 1918: Jan Kucharzewski
October–November 1918: Jozef Swierzynski
November 1918: Wladyslaw Wroblewski
November 1918: Ignacy Daszynski
November 1918–January 1919: Indrzej Morakzewski
January–December 1919: Ignacy Jan Paderewski
December 1919–June 1920: Leopold Skulski
June–July 1920: Wladyslaw Grabski
July 1920–September 1921: Wincenty Witos
September 1921–June 1922: Antoni Ponikowski
June–July 1922: Stanislaw Sliwinski
July 1922: Wojciech Korfanty
July–December 1922: Julian Nowack
December 1922–May 1923: Wladyslaw Sikorski
May–December 1923: Wincenty Witos
December 1923–November 1925: Wladyslaw Grabski
November 1925–May 1926: Aleksander Skrzynski
May 1926: Wincenty Witos
May–October 1926: Kasimierz Bartel
October 1926–June 1928: Jozef Pilsudski
June 1928–April 1929: Kasimierz Bartel
April–December 1929: Kasimierz Switalski
December 1929–March 1930: Kasimierz Bartel
March 1930–May 1931: Walery Slawek
May 1931–May 1933: Aleksander Prystor
May 1933–May 1934: Janusz Jedrzejewicz
May 1934–March 1935: Leon Kozlowski
March–October 1935: Walery Slawek
October 1935–May 1936: Marian Zyndram-Koscialkowski
May 1936–September 1939: Felician Slawej-Skladkowski
September 1939–January 1945: German occupation
January 1945–February 1947: Edward Osobka-Morawski
February 1947–November 1952: Jozef Cyrankiewicz
November 1952–March 1954: Boleslaw Bierut
March 1954–December 1970: Jozef Cyrankiewicz
December 1970–February 1980: Piotr Jaroszewicz
Feburary–August 1980: Edward Babiuch
August 1980–February 1981: Jozef Pinkowski
February 1981–November 1985: Wojciech Jaruzelski
November 1985–August 1988: Zbigniew Messner
August 1988–August 1989: Mieczyslaw F. Rakowski
August 1989–   : Tadeusz Mazowiecki

Communist Party Leaders (from 1945)
(Secretary–General 1952–4; First Secretary since 1954)

January 1945–September 1948: Wladyslaw Gomua
September 1948–March 1956: Boleslaw Bierut
March–October 1956: Edward Ochab
October 1956–December 1970: Wladyslaw Gomua
December 1970–September 1980: Edward Gierek
September 1980–October 1981: Stanislaw Kania
October 1981–   : Wojciech Jaruzelski

CABINET LIST

President: Wojciech Jaruzelski
Prime Minister: Tadeusz Mazowiecki
Deputy Prime Minister: Leszek Balcerowicz
Deputy Prime Minister: Czeslaw Janicki
Deputy Prime Minister: Jan Janowski
Deputy Prime Minister: Czeslaw Kiszczak
Minister of Agriculture and Food Industries: Czeslaw Janicki
Minister of Culture and Art: Izabela Cywinska
Minister of Domestic Trade: Aleksander Mackiewicz
Minister of Environmental Protection and Natural Resources:
   Bronislaw Kaminski
Minister of Finance: Leszek Balcerowicz
Minister of Foreign Affairs: Krzysztof Skubiszewski
Minister of Foreign Economic Relations: Marcin Swiecicki
Minister of Health and Social Welfare: Andrzej Kosiniak-
   Kamysz
Minister of Industry: Tadeusz Syryjczyk
Minister of Internal Affairs: Czeslaw Kiszczak
Minister of Justice: Aleksander Bentkowski
Minister of Labor, Wages and Social Policy: Jacek Kuron
Minister of Land Use Management and Construction: Aleksander
   Paszynski
Minister of National Defense: Florian Siwicki
Minister of National Education: Henryk Samsonowicz
Minister of Transportation and Navigation: Franciszek Wieladek
Minister, Chairman of the Office of Central Planning: Jerzy Osia-
   tynski
Minister, Chief of the Office of the Council of Ministers: Jacek
   Ambroziak
Minister, Chief of Office of Scientific and Technical Progress and
   Implementation: Jan Janowski
Minister Without Portfolio: Artur Balazs
Minister Without Portfolio: Aleksander Hall
Minister Without Portfolio: Marek Kucharski
Minister Without Portfolio: Witold Trzeciakowski
President, Polish National Bank: Wladyslaw Baka

FREEDOM & HUMAN RIGHTS

In 1989 Poland was passing through a critical transitional stage in its postwar history as a Communist nation. The transition has been made more difficult because it coincides with a serious economic downturn caused by decades of mismanagement. Although economic reform and market stabilization are regime priorities, the economic managers have not been able to reverse the tailspin into which the economy dived in the early 1980s. Even as the second stage of the economic reform was launched in October 1987 with the stated goal of encouraging private initiative and increasing reliance on market mechanisms, bureaucratic controls continued to operate, preventing the reform from taking hold. A new set of economic reforms was introduced in 1988. The focal points for private economic activity are the small private farms, which form 75% of total agricultural land, and the growing small-business sector, which accounts for 8% of the nonagricultural sector. Meanwhile, the economy is plagued with a high debt-servicing burden, inefficiency, shortages of essential foodstuffs and consumer goods, worker discontent and various other malaise. The government's loose-credit policy, failure to restrain income growth and attempts to adjust prices of food and energy have sent the annual inflation rate up to 70%.

In the context of the economic morass, the exercise of human rights remains restricted, although Poland is undoubtedly the freest country in the Communist bloc. Technically all the fetters on freedom are in place, but few of them are being enforced. Censorship is officially in force, but opposition views are openly expressed, even in the party-controlled press. The Solidarity union, which has spearheaded Poland's move to the center, meets openly without harassment. A number of independent associations have been legalized since 1988. Religion, which never suffered the kind of persecution it did in other Communist countries, flourishes, and the Polish Catholic hierarchy wields an influence that even its counterparts in the West cannot match. There are no political prisoners in Poland for the first time since Gen. Pilsudski came to power in 1926. Certain political offenses are treated as misdemeanors subject to fines and short detention. Striking workers sometimes lose their apartments and jobs, but such instances are increasingly rare. Demonstrators may be detained by the police for several hours to two days and may suffer verbal abuse or blows with billy clubs.

Polish law allows for a 48-hour detention before the authorities are required to bring formal charges. After presentation of the legal basis of formal investigation, arrestees may be held in indefinite investigatory or temporary arrest until the investigation is completed and the indictment is filed. After the formal indictment is filed, the accused is granted the benefit of an attorney. Legal provisions for bail are rarely used, but suspects may be furloughed for humanitarian reasons.

After the 1986 amnesty, fewer persons were detained for long periods on vague or unspecified grounds, as in the past. However, the number of brief detentions, usually up to 48 hours, remains high. The 48-hour detention is often used as a deterrent against opposition activists. The legal 48-hour detention period sometimes is effectively extended by the police into periods of 96 hours or longer, often by releasing a person for an hour and then rearresting him for a second period.

Most cases are tried in open court. Defendants receive adequate legal aid and counsel, and defendants have the right of appeal. Political offenses may be treated as felonies or misdemeanors; in the case of the latter the accused often does not have the benefit of defense counsel.

Mail and telephone calls are selectively monitored. Overt censorship of the mail and announced monitoring of telephone calls ceased with the suspension of martial law in 1983. Packages mailed abroad are subject to inspection by postal workers. It is believed that the old network of informers survives in a reduced and different form. Searches may be performed legally only with warrants, but unauthorized searches sometimes occur. Jamming of foreign broadcasts has ceased. Western journals are not available widely due more to lack of foreign exchange than censorship.

The Polish Constitution provides for freedom of speech. Formerly, the exercise of this freedom existed only clandestinely, but it is becoming more open. For example, the Human Rights Conference sponsored by

Solidarity and Freedom and Peace Movement in August 1988 was attended by over 800 people from Eastern and Western Europe and North America, and government interference with the conference was minimal. The conference was held in a Catholic church, where opposition publications were openly distributed. Many churches sponsor or permit alternative cultural and other activities on their premises with little direct reprisal.

The Main Office of the Control of Press, Publishing and Public Performances oversees censorship of all media. Theoretically, Polish citizens may be arrested and fined for writing, printing, distributing or possessing publications not approved by the authorities. However, in actual practice a wide variety of opinion is printed and broadcast on previously forbidden topics, such as criticism of the Soviet Union over the Katyn Forest Massacre of Polish Army officers by the Red Army, and the Soviet invasion of Poland in 1939.

Poland has a diversified press. While following the approved government line on international issues, the press serves as a lively forum for debate on national issues. The range of opinion and ideology extends from the Catholic weekly *Tygodnik Powszechny* to the independent, private *Res Publica*, the official daily *Zycie Warszawy*, the hard-line party weekly *Rzeczywistosc* and the liberal party weekly *Polityka*. Many publications publish interviews with and articles by opposition leaders. The underground press continues to thrive, producing publications of uneven quality, but most of them appear regularly, indicating absence of direct official inferference. Many are sold openly. Also thriving is an underground video market. Satellite television is openly received and has become so common that the official daily military newspaper *Zolnierz Wilnosci* publishes program listings at the beginning of each month. In radio, television and cinema, politically controversial programs appear with impunity, including excerpts or unedited versions of Western programs.

Poland is the home of Eastern Europe's only private university, the Catholic University of Lublin, which counts Pope John Paul II among its former faculty. There also are a number of diocesan seminaries. Certain 1985 amendments to the Higher Education Law were widely feared as directed toward curbing the independence of universities, but this fear has not been realized.

Freedom of peaceful association and assembly is at government suffrance and subject to tight restrictions. Permits are required to hold public meetings or rallies. Requests for permits for protest meetings are routinely denied, but unofficial discussion groups and alternative cultural events take place in private homes and churches with the acquiescence, if not the approval, of the authorities. Major demonstrations in recent years have taken place within church property, including demonstrations in St. Stanislaw's Church in Warsaw, St. Brygida's Church in Gdansk and Jasna Gora Monastery in May, August and September, respectively, of 1988.

Under law, associations and clubs need official permission or sponsorship to function legally. The most important of these clubs is the Catholic Intellectuals' Club (KIK), the Polish Pen Club, the Warsaw Dziekania political club and Young Poland. Certain nonprofit,

independent foundations for charitable, social and health purposes are legally sanctioned.

Freedom of religion is actively enjoyed by the Poles in theory and practice, although party members are discouraged from overtly participating in religious activities. There is no official discrimination against minority religions, but they face practical difficulties in a country that is traditionally Catholic. The largest minority, the Orthodox Church, with 350 places of worship, has recently begun a program of church building and monastery renovation. It also has received back from the government some religious buildings previously under state control.

There are no legal restrictions on travel within Poland or change of residence and work. However, the acute housing shortage makes this freedom a dead letter. In 1987 the government liberalized its policy on issuance of passports, and now 97% of all passport applications are granted. Low-level opposition leaders and criminals are among those most frequently denied passports. The 1987 liberalization also made it easier for those who left Poland illegally to return without fear of reprisal. Most applicants for emigrant passports eventually obtain them. However, there are stringent requirements to be met first, such as the disposal of all real property. Thus most emigrants leave on tourist visas and validate their status later. Citizenship is rarely revoked.

The rubber-stamp function of the Sejm is being increasingly replaced by active debates on critical issues, leading to outcomes not entirely to the government's liking. Such debates are uncensored and are published in the official press. Legislation creating the office of ombudsman or spokesman for citizens' rights was passed by the Sejm in 1987 and went into effect in January 1988. The ombudsman has the right, in theory at least, to review and reverse administrative and legal decisions appealed by private citizens. The ombudsman has been hampered, however, by a deluge of petitions and insufficient responsiveness from the government.

In 1988 a new electoral law was passed. Its main features were: multiple candidacies, the candidates being listed alphabetically rather than as before in the descending order of official acceptability; and voters being permitted to mark their ballots.

Polish women do not as yet play an active role in public life, reflecting history rather than the working of socialist ideology. The heavy loss of male manpower during World War II forced women to fill more jobs in all economic sectors, but women rarely rise to the top or earn as much as their male colleagues. Poland has a liberal maternity and child care leave policy, dating from the Solidarity-inspired Gdansk accords. Women are entitled to four months of paid maternity leave and up to three years of unpaid leave with a guarantee of the same or similar job on return to work.

CIVIL SERVICE

As elsewhere in Eastern Europe, the Polish government has no Office of Personnel Management, as in the United States. The Council of Ministers directs the organs of administration, and its Office or Chancery plays a coordinating role. Each ministry has the equivalent of a personnel office (*wydzial kadr*).

The PUWP's power in the society, government and in personnel matters was reduced drastically following the formation of the government by Solidarity. On January 29, 1990, the PUWP was dissolved, but Solidarity found it difficult to eliminate *nomenklatura* at every level, with appointees numbering 1.2 million. According to a senior Polish official, 100,000 of these are secret service agents. A commission has been set up to oversee the dissolution of the intelligence service. In November 1989 Minister of Foreign Affairs Krzysztof Skubiszewski remarked that the government wishes to organize a civil service structure like the British and replace the present cadre, which were installed from the PZPR's *nomenklatura* channels.

Poland has no particular educational or training institution to prepare students for public service. The normal sources are the 11 universities, 18 technical universities, other specialized institutions and secondary schools. General and specialized training is conducted during employment. The government maintains contact with educational institutions to facilitate the transition from school to employment. The more prominent universities are: Warsaw, Jagiellonian (Krakow), Adam Mickiewicz (Poznan), Silesian (Katowice), Gdansk, Maria Curie-Sklodowska (Lublin) and Lodz.

LOCAL GOVERNMENT

Until the local government reforms of 1972 and 1975 Poland had been divided into 22 voivodships, 391 counties and 4,671 villages. As a result of the reforms the three-tier structure was replaced by a two-tier framework with 49 voivodships and nearly 3,000 basic administrative units consisting of 799 towns, 21 urban districts (seven in Warsaw, four in Krakow, five in Lodz and five in Wroclaw) and 1,533 communes.

Popularly elected people's councils function as the legislative units at both voivodship and local levels. Until 1973 the council elected a presidium from its own members, but since then these two organs have been separate. At the voivodship level, these bodies are now headed by a voivod (prefect or governor), except in the three municipal voivodships of Warsaw, Krakow and Lodz, where the highest officials are called city presidents. Other cities with populations of over 50,000 also have presidents. Communities of smaller populations have town chiefs, and city districts and rural communes have chiefs. These local officers are appointed by the supervising voivod or city president in consultation with the local people's council.

Voivods, city presidents and their deputies are appointed by the prime minister. Their terms of office are indefinite, and they are in effect professional administrators who regard themselves as answerable not only to the council but also to the Ministry of Administration, Local Economy and Environmental Protection. Until 1981 people's councils at both levels were chaired by the regional or local first secretary of the PZPR, and the two deputy chairmen were from the United Peasant Party and the Democratic Party. Commune councils have elected members of other parties and even non-party members as their chairmen.

Elections to the people's councils for four-year terms normally are held concurrently with elections to the Sejm. Multiple candidacies are now permitted, and voters may mark their ballots. The councils exercise their oversight functions in several ways. They must approve annual budgets and plans, adopt guidelines for officials and review their performance. In each voivodship 19 administrative departments are concerned with matters such as the local economy, agriculture and forestry, finance, trade and services, public transportation, labor and social welfare. The plans of locally managed enterprises must be synchronized with national and regional plans. To reduce the possibility of friction, heads of leading industrial enterprises are often coopted into commissions of the local administration or are members of the people's councils. Centrally directed enterprises and state institutions such as universities, prisons, banks and police are exempt from voivodship control.

At the commune level the administrative structure is simpler. Its secretariat, headed by the commune secretary, supervises departments of general administration and of agriculture and a registrar's office. Communes are responsible for utilities, sanitation, road building and maintenance, administration of apartment blocks, encouragement of private farming, farm deliveries and retail trade. In town they also may supervise schools, clinics, cultural clubs, libraries and theaters.

The administrative reforms of the early 1970s had some progressive features, but on the whole their impact has been to widen the gap between the community and the local organs of administration, to make the councils even more subservient to Warsaw. The autonomy of the voivods was curtailed, and they were required to carry out the instructions of the central government implicitly.

The Law on Local Self-Government of March 19, 1990, stresses that the basic administrative district or *gmina* is a "self-governing community." The relevant chapter of the Polish Constitution no longer speaks of "local agencies of state authority and administration" but of "local self-government." The new law states that the *gmina* engages in public activity on its own behalf and is fully responsible for its own actions. The law endows the *gmina* with legal status and ensures that its autonomy is legally protected. Each *gmina* is to be governed by its own statutes and to encompass an area as homogeneous as possible in terms of its population, geography and economy. The formation of each *gmina* belongs to the jurisdiction of the central government but is subject to consultation with local inhabitants. Although some reorganization of the existing territorial administrative divisions is anticipated in the future, the forthcoming local government elections will take place on the basis of existing boundaries.

The *gmina* is the legal owner of communal property, which it is required to manage in accordance with the law and for which it bears fiscal responsibility. It is empowered to engage in economic activity and is bound to balance its annual budget and achieve financial self-sufficiency. The *gmina* draws its income from taxes, duties, revenue from its assets and a central government grant. It can also draw on its budgetary surpluses, central government financing for specific projects, special taxes levied with public consent, loans and bonds as well as bequests and donations. Its finances are open to public scrutiny and checked by regional auditing chambers whose chairmen are appointed by the prime minister.

Each *gmina* is called upon to satisfy local public needs in the following spheres: land management and environmental protection; roads and traffic; water and energy supply; sewage and waste disposal; public transportation; health care; social welfare facilities; public housing; preschool, primary and vocational education; cultural and sports facilities; marketplaces; cemeteries; and fire fighting. It also has local responsibility for the maintenance of public buildings and public order. It is obliged to fulfill these tasks within its own budgetary possibilities. In addition, each *gmina* performs specific tasks "commissioned" by the central government, at the government's cost.

The inhabitants of the *gmina* express their will through referendums or through their representatives elected by universal suffrage for a four-year term. These representatives make up the local council, the *gmina's* constituent and controlling authority, which is responsible for the *gmina's* statutes, finances, policies and programs. The size of each council varies, from 15 to 100 councilors, according to the number of inhabitants. The councilors choose from among themselves a chairman, his deputies, and an executive of some four to seven members. A local government office aids the executive in the running of day-to-day affairs. The head of this office in rural districts is known as a *wojt*, in small towns is a town mayor, and in municipalities with over 100,000 inhabitants is a city president. This individual, who may but need not be a councilor, is appointed by the council and subject to its control. He may not simultaneously occupy the post of council chairman.

Every *gmina* belonging to a particular voivodship delegates one or more representatives to a voivodship *sejmik*. This body acts as the link between the local and central government administrations. The *sejmik* evaluates local government activity within the voivodship. It serves as a forum for sharing practical experience and ideas. It mediates in conflicts between districts and steps in when any *gmina* council is unable to perform its statutory tasks. It represents the interests of local government with regard to both central government and the government's local representative, the voivod. The *sejmik* also assesses the work of the voivod's office and advises the prime minister on candidates for the voivod's office. It is empowered to make formal requests that the government overrule any of the voivod's decisions that are deemed to violate local interests.

The election law of March 19, 1990, provides for a mixed electoral system, with both majority voting, in constituencies of less than 40,000 inhabitants, and proportional represenation, in those of 40,000 or over. The rationale for this distinction was that in small communities individual candidates would be well known to most of the electorate, while in larger communities, particularly within cities, individuals would be less well known than the parties or groups they represented. Therefore, the members of small local communities will be asked to trust the individual candidate, while those belonging to larger communities will have to place their trust in political parties and their programs. Individual candidates require 15 and party lists 150 signatures in order for nominations to be registered as valid by the constituency electoral commissions.

The smaller constituencies will be represented by a single councilor, the one who wins the most votes in a straight contest; while the larger ones will be represented by from 5 to 10 councilors with the winners being identified according to the Sainte-Lague vote counting system (used in Scandinavian countries) that gives even small parties with some 7–12% of the vote a chance of winning a seat. In both cases, the voter has one vote, which he gives to one candidate, the difference being that in the smaller constituencies the ballot consists of a number of individual candidates, whereas in the larger constituencies the voter is confronted with a number of lists of candidates, and he or she must first choose the list (that is, party, movement or coalition) to which he wishes to give his vote, and then, on that list, mark the name of his desired candidate. The number of votes cast for each of the lists is the basis on which the proportional distribution of seats will be calculated. The seats accruing to each of the lists will then be given to candidates on that list with the highest consecutive numbers of votes.

FOREIGN POLICY

Throughout the centuries, Poland has been deeply involved with foreign countries, and its territory frequently was a political or a military battleground. Poland was a mighty power, and it was powerless. Following the reestablishment of its independence after World War I, Poland immediately became embroiled in territorial disputes with its neighbors. In 1919 the Red Army, advancing into Poland, was repelled by the Polish military forces led by Gen. Jozef Pilsudski. Lenin had considered the destruction of the Polish army essential for Communist revolution in Western Europe. The Riga Treaty of March 1921 ended the Polish-Russian War and fixed the boundary between the two countries. Plebiscites and the League of Nations determined boundaries with Germany and Czechoslovakia.

Historically, religiously and culturally, Poland was drawn toward the West. Essentially, its independence and security were entrusted to France through political and defense agreements. However, Pilsudski's attempts to achieve a leadership position in Eastern Europe failed. After Hitler achieved dominance in Germany, Poland proposed a treaty to Czechoslovakia, but the latter's minister of foreign affairs, Edvard Benes, who had rejected Warsaw's overtures in the early 1920s, rejected this offer. Conscious of potential danger from Poland's eastern and western neighbors, Pilsudski attempted to maintain favorable relations with both. Ac-

POLITICAL SUBDIVISIONS				
		Area		Population
Provinces	Capitals	Sq. Km.	Sq Mi.	(1986 est.)
Biala Podlaska	Biala Podlaska	5,348	2,065	297,900
Bialystok	Bialystok	10,055	3,882	671,600
Bielsko	Bielsko Biala	3,704	1,430	873,600
Bydgoszcz	Bydgoszcz	10,349	3,996	1,083,800
Chelm	Chelm	3,866	1,493	240,800
Ciechanow	Ciechanow	6,362	2,456	418,100
Czestochowa	Czestochowa	6,182	2,387	767,400
Elblag	Elblag	6,103	2,356	466,700
Gdansk	Gdansk	7,394	2,855	1,401,500
Gorzow	Gorzow Wielkopolski	8,484	3,276	482,200
Jelenia Gora	Jelenia Gora	4,378	1,690	510,300
Kalisz	Kalisz	6,512	2,514	696,400
Katowice	Katowice	6,650	2,568	3,916,400
Kielce	Kielce	9,211	3,556	1,107,900
Konin	Konin	5,139	1,984	459,300
Koszalin	Koszalin	8,470	3,270	489,800
Krakow	Krakow	3,254	1,256	1,209,300
Krosno	Krosno	5,702	2,202	475,200
Legnica	Legnica	4,037	1,559	490,600
Leszno	Leszno	4,154	1,604	375,600
Lodz	Lodz	1,523	588	1,149,100
Lomza	Lomza	6,684	2,581	338,700
Lublin	Lublin	6,792	2,622	985,400
Nowy Sacz	Nowy Sacz	5,576	2,153	667,400
Olsztyn	Olsztyn	12,327	4,759	725,700
Opole	Opole	8,535	3,295	1,013,700
Ostroleka	Ostroleka	6,498	2,509	384,200
Pita	Pita	8,205	3,168	465,400
Piotrkow	Piotrkow Trybunalski	6,266	2,419	633,100
Plock	Plock	5,117	1,976	509,300
Poznan	Poznan	8,151	3,147	1,298,000
Przemysl	Przemysl	4,437	1,713	395,900
Radom	Radom	7,294	2,816	729,700
Rzeszow	Rzeszow	4,397	1,698	691,300
Siedlce	Siedlce	8,499	3,281	636,500
Sieradz	Sieradz	4,869	1,880	401,200
Skierniewice	Skierniewice	3,960	1,529	409,500
Slupsk	Slupsk	7,453	2,878	396,100
Suwalki	Suwalki	10,490	4,050	449,000
Szczecin	Szczecin	9,981	3,854	942,600
Tarnobrzeg	Tarnobrzeg	6,283	2,426	580,500
Tarnow	Tarnow	4,151	1,603	641,500
Torun	Torun	5,348	2,065	640,600
Walbrzych	Walbrzych	4,168	1,609	735,800
Warszawa	Warszawa	3,788	1,463	2,412,200
Wloclawek	Wloclawek	4,402	1,700	425,900
Wroclaw	Wroclaw	6,287	2,427	1,113,900
Zamosc	Zamosc	6,980	2,695	487,900
Zielona Gora	Zielona Gora	8,868	3,424	646,000
TOTAL		312,683	120,727	37,340,500

gression pact, with its secret protocols, led to Germany's massive invasion of Poland on September 1, and the Red Army's on September 17, which resulted in approximately 200,000 Polish POW's. Poland was again divided, with the Soviet Union annexing substantial territory in the East. A government-in-exile was established in France in October where Gen. Wladyslaw Sikorski, its prime minister, organized Polish troops. The Polish force in the West, numbering 200,000, fought valiantly and with distinction in France, the Battle of Britain, Norway, North Africa, Italy (Monte Casino), Normandy, Belgium, Holland and finally in Germany.

Following the June 22, 1941, German invasion of the Soviet Union, Stalin undertook negotiations with the Polish government-in-exile, now in London, regarding the organization of Polish military forces in the USSR, numbering some 110,000 prisoners of war and labor camp inmates under the leadership of Gen. Wladyslaw Anders. However, unresolved differences resulted in the departure of the Polish troops in early 1942 to the British Eighth Army in the Middle East. Polish-Soviet hostility continued during the war. Considering their objectives, the differences were irreconcilable. When in 1943 the exiled prime minister requested the International Red Cross to investigate the Katyn mass graves of Polish officers, Moscow severed diplomatic relations with the London government-in-exile and established the Union of Polish Patriots as the future political force in the country.

Justifiably, the Allies devoted considerable attention to Poland, which assisted the Allied cause greatly by military forces and in the underground. However, Soviet designs on the country remained unaltered. On July 22, 1944, the Polish Committee of National Liberation was formed in Lublin with Communist veteran Boleslaw Bierut as its chairman. Warsaw's uprising against German occupation forces from August 1 to October 2 was unaided by the Red Army, and Poland sustained irreparable physical damage and loss of life once again. Subsequently Soviet forces occupied the entire country. In January 1945 Moscow recognized the Lublin Committee officially as the Polish government and demanded the annexed eastern territories of Poland. The Yalta Conference of February 1945 provided for "free and unfettered elections as soon as possible," which were audaciously violated by the Soviet Union and the Polish Communist officials. However, with the participation of non-Communists led by Wladyslaw Mikolajczyk, head of the Peasant Party, Great Britain and the United States recognized the Communist-dominated coalition government in July 1945 and withdrew their recognition of the Polish government in London.

The Allies discussed postwar boundaries of Poland at Teheran in November 1943, Yalta, and at Potsdam from July 17 to August 2, 1945. The latter specified Poland's western boundary from the Baltic, east of the Oder and Neisse rivers to Czechoslovakia "pending the final determination of Poland's western frontier," a gain of over 100,000 sq. km. (38,600 sq. mi.). Warsaw was given authority to transfer the German population from the former German territories to Germany. The USSR had incorporated 180,000 sq. km. (69,480 sq. mi.) of Poland's

cordingly, he responded to overtures, and Warsaw signed nonaggression treaties with the Soviet Union and Germany in 1932 and 1934, respectively.

Following the Munich Conference of September 1938 that ceded the Sudetenland to Germany, Poland occupied Cieszyn (Tesin). After the Nazis established a protectorate over Bohemia-Moravia in March 1939, Poland signed a mutual assistance treaty with Great Britain the following month. Hitler's increased demands on Poland were rejected by Warsaw, and Hitler renounced his treaty with Warsaw in August 1939.

Poland became a tragic victim of the Nazi-Soviet division of Eastern Europe. Their August 23, 1939, nonag-

prewar territory, and the Polish population was transferred to the western areas.

Poland's security and the inviolability of its frontiers were entrusted to the Soviet Union. On April 21, 1945, the provisional government signed a treaty of friendship, cooperation and mutual assistance with the Soviet Union. The Polish Workers' Party was a founding member of the Communist Information Bureau (COMINFORM), established October 11, 1947, in Poland. That Poland was firmly under Moscow's control was already clear. Wladyslaw Gomulka was deposed for objecting to the conference to establish the COMINFORM, and Stalin decided against Warsaw's participation in the Marshall Plan.

Poland was one of the six original members of the Soviet-sponsored Council for Mutual Economic Assistance (CMEA) in January 1949. As Moscow's response to the Marshall Plan, the CMEA subsequently became a Soviet-controlled mechanism for coordinating the economies of its members. Following membership of West Germany in NATO, Warsaw hosted the conference that established the seven-nation Soviet bloc military alliance on March 14, 1955, the Warsaw Treaty Organization or Warsaw Pact. The pact was extended in 1975 for 10 years and in 1985 was renewed for another 20 years. The Warsaw Pact has a Political Consultative Committee; a Foreign Ministers' Committee; a Defense Ministers' Committee; and joint armed forces, with a Soviet marshal serving as commander in chief.

Amid rioting in Warsaw and other cities in 1956, plans to install Gomulka as first secretary of the PZPR prompted an uninvited Khrushchev-led Kremlin delegation to Warsaw October 19. Poles became increasingly concerned that Soviet armed forces—tank units were on the move—would be deployed to Warsaw. This possibility proved unnecessary as Gomulka's leadership, effective October 21, succeeded in quieting the population, and the Soviet delegation returned to Moscow. In addition to internal changes, Soviet Marshal Konstantin K. Rokossovsky, Poland's minister of defense since 1949, was reassigned to Moscow, together with other high-ranking Soviet officers. The Polish events had a profound effect on Hungarians, whose demonstrations became revolutionary. As additional insurance to continuing to maintain its troops in Eastern European countries, Moscow concluded status-of-forces treaties in subsequent months; a pact with Poland to this effect was signed in December 1956.

In line with the principle of fraternal relations with the Soviet bloc countries, Poland concluded treaties of friendship, cooperation and mutual assistance with Czechoslovakia on March 1, 1967; East Germany on March 15, 1967; Bulgaria on April 6, 1967; Hungary on May 16, 1968; and Rumania on November 12, 1970. The 1945 pact with the Soviet Union was extended another twenty years on April 8, 1965. This treaty proclaims the "inviolability" of Polish frontiers and provides for the transit of Soviet troops and matériel across Poland to East Germany. Poland's forces were included in the August 1968 Soviet-directed Warsaw Pact invasion of Czechoslovakia. The invasion was supported by Gomulka and doomed Alexander Dubcek's "Prague Spring."

According to Minister of Foreign Affairs Krzysztof Skubiszewski, at a meeting of the heads of state of the WTO on December 4, 1989, in Moscow, "The adoption of a resolution acknowledging the intervention in Czechoslovakia in 1968 was an illegal act and a political, harmful mistake." The delegation, led by the prime minister, caused the resolution to carry the entry that the Warsaw Treaty is no grounds for intervention in the internal affairs of states. This important provision was adopted by the whole WTO.

In November 1968 Leonid Brezhnev declared in Warsaw the right to intervene in "friendly socialist countries" by Warsaw Pact military forces if a Communist regime is determined to be in danger. The Brezhnev Doctrine was on the minds of Poles during the 1980–81 appearance of Solidarity, and again in 1989, when the PZPR regime was in danger of losing control. During negotiations for a new government, President Jaruzelski told Solidarity leaders in July 1989 that Warsaw Pact members—specifically the Soviet Union, Czechoslovakia and East Germany—looked with disfavor on Solidarity leading the government. However, as negotiations developed, the PZPR was not only included in the government organized in September but also received the powerful Ministries of Defense and Internal Affairs. Under the circumstances, and with Gen. Jaruzelski as president, Gorbachev decided the events were an "internal affair." In August the Sejm condemned the 1968 Warsaw Pact invasion of Czechoslovakia. However, there was no evidence of Soviet intention to intervene militarily in Poland during the momentous events in 1989 culminating in the defeat of the Communist regime by Solidarity. Also, the Soviets have not changed their position on the Katyn massacre. On December 5, 1989, Prime Minister Mazowiecki said he believed that a full clarification of the Katyn issue would be made soon.

In his December 7, 1988, address before the U.N. General Assembly, Gorbachev announced Soviet troop reductions within two years, including 5,000 tanks, 50,000 troops, artillery and aircraft from East Germany, Hungary and Czechoslovakia. Poland was not specifically mentioned. Early in 1989 Soviet troops in Poland were estimated at 40,000. In mid-1989 the Soviet Northern Group of Forces announced withdrawal from Poland of one truck battalion and a tank regiment. Also, in accordance with "international detente," it said it would return to the Soviet Union an antichemical defense battalion, an antiaircraft missile regiment and a helicopter regiment, altogether numbering 90 tanks, about 50 aircraft and over 60 helicopters. However, Poles prefer to be free of Soviet forces, which they consider to be an occupation force. This was the clear message of the Polish demonstrators on September 17, 1989, marking the 50th anniversary of the Soviet invasion.

On February 4, 1990, General Jaruzelski, speaking before the World Economic Forum in Switzerland, ruled out Soviet military withdrawal from Poland until Poland received "a definitive, clear and unequivocal statement of the inviolable character of Poland's borders" from West Germany. Jaruzelski objected to references in the West German Constitution that he said called for a return to the borders of 1937 Germany. On

February 11, the Soviet government indicated its willingness to begin negotiations on the withdrawal of more than 40,000 Soviet military forces in Poland if Warsaw requests their pullout. Moscow was already negotiating with Hungary and Czechoslovakia.

In addition to the close bilateral and multilateral political and military alliances, Poland has extensive trade and other relations with Soviet bloc countries. Over the decades the major portion of Poland's foreign trade has been with CMEA members. The Soviet Union has by far been its largest trading partner, with Poland dependent on its petroleum products. On April 21, 1987, Jaruzelski and Gorbachev signed the Declaration of Polish-Soviet Cooperation in the Fields of Ideology, Science and Culture; it serves as a model for Poland's bilateral relations with other East European countries. Strategically, militarily and economically, Poland's other neighbors—Germany and Czechoslovakia—are the most important.

The inviolability of its Oder-Neisse frontier with Germany was and is of great concern to Poland. Thus this provision was not only in the Polish-Soviet treaty but also in bilateral treaties with other East European countries, the 1950 pact with East Germany being of particular significance. However, despite formal pledges of fraternal cooperation, Poland has experienced uneasiness with East Germany. For example, it took three years to reach agreement (signed May 22, 1989) on a border dispute concerning Pomeranian Bay, and decades for East Germany to acknowledge the secret protocol of the 1939 Nazi-Soviet nonagression pact. The long-delayed admission, coming after Moscow's, appeared in the daily *Junge Welt* on August 23, 1989. That same day, the Sejm, marking the pact's 50th anniversary, unanimously condemned the pact as "infamous" and the secret protocols as "immoral." The PZPR Politburo denounced it as a violation of international law.

Polish-Czech relations were strained during the interwar period over Cieszyn (Tesin), which was annexed by Czechoslovakia with the concurrence of the Allies during the Polish-Russian War of 1919–21. In turn, Warsaw seized on Prague's troubles with Nazi Germany to annex the territory in October 1938. In addition, Foreign Minister Benes of Czechoslovakia rebuffed Warsaw's interest in the Little Entente and in other security arrangements. In 1945 Stalin restored Cieszyn to its interwar division, not entirely a satisfactory arrangement for Poland. In August 1968 Warsaw participated in the Warsaw Pact invasion of Czechoslovakia. During the 1970s many Poles traveled to Czechoslovakia and to East Germany not only as tourists but also to purchase goods unavailable in Poland, creating negative Czech and German reactions. The Milos Jakes leadership viewed the 1989 Solidarity develoments as duplicative of Dubcek's "Prague Spring." However, the non-Communist government in Czechoslovakia sought to improve relations with Poland. On January 25, 1990, the president of Czechoslovakia, Vaclav Havel, addressed a joint session of the Polish legislature. Havel proposed the return of Czechoslovakia, Poland and Hungary to Western Europe and the dissolution of NATO and the WTO. His proposal was well received by the Polish government. Czechoslovakia is Poland's third-largest trading partner.

Poland has had friendly relations with Hungary, the latter's population demonstrating in support of the Polish people's strikes and demonstrations in 1956 and during subsequent years, including 1989, when Budapest's reform-minded leaders approved of Solidarity. A nonbloc member, Yugoslavia, was the sole East European country to send a delegation to Solidarity's Congress in 1981. Warsaw's policy toward Communist China has reflected Moscow's. Diplomatic representation was elevated to the ambassadorial level in 1970. Since the early 1980s trade has increased substantially between the two countries.

Since the Communist takeover of power, Poland has given unstinting support to the Soviet Union in unilateral declarations and in international forums on a wide range of issues: regional disputes and conflicts, anti-U.S. (and anti-Western) propaganda, the peace campaigns, nuclear-free zones, détente and arms control. Warsaw has been an active participant at the United Nations, its specialized agencies and in other international organizations, numbering about 1,500. Poland maintains diplomatic relations with 129 countries and is a founding member of the United Nations, serving four times on the Security Council and serving on other major bodies, including the Disarmament Commission in Geneva. Poland was a member of the Korean Truce Commission and the Indochina Truce Commission. Warsaw's membership includes UNESCO, IAEA, UNIDO, WHO, ILO, FAO, UNCTAD, IHO, ITU, International Monetary Fund (IMF), World Bank (IBRD), General Agreement on Tariffs and Trade (GATT), International Council for the Exploration of the Sea (ICES) and the United Nation's environmental program.

Poland has supported increased cooperation between East and West. It was a supporter of the 1975 Helsinki Conference on Security and Cooperation in Europe (CSCE) and has participated in all of its follow-up meetings. Warsaw has had an active delegation at the NATO-Warsaw Pact Mutual and Balanced Force Reduction (MBFR) negotiations in Vienna (1973–89) and is involved in the Conventional Armed Forces in Europe (CFE) talks.

Poland's disarmament proposals include those regarding nuclear-free zones in central Europe, exemplified by the 1957 Rapacki Plan and the 1987 Jaruzelski Plan. While allied with the Soviet bloc, Poland has maintained and developed, albeit unevenly, relations with the Western countries, partly for national reasons and partly in response to the Krelmin's policy of detente in the 1950s, the 1970s and under Gorbachev. The West applauded the 1980–81 independence movement in Poland and denounced Jaruzelski's martial law and the regime's repressive measures; among the critics were, with the exception of the French, the Communist parties in Western Europe.

Perhaps the highlight of Poland's postwar foreign policy was the conclusion in December 1970 of a treaty with West Germany providing for recognition of the Oder-Neisse line as Poland's western boundary with no future territorial claims, renunciation of force in settling disputes and normalization of diplomatic relations. In 1975 the two countries agreed on other outstanding problems, including the emigration of 125,000 ethnic Germans from Poland, West Germany's extension of credit, and compensation to Poles for pre-1945 labor. Trade between them increased so dramatically that within a few years West Germany became Warsaw's second most important trading partner, which it remained throughout the 1980s. In mid-1989 West Germany also was Poland's largest creditor. Nevertheless, Poland's western frontier continued to be of concern to the Poles living in that region. Apparently Chancellor Kohl's comment about the Western border was considered inadequate. On December 8, 1989, speaking before the European Community, Kohl accepted Poland's western border on the Oder and Neisse rivers. This was the chancellor's first public acceptance. However, on December 13 President Kosakiewicz of the Sejm characterized Kohl's position as ambiguous.

The vast majority of Poles are Roman Catholics whose religiosity, combined with strong nationalism, make them a unique force in the Soviet bloc and perhaps in the world. Logically, on July 17, 1989, Poland became the first Soviet bloc country to reestablish diplomatic relations with the Vatican. Relations with the Holy See were first established in 1555 and continued until the third partition of Poland, in 1795. Official representatives were not exchanged until Poland regained its independence after World War I, with a concordat concluded in 1925. The papal nuncio left Warsaw on September 5, 1939, following the German invasion, and the Communist-controlled provisional government renounced the concordat in 1945.

Following the Communist seizure of power, with its repressive policy toward religion, the Catholic Church had no legal status, and the regime's hostility toward it and the Vatican resulted in nonexistent relations. The 1956 "thaw" brought limited liberalization to the faithful, but it was not until 1967 that a Vatican representative, Msgr. (later Cardinal) Agostino Casaroli, visited Poland, and a protocol was signed on July 6, 1974, providing for "delegates." Subsequently discussions concerned diplomatic relations, but several problems required solution, especially the legal status and complete rights for the Church. The election of a Polish pope, the Solidarity movement, and the visits of Pope John Paul II were instrumental in furthering normalization. The resurgence of Solidarity in 1989 and the resulting legislation of May 17 giving legal status and other rights to the Church satisfied the Vatican's requirements for formal links. According to the July 17 short joint communique, the Holy See and Poland "reestablished" diplomatic relations at the apostolic nuncio-ambassadorial level. During the visit of Prime Minister Mazowiecki to Rome, the pope consecrated a Polish bishop October 20 to be the papal nuncio in Warsaw. These precedent-setting diplomatic relations between the Vatican and a Soviet bloc country were immensely important, not only for Poland but also as a model for other Soviet bloc countries. On December 15 the papal nuncio presented his credentials to the Polish government.

The Polish patriots Pulaski and Kosciuszko are known to all American schoolchildren studying the American Revolution. The United States played a major role in the reestablishment of an independent Poland during World War I. The 13th of President Woodrow Wilson's Fourteen Points called for independence for Poland, and the United States supported Warsaw during the Versailles Peace Conference. The two governments established diplomatic relations in 1919. The United States has had a special interest in maintaining favorable relations with Poland, partly because of the large American population of Polish heritage (perhaps 8.5 million, according to Warsaw). As a result, Poles have a favorable perception of America. The United States denounced the Nazi invasion of Poland in 1939; extended Lend-Lease to the fighting Poles during the war; and at the Teheran, Yalta and Potsdam conferences supported Polish independence and its western frontier.

During World War II the United States maintained diplomatic relations with the Polish government-in-exile in London. On July 5, 1945, it recognized the Communist-controlled provisional government, following inclusion of non-Communists, as provided by the Yalta Conference. Washington protested the violation of Yalta that called for "free and unfettered" elections, not held until January 1947, when Communists established complete control over Poland. Relations deteriorated as the United States, and the West generally, became objects of Polish and Soviet bloc attacks.

U.S.-Polish relations improved during the period of East-West "thaw" and Gomulka's liberalization policy, which the United States welcomed, beginning with cultural exchanges, reuniting divided families and trade. As East-West relations cooled in the 1960s, so did U.S.-Polish relations. After Edward Gierek replaced Gomulka as the PZPR's first secretary in 1970, he indicated improvement in bilateral relations with the United States. Washington's positive response included President Richard Nixon's visit to Poland of May 31–June 1, 1972 and the signing of a consular convention. Later in the year ranking Polish officials visiting Washington agreed to reimburse American holders of prewar Polish bonds. Gierek's visit to the United States in October 1974 led to agreements on a joint research board, coal research, an income tax convention, health and the establishment of the U.S.-Polish Economic Council under chambers of commerce. President Gerald Ford visited Poland on July 28–29, 1975, and President Jimmy Carter did so on December 29–31, 1977.

During the 1980–81 period of Solidarity, Washington avoided interfering in Polish internal affairs while encouraging liberalization and extending $765 million in agricultural aid in 1981. Ten days after imposition of martial law on December 13, 1981, President Ronald Reagan denounced the regime's action as "betrayal" of its people and a violation of the U.N. Charter and the Helsinki accords. He suspended major economic elements of the U.S. relationship with the Polish government. The president designated January 30, 1982, as Solidarity Day. On December 29, charging the Soviet Union with "heavy and direct responsibility," Reagan applied several measures against the USSR. Moreover, the United States ceased support for Poland's membership in the IMF and in October 1982 suspended Poland's most favored nation (MFN) tariff status. Because Warsaw refused to accept the new U.S. ambassador in 1983, the U.S. embassy was headed by a charge d'affaires. Gradually Washington responded favorably to internal progress. The president rescinded the economic sanctions on February 19, 1987, restored MFN tariff treatment and lifted the ban on Poland's eligibility for official U.S. credits, Official exchanges were extended, and diplomatic representation was elevated to the ambassadorial level. Among other programs, the Science and Technology Cooperation Agreement was renewed, the Joint Trade Commission revised, and a civil aviation agreement signed.

On the eve of President George Bush's visit to Poland in 1989, U.S.-Polish relations were favorable and trade active. During 1988 U.S. exports to Poland totaled $304 million—the largest East European market—and imports from Poland $378 million. Moreover, Polish reforms encouraged growth. For example, as of January 1989 Western investors were permitted to acquire entire enterprises in Poland.

In July 1989 President Bush visited Poland and Hungary. In his July 10 address before the Sejm he promised to support Western aid and technical assistance for Poland to complement those of the World Bank, the Paris Club and the IMF; ask Congress for $100 million for the Polish private sector; encourage the World Bank to proceed with $325 million in loans to upgrade agricultural and industrial production; request Western allies to support rescheduling of the Polish debt; request Congress for $15 million for a joint undertaking to fight air and water pollution in Crakow; and establish a U.S. cultural center in Warsaw—and for Poland, a similar center in the United States—outside of embassies and consulates.

The ensuing 15th economic summit of the industrialized nations, held in Paris July 14–16, noted progress for reform in Poland and Hungary and pledged economic assistance to these countries, including the areas cited by President Bush. Subsequently the European Economic Community (EEC), in addition to $130 million in emergency food aid, approved a $315 million aid package, including credit. By September the EEC had requested $600 million from 24 non-Communist governments in new aid. Poland was indeed in dire need of economic assistance. In September 1989 inflation was climbing to 100% yearly and its foreign debt was nearly $40 billion. The Polish government requested $1 billion in stabilization loans, and Lech Walesa told President Bush that Poland would need $10 billion in aid during the next three years. Warsaw was establishing more active relations with Western countries in general and with the EEC and the United States in particular. During the fall all were considering economic assistance substantially in excess of the July figures to meet Poland's request.

On December 13, 1989, Western governments, meeting in Brussels, announced plans to increase economic assistance to Poland. A task force of foreign ministers considered the completion of pledges to a $1 billion emergency fund for Poland. Loans and donations toward zloty stability were disclosed as follows (in 000 U.S. dollars):

Country	Loans	Donations
Turkey	750	—
Portugal	5,000	—
Austria	—	20,000
Spain	20,000	—
Canada	—	25,000
Switzerland	30,000	—
Great Britain	—	100,000
France	100,000	—
Italy	100,000	—
Japan	150,000	—
United States	—	200,000
West Germany	250,000	

Source: *The New York Times*, December 14, 1989, p. A22. Excluding food assistance, Warsaw expected $3.2 billion to $3.5 billion in aid during 1990. Poland Promised to reduce its 900% annual inflation rate and reduce budget deficits.

PARLIAMENT

Generally, Poland's Sejm (Parliament) conducted itself from the end of World War II until 1989 as did legislatures in other Soviet bloc countries—in the Sejm's case, meeting twice annually for short periods to approve the PZPR's proposals formally. Exceptions to the Sejm's pro forma activities occurred during the revolutionary period of 1956; during the crisis of 1971 when, among other progressive steps, the Sejm's committee system was strengthened and expanded; during the debates over the controversial constitutional amendments in 1976; and during the dramatic rise of the Solidarity movement in 1980–81.

The promising events in 1980–81 were summarily halted on December 12–13, 1981, with the imposition of martial law by Gen. Jaruzelski, who obtained the Sejm's approval only ex post facto. The Sejm reverted to its normal formalistic role and in February 1984 extended its term of office. Elections were held in October 1985. A new electoral law permitted a choice of two candidates for 410 of the 460 seats. The other 50 were on a single list of candidates. Solidarity, which encouraged a boycott, challenged the regime's reported vote turnout of nearly 80 percent. Jaruzelski resigned as prime minister to become chairman of the Council of State (i.e., head of state or president). He organized a 56-member Consultative Council, attached to the Council of State, allegedly to provide a public voice to non-Communists.

The Sejm was reactivated with renewed vitality in 1989. Agreement was reached in April 1989 between the PZPR-led government and the Solidarity-led opposition. The agreement "What Unites the Poles" was a compromise on a range of topics, especially national elections, a beginning that augured well for progress toward democracy. At stake were the 460-member Sejm, the lower house; and the 100-member Senate, the upper house. Creation of the Senate was proposed by the regime, which also proposed a single presidency to replace the Council of State. Accord was also reached, at Lech Walesa's insistence, on restoration of legality for Solidarity. The Sejm legalized Solidarity on April 17, but the PZPR made clear its intention to maintain control of the country.

Elections were to be "nonconfrontational." Solidarity agreed to a limit of 35% of the Sejm delegates (161), with the PZPR-controlled government coalition to have the controlling 65%. A "national list" of 35 delegates was to be unopposed. Subsequently an electoral law, applicable only for these parliamentary elections, permitted an unlimited number of candidates for the Senate or the 161 Sejm seats allocated to opposition or independent candidates. The electoral law permitted participation of groups in nomination of candidates. Thus Solidarity's Citizen's Committee coordinated the list and conducted the campaign. The government's proposal for a "national list" of unopposed candidates for the Senate was rejected by Walesa, as was the idea for a common platform. Candidates who received a minimum of 50% of the votes in the first round were elected. If none received the required 50% the two highest vote-getters competed in a runoff election.

Elections held on June 4, 1989, resulted in a resounding victory for Solidarity and humiliation for the PZPR. Despite disadvantages, Solidarity-supported candidates won 160 of the 161 seats for the Sejm; 92 of the 100 for the Senate; and 33 of the 35 names of the party's uncontested candidates were crossed out, including those of Prime Minister Rakowski, Defense Minister Florian Siwicki and Minister of the Interior Czeslaw Kiszczak, a further embarrassment for the PZPR.

In the runoff elections on June 18 the PZPR-led coalition suffered another humiliating defeat. Solidarity won the remaining one seat for its sweep of the 161 maximum competitive seats, and increased to 99 its members in the Senate, for a total of 260 of a possible 261 competitive seats in the two houses. Nevertheless, by prior agreement, the government coalition was assured a 65% majority in the Sejm. The breakdown by party affiliation for this coalition was: PZPR, 173 deputies; United Peasant Party (UPP), 76; Democratic Party (DP), 27; and three progovernment Christian parties, 23. The two sides agreed that the next elections, to be held in four years, are to be totally competitive.

According to the Constitution, the Sejm is the supreme organ of state power. It legislates laws, adopts resolutions and exercises control over executive and administrative bodies. Before June 1989 the Sejm was a unicameral legislature. It is composed of 460 deputies elected for a four-year term by universal, equal, direct suffrage and secret ballot. It was convened by the Council of State at least twice annually. The body elects from among its members a speaker, deputy speakers and committees. The speaker, or his deputy, presides over the sessions and supervises the legislative process. The Sejm's deliberations are public. Additional responsibilities are to adopt the national socioeconomic multi-year plan and the annual state budget and to appoint committees to examine specific tasks. Draft legislation was proposed by individual deputies, the Council of State and the government.

At the April 1989 Round Table the regime proposed, and Solidarity agreed, to establish an upper house, the Senate, consisting of 100 deputies. The Senate can propose legislation and veto laws passed by the Sejm. However, the latter can override the veto by a two-thirds vote, a higher majority than the three-fifths proposed by the regime.

According to the Constitution, before June 1989 the Sejm from among its members elected a collective presidency, the Council of State, to a four-year term. The Council was composed of the president, four vice presidents, a secretary and 11 members. The Council, acting on behalf of the Sejm between its sessions, could call for elections, convene sessions of the Sejm, interpret laws, issue decrees, appoint and recall diplomats, receive foreign diplomats, ratify treaties and issue pardons. The Council was represented by its president or a vice president. Whether the president, as chief of state, went much further than performing a ceremonial role depended on his stature in the PZPR, the real policy-setting body.

The April 1989 government-Solidarity agreement provided for a single president to be elected by a joint session of the Sejm and the Senate. Given extensive authority, the president can dismiss both houses and order new elections. He is commander in chief of the armed forces. He can declare martial law; propose and veto legislation; nominate the government; ratify treaties; and declare a state of emergency, during which he can neither dismiss the legislature nor change the electoral law. The prime minister must countersign presidential acts of major importance in spheres other than foreign affairs and defense policy. The president is not given, as had the Council of State, the right of interpretation of laws; the Constitutional Tribunal is assigned this responsibility.

Following the second, runoff elections of June 18, the two houses voted for the new president. Gen. Jaruzelski delayed a decision on his candidacy until the day before the election. In a joint session of the Sejm and the Senate on June 19, Jaruzelski obtained a one-vote margin required for election: 270 votes for, 233 against, 34 abstentions, and seven votes invalid. With 299 seats in the Sejm held by the regime's coalition, the result indicated negative votes from Jaruzelski's own coalition. The April 1989 Solidarity-government agreement provided for the popular election of the president by 1995.

The next national elections are to take place in 1993.

POLITICAL PARTIES

The roots of political parties in Poland were established in the late 19th and early 20th centuries in all three partitioned areas. The parties stemmed from political activities conducted primarily by the intelligentsia, small urban bourgeoisie; emerging workers; and activists speaking on behalf of the peasantry. For example, the Union of Farmers' Circle, a peasant movement, was founded in 1877, the Polish Socialist Party in 1892 and its rival Social Democratic Party in 1895, the same year a peasant party was organized in Galicia. The National Democratic Party appeared in the territory under Russia. During World War I these parties played a role organizing national committees to promote the Polish cause, and in 1917 the Polish National Committee in Paris was recognized by the Allies as representing the Polish nation.

A number of political parties functioned when Poland achieved independence in November 1918, and the provisional chief of state was Marshal Josef Pilsudski, a former Socialist and a hero who successfully headed the Polish military forces against Soviet Russia. Among the parties were the conservative National Democratic Party (ND), the centrist Polish Peasant Party (PPS) and the Communist Party. Despite drawing up an impressive democratic Constitution in 1921, the competing parties were unable to overcome strong differences. First, political frustration prompted the highly regarded nonparty prime minister, Ignacy Jan Paderewski, to leave the country; then in 1926, out of retirement, Marshal Pilsudski engineered a coup d'état. Thereafter, although parties functioned, their importance diminished as political power was exercised by Pilsudski and, after his death in 1935, by the "colonels."

Following the Nazi-Soviet invasion and partition of Poland in September 1939, a government-in-exile was formed on October 1 in Paris with Gen. Wladyslaw Sikorski as prime minister; he organized the Polish armed forces. A National Council, with Paderewski as chairman and with representatives from various political parties, acted as the legislature. The Polish underground, with a Home army, was established by leaders of the Peasant, Socialist, National and Christian Labor parties. Following the defeat of France, the Polish government and the National Council moved to London. This government-in-exile was officially recognized by the Allies, but the Soviet Union severed diplomatic relations with it in 1943 over the Katyn Forest massacre. Gen. Sikorski died in a plane crash on July 4, 1943, and was succeeded as prime minister by Stanislaw Mikolajczyk, leader of the PPS.

Meanwhile, on July 21, 1944, the Communists organized the Polish Committee of National Liberation (PKWN), under the leadership of veteran Communist Boleslaw Bierut, as the postwar government of Poland. Control of the 16-member PKWN, with representatives from six parties, including the Peasant and Socialist, was undeniably in Communist hands. The mass murder of thousands of Polish officers at Katyn and the heavy death toll of the August 1–October 3, 1944, uprising in Warsaw by the Home Army, unaided by the Red Army, destroyed non-Communist leadership inside the country.

The Yalta Conference provided for a "broader democratic basis" of the PKWN, which had been recognized by Moscow in January 1945 as the government. The Polish government in London refused to participate in this Soviet-sponsored coalition, but Mikolajczyk decided inclusion was preferable to opposition from abroad and resigned as prime minister. He became the second deputy premier and secretary of agriculture in the Polish Provisional Government of National Unity, formed June 28, 1945. It was recognized by the United States and Great Britain on July 5. Others added were a socialist from London and two from the Peasant Party inside Poland. However, the Communist bloc retained the most, and more important, positions.

Yalta's provision for "free and unfettered elections as soon as possible" was willfully violated by the Communists and the Soviet Union. To reach their objective of ensuring victory in the January 1947 national elections, they embarked on eliminating non-Communist parties and leaders, especially Mikolajczyk and the popular PPS, but including others as well. In addition to the use of terrorism, coercion and intimidation, the elections were conducted and manipulated by the Communists, who announced overwhelming victory for the government bloc—Communists, and leftist socialist, peasant and democratic parties. Mikolajczyk charged the elections to be falsified, claiming his Peasant Party won about 80% of the votes. Learning of his fate—to be sentenced to death by the Military Court—Mikolajczyk fled the country in October 1947, by which time the Communists consolidated their seizure, to the exclusion of all opposition.

Only three parties were to function. In December 1948 the Polish Workers' Party forced a merger with the Polish Socialist Party, headed by Jozef Cyrankiewicz, becoming the Polish United Workers' Party (Polska Zjednoczona Partia Robotnicza, PZPR); Cyrankiewicz was appointed prime minister. The Peasant Party was forced to merge with the Communist-leaning Peasant Party into the United Peasant Party (Zjednoczone Stronnictwo Ludowe, ZSL) in November 1949. The Democratic Party (Stronnictwo Demokratyczne, SD), which had fallen under leftist leadership during the war and was safely within the government bloc, continued in this role. The Constitution was to cite the "alliance and collaboration" of the PZPR, the ZSL and the SD in the "building of socialism," a provision that remained until the fall of 1989. However, a new force emerged on the political terrain of Poland: Solidarity.

Throughout its history the Communist Party has experienced numerous convulsions. The party had its genesis in the socialist movements of the 1880s. Marxists, including Rosa Luxemburg, founded Social Democracy of the Kingdom of Poland and Lithuania in 1895. In December 1918 its left wing merged with leftists of the Polish Socialist Party (Polska Partia Socjalistyczna, PPS) to establish the Communist Workers' Party of Poland, which was renamed the Communist Party of Poland (Komunistyczna Partia Polski, KPP) in 1925. The KPP operated in an unfriendly society—a people strongly Catholic and nationalistic, a large individualistic peasantry devoted to their land with hatred for collectivization, anti-Russian and oriented toward the West. In 1919 the KPP became a member of the COMINTERN, which was controlled by Soviet leadership. The nationalistic and anti-Russian Marshal Pilsudski drove this Moscow-controlled revolutionary party underground when he seized power in 1926. The KPP held its congresses in the Soviet Union, and its Central Committee (CC) meetings in Berlin until 1933, then in the

Free City of Danzig. Although underground, the KPP promoted candidates for the Sejm through other organizations. In 1922 the party elected two deputies and in 1925 a total of 18 of the 444-member Sejm. Pilsudski did not reciprocate his support by Communists in 1926, and the party's showing in subsequent elections diminished.

During the interwar period the KPP was beset by internal problems, including leadership, organization, factionalism, doctrinal differences and Stalin's enmity. Sparked by espionage charges, a massive purge conducted in the late 1920s affected the entire party. Most of those in Moscow were executed or dispatched to gulags during Stalin's purges in the 1930s and, at the behest of the Soviet dictator, the KPP was dissolved by the Comintern in May 1938.

The future Polish Communist leaders emerged during the 1939–41 Nazi-Soviet occupation of Poland. Most fled to the Soviet Union after the German invasion in 1941. The small number remaining inside Poland organized pro-Soviet groups, maintaining contact with Moscow. The party was reestablished on January 5, 1942, as the Polish Workers' Party (Polska Partia Robotnicza, PPR). Its first leaders were killed, but in November 1943 Wladyslaw Gomulka, from inside Poland, became its first secretary. After Stalin's break with the Polish government-in-exile in London, the Moscow group became the Union of Polish Patriots under the leadership of Boleslaw Bierut in June 1943. On June 21, 1944, the Communists organized the Polish Committee of National Liberation near Lublin, which became the basis of Poland's postwar government. Many of the pro-Soviet Polish military leaders in the USSR were to become prominent in the postwar Polish defense structure.

Following their seizure of power, the Communists in December 1948 forced the merger with the socialists into the Polish United Workers' Party. A massive purge of unreliable elements in the party, the army and throughout the society followed. The suspects included "native Communists"—those who were inside Poland during the war. Among the victims was Gomulka, who in 1948 was replaced by the Stalinist Bierut, who headed the PZPR until 1956. Significantly, purged Polish Communist leaders did not experience the fate of "Titoists" in other Soviet bloc countries: execution.

The Stalinist course plunged Poland into economic crises and public demonstrations. With Bierut's death in March 1956, his associate Edward Ochab became Communist Party leader (now called first secretary). Khrushchev's de-Stalinization in 1956 served as the spark for intellectuals and students to demand reforms. They were joined by workers in Poznan and other cities. The resulting strikes and riots led to Gomulka's rehabilitation and reappointment as first secretary in October. He was instrumental in preventing possible Soviet military intervention, such as crushed the Hungarian uprising that October.

In a sense Poland's history since the war has been on a continuum of economic crises. Forced collectivization had been a failure, and in 1956 the peasants initiated decollectivization, which the shaken PZPR leadership was unable and somewhat unwilling to halt. However, Gomulka failed to implement his reform program, purging instead both reformists and Stalinists. His popularity plummeted. In the late 1960s several events led to instability. Intellectuals and students again took the lead in campaigning for reforms (e.g., over censorship). A hard-line element of the party—the "partisans"—led by the interior minister, Gen. Mieczyslaw Moczar, and supported by a segment of the armed forces and the police, employed anti-Semitic and nationalistic tactics to achieve power. Gomulka mobilized his supporters to prevent his overthrow but was unable to cope with another crisis: price increases leading to workers' strikes in 1970. He was succeeded as party leader by Edward Gierek, who rescinded the rises, dismissed Moczar and made new appointments to the Politburo. The leading position of the PZPR in Polish society was enshrined in the Polish Constitution by a 1976 amendment. During the decade of his leadership, Gierek faced opposition both within the party and outside it. Party challenges and an economic crisis in the late 1970s, with another cycle of price rises and strikes in 1980, combined to force Gierek's downfall in September 1980.

Gierek was replaced by Stanislaw Kania, who also was beset by critics within and outside the party. There was one significant difference: the historic rise of Solidarity, the independent union that attracted widespread membership numbering 10 million at its height, including a goodly number—perhaps one-fourth—from the PZPR's ranks. The party's anti-Solidarity hard-liners were strengthened by Moscow's support. A new party faction—the "horizontalists"—favored some more extensive changes within the party. An extraordinary Party Congress, elected by open nominations, was held July 14–20, 1981. With precedent-setting procedures the composition of the 1,955 delegates, elected by secret ballot, was unusual: about one-fifth were Solidarity members and many were elected for the first time. Also unprecedented was the election of the Central Committee by secret ballot; 275 candidates competed for 200 positions. The result was a stunning setback for the PZPR leadership. Failing to win reelection were five Politburo members, three deputy members and four CC secretaries. The CC itself was dramatically altered, with 90.5% new members. Nevertheless, the "horizontalists," other reformers and would-be leaders were outmaneuvered, and Kania retained enough support to be reelected, also by secret ballot, as first secretary. However, he was incapable of overcoming the serious problems in the country and the deterioration of the PZPR's control. Moreover, Moscow became concerned and he was replaced in October 1981 by Gen. Jaruzelski, who retained the positions of prime minister and defense minister.

Gen. Jaruzelski promised to continue Kania's "strategy of socialist renewal" on the principle of Marxism-Leninism. In October the CC increased the Secretariat staff and promoted Jaruzelski's supporters, such as Soviet-educated Florian Siwicki as deputy member of the Politburo. As discontent continued, Solidarity's development into a potent mass organization was perceived as a potential threat to the PZPR's control. In October Solidarity held its first National Congress, and in November, it called for democratic elections and a vote on the party's leading role. Rather than hold elections, Jaruzelski imposed martial law on December 31, 1981. The regime immediately resorted to the army and riot police to neutralize Solidarity, and interned Walesa, other leaders and intellectuals, numbering approximately 10,000. The de facto banning of Solidarity and other unions was formalized by the Sejm in October 1982. Certain party members were purged, and some were tried for various violations. Walesa was released in November.

Slowly returning to "normalization," Jaruzelski's regime officially ended martial law in July 1983, and an amnesty was granted to most Solidarity prisoners. However, Solidarity continued to be an object of repression for the security forces, whose victims included a Catholic priest who was kidnapped and killed in October 1984. At a public trial, four defendants were declared guilty in February 1985, but their sentences were subsequently reduced.

Discontent over the economic performance, lower living standards and the PZPR's dictatorial rule caused mounting agitation for economic, social and political reform. Solidarity called for a boycott of the October 1985 elections and challenged the official results. In November 1985 Jaruzelski resigned as prime minister to become head of state. In February 1986 the regime's charges against Walesa for slandering election officials were withdrawn to preclude serious disorders in the country. However, in May Solidarity leader Zbigniew Bujak was apprehended and other Solidarity activists were arrested. In this unsettling environment a large party turnover occurred at the PZPR's 10th Party Congress, (in mid-1986). By mid-September the remaining thousands of prisoners, including political prisoners such as Bujak, were released.

In 1986 Solidarity formed a council to achieve reinstatement, but it was banned by the government, which was conducting an anti-Solidarity campaign. The following year witnessed further demonstrations, with resulting arrests, a call by the visiting Pope in June for civil rights, a U.S. Congressional aid package for Solidarity, and the visit of Vice President Bush in September. Attempts at economic and political reform, including restructuring of the government, were inadequate, producing no systemic changes. A November referendum on political and economic reform, boycotted by Solidarity, failed to receive approval of the required majority of the electorate. The regime allowed no opposition party, such as the Socialist, to function.

In early 1988 another cycle of price increases, demonstrations, strikes and demands for higher wages combined to perpetuate an explosive situation. Challenges to PZPR rule became increasingly vocal while the regime appeared determined to pursue its policy of innocuous reforms within the bankrupt Communist system. Personnel changes within the party, including the powerful Politburo and Secretariat, implied a more flexible approach although no reduction of power. However, the 10th CC Plenum, from December 1988 to January 1989, admitting that "profound reform" of the party and political and trade union pluralism was required, agreed to the inclusion of "constructive opposition" to the political system, including Solidarity. Following consultations betweeen Catholic leaders, acting as mediators, and the regime, Solidarity agreed to negotiate with the authorities. The round-table discussions between the government and Solidarity leaders in March produced an agreement—the "indispensable minimum," according to Walesa—toward democracy. Signed April 5, the agreement provided for trade union pluralism with legalization of Solidarity and other groups, such as Rural Solidarity and the Independent Students' Association (NZS). Solidarity agreed to the regime's proposal for a second house of the legislature—the Senate—and a strong president to replace the collective Council of State. Elections were to be "nonconfrontational," with the government assured 65% of the delegates to the Sejm; this provision was limited to the June elections. Political pluralism extended to "freely created associations," although within "constitutional order." The agreement contained access to the media and for other democratic provisions. As promised, the Sejm gave Solidarity legal status on April 17. A month later the Catholic Church was given legal status.

In the June national elections the PZPR sustained a humiliating defeat and Solidarity achieved a dramatic victory. At its July 28–29 Plenum the Central Committee, on the recommendation of Jaruzelski, elected Politburo member and Prime Minister Mieczyslaw F. Rakowski as first secretary of the troubled PZPR. Gen. Jaruzelski, elected president of the republic July 19, was expected to continue to wield the greatest power in the country. Among his other areas of authority, the president is commander in chief of the armed forces and can declare martial law. Rakowski became prime minister in August 1988. However, although he was unable to halt the deterioration of the economy, Rakowski favored the party's program adopted at the 10th Plenum. His task of revitalizing the party appeared difficult.

The formation of the government proved more complicated as well as unprecedented. Jaruzelski's recommendation for Prime Minister, Gen. Czeslaw Kiszczak, minister of the interior, was approved by the Sejm on August 2, albeit not enthusiastically. However, his efforts to organize a "grand coalition," with broad participation but under PZPR contol, was rejected by Walesa, who proposed, instead, a "small coalition" of Solidarity, the ZSL and the SD. Unable to organize a government, Kiszczak withdrew on August 14. The PZPR opposed its exclusion, and subsequent negotiations assigned the important positions of the Defense and Interior ministries, deputy premier and two other ministries to the PZPR. The four parties agreed on the composition, and on September 12 the Sejm gave overwhelming approval to Solidarity's prime minister, Tadeusz Mazowiecki, and his government, a development of historic proportions.

The PZPR organization is contained in the party statutes, adopted at the Third Congress, in March 1959, as amended by later congresses. The party functions on the principle of "democratic centralism"—that is, the organizational units at lower levels are subordinate to the next higher echelons, and decisions made at the higher levels are binding on the lower. Although discussion of issues is formally permitted, once a decision is made by the top leadership it becomes completely binding on all members and subordinate organs. Party discipline is strict. Essentially the PZPR, like its Soviet CP model, is dictatorial.

The PZPR has a pyramidal structure and functions on the national, provincial, city and lower levels. The highest authority is the Party Congress, convened by the Central Committee every five years unless an extraordinary session is scheduled or a crisis dictates a postponement. The First Congress, after the war, was held in December 1945, which provided for congresses at three-year intervals, increased to four years at the Third (1959) and to five years at the Seventh (1975). An extraordinary Congress, the Ninth, was convened July 14–20, 1981, during Solidarity's challenge. As in other Soviet bloc countries, delegates to the Congress are elected at the lower levels.

Major policy statements are made by the leadership, and the Congress considers various reports and adopts resolutions that reflect party strategy. In secret ballots the Congress elects the Central Committee, the first secretary, the Central Audit Commission and the Central Commission of the Party Control; it also amends party statutes. At the 10th Party Congress, in 1986, the PZPR had a changed complexion from the 1981 Extraordinary Ninth in membership (about 1 million fewer members) and in composition. Delegates to the 10th Congress numbered 1,776, of whom 20% were women, and slightly over half (51.5%) were workers or peasants, the result of deliberate effort by the leadership to reflect the class character of the party.

At the 10th Congress, First Secretary Gen. Jaruzelski attacked the United States as an "evil-minded power threatening Poland," while the party program on management efficiency and improving living standards was typically unrealistic. He was reelected as first secretary. Prior to the Ninth Congress these elections were a formality of single candidates selected by the leadership and formally approved by the Congress or the Central Committee. The Ninth Congress had multiple candidates, and the elections were secret. Consequently, elections to the Central Committee, the Politburo and the Secretariat showed surprising and refreshing results.

The Congress elected a Central Committee of 200 members and 70 alternates. The Central Committee is the highest organ between Congresses. Meeting at least every four months, the CC implements the party program, maintains contact with other Communist parties and directs all sectors of party activity. The CC elects from its members by secret ballot the Politburo and the Secretariat. The Politburo is the party's most powerful policy-making body. It oversees implementation of the party's resolutions and policies through the CC's Secretariat, with individual secretaries responsible for day-to-day administration of specific sectors. These include ideology, organization, propaganda, youth, economy and foreign affairs. Also, the Secretariat supervises the selection of cadres and the lower echelons of the party throughout the country.

Along with the People's Councils, PZPR committees function at all lower levels: 49 provinces (voivodships); 818 cities, including 30 major city districts; and 2,122 village districts. Heading the committees are first secretaries. The basic units of the pyramid are organized in villages, institutions, enterprises and residences having a minimum of five party members.

At its July 1989 Plenum the CC redesigned the Politburo and the Secretariat to "rejuvenate" the party leadership. The aggressive Rakowski continued as first secretary, but five Politburo members, including Jaruzelski, resigned. A larger number of younger members replaced incumbents on the Secretariat. The changes appeared designed to reflect rebuilding, unity and a desire for closer personal contact with youth, nonparty organizations and the public.

Despite economic hardships in Poland, the KPP attracted only a limited number of adherents, and of the approximately 12,000 members in 1931 only 1,200 were industrial workers. The majority were intellectuals. Membership was reduced in the 1930s and diminished during the early part of the war. It was about 4,000 in July 1942. When the military element joined with the KPP in 1944, membership still was only 20,000. However, with the liberation of Poland by the Red Army and with the provisional government under Communist control, the party became more attractive. Membership was 30,000 in January 1945 but increased more than twelvefold in the next 18 months, to 364,000 in July 1946. Following Mikolajczyk's departure and Communist seizure of power, the ranks climbed to 848,000 in July 1947.

With the absorption of the Socialist Party in December 1948 the membership swelled to 1,500,000, the height of mass recruitment. With rapid growth came questionable loyalty. Purges followed, especially of Socialists, reducing the membership to 1,129,000 in June 1952. The figure fluctuated only slightly during the next 10 years. The PZPR then embarked on more energetic recruitment, with the membership growing to 1,640,000 by January 1965, increasing to 2,000,000 by May 1967 and to 3,150,000 members and candidates prior to the dramatic appearance of Solidarity in August 1980.

That the PZPR was not particularly attractive to university students and even to workers was disturbing to its leaders. The proportion of the workers fell from 50% in 1950 to about 36% in 1961, while that of intellectuals rose from 29% to 44% during those years. It was precisely workers who demonstrated open hostility with strikes during 1970, which brought Gierek to power. After the 1976 riots, workers were deliberately recruited for membership.

The rise of Solidarity in 1980–81 had a crippling effect on party membership. Perhaps over one-fourth of the PZPR's members became involved in the Solidarity movement, and the PZPR's ranks were reduced drastically—possibly by 800,000 over the next two years, and to 2,186,000 members and candidates by the end of 1983. Following martial law, the PZPR attempted to reestablish normalization, including careful recruitment of loyal members. The 10th Party Congress reported a membership of 2,126,000, and a party spokesman cited 1,168,000 in late September 1989. The composition of the members continued to be unsatisfactory. The 10th Congress reported: workers, 38.2%; peasants, 9.0%; and intellectuals, 51.5%. Youth membership dropped by half. Despite determined efforts, the "workers" party represented only a minority of the country's workers.

Before 1989 the PZPR opposed real political pluralism, permitting only its two collaborationist allies—the United Peasant Party and the Democratic Party—and then certain others as long as they posed no threat to its control. Solidarity has made an indelible impact not only on the trade union movement but also on political parties in Poland. Thus the heretofore compliant allies of the PZPR joined with Solidarity to form the non-Communist government in September 1989.

The round-table discussions provided for trade union and social pluralism. Solidarity and Rural Solidarity were legalized by the Sejm shortly after the conclusion of the talks; other groups and associations required official registration. A number of these organizations began during 1980–81 years of Solidarity, some were formed in subsequent years, numerous others mushroomed since 1988 and still others were being established. The hundreds in existence cover the ideological spectrum. They promote political pluralism, human rights, independence, and reforms in specialized sectors. Some appear apolitical, but the objective of others is to attain legal status as political parties.

The formal name of Solidarity is "Solidarity Independent Self-Governing Trade Union." Founded on August 31, 1980, it was banned in October 1982 and legalized on April 17, 1989. Solidarity is led by Lech Walesa, chairman of the National Executive Commission. Its membership in 1981 was about 10 million, but less than 1 million in 1989. The Second National Solidarity Congress was held on April 25, 1990. It was attended by 487 elected delegates as well as representatives of foreign labor organizations. Lech Walesa was reelected by a large majority, winning almost 80% of the votes. The congress also elected the National Commission, the main policy-making body, the National Audit Commission and the Presidium. The congress amended the union's statutes, removing all restrictions that curtailed the right to strike. Perhaps, the most difficult issue for the congress was defining Solidarity's role in Polish politics. The congress refrained from taking a clear stand on the issue. It formally voted that Solidarity would not set up its own political party, but it stopped short of cutting its links with other political parties. It called for parliamentary elections early in 1991 and for election of the president by direct popular vote. Both motions appeared to be directly linked to Walesa's presidential plans.

At present there are three main contenders for the leadership of the peasant movement: the Polish Peasant Party, a revival of Mikolajczyk's prewar group, the Polish Peasant Party-Renewal and the Independent Self-Governing Union of Farmers-Solidarity.

On the right of the political spectrum is the Polish Independence Party, founded in 1984; it favors Polish independence. The Polish Labor Party (SP) was founded in 1937 along Christian-democratic principles. Suspended in 1946 and reactivated in February 1989, the SP functions as an opposition party. The Confederation for an Independent Poland (KPN), founded in 1979, favors an independent Poland, replacing the PZPR by nonviolent means. Other, more moderate independence groups include Fighting Solidarity (1982), the Polish Socialist Party (1987), Freedom-Justice-Independence (1983), and the Independence Liberal-Democratic Party (1984).

Of the numerous others, the following portray the breadth of associations: Catholic Intelligentsia Clubs, Christian Democratic Club, Committee of Independent Culture, Dziekania Club of Political Thought, Economic Society, Freedom and Peace Movement, Independence Liberal-Democratic Party, "Our Home" Women's Association, Greens Party, Helsinki Committee, "In Our Land" Young Catholics Movement, Liberation Political Movement, National League of Workers in Opposition, League for Human Rights, Independence Committee, Scouts Union of the Republic, Solidarity Christian Group and Solidarity Youth Movement. The Association of Former Political Prisoners was formed in September 1989. Its purpose is to help former political prisoners receive compensation for unjust convictions. By year's end about 500 applications for membership had been received.

A historic event occurred on January 29, 1990. On this date the Polish United Workers' Party (Communist Party) was dissolved, with 1,228 approving, 32 voting against and 32 abstentions. The previous day more than 100 delegates voted to form a new political party, Social Democracy of the Polish Republic, or the Social Democratic Party. This new party elected Aleksander Kwasniewski as chairman and Leszek Miller as general secretary. Also on January 28 a second party was established, by Tadeusz Fiszbach, called the Social Democratic Union. Fiszbach argued that the Social Democratic Party was too linked to the past.

ECONOMY

The Polish economy presents a paradox: One of the 12 largest industrial nations in the world, Poland also is struggling desperately in the 1980s to recover from a decade-long economic crisis characterized by major declines in production; large-scale shortages of consumer and capital goods; and the threat of financial collapse owing to the state's inability to meet payments on a massive foreign debt. Fundamentally, the crisis is but the latest—although the most severe—manifestation of the failure of the Communist regime after three decades of effort to attain, through the mechanisms of central planning based on the Soviet model, national self-sufficiency. Causing this failure were serious economic misjudgments. Poland tried to achieve the kind of progress that the Soviet Union did without considering the different political mood of its people, its moderate natural resources and the lack of a powerful and all-pervasive apparatus to enforce its decisions. A notable example was its inability to collectivize agriculture, as Stalin did in the 1930s; as a result, private farming remains the major part of Poland's agricultural sector.

A persistent priority was accorded development of heavy industry, which according to orthodox Marxist theory is the quickest means to development. However, this was achieved at the expense of greatly reduced investment in agriculture and the light consumer goods sector. Serious shortages that resulted from this policy substantially depressed the standard of living and led to serious crises in 1956 and 1970. In each instance the leadership was reshuffled—coinciding with the rise and fall of Gomulka—but the promised changes were never carried out. The reforms of the early 1970s included some liberalization of economic activities and a new approach to development that involved greatly increased investment for the modernization of industry. Large amounts of Western machinery and technology—including over 200 licenses—were imported to implement this scheme, primarily financed from Western loans that were to be repaid through export receipts. The economy showed considerable improvement in the first few years of the decade. But by the mid-1970s a disequilibrium had developed, in part due to the need to import larger and larger quantities of grain and in part to the first oil shock. Also a factor was the slowdown in productive investment that had occurred as a substantial portion of new Western credits were used to purchase consumer goods. Moreover, the planning bureaucracy had by then reimposed its former style of centralized control over the entire state sector, ignoring the fact that the economy had by then passed the stage in which such controls could function satisfactorily.

By the end of the 1970s shortages had appeared in all categories of goods. The stituation worsened in the early 1980s in the wake of the founding of the Solidarity movement and the cumulative effects of crippling strikes. The government's inability to obtain Western credits for essential imports also contributed to the morass. In 1982 new principles for operation of state enterprises became effective, under which they were to become autonomous, self-financing and self-planning units no longer subject to centralized control. A partially free market and increases in producer prices for certain controlled items also were introduced. However, implementation of these reforms was mixed. At the end of 1987 the government introduced a second phase of economic reforms by reducing the standard of living to about 78% of the 1978 level. Indebtedness to Western creditors increased dramatically in 1987 because of the devaluation of the dollar. By the end of 1988 it exceeded $40 billion, or over 70% of the country's annual income. The amount of indebtedness to the West is expected to increase until 1991 and then stablilize at the range of $43 billion to $44 billion. Inflation for 1988 exceeded 120% as the unofficial value of the dollar increased from about 1,800 zlotys in 1987 to about 4,000 zlotys at the end of 1988. Another fundamental weakness of the economy involves production of defective goods and disregard for safety standards. In 1988 it was reported that 46.1% of the manufactured goods and 23.9% of the food articles had to be withdrawn from the market because of poor quality and that about 40% of food-

stuffs contained dangerous levels of toxic substances. The Central Office of Statistics calculates that the damage due to low-quality production exceeds 105 billion zlotys.

The promarket reorientation of the economy received some encouragement in 1988 when a law authorizing all sectors of the economy to issue, buy and sell bonds cleared by the Sejm. This move should create a 5-trillion-zloty money market out of the forced savings—i.e., cash unsupported by goods held by the public or private sectors. Even more significantly, the Sejm drafted a piece of sweeping legislation stating that "taking up and performing economic activities is free and permitted to anyone on equal rights under conditions defined by law." The law introduced equality for all forms of ownership. Engagement in economic activities in agriculture and manufacturing requires only a notification of authorities. Meanwhile, limits on the size of private enterprises and convertibility of the zloty to hard currency also have been eliminated. Hard-liners within the party have viewed with disfavor the gradual erosion of communism and Communist monopolies implied in these moves.

The economic burden resulting from Poland's efforts to industrialize has fallen on the urban workers rather than on the peasants. Most of the peasants appear to have reached a level of relative comfort, essentially because of their stubborn and successful resistance to government controls. The industrial workers, now a substantially greater proportion of the population than before, have seen their standard of living fall drastically since the 1950s.

The problems now besetting the economy are to some extent carryovers from the previous regimes. The 19th-century partition not only slowed down political and economic development but also complicated unification of the new independent state established in 1918. Each of the three parts of the country had been incorporated into a different economic and monetary system. Transportation systems had been developed to unify each of the three parts with its own occupying power rather than with one another. Under these circumstances, government involvement in the economy became mandatory to unify the country and also because of the scarcity of private capital. World War II brought widespread devastation, but postwar territorial changes were, on balance, not to Poland's disadvantage. The areas ceded by Poland to the Soviet Union were underdeveloped, accounting for one-third of the population but only one-eighth of total prewar industrial employment. By contrast, the German territories acquired by Poland in the West were heavily industrialized, especially in Upper and Lower Silesia and around Szczecin, near the Baltic. In terms of potential production the largest gains resulting from the territorial shift were in coal, lead and zinc. Even in 1946 the new territories supplied 28% of the total electric power output. Important heavy and light engineering industries, cement works and glass and ceramics plants were acquired.

Although comprehensive economic planning along Soviet lines began in 1946, even before the government

PRINCIPAL ECONOMIC INDICATORS, 1988

Gross National Product: $69.970 billion
GNP per capita: $1,850
GNP average annual growth rate (%): 2.5 (1980–88)
GNP per capita average annual growth rate (%): 2.0 (1980–88)
Consumer Price Index (1985 = 100)
    All items: 235.8
Wholesale Price Index (1985 = 100): 238.4
Average annual growth rate (1980–86) (%)
    Public consumption: 3.5
    Private consumption: −1.7
    Gross domestic investment: −0.8
Average annual rate of inflation: 29.2% (1980–87)

BALANCE OF PAYMENTS ($ million), 1988

Current account balance: −372
Merchandise exports: 12,026
Merchandise imports: −11,236
Trade balance: 790
Other goods, services & income: 2,433
Other goods, services & income: −5,160
Private unrequited transfers: 1,565
Direct investment: 4
Other long-term capital: −1,896
Other short-term capital: −144
Net errors & omissions: −7
Exceptional financing: 3,212
Total change in reserves: −797

GROSS DOMESTIC PRODUCT, 1986

GDP nominal (national currency): 12.953 trillion
GDP per capita ($): 1560
GDP average annual growth rate: 1.5 (1980–86)
GDP by type of expenditure (%)
    Consumption
        Private: 62
        Government: 10
    Gross domestic investment: 28
    Gross domestic savings: 30
    Foreign trade:
        Exports: 18
        Imports: −17
Sectoral origin of GDP (%)
    Primary
        Agriculture: 16
    Secondary
        Manufacturing: 49 (includes mining & public utilities)
        Construction: 12
    Tertiary
        Transportation & communications: 7
        Trade: ⎫
        Finance: ⎭ 14
        Public administration & defense: ⎫ 2
        Services: ⎭

had consolidated its political position, the new directions in economic development were called the Polish road to socialism. It emphasized gradualism rather than the ruthless Stalinist collectivization through terror. However, by 1949 the political situation had changed, and the Soviet Union was exerting pressure to make the Polish economy serve its needs rather than Polish needs. Whereas the three-year plan of 1947–49 was relatively mild and leisurely, the six-year plan of 1950-55 contemplated widespread socializaton of all sectors and unrealistic production targets. These goals had to

be scaled down later. After the failure of the six-year plan and the riots of 1956, the new government headed by Gomulka reversed the economy from the Soviet to the Polish road. Gomulka rationalized central planning controls by introducing limited market features and by giving greater initiative to enterprise managers. Gomulka's reforms failed to revitalize the economy, and he was ousted in 1970 in another burst of popular discontent. His successor, Edward Gierek, introduced further reforms, including formation of the large economic unit system and the tying of wage increases to net increases in the value of outputs. However, these reforms were bogged down by regulations and were never fully implemented. As the economy became more and more inefficient, Gierek was replaced as PZPR first secretary in 1980 by Stanislaw Kania, who promised to institute economic stabilization and recovery measures and to develop a set of reform proposals. The resulting *Directions for Economic Reform: A Proposal* was an indictment of the command economy and a call for political reforms to *precede* economic reforms.

Neither the 1982 nor the 1987 phases of economic reforms have achieved tangible results. But the scope of these reforms has grown and now covers prices, taxation, banking and foreign trade. Party organs were neither to interfere in day-to-day management nor to assume the functions of state agencies. The productive enterprises were given the right to draw up plans independently and given financial responsibility for achieving their own targets. The direct control exercised by the central planning mechanism was removed, and direct instruments—prices, taxes, interest rates and others—were introduced to influence economic activities. The government also has called for greater credit discipline, but by 1989 there have been relatively few bankruptcies as a result of such discipline.

In 1988 the government tried again to rationalize the price structure, by significantly raising prices for food and energy products. These increases triggered another wave of labor unrest, and enterprise managers agreed to wage increases to mollify the workers. The government's inability to hold the line on income growth contributed to both open inflation and to an increase in the stock of money held by the public. At midyear retail prices were up 50% and demand for consumer goods continued to outstrip supply. To hedge against inflation Poles have resorted to holding material assets and foreign currencies. The market rate for hard currency is several times the official exchange rate. The more affluent depend on the thriving parallel economy, where they can purchase otherwise unavailable goods for hard currency. As a result, the gap in living standards between Poles with access to hard currency and those without is growing.

Poland's trade surplus and inflow of remittances—estimated at $1.4 billion annually, which is more than the balance of trade—are insufficient to meet its debt service obligations. The current-account deficit totaled $417 million in 1987 and about the same amount in 1988. During the 1987 principal and interest due on external debt totaled $3 billion, while actual payments were limited to $920 million. Hard-currency debt reached $38 billion and soft-currency debt with socialist countries 6.9 billion transferable rubles. Debt service obligations measured against export earnings make Poland one of the most debt-burdened countries in the world. In 1988 Poland signed its seventh debt-restructuring agreement with Western banks.

In an effort to help Poland tide over its economic crisis wealthy Western nations have promised in 1989 over $2 billion in aid packages, including short-term and stand-by loans. This includes $642 million from France, $400 million from Italy, $42 million from Canada, $38 million from the United States, $1.9 billion from West Germany, $150 million from Japan, and $77 million from the United Kingdom. In addition, the IMF and the World Bank have extended credits, the former for $500 million and the latter for $1.67 billion.

The economic recovery plan adopted by the post-Communist Mazowiecki government was based on the so-called Sachs Plan—proposed by two Harvard specialists, Jeffrey Sachs and David Lipton. Their shock treatment for the Polish economy involves an immediate end to the state monopoly of production and distribution, full covertibility of the zloty according to the market rate, immediate elimination of all subsidies and price controls, freedom of export and import, freedom to develop and operate private enterprises, and a suspension of the repayment of foreign debts. This economic recovery plan is known in Poland as a "leap into the abyss," in contrast to the alternative "long staircase" scenario that would prolong the crisis over several years. While most observers are agreed that the introduction of a free market would turn the economy around, the political costs would be heavy. Further, Poland has neither the managerial system nor a socio-economic class capable of providing the expertise and leadership necessary to make a swift transition from a socialist to a capitalist economy.

In 1989 Poland embarked on the first stage of its transition to a free-market economy. The first stage tackled only two issues, namely, hyperinflation and state monopoly of production. Wages were frozen while prices were allowed to rise; limits were set on indexation; and labor unions were asked to forgo their right to strike. The second stage of the plan was divided into three parts; beginning with *Sejm*—supervised privatization of ownership—followed by the introduction of the market sovereignty principle and the full convertibility of the zloty. Poland also entered the global economy with a Western-style banking system and a new taxation law. The social price of these evolutionary changes included a 20% rate of unemployment and the sacrifice of many social programs and benefits. The reform package also included draconian price increases ranging from 40% for bread to 400% for electricity and gas and 600% for coal. It called for a 2–3% reduction in GNP and also an end to subsidies for inefficient state enterprises. Massive economic aid to Poland from the West was a key element of the entire package. Such foreign aid, however, fell far short of Polish expectations.

On January 1, 1990, the Polish Government introduced an unprecedented economic reform program. Convinced that piecemeal, gradual reform would not work, Poland's new economic leaders aim to quickly dismantle Soviet-style central planning and replace it with a market economy based on free prices, private property and unrestrained competition.

The program imposes substantial short-term hardship as the price for long-term recovery. Polish officials project that in 1990 living standards will drop 20%, at least 400,000 workers will lose their jobs (5% of non-farm public sector employees), and GDP will fall 5%. The population so far seems to have accepted the trade-off inherent in the program: a decline in living standards this year in exchange for a solid foundation for future economic growth. The pain of transition should be eased somewhat by generous foreign assistance, a labor (unemployment) fund financed by a 2% tax on company payrolls and changes in pensions and family allowances.

The program pursues two central, interdependent goals. First, the economy will be stabilized by bringing inflation under control. Annual inflation in 1990 is projected at upwards of 150%, with a monthly rate near 1% in the second half of the year. Second, the economy will be restructured on a free-market basis by freeing prices, opening the foreign trade system and introducing fundamental structural changes over the next two years.

1. *Stabilizing the Economy:* The stabilization component rests on three main pillars: braking hyperinflation through exchange rate and wage policies, restoring balance to government finances and tightening money and credit.

Exchange Rate: On January 1, 1990, the zloty was devalued by 31.6% against the U.S. dollar, to Z1 9,500=U.S.$1. This rate was unchanged during the first five months of the year; a $1 billion stabilization fund from Western governments exists to backup the zloty, but these funds have not been tapped to date. Households can keep foreign currency accounts and still have access to private exchange dealers. The government has set a target to keep the parallel exchange rate within 10% of the official rate. Both enterprises and households may now obtain foreign exchange at the unified rate without restrictions.

Wages: A harsh wage tax aims to keep wage growth well below inflation. In the first four months of 1990, firms will be taxed 200–500% on any increase in their wage bills exceeding 30% of the rise in consumer prices in January and 20% of the rise in February, March and April. Lower inflation will permit a higher wage target, not exceeding 60% of inflation, in May and June. The rate for the second half of the year will be determined later in consultation with the International Monetary Fund. Polish officials expect real wages to drop almost one-third between 1989 and 1990, with most of the reduction in the first quarter. By the end of the year, real wages should be some 15% below their 1987 level.

Government Finances: The state budget deficit will drop from over 8% of GDP in 1989 to less than 1% in 1990. About half of this will come from spending cuts. Subsidies will be lowered by 8% of GDP, with the virtual elimination of subsidies for food and agricultural inputs and a sharp cut in coal subsidies.

Money and Credit: Credit policy has been tightened to check demand growth, discipline companies and restore confidence in the zloty. Legislation has been passed making the National Bank of Poland (NBP) a fully independent central bank, responsible for maintaining a stable currency. The government has also pledged as of January 1 not to borrow, either directly or indirectly, from the NBP. During the course of 1990, banks' credit ceilings will be lifted, positive real interest rates introduced, and interest rates, not administrative rationing, relied on to allocate credit. Preferential interest rates on new credit for exports, energy conservation and environmental protection have been abolished. Interest rate subsidies for housing and agriculture have been greatly reduced, and their cost transferred directly to the budget. A capital market will be created in 1990, and new accounting and supervisory rules introduced.

2. *Transition to Free Markets:* The initial move to a free market came in the areas of prices and foreign trade. In January, the percentage of prices set by the state fell from 50% of output to 3-5%—mainly rents, utilities, public transportation fares, coal and electricity. Another 5% of prices are subject to obligatory advance notification. Energy prices were hiked substantially to cover the cost of production (although they are still well below world prices): coal prices rose 400% for industrial users and 600% at the retail level, and electricity prices rose 300% for industry and 400% for households.

In the foreign trade system, a single exchange rate of 9,500 zlotys to the dollar has replaced the previous three-tiered system of official, auction and market exchange rates. Companies must now surrender all foreign exchange receipts; in return, they can purchase foreign exchange without restriction for most current transactions, including merchandise imports and related services. The government also removed restrictions on imports from hard-currency countries by eliminating most forms of import licenses.

A unified customs tariff for business and personal imports has been introduced, with temporary surcharges on imports of alcohol, tobacco, cosmetics, automobiles, consumer electronics and some textiles. The percentage of exported commodities subject to quota has been reduced from 99 to 50, and export trade simplified. Trade is being aligned more closely with standards of the General Agreement on Tariffs and Trade (GATT), and Poland has applied to the GATT to renegotiate its terms of accession received when it joined in 1967 (Poland at that time undertook to increase imports from GATT members by 7% annually, a commitment it has been unable to meet.)

Under the amended foreign investment law, foreign investors can own from 20–100% of a venture, with a minimum contribution to registered capital of $50,000 in hard currency, its zloty equivalent, or in kind (goods or rights). Investors can repatriate all hard currency profits, but only 15% of 1990 net zloty profits as of January 1, 1991 (under the terms of the recently signed U.S.–Polish Business and Economic Treaty, this percentage would increase to 100 by 1995). Government approval for investment proposals, while rarely denied, is still required. By mid-February 1990, 1,000 joint-venture permits had been issued, with some 250 joint ventures in operation.

3. *Structural Changes:* The 1990 program also initiates broad-based reforms to restructure the economy and introduce market mechanisms over the next two years. The government has introduced legislation to begin privatizing most of Poland's state enterprises, mainly through public offerings or auctions. Foreign investors will be able to buy stock in Polish companies, become major shareholders and set up wholly foreign-owned firms.

Also in 1990, a securities exchange will be established and a capital market developed. The authorities have recently enacted legislation to toughen Poland's bankruptcy laws and streamline bankruptcy procedures. A new anti-monopoly law has been passed and a number of the most egregious monopolies have been broken up. The banking system will be modernized, and competition (domestic and foreign) will be introduced; private banks and banks with foreign participation or ownership are now allowed. The budget and tax system will be simplified in 1991–92, with the main elements expected to be a broad-based personal income tax, a value-added tax, a uniform corporate income tax and a new budget process.

After the first three months of the reform program, the Polish Government has registered some initial successes. Prices rose by 78.6% in January—much higher than predicted—but the government's tight money program has succeeded in bringing the pace down to 23.9% in February and 4.7% in March. The introduction of partial convertibility of the zloty at a unified exchange rate has also been a success. Poland's foreign exchange reserves actually increased slightly thus far in 1990, the result of a better-than-expected export performance. The government budget was slightly in surplus for the first quarter of 1990.

However, these gains have been achieved at the cost of a sharp drop in production and retail sales: industrial sales during the first quarter of 1990 were 27% lower than during the same period one year earlier. Unemployment affected 267,000 on March 31, about 1.5% of the total work force. Many voices have begun calling on the government to begin stimulating the economy, but it has resisted pressures to ease its stabilization measures, risking renewed inflation.

PUBLIC FINANCE

The state budget is prepared by the Ministry of Finance, which, assisted by the Ministry of State Control, supervises its implementation at all levels of the economy. The government presents the budget to the Sejm, which usually approves it with minor changes. The fiscal year is the calendar year.

Since 1950 the state budget has been the central financial plan for the whole economy, including state enterprises, which, however, are expected to operate as self-sufficient units. Since 1951 the state budget also has included the budgets of the local governments, the social insurance programs and various social funds.

Appropriations to finance the national economy have risen from about one-quarter in the immediate postwar years to about half. These expenditures constitute most of the capital investments called for in the national plans, working capital to expand production in existing industries, and subsidies to cover operating losses.

Approximately 70% to 80% of total revenues are now derived from the socialized sector of the economy; only a small part comes from the private sector. Revenues from the socialized sector are derived from three main sources: turnover taxes, imposed as a percentage levy on the wholesale price of consumer goods; profits earmarked for contributions to investment; and profit taxes. Some, like the turnover tax, are levied for the central budget; others, such as taxes on real estate and fees for licenses, are levied for the budgets of local administrative units. Customs revenues are relatively unimportant, since all foreign trade is under state control. At times the state has levied special nonrecurring taxes, such as the National Tribute (Danina Narodowa) in the late 1940s for the reconstruction of territories ceded by Germany.

Direct taxes consist of income taxes on wages and salaries; general income taxes; profits taxes; and land taxes. The first is levied on employees, the remainder on self-employed people, small businesses and income from real property and investments. Land taxes are a legacy from the past and have been revised on a scale that favors collective farmers.

Payments by state enterprises into the budget include amortization allowances, surpluses in price equalization funds and excess working capital. Other sources include the proceeds of domestic and foreign loans and deposits of insurance organizations, which are considered current revenues rather than liabilities, as they would be in the United States. Individuals and private enterprises must make deposits in the National Savings Fund.

Immediately after the war Poland repudiated its prewar debt, but since 1945 has launched a number of public loans. Although described as voluntary, minimum subscription quotas are assigned to all population groups according to their earnings.

A major burden on the budget is the system of food subsidies, which amounted to 1.279 trillion zlotys in 1987. These subsidies are partly responsible for the chronic deficits in the national budget, estimated at 369 billion zlotys in 1988.

CURRENCY & BANKING

The national monetary unit is the zloty, divided into 100 groszy (singular: grosz). Coins are issued in denominations of 1, 2, 5, 10, 20 and 50 groszy and 1, 2, 5, 10, 20 and 50 zlotys and notes in denominations of 10, 20, 50, 100, 200, 500, 1,000, 2,000, 5,000 and 10,000 zlotys.

The zloty was devalued by 32% as part of the economic reform package implemented in January 1990. Fifteen industrial nations have established a $1 billion fund to help stabilize the zloty and make it fully convertible with Western currencies.

Even before World War II, private banking was weak and long-term credit was almost entirely in the hands of state institutions. After the war this trend culminated in the virtual elimination of private banking and the nationalization of all credit institutions. As a result, the National Bank of Poland, founded in 1945, is the country's sole general bank. Four smaller banks deal with specialized sectors: the Bank of Food Economy, the Export Development Bank, the State Savings Bank and the Foreign Exchange Bank.

The National Bank of Poland, and the specialized banks not only control and distribute investment funds granted to the various sectors but also control all financial transactions under the national plans. The National Bank, for example, supervises each enterprise's financial plan, examining all the contracts signed by the firm for the delivery of raw materials and the sale of products. Bank directives lay down the maximum level of inventories and prescribe the number of workers in a given operation. However, they cannot exercise their power to withhold wage payments or credits to plants violating financial discipline.

In 1990 the National Commercial Bank was reactivated and authorized to make investments as in a market economy and to act as a commercial bank in lending and credit activities.

CENTRAL GOVERNMENT EXPENDITURES, 1987

% of total expenditures
Defense: 9.1
Education: 13.1
Health: 12.2
Economic services: 46.1
Other: 19.5
Total expenditures as % of GNP: 40.1
Overall surplus or deficit as % of GNP: −1.7

CENTRAL GOVERNMENT REVENUES, 1987

% of total current revenues
Taxes on income, profit & capital gain: 27.5
Social Security contributions: 25.8
Domestic taxes on goods & services: 29.9
Taxes on international trade & transactions: 6.7
Other taxes: 4.0
Current nontax revenue: 6.2
Total current revenue as % of GNP: 38.7

EXTERNAL PUBLIC DEBT, 1988

Total: $42.135 billion
  of which public (%): 66.1
  of which private (%): 33.9
Debt service total: $2.610 billion
  of which repayment of principal (%): 51.6
  of which interest (%): 48.4
Debt service ratio: 18.5
External public debt as % of GNP: 55.7
Debt service as % of GNP: 3.0
Debt service as % of exports: 14.7
Terms of public borrowing:
  Commitments: $558 million
  Average interest rate: 6.5
  Average maturity: 6 years
External financing requirement ($ million); 1,109

FINANCIAL INDICATORS, 1988

International reserves minus gold: $2.055 billion
  SDR's: 0.1
  Foreign exchange: $2.055 billion
Gold (million fine troy oz.): 0.472
Central bank
  Assets (%)
    Claims on Government: 24.9
    Claims on banks: 69.8
    Claims on foreign assets: 5.3
  Liabilities (%)
    Reserve money: 73.1
    Government deposits: 21.6
    Foreign liabilities: 4.1
    Capital accounts: 1.2
Money supply
  Stock in billion national currency: 2.989 trillion
  M¹ per capita: 79,600
Private banks
  Assets (%)
    Loans to government: 52.0
    Loans to private sector: 33.8
    Reserves: 9.3
    Foreign assets: 4.9
  Liabilities (%)
    Deposits (billion national currency): 13.722 trillion
    of which
    Demand deposits: 13.3
    Savings deposits: 19.1
    Government deposits: 0.2
    Foreign liabilities: 44.7

EXCHANGE RATE
(National Currency per U.S. Dollar)

1979	1980	1981	1982	1983	1984	1985	1986	1987	1988
33.2	33.2	33.2	88.0	95.0	122.0	151.0	205.6	342.7	430.55

GROWTH PROFILE (Annual Growth Rates, %)

Population, 1985–2000: 0.7
Crude birth rate, 1985–90: 16.5
Crude death rate, 1985–90: 9.0
Urban population, 1980–87: 1.5
Labor force, 1985–2000: 0.7
GNP, 1980–85: 2.5
GNP per capita, 1980–88: 2.0
GDP, 1980–86: 1.5
Inflation, 1980–87: 29.2
Agriculture: N.A.
Industry: N.A.
Manufacturing: N.A.
Services: N.A.
Money holdings, 1980–86: 23.3
Manufacturing earnings per employee: N.A.
Energy production, 1980–87: 1.9
Energy consumption, 1980–87: 0.9
Exports, 1980–87: 4.3
Imports, 1980–87: 1.2
General government consumption: N.A.
Private consumption, 1980–86: −1.7
Gross domestic investment, 1980–86: −0.8

AGRICULTURE

The agricultural sector includes crop production and livestock raising but excludes forestry and fishing. The sector consists of both state and private farms; the former includes three types of socialized farms: state farms;

collectives, referred to in Poland as agricultural cooperatives; and agricultural associations or circles, which were formed originally as private cooperative undertakings. Private farms play a substantially larger role in Poland than in any other East European country.

About 62% of the total land area of 312,677 sq. km. (120,725 sq. mi.) is classified as agricultural land. Of this area, cropland makes up 77.0%, meadows and pastures 21.5% and orchards the remaining 1.5%. The largest area of cropland lies in a broad east–west zone in central Poland, the country's historic heartland. Extensive areas also are found in Silesia and in the Southwest. In these three regions, cropland occupies 50% to 60% of the land area. Meadows, usable for livestock raising, occur in less well drained areas in the broad river valleys and in the Northeast. Upland areas commonly are used as pastures. The variety of crops that can be grown is wide, though not as wide as in Western or southern Europe. Vegetable and fruit production, for example, is more limited than in Germany, Czechoslovakia or Hungary, and with less satisfactory yields. Corn, soybeans, grapes and peaches can be grown in southern Poland, but the risk of failure is high. A fairly short growing season keeps yields down. Cattle can be kept outdoors for only five months a year. Seasonal variations in egg and milk production are high. Late spring frosts often damage crops, particularly vegetables. Early frosts in the fall are a threat to potatoes and sugar beets.

The richest black soil and loess in southeastern Poland were lost to the Soviet Union in 1945. The land acquired in the West has mainly light soils, which give high yields with heavy applications of fertilizer. The southern soils are more fertile than in the North. The soils of the northern and central lowlands are largely podzols with a low humus content. Erosion is not a major problem, but despite moderate rainfall, most soils need draining because of impermeable subsoils. Diversity of farming operations ranges from highly developed intensive farming in western Poland to subsistence cultivation. With increased fertilizer supply and greater emphasis on animal husbandry, these variations are being evened out.

In prewar Poland, grains, of which rye was the most important, covered two-thirds of the crop area and accounted for 42% of the production. Since the war the area under grain has declined, forcing Poland, once an exporter of wheat, to import it. The major crops, known as the "four cereals" in Poland, are rye, wheat, barley and oats. Rye grows well in the light, sandy soils of the central plains and in the North. It is the principal market and feed grain. Wheat is grown more widely in the southern areas, with better soils and a somewhat warmer climate. Oats are grown mainly in the poor soils of the northern lake region, and barley (much of it used to brew beer) in the central and southeastern areas. Corn, much of it cut green for silage, is limited to the warmer, more sunny southern region.

Poland is the world's third-largest producer of potatoes, after the Soviet Union and China, and Poland's annual output is almost as large as the total production of Western Europe. Potatoes are a principal staple in the rural diet and a major fodder for hogs and are grown throughout the country. Legumes (peas and beans) are relatively minor crops because of economic considerations, including the greater amount of labor required for their cultivation and the lack of government subsidies. The chief oilseed is rape, but its production meets only part of the demand for edible vegetable oils.

The most important industrial crop is sugar beet. In terms of area sown for sugar beets Poland ranks as the fourth-largest in Europe, but in yield per hectare only the 17th. Traditionally, sugar beets are grown in the western parts of the country in a zone extending roughly from Gdansk southward through Bydgoszcz and Poznan to Wroclaw, but cultivation has been extended to the Lublin area and southeastern Poland. Sugar is produced from sugar beets in over 79 factories, most of them over 50 years old.

Unlike the Soviet Union, the Polish Communist regime did not wage a brutal war against the peasantry to achieve collectivization. As a result, the private farmer is more secure in Poland than in other East European countries. The peasantry is officially classified into three groups: (1) poor or small peasants owning parcels of land up to 5 ha. (12.4 ac.); (2) medium peasants holding 5 to 15 ha. (12.4 to 37 ac.); and (3) "the village rich" or kulaks, owning farms larger than 15 ha. As a result of redistribution of agricultural land, the share of the kulaks in the total farm sector has dropped appreciably over the years. Apart from the former German territories, where kulak farming never was important, two major types of kulaks existed at the end of the war. The first, encountered in the midwestern region (Poznan and Bydgoszcz provinces), had relatively large landholdings, with extensive machinery and hired labor. The second type, mostly in the East and South (Bialystok, Warsaw, and Lodz provinces), were smaller, less advanced, used little hired help and employed various tenancy arrangements. The socialization of agriculture has adversely affected the first type of kulak more than the second, thus impairing the more productive units. The latter's productivity also was affected by the tendency of the hired labor to drift to industrial employment in the nearby cities. On the other hand, the midwestern kulaks have been more loyal to the regime than the southeastern ones, and thus the regime has had no reason to pursue a harsh policy toward the midwestern kulaks.

The private farm sector produces about 80% of the "four cereals," 93% of the potatoes and 81% of the sugar beets. It farms nearly 76% of the land sown to crops. In terms of yields per hectare the private sector is more productive than the state sector, although the former receives much less investment aid, fertilizers, pesticides and farm equipment.

Land reform has a long history in Poland. It began in the 19th century with the emancipation of the serfs and was continued in the 1920s to curb peasant unrest inspired by the Soviets. Nearly 8 million acres were transferred from large to small farmers during the interwar period. By 1939 only one-seventh of the arable land was in the hands of the big landlords and six-sevenths of the farms comprised less than 49 ha. (120 ac.).

Expropriation of the remaining large holdings and distribution of the land to the peasants were important planks of the Communist program in the immediate postwar period. The Land Reform Decree of 1944 expropriated all properties exceeding 100 ha. (247 ac.) and all arable land over 50 ha. (123.5 ac.). In addition, all land belonging to German nationals or to collaborationists was confiscated. Of the 3.2 million ha. (7.9 million ac.) thus expropriated, about 1.2 million ha. (3 million ac.) were distributed to peasants; the remainder was converted to state farms.

An abrupt change occurred in 1949, when the government revised its policy under Soviet prodding to one calling for full collectivization. It was to be a slow process and entirely "voluntary," and the peasant was given a choice of three types of collectives. Initially some 10,000 collectives were set up. But the Polish peasant proved more recalcitrant than his counterparts in other East European countries, and his opposition led to the political upheaval that brought Gomulka into power in 1956 with the promise of more liberal policies. Under the new policies, peasants withdrew en masse from the collectives, whose number came down to 2,000. Acquisition of land for the state sector continued through less direct means, especially through the State Land Fund, which acquired farms from old peasants with no heir or who relinquished their holdings in return for a state pension. Some private farms taken over by the state because of low levels of productivity were returned to their owners in the early 1980s. Actually, the peasant began to fare worse than in prewar times. He had to contend with high obligatory deliveries, low prices, discriminatory high taxes and a low priority in investment allocation.

The collapse of the collectivization program in 1956 was followed by the promotion of agricultural associations or agricultural circles. The circle, encompassing one or two villages, was represented as a revival of the voluntary agricultural cooperative organizations first founded in the mid-1800s. The concept offered the government two advantages: first, as a hidden step toward collectivization that would not provoke immediate farmer opposition; and second, as a mollifier to Communist states that were disturbed by Poland's reluctance to suppress private farming. The circles were permitted to buy tractors and combines through the Agricultural Development Fund set up from part of the receipts from the obligatory food deliveries. However, in 1965 these tractors and combines were removed from the circles and assigned to newly established service centers. These centers soon became business operations more interested in the profitable large holdings than in small private holdings. In 1972 the government formed cooperatives of agricultural associations from groups of circles and the service centers. According to official statistics for 1981, there were 30,000 circles with 2.2 million members.

In 1971 the sector was reorganized under a new phase of reforms. These reforms were based on the newly accepted principle that state agriculture would not receive any preferential treatment and that its performance would be based solely on profitability. Centralized direction was abolished, and state procurement prices were raised to help farms turn a profit. Subsidies were eliminated except for certain activities, such as seed production and raising pedigreed stock. Investment was to be covered out of profits or from bank loans. Farm employees were to share in the profits, and their remuneration was tied to the farm's financial outcome. Intensive farming was encouraged through incentives such as greater depreciation allowances and favorable tax rates. Unprofitable farms were shut down unless they could recover in three years with the help of bank loans.

The progress of the reform in achieving its stated goals was meager because farm managers and farm personnel were averse to the new set of responsibilities.

AGRICULTURAL INDICATORS, 1988

Agriculture's share of GDP (%): 16
Cereal imports (000 tons): 2,962
Index of Agricultural Production (1979–81=100): 116 (1986)
Index of Food Production (1979–81=100): 116 (1986)
Index of Food Production Per Capita (1979–81=100): 108 (1985–87)
Number of tractors: 989,503
Number of harvester-threshers: 60,853
Total fertilizer consumption (tons): 3,412,600
Fertilizer consumption (100 g. per ha.): 2,342
Number of farms: 3,952,000
Average size of holding, ha. (ac.): 4.8 (9.9)
Size/class
  Below 1 ha. (2.47 ac.): 52.0
  1–5 ha. (2.47–12.35 ac.): 19.5
  5–10 ha. (12.35–24.7 ac.): 17.5
  10–20 ha. (24.7–49.4 ac.): ⎤
  20–50 ha. (49.4–123.5 ac.): ⎬ 10.9
  50–200 ha. (123.5–494 ac.): ⎦
  Over 200 ha. (494 ac.): 0.1
Tenure (%)
  Owner-operated: 76.5
  Socialized/collective: 23.5
% of farms using irrigation: 1
Total land in farms, ha. (ac.): 18,804,000 (46,464,684)
Farms as % of total land area: 60.1
Land use (%)
  Total cropland: 86.7
    Permanent crops: 1.6
    Temporary crops: ⎤
    Fallow: ⎦ 98.4
  Meadows & pastures: 13.3
Yields, kg./ha. (lb./ac.)
  Grains: 3,107 (2,773)
  Roots & tubers: 18,744 (16,730)
  Pulses: 1,709 (1,525)
  Milk, kg. (lb.)/animal: 2,958 (6,521)
Livestock (000)
  Cattle: 10,919
  Sheep: 6,991
  Hogs: 18,949
  Horses: 16
  Chickens: 53,000
Forestry
  Production of roundwood, 000 cu. m. (000 cu. ft.): 24,296 (858,013)
    of which industrial roundwood (%): 81.7
  Value of exports ($ 000): 158,585
Fishing
  Total catch (000 tons): 645.2
    of which marine (%): 95.4
  Value of exports ($ 000): 103,879

After two decades of decline, the collectives have experienced an upturn from the later 1970s. The number of collectives rose from 1,092 in 1975 to 2,350 in 1981; the number of families operating the collectives rose from 41,000 to 130,000; and total collective holdings rose to 857,000 ha. (2,116,790 ac.), making up 4.1% of the country's total agricultural land. There are four types of collectives. Ranked in degree of socialization, they are: (1) land tillage associations, (2) agricultural cooperative associations, (3) agricultural production cooperatives and (4) agricultural cooperative collectives. All types of collective farms require a stipulated minimum of communal labor from their members. Use of hired help is prohibited. In a land tillage association, the least socialized form of collective, all means of production brought into the group, including land, not only belong to the member but also remain in his individual possession and are pooled for certain periods of the year only. In the other three types farmlands are continuously pooled, though members do not lose the right of ownership to the land they brought in as their dower. The only private piece of land is a garden plot 0.3 to 1 ha. (0.75 to 2.5 ac.) on which each farmer may keep pigs, chickens, and two cows and their calves. In some cases the state assigns lands to the collectives without charge.

Income is distributed to members on the basis of the number of workday units put in by each member. Each farm operation is divided into workday units on the basis of published tables of standard norms. Premiums are given for doing more than one's daily work norm. The work on the farm is carried out in teams called brigades, whose composition and size vary because most members take time off to work on their individual plots or to perform nonfarm work outside the farm.

The Polish collectives have acquired a certain notoriety for their inefficiency. Their weakness stems primarily from the fact that the peasants were forced to join them and hence try to take as much and give as little as they can. They devote their prime time to their own private garden plots and animals, which are often much more than permitted under the regulations. These infractions are facilitated by the lack of stables for collectively owned livestock, which consequently are kept on the household plots. Sometimes the animals are secretly slaughtered and sold on the black market. The affairs of the collective are managed by a small group, most of whom lack experience in running farms. To cover their mistakes they often ignore cost accounting principles and use fictitious figures.

State farms are operated by the Ministry of State Farms. The over 2,700 state farms have an area of 4.2 million ha. (10.4 million ac.). They are the major supplier of seeds for the entire farm sector and of pedigreed animals for the livestock sector. Their track records are just as bad as those of the collectives, although in official literature they are described as the "highest form of socialized agriculture," and they get priority in the supply of equipment, fertilizers and trained personnel. Only state farms own farm equipment. Private and collective farms have to rely on State Machine Centers (POM). The rates payable for the services of these centers are discriminatory, with the collectives paying less than the private farms. Frequently payments are in kind. POM's provide technical assistance as well as politicoeconomic guidance and also supervise the annual accounting of the farms they service.

Until recently, compulsory deliveries of agricultural produce to the state was the one feature of agricultural policy most resented by farmers. These deliveries were based on "accounting hectares," and payment was made according to state-set prices. Beginning in 1955 the government began to relax the program, offering a broad range of exemptions, permitting substitutes, raising prices and abolishing penalties for nondelivery. In many cases the amount of deliveries was cut and some items were abandoned altogether.

Contracting for grain and livestock production is another important element in agricultural policy. Certain crops are entirely on contract. In the case of industrial crops, the government contracting organization provides technical direction and pays advances. Prices depend in part on quality and in part on exceeding the planned delivery total or the planned yield per hectare. Contracting farms also receive bonuses for excess deliveries and needed industrial supplies at low cost.

Mixed farming with animal husbandry as a strong profit-maker has been the rule in Poland for centuries. Because of heavy war losses, the national herd was below optimum level until the 1970s. Cattle account for over one-quarter of the gross income of farms. Dairy cattle now predominate, and the all-purpose cattle of what was formerly southeastern Poland now belong to the Soviet Union. Hogs and sheep increased much faster than cattle after the war, and the composition of the livestock population has changed accordingly in favor of hogs and sheep. With the rapid development of the bacon industry and the growing popularity of Polish ham in the United States and Europe, hogs became a major enterprise on larger and medium-size farms. Sheep are kept by peasants and highlanders in the Carpathian Mountains, and the sheep population has grown in response to rising wool prices. Before the war Poland was one of the largest horse-breeding countries in the world. They are used mostly by private farmers for plowing and hauling.

The Polish diet includes a substantial quantity of meat. As personal income grew, consumption of meat grew accordingly, and the government found it necessary to impose rationing and hike prices, both highly unpopular with urban consumers.

Less than one-fourth of Poland is under forest and only a few areas contain primeval forest. Deciduous trees predominate in the South, the central plains and the Lake District, whereas conifers are the main forms in the northern glacial moraine region and in the far Northeast. Conifers also occur at the upper elevations of the higher mountains in the South. Some 82% of the forests are state-owned; the remaining 18% are owned by agricultural collectives or circles.

The fishing industry occupies a minor place in the agricultural economy. The private fishing sector was almost entirely eliminated soon after the war. The basis of the marine fishing industry is the deep-sea fleet of over 100 trawler factory ships. These trawlers operate not only in the Baltic but also in fishing grounds as far as Australia and South America. Widening operations have led to increased costs, especially for fuel. Fishing in the Baltic, which accounts for some 25% of the marine fish catch, is constrained by agreements limiting the catch of certain types of fish. These species have short harvesting periods, resulting in idle processing facilities for most of the year. The distribution of fish throughout the country is hampered by lack of adequate refrigerated transportation and storage facilities for fresh fish; therefore little if any is available outside the larger urban centers. Salted herring, a Polish favorite, is the major imported fish.

MANUFACTURING

In 1918 the new Polish state inherited its industrial sector from the three former occupying powers. Included were the large textile industry in the Lodz-Lublin region of Russian Poland as well as some iron and steel plants, oil wells in Austro-Hungarian Galicia, coal mines and metal industries in Upper Silesia and food processing plants in Germany. The Great Depression, which followed within a decade and World War II within two decades, not to speak of political instability in the interwar period, frustrated government efforts to build on this industrial base. After World War II the westward shift of Poland's borders resulted in only a negligible loss of industrial enterprises; on the other hand, it gained from Germany an industrially advanced region with numerous manufacturing plants and mines. The first few postwar years were devoted to rebuilding existing plants, but starting in 1950 the government launched a massive industrialization program that doubled the industrial share of the NMP from 26.3% in 1950 to 53.9% in 1980. At the same time, following the Soviet model, private industrial activity was first reduced, then virtually eliminated by regulations limiting the size of the plants and the type of output.

The groundwork of the industrialization program was laid in the six-year plan of 1950–55. The plan organized three industrial districts. The first was the old industrial center of Upper and Lower Silesia and the area around Lodz. Katowice Province was to remain the chief industrial area. Newer plants were to be outside the coal basins to limit undesirable congestion. A similar development based on mineral resources was scheduled for the Walbrzych and Dzierzoniow areas. The second industrial district, including Cracow, Czestochowa and Opole, was to be expanded. The Cracow area was second only to Upper Silesia in the magnitude of investment under the plan. Expansion of the industrial center in Czestochowa was to be based on the existing metallurgical and metal goods industries and that at Opole on the cement industry. Various manufacturing industries were to coalesce around Warsaw, while Gdansk, Szczecin and Gdynia were to concentrate on shipbuilding. The third group comprised centers in which new industries were to be started. It included the Konin and Klodawa regions, where industrialization was to be based on local deposits of potassium and lignite. In eastern Poland the plan envisaged industries based on agricultural raw materials, food processing, textiles and other light industries.

As a result of these efforts, the industrial capacity has been greatly expanded. In 1989 the range of semifinished and finished goods produced in the country included iron; steel; copper; lead; zinc and related products; chemicals; transportation equipment (automobiles, trucks, buses, vans, railroad rolling stock, aircraft and ships); electrical and nonelectrical machinery; and precision equipment, including electronic, automation and data processing equipment, computer hardware and others. The principal light-industry subsector, textiles, is based in Lodz.

Among the heavy industries, the iron and steel sector is the largest and most important. Before the crisis caused by inadequate coal supply caused a decline in output, the production of steel was ranked eighth in the world and second in the COMECON area, after the Soviet Union. The industry also suffers from a high dependence on imported ore. The industry comprises some 27 plants, of which only two have been built since World War II: the Katowice Iron and Steel plant, which started operations in 1976, and the Lenin Iron and Steel plant at Nova Huta, which started operations in 1954; both were built with Soviet aid. Some modernization of older plants has been carried out, notably the Bierut Iron and Steel plant at Czestochowa, and the Warsaw plant, which produces high-grade special steels. Most of the other plants are characterized by low productivity and poor working conditions.

The Mazowiecki government has dismantled regulations against private foreign investment in the country and opened the economy for the first time since 1939 to multinational investors. However, because of the troubled state of the Polish economy only small-scale investment activity was reported in 1989.

The chemicals industry, which accounts for about 10% of the gross value of industrial output, is one of the best developed in Eastern Europe. Based largely on domestic raw materials, its production is concentrated on less complex chemicals, including sulfuric and nitric acids, sodium hydroxide, calcined soda, carbon disulfide, carbide and fertilizers. It also produces plastics and synthetic fibers, but its strength is in basic chemicals. Much of the industry is in the southern part of the country, particularly Upper Silesia. The principal petrochemical facility is at Plock in the central region, and the major phosphatic fertilizer plant is at the port of Szczecin. The industry's main development was based on large-scale investment from 1946 through 1975. Since 1975 expansion has slowed measurably as a result of long delays in construction of new facilities.

The motor vehicle industry's development dates from the 1970s. Fiat cars and trucks had been assembled near Warsaw before World War II, but these plants were completely destroyed during the war. In the 1950s Poland began assembling a Soviet model car called the Warszawa. Several years later the Polish-designed Syrena was added. In the 1960s the Polski Fiat replaced the Warszawa. In 1978 the Warsaw plant began manufacturing a new standard Polish-designed car, the Po-

lonez. Almost half of the annual production is exported, mostly to the Soviet Union and other COMECON countries.

Shipbuilding, which began in 1938, has become a major Polish industry, although its prospects have dimmed as a result of the proposed closure of the Lenin Shipyard in Gdansk. The principal shipyards at Gdansk, Gdynia and Szczecin produce a diversified range of vessels. The Northern Shipyard, also in Gdansk, specializes in construction of large fishing vessels, and a shipyard at Ustka produces small fishing vessels. In the industry's peak year in 1975 it produced over 1 million dwt. Following the worldwide shipping slump in the late 1970s, production steadily declined, to 322,000 dwt. in 1982. The Lenin Shipyard was the scene of considerable labor unrest in the early 1980s and is best known as the birthplace of the Solidarity movement.

Light aircraft has been manufactured since 1960, based mainly on Soviet models and containing a substantial proportion of materials and semifinished parts from the Soviet Union. The output ranges from light planes to trainers and helicopters. Planes are fabricated at Warsaw and Mielec and helicopters at Swidnik, near Lublin.

The organization of industrial enterprises has been changed from time to time but never has undergone a complete overhaul. Generally, each industrial ministry has a central board that combines enterprises in the same or in a related group of activity on a national or regional basis. The central boards are responsible for translating the principles of the national economic plan into goals for their subordinate units; for reviewing the drafts of plans of lower units and combining them for integration into higher departmental plans; and organizing and supervising the accounting, statistical and operational reporting of the subordinate enterprises. They also are concerned with the introduction of new technology and improved methods. When the number of enterprises involved is small, the central board administers them directly. If the number is large, there are intermediate organs, such as associations or trusts. The most important enterprises are directly subordinate to the ministries, omitting all intermediate levels of administration. Local industries are under the control of provincial authorities, municipalities, or Ministry of Small-Scale Production and Handicrafts.

In theory, individual enterprise managers have limited scope for innovation or independent decision-making. In practice, however, their discretion is much greater than legal provisions suggest, because controls from above are imperfect and managers have learned to cut corners and improvise when things go awry. They may manipulate delivery dates as long as they adhere to quotas fixed by the appropriate ministry. They may set prices for minor products and accept outside orders as long as they do not interfere with the fulfillment of plan targets. Although managers may not make investment without authorization, they may undertake capital repairs; modernize equipment or purchase new machinery without authorization. In matters of internal organization they may appoint department heads and merge existing departments or create new ones. Within the framework of the general pay scales they may manipulate labor norms, grant bonuses and extra payments for special tasks and engage consultants. Managers themselves receive bonuses for overfulfillment of quotas, and as a result they tend to encourage production gains at the expense of cost reduction.

Although Poland has succeeded in its efforts to become an industrial nation, the cost has been heavy in terms of neglect of the other sectors and the sharp decline in the standard of living. Some of the economic failures are common to all East European countries that followed the Soviet Union in its single-minded pursuit of industrialization regardless of the human costs. In the case of Poland, additional factors made any kind of regimentation unworkable in the long run. Industrial investment is plagued with waste of equipment and labor at every stage, raw material shortages and a tendency to overestimate supplies and underestimate potential bottlenecks. Material balances often exist on paper only. State-established norms become irrelevant given the complexity of modern industrial processes. Norms often are ignored in a society in which excuse-making has become an art. The system also tends to stifle innovation, and funds are wasted on R&D that already has been done abroad. Inefficiency and backward technology are more prevalent in the larger heavy industries such as automobiles and thus tend to act as a drag on the entire sector.

In 1990 the government launched the most far-reaching privatization program in Eastern Europe. The program consisted of four elements. The first established a government agency to oversee privatization. The second established the Sejm's role in determining the overall value of the enterprises to be sold. The third ended the privileges enjoyed by the socialized sector. The fourth ended restrictions on the sale of land. Under the legislation, foreigners were permitted to buy up to 10% of the shares on sale in a state-owned company.

MANUFACTURING INDICATORS, 1988

Share of GDP: 47.3%
Labor force in manufacturing: 24.3%
Value added in manufacturing (%)
    Food & agriculture: 15
    Textiles: 16
    Machinery: 30
    Chemicals: 6
Index of Manufacturing Production (1985 = 100): 113.5 (1988)

MINING

Poland's principal solid mineral is coal. It ranks as the fifth-largest coal producer in the world, and its bituminous coal deposits are the third-largest in Europe and the sixth-largest in the world. Documented minable reserves of hard coal are estimated at 62 billion tons at a depth of less than 1,000 m. (3,281 ft.) and 130 billion tons at a depth of more than 1,000 m. Brown coal reserves are estimated at 16 billion tons. About three-quarters of the hard coal is in Silesia; the remainder is in

the Lublin region. Major brown coal deposits are in the Zielona Gora voivodship in the West and the Konin and Piotrkow voivodships in the center. Upper Silesia produces about 97% of the hard coal output. Mining in the Lublin area started only in 1975, in a coal basin that covers 8,000 sq. km. (3,088 sq. mi.). Since the 1970s coal output has been running behind plan targets, leading to the introduction of rationing and a conservation campaign. Annual production from 1983 to 1986 was in the range of 192 million tons, about 14 million tons below target. The government attributed the decline to strikes and reductions in worktime forced by the Solidarity movement. In the context of the economic uncertainties of Polish industry, the government's annual target of 300 million tons was unrealistic and attainable only through reckless exploitation of labor.

Brown coal, which is produced primarily for electricity production at thermal plants, is mined at the Turoszow Basin in western Poland, in the former German territory. After World War II two additional deposits have been mined: at Konin in the 1950s and at Belchatow in Piotrkow voivodship in the 1960s. All brown coal is strip-mined.

The major metallic minerals are copper, lead and zinc. In 1957 one of the largest copper deposits in Europe was discovered in Lower Silesia. Production of electrolytic copper rose to 398,000 tons in 1985. Poland's deposits of lead and zinc are ranked about the

---

MINERAL PRODUCTION, 1984–86

Mineral		1984	1985	1986
Hard coal	000 metric tons	191,592	191,600	192,100
Lignite	000 metric tons	50,378	57,800	67,300
Iron ore[1]:				
gross weight	000 metric tons	10.9	11.3	8.8
metal content[2]	000 metric tons	3	N.A.	N.A.
Crude petroleum	000 metric tons	189	194	167
Rock salt	000 metric tons	1,185	1,200	1,222
Evaporated salt	000 metric tons	3,526	3,665	4,197
Native sulfur (per 100%)	000 metric tons	4,990	4,876	4,894
Copper ore[3]	metric tons	398,300	398,500	N.A.
Lead ore[2,3]	metric tons	52,800	51,400	N.A.
Magnesite (crude)[2,3,5]	metric tons	20,600	N.A.	N.A.
Nickel ore[2,3]	metric tons	2,100	N.A.	N.A.
Silver[3]	metric tons	774	831	829
Zinc ore[2,3,4]	metric tons	190,700	N.A.	N.A.
Natural gas[6]	million cu. m. (million cu. ft.)	6,087 (214,962)	6,390 (225,663)	5,824 (205,674)

[1]Including the iron content of iron pyrites.
[2]Source: UN, *Industrial Statistics Yearbook.*
[3]Figures refer to the metal content of ores.
[4]Estimated by Metallgesellschaft Aktiengesellschaft, Frankfurt am Main.
[5]Estimated by U.S. Bureau of Mines.
[6]Including gas repressured.

fifth in size in the world. They lie along the northern edge of the Upper Silesian coalfields, with the main operating mines in the vicinity of Olkosz.

Other metallic ores include iron ore, deposits of which are found in several places. The iron content is only moderate, and the ores are enriched before use. The main mines, at Czestochowa, account for about four-fifths of the total production. Small amounts of cadmium and silver also are produced.

Nonmetallic minerals include barite, gypsum, limestone, rock salt and sulfur. The most important is sulfur, deposits of which were first discovered in 1953 near the confluence of the Vistula and San rivers. Strip-mining began in 1958. About 80% of the output is exported either in the form of ore or as processed sulfuric acid.

Poland's deposits of rock salt are estimated at 43.5 billion tons, and it is the oldest of all mineral products in Poland, actively mined from the 13th century. One mine in the Wieliczka area that started producing in the 14th century still is in operation.

A total of 4.2% of the labor force was in mining in 1988.

ENERGY

Poland's predominant domestic energy resource is coal (see the Mining section). Known petroleum resources are small. Natural gas exists in moderate quantity, but domestic production does not meet demand. Peat occurs rather extensively, especially in the North, but is not a significant source of energy. The hydroelectric potential also is small. The exploitation of nuclear energy has met with increasing opposition from environmentalists.

In 1982 the principal known deposits of petroleum were discovered in southeastern Poland in the Carpathian Mountains between Novy Sacz and the Soviet Border. A second but less important deposit is in the West, south-southwest of Poznan. Domestic crude accounts for only about 5% of consumption; the rest is imported from the Soviet Union and the Middle East. Soviet oil is delivered through the Druzhba (Friendship) Pipeline, completed in 1966, which enters Poland near Brest and then proceeds to Germany through Plock, where a major refinery is located. There is a second major oil refinery near Gdansk.

The largest known natural gas deposits are in the Carpathian foothills. Domestic production accounts for a considerably larger share of total consumption than does oil, but even so, more than half of gas consumption is met by imports from the Soviet Union.

About 70% of the electric power is generated by thermal plants using hard coal, 27% by plants using brown coal and the remaining 3% by hydroelectric stations. The largest power plant is at Belchatow, with an installed capacity of 4,300 mw. Almost all the hydroelectric plants are quite small. Electricity is distributed through a national grid connected to COMECON's Unified Power Grid. Shortages of electric power are frequent, reflected in darkened urban streets, cutbacks in industrial usage and cutoffs in rural areas.

ENERGY INDICATORS, 1988

Primary energy production (quadrillion BTU)
    Crude oil: 0.01
    Natural gas, dry: 0.21
    Coal: 5.43
    Hydroelectric power: 0.04
    Total: 5.69
Average annual energy production growth rate (%): 1.9 (1980–87)
Average annual energy consumption growth rate (%): 0.9 (1980–87)
Energy consumption per capita, kg. (lb.) oil equivalent: 3,386 (7,465)
Energy imports as % of merchandise imports (%): 15
Electricity
    Installed capacity (kw.): 29,773,000
    Production (kw.-hr.): 140.294 billion
        % fossil fuel: 97.3
        % hydro: 2.7
    Consumption per capita (kw.-hr.): 3,744
Natural gas, cu. m. (cu. ft.)
    Proved reserves: 118 billion (4.167 trillion)
    Production: 5.746 billion (203 billion)
    Consumption: 12.625 billion (446 billion)
Petroleum, bbl.
    Proved reserves: 12 million
    Years to exhaust proved reserves: 12
    Production: 1 million
    Consumption: 106 million
    Refining capacity per day: 385,000
Coal, 000 tons
    Reserves: 42,700,000
    Production: 259,338
    Consumption: 225,874

LABOR

In 1988 the labor force was estimated at 18.6 million, compared to 16.5 million in 1981. The growth of the labor force since 1945 has been characterized by two features, both common to other Communist countries: the substantial rise in the number of those employed in the socialized sector; and the equally impressive growth of those employed in the industrial sector, which, according to Polish classification, includes manufacturing, mining, power and marine fisheries. As a result of the economy's expansion it was able to absorb a great deal of unskilled labor, but it suffers from a severe shortage of skilled workers. Unemployment is limited to unskilled workers, who still pour into the cities from the countryside.

The productivity of Polish industrial labor always has been low, and it has declined even further in recent years. This situation is due to a number of factors, including a traditionally negative attitude toward work as well as inefficient manpower planning and work. The low productivity also reflects overall political apathy, the severe shortage of essential goods and services and the lack of material incentives.

Polish peasant women always have worked with livestock and in the fields. During the interwar years some women were drawn into the textile mills and food processing plants. Only since World War II have women entered the labor force in large numbers. Although the recruitment campaigns stressed women's contributions to building socialism, the main motivation of women in accepting jobs has been economic. Most women are employed in light industries and in the service sector; heavy industries still are dominated by males. A total of 45.9% of the labor force was female in 1988.

The trade union movement has had a longer development in Poland than in any other country in Eastern Europe except Czechoslovakia. With roots in a highly developed craft guild organization, the development of trade unions began in the 1870s and proceeded rapidly and legally in the German and Austrian areas and illegally in the Russian area. After independence and during the interwar years, the trade unions developed a strong political orientation in the French and German traditions. The central organization during this period was the Central Committee of Labor Unions, which dominated the labor scene. The usual organization was on an industry basis. Strikes were common among agricultural laborers, particularly *fornals* or *bandos* (landless peasants hired on annual basis), who were organized by the Polish Socialist Party (PPS). The PPS took the lead in initiating a wide range of labor legislation, limiting weekly working hours to 46, regulating employment of women and minors, setting safety and health standards and providing basic Social Security benefits.

When the Communists seized power after the war, they lacked the political clout to suspend free trade union activity. However, they gradually infiltrated the movement, and by 1949 President Bierut announced that trade unions were henceforth to serve as "transmission belts of the Communist Party." The new Trade Union Act passed in that year reorganized the trade unions on the basis of "democratic centralism," which meant that they were simply to carry out the dictates of the party. Elections became "unanimous," and local and provincial unions lost their voice in the national federation. For the next 31 years, the CRZZ (Centralna Rada Zwiazkow Zawodowych, Central Council of Polish Trade Unions) functioned as a cog in the Communist machine. But a radical break came in 1980, when the striking workers at the Lenin Shipyard in Gdansk formed an alternative union, Solidarity (Solidarnosc), which wrested recognition from an unwilling government. This legitimation of a non-Communist trade union was a landmark in the evolution of trade unionism not only in Poland but also throughout Eastern Europe. Upon declaration of martial law in 1981 all trade unions, including the CRZZ, were suspended, although Solidarity continued to flourish illegally. Under legislation passed in 1982 all existing unions were dissolved and were replaced by factory-level representation, initially without a national coordinating body. New unions were to be registered by the provincial courts. In 1984 the National Trade Union Alliance (OPZZ) was formed, enrolling 126 of the 134 trade union organizations. Trade union pluralism—the existence of more than one union in an individual enterprise—was vehemently opposed by the Communist trade union leadership.

The 1982 strike law severely circumscribed the right to strike. Nevertheless, work stoppages ranging from a few hours to full-scale strikes at the dock of Szczecin, the Gdansk shipyard and the mines of Silesia occurred in 1988. Both leaders and workers participating in strikes faced dismissal. These and other anti-union measures were condemned by the ILO, from which Poland withdrew from 1984 to 1987. Poland was found to be in violation of ILO Convention 87, on freedom of association, and Convention 98, on the right to organize and collective bargaining.

In 1989, following talks between the government and the opposition, the former legalized again not only Solidarity but also Rural Solidarity, a farmers' union. With the establishment of the first non-Communist government in Poland since World War II, labor legislation is expected to undergo radical revisions, and the role of the Communist-led OPZZ is expected to diminish accordingly.

Under 1980 legislation, persons who are registered as unemployed and who refuse to seek employment without adequate reasons may be listed as "habitual parasites" and compelled to accept assigned employment, usually in street cleaning, park maintenance or garbage collection. This law has not been effectively implemented. The Labor Code forbids employment of minors under 15. The length and distribution of work hours are regulated by the Labor Code and meet generally accepted international standards. Wages are calculated according to a very complex formula based on a base wage, bonuses and overtime and production quotas. In 1988 the base wage was $35 to $50 per month.

LABOR INDICATORS, 1988

Total economically active population: 18,633,000
As % of working-age population: 82.5
% female: 45.9
% under 20 years of age: 4.2
% unemployed: N.A.
Average annual growth rate, 1985–2000 (%): 0.7
Activity rate (%)
  Total: 47.9
  Male: 53.4
  Female: 42.7
% organized labor: 46.7
Hours of work in manufacturing: 38 per week
Employment status (%)
  Employers & self-employed: 13.2
  Employees: 74.0
  Unpaid family workers: 12.1
  Other: 0.7
Sectoral employment (%)
  Agriculture, forestry & fishing: 28.1
  Mining: 4.2
  Manufacturing: 24.3
  Construction: 7.3
  Transportation & communication: 5.7
  Trade: 8.2
  Finance, real estate: 2.5
  Public administration & defense: 1.5
  Services: 13.4
  Other: 4.9

FOREIGN COMMERCE

Foreign trade is a state monopoly and has been so since 1945. The Ministry of Foreign Trade was established in

1949. It coordinates the activities of the sales and supplies offices of the central industrial boards, which handle imports and exports, analyze foreign markets, seek out competitive sources of supply, arrange transportation, set prices on goods sold and maintain liaison with production enterprises. Also active in these processes are the Polish Chamber of Foreign Commerce and consular establishments, special trade missions and trade delegations.

Export and import prices are largely insulated from world market prices by special accounts or subsidies. Exporters are paid internal prices, which generally are lower than the foreign currency receipts; the reverse takes place in the case of importers. To balance foreign trade accounts the state pays a subsidy to make up the difference between the import price and the resale price to the enterprise. The foreign trade accounts also receive profits from the resale of export commodities purchased at lower prices from Polish industry. This system of accounting necessitates a conversion rate between the zloty and foreign currencies.

The economic reforms of 1981 and 1982 also legislated important changes in foreign trade operations. Under the new laws, any enterprise in the socialized economy, any social organization involved in economic activities or any authorized person in the private sector engaged in production, trade or service functions could obtain permission to conduct foreign trade. A decision on the application for authorization had to be made by the ministry within three months.

The reforms introduced major changes in import financing procedures. Earlier, foreign exchange availability had been based ultimately on allocations decided by the ministry. The size of the allocation depended on "political factors," a Polish euphemism for illegal and corrupt practices. The exchange secured had to be used within the stipulated year or lost. The 1982 legislation established the foreign exchange retention quota system. This permitted enterprises to retain a share or quota of their foreign exchange earnings for use in importing materials, spare parts, items for modernization and the like needed to produce further export goods. The quota was based on the enterprise's exports and imports for the previous three years and was deposited in a bank account established for this purpose. The funds were usable by the enterprises at their discretion and could be carried forward and expended over an extended period.

Foreign trade is conducted with over 100 countries. During the interwar period trade was conducted mostly with the West, and little trade was conducted with the Soviet Union. In the immediate postwar period, imports were shared almost equally between the West and the East, with the latter taking in a larger share of exports. After the Communist consolidation of power in the late 1940s, trade with the East, especially the Soviet Union, became substantial for political reasons and remained so until 1972. Beginning in that year and stimulated by the Gierek modernization program, purchases from the West increased again, reaching 45% of imports by the late 1970s. Since then, however, as Poland experienced hard-currency shortages, imports from the West have declined and those from the Eastern bloc have risen correspondingly. The export pattern has remained relatively stable since 1950, with over 60% going to the Eastern bloc and 30% to the West. Exports to the Soviet Union account for well over half of exports to the Eastern bloc and almost a third of total Polish exports.

Through 1971 Poland's trade with the West was roughly in balance. In that year Poland's hard-currency debt amounted to only $674 million, or 15% of export earnings. The 1971 modernization program called for the import of massive quantities of machinery and equipment, to which was added large unanticipated grain imports because of domestic shortfalls. By 1975 imports from hard-currency areas totaled $5 billion, over six times their value in 1971. Exports to the West also increased, but at a slower rate than for imports, and as a result the trade deficit in 1975 was $2.2 billion and the total hard-currency external debt $7.4 billion.

Government planners had anticipated that loans available from hard-currency areas to finance imports could be repaid with export receipts. The results did not materialize, in part because of major policy miscalculations and in part because of exogenous factors, such as a recession in Western economies; the introduction of trade barriers, including quotas, especially in the EEC; competition in Western markets from several other East European countries; and the effects of poor weather on domestic agricultural production. There also was an important failure to restrain wage increases and to adjust food prices to control the rise in consumption. This led both to a drop in exports (by necessitating diversion to the domestic market) and to an increase in imports of food grains and cereals. The scope of export diversification was too broad, and insufficient allowance was made for the import of materials to sustain expanded production facilities.

After 1976 the foreign trade managers lowered growth targets for both exports and imports, resulting in lower trade deficits: $1.5 billion in 1979, $900 million in 1980 and $60 million in 1981. However, by that time increasing debt service payments were added to the hard currency borrowings required to finance the negative balance of trade. More than any other factor, the burden of debt service continued to depress the Polish economy in the 1980s.

Meanwhile, foreign trade had recovered from the slump of the early 1980s. In 1987 Poland ran a merchandise trade surplus of $1.265 billion with hard-currency areas. Exports to the West increased by 8.4%, compared to 7% for imports. Poland also enjoyed a $1.4 billion surplus on transfers and services during 1987. In trade with socialist countries, Polish exports increased by 5.1%, while imports increased by only 1.5%. As a result, Poland ran a trade surplus of 16.7 million transferable rubles with its COMECON partners, its first surplus since 1980. In 1988 Poland's exports to the West topped $8 billion, and its trade surplus was $1.5 billion. One of the reasons for this growth has been an active exchange rate policy, with the zloty being adjusted weekly against the dollar. Polish exporters also have been granted significant tax incentives and have been permitted to retain up to 50% of their export earnings. Import of capital equipment has been reduced and now accounts for only 10.4%. The sectors with the strongest export performance are metallurgical products, timber and paper products, building materials, chemicals and engineering products. Poland continues to be a net exporter of food products.

The Poznan Fair is the principal trade fair.

FOREIGN TRADE INDICATORS, 1988

Exports: $26.0 billion (1987)
Imports: $24.3 billion (1987)
Balance of trade: $1,700 billion (1987)
Annual growth rate (%), exports: 4.3 (1980–87)
Annual growth rate (%), imports: 1.2 (1980–87)
Ratio of international reserves to imports (in months): 1.4
Value of manufactured exports ($): 8.188 billion
Terms of trade: 112
Export Price Index (1985 = 100): 296.3 (1988)
Import Price Index (1985 = 100): 277.4 (1988)
Exports of goods as % of GDP: 17.4
Imports of goods as % of GDP: 15.5

Direction of Trade (%)

	Imports	Exports
EEC	19.3	21.3
U.S.A.	0.6	2.1
East European countries	46.2	39.0
Japan	1.1	0.3

Composition of Trade (%)

	Imports	Exports
Food & agricultural raw materials	14.3	12.0
Ores & minerals	3.4	3.4
Fuels	20.7	13.2
Manufactured goods	61.6	71.4
of which chemicals	9.6	6.4
of which machinery	32.3	34.7

TRANSPORTATION & COMMUNICATIONS

Poland inherited a transportation from its former occupying powers that was highly developed in the West and South (formerly under Germany and Austria, respectively) and poorly developed in the East (under Russia). In the interwar years the system was expanded somewhat, chiefly in the central region, but little was done to improve the road network because of lack of funds. Both rail and road networks were destroyed or damaged during World War II, and the system that Poland inherited from the German territory it acquired after 1945 was even more heavily damaged. Reconstruction began in 1946, and by the 1950s the system had been wholly restored.

The rail system, operated by the Polish State Railways (Polskie Koleje Panstwowe, PKP), is third in size in Europe, after France and West Germany. Of the system's total length of 27,092 km. (16,838 mi.), 23,961 km. (14,892 mi.) are of standard-gauge, 397 km. (247 mi.) are broad-gauge and 2,734 km. (1,699 mi.) are narrow-gauge. Track in the old Russian Poland had been broad-gauge but had been converted in the interwar years to standard-gauge common to the rest of Europe. The difference in gauges at the Polish-Soviet border poses a major transshipment problem only partially eased by the construction of a broad-gauge line from Zawiercie

in the Katowice region to Hrubieszow on the border. Early planning after World War II had envisaged construction of a considerable length of new track, but only some of the plans have been completed, such as the new line connecting Upper Silesia with Warsaw. Some 8,902 km. (5,533 mi.) have been electrified, mainly lines radiating east, west and south from Warsaw and the line from Upper Silesia to Gdansk and Gdynia. A factor contributing to progress in electrification is the domestic production of electric locomotives. The length of double track is 8,964 km. (5,571 mi.).

Major improvements in the national highways began in earnest in the 1970s and led to construction of 300 km. (186 mi.) of superhighways. The program was stimulated by the growing private ownership of motorcars—Poland's most highly desired consumer item. The urge to own an automobile is evidenced by the fact that in the mid-1980s over 1 million Poles had paid for vehicles in advance of delivery dates scheduled for the 1990s. However, with adverse economic conditions from 1981, much of the road-building programs have been shelved.

Public passenger and freight transportation is the monopoly of Polish Motor Communications (Panstwowa Komunikacja Samochodowa, PKS), a state enterprise. Bus routes cover a total of 118,000 km (73,278 mi.). Peakes Enterprise (International Road Company) organizes tourist and freight transport to Western and Eastern European countries.

The domestic air service is the state-owned Polish Airlines (Polskie Linie Lotnicze, LOT), established in 1929. LOT is one of the world's least-known airlines and, further, its international flights, including those to the United States, were disrupted after the imposition of martial law in 1981. The principal international airport is the Okecie Airport near Warsaw.

A total of 3,989 km. (2,479 mi.) of inland waterways are navigable by regular transportation services, with about 60% on the Vistula and the remainder on the Oder. The two systems are connected in north-central Poland by Kanal Bydgoski. The Vistula is navigable from its mouth at the Baltic Sea to its confluence with the San River in southwestern Poland and technically upstream as far as Crakow. However, much of the river is affected by shifting sandbars and changing water levels. The Oder is navigable to Kozle in Upper Silesia, where it is connected to the industrial area of Katowice by Kanal Gliwicki. The Vistula takes in barges of up to 400 tons and the Oder barges of up to 500 tons.

Historically, Poland was never a maritime nation. In the prewar period, exports from Gdansk (then Danzig) had been handled by British, Dutch and French shipping. The territorial acquisitions after the war, greatly lengthening the coastline and, more importantly, giving Poland the major ports of Szczecin, Gdansk and Gdynia, provided the impetus for the rapid development of a national merchant marine. There are several smaller ports, Swinoujscie and Kolobrzeg among them. The North Port at Gdansk provides bulk cargo handling facilities. Polish Ocean Lines provides regular passenger services to most parts of the world, and the Polish Steamship Company provides tramp steamer services.

TRANSPORTATION INDICATORS, 1988

Roads, km. (mi.): 254,000 (158,000)
  % paved: 61
Motor vehicles
  Automobiles: 3,961,953
  Trucks: 912,984
  Persons per vehicle: 7.7
  Road freight: tonne-km. (ton-mi.): 37,029 (25,363)
Railroads
  Track, km. (mi.): 27,092 (16,838); electrified, km. (mi.): 8,902
    (5,533)
  Passenger traffic, passenger-km. (passenger-mi.): 48.526 bil-
    lion (30.153 billion)
  Freight, freight tonne-km. (freight ton-mi.): 120.712 billion
    (82.681 billion)
Merchant marine
  Vessels: 719
  Total deadweight tonnage: 4,728,400
  No. oil tankers: 7   GRT: 318,000
Ports
  Number: 4 major
  Cargo loaded (tons): 31,608
  Cargo unloaded (tons): 17,388
Air
  Km. (mi.) flown: 26.2 million (16.2 million)
  Passengers: 1,587,000
  Passenger traffic, passenger-km. (passenger-mi.): 2.196 billion
    (1.365 billion)
  Freight traffic, freight tonne-km. (freight ton-mi.): 12 million (8.2
    million)
  Mail ton-km. (mail ton-mi.): 2.9 million (1.8 million)
  Airports with scheduled flights: 12
  Airports: 140
  Civil aircraft: 42
Pipelines
  Crude, km. (mi.): 1,986 (1,233)
  Refined, km. (mi.): 360 (223)
  Natural gas, km. (mi.): 4,500 (2,794)
Inland waterways
  Length, km. (mi.): 3,989 (2,479)
  Cargo, tonne-km. (ton-mi.): 1.620 billion (1.110 billion)

COMMUNICATIONS INDICATORS, 1988

Telephones
  Total (000): 4,418
  Persons per: 8.5
Phone traffic (000 calls)
  Local: }
  Long distance: } 1,139,248
  International: 4,103
Post office
  Number of post offices: 8,297
  Pieces of mail handled (000): 1,679,062
Telegraph; total traffic (000): 18,651
Telex:
  Subscriber lines: 30,733
  Traffic (000 minutes): 9,236
Telecommunications
  1 satellite ground station

TOURISM & TRAVEL INDICATORS, 1988

Total tourism receipts ($): 136 million
Expenditures by nationals abroad ($): 186 million
Number of tourists (000): 3,436
  of whom (%) from
    USSR, 27.1
    East Germany, 20.9
    Czechoslovakia, 16.3
    West Germany, 8.7
Average length of stay (nights): 3.3

DEFENSE

Under President Jaruzelski, himself a military man, the Polish People's Army plays a critical role in the transition of Poland from a hard Communist nation to a soft one. The minister of national defense serves as the supreme commander of the army and the chief of operations. The minister is supported by five deputy ministers: the chief of the General Staff, the head of the Main Political Administration and the commanders of the Main Inspectorate of Training, the Main Inspectorate of National Territorial Defense and the Inspectorate of National Civil Defense.

Organizationally the Polish People's Army includes naval and air defense forces, but the chiefs of the naval and air forces report directly to the minister rather than to the chief of the General Staff. Some confusion prevails about the lines of command because the General Staff sometimes takes actions binding on other services, and sometimes the air force and navy are referred to as separate services. The armed forces are divided into the operational army and the National Territorial Defense. The operational army is an integral part of the Warsaw Pact forces. The National Territorial Defense, on the other hand, operates only in Poland and is not part of the Warsaw Pact. Included in it are the Territory Defense Units, Frontier Defense Forces, Internal Defense Forces and the National Air Defense Force.

Operationally the ground forces are organized into three military districts: the Warsaw Military District, with headquarters at Warsaw; the Silesian Military District, with headquarters at Wroclaw; and the Pomeranian Military District, with headquarters at Bydgoszcz. The 15 ground forces divisions include five tank divisions, eight motorized rifle divisions, one airborne division and one amphibious assault division. Divisions in the two western military districts are considered Category I units and are maintained at 70% of their authorized strength, while those in the Warsaw Military District are considered Category II units and are maintained at 50% of their authorized strength. Authorized strength of a motorized rifle division is 10,800 men and that of a tank division 8,700 men. Motorized rifle divisions replaced World War II infantry divisions. Each division includes an artillery regiment, two rocket artillery battalions, one tank regiment (with 266 tanks) and three motorized rifle regiments. These units are equipped with surface-to-surface missiles and rocket launchers. Poland is the only member of the Warsaw Pact other than the Soviet Union with airborne and amphibious assault units of division strength.

Poland has the largest air force among the Warsaw Pact nations outside the Soviet Union. It functioned as a virtual arm of the Soviet air force until 1962, when it became autonomous. The operational air force, headquartered in Poznan, is responsible for fighter-bomber, reconnaissance and transportation units. The National Air Defense Force is responsible for interceptor aircraft, air defense radar and communications units and SAM systems. Both are organized into divisions, each having three to four regiments of three to four squadrons apiece. The squadrons, with 12 aircraft each, are based at 35 to 40 military airfields scattered throughout the country.

The Polish navy operates at bases from Gdynia, Hel, Kolobrzeg, Ustka and Swinoujscie. It is a small force incapable of fighting alone in a major naval action. Its principal units consist of one destroyer, some submarines and minesweepers, and landing ships. The navy also possesses naval aviation.

Military training is directed by the Main Inspectorate of Training. All male Poles are liable to conscription, and preconscription military training including ideological training. Military service is compulsory for all boys for two years, from age 19. Conscription training involves winter and summer programs and culminates in Warsaw Pact maneuvers, usually held in early fall. Most of the conscripts serve out their time as privates, but a few are promoted to higher grades. Nearly all who become NCO's are chosen at the time they enter the service and are given specialized training. NCO's usually sign up for four additional years of service, warrant officers for six additional years and officers for 12 additional years. Obligations are until age 50 for Army and Navy personnel and until age 60 for air force personnel.

Higher officer candidate schools are the major source of career officers for the army, although a few come from civilian schools and stay on active duty after completing their obligatory military duty. There are 14 such military schools, including the Higher Air Force Officers' Schools, the Westerplatte Higher Naval School, the Higher Officers' School of the Tank Troops and the Higher Officers' School of the Antiaircraft Troops. Specialized postgraduate programs are offered at the Technical Military Academy, the Polish Armed Services General Staff Academy and the Academy of Political and Military Sciences.

The Northern Group Force of the Soviet Western TVD (Major Theater of Operation) was stationed at Legnica in Poland. Until 1990 it consisted of 40,000 troops in one tank and one motor rifle division. Until 1989 the Polish defense forces received considerable aid from the Soviet Union through the Warsaw Pact, mostly in the form of hardware and equipment.

Poland's arms industry, although relatively small, is second only to Czechoslovakia among Warsaw Pact nations outside the Soviet Union. Defense industry production consists mainly of small arms, antitank weapons, artillery, antiaircraft, tanks, aircraft and missiles, all of Soviet or Czech design.

EDUCATION

The history of Polish education is as checkered as that of the nation. Between 1364, when the University of Crakow was founded, and 1773, when the National Education Commission, the first state educational body in the world, came into existence, a variety of educational institutions had been founded in the country, mostly by the Jesuits. The National Education Commission reformed the Universities of Crakow and Wilno, reorganized secondary schools, expanded parish schools for the children of the peasants, issued detailed school regulations and promoted the writing and publication of modern school textbooks. The commission continued until the third partition of the country, in 1795, suspended educational evolution for over a century. In the three sectors, attempts were made to Russianize, Germanize or Austrianize education, but with dismal results. The situation in German Poland was aggravated by Bismarck's *Kulturkampf* waged against the Catholic Church, the principal dispenser of education in Poland. Austrian Poland fared better. In Galicia secondary schools, seminaries and the universities of Crakow and Lwow resumed teaching in Polish from 1867. The Polish Academy of Sciences was founded in Crakow in 1873. It was from Crakow that the Polish cultural revival began to spread to other sectors. Before much was done in the educational field after the establishment of a free Poland in 1918, World War II intervened, followed by the Communist seizure of power. Thus for the past 200 years a free educational system may be said to have flourished in Poland for just 20 years.

Article 72 of the Polish Constitution states that all citizens have equal educational rights. This constitutional foundation is buttressed by a series of legislative acts and party resolutions giving a socialist hue to the system and socializing its curriculum and institutional framework. Notable among these acts are the 1961 Resolution on the Development of the System of Education, the 1971 Resolution of the Sixth Congress of the

---

DEFENSE INDICATORS, 1988

Defense budget ($): 4.35 billion
   % of central budget: 22.6
   % of GNP: 6.0
Military expenditures per capita ($): 381
Military expenditures per soldier ($): 10,729
Military expenditures per sq. km. (per sq. mi.) ($): 13,931
   (36,091)
Total strength of armed forces: 406,000
   Per 1,000: 10.7
Reserves: 491,000
Arms exports ($): 1.1 billion
Arms imports ($): 650 million

Personnel & Equipment

Army
   Personnel: 230,000
   Organization: 3 military districts/army headquarters—1 with 3 tank and 2 motorized rifle divisions; 1 with 2 tank and 3 motorized rifle divisions; 1 with 3 motorized rifle divisions: 1 airborne division; 1 amphibious assault division
   Equipment: 3,950 main battle tanks; 100 light tanks; 800 reconnaissance vehicles; 900 mechanized infantry combat vehicles; 2,700 armored personnel carriers; 2,025 towed artillery; 360 multiple rocket launchers; 88 SSM launchers
Navy
   Personnel: 19,000
   Bases: Gydnia; Hel; Swinoujscie; Kolobrzeg; Gdansk
   Equipment: 4 submarines; 1 destroyer; 1 frigate; 3 corvettes; 12 missile craft; 30 mine warfare vessels
   Naval aviation: 45 combat aircraft; 15 armored helicopters
   Coastal defense: 6 artillery battalions; 3 SSM battalions
Air force
   Personnel: 92,000
   Organization: 6 air divisions; 33 squadrons
   Equipment: 625 combat aircraft; over 30 armored helicopters; 225 ground attack fighters, 400 MiGs; 3 reconnaissance squadrons; 2 transportation regiments

Polish United Workers' Party and the 1973 Sejm Resolution on the National System of Education.

The academic year runs from October through June and is divided into two semesters: October through February and March through June.

Preschool education begins at age three and lasts until age seven. Preschools generally are open 10 months in a year, but some operate year-round. Parents are expected to pay fees on the basis of parental income and the number of children in the family. At age six preschoolers are taught the rudiments of writing and reading and some arithmetic.

Primary school consists of eight grades and is compulsory for all children from age seven. Unlike preschools, education is free. The primary level is divided into two cycles, the first consisting of grades one through four and the second of grades five through eight. The former small one-teacher rural schools have been closed and replaced by larger community schools, to which children from distant areas are bused. There are no qualifying or final examinations at the primary level, and pupils move from one grade to the next on the basis of continual assessment. Academically backward children are given vocational training in the last two years of primary school.

Secondary school consists of several types of establishments: secondary general education; secondary vocational; basic vocational; and secondary technical. There also are regular evening schools for those who have taken up apprenticeships.

The secondary general education schools, known as *lycées*, prepare students for higher education. At the end of the secondary cycle, all students take the *matura* or final examination, on passing which they receive a certificate of maturity. Those who fail receive a completion certificate, entitling the holder to enroll in a postsecondary vocational school.

A major part of the secondary curriculum is devoted to specialized subjects, such as mathematics-physical sciences, biological-chemical sciences, foreign languages or humanities. Secondary vocational schools train technicians, and basic vocational schools train lower-grade specialists and workers. Students who complete the latter school may then proceed to secondary technical schools.

There are 92 institutions of higher education in Poland, all of which are under state control except for the historic Catholic University of Lublin and two theological colleges. Seven universities existed in 1939; all others are of post-World War II origin. The highest enrollments are reported in Warsaw Technical University and Warsaw University, founded in 1898 and 1913, respectively. There are no private schools below the tertiary level.

Entrance to higher education is by means of competitive entrance examinations, and children of peasants and workers are given special preference. The first degree, Magisterium takes four to five years, depending on the subject. There are two types of doctoral degrees: The first takes four years; the second, the advanced doctoral degree (Doktor Habilitowany), involves completion of additional research. Each university is head-ed by a rector nominated by the minister of education, who also appoints the professors. In academic matters the rector is assisted by a senate made up of representatives of the councils of academic departments, lecturers, assistant lecturers and the student body. Each academic department is headed by a dean of studies.

EDUCATION INDICATORS, 1988

Literacy
  Total (%): 99.2
First level
  Schools: 17,553
  Teachers: 262,500
  Students: 5,007,800
  Student–teacher ratio: 19:1
  Net enrollment rate (%): 99
  Females (%): 48
Second level
  Schools: 898
  Teachers: 21,000
  Students: 353,100
  Student–teacher ratio: 17:1
  Net enrollment rate (%): 73
  Females (%): 51
Vocational
  Schools: 6,635
  Teachers: 78,500
  Students: 1,327,300
  Student–teacher ratio: 17:1
Third level
  Institutions: 92
  Teachers: 57,700
  Students: 261,100
  Student–teacher ratio: 5:1
  Gross enrollment rate (%): 16.5
  Graduates per 100,000 age 20–24: 1,221
  % of population over 25 with postsecondary education: 5.7
  Females (%): 55
Foreign study
  Foreign students in national universities: 2,885
  Students abroad: 3,081
    of whom in
      United States, 557
      West Germany, 1,086
      Austria, 246
      Vatican, 218
Public expenditures (national currency)
  % of GNP: 4.7
  % of national budget: 11.4

GRADUATES, 1983

Total: 112,917
Education: 22,914
Humanities & religion: 5,045
Fine & applied arts: 1,436
Law: 1,933
Social & behavioral sciences: 1,618
Commerce & business: 21,024
Mass communication: 659
Home economics: 69
Natural sciences: 3,196
Mathematics & computer science: 771
Medicine: 16,183
Engineering: 16,971
Architecture: 436
Industrial programs: 5,761
Transportation & communications: 881
Agriculture, forestry, fisheries: 11,635
Other: 2,385

Educational administration is the responsibility of the Ministry of Education assisted by the Council of the Ministry of Education, the Interministerial Council for Vocational Education and the Council for Educational Affairs. At the voivodship level, schools are supervised by educational curators as well as school directors and inspectors.

Nonformal education is concentrated in "permanent education" programs, such as those conducted by the Central Technical Organization and radio and television.

Teachers for schools of all types are trained at higher educational establishments. Prospective teachers study at one of the nine universities; 12 higher pedagogical schools; seven academies of physical education; or over 50 technical, economic or artistic higher schools. Studies last four or five years. Vocational and preschool teachers have specialized courses adapted to their pedagogical needs.

LEGAL SYSTEM

Polish law is based on a mixture of continental (Napoleonic) civil law and Marxist legal theory. Laws are systematized in various codes, such as the Administrative Code, the Family Code, and the Labor Code. An entirely new Civil Code was adopted in 1970. Judicial decisions are not regarded as a source of law, although Supreme Court decisions influence lower court decisions.

Justice is administered by a hierarchy of courts consisting of district courts, voivodship courts and the Supreme Court. Outside of this system are informal misdemeanor boards under local organs of administration and headed by laymen. They administer fines of up to 5,000 zlotys and three months' imprisonment for infractions such as traffic offenses or drunkenness.

District courts are the courts of first instance for more serious but not major civil or criminal cases. Their jurisdiction embraces several towns and communes. There are 261 district courts, from two to 20 in each voivodship. Judicial hearings take place before a professional judge and two people's assessors, elected by people's councils for four-year terms. A leading role is played by the public prosecutor or procurator, whose purpose is to ensure strict observance of the law, to indict suspects after conducting preliminary investigations, and to act as the public accuser at trials. Prosecutors' offices at the voivodship and district levels are units of the prosecutor general's office at Warsaw, which is independent of the Ministry of Justice and responsible directly to the Council of State.

Voivodship courts function as courts of first instance for major civil or criminal cases and as appellate courts in relation to lower courts.

The Supreme Court is composed of four divisions: criminal, civil, labor and social insurance, and military, each with its own president. Its justices are appointed by the Council of State for five-year renewable terms. In addition to reviewing judgments of lower courts, the Supreme Court lays down guiding principles for the administration of justice to ensure uniformity or to clarify difficult issues.

All trials are public except those in which national security or other sensitive considerations are involved. Defendants are entitled to counsel. Attorneys are organized into collectives in which profits are partially shared. Although judges are ostensibly independent of the government, they are subjected to considerable pressure from the executive in cases with political overtones, and defendants with political connections receive favorable treatment. However, judges enjoy considerable latitude and are known to resist political pressures and either drop charges against or impose lesser sentences on dissidents. Judicial review of administrative regulations is authorized by law. The Supreme Administrative Tribunal in Warsaw hears appeals against administrative authorities in areas such as housing construction, taxes, real estate, education, welfare, employment and other matters.

A constitutional amendment passed in 1982 provides for the Tribunal of State to monitor the official actions of individuals in key posts (except top party officials). This tribunal is linked to the Sejm by a parliamentary committee on constitutional responsibility. The tribunal consists of a chairman and deputy, 22 regular members and five deputy members, only half of whom need be lawyers. First hearings are before the chairman and six members, and the full court sits only for appeals against the verdict of the smaller body.

The same constitutional amendment withdrew from the Council of State the right of review over the constitutionality of laws and stipulated that a constitutional tribunal should be formed to assess the conformity of laws and legal acts with the Constitution. This Constitutional Tribunal began work in January 1986. In the next two years it reviewed 17 laws, 10 governmental decrees and two ministerial orders. Nine of these acts were rescinded or returned for changes.

The prison system is run by the Main Bureau of Penal Institutions of the Ministry of Justice. Prisoners are subject to one of four regimens: mitigated, basic, intense and severe, each with varying restrictions and privileges. All penal institutions are considered rehabilitative and productive centers. Those serving sentences of less than five years are placed in semiopen labor centers, and those serving longer sentences in penal institutions. Inmates nearing the end of their sentences are sent to transitional institutions. Other facilities exist for multiple recidivists and for prisoners under age 21. Roman Catholic clergymen have access to prisoners. Prisoners are required to engage in productive work, for which they receive standard wages but no Social Security benefits.

The system of justice is being reformed. Judges may no longer be politically appointed but are nominated by a National Judiciary Council. The law courts are being reorganized. The prosecutor's office has been subordinated directly to the Minister of Justice in order to sever the old connections between the local security police offices and the prosecutor's office. After ugly prison riots in December 1989, a commission was established to study conditions in prisons. Its findings revealed widespread human rights abuses. A new Director of Prison Administration was appointed in April 1990 to oversee a reform of the prisons. Many of the repressive provisions of the Penal Code have been amended or have fallen into disuse.

LAW ENFORCEMENT

A national police had existed in the Polish Republic from 1918 to 1939, but in the aftermath of World War II it was dissolved by the Communist regime and replaced by regular forces known as the Citizens' Militia (Milicja Obywatelska, MO) and the Security Service (Sluzba Bespieczenstwa, SB), known in its early years as the Security Bureau (Urzad Bezpieczenstwa). The MO is the basic police force at the voivodship and local levels. Although organized on a regional basis, it has a centralized command in Warsaw. MO units consult and coordinate extensively with local authorities. As a paramilitary force, the MO is run on military lines, sharing training facilities and equipment with the army. Militiamen are generally armed. Warsaw, Lodz and Crakow have their own MO commands controlling a number of commissariats.

The MO is not directly involved in controlling riots and demonstrations, which duty fell upon, particularly in the early 1980s, its motorized units (Zmotoryzowane Oddzialy Milicji Obywatelskiej, ZOMO). Because the ZOMO was used to control pro-Solidarity demonstrations, to storm factories occupied by workers and to patrol tense areas, it became highly unpopular and intensely disliked.

Another unit of the MO is the Volunteer Reserve (Ochotnicza Rezerwa Milicji Obywatelskiej, ORMO), which absorbed most of the former industrial guard units. Usually equipped with armored vehicles, they serve only in emergencies and augment the MO at major trouble spots. During the civil disturbances of the early 1980s, many of them were suspected of being pro-Solidarity and thus were not assigned to high-risk areas.

The Security Service (Sluzba Bezpieczenstwa, SB) is the secret police force. Not only is it modeled after KGB, but also it remains the institution most sympathetic to and most thoroughly penetrated by the Soviets.

In May the Sejm passed, albeit with some misgivings, a package of laws that provided for the reorganization of the police along nonideological lines. The security police was abolished and replaced by a State Protection Office. A strict screening procedure has been instituted for its staff. Such screening will not apply to the regular police force, however, which is to become simply a crime-fighting organization. A number of senior police officials have recently been retired or dismissed, but there is no reliable information by which to judge the moral qualities, competence and loyalties of the new appointees, who come, inevitably, from the old organization. The police have on the whole kept a low profile. The new riot police have not yet been used to quell public unrest. Police officials have responded to demands for change by complaining about the mounting crime wave and their lack of personnel and resources. Many local police stations no longer react or react slowly to public requests for assistance, with the result that crime has increased still further and the population feels threatened.

The crime rate always has been high. There are two parallel trends. The positive trend is the 15% reduction since 1986 in the number of offenses committed in public places. The negative side is the 10% rise in robberies and thefts. The detection rate ranges from 56% to 78%. The overall crime index is 1,350 per 100,000 inhabitants.

HEALTH

Measured by standard indexes, the health of the Polish people has improved since World War II. But the rate of improvement has not been as high as in Western Europe, and further, it began to level off by the early 1970s, and by the 1980s some of the indexes indicated a decline. The reason lay partly in the low rate of capital investment in new facilities and medical infrastructure. The number of general practitioners has not kept pace with the growth of population. There also is a marked neglect of environmental and preventive medicine. A special problem, increasingly acute, is alcoholism.

World War II was responsible for the virtual crippling of the prewar health care delivery system. Most of the hospitals were damaged or destroyed, and of the stock of health professionals and doctors (50% of whom were Jewish), only half survived. Health received little attention in the immediate postwar period, and its rebuilding was largely uncoordinated and haphazard. Hospitals were separately administered, leading to many inefficiencies. The Ministry of Health and Social Welfare was one of the weakest ministries in the government and received one of the smallest pieces of the budgetary pie. Only in one area did health receive adequate priority, and that was in the education of health care workers, including secondary-level physicians, known as *feldshers*, on the Soviet model. However, the pay of health personnel of all kinds has tended to be low. Physicians and dentists may supplement their incomes by working extra hours in a medical cooperative or in private pratice.

The Polish health service was established by law in 1948 as a social insurance program. Health care is provided in state hospitals and by state physicians or by medical cooperatives who provided service in their own clinics at rates approved by the Ministry of Health and Social Welfare. State physicians also may engage in private practice, but they are more heavily taxed and their patients must pay full price for prescriptions. A 1970s reorganization in the public health care system made the family doctor at the local clinic rather than the specialist the key figure in the system and abolished the differentiation between outpatient and inpatient facilities. Both were subordinated to area health communities (*zespol opieki zdrowotnej*, ZOZ). A ZOZ covers an area containing either a number of rural communes or one or more towns or the whole or part of a larger urban area. Included in a ZOZ are a number of primary-care clinics, a general hospital and one or more polyclinics. Primary care is defined as including general medicine, obstetrics and gynecology, pediatrics and dentistry. In addition to community ZOZ's, industrial ZOZ's are attached to large industrial complexes.

Despite the creation of ZOZ's, health services continue to perform poorly. Clinics and hospitals are overcrowded, and medical technology and pharmaceuticals are in chronic short supply. The medical profession is underpaid and overtaxed. According to the journal *Poland Today*, the public is divided into two classes: those who can afford proper medical care and those who cannot. Included in the former category are the senior party and government officials who receive access to facilities and treatment denied to others. The use of bribes to secure good medical attention is fairly common. The crowded conditions in public facilities are in part due to the low level of capital investment in this sector. More than 60% of all hospital beds are in prewar buildings, and the average age of hospitals is more than 70 years. The heavy overuse of hospital facilities has led to beds in corridors and poor sanitation and to a high incidence of hospital-induced infection. Contributing to this problem is a shortage of disposable syringes and consequent use of unsterile equipment.

The Ministry of Health and Social Welfare is advised by the Expert Committee on Health Care. Medical research is conducted at the Medical Academies of the State Institute of Hygiene and at 13 special institutes.

HEALTH INDICATORS, 1988

Health personnel
  Physicians: 75,473
    Persons per: 498
  Dentists: 17,391
  Nurses: 178,387
  Pharmacists: 16,109
  Midwives: 20,773
Hospitals
  Number: 706
  Number of beds: 247,276
  Beds per 10,000: 53
  Admissions/discharges
    Per 10,000: 1,272
  Bed occupancy rate (%): 80.5
  Average length of stay (days): 17
Type of hospitals (%)
  Government: 100
Public health expenditures
  Per capita: $182.30
Vital statistics
  Crude death rate per 1,000: 10.1
  Decline in death rate: 29.7 (1965–84)
  Life expectancy at birth (years): males, 66.8; females, 75.1
  Infant mortality rate per 1,000 live births: 17.3
  Child mortality rate (ages 1–4 years) per 1,000: Insignificant
  Maternal mortality rate per 100,000 live births: 14.2
Causes of death per 100,000
  Infectious & parasitic diseases: 9.6
  Cancer: 181.8
  Endocrine & metabolic disorders: 16.6
  Diseases of the nervous system: 9.1
  Diseases of the circulatory system: 515.4
  Diseases of the digestive system: 31.7
  Accidents, poisoning & violence: 70.3
  Diseases of the respiratory system: 53.5

FOOD & NUTRITION

The traditional Polish diet is high in starches and low in protein. Fruits and vegetables are eaten only in season. Relatively little canned or frozen food is available in urban areas. Peasants and urban workers eat much the same food. Potatoes are the staples of the diet. Grains—predominantly rye and wheat with some millet—are next in importance. Both potatoes and grains in some form are served at all meals—as soup, dumplings, noodles, porridge or bread. Black rye bread is the usual fare; white wheat bread is generally reserved for special occasions. Very small quantities of beef, pork, poultry or fish are consumed, usually added to one of the starchy dishes. The peasants use little milk except in the form of sour cream and cheese; in urban areas milk is in short supply and is almost entirely reserved for children. Eggs appear on the dining table only on special occasions.

MEDIA & CULTURE

The printing press came early to Poland just 20 years after Gutenberg published his first Bible. But newspapers did not develop for another 200 years because of the unsettled political conditions, and they did not last long for the same reason. The country's first newspaper was the weekly *Merkurjusz Polski*, which appeared in Crakow in 1661. It and its immediate successors had only brief lives, and the press developed slowly. In 1729 two papers, *Kurjer Warsawski* and *Kurjer Polski* of Crakow, were founded and were able to survive for some time by forgoing political comment. Press historians date the real beginning of the press to the Constitution of 1791, which provided for freedom of the press. One of the papers founded in this period, *Gazeta Warsawski*, survived until 1939.

The Polish press had a checkered history in the interwar independent Poland, when newspapers came and went as parties rose and fell. Under Pilsudski's dictatorship a free press was effectively suppressed; nevertheless, at the beginning of World War II, a total of 165 newspapers were being published in the country.

The subsequent Nazi and Communist eras were equally dark and troubled. After a brief spell of relative freedom, the Communists clamped down on the press, and it was not until the late 1950s that the press regained some measure of its natural vigor. Weeklies such as *Nova Kultura* and *Po Prostu* led a drive for greater liberalization of the regime, which culminated in the return of Gomulka to power. The small glimmer of freedom was soon extinguished, but things never slipped back to the grim pre-1956 conditions. Although censored and tightly controlled, the Polish press remained freer relative to its counterparts in Eastern Europe. The Roman Catholic Church, publishing its own periodicals, was able to relieve the unmitigated ideological slant of the official press.

With the rise of Solidarity, the press was able to wrest greater autonomy. Solidarity itself was granted the right to publish a paper, the first issue of which appeared on April 3, 1981. However, it was suppressed later that year when martial law was imposed. It reappeared in 1989 as *Gazeta Wyborcza* and played a major role in the final collapse of the Communist regime in Poland.

According to the Constitution both print and electronic media belong to the state. The right to publish is given only to political parties, civic organizations and institutions, the church being included in the latter category. The effect of this concentration is multiplied by the fact that RSW Prasa has a monopoly of all distribution.

Except for a German-language biweekly, all papers are published in Polish. They are published in all major cities and towns, with the largest concentration in Warsaw. Most are of broadsheet size, although a few appear in tabloid. There are no Sunday newspapers, and most dailies print only six days a week. Most are morning papers, although some afternoon papers, such as *Express Wieczorny* (*Evening News*) of Warsaw, claim impressive circulations. The largest-selling and the most influential daily is *Trybuna Ludu*, the official party organ, which is required reading for all party members. Almost all papers are serious publications, with only minor concessions to light news. Only *Express Wieczorny* could be characterized as popular. Although *Trybuna Ludu* ranks first in circulation, both the Catholic *Tygodnik Powszechny* and the party *Polityka* are heavyweights, considered as authoritative at either end of the political spectrum.

The media are regarded as necessary organs of government, serving its information and propaganda needs, and thus are not affected by economic considerations of sales or revenues. The ups and downs of party ideology may affect the contents of the papers but not their economics. RSW Prasa, which enjoys a distribution monopoly, turns over the greater part of its income to the party, but most other media operations are heavily subsidized. Circulation is based not on actual or potential sales but on the newsprint allocated by the government to each paper. The allocation of newsprint also reflects the government's pleasure or displeasure with the editorial contents of each paper. Advertising—as much as 30%—is more evident than in any other East European nation except Hungary. Most are small classified ads, but displays for consumer durables such as automobiles are not uncommon.

The majority of journalists are members of the Polish Journalists' Association, an unofficial or "creative" trade union not affiliated with the official National Trade Union Alliance (OPZZ). Less than half of its members are Communists. Journalists customarily are paid on a "string"—i.e., so much per story. As a result, the better-known reporters enjoy higher incomes than the juniors.

The basic press law is not of Communist origin; it predates World War II and was published in 1938 by the colonels who succeeded Pilsudski. Since this law provides harsh and stringent restrictions on the press, it suited the Communists, who have added only a few minor details. All print publications are under the supervision of the Central Office for the Control of the Press, Publications and Theater, which also is the censorship agency. As in the rest of Eastern Europe, the

FOOD & NUTRITION INDICATORS, 1988

Per capita daily food consumption, calories: 3,301.3
Per capita daily consumption, protein, g. (oz.): 103.3 (3.6)
Calorie intake as % of FAO recommended minimum requirement: 127
% of calorie intake from vegetable products: 67
% of calorie intake from animal products: 33
Food expenditures as % of total household expenditures: 44.6
% of total calories derived from
  Cereals: 34.7
  Potatoes: 6.0
  Meat & poultry: 9.6
  Fish: 1.3
  Fats & oils: 14.6
  Eggs & milk: 12.3
  Fruits & vegetables: 3.5
  Other: 18.1
Per capita consumption of foods, kg., l. (lb., pt.)
  Potatoes: 154.0 (339.5)
  Wheat: 43.3 (95.4)
  Fresh vegetables: 103.0 (227.1)
  Fruits (total): 64.5 (142.2)
    Citrus: 9.9 (21.8)
    Noncitrus: 54.6 (120.3)
  Honey: 0.5 (1.1)
  Fish: 6.0 (13.2)
  Milk: 8.4 (18.5)
  Butter: 8.3 (18.3)
  Cheese: 3.0 (6.6)
  Meat (total): 63.5 (140.0)
    Beef & veal: 15.8 (34.8)
    Pig meat: 34.9 (76.9)
    Poultry: 12.3 (27.1)
    Mutton, lamb & goat: 0.5 (1.1)
  Sugar: 45.4 (100.1)
  Chocolate: 3.1 (6.8)
  Margarine: 5.2 (11.4)
  Biscuits: 2.9 (6.4)
  Beer, l. (pt.): 28.6 (60.4)
  Wine, l. (pt.): 8.5 (17.9)
  Alcoholic liquors, l. (pt.): 4.1 (8.6)
  Soft drinks, l. (pt.): 8 (16.9)
  Mineral waters, l. (pt.): 10.0 (21.1)
  Fruit juices, l. (pt.): 7.0 (14.7)
  Coffee: 0.7 (1.5)
  Tea: 0.9 (1.9)
  Cocoa: 0.5 (1.1)

power of the censor is both positive and negative, both *suggestio falsi* and *suppressio veri*. Since secret information never reaches the press in any case, the main function of the censor is to select for publication the news best serving the state's interest, even if it involves stretching the truth a bit. The result is a lack of media credibility so widespread that most people believe that the truth is the opposite of what is printed in the papers. Censorship is not the only cross that journalists have to bear. Bureaucratic hurdles are placed in the way of gathering even routine information. Thus the media report not so much the whole news but only crumbs of news thrown from the official table.

The principal national news agency is Polska Agencja Prasowa (PAP). It is supplemented by three other specialized agencies: Polska Agencja Interpress, similar to the Soviet Union's Novosti; Centralna Agencja Fotograficzna (CAF), the national photo agency; and Agencjs Robotnicza (AR, the Workers' Agency). All major foreign news agencies are represented in Warsaw including AP, AFP, Reuters Tass, UPI and dpa.

MEDIA INDICATORS, 1988

Newspapers
  Number of dailies: 45
  Circulation (000): 7,480
  Circulation per 1,000: 200
  Number of nondailies: 51
  Circulation (000): 2,846
  Circulation per 1,000: 77
  Number of periodicals: 2,986
  Circulation (000): 39,057
  Newsprint consumption
    Total (tons): 128,600
    Per capita, kg. (lb.); (7.7)
Book publishing
  Number of titles: 7,920
Broadcasting
  Number of employees: 12,290
Radio
  Number of transmitters: 107
  Number of radio receivers (000): 10,512
    Persons per radio receiver: 3.5
  Total annual program hours: 44,253
Television
  Television transmitters: 118
  Number of television receivers (000): 9,692
    Persons per television receiver: 3.9
  Total annual program hours: 8,115
Cinema
  Number of fixed cinemas: 1,757
  Seating capacity: 469,000
    Seats per 1,000: 13.2
  Annual attendance (million): 94.3
    Per capita: 2.5
Films
  Production of long films: 39
  Import of long films: 90
    11.1% from United States
    40.0% from USSR
    3.3% from France
    2.2% from Italy

CULTURAL & ENVIRONMENTAL INDICATORS, 1988

Public libraries
  Number: 10,000
  Volumes (000): 124,266
  Registered borrowers: 7,674,000
  Loans per 1,000: 4,124
Museums
  Number: 537
  Annual attendance: (000): 21,556
  Attendance per 1,000: 574
Performing arts
  Facilities: 149
  Number of performances: 127,184
  Annual attendance (000): 32,965
  Attendance per 1,000: 877
Ecological sites: 15
Botanical gardens & zoos: 26

PRINCIPAL NEWSPAPERS

Newspaper	Circulation
Trybuna Ludu, Warsaw	635,000
Trybuna Robotnicza, Katowice	580,000
Express Wieczorny, Warsaw	470,000
Zycie Warzawy, Warsaw	340,000
Gazeta Pomorska, Bydgoszcz	238,000
Rzeczpospolita, Warsaw	229,000
Gloz Robotniczy, Lodz	220,000
Gazeta Poznanska, Poznan	220,000
Dziennik Zachodni, Katowice	218,000
Sztandar Mlodych, Warsaw	210,000

All broadcasting is directed by the Committee for Radio and Television and is funded by license fees and state subsidies. There are four networks on the Home Radio Service, and two television networks.

SOCIAL WELFARE

The present Social Security system is an extension of that of the interwar government, which was one of the most comprehensive in Europe. The only new feature is family allowance. During the interwar period the cost of benefits was shared by the employer and the employee, but under the Communists it is borne entirely by the employer and the state. Social insurance is compulsory for both blue-collar and white-collar workers in both private and socialized sectors and for collective farmers. As in the past, private farmers and businessmen are not covered. Despite many similarities to the past, the present system has been restructured to serve the party's special goals. Thus contributions from private employers are larger than those from socialized enterprises. The government may withhold benefits from politically unreliable people, and party members who have made special contributions to socialist Poland may receive additional benefits.

In 1955 trade unions were given the responsibility for the administration of social insurance, with the exception of pensions, which were placed in the hands of the Ministry of Health and Social Welfare, which works through provincial, district and local people's councils. There are special systems for miners, railroad employees, police and independent farmers.

The pensionable age is 65 and 60 for men with 20 and 25 years of work, respectively, and 55 and 60 for women with 25 and 20 years of work, respectively. Those in stressful occupations may retire earlier. The major benefits are: old-age and disability pensions, survivors' pensions, family allowances and funeral allowances. There is no unemployment insurance as such, since, technically, a socialist state has full employment. Incidental needs of the unemployed are met from other funds.

There is no private welfare system in Poland.

CHRONOLOGY

1945—Provisional Government of National Unity is installed, with Edward Osobka-Morawski as prime minister and Wladyslaw Gomulka as deputy prime minister.

1947—In elections, the Communist regime wins 80% of the vote; Boleslaw Bierut is named president and Jozef Cyrankiewicz prime minister. . . . The Constitutional Act is passed by the Sejm as an interim Constitution. . . . Gomulka is demoted.

1949—Poland joins COMECON. . . . Soviet Marshal Konstantin K. Rokossovsky is named minister of defense as part of the process of Sovietization. . . . Church-state conflicts erupts as the Vatican excommunicates Communist activists.

1952—New Constitution is promulgated.

1953—The government jails Cardinal Stefan Wyszynski.

1956—Bierut dies. . . . Riots break out in Poznan. . . . Gomulka is restored to power as first secretary of the PZPR.

1968—Poland joins Warsaw Pact powers in invasion of Czechoslovakia.

1970—Bloody riots in Gdansk bring down Gomulka, who is replaced as first secretary by Edward Gierek. . . . Gierek launches crash programs to industrialize the country through massive borrowings from the West.

1976—Food crisis triggers new riots.

1980—Industrial unrest sparked by rising prices and falling wages, leads to wave of strikes, particularly by 16,000 workers at the Lenin Shipyard in Gdansk. Striking workers, backed by the church, form a decentralized independent trade union, Solidarity, led by a 38-year-old electrician, Lech Walesa. . . . Gierek concedes to the workers' demands, enumerated in the Gdansk Agreement. . . . After the conclusion of the agreement Gierek collapses physically and mentally and is replaced as party first secretary by Stanislaw Kania.

1981—As the political and economic crises deepen, Gen. Wojciech Jaruzelski is named prime minister. . . . Jaruzelski proclaims martial law, interns Solidarity leaders and outlaws the trade union. . . . a Military Council of National Salvation takes over the government.

1985—Jaruzelski resigns as prime minister to become chairman of the Council of State (president). . . . Zbigniew Messner is named prime minister.

1987—Government fails to win national referendum on political and economic reforms.

1988—Messner is forced to resign and is replaced by Mieczyslaw F. Rakowski.

1989—Solidarity and Rural Solidarity are legalized following negotiations. . . . Roman Catholic Church is legalized. . . . In first free parliamentary elections in 40 years Solidarity sweeps the polls, winning 99 of 100 Senate seats and all 161 open seats in the Sejm. Leading regime officials fail to win reelection, including Prime Minister Rakowski, Defense Minister Florian Siwicki, Minister of the Interior Czeslaw Kiszczak, government spokesman Jerzy Urban, party economic secretary Wladyslaw Baka and Politburo member Stanislaw Ciosek. . . . Solidarity launches newspaper *Gazeta Wyborcza*, the first independent mass-circulation daily in Poland in 40 years. . . . Jaruzelski is reeleected chairman of the Council of State. . . . Solidarity leader Tadeusz Mazowiecki is elected prime minister, the first non-Communist prime minister in Eastern Europe since the end of World War II.

1990—PZPR is disbanded and replaced by Social Democracy of the Polish Republic and Social Democratic Union. . . . Solidarity is split into pro-Walesa and pro-Mazowiecki factions as Walesa becomes increasingly critical of government.

BIBLIOGRAPHY

Alton, Thad Paul. *Polish Post-War Economy*. New York, 1955.

Ascherson, Neal. *The Polish August: The Self-Limiting Revolution*. New York, 1981.

Barbey, Bruno. *Portrait of Poland*. New York, 1982.

Barnett, Clifford R. *Poland*. New Haven, Conn., 1958.

Bethell, Nicholas. *Gomulka: His Poland; His Communism*. New York, 1969.

Bielasiak, Jack. *Polish Politics: Edge of the Abyss*. Westport, Conn., 1984.

Bogdan, Szajkowski. *Next to God. . . . Poland: Politics and Religion in Contemporary Poland*. New York, 1983.

Bromke, Adam. *Poland: The Protracted Crisis*. New York, 1986.

———. *Poland's Politics: Idealism versus Realism*. Cambridge, Eng., 1967.

Brumberg, Abraham. *Poland: Genesis of a Revolution*. New York, 1983.

Davies, Norman. *God's Playground: A History of Poland*. New York, 1982.

de Weydenthal, Jan B. *The Communists of Poland*. Stanford, Calif., 1978.

Dobbs, Michael. *Poland, Solidarity, Walesa*. New York, 1981.

Garton Ash, Timothy. *The Polish Revolution: Solidarity, 1980–82*. London, 1983.

Halecki, Oscar. *A History of Poland*. London, 1978.

Jazdzewski, Konrad. *Poland*. New York, 1965.

Jedruch, Jacek. *Constitutions, Elections and Legislatures of Poland, 1493–1977; A Guide to Their History*. Lanham, Md., 1982.

Kolankiewicz, George, and Paul Lewis. *Poland*. New York, 1988.

Korbel, Joseph. *Poland Between East and West*. Princeton, N.J., 1963.

Kruszewski, Z. Anthony. *The Oder-Neisse Boundary and Poland's Modernization: The Socioeconomic and Political Impact*. New York, 1972.

Labedz, Leopold. *Poland Under Jaruzelski*. New York, 1984.

Landau, Zbigniew, and Jerzy Tomaszewski. *The Polish Economy in the 20th Century*. New York, 1985.

Lewanski, Richard C. *Poland*. Santa Barbara, Calif., 1984.

Milosz, Czeslaw. *Native Realm: A Search for Self-Definition*, Trans. Catherine Leach. Berkeley, Calif., 1981.

Misztal, Bronislaw. *Poland After Solidarity: Social Movements versus the State*. New Brunswick, N.J., 1985.

Morrison, James F. *Polish People's Republic*. Baltimore, 1968.

Parker, Mauldin W., and Donald S. Aken. *The Population of Poland*. Washington, D.C., 1954.

Piekalkiewicz, Jaroslaw. *Communist Local Government: A Study of Poland.* Athens, Ohio, 1975.

Polonsky, Antony. *Politics in Independent Poland, 1921–39.* Oxford, Eng., 1972.

Rachwald, Arthur R. *Poland Between the Superpowers: Security versus Economic Recovery.* Boulder, Colo., 1984.

Reddaway, William E. *The Cambridge History of Poland.* Cambridge, Eng., 1941.

Rousseau, Jean-Jacques. *The Government of Poland.* Indianapolis, Ind., 1985.

Ruane, Kevin. *The Polish Challenge.* New York, 1984.

Sanford, George. *Polish Communism in Crisis: The Politics of Reform and Reaction, 1980–81.* New York, 1983.

Schmitt, Bernadotte E. *Poland.* Berkeley, Calif., 1947.

Simon, Henri. *Poland, 1980–82.* Detroit, 1985.

Steven, Stewart. *The Poles.* New York, 1982.

Taras, Ray. *Poland: Socialist State, Rebellious Nation.* Boulder, Colo., 1988.

Vale, Michael. *Poland: The State of the Republic.* London, 1981.

Woodall, Jean. *Policy and Politics in Contemporary Poland.* New York, 1982.

Woods, William. *Poland: Eagle of the East.* New York, 1968.

OFFICIAL PUBLICATIONS

Narodowy spis Powszechny z dnia (Census of Poland). Warsaw, 1978.

Rocznik Statystyczny (Statistical Yearbook). Warsaw, 1988.

RUMANIA

BASIC FACT SHEET

OFFICIAL NAME: Republic of Rumania (Republica Rumania)

ABBREVIATION: RU

CAPITAL: Bucharest

HEAD OF STATE: President of the Republic Ion Iliescu (from 1989)

HEAD OF GOVERNMENT: Chairman of the Council of Ministers Petre Roman (from 1989)

NATURE OF GOVERNMENT: Socialist democracy

POPULATION: 23,153,475 (1989)

AREA: 237,500 sq. km. (91,699 sq. mi.)

MAJOR ETHNIC GROUPS: Rumanians, Hungarians, Germans

LANGUAGES: Rumanian, Hungarian

RELIGIONS: Rumanian Orthodox, Roman Catholic

UNIT OF CURRENCY: Leu

NATIONAL FLAG: Tricolor of blue, yellow and red vertical stripes of equal width, with the coat of arms in the center

NATIONAL EMBLEM: A red-gold oil derrick in the foreground against a background of rosy-pink mountain peaks and blue-green forested slopes. A rising sun spreads its rays over the upper portion of the oval shield. Sheaves of wheat on either side frame the device. The sheaves are tied at the base with ribbons of red, yellow and blue, the national colors. Imprinted on the ribbons in white letters is the name: Rumania. The entire emblem is topped by a red star.

NATIONAL ANTHEM: "Te Slavim Ruminie, Pamint Parintesc" ("Hail to You, Rumania, Land of Our Fathers")

NATIONAL HOLIDAYS: New Year's Day (January 1); Union Day (January 24); May Day (May 1); Independence Day (May 9); Liberation Day (August 23); Day of the Proclamation of the Republic (December 30)

NATIONAL CALENDAR: Gregorian

PHYSICAL QUALITY OF LIFE INDEX: 92 (on an ascending scale with 100 as the maximum)

DATE OF INDEPENDENCE: July 13, 1878

DATE OF CONSTITUTION: August 21, 1965

WEIGHTS & MEASURES: Metric

Note: The official spelling is Romania but Rumania is used throughout the encyclopedia in conformity with Facts On File style.

GEOGRAPHICAL FEATURES

Located in Eastern Europe, Rumania has a total land area of 237,500 sq. km. (91,699 sq. mi.) and extends 789 km. (490 mi.) east to west and 475 km. (295 mi.) north to south. It shares its total boundary length of 3,153 km. (1,959 mi.) with four countries: Soviet Union (1,329 km.; 826 mi.), Bulgaria (591 km.; 367 mi.), Yugoslavia (546 km.; 339 mi.) and Hungary (442 km.; 275 mi.). The Black Sea coastline extends 245 km. (152 mi.).

In 1878, when it gained full independence, Rumania was a much smaller country, containing only the provinces of Moldavia and Walachia, south of Bessarabia, and a portion of Dobruja. These boundaries remained unchanged until World War I. At the end of that war Rumania grew by 99,741 sq. km. (38,500 sq. mi.), ceded to it from the dismantled Austro-Hungarian Empire. The added territory included historic Transylvania, a strip along its western side and Bukovina. After the Bolshevik Revolution Rumania acquired Bessarabia from the Soviet Union and enlarged its holdings in Dobruja at Bulgaria's expense. All these gains were lost immediately before World War II, but following the postwar settlement, Transylvania and Dobruja were restored to it, but Bessarabia was lost to the Soviet Union. Rumania has no current border disputes.

The capital is Bucharest, in the region of Muntenia, on a plain on the Dambovita River about 80 km. (50 mi.) north of the Bulgarian border. Formerly the capital of Walachia, it was the seat of the Walachian rulers from the 14th century to 1861. The next largest city, Brasov, is only 17% of the size of Bucharest; there are 16 middle-level cities with populations between 100,000 and 300,000. In spite of their small size, many of the Rumanian cities have long histories. Cities on the Black Sea coast, including Constanta and Mangalia, were founded by the Greeks. Under Roman rule, towns such as Cluj (Napoca), Alba-Iulia (Apulum) and Turnu-Severin (Drubeta) became important military and trade centers. Many of the Roman towns developed from earlier Dacian settlements. As the Roman towns declined, their place was taken by new market towns such as Brasov, Sibiu and Bucharest.

Rumania's three topographical regions—mountains, plateaus and plains—are about the same size. All the mountains and uplands are part of the Carpathian system, which enters Rumania in the North from the Soviet

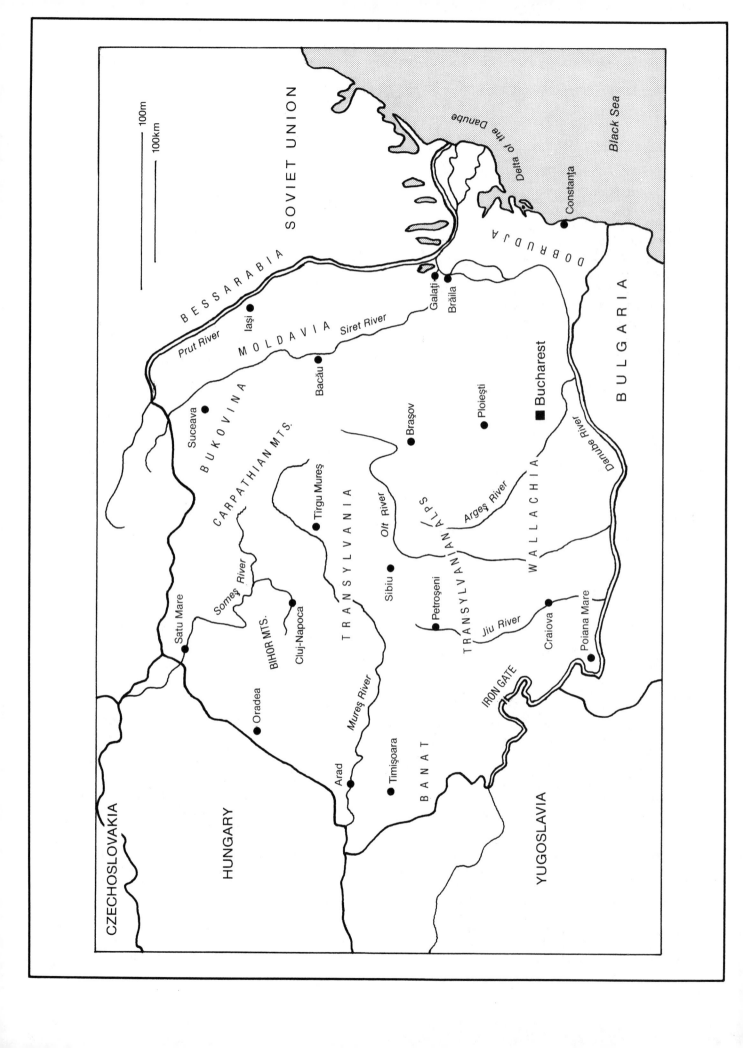

Union and curls in a semicircle around the country. The ranges in the East are known as the Moldavian Carpathians; the slightly higher southern ranges are known as the Transylvanian Alps; and the more scattered but generally lower ranges in the West are known as the Bihor Massif. Ranges in these mountains have peaks that rise to 2,286 m. (7,500 ft.), 2,438 m. (8,000 ft.) and 1,829 m. (6,000 ft.) in the East, South and West, respectively. The Carpathians are characterized by a number of summit passes and river valleys that make movements across them easier than is the case with other European mountains.

Enclosed by the Carpathian ranges is a series of sub-Carpathian hills and plateaus, such as the Moldavian Plateau, the Getic Plateau, the Transylvanian Plateau and the Dobruja Plateau. Moldavia constitutes about one-fourth of the country's land area and is the most extensively forested part of the country. Walachia, in the South, contains the southern part of the Transylvanian Alps—sometimes called the southern Carpathians—and the lowlands that extend between them and the Danube River. West to east, Walachia extends from the Iron Gate to Dobruja. Walachia is divided by the Olt River into Oltenia or Lesser Walachia in the West, and Muntenia or Greater Walachia in the East. Bucharest is approximately in the center of this region. In the West a smaller plains region extends from the Carpathians to the Hungarian border. Called Tisa Plain (Cimpia Tisei), it constitutes the eastern edge of the Great Alfold, a plain extending over most of eastern Hungary. Parts of the Tisa Plain are swampy, but in the Walachian Plain the depressions usually are filled by lakes. There is a third area of flatland—the Danube delta, an area of marshes, sandbanks and floating reed islands.

All of Rumania's rivers and streams drain to the Black Sea and, with the exception of a few minor streams, all join the Danube. Those flowing southward and southeastward from the Transylvanian Alps drain to the Danube directly; those flowing northward and eastward from Moldavia and Bukovina reach the Danube by way of the Prut River. Most of the Transylvanian streams draining to the north and west flow into the Tisza River, which also joins the Danube in Yugoslavia. Dobruja contains most of the Danube River delta marshland. Before reaching the Black Sea the river turns northward, skirts the Dobruja tableland and then turns east again, forming a border with the Soviet Union for some 161 km. (100 mi.). On reaching the delta, the Danube divides into three major channels. Almost three-quarters of the river's flow discharges through the northern channel, but the narrower and deeper central channel (the Sulina Channel) is used for shipping. Two problems reduce the usefulness of the Danube to Rumania: the southerly location of the major length of the river, and a tendency to flooding and swampiness along the banks.

The largest tributaries of the Danube flowing from the North are the Prut, the Olt and the Siret. The Prut is the only one used for transportation, being navigable for about 322 km. (200 mi.) above its confluence with the Danube. The Siret and its tributaries are used mainly for logging, but both the Siret and the Olt are used extensively for hydroelectric projects. A number of rivers flow from the southern Carpathians across the Walachian Plain to join the Danube. The most important are the Jiu, the Arges and the Ialomita. These rivers are used mostly for irrigation. The Mures and the Somes, tributaries of the Tisza, are used for rafting timber from the mountains.

Rumania has over 2,500 lakes, but most are small and occupy only about 1% of the surface area. The largest lakes are along the Black Sea coast and the Danube.

CLIMATE & WEATHER

Rumania has a continental climate characterized by cold winters and hot summers. Weather and rainfall result from the high-pressure systems that predominate over the European Soviet Union and North-Central Asia. Only infrequently and for short spells does Mediterranean weather prevail in the area. Winters are long and cold, with frequent fog and snow. Although summers are hot, they tend to be sunny, with comfortable humidity. This is because the Carpathians confine the humid air masses from the Atlantic to the western parts of the country. The mountains also prevent the movement into Transylvania and the western regions of both hot, dry air masses in the summer from the south and cold, dry air masses from the east in the winter. Consequently, precipitation is much higher, on average, in the Transylvanian Plateau and on the mountains than on the plateaus and plains to the east and south of the Carpathians. The mountainous areas receive more than 1,270 mm. (50 in.) annually, and a record of 2,413 mm. (95 in.) was set in 1941. The countrywide precipitation averages 711 mm. (28 in.). Dobruja, along the lower Danube and adjacent Black Sea coast, averages the least, followed by the lowlands of Moldavia and southernmost Walachia, which usually receive less than 508 mm. (20 in.). The remaining lowlands and the Transylvanian Plateau average between 508 and 762 mm. (20 and 30 in.), with Bucharest receiving 584 mm. (23 in.). In the agricultural regions the heaviest precipitation, most of it from thunderstorms, occurs during the summer growing season. Foothills with all exposures also get more than the country average. Western exposures benefit from the generally eastward movement of the weather systems, while southern and eastern slopes benefit from the clockwise circulation around the high-pressure systems characteristic of the continental climate.

The Carpathian barrier also affects the distribution of temperatures, moderating the continental climate in the western regions. The Transylvanian Plateau rarely experiences the extremes of heat that occur on the Walachian Plain. Bucharest, inland on the southern lowland, is one of the warmest places in summer and has one of the widest variations between the average temperatures of the extreme hot and cold seasons. Its average January temperature is about 27°F; in July it is 73°F. In the eastern lowlands and along the Black Sea the moderating effect of sea winds makes for slightly warmer winters, but the summer temperatures are about the same as in Bucharest. However, there are no places where summer temperatures are oppressively high or winter temperatures intolerably low.

As in many other areas of southeastern Europe, weather conditions are modified by local winds. In winter the eastern part of Rumania is affected by the *crivat*, an easterly wind, which brings low temperatures and causes snowdrifts. The *austru* brings dry air from the Mediterranean to the Southwest in summer, representing the only major Mediterranean influence on the climate. In Transylvania, winter winds from the Atlantic modify the cold, causing fog and thaws, while foehnlike winds from the mountains raise temperatures in Transylvania and the foothills of the southern Carpathians in early spring.

POPULATION

The population of Rumania in 1989 was estimated at 23,153,475, based on the last official census, in 1977, when the population was 21,599,910. Rumania ranks 37th in the world in population and 79th in land area. The population is expected to reach 23,206,000 by 1990 and 25,196,000 by 2000.

Rumania is the second most populous country in the Balkans after Yugoslavia. Postwar demographic statistics reveal a drop in annual growth rates since the turn of the century. In 1930 live births were 34.1 and deaths 19.3 per 1,000, giving a natural rate of increase of 14.8 per 1,000. By 1947 the birth rate had dropped to 23.4 and the death rate had risen to 22 per 1,000, giving a rate of natural increase of only 1.4 per 1,000, the lowest ever recorded in the country. As the population recovered from the effects of World War II, Rumania experienced a baby boom; the birth rate rose again and the death rate dropped sharply, reaching a peak in 1955 when the birth rate was 25.6 and the death rate 9.7 per 1,000, yielding a rate of natural increase of 15.9 per 1,000. In early 1960s the birth rate declined steeply but the death rate declined only slightly. By then, abortion had become widely prevalent. Alarmed by the potential economic consequences of a declining population, the government passed a law in 1966 making abortions and contraceptive devices difficult to obtain, except on legitimate health grounds. This had the effect of raising the birth rate once again, by 1967, to 27.4 per 1,000 and the rate of natural increase to 18.1 per 1,000, the highest ever recorded in Rumania. By 1985 the rates had fairly stabilized, with a birth rate of 15.8 per 1,000, a death rate of 10.9 per 1,000 and a rate of natural increase of 4.9 per 1,000.

Population growth rates have differed widely among the regions and ethnic groups. In general the rate of natural growth increases from west to east across the country. The Hungarian and German populations in Banat Province, for example, have for many years limited their families to one or two children, even in rural areas. On the other hand, birth rates remain high in the predominantly agricultural regions of the Northeast, such as in northern Moldavia. Traditionally, Bucharest had a high rate of natural increase; it no longer does.

The distribution of population is very uneven. Population is most dense in the central portion of Walachia, centering on and west of Bucharest and Ploiesti and along the Siret River in Moldavia. Southwestern Walachia and central and northwestern Transylvania also are more densely settled than the rest of the country. The area around Dobruja, lands of high elevation, and marshlands along the lower Danube are the most sparsely settled areas. However, regions in the Carpathian Mountains support a denser population than comparable areas in the Balkans. The Rumanians are essentially a mountain people, and at one time, under Turkish rule, population densities were much higher in the hilly areas of Walachia than in the plains. The Carpathians are not barren or waterless, as are many mountain areas in Greece or Yugoslavia, and the Carpathian foothills are well watered.

The growth of urban population is a recent phenomenon, and it has not reached the same proportions it has in most Western countries. At the time of the 1899 census, the urban population was 18.4%, and it remained at the same level in 1912. By the end of World War II the percentage had grown by only 3%. The real spurt in urban growth took place between 1945 and 1956, the urban population growing by 2 million to reach 31.3%. More than half of this increase was accounted for by the movement of rural workers into the cities in search of work. Between 1956 and 1966 the rate of growth slowed somewhat, and by the latter year 38.2% of all Rumanians lived in cities. The urban share continued to grow in the next 20 years, crossing the 50% mark in the mid-1980s. Even this figure is low by Western standards as well as in comparison with other Communist countries, such as Poland. The proportion of urban population varies considerably from one part of the country to another. In the predominantly agricultural regions of the Walachian Plain and Moldavia, the rural population still greatly outnumbers the urban. In contrast, the industrialized *judete* of Hunedoara and Brasov show a greater degree of urbanization. The urban configuration also is very uneven. Rumania is predominantly a country of small towns and villages, with Bucharest standing out head and shoulders above all cities in size and importance, accounting for 17% of the urban population. The share of all other cities put together was only 34% in 1985. However, the share of Bucharest declined between 1960 and 1985 from 22% to 17%.

Since World War II several new towns have been built, mainly as industrial centers. Most of them are in Transylvania and the West, with a few in the oil region northwest of Ploiesti. They form the nuclei of considerable potential urban population growth. One of the largest of the new towns is Gheorghe Gheorghiu-Dej, which in a few years rose from a small village to a major town.

Immigration and emigration have played a minor part in demographics. The impact of emigration was strongest in the years immediately following World War II, when Rumania lost between 300,000 and 400,000 persons in various resettlement and population exchange movements. The largest emigration has involved Jews going to Israel. Jews accounted for a major share of all emigration until the late 1960s.

ETHNIC COMPOSITION

Rumania includes elements of virtually every ethnic group in Central and Eastern Europe, but Rumanians, who constitute 88% of the population, are so dominant as to give the country a homogeneous character. The largest minorities are Magyars (Hungarians) and Germans. All other ethnic groups—Serbs, Croats, Slovenes, Ukrainians, Russians, Czechs, Slovaks, Turks, Tatars, Bulgarians, Jews and Gypsies—together make up less than 2% of the population.

The Constitution of 1965 guarantees equal rights to all citizens regardless of nationality or race and bans, under legal penalties, discrimination and instigation of racial or national animosities. National minorities enjoy free use of their mother tongue in schools and the communications media.

The origin of the Rumanians is the subject of two differing interpretations. They are believed to be related to the Vlachs, a pastoral people speaking a language related to Latin and who are found in the mountainous regions of northern Greece and southern Yugoslavia.

According to the Rumanian interpretation, Rumanians are descendants of the Dacians, who inhabited the region before the Christian era. The Dacians were conquered by the Roman legions under Trajan in A.D. 106 and became romanized during 165 years of Roman rule. When Emperor Aurelian abandoned Dacia in 271 in the face of Gothic invasions, the romanized Dacians sought refuge in the rugged Carpathians, where they preserved their language until the 10th century, when they returned to the plains.

The second interpretation, developed by Hungarian historians, denies that the Dacians ever returned to Transylvania and the other regions that today make up Rumania. This theory holds that after the Dacians left in the third century, the region was not settled by any group until the 10th century, when the Magyars moved in from the west.

Hungarians constitute the largest minority, accounting for 7.8% of the population in 1987 compared to 8.4% in 1970. They form the majority population in parts of Transylvania and in pockets along the Hungarian border and a significant minority in the rest of Transylvania and the Banat region. From 1952 to 1968 the areas with Hungarian concentration in eastern Transylvania were designated as an autonomous region, the Mures-Magyar Autonomous Region. The majority of the Hungarians live in rural areas, but several Transylvanian cities, including Cluj, Oradea, Baia-Mare and Tirgu-Mures, have a high percentage of Hungarians. Hungarians first moved into the region in the ninth century, and their presence increased during the eight centuries of Hungarian rule over Transylvania. One interesting segment of Hungarians is known by the name of Szeklers or Szekelys, who were socially and politically distinct from the Magyars during the Middle Ages but who are considered culturally more purely Magyar than most Hungarians.

The German population numbers only half of what it was before World War II and has been steadily reduced since 1945 through repatriation to West Germany. It is

divided into the Saxons and the Swabians. The Saxons settled in the Transylvanian borderlands in the 12th century and built such cities as Sibiu, Brasov and Sighisoara. They formed the majority of the population in a small area. The Swabians settled in Banat in the 18th century to work the lands recently vacated by the Turks. Most Swabians are peasants farming the rich plain around Timisoara.

The Jews are listed in official documents as an ethnic group or nationality rather than as members of a religion. The influx of Jews took place in the first half of the 19th century, when large numbers left the unsettled conditions of Poland and Russia to seek new opportunities in prospering Moldavia and later Walachia. A smaller number of Jews from various parts of Austria-Hungary settled in Transylvania at about the same time. By 1990 Jews constituted more than half of the urban population. Since then their numbers have been decimated by deportations and exterminations under anti-Semitic rulers and emigrations to Israel. As late as 1972 they were estimated to number over 100,000, but their numbers have shrunk considerably since then. About one-fourth of them live in Bucharest.

The principal irritant in interethnic relations is the Hungarian claim over Transylvania. As the former rulers of the region, Hungarians resent the loss of their superior economic and social positions and the constant erosion of their cultural identity. However, the Rumanian Communist Party, which before the war had a high percentage of ethnic minorities, regards itself as the historic protector of minority rights. In 1968 people's councils were established in Hungarian, German and other minority communities to speak for their needs in the Socialist Unity Front. Germans have preserved better relations with the Rumanians and they

PRINCIPAL POPULATION CENTERS
(Est. Population, 1986)

Bucharest, the		Arad	187,744
capital	1,989,823	Bacau	179,877
Brasov	351,493	Sibiu	177,511
Constanta	327,676	Tirgu Mures	158,998
Timisoara	325,272	Pitesti	157,190
Iasi	313,060	Baia Mare	139,704
Cluj-Napoca	310,017	Buzau	136,080
Galati	295,372	Satu Mare	130,082
Craiova	281,044	Piatra-Neamt	109,393
Braila	235,620	Botosani	108,775
Ploiesti	234,886	Resita	105,914
Oradea	213,846		

POPULATION GROWTH, 1899–1966 (000)

Date	Total	Males	Females
1899	5,957	3,027	2,930
1912	7,235	3,656	3,759
1930	18,057	8,887	9,170
1941	16,126	7,989	8,138
1948	15,873	7,672	8,201
1956	17,489	8,503	8,986
1966	19,103	9,351	9,752
1977	21,559	10,629	10,930

Demographic Indicators, 1988

Population: 23,153,475 (1089)
Year of last census: 1977; World rank: 37
Sex ratio: males, 49.34; females, 50.66
Population trends (million)

1930: 14.141	1960: 18.407	1990: 23.206
1940: 15.907	1970: 20.799	2000: 24.196
1950: 16.311	1980: 22.201	

Population doubling time in years at current rate: 80
Hypothetical size of stationary population (million): 28
Assumed year of reaching net reproduction rate of 1: 2030
Age profile (%)

0–15: 24.6	30–44: 19.6	60–74: 10.7
15–29: 22.6	45–59: 18.8	Over 75: 3.7

Median age (years): 32.5
Density per sq. km. (per sq. mi.) 96.9 (251.0)
Annual growth rate

1950–55: 1.39	1975–80: 0.88	1995–2000: 0.69
1960–65: 0.67	1980–85: 0.76	2000–2005: 0.66
1965–70: 1.35	1985–90: 0.71	2010–15: 0.50
1970–75: 0.85	1990–95: 0.71	2020–25: 0.49

Vital statistics
  Crude birth rate, 1/1,000: 15.8
  Crude death rate, 1/1,000: 10.9
  Change in birth rate: −4.7 (1965–84)
  Change in death rate: 20.9 (1965–84)
  Dependency, total: 53.2
  Infant mortality rate, 1/1,000: 22
  Child (0–4 years) mortality rate, 1/1,000: 1
  Maternal mortality rate, 1/100,000: 152
  Natural increase, 1/1,000: 4.9
  Total fertility rate: 2.1
  General fertility rate: 71
  Gross reproduction rate: 1.15
  Marriage rate, 1/1,000: 7.1
  Divorce rate, 1/1,000: 1.4
  Life expectancy, males (years): 67.0
  Life expectancy, females (years): 72.6
  Average household size: 3.1
Youth
  Youth population 15–24 (000): 3,903
  Youth population in 2000 (000): 3,847
Women
  Of childbearing age 15–49 (000): 5,654
  Child-woman ratio (children per 000 women 15–49): 347
  % women using contraceptives: 58
  Rate of abortions per 100 live births: 99
Urban
  Urban population (000): 14,055
  % urban: 1965, 38; 1987, 49
  Annual urban growth rate (%) 1965–80 3.0; 1980–87: 0.3
  % urban population in largest city: 17
  % urban population in cities over 500,000: 17
  Number of cities over 500,000: 1
  Annual rural growth rate: −1.1

have kept aloof from Hungarian irredentism in Transylvania. However, Germans make few efforts to integrate themselves into the national society.

There are no foreign communities as such in Rumania.

LANGUAGES

The national language is Rumanian, a Romance language derived from Latin. Latin word elements make up 85% to 90% of the modern Rumanian vocabulary, and grammar and syntax are purely Romance. Rumanian has been influenced by contacts with other languages, such as Albanian, Slavonic, Hungarian, Greek and Turkish. Of the loanwords, Slavonic are the most numerous. Frequently parallel words of Latin and Slavic derivation exist for a single object or concept and may be used interchangeably. Hungarian is the principal minority language.

RELIGIONS

Tradition holds that Christianity was introduced into Rumania by the Apostle Andrew, and by the beginning of the third century it had established itself firmly. Rumanians were among the martyrs of the persecutions under Emperor Diocletian. At first the liturgy was in Latin, but the introduction of a Slavic liturgy by Methodius and Constantine in Bulgaria influenced the church and drew it into the orbit of the Ecumenical Patriarchate at Constantinople. Old Church Slavonic remained the liturgical language of the Orthodox Church until the late 16th century, when it was replaced by Rumanian. During the period of Turkish rule in Waldachia and Moldavia and of Hungarian rule in Transylvania the Orthodox Church helped to maintain national unity and cultural identity. Under the Turks the church was able to act as a representative of the nation. However, the church was compelled by the Austro-Hungarian rulers in Transylvania to become Uniate under Roman authority while retaining Orthodox liturgy and ritual. Calvinism also was introduced into Transylvania during this period. The dominance of the Orthodox Church was restored only after the advent of the Communist regime, which from 1946 to 1950 forced the Uniates to merge with the Rumanian Orthodox Church and disavow allegiance to the pope.

The Rumanian Orthodox Church became autocephalous in 1865 and was recognized as such by Constantinople in 1885. The revised statutes of the church issued in 1949 differ little from those in effect before that date. Headed by a patriarch, the church consists of five metropolitanates divided into 12 dioceses and 106 deaneries with 8,185 parishes, 2,847 annexes and 11,722 places of worship served by 8,600 priests. Monastic foundations number 114, of which 57 are monasteries (30 for men and 27 for women) and 20 monastic annexes. Annually, ordinations to the priesthood exceed 300 and consecrations of new sanctuaries average over 200. The educational level of the clergy is exceptionally high. There are two theological institutes, at Bucharest and Sibiu, and a seminary at Cluj.

Since 1965 the Rumanian Orthodox Church has been virtually free of persecution. It also exhibits considerable internal vitality, with its seminaries having three times as many candidates as there are clerical vacancies. Participation of the faithful in reception of sacraments and in regular public worship is significantly higher than in many Western countries. Usually there are massive crowds at Easter in most churches. Bibles in Rumanian are locally printed. The educated youth and the working classes are not as alienated from the church as they are in many Western countries. The church administers its own lands, property, presses and factories and also publishes nine religious journals and a large number of books each year.

Officially all present-day Catholics are of the Latin rite only, and in size of membership the Roman Catholics constitute the largest religious minority. Although there are several thousand Moldavian and German Catholics dispersed throughout southern Transylvania and in Bucharest, the majority of Rumanian Catholics belong to the Hungarian minority and live in Transylvania. The well-organized church and its institutions have been a natural vehicle for the promotion of Hungarian interests and the preservation of Hungarian cultural traditions. Catholic schools, which were independent of government control until 1948, most often used Hungarian or German as the medium of instruction. The Concordat of 1927 between the Holy See and the Rumanian state defined the legal position of the church in Rumania until the Communist takeover. It gave the Roman Catholic Church full equality with the Rumanian Orthodox Church and granted the former sole control over all its institutions. It was free from state administrative control and did not receive any financial support from the state. The concordat was abrogated in 1948. Catholic bishops who refused to recognize the supremacy of the state over church affairs as expressed in the General Regulations for Church Affairs of 1948 were imprisoned or otherwise prevented from exercising their administrative or clerical functions. Since 1948 the Roman Catholic Church has had no legal recognition as a religious denomination. All church schools, hospitals and charitable institutions were taken over by the state, and all other church assets were confiscated. All but three monasteries and two convents were disbanded, and even these were not permitted to accept new novices. The church was reduced from six to two dioceses: Alba-Iulia and Bucharest. Since the church does not receive a state subsidy and is forbidden to seek contributions, most clergy support themselves by working at lay jobs. Church buildings have been deteriorating for lack of maintenance, and there are marked differences in appearance between the ill-kept Catholic churches and the well-maintained Orthodox churches.

In 1969 the government began to adopt a more conciliatory policy toward the Catholic Church. The archbishop of Alba-Iulia, the head of the church in Rumania and other clergy were released from prison. Since then, the Catholic Church has enjoyed considerably more freedom of worship. State funds have been allocated for restoration of the historic cathedral at Alba-Iulia.

As a result of its isolation, Roman Catholicism in Rumania tends to be introverted, concentrating its energies on sheer survival. The only impact of Vatican II has been in the language of the liturgy and in a new edition of the missal, in which all feasts of Hungarian saints have been removed. The only Catholic organization is the Status of Transylvania, a pastoral council of laymen and clergy. There are two Catholic seminaries as well as a minor church-run school at Cluj, with a small enrollment. Franciscans, the only religious order permitted, live in a convent at Csiksomlyo, a famous lay pilgrimage center.

The government promoted creation of a national Catholic Church in 1951. It recognizes the pope as the supreme authority on matters of faith, morals and dogma but rejects any organizational connection with the Holy See while recognizing the supremacy of the state over church affairs.

The forced merger of the Byzantine-rite Uniate Catholic Church was accomplished without a major struggle. It was engineered by a synod convened in 1948 at Cluj under government auspices and attended by only 36 of the 1,818 Uniate priests, who ignored the bishop's excommunication. However, a vast number of the faithful still consider themselves attached to Rome, and they are served by several hundred priests.

Protestantism also is closely identified with the German and Hungarian minorities. Numbering over 1.2 million, Protestants are divided into Calvinist, Lutheran, Baptist, Seventh-Day Adentist, Evangelical and Pentecostal churches.

The largest Protestant denomination is the Reformed (Calvinist) Church, with a membership of over 750,000, almost entirely Hungarian. Its center is at Cluj, a Calvinist stronghold since the Reformation. Next in size are the Lutherans, with an estimated membership of 250,000, almost entirely German. Introduced in 1519, Lutheranism spread rapidly but suffered persecution under the Austro-Hungarian rulers. It is represented by the Evangelical Church of the Augsburg Confession, headed by a bishop at Sibiu, and the Evangelical Synodal Presbyteral Church of the Augsburg Confession, headed by a bishop at Cluj. The number of Lutherans in the country has been halved since 1945 through the loss of northern Bukovina to the Soviet Union and through the emigration of Saxons to West Germany in the 1940s. The Baptist, Seventh-Day Adventist and Pentecostal churches were united by government decree in 1950 into the Federation of Protestant Cults. The first Baptist community was established in Bucharest in 1856 among the German community and did not gain its first Rumanian adherents until the 20th century. The church was bitterly persecuted by the Nazis between 1930 and 1945 and by the Communists after 1947. Adventists have been at work in the country since 1911 and have built up a sizable community organized into four conferences. Pentecostals began in 1922, but they remain numerically small. Protestant churches were permitted active association with the World Council of Churches in 1961.

The Jesus Movement of the 1970s resulted in the conversion of a large number of Gypsies. There also are a few hundred Jewish Christians.

Of the non-Christian religions, only Islam, Judaism and Unitarianism are significant. Islam is the religion of the Tatars and Turks in Dobruja. Mosques, a legacy of the Turkish era, are found throughout the region. The seat of the grand mufti, the Muslim religious head, is at Constanta. Once an important ethnic and religious minority, the Jewish community has shrunk since the 1930s as a result of territorial losses, extermination during World War II and emigration. Since most of the rabbis have emigrated, many remaining congregations are directed by laymen. The only rabbinical school was closed in the 1950s. The legally recognized representative body of the Jews is the Federation of Jewish Communities, headed by a chief rabbi.

The Unitarians were established in Transylvania under the protection of the Hungarian nobility, and the church draws most of its members from the Hungarian community. The seat of the church is at Cluj, which also is the location of its seminary.

Before 1948 the Rumanian Orthodox Church was closely identified with the state. In fact, in 1930 the Orthodox patriarch also was the prime minister. This close association ceased to exist after 1945, but it has not been totally severed. The Rumanian Constitution has been revised four times, but the provisions regarding freedom of worship have not been materially altered. Article 30 states that everyone is free to hold or not to hold a religious belief. Freedom of conscience and worship are guaranteed. The internal organization and functioning of religious groups are unhampered by the state, but their finances are regulated by law. Schools are separated from churches, which may run only seminaries.

The state office of religious affairs, the Department of Cults, maintains surveillance over the churches, which is more strict in the case of the Catholic Church than it is over others. The government pays one-third of the salaries of the clergy and the entire salaries of seminary teachers, including those of Catholic seminaries. Seminarians are not subject to military service. Sunday schools operate freely within church buildings.

Relations between church and state have clearly improved since 1965, when Nicolae Ceausescu came to power as general secretary of the Communist Party. In 1974 the courts declared illegal a law prohibiting the reception or distribution of imported Bibles and religious literature. However, the churches still are subject to numerous limitations. For example, under a 1975 law all cultural and artistic treasures in churches were declared to be state property.

HISTORICAL BACKGROUND

Rumania enters history as a region occupied by a Thracian tribe known as the Dacians. By the middle of the first century there was a Dacian state ruled by kings. In their effort to expand their kingdom to the north and west and, most aggressively, to the south, the Dacians came into conflict with the Romans who, during the same period, were attempting to extend their control over the Balkans and to push the northern border of their empire to the natural barrier formed by the Danube. In a series of campaigns between 101 and 106, Emperor Trajan succeeded in conquering the areas known later as Banat, Oltenia and Walachia and in finally reducing the Dacian stronghold in Transylvania. After consolidating his conquests, Trajan fortified the area, and he stationed Roman legions in garrisons at strategic points. Dacia developed rapidly under Roman rule into a prosperous province; colonists were brought in, agriculture and mineral resources were developed and trade flourished. However, by the third century the province was ravaged by periodic barbarian invasions, forcing Emperor Aurelian to abandon Dacia, leaving

two permanent legacies of Roman rule, Christianity and the Latin language.

The 10 centuries after the withdrawal of the Romans are shrouded in mystery. Little is known of the fate of the Daco-Romans during this period. When the region reemerged into recorded history, it was occupied by a Latin-speaking people known as Vlachs. Although historical records are lacking, it is believed that these Vlachs were descendants of the earlier Daco-Romans who had fled for refuge into the Carpathian Mountains to escape the barbarian invaders.

As the invasions diminished, the Vlachs gradually moved farther into the foothills and plains of the Danube Basin and fused with the local population. Two distinct groups eventually emerged, one settling in modern-day Walachia and the other farther to the east and north, in Moldavia. By the 13th and 14th centuries these two groups formed the semi-independent principalities of Walachia and Moldavia.

By this time the Turks had begun their sweep through southeastern Europe and, in the 15th century, both Walachia and Moldavia were forced to accept Turkish suzerainty. However, unlike other areas under Turkish rule, these principalities remained under the control of native princes, who maintained their position by paying a substantial annual tribute to the Turks. The next three centuries were marked by oppression and misrule both by the Turks and the native nobles and princes, reducing the peasantry to complete serfdom. Even the appearance of outstanding leaders such as Michael the Brave of Walachia (1593–1601) and Stephen the Great of Moldavia (1457–1504) did not redeem the harshness and barrenness of this period.

At the beginning of the 18th century, the oppressiveness of Ottoman rule became more intense as the Turks instituted a system of direct collection of tribute through Greek merchants known as Phanariots. Since the Phanariots were interested only in the collection of the maximum tribute in the shortest possible time, conditions became intolerable and led to massive resistance on the one hand and heavy migration of the peasantry to neighboring areas, particularly Transylvania. Transylvania, peopled by the Asian Magyars, who had overrun the region in the ninth century, was then under Hungarian rule. The Rumanian immigrants were treated at first as serfs, and their social and economic statuses were not much better than under the Turks. The Rumanians' Orthodox faith was not recognized, and to gain equality and recognition, many of them gradually abandoned their Eastern Orthodox creed and became Uniates by accepting papal authority in 1698. By this act the Rumanians won many concessions; they began to share in the political life of the province, and education became more widespread. The Uniate Church became an important medium by which Rumanian national identity was fostered in the struggle against foreign assimilation. Young clerics sent to Rome for training helped Rumanians to discover their Roman ancestry and the Latin connection. It led in the late 18th century to a Latinist movement that created the basis for a broad development of Rumanian culture. The Cyrillic alphabet was replaced with Latin, and the first dictionary and grammar in the Rumanian language were published. Meanwhile, in Walachia and Moldavia, French influences introduced initially by the Phanariot princes helped to open the country to Western ideas. Rumanian students sent to France to study in French universities formed, on their return, the nucleus of an intellectual class bent on gallicizing the country.

The confluence of these various trends was the first revolt against the Turks and the Phanariots in 1821 and was led by Tudor Vladimirescu, a former officer in the Russian Army. Although the outbreak was suppressed, it prompted the Turks to abolish the Phanariot regime and to restore Rumanian princes as rulers in the Danubian principalities. After the Russo-Turkish War of 1826–28 Russian forces occupied both Walachia and Moldavia to ensure payment of a large war indemnity by the Turks. Under the ensuing six-year enlightened and competent rule of the Russian governor, Count Pavel Kiselev, the foundations were laid for a new Rumanian state. In both provinces constitutional assemblies were organized, an administrative system was established on the French model, the foundations of an educational system were laid and a national militia was created. After the Russians left, power was restored to the native princes, but the nationalist movement continued to grow and liberal ideas took firm root. The Crimean War provided the opportunity for the first step toward independence. The Congress of Paris of 1858, which ended that war, also created the autonomous United Principalities of Walachia and Moldavia in 1859. Although still subject to Ottoman authority, the United Principalities elected their own ruler, Alexander Cuza. He fused the two principalities under a single administration, with Bucharest as the national capital. Domestic reforms were undertaken and included the emancipation of the serfs in 1864, land reforms, adoption of free and compulsory education, and the institution of a new legal system based on French civil and penal codes. Political parties on the Western pattern also began to take shape.

Although Cuza's reforms were bold and progressive, his methods were harsh and unpopular, and as a result he was forced to abdicate in 1866. He was succeeded as ruler by a German prince, Charles of Hohenzollern-Sigmaringen, who reigned from 1866 to 1914. He extended the reforms initiated by Cuza, gave the country its first Constitution, built the country's first railroad and modernized the army. In 1878 the country's full independence was recognized by the Treaty of Berlin, and in 1881 the Kingdom of Rumania was formally proclaimed with the crowning of Prince Charles in Bucharest as Carol I.

The period from 1878 to 1918 was marked by considerable economic progress, particularly the development of railroads and petroleum resources. At the same time there were some undesirable developments in the political and social fields. The liberal provisions of the Constitution of 1866 were negated by the landed aristocracy, who concentrated much of the power in their own hands. The second problem was the increasing size and economic power of the Jews. Forbidden to own land and subject to many other restrictions, the Jews had settled in urban areas, engaged successfully in commercial activities and gained economic influence out of proportion to their numerical strength. In the rural areas as moneylenders, they became a symbol of oppression. The 1907 peasant revolt was directed as much against them as against the native aristocracy.

After the death of King Carol in 1914 and the accession of his nephew Ferdinand to the throne, Rumania entered World War I on the Allied side in 1916. By December 1917, however, Rumania was forced to conclude an armistice after Austro-German forces on the west and Bulgarians and Turks on the south advanced into Rumania and captured Bucharest and most of Rumania except Moldavia. By the Treaty of Bucharest of 1918, Rumanians ceded Dobruja to Bulgaria and the Carpathian Mountains passes to Austria-Hungary. However, before the armistice was ratified, the ultimate defeat of the Central Powers became apparent, and the Rumanian army, which had not yet been demobilized, reentered the war, liberated Bucharest and occupied much of Bessarabia and Transylvania. After the war both these territories, along with Bukovina, were incorporated into the kingdom, and their incorporation was confirmed by treaties in 1919 and 1920.

Postwar Rumania, often called Greater Rumania because it was double the size of prewar Rumania, witnessed unprecedented political instability. The immediate postwar years were dominated by the Liberal Party, which gave way in 1928 to the National Peasant Party. In the previous year, King Ferdinand had died. Ferdinand's son Carol was excluded from the succession because of his earlier renunciation of all claims to the throne to accept exile with his Jewish mistress, Magda Lupescu. A regency was therefore appointed to rule in the name of Carol's youngest son, Michael. Dissatisfaction with the regency led to Carol's return from exile and his assumption of the crown in late 1930. He soon emerged, in the unstable political conditions of the time, as a royal dictator. His assumption of power was initially aided by the rise of a fanatical fascist and anti-Semitic group known as the Iron Guard (Garda de Fier), led by a Hitler-like personality, Corneliu Codreanu. After the 1937 elections, in which the Iron Guard won resounding victories, Carol turned against them and promulgated a new Constitution, abolishing all political parties, and instituted personal dictatorship. This action was followed by the suppression of the Iron Guard, whose leader, Codreanu, was shot.

As Hitler gained ascendancy in Europe in 1939, Rumania concluded a Treaty of Economic Collaboration with Germany and placed its extensive oil resources at the disposal of the Axis powers. Within months of the outbreak of the war, Rumania had lost all its gains in World War I: Dobruja was seized by Bulgaria, Transylvania by Hungary and Bessarabia by the Soviet Union. The crisis caused by the territorial losses forced Carol to appoint a pro-German cabinet infiltrated with members of the Iron Guard. A national protest against the king culminated in his abdication in favor of his son Michael. The new government led by Gen. Ion Antonescu joined the Anti-Comintern Pact on November 23, 1940.

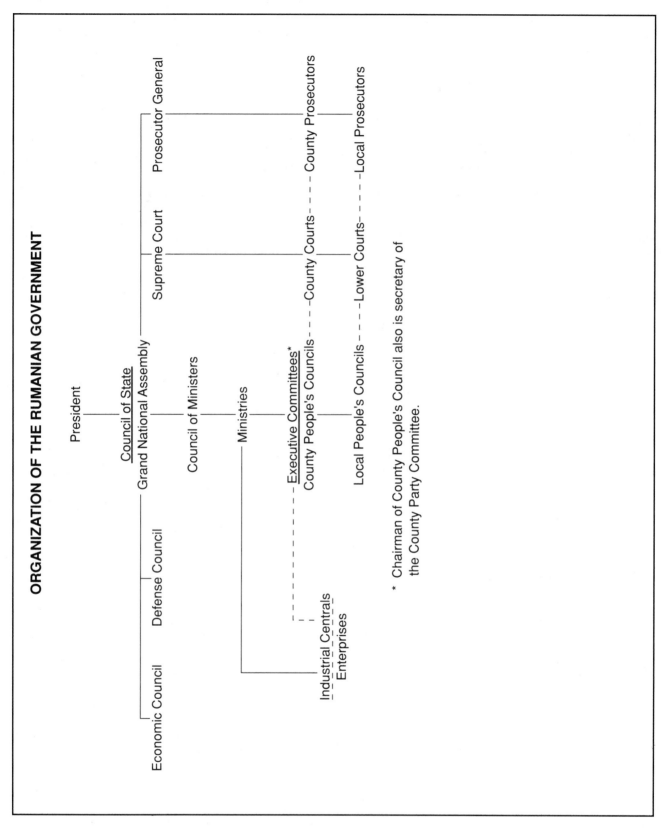

ORGANIZATION OF THE RUMANIAN GOVERNMENT

President

Council of State
Grand National Assembly

Defense Council

Economic Council

Council of Ministers

Supreme Court

Prosecutor General

County Courts- - - County Prosecutors

Lower Courts- - - Local Prosecutors

Ministries

Industrial Centrals
Enterprises

Executive Committees*
County People's Councils

Local People's Councils

* Chairman of County People's Council also is secretary of
the County Party Committee.

In January 1941 members of the Iron Guard, attempting to seize full control of the government, initiated a campaign of terror that was suppressed with much bloodshed by the army. With the continued support of the Germans, Antonescu dissolved the Iron Guard and formed an almost exclusively military dictatorship. Rumania then entered the war against the Soviet Union and incurred heavy losses in the prolonged fighting on the Eastern Front. After the German defeat at Stalingrad, the Soviets swept back the Axis forces and by mid-1944 were on the outskirts of Bucharest. On August 23, 1944, King Michael overthrew the regime of Antonescu, halted all fighting and installed a new government. Under the terms of the armistice that followed, Rumania reentered the war on the side of the Allies, agreed to reparations and accepted Allied occupation of the country until a peace treaty was signed.

The first government set up after the armistice was headed by Nicolae Radescu, but it included the National Democratic Front, a Communist front organization. Bowing to Soviet pressure, Radescu yielded power to Petru Groza, leader of the Plowmen's Front and a long-time Communist sympathizer. This event marked the transition to the takeover of the country by the Communist Party led by Gheorghe Gheorghiu-Dej.

For postwar history, see Chronology.

CONSTITUTION & GOVERNMENT

Throughout its history, Rumania has never known parliamentary democratic government, yet it was the intention of the framers of its first Constitution, in 1866, to establish one. Although modeled on the Belgian Constitution, it gave the right to vote only to propertyholders. In 1923 the Liberal Party introduced a new Constitution, again establishing a parliamentary democracy and a constitutional monarchy. This Constitution was suspended in 1938 by King Carol, who instituted a royal dictatorship. It was restored in 1944 on the eve of the Communist takeover.

Since then Rumania has had three constitutions: in 1948, in 1952 and in 1965. In many ways similar to the initial constitutions of other Eastern bloc countries, the Constitution of 1948 designated Rumania as a "people's republic." It marked the first stage of the transition from capitalism to socialism and created the three basic governmental organs that have survived in the succeeding constitutions: the Grand National Assembly, the Presidium (now the Council of State) and the Council of Ministers. Although not mentioned in the document, the Communist Party functioned as a supragovernmental body, with decision-making powers over and above that of the government. People's communes were established in the regions, counties, districts and communes under the direct control of the central organs of government. The right of ownership of private property was "guaranteed," with the salvo that privately held means of production and financial institutions could be nationalized when the "general interest" so required. Within two months of the passage of the Constitution this clause was invoked to nationalize all banking, industrial, financial, mining and transportation enterprises.

The second Communist Constitution, adopted in 1952, was more patently Stalinist in character. Patterned after the Constitution of 1936 of the Soviet Union, it specifically designated the Rumanian Workers' Party (as the Communist Party was known between 1948 and 1965) as the representative of the working class and the country's "leading political force." The nation's close ties to the Soviet Union were emphasized. Whereas the Constitution of 1948 declared that "the Rumanian People's Republic was born amid the struggle conducted by the people under the leadership of the working class, against reaction, fascism and imperialism," that of 1952 asserted that the republic "was born and consolidated following the liberation of

the country by the armed forces of the Soviet Union." As did the Constitution of 1948, that of 1952 guaranteed full equality to the national minority groups, but the latter document also established an autonomous administrative unit, the Hungarian Autonomous Region (Mures-Magyar), for the Hungarian minority. The Constitution specifically guaranteed citizens' rights, such as the right to work, the right to rest by establishing an eight-hour workday and paid annual vacations, the right to Social Security and the right to education. Similarly, all basic freedoms were guaranteed, including freedom of speech, press, assembly and association as well as freedom of religion. Other rights protected were freedom from arbitrary arrest, the inviolability of the home and secrecy of the mails. The right of citizens to form private and public organizations also was assured, with the exception of fascist organizations.

In March 1961 the Grand National Assembly established a commission to prepare a new draft constitution. At the same time the Constitution of 1952 was amended to transform the Presidium into the Council of State. Although the draft constitution prepared by the 1961 commission was never adopted, it was used as the basis for the work of a second commission, named in June 1965 after the death of Gheorghiu-Dej. The new Constitution, prepared under the leadership of Nicolae Ceausescu, was approved by the Grand National Assembly on August 20, 1965, and came into effect the next day.

The Constitution of 1965 is a nationalist document. To signify Rumania's emergence as a full-fledged socialist state, the title of the nation was changed to the Socialist Republic of Rumania. Unlike its predecessor, the Constitution omits all references to the Soviet Union. Instead, it refers only to the maintenance of friendly relations with all socialists states and, in addition, expresses the intention of promoting friendly relations with nonsocialist states. There also is increased provision for civil liberties, including the right of petition, the right of individual recourse to the courts in the event of illegal acts of state agencies and rights equivalent to habeas corpus. These rights are qualified only when used for "aims hostile to the socialist system and to the interests of the working people." Whereas the Constitution of 1952 had recognized the private sector as one of the three elements of the economic system (along with the socialist sector and small-scale commodity production sector), the Constitution of 1965 omits all references to the private capitalist sector. The Constitution of 1965 declares that the economy rests solely on the socialist ownership of the means of production. However, cooperative farmers, private craftsmen and peasants are permitted limited ownership of land and tools.

One of the most important changes in the new Constitution concerned regional organization. The Hungarian Autonomous Region was disestablished. All of the 16 regional units were subsequently eliminated in a territorial reorganization in 1968, at which time a system of *judete* (counties) was established.

Only minor changes were made in the organizational structure of government. Both the Council of State and the Grand National Assembly are described as "the supreme body of state power" but the former is designated as exercising "permanent activity." The description of the Rumanian Communist Party as the "leading political force" is repeated in the Constitution of 1965.

The head of state is the president of the Council of States, and he is elected by popular vote. Although the Constitution asserts the principle of collective leadership, this principle is virtually moribund in practice. The president's prerogatives are considerable because the Constitution does not require him to submit his decisions for approval by any state authority. In addition to being the ex-officio president of the Council of State, the president also is the supreme commander of the armed forces, chairman of the National Defense Council and chairman of the Supreme Council of Social and Economic Development. If necessary he also may preside over the Council of Ministers. He appoints and revokes ministers or any official at any level of government. When the Assembly is not in plenary session, he appoints the president of the Supreme Court and the general prosecutor.

Under the Constitution, one of the "supreme bodies" of state power is the Council of State. Articles 62 to 69 lists the Council of State's main functions, which are divided into permanent functions and those exercised in the intervals between the meetings of the Grand National Assembly. In the former category are establishment of election dates; appointment and recall of heads of central government agencies except for the Council of Ministers; ratification or denunciation of international treaties; granting of senior military ranks; conferral of honors; granting of citizenship, pardon and refuge; and appointment and recall of diplomatic representatives.

The Grand National Assembly powers that devolve to the Council of State between Assembly sessions include authority to appoint and recall members of the Council of Ministers, members of the Supreme Court and the general prosecutor; establishment of norms having the power of law; control over the application of laws; and supervision of the Council of Ministers and other central administrative bodies and the people's councils at local levels. Although decisions of the Council of State must technically be submitted for approval to the next session of the Grand National Assembly, they take effect as law immediately. Subordinate to the Council of State are two bodies: the Defense Council and the Supreme Council for Economic and Social Development.

The Council of State is composed of the president, six vice presidents and 17 members, all elected by the Grand National Assembly from among its members for an entire legislative term.

Defined in the Constitution as the supreme body of state administration, the Council of Ministers exercises control over the activities of all state agencies on both the national and local levels. The council is composed of a chairman (who as the head of government also is the prime minister), a first deputy chairman, an unspecified number of deputy chairmen, ministers and heads of certain other important agencies and organizations. Unlike the Constitution of 1952, which specified 26 ministries, the Constitution of 1965 fixes neither the number of ministries nor their areas of competence. The Council of Ministers has two categories of membership. The first, nominated by the Grand National Assembly, is composed of the prime minister, first deputy prime minister, deputy prime ministers and secretaries of state. The second is composed of heads of public and administrative organizations whom special legislation designates as members of government.

Formally elected by the Grand National Assembly for an entire legislative term, Council of Ministers members are responsible, both collectively and individually, to the Assembly and, in the interval between the Assembly's plenary sessions, to the Council of State. In 1969 a collegium was established in each ministry consisting of the minister, department heads, certain specialists and representatives of labor unions or other organizations. The purpose of the collegium was to introduce some rudimentary form of collective decision-making and review of ministry activities, but in actual practice it functions as a weak adjunct to the ministry.

FREEDOM & HUMAN RIGHTS

Although one of the first East European countries (outside Yugoslavia and Albania) to abjure Soviet hegemony, Rumania had a troubled human rights record under both Gheorghiu-Dej and Ceausescu. As a highly centralized state fostering a personality cult, dissent was severely suppressed and equated with subversion and treason. In prosperous times, such authoritarianism may provoke little disaffection, but Rumania's economic troubles in the 1970s and 1980s exacerbated both the intolerance of the rulers and the restiveness of the ruled.

The fall of Ceausescu in December 1989 brought to an end the era of active suppression of human rights. But certain vestiges of the past have survived, particularly in three areas. First, the Iliescu regime appears as intolerant of opposition as the one it helped to overthrow. Demonstrations are violently suppressed, opposition leaders are beaten and jailed, and the activities of human rights organizations are curbed. Second, the historic conflict between the Rumanian majority and the Hungarian minority in Transylvania has periodically reached flash point, and the latter generally has experienced discrimination in all sectors of national life. Third, although the Securitate has been formally disbanded, confidence in the impartiality of police and administrative officials has not been fully restored.

Under law, a person may be arrested only with an arrest warrant, but once arrested may be held without trial for up to one month before a hearing, and this period may be extended for up to three months. The court may order further extensions by 30-day increments. There is no limit set by law on the total length of time a person may be held prior to trial. There is no provision for bail.

Religious freedoms are not circumscribed, except in the case of the unrecognized religions, such as Jehovah's Witnesses and Nazarenes, whose members risk being prosecuted for holding unauthorized meetings. They also frequently are charged with being agents of foreign intelligence-gathering organizations and with drug trafficking. Of the 14 recognized denominations, the Rumanian Orthodox Church fares best. The Roman Catholic Church remains without an official charter but enjoys de facto recognition as the religious representative of the Hungarian minority. The principal areas of government interference with religious rights involve: the licensing of clergy; the importation, printing and distribution of Bibles and other religious literature; admission of new students to seminaries; and issuance of church building permits. Extensive urban renewal projects in Bucharest and other cities threaten church buildings of all faiths. Any repair or addition to a church building requires a permit approved by both the local city council and the Department of Religious Affairs.

RULERS OF RUMANIA
Princes (from 1859)
February 1859–May 1866: Alexandru Cuza
May 1866–March 1881: Carol I b. Prince Karl of Hohenzollern

Kings (from 1881)
March 1881–October 1914: Carol I
October 1914–July 1927: Ferdinand
July 1927–June 1930: Michael Regents: Miron Cristea/Gheorghe Buzdugan/Prince Nicolae
June 1930–October 1940: Carol II
October 1940–December 1947: Michael

Presidents (from 1947)
(President of the Council of State since 1948)
December 1947–April 1948: Mihai Sadoveanu (acting)
April 1948–June 1952: Constantine Parhon
June 1952–January 1958: Petru Groza
January 1958–March 1961: Ion Maurer
March 1961–March 1965: Gheorghe Gheorghiu-Dej
March 1965–December 1967: Chivu Stoica
December 1967–December 1989: Nicolae Ceausescu
December 1989–   : Ion Iliescu

Prime Ministers (from 1862)
(Chairman of the Council of Ministers since 1948)
February 1862: Barbu Catargiu
1862: Apostol Arsache
1862–October 1863: Nicolae Cretulescu
October 1863–January 1865: Mihai Kogalniceanu
January–February 1865: Constantine Bosianu
February 1865–1866: Nicolae Cretulescu
1866: Ion Ghica
May–June 1866: Lascar Catargiu
July 1866–March 1867: Ion Ghica
March–November 1867: Nicolae Cretulescu
November 1867–May 1868: Stefan Golescu
May–November 1868: Nicolae Golescu
November 1868–February 1870: Dimitrie Ghica
February–May 1870: Alexandru Golescu
May–December 1870: Manolache Epureanu
December 1870–March 1871: Ion Ghica
March 1871–April 1876: Lascar Catargiu
April–May 1876: Ion Florescu
May–August 1876: Manolache Epureanu
August 1876–April 1881: Ion Bratianu
April–June 1881: Dimitrie Bratianu
June 1881–April 1888: Ion Bratianu
April 1888–April 1889: Teodor Rosetti
April–November 1889: Lascar Catargiu
November 1889–March 1891: Gheorghe Manu
March–December 1891: Ion Florescu
December 1891–October 1895: Lascar Catargiu
October 1895–December 1896: Dimitrie Sturdza (Liberal Party)
December 1896–April 1897: Petru Aurelian
April 1897–April 1899: Dimitrie Sturdza (Liberal Party)
April 1899–July 1900: Gheorghe Cantacuzino

RULERS OF RUMANIA
Prime Ministers (continued)
July 1900–February 1901: Petru Carp (Conservative Party)
February 1901–January 1906: Dimitrie Sturdza (Liberal Party)
January 1906–March 1907: Gheorghe Cantacuzino
March 1907–January 1909: Dimitrie Sturdza (Liberal Party)
January–December 1909: Ionel Bratianu (Liberal Party)
December 1909–1910: Mihai Pherekyde
1910–January 1911: Ionel Bratianu (Liberal Party)
January 1911–April 1912: Petru Carp (Conservative Party)
April 1912–January 1914: Titu Maiorescu
January 1914–February 1918: Ionel Bratianu (Liberal Party)
February–March 1918: Alexandru Averescu
March–November 1918: Alexandru Marghilman
November–December 1918: Constantine Coanda
December 1918–September 1919: Ionel Bratianu (Liberal Party)
September–December 1919: Arthur Vaitoianu
December 1919–March 1920: Alexandru Vaida-Voevod (National Popular Party)
March 1920–December 1921: Alexandru Averescu (People's Party)
December 1921–January 1922: Take Ionescu
January 1922–March 1926: Ionel Bratianu (Liberal Party)
March 1926–June 1927: Alexandru Averescu (Liberal Party)
June 1927: Barbu Stirbai
June–November 1927: Ionel Bratianu (Liberal Party)
November 1927–November 1928: Vintilla Bratianu (Liberal Party)
November 1928–June 1930: Iuliu Maniu (National Peasant Party)
June 1930: Gheorghe Mironescu
June–October 1930: Iuliu Maniu (National Peasant Party)
October 1930–April 1931: Gheorghe Mironescu (National Peasant Party)
April 1931–June 1932: Nicolae Iorga
June–August 1932: Alexandru Vaida-Voevod (National Peasant Party)
August 1932–January 1933: Iuliu Maniu (National Peasant Party)
January–November 1933: Alexandru Vaida-Voevod (National Peasant Party)
November–December 1933: Ion Duca (Liberal Party)
December 1933–January 1934: Constantine Angelescu (Liberal Party)
January 1934–December 1937: Gheorghe Tatarescu (Liberal Party)
December 1937–February 1938: Octavian Goga (National Christian Party)
February 1938–March 1939: Miron Cristea
March–September 1939: Armand Calinescu
September 1939: Gheorghe Artesanu
September–November 1939: Constantine Argetoianu
November 1939–July 1940: Gheorghe Tatarescu
July–September 1940: Ion Gigurtu
September 1940–August 1944: Ion Antonescu
August–December 1944: Constantine Sanatescu
December 1944–February 1945: Nicolae Radescu
March 1945–June 1952: Petru Groza
June 1952–October 1955: Gheorghe Gheorghiu-Dej
October 1955–March 1961: Chivu Stoica
March 1961–March 1974: Ion Maurer
March 1974–March 1979: Manea Manescu
March 1979–May 1982: Ilie Verdet
May 1982–December 1989: Constantine Dascalescu
December 1989–   : Petre Roman

Communist Party Leaders (from 1947)
(First Secretary 1947–65; General Secretary since 1965)
December 1947–April 1954: Gheorghe Gheorghiu-Dej
April 1954–October 1955: Gheorghe Apostol
October 1955–March 1965: Gheorghe Gheorghiu-Dej
March 1965–December 1989: Nicolae Ceausescu
December 1989–   : Ion Iliescu

Governmental displeasure may be measured by the length of the delays for approval. The Orthodox seminaries are full, with 830 students pursuing five-year courses and 504 students pursuing two-year courses. However, other denominations are permitted only a handful of students per year. Leaders of religious denominations generally receive permission to travel abroad without difficulty.

The government's treatment of its Hungarian and German minorities has been the subject of intense international criticism in recent years. Hungarians claim that systematization and Rumanianization have proceeded hand in hand to reduce their cultural identity. In recent years opportunities for minorities in schools, theaters and the media in their own languages have eroded. Schools and newspapers in the Hungarian and German languages still exist, but their numbers have declined. In 1988 the Hungarian consulate in Cluj was closed. Rumanian place names are being substituted for German and Hungarian ones, and Hungarians no longer are permitted to register the birth of their children using Hungarian first names, which have no Rumanian equivalents. Hungarians also claim that the government is using its controls over residence permits, employment and study opportunities to dilute their concentration in their traditional areas.

Women are accorded the same rights as men, and women have equal access to education and employment and enjoy comparable wages. Women are employed in virtually all sectors of the economy, though in smaller numbers at higher ranks.

CIVIL SERVICE

State administration, as the civil service is called in Rumania, revolves around the senior administrative *secretar* attached to every ministry and subnational people's council. The normal entry into civil service careers is through the country's three main law schools, in Bucharest, Iasi and Cluj-Napoca, as well as the Faculty of Economic and Administrative Law in Sibiu.

LOCAL GOVERNMENT

The most extensive reorganization of government since Ceausescu came to power occurred at the subnational level. The Constitution of 1965 had provided for regions and districts, but the 1968 reorganization replaced the existing 16 regions and 150 intermediate districts with a system of 40 counties (*judet*) and 237 independent municipal administrations. At each level, local government bodies known as people's councils were set up. Local councils also were established in all smaller towns, and 2,507 communes in rural areas. A number of the smaller communes were combined to give them a large population basis. Along with the territorial reorganization, party and government functions were combined at the *judet* level so that the same person acted as the party committee first secretary and the people's council chairman.

Deputies to the people's councils are elected for four-year terms, except for the communes, where the term is two years, from single-member constituencies of equal population. Based on population, a *judet* people's council may have a maximum of 231 or a minimum of 141 deputies. The membership of the Bucharest people's council is fixed at 369, and there are 151 deputies on the councils of each of its subdistricts. City people's councils range from 81 to 221 deputies and those of the towns from 35 to 91 deputies. Commune council memberships range from 25 to 71 deputies.

Each people's council delegates its administrative powers to an executive committee and a number of permanent committees. The relationship of the executive committee to the people's council is a replica of the relationship of the Council of State to the Grand National Assembly. The executive committee consists of a chairman, two or more deputy chairmen and an unspecified number of members, who hold office during the council's term. The chairman of the executive committees in the cities, towns and communes is the equivalent of a mayor. The executive committee is required to convene at least once a month. Full council sessions are held every two months on the city, town and commune level and every three months on the *judet* level. The committee's responsibilities include implementation of the laws, decrees and decisions of the central government as well as the decisions of the people's council; preparation of the local budget; drafting of the local economic plan; control of the economic enterprises under its jurisdiction; supervision of the work of the executive committees of the councils subordinate to it; and oversight of public services, educational institutions, medical programs and the militia. Within the offices assigned to the executive committee are also located local specialized organs of state administration, such as finance, agriculture, commerce, education and health. These organs function according to the principle of double subordination, whereby their employees are accountable both to the local political leadership as well as to the corresponding parallel central government ministry. Besides these services, *judet* organizations have four additional responsibilities: administrative offices and bureaus, central organs of control, the provincial inspectorate and administrative services for localities subordinate to it. In practice there is a distinction between the specialized administrative services and the executive committee's own administrative apparatus. Belonging to the latter category are legal services and records, planning and wages, investments, urban planning and architecture, commerce, prices, tourist services and staff services. In the former category are six directorates: agriculture and food industry, commercial activities, schools, worker problems and social services, health services and culture and art. In two areas local government bodies have relatively more autonomy than in others: agriculture and local industries (as distinguished from national industries). The activities of the people's councils are supervised by the National Council for People's Councils. Overall coordination of all economic activities, however, is exercised by the State Planning Committee.

Since executive committees meet only once a month, day-to-day affairs are conducted by an even smaller body, the Standing Bureau.

The responsibilities of the local government have increased as a result of the introduction of the New Economic and Financial Mechanism (NEFM) in 1979. The NEFM is based on two principles: self-sufficiency and self-management. In the early 1980s only 40% of the budget of the people's councils came from its own resources, with the rest funded by direct subventions from the central budget.

FOREIGN POLICY

Under Ceausescu Rumania followed a maverick foreign policy in its relations with the Soviet Union. Rumania was the strongest proponent of the right of each socialist state to follow a foreign policy suited to its interests and traditions and the strongest opponent of the Brezhnev Doctrine, which assigned a hegemonic role to the Soviet Union as a protector of smaller Communist nations. At the same time, Ceausescu repeatedly affirmed Rumania's commitment to the international Communist movement and to the solidarity of the socialist camp.

Disengagement of Rumanian foreign policy from Soviet tutelage was a slow process. Until the death of Stalin, the Rumanians closely hewed to the Soviet line on all international issues. Events following the death of Stalin gave Gheorghiu-Dej the opportunity to make his first cautious moves toward ending Soviet presence in Rumania and asserting an increasingly independent stance. He gained his first concession from the Soviets in 1954 by negotiating dissolution of the joint Soviet-Rumanian industrial enterprises that had been the primary instruments of Soviet economic exploitation during the postwar period. The regime also sought to exploit the population's latent anti-Soviet sentiments by calling for "Rumanian solutions to Rumanian problems." Although Gheorghiu-Dej formally supported the Soviet suppression of the 1956 Hungarian revolt, he exploited the situation to gain additional concessions from the Soviets and to gain recognition of the legitimacy of the "Rumanian road to socialism." His negotiations led to the withdrawal of Soviet troops from Rumania in 1958. When the Soviets revitalized COME-CON in 1955 as an instrument of their foreign economic policy in Eastern Europe, Gheorghiu-Dej rejected its plans for Rumania and proceeded with his own plans for industrial development. To lessen Rumania's dependence on the Soviet Union, the regime initiated a gradual expansion of economic relations with non-Communist states.

The conflict with the Soviet Union became more acute in 1962, after Rumania rejected Soviet collaboration and awarded the contract for the construction of a large steel mill at Galati to an Anglo-French consortium. The Sino-Soviet rift that began at about this time provided Gheorghiu-Dej with an opportunity to increase the distance with Moscow and to find a new ally in Beijing. Rumania's offer to mediate in the Sino-Soviet dispute was turned down by Moscow as arrogant and hostile. Rumanian statements in support of Albania further antagonized Soviet leaders.

When Gheorghiu-Dej died in 1965, Soviet-Rumanian relations were at a low ebb, and under Ceausescu they deteriorated further. Rumanian opposition to Soviet foreign policies was reflected in a number of actions:

• Rumania's refusal to attend a conference of Communist parties except on its own terms.
• Its studied neutrality in the Sino-Soviet dispute and open cultivation of Chinese leadership through frequent exchange of visits by heads of state.
• Its strong ties with the Yugoslav Communist Party and expressions of solidarity with Yugoslav positions.
• Its vigorous opposition to the Soviet invasion of Czechoslovakia and defense of the Czech party's right to construct socialism according to its own dictates.
• Its rejection of the Brezhnev Doctrine of limited sovereignty of all socialist states except the Soviet Union and the concept that the protection of communism in any one Communist state is the legitimate concern of all Communist states.
• Its refusal to follow the Soviet lead in breaking relations with Israel in the wake of the 1967 Arab-Israeli War.
• Its establishment of diplomatic relations with West Germany in defiance of Soviet and East German policy.
• Its refusal to take part in Warsaw Pact military maneuvers and to allow Warsaw Pact troops on its territory.
• Its condemnation of the Soviet invasion of Afghanistan.
• Its equally strong condemnation of the Vietnamese invasion of Cambodia.
• Its strong support of Eurocommunism and friendship with Eurocommunist leaders.
• Its membership in trade and monetary organizations outside COMECON such as the IMF, the World Bank, GATT and UNCTAD as well as Third World organizations such as the Group of 77.
• Its development of trade relations with Western countries.
• Its refusal to follow Soviet president Mikhail Gorbachev's glasnost and perestroika initiatives.
• Its differences with its allies on other issues, such as nuclear nonproliferation and mutual force reductions in Europe.

Having achieved most of its stated goals, Rumanian foreign policy became more muted after 1970. There were no more confrontations with the Soviet leadership, and Rumanian actions became more moderate in tone. The change reflected the relative softening of Soviet positions in the context of détente with the West. It also revealed a greater tolerance of the Soviet leaders to the vagaries of Rumanian policy. Because of Rumania's geographical isolation from the West and close proximity to the Soviet Union, it is not perceived as a military threat. As a result, Rumanian leaders have engaged in foreign policy actions that if taken in Prague might have provoked a far different response from Moscow. The Rumanians realize the limits of this tolerance. Further, Rumania has derived few concrete benefits from its diplomatic moves in the Middle East and other parts of the Third World. Rumania's economic troubles in the 1980s also helped to push its foreign policy initiatives to the background. Significantly, in the light of Rumania's declining energy resources, economic dependence on the Soviet Union is likely to grow stronger rather than otherwise.

Despite the ups and downs of Soviet-Rumanian relations, the two states signed a 20-year Treaty of Friendship, Cooperation and Mutual Assistance in July 1970. The treaty replaced a similar one of 1948 that expired in 1968. The actual signing of the treaty was delayed because of Soviet attempts to insert a clause containing the Brezhnev Doctrine. The treaty was signed only by the prime ministers of both countries, and both Brezhnev and Ceausescu ignored the treaty signing.

Relations with other Communist states, particularly Hungary and Bulgaria, also were subject to periodic strains. Those with Bulgaria are cool because of historical differences over Dobruja as well as Bulgaria's complaints of chemical pollution from Rumania spilling over into Bulgaria. Relations with Hungary are close to being hostile because of alleged Rumanian persecution of its Hungarian minority, who are threatened through the systematization program with the loss of their strongholds in Transylvania. In 1988 a Hungarian protest rally was staged in Budapest involving 50,000 demonstrators, to which Rumania responded by closing the Hungarian consulate in Cluj-Napoca in Transylvania. In an effort to bridge the differences, the Hungarian prime minister, Karoly Grosz, met Ceausescu in the border town of Arad but gained no concessions from the latter. Each country then expelled one of the other's diplomats.

On the other hand, Rumania had close relations with Communist states outside of or opposed to COMECON, such as Yugoslavia, China and North Korea. Yugoslavia and Rumania expressed identical views on important international issues, and it was Ceausescu's desire on Tito's death to take up the latter's mantle of leadership of nonaligned nations. Rumanian emphasis on national independence and sovereignty and divergent paths of socialist development was extremely popular in Tirana and Beijing.

The Ceausescu regime systematically cultivated relations with developing nations, gaining observer status at conferences of nonaligned nations. Both Ceausescu and his wife, Elena, frequently visited Third World countries and held discussions with Third World leaders.

The decommunization of Eastern Europe in 1989 has made it necessary for Rumania to shape new directions in foreign policy. It has been unable to do so because of its inability to break completely with the past. Thus Rumania has become less influential in Eastern Europe as a force for progress and change than neighboring countries, such as Hungary, Poland and Czechoslovakia. In foreign policy, as in domestic politics, the revolution remains incomplete.

PARLIAMENT

The Rumanian national legistaure is the Grand National Assembly (Marea Adunare Nationala, GNA). Its 349 members are elected every five years by universal, compulsory, secret and direct vote. By law it must meet at least twice a year in ordinary sessions lasting no more than a few days.

Under the Constitution, the Grand National Assembly is a supreme state organ, with extensive powers including determination of foreign policy; election, supervision and recall of the members of the Council of State, the Council of Ministers and the Supreme Court as well as the general prosecutor; regulation of the electoral system; formulation of the national plan and the national budgets; supervision of the people's councils; and amending the Constitution. However, few of these powers are ever exercised by the GNA other than in a token fashion. Since 1948 every law proposed to the GNA by the Council of State has been passed unanimously.

The GNA functions under a bureau comprised of a chairman, four vice chairmen and a panel of six executive secretaries. Ten standing commissions study reports, bills and other legislative matters before their submission to the plenary sessions.

All citizens 18 or over have the right to vote. The Constitution provides for multiple candidacies. Elections and counting of votes are supervised by government-appointed officials.

Rumania's first free parliamentary elections in this century were held in 1990. The National Salvation Front gained 67% of the seats; the Magyar Democratic Union, 7.5%; the National Liberal Party, 6%; the National Peasants' Party, 2%; and the minor parties, 17.5%.

POLITICAL PARTIES

Until 1990 the Rumanian Communist Party (Partidul Communist Roman, PCR) was not merely a political party but also a constitutional entity defined as the source of all legitimate power in the state and the leading force in society. Paranoid about potential threats and challenges to its position, the PCR concentrated all political authority in its central bodies.

Originally founded in 1921, the PCR was declared illegal in 1924. Until 1924 it never had more than 1,000 members, mostly non-Rumanian and particularly Jews, Hungarians, Ukrainians and Bulgarians. During the 1930s the PCR openly supported anti-Rumanian causes,

POLITICAL SUBDIVISIONS

Districts	Capitals	Area Sq. Km.	Sq. Mi.	Population (1985 est.)
Alba	Alba Iulia	6,231	2,406	423,600
Arad	Arad	7,652	2,954	502,500
Arges	Pitesti	6,801	2,626	666,300
Bacau	Bacau	6,606	2,551	710,200
Bihor	Oradea	7,535	2,909	653,400
Bistrita-Nasaud	Bistrita	5,305	2,048	316,000
Botosani	Botosani	4,965	1,917	463,300
Braila	Braila	4,724	1,824	398,300
Brasov	Brasov	5,351	2,066	682,400
Buzau	Buzau	6,072	2,344	520,000
Caras-Severin	Resita	8,503	3,283	404,000
Calarasi	Calarasi	5,074	1,959	345,600
Cluj	Cluj-Napoka	6,650	2,568	741,800
Constanta	Constanta	7,055	2,724	698,700
Covasna	Sfintu Gheorghe	3,705	1,431	229,500
Dimbovita	Tirgoviste	4,036	1,559	557,900
Dolj	Craiova	7,413	2,862	771,500
Galati	Galati	4,425	1,708	629,200
Giurgiu	Giurgiu	3,636	1,404	345,500
Gorj	Tirgu Tiu	5,641	2,178	373,600
Harghita	Miercurea-Ciuc	6,610	2,552	356,600
Hunedoara	Deva	7,016	2,709	554,400
Ialomita	Slobozia	4,449	1,718	302,400
Iasi	Iasi	5,469	2,112	784,100
Maramures	Baia Mare	6,215	2,400	538,700
Mehedinti	Drobeta-Turnu-Severin	4,900	1,892	328,600
Mures	Tirgu Mures	6,696	2,585	613,800
Neamt	Piatra Neamt	5,890	2,274	566,500
Olt	Slatina	5,507	2,126	531,000
Prahova	Ploiesti	4,694	1,812	861,500
Salaj	Zalau	3,850	1,486	409,200
Satu Mare	Satu Mare	4,405	1,701	267,200
Sibiu	Sibiu	5,422	2,093	506,300
Suceava	Suceava	8,555	3,303	674,600
Teleorman	Alexandria	5,760	2,224	507,900
Timis	Timisoara	8,692	3,356	716,400
Tulcea	Tulcea	8,430	3,255	267,100
Vaslui	Vaslui	5,297	2,045	455,300
Vilcea	Rimnicu Vilcea	5,705	2,203	424,700
Vrancea	Focsani	4,863	1,878	385,700
Muncipality				
Bucharest	Bucharest	1,695	654	2,239,500
TOTAL		237,500	91,699	22,724,800

including the Soviet annexation of Bessarabia. Its fortunes turned on the Soviet occupation of the country in 1944, and by 1947, under the new name of the Rumanian Workers' Party, it had gained a monopoly of political power. Between 1948 and 1952 the party consolidated its power by eliminating all rivals. Under Gheorghiu-Dej it also shed much of its minority character and became more ethnically Rumanian. After the downfall of the Ceausescu regime in December 1989 the PCR was outlawed and has virtually ceased to exist as a political force.

The ruling party that replaced the PCR is the National Salvation Front. It first emerged as a broad alliance of anti-Ceausescu forces during the critical events that led to the overthrow of Ceausescu. Led by Ion Iliescu, the president of the republic, its core leadership comprises ex-Communists and technocrats who had fallen out of favor with the old regime. Its ideology is described as mild socialism of the Scandinavian variety, but its strong-arm tactics are more reminiscent of PCR.

The main opposition groups that emerged from the rubble of the 1989 revolution are the National Liberal Party and the National Peasants' Party, both whom together were able to garner only 8% of the vote in the 1990 national elections. Minor parties include the Rumanian National Party, the Christian Democratic Union, the Republican Union, and the Social Democratic Party. In Transylvania, the Magyar Democratic Union is strong.

For all practical purposes, Rumania remains a one-party state. Opposition parties suffer from excessive fragmentation; over 40 of them contested the 1990 national elections. They also suffer from lack of access to the state-controlled media, feeble leadership and fragile ideologies.

ECONOMY

Rumania has a highly socialized, centrally controlled and planned command economy. The state owns virtually all industry and shares with collective farms ownership of more than nine-tenths of the farmland. Private artisan shops contribute less than 1% to the industrial output, and private farmers' limited holdings are confined mainly to marginal lands. The state owns all natural resources, controls finance and labor, and has a monopoly of foreign trade and foreign exchange. The economy is directed by comprehensive long-term and annual state plans, which are binding on all sectors. Control over the economy is strongly centralized despite intermittent efforts since 1969 to grant more freedom of initiative to lower management levels in the interests of flexibility and efficiency. Supreme decision-making power rests with the Council of State and is enforced through an administrative hierarchy consisting of three distinct levels: economic ministries, which are responsible for specific sectors; trusts and combines which group enterprises along functional or territorial lines; and the Council of Ministers. Specialized committees with ministerial rank administer certain aspects of economic activity; the chief among these are the State Planning Committee and the Committee for Prices.

Important aspects of the economic organization remain fluid and are subject to frequent restructuring. Officially such reorganizations are designed to keep economic management abreast of the requirements of socialist economic development. The frequency of the changes, however, and lack of clarity in many of the directives have caused a blurring of the jurisdictional lines, with consequent overlapping of functions and conflicts of authority. The organizational problem is compounded by the conflicting motives that have prompted the reforms—granting more discretionary powers to enterprise managers on the one hand, and on the other, strengthening central controls and making economic plan targets compulsory.

Data on gross output and national income in absolute terms are not published. Official statistics on national accounts are limited to a few index series for the overall productive sector and per capita values and a percentage breakdown of gross output and national income by productive sector. The arbitrary nature of the pricing system and differences in statistical methodology as compared to Western practices preclude direct comparison of the growth rates of the economy and its components with similar rates in Western countries. The same holds true for comparisons of economic structure. Independent studies of the economy by Western scholars in Western statistical terms have yielded significantly lower rates of growth and a different structure of economic activities from those published in official Rumanian publications.

Skepticism about the reliability of official statistics arises because Rumania's economic record is among the most incomplete of the East European countries, despite its membership in international organizations such as the IMF and the World Bank. Such incompleteness is not just condoned but officially encouraged to hide the country's economic failures and exaggerate its successes. Much available data are of such poor quality as to be misleading.

Rumania's economy has passed through three cycles. The first began in 1948 with the first socialist industrialization programs and lasted until 1953–54. From then to 1957 national income growth rates and rates of investment were reduced during the new course followed after Stalin's death. A second period of rapid growth lasted until about 1965–66. It saw completion of the agriculture collectivization program in 1962 and the beginning of the shift of foreign trade toward the West. The period ended with the growing problems of managing swollen flows of investment. The last three years of the 1960s were another period of slower development, characterized by a rapid increase in imports from and debt to the West and a generally poor performance of the collectivized agricultural sector. From 1970 to 1978 the country passed through another period of rapid growth and its greatest structural change. Since then, problems of investment management accompanied by massive trade deficits have again caused economic growth to slow.

These cycles of development have been based, first, on the relatively steady and rapid accumulation of capital. For example, the share of imported equipment in total equipment investments has remained at a low 20% to 25% since the early 1950s. Second, the larger share of capital investment has been devoted to industry. The predominant growth of industry has been a direct consequence of the leadership's policy. This policy was reflected in the disproportionately large allocation of investment to industry at the expense of other economic sectors. Within industry, the preponderant emphasis has been on development of the capital goods sector at the expense of consumer goods. One problem was that of the total industrial investment, investment in petroleum took a very large share, resulting in little growth of capital stock. As a consequence of the uneven sectoral growth, the structure of the economy changed significantly between 1960 and 1970, with industry's share of the NMP rising to nearly two-thirds, construction and transport rising moderately and agriculture and trade declining.

Between 1950 and 1977, when Rumania claimed one of the highest growth rates in the world, industrial output grew at an annual rate of about 12.9% and industrial investment averaged 13.0% per annum, while the labor force grew at a rate of 5% and labor productivity at a rate of 8.0%. The proportion of national income allocated to investments grew from 17.6% during 1951–55 to 34.1% during 1971–75 and 36.3% during 1976–80. However, the national income growth rate of 9.3% between 1951 and 1980 was not reflected in the growth of real wages, which was only 4.9% during the same period. The chief victim of this strategy was agriculture, which received only 11.3% of total national investment during the first four five-year plans. Gross agricultural output grew by only 2.2% during the third and fourth five-year-plan periods.

Rumania's economic development policy is based on the Stalinist orthodoxy of industrialization at all costs. With the Soviet aid pipeline turned off, Bucharest not only altered its foreign trade patterns but also turned to the West for credit. Such credit was initially forthcoming with surprising ease because Rumania's debt-service ratio was among the lowest in the CMEA. However, following Rumania's poor economic performance and rising trade deficits, it has lost much of its creditworthiness.

Forced to import oil since 1976 and cut off from Soviet supplies, Rumania increasingly began to cultivate trade links with the Third World, primarily as a source of raw materials. In 1972 Rumania officially declared itself a "socialist developing" country rather than a developed country. Statistics supplied to the United Nations were manipulated to emphasize the country's underdevelopment. Although this declaration contradicted other official pronouncements concerning the regime's achievements in making Rumania an advanced country, it was prompted by the desire to reap the benefits extended to less-developed countries by the advanced countries and by U.N. agencies in matters of trade, energy and raw materials. In addition, the claim to a developing status served the purpose of the regime to demand further sacrifices from the population. After joining GATT in 1971, Rumania signed an agreement with the EC under the system of general preferences available to developing countries.

The intensifying energy crisis in the late 1970s coupled with growing imbalances in trade with the Third World persuaded the regime to adopt harsh measures to ward off an impending economic crisis. A series of austerity measures lowered the national standard of liv-

---

PRINCIPAL ECONOMIC INDICATORS, 1988*

Gross National Product: $151.3 billion
GNP per capita: $6,570
GNP average annual growth rate (%): 2.1
Consumer Price Index (1985 = 100)
    All items: 99.9

*Additional data regarding Rumania's principal economic indicators are not available.

BALANCE OF PAYMENTS ($ million), 1986

Current account balance: 1,408
Merchandise exports: 5,960
Merchandise imports: − 4,043
Trade balance: 1,917
Other goods, services & income: 592
Other goods, services & income: − 1,101
Other long-term capital: − 1,001
Other short-term capital: 184
Net errors & omissions: 21
Counterpart items: − 90
Total change in reserves: − 522

GROSS DOMESTIC PRODUCT, 1988

GDP nominal (national currency): 871.8 billion
GDP average annual growth rate: 4.4% (1980–86)
GDP by type of expenditure (%)
    Consumption
        Private: 58
        Government: 6
    Gross domestic investment: 32
    Foreign trade
        Exports: } 4
        Imports: }
Sectoral origin of GDP (%)
    Primary
        Agriculture: 15
    Secondary
        Manufacturing: 63 (includes mining and public utilities)
        Construction: 8
    Tertiary
        Transportation & communications: 6
        Trade:
        Finance: } 8
        Public administration & defense:
        Services:

---

ing, already among the lowest in Eastern Europe, to levels unmatched since the famine of the post-World War II period. Bread rationing was reintroduced, and measures were taken to limit hoarding basic foodstuffs. Since the people's councils were charged with ensuring local food self-sufficiency, nonresidents and commuters could no longer buy food in town. In 1984 the authorities announced a new program compelling every farmstead to produce strictly specified minimum quotas of agricultural products and to sell them to the state at official prices. The media promoted a scientific diet aimed at reducing per capita consumption of calories. In February 1982 food prices rose by 35% and purchasing power was eroded by 8.8%. The proportion of the family budget spent on food was higher in Rumania, according to a 1983 U.N. report, than anywhere else in the COMECON area. Energy prices rose 300% and brought about further restrictions on the amount of fuel and electric power distributed to the public. The authorities forbade the use of refrigerators, vacuum cleaners and other household appliances and urged the population to store food outside during winter and to refrain from using elevators and central heating. Street lighting, already reduced in 1979, was cut off altogether in the countryside and limited to main streets in the cities.

In 1982 the IMF launched a rescue operation that consisted of a series of proposed reforms, such as cutting back on imports, increasing efficiency in agriculture, stabilizing wages and prices and streamlining statistical data collection and publication. It was the price Rumania had to pay for a rescheduling of its foreign debt in hard currency. The reforms, together with others, became part of the New Economic and Financial Mechanism (NEFM), a revised version of measures adopted by the PCR in 1967. By that time Rumania was the last member of COMECON to adopt a program of economic reform. The program consisted in establishing a new intermediary level between economic ministries and enterprises called industrial centrals, formed of a number of enterprises combined through vertical and horizontal integration. Democratic centralism was not abolished, for the centrals were subject to national planning directives, and one of their main functions was plan fulfillment. They were to draw up plans for their enterprises, allocate materials and investment funds, supervise selling of output and redistribute profits among their component units. Enterprises were allowed to retain part of their profits, which they could use as payments either for incentives or for financing investments. However, as long as there was no reform of the price system or market mechanism, their profits were mere fiction. In actual functioning they were not autonomous units but executants of the ministry programs. The target plans of the centrals were often changed by the ministries, and the role of enterprise managers consisted in mere improvement of technical efficiency, while economic decisions were made at the ministry level.

As economic reforms go in Rumania, these centrals have had a checkered history. Their number was reduced; their powers over investment and foreign trade were curtailed; party and state control was strengthened, not weakened. PCR used a plethora of reformist terminology such as "decentralization," "self-finance" and "self-management," but in practice reserved central planning for itself. At the same time, responsibility for self-sufficiency was off-loaded on local enterprises, giving the leadership an excuse to make scapegoats of local officials for any failure.

The only active principle of the NEFM is self-finance. Cost reductions and profitability are to be achieved under this principle by using net output and commodity production as indicators and by linking material incentives directly to profits. In practice this means that overhead costs and an increasing portion of the social wages are no longer met from the state budget. For this purpose a distinction is made between planned profits and above-plan profits. Enterprise funds are dependent on the latter, which means that mere fulfillment of plan targets brings no bonus to the profit-sharing fund. Where an enterprise's profits are insufficient, loans are provided at penalizing interest rates for a period not exceeding three months. If the enterprise still fails to make profits after this period, it is required to cut staff and revise costs, and should this also fail, the ministry places it under special supervision. The most striking feature of the NEFM is its penalty schedule for underfulfillment of plan targets. Such a penalty is levied not only on the enterprise's profit participation fund but also on its housing and other funds. Individual workers also receive bonuses if their enterprise exceeds plan targets.

Five-year and annual plans form the basic mechanisms for directing and forecasting economic growth. Planning covers not only macroeconomic objectives but also the balancing of supply and demand at each stage of the production process and for each individual enterprise. Most plans fail to meet the set targets. For example, the shortfalls in the 1981–85 plan were as follows:

	Plan %	Actual %
NMP growth rate	7.1	4.4
Industrial production	7.6	5.2
Agricultural production	5.0	2.0

The directives of the 1986–90 plan stress development of energy and raw materials and envisage an average annual growth rate of 9.9% to 10.6% in the NMP, 13.3% to 14.2% in net industrial production, 8.5% to 9.0% in agricultural production and 8.8% in foreign trade. Total plan investment was 1.4 trillion lei (compared to 1.236 trillion lei in the previous plan period), of which 840 billion lei were earmarked for industry.

The publication of the draft annual plans is generally followed by a flurry of contracts between suppliers and producers, and these contracts form the basis for developing the final version of the plan. In the final version most of the contracts are corrected because enterprises tend to overstate their requirements. Despite legal provisions and sanctions, a large number of interenterprise contracts are not concluded on time, and of those that are concluded, thousands are not adhered to. The final stage of the planning process is the assignment to each enterprise of specific tasks known as plan indicators, spelling out capital, labor and materials in minute detail. In the case of large enterprises, the number of indicators runs into the thousands.

PUBLIC FINANCE

The annual state budgets are comprehensive documents covering the whole gamut of the economy and state. Information is not available on the manner in which budgets are prepared, but they are closely linked to the annual economic plans. Budgets are discussed and approved by three bodies: the Council of State, the Council of Ministers, and the Grand National Assembly. The consolidated budget is divided into a central budget and a local budget, the latter making up one-fifth of the total. The fiscal year is the calendar year.

Only summary data are published on the major elements of revenue and expenditure. They show either a small budgetary surplus or a balanced budget every year. Budgetary receipts have increased from (in lei) 58 billion in 1960 to 147 billion in 1969, 259 billion in 1983, 300 billion in 1985 and 433 billion in 1988. The largest source of income appears under the heading "Share of Profits from State Enterprises," and it contributes 37.3%. The second largest revenue item is the turnover tax, which contributes 31.2%. Direct or income tax is relatively minor, contributing only 15%. Social Security contributions account for the balance of the revenues.

Expenditures appear under five headings, of which the broad but undefined category "National Economy" accounts for 61.1%. Social services take up 32% and defense 4.2%, leaving only 2.7% for administration and other items.

CURRENCY & BANKING

The national currency unit is the leu (plural: lei), divided into 100 bani (singular: ban). Coins are issued in denominations of 5, 15 and 25 bani and 1, 3 and 5 lei; notes are issued in denominations of 10, 25, 50 and 100 lei.

The state has a monopoly in foreign exchange, and all foreign exchange realized by private individuals or state agencies from exports must be surrendered to the Rumanian Foreign Trade Bank. Currency transactions by individuals with residents in Western states are prohibited. They may not own foreign securities or currencies or have bank balance abroad without official permission, nor may they import or export Rumanian bank notes.

The leu was devalued in December 1982 and again in July 1983, when a single commercial exchange rate was established. In January 1984 the leu was devalued by 4% against the dollar. However, in November 1984 the leu was revalued by 20% against Western currencies, and further revaluations followed. There is a wide range of official, noncommercial or tourist exchange rates varying from one-third to double the basic rate. In addition, there are over 37 semiofficial rates resulting from multilateral trade and payments agreements.

The banking sector comprises the National Bank (Banca Nationala) as the central bank and four specialized banks: the Investment Bank; the Bank of Agriculture and Food Industry; the Foreign Trade Bank; and the Savings and Consignment Fund, a division of the Savings and Loan Bank. Little information is available on banking operations beyond the formal statement of their basic functions. Data relating to money supply and foreign exchange reserves are state secrets. The National Bank, founded in 1880 and known from 1947 to 1965 as the Rumanian Popular Republican Bank, is the banker for the government and also has the exclusive right to purchase items made of precious metals or stones or items of artistic and historic value. The Investment Bank, created in 1948 and reorganized in 1971, controls all public investment projects outside the agricultural sector.

Interest rates are set arbitrarily as one of the levers to motivate enterprises to achieve greater efficiency. Preferential rates are offered to agriculture and distribution. The credit system is characterized by a schedule of penalties for inefficient enterprises, but apparently no provision exists for bankruptcy.

CENTRAL GOVERNMENT REVENUES, 1987

% of total current revenues
Taxes on income, profit & capital gain: 0
Social Security contributions: 16.5
Domestic taxes on goods & services: 0
Taxes on international trade & transactions: 0
Other taxes: 12.3
Current nontax revenue: 71.2

EXTERNAL PUBLIC DEBT, 1988

Total: $2.2 billion
of which public (%): 48.5
of which private (%): 51.5
Debt service total: $1.602 billion
of which repayment of principal (%): 66.1
of which interest (%): 33.9
Debt service ratio: 11.9
Ratio of external public debt to international reserves: 7.4

FINANCIAL INDICATORS, 1988

International reserves minus gold: $582 million (1986)
Foreign exchange: $582 million
Gold (million fine troy oz.): 3,247
Central bank
Assets (%)
Claims on private sector: 42.1
Claims on banks: 55.9
Claims on foreign assets: 2.1
Liabilities (%)
Reserve money: 28.2
Government deposits: 28.7
Foreign liabilities: 2.9
Money supply
Stock in billion national currency: 179.7
M^1 per capita: 7,860
Private banks
Assets (%)
Loans to government: 30.4
Loans to private sector: 66.1
Reserves: 1.1
Foreign assets: 2.5
Liabilities
Deposits (billion national currency): 670.2
of which
Demand deposits: 6.5
Savings deposits: 25.0
Foreign liabilities: 14.2

EXCHANGE RATE
(National Currency per U.S. Dollar)

1979	1980	1981	1982	1983	1984	1985	1986	1987	1988
18.00	18.00	15.00	15.00	17.17	21.28	17.14	16.15	14.55	14.22

CENTRAL GOVERNMENT EXPENDITURES, 1987

% of total expenditures
Defense: 4.7
Education: 1.8
Health: 0.8
Housing, Social Security, welfare: 21.9
Economic services: 55.5
Other: 15.4

GROWTH PROFILE (Annual Growth Rates, %)

Population, 1985–2000: 0.7
Crude birth rate, 1985–90: 16.8
Crude death rate, 1985–90: 9.7
Urban population, 1980–87: 0.3
Labor force, 1985–2000: 0.7
GNP, 1975–85: N.A.
GDP, 1980–86: 4.4
Energy production, 1980–87: 0.7
Energy consumption, 1980–87: 0.9

AGRICULTURE

Natural conditions are generally favorable for farming. A varied topography has produced diversified weather and soil conditions. Although the winters are cold and the summers warm, the growing season is relatively long, from 180 to 210 days. There are recurrent droughts, but moisture generally is sufficient during the spring growing season. About 20% of the soils are of the chernozem, or black earth, variety, and alluvial soils cover the floodplains of the Danube.

Topography and climate divide the country into five agricultural zones, of which the most important is Walachia, including the rich southern plains, where half the country's grain is grown and where almost half of the vineyards and orchards are located. The region has fertile soils but is subject to droughts.

Transylvania is a largely mountainous area with substantial rainfall but relatively infertile soils. Livestock production predominates on the mountain pastures and meadows. Grains and potatoes are major crops in the central basin. Moldavia, in the Northeast, has poor soils and receives scant rainfall. Corn is the main crop in this zone, followed by wheat and potatoes. The Banat region, on the western border, has the most favorable natural conditions for agriculture. Chernozem soils predominate, and rainfall is more generous. Grain, particularly wheat, is the principal crop, and fruits and vegetables also are important. The Dobruja Plateau is the region least suited for farming, because of inadequate rainfall.

About two-thirds of the country's agricultural area of 15 million ha. (37 million ac.) is arable. The balance is devoted to pastures, meadows, vineyards and orchards. Slightly more than two-thirds of the crop area is under grain. Industrial crops and fodder crops occupy another fourth of the sown area. The remainder is devoted to legumes, potatoes and experimental and seed-producing plots. Half the grain acreage is devoted to corn, which is used both as food and feed, and more than two-fifths is under wheat, the staple food of the Rumanians. The grain acreage has declined in absolute and relative terms after 1960, when it accounted for almost three-fourths of the sown area. All other major crop acreages have increased. Until 1968 there were no restrictions on the conversion of arable land to nonagricultural uses. In that year a law was passed for the protection and conservation of agricultural land, prohibiting the diversion of farm acreages to nonagricultural uses. It revised the Building Code to reduce the land area allowed for individual construction projects, provided for factoring in value of land in construction costs and imposed heavy fines and criminal penalties for infringement of these provisions.

The two principal types of agricultural organization are collective and state farms. Some areas of state agricultural land are operated as subsidiary farms by various industrial and other economic organizations. Some private farms survive, mainly in the mountainous regions, where collectivization is impractical. Of total farmland the state owns 13.7%, collective farms 60.8% and cooperatives 25.5%.

The name "collective" has been dropped by the government, and collective farms are known as "agricultural production cooperatives." They comprise some 3,720 units covering 8.9 million ha. (22 million ac.) of farmland, about 7.3 million ha. (18 million ac.) of which are arable. The average farm has 2,024 ha. (5,000 ac.) or 2.7 ha. (6.7 ac.) per family, including 0.3 ha. (0.7 ac.) of private family plot. The farms are organized along the general lines of the Soviet *kolkhoz* and are run by an administrative and management body under an elected chairman, theoretically accountable to a general assembly. The farm management includes a chairman, a director, a management council, brigade leaders and trained technicians. Farmwork is done by brigades *(brigada de productie)* of various sizes. The peasants in the brigade are paid according to the number of workdays credited to them. The workday *(zi-munca)* is a unit that varies in duration according to the difficulty of the work performed. The value of the workday is calculated at the end of the year from the earnings of the farm after expenses have been deducted and an amount set aside for reinvestment. The net earnings are divided by the total workdays put in by all members during the year. The remuneration of the individual peasant is calculated by multiplying the value of a workday by the number credited to him or her for the year.

Intercooperative councils are charged with responsibility for improving management by initiating and coordinating cooperation at various levels. Cooperative farms are subordinated to the National Union of Agricultural Production Cooperatives and also are subject to the direction of the Ministry of Agriculture.

In theory collective farms are jointly owned by their members, but in practice farm members own only the 11% of land set aside for their personal cultivation and half of the livestock other than horses, which are owned by the collective farms.

Reforms were introduced in the 1970s and early 1980s to strengthen incentives for farmers. They provided for monthly payments on account in cash and in kind and for a share of profits in excess of those planned. If farm revenues turn out to be lower than the amount distributed, the shortage is made up by a bank loan.

The marketing of farm products by the cooperative farms is based on officially fixed prices and the monopoly buying powers of the state procurement agencies and the food processing industry. Products left after compulsory deliveries to the state have been met may be sold in the open market.

The state farms comprise 320 large enterprises, each with an average of 14,008 ha. (34,600 ac.) and including over 3,000 individual farms in an area of over 2 million ha. (5 million ac.). In addition, there are 74 agricultural enterprises for livestock and vegetables subordinated to four trusts. In official terminology, state agricultural enterprises are self-administering and financially self-sustaining. This means that the directors of each enterprise have a certain measure of autonomy and receive income in accordance with the farm's own performance. However, they have no juridical status or bank account. State farm workers are salaried workers of the state and receive all commensurate benefits. State farms concentrate mainly on the production of grain, to which 65% of their cultivated area is devoted. Little livestock is kept on these farms.

State farms receive preferential treatment in allocations of chemical fertilizers. Although state farms occupy only 13.7% of the arable land, they receive 37% of the chemical fertilizer supply. Whereas cooperative farms must hire their machinery from the Enterprise for the Mechanization of Agriculture, state farms own their own tractors and combines, of which their share is 29% and 37%, respectively. State farms also account for 33% of the irrigated land. As a result, per-hectare yields on state farms have generally been higher than yields on cooperative farms.

The bulk of mechanical operations on cooperative farms is performed for payment in cash and in kind by specialized state enterprises. The government has not followed the example of other East European states in selling machinery to the farms. The policy also provides the state with an added lever of control over the farms by extracting a substantial volume of farm produce as payment in kind for services rendered. In 1971 a total of 40 agricultural mechanization enterprises were established throughout the country—one in each of the 39 districts and one in the Bucharest area—with 772 subordinate stations to service an equal number of farm associations and about 4,500 sections to work with individual cooperative farms. These enterprises have become increasingly responsible for agricultural production processes. Mechanized work is carried on by permanent teams, who take over assigned areas in all sectors and are in charge of all operations until the crops are stored.

The agricultural labor force presents a paradox of substantial underemployment coupled with widespread labor shortages, particularly of skilled personnel. The shortages are especially prevalent during the planting and harvesting seasons. The progressive qualitative deterioration of agricultural manpower reflects the transfer of predominantly young male workers into the nonagricultural sector. Another contributing factor is the relatively inferior living conditions on the farms.

Only fragmentary information relating to the farm labor force is published. In 1988 agricultural employment constituted 28.7%, as against 51% in 1969, 65.4% in 1960 and 74.1% in 1950. Published figures relate only to state farm workers, but extrapolations from these data yield an aggregate agricultural work force of 3.062 million. Women constitute the majority of this work force. Not all cooperative farm members participate in the work of the enterprise. Some are permanently employed in the nonagricultural branches of the sector. Most work only a portion of the year because there is not sufficient work for them to be occupied fully. Some 22% put in less than 40 man-days and 55% less than 120 man-days. There are wide variations in the degree of labor participation among regions and among production sectors of a single farm. About 40% of the incomes of the cooperative farm families is derived from nonagricultural pursuits. Underemployment in agriculture is expected to continue because the size of farm labor

AGRICULTURAL INDICATORS, 1988

Agriculture's share of GDP (%): 15
Cereal imports (000 tons): 197
Index of agricultural production (1979–81 = 100): 125 (1986)
Index of Food Production (1979–81 = 100): 125 (1986)
Index of Food Production Per Capita: (1979–81 = 100): 112 (1985–87)
Number of tractors: 194,000
Number of harvester-threshers: 52,000
Total fertilizer consumption (tons): 1,374,000
Fertilizer consumption (100 g. per ha.): 1,301
Number of farms: 4,800
Average size of holding, ha. (ac.): 3,141 (7,835)
Tenure (%)
    Cooperative: 25.5
    State: 13.7
    Collective: 60.8
% of farms using irrigation: 20.4
Total land in farms, ha. (ac.): 15,038,000 (37,158,898)
Farms as % of total land area: 63.3
Land use (%)
    Total cropland: 70.7
        Permanent crops: 6.0
        Temporary crops: 94
    Meadows & pastures: 29.3
Yields, kg./ha. (lb./ac.)
    Grains: 4,949 (4,417)
    Roots & tubers: 24,000 (21,421)
    Pulses: 499 (445)
    Milk, kg. (lb.)/animal: 2,075 (4,575)
Livestock (000)
    Cattle: 7,017
    Sheep: 18,762
    Hogs: 14,711
    Horses: 672
    Chickens: 131,000
Forestry
    Production of roundwood, 000 cu. m. (000 cu. ft.): 24,629 (86,977)
        of which industrial roundwood (%): 81.4
    Value of exports ($000): 290,050
Fishing
    Total catch (000 tons): 271.1
        of which marine (%): 75.7

PRINCIPAL CROPS (000 metric tons), 1984–86

Crops	1984	1985	1986
Wheat and rye	7,627.5	5,711.5	7,385.6
Rice (paddy)	110	138.3	150*
Barley	2,447.7	1,850.1	2,496.8
Oats	94.1	101.7	100†
Maize	13,274.3	15,238.3	20,158.0
Potatoes	6,391.0	7,294.3	9,106.1
Sunflower seed	851.1	709.8	1,003.8
Sugar beet	7,018.5	6,445.6	7,082.1
Grapes	1,751.6	914.4	2,272.4
Plums	876.5	873.7	812.5
Apples	707.8	748.1	1,201.1
Pears	140.5	127.4	118.8
Cherries	96.6	94.7	116.9
Apricots	44.1	45.5	57.8
Walnuts	43.0	41.9	44.8
Peaches	66.6	67.2	94.8
Strawberries	26.2	29.1	30.7

*Unofficial estimate. Source: FAO, *Production Yearbook*.
†FAO estimate.

cannot be adjusted to the needs of production; it is determined by the number of families living on the farm. Each member has the right—indeed, the duty—to participate in the work of the cooperative, and the cooperative has the duty to provide equal opportunities for all its members. As a result, farm work is characterized not only by low incomes but also by low productivity. A series of reforms in the 1970s were aimed at improving the peasants' lot. They included the "global accord" system, which allowed workers to sign contracts with cooperative farms to work in exchange for sharecropping or on a piece-rate basis and also guaranteed peasants a base income with more adequate pensions, paid vacations and some social benefits. However, differentials in remunerations between the agricultural sector and the industrial sector remain substantial.

Investment in agriculture, 1951–82, tended to fluctuate, as follows:

Years	Percent
1951–55	11.3
1956–60	17.2
1961–65	19.3
1966–70	16.0
1971–75	14.4
1976–80	13.7
1981	15.7
1982	13.3

Replacement capital averages about 30% of the investments. The largest part and a rising proportion of the investments is financed by the state; cooperative farms supply the balance out of their own income. Cooperative farms also avail themselves of long-term credits from the Bank of Agriculture and Food Industry. State farms receive a disproportionate share of investment funds. The ratio of cooperative to state farm investment is about 1:4. Cooperative farm statutes require the farms to devote from 18% to 25% of their annual gross income to investment, but about a fourth of all cooperative farms set aside for investment up to 10% more than the maximum legal requirement. About a third of the investment is used for mechanization. Nevertheless, the levels of mechanization and irrigation remain low. Only 16% of the farms use tractors and 20.5% use irrigation.

The growth rate of agricultural production declined from 5.8% during 1970–80 to 1.9% during 1980–85. The growth of farm output has been well below planned levels since the 1950s. The reasons advanced for this poor performance include unfavorable weather conditions, poor planning, shortfalls in fertilizer deliveries, apathy of farmers, and negative effects of the disparity of incomes in the cooperative farm sector. Crop yields are among the lowest in Europe. The greatest advances have been in the output of industrial and fodder crops.

Livestock production accounts for about a third of agricultural production. Livestock numbers have increased very slowly during the past three decades, hampered by an inadequate feed base, poor quality of livestock and inefficient production methods. Private plots account for a substantial share of livestock.

Rumania lost an important fishing region and nearly all its caviar-producing lakes with the loss of Bessarabia to the Soviet Union in 1940. But the Black Sea as well as the Danube and the floodlands remain rich fishing grounds and account for 90% of the Rumanian annual fish catch.

Forests, representing 27% of the national territory, are mainly in the Carpathian Mountains and Transylvania. From 1948 to 1954 forests were administered by a joint Soviet-Rumanian company. Forestry is being developed under a long-term national forestry program (1976–2010), and in 1976–85 580,000 ha. (1.4 million ac.) of forests were regenerated.

MANUFACTURING

A heavy emphasis on industry, particularly heavy industry, has characterized all five-year plans. State control over industry is virtually total. State industrial enterprises employ nearly 95% of industrial labor and account for an equal percentage of output. The remaining employment and output are accounted for by the cooperative sector. Private enterprises exist but contribute only marginally to the economy.

Of the state industrial enterprises, 70% are run by the central government and the balance by local government bodies. Cooperative enterprises are subject to government controls and the economic plans. Many of these enterprises act as suppliers to state enterprises on a contractual basis.

Centrally administered enterprises include all the largest and most important industrial units, employing over 1,000 workers each. Enterprises under local government jurisdiction are smaller, generally employing between 200 and 1,000 workers each. The cooperative enterprises are the smallest, generally employing less than 500 workers each. Industrial enterprises are grouped into combines called industrial centrals. Each industrial central specializes in one area of production. The organizational forms of the industrial centrals and their authority and responsibility vis-à-vis the enterprises on the one hand and the ministries on the other are not clearly defined. Much of the putative autonomy of the industrial centrals is only in the more technical areas; in matters of pricing, investment and new-product development they are subject to a whole range of controls from above. Administratively they function under the industrial ministries, whose number and jurisdictions have undergone an almost continual process of reorganization. In fact, reorganization is the most favorite economic activity of the regime, particularly when things go wrong in any sector.

The internal management of industrial enterprises is vested in management committees, on which trade unions, employee representatives and youth organizations are represented. In 1968 a general assembly of employees was set up in each enterprise as a forum to enlist the effective participation of workers in the decision-making process and in evaluation of performance.

The most important industries are steel, autos, metallurgy, chemicals and engineering. Consumer industries are accorded a low priority in the five-year plans. Steel output, one of the most publicized indicators of industrial development, reached 14.3 million metric tons in 1986.

MANUFACTURING INDICATORS, 1988

Share of GDP: 63% (includes mining and public utilities)
Labor force in manufacturing: 37.3% (including mining)
Value added in manufacturing
    Food & agriculture: 11%
    Textiles: 15%
    Machinery: } 74%
    Chemicals: }
Index of Manufacturing Production (1985 = 100): 106.4

MINING

Rumania is poor in mineral resources. Deposits of coal are small and of low grade. Fields at Petrosani in the Jiu Valley of the southern Transylvanian Alps contain 98% of the bituminous coal reserves, and 90% of the lignite reserves are located in Oltenia, in the southwestern part. Open-pit mining is possible in the lignite area. Coal output increased from 22.8 million tons in 1970 to 38 million tons in 1986.

Workable deposits of iron ore are in the vicinity of Resita and Hunedoara, in the Southwest. Other known deposits, particularly those at Ruschita and Lueta, have a low metal content and harmful radioactive admixtures. Output in 1986 was 2.431 million tons.

All mining in Rumania is under state ownership.

ENERGY

Until the 1950s Rumania was a major European oil producer, and its fields fueled the Wehrmacht in World War II. However, by the late 1970s it had become a net oil importer. Production of crude petroleum fell to 10.1 million tons in 1985 from 11.6 million tons in 1983. Since proved resources will be exhausted in 16 years, geological and drilling activities have been intensified. Petroleum deposits were first discovered in the Rumanian section of the Black Sea in 1981. By 1987 six offshore drilling platforms were operating in the Black Sea, producing both petroleum and natural gas. Energy imports from the Soviet Union rose to 6.3 million tons in 1986.

The installed generating capacity of electrical plants rose from 7.3 million kw. in 1970 to 19.7 million kw. in 1988. Nevertheless, shortages of electricity have reached crisis proportions periodically and have required draconian conservation measures. Thermal pow-

er plants account for 83.1% of the output and hydroelectric stations for the balance. The Iron Gates hydroelectric project on the Danube is operated jointly with Yugoslavia. The 436-mw. Iron Gates 2 was completed in 1986. The first nuclear power station was begun in 1981 with Canadian assistance and started production in 1990.

ENERGY INDICATORS, 1988

Primary energy production (quadrillion BTU)
    Crude oil: 0.47
    Natural gas liquid: 0.03
    Natural gas dry: 1.52
    Coal: 0.60
    Hydroelectric power: 0.12
    Nuclear power: 0
    Total: 2.74
Average annual energy production growth rate (%): 0.7 (1980–87)
Average annual energy consumption growth rate (%): 0.9 (1980–87)
Energy consumption per capita, kg. (lb.) oil equivalent: 3,464 (7,637)
Electricity
    Installed capacity (kw.): 19,682,000
    Production (kw.-hr.): 71.580 billion
        % fossil fuel: 83.1
        % hydro: 16.9
        % nuclear: 0
    Consumption per capita (kw.-hr.): 3,218
Natural gas, cu. m. (cu. ft.)
    Proved reserves: 136 billion (4.803 trillion)
    Production: 35.9 billion (1.268 trillion)
    Consumption: 39.9 billion (1.409 trillion)
Petroleum, bbl.
    Proved reserves: 1.286 billion
    Years to exhaust proved reserves: 16
    Production: 78 million
    Consumption: 191 million
    Refining capacity per day: 617,000
Coal, 000 tons
    Reserves: 3,970,000
    Production: 46,700
    Consumption: 52,000

LABOR

The Rumanian labor force was estimated at 10.69 million in 1988. Since the state controls all means of production, there are few workers outside the socialist sector. Although socialist ideology promises all able-bodied persons a job, significant wage differentials exist between males and females, between urban workers and rural workers and among different sectors. To maintain balance in the sectoral distribution of jobs, the state has taken upon itself the work of allocating manpower without reference to the preferences of the worker. The state not only controls all employment but also such things as vocational education, urban apartments and pay scales, all of which have a bearing on the capacity to earn a living. There are no foreign workers in Rumania.

Urban workers fare best under the socialist system in Rumania. They have access to better jobs, training, living amenities and social networks. Rural workers have advantages of a different order: direct access to food, which always is in short supply, and the right to cultivate small farm plots, where they can raise their own livestock as well as crops. Such secondary sources of income are known as "second shift." The second shift is important not only for the individuals engaged in it but for the socialist sector as well, by adding to the total output without adding to production costs. However, hidden costs are associated with the system, such as unauthorized diversion of time and materials for personal use, and lower productivity caused by frequent absenteeism and tardiness.

The principal mechanism for worker participation in management is the workers' council (Consiliilor Oamenilor Municii, COM). The councils vary in size from nine to 25 members; the majority are elected by the workers, while others represent managerial and technical cadres. General assemblies (adunarile generale) in each enterprise, of which the workers' councils are the de facto executive councils, have a special role in affirming worker self-management.

Workers under 30 are the most alienated group in the labor force. They also are likely to be the least involved in workers' councils and to be most apathetic to production norms and targets. There is considerable tension between the state and industrial labor, of which the miners' strike in Jiu Valley in 1978 was the first manifestation.

Projections by Rumania's planners indicate a tightening of the manpower supply after 1990. This trend is expected to affect the sectoral and social composition of labor. Workers in the services sector as well as private farmers and artisans are expected to increase in number. Females will make up two-thirds of new employees, most of them drawn from rural areas. One of the most important evidence of tightening labor supplies is the delay in implementing a shorter workweek. Rumanians have one of the longest workweeks in the Communist world—46 hours—with only one extra day off scheduled for each month.

Almost all Rumanian workers belong to the General Union of Trade Unions (Uniunea Generala Sindicatlr din Rumania, UGSR), which consists of 12 component labor union federations, 40 area councils and 12,000 local unions.

The Labor Code is silent on the right to strike, except to formulate procedures by which union leadership is required to mediate disputes between workers and management, with recourse to the courts when disputes cannot be settled. In practice the sanctions available to the union make it unlikely that such disputes will reach the courts. Workers who have been dismissed from their jobs may take their case before the civil courts. Nevertheless, when strikes occur they are brutally suppressed. Following a particularly bloody miners' strike in the late 1970s, the ILO declared Rumania to be a violator of generally accepted labor standards. Workers do not have the right to bargain collectively. Despite the existence of general assemblies in all industrial enterprises, the workers have little say on policies affecting their welfare. In practice the primary function of the UGSR is to dispense certain social benefits, such as vacations at union-owned hotels; low-interest loans; and access to cultural, educational and recreational activities.

The Labor Code stipulates that each citizen over age 16 has the right and the duty to work. Unemployment, officially defined as "social parasitism," is a crime. With certain exceptions, such as housewives, full-time students and private farmers, all able-bodied unemployed citizens must report to the government employment bureau for job placement. A 1976 law states that persons who refuse to take up gainful employment may be fined or assigned a compulsory job for one year as a punitive measure. A 1968 law provides imprisonment as a sanction against "social parasites." The ILO has interpreted these laws as constituting forced labor.

There is no specific minimum employment age, although schooling is compulsory to age 16. According to the Labor Code, children over 16 not enrolled in full-time schooling are expected to work. Youths 14 years of age may be employed in temporary jobs, and youths of 15 may be employed in industrial work as long as the employer provides opportunities for further education and the work performed is "appropriate for the age and condition" of the employee. In such cases the law limits work to six hours per day. Children from age 11 may work in the fields or in "patriotic work" as part of a school or other group activity.

The Constitution provides for an eight-hour workday (six hours in the case of arduous occupations), a 24-hour rest period each week, paid vacations and the right to leisure. The Labor Code elaborates on these promises but allows employers to override them "if conditions warrant." Workers usually are required to perform extra, uncompensated labor to make up for lagging production or official holidays. The institution of unrealistic production and sales quotas, and penalties in the form of salary deductions for failure to meet them have led to worker dissatisfaction. Wages and salaries are cut even when shortfalls in production are due to lack of raw materials, or cuts in electrical power. Worker demonstrations in Brasov in November 1987 to protest pay cuts and poor living conditions were swiftly suppressed.

In 1988 pay increases were approved for all workers, starting with those at the lowest end of the salary scale. The new monthly wage is equal to $220 at the official exchange rate. However, because of the government's austerity program and chronic shortages of foodstuffs and energy, this wage level is inadequate to maintain a decent standard of living.

The Labor Code sets down strict theoretical norms for safety in the workplace. An institute devoted to worker safety and health has existed since 1968. However, the Ministry of Labor is lax in enforcing its own standards, and most factories present substantial health and safety hazards because government emphasis on meeting production goals takes precedence over health and safety considerations. Rumania is a signatory to International Convention 81, on labor inspection, but since 1973 has not reported to the ILO on its compliance with the convention.

LABOR INDICATORS, 1988

Total economically active population: 10.69 million
As % of working-age population: 76.5
% female: 44.7
% under 20 years of age: 6.6
Average annual growth rate, 1985–2000 (%): 0.7
Activity rate (%)
    Total: 50.1
    Male: 55.2
    Female: 45.1
% organized labor: 99
Sectoral employment (%)
    Agriculture, forestry & fishing: 28.7
    Mining: ⎫
    Manufacturing: ⎬ 37.3
    Construction: 7.4
    Transportation & communication: 6.9
    Trade: 5.8
    Public administration & defense: 0.5
    Services: 12.0
    Other: 1.4

FOREIGN COMMERCE

Since the 1950s Rumania has adopted a policy of greater reliance on foreign trade as an engine of economic growth. This has led to a rapid escalation of both imports and exports, the former more than the latter. In a bid for economic and political independence from the Soviet Union, the regime reoriented a substantial portion of its trade to the West during the 1960s and to the Third World in the 1970s. Since then, however, the inability to generate enough exports salable in both markets to balance imports has forced the country to turn increasingly to the Soviet Union and other COMECON countries to meet its import needs, particularly for oil.

Foreign trade is a state monopoly conducted through the Ministry of Foreign Trade. Before 1970 only specialized foreign trade enterprises directly subordinated to the Ministry of Foreign Trade could carry on trading activities. Producing enterprises, completely divorced from foreign buyers, delivered their export goods to the foreign trade enterprises at domestic prices without knowing to whom or at what price the goods would be sold abroad. Imports also were obtainable only through these enterprises at domestic prices regardless of their acquisition cost. Foreign trade losses were covered out of the state budget, and domestic enterprises assumed no risk whatever in foreign trade transactions. Producing enterprises had no interest in exports or in making their products competitive in world markets, nor were they interested in using domestic substitutes to avoid the need for imports.

This system was reformed through administrative regulations in 1970 and by law in 1971. Under the new law, authority to engage in foreign trade has been decentralized and granted to some of the industrial ministries, trusts and enterprises. The transfer of authority has not involved a diminution of central control over policy and decision-making. All trade is conducted in accordance with binding state plans and guidelines, and every transaction requires approval by the Ministry of Foreign Trade in the form of an import or export

license. Central controls also have been retained over foreign exchange and over export and import prices. At the same time, the law provides a limited opportunity to producers to develop direct customer relations and encourages them to exercise initiative in seeking out potential customers. Domestic products also receive greater exposure to international competition. In addition, the law created favorable conditions for establishment of industrial enterprises with foreign participation.

Under the law, production for exports has priority. Failure by economic units to discharge their export obligations adversely affects their profits, even if they meet their total output target. The provision applies equally to suppliers and subcontractors of export manufacturers. A positive incentive to exceed export quotas is provided in the form of export bonuses. Manufacturers are entitled to keep for their own use a portion of the above-plan export earnings. However, because the leu is nonconvertible and prices are set arbitrarily by the state, it is difficult to calculate the actual profitability of exports.

Trade with the COMECON countries remains substantial, and about half of this trade is with the Soviet Union. Rumania has more liberal trade arrangements with the West than with the Eastern bloc and was the second East European country, following Poland, to be admitted to GATT. In 1980 Rumania became the first Eastern bloc country to sign a comprehensive industrial trade agreement with the EEC. Among the Western countries, Rumania's most important trading partners are West Germany and France. Trade with the United States has been small, despite the fact that Rumania was granted a most-favored-nation status from 1971 to 1988, when Rumania unilaterally renounced it rather than change its emigration policies.

Imports have been overwhelmingly weighted in favor of capital goods. Exports consist mainly of raw and processed materials and foodstuffs, but the share of machinery, equipment and manufactured consumer goods has risen steadily, in accordance with official policy. In

FOREIGN TRADE INDICATORS, 1988

Exports: $12.5 billion
Imports: $10.6 billion
Balance of trade: $1.9 billion
Ratio of international reserves to imports (in months): 1.9
Exports of goods as % of GNP: 8.2
Imports of goods as % of GNP: 7.0

Direction of Trade (%)

	Imports	Exports
EEC	10.2	24.1
U.S.A.	3.1	5.8
East European countries	43.1	36.1
Japan	1.1	0.6

Composition of Trade %

	Imports	Exports
Food & agricultural raw materials	10.6	12.6
Ores & minerals	} 56.1	} 28.3
Fuels		
Manufactured goods	33.3	59.0
of which chemicals	6.8	10.7
of which machinery	22.2	29.9

most years the balance of trade has been negative. The cumulative hard currency trade deficit with the West is reported to be over $4 billion. Since balance-of-payments figures are never released, it is not known how the trade deficit is financed. Hard-currency receipts from tourism equal only a fraction of the annual trade deficit. The most important trade promotion event is the Bucharest International Fair held annually in October.

TRANSPORTATION & COMMUNICATIONS

Before World War I Rumania had only 3,540 km. (2,200 mi.) of railways. One major trunk line ran south and east of the Carpathians from western Walachia to northern Moldavia, with some feeder lines. There was one bridge across the Danube, at Cernavoda. When Transylvania was annexed in 1918, Rumania inherited the existing railroads built by the Hungarians and set about linking them with the rest of the country. Most of the modern system was completed by 1938, but route mileage increased by another 10% after World War II, including a bridge over the Danube at Giurgiu, south of Bucharest. Current trackage is 11,221 km. (6,974 mi.), of which 3,328 km. (2,068 mi.) are electrified. The first phase of the Bucharest subway was opened in 1979, and the 27-km. (17-mi.) east–west line was completed in 1983. The first section of the north–south line was opened in 1986 and the second section in 1987. The entire network is to be completed in 1990. The railroads are administered by the Department of Railways.

The road network consists of 72,799 km. (45,245 mi.), of which 15,526 km. (9,649 mi.) are concrete, asphalt or stone block; 20,199 km. (12,554 mi.) are asphalt-treated; 27,874 km. (17,324 mi.) are gravel, crushed stone or other surfaces; and 9,200 km. (5,718 mi.) are unpaved.

Of the navigable inland waterways, the most important are the Danube and the Prut. Rapid currents in hilly sections, silting and meandering streambeds in the lowlands, and fog and ice in the winter limit the usefulness of most rivers. Ice stops traffic on the Danube for an average of one month per year and on the other rivers or streams from two to three months. The country's topography does not lend itself to development of an extensive system of canals. There are short canals in the western lowlands, two of which connect to the Tisza River in Yugoslavia. The Danube–Black Sea Canal was opened to traffic in 1984 and the Danube–Bucharest Canal in 1988. Rumania's principal seaports are Constanta, Tulcea, Galati and Braila.

The national air flag carrier is TAROM (Transporturi Aeriene Rumane), which is run by the Ministry of Transportation. Domestic air services have expanded steadily and are heavy during the holiday and tourist seasons. The most important international airport is the Otopeni International Airport near Bucharest.

Most liquid petroleum products and natural gas are moved via pipeline. The largest network of liquid-product lines serves the large oil field in the Ploiesti area and a smaller one, in west-central Walachia, transporting the refined products to the Danubian ports and to Constanta on the Black Sea. Natural gas is piped to

all parts of Transylvania from sources in the center of the province.

TRANSPORTATION INDICATORS, 1988

Roads, km. (mi.): 72,799 (45,245)
  % paved: 64
Motor vehicles
  Automobiles: 250,000
  Trucks 130,000
  Persons per vehicle: 58
  Road freight, tonne-km. (ton-mi.): 5.957 billion (4.080 billion)
Railroads
  Track, km. (mi.): 11,221 (6,974); electrified, km. (mi.): 3,328 (2,068)
  Passenger traffic, passenger-km. (passenger-mi.): 31.082 billion (19.313 billion)
  Freight, freight tonne-km. (freight ton-mi.): 74.215 billion (50.830 billion)
Merchant marine
  Vessels: 430
  Total dead weight tonnage: 4,893,300
  No. oil tankers: 12   GRT: 384,000
Ports
  Number: 4 sea, 4 river
  Cargo loaded (tons): 11,863,000
  Cargo unloaded (tons): 31,055,000
Air
  Km. (mi.) flown: 20.3 million (12.6 million)
  Passengers: 1,216,000
  Passenger traffic, passenger-km. (passenger-mi.): 3.402 billion (2.115 billion)
  Freight traffic, freight tonne-km. (freight ton-mi.): 73 million (50 million)
  Airports with scheduled flights: 15
  Airports: 160
  Civil aircraft: 70
Pipelines
  Crude, km. (mi.): 2,800 (1,738)
  Refined, km. (mi.): 1,429 (887)
  Natural gas, km. (mi.): 6,400 (3,974)
Inland waterways
  Length, km. (mi.): 1,724 (1,071)
  Cargo, tonne-km. (ton-mi.): 2.417 billion (1.655 billion)

COMMUNICATIONS INDICATORS, 1988

Telephones
  Total (000): 1,963
  Persons per: 11
Post office
  Number of post offices: 5,046
  Pieces of mail handled (000): 795,199
Telegraph, total traffic (000): 5,393
Telex
  Subscriber lines: 6,750
Telecommunications
  1 satellite ground station

TOURISM & TRAVEL INDICATORS, 1988

Total tourism receipts ($): 178 million
Expenditures by nationals abroad ($): 57 million
Number of tourists (000): 4,535
  of whom (%) from
    Hungary, 25.3
    Poland, 15.9
    Czechoslovakia, 14.2
    Bulgaria, 10.9
Average length of stay (nights): 3.8

DEFENSE

Rumania is a member of the Warsaw Pact, and technically its forces are integrated into the pact's military structure. But since the 1960s Rumania has not fully participated in its activities and has periodically defied both the Soviet Union and other Warsaw Pact members. As a result, the primary mission of the armed forces is to defend the country against possible threats from the military alliance of which Rumania is a member.

The president, as chief of state, is head of the armed forces and also of the Defense Council. Under him there is a minister of the armed forces assisted by several deputy ministers, of whom one is the secretary of the Higher Political Council and another is the chief of the General Staff. The ministry also controls various directorates, such as training, political affairs and logistics. Area organization includes two military regions, with headquarters at Bucharest and at Cluj. Regional headquarters, which are simultaneously corps headquarters for the ground forces, control support facilities for all services.

The ground forces are commonly referred to as the army, although the Rumanian People's Army (RPA) comprises all the regular armed forces. The combat units of the army include tank and motorized rifle divisions and mountain, airborne and artillery outfits. Divisions are organized on the same pattern as in the other Warsaw Pact countries. Each tank division has one artillery, one motorized-rifle and three tank regiments. Each motorized-rifle division has one tank, one artillery and three motorized-rifle regiments.

The three other arms of service are air and airdefense forces, naval forces and frontier troops, each headed by a command equal in authority to the commanders of the two military regions. The tactical air force includes fighter-bomber and fighter-interceptor, reconnaissance, transport and helicopter squadrons. The naval organization includes a naval base at Mangalia, a minor base at Constanta and stations on the Danube. The navy is a flotilla of old and miscellaneous ships designed to operate along the coast. Until 1971 the Frontier troops were subordinate to the Ministry of Internal Affairs and were indistinguishable, except in their deployment, from the ministry's internal security troops. By a 1971 decree they were merged with the rest of the armed forces and brought under the control of the Ministry of the Armed Forces. On level, dry ground the border strip is about 20 m. (65 ft.) wide. The navy patrols the Danube by boat.

Military service is a national tradition, and conscription is provided for in the Constitution. Young men reaching age 18 are subject to draft. Because of the short duty tours, it is necessary to call up most of the eligible group. The mandatory tour of duty is 16 months for ground and air force personnel and 24 months for navy personnel. All recruits may opt for extra service on a voluntary basis. Conditions of service are reasonably good, and the morale and loyalty of the armed forces are not of concern to the regime. Men released from active duty remain subject to recall until age 50. However, only a small portion of them remain physical-

ly fit and familiar with new weapons to go into action without extensive retraining. Reserve training has low priority. Sometimes a few reserves are called to active outfits for short refresher training.

With the standardization of units, weapons and tactics accompanying the formation of the Warsaw Pact, training follows Soviet manuals, under which the training cycle starts with individual training, then fans out into group training, equipment familiarization and group maneuvers. Rumania participates only occasionally, and even then on a limited scale, in Warsaw Pact field exercises.

The General Military Academy in Bucharest is a fouryear, university-level school whose graduates receive general officer commissions and are expected to serve as career officers. It also offers midcareer command and staff types of courses. The Military Technical Academy is an advanced school offering advanced technical courses in engineering and other technical areas.

In addition to their military function, the armed forces play other important roles in the political education of youth conscripts, large-scale construction projects and ceremonial functions—and also as an instrument of social and political control.

As a socialist developing country, Rumania's economy places constraints on its military policy. Its armed forces consist of lightly armed defensive units rather

---

DEFENSE INDICATORS, 1988

Defense budget ($): 5.473 billion
　% of central budget: 18.0
　% of GNP: 4.3
Military expenditures per capita ($): 233
Military expenditures per soldier ($): 30,490
Military expenditures per sq. km. (per sq. mi.) ($): 23,760 (61,554)
Total strength of armed forces: 179,500
　Per 1,000: 7.8
Reserves: 556,000
Arms exports ($): 180 milion
Arms imports ($): 320 million

Personnel & Equipment

Army
　Personnel: 140,000
　Organization: 4 army regions, 1 with 1 tank and 2 motorized rifle divisions, 1 with 1 tank and 1 motorized rifle division, 1 with 3 motorized rifle divisions and 1 with 2 motorized rifle divisions
　Equipment: 1,860 main battle tanks; 175 assault guns; 325 reconnaissance vehicles; 3,000 armored personnel carriers; 325 multiple-rocket launchers; 30 SSM launchers; 200 mortars; 120 antitank guided weapons; 60 SAM's
Navy
　Personnel: 7,500
　Organization: Black Sea Fleet; Danube Squadron; Coastal Defense
　Bases: Coastal: Mangalia and Constanta; Danube: Braila, Giurgiu, Sulina and Tulcea
　Equipment: 1 destroyer; 1 submarine; 4 frigates; 3 corvettes; 6 missile craft; 38 torpedo boats; 58 patrol vessels; 40 mine warfare vessels
　Coastal defense: 4 sectors; headquarters, Constanta; 10 coastal artillery batteries
Air force
　Personnel: 32,000
　Organization: 3 air divisions; 9 combat regiments
　Equipment: 350 combat aircraft

than the technology-intensive units characteristic of advanced countries. Although absolute military expenditures have steadily increased, they have remained stable and even decreased as a percentage of the GNP and as total annual budgetary expenditures.

EDUCATION

The oldest school in Rumania, the school at the monastery at Cenadul Vechi, dates from the 11th century. Instruction in the early schools was in Latin, Greek or Slavonic. The first school to give instruction in Rumanian was founded in 1522 at Cimpulung, in Walachia. More Rumanian-language schools followed through the 17th century at Sighet, Hateg, Tirgoviste, Jina, Lancram and Turda. The first Moldavian university, the Vasiliana Academy at Jassy, was founded in 1640. The elementary school founded at Blaj in 1640 later developed into a seminary. In Transylvania the Austro-Hungarian rulers fostered the growth of an extensive school system consisting of frontier schools (for the benefit of the frontier regiments) in which the medium of instruction was German, village schools and higher and advanced schools as well as denominational schools run particularly by Catholics and Uniates.

By the 18th century, schools were under the administration of local communities rather than churches. The Hrisovul Law of 1776 established the Bucharest curriculum for schools in Walachia. It had four levels, each of three years. The first schools regulatory laws came into force in Walachia in 1832 and in Moldavia in 1835, adding councils and committees for aiding educators. The Proclamation of 1838 at Islaz declared that education was to be equal for Rumanians of either sex. The first journals dealing with methodology and teaching problems appeared, and the first schools for handicapped students opened their doors. Writing in Latin characters instead of Slavonic or Cyrillic characters was introduced.

With the unification of Moldavia and Walachia in 1859, the stage was set for the rapid growth of education. The University of Jassy, closed because of political unrest under the Turks, reopened with four faculties and the University of Bucharest opened with three faculties in 1860. Legislation in 1864 made four-year primary education free and compulsory and determined that secondary education and higher education would last for seven and three years, respectively.

Other important laws followed. They included a law in 1893 on teacher education and extension of compulsory education; primary and normal education laws in 1896; the Spiru Hiret Law in 1898 on secondary and higher education; the Apponyi Law of Transylvania in 1907; a 1924 law that provided a unified primary education cycle for Transylvania, Walachia and Moldavia; a 1925 law on private education; a 1938 law establishing pedagogical schools; and a 1939 law expanding free and compulsory primary education.

In education as in other spheres, the rise of the Communists to power meant a radical break with the past. One immediate effect was the abolition of all private schools and schools run by religious organizations. Oth-

er changes, equally far-reaching, included the establishment of Marxism-Leninism as the ideological basis of education, the reorientation of the curriculum in favor of technical subjects, the extension of general education to 12 years and growing emphasis on work experience for admission to higher education.

Three articles in the Constitution deal with education: 21, 22 and 30. Article 21 guarantees everyone the right to a free education. Article 22 guarantees the educational rights of minority groups. Article 30, disestablishing churches also takes away from them the right to run schools.

During the next 35 years further educational laws were added to the statute books, clarifying the basic constitutional foundations. The Laws of Educational Reform of 1948, the Law of Education of 1968 and the Education Law of 1978 did not so much reform the system as deepen its moorings in the Marxist educational philosophy.

The 10-year compulsory education program introduced in 1978 is comprised of three levels: a primary four-year program, a four-year gymnasium program and a two-year program as the first cycle of the lyceum. Graduates of the 10-year program then proceed to the two-year second cycle of the lyceum before enrolling in higher-education institutions. Children begin preschool or kindergarten at age three and first grade at six. Most students complete school by age 18.

The academic year runs from September through July. The language of instruction is Rumanian, although some concessions are given to minority-language students to learn in the early years in their own language. The grading system for the entire educational system is based on a scale of 10 to 1, with 5 as the passing grade. The state provides all textbooks free of charge to students. Textbooks and manuals are written by collectives of specialists and edited and published by Editura Didactica and Pedagogica, the state publishing house.

Preschool education is outside the compulsory cycle but is attended by two of every three children between three and six. There are three types of kindergarten programs:

- normal programs of three to six hours daily
- longer programs of eight to 12 hours daily
- weekly programs in which children are taken home on Saturdays and returned on Mondays

Preschool education is free, but children in weekly programs are required to pay for their board and lodging. Kindergartens are organized by educational subdivisions, local popular *judet* councils and economic enterprises. Kindergarten teachers are called *educatoare*.

Primary grades run from one through four and gymnasium grades from five through eight. Work experience programs begin at grade five and are modified to suit the age and physical capacity of the students and the economic activities of the locality. The school year is divided into three trimesters separated by spring and winter vacations. Students receive at least two grades per subject each trimester in addition to a grade for a written assignment. These grades are averaged per trimester for each subject. Those who fail to receive the passing grade of 5 get one more chance before the opening of the next school year. In addition to academic grades, pupils receive grades for conduct, also on a scale of 10 to 1, with a passing grade of 6. Students who receive high grades in conduct are honored, while deviants are subjected to a graduated system of punishments and sanctions. Dropouts at the primary-school level constitute less than 0.5% of the school population.

The secondary school or lyceum is divided into two cycles. The first, which includes the ninth and 10th grades, is part of the 10-year general compulsory education and often is housed in the primary-school building. The second cycle contains the 11th and 12th grades as a day-school program and the 11th, 12th and 13th grades as a night-school program.

Students who have completed the gymnasium are automatically enrolled in the first cycle of the lyceum. Students may select the type of lyceum they wish to attend. If there are not enough places for all applicants, competitive examinations are held, and those with the highest scores are admitted, while others are directed to other lycea. Admission to the second cycle is based on competitive examinations. The principal types of lycea are: industrial; agro-industrial; economics; health services; and science. The specialized lycea offer 32 varieties of curricula, with programs in 98 vocations. Throughout the lyceum cycle, students continue their work practice. Internship programs also are offered, for six to 18 months. Evaluation in the lyceum is similar to that of students in primary schools and the gymnasium, with two exceptions: Students may fail in one to three subjects and may repeat a grade one more time. Upon completion of the lyceum the student receives a certificate of academic studies and a certificate of qualification, as follows: Graduates of the first cycle receive a diploma of completion and a certificate of qualification; graduates of the second-cycle day program receive a baccalaureate diploma and a certificate of qualification; graduates of the second cycle night program receive only a baccalaureate diploma.

Professional schools train workers with special qualifying courses as well as apprenticeship and on-the-job training. The program lasts from a year to a year and a half. There are both day and night professional schools, which work closely with state enterprises.

Vocational schools offer *maistri* (apprentice) education in courses lasting a year to a year and a half in day schools and two years in night schools. Day students spend half their time in on-the-job practice. They are expected to maintain passing-grade annual averages in more than three subjects.

Students in all schools are recruited during free time and vacations to participate in patriotic work activities and to care for historical monuments and natural sites of environmental value as well as to assist in the fall harvest.

Higher education encompasses all forms of education beyond the second cycle of the lyceum and includes universities, polytechnical institutions, conservatories and academies. There are 19 universities and

---

EDUCATION INDICATORS

Literacy
  Total (%): 95.8
First level
  Schools: 14,046
  Teachers: 144,878
  Students: 3,017,339
  Student–teacher ratio: 21:1
  Net enrollment rate (%): 98
  Females (%): 49
Second level
  Schools: 981
  Teachers: 46,124
  Students: 1,196,949
  Student–teacher ratio: 26:1
  Net enrollment rate (%): 74
  Females (%): 47
Vocational
  Schools: 747
  Teachers: 12,420
  Students: 257,196
  Student–teacher ratio: 21:1
Third level
  Institutions: 63
  Teachers: 12,504
  Students: 157,174
  Student–teacher ratio: 13:1
  Gross enrollment rate (%): 11.2
  Graduates per 100,000 age 20–24: 694
  % of propulation over 25 with postsecondary eduation: 4.6
  Females (%): 44
Foreign study
  Foreign students in national universities: 13,068
  Students abroad: 534
    of whom in
    United States, 74
    West Germany, 238
    Switzerland, 67
    Italy, 51
Public expenditures (national currency)
  Total: 17.465 billion lei
  % of GNP: 2.1
  % of national budget: 7.5
  % current expenditures: 96.8

GRADUATES, 1979

Total: 37,834
Education: 3,918
Fine & applied arts: 951
Law: 1,867
Social & behavioral sciences: 4,953
Natural sciences: 1,744
Mathematics & computer science: 786
Medicine: 3,447
Engineering: 16,499
Architecture: 278
Transportation & communications: 301
Agriculture, forestry, fisheries: 3,090

---

44 other institutions of higher education. Higher education is state-controlled and free. Admission is based on competitive examinations in which an average of 35% of

applicants are chosen. The length of the program depends on the kind of institution and varies from three to six years. Enrollment in the evening programs is limited to employed persons. The curricula combine academic studies with projects, research and practice in production. The university academic year is divided into two semesters. Attendance is mandatory. Evaluation is based on academic performance and examinations at the end of each semester. Students may not fail more than three examinations, and students who fail the first year are expelled and may be readmitted only if they take a further entrance examination. Students are permitted to repeat only one year of their studies. A final examination is held at the end of the program, with a minimum passing grade of 6. Final examinations consist of defense of a project or research paper.

Graduates may pursue postuniversity courses in specialized fields or for doctoral programs. The latter are approved by the Council of State.

Overall, education is administered by the Ministry of Education and Instruction. Regional popular councils have a direct responsibility for certain levels of education, such as kindergartens and the curricula of preuniversity education. Part of the educational funding is derived from proceeds of student voluntary labor; the rest comes from the state.

A number of councils, committees and congresses are concerned with education. The Congress of Education and Instruction meets every five years to provide guidelines to the planners on new directions and priorities in education. Generally its resolutions are incorporated into the five-year plans. The Superior Council of Education and Instruction represents a broad spectrum of educators, labor unions, youth organizations, children's organizations, women's groups and others. Its directives are implemented by the Ministry of Education and Instruction.

School inspectorates operate on a county basis and are subject to the Ministry of Education and Instruction and the regional popular councils. Certain areas have school coordinating councils in which parents and youth are represented.

Universities are headed by rectors assisted by an administrative council, a professorial council and a scientific council.

Nonformal education is offered by schools and universities through night classes, conferences and lectures. Rumanian Radio and Television Network transmits special programs for adults.

Teachers are trained in pedagogical institutes attached to universities and are organized into syndicates according to disciplines. Teachers' salaries are dependent on category, rank and tenure. Tenure is obtained after a three-year probationary period.

LEGAL SYSTEM

Like most continental countries, Rumania follows the Civil Law system. Between 1945 and 1990 legal theory followed Marxist interpretation emphasizing the rights of the state rather than those of the individual. Rumania does not accept the jurisdiction of the International Court of Justice. The judiciary and the legal system are governed by the Constitution and the 1968 Law on the Organization of the Court System, which assigned overall responsibility in this field to the Ministry of Justice. The Ministry of Justice is divided into six directorates: civil courts; military courts; studies and legislation; personnel; administration and planning; and accounting. In addition, it includes a corps of inspectors and the office of the state notary.

The Constitution places the nation's top judicial body, the Supreme Court, subordinate to the Grand National Assembly and the Council of State. Members of the Supreme Court are appointed by the Grand National Assembly to four-year terms. The Supreme Court functions principally as an appeals court but in certain matters specified by law may act as a court of first instance. It also may issue directives on legal and constitutional issues for the guidance of lower courts and administrative agencies. The Supreme Court is divided into civil, criminal and military sections, each presided over by a panel of three judges. Plenary sessions are held at least once every three months in the presence of the minister of justice.

Subordinate courts include *judet* courts and the municipal court of Bucharest. Each court is presided over by a panel of two judges and three lay jurors known as people's assessors, and decisions are made by majority vote.

At the bottom tier are the lower courts, presided over by a panel composed of one judge and two people's assessors. In Bucharest there are eight sectional courts under the supervision of the Municipal Court. Military courts also are established on a territorial basis.

In 1968 the Grand National Assembly established judicial commissions as courts of special jurisdiction in the state economic enterprises. Functioning under the control of the enterprise management or municipal executive committees, the judicial commissions are assigned such matters as labor disputes, misdemeanors, property disputes and other violations. As a rule, commissions consist of five elected members, except in the case of labor disputes, in which two additional members are co-opted.

General supervision over the application of the law and the initiation of criminal proceedings is exercised by the office of the prosecutor general, who is elected by the Grand National Assembly for four-year terms. Subunits of the office of the prosecutor general exist in each judicial district. Prosecutors on the *judet* level have a consultative vote in the meetings of the local government agencies when important legal questions are being decided. The prosecutor general also may participate in plenary sessions of the Supreme Court.

The Penal Code in effect before 1968 was one of the most severe in Europe. The Penal Code and the Code of Criminal Procedure that replaced it make some concession to civil rights and even speak of the rights of accused persons. If the possible sentence for an alleged crime is five years or more, the accused is guaranteed counsel, who has access to all findings uncovered by the prosecutors during the investigation of the case. Except in special cases specified in the law, all trials are public. The maximum prison sentence for a first offense is 20 years and for a repeated serious offense 25 years. The death sentence is authorized but generally is commuted to life imprisonment. The most severe sentences are reserved for crimes against the state.

The new codes attempt to reduce court time spent on minor offenses. Those that constitute no significant danger to society have been removed from the list of crimes and placed under the purview of judicial commissions. In other cases, where an act still is classified as a crime, an offender may elect to plead guilty without a trial; then he or she receives half of the minimum punishment.

The prison system consists of correction camps; labor colonies; and military disciplinary units for those subject to military justice. Prisons include penitentiaries, prison factories, town jails and detention facilities. All convicted persons are required to perform useful work. All but town jails have educational facilities. A convict is paid according to the standard wage scales but earns only 10%, with the balance going to the state Treasury. Inmates are segregated according to seriousness of offense, status, gender and age. Drug addicts and alcoholics are isolated wherever possible, and persons held in preventive arrest but not yet convicted are separated from convicted persons. Convict privileges vary with the severity of the original sentence and may be increased, decreased or done away altogether. Consistent good conduct may earn parole, and an exceptional inmate may be pardoned. Disciplinary measures include reprimand, simple isolation, severe isolation or transfer to a facility with a more strict regimen. All convict mail is censored. Conversations during visits is limited to Rumanian unless a translator is present.

LAW ENFORCEMENT

The law enforcement and internal security situation in Rumania has changed radically from the reign of terror and police excesses that characterized the immediate post-World War II years. The internal security troops have receded into the background. Although controls over the population remain strict by Western standards, the average Rumanian does not feel that he is living in an occupied country.

The police or militia are organized under the Ministry of Internal Affairs, which also is responsible for the security troops, fire fighting, special guard units and prisons. A supraministerial body known as the State Security Council oversees all police activities.

The chain of command runs from the minister of internal affairs to the inspector general, who commands the *judet* inspectorates and the municipal district of Bucharest. Local police units and inspectorates also are subordinate, under the principle of dual subordination, to the locally elected people's councils.

The four principal tasks of the militia are defense of the regime; detection of criminal activities and apprehension of criminals; traffic control; and rendering assistance during disasters and emergencies. By law auxiliary police groups may be formed to supplement police personnel. Policemen are recruited from gradu-ates of military schools and from among those selected annually for compulsory military service.

The Securitate, the former national security force, disbanded in 1990, was organized along military lines, and most if not all of its personnel had military rank. Administratively it was under the State Security Council and the Ministry of Internal Affairs.

Criminal statistics are collected but not published. Although reliable data are hard to come by, it is possible to assess the overall crime situation from speeches made by party leaders deploring such rising crimes as begging, vagrancy, prostitution, black-marketing and currency speculation. The vast majority of reported crimes are economic crimes or antisocial crimes. Further, the militia frequently complains of lack of public cooperation in solving crimes.

HEALTH

Health care and medical services are completely socialized under the direction of the Ministry of Public Health and Social Welfare. Private medical practice was abolished in 1959. Under the Communists the general health of the population has improved, and several serious diseases such as malaria have been eliminated. Through social insurance, all employees and other workers, pensioners and members of cooperative farms are covered for medical care and medicine.

HEALTH INDICATORS, 1988

Health personnel
  Physicians: 40,706
    Persons per: 567
  Dentists: 7,356
  Nurses: 81,031
  Pharmacists: 6,471
  Midwives: 12,248
Hospitals
  Number: 437
  Number of beds: 213,560
  Beds per 10,000: 94
Type of hospitals (%)
  Government: 100
Public health expenditures
  As % of national budget: 0.8
  Per capita: $5.00
Vital statistics
  Crude death rate per 1,000: 10.9
  Decline in death rate: 20.9 (1965–84)
  Life expectancy at birth (years): males 67.0; females 72.6
  Infant mortality rate per 1,000 live births: 22
  Child mortality rate (ages 1–4 years) per 1,000: 1
  Maternal mortality rate per 100,000 live births: 152
Causes of death per 100,000
  Infectious & parasitic diseases: 8.4
  Cancer: 128.4
  Endocrine & metabolic disorders: 7.4
  Diseases of the nervous system: 8.3
  Diseases of the circulatory system: 603.7
  Diseases of the digestive system: 50.0
  Accidents, poisoning & violence: 66.3
  Diseases of the respiratory system: 115.4

FOOD & NUTRITION

The quality of available foods has declined steeply in recent years. Even common staples such as eggs, cheese and sausage are in short supply, and even when available, consumers have to wait in long lines to obtain them.

FOOD & NUTRITION INDICATORS, 1988

Per capita daily food consumption, calories: 3,341
Per capita daily consumption, protein, g. (oz.): 102 (3.6)
Calorie intake as % of FAO recommended minimum requirement: 126
% of calorie intake from vegetable products: 76
% of calorie intake from animal products: 24
Food expenditures as % of total household expenditures: 62.7
% of total calories derived from:
    Cereals: 43.2
    Potatoes: 3.9
    Meat & poultry: 8.8
    Fish: 0.7
    Fats & Oils 12.0
    Eggs & milk: 9.1
    Fruits & vegetables: 6.5
    Other: 15.9
Per capita consumption of foods, kg., l. (lb., pt.):
    Potatoes: 286.0 (630.6)
    Wheat: 230.0 (507.1)
    Rice: 5.0 (11.0)
    Fresh vegetables: 140.0 (308.7)
    Fruits, citrus: 2.9 (6.4)
    Eggs: 290 (639.6)
    Honey: 0.5 (1.1)
    Fish: 5.5 (12.1)
    Milk: 180.0 (397.0)
    Butter: 2.1 (4.6)
    Cheese: 4.1 (9.0)
    Meat (total): 71.9 (158.5)
        Beef & veal: 11.0 (24.2)
        Pig meat: 40.5 (89.3)
        Poultry: 17.4 (16.3)
        Mutton, lamb & goat: 3.0 (6.6)
    Sugar: 31.6 (69.6)
    Biscuits: 3.4 (7.5)
    Beer, l. (pt.): 50.0 (105.7)
    Wine, l. (pt.): 35.1 (74.2)
    Alcoholic liquors, l. (pt.): 2.1 (4.4)
    Soft drinks, l. (pt.): 9.0 (19.0)
    Mineral waters, l. (pt.): 7.0 (14.7)
    Coffee: 0.5 (1.1)
    Cocoa: 0.5 (1.1)

MEDIA & CULTURE

Rumanians trace the history of their press to 1829, when Ion Eliade Radulescu founded *Curierul Rumanescu* (Rumanian Courier). Rumania then was nominally part of the Ottoman Empire but actually under Russian military control. For the next 50 years unsettled conditions limited the quality and influence of the press. It was not until the 1880s, after independence, that the press gained freedom and standing. Among the better-known papers of this time were *Universul*, the first national daily; and *Adeverul* (Truth), which was the acknowledged champion of social and economic reform.

Despite the political turmoil of the first four decades of the 20th century, the press flourished. On the eve of World War II Rumania had a large and diversified press, with several dailies enjoying a national reputation. However, with the rise of the Communists to power in 1944, the slate was wiped clean, and a new press took shape on the Soviet model. No prewar dailies survive today except *Scinteia* (Spark), founded in 1931 as the organ of the PCR.

The national press consists of six dailies in addition to *Scinteia:*

- *Elore* (Forward), in Hungarian. Founded in 1944 as an organ of the National Council of the Socialist Democracy and Unity Front. Circulation: 80,000.
- *Informatia Bucurestiului* (Bucharest Information). Founded in 1953 as the organ of the Bucharest Committee of the PCR. Circulation: 210,000.
- *Neuer Weg* (New Way), in German. Founded in 1949 as an organ of the National Council of the Socialist Democracy and Unity Front. Circulation: 31,000.
- *Rumania Libera* (Free Rumania). Founded in 1943 as an organ of the National Council of the Socialist Democracy and Unity Front. Circulation: 430,000.
- *Scinteia Tineretului* (Spark of Youth). Founded in 1944 as the organ of the Union of Communist Youth. Circulation: 235,000.
- *Sportul* (Sport). Founded in 1945 as the organ of the National Council of Physical Education and Sports. Circulation: 445,000.

Scinteia, the Rumanian version of *Pravda*, is the country's largest-selling and most influential daily, with a circulation of 1.4 million.

There is a well-developed regional press, with 56 papers. There also are publications in minority languages such as Greek, Armenian and Yiddish.

Most papers are printed in a somewhat reduced broadsheet size, with relatively few pages. Even *Scinteia* seldom exceeds eight pages. Papers are published six days a week—Tuesday through Sunday, with no issue on Monday. There are no special Sunday editions or sections.

As in other Eastern bloc countries, the periodicals press is characterized by extraordinary diversity. There are specialized publications dealing with everything from culture to farming. The Orthodox Church publishes nine religious journals and a large number of books each year.

Since all publications are state organs, they are not subject to the same economic constraints as their counterparts in the West. Nevertheless, the press is hard hit in times of austerity, and its newsprint supplies have been curtailed since the early 1970s. The government also favors the electronic media over the print media for propaganda purposes and therefore is unwilling to fund new printing equipment and technologies.

The Constitution guarantees freedom of speech and of the press but qualifies them immediately by noting that these freedoms "cannot be used for aims hostile to the socialist system and to the interests of the working people." In any case, since the press and broadcasting are state monopolies (except for religious publications), the constitutional guarantees are moot.

A 1974 press law gave to the Press and Printing Committee of the Council of Ministers the power to oversee all publishing authorizations, newsprint supply and allocation, operation of printing plants, distribution of all publications and issuance of journalists' cards. Among the principal provisions of the law are:

Press organs are not obliged to disclose to those concerned the sources of information on the basis of which they have edited the published material; the undisclosed sources are a professional secret.

For the protection of the interests of society and individuals against the misuse of the right to freedom of expression in the press, it is forbidden to publish and disseminate through the press materials that:

• are contrary to the Constitution

• contain attacks against the socialist social order and the principles of the internal and foreign policy of the party and government

• defame the party and state leadership

• communicate secret information, facts or documents that are defined as such by law

• contain false or alarming information and comments that endanger or disturb public order or constitute a danger for the security of the state

• call for the disrespect of the laws of the state and for the perpetration of criminal offenses

• disseminate fascist, obscurantist or antihumanitarian views, disseminate chauvinist propaganda, incite to racial hatred or national hatred or to acts of violence, or offend national feelings

• offend against good morals or incite to the violation of the standards of ethics and of social life

• give information on current trials and thereby anticipate judgments to be made by the legal organs

• make untrue statements that detract from an individual's reputation or his or her social or professional prestige, or in which insults, libels or threats are uttered against a person

In December 1977 a decree by the Council of State abolished the Press and Printing Committee and transferred its powers to the Council on Socialist Culture and Education. The decree further stated that the council would "guide the publishing houses and exert control over their output," clearly assigning it both pre- and postpublication censorship powers. It also is directly responsible for the import of all books, film and phonograph records and for scheduling professional and amateur artistic performances. The council can suspend offending publications pending final decisions by proper authorities or courts of law. A more important departure was the creation of a new category of journalists called "cooperating journalists." These cooperating journalists are designed to monitor the production and distribution of publications.

The national news agency is the Agerpress (Agentia Rumana de Presa), set up in 1949 and reorganized in 1978 as a "party and state" institution. Only Agerpress is empowered to distribute news to the domestic media. The major foreign news agencies represented in Bucharest are Novosti, TASS, AP, ANSA, ADN, Tanjug, Prensa Latina, and Xinhua.

Both television and radio are of particular concern to the regime—a fact reflected in recurrent personnel reshuffles and reorganization of the electronic media.

MEDIA INDICATORS, 1988

Newspapers
  Number of dailies: 36
  Circulation (000): 3,109
  Circulation per 1,000: 136
  Number of nondailies: 24
  Circulation (000): 122
  Circulation per 1,000: 5
  Number of periodicals: 422
  Circulation (000): 709
  Newsprint consumption:
  Total (tons): 60,000
  Per capita, kg (lb.): 2.6 (5.7)
Book publishing
  Number of titles: 5,276
Radio
  Number of transmitters: 83
  Number of radio receivers (000): 3,192
    Persons per radio receiver: 7.1
  Total annual program hours: 32,812
Television
  Television transmitters: 344
  Number of television receivers (000): 3,856
    Persons per television receiver: 5.9
  Total annual program hours: 5,057
Cinema
  Number of fixed cinemas: 5,454
  Seating capacity: 257,000
    Seats per 1,000: 11.2
  Annual attendance (million): 191.5
    Per capita: 8.3
Films
  Production of long films: 27
  Import of long films: 113
    5.3% from United States
    38.9% from USSR
    3.5% from France
    2.7% from Italy

CULTURAL & ENVIRONMENTAL INDICATORS, 1988

Public libraries
  Number: 6,290
  Volumes (000): 67,379
  Registered borrowers: 4,661,000
  Loans per 1,000: 2,050
Museums
  Number: 459
  Annual attendance (000): 17,108
  Attendance per 1,000: 750
Performing arts
  Facilities: 154
  Number of performances: 49,400
  Annual attendance (000): 17,900
  Attendance per 1,000: 788
  Ecological sites: 9
  Botanical gardens & zoos: 9

Broadcast operations are controlled by the National Council on Radio and TV under the supervision of the Council of State. Actual operations are controlled by the Rumanian Radio and Television Network, headed by a director general and an executive bureau. Radio (Radiodifuziunea Rumana) broadcasts three programs on both long and medium wave as well as FM from its headquarters in Bucharest. In addition, six regional stations not only serve as relay points for the national network but also originate some of their own programming, including broadcasts in Hungarian, Serbo-Croatian and German. About a fourth of the broadcasts consists of news and information programs. Foreign programs are broadcast on one medium-wave and eight shortwave transmitters. The TV service (Televiziunea Rumana) consists of two channels. Until 1971 a sizable share of TV entertainment programming consisted of U.S. and British features, but between 1971 and 1990 the regime banned many of them as representing "the retrograde bourgeois ideology and the decadent philosophy, morals and culture of the contemporary capitalist world."

Book publishing is conducted under the auspices of Centrala Editoriala (Publishing Center), founded in 1962 as a state organization. The average number of titles issued annually has declined to about 5,000 from the peak of 13,500 from 1949 to 1953. There are 26 publishing houses; 21 of them are in Bucharest. Each publishes materials within its own field and is responsible, through its director, for the quality of the works. Distribution and sale of books, both domestic and foreign are vested in the Book Central.

Rumanian libraries are divided into general libraries and documentary or specialized libraries. The two national libraries are the Library of the Academy of the Socialist Republic of Rumania, founded in 1867; and the Central State Library, founded in 1955. The former holds a valuable collection of ancient Rumanian manuscripts, and the latter publishes the *National Bibliography*.

Film production, distribution and exhibition are controlled by the National Center of Cinematography, which operates two production studios: the Alexandru Sahia Film Studio in Bucharest, producing documentaries, cartoons and puppet films; and the Bucharest Film Studio, producing feature films at Buftea, about 24 km. (15 mi.) northwest of the capital. Continuing to reflect their earlier French influence, Rumanian films were noted for their high quality until 1968. However, an ideological purification campaign started in 1971 resulted in a decline in the number and quality of films.

SOCIAL WELFARE

Since 1967, Social Security has been the responsibility of the Ministry of Labor, and many social benefits are administered through trade unions. The principal benefits are free medical assistance and medicine, maternity benefits, old-age pensions, disability pensions, family allowances and funeral allowances. Old-age pensions are granted at age 62 for men and 57 for women, except those performing arduous tasks, who retire at 55 and 50, respectively.

There is no private welfare system in Rumania.

CHRONOLOGY

1946—The National Democratic Front regime led by Petru Groza, leader of the Plowmen's Front, holds rigged elections in which Communists win 379 of 414 seats in the Grand National Assembly.

1947—King Michael is forced to abdicate; the People's Republic of Rumania is declared. . . . Peace treaty is signed with the Soviet Union.

1948—Social Democrats and Communists form a new party called the Rumanian Workers' Party, controlled by the latter. . . . Grand National Assembly adopts new Constitution. . . . All banks, industrial enterprises and farmlands are nationalized.

1952—Anna Pauker and the pro-Soviet group who had been in exile in Moscow during World War II are purged; Gheorghe Gheorghiu-Dej emerges as the undisputed leader of the PCR. . . . New Constitution is promulgated.

1961—Politburo is replaced by the Standing Presidium, and the Presidium of the Grand National Assembly by the Council of State.

1965—Gheorghiu-Dej dies. . . . New Constitution is promulgated. . . . The People's Republic of Rumania is renamed the Socialist Republic of Rumania. . . . Nicolae Ceausescu succeeds Gheorghiu-Dej as PCR leader.

1967—Ceausescu is elected president of the republic.

1979—Ilie Verdet replaces Manea Manescu as prime minister.

1982—Constantine Dascalescu is named prime minister.

1988—Relations with Hungary worsen over Rumania's "systematization" program, aimed at reducing Hungarian concentration in parts of Transylvania. . . . Rather than change its emigration laws, Rumania renounces its most-favored-nation status in trade with the United States.

1989—Massive protests follow the shooting of hundreds of peaceful demonstrators in Timisoara by Securitate troops; clashes spread to Bucharest, where a massive anti-Ceausescu rally of over 150,000 is broken up by the Securitate; unrest spreads to other cities; army refuses to fire on demonstrators. . . . The defense minister, Col. Gen. Vasile Milea, is executed by the Securitate on Ceausescu's orders; military units and civilian rebels join in storming the presidential palace and CP Central Committee building. . . . Ceausescu and his wife, Elena, are captured by rebels while trying to flee and, after a summary trial, are condemned to death and shot. Council of National Salvation is set up as an interim government with Ion Iliescu as president and Petre Roman as prime minister.

1990—Council of National Salvation is dissolved pending free national elections; the Communist Party is banned. . . . In free elections contested by over 40 political parties, the National Salvation Front wins overwhelming victory in an apparent landslide. . . . Iliescu is elected president. . . . Students and opposition parties stage violent demonstrations that are put down by pro-government forces. . . . Private enterprise is legalized. . . . Government declares emergency in Transylvania as ethnic clashes between Hungarians and Rumanians leave three people dead and hundreds injured.

BIBLIOGRAPHY

Fischer-Galati, Stephen. *The New Romania.* Cambridge, Mass., 1967.
_____. *Romania.* New York, 1957.
_____. *The Socialist Republic of Romania.* Baltimore, 1969.
_____. *Twentieth-Century Romania.* New York, 1970.
Floyd, David. *Romania: Russia's Dissident Ally.* New York, 1965.
Graham, Lawrence. *Romania: A Developing Socialist State.* Boulder, Colo., 1982.
Ionescu, Ghita. *Communism in Romania, 1944–62.* London, 1964.

Matley, Ian M. *Romania: A Profile.* New York, 1970.
Nelson, Daniel N. (ed). *Romania in the 1980s.* Boulder, Colo., 1981.
Shafir, Michael. *Romania: Politics, Economics and Society.* New York, 1985.
Staar, Richard F. (ed). *The Communist Regimes in Eastern Europe: An Introduction.* Stanford, Calif., 1967.

OFFICIAL PUBLICATIONS

Anuarul Statistical Republicii Socaliste Rumania.
Recersamintul Populatiei si al Locuintelor.
Rumania Yearbook.

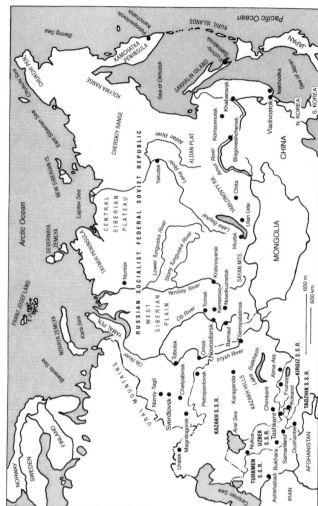

SOVIET UNION

BASIC FACTS SHEET

OFFICIAL NAME: Union of Soviet Socialist Republics

ABBREVIATION: USSR

CAPITAL: Moscow

HEAD OF STATE: Chairman of the Presidium of the Supreme Soviet and General Secretary of the Communist Party of the Soviet Union Mikhail Gorbachev (from 1985)

HEAD OF GOVERNMENT: Chairman of the Council of Ministers Nikolai Ryzhkov (from 1985)

NATURE OF GOVERNMENT: Emerging Socialist democracy

POPULATION: 286,700,000 (1989)

AREA: 22,402,000 sq. km. (8,649,512 sq. mi.)

MAJOR ETHNIC GROUPS: Russian (52%); Ukrainian (16%); over 100 other ethnic groups (nationalities)

LANGUAGES: Russian (national language); more than 200 other languages (18 with more than 1 million speakers); language groups: 75% Slavic; 8% other Indo-European; 12% Altaic; 3% Uralian; 2% Caucasian

RELIGIONS: Officially atheist, estimated at 70% of population; 18% Russian Orthodox; 9% Muslim; 3% Jewish, Protestant, Georgian Orthodox, Armenian Orthodox or Roman Catholic

UNIT OF CURRENCY: Ruble

NATIONAL FLAG: Red with a gold hammer and sickle in the upper left corner surmounted by a five-pointed red star bordered in gold.

NATIONAL EMBLEM: The central figure is a globe bright red for the landmass and blue for the oceans, on which are imposed in gold a crossed hammer and sickle. The globe is illuminated by a rising sun. These elements are displayed on a white elliptical field, above which is placed a gold-edged, red five-pointed star. Surrounding the design is a garland of golden wheat ears tied with red ribbon, on which gold lettering in 14 languages (with Russian at the base) repeats 15 times, one for each constituent republic, the rallying cry of the October 1917 Revolution, "Workers [Proletarians] of the World, Unite." Each of the constituent SSR's has its own emblem, on which the red star and the hammer and sickle appear prominently.

NATIONAL ANTHEM: "Soyuz Nerushimy Respublik Svobodnykh" ("Indestructible Union of Free Republics")

NATIONAL HOLIDAYS: New Year's Day; March 8 (International Women's Day); May 1 and 2 (May Day); May 9 (Victory Day); November 7–8 (Revolution Day); December 5 (Constitution Day); no religious holidays

NATIONAL CALENDAR: Gregorian

PHYSICAL QUALITY OF LIFE INDEX: 94 (on an ascending scale with 100 as the maximum)

DATE OF INDEPENDENCE: C. 900

DATE OF CONSTITUTION: October 7, 1977

WEIGHTS & MEASURES: Metric

GEOGRAPHICAL FEATURES

The Soviet Union is the largest country in the world, with a total area of 22,402,000 sq. km. (8,649,512 sq. mi.), or about one-sixth of the inhabited part of the world's land surface. It extends through 11 of the world's 24 time zones. It occupies the eastern half of Europe and the northern part of Asia, extending 10,944 km. (6,800 mi.) east to west and 4,506 km. (2,800 mi.) north to south. About 5,571,200 sq. km. (2,151,046 sq. mi.) are in Europe and 16,831,000 sq. km. (6,498,466 sq. mi.) are in Asia. The mainland, with its rivers and lakes, makes up 21,781,883 sq. km. (8,410,000 sq. mi.), while inland seas and territorial waters, such as the Sea of Azov and the White Sea, account for an additional 181,300 sq. km. (70,000 sq. mi.). Soviet island groups in the Arctic and Pacific oceans—Franz Josef Land, Novaya Zemlya, New Siberian Islands, Sernaya Zemlya, Wrangel Island,

Commander Islands, Kuril Islands and Sakhalin—total 310,800 sq. km. (120,000 sq. mi.).

The total exterior coastline is 60,085 km. (37,335 mi.), and the total insular coastline is 48,261 km. (29,988 mi.).

The Soviet Union borders on 11 countries, with which it shares a total of 80,302 km. (49,899 mi.) of boundary, as follows:

In the far north, the boundary with Norway extends inland from the Barents Sea for about 193 km. (120 mi.) to the Finnish tripoint at Krokfjell, a few miles west of the Pasvikely River. For most of its length the boundary follows natural water features. The boundary was established by the 1826 Treaty of Petersburg. From the Norwegian tripoint the boundary with Finland extends in a generally southerly direction for about 1,287 km. (800 mi.) to the Gulf of Finland at a point about 161 km. (100 mi.) west of Leningrad. The boundary is delimited

413

for the most part by straight lines, ignoring natural features. The boundary rests on agreements negotiated at the end of World War I, the Winter War of 1939–40 and World War II. The boundary with Poland was established at the end of World War II through the Yalta and Potsdam agreements. From a point on the shore of the Gulf of Danzig, some 48 km. (30 mi.) southwest of Kaliningrad, the boundary runs east and then south for 1,046 km. (650 mi.) to the Czechoslovak tripoint, about 129 km. (80 mi.) southwest of Lvov. Except for 161 km. (100 mi.) where the boundary follows the course of the Bug River, natural features are disregarded. The boundary with Czechoslovakia, extending from Poland to the Hungarian tripoint southwest of the railway junction of Chop, was fixed by the Moscow Agreement of 1945 by which Czechoslovakia ceded Transcarpathian Ruthenia to the Soviet Union. The boundary with Hungary was established at the Paris Peace Conference of 1919. The boundary with Rumania from the Hungarian tripoint to the Black Sea derives from Rumania's cession of Moldavia to the Soviet Union in 1940, recognized by the Treaty of Peace of 1947. The boundary with Turkey begins on the Black Sea coast about 24 km. (15 mi.) southeast of Batumi and follows an irregular course. The boundary was delimited in the 1921 Treaties of Moscow and Kars and demarcated in 1925–26. Beginning at the Turkish tripoint in the center of the main channel of the Araks River about 64 km. (40 mi.) southeast of Yerevan, the boundary with Iran extends for over 1,609 km. (1,000 mi.), of which some 724 km. (450 mi.) lie west of the Caspian Sea. The boundary follows the Araks River until it reaches the Caspian Sea about 241 km. (150 mi.) south of Baku and then follows an irregular course eastward to the Afghan tripoint in the main channel of the Hari Rud River about 161 km. (100 mi.) northwest of Herat. West of the Caspian Sea the boundaries were defined by the 19th-century Treaties of Gulistan and Turkmanchai and to the east by the Tehran conventions of 1881 and 1893. The irregular border with Afghanistan follows a winding course to the Amu Darya (Oxus River) and then follows the Amu Darya and two of its tributaries upstream through high mountains to Lake Victoria (Zorkul), from which it continues along the ridgelines of the Pamirs to the Chinese tripoint. The boundary with Afghanistan is based on several bilateral agreements, particularly the Afghan-Soviet agreements of 1921 and 1946. The boundary with China stretches from the Pamirs in central Asia to within a few miles of the Sea of Japan, and it is the longest boundary in the world. It is divided into two sectors by the Mongolian People's Republic. On the west the Sinkiang-Turkestan section follows main drainage divides for about half its length and then valleys and streamlines for the other half; on the east it follows the Argun, Amur and Ussuri rivers. Although most of this boundary has been delimited by a series of treaties (except the portion in the area of the Pamirs), there are a number of territorial disputes over the exact course of the rivers and the alignments of other features. The boundary with Mongolia extends in an irregular arc south of Lake Baikal and is based on the Treaty of Kyakhta, concluded in 1727 between Russia and China. Extending from the Chinese tripoint to the Sea of Japan, the boundary

with North Korea follows the lower course of the Tumen River.

The capital is Moscow, which also is the largest city in the Soviet Union and the capital of the Russian Soviet Federated Socialist Republic (RSFSR). Founded in the 12th century, Moscow has been the capital of Russia ever since, except during the period after Peter the Great moved his capital to St. Petersburg. There are 21 other cities with over 1 million inhabitants and 31 cities with populations between 500,000 and 1 million. The 21 largest cities are:

Leningrad. Situated at the head of the Gulf of Finland and at the mouth of the Neva River and known formerly as St. Petersburg, or, from 1920 to 1924, as Petrograd. Leningrad is the chief Baltic seaport.

Kiev. Capital of the Ukrainian Soviet Socialist Republic and formerly the capital of the grand princes of Kiev, sacked by the Mongols in 1240 and annexed by Russia in the 17th century.

Tashkent. Capital of the Uzbek Soviet Socialist Republic and the largest city in central Asia, it is situated on the Syr Darya.

Baku. Seaport, capital of the Azerbaijan Soviet Socialist Republic and situated on the Caspian Sea on the southern coast of the Apsheron Peninsula. It is the chief center of petroleum production and refining, a leading naval station and an important rail and pipeline junction.

Kharkhov. Industrial center on the Udi River in the Ukraine, founded by the Cossacks in 1650 and the capital of the Ukraine from 1919 to 1934.

Minsk. Capital of the Byelorussian Soviet Socialist Republic, it is on the main railroad line between Moscow and Warsaw.

Gorky (or Gorki). Formerly Nizhni or Novgorod, about 402 km. (250 mi.) east of Moscow and situated on the junction of the Oka and Volga rivers. Site of a famous annual fair in the 19th century.

Novosibirsk. Chief city of Siberia on the Ob River and the Trans-Siberian Railroad. Founded in the 1890s as a railroad town, but developed rapidly.

Sverdlovsk. Formerly Yekaterinburg. Principal industrial and commercial city of the Urals; founded by Peter the Great in 1723.

Kuybyshev (or Kuibyshev). Chief port of the Volga at the junction of the Samara and Volga rivers.

Tbilisi (or Tiflis). Capital of the Georgian Soviet Socialist Republic; on the Kura River. Chief commercial city in Caucasia; often plundered by the Persians and the Mongols.

Dnepropetrovsk. Formerly Ekaterinoslav. Ukrainian city on the Dneiper River above the rapids.

Yerevan (or Erivan). Capital of the Armenian Soviet Socialist Republic; on the Zanga River.

Odessa. Seaport on the Black Sea; chief seaport in the Ukraine. Founded in 1794 and heavily bombarded during the Crimean War.

Omsk. City in the RSFSR in western Siberia, at the junction of the Om River with the Irtysh. Its historic fortress was founded in 1716.

Chelyabinsk. City in the RSFSR in the southern Urals.

Alma-Ata. Formerly Verny. Capital of the Kazakh Soviet Socialist Republic; at the junction of the Turkestan-Siberia Railroad.

Donetsk. Formerly Stalino. City in the Donbas coal basin; founded in 1870.

Ufa. Capital of the Bashkir Autonomous Soviet Socialist Republic of the RSFSR; on the Belaya River; founded in 1574.

Perm. Formerly Molotov. City on the banks of the River Kama; founded in 1723.

Kazan. Capital of the Tatar Autonomous Soviet Socialist Republic; near the Volga River. Founded in 1437 as a Tartar fortress; capital of a khanate until taken by the Muscovites in 1469.

The great plain that comprises much of the Soviet Union reaches from the western frontiers in Europe to the center of Asia. To the west it is broken by higher ground along the Barents Sea and the border with Finland, extending southward nearly to the Black Sea through the center of European Russia. To the southwest, the hilly region of the Ukraine extends eastward to uplands along the Volga River and southward to the

Country	Km.	Mi.
North Korea	17	11
China	7,520	4,673
Mongolia	3,441	2,138
Afghanistan	2,383	1,481
Iran	1,974	1,227
Turkey	617	383
Rumania	1,307	812
Hungary	135	84
Czechoslovakia	99	62
Poland	1,215	755
Finland	1,313	816
Norway	196	122

MAJOR URBAN CENTERS

(est. population in 1986, in 000)

Moscow (Moskva), the capital	8,703	Zaporozhye	863
Leningrad	4,901	Voronezh	860
Kiev (Kiyev)	2,495	Lvov	753
Tashkent	2,073	Krivoy Rog	691
Baku	1,722	Kishinev	643
Kharkov	1,567	Yaroslavl	630
Minsk	1,510	Karaganda	624
Gorky	1,409	Ustinov (formerly Izhevsk)	620
Novosibirsk	1,405		
Sverdlovsk	1,316	Frunze	618
Kuybyshev	1,267	Krasnodar	616
Tbilisi	1,174	Tolyatti	610
Dnepropetrovsk	1,166	Vladivostok	608
Yerevan	1,148	Irkutsk	602
Odessa	1,132	Barnaul	586
Omsk	1,124	Khabarovsk	584
Chelyabinsk	1,107	Novokuznetsk	583
Alma-Ata	1,088	Ulyanovsk	567
Donetsk	1,081	Doshanbe	565
Ufa	1,077	Vilnius	555
Perm	1,066	Tula	534
Kazan	1,057	Penza	532
Rostov-on-Don	993	Orenburg	527
Volgograd	981	Zhdanov	525
Saratov	908	Kemerovo	515
Riga	890	Astrakhan	503
Krasnoyarsk	885	Voroshilovgrad	503

mountains of the Caucasus. Farther east, the great plain is interrupted by the chain of the Ural Mountains, which traditionally is considered as the dividing line between the continents of Asia and Europe.

South of the Ural Mountains and extending eastward along the Caspian Sea, lowlands extend into Asia as far as the foothills of the high ranges of the Pamirs and the Tien Sha, Altai and Sayan mountains that rise abruptly along the southern border. Lowlands continue to the north beyond Lake Balkhash and the moderately elevated uplands of Kazakhstan and slope as a wide plain across western Siberia to the shores of the Arctic Ocean. Farther east, beyond the Yenisey River, the land rises to form a hilly plateau region across central Siberia that merges into a complex of mountains and drainage basins extending to the eastern seaboard.

The country's northern seacoasts are never completely ice-free except for the northeast coastal region of the Kola Peninsula with the port of Murmansk, which remains ice-free because of the effects of the Gulf Stream. The Pacific seaboard, by contrast, has weather modified by the maritime influence of the Pacific Ocean. Its port city of Vladivostok overlooks Peter the Great Bay, which, although icebound in winter, is free of ice in the summer.

There are four major zones of natural vegetation, with some local variations caused by elevation, amount of sunshine, soil types and moisture. A treeless zone of tundra extends southward from the Arctic seaboard to an irregular line roughly approximating the Arctic Circle except in the White Sea-Kola Peninsula area of the far Northwest. This is a region of permafrost, with only scattered, stunted bushes in the southern part.

South of the tundra is the Taiga, with its great coniferous forest, the largest in the world. In the northern reaches the trees grow slowly and are shorter, but farther south the forest stands are thicker and taller.

A belt of grassland consisting mainly of steppe with natural cover of short, bunched grasses lies south of the forest zone. This belt is widest in European Russia and extends through the Ukraine in a narrowing triangle across western Siberia. This zone has the best agricultural land in the country.

A wide belt of arid steppe and desert extends from the mountains along the southern border westward from central Asia to the northern slopes of the Caucasus. This zone is broadest in western Siberia and Kazakhstan and is characterized by lack of trees, scanty grasses and poor soils. South of the steppe the land becomes a true desert.

Geographers distinguish six major topographic regions: the Baltic-Belorussian region; the Ukraine-Moldavia region; Transcaucasia; the RSFSR in Europe; the RSFSR in Asia; and central Asia.

The Baltic-Belorussian region is made up of a broad glacial plain stretching from the shores of the Baltic Sea southward along the western borders across the lowlands of the Pripet Marches to the Ukraine. Most of the region is below 152 m. (500 ft.) in elevation, and much of the land is either boggy or interspersed with small lakes and swamps. From a low divide that crosses the center of the region, the western Dvina and the Bug rivers and their tributaries drain northwestward to the

Baltic Sea. South of the divide, drainages into the Pripet and Dnieper rivers flow to the Black Sea.

The Ukraine-Moldavia region is a land of broad plains and low, rolling hills, with a few wide river valleys extending across the southern part of Russia in Europe as far as the hilly area north of the Sea of Azov on the western side of the Don River. From the edge of the Carpathian Mountains the land descends to the east. Most of the region is below 457 m. (1,500 ft.) and of nearly featureless relief. Major drainage is to the south and east. The Dnieper River flows to the Black Sea through the center of the region, roughly paralleled on the west by the Dniester and Prut rivers and on the east by the Donets.

Transcaucasia, made up of the republics of Georgia, Armenia and Azerbaijan, is situated between the Black and Caspian seas and includes most of the high ranges of the Caucasus Mountains. Armenia is the most mountainous and arid, while in Georgia mountain meadows and steppes alternate with forests. The southern part of Azerbaijan is subtropical.

The RSFSR in Europe is largely a plain interrupted by a few ranges of hills and wide river valleys that terminate in the Ural Mountains. In the far North a narrow belt of tundra extends inland from the Arctic shoreline. However, most of the northern half of the region has natural vegetation. East of the mouth of the Volga River and northeast of the Caspian Sea begins the great central Asian area of deserts and semideserts.

The RSFSR in Asia is the largest region in the country, stretching eastward from the Ural Mountains north of Kazakhstan to the Lena River and the Pacific Ocean and consisting of the western and northern Siberian lowlands interrupted by the Irtysh, Ob and Yenisey rivers. The last-named marks the beginning of the Central Siberian Plateau. This plateau is, in turn, interrupted by a large triangular plain, the Central Yakutsk Lowlands, formed by a bend of the Lena River. Beyond the Lena River, the high and irregular Verkhoyansk, Cherski and Kolyma mountain systems range northeast toward the Bering Strait. Along its southern borders, the region is delimited by the Altai and Sayan mountains, the Mongolian Desert and the Amur and Ussuri rivers.

South of the RSFSR in Asia and extending eastward some 2,414 km. (1,500 mi.) to the Chinese border is the central Asian region, which includes five republics: Kazakh, Turkmen, Kirghiz, Uzbek and Tadzhik. From the high mountains that rise along the southern and southeastern part of this region, the ground descends to much lower elevations, with drainage to the north. Beyond the foothills the land consists largely of flat to moderately hilly country crossed by a few major river valleys and of lowland plains along the Caspian and Aral seas.

The immense rolling plains dominate Russia to such an extent that its mountains and depressions do not figure prominently in geographic analyses. The best known of these mountains, the Urals, are actually low ranges, and although uplands predominate east of the Yenisey, they seldom rise above 914 m. (3,000 ft.). The highest mountains are in the southern border regions, where Communism and Lenin peaks rise to 7,495 m.

(24,590 ft.) and 7,121 m. (23,363 ft.), respectively. High mountain ranges also separate central Siberia from the Pacific coast; the Pobeda reaches 3,146 m. (10,322 ft.) and the Klyuchevskaya Sopka in Kamchatka Peninsula 4,572 m. (15,000 ft.). In contrast, the Caspian lies 28 m. (92 ft.) below mean sea level. Another great depression is occupied by Lake Baikal, the deepest lake in the world.

Between the Russian Plain and the West Siberian Lowland—two of the most monotonously flat surfaces on earth—lie the Ural Mountains, a series of parallel ranges extending 2,414 km. (1,500 mi.) along longitude 60°E, from the Arctic coast to the Ural River. Their average altitude is 229 to 914 m. (750 to 3,000 ft.), but the highest points rise to over 1,524 m. (5,000 ft.). The system is about 80 km. (50 mi.) wide in the North, much narrower in the center and over 225 km. (140 mi.) wide in the South. The northern range contains the highest point of the whole range, Mount Narodnaya, at 1,885 m. (6,185 ft.). The system here consists of two parallel ranges cut by transverse valleys narrowing toward the north where the Arctic Ural forms a single range with a general elevation of about 610 m. (2,000 ft.). The southern Ural extends from Mount Yurma to the middle reaches of the Ural River, beyond which the ranges die away into the low, rounded Mugodzhar Hills. The ranges comprise several parallel chains. The highest point here is the Yaman Tau (1,656 m.; 5,432 ft.) on the Ural Tau, the eastern range.

The remaining mountain systems may be divided into three main groups. The mountains on the southern fringe of the Central Siberian Uplands, also covering most of northeastern Siberia; the mountains of central Asia; and the alpine ranges of Kopet Dag, the Caucasus and the southern European Russian ranges in the Carpathians and the Crimea.

Of the Siberian mountain systems, the best known is the Altay, which may be divided into the South Altay, a westward extension of the Tabyn-Bogdo-Ola massif; the Inner Altay; the East Altay, which separates the Ob and the Yenisey drainage; and the Mongolian Altay, lying mostly beyond Soviet borders. The highest peaks in these ranges are in the Katyn Belki of the Inner Altay, where the twin peaks of Mount Belukha rise to 4,619 m. (15,154 ft.) to the east and to 4,439 m. (14,563 ft.) to the west.

A probable northern continuation of the Altay is the Kuznetsk Basin, bordered on the west by the Salair Range and on the east by the Kuznetsk Ala Tau and drained by the Tom River.

The Sayan is less known than the Altay. It forms a broad, south-facing arc of mountains between the Abakan River and the Baykalian Khamar Daban Mountains. The system is divided into the Eastern Sayan and the Western Sayan. The former are generally higher than the latter and rise to almost 3,200 m. (10,500 ft.) in Mount Munku-Sardyk, from which several glaciers descend. Except where they have eroded by ice, the mountains have rather flat summits, above which rise bare, domelike peaks (goltsy). Between the Abakan Range and the Kuznetsk Ala Tau is a rich steppe known as the "Granary of Siberia."

Southeastern Siberia consists of wide watershed plateaus dissected into dome-shaped peaks and rounded ridges. Four subdivisions of these plateaus are distinguished: Cisbaykalia, western Transbaykalia, eastern Transbaykalia and northern Transbaykalia. The major ranges are the Khamar Daban Range, the Barguzin Range and the Yablonovyy Range in western Transbaykalia and the Stanovoy Range in northern Transbaykalia. The separate Dzhugdzhur Range forms the coastal mountain belt along the Okhotsk Sea. In the far east, the major ranges are the Tukuringra Range in the north; the Bureya Mountains; and the Sikhote Alin, on the coast of the Gulf of Tartary. On the eastern side of the Gulf of Tartary Sakhalin is a mountainous island formed by two parallel chains with a central depression. Kamchatka has a volcanic belt, which continues on to the Kuril Islands.

Central Asia is ringed on the south and east by mountains. The southern mountains are the Kopet Dag, the Pamir, the Parompamiz and the southern Tyan Shan. The central Tyan Shan continues westward in the Zeravshan, Turkestan and Fergana ranges as well as the Alay, the Dzungarian Ala Tau and the Tarbagatay and eastward in the Kwen Lun. The ranges form a majestic range of high peaks and plateaus, with two major glaciers. East of the Amu Darya, in the Pamirs, are the highest peaks in the Peter the First Range and the Academy of Sciences Range. Earthquakes are particularly common in the western Pamirs.

The mountains of Caucasia are subdivided into the Great Caucasus and the Little Caucasus, the two separated by a broad depression. To the west the depression forms the Colchis (Kolkhiz) Lowlands, a humid coastal plain drained by the Inguri and the Rioni, and to the east the Kura-Araks Lowlands. The two lowlands are separated by a higher depression, itself broken by the sweep of the Suram Range, a granitic massif crossed by the difficult Suram Pass. The Little Caucasus seldom rise over 2,286 m. (7,500 ft.) and generally are composed of rocks younger than those in the Great Caucasus. To the south the Armenian Plateau is cut by the Soviet border along the Araks and Akhuryan rivers. The highest points, the 4,877-m.-high (16,000-ft.-high) twin peaks of Mount Ararat, lie just across the Turkish boundary.

Although Crimea forms a southern and almost detached portion of the steppes of the Black Sea Lowlands, the southern coast is distinguished by three parallel ranges to the west and two to the east. Since the incorporation in 1945 of the extreme eastern districts of Czechoslovakia, the Soviet Union also has included a section of the Carpathian Mountains.

The Soviet Arctic islands have geographically so little in common with the mainland that they must be considered separately. The westernmost is Franz Josef Land, a group of about 800 islands discovered in 1873 and incorporated in 1926. Novaya Zemlya consists of two large and several smaller islands, with the narrow navigable deep channel of Matochkin Shar between the two large islands. There is extensive glaciation in the northern island, with poor tundra vegetation elsewhere. Other islands in the northern waters include Vaygach, Kolguyev, Severnaya Zemlya (consisting of four large and several smaller islands), the New Siberian Islands (an archipelago of over 11 islands), Feddeyev, Kotelnyy, Wrangel and Herald.

Russian rivers are among the longest and largest in the world. They have characteristically long courses and large basins; their flow is quantitatively great, though in relation to basin and area, relatively small. The major control on their use is climate. Frozen for varying periods in winter, they thaw in spring, their great floods hampering navigation and causing much destruction. In the summer, navigation is frequently hampered by low water. Canals linking river basins as well as dams have only partially helped to correct these problems.

The rivers of European Russia flow either north or south across the almost level plain, and their watersheds often are indistinct. The main watershed lies in the northern glacial morainic belt so that the southern-flowing rivers are the longer ones. The rivers are nearly all marked by spring high water, often accompanied by flooding, since their main source is melting snow. Toward summer the northern-flowing streams show a more even regime than those flowing south and have winter low water. The greatest system is the Volga and its tributaries. The Volga rises in the Valday Hills and collects most of its tributaries, including the Kama, in the reaches above the great Samara Bend, where the river flows out into the steppe. The river is frozen from late November until early April, when the *raputitsa* provides a sudden increase in water. The level rises slowly, carrying with it ice floes, which block the river and cause floods. At the Samara Bend, the maximum volume in April and May may be 80 times normal. South of the Samara Bend, evaporation, lack of tributaries and some seepage reduce the river's volume, although not so much as to prevent flooding below Volgograd. Low water in late summer hinders navigation.

The Dnieper also rises in the Valday Hills and flows into the Black Sea. The Dnieper has a longer ice-free period in its lower reaches than most Russian rivers. The 37-m.-deep (120-ft.-deep) reservoir behind the Dneproges Dam, built in 1932, has drowned the former Zaporozhye rapids; and the Kakhovka Barrage, built in 1956, has raised the water level in the lower reaches. Other rivers in European Russia are relatively minor. The western Dvina, the Narva and the Neman, flowing into the Baltic, are short, while the Karelian and Kola rivers have many falls and rapids.

The western Siberian rivers have extremely low gradients. The Ob, for example, is only 91 m. (300 ft.) above sea level over 1,931 km. (1,200 mi.) from its mouth. They are all very slow in the middle and lower reaches. Some, like the Irtysh, are fast-flowing in their upper reaches. The winter freeze also lasts much longer than in Europe, so that in general most Siberian rivers have less than 10% of their flow in winter. The eastern Siberian rivers have a similar regime, as runoff from permafrost areas is rapid. May and June are the high-water period. At high water the Yenisey has 52 times the low-water volume and the Yana has 500 times the low-water volume. Ice floes carried downstream frequently form dams across rivers at narrow bends, and shallows and floods from bursting ice dams can cause serious damage. The rivers are very large: The Yenisey is 5 to 6 km. (3 to 4 mi.) wide in its lower reaches, and the Lena is 13 km. (8 mi.) wide in its middle and lower reaches. The rivers of the Altay and Sayan mountains are tributaries of the major Siberian rivers.

The major rivers in central Asia are the Syr Darya, the Amu Darya and the Ili. In their upper reaches they are fed by snowfields and melting glaciers and by spring rains in their foothill courses. Loss by evaporation is high, and in summer most rivers carry little water or dry up.

The Soviet Union contains some of the world's largest inland waters, truly described as seas rather than lakes, but with the exception of the Caspian, they do not play a major role in the economy comparable to that of the Great Lakes in the United States or Canada. The Caspian Sea, whose surface area exceeds that of the United Kingdom, lies 28 m. (92 ft.) below mean sea level and consists of a shallow northern basin and a deep southern basin. The water is brackish, although the salt content is kept down by the movement of the water into the almost totally enclosed shallow evaporating pan of the Kara Bogaz Gol. Less water is brought into the Caspian than is lost through evaporation, irrigation, etc., with the result that the water level has fallen steadily in the past half century, and the shore outline is changing noticeably.

The Aral Sea is much smaller and shallower, from 18 to 61 m. (60 to 200 ft.). It lies in a gentle downfold bordered on the west by the scarp edge of the Urt Plateau and is fed entirely by the Amu Darya and the Syr Darya. Like the Caspian, the northern part freezes for about three months in winter.

Most of the lakes of northern European Russia, such as Ladoga, Chud (Peipus), Onega and others, are glacial in origin. Lake Baykal, in Siberia, is the deepest lake in the world, at 1,201 m. (3,939 ft.). Over 644 km. (400 mi.) long and 80 km. (50 mi.) wide, it is entirely fresh water. The Selenga and Angara rivers supply 85% of its water. Lake Balkhash is fed by the Ili River; the lake's eastern end is brackish and the western end fresh. Other major lakes are the Issyk Kul (Warm Sea), Kara Kul (Black Sea) and Lake Sevan in Transcaucasia.

The Soviet coastline is two and a half the times the length of the land borders. Nearly all the coastline freezes for varying periods each year. Several of the seas on which the Soviet Union has a frontage have narrow entrances commanded by foreign powers. Examples are the Baltic narrows, the Dardanelles entrance to the Black Sea, the Sea of Japan and the Atlantic and Pacific oceans approaches to the Soviet Arctic coast.

The Arctic coastline is the longest. It is divided into sectors by numerous islands and island groups, while the submarine Lomonosov Ridge divides the ocean into two distinct basins: the relatively shallow Barents Sea and the much deeper White Sea. The Kara Sea overlies a sunken part of the West Siberian Lowland. The most difficult waters to navigate along the northern sea route are those between the Kara Sea and the Laptev Sea, divided by the shallow Vilkitskiy Strait, frequently strewn by grounded ice floes. Shallowness, low salinity, lack of tides and low temperatures all contribute to rapid ice formation in the waters of the East Siberian Sea and the Chukchi Sea.

In the South, the Black Sea and the Sea of Azov provide the coastlines. The Black Sea is geologically young and shows traces of recent submergence. It is connected to the Sea of Azov by the Strait of Kerch. The Siwash Sea lying, behind the Arabatskaya Strelka, acts as an evaporating pan. With the incorporation of former East Prussia into Soviet territory after World War II, the Soviet Union commands the southern shore of the Gulf of Finland. The northern sector is frozen in winter.

In the far East, the Russian Pacific coast lies behind an outer belt of islands facing the Sea of Japan, the Okhotsk Sea and the Bering Sea. The Bering Sea is separated from the Pacific by the Aleutian Islands, the Sea of Okhotsk by the Kuril Islands, and the Sea of Japan by the islands of Japan. The Sea of Okhotsk is more icebound than the other two.

CLIMATE & WEATHER

The Soviet climate is typically continental, with long, cold winters and short, warm summers. Maritime influences on climate are limited by the fact that nearly three-fourths of the country is more than 402 km. (250 mi.) from the sea. The long Arctic coast also influences the climate negatively by exposing the northern parts to cold, frigid air systems. Warmer air from lower latitudes is excluded by the high mountain barriers across central Asia, and Pacific air by the coastal ranges. Cold winter is one of the constants of the Russian climate, even in desert areas of central Asia, where the summers are as hot as deserts in other continents.

Winter is dominated by the intense high-pressure system developed in the polar continental air mass over Mongolia and central Siberia. From this system, intensely cold air streams out as the Asian winter monsoon. A ridge along the 50°N line across southern Russia and central Europe forms the barometric divide, with westerly circulation to the north, so that cyclonic development along the Atlantic polar and Arctic fronts brings occasional winter warm spells to northwestern Russia. To the south, easterly circulation keeps much of southern Russia and Transcaspia under the spell of Siberian cold. Cyclonic movements into this region from the Mediterranean influence the broader pattern only slightly.

As the sun moves north, the central Asian high pressure disappears with the rapid heating of the land and is replaced by an intense low-pressure system from Baluchistan. Although the system draws in warm, moist air from the southern oceans, the Himalayas act as a barrier to the moisture. Cool and damp conditions are limited to the eastern Siberian littoral and the islands. The Soviet Union remains dominated by the warm, dry, tropical continental air. Summer is short, but usually hot, with thundery showers or periods of dry and dusty conditions. After four or five short weeks of autumn, the land is once again in the icy grip of winter, although there are occasional reversions to warmer conditions in

European Russia. But in much of Siberia, where some of the lowest temperatures on earth have been recorded, there is no respite from the cold and the frequent blizzards.

Differences in precipitation are not particularly significant. Precipitation decreases eastward as well as to the south, and to the north away from the central belt of moderate fall. It is lowest in northeastern Siberia and central Asia and around the Aral Sea. The somewhat heavier fall in Amuria compared to the rest of Siberia results from the local southeasterly monsoon. North of 45°N much precipitation is in the form of snow. Throughout most of the country, summer is the rainiest season because, in winter, strong winds blowing from the winter anticyclone in Siberia prevent the penetration of moisture. Over European Russia and Siberia, July and August are the wettest months, with rain brought in by thunderstorms. In the Amur and Ussuri basins the southeasterly monsoons bring summer rain with fine drizzle along the Okhotsk coast. The extreme west and north of European Russia have autumn rain brought by westerly depressions. Although the Crimean and Black Sea coasts have no true dry season, they have a quasi-Mediterranean climate, with late autumn and winter rain. An autumn-winter maximum also is characteristic along the western shore of the Caspian Sea, although in the Armenian Plateau, the maximum is in the late spring. In central Asia the maximum is in March and April, and in the north, along the steppe fringe in May and June, most of it in thundershowers. European Russia has snow between mid-November and March and Arctic Russia between mid-September and early June. Although the winters are harsher in Siberia, the snow cover is lighter, since moisture for its formation is not present in large quantities.

The severity and length of winter over much of the Soviet Union is related to the fact that 47% of its area is covered by permafrost. In some areas permafrost may be found at depths of up to 610 m. (2,000 ft.), but more commonly only several feet. The upper, or so-called active, layer of 0.5 to 2.1 m. (1.5 to 7 ft.) may thaw in summer, with the lower limits in peat bogs and marshy ground. Buried ice is, in certain areas, overlain by more recent terrestrial deposits.

It has been said that the Soviet Union has climate but little weather. This is caused by a monotonous regularity of seasonal conditions. The major climatic belts form remarkably regular latitudinal zones across the country. The transition between these belts is gradual so that the border lines between the regions are arbitrary. The nine major zones are: (1) arctic, (2) subarctic, (3) European forest, (4) western Siberian and central Siberian, (5) far eastern monsoonal, (6) steppe, (7) desert, (8) Transcaucasian and (9) mountain.

The arctic climate is distinguished more by cool summers than by the intensity of winter cold. It is strongest in the central section of the Arctic coast between the Yenisey and the Lena rivers. Summer thaws only the surface layer for two or three months. The winters are bearable as long as the air remains still and the skies clear. Life in the open is impossible during the heavy blizzards.

The southern limit of the subarctic zone extends to the southern limit of permafrost. In the west this regime is characterized by tundra vegetation and in the center and east by wooded tundra and some forest. The western sector, which extends to the Taz River, has more varied and warm winters. Some of the lowest temperatures in the world are recorded in this zone. Generally the weather is clear and bright, but during the occasional *burans*, or violent cyclonic storms, life becomes unbearable. Summers are warm, and temperatures of up to 38°C (100°F) have been recorded. The diurnal range is very great, with a spread of up to 54°F between day and night temperatures.

The European forest zone has warm summers and long, cold winters. In the north and northwest, cyclones help to break the winter cold, and invasions of warmer and more moist Atlantic air cause warm spells *(otepely)*, particularly during November and December, when temperatures may rise to over 7°C (45°F). In the South and Southeast there is a less varied winter. Snow lies for 80 days in the South and for up to 200 days in the north between October and April, and about a third of the annual precipitation comes in the form of snow. Rivers freeze by late December and stay icebound until March. The winter is gloomy and dull, with overcast skies, and the humidity is greater, so that it feels raw. In the spring, when the thaw begins, the rivers flood, and movement becomes difficult. Summer is warm and short, and one-third of the annual precipitation falls during June and August, much of it as thunderstorms, preceded by hot, dusty winds. Autumn is the only bright and pleasant period. Along the Baltic coast, maritime influences temper both the summer warmth and the winter cold. The western slopes of the Urals have a much heavier precipitation than elsewhere.

The western and central Siberian lowlands form a transitional zone between the European forest zone and the far eastern monsoonal zone on the one hand and the steppe zone of the south on the other. Winter cold is intensified under the clear skies but is made bearable by the still air. Because of the low annual precipitation, the snow cover is light. The summer is much warmer than normal for the latitude, but it lasts only about 70 days in the north and about 100 days in the South. Over half the annual rainfall comes in late summer, which is an unpleasant time because of frequent dusty winds, mosquitoes and forest fires.

East of the Stanovoy Range and the mountains of the Okhotsk coast the influence of the southeast monsoons creates the monsoonal zone. The winter temperatures tend to be as low as those of central Siberia, but summer is moist and warm as the Pacific maritime air tempers the weather. Monsoonal rains begin in May and last until September, with the maximum in July. Annual precipitation exceeds 1,016 mm. (40 in.) in parts of Sikhote Alin. The coasts have misty, cool summers. North of the Amur estuary, the high coastal ranges of the Okhotsk coast hinder inland penetration of the monsoons. The Okhotsk coast, the Kuril Islands and Kamchatka have unpleasant, misty and moist summers.

The steppe zone, a transitional one between the forest and the desert, has cold winters but hot summers, with maximum rainfall in spring. The European steppe has warmer winters and cooler summers than the Asian steppe. Dryness increases toward the east and south except in the Black Sea littoral. Precipitation varies from 203 to 406 mm. (8 to 16 in.) a year, but even this is not reliable and falls mostly in heavy showers, so that much is lost by runoff. The resulting gullies create serious erosional problems. Winter frost reduces the friable soil to dust and provides the raw material for later dust storms, and the spring thaw turns it into a sea of mud. Rainfall reaches a maximum in late spring. Vegetation withers toward the end of the hot, dry summer, when the air becomes oppressive with dust storms. The dry *sulkhovy* blowing along the periphery of the anticyclones is another summer hazard.

Toward the south, the steppe becomes drier and drier and finally is transformed into a true desert around the Aral Sea. Summers are intensely hot and dry under the influence of the winds from the South, such as the *afganets*. Summer also is a period of great diurnal change of temperature. Most of the scanty precipitation falls during this period. Winters are cold, and the rivers freeze. Snow cover is rare in the deep south but may last for up to 60 days in the north.

Transcaucasia has a climate not found elsewhere in the Soviet Union. The lowlands have a warm and moist climate, with heavy rainfall and many clouds. There is no true dry season as moist, cool air blows from sea to land in summer and dry, warm air flows out from the interior in winter. The diurnal change of temperature is small. The Armenian Plateau has a continental steppe climate, with cold winters and much snowfall, and maximum precipitation in spring and early summer. Two small areas on the Black Sea coast—around Alushta and Yalta in Crimea and between Sochi and Sukhumi in Transcaucasia—have a Mediterranean climate, making them favorite resort areas.

The mountain climate is found in the Great Caucasus and in the central Asian mountains. The former has a warmer and wetter western face, but Dagestan is particularly dry and sunny in winter. The central Asian mountains have a continental mountain climate. The snow line varies from 3,353 m. (11,000 ft.) on the northern slopes to 5,486 m. (18,000 ft.) on the southern slopes. Winter is raw and foggy, but fohn winds occasionally bring warm conditions. In the Pamirs the snow line lies above 4,877 m. (16,000 ft.), and the atmosphere is rare and dry. The mountains of southern Siberia are warmer than the surrounding lowlands in winter and cooler in the summer. In the high mountains, the snow cover is light, so that permafrost is widespread. Climatic conditions are harsher in the Sayan than in the Altay, and winters are more severe. Mountains in northeastern Siberia have a subarctic climate.

POPULATION

The population of the Soviet Union in 1989 was 286,700,000 according to the last official census, held in that year. The Soviet Union ranks third in size of population and first in land area. The population is expected to reach 290,939,000 by 1990 and 311,637,000 by 2000.

The Soviet Union accounts for only one-seventeenth of the world population, although it accounts for one-sixth of the land surface. This is because the population is concentrated in one-fourth of the territory, while the remaining three-fourths are sparsely populated. Population density is more uneven in the Soviet Union than in any other European country.

Russia was one of the first countries in the world to hold a national population census. Ordered in 1724 by Peter the Great, it enumerated the population of European Russia. Adjusted at various dates, it remained the basis of later population statistics until the census of 1897, which listed all the population of czarist Russia. By this time the Russian colonization of the vast landmass was almost complete. Of particular demographic significance was the fact that the flood of migration to Siberia was changing the historic configuration of population settlements. Although the power of the czars spread from Poland to the Bering Strait and beyond, the population shifts came only slowly. For one thing, most of the imperial acquisitions, such as Finland, Moldavia, Congress Poland in the north and west and Transcaucasia, were fairly well settled and offered little scope for Russian colonization. The main colonization moves were therefore to western Siberia—the fertile wedge between the northern swampy forests and the southern steppes. A great wave of settlement was triggered by the agricultural depression in European Russia in the 1870s and the building of the Trans-Siberian Railway after 1894. The favorite destinations of these migrants were the western lands beyond the Urals; the Altay foothills; the dairying meadows of Tobol, Iset, Tura, Ishim and Irtysh; the steppe fringes near Omsk, Petropavlovsk and Kulunda; and the Amur and Ussuri valleys. During the 19th century over 5 million people settled in Siberia, the population of which rose to 8 million by the end of the century. By 1914 all of Siberia was Russian country.

At the time of the 1897 census the steppe of New Russia, as Siberia was called, was well filled with settlers, in a belt that extended from St. Petersburg to beyond Lake Baikal. Other settled areas included the Kama Basin, where there was forest exploitation; central Ural; and around Vladivostok and the Khanka Plain.

The first census after the October Revolution was in 1926; it was followed by the inconclusive census of 1939, before the war, and the census of 1959, after the war. These censuses revealed continued population shifts in response to civil unrest and new industrial strategies. Migration was officially encouraged by numerous means, such as free housing, extra pay, travel expenses and other benefits. Undesirables were deported or directed to work in less pleasant regions. There also was considerable internal migration, mostly by peasants leaving villages because they did not like collectivization or because the new farm machinery made them redundant. War, pestilence and famine also wrought havoc, reducing the population by several millions in the 1920s. The greatest losses were in the Ukraine, Transcaucasia and the Volga steppes. Immediately before the war there was a shift to the eastern bank of the Volga, where discoveries of rich petroleum deposits heralded great expansion. There also was a strong movement to the new industrial and mining communities and to the Leningrad conurbation.

Development of population between 1945 and 1959 was complicated by the changes in boundaries and the further annexation of territory in the West. Meanwhile, the eastern lands continued to show gains in population, primarily through induced migration.

Rural decline became more extensive after the war except in certain regions, such as central Asia and Kazakhstan, where expanding irrigation and agriculture strengthened the rural sector. By the 1950s urban dwellers constituted more than half the population, and by 1990 their share had grown to 66.4%, or two-thirds. Between 1939 and 1959 the urban population grew by 65%, compared to 19.5% growth in the total population. The increase of over 40 million in the urban population was made up by nearly 25 million migrants from the country, about 8 million by natural increase and 7 million by reclassification of rural as urban settlements. There also was a small addition from boundary adjustments to towns. After the war the larger towns grew more slowly and most of the urban growth came from satellite towns and smaller towns. Wartime damage also slowed the growth of the large cities, many of which had a smaller population after the war compared to 1939. The size of the boom towns also shrank, particularly in the central industrial region and in the Ukraine.

In 1989 there were 2,186 towns compared with 1,694 in 1959, with an urban population of 189 million and 82.6 million, respectively. Over one-third of the urban population lives in the 53 cities with over 500,000 persons. Moscow, the largest city, accounts for only 6% of the urban population, down from 8% in 1960. Of the 52 largest cities, only four are outside Europe: Alma-Ata, Tashkent, Novosibirsk and Omsk.

The Soviet policy of industrial and mining expansion in Siberia is reflected in the growth of urban communities in that region, some of them exhibiting vigorous growth. These core settlements in otherwise thinly populated areas have a heavy urban component. For example, Magadan City accounts for 81% of the population of the Magadan *oblast*. These towns are virtually isolated in tracts of almost virgin country.

Even with the third-largest population in the world, the Soviet Union is thinly settled, with an average density of 12.8 persons per sq. km. (33 persons per sq. mi.) (compared with 233 persons per sq. km; 604 persons per sq. mi. for the United Kingdom and 25 persons per sq. km.; 66 persons per sq. mi. for the United States). Over three-quarters of the USSR, the density is far below even this modest level. Three of four people live in Europe, particularly in a triangle with its base resting between the Black and Baltic seas and its apex in western Siberia. Southward moderate densities are in the Great Caucasus and in piedmont and riverine areas south of the Turanian deserts. Another slender popula-

tion belt extends along the eastern sections of the Trans-Siberian Railway.

Even within the population triangle there are considerable variations in density. The heaviest densities are in the better-watered steppes, the forests of Podolia, the industrial Donbass and around Moscow. Areas of lesser density are lower Dnieper and northern Crimea, Byelorussia, the Baltic republics, northwestern European Russia, the Volga region and the Ural uplands.

For some decades the population has been characterized by an imbalance in the sexes among the adults. The imbalance grew out of the death toll of the two world wars and Stalin's brutal mass massacres, in which proportionately more adult males were killed or otherwise died than females. The 1989 estimates showed that 52.9% of the population was female, compared with 55% in 1959. The overall imbalance is more of a carryover because there is a growing balance among the sexes in the younger generation. Although sex ratios are not available for individual regions, it may be assumed that they are wider in regions where the two world wars were fought than in central Asia or Siberia.

The patterns of development in birth rate, mortality rate, life expectancy and infant mortality closely resemble those of other industrially advanced societies. The limited efforts by the authorities to control population growth have had only slight effect. Nevertheless, other factors have been at work restricting childbirth, the most important being the large-scale employment of women, lack of adequate housing, and abortions. Abortions have been the principal check on population growth. In many years the number of abortions have exceeded births, and the abortion rate for employed women is about 2.5 times that of nonworking women. The influence of the other restraints has not been determined.

Comparisons of the birth rates for the republics indicate that Slavic people are reproducing at lower rates than non-Slavic. Rates in the predominantly Muslim republics are approximately twice those of the RSFSR and the Ukraine. Birth rates are slightly higher in the urban areas than in the country. Reductions in the death rate and in the infant mortality rate were impressive in the first half century after the Bolshevik Revolution. Despite reports of the extraordinary longevity of some Soviet citizens in central Asia and the Caucasus, the Soviet Union still lags behind advanced countries such as Japan and Sweden in average life span.

The Soviet Union has never had an official population policy because Marxist doctrine denies the need for control of population growth under socialism. For many decades Soviet policy was guided by Lenin's principle that each citizen had the basic right to determine whether a child should be born. It explained the liberal abortion laws for the period from 1920 to 1935. On the other hand, provision of day care centers for children of working mothers and support payments for children had the opposite effect. The abortion rate reached such alarming proportions that in 1936 Stalin adopted a restrictive policy, which continued until 1956. Under this policy the number of illegal abortions soared. Abortion laws were made more liberal in 1956, but these changes were promoted as measures to protect the health of women and not as population control per se.

As evidence of the Soviets' increasing concern with demography was the creation of the Coordinating Council for Population Problems in 1964 and the establishment in 1965 of the Problem Laboratory of Population at Moscow University.

DEMOGRAPHIC INDICATORS, 1989

Population: 286,700,000
Year of last census: 1989   World rank: 3
Sex ratio: males, 47.1;   females; 52.9
Population trends (million)
  1930: 179.000   1960: 214.335   1990: 290.939
  1940: 195.000   1970: 241.720   2000: 311.637
  1950: 180.075   1980: 265.542
Population doubling time in years at current rate: 70
Hypothetical size of stationary population (million): 398
Assumed year of reaching net reproduction rate of 1: 2020
Age profile (%)
  0–15: 25.5   30–44: 18.7   60–74: 7.1
  15–29: 24.0   45–59: 18.3   Over 75: 6.4
Median age (years): 31.5
Density per sq. km. (per sq. mi.): 12.8 (33.0)
Annual growth rate
  1950–55: 1.71   1975–80: 0.93   1995–2000: 0.76
  1960–65: 1.49   1980–85: 0.95   2000–2005: 0.69
  1965–70: 0.91   1985–90: 0.91   2010–15: 0.62
  1970–75: 0.95   1990–95: 0.79   2020–25: 0.56
Vital statistics
  Crude birth rate, 1/1,000: 19.8
  Crude death rate, 1/1,000: 9.9
  Change in birth rate: 8.9 (1965–84)
  Change in death rate: 47.9 (1965–84)
  Dependency, total: 52.5
  Infant mortality rate, 1/1,000: 30
  Natural increase, 1/1,000: 9.9
  Total fertility rate: 2.3
  General fertility rate: 74
  Gross reproduction rate: 1.15
  Marriage rate, 1/1,000: 9.8
  Divorce rate, 1/1,000: 3.4
  Life expenctancy, males (years): 65.0
  Life expectancy, females (years): 73.6
  Average household size: 3.9
Youth
  Youth population 15–24 (000): 41,282
  Youth population in 2000 (000): 47,396
Women
  Of childbearing age 15–49 (000): 69,692
  Child–woman ratio (children per 000 women 15–49): 354
  Abortion rate per 100 live births: 230
Urban
  Urban population (000): 201,590
  % urban 1965, 52; 1985, 66
  Annual urban growth rate (%): 1965–80: 2.2; 1980–85: 1.6
  % urban population in largest city: 4
  % urban population in cities over 500,000: 33
  Number of cities over 500,000: 53
  Annual rural growth rate: −0.9%

POPULATION GROWTH (000)

Year	Total	Males	Females
1897	126,367	63,208	63,159
1926	147,028	71,053	75,985
1939	170,467	81,665	88,802
1959	208,827	94,050	114,776
1970	241,720	111,399	130,321

The statistics for 1897 are for the Russian empire excluding Finland. Later statistics are for the USSR. Other official estimates are (000):

Year	Total	Males	Females
1851	65,077	32,212	32,865
1858	67,299	32,839	34,459
1885	106,611	52,996	52,779

P. A. Khromov, *Economic Development of Russia in the 19th and 20th Centuries, 1800–1917* (Moscow, 1950) gives the following estimates at decennial intervals (000):

1800: 35,500
1810: 40,700
1820: 48,600
1830: 56,100
1840: 62,400
1850: 68,500
1860: 74,100
1870: 84,500
1880: 97,700
1890: 117,800
1900: 132,900
1910: 160,700

Statistics for the 50 provinces of European Russia (i.e., excluding Finland, Poland, and the Caucasus) are (000):

Total 94,215   Males 46,448   Females 47,767

The population of the areas of the former empire excluded from the USSR was 21,734,000 in 1897 (excluding Finland).

The population of areas incorporated into the USSR between 1939 and 1945 was approximately 22,200,000 in 1939.

ETHNIC COMPOSITION

During the czarist era and since 1917 under communism the country that became in 1922 the Union of Soviet Socialist Republics has been a vast, multinational empire. There are over 100 nationalities in the Soviet Union, which according to the January 1989 census, has a population of 286.7 million. The Russians, numbering 145.1 million, are now a bare majority (50.8%), reduced from 52.4% in the 1979 census. The Ukrainians, with 44.1 million, are the second-largest, followed by the Uzbeks, at 16.7 million. The accompanying table shows the national composition of the population in the USSR as reported by the 1979 and 1989 censuses.

Over 25 million ethnic Russians live outside the Russian Federation. Over the decades Moscow has encouraged the migration of Russians into the various republics for economic and political reasons. Russians frequently have been given preferential treatment in the non-Russian republics, causing resentment by the indigenous population. For the Kremlin the Russians represent a loyal, more dependable, controlling element.

NATIONAL COMPOSITION OF POPULATION IN USSR, NATIONALITIES OF UNION REPUBLICS (in millions)		
Nationality	1979	1989
Russian	137.4	145.1
Ukrainian	42.3	44.1
Uzbek	12.5	16.7
Byelorussian	9.5	10.0
Kazakh	6.6	8.1
Azerbaijan	5.5	6.8
Armenian	4.2	4.6
Tajik	2.9	4.2
Georgian	3.6	4.0
Moldavian	3.0	3.4
Lithuanian	2.9	3.1
Turkmen	2.0	2.7
Kirghiz	1.9	2.5
Latvian	1.4	1.5
Estonian	1.0	1.0

The accompanying table indicates Russian presence in the Union republics:

ETHNIC RUSSIANS IN UNION REPUBLICS (1989)		
Republic	No. of Russians in the Republic (in 000)	% Russians of Total
RSFSR	119,807	81.3
Ukraine	11,340	21.9
Byelorussia	1,341	13.1
Uzbekistan	1,657	8.3
Kazakhstan	6,226	37.6
Georgia	339	6.2
Azerbaijan	392	5.6
Lithuania	344	9.3
Moldavia	560	12.9
Latvia	906	33.8
Kirghizia	917	21.4
Tajikistan	387	7.6
Armenia	52	1.6
Turkmenistan	334	9.5
Estonia	475	30.3

Of the 44.1 million Ukrainians, 6.8 million live outside the Ukraine, mostly in the RSFSR. The greatest increase of the Ukranians has been in Latvia (38.1% over 1979), Estonia (33.9% over 1979) and Lithuania (38.8% over 1979). The highest number of Ukrainians outside the RSFSR is in Kazakhstan (896,000) and Moldavia (600,000). The greatest increase of Russians between 1979 and 1989 occurred in Byelorussia (18.2%), Estonia (16.2%), Lithuania (13.2%), Moldavia (10.8%) and Latvia (10.2%), giving concern especially to Estonians and Latvians; the Russian population in both Estonia and Latvia is over 30% of the total population. When Ukrainians are included, the proportion of these Slavs (37.2% in Latvia and 34.4% in Estonia) is considered threatening to the national viability of these Baltic nations.

The trends in the central Asian republics and, to a lesser extent, the Caucasus, have been the opposite. Not only outmigration but also the annual rate of growth have given Moscow even great apprehension. Earlier departures by Russians and Ukrainians were motivated by professional and social considerations, with supervisory positions increasingly offered to the indigenous people. More recently, public displays of nationalism—resulting in strikes, demonstrations and violence—have stimulated others to depart. Even more recently, during 1989, legislative recognition of native languages as state languages, where the nonindigenous would be forced to learn a "foreign" language, caused additional Slavs to choose departure. Between 1979 and 1989 the largest proportional decrease of Russians occurred in Armenia (26.7%) and Azerbaijan (17.5%), probably because of the violence over the Nagorno-Karabakh Autonomous Oblast. For the first time the Russians showed a decrease in Uzbekistan, Tajikistan and Turkmenistan; they also showed a lower number in Georgia, a decrease of 8.9%. It should be noted that while the Russians and Ukrainians have decreased in Kazakhstan—from 46% of the total population—the proportion in 1989 (43%) still was disturbingly high.

For many years the proportion of Russians in the USSR has been dropping while that of central Asian and other nationalities has been growing—and ethnodemographic predictions indicate a continuing trend—to such an extent as to cause concern for central authorities. This situation poses political, economic, military and psychological problems for the regime. The largest annual rate of growth during 1979–89 for Russians was only 0.55% (approximately the same as for the Ukrainians and Byelorussians), compared to 3.82% for Tajiks, 2.97% for Turkmen, 2.88% for Kirghiz, 2.18% for Kazakhs and 2.17% for Azerbaijanis. The percentile increase in these nationalities during the decade is astounding: Russians (5.6%), Tajiks (45.5%), Uzbeks (34.0%), Turkmen (34.0%), Kirghiz (32.8%), Kazakhs (24.1%) and Azerbaijanis (24.0%). The result has been a reduction between 1970 and 1989 of Russians from 53.37% to 50.78%, and of Slavs (Russians, Ukrainians and Byelorussians) from 73.97% to 70.3% and an increase of Kazakhs and indigenous peoples of the four central Asian republics from 8.10% to 12.00% of the total population.

In addition to the major nationalities of the Union republics cited above, the numerical strength of other ethnic groups, as reported in the 1979 census (the 1989 figures were not available as of this writing), were as follows, in thousands: Tatars (6,317); Germans (1,936); Jews (1,811); Chuvash (1,751); ethnic groups of Daghestan (1,657); Bashkirs (1,371); Mordvinians (1,192); Poles (1,151); Chechens (756); Udmurts (714); Mari (622); Ossetians (542); Koreans (389); Bulgarians (361); Buryats (353); Greeks (344); Yakuts (328); Komi (327); Kabardinians (322); Kara-Kalpaks (303); Uighurs (211); Gypsies (209); Ingush (186); Gagauz (173); Hungarians (171); and Tuvinians (166).

Adding to the ethnic diversity are foreign students who attend universities, institutes and other educational and training institutions throughout the Soviet Union, in 1990 numbering over 100,000 studying at more than 500 educational institutions.

The Soviet Constitution provides for "equal rights" of races and nationalities (Article 36). However, the provision conditions this right on "all-round development and drawing together of all the nations and nationalities of the USSR by educating citizens in the spirit of Soviet patriotism and socialist internationalism." Before April 1990 Article 70 defined the USSR as an "integral, federal, multinational state formed on the principle of socialist federalism as a result of the free self-determination of nations and the voluntary association of equal Soviet socialist republics." It also states that "the USSR embodies the state unity of the Soviet people and draws all its nations and nationalities together for the purpose of jointly building communism." The USSR consists of 15 republics, each bearing the name of its principal nationality:

Russian Soviet Federated Socialist Republic (RSFSR)
Ukrainian Soviet Socialist Republic (SSR).
Byelorussian SSR
Uzbek SSR
Kazakh SSR
Georgian SSR
Azerbaijan SSR
Lithuanian SSR
Moldavian SSR
Latvian SSR
Kirghiz SSR
Tajik SSR
Armenian SSR
Turkmen SSR
Estonian SSR

Article 72 stated: "Each Union republic shall retain the right freely to secede from the USSR," and according to Article 76, "a Union republic is a sovereign Soviet socialist state" and "exercises independent authority on its territory." These and other articles gave the republics substantial power, but the reality has been the reverse: Power rests with the all-Union government, which is, in turn, controlled by the Communist Party, which ensures the continuity of the Union as also provided in the Constitution.

Twenty nationalities are organized into autonomous Soviet socialist republics (ASSR) within the Union republics of which they are a constituent part. Sixteen are in the RSFSR (population in thousands): Bashkir (3,805), Buryat (1,030), Daghestan (1,768), Kabardin-Balkar (732), Kalmyk (329), Karelian (795), Komi (1,247), Mari (739), Mordovian (964), North Ossetian (619), Tatar (3,568), Tuva (289), Udmurt (1,587), Chechen-Ingush (1,235), Chuvash (1,330) and Yakut (1,034). The Uzbek SSR includes the Kara-Kalpak ASSR (1,139,000) people). The Georgian SSR contains the Abkhasian (535,000) and Adzhar (385,000) ASSR's. The Azerbaijan SSR includes the Nakhichevan ASSR (278,000).

In addition, eight smaller ethnic groups are organized in autonomous regions (*oblast*—AO), also a constituent part of a Union republic or territory. Five are in the RSFSR: Adygei (426,000 people), Gorno-Altai (180,000), Jewish (216,000), Karachai-Circassian (402,000) and Khakass (555,000); one in the Georgian SSR (South

Ossetian AO, with 99,000 people); one in the Azerbaijan SSR (Nagorno-Karabakh AO, with 180,000); and one in the Tajik SSR (Gorno-Badakhshan AO, with 151,000). The lowest ethnic unit is the autonomous area, which is a constituent part of a territory or region; all are in the RSFSR's part of Siberia and the far North. The newest ethnic administration was established October 30, 1989, in the Yakut ASSR, the republic's first national district for the Even group; it is known as the Yakuts-Even-Batagai District.

Many of the nationalities in the present-day USSR have an ancient and proud history. They formed part of czarist Russia through wars, conquests or voluntary association. Their development was starkly uneven. While European nationalities were relatively advanced, numerous other ethnic groups—especially in central Asia and Siberia—were terribly deprived, lacking even a written alphabet. From the beginning of the October Revolution in 1917 the Bolshevik regime, led by Lenin, proclaimed national equality and the right of secession. Neither was without failing. National equality still was unachieved in 1989, and secession was more a tactical miscalculation by Lenin than a meaningful declaration. Moreover, the decision to grant Finland independence, the historical event often cited in defense of the secession issue, was granted (in December 1917) during a revolutionary period when the Bolsheviks were incapable of preventing the Finnish action.

The Treaty of Brest-Litovsk (March 3, 1918) concluded Russia's war with the Central Powers. The Bolshevik regime recognized the separation of Finland, Georgia, the Ukraine and Poland. The Baltic nations of Lithuania, Latvia and Estonia were placed under German suzerainty. The succeeding war with Poland ended with the Treaty of Riga (1921), providing for control over Ukrainian territory by both countries. With the end of World War I and in Russia the civil war, the Communist regime consolidated its control over nations and nationalities still under its control. Finland, Poland and the three Baltic nations, supported by the Western Allies, including the United States, became independent states. The Soviet regime ended any hope of self-determination for the Ukrainians, Byelorussians and others. Georgia's independence (proclaimed in 1918) was crushed by the Red Army in 1921; this was ordered by Stalin, a Georgian, as commissar of nationalities. The Communists succeeded in gaining control, by force, over the entire Transcaucasus. In the Far East, fighting with the Japanese ended when the Communists created the so-called Far East Republic. When the Japanese departed, this republic became a part of what became in 1922 the Union of Soviet Socialist Republics (USSR), uniting under Moscow's, and the Communist Party's, control over the many nations, nationalities and ethnic groups throughout this vast territory. Thus during the 1920s the structure of union republics, autonomous republics and regions evolved. In 1934 the Jewish Autonomous Region was established, and in 1936 the Transcaucasian Federation was abolished and Armenia, Georgia and Azerbaijan became Union republics. In central Asia the Kazakh Autonomous Republic and the Kirghiz Autonomous Republic became Union republics.

As a result of the Nazi-Soviet Non-Aggression Pact of August 1939, with its secret protocol on spheres of influence, the Soviet Union entered the war against Poland on September 17, annexing eastern Poland. In 1940 Moscow engineered the incorporation of Estonia, Latvia and Lithuania, which became Union republics. Farther south, the Soviet Union acquired Bessarabia and northern Bukovina from Rumania in the same year, forming the Moldavian SSR. However, Moscow was less fortunate in its design upon Finland, which defended itself militarily during 1939–40. Following the German invasion of the USSR in 1941, Stalin ordered the deportation of ethnic Germans living along the Volga, Crimean Tatars, Kalmyks, Karachais, Balkars, Chechens and Ingush into Siberia and central Asia. The allegation was suspicion of treason or the possibility of committing treasonable acts. Following the war the Soviet Union retained control over the people of these nations, giving them no opportunity for self-determination. The Western Allies accepted Stalin's territorial demands at Yalta in February 1945. In addition, Stalin acquired still more territory and, of course, people—parts of Finland, Czechoslovakia and Japan.

Following Stalin's death in 1953, the Soviet leadership rehabilitated the Kalmyks, Balkars, Karachais, Chechens and Ingush during 1956–57, permitting these nationalities to return to their former homeland. They were cleared of collaboration with the Germans, as were the Volga Germans (in 1964) and the Crimean Tatars (in 1967). However, the last two nationalities still have not been able to return to their homelands as a group as 1990 draws to a close. The reason given is that their former territories were and continue to be settled by wartime refugees and others. That the rights of these nationalities have been "violated" has been recognized by Gorbachev.

The Crimean Tatars have become increasingly bitter and, unless a satisfactory solution is found shortly, violence can be expected. A USSR Supreme Soviet Commission for Problems of the Crimean Tatars was established to recommend a solution. As recently as 1979 the Crimean Tatars were not listed as a separate census category, but their number is estimated at 450,000. Perhaps over 50,000 have managed to return to the Crimea during the past 20 years. However, there is strong resentment against their return, although charges against them were unfounded. The Crimean Tatars believe they are unjustly discriminated against and demand their just due: to be politically rehabilitated, to be permitted to return to their homeland, to have their autonomy restored and to have their language equal with Russian and Ukrainian. On May 13, the Commission announced a plan for the organized return of the Crimean Tartars to begin in 1991 and to be completed by 1996.

The ethnic Germans appear to have fared somewhat better. On October 19, 1989, the USSR Supreme Soviet Commission on the Problems of Soviet Germans proposed the reestablishment of autonomy in the former Volga German Autonomous Republic. In 1990 128,000 Germans lived in the Altai Kray. The Kray Soviet appealed to Gorbachev to restore their autonomy.

Discontent and grievances among nationalities are not new, but have existed since the 1917 Revolution. In the past strikes, demonstrations, protests and petitions were rejected and repressed, often brutally. *Glasnost* and *perestroika* have provided opportunities for grievances to be aired publicly. Probably every ethnic group in the Soviet Union harbors grievances against another nationality; a nationality on a higher level; and against centralization, which is considered Russification. Previously, more so than now, Russians in non-Russian republics were resented because of their arrogance as well as preferential treatment accorded to them. More recently, the Russians themselves have felt the sting of discrimination, which has given rise to their protest for equality and greater Russian nationalism; for example, they think it unfair to be required to learn Estonian, Armenian or Uzbek.

A particularly bitter dispute exists between Christian Armenians and Muslim Azerbaijanis over the Nagorno-Karabakh Autonomous Oblast (NKAO), which is situated inside Azerbaijan but with a population that is 75% Armenian. In February 1988 the Armenians there proposed annexation with Armenia, resulting in denunciations, demonstrations and ultimately violence, which was put down by Soviet military forces; many casualties were sustained. In January 1989 the USSR Supreme Soviet established a special administrative committee to administer the *oblast*, but it was abolished on November 28. Instead the Supreme Soviet set up an organizational committee, consisting of proportional representation from the two republics, in effect giving Armenia the majority. Azerbaijan is obligated to render "real autonomy" to the NKAO. Among other ethnic problems in the USSR, those in the Georgian SSR are multifaceted. The Abkhaz are promoting the incorporation of their autonomous republic into the RSFSR, the Azerbaijanis are demanding establishment of their own autonomous area and the Ossetians are campaigning for the upgrading of the South Ossetian AO to an autonomous republic.

Initially, the most immediate pressing nationality problem for Moscow was with the Baltic republics, where popular front organizations had developed rapidly into popular and powerful political forces. Their demands had escalated from supporting reforms to demanding outright secession from the USSR. The general secretary and the Communist Party oppose such drastic demands, insisting, instead, on continued USSR federation, a unified Communist Party and equal rights for all citizens along reforms stimulated by *perestroika*. In the longer run, the most important issue is the future of the Ukraine, the second-largest republic in the USSR. Although discontent has existed in the Ukraine for decades, more recent organizations, including the Ukrainian Popular Front, founded in September 1989, have succeeded in rallying mass support that goes far beyond reform of the present system. The Ukrainians, who have been denied the right of self-determination, are a people who have never forgotten their incredible losses in human life and property from Stalin's forced collectivization and induced famine. Moscow understands the importance of the Ukraine for the survival of the USSR, and General Secretary Gorbachev has admitted the gravity of the situation. The change in Communist Party leadership in September 1989 was considered by Ukrainian nationalists as insufficient in their objective of independence from Moscow.

In his report to the Central Committee Plenum on September 19, 1989, Gorbachev declared: "We must do everything to restore the violated rights of the Soviet Germans, Crimean Tatars, Mekhetian Turks, Kalmyks, Balkars, Karachais, Chechens, Ingushes, Greeks, Koreans and Kurds," adding that although difficulties exist, "we must painstakingly search for solutions that will be acceptable to all." At its session on October 4 to review the results of the Plenum, the Politburo instructed the Central Committee Secretariat to develop a program of concrete action for implementing the provisions of the Communist Party's platform "The Party's Nationalities Policy in Present-Day Conditions," to which Gorbachev addressed himself, and to ensure that the nationalities factor is given maximum consideration in all organizational, political, ideological and personnel activities.

The nationalities problem not only continued into the 1990s but reached crisis proportions, threatening the very fabric of the Union. In November 1989 the Presidium of the Supreme Soviet called on the Baltic republics and Azerbaijan to change their laws that violated the USSR Constitution, and in subsequent months other republics were advised as well. In the face of mounting clamor in the republics for drastic changes, the USSR Congress of People's Deputies on April 3 amended the Constitution on secession from the USSR, detailing the mechanics for the procedure.

The new Treaty of the Union, created "a union of sovereign states." All parties to the treaty, to include autonomous ones, have equal rights in "a genuine commonwealth of peoples." As for opting out of the Union, the Congress declared that "it is the duty of Communists to combat the ideology and political practice of national extremism."

The object of the treaty is to maintain a central structure. Neither the new law on secession nor the draft treaty satisfied the republics and by the fall of 1990, 11 of the 15 declared their independence or sovereignty, including Lithuania (March 11, 1990), Estonia (March 30), Latvia (May 4), Russian Republic (June 8), Uzbekistan (June 20), Moldavia, (June 23), Ukraine (July 16), Byelorussia (July 27), Armenia (August 23), and Tadzikistan (August 24). The national movements or fronts in each republic are opposed to the continued central control by Moscow and the CP. Marxism is an alien ideology for them. Their struggle for independence or sovereignty involves a variety of goals: their own political, economic, cultural, educational and social development; the primacy of their language and laws; ability to conduct relations with other republics and, in varying degrees, with foreign countries, directly; and a free, democratic, pluralistic political system. In short, they want to be masters in their own home. The fundamental question, however, is not only what the republics demand but what Moscow will permit. The Gorbachev leadership rejects the idea of dissolution of the USSR—characterizing as "alien," for example, exiled writer Alexander Solzhenitsyn's proposal for the creation of a Slavic state—and is firmly committed to a centrally conducted commonwealth of nations.

LANGUAGES

With over 100 nationalities, the Soviet Union is a multinational and a multilinguistic empire, a veritable polyglot. The USSR Constitution provides for "equality of languages" (Article 34), the right to exercise "national languages" (Article 26) and "opportunity to attend a school where teaching is in the native language" (Article 45). The central, republic and lower authorities frequently have not lived up to these promising provisions.

During the early years following the Revolution, the new regime encouraged ethnic cultural development among substantial groups in their own native language. The Constitution of 1918 provided for equality among ethnic groups within individual republics. However, later constitutions ignored this formal guarantee. Thus, under Stalin, the authority on national questions, the flowering of minority languages withered. The result was greater assimilation, basically the policy of succeeding regimes, except for a short period of the late 1950s and early 1960s when cultures and languages of several small ethnic groups were restored.

Russian has been the lingua franca of the USSR, the language of the central govenment, the Communist Party, foreign affairs and the media. It is the second language in the non-Russian schools where instruction is in the language of the dominant ethnic group. At least one foreign language is part of the school curriculum, beginning in the fifth grade, with English perhaps the most popular, followed by French and German. Command of Russian has been promoted by Moscow and for many is a practical necessity for a successful professional career. Insufficient knowledge of Russian by millions of non-Russians has been a problem for the central regime in various areas, including the Communist Party, the military and industry.

Of the total population of 286.7 million in the USSR, the Russians are by far the largest, numbering 145.1 million, the Ukrainians are next with 44.1 million, and the Byelorussians have 10.0 million. They are the three major eastern Slavic nationalities living in the western and southwestern or European part of the country and each speaks its own language. There are a small number of western (Poles, Slovaks and Czechs) and eastern (Bulgarians) Slavs speaking the language of their brethren in their ancestral countries. The historic Church Slavonic continues to be used by the Russian Orthodox Church. The other major language groups are Turkic, Finno-Ugric, Caucasian and Mongol. Arabic and Hebrew are used by Muslims and Jews, respectively, in religious services. Dialects are numerous throughout the country.

Russian, Ukrainian and Byelorussian belong to the eastern group of Slavic languages. They are related but separate languages, and all three are written in the Cyrillic alphabet. The other Indo-European languages in the USSR include the Baltic (Lithuanian and Latvian);

Iranian, spoken in the Caucasus and central Asia (Ossetic of the western branch and Tajik, Kurdish, Talysh, Baluchi, Yagnoh and Pamir); Romance (Moldavian, related to Rumanian but written in Cyrillic); German; Armenian (eastern dialect); small groups speaking Greek; and Gypsy or Romany. An undetermined part of the Jewish population—only a minority cites Yiddish as their native language—has retained Yiddish but publicly uses Russian and/or the language of their residence. Yiddish is the official language of the Jewish Autonomous Region, which has a population of 216,000.

Finno-Ugric, a branch of the Uralic languages, is spoken by people living in northern territories from the Baltic to Siberia and includes Estonians, Finns, Karelians, Livonians and Lapps of the western Finnic; the Mari and Mordvinians of the eastern Finnic group; and those of the Permian branch, which includes the Komi, Udmurt and Permyak who live west of the Urals. The western branch of the Ugric languages includes Magyar (Hungarian) and the eastern Ostyak, and Vogul, spoken by groups who live, together with those using Samoyedic tongues, in northern European Russia and Siberia. The Turkic languages, second only to the Slavic in numbers, consist of the Uzbek (the most numerous, with 16.7 million), Kazakh, Kirghiz, Kara-Kalpak, Turkmen and languages of others living in central Asia; Azerbaijani in the Caucasus west of the Caspian Sea; Bashkir, Chuvash, Gagauz, Tatar and languages of others in the Caucasus and along the Volga River; and Yakut, Tuvinian and Dalgan, spoken in Siberia. Mongol languages are spoken by people in the Caucasus and Siberia, the better known of these languages being Kalmyk and Buryat. The Tungusic tongues are spoken in Siberia and Asia, while Korean is spoken in central Asia and by a goodly number on Sakhalin Island.

The Caucasian languages consist of the northern and southern groups, the former consisting of Circassian, Abkhaz, Ubykh, Chechen, Ingush and the Dagestan group (Avar, Darghin and Lezghian, among others). Of the southern branch, the most important are Georgian, Mingrelian, Svan and Laz. There are, in addition, ethnic groups of various sizes throughout the Asian republics and Siberia who speak Paleo-Asian languages, including Chukochi, Koryak, Itelmen, Eskimo, Aleut, Yukagir (in Yakut) and Gilyak (on Sakhalin Island). There are still other tongues—e.g., Dungan, related to Chinese and which is spoken by a Muslim group.

Up to World War I, illiteracy in Czarist Russia was over 60%. The Bolsheviks addressed this problem aggressively, reducing illiteracy to 20% by 1939. The Soviet leadership emphasized a unitary state while encouraging the development of minority cultures and languages, some of which previously had no written alphabet. Thus the Communist regime began to establish alphabets, ultimately numbering about 50 out of a total of almost 75 in the USSR. However, only 39 languages were employed in schools throughout the country in 1989, an unsatisfactory situation that Gorbachev's leadership has been discussing in applying *perestroika* to the national question.

Seventy years earlier, the Bolsheviks attributed great significance to the print medium for propagandizing the population. Stalin stressed Russian centralism. In the 1930s his regime imposed the Cyrillic alphabet on the Turkic and Tajik languages. The attempt in the latter 1930s to Latinize Arabic alphabets was strongly opposed by the ethnic groups, and the scripts were changed to Cyrillic. With the establishment of the Moldavian Republic in 1940 the Latin alphabet was replaced by Cyrillic. The exceptions to Cyrillic are Yiddish; the Baltic languages of Estonia, Latvia, Lithuania and others who use Latin; and the languages of the Georgians and Armenians, who have had their own scripts since the fourth and fifth centuries, respectively.

The teaching of Russian has been mandatory in all Soviet schools since 1938. Where there are Russian schools in the republics, the native language is taken as a second language, and in republics where other non-Russian languages are spoken, Russian may be neglected. The result has been the teaching of indigenous languages and an inadequate fluency in Russian, which is the official national language of the USSR. The indigenous languages of the non-Russian Union republics, the autonomous republics and the autonomous regions also are official languages with Russian in those places.

The 1989 census confirmed that nationalities in the all-Union republics continued the natural inclination of speaking their mother tongue. Most were above 97%, with Russian the highest, with 99.8%. Surprisingly, some were much lower, with Byelorussians reporting the lowest, at 70.9%, a reduction from the 1979 census (74.2%); the Ukrainians 81.8%; and the Armenians 91.6%. However, Armenian was higher than 10 years earlier, as was Estonian, the only two republic nationalities that showed an increase, probably the result of recent nationalistic exuberance. For Moscow, fluency in Russian as a second language in the republics continued to be disturbingly low. The range of "good" knowledge of Russian in the 14 non-Russian republics was from a high of 64.4% by Latvians to a low of 23.8% by Uzbeks, a decrease by the latter from 49.3% in 1979. Lithuanians also showed a marked decrease during the decade, from 52.1% in 1979 to 37.9% in 1989, while Estonians reflected an increase, from 24.2% to 33.8%. These differences can be attributed to earlier inflated reporting and to increased nationalistic openness.

Under Gorbachev's policy of *perestroika* the nationalities question has been given more serious attention than previously. The 19th All-Union Party Conference, in 1988, considered this problem. The result was the December 1, 1988, Law of the USSR on national equal rights. In August 1989 the Communist Party cited as an objective of improving interethnic relations the free development of national cultures and languages. All republics discussed the language question but they took independent initiatives, uncertain of Moscow's tolerance, to bolster their language.

Estonia led the way when on January 18, 1989, its Supreme Soviet passed legislation providing for Estonian to be the state language of the republic. This action was followed by similar laws enacted by Lithuania (January 25) and Latvia (May 5). In Moldavia mass demonstrations resulted in an extraordinary four-day Supreme Soviet session dominated by emotional controversy and that adopted a constitutional amendment and legislation on August 31 providing for Moldavian as the state language. Draft legislation had sparked protests and strikes by ethnic Russians in Moldavia (12.9% of the population), who were supported by Moscow, which characterized the Moldavian initiative as "nationalist" and "anti-Russian." A personal intervention by Gorbachev resulted in a revision of the draft to make Russian the language of "interethnic communication" in the republic. The change was opposed by the majority of the deputies, but a compromise provided for both Moldavian and Russian to be languages of interethnic communication. Moldavian was unchanged as the state language.

On September 23 the Kirghiz Supreme Soviet passed a law making Kirghiz the official language of the republic with Russian, the language of interethnic communication. In the Ukraine the impetus for cultural and linguistic development was given by writers and other cultural activists, who in January 1989 established the Taras Shevchenko Ukrainian Language Society. Their advocacy contributed to a draft law on languages, published in early September, by the Presidium of the Ukrainian Supreme Soviet calling for Ukrainian to be the state language and Russian the language of interethnic communication.

The emotional language controversy was no less heated in Uzbekistan. A draft law was published on June 18 and immediately caused an uproar. As in Moldavia, Russians comprise a sizable minority—1.7 million, or 8.3% of the total population. The Uzbek Supreme Soviet postponed a decision on the draft from August until October 21, when it made Uzbek the official language, with "free and equal" Russian the language of interethnic communication. Tens of thousands of Uzbeks demonstrated in favor of a law to make Uzbek also the official language of interethnic communication. Earlier, in July, the Tajik Supreme Soviet made Tajik the state language of the republic, prompting thousands of Russians and other non-Tajik minorities to emigrate. The major reason for their decision was that living and working conditions would be virtually impossible, this despite a provision for the right to use other languages.

Another important linguistic ingredient in the nationalist movement is the restoration of historic, non-Cyrillic alphabets, especially for the Turkic, Tajik and Moldavian languages. Moldavia initiated the process. On May 21, 1989, the republic published draft legislation to restore gradually the Latin alphabet by 1995. Even without formal legislation, certain publications in Moldavia, Tajikistan, Uzbekistan, Kazakhstan and the Tatar ASSR began appearing, in whole or in part, in Latin or Arabic alphabets. This development was expected to continue, but the process was considered to be of long duration. In addition to problems such as costs, an educational program would be essential given the generational use of Cyrillic and the accompanying neglect of the indigenous script.

The language controversy continues. On November 13, 1989, the All-Union Supreme Soviet Commission on Nationalities Policy and International Relations reported a draft law on nationalities that, among other elements, provided for Russian to be an all-state language. The first reading by the national Supreme Soviet was conducted two days later. Toward year's end the exact formulation had not been decided, but republics feared legislative passage would denigrate native languages.

RELIGIONS

Religion occupies a special, if negative, place in Communist doctrine and the Soviet state, particularly as it represents an area of signal failure. The survival of the Christian church in the Soviet Union, after over 70 years of intense persecution, is one of the great miracles of the 20th century and attests to the strength of its historic roots and its institutional vitality.

Christianity is represented by Russian and Georgian Orthodox, Armenian Gregorian, Roman Catholic and various Protestant denominations and comprises the major religious identification of the people. Of these denominations, the oldest is the Armenian, which was established, according to tradition, by the Apostle Thaddeus a few years after Pentecost. Armenia was the first nation in the history of the church to accept Christianity as its state religion. Georgia was Christianized soon after, and by the third century there were churches in Crimea.

The largest denomination, and one most influential in Russian history, is the Orthodox Church, or the Eastern Orthodox Church, as it sometimes is called. The church dates from the conversion of the Slavs by missionaries from Byzantium, led by Sts. Cyril and Methodius. In 988 Vladimir of Kiev was converted to the Orthodox faith, thus marking the beginning of Christianity as the official religion of the land. The metropolitan of the church was first headquartered in Kiev and later in Moscow. After the fall of Constantinople in 1453, the Moscow Patriarchate was instituted in 1589, and thereafter the church considered itself as the third Rome. In 1721 Peter the Great, by his Ecclesiastical Regulations, deprived the church of its autonomy by abolishing the patriarchate and placing the church under the administration of the Holy Synod, composed of clerics and laymen chosen by the state. The czar was represented in the synod by the high procurator, without whose approval no action could be taken.

For the next two centuries the church became a tool of the state. The church's influence reached a nadir during the years immediately preceding the Bolshevik Revolution, when the charlatan Grigory Rasputin, an unordained starets possessed of hypnotic powers, gained ascendancy over the czarina.

Three crucial events affecting the church took place in the immediate aftermath of the October Revolution, First the patriarchate was restored in 1917 and the six-man synod was abolished. Second, the Soviet Constitution of 1918 guaranteed freedom of belief (later changed to freedom of worship) and simultaneously freedom of antireligious propaganda under official aegis. Third, the decree of separation of church and state deprived the church of its property, allowing churches to be used for worship only at the discretion of local authorities. All convents, monasteries and seminaries were closed. Many parish churches were closed, and cloisters were converted into hospitals or schools. The church suffered great losses in both membership and facilities and was forced to accommodate itself to the regime to preserve what remained.

Patriarch Tikhon died in 1925, and Stalin refused to permit the election of a new patriarch until 1944. In 1927 Metropolitan Sergius of Nizhny Novgorod was allowed to set up a central administration without the title of patriarch. Sergius called upon believers to renounce hostility to the regime and ordered prayers for Soviet leaders.

With the advent of Stalin's forced industrialization and collectivization of agriculture in 1928, an all-out attack on religion was begun. The church was considered to be a center of opposition against Stalinism. The ranks of the clergy grew thinner as many of them were imprisoned and exiled to labor camps. The most virulent of the antireligious organizations during this period were the Komosomol, the League of the Militant Godless and the trade unions. As the excess of antireligous propaganda alienated many people, the government softened its campaign. But violence against the church and clergy continued until the German invasion in 1941 opened the way for partial reconciliation between church and state. In return for support for the war effort, the state permitted the election of a patriarch and Holy Synod, the establishment of theological seminaries and the publication of an ecclesiastical periodical.

The wartime detente continued until the mid-1950s, and until Stalin's death active persecution was not resumed. By the time Khrushchev achieved full power in the late 1950s the ideologues were again calling for militant atheism, and the Khrushchev era was marked by worse excesses against the church than those that marked the 1930s. The Society for the Dissemination of Political and Scientific Knowledge, successor of the League of the Militant Godless, increased its attacks on religion. Legal codes were revised and strengthened to prohibit religious teachings and propaganda. Churches and seminaries were closed by the thousands, and clergy were imprisoned or confined to mental institutions. Khrushchev himself declared that religion would completely disappear in the Soviet Union by 1980! To achieve that goal the Soviet Union sponsored the Institute of Scientific Atheism, and cells were established in every government agency to coordinate antireligious efforts. The attacks against the church continued relentlessly through the 1960s and 1970s until the assumption of power by Gorbachev, when the celebrations of the millennium of Russia's "baptism" in 1988 heralded a thaw. Meanwhile, the official atheist magazine, *Science and Religion*, continued to report more ideological campaigns against the right of parents to instruct their childen in the faith and against the right of those openly religious to hold public office. Generally, the church has accepted these pressures with silence. However, there is growing unrest among the clergy and lay believers against the passivity of the church and its acquiescence in the brutal suppression of its civic rights. Such protesters are eventually arrested, dismissed from their jobs or exiled.

The Russian Orthodox Church is autocephalous under the authority of an elected patriarch and Holy Synod. Each of the church's 70 dioceses is large—several thousand square miles in size. The internal organization of the church is governed by regulations adopted by the Church Assembly in 1945. All bishops are selected by the patriarch and may be removed or transferred by him. Each of the 70 bishops takes his title from the cathedral town. Generally he is an unmarried monastic. Orthodox clergy may marry before or after ordination but may not be promoted above the rank of priest. There is no prohibition against the selection of a bishop from the laity, but this is rarely done. Dioceses are divided into districts headed by provosts appointed by the bishop. Priests are ordained by bishops and are subject to their theological and administrative supervision. Village priests generally are married and typically are undereducated.

Even more than the clergy, the monks and holy men (startsy) represented the most influential group within the church. Monasticism and asceticism were traditionally held in very high regard by the common people and served as reservoirs of Russian spirituality. The monastic community was especially important in preserving the heritage and traditions of the church. The monks were generally better educated and more committed to prayer than were the clergy.

As the pressures against believers have grown, so have the number of crypto-Christians—those who practice their faith in secret. According to official Soviet publications, there are party members in good standing who are covertly baptizing their children and committing other antisocialist acts.

The 70-year persecution of the church has left the church much debilitated. The number of churches declined from 80,792 in 1913 to 39,000 in 1925 and to 1,000 in 1939, rising to 16,000 in 1945 and 20,000 by 1957. They declined again, to 5,100 by 1973, and hovered near 10,000 in the 1980s. Reportedly many churches have been returned to believers in the Gorbachev era.

The other Orthodox church in the Soviet Union, that of Georgia, is under the Moscow Patriarchate. It has been as bitterly persecuted; as a result there are only about 100 churches left, and there is no seminary.

The Armenian Apostolic Church, usually termed Monophysite because of the absence of Armenian representatives at the Council of Chalcedon in 451, is headed by the Catholics of Etchmiadzin, whose jurisdiction extends throughout the world. It is not only one of the oldest but also one of the distinctively national churches, where membership in the church and the Armenian nationality are coextensive. The number of churches fell from 1,446 in 1917 to 89 by 1954, but this has not affected the vitality of the church. The monastery of Etchmiadzin plays a leading administrative role, and the theological institute, opened in 1945, attracts a number of students.

The Roman Catholic Church is distinctively a minority church as well as a persecuted church. Most of the Catholics are in Lithuania, Latvia and in the western parts of Byelorussia and the Ukraine. Unlike the Orthodox Church, the Catholic Church has not been allowed to create a central ecclesiastical authority, although the church in Lithuania and Latvia has been allowed to organize itself into a diocese. Catholics in Byelorussia and the Ukraine are under the jurisdiction of the archdiocese of Riga or Kaunas.

Even under the czars, Roman Catholicism fared poorly because it clashed with the dominant Orthodox Church. Few ethnic Russians were Catholics, and ethnic animosities reinforced anti-Catholicism. In addition, there were millions of Uniates who retained Russian Orthodox ritual and liturgy while acknowledging the pontiff as the head of the church.

Bolshevik anti-Catholicism was particularly intense because of the nationalist dimension. As the Catholics openly rejected decrees that nationalized church property and forbade the teaching of religion to children, the Bolsheviks responded with arrests, exiles and executions of Catholic clergy and the closing of churches, monasteries and seminaries. The 1920s and 1930s were black decades for the Catholic and Uniate churches. The Great Purge brought destruction and desecration of churches and mass disappearances of clergy and laity. After a brief wartime truce, the campaigns against the Catholic Church—or what was left of it—resumed and bloomed into a full-scale offensive under Khrushchev. Even more than for the Orthodox Church, survival became a struggle. The Uniates fared worse and went under, and between 1946 and 1950 ceased to exist. Most were coopted forcibly into the Russian Orthodox Church.

The Catholic Church in Lithuania is perhaps the largest and most influential of the Soviet Catholic communities. This is because the Catholic Church served since 1794 as the principal guardian of Lithuanian nationalism and cultural identity, and the Lithuanian clergy spearheaded resistance to Russification. As a result, the church came under Communist assault after the country was taken over by Stalin. In 1940 the papal nuncio was expelled and the concordat between Lithuania and the Vatican was abrogated. In the 1940s four of the six dioceses were left bishopless as several bishops were imprisoned or shot. After 1953 the church administration hardly functioned. The church responded by going underground and keeping up a barrage of petitions and letters. The Lithuanian Catholics also began publication in the 1970s of a *samizdat*, *The Chronical of the Catholic Church in Lithuania*, which became a record of the "Church of Silence and Suffering." Pope John Paul II has taken a keen interest in Lithuanian church affairs and has won some minor concessions.

The position of the Catholic Church in Byelorussia is far weaker because only 25% of the population is Catholic. There are no bishops in this region; there is only one seminary. There are 112 churches in the western part, compared to one in the eastern part. The church in the Ukraine is even smaller, and it is more underground than open.

Despite relentless persecution, Catholic religous life persists, especially in the more remote areas, much to the chagrin of the official tormentors. There are only five official Catholic churches in the country—in Moscow, Leningrad, Odessa, Frunze and Tiflis—but for the most part religous services and ceremonies are celebrated clandestinely. Although there are no resident bishops, there are titular archdioceses, six dioceses and one apostolic exarchate. Services often are performed in the priest's living quarters. Priests continue to officiate at weddings, baptisms and funerals, and the congregations grow yearly. Since priests are forbidden to receive money for their services, parishioners donate food, clothing and other articles.

The Evangelical Christians and Baptists constitute the second-largest Christian group in the Soviet Union. Estimates of their adherents vary from 1 million to 5 million. Protestantism entered Russia with the establishment of the Russian Baptist Union in 1884 and the Union of Evangelical Christians in 1908. The two groups merged in 1944. Before and immediately after the Bolshevik Revolution these groups were favored by the Communists, since they represented a means of discrediting the Orthodoxy. Because of official tolerance the two groups gained new members rapidly. By 1923 the government ended its official favor and began to subject them to the same hostile acts directed against other religious groups. Central to the religious life of these two groups were prayer meetings and farming communes. In the 1930s the Communists outlawed both. Believers were scattered and clergymen were arrested and exiled. During the war the Baptists, like other religious groups, enjoyed a brief interlude of official tolerance. The cycle of repression returned with Khrushchev, when many members were charged as American spies. In 1961 the church was split in a schism between the official Baptist leadership and a reform or "initiative" movement, the latter calling for a spiritual revival and an end to state interference in church affairs. The "initiative" communities have been refused registration and subjected to considerable harassment. Their leaders, such as Georgi Vins, have been sentenced to many years in prision. Their main printing press was seized and destroyed for having printed 40,000 copies of the New Testament, hymnbooks and other materials.

The Lutheran Church is the next-largest Protestant denomination, mainly concentrated in Latvia and Estonia. Soviet Pentecostals were banned under the Instruction on the Application of the Law of Cults of 1961. Some of the Pentecostal groups are registered, but most are unregistered. A strong emigration movement among the unregistered Pentecostals was suppressed, and their leaders have been imprisoned and denied emigration. One such family took refuge in the U.S. Embassy in Moscow in 1978. Lesser Protestant denominations include Seventh-Day Adventists, Mennonites and Molokans. The latter sect, dating from the 17th century, rejects all rituals.

One feature of the religious scene, particularly troubling to the regime, is the existence of a vast underground church, called by various names—the Catacomb Church, the Church of Silence or the Church of the Martyrs—comprising over 34 unregistered and clandestine organizations with a membership exceeding 1 million. They belong to all three streams—Orthodox, Catholic and Protestant—but are united in their common rejection of the Soviet regime and the registered churches that collaborate with it.

Next to the Russian Orthodox Church, Muslims comprise the most numerous religious group in the Soviet Union. Estimates vary, but their number may be as high as 18 million. They are in three main areas: central Asia, with 75%; the northern Caucaus and eastern Transcaucasia, with 12%; and the Middle Volga region and the southern Urals, with 13%. Small Muslim groups exist in western Siberia (Siberian Tatars), in central Asia (Kasimov Tatars) and in Lithuania (Lithuanian Tatars). A total of 75% of Muslims are Turks; the rest are divided equally between Iranians and Ibero-Caucasians. There is a small group of Muslim Semites, such as the Arabs of Samarkand, the Chalas and the Bukharans, who are crypto-Jews. There also are Chinese Muslims (Dungans), and two northern Caucasian nationalities, the Abkhazians and the Ossetians, at least half of whom are Muslims.

The most significant fact about Muslims is that with a higher birth rate than non-Muslims, they are a growing minority. It is believed that by 2000, based on current demographic trends, one in every three Soviet citizens will be of Muslim origin.

Initial Soviet policy toward Muslims, as toward members of other religious groups, was one of repression. Most of the 25,000 mosques in 1917 were closed along with Shari'a courts and madrasahs, or Koranic schools. The institution of wakf (charitable endowments) was ended, as was the hajj or ritual pilgrimage to Mecca. Printing and distribution of religious materials also was banned. New religious laws introduced in 1928 abolished the Arabic script and the use and teaching of Arabic.

After World War II the official policy moved in the direction of breaking up the old tribal and extended family society in order, initially, to draw Muslims closer *(sblizhenie)* to other national nationalities and eventually to merge them *(sliyanie)* with the Russian nation. This policy did not achieve any of its goals. Muslims have shown no inclination to intermarry, to migrate or to abandon their social practices.

To enforce the laws governing the religious life of Muslims, the government has set up four spiritual directorates, in (1) central Asia and Kazakhstan, (2) European RSFSR and Siberia, (3) Northern Caucasia and Daghestan and (4) Transcaucasia. All directorates come under the control of the Council for Religious Affairs, headquartered at Tashkent, where the only major Islamic library also is located. There are two madrasahs, which produce about 20 mullahs, or religious leaders, annually. A few more mosques have been opened in recent years, but the total number of mosques is estimated at less than 500.

In the past the Muslim clerics have neither protested against the antireligious propaganda nor the atheistic character of the regime. Because Muslims are permitted by the Koran to adopt the practice of *taquiyah* (dissimulation in a hostile environment), they appear com-

pletely loyal to the regime and even play an active role in the Communist Party. Both sides have paid a high price for such a situation. The Soviets have had no success in their efforts to engineer social change in Muslim areas. The Muslims have been forced to carry out most of their religious activities clandestinely.

Although Jews played a disproportionately important role in the October Revolution (Trotsky and a number of Lenin's closest aides were Jews), they were not exempt from the persecution of religious groups. They were deprived of a central organization; most of the rabbis were either imprisoned or killed; and Jewish festivals and traditions were forbidden.

Jewish settlements in the territory of the present-day Soviet Union date from the early pre-Christian period. The state of Khazaria in the lower Volga region had Jewish settlements in the seventh century. Many of these colonies were scattered by the Tatar invasions, and most Jews migrated to the western areas of the present-day Ukraine, Byelorussia and Poland, and some settled in the Moscow area.

The Jews suffered severe discrimination is czarist Russia, particularly after Catherine the Great instituted the "Pale of Settlement," which restricted Jewish residence to certain areas. Her son Alexander I forbade Jews to live in rural areas or engage in farming. A highly restrictive quota system limited the number of Jewish youth allowed into secondary and higher schools. In addition to periodic pogroms, the Jews were under constant pressure to assimilate. After the Revolution, the New Economic Program reduced the Jews, who were mostly small shopkeepers and merchants, to dire poverty. In 1934 the Soviet government established the Jewish Autonomous Region in far eastern Siberia, in a remote area with a harsh climate. Few Jews responded to this offer of a "homeland," and they never constituted more than 10% of the population of this region. The purges of the 1930s wreaked havoc among Jews and eliminated many well-known Communists, such as Lev Kamenev and Grigory Zinoviev. Just before his death, Stalin was preparing for another anti-Semitic drive following the alleged discovery of a plot by his Jewish doctors.

After the exit of Khrushchev, much of the open anti-Semitism subsided, and thousands of Jews were permitted to leave for Israel or the United States on a selective basis. There were also some minor concessions in response to the efforts of the World Jewish Congress.

The number of Jews in the Soviet Union in 1990 is estimated at 2.1 million, excluding some 1 million secularized Jews. This contrasts with 5.2 million Jews in 1897 and 3 million Jews in 1939. Over 1.3 million Soviet Jews were massacred by the Nazis during World War II. Soviet Jews are generally divided into western Jews and eastern Jews, the former found in Moscow, the Ukraine and Byelorussia and the latter in Crimea, Georgia and central Asia.

Buddhism has been virtually wiped out in the Soviet Union, but vestiges survive in the Buryat Autonomous Republic. In addition to the Buryats, most Buddhists are Kalmyks, Tuvins or Koreans.

Church-state relations are governed by both constitutional provisions and decrees. Article 124 of the Stalin Constitution of 1936 separates church and state but grants, ironically, the right of freedom of worship and also the freedom of antireligious propaganda. Although the Lenin Constitution of 1918 guaranteed the right of religious instruction, this right was taken away by decree in 1929. The same decree makes mandatory the registration of religious associations and also introduces a number of prohibitions limiting religious activity to worship services only. The hardening of state attitudes after 1960 was reflected in modifications to the Penal Code, prescribing harsh penalties for infractions of laws relating to religion. A new law concerning marriage and the family permits the removal of children from believing parents. In 1976 a Soviet publication for official use only, titled *Legislation on Religious Cults*, was leaked to the West. Since 80% of all Soviet decrees remain unpublished, this publication was a valuable source on the thousands of regulations on which the regime bases its persecution of the church. The chief agency responsible for conducting the campaigns against the church and applying the draconian laws for this purpose is the Council for Religious Affairs, which invariably is headed by a noted atheist. It operates, as far as is known, without any official statute, and its principal duty is the registration of cults and religious acts.

HISTORICAL BACKGROUND

The origin of the Slavs is a subject of great controversy among historians. They were perhaps the last of the many tribes that held sway over Eastern Europe from a very early time: Scythians, Sarmatians, Goths, Huns, Khazars and Avars, among many others. When they appear on the stage of history around the eighth century, they were already divided into three groups: West Slavs (Poles, Czechs and Slovaks); South Slavs (Serbs, Croats, Macedonians, Slovenes, Bulgars and Montenegrins); and East Slavs (Russians, Ukrainians and Byelorussians).

In about 862 the East Slavs sought and received the protection of a Viking group known as Varangians, whose king, a Dane named Rurik, is the first king in Russian history. He founded a dynasty that was to rule Russia for 700 years, and it is possible that the term Rus (or Russian) was derived from his name. Rurik himself settled in Novgorod, but his son Oleg moved south and established himself as the prince of Kiev. Kiev, which was the first truly Russian state, encompassed a vast territory that included several large trading centers. By the 10th century Vladimir, prince of Kiev, had accepted the Orthodox faith, and it became the richest legacy of Kiev to Russian civilization. In addition, Russia also inherited from Kiev an extensive commercial system, settled agriculture, a money economy and a military tradition.

The Kievan state was in an advanced stage of decline when the last great mass movement from Asia swept over the land, led by the Golden Horde of the successors of Chingis Khan. The horde destroyed the city of Kiev in 1240, overthrew the Kievan princes and held Russia in bondage for over 200 years, laying waste the cities and slaughtering thousands. After the first wave of devastation, the Mongols adopted a policy of indirect rule.

The first Mongol reverse was the Battle of Kulikovo in 1380, in which a Russian army led by a prince of Moscow gained a victory over their oppressors. However, the tributes to the Mongols continued for another century until the time of Ivan the Great. During the Mongol period all principalities were ruled by princes, but the rulers of Kiev, Novgorod and Tver were known as grand princes. In 1325 Ivan I of Moscow, a small town first mentioned in Russian chronicles only in 1147, persuaded the khan to name him grand prince. Ivan also persuaded the metropolitan of the Russian Orthodox Church to shift his metropolitanate to Moscow. These moves helped to enhance the power of Ivan I to such an extent that his immediate successor assumed the title of Grand Prince of All the Russians. When Ivan III, also known as the Great, came to power in 1462, Moscow (or Muscovy) was as large as Kiev had been in its heyday. During his 43-year reign Ivan III strengthened central control, created a bureaucracy, ended Mongol domination, regained large territories in the West from the Polish-Lithuanian kingdom and incorporated Novgorod, Tver and Ryazan into Muscovy. Ivan III was the first to call himself czar, or Sovereign of All Russia.

Ivan III's grandson Ivan IV, also known as the Terrible, dominated Russian history in the 16th century. Ivan was a child of three when he succeeded to the throne, and he was crowned when he was 17, in a glittering ceremony. For the next 37 years he ruled Russia with an iron fist. The first to feel that iron fist were the boyars, or the nobles, who had wielded extensive powers at the court. They were excluded from the advisory council. During the early years of his reign Ivan initiated various enlightened reforms, which contrasted with the mad excesses during the latter part. These reforms included a new legal code and church regulations and the calling of the first national assembly (Zemsky Sobor). He conquered the three Mongol khanates of Siberia, Kazan and Astrakhan and incorporated them into his domains. To foil opposition to his policies, Ivan created a 6,000-man political police, the first in Russia, and unleashed a reign of terror. Entire cities suspected of disloyalty, such as Novgorod, were destroyed. Eventually Ivan turned mad and killed his own son and heir apparent. The surviving son, Fyodor I, died without an heir, thus ending the line of Rurik and setting the stage for a dynastic struggle known as the Time of Troubles, which lasted from 1605 to 1613. The struggle for the crown among a succession of pretenders, charlatans and foreign princes was marked by absolute anarchy in the land, giving free rein to Cossack freebooters and marauders. In 1610 Polish armies occupied Moscow. At this point the tide turned as the patriarch of Moscow rallied the people to drive out the foreign troops and defend Holy Russia. In 1613 the interregnum ended with the election by a Zemsky Sobor of Czar Michael Romanov, the first of a new dynasty that would rule Russia for 304 years.

The first three Romanov czars were weak rulers, and

boyar intrigues, peasant uprisings and foreign wars continued to plague the land. Gradually some semblance of internal order returned. The Cossacks were won over by treaty, resulting in the annexation of the Ukraine. The Poles and the Swedes were bought off in the West. A new code legalized the institution of serfdom. Finally, a schism in the Orthodox Church led to a gradual usurpation of church prerogatives by the tsars.

Near the end of the 17th century the most powerful of the Romanovs ascended the throne—Peter I, also known as the Great. Under him Russia was transformed from a backward medieval principality into a modern empire. He was a man of furious energy, and there was no area of Russian national life that he did not alter. He modernized the army and built a navy. He established a table of ranks for the military and civil service in which ability rather than heredity determined position. He abolished the office of patriarch, creating a Holy Synod in his stead, and placing a lay official in charge of church administration. Among his other achievements, he changed the ancient Russian calendar, introduced Arabic numerals, revised the Cyrillic alphabet, published the first newspaper, established compulsory schools for the children of the gentry and founded an academy of sciences. In a series of foreign wars that engaged 40 of the 42 years of his reign, he eliminated Sweden as a power in northern Europe and obtained his long-sought outlet to the sea and "window on Europe," as he termed his new capital of St. Petersburg. He also made several inroads into the Ottoman Empire.

With all his reforms, Peter was a typical feudal monarch, and during his reign the position of the serfs became worse. Like Ivan the Terrible, he used terror and executions to cow his subjects and tortured to death many, including his own son.

The next great ruler of Russia was Catherine the Great, a princess of the small German state of Anhalt-Zerbst who had married the grandson of Peter the Great and converted to Orthodoxy. By the force of her personality and her skill in court intrigue, she managed to depose her husband, bypass her son and proclaim herself empress of Russia. Initially a friend of Voltaire and other philosophers of the Enlightenment, she turned a reactionary after the French Revolution. During her reign the serfs lost all human rights and under a new law were listed as chattels. With nothing to lose, they exploded into Russia's most famous serf rebellion, led by Yemelyan Pugachev, a Don cossack. Doomed to failure by poor leadership, the revolt, which lasted from 1773 to 1775, frightened the gentry class and fostered further repression. In foreign affairs the empire expanded at the expense of Turkey and Poland, acquiring in the process the Ukraine, Byelorussia and Crimea. Catherine was succeeded by her son Paul, who within five years turned mad. He was murdered in a palace revolt, and his son Alexander I succeeded him on the throne.

Alexander began his reign auspiciously, sponsoring some liberal reforms. In the spirit of the age, he opened education to all classes and built many universities. But the bureaucracy proved too cumbrous, and the high promise of his early years was worn down by the size of Russia's problems. Externally, the highlight of his reign was the invasion of Russia by Napoleon. Two years later, Alexander rode triumphantly into Paris along with his victorious allies, and he played a leading role at the Congress of Vienna in 1815. He drew up a constitutional plan for Russia, but before anything was done with it, died in 1825. In the confusion that followed, another abortive revolution took its bloody toll. The so-called Decembrist uprising, although brutally suppressed, remained a symbol until 1917 for both the radicals and the reactionaries of their mutual conflict. Nicholas I, brother and successor of Alexander, devoted his 30-year reign to the suppression of liberal ideas, both at home and abroad. In the latter years he blundered into the Crimean War against France and Great Britain; the war ended in a humiliating defeat for Russia. Nicholas died in 1855 before the war was over and was succeeded by his son Alexander II.

Although as conservative as his father, Alexander II was more pragmatic. Concerned with the over 1,500 peasant uprisings in the first 60 years of the 19th century, he issued an imperial proclamation in 1861 freeing the serfs. For this act he is known in history as the Liberator and as the Great Reformer. Although the economic condition of the serfs did not materially alter, the proclamation ended one of the social anachronisms that had troubled the Russian conscience. He also carried through a number of other reforms in the judicial system, local government, education, military organization and the fiscal system, all without diluting his own power. On the international scene, Alexander completed the expansion of the empire to its farthest extent by conquering the remaining khanates and securing the trans-Caspian region and the Caucasus mountain region. Despite the reforms, Russia remained a troubled country spawning scores of radical movements. Extremists turned to acts of terrorism, making several attempts on the life of the czar, who finally was killed by a terrorist bomb in 1881.

The reigns of Alexander III and Nicholas II, the two last Romanovs, represented a time of reaction. Seeking to perpetuate their absolutism, they turned Russia into a police state. The onset of industrialization brought with it even more serious economic problems, such as urban slums, unemployment and worker exploitation. Political repression and economic uncertainty created conditions ripe for a revolution.

The first revolution, that of 1905, was sparked when a peaceful workers' demonstration was fired on by the militia at close range. The resulting massacre, known as Bloody Sunday, was a prelude to mass disturbances, strikes and civil strife that lasted for a whole year, and it almost brought the imperial government down. Nicholas survived by making some minor concessions and by calling a Duma (legislature), which for the next 12 years set the stage for an experiment in parliamentary government. Until 1911 the Duma was dominated by a strongman, Peter Stolypin, a monarchist who tried to pacify the malcontents by introducing limited land reforms while at the same time sending radical revolutionaries to the gallows. With Stolypin's assassination in 1911 the reform movement languished. Within three years Russia was caught in the vortex of World War I.

Nicholas's first war, the Russo-Japanese War, had ended in 1904 disastrously and had precipitated the 1905 Revolution. World War I was no different and helped to deliver the coup de grace to the Romanov dynasty. Although the Russian army, over 1 million strong, fought valiantly and inflicted serious defeats on the Turkish and Austrian forces, the casualties were enormous, and the supply lines broke down many times. Morale at the front deteriorated as the Germans continued to advance, and the revolutionaries made political capital of every reverse, particularly after Nicholas assumed personal command of the army. At home, the unpopular Queen Alexandra and her Svenga-li-like adviser Grigori Rasputin scandalized the nation and brought the monarchy into disrepute.

Finally, even as the war was dragging on in the West, a new revolution broke out in March 1917. It was not led by the radical revolutionaries but by common people, workers and housewives who took to the streets. Troops ordered to suppress the demonstrators joined them instead. Four days later, Nicholas II abdicated the throne. Russian monarchy had lasted 1,055 years.

In the first days of the Revolution there was chaos in Petrograd. Two governments were formed, one the Provisional Government led by Alexander Kerensky and the other a Soviet (Council) of Workers and Soldiers' Deputies. The most prominent revolutionaries of the time were not present in Petrograd at this time but were abroad or in exile. Lenin was in Switzerland, Trotsky in New York and Stalin in Siberia. The events of March had surprised them, and all three returned to Petrograd posthaste. Lenin (born Vladimir Ilich Ulyanov) with his wife and two lieutenants (Karl Radek and Grigory Zinoviev) were transported by the German government in a sealed train in the hope that Lenin's disruptive influence would lead to Russia's withdrawal from the war. When Lenin arrived at Finland Station, he was greeted by the Petrograd Soviet leaders. Shortly the Bolsheviks took over the Petrograd Soviet as well as 350 other soviets in other major cities and towns. Meanwhile, the Provisional Government continued to keep Russia in the war, which helped to make Lenin, with his call for immediate peace, popular. In July 1917 the Bolsheviks made an abortive bid for power. The Provisional Government survived the insurrection, but its days were numbered. After a summer of confusion in which Kerensky was beset by the right and the left, the Bolsheviks made another bid for power in November, and in a swift coup succeeded in seizing complete power.

The new era in Russian history that began on November 7, 1917, was not the result of a mass movement, unlike the March 1917 Revolution. It was a revolution in which power was seized by a well-organized party, perhaps the only group with unity of purpose and leadership at that time in Russia. The prime mover of the Bolshevik success was Lenin, without whom, as Trotsky said later, the revolution could not have succeeded.

The new government called itself the Soviet of People's Commissars, with Lenin as chairman, Trotsky as commissar of foreign affairs and Stalin as commissar of nationalities. The many years the new leaders had operated underground, from prison or from exile, colored the operation of the government, in which secrecy and conspiratorial methods were fundamental. Within a month a secret police was established under the name Special Commission for the Fight Against Counterrevolution, which in another two weeks became the All-Russian Extraordinary Commission to Fight Counterrevolution, Sabotage and Speculation, whose long title usually was shortened to Extraordinary Commission (Chrezvychaynaya Kommisiya, or Cheka), an agency of terror more infamous than the secret police of Ivan the Terrible. The Bolsheviks constituted only a small political minority, and Lenin's immediate efforts were directed toward eliminating their rivals. In the election to the Constituent Assembly, the first and only free elections in Russian history, the Bolsheviks won only 24% of the vote. It held only one stormy meeting, which ended when Lenin ordered his Bolshevik Guard to dissolve the Assembly. Lenin's next pressing problem was ending the war. In March 1918 he concluded the Treaty of Brest-Litovsk with the German High Command as quid pro quo for their role in securing his passage to Russia a year earlier. According to the terms of this treaty Russia gave up one-quarter of its population, one-third of its industrial capacity, one-quarter of its railway system and one-third of its arable land. The terms were so harsh as to make it a virtual capitulation. In another move Lenin moved the capital of the republic to Moscow, to signalize the break with the imperial past.

After Brest-Litovsk, civil war swept through the land, and former Allied forces, particularly, from France, Britain, the United States and Japan, sent forces of intervention, ostensibly to guard the huge stocks of military supplies from falling into German hands. Although foreign troops did not play a decisive part in the civil war, conflict raged with varying intensity on many fronts across the length and breadth of Russia. Admiral Alexander Kolchak commanded a large White Russian (an anti-Bolshevik) army, with headquarters at Omsk. He was assisted by a Czech legion of 40,000, who controlled most of the major towns along the Trans-Siberian Railway. Gen. Anton Denikin, chief of staff under the Provisional Government, organized cossack troops in the Don region in the South. Denikin later subordinated his troops to Baron Peter Wrangel. From the Baltic region a White Russian army commanded by Gen. Nikolai Yudenich attacked Petrograd but was beaten back at the outskirts by the Bolsheviks. The Bolsheviks were hemmed in to a small territory for much of 1918, but their fortunes changed abruptly with the end of World War I in November of that year. Soon thereafter the Allied troops in Russia withdrew and the Red Army pushed toward ultimate victory. The Revolution had been saved from extinction by the organizational genius of Trotsky, now commissar of war, and emerging military leaders such as Frunze, Voroshilov, Tukachevsky and Budyenny.

Although the civil war was over, it took several years to heal the land ravaged by the armies on both sides. The end of the war did not bring an end to the depredations and pillages of outlaw bands. Estimates of the number of homeless children ranged between 7 million and 9 million, and most of them roamed the land in a terrible struggle for survival.

In the wake of the civil war came epidemics of cholera and typhus, and a famine in 1921 added to the catalog of catastrophes. Some relief was afforded by domestic as well as foreign agencies, such as the American Relief Administration, led by Herbert Hoover, which was feeding 10 million Russians daily in 1922.

The large-scale human suffering precluded the immediate enforcement of socialism. Lenin therefore prescribed a small dose of capitalism, called the New Economic Policy (NEP), to cure the country's troubles until the time was ripe for full-fledged socialism. However, the state took over the "commanding heights of the economy"—banks, mines, transportation and large factories.

On December 30, 1922, over five years after the Revolution, the Union of Soviet Socialist Republics (USSR) was formally established as a federation of four independent socialist republics—the Russian (first set up on November 15, 1917), Ukrainian, Byelorussian and Transcaucasian, the last split up in 1936 into the Georgian, Azerbaijan and Armenian SSR's. All political parties other than the Communist Party were outlawed. In 1924 the Second All-Union Congress of the Soviets formally approved the federation, inserting, tongue in cheek, a provision for free secession from the union. The Turkmen and Uzbek SSR's were formed in 1924; the Tajik SSR in 1929; the Kazakh and Kirghiz SSRs in 1936; and the Latvian, Lithuanian, Estonian and Moldavian SSR's in 1940.

In 1922 Lenin, then aged only 52, suffered a stroke and in the following two years was paralyzed by several more until his death in 1924. Trotsky was the heir apparent, but Stalin (born Joseph Vissarionovich Dzhugashvili), holding the key post of general secretary, took over complete control of the party within four years of Lenin's death. Trotsky was hounded out of the country and pursued by Stalin's agents relentlessly until his assassination in Mexico in 1940.

The Stalin era may be divided into two periods: that from 1929 to 1941, when the war broke out, and the second from 1941 to Stalin's death in 1953. During the first period Stalin unleashed one of the most monstrous bloodbaths in Russian history, killing millions of kulaks (wealthy peasant farmers) who opposed his collectivization plans. The kulaks were eliminated as a class and forced labor was made commonplace, but the difference between labor camp inmates and free workers was marginal at best. After this was accomplished Stalin turned to the party itself. In the lexicon of communism, the word "purge" had a special significance, as a means of keeping the party "pure" of opportunists and ideologically weak members. Stalin gave an extended meaning to this term, as he not only expelled those unworthy of party membership but also executed them. Among those who fell to the firing squad were Lenin's close associates Lev Kamenev and Grigory Zinoviev; Marshal Tukachevsky, a hero of the civil war; five other marshals; 13 to 15 army commanders; 57 of 85 corps commanders; and 110 of 195 division commanders. Genrikh Yagoda, the chief of the security police who had been the overseer of the early purges, was himself purged and replaced by Nikolai Yezhov. The latter administered the terror so efficiently that the period from 1936 to 1938 is known in Russian as Yezhovshchina, a time of infamy and terror unequaled in Russian history. In 1938 Yezhov disappeared and was replaced by Lavrenti Beria. Even common people did not escape, as they found themselves swept up in police nets and herded into labor camps. The number of forced laborers is placed between 12 million and 15 million; arrests were rapid, trials were abolished and sentencing became a police function. To add insult to injury, Stalin published in 1936 a "democratic constitution" guaranteeing all civic and human rights. Its promulgation signaled the fact that Stalin felt completely secure now, having achieved absolute control of the nation and having eliminated all opponents.

Meanwhile, Hitler's star had arisen in Germany and the two dictators concluded the infamous Non-Aggression Pact of 1939. For Stalin this was an opportunity to swallow half of Poland, as well as Estonia, Latvia and Lithuania. He also invaded Finland. In the midst of these military adventures he was surprised by the German invasion of June 22, 1941. In 1941 Stalin for the first time made himself prime minister, and later as the commissar of defense and commander in chief took the title of generalissimo. The Great Fatherland War was Stalin's finest hour as he rapidly made peace with the Orthodox Church, abolished the Comintern and united the Russian people against the invaders. German troops, over 330,000 strong, quickly swept over the Ukraine but failed to achieve their three principal targets: Leningrad, Moscow and Stalingrad (now Volgagrad). In February 1943 Field Marshal Paulus surrendered to the Soviet defenders of Stalingrad. Two years later Russian troops were in Berlin, and the worst war in world history was over. Stalin and Stalinism emerged from the war much stronger than ever. The Allies parceled out Eastern Europe as a Soviet fief, and Russia gained in Poland, Finland and elsewhere more than it had lost at Brest-Litovsk. In the Far East it gained the lower half of Sakhalin and the Kuril Islands. The war had cost the lives of 20 million Russians, but with reparations from Germany and Japan, Stalin quickly rebuilt Soviet industry.

CONSTITUTION & GOVERNMENT

Czar Nicholas II was forced to abdicate in March 1917. A Provisional Government of moderate convictions was established and overthrown in Petrograd on November 7 (the "October Revolution") by the Bolshevik ("Majority") wing of the Social Democratic Party. Led by Lenin, the Bolsheviks established a "dictatorship of the proletariat," created the "Soviet state" and embarked on "building socialism." The Communist Party (CP), claiming to be the "vanguard of the proletariat," assigned to itself the leading role in the society and a monopoly of political power. Marxism-Leninism was the foundation for the party's rule.

On November 8 the Second Congress of Soviets established the Council of People's Commissars (Sovnarkom), and on November 15 the Council created the Russian Soviet Federated Socialist Republic (RSFSR). During succeeding years republics, regions and areas were established to reflect various nations and nationalities. On the principle of "united and equal," Lenin's plan was adopted into law on December 20, 1922, by the First All-Union Congress of Soviets creating the Union of Soviet Socialist Republics (USSR). During 72 years of its existence (1917–89) the Soviet Union has functioned under four constitutions—those of 1918, 1924, 1936 and 1977. In 1989 a new constitution was being drafted to codify developments generated by General Secretary Mikhail Gorbachev's policies of *glasnost* and *perestroika*.

The first constitution under Communist control was promulgated on July 10, 1918, by the First All-Russian Congress of Soviets, shortly after Russia had withdrawn from the First World War and during the civil war. The Congress created the RSFSR and formalized a structure and programs already decreed into existence. Although the CP was not mentioned in the Constitution of 1918, it controlled the government's mechanisms. Within a short time competing political parties were not allowed to function. The principle of separation of legislative, executive and judicial power was abhorred. The basic law consisted of two parts: Declaration of the Rights of Toilers and Exploited People, and the governmental structure. Lower soviets (councils) were subordinate to the higher in a state structure reflecting a multinational society, theoretically a federation with the right of "free secession." In fact, power was centralized in Moscow. Similarly, an array of human rights was coupled with duties, and citizens soon learned the limits of professed freedoms. Suffrage, denied to many, was indirect and unequal, with the urban proletariat heavily favored over the independent-minded peasantry.

Under the Constitution the supreme organ of state power was vested in the unicameral All-Union Russian Congress of Soviets. The Congress elected the All-Russian Central Executive Committee of some 200 members to conduct legislative and executive functions between its sessions. The Committee, in turn, selected the Council of People's Commissars as the executive arm and assigned it enormous powers, although it was responsible to the Congress and the Committee. The previous judicial system was abolished and replaced by a system—Supreme Court, lower courts and the procurator-general—to enhance the CP's rule. The Constitution provided for a hierarchical system of soviets at lower levels—republic, regional, district and local.

The creation of the USSR in 1922 necessitated revision of the Constitution. Lenin suffered a stroke in the fall of 1922 and died in January 1924. The draft was developed by a commission headed by Josef Stalin and was codified on January 31, 1924, by the Second All-Union Congress of Soviets, which gave the USSR its constitutional imprimatur. As previously, the republics were given the right of secession and a variety of other rights. Although not again mentioned in the Constitution, the CP continued to have a monopoly of power in directing the governmental structure and in setting policy.

The Communist ideological outlook was a world of irreconcilable antagonists: socialists and capitalists. Political power in the USSR was centralized in a "Union State" consisting of the RSFSR and the Ukrainian, Byelorussian and Transcaucasian republics, bound by treaties. The republics were left with residual powers. Formally supreme power was vested, as under the Constitution of 1918, in the All-Union Congress of Soviets, a unicameral body of over 2,000 deputies meeting annually; after 1927 the sessions were to be held twice yearly. Also repeated was the election by the Congress of the Central Executive Committee, to act on its behalf between sessions. However, the Committee was now bicameral—to give the nationalities a heightened sense of representation and participation. This body of 750 members, in turn, elected a 27-member Presidium to carry on day-to-day activities. The Central Executive Committee selected the Council of People's Commissars, or Sovnarkom, as the executive and administrative organ. Sovnarkom was responsible to the Committee and the Presidium. All positions of authority on the Council were held by CP leaders and, increasingly, this body accumulated power while that of the Supreme Soviet diminished. The Congress's Executive Committee elected the Supreme Court and the procurator-general. The Constitution assigned to the Supreme Court authority to decide on the constitutionality of laws passed by Union republics but not on all-Union laws. The procurator was given the right to challenge the Supreme Court's rulings before the Council of People's Commissars, which now was invested with legislative, executive and judicial power.

A number of amendments were legislated following the adoption of the Constitution of 1924, additional republics were established, some changes occurred in the government, forced collectivization was instituted and Stalin emerged as the leader in the power struggle. In February 1935 the Central Committee of the CP proposed a new constitution drafted to reflect current "correlation of class forces" in the USSR. The All-Union Congress of Soviets gave proforma approval and the Executive Committee established a constitutional commission directed by Stalin, Nikolai Bukharin and Karl Radek to formulate a draft of a new constitution. The draft was published on June 12, 1936. Discussions and proposals for amendments were encouraged, but changes to the draft were minor. The document was promulgated by the All-Union Congress on December 5, 1936, and became known as the "Stalin Constitution," which lasted until 1977 and which was to serve as a model for East European Communist regimes following World War II. The primacy of the CP was noted in the Constitution as "the leading core of all organizations of the working people, both public and state."

This was a comprehensive document that established economic and social principles as well as the structure of the government. According to Chapter 1, the USSR was proclaimed a "socialist" state of workers and peasants with socialist means of production. State ownership was extensive, private property was severely limited and the economy was to be developed according to state plans. The state was characterized as a federation and union of 15 equal republics which, as in previous constitutions, had a right of secession (Article 17). Prior to General Secretary Gorbachev's leadership, this provision was never seriously tested, but any attempt would have been summarily rejected. The article was a useful propaganda claim, however. Union republics were consigned to a secondary position, having residual powers (Article 15), with the preponderance of jurisdiction as the province of the central government (Article 14). The only similarities between the Union and the Union republics were the governmental structures.

The highest organ of state power was the Supreme Soviet, consisting of two chambers: the Soviet of the Union and the Soviet of Nationalities. The Constitution designated the Supreme Soviet as the principal legislative body. It was elected every four years by citizens age 18 or over on the basis of universal suffrage and direct and secret ballot. Candidates qualified at age 21 and were selected by a CP-controlled electoral commission. A single list was presented to the voters, who were not only encouraged but also pressured to vote for the approved slate. Some candidates, especially at lower levels, were non-CP members—mostly for propaganda purposes—but all owed allegiance to the party, and the results always were either unanimous or over 99%.

The Soviet of the Union had one deputy for every 300,000 people; thus, approximately 800 deputies at that time. Deputies to the Soviet of Nationalities were elected by Union republics (25 each), autonomous Union republics (11 each), autonomous oblasts (five each) and national *okrugs* (one each). Thus the Soviet of Nationalities had 652 deputies. The sessions were held twice yearly for short periods of time, at which the Supreme Soviet adopted the annual budget and approved laws and decrees previously issued or newly submitted by the Council of Ministers and the Presidium. At a joint session of the Chambers the Supreme Soviet elected from among its members a Presidium, which acted on its behalf between sessions, when it assumed the role of the highest organ of state power and issued decrees. The Presidium consisted of a chairman, who represented the state; 15 deputy chairmen (one from each Union republic), 16 permanent members and a secretary.

The highest executive and administrative organ of the state was the Council of Ministers (the name was changed from Council of People's Commissars in March 1946), which, however, no longer possessed formal legislative authority, as it did previously, but continued to prepare legislative drafts. Appointed by the Supreme Soviet and responsible to it and the Presidium, the Council of Ministers was headed by a chairman or the prime minister and consisted of deputy chairmen, all-Union and Union republic ministers, chairmen of designated central committees and heads of special agencies. Also included as ex officio members were chairmen of the Council of Ministers of Union republics. Altogether the Council numbered as many as 75 or more members.

The Council of Ministers operated by issuing ordinances and making decisions in implementing laws and, more meaningfully, by carrying out policies established by the CP in which Council members held high positions. Given such a large, unwieldy body of members, a smaller Presidium, composed of the chairman and deputy chairmen, and a Bureau of the Presidium conferred more frequently and established policies. For many years Moscow did not reveal the existence of these executive organs, but following Stalin's death in 1953 it announced their replacement by the Presidium of the Council of Ministers.

The court system reflected the hierarchical structure of the government—the Supreme Court on the all-Union level, the Supreme Courts of the Union republics, and courts at lower levels. The Supreme Soviet elected the Supreme Court to a five-year term and the procurator-general to a seven-year term. All cases, except those exempted by law, were heard by a body consisting of a judge and people's assessors, the latter elected by the Supreme Soviet to two-year terms. The procurator-general—the most powerful and at times most notorious enforcer—and his bureaucracy supervised the enforcement of laws and the regime's policies.

Chapter 10 contained a panoply of fundamental rights of citizens, including employment, pay, leisure, health, education, equality of sexes, religion, speech, press, assembly and demonstrations. However, the rights were coupled with duties and conditions such as duty of work discipline and respect for socialist society. The Constitution provided for antireligious propaganda, and the regime pursued policies designed to create an atheistic society. Rights of speech, press, assembly and demonstrations were restricted to serve the socialist system as decided by the authorities. And the Constitution simply ignored judicial review.

Dramatic events marked the 41-year passage between the Stalin Constitution and the Constitution of 1977—Stalin's purges, World War II, extension of the Soviet empire, nuclear weapons, "Titoism," the Cold War, Stalin's death, de-Stalinization, the Hungarian uprising, space flight, the Berlin Wall, discontent within the empire, Dubcek's "Prague Spring" and the Soviet claim of achievement of a "developed socialist society." The Constitution of 1977 was promulgated on October 7, at a special session of the Supreme Soviet. It is a lengthy document of nine sections, 21 chapters and 174 articles.

The first section establishes the principles of the socialist structure and the policy of the USSR. The Soviet Union is a "socialist state," organized on the principle of "democratic centralism." The foundation of the economic system was restated to be the socialist ownership of the means of production, with state property and collectivization of farms.

As in the Constitution of 1936, the Constitution of 1977 enumerated a comprehensive set of basic rights, freedoms and duties. Citizens have a constitutional right to work (i.e., guaranteed employment and pay); rest and leisure; health protection; maintenance in old age, sickness and disability; housing; education; cultural benefits; freedom of scientific, technical and artistic work; participation in state and public affairs; freedom of speech, press, assembly and demonstrations; association in public organizations; freedom of religion; inviolability of person and home; privacy and protection of correspondence and communications; and freedom to lodge complaints against officials and state organs.

The rights, freedoms and benefits, however, must not be to the "detriment of the interest of society or the state." Employment considerations must meet the "needs of society," thus denouncing labor strikes, while rest and leisure are subject to availability of facilities. Health and medical facilities often are substandard, and housing continues to be in a deplorable condition. Higher education often is available only to those with class and CP credentials. The basic rights of speech, press, assembly and demonstrations must be "to strengthen and develop the socialist system" and thus have been severely violated; only under Gorbachev's *glasnost* has the CP permitted greater freedom of expression and demonstrations, while the limits of public organizations still are to be determined. Generally, travel to non-Communist countries and emigration have been severely limited, although relaxed in 1989. The Soviet history of combating church and religion is well known. The Constitution provided for "atheistic propaganda." However, the regime's attempt to create an atheistic society failed, and Gorbachev's administration has adopted a more liberal attitude toward believers. The rights of families, individuals, home and correspondence often had been violated by the feared KGB (Committee for State Security) and other officials.

In addition to rights, the Constitution lays down a litany of duties to observe the Constitution and other laws and to "comply with the standards of socialist conduct." These include the duty to work "conscientiously"; to "preserve and protect socialist property"; to safeguard the interests of the Soviet state, as the defense of the "Socialist Motherland is the sacred duty" of citizens; of military service; and to raise children as "worthy members of socialist society."

Chapter 20 covers the judicial system, with the following courts: Supreme Courts of the USSR, Union republics and autonomous republics; territorial, regional and city courts; courts of autonomous regions; courts of autonomous areas, district people's courts; and military tribunals. All are elected by the voters. The Supreme Court of the USSR is the highest judicial body and supervises the administration of justice by USSR and Union republic courts. It is elected by the Supreme Soviet to a five-year term, as are the Supreme Courts by the legislative bodies at lower levels. The bulk—perhaps 98% to 99%—of cases are tried by district (city) people's courts, which are composed of people's judges (elected directly by the voters for five years) and lay, people's assessors (elected directly for two and one-half years). Judges of military courts are elected to five-year terms by the Presidium of the Supreme Soviet and people's assessors of these courts for two and one-half years by military service personnel. In the 1987 elections, 12,000 people's judges and 850,000 people's assessors were elected. As previously, supervision of compliance of laws and decisions is the province of the proc-

urator-general. This powerful official is appointed by the Supreme Soviet to a five-year term. Procurators at the Union republic and lower levels are appointed by the procurator-general of the USSR, also for five years. In appeals and demonstrations what the population demands is the government's—and thus the CP's—compliance with the constitutional provisions.

Toward the end of 1989 Soviet authorities continued discussion over the necessity of revising the legal system. In 1988 Gorbachev expressed the need for "increasing the role and prestige of the Soviet court," and the CP in that year declared that "Constant concern with strengthening the guarantees of Soviet citizens' rights and freedoms is the duty of the state." The 19th All-Union Party Conference, in June 1988, endorsed that idea. During 1989 various draft laws were considered and several passed into law.

Amending the Constitution has not been a difficult task in the Soviet Union, and it has been amended frequently. The Constitution of 1977 provides for passage of amendments by the Supreme Soviet by a majority of not less than two-thirds of the total number of deputies of each chamber. Nearly always amendments were adopted by unanimous vote, but the temperament of the reconstituted Supreme Soviet in 1989 promised less than automatic unanimity.

The USSR is described (Article 70) as an "integral, federal, multinational state," which embodies "state unity" for "jointly building communism." Fifteen Union republics comprise the USSR (see Ethnic Composition). As in previous constitutions, each republic is given "the right freely to secede from the USSR" (Article 72). Also, as previously, the USSR is given extensive powers (Article 73), with the republics having residual powers (Chapter 9). According to Article 73 the jurisdiction of the USSR embraces the following: admission of new republics into the USSR; determination of the state boundaries and approval of changes in the boundaries between Union republics; establishment of principles for organization and functioning of republics and lower bodies; ensuring uniformity of legislation throughout the USSR; determining economic, social, scientific, technological and other programs; drafting and approval of the state budget; war and peace, defense, safeguarding of frontiers and territory, and direction of the armed forces, state security; foreign affairs; coordination of relations of Union republics with other states and international organizations; foreign trade and other external activities; observance of the USSR Constitution and ensuring conformity of constitutions of Union republics with that of the USSR; and other all-Union matters.

Although the Constitution declares that the Union republics are "sovereign," their residual powers outside the jurisdiction of Article 73 are severely limited. The republics have their own constitutions, which must conform to that of the USSR. They are allowed to participate in the decision-making of the USSR Supreme Soviet, its Presidium and the central Council of Ministers or the government. In their economic and social development the republics must cooperate and coordinate with USSR authorities. Any boundary changes between republics must be ratified by the USSR. Union republics are given the right to conduct relations with foreign states, conclude treaties, exchange diplomatic and consular representatives and participate in international organizations.

The rash of declarations of sovereignty and independence prompted Gorbachev's leadership, despite its reluctance, to fashion a new Treaty of the Union with which to prevent secessionist tendencies in the Union Republics. The 28th Congress, meeting July 2–13, 1990, acknowledged a nationality crisis that "threatens the break-up of our society," and the "right of self-determination," and resolved as a solution "the preparation and conclusion of a new Treaty of the Union." The Congress stressed that this should be a "union of sovereign states." However, despite its recognition of need to transform the USSR from a "unitary State into a genuine commonwealth of peoples," Congress' Resolution declared that "It is the duty of Communists to combat the ideology and political practice of national extremism."

Outside of the Ukraine and Byelorussia, which, along with the USSR, were original members of the United Nations, no other Union republic has availed itself of this constitutional provision. Pressures on Moscow from various republics—especially the Baltic states, the Ukraine and Moldavia—have been escalating from reforms to outright independence. Forces in the Baltic states have demanded that the secret protocols of the 1939 Nazi-Soviet Non-Aggression Pact be declared "null and void." At the same time, there is concern regarding the limits of Moscow's tolerance. What these limits are and what success the Union republics will have in their march toward independence still remained a question in the fall of 1990. A year earlier, in November 1989, the Presidium of the Supreme Soviet called on the Baltic republics and Azerbaijan to change their laws that violate the USSR Constitution, and in subsequent months other republics were advised as well. However, in the face of mounting clamor in the republics for drastic changes, the USSR Congress of People's Deputies on April 3, 1990, amended the Constitution on secession from the USSR and the Gorbachev leadership was preparing a new Treaty of Union with the objective of maintaining a central structure. Neither the new law on secession nor the draft treaty satisfied the republics and by the fall of 1990 almost all declared their independence or sovereignty, (see Ethic Composition).

For a discussion of the electoral system (Chapter 13) and the Supreme Soviet (Chapter 15), see the Parliament section. Chapter 16 is devoted to the Council of Ministers, or the government—the highest executive and administrative organ in the USSR, elected by a joint session of the Soviet of the Union and the Soviet of Nationalities of the Supreme Soviet. The Council consists of the chairman (or prime minister), first vice chairmen, vice chairmen, ministers and chairmen of state committees. The chairmen of the Council of Ministers of Union republics, as in the Constitution of 1936, are ex officio members. The chairman (hereafter prime minister) may recommend to the Supreme Soviet heads of other organs of the USSR. The government tenders its resignation to a newly elected Supreme Soviet. It should be noted that the head of state is the chairman of the Supreme Soviet, currently Mikhail Gorbachev.

The Council of Ministers is responsible to the Supreme Soviet and, between its sessions, to the Presidium of the Supreme Soviet; also, the government is obliged to submit reports to the Supreme Soviet or the Presidium on a regular basis. The Constitution assigns to the Council of Ministers jurisdiction over all matters of administration outside the competence of the Supreme Soviet or the Presidium of the Supreme Soviet. The Council of Ministers:

• ensures the direction of economic, social and cultural development
• drafts and executes current and long-term state plans for economic and social development and the budget
• defends the interests of the state, protects socialist property, maintains public order and guarantees and protects citizens' rights and freedoms
• ensures state security
• directs the development of the armed forces
• directs foreign relations; foreign trade; and economic, scientific, technical and cultural cooperation with other countries
• establishes committees, boards and departments under the Council of Ministers in economic, social, cultural and defense spheres

For the day-to-day functioning of the Council of Ministers, the Constitution provides for a Presidium, consisting of its Chairman, first vice chairmen and vice chairmen, which is responsible for guiding economic and other areas of administration. In implementing the laws of the USSR and the decisions of the Supreme Soviet and its Presidium, the government issues binding decisions and ordinances and is responsible for their execution. The USSR's government is empowered by the Constitution (Article 134) to suspend execution of decisions and ordinances of the Council of Union Republics, as well as to rescind acts of its own ministries, state committees and other organs.

The Council of Ministers coordinates and directs activities of the all-Union and Union republic ministries, state committees and other bodies. The all-Union ministries and state committees direct the work of the branches assigned to them or of interbranch administration throughout the USSR, while Union republic ministries and state committees direct the work entrusted to them, including direct administration of enterprises and amalgamations. Any transfer of the latter is determined by the Presidium of the Supreme Soviet of the USSR. Ministries and state committees of the USSR issue orders and other acts in administering their areas of responsibility in accordance with laws of the USSR, decisions of the Supreme Soviet and its Presidium and of decisions and ordinances of the Council of Ministers.

Before Gorbachev the Council of Ministers was a large body that in 1984 numbered 111, including eight without portfolio, with a staff of approximately 2,000.

Moreover, many ministers were veterans of the ancient regimes with a questionable record of effectiveness and little enthusiasm for the new general secretary's policy of *perestroika* or restructuring. To administer his ambitious policy Gorbachev needed not only loyal supporters but also competent, qualified ministers. Accordingly, drastic measures were required and were made. The number of ministries was reduced in the reorganization, and since March 1985, when Gorbachev assumed power, and the fall of 1989, very few of the previous ministers remained. This was an unprecedented turnover. In addition to their support of *perestroika*, the new appointees were selected for their proven competence rather than their standing in the CP. Outstanding economists were especially in demand.

An extraordinary innovation unfolded in the confirmation process. Rather than giving pro forma approval to the nominees, as in the past, the committees of the Supreme Soviet as well as the entire Supreme Soviet scrutinized the candidates seriously. Consequently, the prime minister's list of 71 candidates, submitted to the first session of the new Supreme Soviet in 1989, was not automatically approved, including Gorbachev's personal choices. Also striking was the length of the period devoted to the nominations (June to July). One of the ministerial posts was not submitted because Premier Nikolai Ryzhkov was unsuccessful in finding a suitable person who would accept the portfolio of chairman of the State Committee for Environmental Protection. Interestingly, the post subsequently was filled by a scientist, Nikolai Vorontsov, who apparently is the first non-CP official of ministerial rank. Of the 71 candidates a number were unconfirmed by the committees and the Supreme Soviet. Surprisingly, only two appointees were confirmed unanimously: Foreign Minister Eduard Shevardnadze and Minister of Justice Veniamin Yakovlev. The process indicated increased legislative authority for the Supreme Soviet.

In the fall of 1989 the Council of Ministers consisted of Chairman Ryzhkov, the head of government (since September 1985); three first deputy chairmen; 10 deputy chairmen; 40 all-Union ministers; 15 Union-Republican ministers; 25 state committee chairmen, 10 ex officio members and three others of ministerial rank (chairman of the USSR State Bank—Gosbank; administrator of affairs of the Council of Ministers; and deputy chairman of the Military Industrial Commission); and the 15 ex officio chairmen of the Union republic Councils of Ministers. The Presidium of the Council of Ministers consists of the chairman, first deputy chairmen, deputy chairmen and three of the state committee chairmen.

Among those scrutinized were the minister of defense and the chairman of the Committee for State Security (KGB). The reappointment of Defense Minister Dimitri Yazov (since May 1987) involved Gorbachev's personal appeal to the Supreme Soviet. The Ministry of Defense and the Soviet armed forces have been of particular importance to the CP since the Revolution. The armed forces are undergoing restructuring also, and on July 3, 1989, Yazov denied rumors of a military coup, saying the USSR Defense Council made that "irrelevant." Formed by the Supreme Soviet, the Defense Council is headed by Gorbachev as general secretary of the CP and commander in chief of the armed forces. Furthermore, the CP's Central Committee continues to exercise its authority over the armed forces through the Main Political Administration of the Soviet army and navy. The chairman of the dreaded KGB, Vladimir Kryuchkov, (since October 1988 but in the Ministry from 1967), is in control of internal security forces, including the secret police and frontier troops, and is pursuing the reorganization of the Ministry and attempting to acquire a positive image through greater openness and public relations. On June 10, 1989, the Supreme Soviet established the Committee for Defense and State Security, whose composition was completed June 26. Chaired by Vladimir Lapygin, a space scientist, the committee's oversight responsibility over such powerful defense and state security institutions is potentially of great significance, but the degree of its effectiveness remains to be seen.

In November 1989 Gorbachev presented an assessment of *perestroika* and proposed the creation of a single president endowed with power to deal effectively with affairs of state. The new presidency was to be the center of power rather than the CP Politburo. Following consideration by the CP organs and discussions in the Supreme Soviet, which approved the proposal, the latter called an extraordinary session of the Congress of People's Deputies. The Congress amended the Constitution (Chapter 15 (1)) creating a president possessing extensive power.

- Article 127. The head of the Soviet state is the president.
- Article 127(1). Any USSR citizen between 35 and 65 years of age can be elected president by universal and equal suffrage by secret ballot for a five-year term for a maximum of two terms; the number of candidates is not limited; the candidate receiving a majority of votes in the USSR as a whole and in the majority of union republics is elected;
- Article 127(2). Upon inauguration the president swears an oath at the session of the Congress of the People's Deputies.
- Article 127(3). The president:

  1) is the guarantor of observance of Soviet citizens' rights and freedoms, and of the Constitution and laws;
  2) protects the sovereignty of the USSR and union republics and the country's security and territorial integrity; implements the principles of the national-state structure;
  3) represents the USSR internally and in international relations;
  4) coordinates supreme organs of power and management;
  5) submits to the Congress of People's Deputies annual reports on the state of the country, and briefs the Supreme Soviet on important domestic foreign policy;
  6) proposes to the Supreme Soviet for confirmation candidates for chairmen of the Council of

Ministers [prime minister of the government or cabinet], People's Control Committee, Supreme Court, prosecutor general and chief state arbiter; informs the Congress and the Supreme Soviet of, with the exception of the chairman of the Supreme Court, their release from duties;

7) appoints and submits for confirmation to the Supreme Soviet members of the cabinet, and dismisses ministers;

8) signs laws; within two weeks may refer a law with objections to the Supreme Soviet, which can reconfirm its decision by a two-thirds vote in each chamber;

9) can suspend the operation of government's resolutions and instructions;

10) ensures the defense of the country; is the commander-in-chief of the armed forces, appoints and replaces the supreme command, confers the highest military ranks; appoints judges of the highest military tribunals;

11) holds talks and signs international treaties; accepts credentials and letters of recall of foreign diplomats; appoints and recalls diplomats; confers the highest diplomatic ranks and other special titles;

12) awards orders and medals, and confers honorary titles;

13) decides questions of citizenship and asylum; grants pardons;

14) declares mobilization; declares a state of war in case of a military attack on the USSR and immediately refers the question to the Supreme Soviet; in accordance with law declares martial law in particular locations in the interest of the defense of the USSR and security of its citizens;

15) warns of a declaration of state of emergency in particular localities and, if necessary, introduces it at the request or with the consent of the Supreme Soviet Presidium or supreme organ of state power of the corresponding union republic; in the absence of consent, introduces the state of emergency and submits the decision without delay for ratification by the Supreme Soviet by two-thirds vote of all its members; the president can introduce temporary rule while observing the sovereignity and territorial integrity of the union republic;

16) in case of impasse between the Soviet of the Union and the Soviet of Nationalities, the president can recommend solution; if unsuccessful and a threat exists in disrupting government activity, he can propose to the congress of People's Deputies the election of a new Supreme Soviet.

• Article 127(4). The president heads the Council of the Federation, which comprises the supreme state officials of the union republics; The Council:

—examines compliance with the union treaty;
—elaborates measures to implement the state's nationalities policy;

—recommends to the Soviet of Nationalities resolution of disputes and settling conflicts in inter-ethnic relations; and
—coordinates the union republics' activity and ensures their participation in resolving unionwide significance within the competence of the President.

The Council examines questions affecting people who do not have their own national state with the participation of these people.

The chairman of the Supreme Soviet and chairmen of the chambers can participate in sessions of the Council.

• Article 127(5). Operating under the president, USSR Presidential Council elaborates measures to implement the main directions of the domestic and foreign policy and ensures the country's security.

Council members are appointed by the president; the prime minister is an *ex officio* member.

The chairman of the Supreme Soviet can participate in sessions.

• Article 127(6). The president holds joint sessions of the Council of the Federation and the Presidential Council.

• Article 127(7). Within the constitution and laws, the president issues decrees.

• Article 127(8). The president has the right of inviolability and may only be replaced by the Congress of People's Deputies on its own initiative or the Supreme Soviet by two-thirds vote of the total number of deputies, taking into account the findings of the Constitutional Oversight Committee.

• Article 127(9). The president may entrust the execution of his duties under points 11 and 12 of Art. 127(3) to the chairman of the Supreme Soviet and the prime minister, and the duties under point 13 of that article to the chairman of the Supreme Soviet.

• Article 127(10). If the president is unable to execute his duties, his powers are transferred to the chairman of the Supreme Soviet or, if not possible, to the prime minister until the election of a new president which must be within three months.

Gorbachev, as expected, was elected president by the Congress by a vote of 1,329 to 495. Although Gorbachev's March 14 victory was expected, his 59.2% of total votes was a radical departure from previous CP-controlled elections in which a 100% or near unanimous vote was the norm. Hereafter, the president is to be elected by direct vote of the citizens. President Gorbachev took the following oath of office before the Congress of People's Deputies:

I solemnly pledge faithfully to serve the peoples of our country, strictly to abide by the Constitution of the USSR, to guarantee citizens' rights and freedoms, and diligently to fulfil the high duties of President of the Soviet Union placed upon me.

Among his vast powers, the president issues decrees *(ukazy)*. After his inauguration Gorbachev said he intended to exercise his new authority especially to "radicalize *perestroika*"—that is, economic reforms. During the first several months a number of decrees were issued. In a society conditioned to a continuing flow of decrees and directives from government and CP bodies, the record of compliance with Gorbachev's decrees was disappointing. When they affect the Union republics, presidential decrees have caused additional complications with one—annulling Union-republic laws—questioned by the RSFSR as unconstitutional and ignored by other republics.

Gorbachev admitted that the system of executive power was not functioning. On September 24 the Supreme Soviet considered a resolution granting the president emergency powers to stabilize the erratic and dangerous period of transition from command to a free-market system. The vote for the "500 Day Plan" was 305 to 36, with 41 abstentions, empowering Gorbachev to issue decrees having the force of law.

Article 127(5) of the constitutional amendment establishing the presidency provided for a Presidential Council to function under the president. The Council's responsibility is to elaborate measures on Soviet domestic and foreign policy and ensure the country's security. The president is given the authority to appoint an unspecified number of its members, with the prime minister serving as an *ex officio* member while the right of participation in sessions is granted to the chairman of the Supreme Soviet.

The establishment of the Presidential Council is perhaps the clearest evidence of the political shift from the party to the presidency under Gorbachev's leadership. Its responsibility had been the province of the CC's Politburo and the Secretariat while security was with the Defense Council. Marshal Sergei Akhromeev reflected the official consensus that "ultimately real executive power will rest with the President and his Council." President Gorbachev is unrestrained, empowered as he is to appoint and dismiss Council members without confirmation. The Council is not a consultative body, as it appeared when it was established, but its members have sectors of responsibilities (see table), similar to previous CP Secretarial assignments. According to Gorbachev, the Council is the "president's working organ." Nationalities are better represented on the Council than on past central bodies, but Russians still predominated with over two-thirds.

Name	Original Position	Council Responsibility
Aitmatov, Chingiz T.	Writer	Culture
Bakatin, Vadim V.	USSR Minister of Internal Affairs	Public Order
Boldin, Valeriy I.	Former Assistant to Gorbachev; Chief of Staff of the Council	Staff work
Kauls, Albert E.	Chairman, agricultural combine Adaji, Latvia	Agriculture
Kryuchkov, Valdimir A.	Chairman, USSR State Security Committee (KGB)	State Security
Maslyukov, Yuriy D.	Chairman, USSR State Planning Committee	Economic Planning
Medvedev, Vadim	Former Politburo Member	Ideology
Osipyan, Yuriy A.	Vice President, Academy of Sciences	Science and Technology
Primakov, Evgeniy M.	Academy of Sciences; former Chairman of the Council of the Union	Foreign Policy
Rasputin, Valentin G.	Writer	Ecology, Culture
Revenko, Grigoriy I.	First Secretary, Kiev Regional CP Committee of the Ukrainian CP	Nationality Questions
Shatalin, Stanislav S.	Academician, Academy of Sciences	Socioeconomic Policy
Shevardnadze, Eduard A.	USSR Minister of Foreign Affairs	Foreign Policy
Yakovlev, Aleksandr N.	Member of the Politburo	Law-enforcement bodies, ideology
Yarin, Veniamin A.	Worker from Nizhni Taghil, Urals; head of the United Front of the Working People of Russia	The Workers' Movement
Yazov, Dmitriy T.	USSR Minister of Defense	Military Affairs
Ryzhkov, Nikolai I. (*ex officio*)	Prime Minister	Overall economy
Lukyanov, Anatoli	Chairman, Supreme Soviet	(may participate

USSR COUNCIL OF THE FEDERATION
June 1990

Dementai, Nikolai Ivanovich
Yeltsin Boris Nikolaevich
Gorbunov, Anatolii
Gumbaridze, Givi Grigor'evich
Ivashko, Vladimir Antonovich
Karimov, Islam Abduganievich
Landsbergis, Vytautas
Makhkamov, Kakhar Makhkamovich
Masaliev, Absamat
Mutalibov, Ayaz Niyazi ogly
Nazarbaev, Nursultan Abishevich
Niyazov, Saparmurad Ataevich
Snegur, Arnold
Snegur, Mircea Ion
Voskanyan, Grant Mushegovich

FREEDOM & HUMAN RIGHTS

Human rights represent historically the area where the most abuses have taken place in modern Soviet history. This is because Communist political ideology is structurally incompatible with the full exercise of human rights. The monopoly of political and economic power in one party; the existence of a powerful and unchecked secret police; intolerance of dissent, which is equated with disloyalty and treason; the fear of reform; doctrinaire hostility to religion and other philosophical systems all were conducive to an authoritarian state in which human rights could not flourish. The history of Russia from the time of Rurik has been one characterized by the absence of freedom. Russia is perhaps the only nation in Europe to suffer from such unmitigated and continuous tyranny.

However, since 1985, from the assumption of Mikhail Gorbachev to power, first as general secretary and later also as president, there has been a cautious opening up (*glasnost* in Russian) of many areas of public life whose actual scope and extent can be assessed only several decades hence. Such a *glasnost* is accompanied by a restructuring (*perestroika* in Russian) of institutions and administrative structures that also has progressed with typically Russian slowness. Both processes are characterized by a slow relaxation of restrictions and regulations so built into the fabric of government that their very removal is threatening to cause a whole new range of problems. Historic traditions of authoritarianism, sustained and reinforced by the requirements of Communist orthodoxy, have made *glasnost* and *perestroika* difficult goals to achieve without a radical break with the past.

The major reforms that have been proposed are more far-reaching than the changes that have been implemented by 1990. These have included abolition of the CP's monopoly of power, extension of the limits of dissent, reduction in the punishment meted out to dissenters, and an acknowledgment of the right of limited private enterprise. Even these changes have come mainly as a result of political decisions at the top rather than from the bottom. They have yet to be reinforced by the adoption of laws, administrative regulations and bureaucratic procedures. Moreover, the citizenry itself is unused to defending its rights against encrusted traditions of state repression.

Since the death of Stalin, the more brutal aspects of political repression have become uncommon. Political killings and disappearances have not been reported for a number of years and probably are no longer actively employed. In May 1987 the Soviet Union made a historic commitment to the International Convention Against Torture. Accordingly, the Presidium of the Supreme Soviet has rescinded a paragraph of the Penal Code stipulating reduced rations for labor camp inmates who undergo punishment in solitary confinement. However, most Soviet prisoners suffer mental and physical abuse and mistreatment during interrogation, trial and confinement. Prison and labor camp conditions have not improved and continue to be marked by compulsory hard labor, beatings, and poor diet and nutrition. Many political prisoners are confined to psychiatric hospitals, a practice that has led to the expulsion of Soviet psychiatrists from international bodies of psychiatrists. Political prisoners in psychiatric hospitals are given sedatives, antipsychotics and other unnecessary drugs, although they do not suffer beatings as often as before. Even when released from mental hospitals, these persons are prohibited from certain activities, such as driving. Official attention to the problem of psychiatric

abuse has led to considerable reduction in its incidence. In 1988 a new decree banned forced commitment to mental hospitals and made psychiatrists personally and financially liable for any malpractice. A commission was appointed to review the cases of many patients who were thereupon removed from the register of the mentally ill. According to independent observers more than 50 political and religious dissidents were released from psychiatric hospitals in 1988 as a result of the new policy. Routine beatings of demonstrators, common in the past, have decreased. Militia units in charge of controlling demonstrations appear to operate on the principle of minimum rather than maximum force.

Soviet criminal laws mostly drafted under Stalin, violate internationally accepted human rights. Among them are:

• Article 70: Seven years of imprisonment and five years of internal exile for "anti-Soviet propaganda and agitation."
• Article 142: Three years of imprisonment for violation of laws on the separation of church and state and church and school.
• Article 190-1: Three years of imprisonment for "dissemination of deliberately hostile fabrications defaming the Soviet state and social system."
• Article 190-3: Three years of imprisonment for the "organization of, or active participation in, a group actively violating public order."
• Article 227: Five years of imprisonment for "performing religious ceremonies."

A draft of a new criminal code calls for the elimination of internal exile, reduction of the number of crimes punishable by death to six, abrogation of Articles 190-1 and 227 and modification of Articles 70 and 142. Article 70 was invoked against a number of political dissidents in 1988. Political activists without full-time employment are generally charged with parasitism and, sometimes, hooliganism, although both charges are used less frequently.

Under the Criminal Code authorities may detain citizens for three or four hours for questioning; after this period, detainees must either be charged or released. Pretrial detention may last as long as nine months, and such detainees may not consult a lawyer until shortly before trial. An addition to the Criminal Code empowers authorities to sentence to an additional three years those guilty of "malicious disobedience" in a labor camp. Internal exile is a form of punishment the Communists inherited from the czarist regime and that they have used unsparingly. Exile often is in addition to and following the prison term, and the places of exile generally are those with the harshest climate, where food is scarce and accommodations primitive. Such exilees are expected to find work (usually menial) to support themselves, although they may receive food packages from family members. In 1987 the government announced that it was planning to end the use of internal exile as a form of punishment. Released exilees, however, are not allowed to return to their former place of residence or to visit Moscow or its environs.

Soviet courts were notoriously subservient to the state, and judges were expected to pass sentences according to political directives. The deficiencies of the system received much attention in the Soviet press, and a draft new law on the courts was published in 1989. Worse than judges, lawyers acted as minions of the party and refused to take on politically sensitive cases. About 60% of attorneys were party members. Moreover, attorneys had to have special clearance to act as defense counsel in political cases. Since the beginning of *perestroika* there have been a few cases where judges have been bold enough to acquit political activists.

Government interference in private life, pervasive under Stalin and his successors, is diminishing, but, nonetheless, quite prevalent. Internal security troops may enter private homes and conduct searches without warrants. Electronic monitoring of residences and telephones of certain types of citizens and foreigners is done routinely. Through the control of mail and electronic circuits, the authorities selectively restrict contacts between citizens and foreigners. This practice has become less frequent than in the past, and a resolution of the 19th Communist Party Conference called for guaranteeing the privacy of private communications. Contacts with foreigners continue to be discouraged, although less actively than in the past.

During 1988 jamming of Western broadcasts, including that of Radio Liberty, ended. The jamming of Voice of America broadcasts ended in 1987.

One freedom that has significantly gained under glasnost is freedom of the press and speech, although this freedom falls far short of what avails in the West. Television coverage of party debates is extensive, and more importantly, balanced. Most observers found rudimentary signs of "adversary politics" at the 19th Communist Party Conference, where unorthodox opinions were freely expressed and publicized. Concomitantly, the media have grown livelier. No longer are publications, films and television and radio scripts submitted in advance to the dreaded Main Administration for Safeguarding State Secrets in the Media. A new breed of investigative reporters has appeared, such as those of the illustrated weekly *Ogonek*. Signed articles on formerly taboo subjects, such as strikes and demonstrations, have delighted readers and discomfited officials.

The *samizdat* press (one of the Soviet Union's enduring contributions to the media lexicon) has grown in number and sophistication. To mark its coming of age, 50 editors of *samizdats* assembled in Moscow in 1988 to discuss common problems. Currently *samizdats* are published not only in Moscow and Leningrad but also in smaller provincial cities such as Lvov, Pskov, Sverdlovsk and Kuybyshev. One of the best known of these *samizdats*, *The Express Chronicle*, also is the most reliable source on human rights in the Soviet Union.

The government has relaxed somewhat the obstacles to foreign journalists. Official press conferences have become regular features, and Western journalists' access to Soviet officials has considerably improved in recent years. Overt censorship of wire and satellite transmissions of news stories out of the country has become very rare.

Restrictions on researchers similarly have been relaxed. Access is being granted to many previously closed archives, and many books formerly banished to closed stacks have been moved back into open library shelves. A significant number of previously banned books and plays have been published or staged, including *Doctor Zhivago* and *Life and Fate*. Political satire has become sharper, although generally within officially approved limits.

Until 1985 demonstrations and unauthorized meetings were crimes and were never reported in the press, if they did take place. Since then reports on demonstrations and rallies have become staples of the Soviet media. In 1988 the Ministry of Justice counted 250 unauthorized rallies and the Ministry of Internal Affairs 600 rallies, including authorized ones. Some of them were very large—that at Yerevan on March 8, 1988, was over 700,000 strong, and one in Estonia in October 1988 was over 300,000 strong. In 1988 the Presidium of the Supreme Soviet issued a decree, "Procedures for the Organization and Conduct of Meetings, Rallies, Street Marches and Demonstrations in the USSR." According to its provisions, organizers must apply to the local soviet 10 days before the scheduled meeting, and the officials must notify them of their decision at least five days before the meeting. Stiff penalties are provided for violations, ranging from a fine of about $500 and/or administrative jail for up to 15 days up to a fine of $3,300 and deprivation of freedom for up to six months and corrective labor for up to one year. Generally the sentences have been closer to the lower range. There has been no consistency in the administration of this law. The same type of demonstration may be permitted at one time and denied at other times.

The Constitution grants citizens the right to associate in public organizations "in accordance with the aim of building communism." This right, long a dead letter, came to life in the late 1980s as a large number (reportedly over 30,000) of informal and unofficial organizations came into being, mostly related to uncontroversial issues. Many of these clubs produce journals or bulletins and organize networks providing an alternative to party networks. In 1988 the movement took a major step forward when large organizations for political action were formed in Estonia, Latvia, Lithuania, the Ukraine, Moldavia, Georgia and Byelorussia as well as Moscow, Leningrad and Yaroslav. Most of them have a nationalist orientation. The Estonian People's Front for the Support of *Perestroika* claims over 100,000 members. A self-avowed opposition political party, the Democratic Union, founded in Moscow in 1988 found less favor in the Kremlin, but the group itself has not been suppressed.

Religious freedom was one of the earliest casualties of Leninism. However, significant changes have taken place in regard to this freedom, and they were legalized in 1989. Gorbachev has taken a more sympathetic view of the Orthodox Church than his predecessors. The state was a full participant in the celebration of the Millennium of the Baptism of Kievan Rus in June 1988. On this occasion Gorbachev remarked that believers are patriots and not second-class citizens. The media gave favorable coverage to the Millennial celebrations, and a portion of the Easter service was broadcast over state television! Overall, articles on religious themes have become commonplace. Worshipers at Easter services are not harassed, as they were in past years. Gorbachev also has opened the door for improved relations with the Vatican with a visit to the pope. Pressure on the Roman Catholic Church in Lithuania also eased somewhat in 1988. The cathedral at Vilnius, which had been converted into an art gallery in 1950, was returned to religious use, and several Catholic bishops were allowed to visit the Vatican.

In 1990 the lessening of restrictions manifested itself in various ways, culminating in the historic passage October 1 of Supreme Soviet legislation on freedom of religion. By the overwhelming vote of 341 to 1 the law forbids government interference in religious activities, grants legal status to religious organizations and grants to citizens the right to study religion in homes and private schools. The government is prevented from financing atheist propaganda as well as religious activities, although atheism continues to be the party's doctrine. While this development was welcomed inside the country and abroad, many recalled past violations of constitutional provisions but now were more optimistic about official compliance with the new law.

ORGANIZATION OF SOVIET GOVERNMENT
GENERAL ORGANIZATION

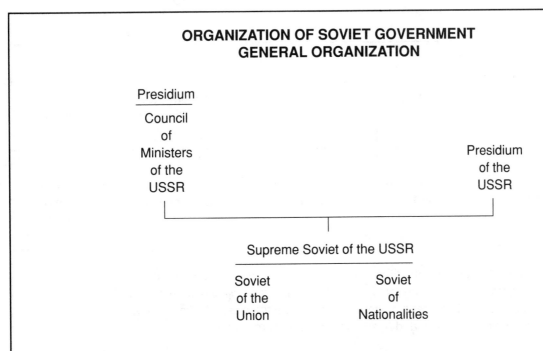

Presidium

Council of Ministers of the USSR

Presidium of the USSR

Supreme Soviet of the USSR

Soviet of the Union

Soviet of Nationalities

Note: Presidium includes chairman and deputy chairmen of the Council of Ministers.

LEGAL SYSTEM

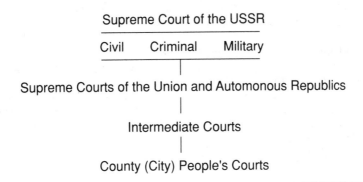

Supreme Court of the USSR

Civil   Criminal   Military

Supreme Courts of the Union and Automonous Republics

Intermediate Courts

County (City) People's Courts

ADMINISTRATIVE AND NATIONAL STRUCTURE

USSR				
Republics	Union Republics			
		Autonomous Republics		
Regions and Regional Equivalents	*Kraya*	*Oblasti*	Autonomous *Oblasti*	The Largest Cities
Districts	National *Okruga*	Rural *Rayony*	Medium-Size Cities	City *Rayony*
Lowest Governmental Level	Small Cities and Towns	Groups of Villages	Workers' Settlements	Agricultural Settlements

Note: Vertical differentiation of the blocks indicates the relative importance of a unit within its administrative category. For example, the *kray, oblast* and autonomous *oblast* regions are of descending importance. Since the sizes of cities vary widely, their governments are included at all levels of local administration.

The growth of Muslim fundamentalism elsewhere in the world is a matter of official concern, and the government is accordingly cautious in allowing more religious freedom in Muslim areas. Islamic radio broadcasts, especially from Iran, are jammed. In an effort to bolster atheism, the government has encouraged the adoption of secular life cycle ceremonies for religious ones.

Books in Hebrew may not be printed in the Soviet Union, but the ban on teaching Hebrew was relaxed in 1988. There is a severe shortage of synagogues and Jewish cemeteries. Ritual articles such as phylacteries may not be imported, and no training facilities exist to teach the scribal arts needed for their domestic manufacture. The two-million-strong Jewish community is served by one yeshiva with 10 students. There is no rabbinical seminary.

Only a few religious publications of controlled content, such as *Vestnik* of the Russian Orthodox Patriarchate, are officially allowed to appear. Two unofficial Orthodox publications appeared in 1987: *The Bulletin of the Christian Community* and *Choice*. The printing and importation of Bibles and other scriptures are limited by various laws.

Freedom of movement is not guaranteed under Soviet law. All adults are issued identity documents or internal passports, which must be carried on their persons during travel and used to register with the local authorities visits of more than three days. Citizens generally are free to move about within the country, but travel in certain areas, such as frontier regions, requires special permission. About 20% of the national territory is officially closed to travel by foreigners, but outside urban areas the rest of the country is de facto off-limits to foreigners.

Every Soviet citizen is required to register his or her

CABINET LIST
(July 1990)

Chairman, USSR Council of Ministers: Nikolay Ivanovich Ryzhkov

First Deputy Chairman, USSR Supreme Soviet: Anatoliy Ivanovich Luk'yanov

Deputy Chairman, USSR Supreme Soviet: Tashtanbek Akmatovich Akmatov

Deputy Chairman, USSR Supreme Soviet: Vitautas Stasevich Astrauskas

Deputy Chairman, USSR Supreme Soviet: Roza Atamuradovna Bazarova

Deputy Chairman, USSR Supreme Soviet: Otar Yevtikhiyevich Cherkeziya

Deputy Chairman, USSR Supreme Soviet: Anatoliy Valer'yanovich Gorbunov

Deputy Chairman, USSR Supreme Soviet: Mirzaolim Ibragimovich Ibragimov

Deputy Chairman, USSR Supreme Soviet: Mircha Ivanovich Snegur

Deputy Chairman, USSR Supreme Soviet: Gaibnazar Pallayevich Pallayev

Deputy Chairman, USSR Supreme Soviet: Arnol'd Fedorovich Ryuutel'

Deputy Chairman, USSR Supreme Soviet: Makhtay Ramazanovich Sagdiyev

Deputy Chairman, USSR Supreme Soviet: Valentina Semenovna Shevchenko

Deputy Chairman, USSR Supreme Soviet: Nikolay Ivanovich Dementey

Deputy Chairman, USSR Supreme Soviet: El'mira Mikhaylovna Kafarova

Deputy Chairman, USSR Supreme Soviet: Vitaliy Ivanovich Vorotnikov

Deputy Chairman, USSR Supreme Soviet: Grant Mushegovich Voskanyan

First Deputy Chairman, USSR Council of Ministers Presidium: Yuriy Dmitriyevich Maslyukov

First Deputy Chairman, USSR Council of Ministers Presidium: Vladilen Valentinovich Nikitin

First Deputy Chairman, USSR Council of Ministers Presidium: Lev Alekseyevich Voronin

Deputy Chairman, USSR Council of Ministers Presidium: Leonid Ivanovich Abalkin

Deputy Chairman, USSR Council of Ministers Presidium: Igor' Sergeyevich Belousov

Deputy Chairwoman, USSR Council of Ministers Presidium: Aleksandra Pavlovna Biryukova

Deputy Chairman, USSR Council of Ministers Presidium: Vitaliy Khusseynovich Doguzhiyev

Deputy Chairman, USSR Council of Ministers Presidium: Vladimir Kuz'mich Gusev

Deputy Chairman, USSR Council of Ministers Presidium: Nikolay Pavlovich Laverov

Deputy Chairman, USSR Council of Ministers Presidium: Pavel Ivanovich Mostovoy

Deputy Chairman, USSR Council of Ministers Presidium: Lev Dmitriyevich Ryabev

Deputy Chairman, USSR Council of Ministers Presidium: Stepan Aramaysovich Sitaryan

Other Member, USSR Council of Ministers Presidium: Valentin Sergeyevich Pavlov

Other Member, USSR Council of Ministers Presidium: Mikhail Sergeyevich Shkabardnya

Chairman, Bureau for Chemical and Timber Complex: Vladimir Kuz'mich Gusev

Chairman, Bureau for Fuel and Energy Complex: Lev Dmitriyevich Ryabev

Chairman, Bureau for Machine Building: Ivan Stepanovich Silayev

Chairwoman, Bureau for Social Development: Aleksandra Pavlovna Biryukova

Chairman, Commission for Arctic Affairs: Yuriy Dmitriyevich Maslyukov

CABINET LIST (continued)

Chairman, Military Industrial Commission: Igor' Sergeyevich Belousov

Chairman, State Commission for Extraordinary Situations: Vitaliy Khusseynovich Doguzhiyev

Chairman, State Commission on Food and Procurements: Vladilen Valentinovich Nikitin

Chairman, State Foreign Economic Commission (GVK): Stepan Avramysovich Sitaryan

Chairman, State Commission on Economic Reform: Leonid Ivanovich Abalkin

Minister of Automotive and Agricultural Machine Building: Nikolay Andreyevich Pugin

Minister of Aviation Industry: Apollon Sergeyevich Systsov

Minister of Chemical and Petroleum Refining Industry: Nikolay Vasil'yevich Lemayev

Minister of Civil Aviation: Boris Egorovich Panyukov

Minister of Coal Industry: Mikhail Ivanovich Shchadov

Minister of Communications: Erlen Kirikovich Pervyshin

Minister of Construction of Petroleum and Gas Industry Enterprises: Vladimir Grigor'yevich Chirskov

Minister of Culture: Nikolai Gubenko

Minister of Defense: Dmitriy Timofeyevich Yazov

Minister of Defense Industry: Boris Mikhaylovich Belousov

Minister of Electrical Equipment Industry and Instrument Making: Oleg Georgiyevich Anfimov

Minister of Electronics Industry: Vladislav Grigor'yevich Kolesnikov

Minister of Finance: Valentin Sergeyevich Pavlov

Minister of Fish Industry: Nikolay Isaakovich Kotlyar

Minister of Foreign Affairs: Eduard Amvrosiyevich Shevardnadze

Minister of Foreign Economic Relations: Konstantin Fedorovich Katushev

Minister of General Machine Building: Oleg Nikolayevich Shishkin

Minister of Geology: Grigoriy Arkad'yevich Gabrielyants

Minister of Health: Igor Nikobevich Denisov

Minister of Heavy Machine Building: Vladimir Makarovich Velichko

Minister of Installation and Special Construction Work: Aleksandr Ivanovich Mikhal'chenko

Minister of Internal Affairs: Vadim Viktorovich Bakatin

Minister of Justice: Veniamin Fedorovich Yakovlev

Minister of Machine Tool and Tool Building Industry: Nikolay Aleksandrovich Panichev

Minister of Maritime Fleet: Yuriy Mikhaylovich Vol'mer

Minister of Medical Industry: Valeriy Alekseyevich Bykov

Minister of Metallurgy: Serafim Vasil'yevich Kolpakov

Minister of Nuclear Power Generation and the Nuclear Industry: Vitalii Fedorovich Konovalov

Minister of Petroleum and Gas Industry: Leonid Ivanovich Filimanov

Minister of Power and Electrification: Yuriy Kuz'mich Semenov

Minister of Radio Industry: Vladimir Ivanovich Shimko

Minister of Railways: Nikolay Semenovich Konarev

Minister of Shipbuilding Industry: Igor' Vladimirovich Koksanov

Minister of the Timber Industry: Vladimir Ivanovich Melnikov

Minister of Trade: Kondrat Zigmundovich Terekh

Minister of Transport Construction: Vladimir Arkad'yevich Brezhnev

Minister of Water Resources Construction: Vacant

Chairman, State Committee for Administration of Quality Output Control Standards: Valerii Vasil'evich Sychev

Chairman, State Commission for Cinematography (Goskino): Aleksandr Ivanovich Kamshalov

Chairman, State Commission for Computer Technology and Information Science: Boris Leont'yevich Tolstykh

Chairman, State for Construction Committee (Gosstroy): Valeriy Mikhaylovich Serov

Chairman, State Commission for Forestry: Aleksandr Sergeyevich Isayev

CABINET LIST *(continued)*

Chairman, State Commission for Hydrometeorology: Yuriy Antoniyevich Izrael'

Chairman, State Commission for Labor and Social Problems: Vladimir Ivanovich Shcherbakov

Chairwoman, State Commission for Light Industry: Lyudmila Yel'matovna Davletova

Chairman, State Commission for Material and Technical Supply (Gossnab): Pavel Ivanovich Mostovoy

Chairman, State Commission for Output Quality Control and Standards: Valeriy Vasil'yevich Sychev

Chairman, State Commission for Physical Culture and Sports (Goskomsport): Nikolay Ivanovich Rusak

Chairman, State Planning Commission (Gosplan): Yuriy Dmitriyevich Maslyukov

Chairwoman, State Committee for Light Industry, attached to State Planning Commission (Gosplan): Lyudmila Yel'matovna Davletova

First Deputy Chairman, State Planning Commission (Gosplan): Vladimir Aleksandrovich Durasov

Chairman, State Commission for Press (Goskompechat): Nikolay Ivanovich Yefimov

Chairman, State Commission for Prices: Vyacheslav Konstantinovich Senchagov

Chairman, State Commission for Protection of the Environment: Nikolay Nikolayevich Vorontsov

Chairman, State Commission for Public Education: Gennadiy Alekseyevich Yagodin

Chairman, State Commission for Science and Technology (GKNT): Nikolay Pavlovich Laverov

Chairman, (State) Commission for State Security (KGB): Vladimir Aleksandrovich Kryuchkov

Chairman, State Commission for Statistics: Vadim Nikitovich Kirichenko

Chairman, State Commission for Safety in Industry and Atomic Power Industry: Vadim Mikhaylovich Malyshev

Chairman, State Commission for Television and Radio Broadcasting: Mikhail Fedorovich Nenashev

Chairman, Commission of People's Control: Gennadiy Vasil'yevich Kolbin

Administrator of Affairs for the Council of Ministers: Mikhail Sergeyevich Shkabardnya

Chief Arbitrator, State Board of Arbitration: Yuriy Gennad'yevich Matveyev

Chairman, Board, State Bank (Gosbank): Viktor Vladimirovich Gerashchenko

Chairman, Armenian SSR Council of Ministers: Vladimir Sureni Markaryants

Chairman, Azerbaijan SSR Council of Ministers: Fadei Tachatovich Sarkisyan Gasan Neimat ogly Seidov

Chairman, Belorussian SSR Council of Ministers: Mikhail Vasil'yevich Kovalev

Chairman, Estonian SSR Council of Ministers: Bruno Eduardovich Saul

Chairman, Georgian SSR Council of Ministers: Nodar Amrosiyevich Chitanava

Chairman, Kazakh SSR Council of Ministers: Uzakbay Karamanov

Chairman, Kirghiz SSR Council of Ministers: Apas Dzhumagulovich Dzhumagulov

Chairman, Latvian SSR Council of Ministers: Vilnis-Edvins Gedertovich Bresis

Chairman, Lithuanian SSR Council of Ministers: Vitautas Vladovich Sakalauskas

Chairman, Moldavian SSR Council of Ministers: Ivan Petrovich Kalin

Chairman, RSFSR Council of Ministers: Aleksandr Vladimirovich Vlasov

Chairman, Tajik SSR Council of Ministers: Izatullo Kh. Khayeyev

Chairman, Turkmen SSR Council of Ministers: Annamurad Kh. Khodzhamuradov

Chairman, Ukrainian SSR Council of Ministers: Vitaliy Andreyevich Masol

Chairman, Uzbek SSR Council of Ministers: Gairat Khamidullaevich Kadyrov

COUNCIL OF MINISTERS

Chairman
First Deputy Chairmen 3
Deputy Chairmen 10
All-Union Ministers 40
Union-Republican Ministers 15
Chairmen of USSR State Committees 25
Ex officio 10
Chairmen of the Union Republic Council of Ministers 15

place of residence. In large cities, in an effort to prevent overcrowding, the authorities limit the number of residence permits. Intending emigres lose their residence permits, thus adding to their problems. Citizens convicted of certain political offenses are excluded from the city of Moscow.

Travel abroad became easier for Soviet citizens in the late 1980s, but routine issuance of passports is far from commonplace. Lengthy formalities and bureaucratic delays discourage all but the most persistent. In additon to a passport, Soviet citizens need an exit visa, which, since 1988, does not specify the duration of the trip. For private visits, Soviet tourists need a friend or relative in the West who undertakes all financial responsibility for the trip. Currency regulations and the requirement to purchase tickets in rubles also prove cumbersome.

The right to emigrate is restricted, as Soviet law does not recognize such a right. Although the Soviet Union has signed the Helsinki Final Act in which this right is recognized, it continues to put official roadblocks in the path of those who apply for emigration. In 1987 these restrictions were codified, although substantial numbers of Jews, Germans, Pentecostals and Armenians emigrated in 1988 without regard to this requirement. A number of former political prisoners also were permitted to emigrate in 1988 without any claim to family reunification. The most frequently used barrier to emigration is the requirement that the prospective emigrant should have had no access to official secrets. Application of this restriction often is quite arbitrary. Another barrier is the requirement that family members sign release forms for their children. In 1988 the major groups of emigrants were 19,292 Jews, 10,000 Armenians and 45,000 Germans. In 1990, over 100,000 Jews were permitted to leave for Israel.

Although political power is no longer a monopoly constitutionally vested in the Communist Party, it is concentrated in a small, elite group. Trotsky's prophesy in the early 1920s that the Leninist system of government would be disguised dictatorship was borne out by later events. The Soviet parliament has not functioned well even as a rubber stamp. Some electoral reforms, such as secret balloting and multiple-candidate elections in some constituencies introduced in 1989, appear to harbinger further enhancement of parliamentary activity and control of government.

Gorbachev has adopted a more forthcoming approach to foreign criticism of the Soviet human rights record, acknowledging the problem and stating his desire to make Soviet society more humane. He has permitted some foreign groups, such as Christian Solidarity International and the International Society

RULERS OF RUSSIA AND THE SOVIET UNION
Grand Dukes

1328–March 1341: Ivan I
March 1341–1353: Simeon
1353–9: Ivan II
1359–May 1389: Dmitri I
May 1389–February 1425: Vasily I
February 1425–1434: Vasily II
1434: Yuri
1434–46: Vasily II
1446–7: Dmitri II
1447–March 1462: Vasily II
March 1462–October 1505: Ivan III
October 1505–December 1533: Vasily III
December 1533–January 1547: Ivan IV (Regent: 1533–38, Yelena)

Czars/Czarinas

Jan 1547–March 1584: Ivan IV
March 1584–January 1598: Fyodor I (Regent: 1584–98, Boris Gudunov)
Jan 1598: Irina
February 1598–April 1605: Boris (B. Gudunov)
April–June 1605: Fyodor II
June 1605–May 1606: Dmitri III
June 1606–July 1610: Vasily IV
July 1610–February 1613: Interregnum
February 1613–July 1645: Mikhail
July 1645–February 1676: Aleksei
February 1676–April 1682: Fyodor III
April 1682–January 1696: Peter I/Ivan V (Regents: 1682–89, Sophia Aleksevna: 1689–96, Natalia Naryshkin)
January 1696–November 1721: Peter I

Emperors/Empresses

November 1721–February 1725: Peter I
February 1725–May 1727: Ekaterina I
May 1727–June 1730: Peter II
June 1730–October 1740: Anna
October 1740–December 1741: Ivan VI (Regents: October–November 1740, Ernst Biron; November 1740–December 1741, Anna Leopoldovna)
December 1741–January 1762: Elisaveta
January–July 1762: Peter III
July 1762–November 1796: Ekaterina II
November 1796–March 1801: Pavel
March 1801–November 1825: Alexander I
December 1825–March 1855: Nicholas I
March 1855–March 1881: Alexander II
March 1881–November 1894: Alexander III
November 1894–March 1917: Nicholas II
March–November 1917: Provisional Government.

Presidents

Chairman of the Central Executive Committee, 1917–37; Chairman (President) of the Presidium of the Supreme Soviet since 1937

November 1917–March 1919: Yakov Sverdlov
March 1919–March 1946: Mikhail Kalinin
March 1946–March 1953: Nikolai Shvernik
March 1953–May 1960: Kliment Voroshilov
May 1960–July 1964: Leonid Brezhnev
July 1964–December 1965: Anastas Mikoyan
December 1965–June 1977: Nikolai Podgorny
June 1977–November 1982: Leonid Brezhnev
November 1982–June 1983: Vasily Kuznetsov (acting)
June 1983–February 1984: Yuri Andropov
February–April 1984: Vasily Kuznetsov (acting)
April 1984–March 1985: Konstantin Chernenko
March–July 1985: Vasily Kuznetsov (acting)
July 1985–October 1988: Andrei Gromyko
October 1988–   : Mikhail Gorbachev

RULERS OF RUSSIA AND THE SOVIET UNION
(continued)
Chief Ministers

1812–16: Nikolai Saltykov
1816–27: Pyotr Lopukhin
1827–32: Viktor Kochubei
1832–38: Nikolai Novosiltsev
1838–47: Ilarion Vasilchikov
1847–48: Vasily Levashov
October 1848–1856: Aleksandr Chernyshev
1856–January 1861: Aleksei Orlov
January 1861–March 1864: Dmitri Bludov
March 1864–January 1865: Pavel Gagarin
January 1865–1872: Post abolished
1872–77: Pavel Ignatyev
1877–October 1881: Pyotr Valuyev
October 1881–January 1887: Mikhail Reutern
January 1887–June 1895: Nikolai Bunge
June 1895–June 1903: Ivan Durnovo
June 1903–October 1905: Sergei Witte

Prime Ministers

Chairman of the Council of People's Commissars, 1917–46; Chairman of the Council of Ministers since 1946

October 1905–May 1906: Sergei Witte
May–July 1906: Ivan Goremykin
July 1906–September 1911: Pyotr Stolypin
September 1911–February 1914: Vladimir Kokovtsev
February 1914–February 1916: Ivan Goremykin
February–November 1916: Boris Sturmer
November 1916–January 1917: Fyodor Trepov
January–March 1917: Nikolai Golitsyn
March–July 1917: Georgi Lvov
July–November 1917: Aleksandr Kerensky
November 1917–January 1924: Vladimir Lenin
February 1924–December 1930: Aleksei Rykov
December 1930–May 1941: Vyacheslav Molotov
May 1941–March 1953: Joseph Stalin
March 1953–February 1955: Georgi Malenkov
February 1955–March 1958: Nikolai Bulganin
March 1958–October 1964: Nikita Khrushchev
October 1964–October 1980: Alexei Kosygin
October 1980–September 1985: Nikolai Tikhonov
September 1985–   : Nikolai Ryzhkov

Communist Party Leaders

General Secretary, 1922–53 and since 1966; First Secretary, 1953–66

March 1922–March 1953: Joseph Stalin
March 1953: Georgi Malenkov
March 1953–October 1964: Nikita Khrushchev
October 1964–November 1982: Leonid Brezhnev
November 1982–February 1984: Yuri Andropov
February 1984–March 1985: Konstantin Chernenko
March 1985–   : Mikhail Gorbachev

willing to communicate officially with Amnesty International and has suppressed its Moscow chapter as an agency of the CIA.

At the 19th Communisty Party Conference Gorbachev admitted that earlier Soviet claims that there were no minority or nationality problems in the Soviet Union were false. The Soviets recognize more than 100 nationalities, and although the Soviet federal system is based on nationalities, some 55 million Soviet citizens live outside their nationality's administrative region or belong to a nationality that has none. Russification is a major plank in national policy, and the Russian language and culture have tended to displace those of the minorities. Russification has strangled the cultures of not only smaller minorities but also larger ones, such as the

for Human Rights, to meet freely with dissidents, *refuseniks* and others. However, the Soviet Union is not yet

Ukrainians. The increase in ethnic German emigration also is related to the fact that ethnic antagonisms are stronger than official assertions of the equality of all ethnic groups.

During the Brezhnev period, a quota system was used extensively as part of a broader nationality policy. This system benefited central Asian Muslims. Gorbachev has abolished the system in a move that has benefited the Jews. In other areas, too, there has been an easing of the restrictions against Jews and a greater official tolerance of expressions of Jewish culture, such as a Jewish library and a Jewish museum, both in Moscow. The nationalist and virulently anti-Semitic Pamyat Society has been officially disbanded.

The three nationalities most vocal in their efforts to set aright historic injustices are the Crimean Tatars, Armenians and Estonians. The Armenian demand was for the incorporation of Nagorno-Karabakh in Azerbaijan in the Armenian SSR. The nationalities in the Baltic republics have gone so far as to call for secession. The Crimean Tatars, a Muslim minority, forcibly deported from their Crimean homeland to central Asia in 1944, continue to seek repatriation and establishment of a Crimean autonomous region.

Constitutionally women enjoy equal rights with men. An extensive system of day-care service and maternity-leave benefits enhance their rights in the workplace. However, women bear the main brunt of the hardships of Soviet daily life, such as waiting in the long lines in supermarkets. Women hold a disproportionate percentage of low-level jobs, such as street-sweeping. Men occupy the great majority of the leading positions in most professions, above all in politics. There are no women serving as full Politburo members or as secretaries of the Central Committee. Only 12 of the 305 full members of the Central Committee are women, and only one of the hundreds of ambassadors is a woman.

Although described as an egalitarian society, the party, the military, the diplomatic service, the scientific-technical intelligentsia and the cultural and sports establishments have formed a privileged elite with perquisites rivaling those of the nobility before the Revolution. Not only are they shielded from the hardships to which the ordinary citizen is exposed, but also they have greater access to quality food and consumer goods, special medical facilities, the best schools, foreign travel benefits, automobiles, *dachas* (country houses), and paid vacations at choice resorts. However, these bastions of privileges are being phased out gradually. Many clinics and stores that formerly served only the party elite are being opened to the general public in a move that further demonstrates the winds of change blowing through the Soviet Union.

CIVIL SERVICE

The Soviet civil service is an enormous bureaucracy when government employment is considered, for most—perhaps two-thirds—of the total number of Soviet employees are on the government payroll; this includes the state-owned economic sector but excludes collective farmers. Of these, employees in state admin-

istration are comparable to a degree to civil servants in the United States and other Western countries. However, the Soviet Union, as in the East European bureaucracies, has no Office of Personnel Management, as in the United States, with recruitment standards, rules, regulations, rights and promotion procedures.

Placement of incoming state administration employees, especially at the higher levels, was radically different from Western procedures. As indicated earlier, the Constitution, in Article 6, designated the Communist Party as the "leading and guiding force of Soviet society and the nucleus of its political system, of all state organizations and public organizations." Accordingly, the CP, which assigned that primacy to itself, was deeply involved in all phases of personnel matters, not only with its own party apparatus, but also in all state organs and at all levels, from the all-Union to the lowest. Article 6 had come under criticism recently by people, including reformist party members, who demanded that the CP's leading role be removed. Article 6 was removed from the Constitution in March 1990 by the Congress of People's Deputies.

For appointment of officials especially at the higher organs of government, the party relied on lists of positions and names, known as *nomenklatura*. Every echelon of the party had such a listing, which controlled its appointments. Another list consisted of party-designated individuals to fill designated positions. At the highest level, of course, appointments were made by the general secretary, Politburo members, the secretaries and the Secretariat. In the Council of Ministers, individual ministers and chairmen of committees propose appointments subject to confirmation of the officials just stated. The Council of Ministers has a coordinating responsibility for employment, including the salary and wage structure. It should be remembered that the Soviet method has been a parallel system of party and government bodies and that all the government officials had been simultaneously in influential party positions.

The ministries and committees have their individual personnel offices (*otdel kadrov*), which handle various personnel matters. Collegiums, consisting of the minister, deputy ministers and heads of departments, are responsible for planning and policy. Legislation, decrees and directives guide recruitment by employing agencies, which are formally obliged to comply with certain standards, such as prohibition of discrimination, and to consider professional qualifications. In reality, however, the most important principle before 1990 had been the provision on political qualifications—i.e., the candidate's party orientation. As noted, the final decision for hiring had been made by the CP committees.

Although there is no central institution specifically designated to prepare students for government employment, the Soviet Union has numerous sources for a steady supply of recruits. The country has over 900 institutions of higher education. The system is under ministerial as well as the party's control. The most productive are the universities, institutes and technical institutes for professional ranks, and high schools for lower-level positions. The state universities are in the major cities throughout the country. Moscow State University, founded in 1755, is the largest and best-known, with many faculties and departments. Some of the other prominent universities are in Leningrad, Kiev, Tbilisi, Odessa, Alma-Ata, Tashkent, Kazan, Kharkov, Gorky and Vladivostok.

The Cirminal Code for government employees is strict and harsh, exacting severe penalities for malfeasance and dereliction. On the other hand, loyalty and good performance are rewarded. Salaries and pensions are above average, and perks, especially at the higher levels, are beyond the reach of ordinary people.

The many institutes provide graduates for specialized branches of industry and agriculture, while some are for a particular central government activity. For example, graduates from the Institute for Foreign Relations are well suited for the Foreign Ministry and other foreign-oriented agencies. To improve qualifications of management, Moscow established the Academy of the National Economy for training managerial personnel under 45 years of age. Students are directors of large enterprises and associations, and higher-ranking officials from ministries and departments. Gorbachev's *perestroika* applies to education as well, with the objective of establishing closer ties with industrial and research centers.

Economic and technological development efforts were occasionally made in the past, at least formally, to respond to special needs of these newly developing branches. The policy affected educational institutions and recruiting as well as on-the-job training.

Gorbachev's *perestroika* especially requires restructuring of the bureaucracy. One of the resolutions of the 19th Communist Party Conference, in June 1988, was "On Combating Bureaucracy." The resolution noted that the June 1985 Central Committee Plenum and the 1966 Party Congress "launched an offensive against bureaucracy and its uglier manifestations such as *diktat*, arbitrary administrative action in the economy, in the social, intellectual and cultural spheres, bureaucratic indifference to people's rights and needs, and high-handed dismissals of public opinion of the social experiences of working people." The resolution, unquestionably spawned and approved beforehand by Gorbachev, demanded "radical reforms." The managerial apparatus, it said, remains unreasonably cumbersome, and the organizational structure must be reformed. The resolution reiterated previous party decisions to "restructure the managerial system, abolish some of its redundant elements and reduce the size of its apparatus." The resolution stressed the need for immediate implementation. "A well-ordered, smoothly functioning and flexible managerial apparatus is to be an effective working tool of *perestroika*," the resolution held. Government and public bodies were directed to be fully accessible to people, with ministers and other senior officials personally available.

However, there was no diminution of the party's control. The resolution placed the responsibility for the radical changes in the bureaucracy especially on party leaders and organs, but its direction is the elimination of shortcomings to pursue more effectively the party's and Gorbachev's policies. In the restructuring, the resolution was clear in indicating that replacement of "democratic centralism" by "bureaucratic centralism" is to be "firmly rebuffed."

Under intense pressure the CP not only decided in early 1990 to abolish Article 6 of the Constitution but in its policy statement the 28th Party Congress (July 2–13, 1990) "renounces . . . the *nomenklatura* approach in its personnel work." The Congress went on to say that state bodies and management "enjoy the full jurisdiction in making personnel decisions." Abrogating its *nomenklatura* affected as many as 23 million positions. Officially CP monopoly is broken and the government is in the process of decentralization. The *locus* of power has shifted from the CP to the government—the executive presidency, the Presidential Council and the Council of Ministers. The government bureaucracy is still dominated by Communists but increasingly they were reformists supporting Gorbachev and his policies. Some appointments to even top-level positions are going to non-party professionals. However, with decentralizations, the republics and lower government echelons as well as the numerous enterprises are given authority over their personnel. By late 1990 more employees were hired on their qualifications than previously, but the changes in personnel, as well as in the economy, were excruciatingly slow. The conservative bureaucracy, experienced and still within CP organizations, was well entrenched.

LOCAL GOVERNMENT

As the largest nation on earth, the Soviet Union has a number of levels of local government. At the top there are 14 soviet socialist republics (SSR) and one soviet federated socialist republic (the RSFSR). Each of these 15 republics, called Union republics, has its own constitution, a clone of the Soviet Union's Constitution; a supreme soviet; and a supreme court, the latter two as powerless as the ones in Moscow. Incidentally, the Ukraine and Byelorussia are independent members of the United Nations, with voting rights there.

Contained within and subordinate to some of the union republics are 20 so-called autonomous republics (ASSR) and various levels of local governments, ranging from villages to regions. These subdivisions are either national or administrative. The administrative local government units include *kraya* (territories) and *oblasti* (provinces), regional subdivisions; *rayony* (districts); towns; settlements; and villages. The village is the smallest area that merits a soviet. *Kraya* and *oblasti* are directly subordinate to SSR's.

District-level governments include the rural *rayon* (equivalent to a county), medium-size cities and the boroughs of large cities. The lowest level of local government is the village, of which there are over 40,000. An additional 3,000 to 3,500 populated areas are referred to as workers' settlements or agricultural settlements.

The three types of autonomous units—republics, *oblasti* and *okruga* (a national area subordinate to a *kray* or *oblast* and created to recognize a small national minority) enjoy a descending order of self-determination. All of them are represented in the Soviet of Nationalities. Of these, the least important are the *okruga*, which are sparsely populated.

Governments throughout the entire system are structurally similar. Basically all are soviets, but local soviets cannot use the title *supreme*. Republic ministries and state committees are replaced in local governments by administrations or departments, and councils of ministers and presidiums by executive committees. As a result, each government unit operates in triple subordination: to the soviet and presidium or executive committee at that level, to the parent agency in the government at the administrative level above and to the corresponding unit of the Communist Party.

The requirements for an area to become a union republic were set by Stalin. He declared that it must be on the frontier, with a population of over 1 million belonging predominantly to the nationality for which it is named. The constitutional status of these republics is grand and imposing and bears no relation to reality. They are "free" and "independent" with a right to secede, conduct foreign relations and maintain their own army. Of the union republics apart from the RSFSR, only the Kazakh SSR, Byelorussia and the Ukraine are relatively large; Armenia is the smallest in size and Estonia the smallest in population.

Each SSR has a constitution that is approved by the USSR and cannot contradict the constitution of the Union. All actions taken by any organ of the SSR are subject to review and possible reversal by the Supreme Soviet, the Presidium or a USSR ministry. All supreme soviets in the constituent republics are unicameral, as are all legislative bodies below the USSR level. These supreme soviets are required to meet twice a year, but they meet far less frequently than that. Each SSR has only a Union republic type of ministry subordinate to the corresponding ministry at the Union level and to its own Presidium. In addition to the Union republic ministries, each republic also has a number of republican ministries that have no counterpart at the Union level. These ministries are concerned exclusively with local affairs and are subordinate only to their own governments.

Each SSR sends 32 deputies to the Soviet of Nationalities. Together the 480 SSR deputies constitute a majority in the 750-member chamber. The revenues of the SSR are derived primarily from two sources: a percentage of the income from enterprises and a percentage of the direct national taxes collected within their borders. In addition, they are allowed to levy minor taxes.

Kraya are administrative subdivisions of SSR's consisting of large, thinly populated areas without special ethnic character or economic significance. Five of the six *kraya* have autonomous *oblasti* within them. All are in the RSFSR; two of them, Khabrovsk and Maritime, are on the far eastern periphery; the largest, Krasnoyarsk, is at the eastern-western center; Altay is in south-central Siberia bordering Mongolia; and the two smallest, Krasnodar and Stavropol, are in the Caucasus. Although they average more than twice the size and population of the typical ASSR, *kraya*, as administra-

tive and not political units, have neither autonomy nor representation in the Soviet of Nationalities. They do not have supreme soviets or supreme courts. *Kray* soviets are considered local soviets and have executive committees in place of presidiums and councils of ministers, and administrations or departments in place of ministries or state committees.

Oblasti are administrative subdivisions covering about half of the entire Soviet territory. Territorial breakdowns below the republic level have been fluid throughout Soviet history, and *oblasti* have been created, abolished, combined or subdivided to conform with growth of population, changes in the economy or governmental reorganization. Overall, their number has been reduced from a peak of 145 in 1953 to about 100, half of them in the RSFSR. *Oblasti* are economic or geographical units rather than ethnic ones. On the average, an *oblast* has about 1 million inhabitants; the most populous is the Moscow *oblast*, followed by the Leningrad *oblast*. All of them are subordinate to the union republics. *Oblasti* are subdivided into rural *rayony* and also may contain national *okruga*, which exist at a level between the *oblast* and the *rayon*. *Oblasti* generally contain towns of *oblast* status that are directly responsible to the SSR. Of the nine largest cities, only Baku is not also the center of an *oblast* named for it.

Oblasti and *kraya* are considered regions and therefore have soviets. Executive and administrative functions are carried out by the executive committee and various departments and administrations.

The *rayon*, or district, is a subdivision of the smaller union republics, ASSRs, *kraya*, *oblasti*, autonomous *oblasti* and national *okruga*. Districts may be either rural *rayony* or city *rayony*, the former including workers' and agricultural settlements and the latter large and medium-size towns. There are about 1,800 rural *rayony*, nearly the same number of cities and towns of *rayon* status and 400 city boroughs. *Rayon* governments are similar to but scaled down from those of the *oblasti*. *Rayony* have soviets scheduled to meet for a session at two-month intervals. The administrative functions are discharged by executive committees, departments and standing committees.

Cities or towns, depending on their size, are administered at any level below the republic. The smallest, sometimes referred to as urban-type settlements, are subordinate to the *rayony*. The largest have governments of *oblasti* equivalence and are directly responsible to their SSR's. They have boroughs or city *rayony* within them. Large cities, such as Moscow, have large soviets with hundreds of deputies. Administrative status changes with urban growth. Growing cities, initially responsible to the *rayony*, may achieve *rayon* status themselves and become responsible to the next higher regional or republican government. Larger cities have departments and administrations, but smaller ones have far more modest staffs.

The village or settlement soviet forms the lowest rung of the local government ladder. It may comprise a group of villages or a large workers' or agricultural settlement. Although the number of village soviets has declined by almost half since 1953, over 1.5 million deputies are involved at this level, making them members of the level of government with the broadest popular base. Daily administration in most cases is conducted by a committee of three persons. Village soviets ordinarily are subordinate to the *rayony*.

Autonomous republics form a distinct group of territorial governments. Their constitutions refer to autonomy, as opposed to the sovereignty and independence ascribed to the union republics. ASSR's are considered "national states within the republics" and as such are physically within and subordinate to the union republics. The autonomy they enjoy is roughly comparable to that of the SSR's in relation to the USSR. At the minimum, such autonomy entails the right of the national group to retain its local language, courts, news media, local business and local administration and also to foster national manners and customs.

Sixteen of the 20 ASSR's are in the RSFSR, two in Georgia and one each in the Azerbaijan and Uzbek SSR's. In the RSFSR five of the smaller ones are in a cluster east of Moscow between the city and the Urals. Four other, smaller ones are in the Caucasus between the Black and the Caspian seas. One is in the south-central USSR, roughly surrounding the southern half of the Aral Sea. Two are in southern Siberia, bordering Mongolia, and two are in the northern part of the European RSFSR. The Yakut ASSR, constituting a large portion of east-central Siberia, is the largest, with 3,103,200 sq. km. (1,197,835 sq. mi.). At the other end, the Adzhar ASSR has only 3,000 sq. km. (1,158 sq. mi.). Initially the ASSR's were named for the majority nationality in each republic (except for Dagestan, which was a geographical region with over 30 minority groups), but in the course of time, population shifts and migrations altered their ethnic composition. Thus the Yakuts and the Komis are no longer in the majority in the republics named after them.

The ASSR's have governments structured almost identical to those of the USSR and SSR's, with comparable constitutions, supreme soviets, councils of ministers, presidiums and supreme courts. The supreme soviets are unicameral and have a typical membership of 150. Each ASSR sends 11 deputies to the Soviet of Nationalities. A minimum of 12 ministries is provided for in all ASSR constitutions, and others may be added if needed.

Autonomous *oblasti* usually contain minority groups in areas that are not important enough to constitute distinctive and integral economic regions. There are eight such AO's. The autonomy granted to them is purely cultural and enables them to maintain their languages in schools, courts, news media and local government offices and also to retain their local customs. AO's are subordinate either to the *kray* or to the union republic in which they are located. Each sends five deputies to the Soviet of Nationalities.

Five of the eight AO's are within the RSFSR; the other three are in Georgian, Azerbaijan and Tadzhik SSR's. Of those in the RSFSR, two are in the Caucasus, two are in south-central Siberia and one is in the far eastern area. Each is within a *kray* and is subordinate to it except in the smaller SSR's, where AO's are directly responsible to the republic governments. Generally, AO's are in the more remote areas and are thinly populated.

National *okruga* are large territorial subdivisions with sparse populations. They are parts of *kraya* or administrative *oblasti* and are subdivided into *rayony*. Local autonomy is limited, but each NO sends one deputy to the Soviet of Nationalities. All 10 NO's are in the RSFSR. As in ASSR's, each NO had formerly a predominant nationality, but population changes have reduced ethnic concentration in all of them.

FOREIGN POLICY

The foundations of Soviet foreign policy were established by Lenin, are enshrined in the Constitution (Chapter 6) and are formulated by the Politburo of the Communist Party. These three sources coalesced as General Secretary Mikhail Gorbachev's *glasnost* (openness) and *perestroika* (restructuring) evolved into Soviet foreign policy initiatives. According to Article 28 of the Constitution of 1977, "The USSR steadfastly pursues a Leninist policy of peace and stands for strengthening of the security of nations and broad international cooperation." Also, the foreign policy is designed to achieve favorable international conditions for building communism, safeguarding state interests, consolidating the gains of world socialism, supporting the struggle of peoples for national liberation, achieving disarmament and implementing the principle of peaceful coexistence. Lenin's principle of "peaceful coexistence" has been invoked at critical periods, including the latter 1950s by Nikita Khrushchev, in the 1970s by Leonid Brezhnev and currently by Gorbachev as part of his "new thinking."

The policy of peaceful coexistence or of detente, as it is occasionally called, has not always been understood. Soviet ideologues have consistently considered it in characterizations such as: "This principle is nothing but the highest form of the class struggle between two antagonistic systems—socialism (communism) and capitalism." Accordingly, Soviet foreign policy toward the West has shifted from confrontational to nonconfrontational, with emphasis on disarmament and foreign trade. With its Warsaw Treaty Organization (WTO or Warsaw Pact) allies, Moscow seeks to maintain bilateral as well as multilateral binding ties while permitting them greater autonomy in domestic affairs and in foreign relations. Its support for Third World insurgencies lessened militarily and financially after Soviet armed forces withdrew from Afghanistan.

With a revolutionary ideology the Soviet Union has been embroiled in world affairs since the 1917 October Revolution, when the goal of world revolution—unrealistic as it proved to be—was perceived attainable, at least by some Bolshevik leaders such as Lenin and Leon Trotsky. World War I still was in progress, and the new Soviet (Council) regime withdrew from the conflict with the conclusion of the Treaty of Brest-Litovsk with the Central Powers on March 3, 1918. This helped the Bolsheviks consolidate their political position, as they were forced to engage in another war—a civil war—not only against anti-Communists ("Whites") but also against foreign military contingents, including French and British. The Red Army emerged victorious by 1920 but continued its offensive against Poland to extend the revolution beyond, to Germany. This campaign ultimately failed, and by the Treaty of Riga in 1921 Poland became an independent state with areas containing large Ukrainian and Byelorussian populations. Also achieving sovereignty were the Baltic republics of Lithuania, Latvia and Estonia, as well as Finland. Bessarabia was awarded to Rumania and Kars and Ardahan to Turkey. The Bolsheviks thus lost territories formerly part of the Russian czarist empire, but they achieved complete control of a major country, a base for revolutionary operations.

To attain the goal of world revolution, or establishment of Communist rule in various countries, the Bolsheviks created in Moscow the Communist International (Comintern) in March 1919. Originally the membership was small, consisting of the Russian Communist Party (CP), the German CP and several other leftists and radicals, but in subsequent years Communist parties from many countries, where they were organized, became members. Comintern congresses were held in Moscow, where strategy and tactics were formulated and policies were implemented by committees. The organization was instrumental in forming Communist or workers' parties throughout the world. Because of their objective of overthrowing governments and interfering in affairs of states, the Comintern and its agents were anathema to governments.

Domestically, "war communism" ended in 1921, and Lenin inaugurated the New Economic Policy (NEP), which was prompted by an economic crisis resulting in a disastrous famine. The NEP permitted a limited market economy and attracted foreign aid and trade. It was abolished in 1929 by Stalin. The Union of Soviet Socialist Republics (USSR), organized in 1922, was constitutionally legalized in 1924, and the regime struggled to achieve legitimacy. Its diplomatic isolation appeared near its end when the European powers invited Moscow to participate in the Genoa Conference, its first international meeting, on reconstruction of the European economy. Immediately following Genoa, rapprochement was established with Germany with the conclusion of the Treaty of Rapallo on April 16, 1922, providing for diplomatic and commercial relations. Beginning in 1924, numerous countries extended official recognition to the Soviet regime, but the United States delayed until 1933. However, in 1927 London severed diplomatic ties with Moscow, charging Soviet interference in British internal affairs. The breach lasted until 1929.

Lenin's death in 1924 resulted in a leadership power struggle that was not resolved until the latter 1920s. With the defeat of Trotsky and his "permanent revolution," Stalin embarked on building "socialism in one country." Moscow's diplomatic pursuits with European countries resulted in non-aggression treaties with France, Poland, Finland and the three Baltic states, all in 1932. In 1934 the Soviet Union was admitted to the League of Nations. With the anti-Communist Hitler's rise to power in 1933, the Soviet Union and the Comintern in 1935 adopted a "Popular Front" policy of cooperating with previously hated socialist and other parties against fascism. Moscow signed mutual assistance pacts with France (May 1935) and with Czechoslovakia (also May 1935), the latter conditioned on first French aid, a provision that was to play a significant role at the

POLITICAL SUBDIVISIONS					
Soviet Federated Socialist Republic	Area		Population (1989 Census)	Capitals	Population of Capital (000 1989 Census)
	Sq. Km.	Sq. Mi.			
Russian S.F.S.R.	17,075,400	6,592,800	147,386	Moscow	
Soviet Socialist Republics					
Armenian	29,800	11,500	3,283	Yerevan	1,199
Azerbaijan	86,600	33,400	7,029	Baku	1,757
Byelorussian	207,600	80,200	10,200	Minsk	1,589
Estonian	45,100	17,400	1,573	Tallinn	482
Georgian	69,700	26,900	5,449	Tbilisi	1,260
Kazakh	2,717,300	1,049,200	16,538	Alma-Ata	1,128
Kirgiz	198,500	76,600	4,291	Frunze	616
Latvian	63,700	24,600	2,681	Riga	915
Lithuanian	65,200	25,200	3,690	Vilnius	582
Moldavian	33,700	13,000	4,341	Kishinyev	665
Tadzhik	143,100	55,300	5,112	Dushanbe	595
Turkmen	488,100	188,500	3,534	Ashkhabad	398
Ukrainian	603,700	233,100	51,704	Kiev	2,587
Uzbek	447,400	172,700	19,906	Tashkent	2,073
TOTAL LAND AREA	22,274,900	8,600,400	286,717		
INLAND WATER	127,300	49,100			
TOTAL	22,402,200	8,649,500			

Note: Moscow 1989 population 8,967

POLITICAL SUBDIVISIONS *(continued)*

Autonomous Republic	Area Sq. Km.	Sq. Mi.	Population (000, 1989 Census)	Capital	Population of Capital (000, 1989 Census)
Within RSFSR					
Bashkir	143,600	55,430	3,952	Ufa	1,083
Buryat	351,300	135,602	1,042	Ulan-Ude	353
Chechen-Ingush	19,300	7,450	1,277	Grozny	401
Chuvash	18,300	7,064	1,336	Cheboksary	420
Dagestan	50,300	19,416	1,792	Makhachkala	315
Kabardino-Balkar	12,500	4,825	760	Nalchik	235
Kalmyk	75,900	29,297	322	Elista	85*
Karelian	172,400	66,546	792	Petrozavodsk	270
Komi	415,900	160,537	1,263	Syktyvkar	233
Mari	23,200	8,955	750	Yoshkar-Ola	242
Mordovian	26,200	10,113	964	Saransk	312
North Ossetian	8,000	3,088	634	Ordzhonikidze	300
Tatar	68,000	26,248	3,640	Kazan	1,094
Tuva	170,500	65,813	309	Kyzyl	153
Udmurt	42,100	16,251	1,609	Izhevsk	635
Yakut	3,103,200	1,197,835	1,082	Yakutsk	187
Within Azerbaijan					
Nakhichevan	5,500	2,123	295	Nakhichevan	51*
Within Georgia					
Abkhasian	8,600	3,320	537	Sukhumi	174
Adzhar	3,000	1,158	393	Batumi	136
Within Uzbekistan					
Kara-Kalpak	165,600	63,922	1,214	Nukus	169

*In 1987.

Autonomous Region	Area Sq. Km.	Sq. Mi.	Population (000, 1989 Census)	Capital	Population of Capital (000, 1989 Census)
Within RSFSR					
Adygei	7,600	2,934	432	Maikop	149
Gorno-Altai	92,600	35,744	192	Gorno-Altaisk	40*
Jewish	36,000	13,896	216	Birobidzhan	82*
Kharachayevo-Cherkess	14,100	5,443	418	Cherkessk	113
Khakass	61,900	23,893	569	Abakan	154
Within Azerbaijan					
Nagorno-Karabakh	4,400	1,698	188	Stepanakert	39*
Within Georgia					
South Ossetian	3,900	1,505	99	Tskhinvali	35*
Within Tadzhikistan					
Gorno-Badakhshan	63,700	24,588	161	Khorog	12*

*In 1987.

four-power Munich Conference in September 1938, which excluded the Soviet Union as well as Czechoslovakia. In a continuing effort to check Hitler the Soviet representative at the League of Nations sided with the opposition to the Nazi remilitarization of the Rhineland, but Paris and London demurred on the necessary action.

The most active bilateral relations the USSR had before World War II were with Germany, with long-lasting consequences. Following Rapallo, the Soviet Union concluded with Germany the non-aggression and neutrality Treaty of Berlin in April 1926, and three years later they agreed on a conciliation convention. Throughout the 1920s the governments engaged in military cooperation, the result of secret agreements in violation of the Treaty of Versailles. In May 1933 the Treaty of Berlin was renewed, but such cooperative relations subsided when Hitler came to power. However, the most damaging, and to many incomprehensible, of the bilateral agreements was the Nazi-Soviet Treaty of Non-Aggression, signed August 23, 1939, for ten years by these ideologically antagonistic dictatorships. Also known as the Molotov-Ribbentrop Pact after the foreign ministers of the two countries, the treaty hastened World War II and victimized neighboring nations. That it violated the Franco-Soviet Treaty of 1935 seemed immaterial.

The publicly announced document contained the standard diplomatic formulation: non-aggression, consultations, peaceful settlement of disputes, plus the provision (Article 2) that if either became "the object of belligerent action by a third power, the other . . . shall in no manner lend its support to the third." In addition, Nazi Germany and the Soviet Union concluded secret protocols on spheres of influence that affected a number of countries. The secret protocol of August 23 assigned Finland, Estonia, Latvia and Bessarabia (then a part of Rumania) to the Soviet sphere, Lithuania to Germany's and partitioned Poland between them. On September 1 Germany invaded Poland, followed by the Red Army on September 17, conquering that beleaguered country. On September 28 Moscow and Berlin concluded the Boundary and Friendship Treaty, which divided Poland between them. On the same date they signed a secret supplementary protocol assigning most of Lithuania to the Soviet sphere in exchange for additional Polish territory to Germany.

Although the Soviet Union had a non-aggression treaty with Finland, the Red Army invaded that country, which the secret protocol made possible, in November 1939. Finland displayed impressive courage in the Winter War, but the Soviet military overwhelmed the relatively undermanned Finnish defense forces. By the March 12, 1940, armistice, Finland was forced to cede part of its eastern territory and provide military and naval bases to the Soviet Union. The three Baltic countries were annexed into the USSR in June 1940 as Union republics, and in the following month Bessarabia and northern Bukovina were incorporated into the Moldavian Republic. Diplomatic and economic relations between Germany and the USSR continued to their mutual advantage, including discussions of further expansion, Moscow into the Balkans, until Hitler attacked the USSR on June 22, 1941. The Soviet Union became one of the Allies of the United States and Great Britain during World War II against the Axis Powers.

The Soviet Union suffered incredible loss of life and devastation in the war, the most of any country—over 7 million military and nearly 20 million civilians perished. It received American Lend-Lease and other aid. The Comintern was officially dissolved in 1943 by Stalin to dispel suspicions of subversion by Allies fighting a common enemy, but doubts lingered. Stalin was a participant with President Franklin D. Roosevelt and Prime Minister Winston Churchill in the major Allied conferences—Teheran (1943), Yalta (1945) and with President Harry S. Truman at Potsdam (1945)—at which decisions were made on the military conduct of the war, on the East European countries and on Germany. Even while engaged in critical military operations the Soviet leadership was simultaneously preparing for the postwar political arrangements in Eastern Europe.

During the war and immediate postwar period Stalin was unalterably opposed to reestablishing independence for the Baltic states, returning Bessarabia and northern Bukovina to Rumania or the areas exacted from Finland, or giving up the formerly eastern territory to Poland. In addition, Moscow acquired territory from defeated Germany and Japan as well as from friendly Czechoslovakia—the eastern province of Podkarpatska Rus or Ruthenia, which became part of the Ukrainian Republic. Now, unlike prewar, the USSR had a common border with Czechoslovakia and Hungary. Soviet armed forces liberated much of Eastern Europe, with the exception of Yugoslavia, and remained in occupation. By February 1948, when Communists seized power in Prague, all of Eastern Europe, Yugoslavia again excepted, was dominated by Soviet Communist allies it had supported in achieving control with tactics brazenly in violation of the Yalta Agreement.

The Western countries responded initially with protests but later established the Marshall Plan for economic recovery, and NATO as a defensive organization to contain communism. Stalin rejected the Marshall Plan even for his allies and the Cold War began, exacerbated by Moscow's design upon West Berlin. The Soviet Union welcomed the victory of communism in China, became an atomic power and formed the Council for Mutual Economic Assistance (CMEA), all during 1949, and the following year helped engineer North Korea's invasion of South Korea, to which the United Nations responded with military forces led by the United States. Following Stalin's death in 1953, First Secretary Nikita Khrushchev was instrumental in establishing in 1955 the WTO, which bound the East European satellites to the Soviet Union militarily. His "de-Stalinization" policy was extended into Eastern Europe, but Soviet armed forces crushed the Hungarian uprising in 1956. Lenin's policy of "coexistence" was refurbished, signifying a shift in Kremlin's approaches toward the West. This led to the Big Four summit conference (1955) in Geneva, which included President Dwight D. Eisenhower. Khrushchev visited the United States in 1959.

Khrushchev was deposed by Leonid Brezhnev as party leader in 1964. Four years later the Soviet-led WTO invaded Czechoslovakia, crushing Alexander Dubcek's "Prague Spring." In the 1970s Brezhnev adopted a policy of detente, or relaxation of tensions, toward the Western countries. As with coexistence policies in the past, relations improved politically and economically. The first major arms control negotiations were concluded in 1972: SALT I. Moscow engaged in others (e.g., MBFR and those at the United Nations) and participated in the process leading to the Helsinki Accords (1975).

At the same time, detente helped the regime to strengthen its military forces and promote insurgencies in Third World countries. This was climaxed by the Soviet invasion of Afghanistan in 1979, which led to condemnation by the Western world and the end of detente. A period of transition followed Brezhnev's death in 1982 as successors Yuri Andropov and Konstantin Chernenko each lived only a short time. During the former's leadership the bilateral U.S.-Soviet START (strategic arms reduction talks) and INF (intermediate-range nuclear forces) negotiations were suspended in Geneva. However, the multilateral NATO-WTO talks continued in Vienna.

On March 11, 1985, the Communist Party elevated a relatively young and, in the West, largely unknown official as Soviet general secretary—Mikhail Gorbachev, then 54 years of age and a full member of the Politburo since only November 1980. The new party leader responded rapidly with critically needed reforms. Among the many personnel changes, Gorbachev removed veteran foreign minister Andrei Gromyko and appointed a newcomer to the international scene, the more personable Eduard Shevardnadze, a Georgian. The general secretary's policies of *glasnost* and *peres-*

troika have affected not only domestic developments but also have made a dramatic impact on foreign relations.

Gorbachev's policies were endorsed by the Party's 27th Congress in 1986 and, more importantly, by a rarely convened conference—the 19th All-Union Conference—which Gorbachev arranged and held in Moscow June 28–July 1, 1988. The general secretary's policies of *glasnost* and *perestroika* became clearer and, despite opposition from the conservative wing, received the appropriate Party support for their continuation. In 1987 his book *Perestroika: New Thinking for Our Country and the World* provided additional insights on current Soviet foreign policy.

At the conference Gorbachev made a surprisingly candid admission: "We have to acknowledge that command methods of administration did not spare the field of foreign policy . . . even decisions of vital importance were made by a narrow circle of people. . . . This led to an inadequate reaction to international events and to policies of other states. . . ." Gorbachev embarked on refashioning the direction of Soviet foreign policy in an increasingly interdependent world of nuclear arms. Admitted, too, is that in the past the principle of peaceful coexistence was a form of class struggle, but Moscow claims this is no longer the case. In view of historical experiences, foreign officials and observers were skeptical at first. Within the party conservatives were critical of Gorbachev's seeming departure from the class principle and Communist internationalism.

As already noted, during 1939–40 the Soviet Union extended control over several nations that were incorporated into the USSR, and over East European countries following World War II. With Moscow's political and military assistance, Communists seized power in Poland, Czechoslovakia, Hungary, Bulgaria and Rumania. According to the Allied Agreement the Soviet Union occupied and administered a zone of the defeated Third Reich that in 1949 became the German Democratic Republic (GDR, East Germany). Although the Red Army entered Yugoslavia toward the end of World War II, and Moscow claimed to have participated in its liberation, the fact is that Yugoslavia in the main liberated itself. As a result, that Balkan country, headed by Partisan leader Marshal Jozip Broz Tito, rejected Stalin's control and embarked on an independent course, with its own brand of communism. Albania's indigenous Communists seized power when occupation armies departed.

With Communist regimes in control in Eastern Europe, the Soviet Union then sought to tighten its grip through bilateral and multilateral arrangements. Since Stalin had dissolved the Comintern during the Second World War, no international Communist mechanism existed until October 1947, when the Communist Information Bureau (Cominform) was established. The founding meeting of Communist leaders was held in Poland, but the Cominform's capital was to be, ironically, Belgrade. The strange title of its publication, reportedly decided by Stalin although he did not attend, was *For a Lasting Peace, for a People's Democracy.* The original members were all East European parties, in-

cluding Yugoslavia and Albania, but not East Germany, plus the French and Italian parties. Although formally its decisions were not binding on its members, as were those of the Comintern, the Cominform was a channel for Moscow's policies, now disseminated worldwide. It also became the instrument for expelling Yugoslavia from the Soviet bloc in 1948 following Tito's dispute with Stalin on the pretext of Marxist-Leninist deviation, but in reality it was over control of Yugoslavia. With this move, and the economic blockade of Yugoslavia by its former Allies, Stalin hoped to depose Tito. The Yugoslav leader maintained his independent attitude, received Western aid and survived. Tito's national Communist posture became known as an "independent road toward socialism" and "Titoism." The latter was applied as stigma to numerous Communists throughout Eastern Europe who were in real or imagined opposition to Moscow's domination. Cominform's capital was moved to Bucharest and remained in Rumania until the organization was dissolved by Moscow in April 1956 as part of Khrushchev's "de-Stalinization" policy.

The Soviet Union's instrument for eventual economic integration of its empire was the Council for Mutual Economic Assistance (CMEA). It was established on January 25, 1949, at a conference in Moscow attended by all East European countries except Yugoslavia and Albania, the latter joining shortly after the meeting. The GDR had not yet been established and became a member in September 1950, but Albania has not participated since 1966. Later, Cuba, Mongolia and Vietnam became members. Created in response to the Marshall Plan, the CMEA's progress for a number of years was unimpressive, but at a meeting in 1954 the members agreed to a Soviet proposal for coordinating their economies, including their economic plans. The CMEA became a structured organization, with its policy-making, ministerial-level Council meeting yearly. There are numerous committees, commissions and functional organs, as well as an Executive Committee. Its Secretariat, in Moscow, administers the day-to-day activities of the CMEA's vast bureaucracy. Greater coordination and integration developed among these centrally planned economies, and most trade was within the CMEA. However, trade with non-Communist countries, especially by Rumania, Poland and Hungary, became significant in the 1980s. The CMEA became stagnant, and members established contacts with the European Community, thereby weakening Moscow's control. Trade with Western countries was expected to increase substantially during the 1990s.

In addition to political and economic control, the Soviet Union created a military alliance system consisting of a multilateral organization and bilateral treaties with its East European allies. Establishment of the Warsaw Pact in 1955 purportedly was in response to West Germany's adherence to NATO. A more compelling reason was to establish an international legal basis for the Soviet Union's continued maintenance of its military forces in those countries. With the signing of the Austrian State Treaty in 1955, Moscow would have been obliged to withdraw its troops from Hungary and Rumania. Moreover, the Warsaw Treaty Organization (WTO), or the Warsaw Pact, as it is commonly known, applied to Soviet forces in Poland and East Germany as well. Moscow had withdrawn its troops from Czechoslovakia in the spring of 1946. The Warsaw Pact signatories were the USSR, Albania, Bulgaria, Czechoslovakia, East Germany, Hungary, Poland and Rumania. The WTO was extended automatically in 1975 for an additional 10 years, and in 1985 the members renewed it for another 20 years, which Gorbachev characterized as crucial.

The highest decision-making organ of the WTO is the Political Consultative Committee (PCC), which is composed of the party leaders of member states. Ministerial meetings are held by the Foreign Ministers' Committee and the Defense Ministers' Committee. The Warsaw Pact provides for joint or combined armed forces, with a Soviet marshal or general as commander in chief. The elaborate structure, in addition, has a Joint Secretariat, a Military Council and various other elements. Until late 1989–1990 there was no question regarding the totality of Soviet control, from the general secretary of the party, through the Ministry of Defense and the General Staff of the Soviet armed forces down to individual Soviet groups of forces in East Germany, Poland, Czechoslovakia and Hungary. Early in 1989 General of the Army Petr Lushev replaced Marshal Victor Kulikov, becoming the fifth commander-in-chief of the joint armed forces since 1955. The chief of the General Staff also was a Soviet officer, and Soviet military advisers were attached to the high command of member armed forces.

Combined military exercises began in 1961, increasing over the years in magnitude and performance. Such maneuvers were held in August 1968—they had been used by Moscow for psychological purposes as well—when during the night of August 20–21 Soviet-led WTO military forces invaded Czechoslovakia to suppress Alexander Dubcek's program known as "Prague Spring." Rumanian territory had not been used for these WTO maneuvers, and its forces did not participate in these exercises. Bucharest criticized the invasion along with Yugoslavia and Albania, the latter withdrawing from the Warsaw Pact in protest. The successor to Dubcek, Gustav Husak, justified the invasion as "rendering international assistance" against "counterrevolutionary forces." All foreign troops later withdrew except the Soviet military forces.

In October 1968 Moscow concluded a status-of-forces treaty with Prague for continued stationing of Soviet troops in Czechoslovakia. Such treaties were signed by the Soviet Union with its allies during the 1950s: Poland (December 1956), East Germany (May 1957), Rumania (April 1957) and Hungary (May 1957). Soviet troops withdrew from Rumania in June 1958. Another network of treaties—bilateral friendship, cooperation and mutual assistance—was concluded among the Warsaw Pact countries. The Soviet Union entered into such treaties as follows: Poland (April 1965), Bulgaria (May 1967), Hungary (September 1967), Czechoslovakia (May 1970), Rumania (July 1970) and East Germany (October 1975).

While the Hungarian uprising was suppressed by Soviet armed forces alone, the invasion of Czechoslovakia was the first WTO multilateral military action. The question of when Soviet and other Warsaw Pact forces would be militarily engaged in allied countries was answered by Brezhnev. In November 1968 the general secretary declared in Warsaw the right to intervene in "friendly socialist countries" by WTO military forces when a regime is considered to be in danger. This became known as the "Brezhnev Doctrine" of limited sovereignty. The logic of its applicability was raised repeatedly in light of *perestroika*. Based on Gorbachev's policies of greater autonomy for East European countries and his comments that another Czechoslovakia, or Afghanistan, cannot be repeated, journalists, academicians and officials concluded that "the Brezhnev Doctrine is dead." Gorbachev, the Politburo and the CC were slow to renounce the doctrine, but on December 4, the Soviet Union together with Poland, East Germany, Hungary and Bulgaria, condemned their 1968 invasion as "illegal," pledging not to interfere again in each others affairs.

In 1989 Soviet military forces in Eastern Europe numbered as follows: East Germany (380,000), Czechoslovakia (80,000), Hungary (62,000) and Poland (40,000), for a total of 562,000. As a result of the U.S.-Soviet INF Treaty of December 1987, Moscow withdrew those weapons affected by the INF from East Germany and Czechoslovakia the following year. In December 1988 Gorbachev announced before the U.N. General Assembly Soviet plans to reduce its military forces within two years. He cited 5,300 tanks in six divisions, 50,000 troops, artillery and aircraft to be withdrawn from East Germany, Hungary and Czechoslovakia, with reductions in Poland later. During 1989 reductions in the various categories were reported in the several countries.

Following revolutionary changes in 1989 and 1990 Hungary and Czechoslovakia demanded total withdrawal of Soviet troops. On February 26 President Vaclav Havel of Czechoslovakia and Gorbachev agreed on a three-stage pullout of the 73,500 Soviet troops and equipment to be completed by July 1, 1991. The following month, on March 10, Hungary and the Soviet Union signed an agreement calling for a complete withdrawal of the 50,000 Soviet forces by the same date, and began the reduction March 11. The four World War II Allies (U.S., U.K., France and the USSR) and the two Germanys concluded the "Two-plus-Four" treaty providing for, among other things, Soviet troop withdrawal from the then East Germany by the end of 1994. The following day Moscow concluded a treaty with the FRG that obligated the latter to DM 13 billion (about $10 billion) through 1994 to finance Soviet troops and their 220,000 dependents, and to construct 36,000 apartments to accommodate returning Soviet personnel (see Foreign Policy in East Germany for more information on German unification). During 1990 the Soviet Union promised to complete the reduction of 10,000 (of its 58,000 total) troops, two helicopter divisions and a fighter regiment from Poland.

While the Soviet Union established economic, political and military instruments for control, and there was no question of its dominance over Eastern Europe, the history of Soviet-East European relations has been replete with events signifying dissatisfaction with internal Communist rule and Soviet domination. In addition to the Hungarian uprising in 1956, the WTO invasion of Czechoslovakia and Yugoslav as well as Albanian defections already cited, numerous other eruptions occurred during the decades. Several are listed here. In June 1953 demonstrations and strikes in East Berlin were suppressed by East German police and Soviet troops. Rumania embarked on basically an independent foreign policy course beginning in the early 1960s and, as noted above, was critical of the WTO's incursion into another East European country. Unfortunately, internally Ceausescu exercised brutal control. The Kremlin threatened Poland militarily in 1956 and during the evolution of Solidarity in 1980–81, leading to imposition of martial law.

Western officials and scholars discussed the "disintegration" of the Soviet empire, but Gorbachev spoke of safeguarding "socialism" amid diversity while his conservative detractors used more threatening language.

Military transformation of Eastern Europe accompanied political and economic changes. The very question of continued existence or dissolution of the WTO was raised at highest levels. Was the Pact still viable and relevant? To Moscow the answer was yes, but Hungary threatened resignation and all favored reorganization. The Pact's leaders agreed to change the character of the organization from confrontational to "constructive cooperation" with NATO and other European countries. Accordingly on June 7, 1990, the PCC announced "the formation of a new, all-European security system and the creation of a single Europe of peace and cooperation." The leaders renounced the Pact's "ideological enemy image" of NATO and decided "to review the character, functions, and activities of the Warsaw Treaty."

The members pledged to begin the transformation of WTO into a "treaty of sovereign states with equal rights, formed on a democratic basis." A commission was created to prepare "concrete proposals" for the PCC in October for that body to examine them in November 1990. The transformed WTO was to become a greater political alliance. However, not all Soviet military leaders were enamored with the changes. The defense minister charged NATO strategy to be "aggressive" and spoke of the continued need "not to slacken our allied ties." In mid-September, with German unification near, the East Germans departed from the Pact's headquarters in Moscow and on September 24 formally ended their membership. East Germany's departure reduced the WTO to six members.

Ideologically the Western democratic countries with their "capitalistic" systems had been portrayed as communism's mortal enemy, a system that is doomed by history and if it doesn't collapse must be overthrown. Also, the capitalists were "imperialists" seeking the destruction of communism. Politically the Soviet Union, the leader of international communism, has pursued other than militant policies toward the Western countries, although its historical objectives, even under Gorbachev, have never been repudiated. As indicated earlier, tactics and policies are changeable, depending

on the international situation, with the policy of coexistence continually revived. That is the policy in Gorbachev's "new thinking" toward the West.

Soviet relations with the United States have been the most important during the nuclear age, but Washington delayed diplomatic recognition of the Bolshevik regime until 1933. Relations between the two countries, contrary to Soviet hopes, had been minimal and marred by suspicions. The United States has never recognized the Soviet incorporation of Lithuania, Latvia and Estonia. The United States and the USSR were allies during World War II, and Washington extended $11 billion in material aid under the Lend-Lease program to the Soviet Union during the war. The Roosevelt-Churchill-Stalin conferences during the war were of historical proportions, as they decided the fate of postwar Europe. However, disillusionment followed quickly as the Soviet Union violated provisions in their agreements, especially the Yalta document, which provided for "free and unfettered" elections in Eastern Europe. Instead Moscow imposed Communist dictatorships, including East Germany, and forced the division of Germany. The result was the Cold War between East and West.

The United States established a policy of "containment" to halt the spread of communism. With the Greek Civil War as an impetus, U.S. President Harry S. Truman enunciated his Truman Doctrine in March 1947, pledging assistance to threatened governments. The Marshall Plan was announced by Washington in June 1947 for European recovery, but Stalin reacted angrily, forbidding Czechoslovakia and Poland to participate in this beneficial program. As Churchill expressed it in Fulton, Missouri, on March 5, 1946, "An iron curtain has descended across the Continent." In June 1948 the Soviet authorities imposed a complete blockade of West Berlin. Immediately a massive Western airlift was undertaken, which sustained the inhabitants. After 11 months Moscow lifted the blockade, its effort frustrated. A defensive organization was established by the Western countries in Washington on April 4, 1949, with the signing of the North Atlantic Treaty creating NATO. The North Korean invasion of South Korea was instigated and supported by the Soviet Union, to which Western countries through the United Nations responded militarily, preventing the takeover but exacerbating the already poor East-West relations.

Following Stalin's death and the suppression of the Hungarian uprising, Soviet leader Nikita Khrushchev's policy of "peaceful coexistence" thawed East-West relations. His objective was, as he phrased it, to catch up and overtake the United States. In addition to high-level contacts, the Soviet Union and the United States agreed in 1956 on exchanging magazines—the Russian-language *America Illustrated* and the English-language *Soviet Life*. Other informational, cultural and educational exchanges were to follow, beginning in 1959 when Vice President Richard Nixon and party leader Khrushchev engaged in their famous "kitchen debate" at an American exhibit in Moscow. However, East-West relations were plagued by several incidents, including the Moscow-generated Berlin crisis in 1958 and the Soviet downing of an American U-2 reconnaissance plane, which resulted in the cancellation of President Eisenhower's invitation to visit the Soviet Union in 1960. Khrushchev visited the United States in September 1959. His schedule included talks with President Eisenhower at Camp David. However, U.S.-Soviet relations suffered a setback over the Cuban missile crisis. In 1962 Moscow secretly installed medium-range nuclear missiles in Cuba, which created a confrontation of major proportions. President John F. Kennedy demanded immediate withdrawal or Cuba would be blockaded. Rather than test Kennedy's resolve, Khrushchev ordered that the offensive nuclear weapons be removed and not reintroduced.

The Soviet Union entered into multilateral arms control negotiations, resulting in the Antarctic Treaty in 1961 and the Limited Nuclear Test-Ban Treaty in 1963. Talks continued under Khrushchev's successor Leonid Brezhnev, which materialized in the Outer Space Treaty in 1967, the Nuclear Nonproliferation Treaty in 1968 and the Biological and Toxin Weapons Convention in 1972.

Brezhnev's announced policy of "détente" in the 1970s gave hope to many in the Western world, including the United States, for real relaxation of tensions. Meetings between American presidents and party leader Brezhnev reflected the improved relations. Only one so-called summit meeting materialized during the 1960s—between John F. Kennedy and Khrushchev in June 1961 in Vienna—but President Lyndon Johnson met with Premier Alexei Kosygin in Glassboro, New Jersey, in June 1967. However, six highest-level meetings were held during the 1970s between an American president and Brezhnev: with Nixon in May 1972 in Moscow, June 1973 in Washington and June–July 1974 in Moscow and Yalta; with Gerald Ford in November 1974 in Vladivostok and in July–August 1975 in Helsinki; and with Jimmy Carter in June 1979 in Vienna.

East-West relations improved. Several significant agreements were reached between the Soviet Union and Western countries and bilaterally with the United States. In 1970 the Soviet Union concluded a treaty with the Federal Republic of Germany, and the following year a Quadripartite Agreement was reached on Berlin. SALT I, the first Strategic Arms Limitation Talks was signed on May 26, 1972, by Nixon and Brezhnev during the president's visit to Moscow. The agreement included a treaty limiting antiballistic missile systems (ABM). In 1973 the Soviet Union and its WTO partners began negotiations with 12 NATO countries on the Mutual and Balanced Force Reductions (MBFR) in Vienna. These talks were intended to reduce conventional forces in central Europe. From the beginning the negotiators faced two obstacles: data (i.e., the present level of Warsaw Pact forces in the area) and associated or verification measures.

In promoting an all-European approach to international problems, Moscow was an active participant in the Conference on Security and Cooperation in Europe (CSCE), signed in Helsinki in 1975. Known as the Helsinki Final Act or the Helsinki Accords, the agreement was signed by Brezhnev, apparently unfazed by its provisions on respect for human rights, given the history of Soviet violations. Reforms in the Soviet Union and in Eastern Europe were expected as a result. Unfortunately, until late 1989–early 1990 reforms were minimal, and Moscow was criticized by Western officials.

The Soviet Union continued to be an active participant in the subsequent review conferences and to be a major negotiator, representing the Warsaw Pact members, in the Confidence- and Security-Building Measures and Disarmament in Europe Conference (CDE). The conference began in January 1984 in Stockholm and ended with an agreement effective January 1, 1987. The objective was to adopt confidence-building measures to reduce the risk of military confrontation in Europe. Since the Soviet Union had been sensitive to intrusive verification measures, the agreement at Stockholm was unprecedented. The signatories agreed to "binding" compliance, the area of applicability from the Atlantic to the Urals, and on-site inspection on demand. There was understandable skepticism about verification, which the United States considered to be of "critical importance." Washington released documentation of Soviet noncompliance with the arms control agreement. In recent years the Soviet Union has allowed intrusive on-site inspections and admitted to certain past violations, such as the Krasnoyarsk radar installation. The MBFR negotiations, while providing much experience for both WTO and NATO delegations and a modicum of understanding, were unable to produce a treaty on conventional troop reductions. These negotiations concluded in early 1989, but reduction of conventional armed forces continues to be discussed by the expanded Conventional Armed Forces in Europe (CFE) negotiations, also in Vienna. The area has also been expanded—from the Atlantic to the Urals.

In comparison with the many years of frustrating MBFR negotiations, CFE's progress has been impressive. The Soviet economic crisis and Gorbachev's "new thinking" had an obvious impact on the latter talks. In his 1990 State of the Union message President Bush proposed the lowering of U.S. and Soviet ground and air force personnel in Central and Eastern Europe to 195,000, which received Soviet acceptance in February in Toronto. By June 26, 1990, the 23 NATO and WTO negotiators agreed to definitions of categories of arms reductions, including battle tanks, armored combat vehicles, artillery, combat aircraft and attack helicopters; also on the need for regional and individual sublimits of equipment; and on the need for on-site inspection for monitoring. Moreover, there was agreement on the limits of tanks and armored combat vehicles. The U.S. demand for additional 30,000 troops on the periphery was, reluctantly, approved by Moscow.

Hope was expressed by both East and West about concluding a treaty during 1990. On October 4 CFE (22 delegations without East Germany) reached agreement on the bulk of the differences with the remainder (e.g., aircraft) to be concluded in time for the November 19–21 Paris CSCE conference. Altogether the June–October decisions, considered a breakthrough in East-West negotiations, set NATO and WTO ceilings as follows: 20,000 battle tanks, 30,000 armored combat vehicles and 2,000 attack helicopters. Within these limitations for each side, one country can have up to 13,300 tanks, 13,700 artillery pieces and 1,500 helicopters. The result is that the burden of destruction of weapons falls on the Soviet Union. Secretary of State Baker cited tanks as an example, with NATO demolishing about 4,000 and the WTO some 19,000 and thousands more of the other arms.

The agreement did not include ceilings on military personnel and, since the Baker-Shevardnadze understanding in February, the treaty on German unification provided for Soviet withdrawal of its troops from former East German territory by 1994. Because of Moscow's insistence, due to defense reductions in Eastern European countries, the Soviet Union was allowed to have about one-third of the WTO arsenal.

Soviet negotiations with the United States extended beyond SALT I. Continuing talks led to the SALT II Treaty, signed by Brezhnev and President Jimmy Carter in June 1979. Confirmation of the treaty was not concluded when on December 27, 1979, the Soviet Union invaded Afghanistan. SALT II was withdrawn from consideration, but SALT I continued to be observed. Washington gave its assurance regarding this in 1982 as long as the Soviet Union reciprocated, and this was reaffirmed in 1985 by President Ronald Reagan.

During the period of détente in the 1970s Moscow continued to modernize and strengthen its military capability, especially in nuclear arms, while the West seemingly relaxed, as that principle suggests. Significant quantitative and qualitative improvements were made in both strategic and intermediate-range nuclear forces (INF), the latter SS-20s deployed beginning in 1977. In response to this threatening move, NATO responded by proposing in December 1979 a "dual-track" approach—i.e., U.S.-Soviet negotiations to eliminate the Soviet INF missiles and, if this failed, to have the United States deploy Pershing II and ground-launched cruise missiles (GLCM). U.S.-Soviet INF negotiations began in February 1982 in Geneva, with the United States proposing the "zero option," the elimination of the missiles or parity at the lowest level. The Soviet representative rejected this, claiming that parity already existed. Consequently, Washington proceeded with the second NATO track, the deployments beginning in December 1983, whereupon the Soviet delegation walked out of the Geneva negotiations. The Soviet delegation also discontinued the strategic arms reduction talks (START), which were initiated in June 1982, also in Geneva.

With U.S. intermediate-range deployments in Europe and a new attitude in Moscow, U.S.-Soviet arms negotiations were resumed in Geneva March 12, 1985, one day after Gorbachev became general secretary, but with three, not two, delegations concerned with intermediate-range, strategic, and defense and space arms. During the negotiations the Soviet Union continued to develop alternative systems to INF and probably calculated that in mutual reductions, it would benefit from the U.S. missiles' removal from Europe.

Gorbachev's "new thinking" gave disarmament high priority. Not surprisingly, then, Soviet representatives negotiated more seriously in Geneva, especially on INF.

Gorbachev met with President Reagan at a summit in Geneva in November 1985 and in Reykjavik in October 1986, but these produced no arms agreement. Their third summit, in Washington, did, with the signing on December 7, 1987, of the INF Treaty. This treaty eliminates all U.S. and Soviet intermediate-range nuclear missiles with ranges from 500 to 5,500 km. (311 to 3,108 mi.); it also provides for "effective" verification measures by the United States. According to Washington, "The INF Treaty is in the security interests of the United States and our allies." For Moscow, it meant eliminating American INF from Europe and the beginning of further reductions.

Negotiations in the other two areas continued into 1990. The Soviet Union favors phased elimination of all nuclear weapons by the year 2000 and the withdrawal of troops and elimination of military bases overseas. For many years, too, Moscow and its allies have proposed the elimination of both NATO and WTO. Achievement of these objectives would give the Soviet Union a devastating military advantage. Its next immediate goal is a 50% reduction in strategic offensive nuclear arms.

Obviously East-West and U.S.-Soviet relations have improved since Gorbachev's leadership began in 1985. He met with outgoing President Reagan once more—at a Moscow summit, May 29–June 2, 1988, during which several agreements were signed, including pacts on joint verification experiments; peaceful uses of atomic energy; transportation, science and technology; maritime search and rescue; fishing; outer space; and cooperation and exchange. The latter were for the period 1989–91 and expanded the U.S.-USSR General Exchanges Agreement signed November 21, 1985, in Geneva by Secretary of State George Shultz and Foreign Minister Shevardnadze at the Reagan-Gorbachev summit for the period 1986–91. The 1985 agreement followed a hiatus of five years due to the Soviet invasion of Afghanistan.

During the first two years of George Bush's presidency, in 1989–90, U.S.-Soviet and East-West relations appeared more favorable than at any time since the 1917 October Revolution, despite the disarray in the Soviet empire and Gorbachev's manifold problems at home. Ministerial-level contacts continued following the departure of President Reagan, and the first summit between Bush and Gorbachev took place in early December 1989 on U.S. and Soviet ships and in Malta. Although no dramatic treaty was signed, they reached agreement on a summit in June 1990. The leaders decided to pursue negotiations leading to treaties on conventional troop reductions and START. President Bush pledged support of observer status to the Soviet Union at the General Agreement on Tariffs and Trade (GATT) talks, which Moscow requested in 1986, and to waive the Jackson-Vanik amendment, restricting trade until the Supreme Soviet legislated for free emigration. Bush voiced concern about Central America, and Gorbachev suggested negotiations on withdrawal of U.S. and Soviet navies from the Mediterranean Sea, the latter a contentious issue rejected by the United States.

Perhaps of greater importance than the agreements were the unrestrained and public expressions by the two leaders. Bush said: "With reform under way in the Soviet Union, we stand at the threshold of a brand-new era of U.S.-Soviet relations. It is within our grasp . . . to overcome the division of Europe and end the military confrontation there." Gorbachev declared that "The arms race, mistrust, psychological and ideological struggle, all those should be things of the past."

As pledged in Malta, the two leaders held a summit in Washington May 30–June 3, 1990. Among the joint statements issued was one on START, evidence of progress in strategic arms negotiations. An agreement was reached on limits in significant categories—1,600 nuclear delivery vehicles and 6,000 warheads—and on sublimits of various delivery systems. Moreover the total throwweight of deployed Soviet levels would be reduced by 50%. The two presidents pledged to complete negotiations on the START treaty by the end of 1990. Of continuing concern to U.S. defense officials, however, are the unfavorable record of Soviet treaty violations, the Backfire bomber, SS-18 (heavy ICBM) modernization and "agreement provisions that could affect U.S. alliance relationships."

Bush and Gorbachev also made a Joint Statement on Follow-on Strategic Negotiations committing the two sides to continue the Defense and Space Talks (DST) designed "to implement an appropriate relationship between strategic offense and defense." Also, at the summit the two presidents signed an agreement on chemical weapons (CW) calling for their destruction—to begin by the end of 1992 and to conclude by 2002. Neither country is to produce more CW. The Soviet Union, with admitted stocks at least 40,000 tons, has acquired the greatest chemical warfare capability in the world.

Also at the summit, the two presidents signed agreements on the following: commercial cooperation; a protocol to a treaty on nuclear testing; a protocol to a treaty on nuclear explosion for peaceful purposes; cooperation in the peaceful uses of atomic energy; and university student exchanges. Their other joint statements were on the CAF talks and the creation of a U.S.–Soviet park across the Bering Straits. Secretary Baker and Foreign Minister Shevardnadze signed agreements on the demarcation of oceans, ocean studies, civil aviation, maritime transportation and grain sales.

Iraq's invasion of Kuwait precipitated a one-day summit, held in Helsinki, Finland, September 9. The presidents issued a joint statement pledging to act individually and jointly to resolve the Persian Gulf crisis. The leaders differed on specific actions but appeared resolute on ending Iraq's aggression.

The Persian Gulf crisis was potentially a disruptive element in East-West relations—some Soviet military leaders criticized U.S. deployment of forces—but the Bush-Gorbachev agreement seemed to symbolize, in Gorbachev's word, "solidarity" in dealing with Iraq's aggression.

Moscow maintains trade relations with over 140 countries, with energy and raw materials the Soviet major exports. In 1986 a new coordinating body was formed—the State External Economic Commission—to oversee the restructuring of external trade. About 60% of Soviet trade is with CMEA countries.

The Soviet intention to continue integration of CMEA economies went awry during the 1989–90 revolutions in Eastern Europe. These countries are not only implementing *perestroika* toward market economy but are energetically seeking to establish close economic relations with West European countries and institutions. The question in 1990 was not CMEA integration but reform and possible disintegration. East Germany automatically ceased membership with German unification, October 3. Moscow preferred reform to dissolution and began to introduce new mechanisms, such as payments in dollars, rather than rubles, at world market prices. However, the attraction of full membership in the EC to East European countries is not diminishing. Complicating developments for the USSR are pressure from its republics for sovereignty, and its own unfavorable economic and foreign trade performance, including cutbacks of oil exports to its CMEA partners.

Trade relations with Western or capitalist countries have been uneven and modest, with West Germany, Finland, Italy, Japan, France, Great Britain and the United States the major trading partners; but in recent years, especially since *perestroika*, Moscow has sought to increase trade and commercial contacts with the West. The summit meetings have given the effort a boost. The U.S.-USSR Trade and Economic Council has coordinated commercial relations between the two countries. European firms have hundreds of contacts with the Soviet government and enterprises. Moscow has eased licensing, and in December 1988 the Council of Ministers liberalized the rules. Thus in 1989 a total of 191 joint ventures were operating worldwide, including 27 with CMEA countries, 16 with West German companies, 10 with U.S. companies and six with Japan.

In addition to observer status with GATT, mentioned by President Bush at Malta, the Soviet Union desired association with the World Bank, the IMF and various development banks. In 1990 Moscow applied for observer status in GATT but its long-term objective is to become a full member of GATT; to conclude a substantial agreement on trade and cooperation with the European Community; and to establish business contacts with EFTA, OECD, the IMF and the International Bank for Reconstruction and Development. An impediment to expansion of international financing has been the nonconvertibility of the ruble; prospects for its convertibility were not promising until 1990, when Moscow reversed its policy and decided for conversion. Gorbachev was not concentrating solely on the United States but proclaimed the policy of "our common European home." Even before he became general secretary, Gorbachev visited Great Britain in December 1984, when he was complimented by Prime Minister Margaret Thatcher. His first official visit after becoming general secretary was to France in October 1985, where he also made a favorable impression. He continued his visits abroad with a public-relations style not previously exhibited by any Soviet leader, with the result that he became in some countries, surveys revealed, the most popular world leader. However, his official visits to Western Europe ceased after Paris in 1985, but in 1989 he was unusually active. In 1989 Gorbachev visited Great Britain in April, West Germany in June, France in July, Finland in October and Italy in December. While in Italy he shattered a 70-year record of antagonism by meeting with Pope John Paul II, the first Soviet CP leader to do so, voicing a "need" for "spiritual values"; "envisioning Europe as a commonwealth of sovereign democratic states"; and, on communism, declaring, "We have abandoned the claim to have a monopoly on the truth." Among other things, Gorbachev pledged the restoration of the Roman Catholic Eastern Rite Church in the Soviet Union; that church is primarily in the Ukraine. In 1990 Moscow reestablished "permanent official relations," (short of full diplomatic ties) with the Vatican.

Western countries, including the United States, welcome *perestroika* and *glasnost*, but some experts and officials are concerned about assisting *perestroika* to a degree that may be threatening to the national interest of Western countries.

Japan is not entirely a "Western" country from Moscow's perspective. History reminds them of a military defeat in 1904–5 and that Japan was a military power during World War II and today is an economic giant with a military potential that is perceived to be a security threat to the Soviet Union. Their relations since the war have been strained, partly because a peace treaty has not been signed, and because of former Japanese islands under Soviet control that Japan considers to be Japanese "northern territories." Moscow maintains that it has a right to the islands by virtue of the 1945 Yalta Agreement, the Potsdam Declaration and the September 1951 peace conference in San Francisco. The two countries conducted negotiations in 1956 with a joint declaration providing for restoration of diplomatic relations, which, however, have not materialized. Moscow protested that the 1960 U.S.–Japanese treaty, which returned full sovereignty to Japan in defense matters, "violated the 1956 declaration." For Gorbachev's reforms Japan has the potential for contributing significantly to Soviet economic development. To improve relations, Gorbachev sent to Tokyo in November 1989, a Supreme Soviet delegation led by Politburo member Aleksandr Yakovlev. No agreement was signed, but the discussions were considered in positive terms. Soviet improvement of relations in Asia-Pacific includes greater cooperation with the Association of Southeast Asian Nations (ASEAN) as well as with individual countries and regional economic institutions. Despite Moscow's announcement to reduce its military forces east of the Urals by 40% by January 1991 and its efforts to resolve the Cambodian conflict, some countries—particularly Japan and South Korea—are concerned about Soviet naval and air forces near them.

Although a world revolution had not materialized after World War I, revolutions did expand Communist control after World War II, first in Eastern Europe then in October 1949 in China. The Kremlin hailed these as victories for international communism. A few months later, on February 14, 1950, the two regimes concluded a 30-year friendship and alliance treaty. However, by the 1950s ideological, tactical and personality differences resulted in the historic Sino-Soviet split. In addi-

tion to their ideological quarrels, Moscow and Beijing competed for leadership in the international Communist movement. Beijing set off a nuclear explosion in 1964, and the two antagonists increased their military forces along their common border, resulting in numerous incidents. Their relations were exacerbated when Beijing improved its relations with Western countries, including Japan, ushered in by the visit of President Nixon to China in 1972. China denounced Moscow's invasion of Afghanistan in 1979, and its support of Vietnam's invasion of Cambodia and operations in Laos were further impediments. However, attempts for a rapprochement beginning in 1982 bore fruit, especially when Gorbachev assumed power in the Soviet Union.

The general secretary embarked upon improvement of relations with China, beginning with a visit of Soviet deputy foreign minister Mikhail Kapitsa in December 1985. Gorbachev signaled flexibility on their border dispute, on which talks were resumed, after nine years, in February 1987. A five-year trade agreement was signed, and their scientific-technical-cultural program was expanded. East European leaders were encouraged to visit Beijing, and Soviet high-level contacts increased. These were crowned by Gorbachev's summit visit to Beijing in May 1989 during demonstrations on Tiananmen Square. Sino-Soviet bilateral relations continued, including Soviet sale of military aircraft, despite Beijing's disapproval of Soviet reforms.

The Soviet Union invaded Afghanistan on December 27, 1979, to maintain a Communist government in danger of collapse. It established a loyal regime and calculated a rapid victory. Instead, the Afghan resistance fighters, *mujahidin*, resisted heroically, and Moscow increased its armed forces to about 115,000. The invasion drew universal criticism, including condemnation by the United Nations. After over nine years the Soviet Union in February 1989 ended the fighting and withdrew its military forces from Afghanistan. The Gorbachev leadership places the blame on the Brezhnev era and pledges that an Afghanistan and a Czechoslovakia will not be repeated. In addition to Soviet military misfortunes and the drain on the Soviet economy, Gorbachev recognized that his "new thinking" policy for improved East-West and other relations would be hindered by continued operations in Afghanistan. Before its withdrawal Moscow and Kabul signed an economic agreement, and the Kremlin continues to support the Communist regime in Kabul politically and with large military supplies, thus perpetuating the civil war.

Vietnam is an important constituency for the Soviet Union, bordering strategically on China and providing air and naval facilities. The former U.S. facility at Cam Ranh Bay has been modernized into the largest Soviet naval base abroad. Reciprocally Moscow extends enormous financial and military assistance to Vietnam, a burden it can ill afford.

Another important but financially the most burdensome client state is Cuba, a country the Soviet Union has been subsidizing for decades. As mentioned previously, in the early 1960s Moscow secretly deployed offensive intermediate-range nuclear missiles that led to the Cuban missile crisis and eventual Soviet withdrawal. The annual outlay had been estimated at over $10 billion several years ago; in 1988 it was approximately $1.5 billion for military assistance and $4.0 billion in economic aid. Current (1990) Soviet economic assistance is at the $5 billion level, a continuing drain on the Soviet budget, but may be reduced. Moscow's policy has been to extend its influence throughout Latin America overtly and covertly. It has supported coups, and the Castro regime has played a major role in aiding insurgencies throughout the region, especially in Central America. Havana had been supplying military equipment to Nicaragua, some of which, in turn, was earmarked for guerrillas in El Salvador. Moscow continued to extend commercial aid to the democratic government in Nicaragua but at lower levels. In addition, Cuba has participated militarily in African campaigns. Gorbachev visited Havana in April 1989 in an unsuccessful attempt to impress on Castro the need for economic reforms. In 1990 Moscow informed Castro that their trade will involve Cuban payments in hard currency at world market prices.

For years the Soviet Union has supported insurgencies in Africa as well. The Constitution of 1977 supports "national liberation and social progress." Accordingly, Moscow annually committed huge outlays in economic and especially military assistance. During the years 1954–84 Soviet economic aid totaled $14 billion in economic aid and $75 billion in military aid. By early 1980s Moscow became the largest supplier of arms transfers to the Third World, totaling $55 billion during 1980–85. In 1990 Soviet military aid was over $8 billion yearly, a level expected to be maintained into the 1990s despite Moscow's economic crisis. In addition, many thousands of advisers, including military, have been assisting in economic development and military training. Moreover, the Soviet Union has underwritten study and training programs in the Soviet Union for Third World students; they numbered over 100,000 in 1989–90. The objective is to cultivate potential future leaders. WTO members added substantially to this amount. Supported insurgencies included those in South Africa, Mozambique, Angola, Nicaragua and Ethiopia. Although Soviet-aided insurgencies continued under Gorbachev, there has been quantitative retrenchment in African countries. It was instrumental in removing Cuban troops from Angola and has encouraged the latter and Ethiopa to resolve their civil wars. However, Moscow continues to aid the Marxist-Leninist regimes in sub-Saharan Africa.

For the Soviet Union the Middle East is of importance strategically, ideologically, politically and economically, with oil not the least of the reasons. Moscow has exploited the Arab-Israeli conflict and has assisted Arab insurgents. Despite aid to Egypt the Soviets were expelled from that country in 1972 for interfering in its internal affairs. Moscow continues to assist insurgencies as well as governments in power, especially in Syria and Iraq. Brezhnev proposed the establishment of an independent Palestinian state, to which Israel and other countries object because it does not conform to U.N. Resolution 242. Soviet massive military supplies to Libya support international terrorist activities, which have been denounced throughout the world. The Gorbachev regime has become more involved in the Middle East diplomatically, including peace settlements. Its foreign minister visited the area in February 1989 to improve relations with Israel, the PLO and Iran. He proposed U.S.-Soviet efforts to solve disputes. Bush and Gorbachev expressed support for an agreement in Lebanon.

The Soviet Union encouraged a U.N. approach to Iraq's August 2, 1990, invasion of Kuwait. Moscow had invested heavily in economic and military assistance to Iraq and its policy of accepting U.N. decisions and suspending arms deliveries to Iraq received plaudits from the United States and other countries. At the time of the invasion Moscow had thousands of personnel in Iraq, including military advisers with families, and hundreds in Kuwait; also, 178 Iraqi military trainees were in the Soviet Union. While the bulk of Soviet citizens were evacuated during the first weeks following the invasion, the advisers were to remain until the expiration of their contracts. This drew a rebuke from the U.S. State Department as "inappropriate." While complying with U.N.'s arms embargo and naval blockade against Iraq, Moscow declined to employ its own military forces in the trade embargo. Instead, Soviet leaders undertook a mediator's role. President Bush and President Gorbachev, meeting September 9, 1990, in Helsinki, issued a communique signifying a cooperative approach to end Iraq's aggression.

The Soviet Union has cultivated friendly relations with India since the latter's independence. In addition to its ideological, political and economic interest in India, Moscow shares with New Delhi common perceptions of China. Accordingly, the Soviet Union has rendered economic and military assistance and supported India in the Kashmir dispute. In 1971 the countries concluded a 20-year treaty of peace, friendship and cooperation. In reciprocating, India did not condemn the Soviet invasion of Afghanistan, but instead called for an end to U.S. support for the resistance fighters. Gorbachev visited Delhi in November 1988 and signed, with Prime Minister Gandhi, a wide-ranging statement. The leaders characterized the 1971 treaty as an "outstanding milestone" in their relations. The two leaders pledged to increase their trade relations and to formulate a long-term program for economic, trade, scientific and technical cooperation until the year 2000.

Soviet withdrawal from Afghanistan has had a salutary effect on its relations with Pakistan, the country that received Afghan refugees and that was the link for foreign aid to the resistance fighters.

PARLIAMENT

The parliament was not a time-honored institution in Czarist Russia, nor has it been significant under Communist rule, at least not until 1989. The general unrest in Russia forced Czar Nicholas II to establish a legislature (Duma). Elections were held, and a constitutional monarchy appeared promising. However, political differences and legislative-executive clashes led to the dissolution of the first Duma. The second was no improvement, and the succeeding Dumas were reduced to compliant bodies of no political consequence. Following the overthrow of the Czar in March 1917, however, the Duma organized a Provisional Government, but the Bolsheviks (Communists) seized power on November 7, 1917. The Communists had earlier revived a 1905 group, the Soviet of Workers' Deputies. The 1917 slogan "All power to the soviets" was their battle cry for placing control into the hands of soviets (councils), from the highest state level to the lowest. Separation of power was rejected by Communist ideologues.

Also on November 7 elections were held for a Constituent Assembly, with the Bolsheviks receiving only 24% of the vote. In January 1919 they abolished the Constituent Assembly. Following the Communist coup the Second Congress of Soviets created the Council of People's Commissars, with Lenin as chairman. Theoretically the Congress and, between sessions, its Executive Committee (see Constitution & Government section) were the highest state authorities, but henceforth real political power was to be exercised by the Communist Party through the Council of People's Commissars and lower councils (soviets) throughout the country. The 1917 promise of representative soviets did not materialize. Consequently, legislation became generally the province of the Council rather than of the Supreme Soviet, formally the legislative body. (This development prior to 1977 was covered in the Constitution & Government section.)

Under the Constitution of 1977, the highest body of state authority was the bicameral Supreme Soviet—the Soviet of the Union and the Soviet of Nationalities. Each had 750 deputies, and both were equal. Delegates to the Soviet of the Union were elected by constituencies with equal populations, while those to the Soviet of Nationalities were elected to reflect national areas: 32 deputies from each Union republic, 11 from each autonomous republic, five from each autonomous region and one from each autonomous area. Each chamber elected a chairman and four vice chairmen. When in joint session, the chairmen alternate as presiding officers. Legislation was adopted by a majority of the total deputies in each chamber.

The Supreme Soviet was obliged to meet at least twice yearly, usually for short periods of time (two to three days), and special sessions might be called by the Presidium, by a Union republic or by at least one-third of the deputies of a chamber. Each chamber had standing commissions, and the Supreme Soviet its own commissions. In session for short periods, the chambers were ill prepared to conduct legislative matters except to confirm legality on past decrees and on drafts presented currently. The right to initiate legislation was assigned to the Supreme Soviet, to each chamber, the Presidium of the Supreme Soviet, the Council of Ministers, the Union republics, the commissions of the Supreme Soviet, standing commissions of each chamber, deputies of the Supreme Soviet, the Supreme Court and the procurator-general. Each chamber had 16 commissions, each with 35 deputies, except the Planning and Budget commissions, which had 45. The preponderance of legislative preparation was accomplished by the full-time staffs of the Council of Ministers, individual ministries and the Presidium of the Supreme Soviet in coordination with the Secretariat of the Communist Party's Central Committee.

A Presidium was elected by the Supreme Soviet from its deputies to conduct legislative activities between sessions. It consisted of a chairman, first vice chairman, 15 vice chairmen (one from each Union republic), a secretary and 21 members.

Articles 121–23 of the Constitution enumerated the Presidium's responsibilities, including the following: to coordinate the work of the standing commissions; ensure observance of the Constitution of the USSR; interpret laws; ratify treaties; revoke resolutions and ordinances of the Council of Ministers of the USSR and of Union republics; issue amnesties and grant pardons; appoint and receive diplomats; form the Council of Defense and confirm its appointments; appoint and dismiss the command of the armed forces; proclaim martial law; order mobilization; and proclaim a state of war. Also, the Presidium might amend laws; form and abolish ministries and committees; and appoint and dismiss ministers, the latter two on recommendation of the Council of Ministers and its chairman, respectively. Finally, the Presidium could promulgate decrees that were confirmed as laws at the next session of the Supreme Soviet.

These formal powers were recognized as normally associated with a president as head of state and, indeed, the Presidium was a kind of collective presidency represented by its chairman at official functions. The array of powers was deceptively impressive, but the history of the Presidium revealed an institution devoid of real influence, as was its parent organization, the Supreme Soviet. The greater authority was the Council of Ministers, and the most powerful political force the Communist Party, whose policies and decisions were given official blessing by the Supreme Soviet.

The era of impotence of the Supreme Soviet and the Presidium appeared ended in 1988 as a result of Gorbachev's policies of *glasnost* and *perestroika*. However, because the impetus for political change was initiated by the general secretary of the Communist Party and promoted by the party, there was little scope for independent initiatives.

Gorbachev pursued political reforms not only through the party, where conservative opposition existed, but also through the governmental structure, especially the legislature. At the 19th Communist Party Conference, in June–July 1988, his proposals for reform were approved almost unaltered. These included a change in the parliamentary structure and a strengthened presidency, both of which necessitated constitutional amendments. The Conference recommended an entirely new legislature: the Congress of People's Deputies.

A draft of the constitutional changes was published in the fall for traditional discussion which, unlike previously, generated concerns of non-Russian nationalities, resulting in adjustments in the draft.

In December 1988 the Supreme Soviet adopted the Law of the USSR on Changes and Amendments to the Constitution of the USSR, and the Law of the USSR on the Election of People's Deputies of the USSR. The

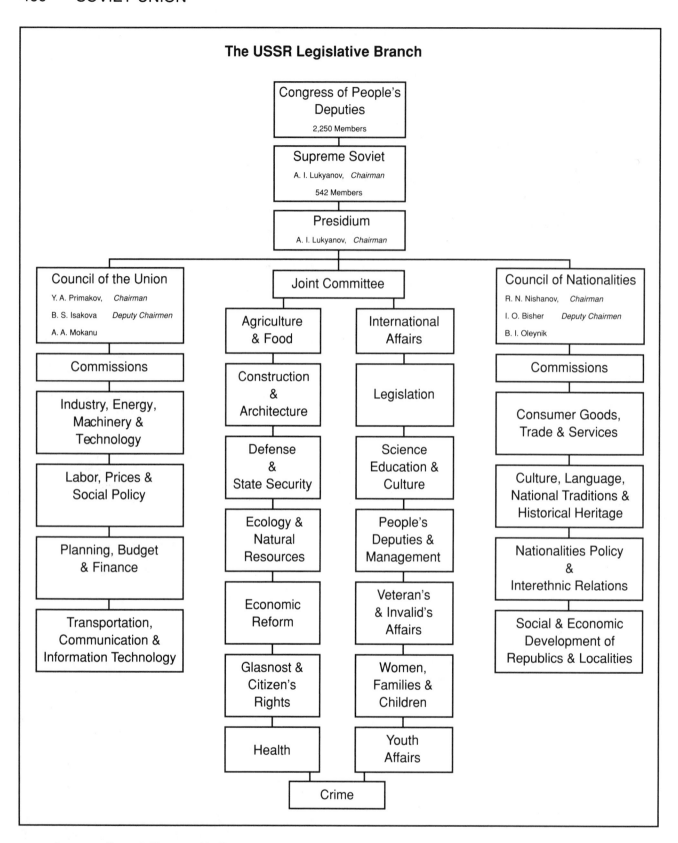

The USSR Legislative Branch

Congress of People's
Deputies

2,250 Members

Supreme Soviet

A. I. Lukyanov, *Chairman*

542 Members

Presidium

A. I. Lukyanov, *Chairman*

Council of the Union

Y. A. Primakov, *Chairman*

B. S. Isakova *Deputy Chairmen*

A. A. Mokanu

Commissions

Industry, Energy,
Machinery &
Technology

Labor, Prices &
Social Policy

Planning, Budget
& Finance

Transportation,
Communication &
Information Technology

Joint Committee

Agriculture
& Food

Construction
&
Architecture

Defense
&
State Security

Ecology &
Natural
Resources

Economic
Reform

Glasnost &
Citizen's
Rights

Health

International
Affairs

Legislation

Science
Education &
Culture

People's
Deputies &
Management

Veteran's
& Invalid's
Affairs

Women,
Families &
Children

Youth
Affairs

Crime

Council of Nationalities

R. N. Nishanov, *Chairman*

I. O. Bisher *Deputy Chairmen*

B. I. Oleynik

Commissions

Consumer Goods,
Trade & Services

Culture, Language,
National Traditions &
Historical Heritage

Nationalities Policy
&
Interethnic Relations

Social & Economic
Development of
Republics & Localities

amendments affected Chapter 12 (System and Principles), Chapter 13 (Electoral System) and Chapter 15 (Congress of People's Deputies and the Supreme Soviet) of the Constitution of 1977. The law did not change the constitutional status of the Soviets of People's Deputies—i.e., "a single system of representative bodies of state authority"—or the term of the deputies, five years. The Congress of People's Deputies elects the Supreme Soviet and its chairman while the local Soviets elect their own chairmen and form their own presidiums.

The Soviets of People's Deputies organize commissions and form executive-administrative bodies whose officials are limited to two consecutive terms. Control bodies are to observe compliance of laws and to combat breaches of discipline, local tendencies, mismanagement, wastefulness and bureaucracy. The Soviets of People's Deputies direct all sectors of state, economic, and social and cultural development directly or through organizations formed by them, and make, implement and verify decisions. The Soviets are to function on the basis of collective, free and constructive discussion and decision-making, of *glasnost*, and reporting by their executive-administrative bodies. The soviets and the organs established are obliged to consider public opinion and systematically inform the citizens.

The amended electoral system (Chapter 13) contains important provisions. Rather than one Communist Party-approved candidate for each position, Article 95 provides for deputies to be elected "in one-candidate and multi-candidate" electoral districts on the basis of universal, equal and direct suffrage by secret ballot. One-third of the deputies are elected from public organizations (Communist Party, Communist Youth League, trade unions, cooperative organizations of women, war veterans, retirees, etc.). The voting age is 18 and for candidates 21. One cannot be simultaneously elected to more than two Soviets, as in the Constitution of 1977. However, members of the All-Union Council of Ministers and those of the Union and autonomous republics, executive committees of the local soviets (except the chairmen) and other designated officials cannot be elected deputies to the soviet that appoints or elects them. An especially significant change, contained in Article 100, concerns the number of candidates. Heretofore the Communist Party engineered the selection of one candidate for each position. Now the "ballots can carry the names of any number of candidates." However, the new law, as the previous one, specifies organizations, cited above, given the right to nominate candidates. While voting still is managed by the familiar election commissions, a new element was added: "meetings of voters at their residence." Also an innovation is the provision guaranteeing to citizens, work collectives and public organizations "free and all-round discussion of the political, professional and personal qualities of candidates" and "the right to campaign for or against a candidate at meetings, in the press, on television and on radio."

In pursuit of Gorbachev's claim of marching toward "democracy," nationwide elections were held March 26, 1989, under the new electoral law for the 2,250 members of the new CPD. These were the first multicandidate elections since November 1917, but not all were contested. Candidates were uncontested in 384 cases, two competed in 953, four in 27 and at least six in 14 others. Voters crossed out names of all except one candidate. The elections were highly touted by the regime and received widespread attention. Although they were an improvement over the single-candidate ballot, the electoral system still is substantially short of "free elections." Most important, perhaps, is the existence of only one party—the Communist Party—and public organizations it dominates. Consequently, the electorate had no choice of parties, and the electoral law, as noted

above, provides for one-third of the deputies to be nominated by public organizations. The electoral commissions screened nominees to ferret out "undesirables," and there were widespread reports of irregularities.

In Leningrad the voters rejected the Communist Party leader and five other high officials as single candidates, a defeat of major proportions for the regime. In the Baltic Republics multicandidate ballots were common, and nominees represented not only the Communist Party but various nonparty organizations, which registered positive results. Overall, the elections created public excitement and afforded an opportunity for public expression. Communist Party candidates polled higher in 1989 (87.6%) than in 1984, when candidacy was determined virtually entirely by the party; workers dropped (from 32.5% to 18.6%), as did women (32.8% to 17.1%). Nearly two-thirds of the winning deputies were from the managerial sector (all levels).

According to Article 108 of Chapter 15 of the amended Constitution, the highest organ of state authority is the Congress of People's Deputies of the USSR, which can "consider and resolve any issue within the jurisdiction of the USSR." The Congress was given the following "exclusive prerogatives" (pertaining to the USSR):

- adopt and amend the Constitution
- decide on questions of national and state structure
- determine state borders and endorse border changes between republics
- establish guidelines for domestic and foreign policies
- approve long-term state plans and important state programs for economic and social development
- elect the Supreme Soviet, the chairman of the Supreme Soviet and the first vice chairman of the Supreme Soviet
- endorse the chairmen of the Council of Ministers, the People's Control Committee, the Supreme Court, the procurator-general and the chief state arbitrator
- elect the Constitutional Oversight Committee
- repeal laws passed by the Supreme Soviet
- decide on nationwide referendums

Article 109 provides for a 2,250-member Congress, elected as follows:

- 750 deputies from territorial electoral districts with equal numbers of voters
- 750 deputies from national-territorial electoral districts
  32 from each Union republic
  11 from each autonomous republic
  five from each autonomous region
  one from each autonomous area
- 750 deputies from all-Union public organizations, their representation established by law

The Congress assembled in May 1989 amid great interest. Its televised deliberations created such massive viewing that subsequent Supreme Soviet sessions were not televised. As expected, the Congress elected Gorbachev as chairman of the Presidium of the Supreme Soviet and, according to its constitutional mandate, that parliamentary body as well. The deputies exercised their new role of actively debating issues, such as economic reform. Their grievances, reflecting the public's, quickly surfaced, as they leveled charges against even the KGB. Among the most emotional was the many-faceted nationality question, with criticism of centrist Moscow. Physicist and human rights activist Andrei Sakharov was himself attacked for his criticism of Soviet involvement in Afghanistan.

In addition to the intense interest in the new Congress, there was public expectation of dramatic accomplishment beyond the debates. In this the Congress did not meet the public's hopes. However, it was the first session, and the role of the Congress was evolving.

Article 111 designates the Supreme Soviet as the "permanent legislative, administrative and control organ of state authority." The Supreme Soviet, with 542 deputies, is elected by the Congress from among its members by secret ballot and is responsible to it. It consists of two chambers; the Soviet of the Union and the Soviet of Nationalities, both having an equal number of deputies (271) and equal rights. The chambers are elected by the Congress. The Soviet of the Union is composed of deputies representing territorial electoral districts and public organizations. The Soviet of Nationalities consists of deputies representing national-territorial electoral districts and public organizations, as follows:

- 11 from each Union republic
- four from each autonomous republic
- two from each autonomous region
- one from each autonomous area

Initially the Congress annually reelected one-fifth of the deputies to the Soviet of the Union and the Soviet of Nationalities. Because the turnover was considered too rapid to retain experienced legislators, an amendment to the Constitution in December 1989 provided for Congress to replace "up to" one-fifth of the Supreme Soviet annually. Each chamber elects a chairman and two deputy chairmen, with the chairmen presiding over their respective bodies. The presiding officer at joint sessions is the chairman of the Supreme Soviet or his first deputy, or alternately the chairmen of the two chambers.

The Constitution provides for an annual session of the Supreme Soviet, convened by its Presidium for spring and fall sessions, each lasting three to four months. The Presidium may convene special sessions on its own initiative, if proposed by the chairman of the Supreme Soviet or of a Union republic, or if one-third of the deputies of a chamber request it.

Article 113 enumerates the extensive powers of the Supreme Soviet:

- establish the date for elections of deputies and approve the Central Electoral Commission
- appoint the chairman of the Council of Ministers, approve his government or make changes in it and establish or abolish ministries and state committees

- form the Defense Council, confirm its composition and appoint and dismiss the high command of the armed forces
- elect the Committee of Public Inspection and the Supreme Court, appoint the procurator-general and the chief state arbitrator and approve the composition of the Board of the Prosecutor's Office and the Board of State Arbitration
- conduct regular hearings of organs and officials
- ensure uniformity and fundamentals (also for Union republics) of legislation
- implement legislation in economic, cultural, social and other spheres of society, and in the exercise of human rights, freedoms and duties
- interpret laws
- establish principles of organization of Union republics and lower organs and determine fundamentals of the legal status of public organizations
- submit and state plans and economic and social programs for ratification by the Congress of People's Deputies and approve state plans for economic and social development and the state budget, overseeing their fulfillment
- ratify and abrogate treaties
- oversee granting of loans and foreign economic and other aid, conclude agreements on state loans and credits from foreign sources
- determine major measures in defense, ensure state security, order mobilization and declare a state of war
- decide on deploying armed forces to meet treaty obligations
- establish military and diplomatic ranks, orders, medals and honorific titles
- proclaim amnesties
- revoke decrees and decisions of the Supreme Soviet Presidium, directives of the chairman of the Supreme Soviet and decisions and directives of the Council of Ministers
- repeal decisions and directives of the Councils of Ministers of Union republics if they contravene the USSR Constitution
- decide all other questions except those within the exclusive competence of the Congress of People's Deputies

The Supreme Soviet can adopt laws and make decisions that do not contradict laws and other acts adopted by the Congress of People's Deputies.

The jurisdiction of the Soviet of the Union and the Soviet of Nationalities can be gleaned from the standing commissions of the two chambers. For example, matters that fall within the province of the Soviet of the Union include social and economic development; the general development of state; the rights, freedoms and duties of citizens; foreign affairs; defense; and state security. Those of the Soviet of Nationalities involve ethnic questions, including equality of nationalities, national and ethnic groups and improvement of interethnic relations.

The Presidium, elected by and accountable to the Supreme Soviet, ensures the organization of the functioning of the Congress of People's Deputies as well as the Supreme Soviet and exercises powers assigned to it by the Constitution and laws of the USSR. The Presidium is composed of the chairman and first vice chairman of the Supreme Soviet, 15 vice chairmen (the chairmen of the Supreme Soviet of the Union Republics), chairmen of the Soviet of the Union and the Soviet of Nationalities, the chairman of the Committee of Public Inspection and the chairmen of the standing commissions of the chambers and committees of the Supreme Soviet. The Presidium is headed by the chairman of the Supreme Soviet.

The Constitution (Article 119) gives the Presidium the following responsibilities:

- convene sessions of the Supreme Soviet
- prepare for sitting of the Congress of People's Deputies and the Supreme Soviet
- coordinate activities of standing commissions of the Chambers and committees of the Supreme Soviet
- assist deputies in the exercise of their powers
- ensure conformity of the constitutions of Union republics with the Constitution of the USSR
- organize the holding of nationwide referendums, and discussions of draft laws and other important state matters
- confer the highest military and diplomatic ranks and other special titles
- award orders and medals and confer honorific titles
- grant citizenship of the USSR, decide on renunciation or deprivation of USSR citizenship and grant asylum
- grant pardons
- appoint and recall USSR diplomats and receive and expel foreign diplomats
- between sessions of the Supreme Soviet, order mobilization, declare a state of war if the USSR is attacked or to meet treaty obligations
- in defense of the USSR and security of its citizens, proclaim martial law or a state of emergency statewide or in localities, the latter considered with the Presidium of the relevant Union republic, and introduce "special forms of government"
- publish laws and other acts approved by the Congress of People's Deputies, the Supreme Soviet, its chambers, the Presidium and the chairman of the Supreme Soviet in the languages of the Union republics

According to Article 120, the chairman of the Supreme Soviet is "the highest-ranking official in the Soviet state and represents the USSR internally and in international relations." The chairman is elected by the Congress of People's Deputies from among the deputies by secret ballot for a five-year term and not more than two consecutive terms. He may be recalled at any time by a secret vote of the Congress of People's Deputies. The chairman is responsible to the Congress of People's Deputies and to the Supreme Soviet.

The powers of the chairman (or the president) of the Supreme Soviet have been greatly strengthened by the amended Constitution. He was, in a sense, an innovation, a departure from the principle of collective presidency. Among other things, the chairman was head of the powerful Defense Council and, externally, negotiated and signs international treaties. At its first session, the new Congress elected Mikhail Gorbachev as the chairman of the Presidium of the Supreme Soviet. Article 120 was nullified with the addition of Chapter 15(1) to the Constitution establishing the post of the President of the USSR (see Constitution and Government above).

The Constitution provides for committees of the Supreme Soviet and standing commissions of the two chambers. The members are elected from among the Supreme Soviet and other deputies. The committees and commissions prepare legislation and work on other relevant matters to be considered by the Supreme Soviet, assist in implementing the laws and resolutions by the Congress of People's Deputies and the Supreme Soviet and observe the application of laws by various organs. As with the Supreme Soviet, one-fifth of the standing commissions of the chambers are replaced annually. Other commissions may be established as necessary. Over 800 deputies were elected to committees and standing commissions in 1989.

The Supreme Soviet has 15 committees: International Affairs; Defense and State Security; Legislation, Legality, and Law and Order; Affairs of Soviets of People's Deputies; Development of Government and Self-Government; Economic Reform; Agrarian Matters and Foodstuffs; Construction and Architecture; Science, Public Education, Culture and Upbringing; Public Health; Affairs of Women, Family, Mother and Child Protection; Affairs of Veterans and the Disabled; Youth Affairs; Ecology and Rational Utilization of Natural Resources; and *Glasnost*, Citizens' Rights and Petitions.

The chambers of the Supreme Soviet form eight standing commissions: The Soviet of the Union has the following: Commission for Planning, Budget and Finance; Development of Industry, Power Engineering, Equipment and Technology; Transportation, Communications and Information Science; and Labor, Prices and Social Policy. The Soviet of Nationalities organized the following: Nationalities Policy and Interethnic Relations; Social and Economic Development of the Union and Autonomous Republics, Autonomous Regions and Autonomous Areas; Consumer Goods, Trade, Municipal and Other Services; and Development of Culture and Language, Ethnic and International Traditions and the Protection of Historical Heritage. At the summer 1989 session the Soviet of Nationalities established commissions on the Meskhetian Turks, the Crimean Tatars and the Volga Germans.

Deputies of Congress who were not elected to the Supreme Soviet as well as those who were elected may be elected to the standing commissions and committees; deputies not elected are nevertheless eligible to participate in the deliberations, including voting, of these bodies.

If the first session of the Supreme Soviet is any indication, the standing commissions and committees may not only be invested with potential powers but also may well exercise those important responsibilities. They performed in a manner not previously observed, especially preparing for the Supreme Soviet information on candidates for the Council of Ministers, the Supreme Court, the People's Control Committee, the procurator-general's staff and the Board of State Arbitration. Confirmation hearings were held, with the candidates frequently examined critically. Six of the 71 ministerial candidates submitted by the prime minister were rejected by the committees, and one withdrew during the hearings; two others were turned down by the Supreme Soviet.

A totally new political body is the USSR Committee for Constitutional Compliance. Elected by the Congress of People's Deputies for a term of 10 years, this committee is composed of experts in politics and law, with a chairman, a vice chairman and 21 members, including representatives from each Union republic. Members of the committee cannot, concurrently, serve on organs whose acts are subject to review by this committee. Officially the members are considered independent, and answerable only to the Constitution of the USSR. The committee's jurisdiction extends to the following: It determines for the Congress conformity of draft laws with the Constitution of the USSR; and it decides on the constitutionality of acts by the Supreme Soviet and the two chambers, and on drafts of their acts. In addition, the committee monitors conformity of the constitutions and laws of the Union republics and the resolutions and ordinances of the USSR Council of Ministers and of the Councils of Ministers of the Union republics with the Constitution and laws of the USSR. Likewise, the committee can decide on the constitutionality of acts of state agencies and public organizations. The committee can propose to the Congress, the Supreme Soviet and the Council of Ministers revocation of acts deemed unconstitutional.

Seemingly in recognition of the value of public relations, and in line with *glasnost*, the Supreme Soviet established a Secretariat with functions not unlike those long common in Western countries. Organized into 10 sections, a press center and a financial and administrative office, the Secretariat's objective is to ensure the successful functioning of the Congress, the Supreme Soviet, the chambers and their bodies. During sessions of the Congress and the Supreme Soviet the Secretariat prepares daily bulletins of speakers' remarks. At the conclusion of sessions, complete verbatim reports are to be published. Acts of various organs and information on their activities are published in the Bulletin of Congress of People's Deputies of the USSR and the Supreme Soviet of the USSR, issued in languages of all Union republics.

The first session of the Supreme Soviet ended after 40 days. Gorbachev, its chairman, declared that the parliament was "an authoritative link in our self-renewing political system." He said a "sound foundation" was established for a "socialist law-governing state" and that parliamentarianism now combined with socialism. Henceforth, the chairman stated, decisions would be made by those elected by the people and not by a "nar-

row circle," and they would be reached publicly. Gorbachev claimed the Supreme Soviet was a success. It approved a government after critical questioning and some rejections, and adopted important legislation, including "presumption of innocence," amelioration of "anti-Soviet propaganda," combating crime, greater economic independence for the Baltic republics and other measures.

Soviet parliamentary experience has progressed from a behavior of total acceptance and unanimity to lively, even acrimonious debates, critical examination of ministerial nominations, and meaningful resolutions, laws and amendments to the Constitution. Considering the inexperience of the new deputies and decades of CP monopoly in decision making, the CPD and the Supreme Soviet have achieved positive—to some, remarkable—results. Constitutional amendments included establishing the presidency, the Committee on Constitutional Compliance, replacing the CP's leading position with a multiparty system, and ownership of private property. Laws were passed on leasing of state enterprises; land reform; emigration rights; freedom of the press, assembly, and religion; and on economy in the Baltic republics. The CPD heard reports on the Nazi-Soviet Pact (1939), privileges for high officials, the Soviet invasion of Afghanistan (1979) and on use of force to suppress an uprising in Georgia (April 1989). The Congress established parliamentary rules for itself and the Supreme Soviet, and its committee system was strengthened. Taking a cue from the U.S. Congress and other Western democracies, electronic voting was installed.

While lacking parliamentary parties, numerous informal opposition groups emerged, along nationality and special interest lines. The most publicized and best-known abroad is the Interregional Group, established in June 1989 with three cochairmen, including Boris Yeltsin. It is a loose, heterogeneous body with perhaps as many as 400 adherents who advocate, among others, implementation of *perestroika*, decentralization of government, direct election of the Chairman of the Supreme Soviet and the right to own property. Leaders of the Interregional Group have considered becoming a political party but this had not developed through September 1990. There were detractors even within the Group who caused abuses such as the use of undue pressure, insufficient freedom to express views, too much complaining and too few legislative initiatives. However, the Group has had an impact on legislation, including Article 6, and on government policies generally. Other groups include: Rossiya, which propagates Russian nationalism; Baltic, advocating with its 50 deputies sovereignty for their republics; and Workers' Agrarian, Greens, Women's, Youth, and Veterans.

The parliament's performance has revealed serious weaknesses. While generally hailed as democratically elected in multicandidate voting, one-third of the deputies were nominated by organizations most of which were controlled by the CP. Entrenched electoral commissions screened candidates, rejecting many on spurious grounds. The Supreme Soviet is not elected by the public but by Congress. There are complaints of too much discussion, debate and argument and insufficient attention to urgent matters in need of legislation, especially to meet the economic crisis. Cited as evidence are the relatively few laws passed by the Supreme Soviet, whose seeming inability to proceed resolutely led Gorbachev to seek—and win—emergency powers from the Supreme Soviet, which, in effect, has abrogated its responsibilities. The legislature has lacked quorums due to persistent absenteeism; two-thirds hold other full-time employment and some take unreasonable advantage of perquisites. The Presidium is said to have inordinate power, as does the Council of Ministers, at the expense of the full legislature. Then there is the Communist Party, which, despite internal differences, has an organization and operates on the principle of "democratic centralism." The public, while favoring democracy and political pluralism, continues to be wary of party politics and appears disenchanted with the parliament's argumentative behavior and lagging legislative action.

POLITICAL PARTIES

According to Article 6 of the USSR Constitution of 1977:

> The leading and guiding force of Soviet society and the nucleus of its political system, of all state organizations and public is the Communist Party of the Soviet Union.
>
> The Communist Party, armed with Marxism-Leninism, determines the general perspectives of the development of society and the course of domestic and foreign policy of the USSR, directs the great constructive work of the Soviet people and imparts a planned systematic and theoretically substantiated character to their struggle for the victory of communism.

Other political parties were neither mentioned nor allowed to exist. Unitl 1990 the Communist Party's monopoly of power in the USSR was complete in its totality of control over the government—legislative, executive-administrative and judicial branches—as well as the country's socioeconomic system, culture, education, security, defense and every other sector of society, down to the lowest level of existence. The Communist Party's Politburo makes policies, and the vast party and government bureaucracies implement them.

Social movements in czarist Russia emerged in the second half of the 19th century, followed by formation of political parties toward the end of the century. Liberalism and reform under the czars were generally resisted, and political opposition was aggressively pursued by the secret police—the Okhrana. Consequently, passive dissatisfaction progressively turned into grievances, discontent and eventually to revolt and revolution. The czars had experienced an earlier revolt—the Decembrist Revolt—staged by army officers in 1825. In the latter 19th and early 20th centuries, however, the revolts were undertaken primarily on behalf of the masses of peasants and the growing number of urban workers. Grievances were vocalized also by the numerous nationalities under czarist rule—e.g., the Ukrainians, Poles and nations in the Baltics—against Russification, as well as by religious sects, students and others. It is worth noting that many revolutionary leaders, including Lenin, operated abroad for many years because of the Okhrana.

In this volatile environment social and revolutionary movements emerged. These covered a wide spectrum of social and ideological beliefs and included socialists, Marxists, terrorists and revolutionaries. Among the early groups were the Narodnik (Populist) movement, which took root in the 1870s, and the radical Zemlia i Volia (Land and Freedom), out of which emerged Narodnaya Volia (Will of the People), which targeted high-ranking officials as well as Czar Alexander II, who was assassinated in March 1881. Several groups achieved greater prominence and importance. The Social Revolutionaries promoted non-Marxist socialist revolution among the peasantry. The liberal Constitutional Democratic Party favored a Western-type parliamentary government. The most enduring was the Russian Social Democratic Labor Party (RSDLP), which was founded at a secret First Congress in 1898 in Minsk. It is in this organization that the Communist Party had its beginning.

At the Second Congress (1903), first in Brussels, then in London, the RSDLP split into two factions: the Bolshevik ("Majority") wing, led by Lenin, and the Menshevik ("Minority") wing, led by J. I. Martov. Initially their differences, in addition to personalities, centered around organization and membership, with Lenin favoring a small number of disciplined, elite revolutionaries, while the Mensheviks visualized a mass, popular organization similar to those in West European countries. Subsequently other differences arose, especially over ideology and tactics. The Mensheviks' outlook was a long-term development toward the establishment of a socialist society, while Lenin and the Bolsheviks perceived a more immediate revolutionary development. Efforts to reconcile factionalism—e.g., at the 1906 Congress in Stockholm—failed because of ideological, tactical and personality differences.

Internal conditions worsened at the turn of the century, the major activities resulting in peasant revolts, workers' strikes and student demonstrations. The Russo-Japanese War of 1904–5 exacerbated the socioeconomic conditions in Russia, and its defeat added fuel to the discontent. In January 1905 peaceful, unarmed workers, demonstrating in St. Petersburg, were fired on. "Bloody Sunday," as it became known, intensified the unrest of workers and peasants, with military elements now joining them. In October a general strike forced Czar Nicholas II to extend civil liberties to the general population and to establish a legislature (Duma), but revolutionary activities continued. In the March 1906 elections a number of political groups and parties participated with the Constitutional Democrats, a moderate liberal group, receiving 178 of the 524 seats. Unfortunately, when the delegates exercised their legislative prerogative in criticizing and petitioning the czar, the government dissolved the Duma. Subsequent sessions met the same fate until the czar and his officials manipulated the Duma into a pliant, ineffective institution. The workers were slighted, the peasantry underrepresented and both classes resented their minor roles. During World War I the czar and the government generally bypassed the Duma, the most representative political body in the vast country.

By early 1917 the populace, involving all segments, including the military and czarist officials, wearied of war and the deteriorating economic situation and were in a revolutionary mood. The czar's attempt again to dissolve the Duma failed, and the czar was forced to abdicate. The Duma established a Provisional Government, with representatives from all political groups. It was provisional until the election of a Constituent Assembly, which would formulate a constitution.

Simultaneously involved with the government and competing against it, Lenin issued his rallying slogan "All power to the soviets," prematurely in April, but it quickly attracted support. The attempt by workers and troops to seize power in July was defeated, and Lenin fled to Finland. Alexander Kerensky, a Socialist, took over the leadership (as prime minister) of the Provisional Government from Prince George Lvov. Kerensky was ineffective in the war and did not achieve progress domestically. His socialism was opposed by many influential leaders. The Bolsheviks, with many freed from prison by Kerensky, gained strength and support and acquired additional arms. In September they became dominant in the Petrograd Soviet, and in October Lenin reappeared. After years of plotting, polemics and intrigue—in the underground inside Russia and abroad—Lenin's militant Bolsheviks seized revolutionary power on November 7, 1917, in Petrograd. The coup became known as the Great October Revolution (November 7 was October 25 in the Julian calendar). The Bolshevik success against the Provisional Government was due in no small part to the organizing skills of Leon Trotsky, second in power only to Lenin. The Bolsheviks triumphed in Moscow, in other urban centers—including factories—and throughout the vast country, setting up local soviets to govern. The czarist Okhrana was replaced by the Soviet secret police Cheka.

The Second All-Union Congress of Soviets elected Lenin chairman (prime minister) of the Council of People's Commissars. Initially other political representatives participated in Lenin's government, but following an intraparty controversy over non-Bolshevik involvement, Lenin's position prevailed, and the Bolsheviks embarked on the elimination of all competing political forces. They first abolished the conservative and centrist parties—e.g., the liberal Constitutional Democratic Party; then, following the dissolution of the legally elected Constituent Assembly, they eliminated the leftist Menshevik wing of the RSDLP and the centrist Social Revolutionaries as well as the leftist Social Revolutionaries. The last had attempted an abortive coup in July 1918. Thus Lenin's party eliminated all effective opposition and achieved total political control rapidly and effectively. Not only political parties but even "factionalism" were banned in 1921 by the 10th Party Congress. In March 1918 the party's name was changed to the All-Russian Communist Party (Bolsheviks).

On March 3, 1918, the Soviet government concluded the Treaty of Brest-Litovsk with the Central Powers and withdrew from World War I. This allowed the Bolsheviks to consolidate their power internally and to conduct a civil war and a war against Poland. In January 1918 a decree, signed by Lenin, established the Workers' and Peasants' Red Army, and in February the Red Navy. In April compulsory military service was reinstituted; the first commissar of war was Leon Trotsky. Trotsky played a prominent role in the Communist victory over the anti-Communists (the "Whites"). Altogether, the wars exacted an enormous price on Russian and other peoples. The country's economy was crippled and a new wave of discontent of workers and peasants erupted. Lenin announced the New Economic Policy (NEP) in 1921, a temporary ideological retreat.

An historic change in leadership developed after Lenin suffered a debilitating stroke in 1922. He was only partially active thereafter and died in 1924. A struggle for leadership in the Politburo ensued. The major competitors were Joseph Stalin, general secretary of the Communist Party since 1922; Leon Trotsky, considered second in standing only to Lenin; Lev Kamenev; and Grigory Zinoviev. There were differences over party tactics, ideology and personalities. Lenin had been unchallenged either as a leader or as the Communist Party's ideologue, but after his demise the party's leadership differed on ideology and revolutionary tactics. Trotsky's wing favored the immediate establishment of socialism in Russia and the promotion of world revolution. Nikolai Bukharin led another group, which also subscribed to Trotsky's view that prospects for socialism in Russia were subject to successful world revolution. However, Bukharin reasoned that since revolutions were not yet materializing in foreign countries, Lenin's New Economic Policy should be continued in Russia.

Stalin's wing held that successful socialism in Russia—popularly known as "socialism in one country"— was not dependent on the success of world revolution. In the struggle for leadership, Stalin occupied the most strategic position. As general secretary he assembled support of central and lower party leaders who realistically visualized their future professional prospects with Stalin. Over the years Stalin's supporters increased, and consequently he strengthened his power over the party's structure.

Stalin's tactics for acquiring total leadership were classic. With the help of others, he defeated Trotsky in 1925. Trotsky was exiled and deported in 1929 and assassinated in Mexico in 1940; he had been tried in absentia and sentenced to death. Then, aligning with Bukharin, Stalin succeeded in ousting his former associates Kamenev and Zinoviev. By December 1927—at the 15th Party Congress—Stalin's victory was almost totally complete. He now shed his earlier position and declared for complete socialism, not unlike Trotsky and others he deposed. The Congress, packed with Stalin's loyalists, adopted his recommendation as the policy for the Soviet Union.

Of Stalin's major competitors for leadership, only Bukharin and his supporters remained, but only until 1929. Now Stalin's victory was so complete that Bukharin and his associates were reduced to signing a kind of *samo-kritika* (self-criticism), confessing their alleged errors about the economy and acknowledging the correctness of Stalin's policies. Lenin's temporary NEP passed into history, and Stalin began the five-year-plans, which have lasted until now; inaugurated policies of nationalization; and started state *(sovkhoz)* farms, forced collectives *(kolkhoz)* and heavy industrialization. Collectivization was strongly resisted. Over 1 million farmers were sent to labor camps, and Stalin induced famine. The death toll was a staggering 20 million lives.

Stalin's aggressive, debilitating policies were opposed by many inside the Soviet Union, including within the party. To eliminate the opposition Stalin, in the late 1930s, inaugurated the infamous "Great Purges." Millions of people were victimized, not only by the secret police but also by informers, including even family members. Party members were not spared. Show trials were organized, with party members subjected to abject confessions. The executed included Kamenev; Zinoviev; Bukharin; and Karl Radek, the latter two having helped draft the "Stalin Constitution" of 1936. Stalin came to exercise dictatorial powers seldom witnessed in history. The purges were declared ended by the 18th Party Congress in 1939.

The Soviet Union suffered enormous losses during World War II, with over 20 million military personnel killed; additional millions of civilians killed added to the enormity of the tragedy, as did physical destruction. The party survived. Stalin fought not only military but political wars as well as the Soviet Union extended Communist control over Eastern Europe. Limited relaxations during the war were replaced by restrictive policies. In 1952 the party adopted its present name of Communist Party of the Soviet Union (Kommunisticheskaia Partiia Sovetskogo Soiuza, CPSU) and ended the use of "Bolsheviks." Suspicions regarding a plan to kill Stalin—the "doctors' plot"—resulted in a new wave of arrests, trials and executions.

With Stalin's death on March 5, 1953, another power struggle materialized. Initially a collective leadership functioned temporarily. The main competitors were Politburo member Georgi Malenkov, long considered Stalin's successor, who was prime minister (1953–55) and immediately became senior secretary; and Politburo member Nikita Khrushchev, who succeeded Malenkov as first secretary on March 14. A third potential contender, Lavrenti Beria, minister of internal affairs (1941–53) and Politburo member, was eliminated by execution for "treason, organizing an anti-Soviet group of conspirators to seize power." Operating from the position of party leader, as Stalin had done 30 years earlier, Khrushchev outmaneuvered Malenkov, forcing the latter's resignation as prime minister in 1955. However, unlike in Stalin's time, Malenkov was neither executed nor even put on trial, continuing as deputy premier (until 1957), then as director of a power station. He was succeeded as prime minister by Politburo member and Deputy Premier Nikolai Bulganin, but Khrushchev appeared to be the undisputed party leader despite having enemies.

An unexpected event took place at the 20th Party Congress in 1956, when at a closed session Khrushchev delivered a blistering attack against Stalin, characterized later as "de-Stalinization," accusing the former dictator of a "personality cult" and calling him murderous. Subsequently Khrushchev's dramatic "secret" speech became public, and he continued his policy against Stalinism that, in varying degrees, was pursued by East European regimes. Many party members were shocked by the revelations, and some resented Khrushchev for making them. In addition to alienating a segment of the members with "de-Stalinization," Khrushchev sustained additional loss of prestige and support over the Polish events and the Hungarian uprising later that year. His Politburo opponents wanted his resignation, but in 1957 Khrushchev was supported by the Central Committee and won over the "antiparty group," which included Malenkov, who was removed from the Central Committee. Also in 1957 a successful Sputnik launch was politically beneficial to Khrushchev. In 1958 he became prime minister in addition to his party leadership.

Khrushchev's policy of "de-Stalinization" continued—e.g., at the 22nd Party Congress, in 1961—and Stalin's body was reburied from the tomb in front of the Kremlin wall where it lay alongside Lenin's. Among other modest changes, terrorism was reduced, limited liberalization was allowed and production shifted slightly toward consumer goods. However, Khrushchev's leadership was dealt a blow by the Sino-Soviet split and his retreat during the Cuban missile crisis in 1962; also, his agricultural policies experienced serious problems. In 1964 the Central Committee, the body which supported him against his rivals in 1956, forced him into retirement.

Initially, a "collective leadership" was established. Succeeding Khrushchev was Politburo member Leonid Brezhnev as first secretary of the party and Politburo member Alexei Kosygin as prime minister. At the 23rd Party Congress in 1966, the party leader's title was changed from first secretary to general secretary, and the Central Committee's Presidium was restored to the Politburo. Steadily Brezhnev would acquire stature as the party head and with additional power, which would establish him as the unchallenged leader. In 1977 he was elected chairman (president) of the Presidium of the Supreme Soviet in addition to his position as general secretary. This was contrary to a Central Committee resolution forbidding the simultaneous holding of the two positions.

Economic changes were instituted, but problems in various sectors continued. Stagnation led to inevitable deterioration. Brezhnev's policy of detente, reminiscent of coexistence policies of Lenin and Khrushchev, elevated the Soviet image in the world, but ventures into Third World countries in the name of "national liberation" received negative responses. The most serious of these was the invasion of Afghanistan in 1979, which brought rebuke from the United States and many other countries. Brezhnev managed to avoid a leadership crisis, but his tenure has come to be characterized by the Gorbachev regime as "the period of stagnation."

Brezhnev experienced poor health beginning in early 1979 but continued to function in his leadership roles. The 26th Party Congress, in 1981, reflected the stagnation. Brezhnev died in 1982 and was succeeded as general secretary by Yuri Andropov, member of the Politburo and chairman of the Committee for State Security (KGB). He soon became chairman of the Presidium of the Supreme Soviet or president. Andropov instituted changes in the economy and the party, but he, too, became ill, and died in 1984. He was succeeded by Politburo member Konstantin Chernenko, who also was elected president. However, he was in poor health, and the uncertainty in leadership continued. Domestically the country was in critical need of revitalization, and its foreign involvement, especially in Afghanistan, was continually criticized abroad. Moscow's East European allies were experiencing increasing internal pressures from internal activists and NATO countries countered Soviet nuclear weapons with deployment of American Intermediate-Range Nuclear Forces (INF). Chernenko died in 1985.

The Central Committee elected as general secretary a relatively young and vigorous Politburo member—Mikhail Gorbachev, who immediately inaugurated dramatic changes that impressed not only the citizens of the Soviet Union but governments around the world as well. Outside of the sanctity of Marxism-Leninism, the fundamental Communist system, and the party's role in the Soviet Union, nothing appeared untouched. He openly leveled criticism at corruption within party ranks, questionable discipline, economic problems stemming not only from production but also from productivity, and he looked critically at Afghanistan and other Third World activities and at the confrontional posture against the West. Gorbachev's new policies at home became known as *glasnost* (openness) and *perestroika* (restructuring). In foreign affairs he announced a policy of coexistence, of "new thinking," which resulted in his meeting with President Ronald Reagan at a summit in Geneva in November 1985. In July Gorbachev had appointed as foreign minister Eduard Shevardnadze, a personable Georgian.

Gorbachev's attacks on the party's complacent cadres and the unprecedented rapid changes he initiated were not without opposition, largely from the conservative wing. The 27th Party Congress, in 1986, was an early test for Gorbachev's policies and for himself. If anything, his position was strengthened as the Congress approved his policies. Personnel changes during 1985 were followed by additional dismissals in the ensuing years as Gorbachev moved aggressively in the implementation of his domestic and foreign policies. His policies of *glasnost* and *perestroika* were taking shape. Among other developments, in 1987 physicist and human rights activist Andrei Sakharov was released from internal exile in Gorki and permitted to return to Moscow. Even the dreaded KGB was criticized in the nonofficial media. Resistance by some party officials to the restructuring continued, but for some the pace was not fast enough. The attacks against slowness within party ranks were led by Moscow Communist Party chief Boris Yeltsin, until now a Gorbachev supporter for reform. In November 1988 Yeltsin was dropped from his position but was allowed to continue his criticism. Externally, Gorbachev, who displayed his diplomatic and public affairs skills, scored successes. While Reykjavik in 1986 appeared questionable, the 1988 Moscow summit with President Ronald Reagan resulted in the INF Treaty, which added tremendously to Gorbachev's prestige at home and abroad. The Soviet withdrawal from Afghanistan added to his stature. Shortly after the summit the 19th All-Union Party Conference considered Gorbachev's three-year record and gave its approval for the continuation of his policies.

However, Gorbachev's problems domestically were extended to debate over the primacy of the party in the Constitution and to the many discontented nationalities in the Soviet Union (see Ethnic Composition), the independent tendencies of Communist parties in the Union republics, increasing clamor of reformists for real economic restructuring, and to political pluralism. Despite the opposition of the all-Union Politburo, the Lithuanian Communist Party at its December 1989 Extraordinary Congress declared its independence from the CPSU. Moreover, the Lithuanian Supreme Soviet decided to delete from its Constitution the clause on the Communist Party's leading role. Tendencies in other republics were to follow suit in both cases. The commission preparing the draft of a new all-Union constitution deleted Article 6, on the party's primacy.

With greater permissiveness East European countries—initially Poland and Hungary—were proceeding with reforms that tested Moscow's effectiveness, and perhaps continued determination, of control. These developments were officially considered as "internal matters" by Moscow, but the extent of independence it would allow its allies remained unanswered, even as East Germany and Czechoslovakia removed their conservative party leadership and as Rumanians executed their longtime tyrannical ruler Nicolae Ceausescu. Despite these internal and external pressures, Gorbachev appeared in control of the Communist Party's hierarchy as he pursued the double policies of *glasnost* and *perestroika*.

The Communist Party's rules, a document of 72 articles, prescribes the guiding principles, the rights and duties of members, republic and lower organizations, party-state organizations, operational procedures, admission requirements, behavior of members and party funds. Routinely party rules are discussed, reviewed and amended; new ones are adopted at party congresses; and updated emphasis is given as guidance for implementation of current policy. The last rules were adopted by the 27th Party Congress, in 1986, and a commission established by Gorbachev is drafting (as of the end of 1989) new rules for the 28th Party Congress, scheduled to be held in October 1990. According to the 1939 party rules the Communist Party was the "organized vanguard of the working class." In October 1952 the Party Congress rules characterized it as a "voluntary militant union of Communists holding the same views formed by people of the working class, the working peasantry and the working intelligentsia." The 1977 rules said the Communist Party was the "leading and guiding force of Soviet society," and the 1986 document said it was the "tried and tested military vanguard of the Soviet people which unites, on a voluntary basis, the more advanced, politically more conscious section of the working class, collective-farm peasantry and intelligentsia of the USSR." However, this emphasis on equality was as far from reality in 1986 as it was earlier.

As noted in the Constitution & Government section, Chapter 6 of the Constitution of 1977, repealed in 1990, designated the party in the same language—as the "leading and guiding force of Soviet society and the nucleus of its political system." The rules established clear principles for the party: "Ideological and organizational unity, monolithic cohesion of the ranks and a high degree of conscious discipline on the part of all Communists are an inviolable law of the CPSU." Both the Soviet state (Article 3 of the Constitution) and the Communist Party (rules) were required to be "guided by Marxism-Leninism, organized and functioning on the principle of democratic socialism." The rules designated five elements of the "guiding principle":

• election of all leading party bodies, from the lowest to the highest;
• periodic reports of party bodies to their party organizations and to higher bodies
• strict party discipline and subordination of the minority to the majority
• decisions of higher bodies are obligatory on lower bodies
• collective spirit in the work of all organizations and leading party bodies

The importance of discipline, centralization and unity cannot be overemphasized. They are considered indispensable to the effective functioning, and perhaps even the existence, of the party. To what extent the new rules will reflect Gorbachev's principle of "democratic control" remains to be seen, but the impact on many party members may be traumatic. However, as the draft was being prepared, the application of real democracy into party rules was opposed by conservatives not only at the all-Union level but also throughout the entrenched bureaucracy. Also, the meaning of "democratic control" was not entirely clear—i.e., the extent of real democratization.

The party structure parallels that of the territorial government administrations and extends to the primary organizations that function throughout the country. Party rules designate the organs for various levels. Below the dominant all-Union party bodies are the Union republics, which, with the exception of the Russian Federation, have similar structures; the autonomous republics or territories *(kraya)*; provinces *(oblasti)*; the autonomous areas *(okruga)*; the cities *(gorodni)*; the urban or rural districts *(rayony)*; and the vast number of primary party organizations. With some differences, the party organs at the province, district and city levels resemble the structure of the Union republics—e.g., the latter's highest organ is the Congress, while it is a conference at the lower levels.

According to party rules the "supreme" organ of the Communist Party is the All-Union Congress, convened by the Central Committee not less than once in five years, but an extraordinary or emergency congress can be convoked by the Central Committee or one-third of the previous congress. Party Congresses in the republics are held just prior to the All-Union Congress. Rules specify that party bodies are elected by secret ballot, rather than by show of hands common in the past. Delegates to the Congress are elected from republic and lower party congresses or conferences and meet in the Kremlin's Palace of Congresses. The Central Committee determines the representation. The 27th Party Congress, in 1986, was attended by 4,993 delegates. It was reported that 152 delegates from 113 other countries, representing Communist and workers' parties, attended. Such a large assembly of delegates, meeting for a relatively short period, cannot realistically conduct any meaningful party business themselves. The Congress is an elaborate public-relations production, given domestic and foreign coverage.

However, the Congress cannot be dismissed as insignificant. Party rules give it formal importance, and perhaps under the promise of Gorbachev's policies, it has the potential of developing into a more meaningful institution. At the 27th Party Congress, the first under Gorbachev, its future was uncertain, especially taking into consideration the general secretary's revival of the neglected Party Conference (see below).

According to Article 33 of the rules, the Congress:

• hears and approves the reports of the Central Committee, the Central Auditing Commission and other central organs
• reviews, amends and approves the program and rules
• determines the party's line in domestic and foreign policy
• elects the Central Committee and the Central Auditing Commission

A major event at the Congress is the report of the general secretary on behalf of the Central Committee, inevitably a lengthy document; Gorbachev's presentation of it lasted over five hours. The leader's address is a keynote *tour d'horizon* of the domestic and foreign scene, enumerating achievements, exhorting the assemblage to achieve greater heights and indicating the party's direction. Gorbachev focused on the transformation of Soviet society, on the need for restructuring and accelerating. In a second major speech Prime Minister and Politburo member Nikolai Ryzhkov presented a report on the economy; there were other statements reflecting Gorbachev's current policies. Not surprisingly, the Congress approved the general secretary's new program, including the five-year and fifteen-year plans, the latter setting goals to the year 2000. The Congress adopted new party rules, but changes were modest.

The Congress elected a new Central Committee and Central Auditing Commission. The selection of Central Committee members always has been prearranged by the leadership, but Gorbachev's principle of "democratic control" may be extended to the Central Committee. The Central Committee numbered 307 full members and 170 alternate or candidate (nonvoting) members, compared to 319 and 151, respectively, elected by the

26th Congress, in 1981. The turnover of Central Committee members under Gorbachev was higher (40%) than at the earlier Congress (20%). At the April 1989 Plenum, 110 members of the Central Committee and the Central Auditing Commission were retired, including Andrei Gromyko, former longtime foreign minister; Politburo member; and chairman of the Presidium of the Supreme Soviet. This was another victory for the general secretary over entrenched conservatism. Union republic and lower party secretaries numbered 110 of the members, or about one-fifth. Other members generally are prominent representatives in government, public or other organizations, including chairmen, directors, military officers, scientists, cosmonauts, ambassadors, journalists and a modest number of "workers" and "peasants." Vacancies on the Central Committee are filled by alternate members.

CENTRAL COMMITTEE SECRETARIES
July 1990

Secretary	Responsibility
Gorbachev, Mikhail	General Secretary
Ivashko, Vladimir	Deputy General Secretary
Baklanov, Oleg	Defense Industry
Dzasokhov, Aleksandr	Ideology
Falin, Valentin	International Affairs
Gidaspov, Boris	First Secretary, Leningrad Party
Girenko, Andrei	Nationalities
Kuptsov, Valentin	Sociopolitical Organizations
Manaenkov, Yurii	Secretary, RSFSR CP
Semenova, Galina	Women's Affairs
Shenin, Oleg	Organization
Stroev, Igor	Agriculture
Yanaev, Gennadi	International Affairs

Members of the Secretariat

Aniskin, Viktor	Chairman, Gorky Kolkhoz
Gaivoronsky, Valentin	Worker
Melnikov, Ivan	Secretary, Moscow State University Party Committee
Teplenichev, Aleksandr	Secretary, Novolipetsk Metallurgical Combine in Lipetsk
Turgunova, Gulchakha	Farmer

Article 35 specifies that during the interval of the Congresses, the Central Committee "guides" the activities of the party and the local party bodies; selects and appoints leading functionaries; "directs" the work of central government bodies and public organizations; forms and guides party bodies, institutions and enterprises; appoints editors of central newspapers and journals operating under its control; and distributes as well as controls the party's funds. Moreover, the Central Committee represents the party in its relations with other parties.

The Central Committee must hold plenary sessions at least every six months. Although during 1989 Gorbachev convened Central Committee plenums five times—an unusual frequency due to demands of his policies—normally the CC meets at the minimum interval, twice yearly, and for very short periods (one to three days). In addition, considering the Central Committee's large membership, the rules provide for a Politburo and a Secretariat to conduct the activities of the

CPSU between its sessions. Following its election by the Congress, the Central Committee elects the Politbuweekly and responsible to the Central Committee, the Politburo is the highest policymaking organ not only for the party but for the government and the whole society as well. The rules (Article 38) specify that the Politburo is to "direct" the work of the party between plenary meetings of the Central Committee. The Congress elects the general secretary.

The general secretary possesses enormous power in the Soviet Union. Although in recent years he has been the head of state as well, it is his position as the leader of the party that gives him power few others have. He is head of both the Politburo and the Secretariat, preparing their meetings and chairing them. He, as no other party official, influences if not dictates appointments at the highest levels, including those to the Politburo and the Secretariat. In addition to these, the highest party positions, Gorbachev is president, a head of state with governmental powers substantially enhanced over those previously exercised by the chairman of the Presidium of the Supreme Soviet. Moreover, Gorbachev is, in addition to being commander in chief of the armed forces, chairman of the Defense Council, consisting of the highest political and military leaders and that establishes military policy. As chairman, Gorbachev has revitalized the Defense Council.

Over the years the Politburo has had a varying number of members—party rules are silent on this—and also has been named the Presidium. The 26th Party Congress elected 14 members and eight candidate or Alternate (nonvoting) members. The 27th Party Congress reduced the number to eight and seven, respectively. The backgrounds of Politburo members reflect many years of upward mobility through the party hierarchy and experience in decision-making positions in government and other sectors. At Brezhnev's last Congress (the 26th) all Politburo and secretary members were reelected, an occurrence not recorded in 50 years. Those elected at the 27th were a mixture of former members and Gorbachev's loyalists, but in succeeding years additional changes progressively reflected a Politburo of the general secretary's supporters of his programs. In July 1990 the nine full members of the Politburo were:

Members	Responsibility
Mikhail Gorbachev	General Secretary
Vladimir Ivashko	Deputy General Secretary
Aleksandr Dzasokhov	Ideology
Ivan Frolov	Editor-in-Chief, *Pravda*
Jurii Prokofiev	First Secretary, Moscow Party Committee
Galina Semenova	Women's Affairs
Oleg Shenin	Organizational Matters
Egor Stroev	Agriculture
Gennadi Yansev	International Affairs

In early 1989 Gorbachev focused on the party's reluctance to implement reforms, and during the year several important changes in the Politburo were made by the Central Committee, demonstrating his power in the party. In September three of the 12 Politburo members and two of eight candidates were dismissed. The leader for the past 17 years of the Ukrainian Communist Party, Vladimir Shcherbitski, was deposed, and succeeded in December by Vladimir Ivashko as first secretary. The only Politburo member from the Brezhnev era, outside of Gorbachev, Shcherbitski in controlling the Ukraine had a reputation of conservatism, anti-Ukrainian nationalism, anti-Catholicism and antireformism. Not surprisingly, he was extremely unpopular there. Although of Ukrainian heritage, Shcherbitski spoke Ukrainian only infrequently, which did not endear him to the people over whom he held tight reins. Praised by Gorbachev for his working ability and "principled positions," Ivashko promised to deal with social and economic problems in the republic.

To "direct the current work, chiefly the selection of cadres and the verification of the fulfillment of party decisions," the Central Committee elects the Secretariat, its administrative body. As with the Politburo, the number of secretaries has varied. The 26th Party Congress elected 10 and the 27th elected 11. At the end of 1988 there were eight secretaries, including General Secretary Gorbachev. Of these, only one—Oleg Baklanov—was not simultaneously a member of the Politburo. He is an Ukrainian and was secretary in charge of the defense industry. In 1986 only four of the 11 secretaries were in the Politburo. The 1989 changes in the Politburo affected the composition of the Secretariat, as five new secretaries were elected, none of whom was a Politburo member. Other sections dealt with security and legal affairs, agriculture (under two secretaries), ideology, the economy and cadres. In 1986 the sections dealt with ideology and personnel, the economy, heavy industry, light industry, international affairs, propaganda, ruling Communist parties, agriculture, cadres and culture. As the Politburo, the Secretariat usually meets weekly.

Day-to-day administration is accomplished through the Secretariat's departments, which usually number 20 and are divided into various spheres of activity, such as social, economic, foreign affairs, cultural, propaganda, education, personnel, security and defense. The heads of the departments are party officials of substantial influence as they, with their large staffs, administer the party's policies and decisions throughout all segments of society. The Secretariat has been an organ of immense power in party history, and its functions of supervision and of formulating the political agenda for Politburo meetings were transferred to Central Committee commissions in 1989. This removed, or at least diminished, a possible hard-line impediment to Gorbachev's policies as he determinedly pursues reduction of the party's bureaucracy.

The party rules (Article 40) provide for a seldom-used institution: the Party Conference. Between party congresses the Central Committee can convene an All-Union Party Conference "should the need arise," to discuss "pressing party policy issues." Gorbachev proposed the conference at a Central Committee plenum in January 1987, and it was officially approved by the Central Committee in June of that year. The Central Committee, which determines the procedure, convened the 19th All-Union Party Conference in 1988 to review the record of *perestroika* , discuss problems and adopt policies to enhance the realization of Gorbachev's proposed transformation.

During the early years of Communist existence, conferences were held frequently—seven before the 1917 October Revolution. The 1919 party rules provided for all-party conferences. The 18th was convened in February 1941, after which the rules deleted the provision for conferences. Although the 23rd Congress, in 1966, reinstituted the conference none was convened until 1988. The 19th Party Conference adopted resolutions "on urgent measures for the practical implementation of the reform of the country's political system." They were on:

- progress in implementing the decisions of the 27th CPSU Congress and the tasks of promoting *perestroika*
- democratizing Soviet society and reforming the political system
- combating bureaucracy
- relations among Soviet nationalities
- *glasnost*
- legal reform

The general secretary's tactic to overcome conservatism was to adopt new party rules and achieve a personnel turnover in the Central Committee. He succeeded in neither, but the Conference agreed to the restructuring of the government with a strengthened president and a revitalized parliament (see the Constitution & Government section).

As noted, the Central Committee elects the Central Auditing Commission. Article 36 of the rules assigns the Commission the responsibility of ensuring the appropriate handling of the party's budget and financial accounts, as well as of the Central Committee's enterprises and institutions. The Commission, which reports to the Central Committee, had a membership of 83 in April 1989 when the Central Committee plenum retired 12 of these members.

The Central Committee also elects the Party Control Committee, which is responsible for verifying observance of party discipline by members and which takes action against Communists who violate the party's program and rules, party or state discipline, or party ethics. The Control Committee considers appeals against decisions of central committees of Union republic parties, or of territorial and regional party committees, on expelling members from the party or imposing penalties on them.

As indicated above, the party's organizational structure descends from the all-Union level to the primary party organizations. The Congress is the highest organ in a republic, and the conference in territorial and regional party organizations. The republic congresses are held at least every five years; in practice they are convened just prior to the All-Union Congress. The conferences are convened every two to three years; these and extraordinary congresses or conferences are called by their Central Committee. They hear Central Committee and other reports; discuss party, economic and cultural issues; and elect new Central Committee members, auditing commissions and delegates to the All-Union Congress. The Central Committee elects bureaus, including secretaries of the committees. The Central Committee also forms secretariats to administer current affairs. The Central Committee, meeting at least every four months, directs the area, city and district party organizations. Party organizations in autonomous republics and autonomous and other regions of a Union republic or a territory function under the Central Committee of the Union republic or territorial committees.

The highest body of an area, city or district party organization is the Party Conference or the General Meeting, convened every two to three years. The conferences or meetings hear reports of the committees and the auditing commissions; discuss various party, economic, cultural and other matters within their jurisdictions; and elect committees, auditing commissions and delegates to the regional or territorial conference or Union Party Congress. The area, city or district committees, which meet at least once every three months, elect a bureau that includes the committee secretaries, the chairman of the party commission and newspaper editors. The secretaries, who are required to have a minimum of five years in the party, are approved by the regional or territorial committee or the Central Committee of the Republic.

The area, city or district committees set up the primary party organizations (PPO), direct their work, hear their reports and keep a register of Communist members. Article 52 declares the PPO's to be the "basis of the party." They are formed at places of employment—e.g., factories, state or collective farms, armed forces, offices, educational establishments—wherever there are at least three party members—or at residential sites. To conduct day-to-day activities, the PPO's with 15 or more members elect a bureau for a term of two or three years, while those with less than 15 members elect a secretary and a deputy secretary. These elections are held annually. Secretaries must be party members for at least one year. The rules state that PPO's with less than 150 party members "as a rule" have no salaried functionaries.

The number of party members required for the formation of a committee varies and is specified in the rules. The committees are elected for two- to three-year terms, their composition determined by the General Meeting or Conference. The large PPO's, with over 1,000 party members, may be granted certain rights of a district committee. As at all other levels, the PPO's, "guided" by the party program and rules, rally members around the party, organize them to fulfill tasks of Communist construction and implement the party's personnel policy. Among other functions the PPO's:

- admit new members
- educate members "in the spirit of loyalty to the party cause, ideological staunchness and Communist ethics"
- organize study of Marxism-Leninism

- ensure the growing vanguard role of Communists in work and in sociopolitical life
- exhort workers to achieve higher production
- conduct political education and propaganda work
- by criticism and self-criticism combat bureaucracy, parochialism and violations

The PPO's "enjoy the right to control the work of the administration" of their place of employment, while party organizations at ministries, state committees and other agencies "exercise control over the fulfillment of party and government directives and the observance of Soviet laws by the apparatus."

The CPSU, in line with Article 60, "exercises political leadership of state and public organizations and directs and coordinates their activities." The party organizations are said not to supplant government and public bodies but are instructed to observe compliance and see to involvement of working people in management and in political, economic and social decisions. Party groups are formed at congresses, conferences and meetings sponsored by state and public organizations, and at their elected bodies, when three party members are involved. The objective, again, is to carry out party policy. Party activities in nonparty organizations are guided by the CPSU's Central Committee; by Union republic central committees; and by the territorial, regional, area, city or district party committees.

In addition to the general secretary, the other Politburo and Secretariat members have a strong voice in political appointments. However, the preponderance of personnel or cadre matters is handled by the vast bureaucracy of the Secretariat. Over the years the party's appointments have been dominated by the system known as *nomenklatura*, lists of positions and names at all-Union and lower levels used to fill especially the more influential positions in party, government and public organizations. (Also see the Civil Service section.)

The immense party bureaucracy and its multifaceted activities require a huge budget. The funds are obtained from CP members, party enterprises and "other revenue." How the money is spent is decided by the Central Committee. The assessments are based on the monthly income of members, ranging from 10 kopecks (R0.2) for those earning up to R70, to 1% for those with an income of R101 to R150 and progressively to 3% for people receiving over R300.

Membership in the Communist Party is open to "politically conscious and active citizens." People up to age 25 are eligible only through the Young Communist League (YCL), and 18 is the minimum age. An applicant must have recommendations from three party members who have been in the party at least five years and who have worked with the applicant for one year. The PPO's vote must be approved by the district or city party committee. Termination of membership, after warning and reprimand, can occur for nonpayment of dues and failure to fulfill duties specified in the rules.

A section of party rules is devoted to duties and rights of members. In addition to accepting the party's program and the rules, the members' duties are to:

- implement, firmly and unequivocally, the party's general line and directives
- be a conscientious worker and protect socialist property
- be active politically for socialist government
- master Marxist-Leninist theory; promote people's consciousness and their ideology; and combat resolutely bourgeois ideology, private property mentality, religion and other anti-Soviet views
- abide by standards of Communist morality
- disseminate ideas of proletarian socialist internationalism and Soviet partiotism among the masses
- strengthen Soviet defense
- strengthen the Communist Party's ideological and organizational unity
- develop criticism and self-criticism, exposing shortcomings
- pursue the party's policy undeviatingly
- observe party and state discipline

The Communist Party has changed numerically and in composition, from Lenin's conception of a revolutionary "elitist" group to a massive organization, and from primarily a "workers' organization" to one of white-collar complexion. Prior to the Revolution the party's size was debated by its leaders in the underground and abroad. The membership then was necessarily small. Its strength in early 1917 was estimated at 24,000, but grew rapidly during the year to perhaps 300,000 (estimates vary widely) at the October Revolution. When Lenin died in 1924, the party's ranks were under 500,000, or less than 1% of the population. The party's numbers increased following Lenin's death with infusion of the "proletariat," and again on the 10th anniversary of the Revolution, the 1927. The ranks continued to increase into the early 1930s, with emphasis on the "intelligentsia." The figure rose despite purges during the early and late 1920s. The massive Stalin purges of the 1934–38 period had a debilitating effect on party members.

In 1924 Stalin declared that "party becomes consolidated by purging itself of opportunist elements." The spark for Stalin's purges was the assassination of Sergei Kirov, party leader in Leningrad, on December 1, 1934. This was Stalin's "Great Terror." Its victims existed at all levels and represented all periods, including the prerevolutionary Bolsheviks. Arrests, trials, imprisonment, labor camps and deaths were common. The victims were charged with being Trotskyites, spies and counterrevolutionaries. At the 18th Party Congress, in 1939, Stalin admitted to "grave mistakes" committed during the purges.

During the 1934–37 period the number expelled probably was over 600,000, including many "elites" (this does not refer to the many millions who died as a result of forced collectivization, famine and later repression). Stalin rid himself of competitors and real or imagined opponents, but the society suffered immense losses. The party's four-year period of nonrecruitment, beginning in January 1933, depleted the roster, resulting in an energetic recruitment campaign. Over 1 million joined the party during 1939, increasing membership to

nearly 2.5 million, and to nearly 3.5 million the following year. Membership was nearly 4 million when Hitler invaded the Soviet Union in June 1941.

Party members as well as the military and ordinary citizens sustained heavy losses during the war. An immense number of people were lost, but many continued to join, in an incredible cycle of turnovers. However, during and following the war, membership rules often were relaxed and the party's ranks climbed rapidly, reaching about 6 million in 1946, then essentially stayed at about 7 million by 1953–56 (about 3% of the population) and increased to more than 8 million by 1959. The seemingly inevitable purges, albeit mostly minor, or "cleansing," occurred continually as new members were admitted. Certain periods showed small growth, indicating consolidation or stabilization—e.g., during 1961–66 the growth averaged 6% annually, while 10 years later it was about 2%. The 25th Party Congress, in 1976, adopted stricter admission requirements, which reduced the rate of growth further. This followed a purge directed by the 24th Party Congress, in 1971, requiring a revalidation of party cards. According to General Secretary Brezhnev in 1976, a total of 347,000 had been rejected. In April 1980 the membership reached 17.2 million, or 6.5% of total population. Between the 25th Party Congress, in 1976, and the 26th, in 1981, the membership grew by 1.8 million to 17.48 million, and it was officially reported to be slightly over 19 million at the 27th Congress, in 1986. In April 1988 membership reached a new high of 19.5 million. With the formation of numerous front and other groups during 1988 and 1989, together with the deterioration of the party's control, many members left. Membership at the end of 1989 was 19.5 million, of whom 45.4% were workers, 11.4% peasants in collectives and 43.2% white-collar employees. CC Secretary Georgi Razumovsky reported to the 28th Congress that in 1989 136,000 Communists resigned from the CP and that 82,000 left the party during the first quarter of 1990. Probably more disturbing was the June survey conducted by the CP's Center for Sociological Research whereby 53% of the respondents did not consider the party as the leader in Soviet society. Deputy General Secretary Ivashko announced at the October 8 CC plenum that 371,000 members had left the party during the first six months of 1990 and a further 311,000 during July and August.

The party of the "proletariat" or the working class has become a party of the intelligentsia. The leadership has added the adjective "working" to the latter, but this is specious, as is the continuing identification of high-positioned officials as workers based on origin. Perhaps the appellation "white-collar" better describes this group, which includes intellectuals, professionals, technocrats, managers, military, personnel and others.

Workers comprised about three-fifths of the membership before the Revolution. They continued in the majority into the late 1920s, but after Stalin's purges this category experienced a steady reduction. Peasants, independent by nature and suspicious of the Communists, were reluctant to join the party. They reached a high rate of about 27% of total membership in 1927, but declined rapidly when collectivization was forced on them by Stalin. Millions were driven from their land, and millions died.

The rate for workers also was reduced, to approximately one-third in the late 1940s and into the 1950s, then increased to over 40% in the 1970s. The rate for peasants continued on a downward spiral, dipping to 18% in 1947, to 16% in 1967 and to below 13% in the 1980s. Recruitment of the intelligentsia and developments in education and technology combined with an ever-increasing and entrenched party bureaucracy to produce a "new elite." This new class showed a rapid growth to a dominant position by the latter 1950s, which Khrushchev embraced as a party representative of all people.

General Secretary Brezhnev, on the other hand, placed greater emphasis on recruitment of workers, so that of the 1.8 million new members between the 1976 and 1981 congresses, 59% were reported to be workers. In 1984 the figures were 44.1% for workers, 12.4% for peasants and 43.5% for white-collar workers. In 1988 the figures were, respectively, 45%, 11.8% and 43.2%.

While women live in a system claiming sexual equality and are a clear majority of the population, their ratio in the party reflects a record of inequality. Since the Revolution the leading organs of the party have not only been dominated by males but also have virtually excluded women. The occasional symbolic woman—party leader or cosmonaut—proves the rule. Currently only one woman is a member of either the Politburo or the Secretariat. She is Aleksandra P. Biriukova, who has been a candidate member of the Politburo since September 1988. Since the Revolution women have risen slowly in total membership but have yet to reach 30%. They were 7.4% in 1920, nearly 17% in 1937, almost 20% in 1957, about 25% in 1977, 27.6% in 1984 and approximately 28% in 1989.

In no small measure the party relies on public organizations, cited in the Constitution, to maintain political control. The objective of forming mass organizations is both for effective control of the population and to harness their energies for development of Marxism-Leninism or socialism. The Communist Youth League (Kommunisticheskii Soiuz Molodezhi—CYL on Komsomol), with about 39 million members, is considered by party rules as an "independent [which it is not] public and political organization, an active assistant and reserve of the party," which it is. Komsomol is to assist the party in educating youth "in the communist spirit," how to build the "new society" and raise a generation "prepared to work and to defend their Soviet Motherland." Among those the CYL educates are children who belong to the All-Union Young Pioneer Organization, age 10 to 15 and numbering some 20 million, who are inculcated with ideology, patriotism and the defense of socialism. Those younger (seven to nine) are members of the Octobrists. Under guidance from the CPSU, Komsomol is to "promote party directives in all spheres." The ages for admission into the CYL are 14 to 28, but one can become a member of the CPSU at 18 (21 if not a CYL member), at which time membership in the youth group ceases. The CYL is the normal channel for joining the party, providing up to 70% of new members. However,

Komsomol leaders can be older. Other mass organizations of significance are the All-Union Central Council or Trade Unions (135 million); the Voluntary Society for the Promotion of the Army, Air Force and Navy (over 100 million); and the Union of Soviet Societies for Friendship and Cultural Relations with Foreign Countries (50 million).

As 1989 ended, the Soviet Union continued to be a one-party state, with its leaders resolute in opposing political pluralism. However, under Gorbachev's policies of *glasnost* and *perestroika*, groups, associations and fronts outside the party-controlled public organizations have been allowed to organize and function, albeit within certain parameters not considered seriously threatening to the party's dominance.

Entering 1990 the CP appeared to be in disarray. New groups and political parties were becoming a threat to the CP's seven decade monopoly position, and the factionalism within the all-Union and splits in the Republican parties were potentially destructive. Thus, the CP sought to stem the tide of dissolution and reestablish unity. In preparation for the 28th Congress the CP made public its draft platform in February. Succeeding CC plenums considered the draft, establishing a commission to take into account draft proposals made by the Marxist Platform and the Democratic Platform. Despite some dissident views, characterized as divisive, prompting an open letter from the highest party leaders for unity, an alleged purge was denied but some critics were expelled from the party. Gorbachev and other leaders, while accepting dissent within the party, rejected factions.

The conservative-reformist controversy continued during the July 2–13 28th Party Congress—the 27th was held in 1986—watched by an estimated 100 million television viewers. Gorbachev was the overall individual winner, partly due to his adroit tactics, for he sustained setbacks as well. His proposal for multicandidate elections of deputies to the Congress was defeated by the CC Plenum in March. The CC decided to continue the traditional election practice. Consequently a substantial number of the 4,700 delegates was of conservative persuasian, opposed to or skeptical of Gorbachev's policies. Egor Ligachev, Politburo and Secretariat leader of the conservative block, was the biggest loser. He was defeated for the post of deputy general secretary and not elected to either the Politburo or the Secretariat. His harsh criticism of Gorbachev's policies and antireformist attitude did not receive much support.

While the results of the Congress were inconclusive, it was clear that the political locus of power was being transferred from the CP to the government, with Gorbachev its driving force; that *perestroika* would continue toward a market economy despite current difficulties; that the CP lost its preeminent, monopoly position in the society; and political pluralism had become a fact of life in the USSR. The Congress elected a commission, with Gorbachev as chairman, to draft a new party program by mid-1991 for approval by a party conference tentatively planned for 1992.

The CP was not eliminated, as some had suggested. However, the composition, number and power of the once-powerful Politburo and the Secretariat changed significantly. Gorbachev was reelected by secret ballot of the entire Congress rather than in a secret session of the CC, as had been done in past congresses. Moreover, he was challenged. Eight deputies were nominated but six withdrew. Gorbachev won by a vote of 3,411 to 501, with hundreds not voting—far from a unanimous endorsement. According to the new party rules, the general secretary can be removed from his position only by the next Congress but earlier only by an extraordinary Congress. While in past years the Politburo had an unofficial deputy, the new party rules adopted at the 28th Congress provided for a deputy general secretary. The deputy is responsible for administration of the CC Secretariat and, in the absence of the general secretary, chairs Politburo meetings.

In its resolution the Congress instructed the CC and the Politburo to concentrate on key problems of unity and developing democracy within the party. An indication of the Politburo's reduced role in policy-making and influence was clearly indicated in the election of its members. The membership was reduced to nine, of whom seven did not hold top government positions. Moreover, the participation, in *ex officio* roles, of republican party leaders does not augur well for a harmonious Politburo. The Congress abolished the "candidate" position. Notably absent were Prime Minister Ryzhkov, Foreign Minister Shevardnadze, Defense Minister Yazov, Council of the Union Chairman Primakov and former member Yakovlev, all of whom were on the Presidential Council. Six former full and four candidate Politburo members were not even reelected to the CC. The Secretariat consists of 11 secretaries and five members of the Secretariat, plus General Secretary Gorbachev and Deputy Ivashko. Only two other Politburo members are also secretaries.

In its policy statement, the Congress admitted to "crisis" in the society, rejected the former "command system" and called for "renewal" of the party. Reestablishing "unity" was the objective of the Congress, the CC and Gorbachev. While renouncing political and ideological monopoly, the Congress mapped out the strategy and tactics for "socialist renewal." The Congress defended the party's "world outlook and moral values," renounced the *nomenklatura* system and rejected democratic centralism as previously applied. It seeks democratization of the party instead, with participation at all levels and direct, competitive and secret elections for secretaries and delegates. Control bodies are not excluded. In the renovation of the USSR, the Congress granted independence to republic CPs, which, however, should be dialectically in harmony with the fundamental program and statutory principles of the CP of the Soviet Union. All are obliged to advance the party line in the governmental and the socioeconomic as well as cultural spheres. The Congress stated that the CP strives for cooperation with movements of "socialist orientation" and for dialogue and equal partnership with "all progressive ideological and political tendencies." The party is prepared to form political blocs with these but the Congress considered "impermissible" that Communists be members of groups "propagating chauvinism, nationalism, racism and anti-socialist ideas."

As with the party's platform, the draft of new party rules was equally controversial, requiring a revision. At the Congress, Gorbachev headed the committee on revising party rules, where heated debates continued. The proposal for a party presidium, opposed by Gorbachev, was soundly defeated by the Congress. However, the Politburo was to include the first secretaries of republican parties. The election of the general secretary by ballot of the entire Congress, rather than the CC in secret, was narrowly approved.

The new party statutes, as ratified by the 28th Congress contain the following sections: party membership, their rights and obligations; intraparty democracy; organizational structure; Communists in soviets, state organs and public associations; CP's monetary funds and property; and an appendix. As before, citizens are eligible for membership if 18 years of age, acknowledge the party program and observe the party statutes, work in a primary organization, and support the party materially. Members have a duty to propagandize the ideas of the party. The CP continues to operate on the principle of democratic centralism but now freedom of expression is guaranteed and all party organizations are autonomous. Party organizations and elected party organs operate with *glasnost* or openness.

Leadership, executive and control organs are now to be elected by secret ballot with multiple candidates. Those at the rayon level and above can be elected for only two consecutive terms. Party committees and control commissions are accountable to the organization that established them. Various viewpoints should be considered but final decisions are binding on everyone.

The party is structured on territorial and workplace lines, as before. The primary organization is the foundation of the structure, which moves up through the *rayon*, city, *okrug*, *oblast*, *kray*, autonomous republics and the republican parties. Factions are prohibited. The rayon and city party organizations, which unite primary units, are considered the party's pivotal structural link.

With Soviet CP's objective of unity, the most controversial, emotional and important issue is the position of the republican Communist parties, which is an extension of the more fundamental question of the nation-republics within the USSR. Gorbachev is categorically committed to a CP of the Soviet, as he is to a USSR, with all others subordinate to it. He is opposed to independence of parties or even "federalization" of the party. In the current environment Union republican parties, vying for public support, fear alienation if they do not support the aspirations of their republic's people. According to the statutes, which, for the first time included a section on Union republic Communist parties, the Union republics are "autonomous." They can work up their own programs, decide on their own organizations and pursue the party line within the republic's province. However this must be on the basis of the Soviet CP "fundamental program and statutory principles." In case of a dispute the republic CP CC has the right of appeal to the CC plenum or a joint CC and Central Control Committee plenum of the Soviet CP.

The CP organizations in the armed forces, the KGB, internal troops and railroad troops are subject to the statutes and to their own documents submitted by their conferences and ratified by the CC.

The Congress continues to be the supreme organ. Regular congresses are convened at least every five years, at the call of the CC, which prepares the agenda, decides on the representation and publishes draft documents. Extraordinary or emergency congresses are convened by the CC and other bodies specified in the statutes. The Congress hears reports, adopts the party program, establishes the party line, elects the CC and the Central Control Commission and elects the secretary general and his deputy. Between congresses the CC can convene a party conference to consider urgent problems. Between congresses and conferences the CC implements the decisions of the Congress and the conference and submits domestic and foreign policy proposals to the Congress of People's Deputies and the Supreme Soviet. Also, it directs the activities of party groups in Union representation organs, and draws up and implements cadre policy, creates party institutions and enterprises, and collaborates with socio-political organizations and represents the CP in relations with foreign parties.

In a secret ballot the Congress elected 412 CC members. New rules do not provide for candidate members. The CC is required to meet at least twice yearly to decide on policy and organizational matters. Between its plenums the CC elects the Politburo, the number determined by the CC, which includes the general secretary, his deputy, and the first secretaries of union republic CP CCs. The Politburo, headed by the general secretary, issues decisions to party organizations on behalf of the CC and annually reports on its activities to the CC plenum. The CC also elects the Secretariat, led by the deputy general secretary, which implements the decisions of the congresses, conferences, CC and the Politburo, and directs the work of the CC bureaucracy. Standing commissions are formed from among the CC members and Communists designated as advisers. The committees, headed by CC secretaries, are responsible for defined sectors of CC activity. The Central Control Commission (CCC) oversees compliance with party statutes and Congress's provisions. A Presidium, elected by the CCC acts on its behalf. As the CC, the CCC is required to meet at least twice yearly. A party member cannot simultaneously be a member of both the CC and the CCC. CC and CCC members can participate in each other's plenums on a non-voting basis.

Party organizations and committees are not to exercise functions with state and economic organs but pursue party policies through Communists employed in them. The CP strives for political leadership through elective and other offices, propagating the party's policies. Party organizations can join with other groups, support non-Communist candidates and unite with others in a voting bloc in the soviets. However, Communists are not permitted to organize groups or factions independent of the leading party organs. The party cooperates with social forces, such as the trade unions and mass movements. Here party groups or Communist factions can be established at congresses and conferences of those organizations.

As before, the party assigns the responsibility of working among youths to the Komsomol (All-Union Lenin Communist Youth League), cooperating with other youth organizations with socialist orientation. The statutes recognize Komsomol's organizational autonomy, cite political partnership and ideological commonality of the party and Komsomol, the latter regarded as the immediate reserve to replenish its ranks.

Dues for members are specified as follows, depending on the monthly income: up to 70 rubles—10 kopeks; 71–100—20 kopeks; 101–150—30 kopeks; 151–250—1% of income; and over 250—2% of income. All party organizations are said to be autonomous in controlling their budgets. Up to 50% of the total membership dues are to finance the activities of primary organizations.

Despite the CP's policy statement, the new Statutes, and Gorbachev's pronouncements about anti-factionalism and the reestablishment of unity within the party, the trend in the Soviet Union during 1990 was not only for a multiparty system but pluralism within the CP itself. In the RSFSR the largest republic, there are about 40 parties and groups, and some 58% of all CP members are in Russia, where the greatest splits exist. In January 1990 the CP of the Russian Federation was founded. It is a conservative party opposing Gorbachev's *perestroika* and advocating central planning and a Russian empire.

In the larger all-Union context certain parties have had an impact, especially the Democratic Platform and the Marxist Platform. The former was founded in January 1990, has a membership of over 500,000, and its leadership includes Boris Yeltsin, the president of the RSFSR. This party is probably the most influential, and Yeltsin is Gorbachev's most serious competitor. The Democratic Platform is a left-wing, radical reformist party leading toward socialist democracy. It advocates rapid march toward market economy, eliminating CP control of enterprises, the armed forces and security (e.g., KGB) agencies. The Marxist Platform, founded in April with former Politburo member Egor Ligachev its best-known leader, is conservative, advocating limited application of *perestroika* and a return to CP monopoly of power. The Marxists suffered a serious political setback during the 28th Party Congress. The Marxist-Leninist United Workers' Front (UWF) was established in October 1989 and has a membership of 5,000. It advocates central planning, full employment and a minimum wage. UWF allies with and closely resembles the Marxist Platform, drawing on its major support in large industrial cities.

The multiparty system in the Soviet Union was given constitutional recognition in March 1990 when the Congress of People's Deputies amended the Basic Law permitting political parties and groups. Some of the groups are in effect parties. A number, such as national groups, were already in existence and others were to be and are being established. Organizations proliferated representing the political and socioeconomic spectrum as well as the numerous nationalities in the USSR. One of the earliest was Democratic Union, established in May 1988 at a time when anti-Communists faced overwhelming KGB power. Its influence was greater in the past than today with the emergence of other parties.

Of the approximately 150 popular fronts in the RSFSR, the largest are in Moscow and Leningrad. The Leningrad Popular Front, which claims over a million adherents, won impressively in the March 1990 municipal and district elections. The Russian Popular Front (RFP), founded in December 1988, also has a large membership with branches in over 60 cities, advocates Western-type free-market economy and democratic and spiritual values. Opposing Marxism and CP policies, the RPF favors denationalization of property and the return of the land to the peasants. The RPF flies the flag of St. Andrew at demonstrations and some of its supporters are ideologically similar to the Russian nationalist Pamyat (see below). The left-of-center Democratic Party was formed in January 1989 by a faction of the Democratic Union.

The Socialists too have reemerged as the center-left Social Democratic Party of Russia (SDPR), founded in May 1990. The SDPR, with a membership in some 75 organizations, maintains contact with West European socialist democratic parties and with Soviet CP reformists. It collaborates with the Estonian Social Democratic Association. The party's ideology is democratic socialism and its tactics are to gain influence through elections to legislatures. SDPR scored early successes, having 70 delegates in the USSR Supreme Soviet and 50 in the RSFSR Supreme Soviet.

The Socialist Party (SP), dating from June 1990, is linked to the strike committee of the unofficial trade union movement. Its socialist ideology promotes transforming state property and economic controls to local governments. Leftist socialists organized into the Moscow Committee of New Socialists (MCNS), which reflects objectives between socialism and communism. MCNS favors mass support of the workers, labor movement and independent trade unions, but short of state socialism. It rejects complete privatization of property and supports the state's leading role in creating a market.

The Christian Democratic Union (CDU), founded in April 1989, is a center-right, anti-Communist party with ties to West European Christian Democrats. CDU is highly regarded, partly because its founder and chairman, Aleksandr Ogorodnikov, is a former religious dissident. CDU has over 80 organizations with branches in the RSFSR, Ukraine and Byelorussia. In September 1989 it became a member of the Christian Democratic International. CDU upholds Christian values, freedom and favors a free-market economy with some limitations. It cooperates with the Russian Popular Front and the independent trade unions.

The liberal democratic movement was personified by the late physicist and human rights advocate Andrei Sakharov. Perhaps the best known is the Union of Constitutional Democrats (UCD), founded in October 1989. Its objective is a democratic state based on the rule of law with individual freedom, a mix of ownership and ideology separated from the state. The Constitutional Democratic Party, founded in May 1990, patterns itself on the UCD. It is center-left persuasian. The Liberal

Democrats split from the Democratic Union in March 1990. They have no particular ideology and are guided by common sense, favoring a free-market economy.

Patriotic movements existed underground during the repressive decades, emerging in recent years as organizations in all republics. Radical groups in the Russian republic date from the 1960s with open and *samizdat* publications. The nationalists advance a strong Russian state and national revival. The major groups are the Spiritual Revival of the Fatherland, the Russian Patriotic Center (in Leningrad) and the well-known Pamyat. The last is an umbrella organization for numerous such groups, claiming to promote the unification of the national patriotic and democratic forces. Pamyat rejects charges of racism.

Although they have no tradition to draw on, the environmentalists function in some 20 groups in the USSR. The Greens believe that the greatest ecological impact can be made through political change. The largest of the groups is the Socioecological Union. Activists in the Movement for the Creation of a Green party were engaged in its realization in the fall of 1990. The aim of the Movement is to create a "communitarian" society, one composed of self-governing rural and urban communes, best achieved through legislative action but, in addition, employing demonstrations and strikes.

The traditional Russian anarchists advocate total abolition of the state. However, the Confederation of Anarcho-Syndicalists (CAS) maintains that it is campaigning for distribution of power, which should come from the bottom rather than from the top. Accordingly, CAS demands the abolition of ministries and their replacement by self-financing territorial economic planning centers. CAS was founded in January 1989 and by mid-1990 was operating in 38 cities.

The restoration of the monarchy was always attractive to some people. On May 19, 1990, the birthday of Nicholas III, the Orthodox Constitutional Monarchy Party was organized. It favors joining of the Russian Orthodox Church, the army and the KGB in a restored constitutional monarchy. The party's members take an oath of allegiance to Grand Duke Vladimir Romanov. Other monarchists prefer the czar's election by a national assembly.

In addition to these political parties and groups, numerous others are already functioning or in the process of being organized. New ones can be expected. Each republic has organizations advocating self-determination, sovereignty and even complete independence from the USSR. The attempt—e.g., by Gorbachev—to maintain CP unity has been increasingly ineffective as Communists on the republic and lower levels distance themselves from the all-Union CP in competing for parliamentary representation. As independent parties and groups become stronger and gain in influence, the CP will simultaneously become weaker and ineffectual.

Desires for human rights, freedoms and political pluralism always have existed, as have grievances against violations. However, the long, brutal, repressive regime of Stalin silenced the voices of reform. The modest liberalization under Khrushchev permitted limited expression and ennobled courageous people to voice dissatisfaction. The origins of dissident groups date from the early 1970s. The early objectives were to promote human rights and freedoms contained in the Soviet Constitution and inform people internally but especially abroad of infractions and violations. Since publishing facilities were completely denied to all but Communist Party-approved organizations, the dissenters turned to *samizdat* (self-publishing), which continues to be active.

Dissent and reform were expressed by individuals and a small number of groups. The better-known individuals were writer Aleksandr Solzhenitsyn, who was expelled from the country; Andrei Sakharov, who was sent into internal exile; and Roy Medvedev, a Marxist historian who was stripped of party membership but not jailed. Sakharov was freed and was elected a deputy to the Congress of People's Deputies; he died in December 1989. The first groups, dating from the early 1970s, were small underground organizations such as the Party of the Communists, the Marxist Party of a New Type and New Left, all advocating reform within the Communist system. The Helsinki Final Act, to which Moscow was a signatory, provided another forceful argument for the continuation of dissidence.

The impetus for the recent flowering of groups came under Gorbachev, especially during 1988 and 1989. At first groups moved cautiously, uncertain of the political terrain. Thus they proposed modest changes and limited reforms within the existing system, concentrating on those issues their precedessors in the underground proposed during the 1960s and 1970s. Hundreds, then thousands of groups were formed, and during 1989 they doubled to perhaps 60,000. Some are small, but others number in the thousands. They represent the spectrum of human activity, from general to narrowly specialized issues. For the preponderance the common bond is advocacy for reform—social, economic, political—but some have been formed to oppose change and reform. In addition to the incredible increase in their number, their advocacy has taken a quantum leap—from modest reforms within the Soviet system to outright independence and even secession of Union republics from the USSR.

Perhaps the most rapid and the greatest impact on the political scene has been made by popular fronts, which originated in the Baltic republics in 1988 and whose political objectives challenged the very structure of the USSR, prompting a personal visit by General Secretary Gorbachev to Lithuania in January 1990. These groups cannot be classified as political parties, which (except for the Communist Party) are forbidden to exist in the Soviet Union, but unquestionably that is precisely their outlook.

The most aggressive popular fronts emerged in the Baltic republics, where they participated in elections and scored impressive victories. In August 1989 Sajudis, a Lithuanian restructuring movement organized in 1988, declared in favor of the country's independence. The Lithuanian Communist Party (LCP) Congress on December 20, 1989, declared its independence from the CPSU, and the Lithuanian Supreme Soviet on December 7 deleted from its Constitution the provision (Article 6) on the leading role of the LCP. This made a

multiparty system possible in the republic. Lithuania became the first republic to take this momentous step. Prior to this action Soviet officials and the central media conducted a campaign, repeated against other republics, denouncing such extreme moves. The Lithuanian first secretary explained that only with Lithuania's independence can the LPC successfully compete with other political forces, and that victory can be gained only through democratic elections. Egor Ligachev responded that "grief will descend" on Lithuania.

Similarly, a draft proposal for a constitutional deletion of the primacy of the Communist Party of Estonia from the republic's constitution was presented, but the Estonian Supreme Soviet in its December 15, 1989, session delayed taking action. At the same time, leading members of the Estonian Popular Front announced the formation of a new political party—the Estonian Social Democratic Independence Party—whose objective is to achieve an independent and democratic Estonia. The People's Front of Latvia was founded in October 1988 of individuals and organizations, as in the other Baltic republics, and within a year reported a membership of 250,000 and support of over half the total population. Opposition to the front came, in addition to Moscow, from the conservative wing of the Latvian Communist Party and the numerous ethnic Russians in Latvia. The front's advocacy changed in 1989 from reform within the USSR to an independent democracy.

Influenced by the success of the popular fronts in the Baltic republics, similar movements were fashioned in the other republics. While they may have different immediate objectives and employ differing tactics, the popular fronts desire democratic reforms leading toward autonomy and independence. Moldavia established its National Front in May 1989 and received official recognition in October. The front in Azerbaijan was first discussed in November 1988 to help implement the principles of *perestroika* and thus achieve democracy. The front's founding conference was held in July 1989. The front organized mass demonstrations, with hundreds of thousands participating, and strikes, which influenced political action. Because of official opposition the Byelorussians established their Popular Front of Byelorussia for *Perestroika* in Vilnius, the capital of Lithuania, in June 1989. The Uzbek Popular Front Birlik was formed in May 1989 with a modest *samizdat* monthly newsletter titled *Birlik*.

Gorbachev was especially concerned with independence movements in the Ukraine, the second-largest republic, which he considers crucial. A number of groups and associations have been established in recent years. The Helsinki Union was created in 1976 but ceased operations and its leaders were jailed. Not considered political, this group represented human rights groups in the Ukraine. It was reactivated in 1988 and amended its Declaration of Principles in May 1989 in favor of Ukrainian statehood in a political realignment of the USSR, with complete independence as one alternative.

Sponsored by the Ukrainian Writers' Union, the Popular Movement of Ukraine for *Perestroika* (Rukh) was discussed in October 1988 in Kiev, voicing concerns covering a wide spectrum. An organization was created, many groups were established and the founding congress was held in September 1989 in Lvov. Rukh promotes economic and political reforms and demands guarantees for religious freedom and human rights. Its stated major objective is economic independence for the Ukraine. Moscow criticized Rukh and its leaders for their anti-Sovietism but decided to maintain a dialogue with the influential organization.

The Ukrainian Language Society, established in June 1988 in Lvov, is represented by leading intellectuals in support of Ukrainian nationalism. In October 1987 the Ukrainian Association of Independent Creative Intelligentsia was formed by dissidents and former political prisoners. The Association represents "the fullness of the spiritual, literary, cultural and public process." The Ukrainian Democratic Union, founded in May 1988 in Moscow, is a political opposition party. Initially a branch of the Russian Democratic Union (RDU), it became independent in 1989, with branches in various cities. As in the RDU, it is organized into political factions (liberal democratic, Christian democratic and social democratic). In February 1989 it changed its name to the Ukrainian People's Democratic League; it seeks to achieve a multiparty system in an independent Ukraine.

Others include the Social Democratic Federation, which calls for an independent, socialist and democratic Ukraine; the Ukrainian Christian Democratic Front, which supports a multiparty system in an independent Ukraine; student organizations (e.g., Hromada), which are considering organizing an independent Ukraine-wide association; and hundreds of other groups.

Numerous independent, unofficial groups are functioning in the Russian Federation. Before Gorbachev, fledgling groups were suppressed, but in recent years Russian nationalists have emerged, some with radical programs. Some pose as an alternative force to the Communist regime, while many have special interests concerned with developing the economy, culture and the environment. Still others are concerned with past injustices for all people and campaign for reforms generally. For example, the anti-Soviet Democratic Union was critical of Moscow's military action in Armenia, opposes the Soviet "occupation" of the Baltic republics and supports the Crimean Tatars.

Russian intellectuals have become deeply involved in political as well as cultural activities. In October 1988 the *Moscow Tribune* was established by a group of reform-minded intellectuals. Their objective is "the radical transformation of society." Russian nationalism was the catalyst for the creation in November 1988 of the Association of Russian Artists, which calls for efforts to "strengthen the national self-awareness and spiritual powers of the Russian people." The Association opposes "separatist minority nationalist tendencies" that threaten the Soviet Union. In March 1989 patriotic groups from Russian cities founded the Union for the Spiritual Revival of the Fatherland, with indications of official support. An organization promoting pan-Slavic sentiments—the Foundation for Slavic Writing and Slavic Cultures—was established in 1989. In August 1989 the Christian Democratic Union of Russia held its founding conference in Moscow. Its principles propose a parliamentary democracy with a multiparty system.

Among the more radical groups the anti-Semitic Pamyat (Memory) is a self-proclaimed "national patriotic front" with branches in numerous cities. Pamyat has experienced schismatic tendencies, with new groups forming, such as Pamyat II. Pamyat stands for the reestablishment of the monarchy and a state Orthodox Church, with citizens having consultative expression through a parliamentary body or bodies.

In 1989 a development among "workers" and "peasants" may be of greater significance in the long run. Arising out of the successful miners' strikes in July were standing "workers' committees," which considered the possibility of becoming independent trade unions and workers' movements. A Moscow conference in late July founded the Association of Peasant Farms and Agricultural Cooperatives. With the regime's support, the Association is designed to unite peasants and farms leasing cooperatives. The potential for developing political power among people in agriculture—outside the state farms and collectives—was not underestimated and suggested the possibility of a political party in the future.

Not only reformists but also conservatives established organizations. Some of these—e.g., in opposition to the popular fronts—were supported by Gorbachev's regime, but others—e.g., those critical of the general secretary's policies—were not. The day following the establishment of an independent Lithuanian Communist Party in December 1989, a group of those opposing the move formed an alternative party: the Lithuanian Republic Organization of the CPSU. In the summer of 1989 the United Front of Workers was initiated by Leningrad's deposed first secretary, Yuri Solvev, who criticized *perestroika* as contrary to Marxism-Leninism. Such united fronts were subsequently organized in other cities. In September 1989 these established the United Front of Workers of Russia. The leaders leveled criticism at both the popular fronts and the International Group of Deputies and were preparing for elections.

An interesting and potentially significant organization developed at the first session of the Congress of People's Deputies (CPD) in July 1989. Boris Yeltsin and other reform-minded deputies formed the International Group of Deputies, the first faction in the history of the USSR Supreme Soviet. The group failed to delete Article 6, but the vote at the December 1989 session to place it on the agenda was close. According to Yeltsin, the group, which has been attacked by conservatives, is considering announcing itself as a formal opposition in the parliament. Draft regulations for the Congress of People's Deputies and the Supreme Soviet providing for the right of deputies to form permanent or temporary groups was being prepared at the end of 1989. On September 30 CPD deputies from the three Baltic republics organized into the Baltic Parliamentary Group to "defend the principles of democracy and rights of nations."

ECONOMY

The Soviet Union is the second-largest industrial power in the world, with a GNP of $2.5 trillion in 1988. It has a centrally planned economy in which the dominant sector is public. It also has the largest Communist economy in the world and in this sense towers above all other socialist countries. The Soviet economy also was important for the fact that apart from its significance in a national sense, it was a proving ground and showcase of Marxism. Economic performance provided legitimacy to the ideological foundations of the state. Thus the Soviet Union competed not only against other states for an increasing share of the global economy but also against the capitalist system itself. The successes of the economy were considered as successes of the "system" devised by Marx and Lenin to "bury capitalism." Equally, its failures were closely watched around the world as discrediting the central theses of Marxism: centralized command planning, socialized property, abolition of private enterprise, state capitalism and lopsided industrial growth at the expense of agriculture and services. Unfortunately, the failures have been more numerous than the successes, and, combined with the heavy cost in personal liberty and initiative, have caused even the managers of the Soviet economy to rethink their strategies and pursue new directions and reforms.

However, even the structural deficiencies of the Soviet economic system that became apparent in the 1980s cannot hide the fact that the Soviet Union has made giant economic strides in the more than 70 years since the 1917 Revolution. In 1917, according to Lenin, the Soviet Union was one of the most backward nations in the world, estimated to be 100 to 150 years behind the rest of Europe. The Soviet Union's gross industrial output was only about 17% that of the United States. Although officially described as Marxists, the new leaders could obtain little guidance from Marx, whose economic theories were vague and totally unsuited to the Russia of the time. Further, the regime was faced with a hostile world environment without and an even more hostile peasantry within. The principal features of the Soviet economy bear the impress of those early years of conflict and isolation, and even its harshest aspects were evolutionary mechanisms of survival designed to sustain it through the locust years. Thus the economic managers were forced to take the path of autarky because of the virtual exclusion of the Soviet Union from the world economic community; they were forced to enforce total governmental control because of threats of sabotage by significant sectors of the population; and they were forced to adopt a scale of priorities that favored industry over the other sectors because of the pressing need to catch up with the West in the shortest possible time. The discrimination in resource allocation has produced a two-tier economy in which technologically advanced and highly productive enterprises in priority sectors coexist with obsolete plants in less essential sectors.

Beginning with the death of Stalin, the economic system has lost much of its doctrinaire severity and rigidity without significantly losing its fundamentally socialist nature. Measures introduced by his successors have

---

GROSS DOMESTIC PRODUCT, 1986

GDP nominal (national currency): 576 billion
GDP real (national currency): 563.1 billion
GDP average annual growth rate: 3.7% (1980–86)
GDP by type of expenditure (%)
　Consumption
　　Private: ⎱ 72
　　Government: ⎰
　Gross domestic investment: 26
　Foreign trade
　　Exports: ⎱ 2
　　Imports: ⎰
Sectoral origin of GDP (%)
　Primary
　　Agriculture: 19
　Secondary
　　Manufacturing: 46
　　Construction: 11
　Tertiary
　　Transportation & communications: 6
　　Trade: 18

PRINCIPAL ECONOMIC INDICATORS, 1988*

Gross National Product: $2.5 trillion
GNP per capita: $8,700
GNP average annual growth rate: (%) 1.5
Consumer Price Index (1980 = 100)
　All items: 105 (1986)
Average annual rate of inflation: 5.0% (1988)

*Other data regarding principal economic indicators and balance of payments in the USSR have not been published.

---

granted workers much greater freedom of movement and job selection and have improved the lot of collective farmers by raising government procurement prices for farm commodities. A continuing central problem for the economy has been the maintenance both of work incentives and efficiency at all levels of production and distribution in the absence of a profit motive and of an adequate supply of consumer goods on which workers' earnings could be spent. The enemy of the Soviet economy has not been so much the system itself but human nature.

The economy is organized on a sectoral and hierarchical basis. Overall control is vested in the Central Committee of the CPSU and the USSR Council of Ministers, some of whose members hold positions on both bodies. The Council of Ministers provides direction to a number of Union ministries responsible for individual sectors and subsectors of the economy. Each ministry administers the sector under its jurisdiction through a series of main administrations responsible for groups of enterprises engaged in similar lines of activity. Individual enterprises are managed by state-appointed directors, under the *nomenklatura* system, who have very little autonomy. In a growing number of instances, associations of industrial enterprises form an additional administrative link, intermediate between the individual enterprise and the main administration. A parallel administrative organization, responsible to the Union Council of Ministers, exists in each republic. As a rule the most important enterprises in any one sector are subject to union jurisdiction. Some local enterprises are controlled by lower levels of the CPSU and government structures.

In addition to the control exercised through the ministries and the banking system, close supervision over enterprise performance also is maintained by the CPSU through various means. This is in accordance with Lenin's dictum that politics takes precedence over economics. At the same time, great importance is attached to moral incentives, including titles, honors and favorable publicity, as well as to appeals to patriotism.

Management of the economy has been severely hampered by conflicts between the interests of the state and those of enterprise managers. Motivated by a drive for maximum economic growth, the government has consistently endeavored to set production goals high enough to force managers to exploit to the utmost all available resources. Operating within a system that offers them large rewards for meeting or exceeding planned targets and penalizes them for falling short of the goals by even a very small margin, managers have sought to protect themselves by creating reserves of equipment, materials and labor through underestimating the productive potential of their plants and overstating their resource requirements. The need for such reserves has been accentuated by chronic supply difficulties induced by shortcomings in planning.

In an attempt to eliminate this management practice and to encourage greater efficiency, a much-publicized economic reform was instituted in 1965. Gradually extended throughout most of the economy, this reform introduced charges for interest and rent as a means of stimulating a more economical use of capital and natural resources; it also changed the standard for measuring enterprise performance from volume of output to profits, in order to make managers more cost-conscious. In addition, it reduced by a very small margin the number of performance targets dictated to the enterprise by superiors and allowed the enterprises to use a portion of their profits for the benefit of the work force and for plant improvement.

In practice, the reform did not significantly alter the functioning of the economy, although it provided incentives for more efficient performance. The cumbrous price mechanisms have largely negated its effectiveness.

One of the major deficiencies of the Soviet economy concerns the collection and reporting of statistical data, making analyses difficult and ultimately flawed. Data have never been published either on many of the essential industrial products and armaments or on the number, size and distribution of industrial establishments. Labor force statistics are not sufficiently detailed, and very little information is published on earnings or in other areas where the Soviet Union has a comparative disadvantage. Statistics on national income and the value of industrial and agricultural output are limited to percentage changes of these aggregates from year to year, or to annual totals without adequate breakdowns into constituent parts. Further, a number of industries are treated as classified information, even when they have no true military significance. Definitions often are imprecise, and comparability over a period of time is destroyed by changes in pricing. Even where the Central Statistical Administration reports physical output statistics correctly, they are derived from exaggerated

figures submitted to them by enterprise managers bent on fulfilling plan quotas at least on paper. Other conditions hamper the collection of data in agriculture, and the absolute level and rate of increase in the output of some farm products are invariably overstated.

With regard to the validity of index number series for such items as national and real personal income, industrial production and farm output, there is widespread skepticism among Western analysts, shared in part by some Soviet economists. Statistical results vary greatly depending on the methods of calculation used. It is generally believed that official Soviet indexes reflect statistical practices that yield the most favorable data from the point of view of demonstrating superior economic performance. In other words, good statistics are designed as good propaganda.

There are significant differences between Soviet and Western statistical concepts and methods. Western economists, translating Soviet data into Western terms, have arrived at significantly lower rates of growth and aggregates. The Soviet concept of GNP distinguishes between productive and unproductive activities and excludes most services. Gross output also differs from the Western concept in that it consists of the sum of the gross outputs of all productive enterprises rather than only of the sum of the values added by each enterprise in the productive process. These conceptual differences account very largely for the substantial disparity between Soviet GNP data that appear in official statistics and those published by Western economists.

One of the principal legacies of Stalinism is the overemphasis on industry to the neglect of agriculture. According to official statistics, the gross output of industry has since 1913 risen 24 times faster than that of agriculture. Agriculture has been discriminated against not only by depriving it of needed inputs but also through price structures. Thus the price of industrialization has fallen disproportionately on the farm sector, and living conditions of collective farmers are among the poorest in the country. This neglect is responsible for empty shelves in the supermarkets, inadequate protein content in the average diet and a high import bill in years of poor harvests. The inefficiency of socialized agriculture is demonstrated by the magnitude of the output of the small private plots. With little more than 3% of the sown land, the private sector produces about two-thirds of the potato and egg output; two-fifths of vegetable, meat and milk production; and one-fifth of the wool output.

In contrast, industry is the dominant economic sector, and in size it ranks second only to the United States in the world. Natural resources for industrial development are large, but most of these are unfavorably located. Exploitation of resources east of the Urals poses substantial technical difficulties and entails high labor and transportation costs that are only partly offset by the better quality of these resources. For historic and climatic reasons, most industrial establishments are in the European part of the country, although substantial development has taken place in the eastern regions, especially since World War II. The new industrial centers are mainly suppliers of raw materials and energy and account for only a small portion of the manufacturing output. Workers are unwilling to relocate to the remote regions, even with higher pay and other inducements. Relative emphasis on the development of particular industrial branches has shifted from time to time, but common emphasis has been on investment in primary production—i.e., raw materials, fuels, and power—at the expense of processing industries. Development of light and food industries has been hampered not only by the inadequacy of capital investments but also by their poor utilization. Of the output of consumer goods, one-third is accounted for by textiles, clothing, knitwear, leather goods and footwear. Durable consumer goods such as refrigerators, washing machines, television sets, bicycles and household equipment are produced by heavy-industry enterprises.

Functioning like a giant corporation—or "USSR, Inc.," as it has been called—the Soviet economy is organized on an industrial-territorial basis. There are 18 major economic regions, based on geographic factors. These regions are not administrative units but rather planning zones. Each region has its own mix of industrial and agricultural potentials that are supposed to be developed in concert. Ten of the economic regions are made up of 70 administrative units within the RSFSR, six of them in the European part of the RSFSR. The Ukrainian SSR is divided into three economic regions: The Byelorussian SSR, the Kazakh SSR, the three Baltic republics, the three Caucasian republics and the five central Asian republics each form one. The largest is the Central Economic Region, which includes Moscow, and the smallest the Far East Economic Region.

The structure of the Soviet economy can be understood only in reference to the productive enterprises that make up the economy. Many types of economic activity familiar in the West are not found in the Soviet Union or are illegal there. The laws and regulations governing these activities have changed only slightly since the liquidation of the New Economic Policy in the late 1920s.

It is illegal for any private citizen to employ anyone to produce a commodity for sale—e.g., a private shoemaker may make shoes but may not employ an assistant. In principle, the exploitation of person by person is prohibited by law, although one may employ a domestic servant who "produces" nothing. It also is illegal for an individual to sell anything he has not produced himself. This means that no one may resell anything for a profit. These activities exist but are illegal. Even within the sectors in which private or cooperative activities are nominally permitted, state organs have used and frequently do use the right to refuse the necessary registration permits. Thus if the state does not provide certain services or goods, they are not provided at all.

The principal categories of productive enterprises in the Soviet Union are as follows:

- state enterprises
- nonagricultural cooperative enterprises
- collective farms
- the private sector, subdivided into private farm plots and private craftsmen

A state enterprise belongs to the state and is a convenient unit for the administration of state property. As a juridical person it can sue and be sued, but it owns none of its assets, and its profits belong to the state, which can take away any of its assets without compensation. A state enterprise is under a one-man director, whose primary task is to fulfill, and if possible overfulfill, the output plans and to manage its resources in strict accordance to detailed orders from above. The Soviet system involves a complex interaction between planner-administrators on the one hand and productive enterprises on the other; the former are in command, yet much that happens in Soviet microeconomics is explicable only by the existence of loopholes in the system of rules and orders. The severity of the system is tempered and humanized by its inefficiency. Only the loopholes stimulate and preserve initiative in a system that otherwise has no place for it. In addition to state enterprises in industry, there are other state enterprises, with their own peculiarities. These include building enterprises that do contract construction; state farms; trade and material supply organizations (divided into state shops [torg] and consumer cooperatives); transportation enterprises such as Aeroflot; service undertakings such as laundries and pawnshops, organized by local authorities; and foreign trade corporations. Although the cooperative and private sectors exist formally outside the state system, they are so heavily regulated as to be de facto parts of the state economy.

Economic performance from the end of World War II until the late 1950s was satisfactory from the point of view of the leadership intent on closing the gap between the Soviet economy and the economies of advanced Western countries. During that period the Soviet Union led all other countries in rate of economic growth, with the possible exception of West Germany. Since 1958, however, the economy has steadily deteriorated and has failed to recover even after most Western economies recovered from earlier recessions. In Soviet statistical terms the growth of the national income declined from an average annual rate of 10.9% in the 1951–58 period to about 4% in the late 1980s. Industrial production and farm output also shared in the decline.

The tendency of Soviet leaders is generally to blame external factors for the shortcomings of the economy and not the system itself. Those usually bearing the brunt of the blame are the managers on the one hand and the workers on the other. The initial remedy is to impose more penalties on managers and workers, and when these penalties fail to produce results, the next step is to propose cosmetic reforms, which take over a decade to prove themselves ineffective and thus give the leadership some breathing time.

Although a lag in the introduction and assimilation of technological innovation is a principal cause of such dysfunctions, an even more important one is the labor shortage. Because nearly 20% of the labor force is employed in the agricultural sector (compared with 3% for the United Kingdom and 4% for the United States), industrial labor potentials are accordingly reduced. It is not considered feasible to reduce the labor share of agriculture because of low productivity and poor mechanization. Neither is it possible to enlarge the catchment areas of labor, since the entire able-bodied population of working age is already employed. A declining rate of natural population increase and a growing demand for labor in social services and trade are anticipated to place further pressures on industrial labor supply. At the same time, large increases in capital investment and industrial research appear to be precluded by the continued heavy expenditures on space and military programs and the popular clamor for housing and consumer goods. Thus the only option open to the leadership is to call for increased productivity, but such an improvement is contingent on reallocation of national priorities and better management of technology. This is the thrust of Gorbachev's *perestroika* program, which still is in its incubation stage.

The decline in productivity, which appears to be the central problem for Soviet planners, is attributable to the conjunction of several related factors, such as the resort to marginal labor without proper work experience or training, the progressive obsolescence and deterioration of a large number of the existing capital stock and the depressing influence of the agricultural sector.

Over the years the Soviet Union has consistently devoted as much as one-third of its GNP to investment by controlling consumption and siphoning huge funds into the budget through the turnover tax, levied primarily on consumer goods. Between 35% and 40% of total investment is channeled into industry, and of total industrial investment almost 90% is devoted to capital goods, with the balance to consumer goods. Agriculture receives about 20% of total investment, and its ailing condition has helped to depress consumer goods industries based on farm products. Housing, long one of the nonpriority areas for investment, has only recently received adequate attention.

Pari passu with declining labor productivity is the unfavorable trend in the capital–output ratio—i.e., the amount of new investment needed to produce an additional unit of output. This productivity has declined by more than one-third since 1958. Capital construction has traditionally been associated with great waste of resources. Delays in the completion of construction and the attainment of full-scale operation inevitably resulted in the immobilization of a substantial volume of capital. The volume of construction projects undertaken each year has far surpassed the resources available to complete them. Since capital could be obtained from the budget free of charge and in the absence of a rational price system, the planners have no sound economic criteria for evaluating the relative merits of investment proposals. Individual construction projects have dragged on for years, with machines and equipment awaiting installation. Another reason for the lowering of capital productivity has been the rising portion of gross new investment needed to compensate for the depreciation of existing facilities and the depletion of natural resources. Because much of Soviet machinery is of poor quality, it is short-lived and is in constant need of repair. The productivity of capital also is adversely affected by the failure to translate scientific research findings into improved technological processes and by long delays in assimilating new technologies. Although Soviet scientific capabilities are of a high

order, emphasis is on research rather than on development; further, the best talents and facilities are devoted to military and space research. Also impediments to innovation are the enterprise performance evaluation system, which penalizes slowdowns attendant upon the introduction of new technology; and the industrial price system, under which quality improvements entail a loss in profits.

Consumption as a proportion of the GNP fell from 60% in 1950 to about 50% in the late 1980s, but consumption of goods has risen at a rate of 4.3% per year and per capita consumption of goods has risen at 2.2% per year since 1950. Food as a percentage of the GNP dropped to about 20% in the late 1980s, from 32% in 1950. The standard of living in many Soviet republics is slightly lower than in almost all the advanced Western countries. The average net take-home pay of an industrial worker in the Soviet Union is only one-quarter that of his counterpart in the United States and one-third that of his counterpart in the United Kingdom at the official exchange rates. However, these figures do not measure purchasing power. The ruble rate is artificial; the level of employment in the Soviet Union is higher and the number of wage earners per family larger; income in kind (e.g., low rents, free social services, subsidized meals, etc.) is higher; and prices are lower. Even so, Soviet earned income is less than half the U.S. figure.

Soviet consumption expenditures are historically different from those in capitalist countries. Basic needs (shelter, medical care, transportation, insurance) account for only 15% of Soviet money income, compared with 50% in the United States. Utilities are cheap or are heavily subsidized. Rents have remained virtually unchanged since 1928. It is estimated that the Soviets spend only 5% of their income on housing, fuel, light and power, whereas the average American spends 35%. In most consumer durables the Soviet Union lags behind Western countries and, further, they are often of inferior quality.

A major difference between capitalist and state socialist societies is the absence of price inflation in the latter. Prices are fixed by the government and rise 1% to 2% each year. Thus the Soviet Union is exempt from the rapid escalation of prices suffered by almost all capitalist countries since the 1960s. However, instead of inflation, the Soviets have *defitsits* (shortages). As the demand for goods exceeds the supply of goods at the ruling price, goods vanish when they are put on the market, and services are oversubscribed. A study made in the early 1980s reported that only three of 19 foodstuffs (sugar, bread and vodka) were regularly available in shops in 80 of 102 cities. There are three reasons for this state of affairs. First is price inflexibility; prices are fixed by planners either on estimated market demand or on political considerations. The latter criteria are applied to essential items such as gasoline, meat and butter, which have remained constant for many years. Second, there are temporal and regional shortages created by transportation bottlenecks or shortfalls in the production of certain goods, such as potatoes in times of drought. In such cases prices do not rise to equate demand and supply. Third is the increase in purchasing power, driving up demand.

The consequences of such reverse inflation are as negative as those of inflation. Unless supply responds to meet demand, money loses value and is supplanted by bribery and corruption. When goods are available they are hoarded, eroding confidence in the market and in the government. Just as some goods are priced too low, others are too expensive. Output often is valued by weight of materials, and as a result Soviet goods often are heavy. Producers also try to maximize their total sales by inflating the costs of their products or services.

Just as in capitalist societies, there exists a strong underground economy in the Soviet Union as ingenious citizens have devised a host of ways of compensating for the inadequacies of the official economy. There are parallel or alternative markets of varying degrees of legitimacy and legality, some of them highly specialized in terms of the products handled and their clientele. According to observers, "everyone from plumber to government minister derives illegal rewards through the theft of state goods and services." There is a whole range of "colored" markets ranging from the legal red, pink and white to the semilegal gray and the illegal brown and black. Some of these markets are typically socialist, some are presocialist and many more are universal, such as are found in every society.

The red market is a distribution system that conforms to state prices; the white embraces the legitimate exchange of secondhand goods in the equivalent of flea markets, and the sale of farm produce through collective farmers' markets; and the pink embraces the sale of secondhand goods in commission shops. The gray market embraces the sale of goods and services for which state supply is inadequate: housing, educational tuition, health care, legal advice, repairs, tailoring, shoemaking, all beyond the pale of state control and thus untaxed. Illegal markets are those in which the participants when caught are liable to be prosecuted or disciplined. The most obvious brown market covers items in short supply that are traded *nalevo* (literally, on the left or under the counter) by those with access to them, such as shop assistants or restaurant staff. Another brown market exists for foreign goods, materials stolen from state enterprises by technicians or servicemen, spare parts for cars and other equipment. The black market embraces strictly illegal transactions in which the participants are liable to be prosecuted and jailed. This includes trade in fashions, foreign currency, gold, drugs and prostitutes' services. A more common area of the shadow economy is the practice of doing private work on company time. The scale of the shadow economy has been estimated at 4% to 12% of the GNP.

One of the major contributions of Communist ideology to the Soviet economy is planning, which is the process by which scarce resources are allocated to competing ends. Based on general CPSU directives concerning broad economic goals, the planning authorities formulate long-term (five-year or more) and short-range (annual, quarterly and monthly) plans to achieve specific targets in virtually all spheres of economic activity, although major emphasis is placed on the production of high-priority items and industrial development. The production plans are supplemented by comprehensive plans for the supply of materials, equipment, labor and finances to the producing sector; procurement of farm products by the state; and distribution of food and manufactured products to the population. The economic plans have the force of law. They are worked out in great detail down to the level of the individual economic enterprise, where they are reflected in a set of output goals and performance indicators (called success indicators) that management is expected to meet. The planning process must ensure that each enterprise has at its disposal at the proper time the necessary materials, labor and capital to carry out its assigned task. This planning of material balances is done primarily in physical terms—i.e., in tons of coal or wheat, etc.; in numbers of bulldozers, eggs, etc.; and in man-hours. Corollary financial plans developed through the application of fixed, government-established prices to the physical plans mainly as a means of control over enterprise performance through the banking system.

The immense difficulty of planning the physical flow of productive resources and finished goods in an economy as large and complex as that of the Soviet Union inevitably entails serious planning errors. Bottlenecks in production and distribution, shortages in low-priority sectors, rising inventories of goods for which there is no demand and frequent diversion of resources from agriculture and consumer goods have plagued the system since its introduction in the 1920s. These difficulties are compounded by (1) the rigidity of the planning mechanisms, which do not permit consideration of alternatives and which rely overly on administratively set prices; (2) the lack of autonomy at the enterprise level, and (3) the tendency to set overly ambitious production quotas.

Adherence by enterprise management to the major plan directives is generally assured through inspection procedures and through systems of incentives and sanctions. The former include honors, promotions and bonuses; the latter include reprimands, loss of income and/or position and even criminal prosecution. There are provisions for plan modifications, but these are limited to secondary targets. To achieve their quotas, managers resort to wasteful substitutions and extralegal procurement practices. As a result, overfulfillment of targets by heavy industry and underfulfillment by agriculture and consumer industries have been regular features of Soviet economic performance. In their pursuit of numbers, managers tend to neglect quality, development of new products and technological innovation, all of which may temporarily reduce managerial income and good showing. Even at the Kremlin, there always is the temptation to fabricate numbers and to conceal flaws and failures so as not to mar the record of socialist achievements.

At the top of the planning pyramid is the State Planning Committee (Gosplan), under the Council of Ministers. This agency, comprising a large number of sectoral, functional, technical and statistical departments, is responsible for formulating nationwide plans, aggregating and integrating the more detailed sectoral and regional plans prepared by subordinate planning levels, and supervising plan fulfillment. It also is responsible for assuring a correct balance among the different branches of the economy, searching out means to speed the growth of the national income and raising the level of efficiency in production. Gosplan itself has no productive enterprise under its orders. Formal authority over the enterprises rests with the ministries.

Economic ministries draft plans within the sphere of their own jurisdictions, direct the planning by subordinate enterprises and supervise enterprise performance. Within the ministries the planning task is subdivided among several departments called *glavki*, which deal with functional problems such as finance or procurement, or with regional problems, or with particular product categories, such as woolens.

Individual enterprises at the base of the planning pyramid develop the most minutely detailed plans, covering all aspects of their operations. Generally, enterprises are directly subordinate to a *glavk*, although in some instances there are intermediate organizations in the form of trusts or associations, grouping together several enterprises. These organizations also form a link in the planning chain.

A parallel organizational system for planning exists in each Union republic and autonomous republic. The republic state planning committees are subject to the jurisdiction of both the Republic Council of Ministers and Union state planning committees. The regional system also includes planning agencies created for several major economic regions, extending down to the local district or town level.

The second most important functional organization in planning is the State Committee for Material-Technical Supply (Gossnab). This agency shares with Gosplan control over allocation of essential materials and equipment. Gosplan prepares balances for about 2,000 of the more important products, while Gossnab together with its local organs prepares some 18,000 items considered to be of lesser importance but that have a wider spread of users throughout the economy. However, Gosplan's allocations cover 80% of the *value* of allocated commodities. Other functional agencies include the State Committee for Construction, the State Committee on Labor and Wages, the State Committee for Science and Technology and the Academy of Sciences.

The planning process has never been adequately described, but its broad outlines are clear. The key economic goals are formulated by the Council of Ministers and transmitted to Gosplan. At the same time, a flow of information, requests and proposals reaches Gosplan from many organizations and ministries in the form of *zayvaki* (indents or applications for inputs), which are key features of the planning process. Republican organs and regional bodies, local party functionaries and domestic and foreign trade organs also add their voices. Based on these inputs, Gosplan works out a set of control figures covering major aspects of the economic activity; these figures are then routed back to the participant units for elaboration. The flow then is reversed and the detailed draft plans developed at the lower levels are sent back up the ladder for review, adjustment and integration. This process entails intensive bargaining up and down the line, with Gosplan pressing for higher quotas. After final review and revision by Gos-

plan, the Council of Ministers, the CPSU and the Supreme Soviet, the approved plan containing specific targets is returned to each economic entity. In agriculture, detailed plans for crop and livestock production and production methods are developed and assigned by the planning apparatus to the individual farms.

To have the annual plans for the enterprises completed by the beginning of the operational year, preparation of plans normally begins in March or April of the preceding year. Therefore, planners have to rely on estimates formed many months before actual output levels become known. Planning for material and equipment supplies also must be done in advance, so that enterprises are forced to make detailed requisitions for these items long before they know what their production program will be. Although plans are laws in theory, they are, in fact, guesstimates, and the lack of correspondence between targets and results reflects the problem of timing. Frequent changes of plans in midstream aggravate this discrepancy. Plans frequently reach enterprises well after the beginning of the planning period. The third five-year plan was not completed owing to the outbreak of World War II in 1939. The sixth five-year plan (1956–60) was dropped in its third year and replaced by a seven-year plan (1959–65).

The eighth five-year plan (1966–70) was successfully completed, and in many cases, particularly in the petroleum, nonferrous metal, engineering and mineral industries, targets were exceeded. Net Material Product (NMP or "national income") rose by 41% between 1966 and 1970, and industrial production by 50%; real incomes increased by one-third. The ninth and 10th five-year plans failed to achieve the levels of growth sought in most sectors of the economy, and targets have progressively become more modest. The most significant feature of the 10th five-year plan (1976–80) was a shift of resources to agriculture, with more than one-quarter of investment during the five years being allocated to this sector, resulting in a 9% increase in production, compared with the goal of 14% to 17%. Industrial production rose by 24%, against a target of 35% to 39%, and national income grew by 23%, compared with a planned growth of 24% to 28%. The 11th five-year plan (1981–85) gave priority to the production of consumer goods, representing a shift from the traditional emphasis on heavy industry. Targets for the 11th plan were for industrial production to increase by 26% (with heavy industry attaining a similar rate of growth and the output of consumer goods increasing by 26.2%) and for agricultural production, which accounted for one-third of total investment under the plan, to increase by 13%. Overall, the NMP was to grow by 18%. In 1986 it was announced that industrial production had increased by 20% during the plan period, while agricultural production had increased by only 6% and overall NMP by 17%. Real per capita income was reported to have increased by 11% during this time. The 12th five-year plan (1986–90), announced in 1985, envisaged an increase of 19% to 22% in NMP over the period. Total industrial production was to rise by 21% to 24%: this was to be achieved by increasing labor productivity rather than by massive investment in new projects. In 1986 the NMP reached 590 billion rubles (compared with 577 billion rubles in 1985), a total that was official-ly reported to represent growth of 4.1% in real terms (compared with real growth of 3.5% in the previous year). In 1986 gross industrial output increased by 4.7%, reaching a value of 836 billion rubles, and gross agricul-tural output by 5.1%, reaching a value of 219.2 billion rubles. In 1987 the NMP grew by 3.3%, compared with a planned growth of 4.1%, and gross industrial output rose by 3.8% to 870 billion rubles. Gross agricultural output rose by 0.2%, to 220 billion rubles. Labor produc-tivity, which had grown by 3.8% in 1986, increased by 4.1% in 1987. Targets for the 1988 plan were for an esti-mated increase in industrial production of 4.5%, in the NMP of 4.3%, in agricultural production of 3.4% and in labor productivity of 4.2%. The GNP, which increased by 8% in 1986, grew by 3.3% in 1987 and was expected to rise by an average annual rate of 2% to 3% until 1990.

Long-term plans (five years) and perspective plans (15 years or more) are by their nature development plans and not operational plans because they do not contain specific orders to any industrial manager to produce anything. To make them operational they have to be disaggregated into a more detailed product mix and into orders or instructions addressed to their exec-utants. There also is an operational counterpart, called an investment plan. National five-year plans and annual plans are published in condensed form, presenting un-der appropriate headings the targets for the economy as a whole and for its component branches. Neither quar-terly nor monthly plans are published. Short-term plans are intended to allow for current adjustment of long-term plans in light of changed or unforeseen circum-stances. In actual practice they are more frequently used to eliminate bottlenecks or breakdowns in the supply system due to planning errors.

The method used by planners to achieve internally consistent plans in both a sectoral and a regional con-text is called method of balances. Essentially it consists of preparing balance sheets in which available material, labor and financial resources are listed as assets and requirements based on planned output as liabilities. The task of planners is to equate both sides through trial and error and successive approximations to as-sure that the necessary inputs are provided for the planned output, both overall and for each product. To reduce the task to manageable proportions, the most detailed output goals, investment projects and supply plans are formulated by the Union authorities for the key branches only, with the rest of the plan developed only in relation to these key branches. Implicit in this process are prioritization of sectors and maximum ex-ploitation of available resources so that all high-priority sectors are fully covered and as many of the remaining as possible are covered in descending order. In working out material balances, norms specify for each type of operation the quantity and quality of materials and labor to be used, the intensity of equipment utilization, the time span and other relevant factors. In keeping with Marxist doctrine, these norms are progressive and become more stringent over the years. In each sector there are output norms for workers, rates of growth for labor productivity and centrally determined wage rates for each category of worker.

Separate balances are drawn up for many thousands of items used in production and construction by some 130 branches of industry; all of these balances must subsequently be reconciled through mutual adjustment and integrated into coherent sectoral and regional pro-duction and investment plans. The same method is used in formulating plans for all other aspects of the econo-my, such as trade, procurement, consumer goods and agriculture. The sum total of these plans constitutes the national plan. This planning process is known as a microeconomic approach, in contrast to a macroeco-nomic approach, which deals with broad categories of the national income, such as production, consumption, savings and investment and which plays only a minor role in Soviet planning.

The sheer complexity of planning is a challenge to the ingenuity of the best economists working with the best computers. Availability of both is quite limited in the Soviet Union. Apart from the problems already alluded to, the most serious problems in Soviet plan-ning are: coordination among the thousands of agencies involved in the task; consistency of data; and neglect of unquantifiable factors in all human activity, such as the human elements, weather and local conditions. There also has been a tendency to overexploit natural re-sources without regard to environmental conse-quences. Inevitable duplication leads to waste of re-sources and of labor.

At the enterprise level, the operational plan is embod-ied in a document known as *techpromfinplan* (techni-cal-industrial-financial plan), which specifies in detail the production targets in terms of gross output and val-ue of sales; the product mix; units, materials and equip-ment that may be purchased and their sources of sup-ply; the number of workers who may be employed; and the wage bill. The financial section of the plan trans-lates this program into monetary terms on the basis of set prices and wages and contains assignments for sales, profits and profitability; receipts from and pay-ments into the state budget; and a breakdown of capital expenditures. The plan also provides product quality specifications and directions for the introduction of new products and technology.

Since achievement of plan targets depends heavily on the level of performance, devotion and loyalty of the members of enterprise management, there are moral and material incentives to incite them to maximum pro-ductive effort. Moral incentives have not worked too well in the past. Material incentives consist primarily of bonus payments for industrial managers and distribu-tion of residual farm income among collective farm managers. Since both are based on attainment of output targets, managers maneuver to obtain low production assignments and liberal allocations of resources. Man-agers who exceed their plan targets by too high a mar-gin may be hoist with their own petards when the next plan routinely raises that target by a fixed percentage. Since 1970 a new incentives program has been intro-duced based on the concept of profitability.

At the core of the materials incentives program are three special funds: the materials incentives fund; the fund for social and cultural measures and for housing; and the fund for production development. The amount of deductions from profits for the benefit of these funds is based on sales, profits and the total wage bill. Administration of the program, particularly the task of identifying the individuals and groups entitled to bonus payments and measuring their contribution, entails a heavy burden on the accounting system.

Since the beginning of the Cold War the Soviet Union has become a major source of economic aid for two categories of countries: Communist countries within or without COMECON, and developing countries that are neutral or politically inclined toward Moscow. Aid was a weapon in the Cold War, and the Soviet Union, like Western capitalist countries, has had its successes and failures in this area. In some cases, such as Cuba, the quantum of aid was much higher than the benefits derived; in Egypt, there were tactical misjudgments; in Ghana, the Soviet Union backed the wrong horse; and in China, the aid program was a disaster. Responsibility for foreign economic assistance rests with the State Committee for Foreign Economic Relations. The program is handled exclusively on a government-to-government basis. The bulk of the aid has been channeled into publicly owned industrial plants and the balance into agricultural and infrastructure facilities. The nature of the assistance granted usually is conditioned by the stage of the recipient country's development. The Soviet organization usually accepts responsibility for project research and for delivery of all equipment, spare parts and materials not available locally. It also provides technicians and trains indigenous workers and technical personnel. As a rule, economic aid has been provided in the form of credits rather than outright grants. About a third of the aid commitments are in the form of trade credits and the balance in the form of long-term development credits.

In 1990, the Soviet took the first step on a historic transformation of its economy into a Western-style free market. Dubbed as the Shatalin Plan, after Stanislav S. Shatalin, a liberal economist who is a member of Gorbachev's Presidential Council, the plan is the result of an agreement between Gorbachev and Boris Yeltsin, the reformist president of RSFSR. It represents a radical break with the fundamental tenets of Marxism, and calls for a restoration of private property and economic freedom to Soviet citizens and a devolution of economic decision-making power to the republics. According to the draft, "the program takes away from the state as much as possible and gives it back to the people . . . Everybody should be free to choose for himself his own role: to be an entrepreneur, to work for the government, or to work as a manager in a private company. Freedom of choice is at the basis of personal freedom."

The Shatalin Plan gives the 15 Soviet republics a major role in implementing reform—through the creation of a new agency to oversee compliance—and would reward them with broad economic autonomy when the reform was completed. Each republic would set its own pace in privatizing land and state enterprises.

A central bank, run collectively by the republics, would control the money supply, and thus control both the overall price level and the availability of credit. Even the power to raise revenue for the military would apparently be subject to veto by the republics. The plan also calls for the breakup of giant factories and the introduction of foreign competition.

Under the draft plan, scheduled for completion within 500 days, the first 100 days would be devoted to the passage of laws establishing property rights and financial markets, decentralizing banking and creating a "safety net" for the poorest members of society. The central regime and the republics would raise imports and impose selective wage and price controls to fight inflation. During the next 150 days, state subsidies to agriculture and industry would be ended, central economic ministries would be abolished and the central government would begin a sweeping privatization of land, housing and industry. During the next 150 days private controls would be lifted while bolstering programs for the needy. The final 100 days would be devoted to stabilizing measures, including the use of government reserves to hold down prices. At this point, the plan anticipates that public investment in newly privatized businesses would help counter unemployment.

Meanwhile, the economic system established by Lenin and Stalin is already unraveling before a new one is set up in its place. Shortages were common even in the pre-Gorbachev era, but now they have become universal. The proximate cause of the shortages is the rise in demand and the fall in supplies—too many rubles chasing too few goods. The new managers, undisciplined by either the bureaucrats or market forces, have raised wages—and thus consumer buying power—faster than justified by productivity gains. There is no longer a way to guarantee the delivery of products in the context of the erosion of central authority. Shortages have begotten more shortages, as enterprises, republics and cities resort to barter. Karelia, an autonomous region near Finland, refused to export newsprint until sausages appeared in its shops. Moscow and Leningrad have closed price-controlled stores to non-residents. Factories are making side deals with other factories to supply their own workers everything from shoes to cars, leaving store shelves empty. Collective farms are building inventories in the expectation that grain and meat prices will rise. Enterprises are no longer exchanging all the marks and dollars they earn abroad for rubles, leaving Soviet importing organizations with inadequate funds to pay Western suppliers.

During the past two decades, the creditworthiness of the Soviet Union on international hard-currency markets had been enviably high. Such ratings were attributable chiefly to a low debt-service ratio, the immaculate servicing of debts, steady economic growth, large stocks of gold and known reserves of exploitable and exportable commodities. However, since the late 1980s, Soviet standing in credit markets has begun to dip. Until 1989 the Soviet Union published virtually no data about its transactions on the world financial markets. The first official disclosure of Soviet indebtedness came from Prime Minister Ryzhkov in 1989 when addressing the Congress of People's Deputies; he put the current debt at 34 billion rubles ($57 billion) and the cost of servicing that debt at 12 billion rubles ($19 billion). Although it was believed that Ryzhkov had exaggerated the debt and servicing budens in order to counter those who urged massive imports of finished consumer goods, it was confirmed in November 1989 that the Soviet Union was a creditor nation to the tune of 85.8 billion rubles.

Closely allied to the disintegration of the economy is the disintegration of the Soviet environment. According to Novosti, environmental problems affect 16% of Soviet territory. The content of toxic substances in the air exceeds maximum permissible levels in 103 cities. Although the amount of atmospheric emissions in the Soviet Union is far less than that in the more developed United States, it is estimated as being in excess of 100 million tons annually. Further, the emissions of particulate matter are twice those of the United States. The quality of water in many Soviet rivers and lakes is near crisis levels. This is particularly true of the five seas— Aral, Baltic, Azov, Black and Caspian. In 1988 a state committee for environmental protection was set up and enabling legislation was passed, establishing certain areas—including Lake Baikal, the world's largest freshwater body—as protected regions. A 15-year program has been drawn up to stop all discharge of effluents into rivers or lakes and also reduce industrial emissions by half. During this period R&D for environmental purposes is expected to grow by 50%, with emphasis on waste-free technologies.

The Soviet Union is a founding member of the Council for Mutual Economic Assistance (CEMA, CMEA or COMECON), a rather loose regional organization, without executive authority, that joins the Soviet Union with six East European countries—Bulgaria, Rumania, Poland, East Germany, Hungary and Czechoslovakia—as well as Mongolia, Cuba and Vietnam. Created in 1949 as a counterweight to the Marshall Plan, it was relatively quiescent until 1956, and it adopted a formal charter only in 1960. Its original aim of full economic integration of all socialist countries, successfully opposed by Rumania, has been replaced by one of socialist division of labor. Apart from foreign trade and associated finance, principal COMECON activities include coordination of national economic plans, product specialization, industrial standardization and scientific and technological cooperation.

PUBLIC FINANCE

The financial system of the Soviet Union is an integral part of its planned economy and is subordinate to the national economic plan. Unlike in nonsocialist countries, the national budget is an instrument of the plan and is essentially the financial part of the plan, translating economic goals into monetary terms. Revenues originate predominantly in the operation of the state sector of the economy, which also consumes a large portion of the expenditures. Similarly, financial authorities operate within the bounds of the plan, and their allocation of monies for credit purposes is designed to further the plan. The budget and the economic plan are so closely interrelated that it has become the practice to submit both to the same session of the Supreme Soviet. Another feature of the Soviet budget is its vast scope, without parallel in the West. It is estimated that 40% to 45% of the GNP is channeled through the state budget. The state budget is large also because it comprises some 50,000 various budgets. At the top, the all-Union budget accounts for about half of the total, including nonclassified military expenditures, industries with all-Union status, most transportation and communications, foreign trade, state reserves and certain social services. The republics account for about two-thirds of the remaining expenditures, including much of industry and a major part of specialized and higher education. Local budgets finance small-scale industrial enterprises, trade and services, housing, lower levels of education, health and cultural establishments.

The legal foundations of the budget are in the Constitution of 1918 and various budgetary laws. The present system of taxation is based largely on the reforms carried out in 1930 and 1931. At that time separate systems of taxation were set up for the socialized and private sectors, and a turnover tax and a profits tax were established as the major sources of revenue. The fiscal year is the Calendar Year.

The state budget is drafted in highly aggregated form and handed downward to successively lower levels of governmental units, where it is matched against preliminary draft budgets at each level. After ratification at the top level, the legislative organs at descending levels formally ratify their budgets in rapid succession.

After ratification, operational budgets are prepared, on the basis of which spending takes place. Budgetary credits (actually grants) are established, with branches of the state bank giving spending units the right to make expenditures chargeable to the state budget. Credits are opened for each quarter and may be carried over into the next quarter, but unused credits at the end of the year are returned to the budget. Central surveillance is maintained over revenues and expenditures on the basis of continual reports from each branch bank to the central office and to the Ministry of Finance.

The published version of the state budget is in a highly aggregated and summarized form, making it difficult to appraise real allocations and activity within the major components. Furthermore, large sums are contained in unidentified residuals.

Budget expenditures are broken down into four primary categories: national economy, social and cultural programs, defense, and administration. The 1988 budget was R443.5 billion, of which the national economy accounted for R240.82 billion and defense R20.401 billion. The 1989 budget was R459,814,445,000, of which national economy accounted for 56.4%, social and cultural programs 33.0% and defense 4.1%. The item "national economy" comprises investment in productive facilities, subsidies and reserves. Budgetary investment is restricted to financing new construction, and enterprises finance their own investments from retained profits or bank loans. Expenditures under "national economy" usually are divided into five components, of which the largest is industry and construction. The second-largest is the financing of state agriculture and the maintenance of procurement organizations. Collective farms are not financed from the budget but receive budgetary expenditures through state procurement of agricultural products. A considerable sum of expenditures remains under the "national economy" heading after allocations to the identified components. It is believed that these represent hidden military expenditures. Budget expenditures for science under "social and cultural programs" also may include such hidden military expenditures.

The Soviet defense budget as a percentage of the total budget and as a percentage of the GNP is among the lowest in the world. Western observers are puzzled by the discrepancy between the size of the armed forces and the quality of their equipment and the ruble amounts in the budget. It is possible that either Soviet defense industries are extraordinarily cost-efficient or that many defense expenditures are not included in this category in an effort to deceive Western analysts. In any case, there is no breakdown under this category, and there is uncertainty about what is covered. What is more suspicious is the fact that defense expenditures appear to be extremely stable over the years despite external events such as the invasions of Czechoslovakia and Afghanistan, which must have caused sudden increases.

The category "other expenditures" generally is large. It probably includes reserve funds, interest on state loans, subsidies, foreign trade and wage adjustments. For every year there is said to be a budget surplus, if the budget is not balanced. Deficits are unknown, at least on paper. This claim also is contested by Western observers based on speeches before party congresses indicating substantial deficits in recent years.

Revenues are derived primarily from indirect taxes. Turnover tax receipts and payment out of profits account for about two-thirds of total revenues, and direct taxes form about 8%. The major trend in taxation in recent years has been a shift from turnover taxes to payment out of profits. Payment out of profits is divided into three parts: a capital charge, a rental charge and a remainder. The capital charge is a levy based on an enterprise's fixed and working capital. The rent payment is mainly for enterprises in the extractive industries that have a particularly favorable location. The remainder of profit, after all deductions and payments, is transferred to the budget. This profit remainder accounts for over half of all payments out of profits made to the budget.

The turnover tax is essentially an excise tax on consumer goods, although the tax is levied also on electricity, natural gas and oil. The tax is established in conjunction with the pricing decision and represents the difference between the retail and wholesale prices, allowing for a markup for distribution. In Soviet budgetary classification the tax is considered a revenue from the socialized sector because it is assessed on the producer or on a wholesale organization. The actual rate of tax charged is kept an official secret and is never published, because the official line is that the turnover tax is not a tax, although ultimately it is paid in full by the consumer. Actual rates are believed to be as high as 100% on luxury goods. About 40% of the payments are made by the wholesaling organs of the Ministry of

CENTRAL GOVERNMENT EXPENDITURES, 1989
% of total expenditures

Defense: 4.1
Education:
Health: } 33.0
Housing, Social Security, welfare:
Economic services: 56.4
Other: 6.5

CENTRAL GOVERNMENT REVENUES, 1989
% of total current revenues

Profits from state enterprises: 91.4
Other: 8.6

EXCHANGE RATE (National Currency per U.S. Dollar)									
1979	1980	1981	1982	1983	1984	1985	1986	1987	1988
0.650	0.660	0.720	0.730	0.766	0.853	0.770	0.684	0.602	0.598

Trade and the rest by industrial enterprises and disposal organs under the industrial ministries and also agricultural procurement organs. As a result, the tax is paid even if no one buys the products.

State social insurance receipts form the third-largest revenue source. The state social insurance budget is a separate budget drawn up and administered by the trade unions, but it is consolidated into the overall state budget. When contributions to social insurance by enterprises are not sufficient to cover claims, the difference is made up from general funds.

Organizations not owned and operated by the state—collective farms, consumer cooperatives and producer cooperatives—pay tax on their income. Cooperatives pay higher taxes than collective farms. Other revenues are derived from the sale of bonds, the sale of gold, customs duties, an entertainment tax and other fees. These revenues are not itemized in the published budget but collectively account for a large share of the income.

The principal direct tax is the income tax, paid according to a progressive rate schedule. Income from private activities, such as by physicians, is taxed at a much higher scale. Other taxes on the population include an agricultural tax levied on income from private plots, a tax on privately owned horses, and a bachelor and small-family tax levied on single men between 20 and 50 and childless couples.

The USSR's external public debt was $26.4 billion in 1988.

CURRENCY & BANKING

The national monetary unit is the ruble (R), divided into 100 kopecks. Coins are issued in denominations of 1, 2, 3, 5, 10, 15, 20 and 50 kopecks and 1 ruble and notes in denominations of 1, 3, 5, 10, 15, 50 and 100 rubles.

Although defined by the government as worth .987412 g. (.03 oz.) of gold, the ruble is not redeemable in gold, nor is it freely convertible into any other currency. Gold holdings are never reported, and the Soviet Union is not a member of the IMF. The official rates of exchange are quite arbitrary. Statistics on currency in circulation have not been published since 1937.

The role of money in the Soviet Union as a medium of exchange is quite different from that in free market economies. Money is essentially an accounting unit. The value of ownership of money is circumscribed, as the individual can acquire only consumer goods (assuming they are available) and strictly limited categories of property for personal use.

Monetary payments are of two types: cash and noncash. Payments within the state sector are almost wholly noncash—strictly bookkeeping. Cash payments are used for all transactions between the government and the population and for payments within the private sector. Control over the noncash money supply in the socialized sector is largely through the credit plan. A cash plan prepared annually and quarterly by Gosbank estimates payments and receipts of cash by the bank. Although the amount of currency in circulation is growing, its volume is low compared to Western industrial democracies. The circulation of currency for the most part involves only one basic transaction cycle: It is issued as wages, or spent in retail stores and for state services and returns to Gosbank.

On coming to power in 1917 the new Soviet government did two fiscal things: It repudiated all foreign debts, and it nationalized the banking system. Four years later the new central bank, Gosudarstvennyy Bank, Gosbank, was established. The credit reform of 1930 and 1931 gave Gosbank a monopoly of short-term lending. Since that time the banking and currency system has remained essentially unchanged except for organizational modifications. In 1954 Gosbank was separated from the Ministry of Finance and given a separate ministerial status. The Bank Reform Act of 1959 abolished certain specialized banks, transferring their lending functions to Gosbank. In 1988 the credit system was reorganized once again in line with the self-financing policy *(khozrashchot)* introduced into the commercial sphere in 1987.

The main bank of the Soviet Union, Gosbank, acts as a combination central bank, commercial bank and settlement bank. It is the bank of issue, regulates currency and credit and handles payments between enterprises and organizations. The bank also acts as the fiscal agent for all levels of government, receiving taxes and payments and paying out budgetary appropriations.

Gosbank is organized regionally. In addition to the head office in Moscow there are main offices in the various republics and district offices in the ASSR's, *kraya* and *oblasti,* with a total of 158 regional and town offices and over 4,000 smaller branches in 1989.

Although most of the activities of Gosbank are in the state and socialized sector, it does provide some services for the population. It maintains a small amount of personal deposits and issues long-term loans to individuals, mostly for housing construction. In addition, it furnishes consumer credit through retail stores. Gosbank also fills a unique role as a financial policeman for the Gosplan, monitoring transactions of enterprises to as-

sure fulfillment of production and financial plans, proper use of funds and maintenance of financial discipline. Such control is facilitated by the requirement that nearly all their funds be maintained in noninterest-bearing accounts with a branch of Gosbank. As interenterprise credit is prohibited, virtually all payments are made through these accounts. The bank receives copies of the financial plan and other information concerning the operation of each enterprise and thus is able to verify its transactions on a day-to-day basis. The bank can enforce payment for contracts between enterprises and organizations and assure prompt fulfillment of obligations to the state budget. Another important means of control is payment of wages. A time schedule of cash disbursements for wage payments is maintained by the bank, but actual disbursements are made contingent on the fulfillment of quarterly production goals. Enterprises underfulfilling plans do not receive the wage fund in full.

The 1988 bank reorganization led to the creation of five new banks:

- Agroprombank (Agro-Industrial Bank), which handles credits and settlements in the agro-industrial sector
- Promstroibank (Industry and Construction Bank), which handles credits and settlements in the industrial and transportation sectors
- Sberbank (Savings Bank), which assumed responsibility from Sberkassa (Savings Fund) for public and consumer credit and savings
- Vneshekonombank (Bank of Foreign Economic Affairs), which took over the functions of the former Vneshtorgbank
- Zhilsotsbank (Bank of Housing, Communal Services and Social Development)

A credit plan is prepared quarterly and annually by Gosbank, determining the amount of short-term credit to be made available to the economy. The bulk of credit for working capital is used to carry inventories. Credit sanctions are imposed when loans are used for other than planned purposes. The use of long-term credit is expanding in accordance with the new economic reforms.

There are Soviet-owned banks in foreign countries, such as Narodnyy Bank in London, Banque Commerciale pour l'Europe du Nord in Paris and Voskhod Handelsbank in Zurich. In 1964 Gosbank set up the International Bank for Economic Cooperation to promote multilateral clearances among members of COMECON.

AGRICULTURE

Until the 1930s the Soviet Union essentially had an agrarian economy, as it had been for thousands of years. Some 82% of its population was employed in agriculture. Of the 367 million ha. (906 million ac.) of agricultural land in 1913, about 41% was owned by the aristocracy and the church; an additional 22% by independent farmers; and the remaining 37% by peasants who farmed communal plots. About 11 million peasants were landless. Even with primitive farming methods, harvests were abundant in favorable years, and Russia was a major exporter of foodstuffs.

The day after the November 1917 Revolution, Lenin nationalized all land by expropriation. Between 1918 and the end of World War II, peasants were engaged in a losing conflict with the state in an effort to preserve their private ownership, first during the years of "war communism," when the state requisitioned agricultural produce by decree, and later under Stalin, who massacred millions of *kulaki*, confiscated their property and resettled most of the surviving *kulaki*. The collective farm-state farm system established through such brutal measures has survived with little change to this day. However, the agricultural sector has never truly regained its precollectivization period vigor. The pattern of low procurement prices, underinvestment, erosion of farm labor and inadequate mechanization has made agriculture the Achilles' heel of the Soviet economy.

With its vast size the Soviet Union leads all nations in total acreage under cultivation. The cultivated area, however, represents a relatively small part—about 10% of the total area—as a result of adverse climatic conditions in the frozen North and arid South. Three-fourths of the cultivated area is subject to periodic drought.

The country's main agricultural region forms a roughly triangular area extending from the western border between the Baltic and Black seas eastward more than 5,000 km. (3,108 mi.) to the Yenisei River, near the city of Krasnoyarsk. This region, commonly known as the Fertile Triangle, contains most of the large cities and major industrial centers.

The distribution of arable or crop land is the key to the distribution of agriculture. All land used for farming purposes (excluding reindeer grazing) occupies some 27% of the total area, composed of 16% to 17% meadows or natural pastures and 10% plowed land. The total plowed land is reduced by long fallow and temporary fallow lands. The balance, representing field crops, is known as sown area. The amount of sown area per inhabitant varies greatly from *oblast* to *oblast*—e.g., it is 14 times greater in Kazakhstan than in the Northwest, central Asia or Caucasia, although the sown area is more intensively cultivated in the last two regions. Such contrasts lead to surpluses in some regions and deficits in others. Livestock raising is strongest in the Northwest and the Baltic, where it accounts for 58% of the gross value of agricultural production. In central Asia, where sheep outweigh cattle in importance, meat production is more important than dairying. Cereal production is strongest in Kazakhstan (35%), West Siberia (26%) and the Volga region (26%). Certain regions stand out for industrial crops: central Asia (50%) and Transcaucasia (20%).

Regional variations in farming represent efforts to adjust to natural conditions, notably soil, climate and location; further, there are historic differences between farming among Russian and non-Russian peoples. Mixed farming predominates in the main settled areas. On lands where arable farming is not generally possible, livestock raising predominates. In the northern forests

only patches of agriculture take place amid lumbering, herding and hunting. In some richer mountain valleys and in desert oases, garden *(bakhchi)* farming is common.

GROWTH PROFILE (Annual Growth Rates, %)

Population, 1985–2000: 0.8
Crude birth rate, 1985–90: 18.1
Crude death rate, 1985–90: 19.1
Urban population, 1980–85: 1.6
Labor force, 1985–2000: 0.5
GNP, 1988: 1.5
GDP, 1980–86: 3.7
Inflation, 1988: 5.0
Energy production, 1980–85: 4.5
Energy consumption, 1980–85: 3.2

The northwestern part of the Fertile Triangle is characterized by flax and dairying. Rye and oats also are grown, but the damp climate is not good for wheat. Potatoes are grown, particularly around Leningrad. Livestock raising is based on green corn for silage. The Baltic republics are important for dairying.

The central European region grows potatoes, spring wheat and other grains. In the wooded steppes the more fertile soils combine with warmer and drier summers and milder winters to allow a wide range of crops. Throughout good pasture is found along the sluggish rivers, and fodder is provided by the complex rotations developed since 1917. This is one of the most intensely farmed parts of the mixed farming region, where, since the war, industrial crops have been introduced. Apples and pears are widely grown, notably near Bryansk. The swampy Oka lowlands form a subregion producing soft fruit and vegetables. Poultry and beekeeping form important secondary sources of income.

The wooded steppes of the western Ukraine and Moldavia, with their long, warm summers and annual rainfall of 508 to 610 mm. (20 to 24 in.), are good for sugar beets with rotations of winter wheat, grasses and coarse grains. The southern part of the mixed farming belt stretches across the Ukraine and east of the Volga into Siberia. Associated with the best black earths and chestnut and brown earths, this zone forms the Soviet granary.

West of the Don, winter wheat predominates, while sunflower, corn and industrial crops are grown along with perennial grasses. Where too dry for corn and wheat, millet is grown. Although there is little natural pasture, waste grain, rotation grass and silage provide for stall-fed animals. There also is cultivation of some rice on the flood plains of the Dnieper, Dniester and southern Bug, and vines on the gravel terraces of Moldavia and the Ukraine. Grains are ideally suited to the grasslands climate of long, warm summers and annual precipitation of 381 to 508 mm. (15 to 20 in.), although occasional hot, dry winds damage the crops and strong winter winds blow away the light snow cover and expose the friable soils to erosion.

East of the Don, annual precipitation is light (203 to 305 mm.; 8 to 12 in.) and variable, with a maximum in early summer. Spring wheat predominates, occupying two-fifths of the sown area in the lower Don and northern Caucasus. The region supplies about a fifth of the Soviet wheat, corn and sunflower. Other crops include kenaf, castor seed and rice grown in the flooded backwaters of the Don, Terek and Kuban. On the coastal plains there are two corn crops a year. Vines also are grown.

In the lower Volga and southern Urals the pattern is similar. Wool sheep are important, and millet is found in the driest parts. Near the rivers, fruit growing is prevalent, particularly in the Volga River Valley below Volgograd.

In western Siberia, along the line of the Trans-Siberian Railway, grain growing gives way to dairying. Excellent natural pastures, partly flooded in spring, exist in the river valleys. This still is pioneer country, and since World War II mixed farming has spread farther into the Altay foothills and the Minusinsk steppes as well as eastward, toward Lake Baikal. Scattered farms are found in Transbaikalia and in the far eastern area, where Russian farmers have abandoned traditional Russian methods and use Chinese systems—e.g., grain is grown in ridges to keep it above the water, which stands long in the fields. Transbaikalia grows grain, but the Amur-Ussuri Basin is more varied. Soy beans and perilla are grown by Russians, corn by Chinese and rice by Koreans. Sugar beets introduced in about 1920, flourishes in the Khanka Lowlands.

Pastoral farming occurs where natural conditions prevent arable farming. Pastoral activities differ between the southern lowlands and mountains of the arid belt and the northern forests and tundra, but both have a low density of animals and a seminomadic economy, to which the artels have been adapted. The central Asian poor steppes and semidesert are largely used for sheep breeding, for wool, meat and tallow. Cattle are kept only on the fringe of the cultivated lands and pigs only by Russian settlers. Camels still are found on the eastern shore of the Caspian and along the southern frontier. In the winter the animals are taken from the mountains into the lowlands, and in summer they either return or move to richer steppes. Since the war, wells have been dug to provide drinking pools for the herds, aircraft direct flocks to pastures and weather forecasts of storms or droughts are used to move flocks to safety.

Pastoralism in the central Asian mountains is characterized by seasonal movement of flocks and herds up and down the slopes. Horses generally are kept on the lower slopes, cattle on the middle pastures and sheep on the highest. The Caucasian pattern is more diverse. Extensive movements take place from the Caucasian ranges and the Armenian plateau to the winter pastures in the Kuma Kura steppes and even the Terek and Iori valleys.

In southern Siberia, settled pastoralism is replacing the old migratory habits. The herds also are more varied and include yaks, reindeer, goats, maral, horses and sheep. Tuva has the highest ratio of animals to humans in the country. With the availability of fodder crops, stall feeding is common.

Irrigation is important in central Asia, where oases lie in sheltered valleys. Conditions make possible the raising of two crops each year, and where precipitation is adequate, dry farming is practiced. Industrial crops are preferred, particularly cotton, which cannot be grown satisfactorily elsewhere. Rice and grapes also are grown. Few animals are kept because of the lack of fodder and pasture, although trees are planted for shade and wood. There are three types of oases: those almost surrounded by a desert, such as Murgab and Tedzhen; oases on the mountain footslopes, such as Fergana and Tashkent; and oases in the higher foothills, such as Vaksh and Kashkadarya. Oases on the plains and lower foothills concentrate on cotton, vines and fruit, while those on the higher foothills produce fruit, vegetables and even grain. Sheltered and irrigated valleys in Dagestan and other parts of Caucasia produce a wide range of crops, but the main centers of subtropical crops are the Kolkhiz Lowlands and the western slopes overlooking the Black Sea. Adzharia supplies three-quarters of the Soviet Union's citrus fruits, while tea comes from Georgia around Makharadze and terraces overlooking the Black Sea. Grapes grown here form the basis of a well-developed wine industry.

Grains occupy almost two-thirds of the sown area. Official policy had been to reduce specialization in any one area where crop failure might affect the national harvest seriously. Wheat, formerly limited to black and brown earths, now is grown as far east as Baykalia and the far eastern area. New quick-ripening and frost-resistant strains of wheat have been introduced as far north as 60°N. Winter wheat, which gives a better yield than other strains, is the most important grain in the Ukraine, northern Caucasia and the Crimea and has been introduced into Siberia. Rye, the traditional forest belt cereal, is almost entirely a winter crop in northern European Russia and a spring crop in northern and eastern Siberia. Oats form a fodder crop in the central and northern districts, while barley is cultivated in Karelia and the lower reaches of the Ob and the Yenisey. Spring barley is grown in the Black Sea littoral, northern Caucasia and the central Asian foothills. Corn is grown for grain, green fodder and silage, but the proportion for grain is very low (3.5% versus 32% in the United States). The main corn centers are the southern Ukraine and northern Caucasia as well as Moldavia and the central black earth belt. Millet, which is resistant to drought although susceptible to frost, is grown in the drier parts of the Ukraine and the central black earth belt; it also is grown in central Asia, where it has been put in rotations in place of wheat. Rice, mostly of lowland types where irrigation is available, is grown in central Asia. Rice paddies also are found in the Amu Darya River Delta. Koreans have developed growing of rice in the Vladivostok area. Favored valleys along the Black Sea littoral also grow rice.

Among industrial crops, one of the most important is cotton, grown in central Asia, where nilotic conditions prevail in sheltered valleys with abundant water, plentiful sunshine and freedom from frost. The Uzbek SSR has over half the area under cotton. Russia is a major producer of flax, which is grown on a wide range of soils with cool, moist summers, but because it rapidly exhausts the soil, it is grown in rotation with other crops. Northern flax is largely for fiber and southern flax for seed. Other fiber crops include hemp, kenaf, jute, ramie (Chinese nettle) and kendyr. Sunflower, the most important oil-bearing plant, is widely grown in the black earth belt, the Ukraine, northern Caucasia and the northern Kazakh SSR. Soybeans, a recent introduction, come almost entirely from the Far East, with half the sown area in the Amur District.

Sugar is derived principally from beet but also is an industrial crop producing alcohol. Almost two-thirds of the area is in the Ukraine and most of the remainder in the black earth belt in northern Caucasia and the middle Volga as well as Moldavia. In the Ukrainian wooded steppes about a tenth of the area is under beet.

About two-fifths of the vegetable production and two-thirds of the potato production come from private plots of collective farm workers. Fruit growing is found on collective farms as well as private plots throughout the country. In northern European Russia the most common fruits are apples, pears, plums and soft berries, and south of Moscow cherries and apricots. Melons are important along the Volga below Kazan and dried fruits in the lower Volga. Citrus fruits are grown on the Black Sea coast, in western Georgia and in Azerbaijan. Armenia has persimmon, peaches and apricots, while the Megrisk district is noted for almonds. Central Asia is the home of many varieties of figs, grapes, peaches, pears, melons, quince, pomegranates and apples.

Russia is not noted for its wines, which are mostly of mediocre quality. The best sparkling wines are produced in Moldavia; the best white wines on the southern shores of the Crimea, particularly the former imperial estate near Massandra, near Yalta; and the best red wines from Caucasia. Georgia is the largest producer of red wines. The champagne factories around Kutaisi and Tbilisi produce about a quarter of the Soviet output. Dry wines come from Azerbaijan and cognac, liqueurs, sherry, madeira and muscat from Yerevan.

Tea is grown in western Georgia and tobacco in southern Russia, but both are of poor quality. However, the best Crimean and Caucasian tobacco is reputedly as good as Balkan tobacco. Makhorka, an inferior type of tobacco, is cultivated in the northern climes.

Land reclamation has played an important role in the development of agriculture. One of the boldest—if ill-fated—projects in this area was the virgin lands program, which brought into cultivation at heavy ecological cost some 40 million ha. (99 million ac.) of semiarid land between 1954 and 1962. By the late 1960s the reclaimed area there represented about 17% of all arable land. Much land also has been brought into the sown area through drainage of swamps and construction of irrigation facilities. Most swamps are in the European part of northern Russia and in the Baltic region. The Hungry Steppe—a vast plain at the junction of Uzbek SSR, the Kazakh SSR and the Tadzhik SSR—is an example of the large-scale irrigation projects sponsored by the Soviet government. It includes the canal system based on the Syr Darya and the Kara Kum Canal, 850 km. (528 mi.) long and equal to the largest rivers of Central Asia in volume of flow.

Although under Soviet law all land is the property of the state, agriculture is imperfectly socialized and consists of three levels of productive units: the state farm (*sovkhoz*), the collective farm (*kolkhoz*) and the private plot.

The state farm is the agricultural homologue of the industrial enterprise and has a similar status and organization. State farms were established in 1918–19 to prevent fragmentation of the larger expropriated private estates. Many of them were made adjuncts of industrial plants and later were designed to serve as models of efficiency in the farm sector. As a result, most of them are large units, averaging 24,291 ha. (60,000 ac.) each. The grain farms average 40,486 ha. (100,000 ac.), while the largest state farms, those for raising caracul, average 133,603 ha. (330,000 ac.). Most state farms specialize in one or two types of crops (such as grain and/or cotton), livestock breeding, dairy products or vegetable growing. Their location and output are determined by geography: Grain-producing farms are in black earth and virgin land areas; dairy and vegetable units are close to towns; and livestock farms are scattered in almost all regions. As state firms, state farms receive preferential treatment from the state in access to inputs. They operate their own tractors and receive fertilizers and other supplies at wholesale prices. Wage payments are guaranteed, and deficits are met out of the budget. Each farm is managed by a director appointed by the republic's agricultural ministry. He hires all workers, except for his deputy and other agricultural specialists, who are appointed by higher authorities. As in industrial enterprises, there are appropriate functional and operational departments. Each state farm is divided into a number of basic production units, such as tractor brigades or livestock brigades. In accordance with state and regional planning directives and on the basis of its contracts with procurement, trade and marketing organizations, the management establishes targets for sales, profits, costs and capital construction subject to indices and limits set by higher authorities. The state farm operates on the basis of "full cost" (including fixed costs), pays capital charges and is authorized to retain various shares in profits for statutory funds, insurance and farm expansion. On the basis of these decisions, a number of plans detail output, sales and deliveries, costs (including labor and wages) and finance (including capital investments and repairs). If the sales plan is fulfilled, a percentage of the profits is distributed as a premium among the personnel, with the director receiving a sizable share. Workers are paid some 70% to 80% of their wages according to output, with the rest according to assorted norms. Each worker is provided with a plot of land slightly larger than .4 ha. (1 ac.), but the produce of these plots may not be marketed.

The collective farm (artel or *kolkhoz*) is a pseudocooperative designed to supply agricultural produce to the state at minimum cost while at the same time giving the illusion of self-management to the restive peasants, who historically have been a thorn in the side of the state. Work on the collective sometimes is described by the term *barshchina*, which was the term applied to serf service in medieval manors. The collective farm is discriminated against in a number of ways, such as low prices for compulsory deliveries of produce and restrictions on access to inputs and equipment. At the same time, there is a growing trend to bring closer together the *sovkhozy* and the *kolkhozy* by involving them in joint enterprises and other activities.

Up to the late 1960s the operation of each collective farm was governed by a charter based on a model statute adopted in the 1930s. The statute emphasized the principle that the collective is a "voluntary" organization, although Stalin killed millions to form them. The governing body of each collective is an assembly of elected delegates who "elect" a chairman and an executive board. In practice, the party "recommends" the chairman, dismisses or transfers him and places whom it wishes in key administrative posts.

AGRICULTURAL INDICATORS, 1988

Agriculture's share of GDP (%): 20.6
Cereal imports (000 tons): 25,473
Index of Agricultural Production (1979–81 = 100): 115 (1986)
Index of Food Production (1979–81 = 100): 117 (1986)
Index of Food Production Per Capita (1979–81 = 100): 108 (1984–86)
Number of tractors: 2,854,000
Number of harvester-threshers: 849,000
Total fertilizer consumption (tons): 25.387 million
Fertilizer consumption (100 g. per ha.): 1,093
Number of farms: 49,600
Average size of holding, ha. (ac.): 12,300 (30,393)
Tenure (%)
  State: 46.2
  Cooperative: 53.8
Activity (%)
  Mixed: 100
% of farms using irrigation: 3.1
Total land in farms, ha. (ac.): 608 million (1.502 billion)
Farms as % of total land area: 27.2
Land use (%)
  Total cropland: 37.5
    Permanent crops: ⎫
    Temporary crops: ⎬ 92.2
    Fallow: 7.8
  Meadows & pastures: 61.6
  Woodlands: ⎫
  Other: ⎬ 0.9
Yields, kg./ha. (lb./ac.)
  Grains: 1,863 (1,663)
  Roots & tubers: 12,086 (10,787)
  Pulses: 1,254 (1,119)
  Milk, kg. (lb.)/animal: 2,415 (5,324)
Livestock (000)
  Cattle: 120,888
  Sheep: 140,850
  Hogs: 77,772
  Horses: 5,800
  Chickens: 1,130,000
Forestry
  Production of roundwood, 000 cu. m. (000 cu. ft.): 377,600 (13,334,932)
    of which industrial roundwood (%): 77
  Value of exports ($000): 2,858,775
Fishing
  Total catch (000 tons): 11,260
    of which marine (%): 91.8
  Value of exports ($000): 587,081

According to its charter, each collective farm holds its land in perpetuity. The land cannot be sold or leased; it can be taken by the state, but only if proper compensation is made. The capital funds of the collective, called indivisible funds, are composed of the original contribution of the members augmented by annual deductions from current income. Collective farms may obtain long-term state credits.

A collective farmer may be expelled from the collective for slack work, or he may leave it of his own accord with the authorization of the management. In the latter case, his share is returned to him.

Since 1958, when the Machine Tractor Stations (MTS) were dissolved, the collective farms have had, at least in theory, the right to order, purchase and own machinery. However, this freedom is limited by a group of inspectors attached to the regional executive committees, whose guidance on investment is decisive.

A collective may establish long-term and short-term plans. The former deal with soil improvement, livestock breeding, fodder supply, labor force and productivity, and capital formation. The latter deal with patterns of cropping, technical improvements, construction and repairs, purchases of inputs, labor inputs, and income distribution. The former compulsory deliveries have been replaced since 1958 by state purchases with quotas for basic produce. Also since 1958, collective farm workers are paid a monthly wage based on the rates of pay of corresponding categories of state farm workers and on the volume of work performed. Wages have priority in the disbursement of earnings, and when collective farms lack funds for making wage payments, Gosbank must grant them credit, which must be repaid within three years. Most farmers supplement their incomes by doing supplementary work, but most importantly, by working intensively on their own small plots and selling their own produce at free-market prices in the collective farm market. To ensure that the collective work is not neglected, each member must devote a minimum number of workdays annually to the collective. Those who do not do so may be expelled and otherwise punished.

Agriculture has been made an integral part of the "agro-industrial complex" by a decree adopted in 1985. The reason for this major reorganization was the growing size of agricultural investment, which reached over R50 billion, or 26% of all investment, in 1988. Despite such investment, the outcome was quite unsatisfactory. Observers attributed the lack of progress to a number of reasons, such as the poor quality of farm machinery, which tended to break down often; shortage of facilities for storage, packing and transportation; neglect of infrastructure; the inefficiency of the so-called service organizations, especially those that handled chemicals, land improvements and workshops; and bureaucratic disregard for local conditions of livestock and fodder. To correct this situation, a new hierarchy was created under a deputy premier at the center, and joint agro-industrial organizations were created in the republics, *oblasti* and *rayony*. The last and basic unit was known as RAPO (Rayonnoye Agro-Promyshlennoye Obyedineniye). These RAPO's were unified under the State Agro-

Industrial Committee of the USSR, into which the Ministry of Agriculture and a number of other ministries were merged. Gorbachev also has backed the idea of state and collective farms assigning land to families and using autonomous work groups or contract brigades.

The Soviet Union has the largest forest resources in the world. The principal forest areas are in the Urals, the Siberian and far eastern regions and the Northwest. Coniferous forests constitute more than half the timber resources. Of the deciduous varieties, oak, birch and beech predominate. Conifers dominate in the far eastern region, eastern and western Siberia, the Urals and the Northwest. The deciduous stands are more frequent in the less-forested areas of central and southern European Russia, the Caucasus and the extreme South of central Asia. Hardwoods are relatively scarce. The Soviet Union is the world's largest timber producer. About 50% of the timber is floated along the 140,000 km. (87,011 mi.) of waterways. Hunting also provides full- or part-time employment to several million persons. Fur farming, a related enterprise, provides the furs of mink, silver-black foxes and light blue polar foxes.

The Soviet Union has developed an extensive fishing industry since the end of World War II. Of its total catch, less than one-fifth comes from fresh water; the rest comes from open-sea fisheries of the Atlantic and Pacific. The open-sea fishing fleet is one of the most advanced in the world, equipped with sonar and other devices and containing facilities for freezing or otherwise preserving their catch. The main fishing centers are Murmansk; Kaliningrad; Astrakhan; Vladivostok; and Petropavlovsk, on the Kamchatka Peninsula.

On the Pacific coast, herring and sardine are taken in the shallow bays around Vladivostok and Sakhalin. Pacific cod comes mainly from Kamchatka, the Commander Islands and Anadyr Bay. The western coast of Kamchatka is renowned for crabs. In the Atlantic and Arctic waters the catch is largely cod, sea perch and herring. The inland seas, particularly the Black, Aral and Caspian, and the Sea of Azov and Lake Balkash abound in fish. In the Caspian and the Volga the most important species are sturgeon, salmon, beluga, whitefish and herring, but the most common is the Caspian roach. However, the size of the annual catch has been adversely affected by the falling level of the Caspian Sea. The catch in the Danube River Delta is handled at Izmail. Despite international opposition, the Soviet Union remains the world's leading whaling nation.

MANUFACTURING

The Soviet Union is the second-largest industrial power in the world. Its industrial achievements are among the most publicized by the regime as evidence of the superiority of the socialist system in transforming a backward country into an industrial giant. Industry is a priority sector, receiving massive investments from the budget, particularly since World War II. This policy conforms to orthodox Marxist doctrine as modified by Stalin. Within the industrial sector, production is heavily weighted in favor of capital goods, to the neglect of consumer goods.

As a super industrial power, the Soviet Union possesses discernible advantages and disadvantages. The advantages include a vast landmass containing virtually all the mineral, forest and water power resources essential to modern industry. A similarly large labor force cowed into abject obedience to the regime over most of this century exists to do the will of the planners without regard to free preferences. The normal laws of the labor market place, such as supply, demand and incentives, do not apply in such a situation. But both these advantages have their corresponding disadvantages. The bulk of the natural resources is away from the major population centers and located in regions subject to harsh climatic conditions. Exploitation, therefore, presents considerable difficulty and necessitates costly transportation of raw materials and finished products over long distances. Similarly, while regimentation produced rapid rates of growth over the short haul, it has created a highly imbalanced industrial structure whose problems have become intractable and whose size has become unmanageable for planners accustomed to conventional principles of Marxist planning. An emphasis on numbers and quantity has led to a widespread deterioration in quality, both of the products and of the environment. The hidden social and environmental costs of rapid industrial growth are expected to hamper the efficient performance of this sector in the 1990s and beyond.

Rapid technological progress has been achieved in large measure through heavy reliance on foreign research and extensive borrowing of foreign techniques. Available resources have not been adequate to provide civilian industry with advanced technology comparable to that introduced in the high-priority defense sector. Innovation at the enterprise level has been inhibited by institutional factors, including production quotas, pricing and financing.

Traditionally, Soviet industrial enterprises have tended to hoard labor as a safety measure to meet unanticipated increases in production quotas. A tightening of the supply of new industrial labor has led to measures for raising labor productivity through improved organization, increased mechanization and stricter labor discipline. These measures have not proved effective, and labor productivity has actually declined since 1967.

Industry is organized along predominantly functional lines, with individual branches such as coal, chemicals, textiles and food administered by separate ministries through specialized departments. Most enterprises tend to be self-contained, although some progress has been made toward a greater degree of specialization and the integration of small enterprises producing similar products into single large firms with subordinate branches. Managers of these enterprises enjoy only limited autonomy despite a greater latitude in decision-making granted since the 1960s.

Information on the structure and output of industry is fragmentary because of statistical gaps and official secrecy regarding strategic industrial sectors. There is a virtual statistical vacuum in certain areas, such as nonferrous metals, defense, aviation and electronics. As a result it is difficult to assess overall industrial performance and trends, except in broad terms. An industrial census has never been published; neither has information on the number of enterprises and available capacities in the major branches. Data on the distribution of enterprises by size are given only in percentage terms, and the size groupings are not uniform for all branches. Data on the concentration of industrial output are equally unsatisfactory. Production statistics do not separate extractive from manufacturing industries and include production of forestry and fisheries, which properly are part of agriculture. Data on rates of growth of individual industrial branches are not comparable, first because of distortions introduced through the exclusive use of gross value of output rather than value added in measuring production, and second because of frequent changes in accounting methods and industrial classifications. With only a few minor exceptions, information on regional distribution is limited to a breakdown by republics rather than by industrial regions. Construction is treated as a separate branch of the economy, although production of building materials is included in industry.

Available data indicate that the largest enterprises in terms of employment (excluding metallurgy and papermaking, on which information is lacking) are in machine building, chemicals and textiles, some of them employing over 20,000 persons. In terms of gross output the largest enterprises are in ferrous metallurgy, machine building and oil refining. There is a heavy concentration of output in the large sectors, a characteristic quite in keeping with the Soviet preference for giant enterprises. Thus 3.5% of machine-building plants produce over one-third of the total output, 2.1% of the chemical plants over one-quarter of the total output and 3.2% of the textile plants over one-third of the total output.

The legacy of past industrial policies is reflected in the high degree of vertical integration, involving all production stages from raw materials to finished product. This tendency has been reinforced by the unreliability of supplies and poor planning of production assignments. As a result, most plants produce a heterogeneous assortment of products, and specialization in any product category is uncommon. Mass production involves only one-third of the industrial output. In the case of many products, output is widely scattered throughout several branches under the jurisdiction of several ministries. Light industry produces only about a third of the total volume of consumer goods; the balance is manufactured by heavy industrial plants as supplementary product lines. In many enterprises the number of manufactured items runs into the hundreds, most of them with short production runs. This entails frequent machinery changeovers, with resultant high costs. Although the economies of scale flowing from specialization are widely acknowledged by industrial managers, they are reluctant to increase their dependence on outside supply sources, considering their own stake in meeting production quotas. The many jurisdictional authorities also have divergent interests, which run counter to the development of specialization.

The Soviet Union has one of the largest labor pools in the industrialized world, estimated at 38.1 million, or 29% of the total labor force (including those in mining), up from 31 million in 1969 and 15 million in 1950. Although industrial employment has been expanding fairly rapidly, the supply of new labor is shrinking, and shortages are reported in a number of areas. This is reflected in the declining share of annual output growth, attributable to the increase in the number of workers as against the share of output increase achieved through a rise in productivity. Manufacturing is heavily concentrated in the more populous areas of the country, particularly in the central region around Moscow, the Donetsk-Dnieper area, the Northwest and the Baltic states. Development of the areas east of the Urals is hampered by difficulty in attracting workers.

Productivity is a frequent topic in the Soviet media and is estimated at less than half that of the United States. In most years the productivity rise is below that of wages. Ironically, under the current industrial structure enterprises have a vested interest in keeping productivity low. A planned reduction in the number of workers concomitant to a planned rise in productivity entails a reduction in the wage fund and the incentive funds. In many sectors, including the officially favored machine-building and metalworking branches, mechanization is at a low level, particularly of auxiliary operations. Labor turnover also is a major problem, although figures on its magnitude are not published. The instability of labor is ascribed in part to job dissatisfaction among the young and in part to the lack of adequate amenities in new as well as older industrial areas. Judging by reports in the media, industrial labor is characterized by a widespread disregard for discipline, poor workmanship, absenteeism and late arrival at work. The prevalence of such indiscipline is a matter of great concern for the regime, reflected in the over 200 institutes working on the problems of labor and in numerous experiments carried out at various enterprises introducing innovative work systems. Some of these experiments relate increases in the wage fund to productivity; other involve increases in work loads and a more rational organization of labor; others call for more intensive use of machinery; and still others increase penalties for defective workmanship.

Outside the area of the space and military industries, many Soviet plants are obsolescent or even obsolete. A large volume of the current capital equipment was obtained from Germany and East Europe in the form of reparations. In most plants, mechanization is limited to the basic production processes, while auxiliary operations, such as loading, are performed manually. This is not due to a shortage of scientists and technicians. On the contrary, the Soviet Union has a large cadre of extremely competent scientists and engineers, but the majority of them are channeled into the high-priority sectors. The results of this policy are evident in the sharp contrast between the Soviet achievements in space and the poor quality of consumer goods—can openers that do not work, pens that leak, shoes that lose their heel at the first wearing and chairs with loose legs.

In civilian industry, several factors inhibit innovation of products and technology. Innovation involves risk, and Soviet industrial hierarchs are among the most conservative in the world. Existing regulations do not allow for any departures by the enterprises from its approved annual production plan. Enterprise managers and engineers have nothing to gain and everything to lose through innovation, which offers little prospect for reward but heavy penalties for failure. Financing constitutes another difficult hurdle for innovation. The capital investment required for innovation has to come from the state budget. Prolonged administrative procedures are required to obtain the necessary funds from this source and even more complex procedures for changing current priorities. Delays of many years are common as several scientific and technical organizations, ministries and agencies review and debate the proposal, and even when official authorization is forthcoming, there may be further delays in obtaining materials. According to the State Committee for Science and Technology, the lead time between conception and operation is eight to 12 years. Many products and techniques thus become obsolete by the time they are introduced.

Enterprises have no control over the prices of the products they manufacture. They are sold at wholesale prices established by higher authorities, who are found at Union, regional and local levels, often with overlapping and conflicting jurisdictions. Although enterprises do not set prices, they are the ones most directly affected by such prices, which have a bearing on their sales, profits and the size of their incentive funds. The officially set prices have little correlation with costs of production or scarcity of supplies. They are inflexible over the short term and lack sufficient differentiation with regard to product quality. To maximize sales volume, managers concentrate output on high-priced items at the expense of lower-priced ones; use high-cost materials to inflate the value of the output and thus the volume of sales; and, when producing any one of a group of goods with uniform prices, favor the one with the lowest cost. Although some price differentials for quality were introduced in 1965, they have not been large enough to compensate for the extra cost of manufacturing a better product. In the absence of effective penalties, a considerable volume of substandard goods continues to be produced. Consumers, however, are not easily fooled, and there are long lines for quality products in contrast to a glut of shoddy merchandise, even at reduced prices. Inflexible prices also discourage innovation.

The bulk of Soviet industry lies in the Urals and European Russia, which together contain three-quarters of the total, with Moscow-Gorky, the South (the Ukraine and the eastern Donbass) and the Urals as the three largest concentrations, but smaller groupings lie around Leningrad and in the Volga River Basin. Outside European Russia, western Siberia is the most important group, with smaller industrial pockets in northern Caucasia, Transcaucasia, the central Asian oases, eastern Siberia (the Cheremkhovo-Irkutsh region) and the far eastern region in the Ussuri Valley-Vladivostok areas.

The European South contains three subregions: the Donbass coalfield, the Dnieper Bend and the iron-mining districts of Krivoy Rog. This region is linked to the large industrial town of Kharkov to the north and the metallurgical industries of Zhdanov and Kerch to the south. The availability here of iron ore, coal and fuels has led to the development of a major iron and steel industry. The central industrial region may be divided into Moscow and its suburbs, the textile towns of Klyazma, the lignite mining district of Tula and the industrial node around Gorky. Industry is not spread evenly in the Urals region, but several clusters occur. To the north, around Serov, there are mining and metallurgical towns, with another large group centered on Nizhniy Tagil and a cluster of towns around the transportation and engineering capital of Sverdlovsk; farther south are Chelyabinsk, Magnitogorsk and Orsk-Khalilovo; on the western slope there is an industrial subregion in the Upper Kama, near Berezniki-Solikamsk, on the Kizel coalfield and at Perm; still farther south, industrial and mining towns lie along the Belaya River Valley south of Ufa-Chernikovsk. Industry in the Urals is comprised primarily of iron and steel, heavy chemicals, engineering, transportation equipment, electrical equipment and paper. The industrial towns of western Siberia lie mostly in the valley of the Tom, on the Kuzbass coalfield, but there are big industrial outliers at Novosibirsk, Barnaul and Rubtsovsk. The industrial structure of the Volga is formed of a widely scattered yet related industry based on petroleum, natural gas and salts. Leningrad produces a wide range of machinery and transportation equipment, chemicals, textiles and consumer goods. The industries of the northern Caucasus and Transcaucasia are similar to those of the Volga region. Central Asian industry is a product of Soviet times and is based on ferrous and nonferrous ores and nonmetallic minerals as well as local coal and petroleum. Cultivation of cotton and silk is the basis of a modern textiles industry, with large mills at Tashkent. The principal industrial centers are the republic capitals. In eastern Siberia the Cheremkhovo-Irkutsk region makes mostly heavy chemicals and engineering goods, while the Amur-Ussuri region produces semifinished articles and wood by-products. Food processing, particularly canning fish and crab, is an important element in the region's economy.

MANUFACTURING INDICATORS, 1988

Share of GDP: 43.9% (includes mining)
Labor force in manufacturing: 29% (includes mining)
  Food & agriculture: 20.3%
  Textiles: 17.4%
  Machinery: 46.6%
  Chemicals: 15.7%
Index of Manufacturing Production (1980 = 100): 126 (1986)

MINING

The Soviet Union is one of the richest nations in the world in mineral resources, which is not surprising, considering its extent. Few nations come as close as it

MANUFACTURING, MINING AND CONSTRUCTION ENTERPRISES (1982)			
	No. of Enterprises	No. of Employees	Monthly Wages as a % of Avg. of All Wages	Annual Gross Output (000,000 rubles)
Manufacturing				
Machinery and metal products	8,180	15,011,000	111.2	182,400
Food products	7,538	2,717,000	99.2	104,100
Chemicals and chemical products	1,493	1,148,000	112.8	75,500
Textiles	1,996	2,210,000	88.4	72,700
Clothing	5,118	2,250,000	88.4	30,900
Nonmetallic products	3,200	2,088,000	103.8	24,800
Wood, furniture and paper	2,275	1,619,000	112.8	22,300
Beverages	1,726	374,000	95.5	7,700
Iron and steel	408	1,044,000	131.1	6,200
Footwear	406	494,000	95.8	5,500
Leather and leather products	266	199,000	95.9	4,200
Tobacco	88	40,000	95.5	3,800
Glass and pottery	333	376,000	99.3	3,300
Building materials	3,938	N.A.	107.1	2,300
Rubber and plastic	N.A.	433,000	103.5	N.A.
Mining				
Petroleum and gas	853	1,105,000	161.1	34,400
Coal			153.9	
Metal ores	1,070	194,000	153.9	15,900
Construction	N.A.	11,299,000	103.3	N.A.

does to self-sufficiency in minerals, and, further, most deficiencies are made up by imports from friendly countries in the Communist bloc. However, a serious problem is the unfavorable geographical location of several of the scarcer minerals in the climatically trying regions of Siberia and the Arctic regions. Only in a few metals, such as cobalt and tungsten among the ferrous metals, is domestic production deficient.

The Soviets rarely publish full and adequate statistics on their mineral output or on deposits. Both are treated as classified information. The situation is further complicated by doubtful estimates. New deposits are constantly being claimed, mostly from remoter parts. The uncertain data may not be willful misinformation but rather a reflection of the fact that the Soviet Union still is in a pioneering state of knowledge regarding mineral resources. It was only in 1945 that the initial geological survey of the country was completed, and potential resources could well outweigh the proved ones.

The Soviet Union ranks first in the world in iron ore resources. The most important deposits are in the South (Krivoi Rog and Kerch, 33%), the Urals (19%) and Kazakhstan (20%). Large deposits also exist in the central districts (the Kursk magnetic anomaly and the Tula and Lipetsk districts), the Northwest (the Kola Peninsula and the Karelian ASSR), eastern Siberia and in the far eastern region. The deposits vary in composition and technological properties. More than 12% are high-grade ores, with an iron content of more than 46%; another 57% is medium-grade, with an iron content of 16% to 33%; the remainder are low-grade, needing dressing. Titanium deposits are in the Urals and in Karelia as well as in the Ukraine and western Kazakhstan.

The Soviet Union ranks first in the world in manganese deposits. The most important are in the South—the Chiatura deposits in Georgia and in the Nikopol

Basin in the Ukraine, both of which contain very-high-grade ores. Manganese ores also are in the Urals, western Siberia, Kazakhstan and other regions. Large reserves of high-grade chromite ores are concentrated in the Urals and in Kazakhstan; the deposits in the central Urals have long been known, but the latter are of more recent discovery.

Available supplies of nonferrous ores permit production of more than 60 nonferrous and rare metals. The ores generally are complex and of low quality—from 5% to 2% for copper and somewhat higher for lead and zinc. Therefore ore-separation and concentration facilities have been built at all mining sites. A relative shortage of bauxite, the usual source of aluminum, has led to development of methods for the utilization of nepheline and alunite, which are inferior to bauxite. However, these methods also yield cement, soda and potash, which help offset the higher cost of processing the low-grade ores. The principal copper regions are Kazakhstan, the Urals, central Asia and the Caucasus. The largest are the Dzhezkazgan deposits in Kazakhstan; deposits in the Altai Mountains; and the Alavardi deposits in Armenia, which have been worked since 1790. The largest deposits of cupriferous sands are in the Udokan Mountains in eastern Siberia. Proved resources of lead and zinc also are the highest in the world, located mostly in Kazakhstan and the central Asian republics. Silver, gold, sulfur and various rare elements are found together with copper and zinc in these deposits. Bauxite deposits were first discovered in 1917 in the Tkhvin region, followed by other discoveries in the Urals, Kazakhstan, western and eastern Siberia and the Ukraine. The principal tin deposits are concentrated in eastern Siberia and the far eastern region as well as in Kazakhstan. The most important deposits of nickel ore are in the Krasnoyarsk region, the Kola Peninsula, the

Urals and Kazakhstan. Tungsten deposits are in central Kazakhstan, central Asia and the Buryat ASSR. The Soviet Union ranks second in the world in molybdenum, the principal deposits of which are in Transcaucasia, the northern Caucasus, Kazakhstan and Transbaikalia. The most important deposits of mercury ores include those discovered in 1878 in Nikitovka in the Donets Basin, and in Khaidarken in the Kirghiz SSR, with smaller pockets and veins in the western Ukraine, the Caucasus, central Asia, the Altai Mountains and the Kamchatka Peninsula. The Soviet Union share with China first place in antimony deposits, which are found mostly in the Kirghiz and Tadzhik SSRs.

Among the noble metals, the Soviet Union has one of the world's largest reserves, believed to exceed those of South Africa. Commercial gold mining began in the Urals in 1814 and later was followed by mining in Siberia. Most important are the Lena-Vitim and Aldan fields, worked since the late 19th century and now highly mechanized. Lodes and placers also are worked in Transbaikalia, in the Urals, around Dzhetygara and Stepnyak in Kazakhstan and on the eastern bank of the Yenisey. In eastern Siberia the Allakh Yun field was developed during the war years. Silver, associated mostly with polymetallic ores as a secondary metal, comes from main producers in the southern Urals and the Altai Mountains. Diamonds were discovered in 1829 in the Urals. In 1954 large deposits of kimberlite pipes were discovered in central Siberia, but the most important are Mirniy, Udachnaya and Aikhal on the Sokhsolookh River. There also are placer workings. The stones, generally small but with gems up to 32 carats, are graded and sorted at Nyurba. Amber is worked in open-cast pits on the former East Prussian coast, chiefly at Yantarnyy. Precious stones come from the Urals and Altai-Sayan.

Coal supplies about 45% of Soviet energy requirements. The Soviet Union is believed to possess about one-fifth of the world's known reserves, sufficient to last for several decades at present rates of extraction. About a sixth of the reserves are lignite. Some of the older mines are nearing exhaustion, leading to the working of poorer seams. In the early decades of this century the Donbass was the main producer, but it has declined compared to newer fields in the Kuzbass and Karaganda. During the war the rich but inaccessible Pechora field in northeastern European Russia was developed. The proportion of output from the Moscow lignite field also has greatly increased.

Coal is mainly used in industry as a boiler fuel or metallurgical coke as well as in steam engines of railways. Lignite and poorer coals are used in electricity generation. Siberian coal, although cheaper to mine, is a low-grade coal with a high moisture and a low heat content and therefore unsuitable for metallurgical purposes. Substantial costs are incurred in coal transportation. The average length of haul is over 600 km. (373 mi.), but larger quantities are hauled over distances as great as 2,200 km. (1,367 mi.).

The nonmetallic resources of the Soviet Union are as abundant as those of minerals. It has the world's largest resources of potash salts, apatites and phosphorites

and is one of the largest producers of fluorspar, mica, asbestos, refractory materials, magnesite, kaolin, graphite, native sulfur, borates, barites and witherites. Potash salts are concentrated in the western slopes of the Urals, where in 1925 the vast upper Kama deposits were discovered, occupying an area of over 5,000 sq. km. (1,930 sq. mi.). There are other considerable deposits in the western Ukraine, Byelorussia, Turkmenistan and in the pre-Urals near Aktyubinsk. Phosphorus resources are distributed unevenly. In the greater part, they are concentrated in the Kola Peninsula, where they include the noted Khibin deposits. The world's largest deposits of phosphate ores were discovered in southern Kazakhstan in 1933–36. Other larger deposits have been discovered in the central districts, such as the Vyatka-Kama deposits in the Kirov region. The largest fluorite deposits are in the Primorye, eastern Transbaikalia and central Asia. The Naurgazan and Takob deposits in the Tadzhik SSR also are important. The principal industrial varieties of mica are muscovite (potash mica) and phlogopite (magnesium mica). The most important mica deposits are in eastern Siberia, from the Vitim estuary to the Yenisey. The Mama deposits in the Irkutsk region lie in the extreme northeastern part of the belt along the Mama and Bolshaya Chuya rivers. The Bukachan, Akukan and Priolkhon deposits lie farther to the southwest, on the northwestern bank of Lake Baikal. The principal serpentine asbestos deposits are in the Urals in the Sverdlov region; others are in Bashkiria; in Al-Dourak (in the Tuva ASR); and in Dzhetygara, in the Kustanai region of Kazakhstan. Deposits of refractory clays abound in the Donbass, Kuzbass and Moscow basins, all associated with coal seams, and in Kazakhstan. The largest deposits are in the Novgorod region. Dinas bricks, which are another important refractory, are made from quartz sands and quartzites, deposits of which are in the central and southern Urals, Sverdlovsk, the Ukraine, western Siberia and the Chelyabinsk region. Deposits of both crystalline and amorphous magnesite are in the Urals, Siberia and the far eastern region. In the Chelyabinsk region there are large reserves of high-grade crystalline magnesite in the Satka deposits on the western slopes of the southern Urals. Amorphous magnesite is at Khalilovo in the Orenberg region. The most important kaolin resources are in the Ukraine and in the Urals. There are also several important deposits in western Siberia and eastern Siberia, particularly Yevsino, Balai and Troshkov. The most important deposits of graphite are in the far eastern region, Siberia, the Urals and the Ukraine; of native sulfur in the Kuibyshev region, central Asia and the Carpathians; of borates in the northern Caucasus, the Kerch and Taman peninsulas and in the Lake Inder region in Kazakhstan; and of barites in Transcaucasia, western Siberia and the Urals.

ENERGY

Information on energy is considered to be a state secret, although unofficial data are available on output and consumption. One feature of energy resources is their abundance on the one hand and their limited avail-

MINERAL PRODUCTION IN THE USSR

Mineral		1984	1985	1986
Hard coal	000 metric tons	556,000	569,000	588,000
Brown coal (incl. lignite)	000 metric tons	156,000	157,000	163,000
Peat[1,2]	000 metric tons	50,000	45,000	45,000
Iron ore:				
Gross weight	000 metric tons	247,104	247,639	250,000
Metal content	000 metric tons	134,809	136,000	137,000
Bauxite[2]	000 metric tons	4,600	4,600	4,600
Chromium ore[2,3]	000 metric tons	2,940	2,950	3,100
Copper ore[3,4]	000 metric tons	1,020	N.A.	N.A.
Ilmenite concentrates[2]	000 metric tons	440	445	450
Lead ore[2,3]	000 metric tons	440	440	440
Magnesite[2]	000 short tons	2,400	2,400	2,400
Manganese ore[2,3]	000 metric tons	2,994.4	2,900	2,800
Zinc ore[2,3]	000 metric tons	810	810	810
Fluorspar (excl. precious stones)[2,5]	000 metric tons	550	560	560
Gypsum (crude)[2]	000 metric tons	4,900	4,900	5,000
Salt (unrefined)	000 metric tons	16,545	16,100	N.A.
Phosphate rock[2]	000 metric tons	32,500	32,600	32,900
Potash salts[6]	000 metric tons	9,500	10,400	10,200
Native sulfur[2]	000 metric tons	1,800	1,700	1,700
Asbestos[2]	000 metric tons	2,250	2,250	2,300
Crude petroleum[7]	000 metric tons	612,710	595,291	615,000
Antimony ore[2,3]	metric tons	9,300	9,400	9,500
Cobalt ore[2,3]	metric tons	2,600	2,700	2,800
Molybdenum ore[2,3]	metric tons	11,200	11,300	11,400
Nickel ore[2,3]	metric tons	175,000	180,000	185,000
Rutile concentrates[2]	metric tons	10,000	10,000	10,000
Tin concentrates[3,4]	metric tons	17,000	N.A.	N.A.
Tungsten concentrates[2,3]	metric tons	9,100	9,200	9,200
Mercury (incl. secondary)[2,3]	76 lb flasks	64,000	65,000	66,000
Gold[2,3]	metric tons	269.0	270.0	275.0
Silver[2,3]	metric tons	1,475	1,490	1,500
Diamonds[2]	000 metric carats	10,700	10,800	11,000
Natural gas	million cu. m. (trillion cu. ft.)	587(20.7)	643(22.7)	686(24.2)

Sources: United Nations, *Industrial Statistics Yearbook* and *Monthly Bulletin of Statistics*; R. Levine (U.S. Bureau of Mines).

[1]Peat for fuel, excluding peat gathered for agricultural use.
[2]Estimated data (Source: Bureau of Mines, U.S. Department of the Interior).
[3]Figures refer to the metal content of ores and concentrates.
[4]Estimated data (Source: Metallgesellschaft Aktiengesellschaft, Frankfurt am Main, Federal Republic of Germany).
[5]Acid and metallurgical grade.
[6]Figures refer to the potassium oxide content of salts.
[7]Including gas condensates.

ability in certain regions. Only the Ukraine, among the regions, possesses good energy resources. The central, western and northwestern areas of European Russia have large energy deficits, as do the Urals. The movement of fuels and power from producing to consuming regions necessitates a huge volume of transportation, adding to the energy costs.

There are several distinctive features of the Soviet energy scene:

1. The Soviet Union is one of the world's major energy exporters. Energy exports grew faster than energy consumption in 1975–80 and increased their share in total production.

2. Electric-power stations account for a very large share of all primary energy consumption.

3. Industry is the dominant final consumer, and its share has been increasing since 1975.

4. Cogeneration is employed on a much larger scale in the Soviet Union than in the West. The electric-power industry utilizes more of the energy of the fuels it burns in the form of by-product heat.

5. Gas is used in a different way than in most other countries. It is heavily utilized in boilers and less in households. Whereas in the United States 32% of gas is used for residential and commercial heating and 18% in electric power stations, the relative proportions in the Soviet Union are 18% and 32%, respectively.

6. Soviet requirements of high-value uses of petroleum, such as motor fuels and petrochemicals, are much less than those in Western countries. This gives the Soviet Union room to maneuver in dealing with oil shortages by improving the way it uses oil.

7. The Soviet Union has not gone as far as the West in pushing solid fuel out of the fuel balance. Soil fuel still covers about a third of primary energy consumption, compared to 20% in the United States. The Soviet Union has done so by accepting low quality in solid fuel.

8. Evidence is mounting that energy is used wastefully in the Soviet Union. Enough gas is wasted to supply

the needs of a small country; oil and coal are wasted in transportation and storage, and electricity is generally not metered.

Modern development of petroleum came in 1833, when petroleum was obtained from deposits near the surface at Groznyy. Commercial exploitation began in the 1890s with the help of foreign capital, and by 1903 Russia was the largest oil producer in the world, with most of the supplies coming from Baku. After the Revolution output dwindled to one-quarter of the 1903 production, and no new fields were opened until 1929, when oil was discovered at Chusovoy, on the western flank of the Urals. By 1937 the Ural-Volga fields came on stream, although they did not surpass Baku until 1953. After 1945 output increased through annexation of the western Ukraine and the Japanese concessions in Sakhalin.

Despite such progress, the Soviet petroleum industry lagged for a long time behind the West in technical performance. Equipment was outmoded, and drilling wells were poor and shallow. Until 1945 wells were operated by natural pressure, resulting in low recovery rates.

The rapid change in the early 1950s in the geographical distribution of crude petroleum production led to development of a refining and petrochemicals industry in the Volga region and in western Siberia, linked to consumers and producers by pipelines. Further discoveries of oil are possible, as the Soviet Union includes about a quarter of the world's potentially oil-bearing areas, and 45% of its own area is composed of sedimentary formations. Over 80% of the known reserves are in the Ural-Volga fields and 10% in Azerbaijan. Offshore drilling has expanded in Baku, accounting, possibly, for one-quarter of the output. From Baku the oil is piped to Batumi for shipment from Black Sea ports. Among other important producers in this area are Neftechala, and Pirsagat in the Kura Depression.

In the Caucasus the principal fields are the Kuban and the Groznyy-Dagestan. There are refineries at Tuapse, Krasnodar, Groznyy and Makhachkala. Natural gas from Stavropol is piped to central Russia. The wells are shallow but slow producers. On the northern Caspian shore, the small Emba oil field sends most of its high-quality crude by pipeline to the Orsk refinery for use in the Urals and Kazakhstan. Further oil deposits exist in northwestern Kazakhstan. The southeastern shore of the Caspian Sea contains the Nebit Dag and Cheleken deposits. The central Asian oil fields are growing in importance, chiefly those in the Fergana Valley and near Termez and Frunze. At Gazli, north of Bukhara, a large gas field is linked to Sverdlovsk by pipeline. Siberia receives oil from western producers by rail or pipe, particularly the large Omsk refinery. Natural gas from Berezovo and Shaim is piped to the Urals, and from Taas-Tumus at the Vilyuy mouth to Yakutsk. A pipeline from the Urengoi field in Siberia to Western Europe was completed in 1983. Sakhalin supplies the far eastern region and eastern Siberia from wells in the northeastern part of the island. Khabarovsk is the main refinery.

The Soviet Union annexed the petroleum-bearing Polish territory on the northern slope of the Carpathians between Przemysl and Chernovtsy in 1945. Here Borsilav and Stryy are oil producers, and Dashava produces natural gas piped to Moscow, Kiev, Minsk and Vilnius. In northeastern European Russia, Ukhta produces oil and Voy-Vozh and Dzhebol produce natural gas.

Although new discoveries are constantly changing the geographical distribution of oil, the most important oil-producing district is at Ural-Volga from the Upper Kama around Perm to the lower Volga near Volgograd, covering some 492,228 sq. km. (190,000 sq. mi.). The oil is generally poorer than in the Caucasus, with a high sulfur content. About half the Soviet refining capacity is in this area. Over half the Soviet output comes from areas around Almetyevsk in the Tatar ASSR and Oktyabrskiy in the Bashkir ASSR. There are marginal fields around Perm in the North and Volgograd in the South. Fields near the great Samara Bend of the Volga began producing in the 1930s. Farther south, western bank producers are mainly for gas, including Yelshenka, Kotovo and Frolovo, from which it is piped to Moscow, Kamyshin and Volgograd, respectively. Oil shale reserves have been exploited to a limited extent only. The main worked deposits are around Lake Peipus, and there are other deposits in Ural-Volga; the Orenburg *oblast*; on the Izhma River near Pechora, in Siberia; and in eastern Kazakhstan. The Peipus oil shales extend over 3,886 sq. km. (1,500 sq. mi.) with an average depth of 2.1 m. (7 ft.) and a maximum depth of 10 m. (33 ft.). Oil content varies from 20% to 29%.

The Soviet reserves of natural gas are known to be huge, although no precise data have yet been published. As in the case of other energy resources, most gas deposits are far from consuming centers and require costly transportation, and their exploitation is further complicated by climatic and terrain difficulties. Nevertheless, gas is perhaps the most successful of the energy sectors. From a share of less than 3% of the fuel balance in 1950, it expanded to over 31% in 1983. The main producing regions are western Siberia (accounting for over half of the total output), Turkmenistan, the Ukraine, the Uzbek SSR and Azerbaijan. Although production is declining in the Ukraine and the northern Caucasus, new discoveries at Orenburg have more than made up for the shortfall. The Vutkyl field in the Komi ASSR began production in the 1960s, and outputs in Turkmenistan and Azerbaijan also have risen substantially. The major difficulties are the lack of infrastructure in Siberia and the need for further rapid construction of pipelines. The towns of Nadim and Novi Urengoi are essentially natural-gas towns. Construction in Novi Urengoi in 1981–85 alone cost as much investment as for the whole of the western Siberian gas industry in the previous five years. By 1988 pipelines from Novi Urengoi to the European centers and the Urals had added another 64,000 km. (39,776 mi.) to the existing length of 131,000 km. (81,417 mi.).

Since the inception of the Soviet state, development of electric power has been given high priority, in accordance with Lenin's formula "Communism equals Soviet power plus the electrification of the entire country."

The share of thermal power declined from 86% in 1975 to 80% in 1980, while hydroelectric power and nuclear power expanded to 14% and 6%, respectively, in the same period. The country's hydroelectric potential is estimated at 340 million kw. The trend is toward ever larger capacities, exemplified by the 6,000-mw. station in Krasnoyarsk and the 4,500-mw. station in Bratsk. Other powerful stations are on the Dnieper, Volga, Kama, Kuban, Angara, Yenisey and other rivers. Although output has risen dramatically, per capita consumption is only 5,582 kw.-hr., about half of the U.S. per capita consumption of 11,430 kw.-hr. However, the share of industrial consumption is closer to the U.S. figure. About 60% of power production is from 75 giant plants, including 56 thermal, 14 hydroelectric and five nuclear stations. Combined heat and power plants are widely used to supply heating to housing blocks. There are about 1,000 such stations some of them nuclear, in 800 cities. The Soviet Union is linked by a unified power grid, which is of considerable advantage in coping with peak demands in a territory so vast that when it is noon in Moscow, it is 7:00 P.M. in Khabrovsk.

Efforts to boost the share of nuclear energy to above 14% by 1990 have fallen behind schedule because of the Chernobyl accident in 1986. The Soviet Union built the world's first atomic power station, with a capacity of 5,000 kw, in Obninsk in 1954. The first fast-breeder reactor opened in Dimitrovgrad in 1969 followed by one in Shevchenko in 1973. By 1983 there were 15 nuclear power stations in operation with a total capacity of 3.5 million kw., and a further 14 were under construction. Despite the two accidents—the first one at Atommash plant in Volgodonsk in 1983—plans call for expansion of nuclear power generation to 100 million kw., accounting for 25% of total electric power output by 2000.

LABOR

In 1988 the Soviet labor force was estimated at 151 million, the third-largest in the world. Because of the ideological basis of the Soviet state, this labor force presents peculiarities not found in the Western world.

Following Marx's division of labor into productive and unproductive, the Soviets distinguish between those engaged in material production—i.e., creating physical commodities—and those engaged in branches of endeavor other than material production and thus not of creative value. A doctor or teacher or lawyer is considered nonproductive, although at least the first two are carrying out "useful" functions. The distinction does not equate productive labor with physical labor. Certain types of nonmanual work, such as that of clerk or bookkeeper, are considered productive because they are combined with other activities that produce physical goods. This basic distinction lies at the heart of Soviet formulas concerning cost, gross value of output, income and labor statistics. Soviet statistics group as productive all those in the primary and secondary sectors but exclude those engaged in civil service, education, public health, etc.

Other contrasts emerge when comparing patterns of employment in the Soviet Union with those in the West. First, the share of agricultural and related employment is much greater and the share of services much lower. The 18.9% in agriculture, forestry and fishing is the highest and the 18.2% of service employment the lowest of any industrialized country. This is the result of deliberate official policy, which is more concerned, out of ideological considerations, with preserving near-full employment levels than in allowing market forces of labor supply and demand to operate freely. The demand and supply of labor are governed, on the other hand, by planned output targets. It is advantageous for enterprises to hoard labor and to maintain a sufficiently flexible supply of rural labor, from which their demands for manpower could be met. Instead of seeking to facilitate labor mobility among branches, sectors and regions, the authorities are inclined to check the tendency toward higher labor turnover, called labor instability in official jargon. The use of wage differentials to redeploy labor among sectors, enterprises and regions is used only selectively. The only exception is the encouragement of migration to Siberia through incentives such as tax grants, tax exemptions and free transportation. Formerly, prisoners provided an inexpensive source of labor supply for these regions, but this source has dried up since the 1970s.

The system of recruitment also presents peculiarities. It mainly involves a system called Organized Recruitment of Workers, which recruits unskilled workers

ENERGY INDICATORS 1988

Primary energy production (quadrillion BTU)
  Crude oil: 24.93
  Natural gas, liquid: 1.02
  Natural gas, dry: 22.50
  Coal: 13.95
  Hydroelectric power: 2.19
  Nuclear power: 1.90
  Total: 66.49
Average annual energy production growth rate (%): 4.5 (1980–85)
Average annual energy consumption growth rate (%): 3.2 (1980–85)
Energy consumption per capita, kg. (lb.) oil equivalent: 4,949 (10,910)
Electricity
  Installed capacity (kw.): 321.671 million
  Production (kw.-hr.): 1.598 trillion
    % fossil fuel: 76.4
    % hydro: 13.5
    % nuclear: 10.1
  Consumption per capita (kw.-hr.): 5,582
Natural gas, cu. m. (cu. ft.)
  Proved reserves: 41.003 trillion (1.448 quadrillion)
  Production: 727.005 billion (25.674 trillion)
  Consumption: 614.473 billion (21.700 billion)
Petroleum, bbl.
  Proved reserves: 58.7 billion
  Years to exhaust proved reserves: 13
  Production: 4.554 billion
  Consumption: 3.222 billion
  Refining capacity per day: 12,260,000
Coal, 000 tons
  Reserves: 244,700,000
  Production: 704,683
  Consumption: 689,391

on behalf of contracting ministries. Recruitment through the market and assignment through schools tend to overlap, so that at certain times supply may exceed demand for certain types of workers in given areas, whereas the reverse situation may occur in other regions. Shortages generally tend to affect the nonpriority branches of industry more.

There are no organized employment agencies in the Soviet Union. A worker who has lost his job or who wishes to change employment is on his own in his search for a new one. For the skilled worker, reentry into the labor market is not a severe problem, but it presents difficulties for unskilled workers and workers in small towns or villages. Theoretically unemployment does not exist in the Soviet Union but there are pockets of unemployment that do not appear in official statistics. References to "unoccupied people" (*nezanyati*) and to citizens needing labor placement (*trudoustroistvo*) appear frequently, but these people are not called unemployed. The concept of seasonal unemployment also is not explicitly recognized. The legal setting for such a situation is the citizen's constitutional duty to work, and, on the flip side, his guaranteed right to work. The duty to work means his obligation to engage in "socially useful labor" and not to live on unearned income from private profit or speculation, nor to be idle. Only for women with young children is it legal not to participate in the labor force. There are laws against "persons who avoid socially useful labor and lead a parasitic way of life."

Central planning determines the nature and location of jobs and provides the needed labor. Annual production plans include limits on the number of workers to be employed, the wage fund, average wages and expected increase in labor productivity. Manpower planning begins with the enterprise and then fans out into cities, regions and republics. The system does not work well in practice for many reasons. Individual plants have unnecessary workers because of poor organization, and when they are made redundant through mechanization or other reasons, it is virtually impossible to dismiss them, even though productivity may be adversely affected. Chronic underutilization of workers is a standard feature of Soviet industry.

The relative shortage of adult males—the result of civil war and strife during the first half of this century—caused a systematic resort to female labor in a way unknown in the West. The low wages of the male heads of households also forced women to enter the labor market through sheer necessity and to accept all kinds of demeaning work. In the course of time, certain fields came to have substantial percentages of or to be dominated by women: construction (30%), industry (46%), administrative jobs (55%), education (71%) and public health (86%). In the last case, 75% of physicians and 90% of nurses and laboratory staff are women. Over 52% of all graduates employed are women. Women scientists and engineers are numerous, and women also dominate in banking, insurance and in "the apparatus of the organs of state and of economic administration and of cooperative and social organizations." All this appears satisfactory but for the fact that with few exceptions, women occupy in every case the lower end of the scale in terms of both salary and responsibility. The proportion of women diminishes with every ascending rung of the professional ladder. Even in agriculture, the better-paid mechanizers are nearly all men, while the underpaid field-workers are nearly all women.

The proportion of women workers is highest in the western parts, particularly in the Baltic republics. The proportion diminishes eastward and reaches its lowest in the Tadjik, Azerbaijan, Turkmen and Armenian SSRs.

The law prohibits employment of women in certain arduous or hazardous jobs, including underground mining, fishing boats and carrying loads over 20 kg. (44 lb.). However, the sight of elderly women doing menial jobs in unpleasant conditions is a familiar one in many Soviet cities. In view of the burdensome demands on women workers, the government has taken a number of measures to safeguard their health and welfare. They retire five years earlier than men and perform less night work: Pregnant women may not be dismissed, are exempt from overtime and night shift work and have the right to lower work quotas; they also receive paid leave of absence from work 56 days before and 56 days after childbirth and additional unpaid leave until the child is one year old and also get paid time off every workday for breast-feeding.

Some 3% of the labor force is involved in migration each year. This migration is of three kinds: from rural areas into cities; induced migration from developed areas into hardship areas in Siberia and the far eastern region; and voluntary migration from hardship areas back into developed areas. Because of the government's inability to control migratory flows—internal passports have been phased out—there are severe shortages of labor in certain areas, hampering the full exploitation of natural resources.

More than in Western countries, education is fostered primarily as contributing to the creation of a pool of skilled manpower. Educational enrollments are fine-tuned to reflect the future manpower needs of the economy. There are special commissions for each of the four basic divisions of the educational system that serve as links between employers and institutions, all with long names that the Soviets are so fond of: Commission for the Labor Participation of Youths of the Local Soviets of Workers' Deputies; the State Committee for Professional and Technical Education; and the Commission for the Personnel Distribution of Young Specialists. Extensive on-the-job training is conducted on an ongoing basis by the enterprises.

Productivity was not a major concern of Soviet ideologues until the 1970s, when wastefulness in labor utilization was found to have a serious impact on output. The Soviet Union has one of the lowest productivity rates of all industrialized countries, although rising productivity under Marxism has been one of the boasts of the regime. The economic reforms of the 1960s and the 1980s have led to chaotic conditions in some sectors because of the arbitrary establishment of wages, prices and incentives. Efforts to increase productivity consist of measures to accord managers greater power to hire and fire employees and pay bonuses to workers from the material incentives fund. The most famous experiment, often cited in the Soviet media, is that of the Shchekino Chemical Combine in Tula, which in 1967 fired a substantial number of its workers, yet achieved an 87% rise in productivity through utilization of wage savings as incentive pay for the remaining workers. The extension of this experiment to other enterprises has met with only limited success. Productivity is a complex of many factors other than purely ergonomic. Regimentation itself has a profoundly negative influence on productivity.

The Soviet system of labor control has two interlocking aspects: setting standards of attitudes and performance, and maintaining those standards by a system of Pavlovian rewards and penalties. Productivity is regulated by work norms and technical norms, measurement units representing minima in statistical terms. There are incentives and bonuses for those who fulfill or overfulfill these norms. Socialist competition (also called socialist emulation, socialist innovation or Stakhanovism) is one of the devices used by the regime to prod workers to overachieve their norms. First initiated among groups in 1929, it soon was extended to individual workers. The shock worker was exemplified by Aleksey Stakhanov, who became a national hero by cutting 15 times as much coal as the normal output per man-shift. Although he accomplished this with the help of a team, the achievement was played up as that of one man. Stakhanovites became like a secular order of socialist knights receiving celebrity status and associated perquisites, although some of their achievements were staged performances and much of the socialist innovation consisted of fabricating records and data. After the death of Stalin the use of the term Stakhanovite was dropped. Currently the emphasis is on improvement of processes, and individuals and groups are encouraged to develop such improvements and put them into effect throughout the plant.

Responsibility for administering labor matters rests with a number of agencies. The State Committee on Questions of Labor and Wages, established in 1955, is concerned primarily with productivity and wages. Operating directly under this committee is the Scientific Research Institute of Labor. The state committees on labor resource utilization, at the republic level, operate under the central direction of the Labor Resources Department of the State Planning Committee. Their main functions involve labor recruitment, placement and resettlement. There is no central agency for recruitment of personnel, which is carried out by individual agencies and ministries. However, under the *nomenklatura* system, the Communist Party has the right to appoint all key personnel in the government and in the state and cooperative sectors.

The legal foundations of Soviet labor are in the Labor Code and in many decrees, statutes and regulations rather than in the Constitution. The Labor Code is highly uniform, as the RSFSR code is followed in all the remaining 14 republics. The original Labor Code, adopted in 1922, has been amended a number of times; amendments after 1955 were used to soften the harsher features of the Labor Code, dating back to Stalinist days. The Labor Code deals with trade union rights, the length of the workweek, pensions and labor disputes. Model work rules were issued in 1957 on hiring, dismissal procedures, attendance, safety clothing, sanitation and penalties for violation of labor discipline. Reflecting the paternalistic character of the Soviet state, the Labor Code is as much an educational as a legal document. Although the bargaining rights of workers and unions are circumscribed, workers' basic rights are respected and protected under law. Penalties are prescribed for violations of rules in the workplace as well as for avoiding socially useful work or leading an antisocial or parasitic way of life. Violations of rules result in warning, reproof, reprimand, demotion, or reduced pay for a specified period; absence from work without sufficient reason or persistent breach of rules may result in dismissal. The director of an enterprise may take action, or he may turn the violation over to a comrades' court, which is not part of the regular court system. In case of dismissal the worker may appeal directly to the civil courts.

Little government machinery is provided for settlement of labor disputes. At the enterprise level, the factory disputes commissions and the factory committees are the primary means to settle disputes. Workers may appeal their decisions to the local people's court. Labor laws may not be challenged, but workers could dispute the fairness with which laws were applied. Generally, factory commissions and factory committees are more concerned with promotion of production and good relations with managers than with the interests of the worker. In the negotiation of contracts and other matters, the trade unions are subject to the dictates of the party. Under Gorbachev, trade union officials are recognizing that they had been remiss in protecting workers' rights and thus had contributed to a massive erosion of workers' rights since the 1920s.

Soviet theory holds that in a system of public ownership of the means of production there are no contradictory class interests to cause labor conflicts. The director of the enterprise is the chief authority, but he works under strict control of regulations and instructions from above. Although the reforms after 1956 have given him more autonomy, they also have increased the rights in the plants of union committees, whose consent is required on many points affecting overtime, discharge, transfer or penalty. Joint decisions are required on housing, socialist competition and the enterprise fund. Also subject to joint agreement are vacations, wages and production standards. Collective agreements limit management authority in other respects. The committee is authorized to verify observance of labor legislation, safety regulations and collective contract obligations.

Collective contracts, dormant during the Stalin years, were reactivated by the reforms since 1956 and now play an important role in regulating wages and working conditions. Negotiations give workers an opportunity to criticize management. A typical contract deals with (1) obligations for fulfilling the state output plan and developing socialist competition; (2) wages and production standards; (3) training of new workers; (4) state and labor discipline; (5) protection of labor, a phrase that in Soviet terminology refers to the health and safety of workers; (6) housing and living conditions; and (7) procedures for monitoring observance. Commitments made by management are legally enforceable, while those of the union committee have only "moral force." Among the most unusual features of these contracts is the joint responsibility for production as well as protection. Factory committees also have a key role in enforcing the legal protections against discharge.

LABOR INDICATORS, 1988

Total economically active population: 151 million
As % of working-age population: 72.7
% female: 49.9
% under 20 years of age: 6.5
% unemployed: N.A.
Average annual growth rate, 1985–2000 (%): 0.5
Activity rate (%)
    Total: 51.7
    Male: 55.7
    Female: 48.1
% organized labor: 98
Hours of work in manufacturing: 40.3 per week
Employment status (%)
    Employees: 82.8
    Other: 17.2
Sectoral employment (%)
    Agriculture, forestry & fishing: 18.9
    Mining: } 29.0
    Manufacturing: }
    Construction: 9.1
    Electricity, gas & water: 3.9
    Transportation & communication: 9.3
    Trade: 8.0
    Finance, real estate: 0.5
    Public administration & defense: 1.5
    Services: 18.2
    Other: 1.6

Industrial disputes may be either collective or individual but may relate only to actionable disputes—i.e., those concerned with enforcement of laws or regulations. The major issue of wage levels is outside the scope of labor-management decision, since, in the Soviet system, wages are determined by central authorities. For the most part disputes deal with violations of rights, and the largest number deal with discharges.

Strikes are not specifically prohibited by law in the Soviet Union, although laws against public disorder or weakening the state could possibly be used against strikers. However, strikes are effectively proscribed. This does not mean that they do not occur, although the Soviet media rarely report them. Most strikes are protests against poor living conditions or pay, although there are rare instances of mass protests, such as the 1989 miners' mass strike. In the 1970s strikes are known to have occurred in Kiev, Vitebsk, Vladim, Sverdlovsk, Chelyabinsk, Baku, Dnepopetrovsk, Kaunus, Kamyanets-Podilsky, Riga and Tolyatti, and in the 1980s in Tolyatti, Gorki and Kiev. Workers rarely participate in political strikes. There is little support in the Soviet Union for the Polish-style Solidarity political action, and nearly 44% of Soviet workers are reported to oppose liberalization. The average number of strikes every year is a matter of speculation, but *Pravda* in 1978 gave the figure of "a few dozen per year." There also is evidence that strikes are extremely effective in bringing quick redress to workers' grievances.

Working conditions are governed by laws as well as collective agreements. Union membership is not a precondition for employment, although it is desirable. Written agreements are required for employment only in the far North and other remote areas.

The standard workweek is a five-day, 41-hour one, with a shorter workweek for those in hazardous occupations, for youths 16 or 17 years of age and for groups such as teachers or doctors. Overtime is permitted under special conditions but is limited to 120 hours per year. Refusal to work overtime is considered a breach of labor discipline and is punishable. Paid annual vacations vary from 15 to 48 workdays. Increased or bonus leave is permitted to those in hazardous jobs. *Kolkhoz* peasants are not entitled to paid vacations. All workers, including *kolkhoz* peasants, receive pensions, with a ceiling and a floor of R120 and R50 per month, respectively.

In classic Marxism the wage system is based on the principle "From each according to his ability, to each according to his need." However, the actual application of this principle is highly complex in the Soviet Union. Wages and salary scales are laid down by decrees issued on the authority of the Council of Ministers on the advice of the State Committee on Labor and Social Problems. Between the abolition of the People's Commissariat (Ministry of Labor) in 1933 and the setting up of the State Committee in 1955, there was no central state body responsible for labor and wages and no general review of wage scales. There were several ad hoc revisions within particular ministries and across-the-board increases, such as in 1946. As a result, several anomalies developed. Similar work was paid at different rates, and there was a widening gap between basic rates and take-home pay. Different ministries adopted several zonal differentials. It took many years for the State Committee on Labor and Wages to bring order into this chaos. There is now one national grading program, applicable to all types of work that occur in many industries, as well as separate programs for specific trades found only in certain industries. Analogous grading programs, with definitions and responsibilities for each category of job, are issued for engineer-technical and clerical-administrative staffs. When the reform began in 1955 there were 1,900 different wage scales, with several thousand wage rates for the lowest grade of skill. The number was reduced to 10 by 1960 and eventually will be reduced to three. The number of wage rates for the lowest grade of skill was reduced to 17. The income of engineer-technical and clerical-administrative staffs was determined on the basis of their rank as well as the size and importance of the enterprise or office they administered. The number of different staff salaries was reduced from 700 to 150. Personnel of priority sectors receive higher salary scales than those in nonpriority sectors. In each case of workers, the various categories of skills are arranged into a series of grades, from I (unskilled) to VII (most skilled), with ratios determined for each grade.

The wage structure consists of a basic rate *(stavka)* for the lowest grade and schedules *(setka)* of percentage increases for the higher grades for each occupation. However, wages constitute only part of a worker's earnings. There are incentive programs, bonuses, piece rate programs and regional differentials that double, triple or quadruple the basic wages. Before the 1955 wage reform, differentials for skills were very large, and the base rates in the top grades in many schedules were 1.8 to four times the rates for the lowest grades. To attract and hold workers, managers established low production standards and piece rates that permitted high earnings, sometimes four to eight times the base rate for the unskilled. As rising levels of education and mechanization reduced the differentials, the disparities became less marked. Minimum wages were raised and basic rates were adjusted to give substantial increases to the lower grades. In most branches of industry the post-1956 schedules provide a range of rates that gives the most skilled group only 1.8 to two times the lowest rate. Thus wage differentials have been decreasing since the 1960s and are expected to be reduced to 60% to 80% above the lowest rates.

In addition to skills differentials, there are industrial and regional differentials that go back to the 1920s. Such differentials tended to increase in the massive industrialization drive of the 1950s and 1960s. In 1960 a ranking of a group of 17 industries by average wages showed coal at the top, followed by iron and steel, oil, paper and pulp, chemicals, machinery and electric power production. Farther down were textiles, woodworking, printing and footwear, and at the bottom food processing and garment manufacturing (incidentally, the last two with a predominance of women workers). Industrial differentials also have been declining as high-priority industries face less severe labor shortages.

Regional differentials continue to be emphasized as a matter of policy because of the need to disperse industries. In 1956 a start was made toward a uniform system of regional coefficients. The coefficients ranged from 1.00 in the central, southern and western parts of European Russia to 1.10 to 1.20 in the Urals, southwestern Siberia, Kazakhstan and Middle Asia and up to 1.50 to 1.70 in the far nothern region. The highest coefficient for the far North is said to include 10 points for the arduous nature of the work, 40 points for the poorer living conditions and higher consumer prices and 10 points for the relatively smaller supplements to wages from government services. In 1960 personnel in the far North were given further incentives. On top of the regular coefficients workers receive supplements to monthly pay, depending on the length of service, in addition to extra vacations and disability pay. One year's work in these regions is counted as 1.5 years for pension purposes.

The Soviet planned wage system thus is not entirely different in its operation from that of a free labor market. Through manipulation of incentives, differentials and other premiums, the market responds to changes in the supply and demand of labor. Groups strategically placed in relation to demand receive higher wages, and areas with labor shortages have higher labor costs.

In other ways, too, the market influences the wage system. The system is based on skill classification and payment according to a centrally determined tariff rate upon 100% fulfillment of the norm by a worker in a given grade. However, the norm itself tends to change, thus causing a wage drift through a gradual increase in the extent of overfulfillment of norms. Under the piece-rate system many industrial workers had actual earnings many times their basic wages because of overfulfillment of norms. The wage revisions begun in 1956 led to a sharp rise in both tariff rates and norms, designed to bring the basic rates much closer to actual earnings. The proportion of workers on piece rates fell, and the average percentage of overfulfillment of norms also fell sharply. However, considerable variations remain as a result of bonus programs and illegal regrading of workers. Although the state tries to maintain control over the wage system through the planned wages fund for each enterprise, such control is de facto ineffective at the individual worker level, where output norms, bonuses, grading and differentials play more decisive roles.

Disparities and distortions among the earnings of different occupations have survived the reforms of the 1950s. White-collar staffs, teachers and other nonindustrial workers have suffered an erosion in their incomes relative to those of the workers. Even junior engineers, foremen and managers receive some 30% less income than skilled workers of grade IV on piecework. However, at the higher levels the proper measure of real income is complicated by various extras and perks, such as the use of a car, a better apartment, lavish travel expenses, access to goods and services in closed shops, imported liquors, scarce foodstuffs and others too numerous to list. In a society where shortages are universal, such perks are more valuable than additional cash income. There also are extralegal earnings from the second economy, and the proceeds of various kinds of corruption at the highest circles.

Minimum wages are fixed unionwide by the Council of Ministers on the advice of the State Committee on Labor and Wages. These are not guaranteed monthly earnings, and some workers earn less. If a piece-rate worker fails to fulfill his production standard through his own fault, he does not receive the full wages. If he is not at fault, the guarantee is two-thirds of the base rate, and in case of stoppages one-half to two-thirds of the base rate. Wage rates are differentiated for time work and piecework, with higher rates for the latter.

Some relief from the problems of piece-rate systems is offered by the growing use of "brigades," including workers of different skills, with pay according to the final result of the work of the group. These brigades are widely used in coal mining, metallurgy, chemicals and construction. The wages for the entire group depend on the collective net result, such as tonnage mined, and the total sum is divided among the workers according to their grades and the time worked. In some cases individual piece rates are combined with a collective piece system. The use of brigades has had a positive impact on output in most cases requiring cooperative efforts and has led to an improvement in labor discipline.

The role of trade unions in the post-Stalin era was set forth in a lengthy resolution of the party's Central Committee in 1957. The organization and regulations for the operation of trade unions were updated in the constitution adopted by the 13th All-Union Congress of Trade Unions in 1963. The basic principles governing trade union activity are established by the party and are embodied in Lenin's dictum "The unions must carry on all their activities under party leadership." The party not only issues directives to unions, but also party members dominate union leadership. The functions of trade unions are first to develop Communist attitudes among the working people and to promote cooperation and participation in the building of communism, and second to protect the rights and interests of workers that are accorded by law. Unions do not conduct collective bargaining in the Western sense but rather negotiate and cooperate with managers in working out agreements within the framework established by the state. Unions also have a function in monitoring fulfillment of management obligations under these agreements, in setting up production standards and in grading workers according to established occupational categories. Unlike in the West, unions play and important role in production by fostering socialist competition. A second difference with the West consists in the membership of the supervisory staff in the enterprise union committee. All labor awards, numbering over 200,000 annually, are made on the recommendations of local unions. Trade unions also manage a massive recreation program, including several thousand "palaces of culture," each comprising sports stadia, clubs, cinemas, theaters and libraries. Such well-known soccer teams as Moscow Spartak and Riga Vef are part of the unions. Unions also conduct educational activities through nearly 8,000 "people's universities." Health resorts and vacation accommodations supported by social insurance funds are included in the list of benefits unions extend to their members. Trade unions also administer social insurance, a function they acquired in 1933 when the Commissariat of Labor was disbanded. Along with Social Security, unions administer disability and maternity benefits and related programs. They check on housing and the allotment of apartments.

Under the central trade union organization, the All-Union Central Council of Trade Unions (AUCCTU), there are 30 branch trade unions, as follows:

• Agricultural and Food Workers' Union
• Aircraft Engineering Workers' Union
• Automobile, Tractor and Farm Machinery Industries Workers' Union
• Automobile Transportation and Highway Workers' Union
• Chemical and Petrochemical Workers' Union
• Civil Aviation Workers' Union
• Coal Mining Industry Workers' Union
• Communication Workers' Union
• Construction and Building Materials Industry Workers' Union
• Cultural Workers' Union

• Educational and Scientific Workers' Union
• Engineering and Instrument-Making Industries Workers' Union
• Fishing Industry Workers' Union
• Geological Survey Workers' Union
• Heavy Engineering Workers' Union
• Local Industries and Public Services Workers' Union
• Medical Workers' Union
• Metallurgical Industry Workers' Union
• Oil and Gas Workers' Union
• Power and Electrical Workers' Union
• Radio and Electronics Industry Workers' Union
• Railway and Transportation Construction Workers' Union
• Sea and River Workers' Union
• Shipbuilding Workers' Union
• State Institutions Workers' Union
• State Trade and Consumer Cooperative Workers' Union
• Textile and Light Industry Workers' Union
• Timber, Paper and Woodworkers' Union
• Cinematographers' Union
• Theatrical Workers' Union

There also are professional associations with 105,000 members outside the organizational structure of the trade unions.

Total membership in all the unions is estimated at 140 million. Membership is voluntary, but workers are required to pay a subscription of 1% of their earnings. Workers are organized by industry and not by craft. Thus an electrician in a coal mine belongs to the coal miners' union and not to the electricians' union.

The principle of democratic centralism applies to trade unions as much as to the political system. This means that AUCCTU directives are carried out by member unions and their locals, just as the AUCCTU itself carries out the dictates of the party. By statute the AUCCTU Congress is required to meet every four years, but it has not always done so. This Congress, like other legislative organs in the Soviet Union, has a perfect record of unanimous approval of every decision made by the Central Council of the AUCCTU. The Central Council itself delegates much of its directive functions to the Presidium and Secretariat of the AUCCTU. Invariably, the head of the Central Council and its Politburo is also a member of the Politburo of the Communist Party.

The Central Council controls the operations of the Interunion Trade Union Councils, the Regional Interunion Trade Union Council and the national industrial unions. Each of the national industrial unions has a central committee in Moscow. The authority of these central committees is transmitted through its regional offices to factory, plant or local committees, which in turn transmit it through the shop committees to the trade union groups. At the center are a number of commissions, each dealing with one particular responsibility. There are 13 such commissions, covering the following areas: (1) production; (2) organization; (3) pensions; (4) labor protection; (5) culture; (6) family and school; (7)

youth; (8) housing; (9) elections; (10) labor disputes; (11) consumer services; (12) women's services; and (13) international relations.

As the "school of communism," the trade unions have a strong political function in keeping the ideological fires lit in every workplace and plant through banners, campaigns, meetings and club activities. *Trud*, the principal trade union publication, is one of hundreds of publications issued by the AUCCTU and its branches.

At the factory level, the highest authority of the union is the general meeting. The factory or plant committee provides the leadership and carries out the administrative functions. One paid union worker is authorized for plants with 500 to 2,500 workers, and in larger enterprises one for every 3,500 workers. The factory committee sets up permanent commissions for various facets of their work. The trade union group is the basic element of the union. It elects a group organizer and other leaders for the various union activities. In small plants the group may carry out the functions usually performed by the factory committee under the direction of the district headquarters of the national union.

Trade unions have a direct obligation to spur new technology and innovations in production. Scientific-technical societies and societies of inventors and rationalizers within the unions play important roles in generating innovation within industry. The AUCCTU maintains several research institutes to study labor problems and also two schools, one in Moscow and the other in Leningrad, to train union personnel.

FOREIGN COMMERCE

Foreign economic relations did not play a major role in the Soviet economy until the 1970s. From 1917 untill World War II the Soviet Union was treated as a pariah by the capitalist nations and was excluded from the principal channels of international trade. For their part, the new Soviet leaders pursued, from inclination as well as necessity, a policy of autarky for creating "communism in one country," self-sufficient, defiant and isolated from the world. The internal strife during the 1920s did not favor the achievement of such autarky and, in any case, World War II intervened before a viable economy could be established. Emerging after the war as a superpower, the Soviet Union found a new pattern of foreign economic relations superimposed on its role as leader of the Communist world. This pattern had two aspects: (1) hegemonic relations with a growing number of Communist countries, linked together in COMECON, and (2) trade with combined with aid to developing countries either as a means of weaning them away from association with capitalist countries or to promote indigenous Marxist movements. Trade with the West was limited until the 1970s by the rivalries of the Cold War.

Even after *glasnost*, this pattern of foreign economic relations has changed only slightly. Despite an increasing reliance on imported Western technology, significant restrictions remain on full and free trade between the two blocs. Trade with the West has been consistently negative for most years since 1967. There are further

problems because the bulk of Soviet trade is conducted on the basis of bilateral clearing agreements, with mutual balancing of trade in terms of merchandise without the use of foreign exchange. Hard currencies, however, are essential in settling balances with non-Communist trading partners. A lack of adequate foreign exchange reserves has necessitated the partial settlement of these trade deficits through the sale of gold.

Foreign trade is a state monopoly exercised through the Ministry of Foreign Trade. The ministry is an administratory and regulatory body without direct responsibility for trade transactions. Among its major functions are negotiation of trade and payments agreements with foreign countries; direction of the customs service and of the transit trade; and issuance of import and export permits. The ministry is composed of five departments organized on a regional basis and seven specialized departments concerned with the export or import of specific groups of commodities.

The direct conduct of foreign trade is the bailiwick of a number of all-Union foreign trade associations and officials. In accordance with the foreign trade plan, these organizations buy export goods from producing organizations and arrange for their sale in foreign markets. Similarly, they act as import agents for domestic enterprises and also import from abroad products approved by the plan. Each of these organizations is authorized to handle a specified list of products and services and may engage in imports or exports or both. One of the associations handles patents and licenses. In most instances products handled by individual associations cut across industry branch lines, and the trade of a single industry branch may be handled by more than one organization. Associations that export machinery also are responsible for after-sales service. A national chamber of commerce serves to foster economic relations with foreign countries, holds international trade and industrial expositions and conducts foreign and maritime trade arbitrage. Associations conduct their operations in accordance with national plans. During export contract negotiations they call on industrial specialists familiar with the products and foreign markets. In 1967 councils on export problems were created by law to coordinate the efforts of the associations and the producers. These councils are permanent consultative bodies and include high-level representatives of industry and domestic sales organizations. Among their main concerns are the improvement of the structure and profitability of foreign trade and of the quality of export goods and services, and the timely and efficient fulfillment of export contract obligations.

There are 44 foreign trade associations and five offices.

As a rule, trade with other countries is conducted on the basis of bilateral commercial treaties or agreements. Most of these treaties are negotiated on a long-term basis, preferably for a period of five years coinciding with the five-year economic plans. Those with the Communist countries are comprehensive and outline prices and quantities, freight, customs tariffs and other conditions. Those with non-Communist states are less comprehensive and merely contain a list of commodi-

MAJOR SOVIET TRADE FAIRS		
Place	Theme	Generally held in
Moscow	Robots	February-March
Moscow	Metrology	March-April
Tashkent	Medical Apparatus	March-April
Moscow	"Syvaz"(Communications)	April
Tallin	"Cottage" (Prefabricated Materials)	May
Minsk	Powder Metallurgy	May
Moscow	"Elektro"(Electrotechnical equipment)	June
Kiev	"Stroymaterialy" (Building materials)	June
Moscow	Rail Transport	July
Moscow	"Chempharmindustria"	July
Moscow	"Litkontrolmaterialy" (Moulding, welding)	July-August
Moscow	"Khimiya" (Chemical fibers, plastics)	September
Leningrad	"Interport" (Port equipment)	September
Erevan	Stone processing	October
Moscow	"Nefta-Gaz" (Oil, gas, petrochemicals)	October
Moscow	Optics	October
Moscow	Books	Date varies

ties. The treaties and agreements are supplemented by annual protocols. Provisions concerning payments are included in the basic agreements or made the subject of separate agreements. Under treaties with Communist countries, mutual delivery schedules are obligatory.

Prices in trade with COMECON members are negotiated on a bilateral basis for the duration of the trade treaties, although the prices of machinery may be reviewed annually. These prices are based on the average world prices for a period of several years. In the case of certain strategic commodities such as oil, the Soviet Union charges it partners considerably less than world market prices.

In intra-COMECON trade the predominant form of settling trade balances is through the medium of bilateral clearing accounts or barter. These accounts are balanced through additional commodity shipments. The transferable ruble serves as a unit of account in trade bookkeeping but is not used as a means of payment. Deficits with non-Communist trading partners at the end of an agreement period usually are settled in convertible currency or gold or carried over as an overdraft to the next period.

Even though foreign trade is a state monopoly, there is a customs tariff system, with maximum, minimum and ad valorem rates. The reason for such a tariff is not known. The usual functions of a tariff—protection against imports, and revenue for the government—are irrelevant in a situation where the government pays and collects the tariff.

As in other areas, Soviet data on trade are highly deficient. A balance of payments is not published. In regard to trade with all capitalist countries, both developed and developing, only indices are published, intermingling different sets of data. The foreign trade yearbook reports data only on the current ruble value of trade in selected commodity groups (omitting many important

ones), and these are divided not by country but by two groups: socialist and nonsocialist. Such practices make a study of long-term trends in Soviet trade subject to a high degree of error.

FOREIGN TRADE INDICATORS, 1988		
Exports: $107.7 billion		
Imports: $96.0 billion		
Balance of trade: $11.7 billion		
Direction of Trade (%)		
	Imports	Exports
EEC	11.4	14.4
U.S.A.	1.5	0.4
East European countries	56.5	50.4
Japan	2.7	1.4
Composition of Trade (%)		
	Imports	Exports
Food & agricultural raw materials	18.6	6.7
Ores & minerals		2.3
Fuels	2.7	46.4
Manufactured goods	78.8	44.5
of which chemicals	7.9	3.0
of which machinery	41.4	15.5

The two principal trends in Soviet trade since 1960 are (1) the dramatic shift in the geographical direction of trade away from socialist countries and toward capitalist countries and (2) the equally dramatic increase in imports, particularly of high-technology goods, from the West. However, it is difficult to gauge the extent of these shifts because the Soviets use one ruble/dollar ratio for imports and another for exports. Again, trade figures with Communist bloc countries bear little relation to the world prices on which trade figures for non-Communist countries are computed. Further, because domestic prices are substantially lower than world prices, the relative magnitude of trade flows cannot be stated in terms of the net material product.

Even with these caveats, changes in the commodity composition of Soviet trade are more easily perceived than changes in the geographical direction of trade. In 1913 the top five foreign currency earners in the exports of czarist Russia were grain, sawn timber, eggs and egg products, cotton fibers and logs. Three of these product groups remain among the top earners of foreign currency today: sawn timber, logs and cotton. The other top exports also are primary products: petroleum and petroleum products, natural gas, coal, iron ore, rolled ferrous metals and nonferrous metals. These products account for about three-fourths of Soviet merchandise exports to the hard-currency area. *Pari passu*, the share of machinery and equipment in Soviet imports has risen steadily over the past two decades and now comprises over half of the value of imports from Communist countries and 40% of the value of total imports.

The heavy reliance on a few primary products, generally a characteristic of a developing rather than a developed economy, illustrates the regressive nature of the industrial system, which emphasizes quantity over quality and known technology over new technology. The same factors favor primary commodities that require no after-sales service, that can be easily produced in great quantities and that are less dependent on technological advances.

In addition in petroleum, which is by far the most important of the primary products used to earn hard currency, the Soviet Union has another potentially important source of hard currency: gold. Gold sales have been substantial for many years and by 1980 were yielding almost half of the value of petroleum sales. Since no official information is published on gold sales, production, stocks or prices, all that is known with acceptable accuracy is sales tonnage, as reported by Western gold traders. On this basis the Soviet Union is the world's second-largest gold seller (after South Africa) and plays an important stabilizing role on world gold markets, selling when prices are high and holding back when prices are low.

Sales of military goods have, since 1973, become an important source of convertible currency for the Soviet Union, providing about 11% of hard-currency earnings from merchandise trade. Shipping and other transportation services also are becoming important sources of net convertible currency earnings.

In 1987 total volume of trade was R128 billion, including imports of R61 billion and exports of R67 billion. Trade with COMECON countries accounted for 62% of the total. In 1986 trade deficit with nonsocialist countries widened to $1.9 billion and net external debt to $24 billion. In 1987 new legislation was enacted whereby Western companies were permitted to participate in joint ventures with Soviet companies.

TRANSPORTATION & COMMUNICATIONS

The sheer size of the Soviet Union has influenced the development of its transportation system into the largest in the world. In terms of length it leads the world in rail trackage, roads, navigable inland waterways and air routes. But there are significant variations in the relative importance of each of these systems. The greatest contrast with Western countries is the primacy of railways and the relative underdevelopment of road transportation for long distances. This is not due to lack of investment in roads but rather to the peculiar suitability of railways to Soviet conditions. Further, with a much smaller per capita ownership of motor vehicles, public transportation is dominant in all cities, thus reinforcing the communal nature of Soviet society. Other characteristic features of the transportation system are its east–west orientation and the relative importance of maritime traffic.

The Soviet Union inherited an extensive rail network from czarist Russia. The first railway opened in 1837, from Tsarkoye Selo (now Pushkin) to St. Petersburg. It was followed by the Moscow–St. Petersburg line (1843–51) and the St. Petersburg–Warsaw line (1848–61). By 1872, tracks reached the Volga and by 1874 Konigsberg. Following the war with Turkey the line was extended from Tbilisi to Poti by 1872 and to Baku in 1883. The Urals appeared on the railway map with the building of the Perm–Chusovoy–Sverdlovsk line in 1878. By 1904 the Donets coalfields were connected via Dno with St. Petersburg. The turn of the century saw the pioneering expansion of the system into Siberia and central Asia. By 1888 Ufa had been reached and by 1892 Chelyabinsk, the starting point of the legendary Trans-Siberian Railway. Building across the open steppe was easy, but work slowed in the bitter winters. Omsk was reached in 1894, Krasnoyarsk in 1897 and Irkutsk in 1898. Meanwhile, the Ussuri railway connected Vladivostok with Khabarovsk. In 1916, a year before the Revolution, the final section between Kuenga and Khabarovsk was completed, thus linking Vladivostok with Moscow over Russian territory.

Building railways in central Asia was more difficult because of the terrain. The Trans-Caspian Railway joined Ashkhabad, Tashkent, Bukhara and Samarkand by 1899, and in 1905 the Trans-Aral Railway joined the Volga to these towns. By 1915 Murmansk and Arkhangelsk in the north also had been joined to Moscow. By 1917 the route length was 70,291 km. (43,686 mi.), of which 80% was in European Russia. Because the land is low and open, construction had been speedy and costs moderate.

Under the Soviets, railway development has been mainly in the East and South, particularly the construction of feeder lines, double tracks and interregional supertrunk lines and the installation of electrification.

TRANSPORTATION INDICATORS, 1988

Roads, km. (mi.): 971,500 (604,000)
  % paved: 84
Motor vehicles
  Automobiles: 8,255,000
  Trucks: 7,254,000
  Persons per vehicle: 17
  Road freight, tonne-km. (ton-mi.): 142 billion (97 billion)
Railroads
  Track, km. (mi.): 145,600 (90,491); electrified, km. (mi.): 51,700 (32,105)
  Passenger traffic, passenger-km. (passenger-mi.): 390 billion (242 billion)
  Freight, freight tonne-km (freight ton-mi.): 3.834 trillion (2.626 trillion)
Merchant marine
  Vessels: 6,705
  Total deadweight tonnage: 28,555,700
  No. oil tankers: 262   GRT: 5,337,000
Ports
  Number: 15 major; 11 inland
  Cargo loaded (tons): 164,670,000
  Cargo unloaded (tons): 834,830,000
Air
  Km. (mi.) flown: 113 million (70.1 million)
  Passengers: 112,283,000
  Passenger traffic, passenger-km. (passenger-mi.): 196 billion (121.8 billion)
  Freight traffic, freight tonne-km. (freight ton-mi.): 3.384 billion (2.317 billion)
  Mail tonne-km. (mail ton-mi.): 507 million (314.8 million)
  Airports with scheduled flights: 52
  Airports: 6,890
  Civil aircraft: 4,750
Pipelines
  Crude, km. (mi.):
  Refined, km. (mi.): } 81,500 (50,611)
  Natural gas, km. (mi.): 195,000 (121,193)
Inland waterways
  Length, km. (mi): 123,200 (76,550)
  Cargo, tonne-km. (ton-mi.): 255.630 billion (175.081 billion)

COMMUNICATIONS INDICATORS, 1988

Telephones
  Total (000): 31,000
  Persons per: 9.0
Phone traffic (000 calls)
  Long distance: 1,454,400
  International: 2,130
Post office
  Number of post offices: 94,750
  Pieces of mail handled (000): 58,831,000
Telegraph: total traffic (000): 541,012
Telex
  Subscriber lines: 1,704
  Traffic (000 minutes): 9,581 (international only)
Telecommunications
  N.A.

TOURISM & TRAVEL INDICATORS, 1988*

Number of tourists (000): 2,036

*Additional data regarding tourism to the Soviet Union and expenditures by Soviet nationals abroad are not available.

In 1988 the total length of track was 145,600 km. (90,491 mi.), an increase since 1917 of 75,309 km. (46,805 mi.), of which 20,434 km. (12,700 mi.) had been added through territorial expansion rather than through construction. Except for some 6,436 km. (4,000 mi.), the entire length is broad-gauge. Despite Soviet commitment to ending territorial disparities in transportation development, about a third of the length is in Asian Russia and the Urals, another third in the center and only one-eleventh in the far eastern region and eastern Siberia. The best-served region is the Baltic, although the eastern regions have a high rate of inhabitants to track length because of their low population densities. The bulk of the tracks run along easy, open terrain, although some lines traverse exceptionally difficult country, such as the Frunze–Rybachye line and the Mointy–Chu line. There are only a few sections where express trains are prohibited, such as the Ulan Ude section, the Suram Pass and the Chu–Ili mountain section. About two-thirds of the track length is straight track, although some lines in the Urals and Karelia have bad curves. Tunnels are the exception, except along the 68-km. (42-mi.) route along the southern shore of Lake Baikal; this route has 38 tunnels. The longest bridges are those crossing the Volga at Batraki (1,432 mi; 4,700 ft.), the Irtysh (640 mi; 2,100 ft.), the Ob (814 mi, 2,670 ft.) and the Yenisey (853 mi, 2,800 ft.). The major problems in construction have been marshes and swamps in European Russia and permafrost in Siberia.

Because of the abundance of coal supplies, steam trains still are in service. However, coal has low thermal efficiency in arid central Asia, and in the extremely low winter temperatures of Siberia loss of heat raises fuel consumption by over 70%. As a result, both diesel and electric power are supplanting coal as motive power. With the use of electric and diesel traction, train weights have risen. Soviet trains are essentially built to carry freight, and the average hauls have tended to increase and now are over 965 km. (600 mi.). Freight and passenger movements do not, however, take place with equal intensity over the entire system but are con-

centrated on a few supertrunk lines, all of which are double-track. About 50% of the railways carry 86% of the traffic.

Passenger traffic is secondary to freight traffic. About one-quarter of the traffic and 85% of the passengers are suburban, with an average journey length of 31 km. (19 mi.). Because of the great distances on the major trunk lines, most principal connections take several days, and sleeping cars are a very common feature. The longest journey, from Moscow to Vladivostok on the Trans-Siberian Railway, takes up to seven days, and that from Moscow to Leningrad six hours by express.

In 1984 the laying of track was completed on the 3,145-km. (1,955-mi.) Baikal–Amur line, the most ambitious construction project undertaken by the Soviets; it was begun in the 1930s and almost abandoned several times. A branch of this route, to Yakutsk, was completed in the late 1980s along with a new Trans-Caucasian Railway route, from Tbilisi to Yerevan.

In addition to the mainline rail network, there are subways in 12 cities, including the Moscow Subway, opened in 1935 and one of Stalin's showpieces. It is 216 km. (134 mi.) long and has 135 stations.

In terms of traffic, the rivers are important arteries, although the share of inland water transportation in total transportation has fallen considerably since 1917. The major navigable rivers are the Volga, Dnieper, Don, Ob, Yenisey, Lena, Amur and Amu-Darya. Historically these rivers served to open up the interior to Russian colonization, but their principal disadvantages have become obvious in modern times. Almost all of them flow north to south, whereas the predominant population movement is east to west. Even without their seasonal fluctuations, their navigability is limited by low water in summer and ice in winter, and the northern rivers discharge into the Arctic. The archetypal Soviet river is the Volga, which has played the same role in Russian history as the Ganges in India, the Amazon in Brazil, the Nile in Egypt and the Yangtze in China. With the Volga's Kama, Oka and Belaya tributaries, it serves a basin inhabited by 100 million people. Through numerous artificial canals, the Volga is joined to other river systems, and through these canals Volga traffic may reach the Baltic and White seas. Soviet textbooks claim that Volga traffic is equivalent to that of 10 to 12 main line railways, even though navigation is limited to about six months on the upper reaches and seven to eight months on the lower reaches.

The second most important river is the Dnieper, whose navigation has increased since the completion of the Dnieperoges Dam in 1932 made possible navigation of the 85-km.-long (53-mi.-long) rapids between Dnepropetrovsk and Zaporozhye, while movement in the lower reaches has been eased by completion of the Kakhovka Barrage. The Dnieper has a navigable season of 265 days at Kiev.

The rivers in the European northwest and north are important only for the movement of timber. The greatest limitation is the short shipping season. On the Northern Dvina it lasts 170 days; on the Pechora, 140 days. There is a close relationship between the development of forest resources and river systems in the north. The great rivers of Siberia are little developed for transportation, although some are so large that sea-going ships can sail up them. They also suffer from short annual navigation seasons: 152 days on the Ob at Salekhard; 189 days on the Irtysh at Tobolsk; 88 days in the north and 145 days in the south on the Lena, and 197 days on the Yenisey at Krasnoyarsk. Riverboats can sail up the Irtysh to Semipalatinsk, up the Ob to Novosibirsk and up the Yenisey to Minusinsk. The main route from southern Siberia to Yakutia is along the Lena, on which ships may sail in the high-water season to Kachuga. In the far eastern region the Amur is navigated upstream and along its Shilka tributary to Sretensk.

The Soviets are noted for their canal-building, and there is a maze of canals connecting most every river with others. The principal ones are:

- Moscow–Volga Canal, 128 km. (80 mi.)
- White Sea–Baltic Canal, 227 km. (141 mi.)
- Dnieper–Bug Canal, 202 km. (126 mi.)
- Kara–Kum Canal, 850 km. (528 mi.)
- North Crimean Canal, 400 km. (249 mi.)
- Volga–Baltic Canal, 362 km. (225 mi.)
- Volga–Don Canal, 101 km. (63 mi.)
- Donests–Donbas Canal, 120 km. (75 mi.)
- Golodnaya Steppe Canal, 1,300 km. (808 mi.)

Even with one of the longest coastlines of any nation, the Soviet Union has only limited access to the open seas or warm-water ports. The greatest share of maritime traffic is that of the Black Sea and the Sea of Azov (35%); Caspian traffic amounts to another third; the far eastern ports for a sixth; Baltic ports for 8.9%; and the long northern sea route for 7.1%. The Black Sea and its adjacent waters have vigorous coastal traffic, particularly oil, ores, coal and grain. The principal port, Odessa, has a short season but can be kept open most years with the help of icebreakers. It is the second-largest Soviet port and the port of entry for the Mediterranean Sea and Atlantic and Indian oceans. Other important Black Sea ports include Kherson; Nikolayev, the naval base of Sevastopol; Taganrog; Zhdanov; Rostov on the Don; and Azov. Passage to the Sea of Azov is through Kerch Strait, through which navigation is difficult in certain seasons. The ports of the Caucasian coast are generally not troubled with ice. The best are Novorossiysk, Tuapse, Batumi and Poti.

The Baltic has more severe icing conditions than the Black Sea, particularly in the Gulf of Finland. Ice lasts 130 to 170 days in the eastern parts of the Gulf of Finland and about 90 days at Tallinn. Coastal trade is less important on the Baltic. The most important port is Leningrad, which generally is closed because of ice between the last week of January and the first week of May. Tallinn, the next important port, usually is kept open in the winter by icebreakers and is the winter port for Leningrad. Navigation in the Bay of Riga is difficult in winter because of the presence of ice, aggravated by wind driving the ice inshore or out to sea. The port of Riga is restricted in size, as it needs constant dredging to keep the roadsteads clear of silt. The other important Baltic ports are Klaypeda (formerly Memel), Kalinin-grad (formerly Konigsberg) and Baltisk (formerly Pillau).

The Northern Sea Route is a 4,827 km.-long (3,000 mi.-long) route that is "all Red," as it is free of any interference from other nations. First navigated by Nordenskjöld in 1878–79, it is the most difficult sea route in the world. Ice persists for seven to 10 months, and frequent fog makes navigation difficult in the remaining months. Running the route calls for several ancillary services, such as weather forecasting and study of ice movements; these services are controlled by the Chief Administration of the Northern Sea Route, with headquarters at Leningrad. The season opens in Kara Bay, and entry is made via the Kara Gates, an easy if narrow passage through which ships sail to the lower Ob. The principal ports are on the Yenisey, Dikson and Igarka. Navigation eastward becomes increasingly difficult along the Laptev coast, particularly the Vilkitskiy Strait, where even icebreakers can navigate only rarely and which may be blocked all summer by grounded icebergs. To the east the major bases are Nordvik on the mouth of the Khatanga and Tiksi Bay on the Lena. The first Pacific port is Provideniya Bay.

At the western end of the route lie two major ports: Murmansk, on the southern bank of the Kola Inlet and 40 km. (25 mi.) from the Barents Sea; and Arkhangelsk, the largest timber port. Under the influence of the North Atlantic Drift, Murmansk does not freeze and is easily kept open all winter with the help of icebreakers. Arkhangelsk is less fortunate, as the shipping season lasts from May 15 through November 25 only, and navigation is further restricted by silt.

The long far eastern coast also suffers from ice and accounts for only a small share of the total maritime traffic. Okhotsk Sea ports may be icebound for up to 200 days a year, and ice may persist up to July. The principal port of Vladivostok, founded in 1860 and the base for the Russian Pacific Fleet after 1872, stands at the southern end of Muravyev Peninsula on the deep and well-protected bay of the Golden Horn, sheltered from the cold western and northwestern winds. Ice persists for three to four months in the winter, but the port is kept open. More recently, Nakhodka, a good natural harbor that remains ice-free longer than Vladivostok, has been developed. Along the Sikhote Alin coast Soviet Harbor and Vananino have replaced Nikolayevsk as the principal ports for the lower Amur. Movements through the Straits of Tartary are hampered by ice between December and March. Petropavlovsk-Kamchatskiy is the principal port of Kamchatka in the sheltered Avacha Bay and is the winter harbor for boats working on the Northern Sea Route.

Most ports on the Caspian Sea lie on the western shores, as the eastern shores are largely desert. In the southern basin, Baku is the chief port. A ferry crosses to the eastern shore at Krasnovodsk, the terminus of the Trans-Caspian Railway. Astrakhan, although more of a Volga River port, is the focus of traffic on the northern Caspian.

Unlike in the West, road transportation developed late, and its contribution to total transportation is small. Road transportation is not particularly well suited to the extreme climatic conditions. Prolonged ice and snow wreak havoc on any kind of surface, especially when followed by floods in spring. Paradoxically, winter is the best time for road transportation, since even heavy vehicles can drive over the hard, frozen ground or rivers. About 88% of the roads are considered local; only 12% are suited for interregional traffic. Mountain roads are characteristic in Caucasia and central Asia. The best-known of these mountain roads is the Pamir Highway, over the world's longest lofty terrain. Many of these roads follow medieval caravan routes, such as the legendary Silk Road. In Siberia, roads supplement rail and river transportation. The best-known of the Siberian roads are the Chuya Highway, the Usa Highway, the Ussuri Highway and the Kolyma Highway. The vast northern part of Siberia is generally roadless. Horses and sleds drawn by reindeer are more common here than cars.

The Soviet Union releases little information on air transportation. All civilian air transportation is controlled by the Ministry of Civil Aviation, which operates the world's largest airline, Aeroflot. In many areas of the country air transportation provides the only regular means of travel. Most of Aeroflot's services are for passengers. Its domestic services cover 6,855 population centers and all republic capitals, while its international flights cover 122 destinations in 97 countries. According to unofficial estimates in *Flight International*, its fleet consisted in 1987 of 4,750 aircraft of all sizes.

DEFENSE

According to most contemporary observers, the Soviet Union is the most powerful military power on earth, with a larger defense establishment than its nearest rival, the United States. The quest for national security has been the dominant theme in Soviet history since the Revolution, and it towers above all other goals and priorities. The regime has sought to achieve not merely parity with but superiority over capitalist powers led by the United States. Locked into a competitive arms race with the latter, the Soviet Union has developed a military doctrine and strategy that stresses massive retaliatory power as the means to maintain its own status as a superpower and to deter its enemies from launching an attack against itself or its allies in the Warsaw Pact. Despite periodical changes in emphases, this doctrine has remained unchanged through the years.

Supreme leadership in the Soviet armed forces (the use of "Red Army" and "Red Navy" was discarded soon after World War II) is vested by the Constitution in the Communist Party and the highest bodies of the Soviet goverment—the Presidium and the Council of Ministers. Party control over the military is exercised through the Defense Council chaired by the CPSU general secretary. Senior military officers, under the *nomenklatura* system, are nominated by the party, and their performance is constantly evaluated in the light of party directives and decisions.

Operational control of the Soviet armed forces rests with the Ministry of Defense, headed by an officer with the rank of marshal. The Ministry of Defense collegium, the Defense Council, functions as a consultative body and policy review board. Its membership includes the 14 deputy ministers of defense and the chief of the main political directorate as well as top military brass. Of the 14 deputy ministers, three are known as first deputy ministers, one of whom is the chief of the general staff and the other the commander of the Warsaw Pact forces. Five of the deputy ministers are commanders in chief, respectively, of the services: the strategic rocket force, the army, the navy, the air defense command and the long-range air force. The other six are in charge, respectively, of civil defense, rear services, the main inspectorate, construction and billeting, personnel, and armaments.

Separate administrative structures have been created for peacetime operations and wartime command and control. The peacetime structure of the Supreme High Command (Verkhovnoe Glavnokomandovaniye, VGK) functions under the General Staff. The General Staff is responsible for coordinating the activities of the main staffs of the five services, four fleets, rear services, the staffs of the 16 military districts, four groups of forces, the civil defense force and the main directorates of the Ministry of Defense.

Territorially, the Soviet armed forces within the Soviet Union are organized into 16 military districts (MD's). An MD is a high-level administrative command that contains military units up to army level, training institutions, recruitment or mobilization offices or military commissariats, and other military establishments. Soviet forces stationed in Eastern Europe were organized until 1990 into four groups of forces, headquartered, respectively, in Poland, Hungary, Czechoslovakia and East Germany. Soviet naval forces are assigned to four fleets. MD's, groups of forces and fleets have their own organic staff elements and officers who serve as chiefs of their respective service components. The same structure extends to non-Soviet Warsaw Pact forces, which are fully integrated into the Soviet military strategy.

In the event of war the Defense Council would take over operational control of the Soviet armed forces. In such an event the Council would be expanded and its chairman, as general secretary of the CPSU, would assume the leadership role of supreme commander in chief of the VGK and of its General Headquarters (Stavka). The General Staff would serve as operational agent of Stavka VGK. To decentralize battle management the Soviets employ the concept of theaters of military operations (Teatr voennykh deistvii, TVD). On a global scale the Soviets have identified six continental TVD's and four oceanic TVD's. These are

- Western TVD, including NATO central region, Baltic approaches, East Germany, Poland, Czechoslovakia and western Soviet Union
- Northwestern TVD, including Scandinavia, Iceland and northwestern Soviet Union
- Southwestern TVD, including NATO southern region, eastern Mediterranean, Hungary, Rumania, Bulgaria and southwestern Soviet Union
- Southern TVD, covering southwestern Asia and in-

DEFENSE INDICATORS, 1988

Defense budget ($): 32.08 billion (official); unofficial estimates range up to $275 billion
% of central budget: 49.6 (unofficial)
% of GNP: 12.5
Military expenditures per capita ($): 956
Military expenditures per soldier ($): 58,545
Military expenditures per sq. km. (sq. mi.) ($): 10,062 (26,067)
Total strength of armed forces: 5,096,000 (reportedly reduced by 500,000 in 1989)
  Per 1,000: 17.8
Reserves: 6,217,000
Arms exports ($): 18 billion
Arms imports ($): 1.1 billion

Personnel & Equipment

Strategic nuclear force
  Personnel: 298,000
  Navy:
    Personnel: 15,500
    Equipment: 978 missiles in 75 submarines; 63 SSBN's; 12 SSB's
Strategic rocket force
  Personnel: 298,000
  Organization: 6 rocket armies; 28 "fields"; 300 launch control headquarters; 3 missile test centers
  Equipment: 1,386 ISBM's, 2,500 missile launchers; 608 IRBM/MRBM launchers to be eliminated in accordance with INF Treaty
Strategic aviation
  Personnel: 90,000
  Organization: 5 armies (Moscow 1, West TVD 2, Southwest TVD 1, Far East TVD 1)
  Equipment: 1,400 combat aircraft; 1,195 bombers, of which 175 long-range, 570 medium-range, and 450 short-range; 50 reconnaissance; 205 fighters; 140 electronic countermeasures aircraft; 75 tankers
Ground force
  Personnel: 1.9 million
  Organization: 5 major theaters of operations (TVD); 1 strategic reserve theater; 16 military districts (MD); 2 unified army corps (each equivalent to about 2 divisions); 52 tank divisions; 150 motorized rifle divisions; 7 AB divisions; 18 artillery divisions; some 10 air assault brigades; special forces (spetznaz); 16 brigades/3 regiments
  Equipment: 53,300 main battle tanks; 1,200 light tanks; 8,000 reconnaissance vehicles; 28,000 mechanized infantry combat vehicles; 28,400 armored personnel carriers; 22,300 towed artillery; 9,000 self-propelled artillery; 7,000 multiple-rocket launchers; 10,400 mortars; 1,657 nuclear-capable SSM launchers; 7,250 antitank guns; 11,300 air defense guns; 4,600 SAMs; 4,800 helicopters
Air defense troops
  Personnel: 520,000
  Organization: 5 air defense armies
  Equipment: 16 ABM's; 2,300 fighters; 9,000 SAM launchers in 1,200 sites; 4,600 tactical SAM launchers; 10,000 air defense radars
Warning systems
  Equipment: 9 satellites; 3 over-the-horizon (backscatter) radar systems (2 near Kiev and Komsomolsk and 1 near Nikolayev-na-Amur); 9 ABM-associated phased array systems, at Baranaovichi, Skrunda, Mukachevo, Olnegorsk, Krasnoyarsk, Lyaki, Sary-shagan, Pechora and Mishelevka; 11 Hen House series ABM's
Air force
  Personnel: 444,000
  Equipment: 4,400 combat aircraft (2,500 fighter ground attack; 1,900 fighters); 400 reconnaissance planes; 100 electronic countermeasure planes; 2,000 training planes
  Military transport aviation
    Personnel: 40,000
    Organization: 5 divisions

DEFENSE INDICATORS, 1988 *(continued)*

Navy
  Personnel: 458,000
  Equipment: 338 submarines (75 strategic submarines, 263 tactical submarines); 268 principal surface combatants (4 carriers, 36 cruisers, 62 destroyers, 166 frigates); 408 patrol and coastal combatants (59 corvettes, 97 missile craft, 40 torpedo craft, 212 patrol craft); 453 mine warfare vessels (3 minelayers, 370 mine-countermeasure vessels, 80 amphibious vessels); 600 support and miscellaneous vessels
Naval aviation
  Personnel: 70,000
  Organization: 4 fleet air forces
  Equipment: 400 bombers; 220 fighter ground attack planes; 225 antisubmarine warfare planes; 205 maritime reconnaissance/electronic warfare planes; 70 tankers; 425 transport/training planes
Naval infantry (marines)
  Personnel: 17,000
  Organization: 1 division; 3 independent brigades; 4 fleet special forces, including 3 underwater
Coastal artillery and rocket troops
  Personnel: 7,500

cluding Afghanistan, Iran, eastern Turkey, the Caucasus and the Turkestan region of the Soviet Union

• Far Eastern TVD, covering Siberia and the Soviet far eastern region, Mongolia, China, the Koreas, Japan and Alaska

• North American, South American, African, Australian and Antarctic TVD's

• Arctic Ocean TVD, covering the Arctic Ocean and the Barents and Norwegian seas

• Atlantic Ocean TVD, covering the Atlantic Ocean south of the Greenland-Iceland-United Kingdom gap

• Indian Ocean TVD

• Pacific Ocean TVD

The Soviets also have created an elaborate system of emergency relocation facilities designed to protect high-level military, party and government leaders. In addition, essential personnel of critical industries would be evacuated along with critical machinery out of urban areas and away from immediate battle areas to emergency locations. The non-Soviet Warsaw Pact forces would be placed in complete subordination to Stavka VGK.

The five arms of service are: the army, the navy, the long-range air force, the air defense command and the strategic rocket force. They are administratively co-equal, although the army is predominant in size and influence. The navy is the next senior service, although the Kronstadt Mutiny of 1921 gave the service a bad name in Bolshevik books that never has been totally erased. The long-range air force contains only strategic aircraft and is the equivalent of a bomber command or strategic air force in other countries. Tactical aviation, which includes most of the military air transportation capability and the air defense aircraft required to maintain air superiority on the battlefield, is incorporated in the army. Naval aviation is a part of the Soviet navy. The newest arm is the strategic rocket force, controlling long-range missiles employed in a strategic as opposed to a tactical role. (The former includes permanent military bases and industrial and population centers, while the latter includes troop formations and moving targets during a conflict. Strategic targets are selected prior to hostilities, while tactical targets are selected according to the military situation during battle.)

The Soviet army has two unified army corps (each equivalent to about two divisions) and 227 divisions, about half of them at full strength and in a combat-ready status. Approximately half of the remainder could be ready for action at 24 hours' notice. The rest are maintained only at cadre strength. On the basis of their status, the divisions are divided into categorys I, II and III. A total of 30 divisions are maintained in Eastern Europe; 88 divisions in European Russia, particularly around Moscow and Leningrad; 30 divisions in central Asia; and 53 divisions in the far eastern region.

The motorized rifle divisions, successors to the old rifle divisions, have about 13,000 men each. A typical division has about 200 medium tanks, an equal number of artillery pieces, 500 armored personnel carriers and 2,000 other motor vehicles. It contains three motorized rifle regiments, a tank regiment, an artillery regiment and an antiaircraft artillery regiment plus service and support units. Each tank division has about 11,000 men and 300 to 400 tanks, and artillery approximately equivalent to that of a motorized rifle division. It has three tank regiments, one each of motorized rifle, artillery and anticraft artillery regiments, and the necessary support and service units.

Each airborne division has about 7,000 to 8,000 men, and all divisions are maintained at nearly full strength.

At lower levels army organization is conventional, with some variations. Thus a squad might comprise eight to 12 men, four of whom form a platoon led by a junior lieutenant. Three platoons make up a company, three companies a battalion, three battalions a regiment and three regiments a division.

After a long period of neglect, particularly under Stalin and Khrushchev, both of whom had little regard for naval power, the Soviet navy developed rapidly and now is one of the strongest in the world. A large number of the destroyers and cruisers are new, and most of the submarines are nuclear.

The four fleets are distributed by the principal ocean frontiers: Black Sea (including Mediterranean Sea and Indian Ocean), Baltic Fleet (including the Atlantic), Northern Fleet and Pacific Fleet. The number of vessels are as follows:

Vessels	Black	Baltic	Northern	Pacific
Aircraft carriers	0	0	1	2
Principal surface combatants	79	45	73	83
Other combatant ships	99	95	78	120
Submarines	35	45	180	115
Naval aviation	450	260	425	510

A small marine force, literally translated as naval infantry, was formed in 1964. It is considered an elite force and frequently is called "Black Death." The men wear black berets and black uniforms.

The worldwide Soviet naval presence is imposing. The Mediterranean squadron of the Baltic Fleet forms a powerful counterforce to the U.S. Sixth Fleet. Soviet ships shadow all NATO fleet maneuvers, and 12 intelligence trawlers remain permanently on station off the U.S. coasts and U.S. Pacific Ocean territories such as Guam. Even the expanding merchant marine is designed to supplement the fleets in moving forces in time of war.

The long-range air force, with medium and heavy bombers, has intercontinental range, but since the deployment of ICBM's has been relegated to second-strike/reconnaissance missions.

The air defense command maintains all fighter aircraft, surface-to-air missiles, antiballistic missile systems and the associated warning and aircraft control radar. The force is organized into air defense districts, which are similar to but not coterminous with MD's. It is responsible for the defense of cities, industries and other permanent installations.

The strategic rocket force's mission is nuclear strike. The Soviet Union possesses the world's largest nuclear force, comprising the fifth generation of intercontinental ballistical missiles (ICBM's), with their road-mobile and rail-mobile versions. The Soviet strategic nuclear-powered ballistic missile submarine (SSBN) force remains the largest in the world, with the long-range submarine-launched ballistic missile (SLBM) operational in Delta IV and Delta III SSBN's. The Soviet Union has three manned intercontinental-capable bombers. By 1990 it had 2,500 missile launchers and heavy bombers with deployed warheads ranging from 12,000 to 20,000, depending on how it respects the limits of SALT II.

Since 1960 the Soviet Union has followed a consistent and relentless policy for the development of forces for nuclear attack. These include ICBM's, longer-range intermediate-range nuclear forces (LRINF), land- and sea-based cruise missiles, shorter-range ballistic missiles (SRBM's), free rocket over ground (FROG), air-launched cruise missiles (ALCM's), antisubmarine warfare (ASW) forces, surface-to-air missiles (SAM's) and antiballistic missiles (ABM's).

The five air armies subordinate to the VGK are: Smolensk, Legnica, Venitza, Irkutsk and Moscow. The assets of these armies include Bison and Bear bombers, medium-range Blinder and Badger bombers and shorter-range Fencer strike aircraft. Each of these armies covers one TVD and yet retains flexibility to reallocate aircraft as necessary during wartime.

Over the past 25 years the Soviets have increased both their passive and their active defenses. The former include civil defense and structural hardening to protect important assets from attack. In the area of active defense, the Soviets have made significant advances in ABM systems. The Soviet Union maintains the world's only operational antisatellite (ASAT) system. It has also conducted extensive research into advanced ABM technologies, including laser weapons, particle beam weapons and kinetic energy weapons. The modernized Moscow ABM system consists of a two-layer defense with silo-based interceptors and launchers. The system for detection and tracking consists of a launch detection satellite network, over-the-horizon radars and a series of large phased array radars. The network can provide about 30 minutes warning after any U.S. ICBM launch and can determine the general origin of the missile.

The Soviets are increasing their efforts to develop and deploy space systems to support military operations. They operate several space-based reconnaissance and surveillance systems, two of which have no U.S. counterpart. These are the nuclear-powered radar ocean reconnaissance satellite (RORSAT) and the electronic intelligence ocean reconnaissance satellite (EORSAT). They also operate an extensive network of satellites for missile launch detection and attack warning missions. The Soviets have two new launch systems—one a heavy-lift booster system and the other a medium-lift booster system—to conduct military operations in space. Soviet cosmonauts aboard a space station in low earth orbit can observe large areas of the earth's surface with great clarity and transmit real-time information to military forces below.

The Soviet strategic air defense network is potent and increasingly capable of limiting the retaliatory capability of U.S. strategic bombers and cruise missiles flying at high, medium or low altitudes. The Soviets have over 9,000 strategic SAM launchers, over 4,600 tactical SAM launchers 10,000 air defense radars and 4,000 interceptor aircraft.

The Soviet Union maintains the world's largest stockpile of chemical warfare agents. Virtually all Soviet conventional weapons systems—mortars, artillery, helicopters—can deliver chemical munitions in the forward battle zones. Furthermore, Soviet research institutes are engaged in developing chemical agents with even greater lethality and are investigating binary weapons that would reduce the hazards associated with handling and storage. The Shikhany Chemical Warfare Proving Ground is one of the primary chemical weapons test areas. Chemical warfare is directed by Headquarters, Chemical Troops in the Ministry of Defense and is headed by a three-star general and with more than 45,000 personnel and 30,000 vehicles for decontamination and reconnaissance. The Soviets also maintain offensive biological warfare capabilities.

Military Transport Aviation (Voyennotransportnaya Aviatsia, VTA) is charged with maintaining the mobility of Soviet fighting forces. In wartime, VTA forces would support airborne operations and provide logistic airlift to the armed forces. This force is comprised of about 600 aircraft, but in wartime its capacity could be significantly increased by mobilization of the state-owned airline Aeroflot, with its 4,750 aircraft.

Soviet military doctrine asserts that its armed forces must be maintained at a high state of combat-readiness to ensure expeditious deployment under any conditions. However, in peacetime most ground-force units are manned at levels below their planned wartime strength. These "not ready" units make up 60% of Soviet forces and include all the groups of forces stationed in Eastern Europe. These units require extensive mobilization and preparation.

The survivability of Soviet weapons systems and personnel is enhanced by a very comprehensive dispersal system that would be executed during the transition to actual warfare. Ground forces would disperse and camouflage themselves, while aircraft would proceed to alternate airfields, and surface ships and submarines would depart from their main operating bases. Alternate command posts have been constructed and hardened mobile communication links have been established throughout the country.

The majority of the armed forces personnel are conscripts. The ratio of conscripts to regular personnel varies among operational branches, but in the army it is 65:35. Under the Soviet Constitution, every citizen is liable for military service, and the Military Service Law of 1967 provides the legal framework for conscription. The call-up period is two years in the ground forces and three years in the navy and the KGB. There are two call-up periods each year: May–June and November–December. Deferment is granted on a variety of grounds, with schooling the most common. About 1.3 million conscripts, perhaps half the available total, are called up each year.

Most officers are recruited by way of the Military Schools (VU) or the Special Military Schools (VVU). Applicants may come from civilian life or from the ranks of conscripts. Sons of military officers or party officials may attend the Suvorov or Nachimov schools (for army and navy, respectively) and then move to a VU or a VVU. Servicemen who have extended their enlistment or conscripts nearing the end of their service could reenlist as *praporschchiki*, roughly equivalent to a warrant officer. A high proportion of *praporschchiki* attain commissions either in the regular forces or in the reserves. This grade has improved the senior NCO structure by offering the better conscripts appropriate rank and status.

Compulsory preconscription military training was introduced in 1967. It consists of about 140 hours of training spread over 12 to 18 months. The instructors are serving or retired officers. The conscript training year is divided into two cycles of 26 weeks each, coinciding with the arrival of the two annual recruit intakes. After about 10 weeks of induction and basic training, conscripts are assigned to their units and after a six-month course emerge as junior sergeants. Most conscripts are required to qualify in at least one main and one supplementary trade. Officer training is more thorough and lasts three years at a VU and four or five years at a VVU. In addition to extensive academic and political training, the officer cadets spend much of their time in the field in simulated battle conditions. After receiving their commission, officers undergo periodic training of three to five years duration, and the most promising officers receive special training at the General Staff Academy.

Officers cadets and officers are constantly exposed to indoctrination. Political indoctrination also is carried on in a variety of disguised forms, such as sports and culture. Officers are encouraged to join the party or, if they are under 25, Komsomol.

The 1967 law reduced the training time but increased the throughput of trained soldiers. About 1.3 million recruits pass into the reserves each year, and they retain their reserve liability until age 50. Generals go into the reserves on retiring at 60 and remain in the reserves until 65.

Officers are well paid. The salary of a doctor in the armed forces is twice what he could expect in civilian life. A marshal receives about 115 times the salary of a new conscript. A major normally has a full-time orderly, and a general has a complete household staff. Officer strengths are maintained at levels considerably beyond organizational requirements, allowing a liberal percentage to engage in advanced educational programs.

The Soviet Union has a highly developed armaments industry backed up by one of the strongest R & D establishments in the world. Technological gains in Soviet weapons systems rely not only on contributions from the indigenous R & D base but also on the acquisition, most often through espionage and other illegal means, of Western technology and its incorporation into Soviet weaponry. The Military Industrial Commission (VPK) is a powerful supraministerial agency that coordinates all the efforts of the defense industrial ministries and centrally supervises all weapons programs. Operating across ministerial lines, the VPK is charged with implementing the joint resolutions of the Politburo and the Council of Ministers, approving multiyear weapons programs and coopting any state asset for these programs. Under the VPK there are nine defense industrial ministries, whose relative importance has varied over the years; some have received special emphases because of leadership perspectives of foreign threats, mission requirements or high-level patronage. The system integrator in the military R & D structure is the Design Bureau within each industrial ministry designed to build the system. Soviet weapons designers have historically adhered to strict industrial standards and employed proven design methods. Technological advances usually are assimilated in small steps. As a result, the Soviets produce many more new and significantly modified weapons systems than the United States. The Soviet Union has not only eliminated the qualitative U.S. lead in weaponry but also has acquired an edge in certain areas. The Soviet Union has consistently allocated a larger share of its national resources, both natural and industrial, to the peacetime production of military systems than any other country in modern history. It turns out roughly half of all weapons systems produced in the world and up to three-quarters of some types of military-related matériel. The vast numbers of industrial facilities committed to military requirements ensure that most production goals are met. At present there are over 150 major factories and shipyards producing weapons, armored vehicles, ships, aircraft, missiles, ammunition and explosives. Additionally, 150 other plants manufacture combat-support equipment such as radar, trucks and communication gear. In turn, these facilities, draw on literally thousands of parts and components factories. These facilities are continually being expanded and have increased in size by over 50% since 1970. An example is the Severodvinsk Shipyard, the world's largest submarine production yard, which has expanded by 85% in building area since 1965. Despite *glasnost*, the emphasis on modernizing the military-industrial sector is likely to continue, with heavy investments in electronics, computers and robotics.

Although official data on military aid are not published, and although the aid program is being phased out under President Gorbachev, it is known that Soviet Union provides substantial aid to at least seven countries: Vietnam, Cuba, Ethiopia, Yemen, India and Mongolia as well as Afghanistan. Military aid is mostly in the form of equipment at concessional prices as well as loan of technical personnel.

EDUCATION

Education developed in ancient Russia with the advent of Christianity in the 10th century, and it remained largely in the hands of the church until the time of Peter the Great (1682–1725), whose reign was marked by the establishment of the Academy of Sciences, the School of Mathematics and Navigation and the Engineering and Artillery School. The expansion of education was associated with the Westernization movement, which continued under Peter's successors. An important landmark was the founding of the University of Moscow in 1755. The reign of Catherine the Great witnessed great strides in Russian education. Among the new educational institutions were the Smolny Institute in Moscow and the Yekaterinskiy Institute in St. Petersburg, the first schools exclusively for women. In 1782 Catherine set up the Commission for the Establishment of Schools, which was given the responsibility of creating a public school system in the country.

The 19th century was a turbulent century for Russia, and the political turmoil was reflected in the halting progress of education, marked by cycles of growth alternating with repression. The periods of growth were the reigns of the liberal monarchs Alexander I (1801–25) and Alexander II (1855–81). Alexander I created the Ministry of Public Culture, Youth Education and Dissemination of Science, which was given control of most secular educational institutions. Among the new institutions of higher education were the Universities of Kharkov, Kazan, Odessa and St. Petersburg and the Pedagogical Institute. Under Alexander II the limitations on the number of university students were abolished, private schools were reopened and secondary education facilities for women were enlarged. Universities received their autonomy, more gymnasiums were built and adult education for peasants was introduced. The repression following Alexander's assassination in 1881 lasted until the overthrow of the Romanov dynasty in 1917.

The October Revolution turned the newly established Soviet Union into an educational laboratory for Marxist ideas. After the initial reforms, such as the abolition of all religious influences in education, the introduction of universal compulsory education and the abolition of school fees, there followed a period of confusion that was ended only with Stalin's takeover of the Communist Party. By then the school system was regarded more as an instrument of indoctrination than an arena for learning and free inquiry. On the one hand, the new ideologues were motivated by utopian visions of a class-less society and of a new Soviet man inspired by a collectivist, atheist and scientific materialist outlook. On the other hand, in a land devastated by revolution, civil war, famine and disease, these ideas met with scant success. While the new harmonious and scientific school system was being designed on paper, millions of children were destitute and homeless, and it was not possible to enforce even compulsory primary schooling for all children.

This phase ended with the rise of Stalinism. A new mass campaign against adult illiteracy and for compulsory primary schooling was launched in 1928. The intensified drive toward industrialization under the five-year plans created a soaring demand for skilled workers and specialists. A party decree of 1931, aimed at the stabilization of the school system, declared a thorough general education to be the basis of socialist education. The Leninist emphasis on projects was abandoned, and subjects were restored. In the following years, standardized obligatory curricula, syllabi and textbooks were developed under the close scrutiny of the party, with instruction centered on classroom lessons. A five-point grading system was introduced to assess achievement. The school became authoritarian, performance-oriented and academic, retreating to a considerable extent to prerevolutionary characteristics and practices, such as school uniforms. By 1937 polytechnical education, the centerpiece of Leninist pedagogics, had disappeared altogether from the educational scene. By 1934 the basic structure of schooling had been established in a form that survives to this day: a four-year primary school followed by a six-year secondary school for a total of 10 years, of which seven years were compulsory then. The system of higher education underwent a similar drastic reorganization. The specialized *vysshee uchebnoe zavedenie* (higher education institutions, VUZ) as well as the universities were placed under the All-Union Committee for Higher Education, set up in 1936 and upgraded to ministry level in 1946. New degrees were introduced, such as Candidate of Sciences and Doctor of Sciences as well as a postdiploma three- or-four-year course of study known as *aspirantura*. On the eve of World War II, lower-level vocational education also was thoroughly reorganized with the establishment of state labor reserve schools operated in quasi-military fashion, with 14- to 17-year-olds being drafted. Courses lasted six months to two years, and dropouts were treated as deserters. During the eight Stalinist years after the end of the war, the heavily damaged educational system was swiftly repaired and enrollments began to surge ahead.

The Khrushchev period, lasting for 11 years after Stalin's death, was marked by a return to the polytechnical emphasis of the Leninist era. The educational reform law of December 1958 combined polytechnical instruction in the general school with training for specialized skills, thus linking education with production. In addition, it laid down a number of structural and curricular changes at all levels of the system. By introducing pupils to productive work, the reform was designed to cool out educational aspirations and change social attitudes. The new law extended compulsory education to

eight years. Secondary education was offered in three types of schools: general schools; polytechnical labor schools; and informal schools such as evening, shift or correspondence schools. In secondary schools as well as in higher educational institutions, the curriculum was revised to intensify polytechnical instruction, accounting for up to one-third all weekly lessons in the former. Nearly 80% of admissions to universities were made conditional on two years of full-time work experience after graduating from school.

The Khrushchevian reforms encountered severe opposition from academics as well as industrial managers from the beginning, as they caused organizational problems for schools and factories alike. Academic standards suffered, and the courses involving manual work were unpopular with students. With Khrushchev's dismissal in 1964, most of his educational reforms were dismantled.

In 1966 a new decree was adopted reorganizing secondary education and establishing the Ministry of Public Education. A revised curriculum was introduced for the 10-year general education school. It included "Labor" as a subject but reduced it to a mere two hours a week from the first to the 10th grades, and even in the two senior grades it did not exceed 11% of instruction time. The new conception of labor education was more theoretical in its approach and closely linked with mathematics and science. Vocational guidance and counseling became one of the major functions of labor training in school. Career aspirations were developed through practical work in school workshops and in interschool training and production combines set up by enterprises and educational authorities in a given district. Another innovation was the introduction of electives beginning in grade seven. Special schools and special profile schools were set up catering to the special interests and abilities of students and providing better chances of entry into higher education.

On the basis of the new curriculum, the syllabi of all subjects were redesigned, a process that was completed only in the 1970s. The curriculum reform was closely related to the central educational policy goal of universal secondary education lasting at least 10 years in the general schools, the technicum or the vocational-technical schools. Thus in principle there were no dead ends for graduates from the eighth year.

As imbalances persisted in the educational system, reforms have continued under Brezhnev's successors. Under Andropov, guidelines for the reform of the general and vocational school were approved in 1984. The most significant feature of the reform was the reinforcement of the position of the vocational-technical school. Skill acquisition was encouraged although not made mandatory, the time for labor training was increased at the expense of other subjects and the time for electives was used for practical work also.

The Soviet Constitution, revised many times since its adaption in 1977, guarantees the citizen certain rights and lists his obligations. The rights are often ignored by the state, but the obligations are strictly enforced. Among the rights is that of education (Article 45), specifically free education from preschool to the end of secondary school. Article 25 defines the purpose of education as the communization of the young and preparing them for the world of work. Article 52 separates church and state. Obligations of citizens include bringing up their offspring in accordance with Marxism as "worthy members of socialist society."

Outside of the Constitution, education is governed by laws and decrees of the Supreme Soviet, one of the most important of which is that of July 1973 titled Legal Principles on Public Education. It provides the legal framework to which the educational laws of the 15 SSR's conform. Contrary to its immediate predecessor, the 1958 education law, it did not herald any major reorganization of the educational system but is more or less a codification of existing legislation. An amendment to the 1973 law extended compulsory education to cover the whole length of secondary schooling. The educational reforms of 1984, however, entailed a more fundamental change in the law. Since the principles and goals of Soviet education have not changed since 1917, only the structure and practice have changed. Great stress is placed on the contrasts with bourgeois education, whose deleterious effects on the human personality is a recurring theme in Soviet educational literature.

Although constitutionally the Soviet Union is a multinational and federal state, in fact the educational system is uniform throughout all the constituent republics, with only minor variations. Schooling begins at age six and lasts for 11 years (12 years in the Baltic republics), all of which are compulsory and free. The academic year runs from September to May or June. With the exception of secondary specialized schools, there are no entry examinations.

Although Russian is not the official language of the Soviet Union in a technical sense, it is the national language, and its use is equated with Soviet patriotism and heritage. For the ethnic minorities, who now almost equal the ethnic Russians in number, Russian is a "second mother tongue," but for all practical purposes, their first mother tongues are used in limited social intercourse only and have declined in currency. The number of languages used as mediums of instruction total about 50. A full range of educational provision in the native language, including higher education, is available in all the non-Russian republics and in certain languages, such as Tatar. Outside the national territories, however, speakers of a minority language receive their instruction in Russian. Since 1970 the use of Russian in schools has been intensified by introducing elementary Russian at the preschool level.

The only nonstate schools that survived the 1917 Revolution were the religious seminaries, which lead a tenuous existence. According to official reports, there are 18 clerical training centers, of which six are run by the Orthodox Church and the others by religious minorities. All schools are free, but private tutoring flourishes as part of the underground economy. Textbooks and transportation also are free, and students of vocational-technical schools are provided with free accommodations and special clothing. However, parents of general school students have to pay for the obligatory school uniforms.

Promotions are based on examinations and on marks earned during the academic year. Written and oral examinations are mandatory at the end of the eighth grade and upon graduation from secondary school. They are administered by the schools and monitored by the local school authorities. The Certificate of Secondary Education, incorporating a skill qualification, is a prerequisite for admission to higher-education institutions. Admission to specialized secondary schools and to higher-education institutions is based on entry examinations. Apart from continual assessments during course work, higher-education institutions hold course examinations, generally at the end of semesters. The final diploma is obtained by passing the state examination, which requires completion of a diploma project or work and oral testing. Candidates who fail in any subject may retake that subject. The grading system consists of a five-point scale, with 5 as excellent and 1 as total failure.

Preprimary education is part of the public education system. Crèches take care of infants aged six weeks to three years, and nursery schools or kindergartens those from three to six years. As a rule these two institutions are combined. In addition, in rural areas there are seasonal institutions that operate during summer months only. Preschool institutions are run by the educational authorities of the local soviets or by enterprises and collective farms that set them up for their own work force. Indeed, preschool education has a social function apart from the educational training of the very young. It releases the female labor force from being tied up in the home, although a recent social program granting women paid maternity leave of up to one year and unpaid maternity leave for an additional year has the opposite effect. Communization is another hidden objective in preschool education. By wresting control of the child at a very early age, the authorities are able to reverse any antisocial—i.e., religious—values imparted by the parents and to inculcate Marxist behavioral norms. A special curriculum has been introduced for the school-preparatory final year of the kindergarten. It places stress on the acquisition of basic literacy and numeracy, physical coordination and nature-related skills.

Primary and secondary education is divided into three successive stages—primary, secondary and senior—lasting together for 10 years. In the complete secondary school with grades one to 10 (in the Baltic republics one to 11) all the three stages are under the same roof. Incomplete secondary schools may have either grades one through eight and nine through 10 or one through three and four through 10. Incomplete schools are mostly in rural areas, which also have lower educational standards, greater lack of facilities, higher teacher turnover and lower teacher qualifications. The curricula for all general education schools are laid down by the republic ministries of public education and are based on union standards listing the subjects to be taught in each grade along with the number of hours to be devoted to each. Overall curriculum development is directed by the Academy of Pedagogical Sciences and in particular by its Institute for the Contents and Methods of Instruction. Developmental work on subject syllabi also involves other institutions and specialists. The school textbooks, generally one per subject, closely follow the structure of the syllabi. A basic tenet of Soviet pedagogy since the 1930s has been "the leading role of the teacher within the classroom." Accordingly, the instruction is predominantly teacher-centered.

At the primary level all subjects are taught by one teacher. About half of the 24 weekly hours are devoted to languages and a further six hours to mathematics. The pace of learning is rapid, and the heavy burden of facts and concepts has led to a high rate of repetition.

The emphasis from grades four to eight or five to nine is on languages and mathematics, and with the completion of the primary stage new subjects are introduced, such as foreign languages, natural sciences, history, social studies (mainly Marxism-Leninism) and the fundamentals of the Soviet state and law. For all senior grade students—boys and girls—premilitary training combined with instruction in the values of patriotism is mandatory. The 1984 reform further increased the number of obligatory subjects in the curriculum, such as Ethics and Psychology of Family Life, including sexual education from a moral rather than a psychological point of view, and Fundamentals of Information Science and Computer Technology. Alongside demanding academic work, a large part of the curriculum is devoted to preparing the young people for work. The labor education programs aim to inculcate a love of manual work, instilling work discipline and preparing young people for the choice of an occupation. Since 1977 labor education has become more vocation-oriented. In the senior grades students are expected to gain a basic knowledge of a specific trade or occupation. Most schools provide extended labor training by using the time allotted for elective courses so that students may spend one whole day a week on labor training and receive a grade job qualification along with their general leaving certificate. The 1984 reform has made training for mass occupations compulsory for the general school. The number of specialties offered in each school is determined by local and regional needs, but the overall list of recognized training occupations contains 760 items, many of them highly specialized. These programs may be undertaken within enterprises or in interschool training and production combines, of which there are over 2,700. In rural areas student production brigades are organized to assist state and collective farms.

Beyond its standardized core the general school curriculum features elective courses as an element of differentiation catering to the students' individual interests and aptitudes. Electives, called "facultative courses," are taught from the seventh grade on, beginning with two weekly hours, and rising to four weekly hours in the senior grades. They are either additional subjects complementing the standard range of courses or supplementary materials for a more extensive and detailed study of basic subjects. Extracurricular activities are fostered either within the school or in extraschool establishments such as the Pioneers.

Gifted children receive special attention in so-called special schools or in special classes within general schools. Because of their prestige and the intensive academic training they offer, these schools enhance their graduates' chances of admission to higher education and to interesting careers so that they are extremely popular among middle-class parents. By the same token, they are controversial as an elitist leaven in a theoretically classless society. Entry is at different ages and is highly selective. The oldest type (also known as special-profile schools) are the foreign-language schools, where instruction in some subjects is in a foreign language. After 1966 special-profile schools or classes with extended teaching of mathematics, physics, chemistry or biology came into existence and are much sought after. There are other special schools, some dating back to czarist times, for those gifted in the fine arts, including music, drama and ballet. While entry into these schools is not officially competitive, there are other special schools for which students are recruited through nationwide competition. These are the physics and mathematics boarding schools; the sports boarding schools for producing top sports performers; the eight Suvorov schools for the army and the Nakhimov school for the navy. Handicapped children are not mainstreamed but placed in special institutions, the majority of which are boarding schools or extended day schools. These schools are organized according to the various handicaps. Yet another type of establishment, also called a special school, caters to delinquent children aged 11 to 15.

One of Khrushchev's innovations was the boarding school, which he envisaged as the school of the future, where children would be totally isolated from the "harmful" influences of their parents. After rapid expansion, the development of residential facilities was stopped because of the costs involved and public opposition. Many of these boarding schools have been converted into children's homes or annexes to rural schools. Since 1960 extended day schools have been taking the place of boarding schools, proving particularly attractive to working parents.

With the implementation of the 1984 reforms, all pupils who complete secondary education are equipped with some kind of marketable skill. However, official policy is designed to enhance vocational educational programs even further, by making the vocational-technical school the backbone of the system and doubling the enrollment of the vocational stream to 50%. The system of vocational training schools (PTU's) encompasses three types of school: (1) the lower vocational-technical school, with one- to two-year courses; (2) the secondary vocational-technical school, offering a three-year course; and (3) postsecondary technical schools, offering one-year courses culminating in a job certificate. Most of these schools are under the authority of the State Committee for Vocational-Technical Education of the USSR and its subdivisions at the republic and lower levels. They not only provide blue-collar workers with their initial job qualification but also retrain production workers in new skills and upgrade their qualifications. The 1984 reform provided for a restructuring of the PTU's in one uniform category, with a standard three-year course of 4,900 hours. Training can be obtained in 1,400 mass occupations of the 7,000 specializations officially recognized within the Soviet economy. In addition to combining vocational training and general education, PTU's stress ideological and citizenship education to counteract the political indifference and lack of social commitment widely prevalent among the young. Graduates of PTU's are employed by the school's basic enterprise for a minimum of two years, and only 10% may apply for admission to full-time higher education directly after completing their course.

Vocational training of a higher level is offered in secondary specialized schools, which offer over 500 specialties. Their graduates are known as specialists. These schools admit graduates from the eighth grade who undergo a three- to four-year program, or graduates from the complete general school or secondary PTU, who undergo a two- to three-year program.

Higher education is closely linked to the economy. Higher-education institutions (VUZ's), numbering 900, are divided into three main categories according to their different functions and the range of disciplines taught and research conducted. At the apex are the 68 universities, which have the right to confer degrees. The 61 polytechnics are large establishments offering only technological specialties, as well as training in law, economics, art, etc. Many of them are entitled to confer degrees. Although all higher-education establishments are supervised by the USSR and individual republic ministries of higher and secondary specialized education, the specialized VUZ's are directly subordinate to the various branch ministries and agencies.

Part-time study plays an important role in higher education, comprising 44% of the student population, with 12% in evening and 32% in correspondence courses. Unions conduct educational activities through nearly 8,000 "people's universities."

A higher-education institution is headed by a rector appointed by the appropriate ministry; there are no limits to his term of office. Prorectors are responsible for specific areas of teaching and research under the direction of the Council of the VUZ. Departments are headed by deans, who are elected for three-year terms of office by the Department Councils. The basic organizational unit of each discipline is the chair (katedra), headed by a senior professor. The teaching staff is divided into several ranks. There is no tenure, and staff members are subject to reappointment every five years, although this is very much a formality.

Admission to higher-education institutions is based on a competitive examination set up by the ministry but administered by each VUZ. Certain types of candidates, such as those who have been awarded a gold medal at school, are exempted from some or all of the entrance tests. School grades are not considered for admission. References by Komsomol or one's employer are important in facilitating admission.

To reduce the disparity between the children of blue-collar workers and those of white-collar workers in university enrollment, preparatory divisions have been set up in most VUZ's to provide full- or part-time courses of eight to 10 months' duration for young workers, farmers and demobilized soldiers who have completed their secondary education. Successful completion of the course replaces the VUZ entrance examination. Women make up the majority in most disciplines, agriculture being among the few exceptions.

VUZ courses last four to six years, the majority being five years. The academic year is divided into two semesters (fall and spring), at the end of which there are tests, failure in which may mean repetition of the year or semester. During vacations, many students are recruited for production work. For the over 450 specialties taught in VUZ's there are approved curricula in

---

EDUCATION INDICATORS, 1988

Literacy
  Total (%): 99
First level
  Schools: 65,500
  Teachers: 2,668,000 (first and second levels)
  Students: 36,800,000
  Student-teacher ratio: See below
  Net enrollment rate (%): 106
Second level
  Schools: 62,000
  Teachers: See above
  Students: 4,600,000
  Student-teacher ratio: 16:1 (first and second levels)
  Net enrollment rate (%): 100
Vocational
  Schools: 4,500
  Teachers: 246,000
  Students: 2,880,000
  Student-teacher ratio: 12:1
Third level
  Institutions: 900
  Teachers: 377,000
  Students: 2,688,000
  Student-teacher ratio: 7:1
  Gross enrollment rate (%): 21.3
  Graduates per 100,000 age 20–24: 1,667
  % of population over 25 with postsecondary education: 11.5
  Females (%): 50
Foreign study
  Foreign students in national universities: N.A.
  Students abroad: 1,146
    of whom in
      United States, 196
      West Germany, 86
      East Germany, 268
      Czechoslovakia, 149
      Hungary, 151
Public expenditures (national currency)
  Total: 37.932 billion
  % of GNP: 6.6
  % of national budget: 10.2
  % current expenditures: 83.7

GRADUATES, 1983

Total: 855,000
Education: 272,500
Fine & applied arts: 9,100
Law: 69,300
Medicine: 64,000
Engineering: 356,800
Agriculture, forestry, fisheries: 83,300

which some elements, such as foreign languages, communism and physical education, are obligatory.

Graduate students take state examinations, which consist of a diploma project or work and oral examinations. Graduates are assigned jobs through their VUZ's and are required to work in those jobs for three years. Postgraduate students doing research for the academic degree of Candidate of Sciences are accepted for *aspirantura*, a three-year full-time or four-year part-time course attached to either a VUZ or a research institute.

International links are mainly with Communist countries within the Soviet bloc or friendly Third World countries. Students from the Third World are enrolled in a special institution created in 1960, Patrice Lumumba University for Friendship Among People.

Real power emanates in the Soviet Union from the Politburo (not from the people, as stated in the Constitution), and education is no exception. Within the Central Committee there is the Department of Science and Education, which formulates educational policy and oversees its execution. However, as a legal formality, party decisions are required to be enacted by the Supreme Soviet in the case of major laws, or by the Council of Ministers in the case of more routine ones. Overall, education is under the jurisdiction of three separate agencies. Preschool education, general education and teacher training are under the control of the USSR Ministry of Public Education and the ministries of education of the constituent republics. At the regional, city and district levels, the responsibility devolves on the education departments of the soviet executive committees. Observance of official regulations, the effectiveness of the schools' work and teacher performance are monitored by the school inspectorates.

Each school is headed by a director, who cooperates with the school's basic party organization and its trade union branch. He also heads the Pedagogical Council, on which parents and the basic enterprises also are represented. Students' self-government is organized through branches of the Pioneer and Komsomol organizations.

Vocational technical schools and on-the-job training are controlled by the USSR State Committee for Vocational Technical Education and its counterparts at the republic and lower levels. It acts in coordination with the State Committee for Labor and Social Questions.

Higher-education institutions and secondary specialized schools are under the jurisdiction of the USSR Ministry for Higher and Secondary Specialized Education and the corresponding republic ministries. Many major universities and VUZ's are administered directly by this ministry, but the majority are subordinate either to the republic higher education ministries or to one of the 70 branch ministries, many of which may have no more than one or two VUZ's under their control. All three ministries are assisted by a number of advisory and coordinating councils. Overall educational planning rests with Gosplan, which factors manpower needs into its annual and long-term plans. The flow of graduates through the three levels of the educational system is regulated by interagency commissions.

The main sources of educational finance are the state budgets of the Union, republics and local units. They provide three-fourths of total expenditures; the other one-quarter comes from state enterprises and state and collective farms.

Within 70 years of the Bolshevik Revolution the Soviet Union has raised the literacy of its people to 99%, a signal achievement by any standard. Adult education programs do not figure as prominently in overall educational programs as they used to before the war. Most are opportunities for upgrading current skill levels and for cultural enrichment in a socialist context. The major elements of these programs are evening (shift) and correspondence schools; retraining programs for workers in enterprises, and allied special-purpose courses for acquainting workers with new production methods and techniques and raising their productivity; and cultural and political mass education programs conducted by Houses of Culture, People's Universities and the All-Union Znanie (Knowledge) and other, similar organizations.

Teachers are trained at two levels: Teachers of general subjects are trained at the 201 pedagogical institutes, and teachers of vocational-technical schools in technical and agricultural VUZ's and in a special engineering pedagogical institute at Sverdlovsk. Most of the teachers for the primary grades along with teachers for labor training and arts subjects are trained in the 437 pedagogical schools, and instructors for practical skills in vocational schools in 73 industrial pedagogical technicums. Nearly 80% of general-education schoolteachers are VUZ graduates. Training in a pedagogical institute takes four years in one subject and five years in two subjects. Teachers are expected to engage regularly in in-service training and participate in formal courses at least once every five years. These courses are provided by the Teacher Qualification Improvement Institutes, of which the central institute is in Moscow, one in each of the 15 Union republic capitals and 188 in the regions. Topical seminars and lectures are given by local "methodological cabinets." Every five years teacher performance is evaluated in a process called attestation, and the more outstanding teachers are awarded honorary titles. Those who fail to receive their attestation may be transferred or dismissed. Although teachers have no formal tenure, labor legislation protects them against arbitrary dismissal.

Despite official rhetoric about teachers being held in high public esteem, the profession has fallen behind in recent decades in terms of social prestige and income. As a result, there is a high turnover, and in areas with unfavorable working conditions, there is an acute shortage of teachers. Consequently teaching is increasingly becoming a female profession. Teachers' salaries are graded according to qualifications and length of employment. The normal weekly work load is 18 hours in grades four to 10 and 20 hours for teachers in grades one through four. The national trade union for teachers is the Trade Union for Workers in Education, Higher Education and Scientific Institutions.

LEGAL SYSTEM

The Soviet criminal justice system has a strong ideological content, which makes it different from the criminal justice systems of non-Communist countries. Its most distinguishing features are the extralegal status of the Communist Party, which not only makes the law but also is outside and above the law; the decisive influence of the economic system on all branches of law; and the use of legal terminology that may have no correlation with actual practice. As an example of the last, according to the Constitution the legal system incorporates the most democratic principles, protecting the "fundamental rights of the citizen," yet almost all these rights are violated by the state with impunity. Institutional terms also may be misleading. Thus the use of the word "cooperative" to refer to collectives is deceptive because collectives are not cooperatives in the accepted sense of the term but rather forced-labor farms little different from medieval baronies. Further, many provisions of the Constitution are not actually applied but have been circumvented and superseded by administrative ordinances and decrees. Soviet jurists blur the distinctions among constitutional provision, legislative enactment and administrative decree or directive. They advance the doctrine of "normative acts" as the source of Soviet law, but define these acts in such abstract terms as to equate them with the arbitrary acts of party functionaries. Thus a Soviet statute is defined as the "expression of the will of the working class and of all toilers," and normative acts as "acts by which the will of the ruling class is elevated to law." Consequently there are no distinctions among legislative acts of the Supreme Soviet; constitutional provisions; edicts of the Presidium; resolutions of the Council of Ministers; orders, instructions and rules issued by individual ministers; regulations of the All-Union Central Council of Trade Unions; and acts of local soviets. All have to be obeyed as "the unshakable dictates of the Soviet government."

Instead of the rule of law, Soviet jurists use the term "socialist legality." This concept is just as vague as that of "normative acts." Socialist legality is not a consistent body of laws but rather an uncoordinated collection of rules enacted at various times and for various purposes and characterized only by revolutionary expediency. Whereas ordinary legality means the supremacy of law, revolutionary legality is the supremacy of the interests of the party. According to Soviet jurists, "In different stages of proletarian dictatorship the content of revolutionary legality is subject to change depending upon the circumstances of the class struggle." This legality is construed as *anything* that enhances the legitimacy or authority of the Bolshevik government and that must, for that reason, be implicitly obeyed by Soviet citizens.

Further, Soviet statute books are cluttered with acts and rules that are inoperable or inapplicable but that never have been formally repealed. There is a further group of statutes that were enacted but never enforced. Thus it is not clear at any given time what the laws are

and which laws must be obeyed. Another feature is the presence of secret laws—i.e., laws enacted but never made public. The resolutions of the Supreme Soviet, which alone are called laws are published in *Vedomosti*, the official gazette. But the edicts of the Presidium, the most important source of Soviet legislation, are never published. The special collection of laws and decrees of the Council of Ministers (called People's Commissars before 1946) was not published from 1949 to 1957. In fact, two laws (of August 22, 1924, and February 5, 1925) expressly provide for secret laws or laws withheld from publication but nevertheless state that they shall have binding force. However, references to these secret edicts abound in Soviet judicial decisions. Particularly, regulations against religion are contained in top-secret codes, the mere possession of which itself is a crime!

There is a group of Soviet statutes called codes. However, the term "code" does not denote what it means in the West. The Soviet codes—the Civil Code, the Code of Civil and Criminal Procedure, the Code of Domestic Relations, the Labor Code and the Land Code—are all issued by the several republics but subject to the basic legislative principles of the Union.

The legal structure in existence when the Bolsheviks seized power goes back to various periods of Russian history. The principal elements of this system were Roman law and canon law, both introduced by the 10th century; Byzantine law (from which the law of contracts and torts was derived), imported by the Orthodox Church; and Muscovite law. The first collection of laws, called the Code (Ulozheniye), appeared in 1649. In 1830 Michael M. Speransky codified the laws then in force, an event followed in 1832 by the 15-volume Body of Laws (Svod Zakonov). The volume in this collection that dealt with private law was based on the French Civil Code.

In 1861, under the direction of Alexander II, a landmark reform of the judicial and legal system was completed with the promulgation of several codes: the Code of Civil Procedure, the Code of Criminal Procedure, Statutes on Judicial Institutions and Code of Laws on Punishments to Be Imposed by Justices of the Peace. Some of the far-reaching innovations introduced by Alexander II included a court system based on the theory of separation of the judicial from the executive and legislative branches; trial by jury in criminal cases; right of appeal to the next higher court on issues of both fact and law, with the exception of decisions of a court with a jury, and an appeal to the court of cassation, as a court of last resort, on issues of law *only;* the introduction of public legal proceedings and oral testimony; the right to be represented by a defense counsel; transfer of jurisdiction in pretrial investigation in criminal matters from the police to an examining magistrate; independence of judges in the performance of their duties, and their removal from office on grounds of misconduct or physical unfitness only; graduation from a university faculty of law as a prerequisite for appointment to a judicial position; creation of a hierarchy of government attorneys headed by the minister of justice and making them custodians of administrative legality as well as prosecutors of crimes; and establishment of the bar, marking the birth of the Russian legal profession. The only other legal events before the Bolshevik Revolution were a new Criminal Code in 1903 and the a new Civil Code in 1913.

The new regime that seized power in 1917 defined itself as the "dictatorship of the proletariat." Lenin described it as "power with no restriction whatsoever, absolutely unbound by any rules of law and based upon violence." The early Leninists considered the Russian legal system to be a by-product of capitalism—a superstructure in the same manner as religion and state erected over the material basis of the productive classes. They expected that both state and law would wither away once a classless society had been achieved.

The very first decree of the Soviet government, Decree 1 of December 7, 1917, abolished the entire prerevolutionary legal system and replaced it with a network of people's courts and revolutionary tribunals, which enforced the "Red Terror." The legal profession was abolished, and anyone who enjoyed civil rights could practice law. Judges had no precedents to follow but were instructed to follow their "social conscience." A parallel system of revolutionary courts dispensed revolutionary justice and was not bound by law. Those accused before them were shot first and tried afterward! The Cheka, nominally a security agency, possessed powers of life and death over all citizens.

A uniform judicial system began to take shape in 1923 under the Judiciary Act. A new Criminal Code and a new Civil Code were enacted, but the courts continued to follow Stalin's directive "not to do away with terrorism." During most of Stalin's regime the courts and the legal system served as instruments of terror. The severity of law was illustrated by the fact that the death sentence could be imposed for any one of 74 crimes. An innocent person could be sentenced in court for the crime of another; a terrorist was denied a defense counsel at his trial and could not appeal his sentence.

The death of Stalin in 1953 marked a gradual return to normalcy in Soviet law. In 1958 the Supreme Soviet adopted the Fundamentals of Legislation on the Judicial System, on the basis of which the Union republics later enacted their own laws.

All courts constitute a single judicial system governed basically by federal legislation. At the apex of the system is the Supreme Court of the USSR. Special criminal courts, with the exception of military courts, were abolished in 1958. The only federal courts are the Supreme Court of the USSR and the military tribunals. All other courts are courts of the Union republics with the power to enforce federal and state laws. Republican courts, called regular courts, include the supreme courts of the SSRs and ASSRs; the provincial, territorial and city courts; the courts of the autonomous regions and the national areas; and the county (city) people's courts.

There is no trial by jury. Cases are tried before a trial bench composed of one professional judge and two lay people's assessors, who decide jointly by a majority vote all questions, both of law and of fact. People's assessors sit in federal courts, including the Supreme Court of the USSR, and in all republican courts whenever they sit as part of a trial court of original jurisdiction. Appeals from an adverse ruling of a lower court by the defendant or by the prosecutor against a sentence that has not become final are reviewed by the next higher court. As a rule, a case may be reviewed only once by a higher court. Appeals are heard by a bench consisting of three professional judges.

The Constitution of 1936 maintained the fiction of judicial independence by asserting that "judges are independent and subject only to law." It is difficult to reconcile this statement either with actual practice or with the contentions of Lenin, Andrei Vyshinsky and others that separation of powers cannot exist in a Communist political system; instead, they talked of a distribution of functions within the "unity of people's power." All judges are members of the Communist Party and receive instructions from the party on how to dispose of political cases and what sentences to impose. However, in nonpolitical cases "socialist legality" is effectively and impartially administered.

Judges and judge-assessors of the Supreme Court of the USSR and members of the military tribunals are named by the Supreme Soviet of the USSR. Judges of the Supreme Court of each republic are named by the Supreme Soviet of the republic; judges of the provincial courts are named by the provincial soviets. Judges of the people's courts are elected directly by the voters, and people's assessors are elected informally at general meetings in work places. Judges are elected for five-year terms and assessors for two-year terms, but all may be recalled by the soviet or electorate that named or elected them before the expiration of their terms.

The lowest regular court is the people's court in each county or in a city not divided into districts. It is a court of limited original jurisdiction, with a collegial trial bench composed of one judge and two people's assessors. The next higher level of courts varies with the size of the republic or region. In the RSFSR and the other larger union republics, the higher courts are established within each territory, region, autonomous republic, national region and national area and in certain cities. In smaller Union republics that are not subdivided into territories and provinces, only the Supreme Court of the Union republic is above the people's court. In the former the provincial and regional courts and the courts of the autonomous republics function as courts of original jurisdiction in more serious criminal cases and in all civil cases beyond the jurisdiction of the people's courts. When acting in their capacity as appellate courts, their decisions are final. Any higher court has the right to assume jurisdiction as a court of original jurisdiction over any case within the jurisdiction of a lower court. The plenary sessions of the Supreme Courts of the Union republics are an important innovation of the 1958 law.

Under the RSFSR Law on Court Organization of 1960, the Plenum of the Supreme Court of the RSFSR has the authority to issue guiding instructions to the lower courts in the application of republican legislation and to initiate legislation. Presidiums in all courts of the Union republics, except in people's courts, examine by way of supervision protested judgments and decisions that already have become final.

Comrades' courts, a feature of the war communism period of the 1920s, were revived under Khrushchev and legalized in 1959. They were established in factories, offices, universities, VUZ's, collective farms, housing collectives and street collectives. Cases in these informal courts are heard in public, generally after working hours. Procedural norms are waived, and the socioeducational aspect of the offense prevails over the judicial one. The court may impose admonitions, reprimands and fines and also recommend to the people's court such penalties as evictions, dismissals and docking of wages. There are no appeals from these decisions.

The Soviet federal courts are off-limits to private citizens. Private parties may, however, use a roundabout method to bring their grievances to the USSR Supreme Court by petitioning the attorney general, the president of the Supreme Court or other officers empowered to do so, to lodge a protest, bringing the case to the highest court.

The Supreme Court of the USSR is composed of its Plenum and three collegia: civil, criminal and military. The functions of the Plenum are as follows:

• hear protests of the president of the USSR Supreme Court, the USSR attorney general, or other empowered officers, lodged against judgments in civil and criminal cases and orders issued by divisions of the USSR Supreme Court

• hear protests of the president of the USSR Supreme Court, the USSR attorney general, or other empowered officers, against decisions of the Supreme Courts of the individual soviet constituent republics in cases where such decisions are in conflict with unionwide legislation or violate the interests of other constituent republics

• give directive rulings to courts on matters raised by the application of legislation in deciding judicial cases

• submit to the Presidium of the Supreme Soviet of the USSR matters requiring a solution by legislation and questions arising from interpretation of laws

• settle disputes between judicial bodies of the constituent republics (however, there is no public record of any such dispute since 1917)

The USSR Supreme Court is composed of a president and varying number of members, who include *ex officio* the presidents of the republican Supreme Courts.

The Soviet procuracy was created in 1922. Organized on a republican basis, it was subordinated to the republican ministers of justice. The federal procuracy was established in 1933, with the procurator general performing some of the functions of the attorney general. In 1936 the republican procurators were detached from the republican ministries of justice and placed under the direct and sole supervision of the USSR procurator general. The organization and functions of the federal procuracy are governed by the law of May 24, 1955, as amended in 1959, 1960, 1964, 1966 and subsequent dates. Under this law the procurator general is the most powerful law officer of the Soviet Union. He is appointed for a term of seven years by the Supreme Soviet of the USSR and reports to that body or, between its sessions, to its Presidium. The 1955 law etablished a hierarchy of government attorneys parallel to the hierarchy of the courts. The procurator general of the USSR appoints the prosecutors of the republics, territories and regions; the Union republic prosecutor, in turn, appoints the area, county and city prosecutors. All are appointed for a term of five years. Thus local prosecutors are insulated from the influence of the local agencies and party units. Within the Procuracy the senior assistant to the procurator general is the chief military prosecutor.

In addition to powers of supervision over lower levels, the procurator general can submit to the plenary session of the Supreme Court of the USSR recommendations requiring guiding directives and instructions on matters of judicial practice for the lower courts.

In criminal proceedings the courts and the public prosecutors have equal authority to order the arrest of a suspect of a crime, the search of a private dwelling or the seizure of private communications.

In pretrial investigations, inquiries and preliminary investigations are supervised by the public prosecutors. In less important cases the inquiry is conducted by the police and in other cases by investigators of state security agencies, whose decisions are subject to approval or reversal by the public prosecutors. The procuracy also may intervene in civil litigations where rights and duties of private persons are involved.

The office of state notary was created in 1947 in the RSFSR and subsequently in other republics. State notaries are public officials who perform quasi-legal functions, such as certification of legal transactions, inheritance cases and matters relating to aliens and stateless persons.

The legal profession distinguishes between advocates (practicing attorneys who represent individual clients in criminal and civil cases) and juriconsults (government employees who consult and represent social enterprises and institutions, primarily in civil cases). Advocates practice law in offices operated by colleges of advocates, which are organized at republican, territorial, regional and city levels. Advocates may not receive fees directly from clients but only through legal consultation offices. Like a bar in other countries, the college of advocates admits new members and disbars those guilty of violating professional ethics.

The Soviet Union is one of the few countries in the world without a Ministry of Justice. The former ministry of justice (before 1946 the People's Commissariat of Justice) was abolished in 1956 and its functions were transferred, first to the individual ministries of justice of the constituent republics, then when they, too, were abolished, to the USSR Supreme Court at the federal level and the republic Supreme Courts at the republic level. The result was to give some freedom to the judiciary from political interference.

The death sentence has become rare since the 1950s. Besides imprisonment and fines there are three types of unusual sentences: corrective labor, exile and banishment. The first involves mandatory performance of "socially useful work" under close supervision and in the convicted person's usual place of work. Such work is not recorded on labor records, does not apply toward pay raises and does not add to vacation time. Under a sentence of banishment a person is sent away from his or her place of residence for a specified time. The court determines the banishment area and adds other prohibited places. The typical sentence is "USSR minus six," meaning exclusion from the home area and the six largest Soviet cities. Exile is banishment to a specified area. This is as severe a punishment as imprisonment at a labor colony because in most cases the place of exile is a labor colony in Siberia. Generally those banished or exiled fall into the category of persons officially described as "parasites."

Soviet penal institutions fall into three categories: prisons, corrective labor colonies and educational labor colonies. Most prisons are designed to detain arrested persons for interrogation before trial rather than to house inmates. Conditions in prisons vary. A few in Moscow are as clean as first-class hotels and often are shown on conducted tours for visiting penologists. Generally, prisoners are segregated by categories: men from women, adults from juveniles and first offenders from recidivists. Dangerous criminals and those awaiting a death sentence are isolated from other inmates.

Labor camps, the notorious invention of Felix Dzerzhinsky, the first head of Cheka, have been discontinued since the death of Stalin and replaced with corrective labor colonies and educational labor colonies. The former fall into five categories: standard, intensified, strict, special and colony settlements. The court sentence specifies the appropriate regime for each convict. One camp complex usually contains colonies with several different regimes. Colony settlements constitute a halfway house program for prisoners who have completed a required portion of their sentence and have demonstrated good behavior and a cooperative attitude. Supervision is minimal and movement within the compound is unrestricted in daytime. Prisoners may work outside unsupervised; wear civilian clothes; and retain money, valuables and personal possessions.

Educational labor colonies for minors under 18 feature more tolerable regimes, additional privileges and considerably greater emphasis on rehabilitation and education. The penal regime includes political indoctrination, socially useful labor, general education and technical or vocational training. There are only two categories of educational labor colonies: standard and intensified; girls are committed to the former only.

Noting not only shortcomings but violations of past laws, the Congress of People's Deputies in December 1989 passed a law on the judiciary that was considered as a major step in legal reform. The new law set up an Institute of Assessors to handle serious criminal cases, enhanced the role of the defense and established specialized courts such as to consider family affairs, the press, patents and minors.

LAW ENFORCEMENT

The Soviet Union is only slowly emerging from being one of the worst police states in history. The internal-security (a term more commonly used to describe the police system than law enforcement) organs are highly active and powerful, even though the philosophy behind them has softened and the repression they administered is history. The average Soviet citizen has less to fear today from a sinister and unpredictable terror machine than had been the case in any period in modern Soviet history.

It was only in 1968 that the present law enforcement agencies took shape, with the Committee for State Security (Komitet Gosudarstvennoy Bezopasnosti, KGB) handling state security and the Ministry for Internal Affairs (Ministerstvo Vnutrennikh Del, MVD) handling internal security. However, both these organizations go back to the earliest days of the Bolshevik Revolution and have evolved through a number of organizations:

EVOLUTION OF THE SOVIET POLICE SYSTEM			
Date	State Security	Internal Security	Combined
1917–22			Cheka
1922–23			GPU
1923–34			OGPU
1934–41			NKVD
1941	NKGB	NKVD	
1942–46			NKVD
1946–53	MGB	MVD	
1953			MVD
1954–60	KGB	MVD	
1960–66			KGB
1966–68	KGB	MOOP	
1968–	KGB	MVD	

Beginning with Cheka, all security organizations have been structurally built into the government system. They are separate from the party, although subject to the party's policy decisions. At the highest organizational level, both the KGB and the MVD are responsible to the Council of Ministers. Each union republic has a KGB and an MVD responsible, at least administratively, to the Council of Ministers of that republic. The KGB, with more of its functions relating to national concerns, has little if any substantive subordination to local governments. The opposite is perhaps true of the MVD, whose operations also are restricted by law to the procedural controls of the procuracy. Such constraints are less effective in the case of the KGB. Thus, despite some overlapping of functions between the two, the KGB is the more powerful of the Soviet security agencies.

The KGB is a state committee, which is a ministry equivalent, under the USSR Council of Ministers, and the chairman of the KGB is one of its core members. All KGB heads have been members of the Central Committee; Yuri Andropov, who headed the KGB in the late 1960s and 1970s, became the first to reach the general secretaryship of the party.

Details about KGB operations and personnel are never made public and must be pieced together from unofficial sources. The organizational structure is subject to change; new sections are constantly being added, and old ones are either abolished or given new titles. The KGB's major subdivisions are called administrations or directorates. There are four chief directorates, four directorates and six independent departments.

Chief directorates:
- Foreign Operations: 10 departments
- Internal Security: 12 departments
- Dissident Activity
- Border Guards

Directorates:
- Armed Forces: 12 departments
- Surveillance
- Communications and Intelligence
- Physical Protection of Government and Party Leaders

Departments are concerned mostly with administrative functions, such as finance. The administrations include collection of economic data. The Mobile Group for Special Operations handles sensitive and clandestine operations and maintains its vast Central Index of Biographical Data. In addition to KGB units in every foreign country there are units in Union republic, regional and local governments; in the armed forces; in the enterprises; in state and collective farms; in Communist Party organs; in the labor camps; and in the armed forces and the Militia. All KGB units report directly to Moscow. In the army, for example, KGB personnel have communications channels to which the military commander has no access.

The principal MVD units include the security police; the Internal Troops; and special units in the regular armed forces, the labor camps and in certain prisons and courts. Guard Troops, Railway Troops and Convoy Troops sometimes are considered part of the Internal Troops and sometimes as separate units. The largest MVD organization is Internal Troops, with main administration headquarters in Moscow and local agencies in the Union republics and possibly in smaller territorial divisions. The other directorates not only have branches in the Union republic and lower-level governments but also perform most of their operations at those levels and are subordinate in varying degrees to the local authorities.

Internal troops were first identified as a separate entity in 1923, when they were part of the OGPU. Before that time there were Cheka units of Special Purpose and GPU Guard Troops dating to 1920. MVD troops are uniquely subordinate both to the Moscow headquarters and to the local authorities. Units are stationed in or near large towns. Operational directorates include the Troops of Special Purpose, elite units guarding the Kremlin and the more important civil and military installations. Normally, they operate in small groups, but they can assemble into sizable formations.

The Border Troops, an administrative unit of the KGB, is responsible for guarding the long frontier.

The frontier zones are of unspecified depth, varying with the terrain and the degree of friendliness or hostility of the neighboring country. Admittance into this area is restricted and controlled by local militia, which share authority with the Border Troops within this zone. There are additional and stricter controls in the narrower frontier strip, where Border Troops have complete control. The frontier strip is up to 2.4 km. (1.5 mi.) wide, and along borders where crossings are prohibited, contains special barriers. Inside the border fence there is a strip that is kept freshly plowed so that footprints would be readily noticeable. A second strip is patrolled by armed guards with dogs. It is kept floodlighted and equipped with rows of barbed wire, traps, automatic firing weapons or land mines. Observation posts may be visible or concealed. The Border Troops control entry and exit of people and goods in border zones and conduct raids, searches and checks. The majority are ground forces known as Land Border Troops. There are smaller Aviation Border Regiments and Maritime Border Troops. The border is guarded 24 hours a day, every day of the year. Border patrol is a hardship post, with duty time of up to 16 hours a day, although the normal schedule is three hours a day. Long absences are not permitted, as most units frequently are below authorized personnel strength. However, Border Troops receive the best food rations in the army and pay that exceeds that of the regular services.

The Soviet Militia (Militsiya) corresponds approximately to the uniformed police organizations of other countries. It is controlled by the MVD and thus is subordinate to republican and local governments. Concerned solely with local law enforcement, it has powers of search, arrest, detention and pursuit. Although it can conduct criminal investigations, those relegated to it are the least important. Militia members are armed but may use their weapons in specified situations only. Among its varied functions is that of maintaining contacts with resident aliens and foreigners, and thus militiamen are the officers with whom tourists are most familiar. Their uniform is blue with red insignia, pipings and bandings. In rural areas, collective farms, industrial enterprises and educational institutions, there are groups variously known as People's Voluntary Militia, Public Order Detachments and People's Squads, composed of party members over 18.

A crime is defined in the Soviet Union as a "socially dangerous act" and a punishment as a "measure taken in social defense." Soviet jurisprudence considers crime to be a "protest against the Communist social order." Since the Communist system is the ultimate ideal, there are continuing efforts to gloss away crime as inspired by foreign agents or as a residue of the old society that requires time to be eradicated. Soviet jurisprudence does, however, distinquish between political and criminal offenses.

No data are available on incidence and types of crimes in the Soviet Union.

HEALTH

Health delivery services are highly centralized under the USSR Ministry of Health, and its republican counterparts. The ministry runs hospitals, clinics and dispensaries; trains and assigns physicians; conducts medical research; manufactures drugs, pharmaceuticals and medical equipment; and compiles medical statistics. A small private medical sector exists, but it is difficult to gauge its extent. Private practice is tolerated, but the proceeds are heavily taxed.

Medical care is financed through the state budget. The citizen does not pay for it directly, nor is there a specific medical care deduction from his wages. Soviet sources estimate that free medical care adds about 7% to real wages.

HEALTH INDICATORS, 1988

Health personnel
    Physicians: 1,232,600
        Persons per: 229
    Nurses: 2,880,000
    Pharmacists: 86,000
Hospitals
    Number: 23,700
    Number of beds: 3,720,000
    Beds per 10,000: 131
Type of hospitals (%)
    Government: 100
Public health expenditures
    Per capita: $227.90
Vital statistics
    Crude death rate per 1,000: 9.9
    Decline in death rate: 47.9 (1965–84)
    Life expectancy at birth (years): males, 65.0; females, 73.6
    Infant mortality rate per 1,000 live births: 30
Causes of death per 100,000
    Cancer: 148.1
    Diseases of the circulatory system: 554.3

Since Word War II the medical budget has generally claimed 5% of the USSR budget. The proportion increases markedly at the lower administrative levels, rising to 20% in the republic budgets and 70% of local budgets.

Medical facilities are organized into two networks: the general or open network for the general population, and the exclusive or closed network for party and government dignitaries, professionals and the intelligentsia. The latter has two important subcategories: establishments reserved for workers in certain elite organizations, such as the army, navy and the KGB; and polyclinics and sanatoriums reserved for the upper echelons of the party and the government.

According to law, all citizens are registered in medical districts, where they are eligible to visit the district outpatient clinic, or if confined to bed, to be visited by the district physician or the *feldsher* (medical assistant), who may refer him to an appropriate polyclinic or hospital. Rural medical districts are large in area and poor in transportation; therefore the quality of medical care tends to lag there. The urban population is much better served. Medical facilities are clustered around a district medical center manned by general practitioners and specialists. Urban areas also have much better access to pharmaceuticals and medical equipment. But even here common drugs may often be in short supply.

The achievements of the Soviet regime in the field of health have been impressive and have led to the virtual elimination of major infectious diseases. Improved water supply and sanitation also have contributed to better health and higher life expectancy. Because health is a noncontroversial subject, the government is able to mobilize popular support more effectively for its medical programs.

FOOD & NUTRITION INDICATORS, 1988

Per capita daily food consumption, calories: 3,425.7
Per capita daily consumption, protein, g. (oz.): 100.7 (3.6)
Calorie intake as % of FAO recommended minimum requirement: 132
% of calorie intake from vegetable products: 74
% of calorie intake from animal products: 26
Food expenditures as % of total household expenditures: 39.1
% of total calories derived from:
    Cereals: 37.2
    Potatoes: 5.8
    Meat & poultry: 9.9
    Fish: 2.0
    Fats & oils: 12.7
    Eggs & milk: 8.6
    Fruits & vegetables: 3.8
    Other: 19.9
Per capita consumption of foods, kg., l. (lb., pt.)
    Potatoes: 110.0 (242.5)
    Wheat: 133.8 (295.0)
    Rice: 1.2 (2.6)
    Fresh vegetables: 104.6 (230.6)
    Fruits (total): 68.1 (150.1)
        Citrus: 1.9 (4.1)
        Noncitrus: 66.2 (145.9)
    Eggs: 12.0 (26.4)
    Honey: 0.7 (1.5)
    Fish: 18.0 (39.7)
    Milk: 302.3 (666.5)
    Butter: 6.0 (13.2)
    Cheese: 6.3 (13.9)
    Meat (total): 62.7 (138.2)
        Beef & veal: 28.0 (61.7)
        Pig meat: 22.2 (48.9)
        Poultry: 9.2 (20.2)
        Mutton, lamb & goat: 3.3 (7.2)
    Sugar: 47.7 (105.1)
    Chocolate: 1.6 (3.5)
    Margarine: 3.7 (8.1)
    Biscuits: 2.9 (6.4)
    Beer, l. (pt.): 42.8 (90.4)
    Wine, l. (pt.): 14.5 (30.6)
    Alcoholic liquors, l. (pt.): 3.3 (6.9)
    Soft drinks, l. (pt.): 13.0 (27.4)
    Coffee: 0.4 (0.8)
    Tea: 0.2 (0.4)
    Cocoa: 0.6 (1.3)

FOOD & NUTRITION

Soviet food consumption patterns vary from region to region. The average diet includes a heavy concentration of cereals, potatoes and starches, with a smaller proportion of dairy, meat and vegetable products; Meat is not only scarce but also expensive. Vegetables are relatively scarce because of the shortage of refrigeration. Fruits are available only in season.

MEDIA & CULTURE

The Soviet press is the largest in the world, with 727 daily newspapers with a total circulation of 96,414,000; 7,603 other newspapers; and 5,275 journals, all in 55 languages. While size is the most prominent feature of the Soviet press, another is the fact that it is not so much a dispenser of news and information as a gigantic propaganda machine for Marxist-Leninist ideology, current party policies, socialist realism and Communist achievements. It wages constant campaigns against real or imagined foreign and domestic enemies punctuated by a special vocabulary, repeated ad nauseam. By Western standards and occasionally acknowledged by Soviet readers and journalists, the Soviet press is dull, repetitious, tendentious and opinionated. It is written in a formal style filled with propaganda clichés. Even the changes brought out by *glasnost* have not helped it to shed these characteristics. Soviet papers also tend to be deadly serious and didactic, with a tendency to preach down to their readers on the virtues of socialist existence. One of the few features that spares the readers such an ideological flogging is the section on readers' letters and replies, but even these are not spontaneous but usually generated by the party or government. There have been some efforts to increase readership by adoption of modern techniques—more appealing layout, typography and illustrations—and by adding special sections for younger readers, singles, etc.

The Soviet press has important traditions rooted in prerevolutionary Russia: those of the social critic, censor, educator, political activist, agitator and organizer. Émigré revolutionary publications began in the 1850s, and the first Russian Social Democratic Labor Party newspapers appeared toward the end of the 19th century. Lenin was a great journalist in his own right, first through his own newspapers, such as *Iskra* (*The Spark*), and later by defining the mission and role of the Communist press as an ideological weapon.

The first legal Bolshevik newspaper was *Novaya Zhizn* (*New Life*), which Lenin helped found in St. Petersburg in 1905. *Pravda* (*Truth*) began publication in 1912, with Stalin as its organizer. Suppressed in 1914, it reemerged in 1917 as the Communist Party's official newspaper, a role it continues to occupy today. One of the first decrees of the Bolshevik government was on the press: It abolished all opposition media and established censorship, and a formal censorship office was established in 1922 in Glavlit. Although the number of newspapers has grown, the structure of the press established in those early days of the Revolution holds good today.

Along with a national press represented by *Pravda*, *Izvestia* (*News*) and others, there is a strong regional press in most of the languages spoken in the Soviet Union at both the republic and *oblast* levels. However, the predominance of Russian-language newspapers is decisive. Over 64% of newspapers are published in Russian and another 16% in Ukrainian. Even some of the republic Communist Party organs are published in Russian.

Soviet newspapers generally are four to six pages long and contain no advertising. *Pravda* runs six pages daily except Mondays, when it runs eight. The weeklies have more pages. The regular newspapers have eight columns and the tabloids six. The republic, *kray*, *oblast* and *rayon* newspapers follow the same pattern of four to six pages, half in regular and half in tabloid format. Various enterprises and institutions publish their own newspapers in a two- to four-page format. On the bottom rung, the wall newspapers are in effect nothing more than bulletin boards. Of the dailies, 95% are morning papers and only 5% are afternoon papers. Generally, morning papers appear six days a week, Tuesday through Sunday, *Pravda* being the only one that appears all seven days. The government organ *Izvestia* is an afternoon paper and includes a Sunday supplement, *Nedelya* (*Week*). Afternoon papers tend to be more informal than morning papers.

Despite the large number of newspapers, none is competitive in the Western sense, but rather complementary. In every republic the Communist Party Central Committee, the Council of Ministers, Komsomol and other organs each have their mouthpieces. Since the newspapers are not dependent on circulations or advertising for their revenues, there are no circulation wars.

With a circulation of 8 million, *Pravda* has the largest readership of any newspaper, not only in the Soviet Union but also in the world. It is the bible of all Communist Party members, and even its name, Truth, has a religious ring to it. It is printed in 45 cities, and its editorials are distributed by Tass to over 50 million readers. The largest-selling newspaper is *Trud* (*Labor*), the organ of the All-Union Central Council of Trade Unions, with sales of 18.9 million, the largest in the world, but it has less influence than *Pravda* on Soviet leaders. Closely following in circulation is *Komsomolskaya Pravda* (17.6 million), the organ of the Young Communist League.

MAJOR SOVIET DAILIES	
Daily	Circulation (million)
Trud	18.9
Komsomolskaya Pravda	17.6
Izvestia	10.4
Pravda	8.0
Selskaya Zhizn (Country Life)	7.5
Sotsialisticheskaya Industriya	5.6
Sovietskaya Rossiya	5.2
Sovietski Sport	5.2
Krasnaya Zvezda (Red Star)	2.4

The economics of the Soviet press is perhaps the least complicated in the world. Newspapers are affected by neither lack of readers nor advertising. The major reason for the closure of publications is rather shortage of newsprint. Despite large circulations, they do not have to cater to readers' tastes. Soviet newspapers also are among the cheapest in the world, priced lower than one-third of their Western counterparts.

Distribution of newspapers and periodicals is the responsibility of Soyuzpechat (an acronym for the Main

Administration for the Distribution of Printed Matter). About 80% of the newspapers are sold by subscription and the rest at newsstands or kiosks, some of which have automatic vending machines.

Most journalists belong to the Union of Journalists; others in the publishing industry belong to the Communication Workers' Union; Timber and Woodworking Industry Workers' Union; or Cultural Workers' Union. Pay scales are not generous even at the higher levels, but editors and journalists may earn substantial extra income and also enjoy much-sought-after perquisites, such as special housing, dachas and at discount stores and clubs.

Freedom of the press and objectivity in reporting are rejected as harmful bourgeois concepts. The basic principles of the Soviet press are party-mindedness (*partinost*), idological content (*ideinost*), patriotism (*otechestvennost*), truthfulness (*pravdivost*), popular

---

MEDIA INDICATORS, 1988

Newspapers
    Number of dailies: 727
    Circulation (000): 96,414
    Circulation per 1,000: 345
    Number of nondailies: 7,603
    Circulation (000): 69,179
    Circulation per 1,000: 251
    Number of periodicals: 5,275
    Circulation (000): 4,279,930
    Newsprint consumption
    Total (tons): 1,174,200
    Per capita, kg. (lb.): 4.3 (9.4)
Book publishing
    Number of titles: 55,565
Radio
    Number of radio receivers (000): 182,790
        Persons per radio receiver: 1.5
Television
    Television transmitters: 2,882
    Number of television receivers (000): 90,000
        Persons per television receiver: 3.1
Cinema
    Number of fixed cinemas: 143,027
    Seating capacity (000): 25,847
    Annual attendance (million): 3,682
        Per capita: 13.7
Films
    Production of long films: 321

CULTURAL & ENVIRONMENTAL INDICATORS, 1988

Public libraries
    Number: 134,165
    Volumes (000): 2,138,179
    Registered borrowers (000): 148,000
    Loans per 1,000: 11,500
Museums
    Number: 1,932
    Annual attendance (000): 195,800
    Attendance per 1,000: 660
Performing arts
    Facilities: 640
    Number of performances: 261,800
    Annual attendance (000): 126,000
    Attendance per 1,000: 449
Ecological sites: 163
Botanical gardens & zoos: 660

---

character (*narodnost*), mass accessibility (*massovost*) and criticism and self-criticism (*kritika i samokritaka*). The Constitution provides for freedom of press and speech among other freedoms, but the inefficacy of this guarantee is attested to by the fact that in the Soviet Union the Constitution is cited more often by dissidents than by the regime. The party monopoly of the press effectively precludes the exercise of press freedom. But to leave matters in no doubt, the Criminal Code is loaded with articles that make freedom of speech a crime. The RSFSR Code's Article 70, most frequently applied against dissidents, states: "Agitation or propaganda carried on for the purpose of subverting or weakening Soviet authority or of committing particular, especially dangerous, crimes against the state, or circulating for the same purpose slanderous fabrications that defame the Soviet state and social system, or circulating or preparing or keeping for the same purpose, literature of such content shall be punished by deprivation of freedom for a term of six months to seven years with or without additional exile for a term of two to five years, or by exile for a term of two to five years." An implied intent to depict Lenin negatively is treated as blasphemy! Criticism is not merely permitted but even encouraged as long as it is directed toward some hapless bureaucrat or some minor lapse in an enterprise.

The severity of press repression has spawned, since the 1960s, an underground press producing countless *samizdats*, a term that has entered the lexicon of journalism—a tribute to some of the most courageous editors and publishers in the Soviet Union. Most of them have short lives until their publishers are hunted down by the KGB and physically silenced; others, such as *The Chronicle of Current Events, Maria* (the first Soviet feminist underground paper) and *Khristianin*, have managed to elude their tormentors for lengthy periods. The authorities are continually on the watch not only for *samizdats* but also for *tamizdats* (literally "published there," meaning the West) and *magnitizdats* (tape recordings).

The most important government censorship agency is The Main Administration for Safeguarding State Secrets in the Press (Glavnoye Upravlenie po Okhrane Gosudarstvennykh Tayn v Pechati; Glavlit). Its functionaries are assigned to all publishing enterprises, with responsibilities for prepublication censorship. The *glavlitchik*, as the censor is called, reads the copy twice before the printing and is the last person to see the final proofs. He is guided by a manual (popularly known as the Talmud) containing lists of prohibited materials; the lists are continually expanded. The KGB also has a vested interest in this field, both in suppressing information and in creating disinformation.

Contrary to the Helsinki Final Act, Western correspondents in the Soviet Union face numerous constraints and hardships. Soviet authorities also restrict citizen contact with foreign press representatives. Import restrictions on foreign publications are exacting. Apart from a few official subscribers, most Soviet citizens have never seen a Western publication.

The Soviet Union has two news agencies: Tass (Telegrafnoye Agentstvo Sovietskovo Soyuza, Telegraph

Agency of the Soviet Union) and Novosti Agentstvo Pechati Novosti, APN, the News Press Agency). The former distributes news to the domestic press, while the latter disseminates news about the Soviet Union to the foreign press and news about foreign countries to the domestic press. Since 1971 Tass has functioned directly under the USSR Council of Ministers, with ministerial rank. Novosti is described as "quasi-official." Almost all major news agencies of the world are represented in Moscow. They include AP, UPI, AFP, Reuters, Efe, ANSA, ADN, dpa, Jiji, Excelsior, Interpress, Kyodo Tsushin, MTI, Tanjug, Prensa Latina, PTI, and Xinhua.

Radio and television broadcasting is under the State Committee for Television and Radio. Radio programs are broadcast daily from Moscow via two channels on long, medium, short and VHF wave bands. Channel I covers the entire Soviet Union, with four duplicate broadcasts transmitted separately for regions in different time zones (the Urals, central Asia and Kazakhstan; western and eastern Siberia; and the Soviet far eastern region). Programs broadcast on Channel II, known as Mayak, rech 80% of the population. There also are radio programs in all the union and autonomous republics, territories and regions that have radio and television committees. Broadcasts are in 71 languages. Radio Moscow has radio broadcasts in 75 languages.

The television relay system covers 90% of the country. A national television network includes telecasting in all the union and autonomous republics, territories and regions. There are 115 television centers. Thirteen television channels transmit programs daily from Moscow. Moscow I and Moscow II are nationwide channels, repeating their programs four times daily in order to transmit them to areas of the country in different time zones.

The Soviet Union is the leading book producing country in the world, with 236 publishing houses and an annual output in 1986 of 83,472 titles, or about one-quarter of all books produced in the world, in 89 languages spoken in the Soviet Union and in 73 foreign languages. The number of copies printed in 1986 was 2.234 billion. In 1973 the Soviet Union became a party to the Berne Convention or the Universal Copyright Law. Almost all books are distributed by Soyuzkniga, which runs 17,500 bookshops and 34,000 book kiosks.

SOCIAL WELFARE

Social insurance (excluding medical services) is supervised by the All-Union Central Council of Trade Unions, the central committees of trade unions and local trade union organizations. Trade union organs draft and approve estimates for social insurance, determine expenditures and formulate policy. The social insurance budget is part of the USSR budget. The main expenditure items in this budget are pensions, sick pay and maternity benefits. No unemployment benefits have been paid since 1931 on the ground that there is no official unemployment.

All employees with over eight years' service are entitled to full earnings during sickness leave. Disabled workers receive allowances of up to 90% of their pay,

and in the event of occupational disease or injury, up to 100%. Full paid maternity leave is granted for 112 days. Unwed mothers and mothers of large families receive monthly allowances.

The age of pension is 60 for men (with 25 years of service) and 55 for women (with 20 years of service), except for those in certain categories of hazardous work, where men are pensionable at 55 or 50 and women at 45 or 50. Old-age pensions average 60% to 70% of earnings. Pensions also are paid to families that have lost their breadwinner.

There is no private welfare system in the Soviet Union.

CHRONOLOGY

1946—The reconstruction of the Soviet Union begins. . . . Marshal Georgi Zhukov is demoted.
1947—Cominform is founded in response to the Truman Doctrine.
1948—Stalin breaks with Tito and blockades Berlin.
1949—First Soviet atomic bomb is tested. . . . COMECON is founded.
1950—Korean War begins.
1952—The 19th Party Congress is held.
1953—Stalin dies. . . . Lavrenti Beria, Georgi Malenkov and Vyacheslav Molotov take over the helm of state. . . . Beria falls. . . . Khrushchev becomes head of the party. . . . Soviet H-bomb is developed.
1955—Malenkov resigns. . . . Warsaw Pact is formed.
1956—The 20th Party Congress is held. . . . De-Stalinization begins with Khrushchev's attack on Stalin's cult of personality. . . . Soviet invaders crush Hungarian revolution.
1957—Malenkov, Molotov and others are purged. . . . Sputnik I is launched.
1958—Khrushchev assumes dual leadership of the party and the government.
1959—The 21st Party Congress is held.
1960—USSR-China quarrel flares into the open.
1961—The 22nd Party Congress is held. . . . Yuri Gagarin becomes the first person in space.
1962—The United States and the Soviet Union come to the brink of war in the Cuban missile crisis.
1964—Khrushchev is forced to retire. . . . Leonid Brezhnev takes over as first secretary.
1966—The 23rd Party Congress is held.
1968—Warsaw Pact forces intervene to restore hardcore Communist government in Czechoslovakia under the Brezhnev Doctrine.
1971—The 24th Party Congress is held.
1972—U.S. president Richard M. Nixon visits Moscow. . . . SALT is held.
1973—Brezhnev visits Washington, D.C.
1975—European security conferences result in the Helsinki accords.
1976—The 25th Party Congress is held.
1977—Under new Brezhnev Constitution, Brezhnev becomes head of state.
1979—SALT II is signed. . . . Soviet forces invade Afghanistan.

1980—The United States and other countries boycott the Moscow Olympics.

1981—The 26th Party Congress is held. . . . Polish crisis erupts.

1982—Brezhnev dies and is succeeded as general secretary by Yuri Andropov.

1983—Andropov's anticorruption drive starts. . . . Korean airliner is shot down over Sakhalin.

1984—Andropov dies and is succeeded as general secretary by Konstantin Chernenko.

1985—Chernenko dies and is succeeded as general secretary by Mikhail Gorbachev.

1986—The 27th Party Congress is held. . . . Gorbachev launches his campaign for *glasnost* and *perestroika*.

1987—President Ronald Reagan and Gorbachev sign INF Treaty.

1988—The Russian Orthodox Church celebrates the millennium of Kievan Rus.

1989—Soviet Forces leave Afghanistan. . . . New electoral law permits nonofficial candidates to run for election. . . . Gorbachev meets with Pope John Paul II in first ever visit by a Soviet leader to the Vatican.

1990—Lithuania declares independence, but following Soviet economic blockade "freezes" the declaration. . . . 28th Communist Party Congress is held. . . . CP monopoly of power is revoked. . . . Gorbachev is granted extraordinary executive powers to combat economic chaos as well as secessionist movements of constituent republics. . . . Boris Yeltsin, leader of the reform movement, is elected president of RSFSR. . . . Soviet Union begins phased withdrawal of troops from Eastern Europe. . . . CP broadcast media monopoly is ended. . . . Press freedom law is passed. . . . A 500-day plan, known as the Shatalin Plan, for converting the socialist economy into a free-market one, is launched. . . . Private property is legalized.

BIBLIOGRAPHY

BOOKS

Abraham, Richard, and Lionel Kocha. *The Making of Modern Russia.* New York, 1984.

Allworth, Edward. *Ethnic Russia in the USSR: The Dilemma of Dominance.* Elmsford, N.Y., 1980.

Armstrong, John A. *Ideology, Politics and Government in the Soviet Union.* Lanham, Md., 1986.

Azrael, Jeremy R. *Soviet Nationality: Policies and Practices.* New York, 1978.

Barghoorn, Frederick C. *Politics in the USSR.* Boston, 1972.

Barron, John. *KGB.* New York, 1974.

Barry, Donald D., and Carol Barner-Barry. *Contemporary Soviet Politics: An Introduction.* Englewood Cliffs, N.J., 1987.

Bassiouni, M. Cherif, and V. M. Savitski. *The Criminal Justice System of the USSR.* Springfield, Ill., 1979.

Berg, L. A. *Natural Regions of the USSR.* New York, 1950.

Bergson, Abram, and Herbert Levine. *The Soviet Economy Toward the Year 2000.* London, 1983.

Bialer, Seweryn. *The Soviet Paradox: External Expansion and Internal Decline.* New York, 1986.

Blackwell, William C. *The Industrialization of Russia.* Arlington Heights, Ill., 1982.

Bornstein, Morris. *The Soviet Economy: Continuity and Change.* Boulder, Colo., 1981.

Brown, Archie. *The Cambridge Encyclopedia of Russia and the Soviet Union.* New York, 1982.

Brown, Emily Clark. *Soviet Trade Unions and Labor Relations.* Cambridge, Mass., 1966.

Brucan, Silviu. *The Post-Brezhnev Era.* Westport, Conn., 1983.

Byrnes, Robert. *After Brezhnev: Sources of Soviet Conduct in the 1980s.* Bloomington, Ind., 1983.

Cave, Martin. *New Trends in Soviet Economics.* Armonk, N.Y., 1982.

Charlton, Michael. *The Eagle and the Small Birds: Crisis in the Soviet Empire from Yalta to Solidarity.* Chicago, 1985.

Churchward, L. C. *Contemporary Soviet Government.* New York, 1975.

Cole, J. P., and F. C. German. *Geography of the USSR.* New York, 1961.

Comrie, B. *The Languages of the Soviet Union.* New York, 1981.

Conquest, Robert. *The Last Empire: Nationality and the Soviet Future.* Stanford, Calif., 1986.

————. *Religion in the USSR.* New York, 1968.

Dallin, David. *Soviet Foreign Policy After Stalin.* Westport, Conn., 1975.

Desfosses, Helen. *Soviet Population Policy.* Elmsford, N.Y., 1981.

Dibb, Paul. *The Soviet Union: The Incomplete Superpower.* Urbana, Ill., 1986.

Dmytyshyn, Basil. *A History of Russia.* New York, 1974.

Dunlop, John D. *The New Russian Nationalism.* Westport, Conn., 1985.

Dziewanowski, M. K. *A History of Soviet Russia.* Englewood Cliffs, N.J., 1985.

Feuchtwanger, E. J., and E. J. Nailor. *The Soviet Union and the Third World.* New York, 1981.

Fitzsimmons, Thomas. *USSR: Its People; Its Government; Its Culture.* New Haven, 1974.

Florinsky, Michael. *McGraw-Hill Encyclopedia of Russia and the Soviet Union.* New York, 1961.

Fothergill, D. *Russia and Her People.* Moscow, 1982.

Gilbert, Martin. *Russian History Atlas.* New York, 1972.

Goldman, Marshall. *The USSR in Crisis: The Failure of an Economic System.* New York, 1983.

GPO. *Labor in the USSR.* Washington, D.C., 1964.

————. *The Soviet Economy in 1980: Problems and Prospects: Selected Papers.* Washington, D.C., 1983.

————. *The Soviet Financial System.* Washington, D.C., 1968.

Gregory, James S. *Russian Land; Soviet People: A Geographical Approach to the USSR.* New York, 1968.

Gregory, Paul R., and Robert C. Stuart. *Soviet Economic*

Structure and Performance. New York, 1986.

Gsovski, Vladimir, and Kasimierz Crzybowski. *Government, Law and Court in the Soviet Union and Eastern Europe*. New York, 1959.

Harcave, Sidney S. *Russia: A History*. Philadelphia, 1959.

Hazard, John N. *The Soviet System of Government*. Chicago, 1960.

Herlemann, Horst G. *Quality of Life in the Soviet Union*. Boulder, Colo., 1985.

Hewett, Edward. *Energy, Economics and Foreign Policy in the Soviet Union*. Washington, D.C., 1984.

Hill, Ronald J. *Soviet Union: Politics, Economics and Society*. Denver, Colo., 1985.

Hoffmann, Erik P., and Robbin F. Laird. *The Politics of Economic Modernization in the Soviet Union*. Ithaca, N.Y., 1982.

———. *The Soviet Polity in the Modern Era*. New York, 1984.

Holzman, Franklyn D. *The Soviet Economy*. New York, 1982.

Hough, Jerry F., and Merle Fainsod. *How Russia Is Governed*. Cambridge, Mass., 1979.

Hutchings, Raymond. *The Soviet Budget*. New York, 1983.

———. *Soviet Economic Development*. New York, 1983.

———. *The Structural Origins of Soviet Industrial Expansion*. New York, 1984.

Jacobs, Everett M. *Soviet Local Politics and Government*. Winchester, Mass., 1983.

Jahn, Egbert. *Soviet Foreign Policy*. London, 1982.

Kaiser, Robert. *The People and the Power*. New York, 1975.

Katz, Kev. *Handbook of Major Soviet Nationalities*. New York, 1975.

Keeble, Curtis. *The Soviet State: The Domestic Roots of Soviet Foreign Policy*. Boulder, Colo., 1984.

Kennan, George F. *Soviet Foreign Policy, 1917–1941*. Westport, Conn., 1960.

Koropeckyj, I. S., and Gertrude E. Schroeder. *Economics of Soviet Regions*. New York, 1981.

Koutaissoff, Elisabeth. *The Soviet Union*. New York, 1971.

Kurt, Michael G. *The Soviet Colossus: A History of the USSR*. New York, 1985.

Kuschpeta, O. *Banking and Credit System of the USSR*. Boston, 1978.

Laird, Robbin F., and Erik P. Hoffman. *Soviet Foreign Policy in a Changing World*. Boston, 1986.

Lane, David. *Soviet Economy*. New York, 1985.

Lane, Peter. *USSR in the Twentieth Century*. London, 1978.

Le Donne, John. *Ruling Russia*. Princeton, N.J., 1984.

Lewin, Moshe. *The Making of the Soviet System*. New York, 1985.

Lisitsin, Y. *Health Protection in the USSR*. Moscow, 1972.

London, Kurt. *The Soviet Union: A Half Century of Communism*. Baltimore, Md., 1968.

Lydolph, Paul E. *Geography of the USSR*. New York, 1951.

Matthews, William Kleesmann. *Languages of the USSR*. New York, 1951.

Maxwell, Robert. *Information USSR*. London, 1962.

McClellan, Woodford. *Russia: A History of the Soviet Period*. Englewood Cliffs, N.J., 1986.

McCrea, Barbara P. *Soviet and East European Political Dictionary*. Santa Barbara, Calif., 1984.

McKenzie, David, and Michael Curran. *A History of Russia and the Soviet Union*. Chicago, 1982.

Medish, Vadim. *The Soviet Union*. New York, 1985.

Mellor, Roy. *Geography of the USSR*. New York, 1964.

Munting, Robert. *The Economic Development of the USSR*. New York, 1984.

Nove, Alec. *The Soviet Economy*. London, 1986.

———. *An Economic History of the USSR*. London, 1984.

Novosti Press. *Soviet Almanac.* San Diego, Calif., 1981.

Pares, Bernard. *A History of Russia*. New York, 1953.

Parker, W. H. *The Soviet Union*. London, 1983.

Paskiewicz, Henryk. *The Making of the Russian Nation*. Westport, Conn., 1963.

Paxton, John A. *A Companion to Russian History*. New York, 1988.

Perlo, Ellen, and Victor Perlo. *Dynamic Stability: The Soviet Economy Today*. New York, 1982.

Pipes, Richard. *U.S.-Soviet Relations in the Era of Détente: A Tragedy of Errors*. Boulder, Colo., 1981.

Pokshishevsky, V. *Geography of the Soviet Union*. Moscow, 1974.

Riasanovsky, Nicholas V. *A History of Russia*. Oxford, Eng., 1984.

Rothman, Stanley, and George Breslauer. *Soviet Politics and Society*. Westport, Conn., 1978.

Saivetz, Carol R., and Sylvia W. Edgington. *Soviet–Third World Relations*. Boulder, Colo., 1985.

Schapiro, Leonard. *The Government and Politics of the Soviet Union*. London, 1984.

Schopflin, George. *The Soviet Union and Eastern Europe*. New York, 1986.

Schwartz, Harry. *Russia's Soviet Economy*. New York, 1958.

Scott, William, and H. F. Scott. *Armed Forces of the USSR*. Boulder, Colo., 1984.

Shabad, Theodore. *Geography of the USSR*. New York, 1951.

Sherman, Howard J. *The Soviet Economy*. Boston, 1969.

Shipler, David K. *Russia: Broken Idols; Solemn Dreams*. New York, 1983.

Smith, Hedrick. *The Russians*. New York, 1974.

Sonnenfeldt, Helmut. *Soviet Politics in the Nineteen Eighties*. Boulder, Colo., 1984.

Spulber, Nicolas. *The Soviet Economy: Structure, Principles, Problems*. New York, 1969.

Starr, Richard F. *USSR Foreign Policies After Détente*. Stanford, Calif., 1985.

Stuart, Robert C. *The Soviet Rural Economy*. Totowa, N.J., 1984.

Szymanski, Albert. *Human Rights in the Soviet Union*. London, 1984.

Tucker, Robert. *The Soviet Political Mind.* New York, 1972.

Vernadsky, George. *History of Russia.* New Haven, Conn., 1961.

Voslensky, Michael. *Nomenklatura: The Soviet Ruling Class.* New York, 1984.

White, Stephen. *Political Culture and Soviet Politics.* New York, 1980.

Whiting, Kenneth R. *Soviet Union Today: A Concise Handbook.* New York, 1966.

Wixman, Ronald. *People of the USSR.* Armonk, N.Y., 1984.

OFFICIAL PUBLICATION

Narodnoye Khozyaystvo (National Economy of the USSR) (annual).

YUGOSLAVIA

GEOGRAPHICAL FEATURES

Located in southeastern Europe, Yugoslavia is the largest Balkan nation. Including its 1,050 islands (six of which cover over 259 sq. km.; 100 sq. mi.), Yugoslavia has a total area of 255,804 sq. km. (98,766 sq. mi.), making it the seventh-largest nation in Europe, excluding the Soviet Union. Yugoslavia's greatest distances are 978 km. (608 mi.) east-southeast to west-northwest and 501 km. (311 mi.) north-northwest to south-southwest. It shares its total boundary lengths of 5,061 km. (3,145 mi.) with seven neighbors as follows: Austria, 324 km. (201 mi.); Hungary, 623 km. (387 mi.); Rumania, 557 km. (346 mi.); Bulgaria, 536 km. (333 mi.); Greece, 262 km. (163 mi.); Albania, 465 km. (289 mi.); and Italy, 202 km. (126 mi.). Yugoslavia's total Adriatic coast line is 2,092 km. (1,300 mi.) long. There are no current border disputes.

The capital is Belgrade, the capital of the former kingdom of Serbia. Belgrade is at the junction of the Sava and Danube rivers on a high bank overlooking the Danubian Plain. Of the other major cities, Osijek and Nis are the only ones that are not the capitals of republics. Sarajevo is the capital of Bosnia and Herzegovina, Skopje is the captial of Macedonia and Zagreb is the capital of Croatia.

MAJOR URBAN CENTERS (1981)			
Belgrade (Beograd, the capital)	1,470,073	Novi Sad	257,685
Osijek	867,646	Split	235,922
Zagreb	768,700	Pristina	210,040
Nis	643,470	Rijeka	193,044
Skoplje (Skopje)	506,547	Maribor	185,699
Sarajevo	448,519	Banja Luka	183,618
Ljubljana	305,211	Kragujevac	164,823
		Subotica	154,611

Geographically, Yugoslavia comprises the coastal and interior highlands and mountains and the Pannonian Plains in the North and Northeast. About 60% of the land area consists of ridges and hills over 200 to 1,000 m. (656 to 3,281 ft.) in elevation, and another 20% consists of high mountains and ranges over 1,000 m. high. Tall mountains are a dominant feature of the landscape in the South and Southeast as well as in the Northwest near the Austrian border.

The mountains can be divided into two groups: the old Rhodope Mountains system; and the younger mountains, which consist of the Alpides and the Dinarides, the two branches into which the Central European Alps divide themselves on Yugoslavian territory. The Alpides emerge from the Yugoslav-Austrian border as the Karavanke, Pohorje and Kozjak mountains and the Kam-

AUSTRIA

HUNGARY

ROMANIA

Maribor

Drava River

Ljubljana

SLOVENIA

Zagreb

CROATIA

Subotica

VOJVODINA

Bečej

Koper

Rijeka

Sisak

Osijek

Novi Sad

100m

100km

Pula

KRK

Karlovac

Danube River

Zrenjanin

CRES

Sava River

Banja Luka

Belgrade

IRON GATE

DINARIC ALPS

Zadar

Tuzla

Šabac

DALMATIA

Zenica

Valjevo

Bor

Šibenik

BOSNIA AND HERCEGOVINA

Kragujevac

Morava River

Adriatic Sea

Split

Sarajevo

Titovo Užice

Svetozarevo

Zaječar

BRAČ

Mostar

SERBIA

VIS

Niš

HVAR

MONTENEGRO

Kosovska Mitrovica

KORČULA

Dubrovnik

Nikšić

PALAGRUŽA

Titograd

Priština

KOSOVO

Cetinje

Lake Scutari

Skopje

ITALY

Tetovo

Titov Veles

MACEDONIA

Prilep

Bitola

Lake Ohrid

Lake Prespa

GREECE

ALBANIA

BULGARIA

29·XI·1943

nik and Savinja Alps, extend through Austria in the shape of an arc to reenter Yugoslavia from Rumania under the name of the Carpathian Mountains and continue into Bulgaria as the Balkan Mountains. The Dinarides run through Yugoslavia into Greece along the Adriatic Sea and then along the Albanian border, first as the Julian Alps into Slovenia, then as the Dinaric Mountains parallel to the Adriatic Sea and finally as the Sar Mountains in western Macedonia. The Julian Alps, which occupy the westernmost part of the country, are among the most rugged in Europe and contain many summits that exceed 1,800 m. (5,906 ft.). One peak, Triglav, has an elevation of 2,846 m. (9,338 ft.), the highest in the country. Eastward the ridges of these mountains become less defined, and their crests decrease in height to about 1,000 m. in the vicinity of Maribor.

Between the Alpides and the Dinarides, from the Greek and Bulgarian borders almost down to the Sava and Danube rivers, lie the Rhodope Massif or Mountains.

The three main topographical regions—Western, Central and Eastern—have their morphological subdivisions. The subregions of the Western region are Adriatic, Alpine, Dinaric and Sar. The Adriatic coastal subregion is a narrow strip of mainland with bays, gulfs, coves, channels, peninsulas, islands and caves. There are two large peninsulas: the Istrian and the Peljesac. The Alpine subregion extends between the Yugoslav borders with Austria and Italy and the Dinaric Mountains. Except for a few valleys, there is little flat land in this subregion. The Dinaric subregion extends from the Soca River on the Italian border to Lake Skadar on the Albanian border and to the Sitnica, Ibar and Kolubara rivers in west-central and southwestern Serbia. In the South it borders on the Adriatic littoral and in the North on the Pannonian Basin. Nearly 700 km. (435 mi.) long and from 50 to 230 km. (31 to 143 mi.) wide, this subregion is a plateau gently descending toward the Northeast. It is traversed by parallel, longitudinal mountain ranges running from Northwest to Southeast. The central part has many karst valleys and depressions.

The Sar subregion extends along the Albanian border in western Macedonia. It originates in the North in the Sar Mountains, which have the second- and third-highest peaks in the country: Korab (2,764 m.; 9,069 ft.) and Titov Vrh (2,747 m.; 9,013 ft.).

The Central region consists of two subregions: the Pannonian Plains and the Rhodope subregion. The Pannonian Plains are a southward extension of the Great Hungarian Plain and consist of the valleys of the middle and lower Sava, the lower Tisza and the middle Danube rivers. Occupying approximately 20% of the country's land area, the region extends about 480 km. (174 mi.) northwest to southeast and has a maximum north-south width of 200 km. (124 mi.). This region, the most fertile in the nation, is the area occupied by the ancient Pannonian Sea, which disappeared as the runoff from the surrounding mountains gradually filled it with alluvial deposits. It is a sedimentary region containing wide valley basins; alluvial plains; sandy dunes; and low, rolling hills covered with fertile loam. The southern edge of the Pannonian Plains ascends gradually through a se-

ries of abrasion terraces. Above these terraces rise isolated mountains, such as Avala, Bukulja, Kosmaj, Vencac, Rudnik, Cer, Majevica and Posara.

The Rhodope subregion is cut from north to south by valleys of the Morava and Vardar rivers, with the main part lying to the east of these valleys. Its highest mountains are the Osogoverske (2,252 m.; 7,389 ft.). The somewhat younger Rhodope Mountains—the Baba, with its highest peak, the Perister (2,600 m.; 8,531 ft.), the Jakupica, with its Solunska Glava peak (2,540 m.; 8,334 ft.); and the Nidze, with its Kajmakcalan peak (2,521 m.; 8,271 ft.)—lie west of the Vardar River.

The Eastern Region comprises the Carpathian-Balkan subregion and the Wallachian Pontian basin subregion. In the Carpathians the highest mountains are the Stara Planina, Suva Planina, Rtanj, Ozren, Miroc, Deli-Jovan and Homolje.

Yugoslavia has about 1,850 rivers and streams over 10 km. (6 mi.) long. The 15 most important are (data for Yugoslavia only):

	Area of Basin, Sq. Km. (Sq. Mi.)		Total Length, Km. (Mi.)	Navi-gable, Km. (Mi.)	
Danube	210,080	(81,091)	591 (367)	591	(367)
Sava	95,719	(36,948)	940 (584)	593	(369)
Drina	19,570	(7,554)	346 (215)	—	
Vardar	17,762	(6,856)	300 (186)	—	
Tisza or Tisa	17,300	(6,678)	151 (94)	151	(94)
Western Morava	15,849	(6,118)	318 (198)	—	
Southern Morava	15,469	(5,971)	298 (185)	—	
Drava	12,033	(4,645)	437 (272)	105	(65)
Kupa	11,484	(4,433)	296 (184)	69	(43)
Bosna	10,457	(4,048)	271 (168)	—	
Ibar	8,389	(3,238)	241 (150)	—	
Una	7,285	(2,812)	255 (158)	—	
Morava	6,126	(2,365)	245 (152)	—	
Neretva	5,582	(2,155)	218 (135)	20	(12)
Vrbas	5,406	(2,087)	240 (149)	—	

The total length of the navigable rivers is about 1,900 km. (1,181 mi.). The major canals are the Veliki Canal, 123 km. (76 mi.) long, which connects the Tisza River with the Danube from Becej to Bezdan; the Mali Canal, 69 km. (43 mi.) long, which connects the Veliki Canal with the Danube from Mali Stapar to Novi Sad; and the Begej Canal, 40 km. (25 mi.) of which is in Yugoslavia and the balance in Rumania.

There are three drainage basins—the Black Sea, the Adriatic and the Aegean—accounting for 69.5%, 21.2% and 8.9% of the water flow, respectively. The Danube has four large tributaries: the Drava, Tisza, Sava and Morava. Of these, the first comes from Austria, and the second from Hungary, while the third and fourth are national rivers. The Sava, which is the largest domestic river, flows into the Danube at Belgrade. Thanks to its gentle gradient—only 45 m. (148 ft.) from Zagreb to Belgrade—the Sava is navigable for almost two-thirds of its length. The Sava's main tributaries are the Drina, Vrbas, Bosna, Una and Kupa. No navigable river flows into the Adriatic Sea. The Neretva is the only river that breaks through the interior ranges to the sea. Aside from the Strumica River, which crosses into Bulgaria, the Vardar with its tributaries, is the only river that drains into the Aegean.

Glacial lakes are numerous but small in size. Most of them are in cirques in high mountains, and some in valleys, such as Lake Bled and Lake Bohinj. Tectonic lakes are larger and deeper than glacial lakes. In this category are the three large Macedonian lakes: Prespa (285 sq. km.; 110 sq. mi.; altitude, 853 m.; 2,799 ft.), Ohrid (367 sq. km.; 142 sq. mi.; altitude, 695 m.; 2,280 ft.) and Lake Dojran (43 sq. km.; 17 sq. mi.; altitude, 148 m.; 486 ft.). Prespa and Ohrid are shared with Albania; Dojran, with Bulgaria. Examples of karst lakes are Skadar in Montenegro on the Albanian border, and Vrana and Prokljan in Croatia. Finally, Lake Palic is an example of a fluvial lake.

CLIMATE & WEATHER

Because of its location, Yugoslavia is exposed to three weather systems: Mediterranean (Adriatic and Aegean), modified Continental and Continental. Most of the variations are determined by proximity to the coast and by altitude. Basically, the climate is moderate, with four distinct seasons. Winters are not too cold and summers are not too hot. Across most of the country, cloudiness is greatest and humidity highest in the autumn and early winter months.

The Mediterranean climate contributes warm summers and mild winters in the southern part of the country. The Adriatic climate is characterized by long, warm summers with little rain, mild winters with much rain, short springs and long and rainy falls. The extent of this climate is limited by the high Dinaric Mountains in the North. The Mediterranean-Adriatic climate prevails in all the islands. On the mainland where the mountains come down almost to the coast, this climate is limited to a narrow strip of land. Where the mountains are more distant, as in the case of Istria, central Dalmatia, the Neretva River Valley and the Skadar Valley, the warmth of the Adriatic climate penetrates deep into the interior. July is the hottest month, with temperatures ranging from 23°C to 26°C (73°F to 79°F) along the coast. In the summer the heat is steady because the sky is clear, the limestone stores up much heat and the Adriatic itself is too warm to cool the mainland. January is the coldest month, with a temperature range of 5°C to 10°C. The amount of precipitation increases with distance from the coast. On the islands it varies from 500 to 1,000 mm. (20 to 39 in.) annually; on the coast from 1,000 to 1,500 mm. (39 to 59 in.); and on the steep slopes of the mountains along the coast from 1,500 to 3,800 mm. (59 to 150 in.), reaching a maximum of 5,000 mm. (197 mm.) under Orjen Mountain, the highest in Yugoslavia. The moisture influence of the Adriatic climate is carried much farther than its warmth and does not diminish until the Pannonian Plain and the Morava and Vardar river valleys are reached. However, the seasonal distribution of rain is not too beneficial to agriculture because it falls mostly in late fall and winter.

The principal winds in this climatic region are the yugo (sirocco) and the bura. The yugo blows from the sea to the land, carrying much moisture and lasting several days. The bura, blowing from the Dinaric Mountains to the sea, is a dry, cold wind that brings pleasant weather even though it is strong and brief. The mistral is a cool breeze from the sea that relieves the summer heat.

The Aegean subclimate is limited to the Vardar River Valley up to the town of Demir-Kapija and the Strumica River Valley. Since this area is rather distant from the Aegean Sea and is surrounded by the Rhodope Mountains, the influence of the Aegean is weakened considerably. Winters are considerably colder than in the Adriatic climate because of the influence of the elevations and of the cold Vardarac wind, which blows from the Sar Mountains and the Skopska Crna Gora Mountains toward the sea along the Vardar River Valley. The summers are warmer than in the Adriatic region. Rain falls in the fall and winter, and the summers are dry. The rate of precipitation is in the 500 to 700 mm. (20 to 28 in.) range, much lower than in the Adriatic region.

The modified continental climate extends over all mountainous areas, except the most elevated regions, and in valleys surrounded by high mountains. It is characterized by moderately warm summers and moderately cold winters. The average temperature in July is between 18°C and 19°C (64°F and 66°F) and in January between 2°C and 3°C (36°F and 37°F). Precipitation is in the range of 1,000 to 2,000 mm. (39 to 79 in.), falling generally at the beginning of summer. Snow is common in winter, helped by northern and northeastern winds. In elevated areas the alpine climate prevails, with short, cool summers and prolonged winters with much snow. The higher the elevation, the lower the precipitation. In the valleys surrounded by high mountains, a subalpine climate prevails, with warmer summers and winters than in the mountainous regions.

The continental climate prevails in the Pannonian Plain, where the influences of eastern and northern Europe are strong. The summers are very warm, the temperature rising to 40°C (104°F). Winters are cold, with temperatures dropping to −25°C (−13°F), so that the rivers become frozen. Precipitation is low—only between 500 and 700 mm. (20 and 28 in.)—but it is well distributed and falls mostly at the beginning of the summer, when crops need it most.

The Rhodope is a subzone of the continental climate and reveals influences of both the continental and the Mediterranean climates. Summers are warmer and drier; winters, much colder. Precipitation is very low, less than 500 mm. (20 in.).

POPULATION

The population of Yugoslavia was estimated in 1989 at 23,724,919, based on the last official census, in 1981, when the population was 22,424,711. Yugoslavia ranks 36th in the world in population and 72nd in the world in land area. The population is expected to reach 23,915,000 in 1990 and 25,608,000 by 2000.

Although the birth rate is low (15.4 per 1,000 compared to a world average of 26.0), the government is actively involved in controlled growth. The General Law on Abortions, promulgated in 1969, offers extensive facilities to women in need of them. The Resolution on Family Planning adopted by the National Assembly in the same year expressed the government's commitment to planned parenthood. The annual growth rate of population varies considerably among the republics. It is highest in Kosovo, where it is 2.4, and lowest in Croatia, where it is 0.3.

The density of population increased from 66 per sq. km. (172 per sq. mi.) in 1953 to 92.2 per sq. km. (238.9 per sq. mi.) in 1988. The density varies among various administrative divisions and is highest in Serbia and lowest in Montenegro. A much wider range of densities prevails among the smaller territorial units, such as the *srezovi*, which correspond roughly to counties. The most densely populated section is a broad belt extending from the Sava River southward along the Morava to Skopje and a shorter strip from the vicinity of Zagreb to the Hungarian border. Other areas of dense population are scattered through Slovenia and Vojvodina and along the Dalmatian coast. In highlands settlement is generally sparse, with higher densities in small basins of fertile soil, where cultivation is possible.

Massive urbanization is a post–World War II phenomenon. At the end of the war nearly 80% of the population lived in the countryside. Between that time and 1970 nearly 4.5 million (or 20% of the population) migrated to cities. The urban population grew by 80% between 1953 and 1971. In 1965 a total of 31% of the population lived in cities; the proportion grew to 48% in 1987. Even so, Yugoslavia ranks as one of the least urbanized countries in Europe.

Roughly one-half to two-thirds of the population in the republic's capitals were born elsewhere. Only 30% of Belgrade's population was born in the city. Thus the proportion of first-generation urbanites is much greater than in most other countries. However, the distinction between urban and rural populations is very tenuous. Nearly one-third of those classified as urban are also agriculturists. The urban populace is distributed among, at one end of the urban scale, republic and provincial capitals, and at the other, numerous hamlets and small cities. In addition to the category of cities *(gradovi)* there is an administrative category known as urban municipalities *(gradski opstine)*, which includes much smaller settlements.

The sex ratio is similar to that found in most Western countries. There is a preponderance of males in the earliest age group and a reversal of that ratio in older ones. The impact of the two world wars on the sex structure has been less severe than in other European countries more directly involved in the hostilities. The aging of the population also is less rapid in Yugoslavia because of a later and slower transition to an industrial society. Significantly, the population of the more developed republics—Croatia, Serbia and Slovenia—is considerably older than those of the less developed ones.

Eight censuses have been taken since the nation came into existence in 1918. The population count was 12.545 million in 1921 and 14.534 million in 1931. The first postwar census was taken in 1948, when the population was 15.772 million. Throughout the interwar period the rate of population growth was higher in

Yugoslavia than in other major European countries. During World War II the population suffered severe losses, estimated at over 1 million. About 100,000 of the prisoners of war never returned to the country. A further 500,000 German-speakers either left or were expelled, and 150,000 Italians were transferred to Italy. Several thousand Poles and Hungarians were involved in population exchanges.

This was only the beginning. The most notable migration trend has been the successive waves of Yugoslavs seeking semipermanent employment as guestworkers *(Gastarbeiter)* in Western Europe. The movement began extralegally in the 1950s and, when emigration restrictions were eased in the 1960s, the response was

DEMOGRAPHIC INDICATORS, 1988

Population: 23,724,919 (1989)

Year of last census: 1981	World rank: 36	
Sex ratio: males, 49.4;	females, 50.6	

Population trends (million)

1930: 14.360	1960: 18.402	1990: 23.915
1940: 16.425	1970: 20.371	2000: 25.608
1950: 16.346	1980: 22.080	

Population doubling time in years at current rate: 99 years
Hypothetical size of stationary population (million): 28
Assumed year of reaching net reproduction rate of 1: 2030

Age profile (%)

0–15: 23.5	30–44: 21.0	60–74: 9.4
15–29: 23.9	45–59: 18.8	Over 75: 3.4

Median age (years): 33.1
Density per sq. km. (per sq. mi.): 92.2 (238.9)

Annual growth rate

1950–55: 1.39	1975–80: 0.89	1995–2000: 0.49
1960–65: 1.09	1980–85: 0.76	2000–2005: 0.37
1965–70: 0.94	1985–90: 0.63	2010–15: 0.18
1970–75: 0.94	1990–95: 0.54	2020–25: 0.14

Vital statistics
  Crude birth rate, 1/1,000: 15.4
  Crude death rate, 1/1,000: 9.1
  Change in birth rate: −21.9 (1965–84)
  Change in death rate: 5.7 (1965–84)
  Dependency, total: 46.7
  Infant mortality rate, 1/1,000: 25.0
  Child (0–4 years) mortality rate, 1/1,000: 2.0
  Maternal mortality rate, 1/100,000: 21.0
  Natural increase, 1/1,000: 6.3
  Total fertility rate: 2.1
  General fertility rate: 60.0
  Gross reproduction rate: 0.96
  Marriage rate, 1/1,000: 6.9
  Divorce rate, 1/1,000: 0.9
  Life expectancy, males (years): 66.0
  Life expectancy, females (years): 74.0
  Average household size: 3.6
  % illegitimate births: 8.4
Youth
  Youth population 15–24 (000): 3,602
  Youth population in 2000 (000): 3,609
Women
  Of childbearing age 15–49 (000): 5,972
  Child-woman ratio (children per 000 women 15–49): 307
  Abortions per 000 live births: 74.0
Urban
  Urban population (000): 12,015
  % urban, 1965: 31; 1987: 48
  Annual urban growth rate, (%): 1965–80: 3.0; 1980–87: 2.6
  % urban population in largest city: 10
  % urban population in cities over 500,000: 23
  Number of cities over 500,000: 5
  Annual rural growth rate: −0.9

POPULATION OF YUGOSLAVIA, 1880–1980 (000)										
							Serbia			
Year	Yugoslavia	Bosnia-Herzegovina	Montenegro	Croatia	Macedonia	Slovenia	Total	Proper	Kosovo	Vojvodina
Absolute Numbers										
1880	8,877	1,158	(207)	2,479	(528)	1,182	3,323	1,896	(240)	1,187
1910	12,962	1,898	344	3,375	876	1,321	5,148	3,147	475	1,526
1921	12,545	1,890	311	3,427	809	1,288	4,819	2,843	439	1,537
1931	14,534	2,324	360	3,789	950	1,386	5,726	3,550	552	1,624
1948	15,842	2,564	377	3,780	1,153	1,440	6,528	4,154	733	1,641
1953	16,991	2,843	420	3,936	1,305	1,504	6,979	4,464	816	1,699
1961	18,549	3,278	472	4,160	1,406	1,592	7,642	4,823	964	1,855
1971	20,523	3,746	530	4,426	1,647	1,727	8,447	5,250	1,244	1,953
1980	22,080	4,034	569	4,595	1,882	1,846	9,155	5,593	1,517	2,045
Indices										
1980/1880	248.7	348.4	274.9	185.4	356.4	156.2	275.5	295.0	632.1	172.3
1980/1921	141.3	163.2	150.2	138.2	153.2	109.0	145.0	149.9	182.9	129.5
1980/1948	139.4	157.3	150.9	121.6	163.2	128.2	140.2	134.6	207.0	124.6
Average Annual Growth Rates (%)										
1880–1910	12.7	16.6	17.1	10.3	17.0	3.7	14.7	17.0	23.0	8.4
1921–31	14.8	20.9	14.7	10.1	16.2	7.4	17.4	22.5	23.2	5.5
1948–61	12.2	19.1	17.4	7.4	15.4	7.8	12.2	11.6	21.3	9.5
1961–80	9.2	11.0	9.9	5.3	15.5	7.8	9.6	7.8	24.2	5.2

Sources: Estimates only for Macedonia, Montenegro and Kosovo for 1880 and 1910. All other data drawn from census findings. Estimates for 1980 by the Demographic Research Center.

Note: In 1971 the "permanent" population included about 672,000 persons temporarily working abroad.

far beyond the authorities' expectations. By the 1980s some 20% of the total labor force was believed to be employed abroad, although precise counts varied. The Yugoslav rate of emigration was second only to Portugal's among European countries. The main centers of emigration were not the poorer regions in the South but the economically developed North and West. Croatia, northeastern Slovenia, eastern Vojvodina and northeastern Serbia contributed a disproportionate percentage of all emigrants. In the beginning emigrants were mostly older skilled males, but by the mid-1970s the process had spread to rural areas and included farmers, unskilled laborers and women. Overall, Yugoslavs are among the most highly skilled guestworkers in Western Europe. The drain was a snowballing process. Guestworkers, returning home on vacation, broadcast the benefits of foreign employment and took many of their friends and family members on their return. Government efforts to limit the flow have been of little avail. Returning guestworkers also have posed a problem for the government, not only because of the inability of the economy to absorb them but also because of the newfangled antisocialist ideas they brought back with them from the West.

No data are available regarding immigration to Yugoslavia.

ETHNIC COMPOSITION

Since 1918 Yugoslavia has been a multinational state, except during World War II. The population is more heterogeneous than in any European country except the Soviet Union.

The ethnic composition of those who declared their ethnic nationality in the 1981 census follows on page 547.

The Yugoslav landscape may seem perplexing as a country of six republics, two autonomous provinces, over 20 nationalities, various languages and a number of religions. The preponderance of the people inhabiting Yugoslavia are Slavs. (The very name Yugoslavia means South Slav.) These are the Serbs, Croats, Slovenians, Montenegrins, Macedonians and Muslim Slavs; Slav "minorities" are Slovaks, Ruthenians/Ukrainians, Czechs, Bulgarians, Poles, and Russians. The Hungarians, Albanians, Turks, Rumanians, Italians and Germans are of the same ethnic stock as their compatriots. The Muslim Slavs live in Bosnia-Herzegovina; Albanians in Kosovo; Hungarians, Slovaks, Rumanians, Germans, Czechs, Poles and Ruthenians/Ukrainians in Serbia but especially Vojvodina; Turks and Bulgarians largely in Macedonia, while the Austrians and Italians live near the border of those countries. Gypsies are largely in the southern areas. Most of the 70,000 Jews perished during the war, and the majority of the 8,000 survivors emigrated.

National rivalries were traditional in the history of the territory comprising Yugoslavia. The Kingdom of the Serbs, Croats and Slovenes (in 1929 the Kingdom of Yugoslavia) was established in 1918, comprised of nation-groups living in the Kingdom of Serbia and Montenegro, and for centuries in the defeated empires of Austria-Hungary and Turkey. Instead of a federal state that such an amalgam suggested, the Constitution of 1921 centralized control that rekindled ethnic animosities, especially between the Serbs and the Croats. The latter were frustrated by denial of autonomy, which came only with the approach of war. Ethnic strife continued even during the war but, under Marshal Tito, Yugoslavia was reestablished as a federal republic. Nationalities were granted greater formal political rights, but the Constitution of 1946 created a people's republic. Control was not only centralized but Communist-dominated as well. Ethnic animosities existed but were suppressed under Tito's strong leadership. Recent eruptions, especially by ethnic Albanians, have focused international attention not only on Kosovo but also on the fragility of the multinational structure of the country.

According to the Constitution of 1974 the six socialist republics ("nations") are constituent parts of the Socialist Federal Republic of Yugoslavia (SFRY). The two provinces are "autonomous" parts of Serbia. Each "nationality" is guaranteed the right to develop its culture and establish organizations to do so. Each republic and autonomous province has its own constitution, which specifies rights and duties. Altogether, the Constitution of the SFRY provides an impressive list of rights for the citizens and nationalities—such as sovereignty, independence, equality, national freedom and national defense.

However, all activities must conform to the Constitution of the SFRY. The country is a "single unified whole," and economically Yugoslavia is a unified market. Demands for political pluralism, the deteriorating economic situation, and labor unrest have contributed to the general discontent of the nationalities. During 1988–89 ethnic tensions and the rise of nationalism posed a serious problem for the federal government, which responded with security measures. A resurgence of Serbian nationalism was spearheaded by its party president, Slobodan Milosevic, who generated mass demonstrations directed especially against ethnic Albanians in Kosovo, the least-developed area. Milosevic engineered a Serbian constitutional amendment imposing greater power over its two provinces. Demonstrations turned to violence and bloodshed, such as during March and April 1989, and have continued into 1990. The Albanian grievances, fanned by Tirana, against the dominant Serbs and Montenegrins include denial of self-rule and violations of civil rights; some agitate for secession.

A bitter intraparty controversy with ethnic undertones unfolded between Slovenia and Serbia over Milosevic's attack on Slovenian pluralism and criticism of Serbian unitarism. Milosevic also attacked Croatia and Vojvodina. A Slovenian constitutional amendment of June 1989 providing for the right of secession exacerbated their relations. Macedonia followed the Serbian example in restricting the rights of ethnic Albanians and Turks. Protests, strikes, riots, demonstrations and counterdemonstrations spread to other areas, including Vojvodina. Altogether millions of people in all republics displayed publicly their general dissatisfaction within their republic, the republics against each other and the provinces against Serbia. This created an explosive climate, which Tito had earlier sought to prevent by constitutional decentralization.

Republics/Provinces	Population (000) (1989 est.)
Total	23,724
Republics	
Serbia (with Kosovo and Vojvodina)	9,776
Croatia	4,679
Bosnia-Herzegovina	4,441
Macedonia	2,088
Slovenia	1,943
Montenegro	632
Provinces (in Serbia)	
Vojvodina	2,052
Kosovo	1,893

	Total Population (million) (1981) 22.4
Nationality	% of Total
Serbs	36.3
Croats	19.8
Moslems	8.9
Slovenes	7.8
Albanians	7.7
Macedonians	6.0
"Yugoslavs"	5.4
Montenegrins	2.6
Hungarians (Magyars)	1.9
Gypsies	0.8
Turks	0.4
Slovaks	0.4
Others (Rumanians, Ruthenians, Poles, Bulgarians, Czechs, Jews, Germans, Austrians, Italians, Ukrainians, Russians)	2.0

LANGUAGES

The numerous nationalities employ their mother tongue, including dialects, in personal communication. Many people, especially the better-educated, are bilingual or multilingual. The languages of the national republics are Serbo-Croatian, Slovenian and Macedonian, all of the southern Slavic family of languages. There is no "Yugoslav" language; all attempts toward unification have failed. Historical and religious differences account for the two alphabets—Latin and Cyrillic. The former is used in Catholic and Protestant areas by the Croatians, Slovenians, Slovaks, Poles, Hungarians and others; the latter by the Serbs, Macedonians and Bulgarians. Those using Latin utilize diacritical marks; with them, the Croatians duplicate Cyrillic sounds. Otherwise Serbo-Croatian is basically the same language with some differences reflecting their historical, religious and cultural characteristics.

The Constitution "guarantees" equality of the nations and nationalities in Yugoslavia, including their languages and alphabets. Across the federation, the languages of the "nations"—the six republics—are to be used officially, while the languages of the "nationalities"—the minorities—are to be used in conformity with the Constitution and federal statutes under conditions established by sociopolitical committees and self-management enactments. The nationalities are assured use of their languages in governmental organs, educational/training institutions, before courts of law, and in the mass media. Implementation of these rights is not totally satisfactory, however. The ethnic Albanians, for example, have protested the June 1988 Macedonian law making bilingual education mandatory in schools where Albanian was the sole language of instruction before.

RELIGIONS

There are some 40 recognized religious communities in Yugoslavia. Most believers are Roman Catholics (Slovenes and Croats), Orthodox (Serbs, Montenegrins and Macedonians) or Muslims (Bosnians and Albanians). A very rough estimate of the membership of each creed would be 30% Roman Catholic, 35% Serbian and Macedonian Orthodox and 12% Muslim. There also are small pockets of Protestants in Vojvodina and Slavonia, scattered groups of Greek or Uniate Catholics, a few members of the Old Catholic Church and a small number of Jews. Finally, there are numerous small groups that do not conform to the common ethnic-religious pattern—e.g., Catholic Serbs on the Montenegrin coast and Catholic Albanians in Kosovo.

Religion has been a critical component in cultural and ethnic identity since the ninth-century conversion of many Slavs to Christianity. However, doctrinal orthodoxy played only a minor role in religious history. It was rife with heresy, the clergy was largely uneducated and the faithful were in the throes of superstition. Even in the 19th century, travelers reported that the clergy did not know the Ten Commandments or the simplest prayers. From the Counter-Reformation onward, however, religion became a standard for the nationalists of each group. Despite the onslaughts of materialism and communism, it continues to do so even today.

The first Christians arrived in Dalmatia and Illyricum near the end of the Apostle Paul's ministry. Both Catholic and Orthodox branches were represented in the country by the middle of the fourth century, but the influence of Byzantium grew in the ninth century through the missionary activity of Sts. Cyril and Methodius, who translated the liturgy into the national language. In 1054 the Great Schism split the people along denominational lines. During the succeeding centuries the Orthodox Church itself regrouped into several autocephalous groups. An autocephalous archdiocese was established at Ohrid in southern Macedonia. In 1219 the

independent Serbian Orthodox Church was formed, and in 1316 the Serbian archepiscopate was raised to a patriarchate at Pec, but it was suppressed by the Turks between 1453 and 1557 and from 1776 to the end of Turkish rule. In 1611 the first Uniates of the Byzantine rite joined the Roman Catholic Church. In 1832 Constantinople granted internal autonomy to the Serbian Orthodox Church. This was followed in 1920 by complete autocephality, with the right of electing its own patriarch.

Although never the official church of the land, the Serbian Orthodox Church was virtually one before the war. It was the church of the ruling dynasty, and its patriarch sat on the royal council. Parliamentary oaths were administered according to Orthodox rites. All these privileges were swept away in 1945, but the church nevertheless continues to exert a dominant influence. The patriarch is the metropolitan of Belgrade-Karlovci and archbishop of Pec. The bishops of Dabar-Bosnia, Montenegro-Coastland and Zagreb also bear the title of metropolitan. Overseas eparchies include three in the United States and one each in England, Hungary, and Rumania. The church is administered by five bodies: the Holy Archepiscopal Council, the Holy Archepiscopal Synod, the Holy Archepiscopal Tribunal, the Patriarchal Council and the Patriarchal Administrative Board. The church has 81 monasteries, 72 convents, 3,368 churches, 1,731 parish halls and 2,404 organized parishes. The church also runs four secondary-level seminaries, one secondary-level monastic school and one postsecondary seminary and publishes a variety of journals.

The Macedonian Orthodox Church became fully independent in 1967. It is headed by an archbishop with his see at Skopje; he oversees 953 churches, 86 monasteries and a theological seminary.

The Roman Catholic Church remains the most comprehensively organized religious community in Yugoslavia. More than two-thirds of the religious press is Catholic, as are 80% of the theological faculties and seminaries. However, in part because of the hierarchy's ultramontane loyalties and partly because of the church's identification with Croatian nationalism, the church has experienced and still experiences greater difficulties in its relations with the state than other religious communities. Croatian Catholics see themselves as Western and European, while Serbs are Byzantine and Eastern. Catholicism is a central element in their political identity, although it is paradoxically combined with a strong anticlericalism. By contrast, the clergy played a critical role in Slovenian politics, particularly the 19th-century agrarian reform movement. Being pastoral and pragmatic, the Slovenian Catholic clergy have fared better in Titoist and post-Titoist Yugoslavia. Of the eight archdioceses and 15 dioceses, only three dioceses are in the East and South. In the diocese of Skopje 80% of the Catholics are Albanians. Although religious convictions have declined overall, Catholics have fared better than the Orthodox in this respect.

The principal Protestant tradition is Lutheranism, which gained entry during the Reformation but suffered heavily during the Counter-Reformation. It was able to reestablish itself during the period of religous tolerance proclaimed by Hapsburg emperor Joseph II. Lutherans are divided into four separate ethnic denominations: Slovak, Slovenes, Croatians and Serbians. The Reformed Christian Church is a Calvinist body, also dating from the Reformation. Disbanded under Turkish rule, it was reestablished as part of the Reformed Church of Hungary. Even though the church is now autonomous, most of the members are Hungarian by origin. Of the new Protestant denominations, the most successful is the Christian Adventist Church, which formed its first community in Belgrade in 1909.

Bosnia-Herzegovina and Albania were the only parts of the Ottoman Empire in which there were large-scale conversions to Islam by a substantial percentage of the urban as well as rural population. The unification of Yugoslavia in 1918 brought Muslims in these three areas together. In 1930 they were united under the authority of a single *ulama* (religious scholar), the *rais-ul ulama* in Belgrade, elected by a Supreme Council composed of representatives of Muslims in Bosnia, Serbia, Macedonia and Montenegro. Muslims follow the Sunnite doctrine and practice as propagated by the Turks.

Church-state relations have undergone many ups and downs, but by and large religion has not been subjected to the same degree of persecution as it has in the Soviet Union. The Constitution of 1974 proclaims equality of rights and duties for all citizens without any discrimination, especially due to religion (Article 154). Article 174, which is devoted to religious questions, stipulates: "The manifestation of religion is free; it is the personal affair of each individual. Religious communities are separate from the state; they are free as far as the exercise of religious affairs and worship are concerned. Religious communities may establish confessional schools only for the training of priests. It is anticonstitutional to abuse religion and religious activities by using them for political purposes. The social community may accord material aid to religious communities. Religious communities may have, within the limits fixed by law, a right of ownership of property." These two articles have been reproduced without change from all the previous constitutions.

Each republic and each commune as well as the federal government at Belgrade has an office for relations with religious communities. Further, there is an ongoing dialogue between religious and Marxist intellectuals at various levels. At the same time, church-state relations are influenced by the activities of conservative hierarchy within the churches and the balance of power held by orthodox or progressive Marxists in the Communist Party.

There have been four successive phases in church-state relations since 1945:

1. There was a period of intense conflict and confrontation between 1945 and 1950.

2. A second period was marked by two contradictory features: a hardening of the official positions vis-à-vis the Catholic Church culminating in the elevation of Monsignor Stepinac to the cardinalate and the subsequent breaking off of diplomatic relations with the Vatican in 1952 and, on the other hand, an improvement of relationships with the Orthodox and Islamic communities and the passage a liberalized law on religion in 1953.

3. A third period, from 1960 to 1972, saw relations normalized with all religious communities, including Catholics. A protocol was signed between the Holy See and Yugoslavia in 1966, giving official recognition to the socialist system of government and repudiating the use of religion for political purposes. This was followed in 1970 by a visit of President Tito to the Vatican.

4. The fourth period, from 1972, has marked a hardening of official attitudes and periodic clamping down on religious activities because of a resurgence of ethnic nationalism in many republics. Local-level Communist officials were often less benign toward believers and clergy than those in Belgrade. Points of contention varied among the republics, but the most persistent ones were religious instruction for children, discrimination against believers in public life, and interdiction against political activity by the clergy.

All republics have enacted laws governing religious communities, in keeping with the provisions of the Constitution of 1974. These laws vary in the latitude afforded to religious communities; the zeal with which local Communist officials pursue antireligious policies also varies. Vigorous complaints by religious leaders to Belgrade often bring redress. Church-state relations are happiest in Macedonia and Slovenia and most complex in Bosnia, Croatia and Serbia. In Herzegovina, the alleged appearance of the Madonna to six children and the resulting pilgrimage of nearly 10,000 believers to the site every day has created problems for the regime in 1981. Initially the regime arrested a Franciscan priest, Father Jozo Zovko, for "concocting" the miracle and jailed him for three and a half years, but later, as the stream of pilgrims continued unabated, the government talked of developing hotels and other tourist facilities in the area to attract hard currency from foreign tourists. Similarly, the spread of pan-Islamic and pro-Ayatollah Khomeini sympathies among Muslims caused the government, generally tolerant to Islam, to adopt a more offensive stand. In 1983 a total of 13 Muslim nationalists were tried in Sarajevo and given jail sentences of five to 15 years for fomenting disaffection toward the regime and for calling for the establishment of an Islamistan in Bosnia.

While the Catholic Church and the Islamic community are in many ways strong, the Serbian Orthodox Church seems to be experiencing a gradual decline. Secularization has hit it hardest. A 1982 opinon poll found that while a third of the youth in traditionally Catholic regions are religious, only 3% were so in Serbian Orthodox regions. Second, the Serbian Orthodox Church has the least favorable ratio of clergy to believers of the three major religions. While there is one imam for every 1,250 Muslims and one Catholic priest for every 2,239 Catholics, there is only one Serbian Orthodox priest for every 5,714 believers. Third, the Serbian Orthodox Church is the least organized in religious instruction to believers. Fourth, the church has been the least successful in obtaining permits to establish new congregations.

HISTORICAL BACKGROUND

The territory that is now Yugoslavia has been inhabited since Paleolithic times. In the sixth century B.C. the Greeks established colonies along the Dalmatian coast, giving the region the name Illyria. From the third century B.C. the Romans began penetrating the Balkan Peninsula, and by 168 B.C. Dalmatia, Macedonia and most of Illyria had become Roman provinces. In A.D. 9 Rome created the huge province of Illyricum, which brought under one administration the present national territory with the exception of Vojvodina. Roman rule lasted for the next five centuries until the arrival of the Slavs and the establishment of permanent Slavic settlements. The early distinctions among the Slavic tribes are not clear, but those who conquered Illyricum split into three main branches; the Slovenes to the northwest, the Croats to their south and the Serbs to the southeast. The native inhabitants, such as the Vlachs, survived for a time as distinct groups, but the majority were Slavicized and absorbed by the invaders. By the end of the sixth century the stage was set for the appearance of the first Slavic states.

In the eighth century the Slovenes submitted to the domination of Franks and were converted by them to Christianity. As German influence increased, the Slovene peasants became serfs under German feudal nobles. The region came under the rule of Hapsburgs in the 13th century and remained under Hapsburg rule until 1918. As a result, the Slovenes became the most Germanized of all Yugoslav ethnic groups. Slovenia was briefly under France between the 1809 Treaty of Vienna concluding Napoleon's campaign against Austria and 1815. It was restored to Austria by the Congress of Vienna.

The Croats were converted to Christianity in the seventh century. Two principal settlements developed during the eighth century: Dalmatian Croatia along the Adriatic, and Pannonian Croatia to the north, centering on the valley of the Sava River. During the first quarter of the ninth century the northern Croats came under the dominion of the Franks and the Dalmatian Croats under the nominal control of the Byzantines. Eventually, in about 924, the two groups shook off foreign hegemony and became united in one kingdom under Tomislav, a powerful *zupan* (tribal leader) who was recognized as king by the pope. The dynasty he founded lasted for almost 200 years, until 1089, when the throne fell vacant. A long power struggle between rival claimants ended in the crown of Croatia being offered to the king of Hungary. For the next 800 years, until 1918, Croatia remained politically tied to Hungary, though with a special status in the united kingdom.

In the 14th century the Ottoman Empire began its incursions into the more northern region of the Balkan Peninsula, and after Bosnia fell in 1463, the sultan's armies pushed into Croatian lands. For the next 60 years the Croats and the Hungarians resisted the periodic Turkish raids, but in 1526 the Hungarian army was defeated in a disastrous encounter, the king was killed and Hungarian resistance ended. The Turks pressed northward and by the end of the 16th century had absorbed much of Croatia and almost all of Slavonia.

In 1578 the Habsburg emperor, the nominal ruler of Hungary and Croatia, established the Military Frontier Province of what remained of Croatia and Slavonia. By 1699 the Hapsburgs had recovered all of Croatia and Slavonia from the Turks, and the Military Frontier Province was extended to include the southern half of Croatia as well as Slavonia and Vojvodina. The land was resettled not only by Croatian peasants but also by Germans and Serbs, whose presence became a controversial issue in 19th-century Croatian nationalism. The Dalmatian coast of Croatia had a slightly different history. From the 15th century to the end of the 18th, most of the coastal area was subordinate to Venice, with the exception of the independent republic of Ragusa, modern Dubrovnik. After a brief period of French control, the Dalmatian provinces passed under Austria, while the rest of Croatia went to Hungary, also part of the Hapsburg Empire. In the second half of the 19th century the principal political development was the founding of the two major Croatian political parties: the National Party, founded in 1841 by Bishop Josif Juraj Strossmayer; and the Party of Rights, founded by Ante Starcevic in the 1860s.

The Serbian tribes settled in the interior of the Balkan Peninsula and east of the Croatian lands during the seventh century. From the eighth through the 11th centuries they were under either Bulgar or Byzantine rulers. In the latter half of the ninth century they were converted by Byzantine monks, the most important of whom were Sts. Cyril and Methodius. Byzantine control, however, was weak, and by the 12th century two independent kingdoms emerged: Zeta in the mountainous region of present-day Montenegro, and Herzegovina and Raska in Serbia proper. Shortly before 1170 Stephen Nemanja, the grand *zupan* of Raska, united the two kingdoms and founded a dynasty that lasted over 200 years. In 1196 Nemanja abdicated the throne and with the help of his son helped found the great monastery of Hilander on Mount Athos in modern Greece. The younger Nemanja gained recognition from the Byzantine patriarch for an independent Serbian archbishopric, and 1219 he became its first archbishop, under the name Sava. The Serbian Empire reached its zenith under its last emperor, Tsar Stephen Dusan (1331–35), when it included all of modern Albania, Macedonia, Epirus and Thessaly.

The Ottoman period in Serbian history began with the defeat of the Serbian army first at Kosovo in 1389 and later at Smederevo in 1459. The Serbian lands were then placed under Turkish military occupation and so remained for the next 350 years. Bosnia fell to the Turks in 1463 and Herzegovina in 1483. The Turks introduced one of the most oppressive feudal systems to keep the Serbs in subjection. All Christians were treated as serfs and forced to pay taxes to the Turkish *spahis* (cavalrymen granted large estates) and administrators and yield their healthiest sons to be sent to Constantinople, converted to Islam and trained as Janissaries. In the absence of a native nobility (all the Serbian nobles having been exterminated or forced to flee to the mountains or into Hungary), the church hierarchy was recognized as the national leadership. The Serbian Orthodox Church became the chief perpetuator of the Serbian tradition and the guardian of the national heritage.

From the late 17th century, the Turks began to face a series of peasant uprisings against their rule. The first successful one was led by a peasant, Djordje Petrovic—known to his followers as Karadjordje or Black George—who established a short-lived government in Belgrade from 1804 to 1813, when he was defeated by the Turks. In 1817 a second revolt, led by Milos Obrenovic, forced the Turks to grant the Serbs a considerable degree of autonomy, although Serbia remained nominally a province to Turkey until 1830. In that year it became an autonomous principality, and in 1878 complete freedom was achieved by the Treaty of Berlin. In 1882 the Serbian ruler took the title of king.

Between 1817 and 1918 Serbia was ruled by two rival dynasties: the Obrenovics, who ruled from 1830 to 1842 and from 1858 to 1903; and the Karadjordjes, who ruled from 1842 to 1858 and from 1903 to 1918. Serbian independence had been created by the peasant masses and not the intellectuals, and peasant politics dominated affairs during the latter half of the 19th century. The new rising force became the Radical Party, led by Nikola Pasic and inspired by Serbia's first socialist, Sviatozar Markovic. By the terms of the Treaty of Paris of 1856, Russia's position as exclusive protector of the Serbs was ended and Serbia was placed under the protection of Austria, Great Britain, France and Turkey. Serbia's relations with Austria deteriorated sharply thereafter, especially following Austrian annexation of Bosnia and Montenegro in 1908. The Serbs also were embroiled in a war with Bulgaria (1913), victory in which led to the acquisition of a large part of Macedonia. Serbian success in this war led to a showdown with Austria. When Archduke Franz-Ferdinand, heir to the Hapsburg throne, and his consort, the duchess of Hohenberg, were assassinated in Sarajevo in Bosnia on June 28, 1914, by a member of a secret pro-Serbian terrorist group, the Austrian government presented Serbia with an ultimatum whose terms were so harsh as to preclude acceptance by the Serbs. Austria declared war on July 28, 1914, and within a week Germany was aligned with Austria while Britain, France and Russia sided with Serbia. The war was to end Hapsburg hegemony over the Balkans and to forge a new Yugoslav state.

Bosnia and Herzegovina were separated from Serbia in the 10th century and experienced a different history. Bosnia is named after the Bosna River and Herzegovina from the German title *Herzog* (duke) assumed by a powerful Bosnian noble, Stephen Vuksic, in the 15th century. The region suffered from constant internal turmoil from the 10th through the 15th centuries, complicated by the spread of a heretical cult, Bogomilism, during the 12th century. The chaos caused by this struggle laid the region open to the Ottoman Turks, who conquered Bosnia in 1463 and Herzegovina in 1483. Many Bogomil nobles and peasants thereupon adopted the Islamic religion of their conquerors. Those who did so retained their lands and privileges, but the Christian peasants were subjected to oppressive rule, against which they periodically revolted. In 1850 Istanbul established a central administration over this troubled region. A general insurrection in 1875 was supported by Serbia and Montenegro in 1876, and the next year Russia entered the fray against Turkey. The Turks were defeated in 1878 and by the Treaty of San Stefano forced to concede autonomy to Bosnia and Herzegovina. The terms of this treaty were modified in 1878 by the Congress of Berlin, which placed both areas under the administration of Austria–Hungary. In 1908 the Hapsburgs unilaterally annexed the two provinces.

In medieval times the area north of Lake Scutari was known as Duklja or Zeta, ruled in the 12th century by Stephen Nemanja of Serbia and his successors. After the Turkish victory over Serbia in the late 14th century, the region, which by now had come to be known as Montenegro (the Venetian variant for the Italian word for black mountain), became a refuge for Serbs who fled the Turks. Although repeatedly attacked by Turkish forces, it was never fully subdued. In the early 16th century it became a type of theocracy with *vladike* (Eastern Orthodox bishops) exercising both spiritual and temporal powers. The *vladike* were elected by local assemblies until 1697, when succession was limited to the family of Danilo Patrovic Njegus. Since the *vladike* were celibates, the line passed from uncle to nephew. The Njegus family ruled as bishops-princes for more than 150 years. In 1851 the offices of bishop and prince were separated, but the Njegus family continued to rule. The 1878 Treaty of Berlin greatly increased the size of the kingdom. Nicholas I, who had become king in 1860, established a parliamentary constitution in 1910, but at the outbreak of World War I he went into exile. In 1918 royal rule was ended when Montenegro became part of Yugoslavia.

Macedonia is divided among the nations of Yugoslavia, Bulgaria and Greece. Since the seventh century the region has been ruled successively by Byzantines, Bulgars, Serbs, Turks and Greeks. Even before the departure of the Turks, there was intense rivalry among the Bulgars, Greeks and Serbians for control of the area, while the local underground independence movement, IMRO, struggled under the slogan "Macedonia for the Macedonians." In the Balkan Wars of 1912–13 Montenegro, Serbia, Greece and Bulgaria joined in a successful campaign to drive out the Turks. However, the victors were unable to reach a satisfactory partition of the region, and Bulgaria attacked the Greek and Serbian forces in Macedonia. Thereupon Montenegro, Rumania, Turkey, Greece and Serbia combined to defeat Bulgaria. The Treaty of Bucharest, which ended this war in 1913, ceded central and northern Macedonia to Serbia, southern Macedonia to Greece and a small portion of eastern Macedonia to Bulgaria.

On the outbreak of World War I the Serbians resisted the Austrian invasion successfully until 1915, when Bulgaria joined the Central Powers. Under combined German-Austrian-Bulgarian pressures, the Serbian defense collapsed and Belgrade fell on October 9, 1915. The Serbians retreated toward the Adriatic, reaching Corfu, where they established a government that lasted from 1916 to the end of the war.

The war gave a powerful impetus to the idea of a federation of southern Slavic states known as Yugoslavia (from *yugo*, south). In 1917 the Yugoslav Committee, representing all the nationalities and the Serbian government of Nikola Pasic, issued the Declaration of Corfu, calling for such a state, presenting the Allies with a united front on the issue. On December 1, 1918, Alexander, king of Serbia, officially proclaimed in Belgrade the formation of the Kingdom of the Serbs, Croats and Slovenes. The treaties of Saint-Germain, Neuilly, Trianon and Rappallo granted most of Yugoslavia's territorial demands with the exception of Scutari and parts of Carinthia, Istria, Styria and Fiume. Yugoslavia had a population of 11.984 million in 1918, making it the 10th-largest nation in Europe.

The new state brought together five peoples (Croats, Slovenes, Serbs, Montenegrins and Macedonians) of three different religions (Catholic, Orthodox and Muslim) living in eight historical provinces (Croatia, Slovenia, Dalmatia, Vojvodina, Bosnia and Herzegovina, Serbia, Montenegro, and Macedonia) speaking three different languages (Serbo-Croatian, Slovenian and Macedonian) and using two alphabets (Latin and Cyrillic). The complexity of this arrangement was reflected in the Constituent Assembly, which took two years, from 1919 to 1921, to pass a new constitution, the so-called Vidovdan Constitution. This constitution was suspended in 1929 by the king, who then imposed a personal dictatorship until 1931. The greatest accomplishment of the regime was one of the most far-reaching agrarian reforms in Europe in the 1920s. In foreign policy the king joined with Rumania, Greece and Turkey to create the Little Entente, directed against the revisionist powers Bulgaria and Hungary.

On October 9, 1934, on his arrival in Marseille, France, the king was assassinated by IMRO. The heir apparent, Peter Karadjordevic, was only 11 years old at the time, and in accordance with the royal will, his cousin Prince Paul was appointed regent.

On the outbreak of World War II the Yugoslav government tried to steer clear of involvement. But faced with an ultimatum from Hitler and being at the mercy of the Axis Powers, Yugoslavia signed a protocol at Vienna in 1941 joining the Nazi camp. In Belgrade the news of the event provoked a strong reaction from the public and the army. A group of officers staged a coup, arrested the government, deposed the regent and proclaimed Peter II king. The German response was an immediate attack on Yugoslavia without even a declaration of war. The Yugoslav Army was ill prepared for war. Its 30 divisions were no match for the 52 German, Italian and Hungarian invading divisions, of which two-fifths were armored and fully motorized. The war started with a massive air strike against Belgrade on April 6, 1941, and a land attack from Bulgaria into Macedonia on April 7. German forces converged from both north and south. The Italians attacked Slovenia and the Dalmatian coast. On April 15 the Yugoslav High Command was captured near Sarajevo, and two days later Yugoslavia capitulated. The country was partitioned among the Axis

Powers with the exception of a puppet state in Croatia headed by leader Ante Pavelic of Ustashi, a political group there.

In Serbia a group of officers of the former Yugoslav Royal Army led by Col. Draza Mihailovic refused to surrender and established a center of resistance in western Serbia. Calling his guerrillas Cetniks after the anti-Ottoman guerrillas of the Middle Ages, Mihailovic adopted Fabian tactics against the Germans. On the contrary, the Communists organized their own guerrilla forces, whose objective was to wage all-out attack on the Germans. Named the National Army of Liberation and the Partisan Detachments of Yugoslavia, the Communist forces were led by Josip Broz, surnamed Tito, who had fought in the Austro-Hungarian Army and later in the Red Army and had been named general secretary of the Yugoslav Communist Party by the Comintern. In 1942 Tito summoned from throughout Yugoslavia a conference of representatives that proclaimed itself the Anti-Fascist Council for the National Liberation of Yugoslavia; the Communist-led National Liberation Front was part of this organization.

Until the summer of 1943 the Partisans survived militarily with great difficulty the combined pressures of the Germans, Italians, Ustashi and Cetniks. The surrender of Italy in June 1943 dramatically changed the entire situation. The Partisans were able to secure most of the war matériel left by the retreating Italians, and after June 1943 the Partisans virtually controlled all of the former Italian zone. Mihailovic's unwillingness to fight the Germans put him at odds with the Allies, and the aid he received from them was diverted to the Partisans. In 1944, under British pressure, the royal government of King Peter declared its willingness to collaborate with the provisional government that had been established by Tito with himself as prime minister. Peter's prime minister, Ivan Subasic, met with Tito on the island of Vis and signed an agreement that provided the legal basis for the creation of a new and democratic government in postwar Yugoslavia. The Partisan position was strengthened even more during the last months of 1944. On October 20, 1944, Belgrade was liberated by Soviet troops, and the provisional government moved into the national capital. The Yalta Conference of February 1945 endorsed the Communist-led regime.

The Communists, still preferring to be known as the National Liberation Front, to delude the Western Allies, organized elections in November 1945 that they contested under the name the People's Front. The election, in which none of the other parties participated, ended predictably in the overwhelming victory of Communist candidates. On November 29, 1945, the Constituent Assembly abolished the monarchy and proclaimed the Federal People's Republic of Yugoslavia, and on January 31, 1946, unanimously approved a new Constitution modeled on the Constitution of 1936 of the USSR. Titoist Yugoslavia had become a reality.

For postwar events, see Chronology.

CONSTITUTION & GOVERNMENT

Yugoslavia, like Czechoslovakia, was an artificial creation following World War I. The new Kingdom of the

Serbs, Croats and Slovenes, with King Alexander as head, was a conglomerate. In addition to these major nations, it contained Montenegro, Bosnia-Herzegovina, part of Macedonia and various other ethnic (e.g., Albanian, Hungarian) and religious (Catholic, Orthodox, Muslim) groups. In this heterogeneous state, however, the Constituent Assembly proclaimed in 1921 a centralized constitution that the Croatian delegation refused to endorse. The Serb-Croatian conflict was the most serious but not the only problem during the interwar period.

The period before 1929 was marked by Serbian political control, numerous government changes, an ineffective legislature and unresolved problems. Croatia withdrew from Parliament in 1928 following the assassination of its leader there. In 1929 King Alexander dissolved the legislature and abolished the Constitution. He assumed dictatorial power and renamed the state the Kingdom of Yugoslavia. Croatian reaction was particularly bitter. In 1931 Alexander proclaimed a new Constitution and restored the Parliament but his power was not diminished. Following Alexander's assassination in 1934, Prince Paul became regent, continuing the problem-ridden system, including Serb domination, but shifting toward Nazi Germany. With the approach of war, Croatia was given a measure of autonomy.

In the spring of 1941 Paul was deposed by Serbian military leaders and exiled. Alexander's 17-year-old son Peter became king, and a new government was organized. However, the German-led invasion of Yugoslavia in April 1941 forced Peter and the government into exile. Yugoslavia was partitioned and a pro-Nazi separatist leadership declared Croatian independence under German and Italian domination.

Following the war Yugoslavia, led by Marshal Josip Broz Tito, was reestablished, still with a heterogeneous population but a coalition government. Communist-engineered national elections in 1945, however, resulted in a Constituent Assembly that, in November 1945, abolished the monarchy and proclaimed the Federal People's Republic of Yugoslavia and on January 31, 1946, a new Constitution patterned on the Soviet model. This Constitution departed from the prewar document in establishing a federal system of six republics: Serbia, Croatia, Slovenia, Bosnia-Herzegovina, Montenegro and Macedonia. The autonomous provinces of Vojvodina and Kosovo were given constitutional recognition within Serbia.

Autonomy had been a highly desired quest, and this Constitution provided for federalism and equality of all the republics. The bicameral People's Assembly included the Council of Nationalities, with 30 delegates from each republic and 20 each from the provinces of Vojvodina and Kosovo. As in Moscow, the Assembly elected a Presidium, which in turn appointed a Council of Ministers or government. The republics repeated the federal system, with people's committees functioning on local levels. The Constitution of 1946 ended Serbian domination of the government, but dominant power continued, now exercised by the Communist Party, led by the strong-willed Tito. Following Yugoslavia's expulsion from the Cominform in 1948, "Titoism" replaced the Stalin-type system with the 1953 amendments to the

fundamental law. Ideologically the new law elevated the state to a "socialist democracy," with emphasis on worker-management, which was particularly meaningful at lower levels. The emphasis on workers was reflected in the Federal People's Assembly, which now consisted of the Council of Producers as well as the Federal Council. Executive and administrative powers were separated, with the creation of the office of the president of the republic, as head of state, and the Federal Executive Council (FEC), appointed by the Assembly.

In 1963 a new Constitution was promulgated; it reflected the developing changes in the country, as did its subsequent amendments. The state became known as the Socialist Federal Republic of Yugoslavia (Socijalisticka Federativna Republika Jugoslavija, SFRY). For the first time the League of Communists of Yugoslavia (Savez Komunista Jugoslavije, LCY) was cited as a "leading organized force" and the Socialist Alliance of the Working People of Yugoslavia (Socijalisticki Savez Radnog Naroda Jugoslavije, SAWPY) as the "broadest base of social-political activity and social self-government" in the country. The legislature, now called the Federal Assembly, was again reorganized, with the termination of the Council of Producers, and consisted of the Federal Chamber with the Chamber of Nationalities, and a second body of four specialized chambers to represent the working sectors.

The 1968 amendments significantly changed the character of the Assembly with the abolition of the Federal Chamber and the elevation of the Chamber of Nationalities to assume its responsibilities; the other chambers also were restructured. A 1969 amendment discarded the vice presidency and established four-year terms for all chambers and a limit of two consecutive terms.

Under the Constitution of 1963 the president, as head of state, retained his considerable power, and the composition of the Federal Executive Council was to reflect the country's national structure. The Council's policies were implemented by various federal administrative organs. However, because of numerous amendments, a new Constitution was promulgated on February 21, 1974. It is an expansive document consisting of basic principles and 406 articles detailing the country's social system, relations within the federation, rights and duties of the federation, organization of the federation, the amending process and transitional and concluding provisions. The federal legislative body was renamed the Assembly of Yugoslavia (see Parliament), and the functions of the president, the FEC and the federal administrative agencies remained the same.

Given the lengthy Constitution, amendments and developments, there is consensus in Yugoslavia for a new, less voluminous constitution to reflect political pluralism and market economy. On September 11, 1989, the LCY announced that the new constitution should "abandon the provision that the party has the leading ideological and political role in society."

The executive branch consists of the president, the Federal Executive Council and the administrative agencies. Because Marshal Tito occupied that office, the president possessed enormous power, not due to the

Constitution but because of his prestige dating to World War II and his international standing. A chapter in the Constitution was devoted to Tito as president "for an unlimited term of office." The president was formally elected by the Assembly of Yugoslavia. He was the president of the republic and of the presidency of the SFRY. He was head of state, commander in chief of the armed forces and chairman of the Council for National Defense. The president represented Yugoslavia at home and abroad, promulgated federal statutes by decree and the election of the FEC, appointed Yugoslav diplomats and received foreign diplomats, determined danger of war and informed the Assembly of domestic and foreign policies. He could delegate authority to the vice president. This phase of decades of one-man rule came to an end with Tito's death on May 4, 1980.

Immediately following Tito's demise, the vice president of the presidency, a Montenegrin, became president. The position of president, as it was under Tito, was abolished according to a provision in the Constitution. Tito intended to preclude a debilitating leadership struggle with the SFRY presidency, the executive and policy-setting body and the collective head of state. Probably the most powerful government body, the presidency consists of nine members—one representative from each republic and autonomous province, and the ex officio president of the LCY, who heads its Presidium for one year. Presidency members are elected by republic and provincial assemblies, in joint session, to a five-year term but for not more than two consecutive terms. Their election is announced by the Assembly. The new president and vice president are elected every year on May 15 from among the eight regular presidency members, on a rotating basis as stipulated in its Rules of Procedure.

The presidency represents Yugoslavia at home and abroad; commands the armed forces; proposes foreign and domestic policies to the Assembly; recommends the appointment of the president and members to the Federal Executive Council; promulgates federal laws by issuing decrees; proposes the president and judges of the Constitutional Court; appoints and receives diplomats; appoints and promotes generals, admirals and other officers; and grants pardons. The president is authorized to represent the collective presidency in the exercise of these various functions, including chairmanship of the Council for National Defense. If the Assembly and the presidency are unable to meet, the president of the presidency is empowered to declare war.

Following Tito's death, the successive presidents have been from: Montenegro (1981), Serbia (1982), Croatia (1983), Montenegro (1984), Vojvodina (1985), Kosovo (1986), Macedonia (1987), Bosnia-Herzegovina (1988) and Slovenia (1989). The April 2, 1989, elections in Slovenia were unprecedented in Yugoslavia. By direct, secret ballot the general electorate, rather than constitutionally stipulated officials, elected Janez Drnovsek, an economist, to represent Slovenia on the presidency and, because it was Slovenia's turn, to be the next president. On April 9 Montenegro followed suit, but these were the only two republics to hold direct public elections. Moreover, the Slovenes were given a choice of two candidates and the Montenegrins three. The multicandidate elections were symptomatic of political pluralism developing in Yugoslavia, especially in Slovenia.

The Federal Executive Council is the executive organ of, and is responsible to, the Assembly of Yugoslavia. The FEC, elected from among Assembly members, consists of a president (equivalent to a prime minister or premier, and the head of government), Council members, federal secretaries, and administrative officials specified by statute. The Council members are elected on the principle of equal representation of the republics and provinces. According to the Constitution of 1974 the president of the FEC is proposed by the presidency and elected by both chambers of the Assembly of Yugoslavia, while the members are proposed by the president of the FEC and approved by the Assembly. No president of the FEC can be elected to more than two consecutive terms. However, a 1981 constitutional amendment reduced this to one term, and all members, including the FEC's president, were to be nominated by SAWPY, the mass organization of political and social organizations and of individuals. SAWPY, with a membership of over half the population, is controlled by the LCY.

A new Council is elected every four years by the new Assembly. Following the May 1986 elections, the FEC consisted of 29 members, with Branko Mikulic as its president. Equal representation on the FEC is achieved by each republic electing two members (secretaries) and each province one; fourteen members are appointed by the FEC's president following consultations with party, government and other organizations. The FEC's constitutional responsibilities are to:

• propose internal and foreign policies to the Assembly of Yugoslavia
• propose laws to the Assembly
• determine social plans
• adopt the federal budget and ensure its implementation
• enforce federal statutes by decrees and regulations
• ensure execution of the Assembly's policies
• ensure execution of defense policy and provide for defense preparedness
• ratify international treaties if not within the Assembly's competence
• direct and supervise the functions of the administrative agencies
• lay down principles of organization of federal administrative agencies and provide resources
• establish diplomatic missions
• conduct any other affairs specified by the Constitution

In the first election (1982) following Tito's death, the president of the federal presidency proposed and the Assembly of Yugoslavia elected Milka Planinc, a Croat, as president of the FEC for a four-year term. She was Yugoslavia's first woman head of government. Planinc

ORGANIZATION OF YUGOSLAV GOVERNMENT

Federal Executive Council (FEC)

Coordinating Commission of the FEC

Interrepublican Committees (with the Executive Councils of the Republics and Provinces) for:

Development Policy
Monetary System
Foreign Trade and Foreign Exchange
Market
Finance

Committees of the FEC for:

Questions of Foreign Migration
Veterans' Affairs
Tourism
Science, Technology, Education, and Culture

Mixed Committees and Commissions for:

Economic and other Forms of Cooperation with Twenty-one Foreign Countries

Permanent Commissions of the FEC for:

Nuclear Energy
The Social Order
Social Planning and Development
Current Social and Economic Policy
Foreign Economic Relations
Sociopolitical and Organizational Questions
Foreign Affairs
Defense Readiness and Social Self-Protection
Cooperation with Developing Countries
Peaceful Use of Outer Space
Cadres Questions
Budget Questions
Production and Marketing of Weapons and Military Equipment
Relations with Religious Communities

Permanent Commissions of the FEC for Cooperation with:

COMECON
EEC and EFTA
OECD

Federal Organs of Administration

Federal Secretariats for:
Foreign Affairs
National Defense
Internal Affairs
Foreign Trade
Markets and Prices — Federal Directorate for Strategic Reserves / Federal Market Inspectorate / Federal Institute for Prices / Federal Directorate for Food Reserves / Federal Directorate for Reserves of Industrial Products
Justice and Organization of Federal Administration
Finance — Federal Foreign Currency Inspectorate
Information

Federal Committees for:
Social Planning
Energy and Industry
Transportation and Communications — Federal Administration for Civil Aviation / Federal Administration for Rapid Communications
Tourism
Economic Cooperation with Developing Countries
Labor and Employment — Federal Bureau for Employment Affairs
Veterans and Disabled Veterans
Health and Social Welfare
Science and Culture
Agriculture

Federal Organizations

Federal Institutes for:
Social Planning
International Scientific, Educational, Cultural, and Technical Cooperation
Statistics
Hydro-Meteorology
Standardization
Patents
Measures and Precious Metals
Geology

Federal Directorates for:
Free Trade Zone

Yugoslav Commissions for Cooperation with:
UNESCO
UNICEF
WHO
ILO
FAO

Federal Constitutional Court — Regional Constitutional Courts

Federal Supreme Court — Regional Supreme Courts — Local (Communal) Courts

Organization of the Federal Executive Council and Federal Administrative Agencies

was followed in 1986 by Branko Mikulic, also a Croat but from Bosnia-Herzegovina. Nevertheless, this appointment by SAWPY and the presidency was criticized by some as a violation of the rotation process.

Aside from the sensitivity of equal national representation in the federal governmental structure, the overlapping responsibilities of the presidency and the FEC have proved to be a continuing problem, especially in the economic sphere, despite the Constitution's five articles devoted to the relations between the Assembly of Yugoslavia and the Council. Although the party is the final arbiter, and all high-echelon officials are LCY members, other factors, such as ethnicity, have contrib-

uted to intraparty controversies over political pluralism and economic ills.

The Constitution in Chapter V provides for federal administrative agencies that are responsible to the Assembly of Yugoslavia and the FEC. Federal secretariats are established for the administration of specific areas determined by law. Other administrative federal agencies, including educational and professional institutions, may be organized. Federal secretaries and officials heading administrative agencies are members of the FEC and are appointed by the Assembly for a four-year term; they can be reappointed and, in exceptional cases, reappointed for a third term.

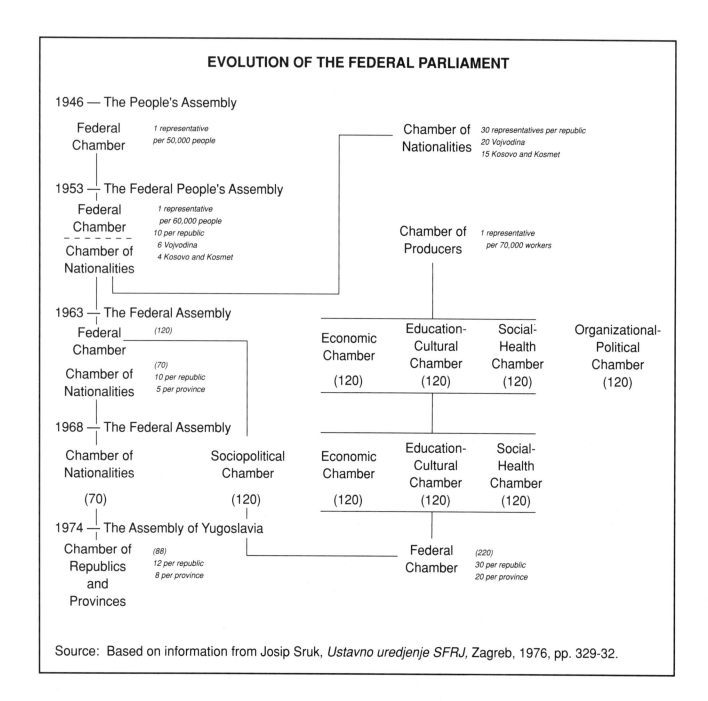

EVOLUTION OF THE FEDERAL PARLIAMENT

1946 — The People's Assembly

Federal Chamber — *1 representative per 50,000 people*

Chamber of Nationalities — *30 representatives per republic / 20 Vojvodina / 15 Kosovo and Kosmet*

1953 — The Federal People's Assembly

Federal Chamber — *1 representative per 60,000 people / 10 per republic / 6 Vojvodina / 4 Kosovo and Kosmet*

Chamber of Nationalities

Chamber of Producers — *1 representative per 70,000 workers*

1963 — The Federal Assembly

Federal Chamber — *(120)*

Chamber of Nationalities — *(70) / 10 per republic / 5 per province*

Economic Chamber (120)

Education-Cultural Chamber (120)

Social-Health Chamber (120)

Organizational-Political Chamber (120)

1968 — The Federal Assembly

Chamber of Nationalities (70)

Sociopolitical Chamber (120)

Economic Chamber (120)

Education-Cultural Chamber (120)

Social-Health Chamber (120)

1974 — The Assembly of Yugoslavia

Chamber of Republics and Provinces — *(88) / 12 per republic / 8 per province*

Federal Chamber — *(220) / 30 per republic / 20 per province*

Source: Based on information from Josip Sruk, *Ustavno uredjenje SFRJ,* Zagreb, 1976, pp. 329-32.

The overwhelming political, social and especially economic problems that plagued his entire tenure contributed to the resignation of Prime Minister Mikulic and his entire cabinet on December 30, 1988, another first under Communist rule. On January 19, 1989, Ante Markovic, a Croat, was selected president of the FEC. He and his FEC members were elected (confirmed) by the Assembly of Yugoslavia on March 16, 1989. In mid-1989 the FEC consisted of its president; two deputy presidents; three members (secretaries or ministers without portfolio); and 12 federal secretaries (or ministers) for agriculture, development, internal trade, energy and industry, finance, foreign affairs, foreign economic relations, internal affairs, legal and administrative affairs, labor and labor relations, national defense, and transportation and communications. There were, in addition, chairmen of federal committees.

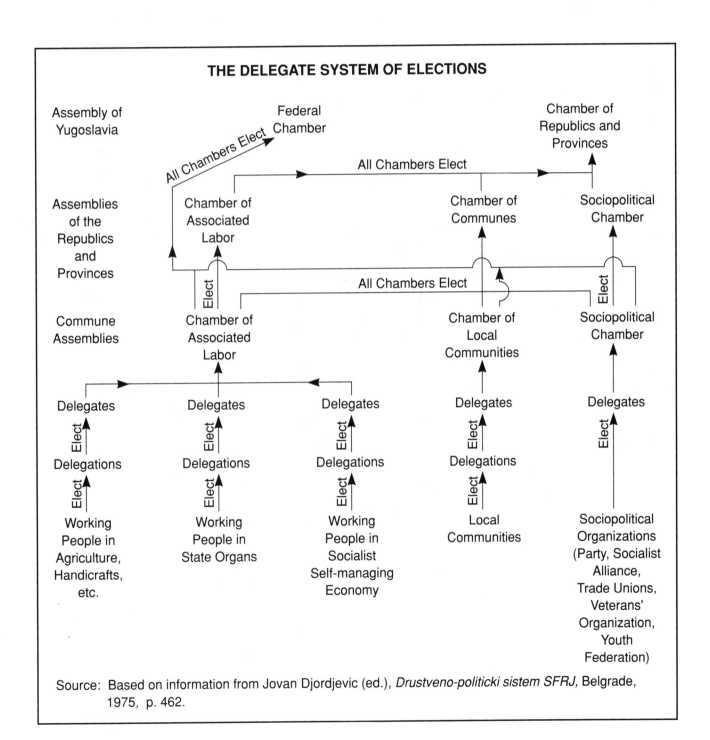

THE DELEGATE SYSTEM OF ELECTIONS

Source: Based on information from Jovan Djordjevic (ed.), *Drustveno-politicki sistem SFRJ,* Belgrade, 1975, p. 462.

FORMAL STRUCTURE OF THE LEAGUE OF COMMUNISTS OF YUGOSLAVIA

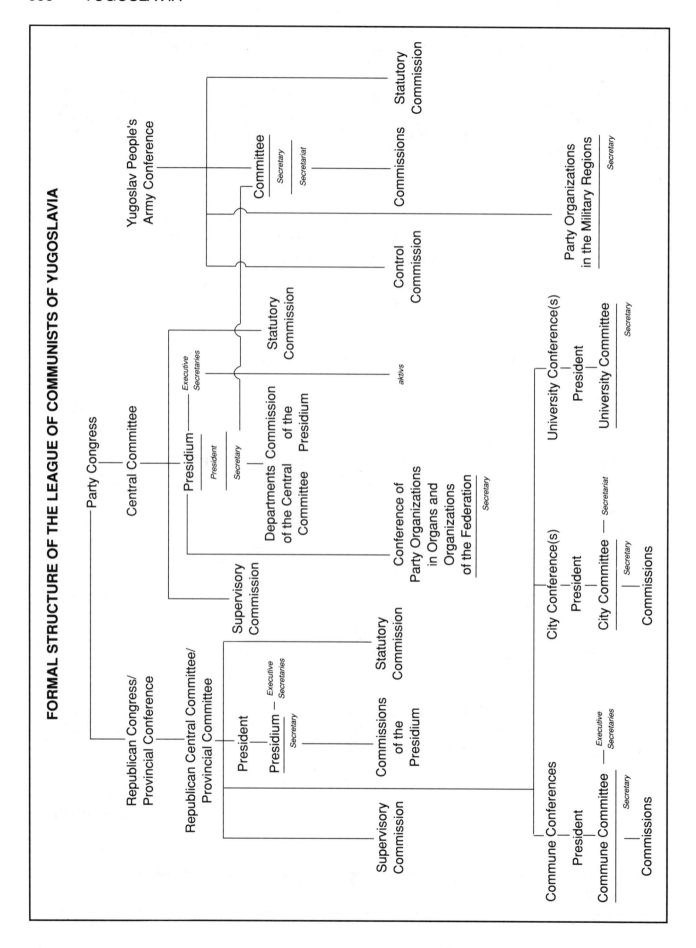

RULERS OF YUGOSLAVIA

Kings (from 1918)

December 1918–August 1921: Peter I

August 1921–October 1934: Alexander

October 1934–April 1941: Peter II (regent, 1934–41, Prince Paul)

April 1941–October 1944: Country occupied by Germany and divided

November 1944–December 1945: Peter II (regency council)

Presidents (from 1945)

President of the Presidium of the National Assembly, 1945–53; president of the federal presidency since 1971

December 1945–January 1953: Ivan Ribar

January 1953–May 1980: Josip Broz-Tito

May 1980: Lazar Kolisevski

May 1980–May 1981: Cvijetin Mijatovic

May 1981–May 1982: Sergej Krajger

May 1982–May 1983: Petar Stambolic

May 1983–May 1984: Mika Spiljak

May 1984–May 1985: Veselin Djuranovic

May 1985–May 1989: Radovan Vlajkovic

May 1989–May 1990: Janez Drnovsek

May 1990–   : Borisav Jovic

Prime Ministers (from 1918)

President of the Federal Executive Council since 1963

December 1918–August 1919: Stojan Protic (Radical Party)

August 1919–February 1920: Ljubomir Davidovic (Democratic Party)

February–May 1920: Stojan Protic (Radical Party)

May 1920–January 1921: Milenko Vesnic

January 1921–July 1924: Nikola Pasic (Radical Party)

July–October 1924: Ljubomir Davidovic (Democratic Party)

November 1924–April 1926: Nikola Pasic (Radical Party)

April 1926–April 1927: Nikola Uzunovic (Radical Party)

April 1927–January 1929: Velja Vukicevic (Radical Party)

January 1929–April 1932: Petar Zivkovic

April–June 1932: Vojislav Marinkovic

July 1932–January 1934: Milan Serskic

January–December 1934: Nikola Uzunovic

December 1934–June 1935: Bogoljub Jevtic

June 1935–February 1939: Milan Stojadinovic (Yugoslav Radical Union)

February 1939–March 1941: Dragisa Cvetkovic

March–April 1941: Dusan Simovic

April 1941–October 1944: Country occupied by Germany and divided

November 1944–January 1945: Ivan Subasic

January–March 1945: Drago Marusic

April 1945–January 1953: Josip Broz-Tito

January 1953–June 1963: Post abolished

June 1963–May 1967: Petar Stambolic

May 1967–May 1969: Mika Spiljak

May 1969–July 1971: Mitja Ribicic

July 1971–January 1977: Djemal Bijedic

February 1977–May 1982: Veselin Djuranovic

May 1982–May 1986: Milka Planinc

May 1986–December 1988: Branko Mikulic

January 1989–   : Ante Markovic

CABINET LIST

President: Janez Drnovsek

Vice President: Borisav Jovic

Member, Presidency: Bogic Bogicevic

Member, Presidency: Nenad Bucin

Member, Presidency: Janez Drnovsek

Member, Presidency: Borisav Jovic

Member, Presidency: Riza Sapundziju

Member, Presidency: Stipe Suvar

Member, Presidency: Vasil Tupurkovski

Member, Presidency: Dragutin Zelenovic

President, Federal Executive Council: Ante Markovic

Vice President, Federal Executive Council: Aleksandar Mitrovic

Vice President, Federal Executive Council: Zivko Pregl

Member, Federal Executive Council: Radisa Gacic

Member, Federal Executive Council: Nikola Gasevski

Member, Federal Executive Council: Petar Gracanin

Member, Federal Executive Council: Franc Horvat

Member, Federal Executive Council: Veljko Kadijevic

Member, Federal Executive Council: Vlado Kambovski

Member, Federal Executive Council: Budimir Loncar

Member, Federal Executive Council: Bozidar Marendic

Member, Federal Executive Council: Stevo Mirjanic

Member, Federal Executive Council:

Member, Federal Executive Council: Nazmi Mustafa

Member, Federal Executive Council: Branimir Pajkovic

Member, Federal Executive Council: Steven Santo

Member, Federal Executive Council: Joze Slokar

Member, Federal Executive Council: Branko Zekan

Member, Federal Executive Council: Veselin Vukotic

Federal Secretary for Agriculture: Stevo Mirjanic

Federal Secretary for Development: Bozidar Marendic

Federal Secretary for Economic Relations with Foreign Countries: Franc Horvat

Federal Secretary for Energy and Industry: Steven Santo

Federal Secretary for Finance: Branko Zekan

Federal Secretary for Foreign Affairs: Budimir Loncar

Federal Secretary for Internal Affairs: Petar Gracanin

Federal Secretary for Justice and Administration: Vlado Kambovski

Federal Secretary for Labor, Health, Veterans' Questions and Social Welfare: Radisa Gacic

Federal Secretary for National Defense: Veljko Kadijevic

Federal Secretary for Trade: Nazmi Mustafa

Federal Secretary for Transportation and Communication: Joze Slokar

Governor, National Bank of Yugoslavia: Dusan Vlatkovic

FREEDOM & HUMAN RIGHTS

Yugoslavia was one of the earliest countries in Eastern Europe to make the transition from the Stalinist political and economic model to that of a gentler and kinder form of socialism without in any way altering the bases or ideology of the state. Relaxation of central controls is particularly marked in the economy, where a system of self-management has been functioning successfully for over two decades. More than 75% of the housing and 85% of agricultural land is privately owned—among the highest percentages in the Eastern bloc—and there is a growing number of private enterprises in services and small-scale manufacturing, particularly in Croatia and Slovenia. Political decentralization varies from republic to republic. Slovenia is perhaps the most liberal. In other republics a more authoritarian climate prevails, and political and civil liberties continue to be circumscribed in varying degrees. Arrests for "hostile propaganda" are common in Kosovo Province, where ethnic Albanians accused of separatism and nationalism are the primary victims. On the other hand, more political issues are openly discussed and more public demonstrations are held without official interference. Public criticism has contributed to the removal of many party leaders, and the corruption of some officials has been exposed and punished. The media also are more vigorous. The well-known dissident Milovan Djilas is able to speak and publish. The role of the League of Communists of Yugoslavia is publicly debated. A Helsinki Watch Group continues to operate as also a human rights committee in Slovenia and a human rights forum at the federal level.

Although torture is constitutionally forbidden, there are reports from former prisoners that people are sometimes mistreated, beaten or threatened during pretrial detention, while serving sentences or while being questioned as possible witnesses. However, unwarranted use of force is not officially condoned.

Yugoslav criminal procedures are based on Napoleonic Law and are generally followed in all, including political, cases. Arrests are conducted pursuant to warrants, and defendants usually are brought before a judge within 24 hours of arrest. Generally, bail is not allowed in political cases. Defendants in civilian courts have the right to independent counsel. The law permits pretrial detention of up to three months, with a further three-month extension in some cases. Access to prisoners in pretrial detention may sometimes be restricted. Persons charged with misdemeanors may be summarily tried and sentenced by administrative courts to up to six months in prison.

The Criminal Code defines a number of criminal acts generally referred to as political crimes. They include not only armed rebellion, terrorism and espionage, as in most countries, but also some broad, imprecise categories such as "hostile propaganda"; arousing national, religious and racial hatred, dissension and intolerance; and damaging the reputation of Yugoslavia. In addition, the provincial and republican criminal codes cover other misdemeanors considered as political crimes, including spreading false rumors. Painting slogans unacceptable to the regime, singing nationalist songs and disturbing the peace also may be grounds for criminal prosecution, although there is wide variation in local practice. Article 133 of the Federal Criminal Code makes it illegal to advocate the overthrow of the socialist self-management system or to make malicious or untrue statements about sociopolitical conditions in the country. However, prosecution for such verbal crimes has become rare. In 1988 the authorities pardoned all prisoners convicted under Article 133. Yugoslav law also permits the arrest and imprisonment of citizens for acts considered criminal offenses even when they are committed abroad and are not crimes in the country in which they take place. The law is directed against the expression of views inimical to the regime and association with antiregime emigre groups.

Although all trials are public and held according to established legal norms, and although the judges have a measure of independence, party officials can and do influence the outcome of some, particularly political, trials. The "moral-political" suitability tests imposed for the election of judges make them susceptible to political or personal influence. Although all defendants have the right to be present at their trials and to be represented by an attorney at public expense, if necessary, authorities sometimes intimidate or chastise attorneys who take political cases. The Constitution allows trials of civilians in military courts in criminal cases relating to defense and national security. This enables the authorities to short-circuit legal procedures, hold the trials in secret and deny the defendants legal counsel.

It is difficult to determine the precise number of political prisoners in Yugoslavia because official statistics treat them as ordinary criminals. The best unofficial estimates place their number at 500 to 1,000, including some 250 prisoners of conscience. In its 1988 report Amnesty International noted that 1,500 ethnic Albanians were charged with political crimes between 1981 and 1987 and a further 6,650 were summarily sentenced for up to six months in prison for political misdemeanors.

Arbitrary interference in private life occurs most often in connection with government efforts to monitor opposition or dissident activity. Judicial safeguards against arbitrary searches sometimes are ignored. Authorities may eavesdrop on conversations, read private mail and tap telephones. Citizens generally are free to receive and read foreign publications, except those published by some Yugoslav emigre groups.

The most important threats to freedom of speech and press are the provisions of the Criminal Code against hostile propaganda and verbal crimes. These provisions are invoked more often in provinces where nationalist activities are extensive. However, press autonomy has increased significantly in recent years, and the range of criticisms now permitted was unthinkable in Tito's time. The Communist Party itself is no longer a sacred cow, and calls are expressed for a dismantling of its virtual monopoly of all sectors of national life. The media in any one republic or province find it easier to criticize the politics and policies of another republic but less often their own. The latitude is broad, but certain topics still are taboo—e.g., any criticism of Tito. Popular rock singer Bora Djordjevic was twice arrested (although later released) for singing a song critical of Tito.

Normally, neither the print nor the broadcast media are censored prior to dissemination of their materials. Government oversight of the media is carried out through publication boards, which include ranking party officials, and through media self-censorship. This type of control is incomplete and varies from republic to republic. There also are important informal channels of control. Editors are named through the Socialist Alliance, and a gadfly may find it difficult to secure suitable employment. Editors may be transferred from one publication to another where they may be less effective or subjected to party discipline. About 80% of journalists are Communist Party members.

Public prosecutors have the power to ban the publication and sale of books or periodicals if judicial authorities hold that the contents are "false" or could disturb the peace. Banning publications is often a local option, and standards of acceptability vary. Police and prosecutors rarely intervene. The works of Soviet and East European dissidents are published in large press runs and sold widely. In 1988 a short story and a biography by Milovan Djilas was published, the first time any work by him had appeared in the country since his fall from grace in 1954. Nevertheless, each year a number of books and periodicals make their way to the list of banned publications.

Public political demonstrations are permitted only by official organizations and generally only in support of government policies. Public gatherings and meetings of private organizations are permitted and must be registered beforehand with the authorities. Because of differing interpretations by the authorities at various levels of what constitutes a threat to public and constitutional order, some rallies and demonstrations are tolerated but others end in violence by the police. In Slovenia, new grass-roots youth and peasant organizations have been permitted that espouse programs at variance with official ideology on issues such as political reform and nuclear energy.

Although Yugoslavia is officially a Marxist state, religious believers are not subject to overt persecution. Religious proselytizing is forbidden. The open practice of a faith is a disqualification for high positions in government and business. A party member who takes part publicly in reception of sacraments of his or her church risks disciplinary action or expulsion from the party. Prisoners and active-duty military personnel are not allowed to be visited by the clergy or to attend religious services, except in Slovenia. Open church-state conflicts are rare. In both Slovenia and Croatia the Catholic Church has harmonious relations with the authorities, and in 1988 the formerly troubled relations between the Serbian Orthodox Church and the authorities improved dramatically as both became allies in the promotion of Serbian culture and identity. The Islamic community, however, is suspect because of its ties with Albanian nationalists on the one hand and Islamic fundamentalists on the other. The official press devotes considerable attention to religious issues, such as the apparition of the Virgin at Medjugorje, the construction of St. Sava Church in Belgrade and religious instruction in public schools. Bibles and Korans are readily available. Foreign contacts by church leaders are extensive and generally are unhindered. Muslims may go on the hajj and undergo theological training in the Middle East. Except in Vojvodina, where no new church buildings have been constructed since World War II, local authorities cooperate in the building of churches, such as the new Roman Catholic cathedral and a Serbian Orthodox church, both in Belgrade.

The churches are not totally excluded from the educational system. The Roman Catholic Church maintains eight secondary schools (about 100 pupils each), two theological faculties, and five seminaries; the Serbian Orthodox Church four high schools and one theological faculty; and the Yugoslav Islamic Association three high schools and one theological faculty.

Freedom of travel within the country is a constitutional right. Passports for foreign travel are routinely available. No exit visas are required to visit the more than 135 countries with which Yugoslavia has diplomatic or consular relations. Milovan Djilas was granted a passport in 1987 for the first time since 1957. Yugoslavia grants both permanent and temporary asylum to refugees seeking its protection.

In the absence of any official opposition parties, the limits of governmental power are subject to a variety of other political forces. The Constitution grants the six republics and the two provinces considerable influence on decision-making. With a few exceptions, no major

initiatives, including constitutional amendments, may be adopted by the federal government without the unanimous consent of the republics and the provinces. The Assembly of Yugoslavia also has been more assertive in recent years and has several times rejected or drastically altered proposals endorsed by the presidency and the Federal Executive Council. The Assembly often is the scene of sharp debates, fully reported in the press. Federal laws must be adopted separately by the provincial assemblies before they can be implemented, and the provincial assemblies wield a virtual veto over federal legislation. Recently adopted amendments to the Constitution provide for a majority of delegates to local, republic and federal assemblies to be chosen directly by their constituents through secret, multicandidate elections. In 1988 there were seven candidates in the Slovenian presidential campaign. Popular political pressures also may be effective in the form of demonstrations, which may bring down governments, as happened in Vojvodina in 1988.

Women are well represented in government. From 1982 to 1986 the head of government was a woman. Two members of the federal cabinet from 1986 to 1988 were women, and women constitute 12% of the membership of the Central Committee. Outside of government, women have not achieved significant gains in the labor market.

Officially, discrimination on the basis of race, sex, religion, language or social status is a crime, and there are constitutional guarantees safeguarding the rights of all nationalities. At the presidency level, the office of head of state rotates among all groups. However, minorities in all provinces and republics complain of some measure of mistreatment, particularly ethnic Albanians, who make up 8% of the population. In Macedonia, Albanians have complained of the downgrading of the Albanian language, and of building codes prohibiting the high walls that traditionally surround Albanian homes.

CIVIL SERVICE

The Constitution declares the League of Communists of Yugoslavia (LCY) to be "the leading organized ideological and political force" of the country. Accordingly, the LCY exercises ultimate executive power at the federal, republic and lower levels throughout the Yugoslav governmental structure. The LCY has its own bureaucracy, operating at all levels of administration. In Yugoslavia, as elsewhere in Eastern Europe, there is no comparable Office of Personnel Management such as that servicing the Executive branch of the U.S. government nor is the term "civil service" in use. The Federal Executive Council establishes general principles for internal organization of federal administrative agencies. The latter conduct administrative affairs in specific sectors, their responsibilities regulated by federal statutes through federal secretariats, committees and other organs.

The LCY's Central committee secretariat is deeply involved in appointments on the federal level and comparable party organs on the republic, provincial and lower levels. Each government secretariat, committee and other organs has a personnel office. Following application to a particular secretariat or committee, the applicant is interviewed and tested. An office of the Federal Executive Council processes employee transfers.

Yugoslavia has no academic institution specifically to prepare students for public service. The normal sources are the universities (best known are Ljubljana, Zagreb, Belgrad, Sarajevo and Skopje), colleges, technical institutes and secondary schools. The secretariats and committees on the federal, republic, provincial and lower levels maintain contact with educational institutions regarding employment in government. The government organizations conduct training programs for their staffs with the assistance of professors, journalists, specialists and experts in particular fields such as diplomats.

Data are not available on the size of the civil service in Yugoslavia.

LOCAL GOVERNMENT

The six republics and two provinces are organized similarly to the federal government. Each has a collective presidency; an executive council; and an assembly composed of three chambers, delegates to which are elected for four-year terms through an indirect system.

The commune (*opstina*) is the basic unit of local government, and the commune assemblies, numbering over 500, are their popular organs. Each commune assembly has three chambers: a Chamber of Work Communities, composed of delegates from workers; a Chamber of Local Communities, composed of representatives from the community; and a Sociopolitical Chamber, composed of delegates from local political and other associations. The commune assembly elects an executive body with administrative responsibilities. Commune assemblies elect the delegations that comprise the assembly of the republic or province.

Local governmental structure is designed to illustrate the Yugoslav concept of decentralized, versus the Soviet concept of centralized, Marxism. According to Tito associate, Edvard Kardelj, the commune is the basic economic cell of society.

FOREIGN POLICY

Before World War I the territory that was to be Yugoslavia was coveted by the great European powers for its geostrategic position. As Yugoslavia, the new country was immediately an object of irredentism. To ensure security against border revisions, Belgrade concluded treaties with Czechoslovakia and Rumania during 1920–21 to form the Little Entente, supported by France, and in 1934 with Greece, Turkey and Rumania to form the Balkan Entente. However, neither these nor other treaties succeeded in deterring Axis aggression. Regent Prince Paul concluded agreements with Bulgaria and Italy in 1937, then signed the German-Italian-Japanese Tripartite Pact in March 1941. He was deposed, and Yugoslavia was invaded and dismembered by the Axis.

POLITICAL SUBDIVISIONS				
Socialist Republics	Capitals	Area		Population (1986 est.)
		Sq. Km.	Sq. Mi.	
Bosnia and Herzegovina	Sarajevo	51,129	19,741	4,356,000
Croatia	Zagreb	56,538	21,829	4,665,000
Macedonia	Skopje	25,713	9,928	2,041,000
Montenegro	Titograd	13,812	5,333	619,000
Serbia	Belgrade	55,968	21,609	5,803,000
Slovenia	Ljubijana	20,251	7,819	1,934,000
Provinces (in Serbia)				
Kosovo	Priština	10,887	4,203	1,804,000
Vojvodina	Novi Sad	21,506	8,304	2,049,000
TOTAL		255,804	88,766	23,271,000

As noted above, the Partisans, led by Marshal Tito, campaigned successfully but suffered staggering losses during World War II. They received support from the Western Allies beginning in 1943 and from the Soviet Union. Marshal Tito concluded an agreement with Ivan Subasic, prime minister of the royal government, in November 1944 on a coalition government that the Yalta Conference approved. This conference provided for free and unfettered elections in all East European countries. However, the future government of Yugoslavia was the Communist-controlled Anti-Fascist Council for the National Liberation of Yugoslavia (AVNOJ). Most of the country was liberated by the victorious National Liberation Army of Yugoslavia, a significant factor in Tito's future relations with Stalin. At war's end the future of Yugoslavia was interwoven with the Soviet Union. Tito became prime minister and concluded a 20-year treaty of friendship, mutual assistance and cooperation in March 1945 with Moscow, followed by similar agreements with East European countries during the next two years. Yugoslavia's enormous devastation required massive economic assistance, for which Tito's regime relied largely on the Soviet Union and Eastern Europe. However, this aid was affected by the Tito-Stalin controversy, as were Tito's discussions with Bulgaria's Dimitrov regarding a future Balkan federation. Also, Tito's involvement on behalf of Macedonian Communists in the Greek civil war came to an end.

Although postwar Yugoslav security was entrusted to the Soviet Union and Stalin was held in the highest esteem, the Tito leadership was determined to maintain an independent course, which was contrary to Stalin's ambitions of establishing control over all East European countries. Differences between the two powerful leaders emerged during the war and continued after cessation of hostilities. Belgrade opposed establishment of joint stock companies, which would have resulted in Soviet control, reorganization of its military forces along the Red Army structure and Soviet intelligence activities inside Yugoslavia. In February 1948 Tito refused Stalin's order to visit Moscow. Moscow recalled its military and civilian advisers from Yugoslavia in March 1948 as relations deteriorated with charges and countercharges in a series of letters. Soviet leaders leveled strong accusations against the Yugoslav leaders, including "deviation," whereas the latter's responses were more reasoned and conciliatory. They professed continued loyalty to the Soviet Union while continuing to rebel against Soviet interference in Yugoslavia's internal affairs. However, Stalin demanded subservience from the Yugoslav Communist Party, as he had from all others. In addition to allegations, Stalin sought to eliminate Tito from power by a series of moves, all of which ultimately failed. Stalin engineered the Yugoslav Communist Party's expulsion, without its being in attendance, from the Cominform in June 1948; instituted an economic blockade with the Eastern bloc; and even generated military activities along the Yugoslav border against the "enemy." Yugoslavia weathered these Soviet pressures, and its future course was to be entirely different from that of the other East European countries. In July 1948 the Fifth Party Congress called for relations among Communist parties on the basis of independence and equality.

Isolated from the East, Yugoslavia's alternative was to establish closer relations with Western countries. The most critical need was economic and financial assistance. Trade agreements were signed, and the United States released Yugoslav assets, extended a loan and made deliveries of surplus grain. During the 1950s Western aid amounted to about $3.5 billion, about half of it from the United States. Other aid came from UNRRA, CARE and other sources. Yugoslavia developed other relations as well. Belgrade concluded a treaty of friendship and cooperation with Greece and Turkey in February 1953 and later a military pact with them. However, consideration of Yugoslavia's adherence to the North Atlantic Treaty Organization (NATO) ended in the mid-1950s as Belgrade embarked on a different course; the nonaligned movement.

Following the expulsion of the Yugoslav Communist Party from the Cominform, the Soviet bloc, according to Belgrade, broke off 46 political, economic, cultural exchanges and other treaties, on top of the trade embargo. Subsequently, relations with the Soviet Union and its satellites fluctuated. After Stalin's death in 1953, Soviet leader Nikita Khrushchev sought to improve relations. Diplomatic missions were elevated to embassies as criticism of Tito lessened and later ceased. In 1955 Khrushchev and Premier Nikolai Bulganin traveled to Belgrade, where the Soviet leader admitted Soviet responsibility for the earlier breach. Their joint declaration called for respect for sovereignty, independence, integrity, equality of states, noninterference in internal affairs and recognition of different roads to socialism. Moreover, they rejected aggression and political and economic domination. During the 1956 Hungarian uprising Tito first opposed interference in Hungarian affairs, but as events escalated, he supported Moscow's military suppression of the revolution. In 1957, Belgrade recognized East Germany.

However, another Soviet-Yugoslav controversy developed when, in 1957, Khrushchev disseminated a document on Communist unity in which he condemned revisionism, a clear reference to Tito's independent Communist course. This led to another cycle of ideological controversy and suspension of Soviet credit, but no diplomatic rupture. Relations between the Soviet bloc and Yugoslavia, while not particularly friendly, continued as they had with the Western world. As a result, Belgrade benefited from both and leaned toward Moscow in support of its policies, such as over Berlin and Communist China's membership in the United Nations. Tito used the nonaligned movement as a forum. However, he approved Alexander Dubcek's program and denounced the Soviet-led Warsaw Pact invasion of Czechoslovakia in August 1968, as well as the "Brezhnev Doctrine." Tito's position regarding Moscow's aggression in Afghanistan in 1979 was the same.

Whatever the ideological or political relations with Belgrade, the Soviet leaders have not again resorted to an economic boycott of Yugoslavia; on the contrary, economic relations between Yugoslavia and the Soviet bloc have been generally favorable. In April 1963 Yugoslavia was given associate status with the CMEA. Belgrade's exports to CMEA countries reached 42% in 1965 and imports 31% but fell to 31% and 24%, respectively, in 1969. Both exports and imports increased during the 1970s. In 1980 Yugoslavia concluded a 10-year economic agreement with the Soviet Union, increasing their trade cooperation substantially. In 1988 the USSR was Yugoslavia's most important trading partner, but its second and third major countries were West Germany and Italy, respectively.

The nonaligned movement became an important factor in Yugoslavia's foreign policy. Tito's ambition was to create a doctrine for new international relations. He was a cofounder of the movement with Nehru, Nasser, Sukarno and Nkrumah at the United Nations in 1960. Having rejected military alliances, Yugoslavia endeavored to organize a powerful political force of nonaligned countries. At the same time, Tito gained international stature. The First Conference of Heads of State of Governments of Nonaligned Countries was held in Belgrade in 1961. The conference, chaired by Tito, established the principles and objectives of nonalignment. Over the years the nonaligned movement served as a forum not only to promote peace but also to criticize, especially Western policies such as arms control. The most recent nonaligned conference, held in September 1989, also was hosted by Belgrade.

Yugoslavia has been an energetic participant in international affairs. It was a founding signatory of the United Nations, which it considers a necessary instrument for peace and international cooperation. At the United Nations' sixth session the Yugoslav representative served as vice president and at the 32nd as president of the General Assembly. Yugoslavia contributed a detachment to the U.N. forces in the Sinai in 1956–67. It participates in all of the United Nations' specialized agencies, among them UNESCO, IAEA, UNIDO, FAO, G-77, ILO and WHO. Also, Yugoslavia is a member of the International Monetary Fund (IMF), the World Bank, the General Agreement on Tariffs and Trade (GATT) and the Organization for Economic Cooperation and

Development (OECD), among others. The sixth UNCTAD session was held in Belgrade in 1964, and Yugoslavia was elected president of the Group of 77 (G-77) developing countries.

Belgrade maintains diplomatic relations with nearly all countries of the world. It severed diplomatic relations with Israel following the 1967 Arab-Israeli War and with Chile in 1974; Morocco broke off relations with Yugoslavia when it recognized the Democratic Arab Republic of the Sahara. Economic relations are conducted with some 140 countries. Yugoslavia has been an enthusiastic supporter of the policies of "détente," "peaceful coexistence" and East-West cooperation. Belgrade played a role in establishing the Conference on Security and Cooperation in Europe (CSCE) in 1975, hosting the first follow-up conference in 1977–78. It was one of the nine European neutral and nonaligned states promoting the principles and aims of the CSCE. Yugoslavia has a delegation at the Conventional Armed Forces in Europe (CFE) negotiations, conducted in Vienna.

U.S. involvement in Yugoslavia dates to World War I, with President Woodrow Wilson championing national self-determination. During World War II the United States delivered critically needed supplies to Tito's Partisans to continue their effective war against the Axis Powers. Since the war Washington has supported Yugoslav independence, unity and territorial integrity. In 1948 an agreement was reached on financial claims by U.S. citizens for nationalized property, paving the way for U.S. assistance following Tito's break with Stalin and the imposition of an economic boycott by the Cominform. Yugoslavia benefits from most-favored-nation tariff treatment and from the Trade and Tariff Act of 1984, providing duty-free exports to the United States. Since 1968 over 30 American firms have made capital investments in joint ventures. The Export-Import Bank and the Commodity Credit Corporation (CCC) have extended credits. During 1949–65 U.S. aid totaled $2.9 billion; economic aid ended January 1, 1967. In 1974 the two countries established the U.S.-Yugoslav Economic Council, a nongovernmental body to promote trade and investment. In 1988 the United States was Yugoslavia's fourth-largest trading partner.

Diplomatic relations with the United States have been at the embassy level, and the United States maintains a consulate general in Zagreb. Yugoslavia has consulates general in New York, Pittsburgh, Chicago and San Francisco as well as a consulate in Cleveland. For decades the United States has had the most active informational and cultural program in Yugoslavia of all East European countries. Yugoslavia is the only Communist-ruled country with an official U.S. Information Service (USIS). With the main operations center in Belgrade, the USIS has a branch office in Zagreb, and information centers have been established in Ljubljana, Skopje, Sarajevo and Titograd. Yugoslavia has a Press and Cultural Center in New York. Moreover, the two countries have one of the largest programs of exchanges in academic, cultural and scientific fields in the world. As with the USIS, Yugoslavia alone of the East European countries has a binational Fulbright Commission to conduct exchanges of students and professors. High-level visits by officials have included presidents: Tito visited the United States on three occasions, and President Richard Nixon was the first U.S. president to visit Yugoslavia.

Relations with Western countries have improved in the past two decades. Rejection of Belgrade's reparation claims by West Germany caused bitterness in Yugoslavia. The Hallstein Doctrine adopted by West Germany affected relations for 10 years. Diplomatic relations were reestablished, and many Yugoslav workers have been employed throughout West Germany, for many years. In 1988 West Germany was Belgrade's second most important trading partner.

Relations with its neighbors have reflected a wide spectrum, from excellent to poor. After the war Tito made territorial claims involving Italy, Austria, Hungary, Bulgaria, Greece and Albania. He succeeded only to a limited degree, partly, he believed, because of insufficient Soviet support. The peace treaty with Italy was concluded in February 1947, delineating their boundary and providing for the Free Territory of Trieste, which, after years of negotiations, was brought into existence in 1954. The city of Trieste was awarded to Italy. Moscow did not support Belgrade's position and did not participate in the agreement. In subsequent years Yugoslavia and Italy concluded a number of agreements involving economic relations, border crossings, exchanges and other matters. In 1988 Italy was Yugoslavia's third-largest trading partner.

Roman Catholics, especially strong in Croatia and Slovenia, make up about a third of the country's population. Thus relations with the Vatican are important. With its seizure of power the Communist Party came into immediate conflict with the church in Yugoslavia and with the Vatican. Belgrade broke off relations with the Vatican in 1952 when Archbishop Aloysius Stepinac, then under house arrest, was elevated to cardinal; he died in 1960. Relations improved gradually. They signed a protocol in 1966 and established full diplomatic relations in 1970. Relations with Austria go beyond favorable economic cooperation. Belgrade was a signatory to the 1955 State Treaty with Austria, receiving guarantees for rights of Slovenians and Croatians living in Carinthia and Burgenland, respectively.

As a Balkan country, Yugoslavia has promoted wide-ranging bilateral and multilateral relations in the area, including a proposal for a Balkan nuclear-free zone. As noted earlier, Tito supported the Communists in Macedonia during the Greek civil war, and Yugoslavia continues to have concerns over the Macedonians in that country. However, agreements with Greece and Turkey during the 1950s laid the foundation for improved relations with these non-Communist countries. Relations with Rumania have been friendly and with Hungary good. Those with Bulgaria, on the other hand, have suffered because of Sofia's policy of denying recognition to its Macedonian minority. This and Bulgaria's past territorial designs are viewed by Belgrade with alarm. The poorest bilateral relations have been with Albania, dating to 1948, over doctrinal differences but largely over Kosovo. Tirana charges the Serbs with chauvinism; Belgrade charges Albania with interference in internal affairs. As a Mediterranean country, Yugoslavia pursues cooperative relations with Middle East countries. Iraq is a major trading partner. Farther away, Belgrade has maintained favorable relations with Communist China.

PARLIAMENT

As seen in Constitution and Government, Yugoslavia has experienced numerous changes in its legislature in attempting to structure a federal body to represent the six republics and the two provinces and, at the same time, to reflect the principle of self-management. According to the Constitution the Bicameral Assembly of Yugoslavia is the supreme organ of power. It consists of the Federal Chamber and the Chamber of Republics and Provinces.

The former is composed of 30 delegates from each republic and 20 from each autonomous province, for a total of 220. The nominating procedures are implemented by SAWPY. Candidates are proposed by self-managing organizations and communities and by sociopolitical organizations. A list of candidates is then prepared by SAWPY. Delegates are elected by the communal assemblies of the republics and autonomous provinces by secret ballot. The Chamber of Republics and Provinces is composed of 12 delegates from each republican assembly and eight from each provincial assembly for a total of 88. The delegates are elected by all chambers of assemblies of the republics and autonomous provinces by secret ballot. All delegates are elected for four-year terms.

Both chambers have working bodies to prepare legislation, regulations and other measures as well as to review implementation of policies and laws. The working groups of the Chamber of Republics and Provinces are formed on the basis of equal ethnic representation. The FEC assists in the adjustment of positions on legislative drafts. The chambers establish a joint commission for elections and nominations and for other common endeavors. The Assembly of Yugoslavia and each chamber elect from their members a president and a vice president for four-year terms.

The rights and duties of the Assembly of Yugoslavia are to:

• amend the Constitution
• establish foundations of domestic and foreign policy
  • enact laws and regulations
  • adopt the federal social plan and the budget
  • decide changes of boundaries
  • decide on war and peace
  • ratify international treaties
  • formulate the policy of enforcing federal laws
  • elect the president of the republic and proclaim the election of the presidency
  • elect the president (prime minister) and members of the Federal Executive Council
  • elect the president and judges of the Constitutional Court, Federal Court and other federal officials

• supervise the work of the FEC and federal administrative agencies
• elect the president and vice president of the Assembly of Yugoslavia
• discharge other duties specified by the Constitution

The Federal Chamber decides on amendments to the Constitution; establishes the principles of internal and foreign policies; adopts federal laws and prescribes their implementation except for those passed by the Chamber of Republics and Provinces; approves the budget; decides on war and peace; ratifies international treaties; decides changes of boundaries; lays down foundations for federal agencies; supervises the work of the FEC and federal administrative agencies; grants amnesties; and discharges other duties outside the jurisdiction of the Chamber of Republics and Provinces. Normally, passage of a law requires a majority vote of members present if a majority is in session.

The Chamber of Republics and Provinces is concerned with matters within the sphere of the republics and provinces requiring their participation. Consequently, proposed laws of the Chamber of Republics and Provinces are sent to the republican and provincial assemblies for an opinion. The Chamber then prepares a final text, which is submitted to the republics and provinces. Only after consensus is obtained is there a final vote on the measure, which then requires a unanimous vote for passage. If unanimity is not achieved, a "temporary measure" can be enacted by a two-thirds vote of all Chamber members if deemed urgent. Among the specific areas requiring federal and republican provincial agreement are the Social Plan, monetary system/currency/foreign exchange, foreign trade and credit, and expenditures of the federal budget. Independently, the Chamber of Republics and Provinces also determines, on the basis of the presidency's proposal, financing the national defense if extraordinary circumstances exist; also, it reviews reports of the FEC and administrative agencies and supervises their work; and it formulates enforcement policy for federal laws, establishing implementation by federal agencies.

Although the Constitution establishes jurisdiction of rights and duties for the federation and the republics/provinces, the functioning of this system encourages pluralism. Consequently, members of the legislative bodies, while LCY members, nevertheless exercise their prerogative of articulating their views in their respective chambers. Delegates and delegations take advantage of the constitutional provision to initiate issues, question the FEC and other federal administrative agencies and make other demands. The chambers not only meet more frequently, and for longer periods, than in other Communist countries, they also frequently conduct themselves as serious deliberative institutions rather than as pro forma legislative bodies convoked to approve the party's programs.

POLITICAL PARTIES

Political parties originated in the territories that later formed Yugoslavia, during the latter 19th and early 20th centuries. The most prominent were the Liberal and Radical parties of Serbia, the Peasant Party of Croatia and Social Democratic parties in several nations. Political parties were active from the establishment of Yugoslavia in 1918. The conservative Serbian Radical Party was the strongest; the Peasant Party of Croatia, which promoted autonomy, was the most influential in Croatia. Others were the Democratic, Agrarian, Slovene People's and Muslim parties, and the Communist Party (CP). At the Unification Congress of April 20–23, 1919, in Belgrade, the Social Democratic parties of Serbia and Croatia joined with the Communists to form the Socialist Workers' Party of Yugoslavia, the predecessor to today's Communist Party. Socialists who eschewed association with the CP and rightists who were ousted by the CP in 1920 formed the Social Democratic Party, together with the Slovenian Party. However, the Social Democrats were unable to solve their numerous problems and concentrated on trade union activities.

In the multiparty system, as frequently happened in other countries, no party attracted majority support, making coalition a practical necessity. The result was an alignment of radical-democratic parties, with the cooperation of others, which together controlled the central government. Also, a serious Serbo-Croatian conflict developed. The Peasant Party of Croatia was the largest opposition party in the country. This party boycotted the Assembly because of centralization, and in 1924 was dissolved by Prime Minister Nikola Pasic, a Serb, who imprisoned its leader, Stjepan Radic, for agitating political reform. Radic was released in 1925 and soon resumed his political crusade.

Following the June 1928 assassination of Radic in the Assembly, the Croatian deputies walked out, and in 1929 King Alexander declared a dictatorship. Some political parties were outlawed and their leaders went into exile. Alexander's centrist policy led to even more radical movements, with the Ustashi demanding Croatian independence. Alexander was assassinated in 1934, and the regent, Prince Paul, continued his policies regarding political parties. Efforts toward satisfying Croatian demands failed until the approach of war prompted Paul to seek a rapprochement with Croatia. An agreement providing for autonomy was concluded with the Croatian Peasant Party in August 1939. Following the German-led invasion of Yugoslavia in 1941, Croatia declared its independence, with the Ustashi leadership under Axis domination. Yugoslavia ceased to exist.

In 1942 the Partisans, led by Tito, created the Anti-Fascist Council for the National Liberation of Yugoslavia (AVNOJ). With representatives from various "democratic" parties and ethnic and other groups, its objective was to prevent the return of King Peter and the royal government-in-exile in London. The following year AVNOJ established a provisional government, appointing Marshal Tito as prime minister. At war's end several non-Communists were included in the provisional government, but AVNOJ held a dominant position. Yalta and Allied pressure forced an increase in representation from prewar political parties and the National Assembly for the Provisional People's Assembly, as the AVNOJ became known. The Government of National Unity, with Tito as prime minister, was composed of representatives from the parties (Croatian Peasant, Serbian Democratic, Independent Democratic and Slovenian Peasant) and from the government-in-exile, but within a short time non-Communist representatives resigned because of Communist repression.

In preparation for national elections the Assembly's electoral law prohibited numerous organizations and individuals. The CP-controlled People's Front prepared a single list of candidates for the November 1945 elections. The many prohibitions and terrorist tactics led to a boycott of the elections by the opposition parties, and the Communists claimed a 96% victory. On November 25 the Constituent Assembly abolished the monarchy and proclaimed Yugoslavia a federal people's republic. On January 31, 1946, a Soviet-type Constitution was announced.

Yugoslavia, as other Communist countries, became a one-party system, with mass organizations under its control. The People's Front became the Socialist Alliance of Working People of Yugoslavia (SAWPY) in 1953, serving a useful function for the regime representing, as it does formally, various organizations it controls.

In the evolution of the CP, the First Congress of the Socialist Workers' Party of Yugoslavia voted for membership in the Communist International (Comintern), accepting its revolutionary principles. The Second Congress, held June 1920 in Vukovar, with Slovenian representatives as well, adopted the name Communist Party of Yugoslavia and a program. Among its objectives was to establish a Soviet Republic of Yugoslavia. The CP participated in the national elections held that year, scoring some local successes and sending 58 of 417 delegates to the Assembly, the third-highest number. The government seized on the abortive attempt on the life of King Alexander and the assassination of the minister of the interior in 1921 to outlaw the CP. It was illegal for the remainder of the interwar period. Thereafter, until seizing power the party was plagued by myriad problems, including ineffective leadership, factionalism, disorganization, ideological differences, police harassment, disaffection and Comintern interference.

Josip Broz (1892–1980) was son of a Croatian peasant father and a Slovenian mother. He was a former Austrian sergeant taken prisoner of war in Russia; later he joined the Bolsheviks and was secretary of the Croatian branch of the CP. Broz, who later became known as Tito, was imprisoned for five years (1928–33) and functioned in the underground. Among his other operations, "Comrade Walter" (Tito) carried out assignments for the Comintern. During its interwar illegal period, the CP was continually embroiled in intraparty strife, and the Comintern dismissed the entire Central Committee in 1932. In 1937 Tito was appointed by Stalin as secretary general of the party. A reorganization and a purge followed, and the CP appeared strengthened, overcoming possible dissolution by the Comintern. As a survivor Tito became a devoted Stalinist.

The foundations for creating a Communist state were laid within the first year of the Axis invasion and dismemberment of Yugoslavia. In 1942 the Tito-led Partisans organized AVNOJ as they fought against the foreign occupiers and the anti-Communist Cetniks. The CP employed successful tactics of promising equality for all nationalities—reminiscent of the resolutions of the Third and Fourth congresses, 1923 and 1928, thus attracting non-Communist adherents and Allied support while destroying all opposition, such as remnants of the prewar government and political parties in violation of Yalta. As early as November 1945 Communist control was nearly complete.

Although Stalin was held in reverence by Yugoslav Communists, including Tito, the Tito-Stalin dispute resulted in Yugoslavia's expulsion from the Cominform in 1948. Tito's regime survived and, isolated by the Soviet bloc, embarked on its own program, contributing "Titoism" to the world's vocabulary. The Sixth Party Congress in 1952, reduced central party control and introduced worker self-management. The party's name was changed to the League of Communists of Yugoslavia (Savez Kominista Jugoslavije, LCY). Ideologically, Tito's independent road to socialism eschewed "national" communism while professing Marxist internationalism. Neither the break with Stalin nor these innovations met with unanimous party support. Tito's most prominent adversaries were, for different reasons, Alexander Rankovic and Milovan Djilas, both considered as possible successors to him. Rankovic was leader of the Serbian CP. He opposed decentralization and was subsequently (in 1966) removed from the Central Committee (CC). Djilas, a Montenegrin and a close associate of Tito since the late 1930s, criticized the "new class" of Communists and was dismissed in 1954 for "heresy"; he was imprisoned two years later. Djilas has continued his critique of Communist behavior, of Tito and of Stalin to the present day. Also, pro-Soviet elements existed within the LCY throughout the post-1948 period, necessitating Tito's intervention in the mid-1970s.

Economic and labor conditions dictated a more extensive liberalization policy of the self-management system. During the 1960s and 1970s decentralization resulted in individual Communist parties in the six republics and the two autonomous provinces. However, demands for further political reforms escalated into open demonstrations, those in Croatia in 1971 of crisis proportions, which Tito suppressed by force. A purge of party leaders followed, not only in Croatia but in other republics as well, including Serbia. Consequently, in May 1974 the 10th Party Congress restored to primacy the LCY's power, as it was recognized in the Constitution of 1974. The party's dominant role in society continues, as it copes with overwhelming economic, social and political problems, as well as those within the party itself. The latter includes severe criticism of members' party-mindedness. LCY ideologist Edvard Kardelj, a Slovenian and party leader since the war, died in 1979, and Tito the following year, creating a vacuum in ideas and power. The collective leadership lacks both.

The LCY is the unchallenged political and ideological force in Yugoslavia, with corresponding LCY organizations in the republics and autonomous provinces. Its statutes establish the responsibilities and behavior of party members and the party structure. The LCY operates on the principle of "democratic centralism," a principle first adopted by the Third Congress in June 1926 in conformity with Comintern precepts. Essentially, democratic centralism requires lower organizations and members to implement party policy and decisions of the leading party organs. Normally the LCY presidency would be the determining authority in Yugoslavia. Between 1937 and 1980 the reality was Tito's authoritarian leadership. However, the decentralized system allows not only discussion of policy but also decision-making by republic and provincial LCY organizations and, occasionally, by lower levels.

Formally, the highest organ of LCY power is the Congress, held every four years. The 13th took place in June 1986 and was attended by 1,553 voting delegates. The Congress hears reports, passes resolutions, establishes policies and elects the Central Committee. The CC consists of 165 members (127 were new): 20 from each republic, 15 from each autonomous province and 15 from the armed forces. The CC, representing the Congress between its sessions, elects from a 23-member presidency (only four were not new), again on the basis of equal national representation: three from each republic, two from each province and one from the armed forces. Fourteen members are elected for the entire period between congresses and nine are ex officio members who are presidents of the LCY organizations in the republics, provinces and the armed forces. These officials are elected for either one or two years and at various times of the year.

The presidency is the policy-making body of the LCY. Tito had been president of the presidency since 1964, but after his death, in compliance with his legacy of collective leadership, the annual rotation system has been in effect. Accordingly, the president is selected from a republic or province in June of every year. At the first Congress following Tito's death—the 12th, in 1982—the election of the president was secret. The president, who convenes and chairs the meetings of the presidency, is the formal leader of the LCY for the year. The presidency has a secretary elected for a two-year term and charged with implementing the LCY's policies. There are seven executive secretaries. In addition, there are five commissions: Propaganda and Information; Appeals; Administrative and Financial Issues; Socioeconomic Relations, Economic and Technical Developments; and Development of Political System of Socialist Self-Government. Recent one-year presidents have been Milanko Renovica, a Serb from Bosnia-Herzegovina, June 1986–87; Bosko Krunic, a Serb from Vojvodina, 1987–88; Stipe Suvar, a Croat from Croatia, 1988–89; and Milan Pancevski, a Macedonian, 1989–90.

The party structure is similar in the republics and the provinces. Prior to the federal Congress, republic and provincial congresses are held; among other things they elect officials to the CC, the presidency and other bodies. Each republic congress selects 20 members and each province and the armed forces 15 for the CC, which is formally elected at the federal Congress. The approximately 530 commune conferences are convened, also quadrennially, and establish functional organs. At the lowest rung are approximately 70,500 basic organizations existing in the self-management units, governmental bodies, local communities and the military. Each is led by a secretariat or a secretary.

The beginning of the Communist Party appeared promising with an impressive membership and showing in the first elections. However, the party's underground existence diminished membership rapidly, to approximately 3,000 in 1928; the number dwindled to several hundred in the early 1930s. Recovery was slow, with 1,500 members in 1937, then picked up to 12,000 at the time of the Axis invasion in 1941. The one-quarter who survived the war included Tito's leadership circle and veterans of the Spanish Civil War. With the military victory of the Partisans and their dominant position in postwar Yugoslavia, as well as the party's need for administrators, membership climbed to 141,000 in 1945, and the party continued to recruit. Membership neared 450,000 in 1948, and 773,000 reported by the Sixth Congress in November 1952.

The LCY conducted purges, especially during crises, while simultaneously recruiting new members, which account for fluctuations in membership. Overall there was a substantial net increase. In 1960 membership was nearly 900,000, reached 1 million within four years and, following Tito's death, went over 2 million by 1981. Membership continued to climb but was reduced to 2.1 million in 1986 and slightly less in 1989, or about 9% of the population. Workers comprise less than one-third of the membership, a diminishing percentage causing concern, and women 27 percent. Over half (55%) of the members are in the economic sector; 25.5% are in public service; and 19.9% are students, retirees, unemployed, housewives or in other categories. Only 3.6% of the members are farmers.

By September 1989 the LCY's, and thus the country's, problems had not diminished. The inflation rate was at 900% annually, the highest in Europe, and unemployment was about 16%. The nationalities continued to express their dissatisfaction publicly. Government leadership was criticized, and the party leadership was undergoing serious introspection. On September 11 the LCY's CC proposed discontinuance of the collective leadership to inject greater authority into the central party apparatus to combat the economic and ethnic crises more effectively. A CC commission suggested an executive organ headed by a secretary elected for a two-year term with a proviso for reelection. Croatian and Slovenian parties were expected to oppose any move toward centralization of power.

These and other issues were considered by the extraordinary 14th Congress held in December 1989 and attended by 1,688 delegates—e.g., division within the LCY, the possibility of the Slovenian party breaking away from the federal LCY, the rehabilitation of former party stalwarts and even "de-Titoization."

While the LCY was the only political party in Yugoslavia in mid-1989, there was not only discussion of political pluralism but also the flowering of numerous organizations. The greatest activity was observed in Slovenia, where, in January 1989, the Slovenian Democratic Alliance—not a party—held its inaugural session; its objective is the establishment of parliamentary democracy. The Social Democratic Alliance of Slovenia was formally founded the following month, although it began activities in December 1987. Also aiming to create parliamentary democracy, this alliance tends to be a political party, the first organization under LCY rule to make such a declaration. These are only two of many general and specialized associations in Slovenia and the other republics that if liberalization permits, may develop into functioning political parties.

On January 22, 1990, at the end of the Party Congress, the LCY renounced its leading role in society guaranteed in the Constitution and proposed to the Assembly of Yugoslavia that it pass a law on political pluralism including a multiparty system.

On February 4, 1990, the Communist Party of Slovenia voted to break away from the ruling LCY. The former's president, Ciril Ribicic, stated that it did not want secession. In the past three years Slovenia has moved to create a pluralist system. The Slovenian Party's new name is Party for Democratic Renewal.

There are no known terrorist groups in Yugoslavia.

ECONOMY

Yugoslavia, one of the poorest nations in Europe before World War II, emerged from it with its economy totally wrecked and its industrial capacity halved. The postwar government, using the Soviet economy as a model, rapidly began reconstruction, emphasizing a high degree of centralization, the collectivization of agriculture, and large-scale industrialization. But the break with the Soviet Union in 1948 necessitated not only a political realignment but also an economic restructuring. Cut off from Soviet development aid and trade with Eastern Europe, Yugoslavia turned to the West, a factor that necessitated an abandonment of the strict Soviet command economy in favor of a somewhat decentralized social self-management, representing a tentative approach to a limited market-oriented economy.

During the first half of the 1970s two further changes were initiated in an effort to institutionalize the self-management concept. The administration of a variety of activities was transferred to self-managed "Communities of Interest," and new production units known as Basic Organizations of Associated Labor (BOAL) were established at the shop level in factories. BOALs within enterprises may remain independent or, in association with other BOALs, delegate certain powers to central self-management groups and thus participate in every level of decision-making, including income distribution, contribution to social welfare, marketing, investment and even foreign trade and international borrowing. Some aspects of overall economic direction involving, for example, credit and monetary policy and coordination and redistribution of resources to less-developed regions remain largely in federal hands, but many broad policies proposed by the central government in the form of planning guidelines are discussed at levels down to the BOALs and back up the hierarchy until a consensus is reached on every issue. Such policies normally are carried out under binding "Social Compacts."

Many of the innovations were incorporated into the Constitution of 1974 and the Law on Associated Labor of 1976. The latter strengthened the role of the BOALs and also provided for a bewildering array of other organs. A number of BOALs can form a Complex Organization of Associated Labor (COAL) with its own council and management. COALs are designed to facilitate vertical and horizontal integration between component units. An enterprise may be a member of more than one COAL in order to benefit from some management functions, such as joint production planning and joint marketing. Reinforcing the social compacts are Self-Management Agreements (SMAs) concluded between self-management organizations in the social sector. Unlike Social Compacts, which are enforceable only through persuasion, SMAs are binding contracts enforceable through the courts. SMAs are used to regulate a wide range of relationships, from funding to distribution of joint income, sharing of risks and investment. Social Compacts and SMAs have substituted for direct action by government in areas such as price controls and income policy.

The transition from a command economy to a social market economy is reflected in the evolution of Yugoslav planning. A central planning agency was established in 1947, and the first five-year plan, covering 1947–51, was based on the Soviet model. In 1951 the role of planning was changed to indicative plans instead of the mandatory targets imposed under the first plan. The economy operated under a series of annual plans until the second five-year plan (1957–61). Under the annual plan a high rate of investment and savings was maintained. The second plan was fairly ambitious, but the investments that preceded it permitted a rapid expansion of output. The plan was fulfilled in 1960, a year ahead of schedule. The third plan (1961–65) was even more ambitious, but it was abandoned after a couple of years because of a poor harvest and a stabilization program that made the plan's targets unattainable.

In the early 1960s the economy faced growing inflationary pressures and balance-of-payments problems. In 1961 a series of measures, hastily drafted and implemented, opened the economy by replacing a system of multiple exchange rates with a single devalued rate, reduced tariffs and quantitative restrictions on imports, restructured financial markets and reduced government control over wage-setting to increase the enter-

---

BALANCE OF PAYMENTS ($ million), 1987

Current account balance: 1,249
Merchandise exports: 11,426
Merchandise imports: −11,343
Trade balance: 83
Other goods, services & income: 4,468
Other goods, services & income: −7,580
Private unrequited transfers: 4,281
Official unrequited transfers: −3.0
Other long-term capital: −894
Other short-term capital: 134
Net errors & omissions: −937
Counterpart items: −98
Total change in reserves: 545

GROSS DOMESTIC PRODUCT, 1988

GDP nominal (national currency): 25.083 trillion
GDP real (national currency): 1.662 trillion
GDP per capita ($): 2,562
GDP average annual growth rate: 1.1% (1980–86)
GDP by type of expenditure (%)
    Consumption
        Private: 48
        Government: 13
    Gross domestic investment: 40
    Gross domestic saving: 40
    Foreign trade
        Exports: 21
        Imports: −22
Cost components of GDP (%)
    Net indirect taxes: 7
    Consumption of fixed capital: 11
    Compensation of employees: ⎫82
    Net operating surplus: ⎭
Sectoral origin of GDP (%)
    Primary
        Agriculture: 11.0
    Secondary
        Manufacturing: 43.0 (including mining)
        Construction: 7.0
    Tertiary
        Transportation & communications; 7.0
        Trade: 11.0
        Finance: ⎫24.0
        Public administration & defense: ⎭
        Other: 8.0
Average annual sectoral growth rates, 1980–87 (%)
    Agriculture: 1.4
    Industry (manufacturing, including mining): 1.4
    Services: 1.6

---

prises' financial interest in productivity. The failure of these reforms touched off a debate about development policies. The debate was won by the liberals, who favored market socialism and between 1964 and 1967 many economic reforms were adopted. They included price adjustments geared to world prices, progressive removal of price controls, devaluation, currency reform, reduced controls on imports and exports, and lower customs duties and export subsidies. These were accompanied by changes in the banking system and reductions in taxes. The net effect of these reforms was to reduce government control over the economy, transfer the main responsibility for the use of investment funds from the state to banks and enterprises, raise the quality of output and raise personal consumption. These reforms were the zenith of the Yugoslav brand of market socialism.

PRINCIPAL ECONOMIC INDICATORS, 1988

Gross National Product: $63.070 billion
GNP per capita: $2,680
GNP average annual growth rate (%): 0.5 (1980–88)
GNP per capita average annual growth rate (%): −2.2
    (1980–88)
Consumer Price Index (1985=100)
    All items: 1,232.3 (1988)
Wholesale Price Index Producers' Materials (1980=100): 6,681
Average annual rate of inflation: 57.2% (1980–87)
Average annual growth rate, 1980–87 (%)
    Public consumption: 0.6
    Private consumption: 0.4
    Gross domestic investment: −0.2
Income distribution: Lowest 20%=6.6%; highest 20%=38.7%

The fourth plan (1966–70) was drafted during the beginning of the reforms. Annual plans were discontinued, and the five-year plans became the standard road maps for the economy. However, many of the targets of the fourth plan were unmet because of dislocations resulting from the reforms.

A radically new system of planning was established by law in 1976 because of the failures of purely indicative planning. Each organization is now required to draft its own plans; BOALs and enterprises prepare microplans, while sociopolitical communities prepare macroplans or social plans. Planning is conducted simultaneously at all levels, there being no hierarchy through which plans pass for approval. The exchange of information and planning process is continuous, with annual assessments and adjustments for changing conditions. Planning starts with the issuance by the federal authorities of a law stating the time period of the plan, the timetable for major steps and the minimum indicators that must be prepared. Although production and social planning start separately, they are harmonized at the various levels. The planning units are obliged to consider broad objectives and trade-offs necessary to meet goals.

During the 1976–80 plan the GDP expanded, in real terms, at an average annual rate of 5.7%, less than projected. Industrial production rose by 6.7%, agricultural production by 1.6% and real income by 1%. During the 1981–85 plan the social product rose by an average annual rate of 3.2%. The 1986–90 plan envisaged an average annual growth rate of 4% in real social product, 4.5% in industrial production, 5% in agricultural production and 6% in exports. Priority was given to the development of small-scale industry.

An important function of the federal government has been its effort to equalize development and income among the regions. The northern republics—Slovenia and Croatia—as well as Serbia proper, plus the province of Vojvodina, are the developed regions; the remaining republics—Bosnia-Herzegovina, Montenegro and Macedonia—plus the province of Kosovo, are the underdeveloped regions. Transfers of resources to the underdeveloped regions began in the 1950s, and in 1966 the permanent Federal Fund for Crediting the Accelerated Development of the Less-Developed Republics and the Autonomous Province of Kosovo was established. Between 1971 and 1975 transfers at concessionary terms contributed about a fifth of fixed-asset investments in the underdeveloped regions, not including other budgetary provisions. Total resource transfers for this period constituted 9.3% of the underdeveloped regions' GMP, or a drain on the developed regions of 2.7% of their GMP. Despite this effort, the per capita income in Kosovo is only one-fifth that in Slovenia. In 1988 the federal budget allotted 446.7 billion dinars to the underdeveloped regions.

Yugoslavia's economic growth since 1960 has been more rapid than that of any other East European country except Rumania and on a par with that recorded by Portugal, Spain and Greece. Between 1952 and 1979 the Yugoslav economy experienced an annual average growth rate of about 7% in GMP, in the process moving from a relatively impoverished agricultural country to a middle-income, semi-industrialized country with a higher per capita income than Portugal or Argentina.

In spite of the high performance of the economy over two decades, there were disquieting signs. Economists discerned cyclical patterns related to too-rapid growth followed by periods of adjustment. The slowdown in economic growth began immediately after the 1965 economic reforms. There were many causes for these changes, some of which were intentional, such as allocating a greater share of income to consumption. The nature of investments and inefficiencies in implementation, however, required increasing sums to yield an additional unit of social product. Investment funds tended to be confined within regions, and access varied greatly among enterprises. The government lost a large degree of control over aggregate demand as planning became regional in scope. Enterprises raised wages faster than productivity and increased inventories and fixed assets with easy credit from banks. Economic decision-making became concentrated in banks and enterprise managerial and technical staffs. A slowdown in emigration of Yugoslav workers led to a worsening of the employment situation and a reduction in workers' remittances from abroad.

By 1980 three major problems had emerged that were to trouble the economy for the rest of the decade: inflation, unemployment and industrial stagnation. Growing import dependency was compounded by slower growth of exports and worsening terms of trade. Output fell short of targets as whole projects fell behind schedule. By 1981 about 597 billion dinars or about half of the GMP was tied up in uncompleted projects. Workers' remittances fell in 1987 to $500 million from $3.450 billion in 1984. About 10% of the GMP was devoted to servicing the external debt. In 1986 the dinar lost 46.2% of its value against the dollar and personal incomes declined by 7%. Inflation reached 79.5% in 1985, 88.1% in 1986 and 167% in 1987, the highest in Europe. In 1988 it fell to 158% but remained serious nevertheless. Unemployment also remained acute, with over 1 million people out of work in 1987. These difficulties have been countered by a series of devaluations, wage and price freezes, and debt rescheduling agreements with creditor nations and commercial banks. The dinar was devalued by 14.6% in 1987 and by 23.9% in 1988. In 1987 the government imposed a new wage freeze, a decision that provoked widespread protests despite federal government threats to use the army to quell the strikes. In 1987 alone the number of strikes totaled 1,570.

The government also was hard hit in 1987 by financial scandals involving AgroKomerc, a major agro-industrial concern employing 13,000 workers in Bosnia-Herzegovina. It had issued illegal promissory notes to the value of $900 million to Yugoslav banks, placing 63 banks in four republics at risk. Official investigations uncovered grave irregularities in the system. Numerous senior politicians and AgroKomerc officials resigned or were dismissed and forced to stand trial. A total of 42 LCY members, including a federal vice president, were expelled, and AgroKomerc was declared bankrupt in November 1987.

Yugoslavia is in the midst of important reforms involving far-reaching reconsideration of basic policy approaches and fundamental principles of economic management. The ultimate goal of most reform projects is to strengthen market mechanisms by introducing penalties for economic failure and rewards for economic efficiency as well as to improve the arsenal of economic policy instruments. Only a few reforms have been fully implemented; others are being debated or await legislative acts—often requiring constitutional change—before they can be realized. Indeed, the economy appears to be caught in a vicious circle of stagflation. The country's fragile balance-of-payments position and its formidable inflation-proneness act as binding constraints to a faster growth of domestic demand. The most serious impediments on the supply side are the predominance of conflicting regional interests, the fragmentation of markets and the relative immobility of capital and labor. On the enterprise level, Social Compacts and SMAs make layoffs extremely difficult if not impossible. Thus even loss-making enterprises are forced to accede to political pressures to increase employment by a certain percentage each year regardless of their economic position. Further, accelerating inflation has dampened productivity as entrepreneurial efforts are focused on protecting the real value of both enterprise income and financial assets.

PUBLIC FINANCE

The fiscal year is the calendar year.

The process of decentralization since the 1960s has reduced the role of the federal government and fiscal policy in management of the economy. Federal expenditures account for only about a fifth of total public-sector expenditures. The federal government's primary expenditures relate to the armed forces and central administration. Moreover, federal expenditures are inflexible relative to revenues and allow little room for maneuver. The process of shedding federal budgetary responsibilities continued well into the 1980s. In 1978, for example, food subsidies were transferred to the republics and export subsidies to the Committees of Interest for Foreign Economic Relations.

Unlike in most federations, income taxes are not collected by the central government and then distributed among the constituent states according to a predetermined formula; rather, it is the reverse. The republics collect income taxes according to rates that vary from republic to republic, and the republics contribute a portion of these revenues to the federal budget. Some of the funds received from the republics are transfer payments.

The federal government may incur surpluses or deficits, but they are usually small and unintentional (due to autonomous and cyclical factors) rather than a method to influence economic activity. In 1985 and 1986 the budgets were balanced at the center and slightly in surplus in the republics.

The bulk of public-sector revenues and expenditures are outside the federal budget; sociopolitical entities

---

CENTRAL GOVERNMENT EXPENDITURES, 1987

% of total expenditures
Defense: 55.1
Education: 0 (education is a state subject)
Health: 0 (health is a state subject)
Housing, Social Security, welfare: 11.2
Economic services: 16.3
Other: 17.3
Total expenditures as % of GNP: 8.0
Overall surplus or deficit as % of GNP: 0

CENTRAL GOVERNMENT REVENUES, 1987

% of total current revenues
Taxes on income, profit & capital gain: 0
Social Security contributions: 0
Domestic taxes on goods & services: 60.1
Taxes on international trade & transactions: 38.4
Other taxes: 0
Current nontax revenue: 1.5
Total current revenue as % of GNP: 8.1
Government consumption as % of GNP: 14.0
Annual growth rate of government consumption: 0.6 (1980–87)

---

account for about a fourth and communities of interest for about half.

The Federal Budget and Resolution of 1987 set restrictive expenditure targets, aimed at reducing or at least stabilizing the public sector's share in the Gross Social Product (GSP). For a number of expenditure categories, representing about a third of total expenditures, strict rules were established, freezing them at the 1986 level and limiting subsequent increases to below the growth of nominal income in the enterprise sector. Laws were passed obliging the other levels of government to comply with these limits, with quarterly controls being established for both federal and state governments. While wage levels and defense expenditures were held down, the other important items, such as pensions, health and Social Security, were planned to rise somewhat faster than the GSP. From 1987 pensions were indexed to wage increases, but the rapid growth in the number of pensioners has made it difficult to place a ceiling on aggregate pension payments.

Balanced budgets are mandatory (revenues exceeding expenditures in any one quarter are to be offset in the next by correspondingly lower taxes, and vice versa). Intervention laws enable the federal government to restrict wages and outlays on services and investment. Additionally, in 1987, the federal government's share of sales tax receipts was raised to 75% from 50%, and the share of the republics was correspondingly lowered.

The Yugoslav tax system suffers from some important drawbacks. Personal income taxes are very small (1.5%, compared to 12% in OECD countries), and tax schedules are not progressive. On the other hand, the share of taxes on enterprise income is twice as high as the OECD average. The authorities are planning to increase taxes on personal income by broadening the tax base and by raising the tax rates and making them progressive. In particular, individuals in the private sector and farmers, who do not pay taxes or who pay only insignificant amounts, are to be taxed. New taxes are planned to cover income from rents, real-estate transactions and income from other activities in the private sector that have expanded considerably in recent years. Moreover, instead of taxing individual incomes separately, family income is to be taxed as a whole. The government also is considering the introduction of VAT, with different rates for luxury goods and for essentials. To reduce the budgetary latitude of regional and local governments, the government also has proposed elimination of certain municipal taxes. To reduce the share of public expenditures to 30% of the GSP by 1990, the number of public-sector employees at all levels of government is to be reduced and certain institutions are to be closed. Investment in buildings and nonproductive sectors also is to be curtailed. A thorough review of retirement pensions is envisaged to bring them into line with the financing capacity of the economy. Criteria for disability and invalidity payments are to be tightened.

In 1983, in addition to its financing of agricultural development projects in Kosovo, the World Bank agreed to a loan of $275 million to assist Yugoslavia's economic stabilization program. In 1987 Yugoslavia's request for a second loan for the same purpose was refused by the World Bank. In 1985 the IMF approved a one-year standby credit enabling Yugoslavia to draw up to $300 million. In the same year Yugoslavia signed an agreement with 17 major foreign creditors deferring $700 million of debt due for repayment in 1986, and a four-year agreement with an international bank consortium on rescheduling payment of medium- and long-term debts totaling $3.8 billion falling due for repayment between 1985 and 1988. In 1986 an agreement on rescheduling repayments of debt principal of $1.4 billion was ratified, and in 1987 a further agreement with the Paris Club of creditor nations on the refinancing of $475 million of debt, due for repayment in 1988, was reached. A further rescheduling took place in 1987 with 16 Western creditor nations and commercial banks. In 1987 the EEC offered Yugoslavia a loan of 550 million ECU over six years to finance various infrastructural projects. In mid-1987, for the first time, Yugoslavia was unable to fulfill its obligations to repay debt principal of $245 million and was obliged to seek a moratorium in addition to a request for an emergency loan of $300 million from the Bank of International Settlements. In 1988 Yugoslavia and the IMF reached a draft agreement on a one-year standby loan of about $400 million, and

creditor banks agreed to reschedule, over 18 years, obligations totaling $6.5 billion. In 1988 legislation was passed permitting debt-for-equity exchanges, and the foreign exchange market was liberalized.

CURRENCY & BANKING

The national monetary unit is the dinar. Coins are issued in denominations of 1, 2, 5, 10, 50 and 100 dinars and notes in denominations of 5, 10, 20, 100, 500, 1,000, 5,000, 10,000, 20,000 and 50,000 dinars.

The Yugoslav credit and banking system is based on the provisions of the Constitution, the Law on the National Bank of Yugoslavia of 1986, the Law on the Basic Principles of Banking and Credit Operations of 1986 and other legislation. Under these laws, the banking system consists of five tiers: (1) the central bank system, including the National Bank of Yugoslavia; (2) commercial banks; (3) the Yugoslav Bank for International Economic Cooperation; (4) savings banks and other loan institutions; and (5) other financial institutions.

The National Bank of Yugoslavia, founded in 1883, together with the six national banks of the republics and the two national banks of the provinces constitute the central bank system. All nine banks constitute an integrated unit, and they discharge the state function of monetary regulation based on the control of liquidity and credit. The normal instruments of monetary policy are the determination of the legal reserve requirements of banks and other financial institutions; issuance and withdrawal of Treasury bills; purchase through banks of short-term securities issued by companies; grant of short-term credits on the basis of bills of exchange discounted by banks; participation in bank credits for specified purposes; buying and selling of foreign exchange; and fixing of active and passive interest rates.

Commercial banks are of three types: internal banks, basic banks and associated banks. Internal banks are the financial counterparts of BOALs. One or more BOALs, enterprises, or communities of interest or of self-management in the social sector (but not governments) may establish an internal bank. It keeps accounts and makes payments for its founders but cannot extend credit. Internal banks maintain deposits in basic banks but not in central banks. It makes investments for its members and prepares investment projects and proposals for borrowing at home or abroad. Since it cannot accept sight deposits, it is not subject to the regulation of the central bank.

A basic bank is a regular and universal banking organization that can accept deposits, extend credit, make investments and conduct all types of banking activities. Basic banks are formed by BOALs, internal banks, enterprises, communities of interest and other organizations (but not governments). Each basic bank is managed by a bank assembly, which determines policy, interest rates and income distribution. The assembly elects the executive board, the credit board and the bank director. A basic bank is required to maintain three compulsory funds: a reserve fund to ensure cur-

---

EXTERNAL PUBLIC DEBT, 1988

Total: $13.173 billion
  of which public (%): 39.5
  of which private (%): 60.5
Debt service total: $1.985 billion
  of which repayment of principal (%): 47
  of which interest (%): 53
Debt service ratio: 11.4
External public debt as % of GNP: 8.8
Ratio of external public debt to international reserves: 8.6
Debt service as % of GNP: 5.1
Debt service as % of exports: 19.4
Terms of public borrowing:
  Commitments: $214 million
  Average interest rate: 8.4%
  Average maturity: 14 years

rent liquidity; a joint and several liabilities fund to cover bad debts; and a business fund to finance fixed assets.

An associated bank performs operations of common interest to members of two or more basic banks, such as credit transactions, international payments, and concentration of domestic and foreign financial resources needed for major development projects.

In 1988 there were 148 basic banks and nine associated banks. Legislation to permit establishment of joint banks by Yugoslav and foreign banks took effect in April 1987.

The Yugoslav Bank for International Economic Cooperation was established in 1978 as a specialized bank for promoting economic cooperation with foreign countries, extending credit for financing of exports of capital goods and underwriting insurance of exports against noncommercial risks.

The savings banks sector includes the Post Office Savings Bank, savings banks and savings and loan cooperatives. Savings banks and savings and loan cooperatives are regulated by the republics and provinces.

In 1989 the government introduced a number of reforms in the banking sector. The main objectives of the reforms were to make banks more independent of the big enterprises and of local political lobbies in allocating financial resources. The measures (1) enabled banks to make transactions for their own benefit rather than solely for the accounts of their clients; (2) made the voting power of the founding members proportional to the capital they have subscribed, with a maximum of 10% to 15%; (3) made the bank assembly the principal decision-making authority; and (4) created new consultative bodies. A law passed in 1987 also increased the independence of the National Bank of Yugoslavia and particularly of its governor. In a number of cases the law permits the governor to make decisions without consulting the governing board (which consists of representatives of the six republic banks and the two provincial banks) and in other cases to veto decisions taken by the board.

FINANCIAL INDICATORS, 1988

International reserves minus gold: $2.298 billion
　Foreign exchange: $2.298 billion
Gold (million fine troy oz.): 1.893
Central bank
　Assets (%)
　　Claims on government: 8.2
　　Claims on private sector: 8.0
　　Claims on banks: 47.6
　　Claims on foreign assets: 36.3
　Liabilities (%)
　　Reserve money: 216.7
　　Government deposits: 1.7
　　Foreign liabilities: 89.6
Money supply
　Stock in billion national currency: 7.643 trillion
　M^1 per capita: 325,000
Private banks
　Assets (%)
　　Loans to government: 0.1
　　Loans to private sector: 55.8
　　Reserves: 38.4
　　Foreign assets: 5.7
　Liabilities, deposits (billion national currency): 44.633 trillion
　of which (%)
　　Demand deposits: 12.1
　　Savings deposits: 47.7
　　Foreign liabilities: 32.8
　Net inflow of publicly guaranteed external capital:
　　−$683 million
　Net workers' remittances: $3.721 billion
　Central bank discount rate: 131.07%

EXCHANGE RATE
(National Currency per U.S. Dollar)

1979	1980	1981	1982	1983	1984	1985	1986	1987	1988
19.163	29.297	41.823	62.487	125.673	211.749	312.805	857.180	736.998	5,210.760

Steps also have been taken to improve and tighten the National Bank's control over the banking sector. In 1987 the compulsory reserve requirements on deposits were reactivated and extended to cover household dinar deposits and long-term dinar deposits of enterprises that previously were excluded.

The authorities also reactivated obligatory bank investments in National Bank bills as a regulatory instrument. Since 1987 overdrafts have been included in credit ceilings. The government also reduced the role of selective credits not subject to quantitative controls and abolished interest rate subsidies on selective credits for exports and agriculture.

AGRICULTURE

Of the total agricultural land area of 14.4 million ha. (35.6 million ac.), 4.3 million ha. (10.6 million ac.) are mostly highland pastures. Of the arable area of 9.9 million ha. (24.5 million ac.), 7.6 million ha. (18.7 million ac.) are cropped, 2.0 million ha. (4.9 million ac.) are meadows and the remainder are orchards, vineyards, woodlands and others. There are three principal belts of cultivation. The middle or cereal-bearing belt comprises the northern, northeastern and central sections from Slovenia and Baranja to Vojvodina and Kosovo-Metohija, including the watersheds of the Danube, Sava

GROWTH PROFILE (Annual Growth Rates, %)

Population, 1987–2000: 0.6
Crude birth rate, 1985–90: 15.2
Crude death rate, 1985–90: 8.8
Urban population, 1980–87: 2.6
Labor force, 1985–2000: 0.7
GNP, 1980–88: 0.5
GNP per capita, 1980–88: −2.2
GDP, 1980–86: 1.1
Inflation, 1980–87: 57.2
Agriculture, 1980–87: 1.4
Industry, (manufacturing, including mining), 1980–87: 1.4
Services, 1980–87: 1.6
Money holdings, 1980–87: 54.4
Manufacturing earnings per employee, 1980–86: −1.9
Energy production, 1980–87: 3.0
Energy consumption, 1980–87: 3.2
Exports, 1980–87: 1.1
Imports, 1980–87: −2.0
General government consumption, 1980–87: 0.6
Private consumption, 1980–87: 0.4
Gross domestic investment, 1980–87: −0.2

and Morava rivers. This belt covers approximately a third of the total territory. The alpine, or mountainous, belt comprises the land west of the central belt to the shores of the Adriatic. Most of this belt is pasture and forests. The Mediterranean, or subtropical, belt is limited to a small section of the Adriatic seashore on the one side and the valley of the Vardar River south of Veles on the other. In the first part of this belt, olives and citrus fruit are grown; in the second, poppies, cotton and sesame seed. Farther down in Macedonia, tobacco, cotton and rice are grown. Over 60% of the crop area is planted in grains, largely wheat and corn. The grain acreage peaked in the 1960s and has since declined as a result of government policies and changing dietary patterns. The decline was partially compensated for by an expansion of the area under vegetables, fodder and industrial crops, such as sugar beets. There also has been a small increase in orchards and a smaller decrease in vineyards.

The bulk of the agricultural land depends on rain for moisture, causing substantial variations in production from year to year. Only about 2% of the agricultural land is irrigated, most of it in Macedonia and Kosovo. Socialized farming accounts for a disproportionate share of irrigated fields using sprinkler systems.

In 1918, when Yugoslavia was born, it was an agrarian nation in which owner-operated small farms were the norm. However, the land tenure systems varied depending on whether the region was under Austrian or Turkish rule. In Serbia and Montenegro small peasant-operated farms had existed for centuries, and there was no need for reform. Feudal holdings (called *kmets* in Bosnia-Herzegovina and *coloni* in Dalmatia) were most common in former Turkish possessions. A system of large estates prevailed in Macedonia, Kosovo-Metohija, Vojvodina, Croatia and Slovenia. A land reform that became law in 1919 redressed some of the worst abuses of the latter two regions and by 1930 had transferred 15% of the agricultural land to about 30% of the peasants.

When Tito seized control in 1945, he was confronted with the task not only of the uncompleted 1919 land reform but also of rebuilding the agricultural sector, which had been devastated by the war. There were other problems as well, such as the low level of agricultural mechanization, the small size of the holdings and rural overpopulation. As in other sectors, the initial solution was the blind adoption of the Soviet model of collectivized agriculture. A 1945 law provided for the expropriation, in many cases without compensation, of all land exceeding certain limits. The upper limit of private holdings was 25 to 30 ha. (62 to 74 ac.), depending on the region. By 1946 some 1.2 million ha. (3.0 million ac.) of farmland and several hundred thousand hectares of forests had entered the public land pool, over 40% of which came from confiscation of property belonging to German nationals who had been forced to flee. Just over half the land so confiscated was turned over without charge to landless or land-poor peasants, many of whom had been Partisans; of the remaining land, nearly half was turned over to state forestry agencies and the rest used to create state farms on the Soviet model. In

1946 the government moved a step closer to collectivized agriculture through a law on cooperatives. The peasants were receptive to cooperatives partly because of a long tradition of communal ownership in Croatia and Serbia. The 1946 law and the subsequent legislation established two forms of cooperatives: the general agricultural cooperative and the peasant working cooperative. The general cooperative, which the older cooperatives became, were basically agencies of the government in the purchase of agricultural produce through a system of compulsory deliveries at low, government-set prices and the distribution of inputs and other goods needed by rural households. The peasant cooperative was more like the Soviet *kolkhoz*, in which the fields were worked collectively and the land and equipment were pooled together. The government favored that latter as the more orthodox type. Both types held title to their land, which could not revert to private ownership.

Because most of the peasants in the cooperatives brought with them little or no land, the government undertook a second agrarian reform, in 1953. It created the Agricultural Land Fund of National Property and decreased the maximum size of private holdings to 10 to 15 ha. (25 to 37 ac.). Land over this maximum was taken over by the fund for distribution to state and collective farms.

Although cooperatives were technically voluntary, considerable pressures were exerted on the farmers to join. Nonetheless, they remained unpopular until the government launched an intensive collectivization drive after the break with the Soviet Union in 1948. In 1950 the number of cooperatives peaked at 16,000, and socialized agriculture held just over one-third of the agricultural land. The momentum of collectivization, however, slackened after 1950, mainly because of strong peasant resistance. Farmers slaughtered livestock rather than join a collective. Additionally, during this period the nation experienced one of its worst droughts.

From 1950 the process of collectivization was partially reversed. Machine tractor stations were dissolved, and compulsory deliveries of farm produce were abolished. Members were allowed to withdraw from collectives and cooperatives. However, the upper limits on private ownership precluded the reemergence of large farms and hired labor, and thus Yugoslavia became, more than before, a land of small farms.

Since 1950 official policy has followed the two-sector approach, with strong support for the socialized sector. The bulk of investments, inputs and technical personnel are channeled to state farms and cooperatives. Although the socialized sector employs only 5% of the farm labor force and controls only 16% of the cultivated land, it accounts for about 27% of the output and about half of the marketed supplies of staple commodities. Because of official favoritism and its substantial holdings of the most fertile land, the socialized agriculture's growth rates have been three to four times those of the private sector. The 2,704 socially owned farms control over 1.6 million ha. (4.0 million ac.). Since the 1960s they have branched out into processing and marketing, becoming agrobusinesses *(agrokombinats)*. About 100 of these complexes, with 5,000 to 100,000 ha. (12,350 to 247,000 ac.) each, farm over 60% of the cultivated land in the socialized sector. In the largest combines, farming accounts for only 25% of activities, while 70% is food processing and 5% is trade. Being vertically integrated enterprises, the *agrokombinats* consist of several BOALs and additional intermediate organizations. They also service the farmers in the vicinity, assisting them with technical expertise and arranging sales and purchases.

In the 1970s, under the Law on Associated Labor, farmers were encouraged to form cooperatives or enter into cooperative arrangements with *agrokombinats*. The intent was to link the private and socialized sectors more closely. The various forms of cooperation arrangements contained many inducements for the peasants to join—such as retaining full title to their land, gaining access to credit inputs and technical services from the socialized sector, guaranteed sales and participation in social sector health and pension programs. However, the independent farmers still were leery of any truck with the socialized sector and preferred to form long-term contractual arrangements rather than cooperative ones.

Despite official discrimination, the private farms form the dominant sector in agriculture, and their existence has saved Yugoslavia from numerous problems that have plagued agriculture in neighboring Communist countries. The private sector in agriculture accounts for 84% of the cultivated land, 73% of the GSP produced by agriculture and 95% of the labor force.

The average private farm is about 3.5 ha. (8.6 ac.) and consists of several separate plots. The extreme fragmentation as well as the small average size inhibit mechanization, while the widely dispersed locations of these farms tax the infrastructure capacity. More than half of the income of private-farm households comes from nonfarm activities. The low income and the lack of amenities cause many farmers, particularly in the South, to seek nonfarm employment. The exodus of young farmers has been substantial over the years. By 1980 some 600,000 ha. (1.5 million ac.) were idle, probably because their owners had become too old to work their fields and their offspring had left to seek employment in the cities. However, cooperative arrangements with state farms enable many farmers to realize higher incomes and increase output and productivity.

Climatic conditions permit a wide range of crops to be cultivated. Cropping patterns are determined by purchase contracts through which the government guides production according to perceived marketing needs. The most important crop, grown in most parts of the country, is corn. Before World War II it was the basic bread grain, but by 1988 nearly 85% of the corn was being used for livestock feed and little for direct human consumption. Corn alone accounts for 15% of total agricultural output and 59% of grain production, although its acreage has declined since 1970 by 500,000 ha. (1.2 million ac.). Yields in the state farms are among the highest in the world, but over 80% of the output comes from private farms, where the yields usually are much

lower. Wheat is the other major crop, and it is grown in many parts. It accounts for about a third the total grain output. Wheat is the basic bread grain, but some of it is used for livestock feed when other fodder is unavailable. Other major crops include potatoes, sugar beets, sunflowers and tobacco. About a third of the tobacco crop is exported in good years. Fruits include plums, grapes and apples.

AGRICULTURAL INDICATORS, 1988

Agriculture's share of GDP (%): 28.7
Average annual growth rate (%): 1.4 (1980–87)
Value added in agriculture ($): 6.815 billion
Cereal imports (000 tons): 782
Index of Agricultural Production (1979–81 = 100): 103 (1986)
Index of Food Production (1979–81 = 100): 102 (1986)
Index of Food Production Per Capita (1979–81 = 100): 100 (1984–86)
Number of tractors: 955,000
Number of harvester-threshers: 9,997
Total fertilizer consumption (tons): 992,000
Fertilizer consumption (100 g. per ha.): 1,275
Number of farms: 2,680,000
Average size of holding, ha. (ac.): 4.2 (10.3)
Size/class
  Below 1 ha. (2.47 ac.): 30.4
  1–5 ha. (2.47–12.35 ac.): 48.4
  5–10 ha. (12.35–24.7 ac.): 16.4
  10–20 ha. (24.7–49.4 ac.): 3.8
  20–50 ha. (49.4–123.5 ac.): 0.9
  50–200 ha. (123.5–494 ac.): } 0.1
  Over 200 ha. (over 494 ac.): }
Tenure (%)
  Owner-operated: 99.9
  State: 0.1
Activity (%)
  Mainly crops: 12.7
  Mainly livestock: } 87.3
  Mixed: }
% of farms using irrigation: 2
Total land in farms, ha. (ac.): 12,462,000 (30,793,602)
Farms as % of total land area: 48.8
Land use (%)
  Total cropland: 52.8
    Permanent crops: 8.5
    Temporary crops: 84.7
    Fallow: 6.8
  Meadows & pastures: 26.4
  Woodlands: 16.2
  Other: 4.6
Yields, kg./ha. (lb./ac.)
  Grains: 3,680 (3,285)
  Roots & tubers: 8,155 (7,279)
  Pulses: 1,201 (1,072)
  Milk, kg. (lb.)/animal: 1,722 (3,796)
Livestock (000)
  Cattle: 5,041
  Sheep: 7,697
  Hogs: 7,821
  Horses: 408
  Chickens: 74,000
Forestry
  Production of roundwood, 000 cu. m. (000 cu. ft.): 16,084 (568,006)
    of which industrial roundwood (%): 73.1
  Value of exports ($ 000): 388,871
Fishing
  Total catch (000 tons): 77.5
    of which marine (%): 66.3
  Value of exports ($ 000): 16,423

There are two markets for agricultural produce: the official or socialized market and the unofficial peasant market, each accounting for about half of the output. In the official market, the government sets purchase prices and guaranteed minimum prices for important products, such as cereals and meat. Minimum but not guaranteed prices are set for a number of other commodities. The official prices, announced at the beginning of the planting season, influence planting decisions. Sometimes the farmers receive premiums from the government to shift production to more socially desirable commodities. Prices in the peasant markets are largely uncontrolled.

The share of livestock in the gross value of farm output has risen from one-third just after World War II to over one-half in response to the demand for more meat. Exports of meat and live animals also provide valuable foreign exchange. The two major constraints on livestock potential are the quality of the stock and the paucity of feed. Further depressing the sector is the fact that 90% of the livestock by weight (and a greater percentage by number) are privately owned. Pigs are the most numerous farm animals next to chickens. The upgrading of cattle herds is reflected in the fact that their body weight has grown faster than their numbers. Sheep, concentrated in the upland and mountainous areas, are raised more for wool than for meat. Macedonia, Serbia proper and Bosnia-Herzegovina are the major sheep-raising regions. Commercial chicken farms are in all republics, but the most important producers are Croatia, Serbia proper, Vojvodina, Slovenia and Bosnia-Herzegovina.

The shortage of feed acts as a major constraint on meat production and exports. Alfalfa, clover and corn are the main supplements to natural pastures. The country depends on imports for high-protein additives, such as fishmeal from Peru and soybean cake from China and the United States.

In spite of the long Adriatic coastline and numerous lakes and rivers, the fishing industry is relatively underdeveloped, principally because fish is not a staple in the Yugoslav diet. Paradoxically, Yugoslavia spent over $51 million in 1987 to import canned and fish products while failing to exploit the Adriatic fisheries.

Yugoslavia has large forest areas, surpassing many of its neighbors. Of the 9.2 million ha. (22.7 million ac.) of woodland, 2.4 million ha. (5.9 million ac.) are in Bosnia-Herzegovina, 2.1 million ha. (5.2 million ac.) in Croatia, 1.8 million ha. (4.4 million ac.) in Serbia and 1.0 million ha. (2.5 million ac.) in Slovenia. Broad-leaved trees are the main source of timber, although the cutting of conifers is increasing. Nearly two-thirds of the forests are state-owned. The forests of Montenegro constitute a separate group because the local tribes have claimed them as their common property since ancient times.

MANUFACTURING

The basic push toward industrialization took place in Yugoslavia during the interwar period, and it was spearheaded by foreign investors. When the Communists seized control in 1945, they immediately set in motion the Stalinist model of development, emphasizing heavy industry. Almost all the large industrial plants were nationalized. From 1945 the major share of fixed investment was diverted to industry at the expense of agriculture, and even the introduction of self-management from the 1950s did not materially alter the flow of funds into industry. Emphasis, however, vacillated among branches of industry, with heavy industry remaining the consistent favorite. By the early 1960s industry surpassed agriculture in contribution to the GSP, and by 1986 the value added by industry was 42%, compared to 12% by agriculture. The large industrial allocations supported by the flow of workers from the rural areas caused industrial output to expand rapidly, although the official Index of Industrial Production invariably overstated the growth rate.

The structure of industry also has changed markedly, from one dominated by food processing in the 1940s. In the decades since then, the fastest-growing branches have been oil and gas extraction, electrical machinery, transportation equipment, chemicals, electric power and oil refining. These were essentially priority branches that started from low levels of production. Other branches that were more developed in the 1940s, such as coal mining, ferrous and nonferrous mining and processing, and metal manufacturing, expanded output considerably, but growth rates were considerably lower. Several nonpriority branches, such as furniture, paper, construction materials and the traditional food and beverage industries, expanded faster than the industrial average. The range and diversity of production also broadened. The aluminum industry, for example, expanded from one of extracting and exporting bauxite to production of aluminum ingots and manufactured products. Manufacturing supplied the increasing domestic consumer market with a wide range of goods, including cars, television sets and refrigerators. In the late 1980s Yugoslavia began to claim a share of the international automobile market with exports of its Yugo car. There also is a significant defense equipment manufacturing sector capable of meeting domestic needs.

Until the mid-1960s the government pumped substantial amounts of investment funds. Since then recourse has been more toward indirect measures, such as credit, tax incentives and commercial policies. Innovations and adoption of advanced technology have been encouraged by various means, including joint ventures with Western industrial firms. The Law of Foreign Investment requires 51% Yugoslav ownership but otherwise leaves the details to be worked out between the participants in the joint venture. The flow of foreign investment has been modest except for a few ventures, such as the large petrochemical complex at the crude-oil terminal on Krk Island.

The focus on energy and the development of basic industries have resulted in an industrial structure consisting of a small number of large facilities with heavy capital costs and offering relatively few jobs. Basic industries (primarily energy, ferrous and nonferrous metallurgy, chemicals and paper) account for 56% of the fixed assets in the socialized sector and contribute 32% of the value added but employ only 21% of the labor force in the socialized sector. Small-scale industries, defined as firms that employ fewer than 125 workers, number over 4,000 but contribute only 10% of the value added in the sector. In addition, there is a small private sector of artisans and handicrafters who are encouraged by the government to form cooperatives. These smaller enterprises are generally efficient, and their production supplements that of the larger ones.

Beginning in about 1970, industrial growth, estimated at 9.9% between 1948 and 1965, began to decelerate; it dwindled to 1.1% between 1980 and 1986. The positive factors that had contributed to the earlier high growth had dissipated as structural flaws surfaced and negative factors became more prominent in the sector. By the 1960s the easily exploited resources and areas of the economy had been largely developed. Additions to industrial output required larger investments and became more difficult to accomplish. The prevailing trend toward decentralization hampered the overall coordination and management necessary for large projects. As a result, both productivity and efficiency suffered. Institutional factors also contributed to the decline. Capital was not mobile because of interrepublic rivalries. Private capital was shy because of uncertainty regarding the government's intentions. Despite official encouragement, investments in underdeveloped regions fell far short of expectations. The growing influence of regional governments resulted in greater politically motivated interventions in economic affairs. Loss-making, antiquated enterprises were not liquidated for fear of ensuing unemployment. Despite an excess of crude oil refining capacity, more refineries were installed in the 1980s. Investments in coal mining and expansion of electric generating and transmission facilities fell behind schedule, thus contributing to a shortage of electricity, affecting industrial production. So also the construction of natural-gas pipelines fell below targets.

The industry worst affected is iron and steel, where production lags behind consumption, thus requiring growing imports to meet domestic needs. The industry consists of about half a dozen independent plants, one in each republic, with a total capacity of 4.3 million tons of crude steel and 5.5 million tons of other products. The units themselves are too small to achieve economies of scale. Although the facilities are being continuously expanded, construction schedules are rarely met and cost overruns are high. Planning and designing of units are oriented toward regional markets, with little coordination among plants. The result is excess capacity in some products and a shortage in others. Many facilities are underutilized because of an irregular supply of inputs. Such inefficiencies require periodic price increases, although the mills complain that the prices are too low. At the same time, domestic steel products are 20% to 70% more expensive than imported ones. Even so, the iron and steel complex in Serbia has required government bailouts more than 22 times to keep it from defaulting on its foreign and domestic debts. Most of the plants are set up to use domestic iron ore, but the mines have not expanded fast enough to meet needs. The industry continues to overproduce cer-

---

MANUFACTURING INDICATORS, 1988

Average annual growth rate, 1980–87: 1.4% (including mining)
Share of GDP: 43% (including mining)
Labor force in manufacturing: 23.6% (including mining)
Value added in manufacturing
  Food & agriculture: 13%
  Textiles: 17%
  Machinery: 25%
  Chemicals: 6%
Earnings per employee in manufacturing: −1.9% (1980–86)
  Growth Rate Index (1980 = 100): 97 (1986)
Total earnings as % of value added: 33
Gross output per employee (1980 = 100): 98 (1986)
Index of Manufacturing Production (1985 = 100): 103 (1988)

---

tain kinds of steel for which there is no market either at home or abroad. With foreign exchange short and imports of iron ore, coking coal and scrap limited, most plants have had to cut down on production. Other branches of industry, such as chemicals, suffer from similar problems.

The total losses of enterprises have grown rapidly since the early 1980s. In 1986 a total of 5% of the enterprises, employing 6% of the labor force, suffered losses amounting to 470 billion dinars. During 1987, rehabilitation programs were applied to 87% of the enterprises, and bankruptcy proceedings were started for 5%. Rehabilitation procedures themselves are not very effective because of the number of competing units in each sector. For example, there are 365 BOALs operating in railways alone. In 1987 a total of 16,000 people were laid off on account of losses incurred in 1986. Moreover, since the beginning of 1987, the application of stricter criteria for defining losses has reduced the loopholes for enterprises to socialize losses either by concealing them or by drawing on public and other social funds.

MINING

Yugoslavia is relatively well endowed in minerals, although only nonferrous minerals are abundant. On the eve of World War II Yugoslavia was the major European producer of bauxite, lead, chromium and antimony and ranked second in the output of zinc, copper and mercury. The reserves of coal are large but of low quality, and iron is scarce. Small amounts of other metals are produced largely as by-products. These include silver, platinum nickel, palladium, bismuth, cadmium, germanium, gold, manganese and selenium.

Yugoslav coal is generally noncoking, but certain varieties may be mixed with imported coking coals. Of the 136 coal basins, the greatest number are in Bosnia-Herzegovina and Serbia. The largest basins are in Rasa in Croatia; Kosovo, Kolubara, Kostolac, Senj-Resava and Aleksinac in Serbia; Kreka, Zenica-Serajevo and Banovici in Bosnia-Herzegovina; and Zagorje-Lasko and Velenje in Slovenia. The vast majority of these mines produce brown coal and lignite. The only two iron ore mines of any importance are those of Vares and Ljubija in Bosnia-Herzegovina. The largest copper reserves are in the Bor and Majdanpek basins in Serbia. Serbia has many other deposits of copper ore, in the eastern part between Krepoljin and Bosiljgrad and in the western part southwest of Zvornik and in the Kapaonik Mountains. Macedonia comes next in size of reserves. Copper also occurs in central Bosnia. Serbia is richest in lead-zinc deposits, found mainly in the Trepca, Rudnik, Veliki, Majdan and Lece basins. In Macedonia lead-zinc is found in the Zletovo Basin and in Slovenia in the Mezica Basin. Yugoslavia is rich in bauxite, and its ore is of high quality. Bauxite deposits occur along the Adriatic coast from Istria to the Albanian border. Yugoslav manganese ore is of poor quality. The principal sources are Cevljanovici, near Sarajevo, in the Ozren Mountains and the Kozara Mountains in Bosnia, in the Kapaonik Mountains and the Rudnik Mountains in Serbia and at Cer near Kicevo in Macedonia. The most important chromium-producing basin is that of Radusa, near Skopje in Macedonia, which supplies almost two-thirds of the output. Serbia and Bosnia have less important deposits. Most of the antimony deposits are in Serbia.

In 1986 production of the main minerals was (in 000 tons): Iron, 6,618; copper, 27,864; lead and zinc ore, 4,588; and bauxite, 3,459.

There is no foreign participation in mining in Yugoslavia.

ENERGY

Domestic sources supply two-thirds of the primary energy consumed. Coal accounts for 63% of the domestic energy supplies, petroleum 19%, natural gas 8%, hydroelectric power 9% and firewood the remainder. Imported oil supplies 28% of the primary energy consumption, and some coking coal accounts for the remainder.

Small deposits of crude oil have been discovered, mostly in 30 fields on the Pannonian Plains. Prospects are considered good for additional finds, and exploration is under way in several areas, including offshore in the Adriatic Sea. Imported oil comes from the Soviet Union, the Middle East and Libya. Soviet oil is shipped by barge up the Danube. The oil terminal at Krk Island in the northern Adriatic serves a pipeline to Hungary and Czechoslovakia as well as to Yugoslavia's seven oil refineries. The refining capacity is considerably in excess of supplies or needs.

Natural gas, some of it associated with crude oil, is found in the Pannonian Plains and in the Adriatic, from where it is transported by pipelines connected to networks leading to Hungary, Czechoslovakia and the Soviet Union. The consumption of natural gas is limited by the lack of distribution facilities and the disinclination of potential consumers to make the necessary conversion investments. The Molve field, opened in 1985 in the Drava Valley, is expected to produce 1 billion cu. m. (35.3 billion cu. ft.) of natural gas annually. Commercial exploitation of gas wells from three wells in the northern Adriatic began in 1988.

Yugoslavia lags behind the Soviet Union as well as many Western European countries in per capita consumption of electricity. Even so, generation of electricity is not meeting demand. The most important source of electric power is hydro, and about 40% to 45% of the hydro potential is being used. The first nuclear power plant, at Krsko in Slovenia, was built in 1981 and has a capacity of 4.4 billion kw.-hr. a year. Long-term plans call for 10 more nuclear power plants to go into production after 1990. The Iron Gates (Djerdap) hydroelectric system on the Danube is operated jointly with Rumania, and by late 1987 a total of eight 27-mw. generating sets at Djerdap II were connected with the Yugoslav grid. Like Rumania, Yugoslavia suffers from chronic power shortages.

ENERGY INDICATORS, 1988

Primary energy production (quadrillion BTU)
  Crude oil: 0.19
  Natural gas liquid: 0.01
  Dry natural gas: 0.09
  Coal: 0.72
  Hydroelectric power: 0.28
  Nuclear power: 0.04
  Total: 1.33
Average annual energy production growth rate (%): 3.0 (1980–87)
Average annual energy consumption growth rate (%): 3.2 (1980–87)
Energy consumption per capita, kg. (lb.) oil equivalent: 2,115 (4,663)
Energy imports as % of merchandise imports (%): 19
Electricity
  Installed capacity (kw.): 16,132,000
  Production (kw.-hr.): 77.381 billion
    % fossil fuel: 56.8
    % hydro: 38.0
    % nuclear: 5.2
  Consumption per capita (kw.-hr.): 3,340
Natural gas, cu. m. (cu. ft.)
  Proved reserves: 84 billion (2.966 trillion)
  Production: 2.283 billion (81 billion)
  Consumption: 5.091 billion (180 billion)
Petroleum, bbl.
  Proved reserves: 200 million
  Years to exhaust proved reserves: 8
  Production: 28 million
  Consumption: 111 million
  Refining capacity per day: 608,000
Coal, 000 tons
  Reserves: 16,570,000
  Production: 68,788
  Consumption: 73,274

LABOR

The national labor force was estimated at 9.6 million in 1988. The principal characteristics of the force are (1) the existence of large migrant force of Yugoslav origin in Western Europe; (2) chronic unemployment, which has been aggravated by the economic downturn of the 1980s; and (3) the relative immobility of labor.

Actual unemployment was about 630,000 in 1987 or 6.5% of the labor force, the lowest in the 1980s. Unemployment is highly regionalized. The less-developed regions have a higher unemployment rate than those that are more developed; Slovenia, the most developed republic, has less than 2% unemployed compared to 27% in Kosovo. However, Yugoslav unemployment data need to be interpreted with some caution. Some of those registering for employment already have some jobs or are students. In addition, unemployment data

LABOR INDICATORS, 1988

Total economically active population: 9.6 million
As % of working-age population: 68.7
% female: 37.8
% under 20 years of age: 9.1
% unemployed: 6.5
Average annual growth rate, 1985–2000 (%): 0.7
Activity rate (%)
    Total: 43.4
    Male: 54.3
    Female: 32.9
% organized labor: 64.5
Hours of work in manufacturing: 45.3 per week
Employment status (%)
    Employers & self-employed: 17.2
    Employees: 65.7
    Unpaid family workers: 10.5
    Other: 6.6
Sectoral employment (%)
    Agriculture, forestry & fishing: 28.7
    Mining: ⎫
          ⎬ 23.6
    Manufacturing: ⎭
    Construction: 7.4
    Transportation & communication: 4.8
    Trade: 8.8
    Finance, real estate: 2.2
    Services: 16.9
    Other: 7.6

are computed on the basis of socialist sector employment only. Further, unemployment is not so much structural as resulting from mismatches between specific regional occupational categories.

The emigrant labor force in Western Europe serves as a safety valve for the Yugoslavian labor market, and the remittances of workers provide valuable foreign exchange. But for the liberalized emigration rules, unemployment would have been even more critical than it is today. However, the exodus had two unintended consequences: It deprived Yugoslavia of some of its most skilled workers at a time of rapid industrialization; and returning workers met with difficulties in reentry to the labor market and related adjustments. There are no foreign workers in Yugoslavia.

Trade unions are organized geographically by republic and province and by trade within these boundaries. Workers do not have the right to form their own trade unions. They are not required to join Communist trade unions, although most do. They elect their own representatives, directly at the local level and indirectly at the upper levels. At the federal level the Confederation of Trade Unions of Yugoslavia (Saveza Sindikata Jugoslavije, SSJ) is the umbrella labor organization. Until the 1980s it maintained only a low profile, but with the austerity conditions prevailing since then, it has become more active in trying to minimize the negative effects of official measures on workers' interests. The Trade Union Organization of Slovenia took the initiative in early 1988 in establishing the country's first postwar strike code. The same organization threatened in September 1988 the first republicwide strike against the steady erosion of worker incomes. In November through a constitutional amendment workers gained the right to strike, the first time such a right has been granted in a Communist state. Instances of police violence against workers are as rare as disciplinary action by firms against strike leaders. In 1988 there were 1,720 strikes (up 2% over 1987) involving 388,000 workers (up 34% over 1987). A growing number of strikes involve only peaceful protest rallies in front of government buildings.

The SSJ has developed bilateral contacts abroad with trade unions of all ideological persuasions, particularly in Austria, Germany and Italy, where Yugoslav workers are most numerous. It is loosely affiliated with the World Confederation of Labor and the European Trade Union Confederation.

There is no collective bargaining in the Western sense, as all firms are socially owned by BOALs, in which workers have a voice in selecting the management and approving major as well as minor business decisions. However, in the 1980s the authority of the BOALs to increase wages was curtailed, forcing workers to strike when their wage demands were not met.

The minimum age of employment is 16. The official workweek is 42 hours, with generous vacation time and sick leave benefits. The republics set minimum wage levels, which vary widely. Given the high inflation rate, these minimum wages hardly serve to maintain a decent standard of life. In Slovenia, for example, the minimum net wage in 1988 was $152 per month. Although there are extensive laws on worker safety in the statute books, they are enforced leniently.

FOREIGN COMMERCE

Since World War II foreign trade has been important to the economy primarily because of the need for imports. In the early years most manufactured goods had to be imported. As the domestic industrial base expanded, the import dependency shifted toward raw and semifinished materials. The ratio of imports to the GDP has remained fairly stable over the years at 21%. Exports also expanded and diversified along with the rest of the economy, but there was no close relationship between economic growth and exports. For most industries, exports were a minor activity, and rapid economic growth tended to diminish the need to export. The ratio of exports to the GDP at 10% is the lowest in the OECD area. Balance-of-payments difficulties are a recurrent problem, causing frequent policy shifts and growing foreign indebtedness.

Until the early 1960s, Yugoslavia retained many of the features of the Soviet model system established in the mid-1940s. One feature was the separation of domestic prices from those in other countries through a variety of buffers. An implicit system of multiple exchange rates provided one of the buffers and also incentives for exports. By 1965 foreign trade was liberalized, and many of the interventions were abolished or reduced. The new goal was alignment of domestic prices with international prices, integration of the country into the world economy and the eventual convertibility of the dinar. These goals still hold in 1990.

The principal components of the foreign trade system established in 1965 were:

• Free disposal of foreign exchange earned by enterprises within the limits set by regulations was established.

• The foreign exchange accounts of enterprises can be established in Yugoslavian banks and used for payments abroad for various business transactions.

• Those firms exporting more than 50% of their production were given the right to use freely their foreign exchange earned by their exports to import raw materials and semifinished goods.

• Enterprises could keep about 20% of their foreign exchange earnings as their retention quota.

• Foreign exchange self-financing was introduced to enable enterprises to enter various forms of credit arrangements with foreign firms and banks.

• An interbank foreign exchange market was introduced to provide a more flexible mechanism for adjusting the economy to changes in world markets.

• All exports were deregulated with two exceptions: An export license is required when there is a shortage of the item on the domestic market, where national health could be endangered or where national security is at stake; and an export permission is required when the free flows of exports could endanger the regional balance of foreign trade.

• Imports, however, are strictly regulated through eight institutional arrangements: (1) Free imports or liberalized imports (LB) are subject to the deposit in dinars of the funds equivalent to the foreign exchange needed. (2) There are conditionally free imports from a nonconvertible currency region. (3) The global foreign exchange quota is an instrument restricting imports on the basis of the total value of the previously achieved level of import transactions. It is distributed to various importers according to certain criteria. (4) The goods contingent quota covers a relatively small category of goods used to improve regional balances in flows of goods. (5) Import license "D" is issued for specific types of imports, such as guns and drugs. (6) Imports are based on export earnings. (7) The import of capital equipment is a global quota distributed among the six republics and two provinces. (8) Import of personal consumption goods is under LB or global quotas.

To promote exports, six measures are applied: (1) a 3% tax benefit for goods exports to convertible currency countries; (2) a 5% tariff compensation for imported inputs used in the production of goods for exports to convertible-currency countries; (3) preferential treatment for credit discounts for capital equipment and ship exports as well as for investment activities abroad; (4) aid from the fund for credits and insurance of export activities; (5) aid from special funds for exports of cattle, meat, etc.; (6) aid from the Fund for Promotion of Economic Publicity Abroad.

In the late 1970s several laws altered the administrative structure of foreign trade. Communities of Interest for Foreign Economic Relations (CIFERs) were set up at the federal, republic and provincial levels. CIFERs draft national and regional balance-of-payments plans, administer the export incentive program, allocate and regulate foreign borrowing rights and allocate and regulate the use of foreign exchange.

FOREIGN TRADE INDICATORS, 1988

Exports: $11.397 billion
Imports: $12.549 billion
Balance of trade: −$1.152 billion
Annual growth rate (%), exports: 1.1 (1980–87)
Annual growth rate (%), imports: −2.0 (1980–87)
Ratio of international reserves to imports (in months): 1.2
Value of manufactured exports ($): 8.320 billion (1986)
Terms of trade (1980 = 100): 116 (1987)
Export Price Index (1980 = 100): 114 (1983)
Import Price Index (1980 = 100): 113 (1983)
Exports of goods as % of GDP: 21.0
Imports of goods as % of GDP: 22.0

Direction of Trade (%)

	Imports	Exports
EEC	40.0	34.8
U.S.A.	5.7	6.4
East European countries	29.6	34.2
Japan	1.4	0.3

Composition of Trade (%)

	Imports	Exports
Food & agricultural raw materials	12.4	12.8
Ores & minerals	2.8	1.0
Fuels	17.4	1.9
Manufactured goods	67.4	84.3
of which chemicals	16.3	11.3
of which machinery	13.5	30.4

Services play a more important role in the balance of payments than the trade balance. The most important inflow is from workers abroad, although these remittances have declined since 1980. Tourism and transportation services also are important as well as service payments from construction contracts overseas won by Yugoslav firms.

Tariffs are generally low. The average effective rate in 1988 was 7% to 8%, with a maximum of 25% (for arms and ammunition) and a low of 1% for minerals.

The relatively low degree of Yugoslavia's integration into the world economy is reflected in the small share of its external transactions in the GSP. Moreover, except for a short period after the first oil shock, the relative trade of merchandise trade has remained roughly the same since 1970, in contrast to marked increases elsewhere.

The most important part of trade is with developing countries and COMECON countries, predominantly on a clearing basis. This pattern is an indication of the difficulty of penetrating OECD markets, given deficiencies in quality, design, technology and marketing. Until 1985 trade on a clearing basis accounted for one-third of the total but fell to nearly one-fourth between 1986 and 1988. This decline is largely attributable to the fall in the oil price, as about half of oil and gas imports are on a clearing basis. Manufactures account for the largest part of exports on a clearing basis. A salient feature of the commodity composition of foreign trade is the small share of finished consumer goods, less than 5%. Finished manufactures dominate exports; raw materials ores and metals and fuels dominate imports. The share of food and agricultural raw materials has shrunk markedly since 1983. On the other hand, the share of manufactures—80% in 1986—is above the OECD average. Even more significant is the large number of exported products. Another indicator is the fact that

Yugoslavia has the smallest concentration index of any OECD or developing country.

In 1988 the government announced a program of import liberalization. The proportion of free imports was raised from 14% to 50%, the proportion of imports under licensing and quota regimes was reduced from 51% to 26% and that under the conditionally free import regime to 34%. The liberalization was completed in 1990.

TRANSPORTATION & COMMUNICATIONS

Railroads in Yugoslavia are owned by eight self-managing enterprises—one in each republic and province. The coordinating body is the Community of Yugoslav Railways. The total trackage of 9,279 km. (5,767 mi.) is standard-gauge; 893 km. (555 mi.) is double-track; and 3,771 km. (2,344 mi.) is electrified. The density is greatest in the North and thins out in the South. Thirty-four rail lines cross the border in the North and Northwest but only four in the South, including a 25-km. (16-mi.) line linking Titograd and Shkoder in Albania that was completed in 1985.

The road network of 119,401 km. (74,208 mi.) includes 807 km. (502 mi.) of superhighways. The most important roads are the main inland route through Lju-

---

COMMUNICATIONS INDICATORS, 1988

Telephones
Total (000): 3,598
Persons per: 6.5
Phone traffic (000 calls)
Local: 3.845 million
Long distance: 7.978 million
International: 2.970 million
Post office
Number of post offices: 3,892
Pieces of mail handled (000): 1,232,839
Telegraph, Total traffic (000): 12,388
Telex:
Subscriber lines: 12,999
Traffic (000 minutes): 316,077
Telecommunications
2 satellite ground stations

TOURISM & TRAVEL INDICATORS, 1988

Total tourism receipts ($): 1.105 billion
Expenditures by nationals abroad ($): 86 million
Number of tourists (000): 23,357
of whom (%) from
West Germany 30.9
Italy 13.1
Austria 9.1
United Kingdom 7.1
Average length of stay (nights): 6.0

---

bljana, Zagreb, Belgrade, Nis and Skopje to the Greek frontier, and the Adriatic highway linking Rijeka, Split, Dubrovnik and Titograd. Work on the 7,864-m. (4.9-mi.) Karavanke road tunnel (of which 3,450 m. (2.1 mi.) are in Yugoslavia) linking Slovenia with Rosenbach in Austria was completed in 1990.

Despite the favorable geographical location and the abundance of good harbors—Rijeka, Split, Koper, Bar and Ploce—the presence of the Dinaric Alps only a short distance from the coast limits the development of maritime transportation. Similarly, the topography works against the development of inland waterways. All rivers flow into the Danube and thus into the Black Sea. No major river flows into the Adriatic. There is no connection between any of the large rivers, and further inland rivers are concentrated in the northern part of the country. A 321-km. (200-mi.) canal connects the Danube and the Tisza.

There are 20 international airports, of which the largest is at Belgrade. The national flag carrier is JAT (Jugoslovenski Aerotransport). Three smaller airlines also serve the domestic air traveler: Adria Airways, Air Yugoslavia and Aviogenex.

DEFENSE

Yugoslav defense forces consist of two distinct elements: the Yugoslav People's Army (YPA) and the Territorial Defense Force (TDF). The latter is essentially a regional command, with each republic and province having considerable autonomy. The TDF is not part of the Federal Secretariat for National Defense-YPA chain of command, although local TDF units fall under the YPA tactical command.

Under the National Defense Law of 1974 the operational head of the armed forces is the federal secretary for national defense, who exercises control through a

---

TRANSPORTATION INDICATORS, 1988

Roads, km. (mi.): 119,401 (74,208)
% paved: 59
Motor vehicles
Automobiles: 2,957,116
Trucks: 283,180
Persons per vehicle: 7.2
Road freight, tonne-km. (ton-mi.): 22.999 billion (15.753 billion)
Railroads
Track, km. (mi.): 9,279 (5,767); electrified, km. (mi.): 3,771 (2,344)
Passenger traffic, passenger-km. (passenger-mi.): 12.398 billion (7.704 billion)
Freight, freight tonne-km. (freight ton-mi.): 27.573 billion (18.886 billion)
Merchant marine
Vessels: 498
Total deadweight tonnage: 4,939,900
No. oil tankers: 12   GRT: 217,000
Ports
Number: 5 major
Cargo loaded (tons): 9,888,000
Cargo unloaded (tons): 25,380,000
Air
Km. (mi.) flown: 36 million (22.3 million)
Passengers: 3.409 million
Passenger traffic, passenger-km. (passenger-mi.): 7.008 billion (4.355 billion)
Freight traffic, freight tonne-km. (freight ton-mi.): 110.7 million (75.8 million)
Mail tonne-km. (mail ton-mi.): 2.9 million (1.8 million)
Airports with scheduled flights: 5
Airports: 184
Pipelines
Crude, km. (mi.): 1,373 (853)
Refined, km. (mi.): 150 (93)
Natural gas, km. (mi.): 2,900 (1,801)
Inland waterways
Length, km. (mi.): 2,001 (1,243)
Cargo, tonne-km. (ton-mi.): 3.926 billion (2.689 billion)

DEFENSE INDICATORS, 1988

Defense budget ($): 2.86 billion
% of central budget: 55.1
% of GNP: 4.94
Military expenditures per capita ($): 121.38
Military expenditures per soldier ($): 15,212.00
Military expenditures per sq. km. (per sq. mi.) ($): 11,180.60 (28,965.28)
Total strength of armed forces: 188,000
    Per 1,000: 8
Reserves: 440,000
Arms exports ($): 60 million
Arms imports ($): 20 million

PERSONNEL & EQUIPMENT

Army
    Personnel: 144,000
    Organization: 6 military regions; 1 maritime military region; 3 corps headquarters; 12 infantry divisions; 9 infantry brigades; 8 independent tank brigades; 3 mountain brigades; 1 airborne brigade; 10 artillery regiments; 6 antitank regiments; 11 AA artillery regiments; 4 SAM regiments
    Equipment: 1,500 main battle tanks; 13 light tanks; 92 reconnaissance vehicles; 360 mechanized infantry combat vehicles; 200 armored personnel carriers; 1,751 towed artillery; 3,000 mortars; 2,300 air defense guns
Navy
    Personnel: 11,000, including 900 marines
    Bases: Lora/Split; Pula; Sibenik; Kardeljevo; Kotor/Trivat
    Equipment: 5 submarines; 3 frigates; 16 missile craft; 15 torpedo craft; 40 patrol boats; 14 mine warfare vessels; 35 amphibious craft
    Coastal defense: 25 coast artillery batteries
Air force
    Personnel: 33,000
    Organization: 12 fighter ground attack squadrons; 9 fighter squadrons; 4 reconnaissance squadrons
    Equipment: 431 combat aircraft; 150 armored helicopters

subordinate, the chief of the general staff. There are seven military districts, based in Belgrade, Skopje, Split, Zagreb, Sarajevo, Ljubljana and Serbia. The two major air commands are based in Zomun and Zagreb. The navy, commanded from Lora/Split, has three regional commands, based in Pula, Sibenik and Kotor/Trivat.

Outside the operational chain of command but overseeing it is the National Defense (or Military) Council, an advisory body to the Federal Executive Council.

The principal source of manpower is the conscription system, which applies equally to all male citizens. Conscientious objection is not legally acknowledged. About 60% of the males who annually reach age 17 are inducted into the service for a 15-month tour of duty. Volunteers are enlisted for three- to nine-year periods. Deferments and exemptions are rare. Noncommissioned officers are selected from two sources: conscripts and qualified applicants directly from the civilian work force. In either case, they undergo training at a noncommissioned officers' school, from which they graduate with the rank of sergeant. Commissioned officers are obtained from two sources: graduates of army, navy and air force academies, and well-qualified noncommissioned officers who have passed a regular officers' examination. Serving in the Reserve Force is part of compulsory military service and the military obligation of all citizens. The Reserve Force includes all male citizens aged 18 to 55 for conscripts and reserve non-

commissioned officers and up to the age of 60 for reserve officers and warrant officers.

Military schools are comparable to secondary, intermediate and higher civilian ones. Noncommissioned officers are trained in secondary military schools in two- to four-year courses. Courses for commissioned officers in the military academies—classified by branch of service—last from three to five years. Above them are command and staff academies, the High Military Political Schools, the National Defense School and the Military Medical Academy. Additionally, there are schools for reserve officers.

EDUCATION

Yugoslavia was educationally underdeveloped before World War II. Except in Slovenia, where the enlightened Habsburgs had established schools, illiteracy was widespread. As late as 1931, a total of 44% of the population over 10 was illiterate. Shortly after seizing control in 1945, Tito began to move against the "bourgeois educational system." Article 38 of the Constitution of 1946 stated, "The state pays special attention to the youth and protects their education. Schools are state-owned. . . ." The Committee for Schools and Science was formed to reorganize the educational system. During the next two decades, particularly after the break with the Soviet Union, education was decentralized and placed under communities of interest. Most laws affecting education are passed by the republics and provinces. Nevertheless, there have been many central laws laying down overall guidelines, such as the General Law on Education of 1959. Congresses of the League of Communists of Yugoslavia also formulate educational policy through decisions that are later enacted by the republics and provinces.

Elementary school is eight years in duration, comprising grades one to eight and is compulsory for all children between ages seven and 15. Attendance at this level is virtually universal, except among Muslim Albanians.

The academic year in schools generally lasts from about the first Monday in September to the middle of June, with only slight variations. For university students the academic year runs from the first week of October to the end of May.

The Constitution provides that each national minority has the right of instruction in its own language. The majority ethnic group in each republic or province has its own schools, and minorities have either separate schools or separate classes within a school. The curriculum of instruction is the same in majority or minority languages. In multiethnic communities, instruction in a class or school may be bilingual. A complete series of textbooks has been issued for both Hungarian and Albanian minority schools, but textbooks are available only for certain grade levels and subjects for the other minorities. In higher grades Serbo-Croatian texts are used; Albanian in Kosovo; Macedonian in Macedonia; and Slovene in Slovenia.

In elementary schools testing takes place frequently throughout the school year, and there are no comprehensive examinations for promotion or graduation. Formerly, all secondary-level students were required to take the matura, but this requirement has been phased out. The grading system is generally on a five-point scale: 5, *odlichen* (excellent); 4, *vrlo dobar* (very good); 3, *dobar* (good); 2, *dovoljen* (satisfactory) and 1, *rkdav* (bad). In the case of some subjects in primary schools, teachers' descriptive evaluations replace numerical grades. Failure of students in elementary grades is strongly discouraged, with the result that there are almost no failures in grades one through four and very few in grades five through eight. Instead, slow students are given supplementary instruction during schooltime in the lower grades and during vacations in the higher grades. Gifted students also receive additional instruction to enable them to skip grades. Grading in higher educational institutional institutions is on a different scale: 10, *deset* (excellent); 9, *devet* (very good); 8, *osam* (good); 7, *sedam* (satisfactory); 6, *shest* (fair); and 5, *pet* (fail).

Except for theological schools for training clergy, there are no private schools in Yugoslavia.

The development of curricula and teaching programs is the responsibility of the education councils at the republican level. Textbooks are published by state publication bodies, such as the Institution for the Publication of Textbooks in Serbia.

Education remains deeply embedded in Marxist philosophy. The emphasis on education for work, the alliance between schools and agricultural and industrial enterprises, and the use of schooltime and premises for agricultural and manufacturing activities are all based on classical Marxist theory and are characteristics that Yugoslavia shares with other Communist countries.

Children from ages three to six may attend a program of preschool education (*predshkolski odgoj*). Attendance is not compulsory, and nurseries are not an integral part of the school system. Nurseries may operate on a half-day or a full-day basis, sometimes in an elementary school and sometimes in separate buildings. Preschool programs generally exist throughout the country, but more of them function in urban areas and fewer in mountainous and remote regions. They may be established by a commune, neighborhood group, elementary school, factory or agricultural enterprise. Tuition fees on a sliding scale are charged in all cases, and financing also is obtained from communities of interest, elementary schools and local sociopolitical communities.

Primary education is essentially the same throughout the country. The elementary school *(osnovna shkola)* is compulsory for all children between ages of seven and 15. Enrollment is virtually universal in the northern republics, but poor attendance is an acute problem in the South.

The typical elementary-school curriculum includes material from the humanities, sciences and mathematics, music and art, physical education and industrial arts. The number of teaching hours with academic content in each grade level varies from 18 to 19 hours in grade one to 25 to 28 hours in grade eight, both weekly. In addition, approximately 70 to 80 hours per year are allotted for courses of a nonacademic nature, including first aid, home economics, sex education, agriculture and career information. All schools include special courses in Marxism. Extracurricular activities of a socialist nature are an integral part of the elementary program, most of them conducted under the auspices of the Pioneers. Participation in patriotic celebrations and community activities also are encouraged.

Secondary education is not compulsory. The secondary institutions are of various types, with programs of study lasting three to four years. The gymnasium (*gimnazija*) is the school of general education, lasting four years. It is divided into three types—classical, scientific and modern languages—although some schools provide the students with the option of mixing these.

One of the aims of Yugoslavian education at all levels is the development of economic competence through acquisition of vocational skills or a profession. Emphasis on this aim begins in nursery school and primary grades. In secondary schools education in labor involves contracting with industry for work for the students to do in the school shop. In addition, there is also what is known as vacation work experience, planned course-related practical work performed by students during summer vacations. Formal vocational training is available by enrollment in a school for the training of skilled workers (usually a two-year program) and at a vocational education center. These latter institutions are of various types, and some are integrated schools that combine regular secondary training with vocational training. The school grade level completed and the level of individual vocational competence are highly interrelated. This system obtains its legal sanction from the Agreement on Unified Bases for Occupational Classification, which divides all vocational and professional activities into eight levels and sublevels of complexity. Marxism is integrated into the curriculum through a course titled "The Basis of Marxism and Self-Managing Socialism." Much emphasis also is placed on military preparedness.

Universities function under provisions of self-management not unlike those of industry. They are considered autonomous work organizations and have the status of self-managing work institutions governed by the working collective—in this case, the academic staff and through faculty elections of deans and rectors. The executive staff of a university consists of the rector and prorectors, who serve generally for two or four years. The University of Zagreb includes a student prorector. The University Assembly, the highest organ, includes representatives of students; deans; professors; and various political, industrial, commercial, scientific and social organizations, including the League of Communists of Yugoslavia and the local city council. Most faculty councils include an executive committee and a council on content and instruction. For an institution to be recognized as a university, at least three faculties must be represented. Under this legal definition, there are 16 universities, of which eight came into existence since 1970, and all but three (Zagreb, Ljubljana and Belgrade) since World War II. Together these universities have 213 faculties. In addition, there are 122 higher schools (*vishe shkole*) below the university level, 19 academies

EDUCATION INDICATORS, 1988

Literacy
  Total (%): 89.6
  Male (%): 95.5
  Female (%): 83.9
First level
  Schools: 12,148
  Teachers: 137,201
  Students: 2,846,845
  Student–teacher ratio: 21:1
  Net enrollment rate (%): 80
  Females (%): 48
Second level
  Schools: 1,212
  Teachers: 62,797
  Students: 952,904
  Student–teacher ratio: 15:1
  Net enrollment rate (%): 76
  Females (%): 47
Third level
  Institutions: 103
  Teachers: 25,629
  Students: 349,013
  Student–teacher ratio: 14:1
  Gross enrollment rate (%): 19.5
  Graduates per 100,000 age 20–24: 1,571
  Females (%): 45
Foreign study
  Foreign students in national universities: 7,982
  Students abroad: 3,736
    of whom in
      United States, 419
      West Germany, 1,864
      Italy, 244
      Austria, 380
Public expenditures (national currency)
  Total: 821.68 billion
  % of GNP: 3.9
  % current expenditures: 90.6

GRADUATES, 1982

Total: 58,790
Education: 7,694
Humanities & religion: 3,720
Fine & applied arts: 645
Law: 5,543
Social & behavioral sciences: 13,602
Commerce & business: 1,785
Mass communication: 61
Home economics: 87
Service trades: 1,005
Natural sciences: 2,245
Medicine: 5,385
Engineering: 10,655
Architecture: 670
Industrial programs: 440
Transportation & communications: 1,918
Agriculture, forestry, fisheries: 2,310
Other: 1,025

or faculties of art, and four specialized higher schools of university rank.

The lecture is the predominant form of teaching. Discussion groups, panels and student reports are almost never used in a formal classroom setting. Students are encouraged to participate in work activities in keeping with the Marxist emphasis on education in labor. Generally tuition is free in institutions of higher education,

although a nominal fee is charged for adult programs. Students provide their own books and supplies as well as their room and board. Sometimes an industry or a commercial organization will sponsor an employee as a student. Because institutions possess considerable internal autonomy, there are differences in the school calendar, programs' length of study and languages of instruction. Minority languages may be used in certain institutions; for example, Albanian and Serbo-Croatian are used at the University of Prishtina, and Hungarian also is used at the University of Novi Sad. Because excessive differences in university practices create problems in mutual acceptability of degrees, there has been a trend toward greater uniformity, primarily under the auspices of the Association of Yugoslavian Universities.

There are four levels of university diplomas. The first-level diploma and professional qualification are roughly equivalent to junior college in the United States. The second-level diploma is a professional title, such as engineer, doctor, attorney, economist or architect. Successful completion of studies at the third level leads to an academic degree of either specialist *(specijalist)* or master *(magistar)*. The highest degree is the doctorate, which is awarded after at least two years of research and study following a *magistar* from which a dissertation has resulted that the candidate has been able to defend successfully.

Academic ranks include the following, although not all institutions have all of them: *redovni professori* (regular professor); *izvanredni professori* (extraordinary professor); *docenti* (assistant professor); *vishi predavachi* (senior instructor); *predavachi* (instructor); *starji assistenti* (senior assistant); and *assistenti* (assistant).

What distinguishes educational administration in Yugoslavia from that in other Communist countries is the principle of self-management. In a school the basic unit of self-management is the workers' council, which consists of representatives of all those with a vested interest in the school, such as teachers, as well as delegates of outside bodies representing the commune; parents; industrial and commercial organizations; the armed forces; and sociopolitical organizations such as the League of Communists of Yugoslavia, the Socialist Alliance of Working People and the Trade Union Confederation. The council appoints the director of the school for a four-year term, but he may be recalled earlier under certain circumstances. Faculty at higher educational institutions may form a BOAL at the *katedra* (departmental) level. The BOAL of this *katedra* may have its own council, especially if the *katedra* is large. In turn, the faculty or school consisting of several departments has an interdepartmental council. The university council generally includes members representing the various schools of the university. The system of self-management requires teachers, administrators and auxiliary personnel to sign one or more self-management agreements, which are binding on all.

Yugoslavia has a decentralized system of education in which education is essentially the responsibility of each republic. The involvement of the federal government is limited to military schools, certain schools for the training of security personnel and international education programs. There is no federal ministry of education.

At the republic level the ultimate responsibility for education rests with its assembly. Most of these functions are delegated to the republican committee or secretariat of education, which maintains an inspectorate service that visits schools and provides consultative services. A second council is an executive body known as the educational council, which reviews and ratifies teaching programs, syllabi and curricula for preschool institutions, elementary schools and gymnasia. A third important body at this level is the institute or council for the advancement of education. This body is primarily responsible for carrying out research. Educational research also is carried out by teacher training institutions and pedagogical faculties of universities as well as separate national organizations such as the University Center for Pedagogical Education and Research of the University of Zagreb and the School of Industrial Pedagogy at Rijeka.

In 1960 the Federal Assembly passed the Basic Law Concerning the Financing of the Educational System. This law introduced a provision whereby 10% of the total levy on the personal income of workers could be allotted to the school funds of the communes and republics. Each commune also was permitted to obtain additional revenues from other sources. The federal government's source of revenue for educational purposes is restricted to funds available to it in the federal budget. In 1966 the Law on Educational Financing was passed that made the schools independent of the commune, province or republic in obtaining funding. Under this law the education tax levied on the personal incomes of workers goes directly to the educational communities of interest. In addition, a certain percentage of the ad valorem tax on goods and services within the commune or republic can be earmarked directly for education.

The financing of education at the republican level differs somewhat from that at the lower level. At the republican level the funds from taxes on the incomes of workers is a minor source and the ad valorem tax is the major source. Overall, the republican share of total educational expenditures is about 25%.

Under the Law on Educational Financing, there is no state salary schedule for teachers. In some schools teachers' salaries are geared to the achievement of stated educational outcomes.

Forms of adult education have existed in some areas since the beginning of the century. In Zagreb a People's University was established in 1907, and it became the forerunner of the so-called people's universities. Workers' universities were formed after World War II. Adult courses generally last one or two years and are scheduled mostly in the afternoon or evening. Admission is open to all adults, but tuition is charged. Basic education for adults also is provided through regular day or evening classes in primary schools. Vocational education for adults is provided in factory training programs and in the regular vocational schools through night classes and extramurally. Few gymnasia have adult education programs.

Preschool teachers (*vaspitaci*) are trained in preschool teacher training institutions of secondary-school status in which the course of study lasts five years. Teachers for primary grades (one through four) are called *ucitelji* and generally obtain their training at secondary-level teacher-training institutions. The program of study lasts five or six years. Teachers in the upper elementary grades (five through eight) are known as *nastavnici* and receive their training in higher teacher training institutions in which the course of study lasts two years. More frequently upper-elementary-school teachers have university training.

Teachers in secondary schools have the title of *professori*. Those teaching academic subjects receive their education in universities. Prospective vocational-school teachers are trained initially in a pedagogical academy and later enroll in special industrial-pedagogical departments of universities, where they receive both industrial training and teacher training.

LEGAL SYSTEM

The Yugoslav legal system is a mixture of a civil law system and Marxist legal theory. The court system, as defined in Chapter V (Articles 217 to 236) of the Constitution, is divided into a federal court, eight regional court systems and constitutional courts for each of the republics and provinces and the federation. The Constitutional Court of Yugoslavia is composed of a president and 13 members (two from each republic and one from each province), who are appointed by the Assembly of Yugoslavia and serve for a nonrenewable eight-year term. The Constitutional Court can judge whether legislation agrees with the federal constitution and whether republican and federal laws conflict with federal law. Republican and provincial laws, however, need not agree with federal laws. The court also can judge the constitutionality of federal regulations; judge whether these regulations and the acts of other bodies agree or conflict with federal law; and resolve disputes between the federation and the regions or federal organs and regional organs, or among the regions (or regional organs) over their respective powers and authority. However, the court cannot become involved in judgments concerning the regional constitutions; these are reserved to the individual constitutional courts of the republics and provinces. Hence the Constitutional Court of Yugoslavia does not serve as a court of appeal above the regional constitutional courts.

The functions of the regional constitutional courts parallel the functions of the Constitutional Court of Yugoslavia, a federal body. To maintain a certain degree of uniformity among the regional legal systems, the constitutional courts of the republics and the provinces hold regular consultative meetings to review their decisions. Through this device an informal but effective link has been established between courts that are otherwise entirely independent of each other. The caseloads of these courts is composed primarily of challenges to the constitutionality of regulations or other acts adopted by self-management enterprises and communities rather than challenges to laws passed by governmental organs. Cases that involve no challenges to the constitutionality of an act or regulation but relate to the nonfulfillment of contracts or agreements are in the jurisdiction of the self-management courts. Decisions of the self-management courts may be appealed to constitutional or regular courts. A system of economic courts serves a parallel function for cases involving economic or financial relations of self-management enterprises or other legal entities other than individuals. The system is headed by a supreme economic court.

The regular court system is divided into local or communal courts and supreme courts in each republic or province. There also is a Federal Supreme Court, whose jurisdiction is limited to federal legislation and other acts administered by federal agencies. The Federal Supreme Court does not serve as a court of appeal above the regional supreme courts, although it does resolve jurisdictional disputes among them. Outside of the regular court system is a system of military courts, with the Supreme Military Court at its head. Regional courts are conducted in the predominant regional language. Judges are elected or dismissed by an assembly—the Assembly of Yugoslavia in the case of federal judges, and republic or provincial assemblies in the case of republic and provincial judges. The Federal Council for the Judiciary exercises overall supervision over the judiciary.

Overall control and supervision of the prison system rests with the Federal Secretariat for Internal Affairs, except for military prisons, which are administered by the Secretariat for National Defense. By delegation of authority, the penal institutions in the republics and provinces are administered by their respective secretariats for internal affairs. Penal institutions comprise penitentiaries, reformatories and jails, in all of which men and women are segregated. Special wards or sections are maintained for categories of prisoners, such as alcoholics, pregnant women, juvenile offenders and political prisoners. All prisoners sentenced to strict imprisonment are required to work, if physically able, and the work schedule is prescribed as eight hours per day, six days a week. Prisoners also are allowed to work outside the prison on a supervised basis but receive reduced wages. Prisoners are authorized to keep only part of their wages, one portion being withheld until discharge and the remainder going toward the support of dependents or relatives.

Prison conditions are strict and harsh but not inhumane. By law prison inmates are entitled to free medical care, the right to correspond and the privilege of receiving parcels and visitors. However, conditions vary considerably among the republics.

LAW ENFORCEMENT

Two major nationwide police organizations—the State Security Service (Sluzba Drzavne Bezbednosti, SDB) and a conventional people's militia known as the Public Security Service (Sluzba Javne Bezbednosti, SJB)—are in charge of public order and internal security in Yugoslavia. The SJB is charged primarily with the customary duties of preserving law and order, but it also cooperates with the SDB in the suppression of political nonconformity or antiregime activity. The two organizations represent modified versions of the earlier security forces created by Tito in the 1940s. Although they ostensibly operate under a decentralized self-management system at the federal, republican and local levels under the Basic Law on Internal Affairs of 1966, the Federal Secretariat for Internal Affairs exercises close and direct control over the operation of both agencies and is empowered to issue binding instructions to their personnel. However, in the republics and provinces, police regulations and procedures are far from standardized. By law, internal security is no longer an area under exclusive federal jurisdiction.

The SDB is organized as a decentralized agency, with units at each level operating under a chief of state security, who is responsible to the respective organs of internal security at the federal or lower levels. All SDB units have a common mission specified in Article 39 of the Basic Law of 1966 as the "gathering of data and other information for the purpose of discovering organized and secret activities aimed at undermining or subverting the constitutionally established order." The Federal Secretariat for Internal Affairs coordinates rather than directs these activities.

The Federal Secretariat for Internal Affairs also is responsible for the supervision and coordination of the SJB, which is organized on a decentralized basis, with units operating at all governmental levels. In addition to regular police functions, the SJB also is in charge of traffic control, fire fighting, the conduct of criminal investigations, the control of movements across borders and the security of prisons and penitentiaries.

The basic SJB unit is the local or commune police, with a varying number of police stations and substations. Posts also are maintained at borders to control smuggling and illegal migration and to assist in customs collection. The SJB is organized and uniformed on military lines. They normally patrol in groups of two or four men, but units of up to company size are available to deal with emergencies. Generally, weapons are limited to sidearms, but in the case of serious disorders billy clubs, rifles, submachine guns, tear gas equipment and protective helmets are available for issue. In 1967 all insignia of rank were abolished within the SJB and substituted by insignia of function or service. Such insignia are displayed on shoulder boards or on the upper left arm. Recruits receive a minimum of three months of basic training, supplemented by periodic refresher courses at police schools. Officers are recruited from the ranks of army officers and reserve officers.

Data on incidence and types of crime in Yugoslavia are not available.

HEALTH

The expansion of health care in the socialist era has been dramatic. In prewar Yugoslavia, malaria, typhus, typhoid, syphilis, dysentery and trachoma were endemic. The kingdom had its highest death rate from tuberculosis. Health care was largely limited to the cities;

HEALTH INDICATORS, 1988

Health personnel
  Physicians: 40,329
    Persons per: 577
  Dentists: 9,278
  Nurses: 67,468
  Pharmacists: 5,047
  Midwives: 7,747
Hospitals
  Number: 425
  Number of beds: 141,039
  Beds per 10,000: 61
Admissions/discharges
  Per 10,000: 1,275
  Bed occupancy rate (%): 85.9
  Average length of stay (days): 15
Type of hospitals (%)
  Government: 100
Public health expenditures
  Per capita: $123.30
Vital statistics
  Crude death rate per 1,000: 9.1
  Decline in death rate: 5.7 (1965–84)
  Life expectancy at birth (years): males, 66.0; females, 74.0
  Infant mortality rate per 1,000 live births: 25.0
  Child mortality rate (ages 1–4 years)/per 1,000: 2.0
  Maternal mortality rate per 100,000 live births: 21
Causes of death per 100,000
  Infectious & parasitic diseases: 15.8
  Cancer: 136.4
  Endocrine & metabolic disorders: 12.4
  Diseases of the nervous system: 7.4
  Diseases of the circulatory system: 486.4
  Diseases of the digestive system: 43.1
  Accidents, poisoning & violence: 59.9
  Diseases of the respiratory system: 64.8

Health Care, representing users, employees and professionals. In general, each commune has a health center, and many communes have established cooperative facilities with neighboring communes.

FOOD & NUTRITION

In 1988 the daily consumption of calories was 3,621.3 per capita and the per capita daily consumption of protein was 102.3g. (3.6 oz.).

MEDIA & CULTURE

Printing presses were set up in Montenegro and Croatia in the last part of the 15th century and later appeared in Bosnia, Serbia and Slovenia. However, these were limited to the production of religious works. In fact, the first periodicals in any of the southern Slavic languages were printed outside the country, beginning with *Slav-*

FOOD & NUTRITION INDICATORS, 1988

Per capita daily food consumption, calories: 3,621.3
Per capita daily consumption, proteins, g. (oz.): 102.3 (3.6)
Calorie intake as % of FAO recommended minimum requirement: 142
% of calorie intake from vegetable products: 77
% of calorie intake from animal products: 23
Food expenditures as % of total household expenditures: 49.4
% of total calories derived from:
  Cereals: 46.0
  Potatoes: 2.7
  Meat & poultry: 7.8
  Fish: 0.3
  Fats & oils: 15.6
  Eggs & milk: 8.2
  Fruits & vegetables: 3.7
  Other: 15.8
Per capita consumption of foods, kg., l. (lb., pt.)
  Potatoes: 55.4 (122.1)
  Wheat: 139.5 (307.5)
  Rice: 1.7 (3.7)
  Fresh vegetables: 90.8 (199.5)
  Fruits (total): 60.8 (134.0)
    Citrus: 2.9 (6.4)
    Noncitrus: 57.9 (127.6)
  Eggs: 175 (385.8)
  Honey: 0.4 (0.8)
  Fish: 3.2 (7.0)
  Milk: 95.9 (211.4)
  Butter: 0.7 (1.5)
  Cheese: 6.6 (14.5)
  Meat (total): 56.5 (124.5)
    Beef & veal: 14.7 (32.4)
    Pig meat: 34.1 (75.2)
    Poultry: 5.4 (11.9)
    Mutton, lamb & goat: 2.3 (5.0)
  Sugar: 38.9 (85.7)
  Chocolate: 2.1 (4.6)
  Margarine: 3.1 (6.9)
  Biscuits: 5.2 (11.4)
  Beer, l. (pt.): 44.2 (93.4)
  Wine, l. (pt.): 29.0 (61.3)
  Alcoholic liquors, l. (pt.): 2.3 (4.8)
  Soft drinks, l. (pt.): 17.0 (35.9)
  Mineral waters, l. (pt.): 23.0 (48.6)
  Coffee: 0.1 (0.2)
  Tea: 0.9 (1.9)
  Cocoa: 0.7 (1.5)

elsewhere there was one physician per 12,000 inhabitants. By the late 1980s, all the major diseases that had ravaged prewar Yugoslavia had been virtually eliminated. There was one physician per 577 inhabitants. Crude mortality rates dropped from 20 per 1,000 to 9.1 per 1,000.

Medical problems remain, although of a different order. The most prominent is the disparity between delivery of health services in urban and rural areas. There also is a marked difference in health-care facilities between the developed and the less developed regions. Although health care has improved in all regions, the gap between the North and the South has remained as wide as before. For example, Kosovo's physician-per-inhabitant ratio is less than half the national average. Yugoslavia's infant mortality rate—25 per 1,000 live births—remains much higher than in developed European countries where it is insignificant. In the less developed regions, the infant mortality rate is two to seven times higher than the national average.

Health care is a constitutional obligation of the state. All citizens are entitled to treatment of infectious diseases and mental illnesses. Pregnant women, infants and children under age 15 (26 in the case of students) receive comprehensive and preventive health care.

A general health insurance program was established in 1945 and gradually expanded until it covers more than 90% of the population today. The program is managed by the Self-Managed Communities of Interest for

eno-Serbski Magazin, which appeared in Venice in 1768, and *Serbskija Novini*, published in Vienna in 1791. The first newspaper to be published within the country's present borders and also the first to be published in Slovenian was *Ljubljanske Novice*, which appeared in Ljubljana from 1797 to 1800. In the 1780s Emperor Franz Joseph II had permitted the publication of a newspaper for Croats called *Kroatischer Korrespondent*, but it was printed in German. Napoleon's administration in Dalmatia witnessed the publication of *Kraljiske Dalmatin* from Zadar on the Adriatic from 1806 to 1810. But the real beginning of the Croatian press dates from 1835, when *Narodna Novine (People's Paper)* was founded by Ljudevit Gaj in Zagreb. The first Serbian newspaper was *Novine Serbske*, which appeared at Kragujevac in 1834, and the first newspaper in Vojvodina was *Vestnik* of Novi Sad, founded in 1848.

The press led a precarious existence in the troubled first half of the 19th century. By the end of the 1850s only eight newspapers survived in all of the southern Slavic lands. One of these was the first Serbian-language daily, *Srbski Dvenik*, which first appeared in Novi Sad in 1852. The climate soon began to change as the Austrians relaxed their controls. The first Croatian daily, *Obzor (Survey)*, was established in 1860. In Serbia, Prince Michael actually encouraged the press. By 1867 a total of 24 Serbian, 20 Croatian and 11 Slovene newspapers and periodicals were on the market. By 1880 newspapers had been founded in other regions as well. The first newspaper in Bosnia-Herzegovina was *Bosanski Vjestnik* (1866), the first newspaper in Montenegro was *Crnogorac* (1871) and the first newspaper in Kosovo-Metohija was *Prizren* (1871). However, freedom of the press was a constitutional reality only in Serbia, where the restoration of the Constitution in 1903 sparked an explosion in the number of newspapers to 775 (including 20 dailies) by 1910. Among the dailies, *Politika*, founded in 1903, led the field in quality and circulation.

With the establishment of the independent Kingdom of the Serbs, Croats and Slovenes in 1918 at the conclusion of World War I, the press entered a new era. Shortly after the formation of the new state there were 61 dailies, and during the interwar years the total number of publications ranged from 648 to 1,108. The immediate postwar years also saw the founding of the first national news agency, Avila.

The political turmoil of the interwar years was reflected in the vicissitudes of the press. Even so, by 1937, on the eve of World War II, 50 dailies were published in six languages in the kingdom. The one with the largest circulation was *Politika* (146,000), followed by *Vreme* (65,000), *Pravda* (45,000), *Novesti* (23,000) and *Jutarnji List* (21,000).

With the seizure of power by Tito and the Partisans the composition and status of the press changed decisively. The former underground Communist papers *Borba* and *Kommunist* became official publications and the mouthpieces of the government. Of the older publications, only *Politika* was permitted to continue publication, principally because its owners, the Ribnikars, had aided Tito before and during the war. A 1946 press law limited the right to publish to the Communist party and its affiliated organizations. Printing presses were nationalized, and newsprint could be obtained only through government channels.

Yugoslavia's rupture with the Cominform in 1948 and the former's subsequent disavowal of Stalinist-type Marxism led to a softening of the rigors of party monopoly of the press. Further, the concept of self-management that replaced Stalinism postulated a relaxation of central controls over all areas of society, including the press. The result was an enlargement of the scope and effectiveness of the Yugoslav press and the latitude permitted to it to present news and views. The party still hovers above the press with a watchful eye, and controls are tightened periodically in response to both internal and external developments. But by and large the Yugoslav media give their readers and listeners a more accurate picture of their country and the world than any comparable system in the Communist world.

A total of 4,537 publications were published in 1989, including 27 dailies, 204 weeklies, 293 biweeklies and 959 monthlies, with a total circulation of 2.5 million. Sixteen of the general dailies are morning papers. Each republic and province has extensive media, including papers in minority languages. There are three minority-language dailies: *Magyar Szo* of Novi Sad in Hungarian, *La Voz del Populo* of Rijeka in Italian and *Rilindja* of Pristina in Albanian. Religious organizations publish more than 127 periodicals. There is no large town or commune or any organization without a publication of its own.

Most newspapers are full size, but several are tabloid, including *Politika* and *Vecernje Novosti*. Compared to newspapers in other Communist countries, they have more pages and run more ads. For example, *Politika* runs an average of 36 to 40 pages an issue on weekdays, including 10 to 15 pages of ads. *Borba* usually prints about 18 pages but devotes far less space to ads. *Oslobodjenje* of Sarejevo, a paper that is important regionally but not nationally, averages 24 to 26 pages per issue, with about a third of the total space given over to ads. There are Sunday editions, but no magazine sections in the Western sense. *Politika* publishes a slick-paper TV supplement in color as part of its Saturday edition. It also publishes *Illustrovana Politika*, which is one of the largest-selling weeklies in the country.

Borba does not appear in the accompanying list because its circulation is a modest 35,000; however, it is the official organ of the League of Communists of Yugoslavia, and as such commands wide attention in the country and abroad, since its editorials offer a clue to government policies and responses to events. One edition of *Borba* is printed in Zagreb in Latin letters and the other in Belgrade in Cyrillic letters.

Commercial self-interest, a rare phenomenon for a Communist country, has revolutionized the Yugoslavian press, resulting in livelier copy, special supplements, color printing and attractive ads. Although there is no formal competition, newspapers do compete for reader interest and against the Western newspapers and periodicals that are freely available in the country. Although circulation has grown since the end of World War II, the number of copies per person still is low compared to other European countries. This is due in part to the historically high illiteracy rates in the South, where about 25% of the population never look at a newspaper.

There is no private ownership, and the founders of most newspapers are tied to the Socialist Alliance or the League of Communists of Yugoslavia. There are far fewer publishing houses than the number of papers would indicate. For example, *Borba* publishes *Vecernje Novosti* as well as the daily *Sport* and a variety of periodicals. In fact, the only Belgrade paper not published by *Borba* or *Politika* is *Privredni Pregled (Economic Review)*.

The concentration is complete in Zagreb, where Vjesnik publishes all the three dailies as well as the popular weekly *Vjesnik u Srijedu*. A total of 90% of the total national circulation is accounted for by 47 enterprises and 80% by the top 10. As a socialized sector, the press enjoys considerable advantages, particularly in the allotment of newsprint. Most full-time journalists are members of republic or provincial professional organizations affiliated with the Yugoslav Federation of Journalists.

MEDIA INDICATORS, 1988

Newspapers
  Number of dailies: 27
  Circulation (000): 2,498
  Circulation per 1,000: 107
  Number of nondailies: 3,036
  Circulation (000): 23,852
  Circulation per 1,000: 1,040
  Number of periodicals: 1,474
  Circulation (000): 4,968
  Newsprint consumption
  Total (tons): 18,500
  Per capita, kg. (lb.): 0.813 (1.79)
Book publishing
  Number of titles: 8,682
Broadcasting
  Annual expenditures (national currency): 14.540 billion
  Number of employees: 19,175
Radio
  Number of transmitters: 919
  Number of radio receivers (000): 4,794
    Persons per radio receiver: 4.9
  Total annual program hours: 385,399
Television
  Television transmitters; 1,061
  Number of television receivers (000): 4,126
    Persons per television receiver: 5.7
  Total annual program hours: 22,734
Cinema
  Number of fixed cinemas: 1,271
  Seating capacity: 437,000
    Seats per 1,000: 19.1
  Annual attendance (million): 78.1
    Per capita: 3.5
  Gross box office receipts (national currency): 2.891 billion
Films
  Production of long films: 24
  Import of long films: 189
    34.9% from United States
    10.6% from Italy
    7.9% from France
    7.9% from USSR

CULTURAL & ENVIRONMENTAL INDICATORS, 1988

Public libraries
  Number: 1,972
  Volumes (000): 26,424
  Loans per 1,000: 1,200
Museums
  Number: 379
  Annual attendance (000): 10,649
  Attendance per 1,000: 497
Performing arts
  Facilities: 123
  Number of performances: 19,496
  Annual attendance (000): 5,610
  Attendance per 1,000: 240
Ecological sites: 20
Botanical gardens & zoos: 19

LARGEST DAILIES IN YUGOSLAVIA

Daily	City	Circulation
Vecernji List	Zagreb	370,000
Vecernje Novosti	Belgrade	363,000
Politika	Belgrade	256,000
Politika Ekspres	Belgrade	227,000
Sportske Novosti	Zagreb	174,000
Sport	Belgrade	125,000
Delo	Ljubljana	105,000
Slobodna Dalmacija	Split	100,000
Vjesnik	Zagreb	95,000
Vecernje Novine	Sarajevo	89,000
Oslobodenje	Sarajevo	74,000

Freedoms of the press, speech and information are guaranteed in the Constitution but interpreted by the government in a narrow way and only to the extent that they serve its purpose. Dissent is tolerated by suffrance rather than as a right, and the same offense may at one point or in one region be ignored while in another time or place call down the wrath of the powers that be.

Three Criminal Code articles have been particularly significant in freedom of information cases. Article 118 makes it a criminal offense to circulate propaganda against the governmental or social order or against political, economic military or other important measures of the people's authority; Article 175 prohibits writings damaging the reputation of a foreign state; and Article 125 bars the distribution of any material that has been banned by the authorities. In 1969 the editor of the Belgrade biweekly *Knjizevne Novine (Literary News)* was sentenced to six months in prison for an article attacking the Soviet invasion of Czechoslovakia, although the regime itself had been highly critical of the invasion. Individual citizens and organizations have the right to demand correction of erroneous or misleading information, and editors are obliged to publish the correction. There is no censorship as such, but there is a variety of informal censorship mechanisms. Top editorial posts generally are held by party members who are well acquainted with the official line and are subject to party discipline. Pressure also can be brought to bear through the social or publishers' councils in each publishing house. Since these councils appoint the responsible editors, they have the right to dismiss them as well, a right often exercised against too liberal or too independent editors. Yugoslavia has figured prominently in several years in the International Press Institute's survey of world press freedom as an offender. Foreign correspondents who wire consistently negative reports on the country also may find themselves persona non grata and expelled, although only rarely jailed. Yugoslavs who voice unacceptable views to foreign newsmen suffer a worse fate. Individual issues of even respected dailies, such as *Politika*, have been banned on occasion.

The national news agency is Tanjug. Founded by the Partisans in 1943, it took over the old Avila agency at the end of the war. Until 1952 it was an arm of the government, enjoying a monopoly of new distribution. Since 1952 it has operated with a greater measure of independence, under its own workers' council. Officially it is autonomous, but the government has a considerable voice in its affairs, since it pays one-third of the agency's income. Tanjug lost its monopoly over news collection and distribution step by step beginning in the 1950s, when newspapers started to send their own correspondents abroad. By the 1960s the larger ones had their own network of correspondents in the main cities of the country and obtained the right to subscribe directly to foreign news services. Today Tanjug is particularly strong in Third World news coverage and is the operating manager of the Nonaligned News Agencies Pool. A third of Tanjug's income comes from the supply of economic and trade information to the nation's commercial and industrial enterprises. Eighteen foreign news agencies are represented in Belgrade including AFP, AP, TASS, dpa, Reuters, UPI and Xinhua.

Decentralization is also a characteristic of Yugoslav broadcasting. Yugoslav Radio and Television (JRT) is a federation, with divisions corresponding to the republics and provinces. These divisions are independent, self-managing organizations financing their activities largely from license fees and income from advertising. They receive, in addition, some state subsidies. JRT is administered at the federal level by a management board and a secretary general; the latter's job has been described as that of an umpire rather than that of a boss.

Each of the larger radio centers broadcasts on several channels. Radio Belgrade operates a shortwave international service and four domestic radio services. Radio Zagreb airs four different services, including one aimed at Yugoslavs working in Western Europe. Radio Sarajevo has four services, and Novi Sad and Ljubljana three each. Novi Sad transmits its programs in Serbo-Croatian, Hungarian, Rumanian, Slovak and Ruthenian; many other stations broadcast in two or three languages.

The eight television centers operate in a similar manner. Belgrade, Ljubljana and Zagreb operate two channels each, and the others—Novi Sad, Pristina, Sarajevo, Skopje and Titograd—one each.

SOCIAL WELFARE

Under the self-management system, the Social Security administration differs markedly from that prevailing in most other countries. Broadly supervised by the Union of Pension and Invalidity Associations on a national scale, Social Security is administered locally by the associations of social insurance in each commune. Each association is headed by assemblies directly elected by the insured persons. General social insurance covers all employees and the self-employed; partial insurance, introduced in 1962, covers farmers. Social insurance funds accrue from the contributions of enterprises and are obtained by levies on the personal incomes of the insured. Maximum contributions vary according to the republic or province.

The principal social insurance benefits are: free health services, sickness benefits, disability benefits, pregnancy and maternity grants, retirement and disability pensions, survivor pensions, children's allowances and funeral allowances. There is no unemployment benefit as such, but unemployed workers applying to the local labor exchange are entitled to compensation equal to 50% of their average earnings in the past three months, payable for up to six months.

There is no private welfare system in Yugoslavia.

CHRONOLOGY (from 1945)

1945—Yugoslavia adopts the name Federal People's Republic of Yugoslavia.

1946—A new Constitution is approved.

1948—Tito's break with Stalin is followed by Yugoslavia's expulsion from the Cominform.

1950—A decentralized system of self-management of economic enterprises is introduced.

1952—The Communist Party is renamed the League of Communists of Yugoslavia.

1953—A new Constitution is adopted, with Tito becoming the president of the federal presidency.

1954—Yugoslavia concedes Trieste to Italy under a new treaty with Italy, the United States and the United Kingdom.

1955—Relations are normalized with the Soviet Union.

1956—Tito hosts a nonaligned summit meeting at Brioni attended by Jawaharlal Nehru of India and Gamal Abdel Nasser of Egypt.

1963—Under a new Constitution that replaced the Constitution of 1953, the country is renamed the Socialist Federal Republic of Yugoslavia.

1974—Yugoslavia adopts a new Constitution.

1979—Tito's close associate, Edvard Kardelj, dies.

1980—Tito dies; the federal presidency takes over as head of state.

1987—Violence erupts in Kosovo, particularly between Serbs and Albanians. As the economy slumps, the government imposes a wage freeze and adopts harsh austerity measures.

1990—Opposition parties win elections in Croatia and Slovenia. . . . Serbia dissolves Kosovo government and takes direct control. . . . Slovenia declares independence and calls for a Yugoslav confederation. . . . Federal government authorizes multiparty elections.

BIBLIOGRAPHY
BOOKS

Borowiec, Andrew. *Yugoslavia After Tito*. New York, 1977.

Burg, Steven L. *Conflict and Cohesion in Socialist Yugoslavia*. Princeton, N.J., 1983.

Byrnes, Robert F. *Yugoslavia*. New York, 1969.

Carter, April. *Democratic Reform in Yugoslavia*. Princeton, N.J., 1982.

Cohen, Leonard, and Paul V. Warwick. *Political Cohesion in a Fragile Mosaic: The Yugoslav Experience*. Boulder, Colo., 1983.

Denitch, Bogdan. *The Legitimation of a Revolution: The Yugoslav Case*. New Haven, 1976.

Dimitrijevic, Dimitrije, and George Masesich. *Money and Finance in Yugoslavia: A Comparative Analysis*. Westport, Conn., 1983.

Doder, Dusko. *The Yugoslavs*. New York, 1978.

Estrin, Saul. *Self-Management: Theory and Socialist Practice*. New York, 1984.

Heppell, Muriel, and Frank B. Singleton. *Yugoslavia*. New York, 1961.

Prout, Christopher. *Market Socialism in Yugoslavia*. New York, 1985.

Ramet, Pedro. *Yugoslavia in the 1980s*. Boulder, Colo., 1985.

Robinson, Gertude Joan. *Tito's Maverick Media: The Politics of Mass Communication in Yugoslavia*. Urbana, Ill., 1977.

Roskin, Michael. *The Other Governments of Europe*. Englewood Cliffs, N.J., 1977.

Seroka, James H., and Rados Smijkovic. *Political Organization in Socialist Yugoslavia*. Durham, N.C., 1986.

Sindic, Milos. *Planning in Yugoslavia*. Belgrade, 1981.

Singleton, Fred, and Bernard Carter. *The Economy of Yugoslavia*. New York, 1986.

Stankovic, Slobodan. *The End of the Tito Era: Yugoslavia's Dilemmas*. Stanford, Calif., 1983.

Wilson, Duncan. *Tito's Yugoslavia*. Cambridge, Mass., 1980.

Zakinovich, M. George. *The Development of Socialist Yugoslavia*. Baltimore, 1968.

OFFICAL PUBLICATIONS

Census of Population and Housing. Belgrade.
Statistical Bulletin. Belgrade.
Statistical Yearbook. Belgrade.

INDEX